Adobe FAQ

Adobe Acrobat 3.0
Adobe After Effects 3.1
Adobe FrameMaker 5
Adobe Illustrator 7.0
Adobe PageMill 2.0
Adobe SiteMill 1.0
The easy way to manage your Web site
Adobe Persuasion 4.0

Adobe® FAQ

Adobe's most

***F**requently **A**sked **Q**uestions*

answered.

ADOBE PRESS SAN JOSE, CALIFORNIA

Library of Congress Catalog No.: 97-70860

ISBN: 1-56830-372-6

10 9 8 7 6 5 4 3 2 First Printing: April 1997

Published by Adobe Press, Adobe Systems Incorporated.

Text design by David Bullen.
Production by Hans Hansen.

Printed in the United States of America.
Pre-press and printing by
GAC Shepard Poorman, Indianapolis, Indiana.

Published simultaneously in Canada.

Adobe Press books are published and distributed by Macmillan Computer Publishing USA. For individual, educational, corporate, or retail sales accounts, call 1-800-428-5331, or 317-581-3500. For information address Macmillan Computer Publishing USA, 201 West 103rd Street, Indianapolis, IN 46290. Macmillan's World Wide Web page URL is www.mcp.com.

Contents

Introduction

Welcome to Adobe® FAQ

This is an official Adobe publication from Adobe Systems Incorporated. It has been compiled by several hundred Adobe employees over the past years—Adobe's Customer Support staff, the editors and writers at Adobe Magazine, and Adobe's Web team of www.adobe.com fame. All have striven to make the material in this book and its companion CD a unique desktop reference to support and accompany your Adobe software.

Adobe provides sophisticated software for the creation of visually-rich graphics, text, page-layout, printing, and motion graphics projects. In this ever-changing converging digital world, a vast array of questions will naturally arise. Combine that digital technology with the creative impulses and vision associated with visually-rich communications, and an even higher, more sophisticated strata of queries occur.

It always has been the creative will and vision of Adobe's users that have pushed the boundaries of our software—new ways of thinking, new ways of working, new combinations and permutations. *Adobe FAQ* attempts to document these trials and errors by our users, as they pioneer how to create, produce, and distribute the world's information.

To accomplish this we have included the entire Adobe technology database from Adobe's Customer Support archives, the past three years of the Q&A section of our sister publication, Adobe Magazine (formerly Aldus Magazine), and a selection of general Adobe tips, articles, Web pages, and even a section on PostScript® troubleshooting from a previous Adobe Press book.

The project faced a massive amount of information—almost 2,100 pages. In the book business, the costs of printing, binding, distributing, and selling that tome would require a retail price of $100 US or greater, not to mention the sacrifice of hundreds of innocent trees. So we made some decisions on how to best serve Adobe users while trying to maintain an air of economy and a degree of utility.

We took the most frequent 20% of all questions and put these in the printed book, feeling that the frequency data justified this inclusion. We also made the decision to feature Adobe Photoshop®, Adobe Illustrator®, and Adobe PageMaker®, with longer chapters on these popular products (increasing the frequency closer to 30%). We included every Q&A and every "tip" from Adobe Magazine because they are superb, and they can only be found in a stack of magazines somewhere in the corner of your office.

For all those 1,300 pages we weren't able to print, because of the constraints (costs) of distributing paper, we created a digital second book, twice as large as this printed book you are hefting around. This second book, which we call the Unabridged FAQ or UFAQ, contains the remaining information. Both the FAQ and the UFAQ are in Acrobat format and are formatted exactly like these paper pages. With the UFAQ we were able to keep the retail price down as best we could but pump up the total amount of content. It requires you to use the CD, but if you have that one nagging question, a quick search using the Acrobat Search features might just solve your dilemma. If you specialize in one particular Adobe product, you might consider printing the UFAQ chapter (and the digital FAQ chapter) for a customized binder on your favorite product. Since all the Adobe products are represented in both FAQ and UFAQ versions, your customization options are as unique as your work habits.

When it came to an index we debated for weeks. What is the most appropriate index for this type of information that contains over a million words in the printed book? A traditional index would take more than fifty pages. We felt it would also be more aggravating than useful. For example, an index entry of "trapping" might be listed in ten of the Adobe product chapters literally hundreds of times. One trapping sub-entry might have a dozen page-number references requiring you to visit each of the dozen pages. This was unacceptable.

So our index resembles a detailed table of contents listing every single question, classified by individual product and by major OS platform (MacOS and Windows). We felt that scanning questions was actually quicker and more insightful than a three- or four-word phrase that required you to visit multiple pages without knowing the context of the question. The Acrobat Search feature of the free Acrobat 3.0 Reader on the CD, or on your existing Acrobat 3.0 Exchange program, will provide a powerful search engine for your proximity inquiries such as "trapping" + "Illustrator" + "color" + "gradient tool", and so forth. Besides, since we put another 1,300 pages or so in the UFAQ, an index to only the paper seemed absurd, because all too often your questions don't fall into the 20% of the most frequently asked.

We took these and many others concerns to David Bullen, one of the finer book designers to be found, and he performed admirably, designing a handsome book that is compact yet accessible. The text face is Adobe Minion and the heads are Adobe Myriad. The optically-adjusted multiple master font technology gave us superior legibility in a dense two-column layout, even at 8- and 9-point sizes. And we choose a natural stock of paper to minimize glare and contrast when reading this text-intensive material.

On the CD we divided the paper book's chapters into separate Acrobat files, accompanied by their sister UFAQ files, to give you a better "hit" analysis for your digital queries. The CD's "home page" was designed to be fast loading and helpful, with built-in hypertext links to www.adobe.com for up-to-date help and product information.

We quickly realized that the book's usefulness would be limited by time. Adobe's Customer Support receives thousands of calls and e-mails a day, and they document the answers to each unique issue. During this book's six-month development period, hundreds of new questions were added each month. We sadly acknowledged that a mere day after the book went to the printer there would be some really useful Q&A arriving at Adobe that should have been included. So we included a section in the frontmatter on how best to use Adobe's Web site (see the section "www.adobe.com") as *the* source for up-to-date information, Q&A, and all things Adobe.

If browsing isn't your idea of fast information or personal help, or you can't or don't care to be connected to the Web, we advocate Adobe's CustomerFirst®—a portfolio of complimentary and fee-based options. Nothing beats a real person trained and schooled in the application about which you are inquiring. We've included information in the frontmatter on Adobe's CustomerFirst program (see the section "Adobe CustomerFirst"). Check the Adobe application package, or the digital media that came with your Adobe product, for information on Adobe CustomerFirst. No book from any publisher can substitute for trained professionals who specialize in your Adobe product.

Nothing, however, beats spending a little time with the manual. Many users shuck the manual to play with their new application, and never return to it. Adobe has striven to make their products as intuitive as possible but doing certain operations "correctly," as documented in the User Guides of your Adobe product, can save time, money, and ultimately, save botched projects from ever happening.

I want to personally thank a few people for their devotion to this reference book project. Hans Hansen produced this book combining several databases. He created a complex set of PageMaker scripts to automate the production of it according to David Bullen's design (see Hans' web site at www.hhansen.com/pmscripting.html). Hans also acted as managing editor and our advocate for user's concerns. Without Hans, this book would have been impossible. Thanks also to Mario Murphy for assisting in the book's production. Brian Turner, of Adobe Customer Support, was instrumental in developing the book's concept, supplying the editors and producers with a constant stream of database entries, and smoothing information flow while maintaining his day-to-day duties. Without Brian, the content of this book would have been severely compromised. Several others at Adobe Customer Support contributed to *Adobe FAQ*, without whose contribution this reference book would have been delayed and inaccurate. The tech notes were created by the Software Support Specialists, Technical Writers, and Technical Editors of the Customer Support division. The CD mastering is due to Tom McIntire. The CD's File Library was created and organziaed by Frank Farm. Editorial assistance provided by Sara Ness. Transposing the Technology Database into workable files was the work of Jim Price, Chris Crossen, Alison MacLellan, Kim Upper, and David Joslin. And the manager of this fine group of Adobe employees is Susan Lang, manager of Service Technology and Operations. From Adobe Magazine, Tamis Nordling, Wendy Katz, Nick Allison, Carla Noble and many, many others over the course of the past three years have not only created a wonderful magazine with a dedicated readership, but have supported the user with a cause and fervor of evangelists. Thank you, Adobe Magazine. And Wendy Govier, Jocelyn Bergen, Francis Poon and all the Adobe.com staff have supplied this book with invaluable information, and act as the virtual Adobe FAQ, 24 hours a day.

Adobe Customer Support is responsible for documenting the material in this book. While tech support groups are often the object of scorn and ridicule, Adobe's Customer Support's devotion to the user is unparalleled in any other industry, and dare I say, company. The material in this book has been developed by literally hundreds of Adobe Customer Support staff, both past and present. We dedicate this book to your ongoing service and commitment to the user.

Finally we dedicate this book to you, the reader. This book's content has been developed because you called, faxed, e-mailed, or hand-wrote your questions to Adobe. Adobe makes the best technological products we can. But we are constantly amazed by what you do with it. Where you go with it. How you twist and bend and struggle to create something unique, something useful. Ultimately, you create the world's information—in print, on the Internet, in video. Adobe is here to help support you in that endeavor.

Patrick Ames
Publisher, Adobe Press
Adobe Systems Incorporated

How to use this book

Using this book

Using this book is easy. First find the chapter for the software application you are interested in, then find the subject topic that you'd like to explore.

This book is first divided alphabetically by primary Adobe software applications: Acrobat, After Effects, FrameMaker, Illustrator, PageMaker, PageMill, Persuasion, Photoshop, PostScript, Premiere, the Adobe Type Library, and Adobe Type Manager. Within these chapters are references to secondary applications, such as Dimensions and Streamline which are covered within the Illustrator chapter. It is easy to locate the primary applications by using the table of contents or the margin thumbtabs.

Chapter article topics:

The articles for each application chapter have been sorted into seven subject topics:

Feature Techniques
Tips and techniques to get specified results.

Unexpected Results
What to do when you get unexpected results.

Application Errors
Troubleshooting application error messages.

System Errors
Troubleshooting system and hardware error messages.

Printing Problems
Diagnosing printing errors and imaging problems.

Installation Issues
Troubleshooting software installation problems.

General Information
Background and specification information.

Each of these topics are sorted by relevant computer platform, first listing articles that apply to all (or multiple platforms), then listing articles for individual platforms in the order of Windows, MacOS, then UNIX.

After the twelve application chapters, an appendix of General System Issues can be found. It contains articles that describe optimizing and troubleshooting Windows, MacOS, and UNIX operating systems for Adobe products. It includes explanations of common system errors and methods for configuring system components, again for Adobe product usage.

Guide to page elements

Use the labeled page elements to help distinguish FAQ chapters, application sections, article topics, and system platform subtopics.

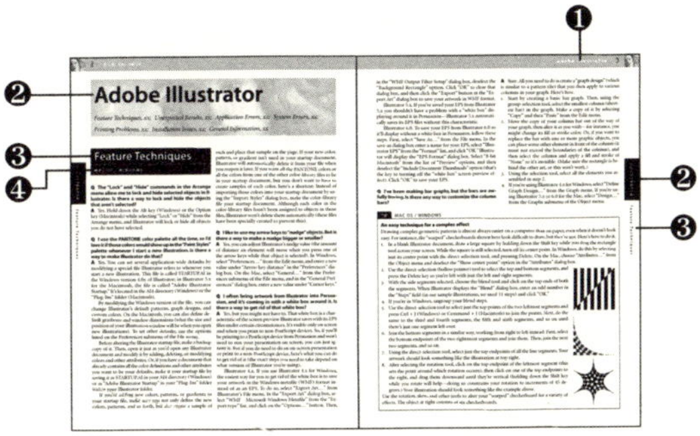

❶ Chapter's primary software application
❷ Software application, chapter section
❸ Article topic within application section
❹ System platform division within article topic

You may also find the book's index a useful way to quickly locate articles. The index lists the title or question of each article within the book so that you can quickly locate articles pertinent to your issue. The "tips" are not listed in the index as some don't have titles or don't indicate what they cover (they originally appeared in various issues of Adobe Magazine).

The Adobe FAQ CD

Only the most frequently accessed articles for each application are printed in this book. However the CD contains an additional 1300 pages, as well as the entire text of this book. This unprinted information is referred to as "UFAQ" or Unabridged FAQ. On the CD chapters are sorted by Adobe application name. Nested within each directory or folder, two files will reside. One will be the paper book's pages, "xxxx_FAQ.pdf", and the other will be "xxxxUFAQ-.pdf" representing the unabridged version.

The CD also contains all the updates and demos of Adobe software available on the Adobe.com FTP site. You can save yourself hours of downloading time by using the CD to quickly get the latest feature and bug-fixing application updates.

See the last page of this book for more information on the contents of the *Adobe FAQ* CD.

Step-by-Step Troubleshooting

To troubleshoot a problem gather as much information as you can and then create simple tests to diagnose and pinpoint its solution. The first part, gathering information, is easy, given this book, this book's CD, and the constantly updated resource at www.adobe.com. The second part, testing to find a solution, can be a bit more tricky. To help with this, follow the steps below to help focus on your problem and test any ideas you have about its cause. Should you feel completely baffled, call Adobe Customer Support (see the section "Adobe CustomerFirst").

Determine the facts

1. **What exactly is the problem?**
   - ❑ I can't do what I should be able to.
   - ❑ I don't get the results I expected.
   - ❑ I can't figure out how to do this.
   - ❑ There should be a better way to do this.
2. **At exactly what point does the problem occur?**
   - ❑ Upon executing a command.
   - ❑ When accessing a file or saving data.
   - ❑ When printing or outputting a file.
   - ❑ When installing software or hardware.
3. **What is the exact text of the error message?**
   - ❑ The message is presented by the application and says…
   - ❑ The message is presented by the system and says…
   - ❑ There is no message, the computer just freezes or blinks.
4. **What is the history or pattern or the problem?**
   - ❑ The problem occurs every time or in all examples.
   - ❑ The problem occurs some of the time or in some of the examples.
   - ❑ The problem is occasional and appears random.
   - ❑ This is the first time I've used this feature and had a problem.
   - ❑ I do this all the time and it hasn't happened before.
5. **What may have changed to cause the problem?**
   - ❑ There is new software or hardware installed.
   - ❑ Software or hardware has been removed or reconfigured.
   - ❑ I've changed the way I commonly use this feature.
   - ❑ The complexity of my work has changed or grown.
6. **Is the computer properly configured to run this software?**
   - ❑ I have enough RAM (memory).
   - ❑ I have enough free hard drive space.
   - ❑ I have the appropriate hardware accessories.
   - ❑ The software was installed properly.

With the answers to these questions you should try to find as much information as you can on the related issues. Develop a hypothesis of your problem's cause, which you can then test. Locate the section of articles in this book which best fit your software and hardware configuration and the general realm of the problem and see if an answer already exists. If you can't find an exact match, try reading about the causes of related problems and see if any seem relevant. When you have a hypothesis to test, be sure to be as scientific as possible by eliminating as many variables as you can, remembering to concentrate on one specific issue at a time.

The Scientific Method

When testing a solution you might consider this time-proven empirical process of investigation:

1. *Observe the phenomena.* Examine all the facts and form a model that accounts for as many variables and characteristics as possible.
2. *Form a hypothesis.* Make a guess about any characteristics you can't define.
3. *Experiment.* Create and execute a controlled test that distinctly proves or disproves your hypothesis.
4. *Modify and Repeat.* Add the results of your test to your observations and reform the model of its variables and characteristics. Repeat this process until you can account for as many unknown characteristics as possible.

This book and CD should answer and confirm your problem and hypothesis. The following three sections of this book provide additional avenues of support beyond the contents of this book: www.adobe.com; Adobe's CustomerFirst; and, Adobe's User Groups. All together, you'll have the total means to answer just about any Adobe question, frequent or not.

www.adobe.com

For the most up-to-date information you should access and use Adobe's Web site (http://www.adobe.com). Adobe.com has beefed up its customer support in a variety of ways detailed below. Whether you need to solve a technical problem, to buy, update, or register an Adobe software product, or to get your creative juices flowing, bookmark www.adobe.com.

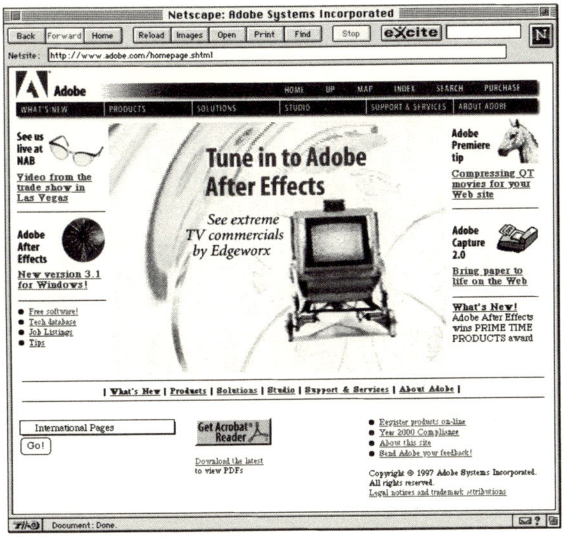

Adobe.com is a one-stop solutions center

Adobe.com continually adds to an already-substantial array of technical information and customer resources that are available. It is free, it is available around the clock, and it is accessible around the world.

"Our Web site is a powerful resource that helps you help yourself on your schedule," observes Wendy Govier, Adobe's Web Publisher/Executive Editor. "Detailed product information and demo versions of software help you choose the Adobe products that best serve your needs. Step-by-step tips will further inspire you and help you master your Adobe software. While *Adobe FAQ* documents the Technical Solutions Database, the actual database changes constantly. Adobe.com is a living book and you should use both this book and CD, as well as Adobe.com, for a tactile yet time-sensitive combination."

Adobe tech support-on-demand

The Technical Solutions Database, the basis for many of the pages of this book, gives customers Web access to the same information that is used by Adobe's own support staff when they answer technical support phone calls from customers. The database also provides the information used in fax-back and email technical support.

A new addition is the Top Issues feature, which is updated monthly and details the most commonly asked technical support questions. Top Issues are broken out by product and platform, with links to specific documents in the Technical Solutions Database. The Top Issues are the material that is printed in the paper version of this book, and they comprise the frequently asked questions.

DEFINING THE PROBLEM

"It's common for customers to not know what the problem is, but they always know what their experience is - I can't print, for example," says Brian Turner. "The more we can do to help customers define the problem the quicker the solution will be discovered."

Your search for a solution will go much more smoothly if you follow these simple steps.

1. Get the facts. Before searching Adobe.com, note:
   - the name of the Adobe product and which version hardware: make and model of personal computer, RAM, peripheral devices that may be involved. If the problem is related to printing, you'll need to know what make and model of printer plus which version of the printer driver software
   - operating system and version number
2. Describe the situation in as much detail as possible: it happens after I do this, when I'm trying to do this, etc.
3. Perform some basic tests.
   In the case of a printing problem, does it happen all the time, in only one particular situation, or only with one document? Does the problem affect other applications? If so, it may be an operating system support issue.

FREE CUSTOMER SUPPORT BY MODEM

Adobe customers can also receive free support by modem and e-mail. Dial into Adobe's bulletin board at 206-623-6984 to download information, technical papers, as well as software updates, drivers, filters, and patches.

FREE E-MAIL SUPPORT

Send e-mail to techdocs@adobe.com to receive an automatic e-mail containing a technical reference document, fact sheet, or answers to common questions. More than 1,000 technical reference documents are available. For complete instructions on how to use this e-mail service, send an initial e-mail with only the word "instructions" in the subject line. There is no need to include other text in the body of the e-mail message.

Free stuff in our File Library

Adobe.com's File Library represents another key customer support resource, containing more than 600 free products, product updaters, plug-ins, filters and drivers, including some 200 PPD (Postscript Printer Description) files. The File Library is included on this book's CD as of April 1997. Be sure to access the Adobe.com File Library for files that are posted after the publication date of this book, but the CD can save you hours of transmission and down-loading time.

Files are organized by version and date, in descending chronological order with the newest at the top. Clicking on the file description leads to a detailed information page including a detailed description of the file's functionality, anything special you need to know to make it work, handling notes to tell you how to handle the compresses file, and links to the companies that provide the decompression utilities. All files are virus-checked before being posted.

Learn from our tips

Adobe.com helps customers master the use of their sophisticated Adobe software tools by offering a rich library of Tips & Techniques articles. Offering detailed, step-by-step instructions, these articles can help produce professional results and increase skills.

Find things fast with our search engine

If Adobe.com's various navigation pathways somehow fail to lead directly to desired information, a powerful search engine permits customers to search the Adobe site using either keywords or a concept. The search engine scans HTML pages and Acrobat PDF (Portable Document Format) files at Adobe.com.

To search by concept, simply enter a group of words (as you would write or speak them) that describe the concept. The search will retrieve documents based on the concept described, even if the document does not contain the exact words in your query. For example, a search on "downloading the free acrobat reader" would list all the pages that included the concept.

Send us your brainwaves!

Found at the bottom of each Adobe.com page, the Feedback Form provides a hot line to Adobe. The form provides pull-down menus to let a customer request information about Adobe's products and services and about the Adobe.com Web site. Customers can also compose and submit questions or comments.

The Adobe.com Web team routes these questions and comments to the appropriate Adobe department. Responding to these messages is taken seriously at Adobe, and represents a high priority. The Feedback Form is a primary channel for customer bug reports and feedback on Adobe product features and capabilities, and they serve to help guide development of future versions of Adobe products.

Buy Adobe products

The Purchasing Adobe Products page directs you where to buy at Adobe.com.

BUYING TYPE

Customers can get U.S. and international type prices and telephone order information at the Type Ordering and Electronic Delivery page; click on the country flag. Order and arrange electronic delivery of fonts at the Adobe Typefaces Center.

Adobe.com's Type On Call Web Service lets customers register a Type On Call CD-ROM (version 4.0 or higher) and receive access keys to your free software at Adobe.com, plus view and purchase any one of the more than 2,100 typefaces included in the Adobe Type Library. The service also lets a customer view a typeface's character set, browse informative type histories, find out about your favorite type designers, access technical information, and take advantage of special offers.

IMAGE CLUB

Image Club Graphics sells a broad range of royalty-free clip art, stock photos, graphical elements for Web site design, and third party plug-ins for Adobe products.

PURCHASE BY TELEPHONE AND FROM RESELLERS

The How to Buy pages provide detailed information about how to purchase Adobe products by telephone and from resellers.

The Adobe Authorized Reseller Search Form lets customers search a database of Adobe Authorized Resellers in the US and Canada, by state or province, postal code, or telephone area code.

Product Registration

Now you can register your Adobe product purchases online. Product registration qualifies customers for technical support (as outlined in product documentation), puts customers on the list for new product announcements and special offers, and enables early notification of product upgrades.

Registering an Adobe product online is a simple matter of linking to the On-line Registration Form and filling it out.

Adobe CustomerFirst®

From the moment you register a product, you have access to our expert support staff and a rich variety of information resources. Adobe CustomerFirst® offers support options that you can mix and match to meet your technical needs.

Adobe CustomerFirst is a portfolio of complimentary and fee-based service options that can increase your productivity, help you with troubleshooting, and expand your software knowledge. Its range of options comes with every Adobe product you buy and register. However you work and whenever you need help, Adobe CustomerFirst provides support you can use.

Complimentary Telephone Support Periods

As a registered Adobe product owner, you receive a period of complimentary, person-to-person support. The support period begins with your first call. You're free to make that call at any time after you register, so you can wait until your need for technical help is greatest. All you pay is the phone charge. The length of the complimentary support period depends on whether your Adobe product is a Level I or Level II product (see below) and whether it's a first-time purchase or an upgrade to an Adobe product you already own.

To start the complimentary support period, dial the technical support number for the Adobe product you own (to look up your Adobe product's technical support number: e-mail to techdocs@adobe.com with 499908 in the "subject line" of the email; or, fax 206-628-5737 and request document 499908; or , call 800-879-3219 and follow the automated directory).

Adobe CustomerFirst Products

Level I products

Adobe Art Explorer ®
Adobe Dimensions ®
Adobe File Utilities
Adobe FrameViewer ®
Adobe Gallery Effects ®
Adobe HomePublisher ™
Adobe PageMill ™
Adobe PhotoDeluxe ™
Adobe Streamline ™
Adobe SuperPaint ®
Adobe TextureMaker ™
Adobe Type Manager ® (ATM ®)/SuperATM ®
Adobe Type Twister ™
Limited Edition (LE) versions of products Not for Resale (NFR) versions of products Type packages and products

Level II products

Adobe Acrobat ®
Adobe After Effects ®
Adobe Font Folio ™
Adobe FrameMaker ®
Adobe FrameMaker+SGML ™
Adobe Illustrator ®
Adobe PageMaker ®
Adobe Persuasion ®
Adobe Photoshop ®
Adobe Premiere ®
Adobe SiteMill ™

First-time Purchase of an Adobe Product Level I products: one incident; Level II products: 90 days.

Note: You can obtain technical support for free products, such as Adobe Acrobat Reader software, only through our pay-as-you-go options or an annual support agreement.

Product Upgrade Purchase Level I products: One incident.

Level II products: 30 days.

Technical Support Phone Numbers: Access the product specific phone number list for the U.S. and Canada only. For International Support see the contents of your shrink-wrapped Adobe product, or visit www.adobe.com for more specifics.

Free Technical Information - Any Time, Any Day

By the Web: the Technical Solutions database and File Library at http://www.adobe.com

By E-mail: Send us an e-mail at techdocs@adobe.com to receive an automatic e-mail containing a technical reference document, fact sheet, or answers to common questions. More than 1,000 technical reference documents are available. For complete instructions on how to use this e-mail service, send an initial e-mail with only the word "instructions" in the subject line. (No need to include other text in the e-mail.)

By Fax: Call our FaxYI line at 206-628-5737 to receive automatic faxes of fact sheets and answers to common questions for any Adobe product. Over 1,400 technical reference documents are available. For an index, follow the phone prompts and have your fax number handy. By Modem Dial up Adobe's bulletin board system at 206-623-6984 to download information, technical papers, as well as software updates, drivers, filters, and patches.

By On-line Services: Go to the Adobe forum on CompuServe, or America Online (AOL) and talk to other Adobe customers to discover solutions and exchange ideas. You'll find software updates, drivers, filters, and patches here as well. CompuServe: Type ADOBEAPP at the GO prompt. AOL: Type ADOBE in the Keyword dialog box (Go To menu).

Pay-As-You-Go Support

When your complimentary support period ends, you can still receive personal service from our qualified support specialists. Because it's often more convenient to pay for occasional help only as you need it, Adobe CustomerFirst offers two pay-as-you-go support options for all Adobe products. If you reside in the US, you can pay by the minute and reach Adobe Technical Support through the product's platform-specific 900 toll number: Windows products (900-555-2200); Mac OS products (900-555-3300); and, UNIX products (900-555-4400). The charge appears on your phone bill. If you live in the US or Canada, you can pay a flat fee that covers all of the support you need for a particular incident (resolve one issue). The fee is charged to your credit card, and you pay the phone charges. Mac OS and Windows products call 206-441-5142 ($25 per incident); UNIX products call 206-441-5142 ($40 per incident).

The best option for extending your person-to-person support, if you reside in the US or Canada, is an Adobe CustomerFirst Alliance annual support agreement. One price buys you a year's worth of toll-free, priority-routed access for any of the Adobe products you own.

Three CustomerFirst Alliance support options are ready to meet your individual or work-group needs:

Alliance: one person wanting support for only one Adobe product

Alliance Plus: one person wanting support for multiple Adobe products

Alliance Premium: for workgroups using multiple Adobe products

For questions or to buy annual support in the US or Canada, call 800-685-3652. For countries outside the US and Canada see the International Support area under "Support and Services" at http://www.adobe.com, or information that came within your shink-wrapped Adobe product.

Adobe User Group Relations and Professional Associations

Because Adobe recognizes the invaluable service that user groups and professional associations provide in raising awareness and building product familiarity among end users, the Adobe User Group Relations and Professional Associations program seeks to support the user group and association community and maintain long-term relationships with its leaders and members.

Register your group with the Adobe User Group Relations and Professional Associations program, and take advantage of a wide variety of free information and services. In addition to the most up-to-date news about Adobe products, we can provide your user group or professional association with product tools, special discounts, and review software. And often, we can even arrange for an Adobe expert to visit your group.

The easiest way to find more on Adobe User Group Relations and Professional Associations program is to visit www.adobe.com.

Log on

Updated product information, current press releases, newest customer spotlights, and more are available from Adobe for publication in your newsletter. To download these documents, check out any of the following on-line services:

Adobe Product Information Area America Online - User Group Forum @ AOL Keyword:UGF or, if viewing with the AOL browser access AOL://1722:aug CompuServe - the Adobe Forum Adobe BBS at 206-623-6984

FaxYI System

Obtain Adobe User Group Relations and Professional Associations program information from the Adobe automated FaxYI fax-response system 24 hours a day, 7 days a week. Simply call 206-628-5737 and follow the prompts to receive an index of available documents. Then, call back and request up to three documents at a time.

Information available by fax includes:

Adobe User Group Brochure
Adobe User Group Relations At-A-Glance
Special Product Offers and Discounts
Adobe Acrobat Products
User Group Program Information
Adobe Internet User Group
Web Publishing Program Information
Speaker/Presentation Request Form and Survey
Review Software Program Information
Adobe User Group Relations Event Calendar
APCUG Membership Information
UGC Membership Information

Vendor Press Release Listserver

Your group's newsletter editor can now subscribe to a Press Release Listserver and receive the latest press releases from vendors who regularly support user groups and professional associations. The ug-pr-pc list features Windows products and the ug-pr-mac list covers Macintosh products. To sign up for the Press Release Listserver, access the User Group Vendor association Web site at http://www.ugr.com/ugva/, follow the User Group Services link to the Press Release Sign-Up form, and subscribe. This service provides up-to-date product information daily!

User Group Vendor association (UGVa)

The User Group Vendor association is an informal group of computer vendor representatives who deal with user groups regularly. The UGVa Web site, http://www.ugr.com/ugva/, outlines the services and activities of the organization for both user groups and vendors. The Web site provides information to user groups about how to contact vendors with User Group Relations programs, how to register user groups for vendor support, and how to request vendor press releases. In addition, the Web site outlines the goals and objectives of the User Group Vendor association, its services and activities, and how vendors may join the association. To register your user group with all the vendors in the User Group Vendor association, complete the User Group Registration form and register on-line.

Association of Personal Computer User Groups (APCUG)

The Association of Personal Computer User Groups is an organization dedicated to fostering communications among and between personal computer user groups as well as assisting groups in fulfilling their educational missions and activities. As such, the APCUG operates as an information network of user group organizations and is structured as a 501(c)(3) non-profit, educational corporation. APCUG membership is open to all microcomputer user groups. At present, some of the members of APCUG are computer societies that serve many different computers; a large number of members are, however, IBM PC-and-compatible user groups.

Because membership in the APCUG is by user group, each user group must have its board of directors or similar governing body approve membership in the APCUG. Once that is done, organizations should fill out the User Group Registration form, the Appointment of Designated User Group Representative form, include a U.S.$50 check for annual dues payable to the APCUG, and mail everything to APCUG, 4020 McEwen, Suite 105, Dallas, TX 75244-5019, USA. You may also register on-line.

User Group Connection (UGC)

User Group Connection is an independent company dedicated to helping user groups and vendors connect with each other. It provides free support and benefits to registered user groups and professional associations. UGC maintains databases of approximately 1,600 PC and 2,200 Macintosh groups, as well as a number of professional associations; organizes monthly mailings; operates a referral service; and provides management assistance to user groups and professional associations.

Groups may register with UGC at no cost, although meeting minimum group requirements is necessary. Organizations interested in receiving UGC monthly mailings and support information may call 408-477-4277 x215 or e-mail info@ugconnection.org.

Chapter One

Adobe Acrobat®

Adobe Acrobat, first issued in 1993, was a ground-breaking product. Now in its 3.0 version, it has the features and bandwidth to provide all the benefits of the latest electronic publishing technology. As corporate intranets and the Web change the way the world communicates, Adobe Acrobat provides a cross-platform, cross-application, cross-media method of creating, sharing, and distributing information. There are several components of Adobe Acrobat—Exchange, Reader, Catalog, Capture, and Distiller—all included here. Acrobat 3 and its native file format, PDF, is quite simply, the world-wide standard for information transfer.

Contents

Adobe Acrobat® PDF

Feature Techniques

MAC OS / WINDOWS/ UNIX

Q What are the advantages of embedding fonts into a PDF file, and how do I do it?

A Acrobat can embed PostScript Type 1, multiple master, and TrueType fonts (Acrobat embeds TrueType fonts and each instance of a multiple master font as individual Type 1 fonts). When you embed fonts into a PDF file, the Acrobat viewers (Acrobat Reader and Acrobat Exchange) will be able to display and print your PDF file with the exact fonts you used in your design, even if they're not installed on the computer you're using to view the PDF.

When you don't embed a font, Acrobat Reader and Exchange must create—on the fly—a simulation of that font if it isn't installed on the computer being used to view the PDF file. The Acrobat viewers create these simulated fonts by reading the metrics (exact character spacing values) of your original font, which the Acrobat PDFWriter or Distiller embed in your PDF. Then the Acrobat viewers, in conjunction with ATM (Adobe Type Manager), use the "AdobeSansMM" and "AdobeSerifMM" multiple-master fonts to synthesize a font with the same metrics as your originals.

Embedding fonts in your PDF files ensures that they'll retain the exact look and fonts of the document from which they were created, but doing so will also increase the size of your PDF files. Not embedding fonts will keep your PDF files relatively small, but they'll take slightly longer to display on screen, since Acrobat and ATM will need to create on-the-fly simulations of your fonts. And although those simulated fonts will retain your original document's layout and line endings, they won't look exactly like the original fonts. Note that by default, both PDFWriter and the Distiller will embed fonts with nonstandard, non-Latin (symbol) character sets—for instance, Zapf Dingbats or the Symbol font—since simulated versions of those fonts won't match the original fonts' characters. (Decorative fonts like display or script faces are not automatically embedded.)

You can control which fonts will be embedded in your PDF files using the font-embedding options in the PDFWriter and in the Distiller. Here's how.

Getting to font-embedding options with the PDFWriter. How you get to the font-embedding options in the PDFWriter depends on what platform you're using. In Windows 3.1, go to the Control Panel, click on the "Printers" icon, select the "Acrobat PDFWriter" device, click on the "Setup..." button, then click "Fonts...." In Windows 95, double-click on the "Acrobat PDFWriter" device in the "Printers" Control Panel, and in the "Acrobat PDFWriter" window, select "Properties..." from the Printer menu. In the "Details" section of the next dialog box, click on "Setup...," then "Fonts..." (at the time of this writing, Windows 95 was not yet released, so this procedure may change).

On the Mac, hold down the Control key while selecting "Print..." from the File menu. In the "Print" dialog box, click on "Setup...," then "Fonts...." (note: Some Macintosh applications, such as Adobe Persuasion and Microsoft Word, provide access to printer-setup options via a "Page Setup" dialog box. In these applications, hold down the Control key while selecting "Page Setup" from the File menu, and in the "Page Setup" dialog box, click on "Fonts....") If neither of these procedures gets you to the "Acrobat PDFWriter Font Embedding" dialog box, check the "PDFWriter Shortcut" Control Panel to make sure it's not disabled or set to use another keyboard shortcut. If the "PDFWriter Shortcut" Control Panel isn't installed, you'll need to select the "Acrobat PDFWriter" printer driver in the Chooser manually.

Getting to font-embedding options with the Distiller. To open the "Acrobat Distiller - Font Embedding" dialog box, select "Font Embedding..." from the Distiller menu.

Using the font-embedding options. With the options in the "Font Embedding" dialog box, you can control which fonts Acrobat embeds in your PDF files. The manual and help files that come with Acrobat provide comprehensive information on using these features—for details, see the

Exchange help file HELP_E.PDF (Windows) or "Help-Exchange.pdf" (Mac), pages 138–40; the Distiller help file HELP_D.PDF (Windows) or "Help-Distiller" (Mac), pages 71–77; or the Getting Started manual, pages 28–32. For technical information on font embedding, refer to FaxYI documents 4406, "How the Adobe Acrobat Distiller and PDFWriter Programs Handle Fonts," and 4408, "Acrobat Viewer Font Management Tables" (see pages 118–19 in this issue for information on how to use FaxYI).

Working With Electronic Mail Systems and PDF Files

PDF files can be enclosures in electronic mail messages. Some electronic mail systems, such as cc:Mail, launch Ac-

TIP MAC OS / WINDOWS / UNIX

Searchable graphics

Acrobat Exchange and Reader let you search for text, but have no built-in feature that'll let you search for graphics. But don't let that stop you—you can create "searchable" graphics as long as you plan ahead.

While you're in your authoring application (whatever program you used to create the document you'll convert to PDF), place some descriptive text behind the graphic you want to be searchable. You can usually do this by typing the text, selecting it, and using a "Send to Back" or equivalent command. Once the PDF is created with either the Distiller or PDFWriter, Acrobat Exchange or Acrobat Reader will "see" the text, even though it'll be invisible to someone viewing the PDF file.

Here are a few tips:

- Use appropriately descriptive text (for instance, "Space Needle" behind a picture of Seattle's Space Needle landmark).
- If you use a small point size, you may be able to include a few different search words. Make sure the text is small enough that it's completely hidden by the graphic.
- To prevent adding a font that'll need to be embedded in your PDF (thereby increasing its file size), use a font that's already on your page, or use a font that Acrobat won't embed—for instance, Times or Helvetica. (Acrobat never embeds Times, Helvetica, Symbol, or Zapf Dingbats, since those fonts get installed automatically with Acrobat Reader and Acrobat Exchange.)

robat Exchange or Reader from within the mail application when users want to view the enclosures. This functionality is set up by the mail application.

If your mail application does not support attachments or enclosures you can still send a PDF file. Since PDF files are text files, they can be viewed in a text editor and their contents pasted into mail messages if enclosures are not possible. The receiver of the messages simply pastes together the contents of the messages in the proper order, using a text editor and saves the combined file out as text. The file can then be opened in an Acrobat viewer.

PDF files can also be enclosures in UNIX mail messages. However, some UNIX mail systems have a file size limit of 30K and do not automatically break messages into smaller units or recombine the pieces. This means that a PDF file larger than 30K needs to be broken into pieces by the sender. The receiver needs to follow the same procedure for putting a PDF file back together, that is, paste together the contents of the messages in the correct order using a text editor and save the combined file out as text.

MAC OS / WINDOWS

Q I've got two PDF documents I'd like to combine into one file. Is there any way to do this in Acrobat?

A Yes, and there are a couple of ways to go about it.

If you want to combine two documents in their entirety, open one of the documents in Exchange and choose "Insert..." from the Pages submenu under the File menu. In the "Select File to Insert" dialog box, navigate to the other document and click the "Select" button. You'll be presented with the "Insert" dialog box, in which you can choose where to insert the pages.

Windows users have a variation on this option that's especially useful for combining multiple PDF files. Open one of the files in Exchange—there must be no others open at the time—and drag one or more PDF files from the File Manager or Windows 95 Explorer window directly onto a page of the open PDF file. You'll get the "Insert" dialog box.

If you instead want to move individual pages from one PDF document into another, or want to control the order in which pages get combined, open both documents with thumbnails displaying (Ctrl/Command + 8), and then choose "Tile Vertically" from the Window menu. Now you can simply grab the page-number indicator under any thumbnail and drag that page into the other document. As you move it around, a black bar appears between existing thumbnails, indicating where the page will get inserted.

Q My clients complain that it takes too long to download PDFs from my Web site. What can I do to make this process go faster?

A The time it takes to download PDF files from the World-Wide Web depends on the PDF's file size, modem (or connection) speed, Internet traffic, and your server's configuration, as well as the kind and version of browser and Acrobat software your clients are using.

Obviously, you can't control all of these factors, but here's a quick list of what you can do.

- You can speed things up by minimizing the file sizes of the PDFs you post. A good reference on how to manage PDF file size is "Have Your Cake and Eat It, Too," by Tamis Nordling, Adobe Magazine, Jan./Feb. 1996, page 55.
- Use Acrobat Distiller 3.0 or the Acrobat 3.0 version of the PDFWriter printer driver to generate your PDFs. Both offer new compression options for images and fonts that'll help you minimize PDF file size further.

- Optimize your PDFs. To do so, you'll need Acrobat 3.0, which includes an "Optimize document" option in the "Save As" dialog box of the Exchange application. The optimization feature organizes the information in a PDF by page, and includes pointers to refer to any recurring graphics, thereby reducing the space such a repeated graphic would occupy.
- Configure your Web server so it can download Acrobat 3.0–optimized PDFs one page at a time. That can make an enormous difference in apparent download times for your customers. It will also enable "progressive" display of PDF files. First the text, then images, and finally embedded fonts will display on your clients' screens so they can begin reading the PDF almost immediately, while the other elements and attributes load in the background. For information on how to configure your server to do this, see "Configuring Your Web Server to Distribute PDF Files" in the "Acrobat on the Web" section of the Adobe Web site (go to www.adobe.com/acrobat).

Q I've heard that PDFs will now open inside Netscape, but it doesn't work for me. Is this true, and if so, what am I missing?

A It is true, and most likely you're just missing the correct version of Acrobat, or possibly the correct version of your Web browser. You need Acrobat 3.0 (Reader or Exchange) in order to open a PDF file inside a Web browser, and the supported browsers are Netscape Navigator version 2.0 or later and Microsoft Internet Explorer version 3.0 or later. You can download the Acrobat 3.0 Reader from the Acrobat section of Adobe's Web site: www.adobe.com/acrobat.

When you install Acrobat 3.0, an Acrobat Plug-in will be added to either of the browsers listed above. Then, when you point your browser at a Web site containing a PDF, Acrobat 3.0 will launch automatically and display the PDF inside the browser application. If you want to save the PDF to your hard drive, choose "Save as..." from the File menu.

Unexpected Results

MAC OS / WINDOWS

Q Sometimes I'll create a PDF file and the fonts will look fine on my computer, but look different on someone else's machine. Why does that happen?

A Chances are that the fonts that looked different on another machine weren't embedded in the PDF file. You were probably able to view your PDF with those fonts displaying as themselves because you have those fonts installed on your computer. But if you give that PDF to someone who doesn't have those fonts on their machine, Acrobat will simulate any missing fonts using multiple-master font technology—and those simulated fonts won't look quite the same as the original fonts.

If you want to get a more accurate preview of your PDF file so you'll know how it might look on another machine, try viewing that PDF file on a computer that has only the following fonts installed: AdobeSans and AdobeSerif multiple-master fonts, plus the PostScript Type 1 fonts Symbol and Zapf Dingbats. (These fonts get installed with Acrobat Reader and Acrobat Exchange, so Acrobat never embeds them. Acrobat also won't embed Courier, Courier Bold, Courier Bold-Italic, Courier Italic, Helvetica, Helvetica Bold, Helvetica Bold-Italic, Helvetica Italic, Times, Times Bold, Times Bold-Italic, and Times Italic—those fonts get installed automatically with Acrobat Exchange.) By viewing your PDF on a machine that has only these fonts installed, you'll see simulated versions of any fonts you did not embed in your PDF file.

Q When I'm browsing the Web with Netscape Navigator, I often want to check out PDF files I find. But when I click on one, it doesn't launch the Acrobat Reader for me—instead, I get a prompt for saving the PDF file to my hard disk. What's going on?

A You just need to tell Netscape Navigator what to do with those PDF files. Follow these steps to configure the Reader or Exchange as a Netscape "helper application."

1. In Netscape 1.1, select "Preferences..." from the Options menu; then in the "Preferences" dialog box, choose "Helper Applications" from the pop-up menu. In Netscape 2.0, choose "General Preferences..." from the Options menu, then click the "Helpers" tab.
2. Click the "New..." button.
3. In the "Create New Mime Type" dialog box, enter "application" in the "Mime type" field, and enter "pdf" in the "Mime subtype" field. Click "OK."
4. Back in the main helper-applications dialog box, click the "Browse..." button. In the resulting dialog box, navigate to your copy of the Acrobat Reader or Exchange application and click "Open."
5. Back once more in the helper-applications dialog box, type "pdf" in the "Extensions" field, and then select "PDF" from the "File type" pop-up menu.
6. Finally, in the "Action" section of the dialog box, click "Launch Application." Click "OK" to close the dialog box, and then select "Save Options" from the Options menu.

There are comparable instructions for configuring other browsers—including several different varieties of Mosaic—on Adobe's Web site, at http://www.adobe.com/Acrobat/acroweb.html#helper.

Q Sometimes when I send PDFs to people via E-mail, the recipients say they can't open them. What's the best way to set up my PDFs for transmission via E-mail?

A There are several reasons, both mundane and not-so-mundane, why you might be having these PDF problems. But before we get into the not-so-mundane reasons, one reminder: When someone reports an unreadable PDF, be sure to ask them if they've tried to open it by launching Acrobat Reader or Exchange, selecting "Open..." from the

File menu, navigating to the PDF, choosing the "Show All File Types" option if necessary, selecting the PDF, and clicking "OK." Chances are they only tried double-clicking on the PDF to open it, and if that PDF was created on a platform other than the one they're using, there's a host of reasons why a double-click might not open the PDF. For instance, if you're using a Macintosh and named your PDF "annual report," someone on a PC or UNIX machine wouldn't be able to open it by double-clicking on it. Most DOS-based, Windows-based, and UNIX-based systems look to a file's three-digit extension to determine what application to launch, and if the PDF is named with anything but a ".pdf" extension, the system won't know how to open it.

If your colleague can't open the PDF using "Open," it may have been damaged in the transfer process. If, when you try to open it, you receive a message saying "File does not begin with %PDF," that's usually the case. The following suggestions will help you prevent this problem. They will also help you make the most easily readable, portable PDFs for transmission to other computers.

Make your files binary. Many people think that the ASCII format is more portable (i.e., universally understood) than the binary format. Actually, ASCII files are more susceptible to damage in transit than their binary counterparts, because some electronic mail systems can't preserve every ASCII character, which causes changes within the PDF code (see "More about the Internet" below). These changes may cause the PDF to appear unreadable. Specifying binary format includes binary information in the file's header, which will often allow it to be encoded during transfers, making the translation process smoother.

Binary is the default in both Acrobat Distiller and PDFWriter. Although there's no visual difference between binary and ASCII PDF files, binary ones are around 20 percent smaller—another benefit of using the binary format.

Smaller is better. It's a good idea to keep your electronically transmitted files as small as possible—your frantic customer with a deadline and your aunt in Hoboken with the 9,600- bps modem will thank you for it. Both the PDFWriter and the Distiller give you compression options for text and graphics—don't be afraid to get in there and bump them up! Concentrate primarily on graphics, which usually occupy far more room in PDF files than fonts, for instance, do.

By default, Distiller downsamples all color and grayscale images to 72 dpi. This makes for manageable file sizes and an attractive, readable graphic for most computer screens. You can set the resolutions differently for grayscale, color, and monochrome images, all within one distillation. If you want to downsample some of your images more than others, you might consider creating separate PDFs with the different graphics settings before combining the distilled pages using Exchange.

More about the Internet. A few more words about transferring PDFs over the Internet. While most E-mail systems are proprietary and therefore standardized to some degree, the Internet isn't—information going over the Internet has to pass through a complex, nonstandardized system or series of systems, which may not transfer your data in a consistent, predictable manner. If you repeatedly have problems transferring a particular file, you can try sending the same file to another recipient to help you determine where the trouble might be. You might also have some success encoding your PDF before you send it (as long as your recipients have software that'll enable them to unencode it later)—BinHex or UUencode, for example, might work.

Acrobat Reader®

Feature Techniques

WINDOWS

Modifying Netscape for Windows to Recognize Acrobat Reader or Acrobat Exchange

ISSUE

When you select a Portable Document Format (PDF) file link on an Internet server, Netscape Navigator 2.02 displays a prompt for downloading the PDF file instead of launching Acrobat Reader 2.0x or earlier or Acrobat Exchange 2.0 or earlier to display the PDF file.

SOLUTION

Configure Navigator 2.02 to use Acrobat Reader or Acrobat Exchange as a helper application:

1. In Navigator 2.02, choose Options > General Preferences.
2. In the Preferences dialog box, click the Helpers tab.
3. Click the Create New Type button.
4. In the Configure New Mime Type dialog box, type "application" in the Mime Type text box, type "pdf" in the

Mime SubType text box, then click OK.
5. In the Preferences dialog box, click the Browse button.
6. In the Source dialog box, navigate to the Acroread or Acroexch directory, select the Acroread.exe or Acroexch.exe file, then click Open.
7. In the Preferences dialog box, type "pdf" in the File Extensions text box.
8. Select the Launch the Application option, then click OK to close the Preferences dialog box.
10. Choose Options > Save Options.

ADDITIONAL INFORMATION

When you select a PDF file link on an Internet server, Navigator 2.02 downloads the PDF file to the Netscape Temp folder. When you configure Navigator to use Acrobat Reader 2.0x or Acrobat Exchange 2.0 as a helper application, Navigator automatically launches Acrobat Reader or Acrobat Exchange to open and display the PDF file it downloaded. After Acrobat Exchange opens the PDF file, you can save the file to your hard disk or other volume by choosing File > Save As.

MAC OS

Modifying Netscape for Macintosh to Recognize Acrobat Reader or Acrobat Exchange

ISSUE

When you select a Portable Document Format (PDF) file link on an Internet server, Netscape 2.02 or earlier displays a prompt for downloading the PDF file instead of launching Acrobat Reader 2.x or earlier or Acrobat Exchange 2.x or earlier to display the PDF file.

SOLUTION

Configure Netscape to use Acrobat Reader or Acrobat Exchange as a helper application:
1. In Netscape, choose Options > General Preferences.
2. In the Preferences: General dialog box, select the Helpers tab.
3. Click the New button.
4. In the New Mime Type dialog box, type "application" in the Mime Type text box, type "pdf" in the Mime Subtype text box, then click OK.
5. In the Preferences: General dialog box, click Browse.
6. Select the Acrobat Reader or Acrobat Exchange application located on your hard disk, then click Open.

MICRO TIP MAC OS / WINDOWS

Ever wish you could scroll around a page, a little at a time, in one of the Acrobat viewers (Exchange or Reader) without using the mouse? You can—just hold down your Shift key while you press the arrow keys on your keyboard.

7. In the Preferences: General dialog box, type "pdf" in the Extensions text box.
8. Select PDF from the File Type pop-up menu.
9. Select the Launch Application option, then click OK to close the Preferences: General dialog box.
10. Choose Options > Save Options.

ADDITIONAL INFORMATION

When you select a PDF file link on an Internet server, Navigator 2.02 downloads the PDF file to the Netscape Temp folder. When you configure Navigator to use Acrobat Reader 2.x or Acrobat Exchange 2.x as a helper application, Navigator automatically launches Acrobat Reader or Acrobat Exchange to open and display the PDF file it downloaded. After Acrobat Exchange opens the PDF file, you can save the file to your hard disk or other volume by choosing File > Save As.

Modifying Mosaic for Macintosh to Recognize Acrobat Reader or Acrobat Exchange

ISSUE

When you select a Portable Document Format (PDF) file link on an Internet server, NCSA Mosaic 2.0 displays a prompt for downloading the PDF file instead of launching Acrobat Reader 2.x or earlier or Acrobat Exchange 2.x or earlier to display the PDF file.

SOLUTION

Configure Mosaic to use Acrobat Reader or Acrobat Exchange as a helper application:
1. In Mosaic, choose Preferences > Options.
2. In the Preferences dialog box, click Apps.
3. Click Helper applications.
4. In the Helper Configuration dialog box, click Add Document Type.
5. In the Type in the MIME Name of the New Document Type text box in the New Document type dialog box, type "application/pdf" and click OK.
6. In the Helper Configuration dialog box, select Application/pdf from the Document Type > Application list and click Set Application.
7. In the Set application dialog box, locate and select the Acrobat Reader or Acrobat Exchange application icon and click Open.
8. In the Pick a File Type dialog, select the PDF icon then click the Launch Automatically option and click OK. Mosaic will display the warning "Changes will not take effect until you restart Mosaic."
9. In the Helper Configuration dialog, click Add Extension.
10. In the Add Extension dialog box, type "PDF" in the Extension text box, choose Application/pdf from the Mime type menu, then click OK.
11. Click OK in the Helper Configuration dialog box.
12. Click Done in the Preferences dialog box.
13. Restart Mosaic.

ADDITIONAL INFORMATION

When you select a PDF file link on an Internet server, Mosaic downloads the PDF file to the Mosaic Temp folder. When Mosaic is configured to use Acrobat Reader 2.x or Acrobat Exchange 2.x as a helper application, after downloading a PDF file, Mosaic automatically launches Acrobat Reader or Acrobat Exchange to display the downloaded PDF file. Once the PDF file is opened in Acrobat Exchange, it can be saved to the local hard drive by selecting File > Save As.

Creating Acrobat Reader Installers Using Acrobat Search for CD-ROMs

Adobe Acrobat Search for CD-ROMs includes a US English version of Adobe Acrobat Reader 2.1 and the Acrobat Reader installer setup utility for Windows and Macintosh. The Reader installer setup utility enables you to create Windows and Macintosh Acrobat Reader installers for inclusion on your CD-ROM. The Reader installer automatically includes your unique Acrobat Reader serial number so others will not need to enter the serial number when they install Reader from your CD-ROM. You may use the setup utilities to customize your Reader installers by adding additional plug-ins (e.g., Acrobat Search, Movie).

CREATING A CUSTOM READER INSTALLER USING THE ACROBAT READER SETUP UTILITY FOR YOUR PLATFORM

To create a custom Reader installer for your platform:

1. Launch the installer setup utility Setup.mac (Macintosh), or SETUP.EXE (Windows). The Setup.mac file is located in the Mac folder in the Search folder in the Acrobat folder. The SETUP.EXE file is located in the acrobat\search\win folder.
2. When prompted, enter your Acrobat Reader serial number in the Setup Utility dialog box.
3. Enter the name of the target folder for the Acrobat Reader installer files.
4. Select plug-ins to include with your CD-ROM's Reader installer.
5. Click install.

CREATING A WINDOWS INSTALLER ON A MACINTOSH

You cannot create a Windows installer on a Macintosh using the installer setup utility. To create a Windows installer on a Macintosh, customize the premade Windows installer located in the example\install folder on the Search CD-ROM.

Customizing the premade Windows installer incorporates your unique serial number in the installer so others do not need to enter the serial number when they install the Reader from your CD-ROM.

It is not necessary to customize the premade Windows installer when you have made a Windows installer using Windows and are transferring the files over a network or some other portable medium.

To customize the Windows installer using a Macintosh:

1. Create a CD-ROM staging area. The staging area is a folder that contains all the files you will burn on your CD-ROM.
2. Copy all folders and files from the example\install\win folder to your staging area.
3. Open the ACROINST.___ file, located in the disk1 folder you copied to your staging area, in an application that can save in a text only format (e.g., Simple Text).
4. Locate the following section:

```
; SerNo=
; Specify the serial number for installation.
; Default: blank
;
SerNo=
```

5. Add your Acrobat Reader serial number to the end of the SerNo= line. For example:

```
; SerNo=
; Specify the serial number for installation.
; Default: blank
;
SerNo=SEW210R0000000-000
```

NOTE: Do not include any spaces when entering the serial number.

6. Save the file and rename it "ACROINST.INI."

CREATING A MACINTOSH READER INSTALLER IN WINDOWS

Because of the differences in file systems between Windows and Macintosh operating environments, it may not be possible to create a Macintosh Reader installer from Windows. The Macintosh file system requires resource forks to identify files. When you create the CD-ROM from a Windows based computer, the CD-ROM burning software may strip out or corrupt the resource fork information, making the files unreadable by the Macintosh.

Creative Digital Research and Corel Corporation each claim to have CD-ROM burning applications that successfully burn Macintosh files onto CD-ROM from Windows. For more information on these applications, contact the respective sofware manufacturer. (See Further Reading for contact information.)

To create the Macintosh Reader installer:

Create the Macintosh Reader installer using Search for CD-ROMs from a Macintosh, and burn your CD-ROM from a Macintosh.

OR: If you're unable to burn a CD-ROM from a Macintosh, create the Reader installer using Search for CD-ROMs for Macintosh, encrypt the installer folder using BinHex, copy it to a Windows-based computer, then burn the CD-ROM.

1. Create the Reader installer using Macintosh Search for CD-ROMs.
2. Use BinHex to encrypt the Reader installer folder.
3. Copy the encrypted file to a Windows-based computer.
4. Burn your CD-ROM.

NOTE: Use BinHex to decrypt the installer file on the CD-ROM before installing Reader.

OR: Use a CD-ROM burning application that can successfully burn multiplatform CD-ROMs. (See Further Reading for contact information.)

NOTE: Adobe Systems has not tested these products with Acrobat Search for CD-ROMs. Adobe Systems does not endorse or recommend the use of these products, and will not provide technical support for these products.

Unexpected Results

MAC OS / WINDOWS

Q Why can't I open the PDF I created with Acrobat 3.0 in Reader 2.1?

A There have been several additions to the PDF format with Acrobat 3.0, such as forms, a wider variety of compression schemes, and the ability to subset both TrueType and Type 1 fonts. Therefore, both the PDFWriter and the Distiller have the option to create PDFs that are compatible only with version 3.0 of Acrobat viewers, or PDFs that are compatible with both version 2.1 and 3.0 viewers. PDFs that are restricted to version 3.0 of the viewers will take advantage of the new features in the PDF format.

If you're not sure what version of the Acrobat Reader your PDFs will be viewed in, you can play it safe by making your PDFs compatible with version 2.1 and higher. Select "Job Options…" from the Distiller menu, and on the "General" tab, select "Acrobat 2.1" from the Compatibility pop-up menu in the "File Settings" area. (You'll find the "Compatibility" setting for the PDFWriter in the compression-settings area.) Be aware, however, that even if you save your files using 2.1 compatibility, your 2.1 users won't be able to see or use any 3.0-specific features; they'll see question marks in the PDF where a form field or other new feature was used. Tell them that this is an excellent reason to download Acrobat Reader 3.0 free of charge from Adobe's Web site (www.adobe.com/prodindex/acrobat/readstep.html). Then you can use the new features with the assurance that everyone who needs to will be able to open and use your files.

WINDOWS

Acrobat Reader Doesn't Launch When You Click on a PDF in Mosaic

ISSUE

When you click on a PDF file link in Mosaic, neither Adobe Acrobat Reader or Acrobat Exchange launch. Instead, Mosaic prompts you to download the PDF file.

SOLUTION

Configure the mosaic.ini file to automatically launch Acrobat Reader or Acrobat Exchange when you click on a PDF file:

1. Make a backup copy of the mosaic.ini file.
2. Open the original mosaic.ini in a text editor that can save in text-only format (e.g., Windows Write, NotePad).
3. To force Mosaic to launch Acrobat Reader when you click on a PDF file, add the following two lines to the [VIEWERS] section:

```
TYPE#="application/pdf"
application/pdf="c:\acroread\acroread.exe %ls"
```

OR: To force Mosaic to launch Acrobat Exchange when you click on a PDF file, add the following two lines to the [VIEWERS] section:

```
TYPE#="application/pdf"
application/pdf="c:\acroexch\acroexch.exe %ls"
```

For example:

```
[VIEWERS]
TYPE0="audio/wav"
TYPE1="image/gif"
TYPE2="application/pdf"
application/pdf="c:\acroread\acroread.exe %ls"
application/x-rtf="write %ls"
```

4. Add the following line to the [SUFFIXES] section:

```
application/pdf=.pdf
```

5. Save the mosaic.ini in text-only format, then restart Mosaic.

ADDITIONAL INFORMATION

When you select a PDF file link on an Internet server, Mosaic downloads the PDF file to the Mosaic Temp folder. When Mosaic is configured to use Acrobat Reader 2.x or Acrobat Exchange 2.x as a helper application, Mosaic then automatically launches Acrobat Reader or Acrobat Exchange to display the downloaded PDF file. Once the PDF file is opened in Acrobat Exchange, you can save it to the local hard disk by choosing File > Save As.

Printing Problems

WINDOWS

Memory Error When Printing to PostScript Printer from Acrobat 2.1

ISSUE

The PostScript error "VMError" or other memory error occurs when you print from Adobe Acrobat 2.1 to a PostScript printer.

SOLUTIONS

Use only one substitution font in Acrobat to increase available printer memory:

1. Choose Edit > Preferences > General.
2. Select Sans Only or Serif Only from the Font Substitution pop-up menu.
3. Click OK.

OR: Print to a PostScript printer with more available memory (RAM).
OR: Add more RAM to your printer.
OR: When printing to a LaserWriter printer, acquire the motherboard upgrade to update your printer's available memory (RAM). See Additional Information for printers requiring updates.

ADDITIONAL INFORMATION
A PostScript error occurs when your printer does not have enough memory available to print a file. Using only one substitution font in Acrobat Exchange makes more memory available at the printer because Acrobat only downloads one substitution font, not two, to the printer's memory when printing.

The following LaserWriter printers generally include 4 MB or less memory, and may require a motherboard upgrade before you can add addition RAM to them: LaserWriter, LaserWriter Plus, LaserWriter NT, LaserWriter II NT, and LaserWriter NTX. Contact your Apple dealer for information on upgrading your printer.

Acrobat 2.1 Prints Slower to PCL Printers From Windows 95 Than From Windows 3.1

Adobe Acrobat 2.1 Exchange and Reader print much slower to PCL printers from Windows 95 then from Windows 3.1.

The slower print times are the result of a conflict between Windows 95 and ATM 3.01 and between Windows 95 and the Embedded ATM, which is optional with Reader 2.1 for Windows.

ISSUE
Some text in a Portable Document Format (PDF) file does not print from Adobe Acrobat Reader 2.x or Acrobat Exchange 2.x to the Apple Personal LaserWriter NT PostScript printer.

SYMPTOM
The text that doesn't print is formatted with a font not available on the system and is being substituted with a multiple master font (i.e., Adobe San Serif or Adobe Serif) by Acrobat Reader or Acrobat Exchange.

SOLUTIONS
Print to a PostScript printer that supports multiple master fonts (e.g., any level 2 PostScript printer, or a level 1 PostScript printer other than the Apple Personal LaserWriter NT).
OR: Upgrade the Apple Personal LaserWriter NT PostScript printer to a Personal LaserWriter NTR Postscript printer.

ADDITIONAL INFORMATION
Adobe Acrobat Reader 2.1 automatically substitutes missing fonts in a PDF file with the AdobeSanXMM and AdobeSerifMM multiple master fonts. The PostScript code used in multiple master fonts is not compatible with the Apple Personal LaserWriter NT's version of level 1 PostScript. When you print a PDF file containing multiple master fonts, use a level 2 PostScript printer (e.g., Apple LaserWriter Pro 630) or a level 1 PostScript printer other than the Apple Personal LaserWriter NT (e.g., Apple LaserWriter II NTX), or upgrade your Apple Personal LaserWriter NT printer to the Personal LaserWriter NTR. For more information on upgrading your printer, contact your printer manufacturer.

To determine whether Acrobat Exchange or Reader is substituting multiple master fonts for fonts used in a PDF file, open the PDF file and choose File > Document Info > Fonts.

MAC OS

Acrobat Reader 2.0.1 Bypasses Background Printing

ISSUE
When you print a PDF file from Acrobat Reader 2.0.1 with background printing on, the computer is unavailable for use until the PDF file has printed.

SYMPTOMS
Acrobat is using a private copy of ATM (i.e., ATM is installed in the Fonts folder located in the same folder as Acrobat Reader and not in the Control Panels folder in the System Folder). QuickDraw GX is not enabled.

SOLUTION
Move ATM from the Fonts folder in the Acrobat Reader application folder into the Control Panels folder in the System Folder, restart the computer and print again.

ADDITIONAL INFORMATION
When using a private copy of ATM, Acrobat Reader 2.0.1 bypasses background printing, making the computer unavailable for use until the PDF file has printed. Acrobat Reader disables background printing because Print Monitor has no way to request font information from the private version of ATM. Without the necessary font information, Print Monitor cannot print the PDF correctly.

Installation Issues

MAC OS / WINDOWS

Q I'm trying to install the Acrobat Reader in Windows and keep getting an error message with the number 0003 in it. Why won't it install?

A You're probably having this problem because your TEMP directory is invalid or the disk it's on is full, making it impossible for the Acrobat Reader to store files in this directory during installation.

When you run the installer application for Acrobat Reader for Windows (ACROREAD.EXE), it makes a copy of the ACROREAD.EXE file in your TEMP directory, which is usually defined in the AUTOEXEC.BAT file's "SET TEMP=" line. When the directory listed in that line doesn't really exist, or you don't have write access to that directory, or that directory's drive doesn't have enough free space, the Acrobat Reader installation fails and returns the error "Error *** 0003 ***."

To prevent this, there are a few things you should do. First, ensure there is at least 4–8 MB of free disk space on the hard drive on which you're installing Acrobat Reader, as well as the hard drive that contains your TEMP directory.

Next, check to see that the "SET TEMP=" line in your AUTOEXEC.BAT file points to a directory that actually exists. If it points to an invalid directory, make a backup copy of your AUTOEXEC.BAT file, then edit the line to point to a different directory—any one will do, as long as that directory really exists, isn't your root directory, and is on a hard drive that you have write access to and has at least 4–8 MB of free space. Furthermore, we recommend designating a directory that will be used only for TEMP files (for instance, C:\TEMP), not a directory you use to store other items. (If you need to create a new directory for this purpose, you can use the Windows File Manager or DOS commands to do so.) When you're done, save your AUTOEXEC.BAT file in text-only format, restart your computer, and try installing the Acrobat Reader again.

One more note: if you've been operating with an invalid TEMP directory, you probably have a few TEMP files (named with .TMP extensions) cluttering up your hard drive. Unless one of those TEMP files might contain valuable data, which is only likely if you've lost an entire document due to a system crash, you can delete them. To do so, exit Windows completely first (this is extremely important, because you should never delete TEMP files while Windows is running—you might delete one Windows is in the process of using). Then, use DOS commands to delete the files.

WINDOWS

Installing Acrobat Reader and Exchange 2.1 on Diskless Workstations or From Disk Images

NETWORK INSTALL SUPPORT FOR ADOBE ACROBAT READER AND ACROBAT EXCHANGE

Adobe Acrobat Reader and Acrobat Exchange can be installed and run on a shared network server. However, when you run Acrobat Reader or Exchange from a shared network server, these applications respond progressively slower for each successive user and ultimately stop responding. For optimal performance, install Acrobat Reader and Exchange on each user's workstation, or when using diskless workstations, install on the unique server location reserved for each user.

INSTALLING ACROBAT READER ON A DISKLESS WORKSTATION

You can install Acrobat Reader 2.1 on a diskless workstation using Acrobat installation disks, CD-ROM, an online file, or Acrobat disk images on a network server.

Acrobat Reader 2.1 includes a built-in version of Adobe Type Manager (ATM) that does not require access to system files. When ATM 3.0 or earlier is installed on the network, update to ATM 3.01, or disable ATM before installing Acrobat Reader 2.1. When ATM 3.0 or earlier is installed on the network, Acrobat Reader 2.1 uses it instead of Reader's built-in ATM.

To install Acrobat Reader 2.1 on a diskless workstation:

1. Choose File > Run (Windows 3.1) or Start > Run (Windows 95).
2. In the Command Line text box (Windows 3.1x) or Open text box (Windows 95) type the path to the Acroread.exe file (e.g., C:\Acroread\Acroread.exe), or click Browse to locate the file, then click OK.
3. Continue the installation by following the on-screen instructions, then click OK to restart Windows when the message appears confirming a successful installation.

To create Acrobat Reader disk images and install Reader from a network server:

1. On the network server, create a new directory called Acroread.
2. Copy the contents of the Acrobat Reader CD-ROM or the downloaded Acrobat Reader installation file to the Acroread directory on the network server.
3. Choose File > Run (Windows 3.1x) or Start > Run (Windows 95).
4. In the Command Line text box (Windows 3.1x) or Open text box (Windows 95) type the path to the Acroread.exe file on the network (e.g., F:\Apps\Acroread\Acroread.exe), or click Browse and locate the file on the network server, then click OK.
5. Continue the installation by following the on-screen instructions, then click OK to restart Windows when the message appears confirming a successful installation.

INSTALLING ACROBAT EXCHANGE 2.1 ON A DISKLESS WORKSTATION

You can install Acrobat Exchange 2.1 on a diskless workstation using either Acrobat installation disks or Acrobat disk images on a network server.

You can install Acrobat Exchange 2.1 with or without ATM. When you install Acrobat Exchange 2.1 with ATM, make sure you review the Techref.wri file on the ATM disk. The section "Using ATM on a Network" explains how to install ATM on different network servers. When you install ATM over a network, first install the network version of ATM, then install ATM locally on each workstation. You can install ATM locally using either ATM installation disks or ATM disk images on a network server.

To install Acrobat Exchange 2.1 on a diskless workstation:

1. Choose File > Run (Windows 3.1x) or Start > Run (Windows 95).
2. In the Command Line text box type the path to the Setup.exe file (e.g., A:\Setup.exe), then click OK.
3. Do not select the ATM install option.
4. Continue the installation by following the on-screen instructions, then click OK to restart Windows when the message appears confirming a successful installation.

To create Acrobat Exchange 2.1 disk images and install Exchange from a network server:

1. On the network server, either create a new directory for each Acrobat Exchange 2.1 disk, and name the directories Disk1, Disk2, Disk3, and Disk4.
2. Copy the contents of each Acrobat Exchange disk to its corresponding directory on the network server.
3. Choose File > Run (Windows 3.1x) or Start > Run (Windows 95).
4. In the Command Line text box (Windows 3.1x) or Open text box (Windows 95) type the path to the Setup.exe file on the network (e.g., F:\Apps\Acroexch\Disk1\-Setup.exe), or click Browse and locate the file on the network server, then click OK.
5. Do not select the ATM install option.
6. Continue the installation by following the on-screen instructions, then click OK to restart Windows when the message appears confirming a successful installation.

AUTOMATING THE ACROBAT INSTALLATION TO INCLUDE ACROBAT SERIAL NUMBER AND COMPANY NAME

To automatically include the Acrobat serial number and your company name, and disable installation prompts in the network disk images:

1. Open the Install._ file, located on Acrobat Exchange 2.1 Disk 1, in a text editor that can save in text-only format (e.g., Windows Write, Notepad).
2. Follow the instructions outlined in the file.
3. Save the file in text-only format and rename it to In-stall.ini.

Removing Acrobat Reader 2.1 in Windows

Adobe Acrobat Reader 2.1 does not include an uninstall application for Windows 95 or Windows 3.1x. To remove Acrobat Reader, you must delete its components and remove references to the Reader from the Win.ini file manually.

To delete the Acrobat Reader 2.1 components:

1. Remove your personal files from the Acroread directory and its subdirectories.
2. Delete the Acroread directory.
3. Delete the Acroread.ini file from the Windows directory.
4. When running Windows 95, delete the Acrobat Reader shortcut file from the Windows\Start Menu\Programs\-Adobe Acrobat directory.

To remove references to Acrobat Reader from the Win.ini file:

1. Make a backup copy of the Win.ini file, which is located in the Windows directory.
2. Open the original Win.ini file in a text editor that can save in text-only format (e.g., Notepad).
3. In the [Extensions] section, remove the line: PDF=c:\acro16\acro16.exe"^.pdf"
4. In the [Adobe Acrobat] section, remove the line: Install path=c:\Acro_16.
5. Save the Win.ini file in text-only format.

MAC OS

Reinstalling Apple Bitmapped Fonts Replaced During Acrobat Exchange and Acrobat Reader Installation

This technical note explains how the installers for the Apple Macintosh versions of Acrobat Exchange and Acrobat Reader handle fonts during installation, the consequences of this behavior, and how you can optionally reinstall fonts replaced during this process.

HOW DOES THE INSTALLER HANDLE FONTS?

Included with Acrobat Exchange and Acrobat Reader are the latest Adobe bitmapped fonts and PostScript font outlines for Courier, Helvetica, Symbol, Times, and Zapf Dingbats. These are used for on screen display and printing to non PostScript printers. Because different versions of these typefaces cannot coexist without potentially causing problems, the installer removes any currently installed versions of these before installing the Adobe versions.

Each time a full installation is performed, the installer searches the System file, the Extensions folder (System 7.0 and higher), and the Fonts folder (System 7.1 and higher) within the active System Folder on the drive designated as the startup drive. The installer relocates any font files and resources associated with Courier, Helvetica, Symbol, Times, Zapf Dingbats, AdobeSerifMM (used for font substitution), and AdobeSansXMM (also used for font substitution) to a new folder outside of the System Folder. This includes bitmapped fonts, PostScript Type 1 font outlines, and TrueType font outlines. The new folder is named De-installed Fonts followed by a number which is incremented depending on whether another De-installed Fonts folder exists. For example, the first time the installer completes a full installation and finds that it needs to remove fonts, it creates a folder named De-installed Fonts 1 and moves the fonts to this folder. Because the installer does not detect the version of any currently installed Courier, Helvetica, Symbol, Times, and Zapf Dingbats fonts, the installer will relocate and replace these fonts regardless of their origin. Therefore, if a full installation is performed even after a previous Acrobat Exchange or Acrobat Reader installation, fonts will be relocated and replaced. If a previous De-installed Fonts folder exists, a new one will be created with a new number to prevent overwriting the existing one. Finally, the Adobe bitmapped fonts and PostScript font outlines are installed in appropriate locations within the System Folder. You can throw away any De-installed Fonts folders if you choose not to replace the newly installed Adobe fonts with the previous versions you had installed.

Apple and Adobe bitmapped fonts give different results The Adobe versions of the Times and Helvetica bitmapped fonts contain different character kerning information (information about the spacing between characters) from the Apple versions of these fonts. As a result, documents created on a machine with the Apple versions of the Times and Helvetica bitmapped fonts may display and print differently on a machine with the Adobe versions of these bitmapped fonts. This can appear as changes in word wrap ping and even the page count of a document. In most cases, Adobe recommends that users standardize on the Adobe bitmapped fonts because they contain more kerning information than those from Apple.

If you output documents to PDF format, you can be assured that document formatting will not change, regardless of the fonts on the viewing system: all formatting informationincluding kerningis contained within the PDF file. For example, a PDF file created using the Macintosh version of Times will display with the same formatting on another machine that has the Adobe version of Times installed.

REINSTALLING APPLE TIMES & HELVETICA BITMAPPED FONTS

If you have a collection of non PDF files created using the Apple versions of the Times or Helvetica bitmapped fonts, or you want to exchange non PDF files using these fonts with other users, you may want to reinstall the Apple bitmapped fonts. The following instructions describe how to remove the Adobe versions and reinstall the Apple versions.

NOTE: These instructions assume that you have a De-installed Fonts 1 folder on your drive containing Apple versions of Times and Helvetica. If you have thrown away your original De-installed Fonts 1 folder, you will need to reinstall the Apple bitmapped fonts from Apple system software diskettes or CD ROM instead of from a De-installed Fonts folder. If you have multiple De-installed Fonts folders, use De-installed Fonts 1.

To reinstall Apple bitmapped fonts on System 7.1:

1. Quit any open applications.
2. Open the System Folder used to startup your Macintosh.
3. Open the Fonts folder within the System Folder.
4. Drag the files named Times and Helvetica to the Trash.
5. Open the De-installed Fonts 1 folder at the root level of your hard drive.
6. Open the Fonts folder within the De-installed Fonts 1 folder.
7. Open the suitcase file named Times.
8. Drag the following files within this suitcase to the Trash: Times, Times (bold), Times (bold, italic), and Times (italic).
9. Close the Times suitcase.
10. Open the suitcase file named Helvetica.
11. Drag the following files within this suitcase to the trash: Helvetica and Helvetica (bold).
12. Close the Helvetica suitcase.
13. Drag the suitcases named Helvetica and Times from the Fonts folder within the De-installed Fonts 1 folder to the Fonts folder within the System Folder.
14. Drag the De-installed Fonts 1 folder to the Trash.
15. Select Restart from the Special menu to restart your Macintosh. You can empty the Trash after restarting.

To reinstall Apple bitmapped fonts on System 7.0:

1. Quit any open applications.
2. Open the System Folder used to startup your Macintosh.
3. Open the System file within the System Folder.
4. Drag the fonts named Times and Helvetica to the Trash.
5. Close the System file. Close the System Folder.
6. Open the De-installed Fonts 1 folder at the root level of your hard drive.
7. Open the System Fonts suitcase within the De-installed Fonts 1 folder.
8. Select the following fonts from the System Fonts suitcase: Helvetica 9, Helvetica 10, Helvetica 12, Helvetica 14, Helvetica 18, and Helvetica 24.
   NOTE: Do not select fonts without a number in their name such as Helvetica (bold). These are True Type fonts that should not be reinstalled because PostScript Type 1 font outlines remain installed.
9. Drag the selected files to the System Folder icon. Click OK to the message that appears.
10. Select the following fonts from the System Fonts suitcase: Times 9, Times 10, Times 12, Times 14, Times 18, and Times 24.
    NOTE: Again, do not select files without a number in their name.
11. Drag the selected files to the System Folder icon. Click OK to the message that appears.
12. Close the System Fonts suitcase. Close the De-installed Fonts 1 folder.
13. Drag the De-installed Fonts 1 folder to the Trash.
14. Select Restart from the Special menu to restart your Macintosh. You can empty the Trash after restarting.

To reinstall Apple bitmapped fonts on System 6.0.8:

1. Quit any open applications.
2. If you are using MultiFinder, switch to Finder and restart your Macintosh (see your system soft ware documentation for details).
3. Launch Font/DA Mover 3.8 or newer. If you have not installed this application on your hard drive, you can find it on your Apple system software diskettes.
4. Select all occurrences of Helvetica and Times from the scrolling list on the left side of the dialog box. Verify that you have highlighted all 38 items.
5. Click Remove. Click OK to proceed with removing these fonts from your System file.
6. Click the Open button under the scrolling list on the right side of the dialog box.
7. Locate and open your De-installed Fonts 1 folder. Select the file named System Fonts. Click Open.
8. Select all occurrences of Helvetica and Times from the scrolling list on the right side of the dialog box.

9. Click Copy.
10. Click Quit.
11. Drag the De-installed Fonts 1 folder to the Trash.
12. Select Restart from the Special menu to restart your Macintosh.

Unable to Install Reader 2.0 on a Macintosh LC Running System 7.5

ISSUE

When you install Adobe Acrobat Reader 2.0 on a Macintosh LC running System 7.5, the Reader installer returns the error "The Software to be installed requires a 68020 CPU, which this system does not have."

SOLUTIONS

Update to Acrobat Reader 2.1 or later.

OR: Temporarily install a previous version of system 7 (e.g., System 7.0, 7.1.x) before installing Acrobat Reader 2.0. Once Acrobat Reader 2.0 is installed, reinstall System 7.5. For instructions, see Additional Information.

OR: When Acrobat Reader 2.0 is installed on another Macintosh on the same network, copy the Acrobat Reader 2.0 components to the Macintosh LC running System 7.5.

ADDITIONAL INFORMATION

The Acrobat Reader 2.0 Installer is not compatible with System 7.5 running on a Macintosh LC. The Acrobat Reader 2.0 application is compatible with System 7.5, and Acrobat Reader 2.0 runs as expected on the Macintosh LC running System 7.5 if installed while running System 7.0 or 7.1.x.

To temporarily install System 7.0 or 7.1.x, then switch back to System 7.5 for installing Acrobat Reader:

1. Restart the Macintosh using System 7.0 or 7.1.x's Disk Tools disk as the startup disk.
2. In the System Folder located on the hard disk, locate the system file named "Finder," and drag the "Finder" file onto the desktop.
3. Rename the original System Folder on the hard drive (e.g., "System 7.5").
4. Copy the System Folder located on the Disk Tools disk onto the hard drive.
5. Restart the Macintosh, which will restart using the System Folder copied from the Disk Tools disk.
6. Install Acrobat Reader 2.0. When installation is complete, the Installer will restart the Macintosh.
7. After the Macintosh has restarted, open the System Folder, and copy the "ATM Font Database" file and into the original System Folder (e.g., "System 7.5").
8. Copy the contents of "Fonts" folder located in the System Folder into the "Fonts" folder located in the original System Folder (e.g., "System 7.5").
9. Move the "Finder" file, located on the desktop, back into the original System Folder (e.g., "System 7.5").
10. Restart the computer, which will restart using the hard drive's original System Folder that contains System 7.5.
11. After the Macintosh has restarted, delete the copied System Folder and rename the hard drive's original System Folder (e.g., "System 7.5") back to "System Folder."

Acrobat Exchange®

Feature Techniques

MAC OS / WINDOWS / UNIX

Using the AutoIndex Plug-in with Acrobat Exchange or Acrobat Search for CD-ROMs

The AutoIndex Plug-in for Adobe Acrobat Exchange 2.x and Acrobat Search for CD-ROMs associates an index (*.pdx file) with a PDF file so that the index is automatically added to the index search list when you open the PDF file. The index is removed from the index search list when the you exit Exchange or the Search for CD-ROMs Reader.

INSTALLING THE AUTOINDEX PLUG-IN

To install the AutoIndex Plug-in, copy the Autoindx.api file (Windows) or autoindx file (Macintosh) into the plug-ins folder inside the Acrobat Exchange or Acrobat folder. The AutoIndex Plug-in is located on the Search for CD-ROMs CD and on Adobe's World Wide Web site. For more information, see Further Reading.

NOTE: "Acrobat Search" must be selected when creating the Search for CD-ROMs Reader installer for the AutoIndex Plug-in to be installed with the Reader.

ASSOCIATING AN INDEX WITH A PDF FILE

To associate an index with a particular PDF file:

1. Open the PDF file to which you want the index to be associated.

TIP MAC OS / WINDOWS

Plugging in more power

The Acrobat family of products—like much of the Adobe product line—features Plug-in technology that allows applications to be enhanced and extended in a variety of ways. There are currently a number of free Plug-ins available for Acrobat, and the best way to get hold of them is via Adobe's Web site. Here's a rundown of the ones that were available at press time. Point your browser to http://www.adobe. com/Acrobat/Plug-Ins/ for the latest lineup. (note: Some of these Plug-ins aren't supported by Adobe Technical Support; they're marked in the list below with asterisks.)

WebLink Plug-in: Allows Acrobat Exchange users to embed links to World-Wide Web URLs within PDF documents, which either Exchange or the Reader can read.

AutoClose Plug-in: Closes the least recently used PDF file before Acrobat's limit of 10 open documents is reached.

SuperPrefs Plug-in:* Adds a "Super Preferences" dialog box to Exchange that, among other things, allows you to customize the way PDF documents will open and creates a "hot list" menu item for quick access to as many as 50 PDF files.

SuperCrop Plug-in:* Adds a cropping tool to Exchange's toolbar, which makes it easier to eliminate unwanted white space from PDF files.

AutoIndex Plug-in: Allows you to attach an index to a PDF document so that when the PDF is opened, a search index is automatically added to the user's search list.

OLE Server Plug-in: Allows Exchange and the Reader to act as OLE servers when PDF files are embedded into other OLE-enabled applications. For example, if a PDF file is embedded in a Word document, double-clicking on its icon launches the Acrobat viewer and displays the PDF.

Monitor Setup Plug-in (Mac only):* Works with ColorSync, Apple's system-level color management system, to help display images in PDF files as accurately as possible on your monitor.

EPS Links:* Not a Plug-in, but a recipe and set of example files for how to create EPS hypertext link buttons that—when placed in a page-layout application and then distilled—become hypertext links.

PDF Type Utility (Mac only):* A Macintosh applet that lets you set the "type" of a file as PDF, so it's recognized by the Mac versions of Exchange and the Reader (especially useful for working with PDF files produced or edited by Windows or UNIX versions of Acrobat).

2. Choose File > Document Info > Index.
   NOTE: Index only appears on the Document info pop-up menu when the AutoIndex Plug-in is installed.
3. Enter the path to the index (*.pdx file) in the AutoIndex dialog box (e.g., c:\Myindex\My.pdx). Or, click on Browse to navigate to the index file. Then click OK to close the AutoIndex dialog box.
4. Save the PDF file.

MAC OS / WINDOWS

Q I have a long PDF file with a lot of links set up in it, but one of the pages contains an error. I know I can use Exchange to swap in a new page, but will I have to recreate all those links?

A Fortunately, no. When you replace a PDF page containing links with a new page, all the links remain intact and in their exact same locations. So if correcting the error won't cause any linked items to move around or off that page, all you need to do is edit the page in your original authoring application, and then make it into a one-page PDF file (to ensure your final document looks consistent, be sure to embed any fonts in your one-page PDF that you embedded in the full-length file). Use Exchange to open the PDF file that contains the error, and choose "Replace..." from the Pages submenu of the Edit menu.

If nothing moved at all on the edited page, you're done. If some items with links associated with them did move around on the page, choose the link tool from the button bar, click on any link, and drag it to its new location.

Q When I copy text in Exchange or the Reader and then paste it into another application, it often comes in with formatting I don't want. What makes this happen? Is there any way to control it?

A Yes, you can control this (at least to some degree)—all you need is a good understanding of how text and its formatting get transferred over the Clipboard. When you cut or copy text to the Clipboard from an application that supports text formatting, that application "posts" the information to the Clipboard in one or more formats, such as:

- The application's native format, which other applications generally can't read;
- RTF (Rich Text Format), an interchange format that supports most text-formatting attributes; and
- ASCII (text-only) format, which does not support any text-formatting attributes.

Then, when you paste that text into another application, that application has to decide which format it'll use. By default, most applications will paste the text in the richest format that it supports—and usually, that's RTF.

Like many applications, the Acrobat viewers (that is, Exchange and the Reader) copy text to the Clipboard in ASCII and RTF. If you paste that text into an application that supports the RTF format, it'll usually paste it as RTF, so the text's formatting should look as it did in Exchange or the Reader. But how well the text pastes into another application can vary depending on how that application interprets RTF and what fonts you have installed on your system. If the fonts a PDF file uses aren't embedded in it, and the system on which you view that PDF also doesn't have those fonts installed, the Acrobat viewer creates substitute fonts, which it uses to display and print the document. When you copy text with simulated fonts to the Clipboard, Acrobat substitutes Helvetica (which is available on virtually all systems)—and that's what you get when you paste the text as RTF into another application.

Sometimes, when you're copying text out of Acrobat Exchange or the Reader, you might not want to paste it elsewhere with any formatting applied. Fortunately, there's an easy way to do this. When you're ready to paste the text into an application, look under that application's Edit menu for a "Paste Special…" command, and if there is one, select it. In the "Paste Special" dialog box, your application should list all the formats in which the Clipboard's contents can be pasted. To paste the text without formatting, select the text-only option (which might be listed as "Unformatted Text" or something similar) and click "OK."

No matter what format you use to paste, you'll probably get a hard return at the end of every line. For long passages, the easiest way to strip these out is to use a search-and-replace routine to swap in spaces for those hard returns.

Q How can I link my PDF to other PDFs on the World-Wide Web?

A By using Acrobat's Weblink Plug-in. Creating a link to a PDF on the Web is hardly different from creating a link from one PDF to another, or from a PDF to another type of file. The difference is that, unlike a link you create by choosing "Open file" or "Go to view," a Web link requires you to type in the Uniform Resource Locator (URL) as the destination. The link function then uses your Web browser to locate the URL address and download the file to your system for viewing, rather than using your system's built-in file structure to find the file.

To create Web links, you'll need to first configure Acrobat Exchange version 2.1 to connect with your Web browser. You'll also need Netscape Navigator version 1.1 or later or Spyglass Mosaic version 2.0.

To configure your Web viewer, choose "Weblink…" from the Preferences submenu of the Edit menu. Click "Select…" to locate your browser application on your hard disk. Select the browser, then click "Open," then click "OK" to close the "Weblink Preferences" dialog box.

To make sure your browser is compatible with and correctly connected to Acrobat Exchange (or to Acrobat Reader, for later viewing), just click on the web-tool button on the Acrobat toolbar. If your browser launches automatically, you're set. If you get an error message about compatibility, replace your current browser with the latest version of a compatible one.

To use the Weblink Plug-in:

1. In an Exchange document, click on the link button or choose "Link" from the Tools menu.
2. Select the area you'd like to associate your link with by clicking and dragging the link tool (+) in your PDF.
3. From the resulting "Create Link" dialog box, choose "World Wide Web Link" from the "Type:" drop-down menu in the "Action" section.
4. Click on "Edit URL…" and enter your PDF's address (for example, http://www.usps.gov/pdf/pub 417b.pdf).
5. Click "OK," then click "Set Link."

You've now successfully set up a link to a URL address. When you click on the hot area, Acrobat will engage your browser and find the PDF at that location. Remember that if the URL address is wrong, or has changed, the link will not function.

NOTE: If you plan to create many Web links to files on the same Web server, you can save time by setting a base URL. Choose "Base URL…" from the "Document Info" drop-down menu on the File menu. Here, you can provide a URL address prefix that will be added to every address entered into the "Create Link" dialog box. For instance, if you type in a base URL of http://www.usps.gov/pdf/, that will be the base URL for that document. Then, whenever you create a Web link in that document, you just enter the remainder of the address. In this example, you need only type *pub-417b.pdf*.

Q *(3.0 only)* **I want to make several edits to text in my PDF file. I've heard that I can do this in version 3.0, but I'm not sure how.**

A You do it by using a Plug-In called TouchUp, which is included with Acrobat Exchange 3.0. You can also use the TouchUp Plug-in to change the appearance of the text, by changing the font used, point size, color, and alignment of selected text.

TouchUp does not allow you to add text where no text previously existed; it allows editing or extending the amount of existing text (one line at a time). Also, be aware that you cannot edit text that's been formatted with either embedded fonts or embedded font subsets.

Here's an overview of text attributes you can modify using the TouchUp Plug-in.

ADDING AND DELETING TEXT.

Open the PDF file you want to edit. From the menu bar, select the TouchUp tool. Move the pointer down onto the PDF file; the pointer turns into an I-beam, like the cursor in a word processor. You can select text with the I-beam or by clicking an insertion point in a text line. To add text, click an insertion point in the text line and type in a few words. The text box will expand to accommodate added text, or shrink if text is deleted from the PDF file. Remember, however, that there is no automatic text wrap; if you enter too much text, it will run off the page.

CHANGING THE FORMATTING OF A TEXT LINE.
With the Touch-Up tool selected, click on a text line, and then drag the I-beam across one character or the entire line until all the desired text is selected (remember that you're limited to one line). Then go to the Edit menu and select "Text Attributes...." The text-attributes dialog box appears with the default tab, "Font," selected. Here, in the "Font" section, you can change the typeface, point size, and color (including outline color) of the selected text. The menus for these choices are simple and fairly self-explanatory; make your changes, and then press Enter. There are several predefined colors for both the body and the outline of text characters, but you can also choose "other," at which point the system color picker or palette will appear, and you can choose or create another color for your text.

CHANGING THE SPACING OF A TEXT LINE.
Still in the text-attributes dialog box, you can click on the "Character" tab to adjust the horizontal scale of a line (in percentage values), the offset of the text from the baseline (in points), and the letter and word spacing (in em/1,000 units). (An em is a measurement unit equal to the point size of given text.)

To increase or decrease the size of a line, enter a value in the scaling text box, and then press Enter.

By default, text will sit directly on its baseline. Use the baseline text box (the bottom left option in the "Character" section) to shift the text up or down from the original baseline by entering the desired point-shift value (in hundredth-of-a-point increments). To shift the text up, enter a positive value; to shift the text down, enter a negative value. To return the text to the original baseline, type in the value 0, and press Enter again.

There are two spacing dialog boxes on the right side of the "Character" section. You can use these to adjust the spacing of a selected text line in hundredths of an em. To change the spacing between all letters of selected text, enter a value in the letter-spacing text box and press Enter. To change the spacing between words uniformly, enter a value in the word-spacing text box and press Enter. A positive value spreads the text apart; a negative value brings the text characters closer together.

ADJUSTING THE ALIGNMENT OF A TEXT LINE.
Click on the "Line" tab to adjust the flow of your text. With your text selected, click on one of the four alignment buttons. The line markers surrounding the text block change position. (If you do not see these line markers, go to the Edit menu and select "Show Line Markers.") With the center-alignment icon selected, new text entered expands in either direction from the insertion point. With the left-alignment icon selected, the new text will be added to the left of the insertion point. With the right-alignment icon selected, new text will be added to the right of the insertion point. With the justi-fication-alignment icon selected, new text will be added to the text block from the insertion point, and the text block will not expand. This may cause text to overlap. If the text begins to overlap, you can select any of the four arrows surrounding the text block and stretch the text line out until the text no longer overlaps.

Use the right- and left-offset margin boxes to shift the entire text line toward or away from the left or right edge of the PDF page (a margin of "0" puts your text at the very edge of the page). To move the selected text line away from either margin, enter a positive value in the appropriate offset margin box and press Enter. Please note that you must have selected the left-alignment icon when you enter a value in the left-offset margin box, and the right-alignment icon when you use the right-offset margin box.

You can also click and drag on the line markers that appear around selected text on the page to move the text to the left or to the right. Click on the justification-alignment icon to stretch or shrink the text line from either the left or right side. The text will justify itself to accommodate the new size of the stretched or shrunken text box.

In short (well, not very), TouchUp's basic editing capabilities will keep you from going back to the drawing board for simple edits—for instance, if you need to fix a misspelled word or adjust punctuation. If you need to make substantial changes to your copy, you'll probably find it easier to go back to the original document. However, you'll find TouchUp handy when you don't have the original file or for making quick or last-minute changes.

Q I've tried to use the Form feature to create a button that will take me from the current page to another page in a PDF, but I've been unable to find a way to do this. Is it possible?

A Yes, but maybe not the way you'd think. Currently, you can't select a "Go to page" command that's directly associated with the Form feature, because field-action types supported in form fields are limited to first-level menu items. (A first-level menu item is one that is not followed by an ellipsis (...) and doesn't open a dialog box.) The menu item to go to another page is not a first-level menu item.

TIP MAC OS / WINDOWS

Acrobat Dictionary Editing

To add or subtract entries from a dictionary, choose "Edit Custom Dictionary..." from the File menu in Capture. Enter any letter of the alphabet, and the custom words beginning with that letter will appear in the list on the right side of the window, below the word "Contents." To remove a word, highlight it in the list, and press "Remove." To add a word, clear the window above the "Add" button, type in the word, then press "Add." The word will be added to the list on your right.

TIP MAC OS / WINDOWS

Every which way

Since most document-creation programs don't support multiple orientations in one document, it's easy to forget that PDF files do. You can combine pages from any number of documents (in any number of orientations) within one PDF, and the pages will retain their various sizes. If you're coming from PageMaker, you can even put spreads in your PDF—our favorite way is to check the "Reader's spread" option in PageMaker's "Print Document" dialog box.

To combine pages of many shapes and sizes within one PDF, use the "Insert Pages…" or "Replace Pages…" command from the Edit menu in Exchange while you're in the destination file, and select a file from which to take new pages. (Inserting will import all the pages in a file, but you can select a range of pages when you use "Replace.") You can also open the source and destination files and drag thumbnails of pages from one to the other. If you click Ctrl (Windows) or Option (Macintosh) while you drag, you will move, not copy, the pages. Drag the new page(s) between thumbnails to insert, on top of thumbnails to replace. When you add pages to a PDF, the PDF page numbers will be renumbered automatically.

However, there's an easy way to tell the Form feature to target a different page in your PDF. Here's how.

1. Create the form field on the "Go to View" destination page. Select the form tool, drag to create the area of the field, and choose the desired field type and appearance in the "Field Properties" dialog box that appears.
2. Assign a mouse action and the "Go to View" action type to your button or other field. Click the "Actions" tab in the "Field Properties" dialog box, select whatever mouse action you prefer, click "Add…," and select "Go to View" from the Type pop-up menu. Click "OK" twice.
   NOTE: If you want the button to take the user to a fixed magnification, you must be in the desired destination view before you create the button.
3. Select and duplicate your newly created field. When the field is selected, anchor points appear at each corner. Select "Duplicate…" from the Fields submenu of the Edit menu.
4. Specify the page(s) on which you want the button to appear. In the "Duplicate Fields" dialog box, fill in the range of page numbers on which you want the form field to appear, and then click "OK."
5. Delete the form field from the page on which you originally created it.

Unexpected Results

MAC OS / WINDOWS / UNIX

Nothing Happens When Clicking on a Link in a PDF File Created in Exchange 2.x and Opened in 1.0

ISSUE

When you click on a link in a PDF file created in Adobe Acrobat Exchange 2.x and opened in Exchange 1.0 or the Acrobat Reader 1.0, the link flashes but does not open the appropriate page.

SYMPTOM

The link was created using Fit Visible magnification option.

SOLUTION

Re-open the PDF in Exchange 2.x and recreate the link using a different magnification option.

ADDITIONAL INFORMATION

Links in a PDF file created using the Fit Visible magnification option in Exchange 2.x aren't maintained when the file is opened in Exchange 1.0 or Reader 1.0. All other magnification options are maintained.

Only One Hit Per Document When Searching in Acrobat Exchange 2.x

ISSUE

When performing an "and" search (e.g., searching for "dogs and cats") using the Acrobat Search Plug-in in Adobe Acrobat Exchange 2.x, the search results in only one hit or find per document (i.e., the status bar at the bottom of the "Search results" dialog states "Document 1 of x: 1 of 1 pages of hits") instead of multiple hits in one or more documents as expected.

SOLUTIONS

When performing "and" searches, deselect the Proximity option in the Adobe Acrobat Search dialog box.

OR: When the Proximity option in the Adobe Acrobat Search dialog box is enabled, perform a different type of search (e.g., search for "dogs or cats").

ADDITIONAL INFORMATION

The TOPIC search engine by Verity Incorporated, which is used by the Acrobat Search Plug-in, is designed to show only the closest hits in a document when the Proximity option is enabled. With Proximity selected in the Adobe Acrobat Search dialog box, words in "and" searches must be within three pages of each other to be found.

For example, when searching for "apples and oranges" with the Proximity option selected in a document containing the text "Apples and oranges, apples and oranges," the second and third words ("oranges, apples") are found (hit) because they are in the closest proximity to each other and therefore are the first set of words with the highest proximity score in the document.

When the Proximity option is deselected, words in "and" searches are found anywhere in a document.

MAC OS / WINDOWS

Cannot Exit From Full Screen Loop Mode in Acrobat Exchange or Reader 3.0

ISSUE

When you display a PDF in Full Screen mode using Adobe Acrobat Exchange or Reader 3.0, you cannot exit the presentation by pressing the Escape key. The Loop preference is enabled, but the Escape Key Exits preference is not enabled, in the Full Screen Preferences dialog box.

SOLUTION

Force quit the application (Windows) or the presentation (Macintosh), then choose File > Preferences > Full Screen, and select Escape Key Exits.

To force quit Acrobat in Windows:

1. Press Control + Alt + Delete.
2. When the Close Program dialog box appears, select your Acrobat viewer application, then click End Task
3. Start Acrobat Exchange or Reader.

To force quit an Acrobat presentation on the Macintosh, press Command + period (.).

NOTE: You do not need to quit the Macintosh Acrobat viewer after pressing Command + period (.).

ADDITIONAL INFORMATION

The Escape Key Exits preference in Acrobat Exchange and Reader enables you to stop a PDF presentation by pressing the Escape key. If you deselect this preference, the only way to stop the presentation is to force quit. This option is only available in Acrobat Reader and Exchange 3.0.

Acrobat Form "Go To View" Action Type Does Not Open a Different Page

ISSUE

When you create a form field in Adobe Acrobat Exchange 3.0 and assign the action type Go To View, you can only select a view on the page on which you are creating the field.

SOLUTION

Create the form field on the destination page (the target of the Go To View action), then copy the field to the page on which you want it to appear.

1. Use the forms tool to create the form field on the destination page, and assign it the Go to View action type.
2. Select the field using the forms tool. (When the field is selected, anchor points appear at each corner.)
3. Choose Edit > Fields > Duplicate.
4. In the Duplicate Fields dialog box, enter the page on which you want the form field to appear, then click OK.
5. Select the original form field and press Delete.

ADDITIONAL INFORMATION

Form field action types in Acrobat Exchange instruct a form field to perform a specific action, such as zoom in on a portion of the page. Field action types are limited to menu items that don't require access to a dialog box. For example, when you choose View > Fit Page, the page view is changed according to the command; no dialog box opens and no other commands are required. However, when you choose View > Go To Page, a dialog box appears that prompts you to select a page. Because Acrobat cannot access dialog boxes via a field action, the Go To View action type in the Field Properties dialog box lists only views for the current page; it does not enable you to "go to" a different page in the PDF.

When you create a Go To View action type on a form field and then copy the field to another page, the field activates the view on the page on which it was created.

Blank Spaces Appear for Used Font in Font Info Dialog Box in Acrobat Viewer

ISSUE

When you open the Font Info dialog box in Adobe Acrobat Reader or Exchange 3.0 or earlier, the Used Font column contains blank spaces where corresponding fonts appear under the Original Font column.

SOLUTIONS

Do one or more of the following:

A. View all the text in the PDF file on-screen. Zoom out on each page of the PDF file so you can view the entire page.

B. View all fonts on-screen in full text mode, instead of in greeked mode. To display fonts in full text mode, either zoom in on all text or change the Greek option. To change the Greek option:
   1. Choose File > Preferences > General (Acrobat 3.0) or choose Edit > Preferences > General (Acrobat 2.x).
   2. In the General Preferences dialog box, click the Greek Text Below option to deselect it.
      OR: Enter a lower pixel value (e.g., 3 pixels).
   3. Click OK to save the changes.
   4. Save and close the PDF file, then open it again to enable the new preference settings to take effect.

C. Open the document in the original application, reformat hidden characters (e.g., space, tab, end of line, end of paragraph) in a font also used for text or non-hidden characters, and then convert the document to a PDF file.

ADDITIONAL INFORMATION

Acrobat Exchange and Reader render font information when they display text on-screen. Exchange and Reader substitute fonts that are unavailable in the PDF file or system. The fonts they use to display text are unknown until they render the text on-screen, so if a specific font on a page that has not yet been rendered, including when they display greeked text or substitute unavailable fonts, that font's name does not appear as a Used Font in the Font Info dialog box. Viewing the entire page by zooming in or out or changing the Greek Text option so it does not greek text (i.e., enter a smaller pixel value) ensures Acrobat Exchange and Reader render all font information in a PDF file and display used fonts.

Hidden characters (e.g. space, tab, end of line, end of paragraph) formatted in a font not used for text or non-hidden characters in the file also cause Exchange and Reader to display blank spaces instead of a used font name in the Font Info dialog box. Reformatting these characters in the fonts used for other text characters prevents blank spaces from appearing for used fonts names.

WINDOWS

PDFs Distilled From Ventura Files Contain Solid Link Boxes or Black Pages

ISSUE

Portable Document Format (PDF) files distilled from Ventura Publisher 4.2 or 5.0 PostScript files containing link information do not display as expected in Adobe Acrobat Reader or Exchange. When you view the PDF using Acrobat for Macintosh, the link boxes are solid rather than an outline as expected. When you view the PDF using Acrobat for Windows, the page containing the link displays black unless the zoom magnification is 400% or more.

SOLUTION

Open the PostScript file in a text editor that saves in text-only format, decrease the link's border line width, then redistill the file:

1. Make a backup copy of the PostScript file, then open the original in a text editor that can save in text-only format (e.g., Macintosh Teach Text or Windows Write).
2. Search for the word "Border" and change the point size of the link border from [0 0 2000] to a value that will create a smaller link border width. For example, use one of Exchange's default link border widths:
   - Exchange's Thin link border width = [0 0 1]
   - Exchange's Medium link border width = [0 0 2]
   - Exchange's Thick link border width = [0 0 3]

   OR: Enter a custom line width for the link border. For example, a border value of [0 0 5] will create a link box with a 5 point line.
3. Repeat step 2 for each link described in the PostScript file.
4. Save the PostScript file in text-only format, then convert it to PDF using Acrobat Distiller.

ADDITIONAL INFORMATION

When you print a Ventura Publisher file to PostScript format, Ventura converts link information in the original file to PDFMarks. Acrobat Distiller uses the PDFMarks to generate links when it converts the PostScript file to a PDF file.

Ventura defines the line width of each link's border as 2000 points. Because Acrobat Exchange and Reader 1.0 only allow for visible or invisible links and do not allow you to change the link border's line width, links created in Ventura 4.2 or 5.0 display as expected.

In Exchange and Reader 2.0 and later for the Macintosh, links defined by Ventura display as solid boxes. In Exchange and Reader 2.0 and later for Windows, the entire PDF page displays black when you view a page containing a link defined by Ventura.

Inherit Zoom Magnification Isn't Maintained With Cross-document PDF Links

The Inherit Zoom magnification attribute of a cross-document PDF (Portable Document Format) link is lost when the link is activated from Adobe Acrobat Exchange 2.x or Reader 2.x for Windows. The external PDF opens at a smaller magnification than the PDF in which the cross-document link is located. When the Inherit Zoom magnification option is applied to a link, the page opened by activating the link should display at the same magnification as that of the PDF in which the link is located.

When the PDF in which the cross-document link is located is displaying in Full Screen or Fit Page view, the external PDF opens and displays at a dramatically smaller magnification. When any of the other page views (i.e., Actual Size, Fit Visible, Fit Width,) is selected in the PDF with the cross-document link, the external PDF still opens and displays at a smaller magnification, but the reduction is not as severe as with the Full Screen and Fit Page views.

Acrobat Form Buttons and Text Fields Display Rotated

ISSUE

Form buttons and text fields created using the forms tool in Adobe Acrobat Exchange 3.0 display on the wrong portion of the page or are rotated 90 degrees in the PDF file.

SOLUTION

Recreate the rotated or incorrectly placed buttons or text fields.

NOTE: When you need to duplicate buttons or text fields throughout a lengthy document, temporarily rearrange the pages, grouping them according to orientation. Once the pages are grouped by orientation, create the button or text field on the first page of each group and duplicate it only within that group. After every page has a new button or text field, reorder the pages in their correct sequence.

ADDITIONAL INFORMATION

The orientation of an Acrobat Exchange form button or text field is determined by the orientation of the page on which it is created. If you rotate the page on which it was created, the button or text field remains in its original position and does not move to adjust to the new orientation. If you copy a button or text field to a page that has a different orientation from the page on which it was created, the button or text field aligns with the original orientation, appearing sideways and on the wrong portion of the page.

For example, when you create a button on the lower left corner of a PDF page, and duplicate it onto other pages of the PDF, it appears on the lower left corner of each page. However, if the page onto which you are copying the button is rotated, the button displays in what was the lower left corner before the rotation. If this page is rotated 90 degrees clockwise from portrait to landscape, the button appears on the upper left corner of the page because that was the bottom left prior to rotation. The button and the text within the button are oriented to a portrait page and appear rotated 90 degrees (sideways). The same things happens when using text fields. When a text field is copied to a rotated page, only a portion of the text in a text field is visible.

Cannot Edit or Delete URLs in Weblink Edit URL Dialog Box in Acrobat Exchange 3.0

ISSUE

You cannot add more than ten URLs (Universal Resource Locators) to the Weblink Edit URL dialog box in Adobe Acrobat Exchange 3.0, nor can you edit or delete URLs already listed in the dialog box.

SOLUTION

Edit the Acrobat URL information in the Registry (Windows 95) or in the Weblink.ini file (Windows 3.1x).

To edit the Acrobat URL information in the Registry:

1. Exit all Acrobat applications.
2. Choose Start > Run.
3. Type "regedit" in the Open text box and click OK.
4. Choose Registry > Export Registry File, specify a location and name for a backup Registry file in the Export Registry File dialog box, then click Save.
5. Navigate to the HKEY_CURRENT_USER\Software\Adobe\Acrobat\Weblink\1.2\OpenURL key (i.e., directory).
6. Double-click on the key you want to edit. The keys specify the following information:
   NumURLs specifies the current number of URLs in the Edit URL pop-up menu.
   URL-x specifies a URL, where x is its position in the pop-up menu. For example, URL-0 represents the first URL, URL-1 represents the second URL, and so on.
   URLLimit specifies the maximum number of URLs that Acrobat can list in the pop-up menu.
7. Click on Default to select the value.
8. If you want to delete a URL, choose Edit > Delete. If you want to edit a URL or change the possible number of URLs, choose Edit > Modify. Then enter the new data in the Value text box and click OK.
9. If you deleted one or more URLs, change the NumURLs value to reflect the new number of URLs. 10. Exit the Registry Editor, which automatically saves your changes to the Registry.

To edit the URL information in the Weblink.ini file:

1. Open the Windows\Weblink.ini file in a text editor that can save in text-only format (e.g., WordPad, Notepad).
2. Locate the [OpenURL] section. This section contains the following lines:
   NumURLs specifies the current number of URLs in the Edit URL pop-up menu.
   URLLimit specifies the maximum number of URLs that Acrobat can list in the URL pop-up menu. URL-x specifies a URL, where x is its position in the dialog box. For example, URL-0 represents the first URL, URL-1 represents the second URL, and so on.
3. Edit or delete the desired URL, or change the limit for the total number of URLs. If you remove one or more URLs, also change the NumURLs value accordingly. For example, the [OpenURL] section might appear as:
   ```
   NumURLs=2
   URLLimit=10
   URL-0=http://www.adobe.com/
   URL-1=http://www.ibm.com/
   ```
4. Save the file in text-only format.

ADDITIONAL INFORMATION

After you create a World Wide Web link in a PDF file, Acrobat Exchange stores the URL information in the Registry (Windows 95) or in Acrobat's Weblink.ini file (Windows 3.1). To edit or delete a URL from the Weblink Edit URL dialog box, or to change the maximum number of URLs that can appear in the dialog box, you must edit the Registry or Weblink.ini file.

Editing or deleting a URL in the Registry or Weblink.ini file does not affect any links that have already been created to the URL.

Movies in PDF Files Don't Conform to Movie Link Box

ISSUE

When you play a movie in Adobe Acrobat Exchange, the movie displays larger or smaller than the link box you defined for it.

SOLUTION

Create a link box that is proportional to the size of the movie.

ADDITIONAL INFORMATION

QuickTime and Video for Windows can't display a movie at dimensions that aren't proportional to the movie's original dimensions. If you create a link box that isn't dimensional to the movie's original proportions, Acrobat uses the smallest dimension of the link box to create a new, proportional link box to display the movie. Although you can create a movie link box with any dimensions, the movie file is limited to dimensions that are proportionate to the movie's original size. For example, if your movie's original dimensions are 2" by 2", create a movie link box that is approximately 2" by 2" or another proportional dimension such as 2.5" by 2.5". If you create a box with dimensions that are not proportional to 2" by 2", such as 2" by 6.5", when you play the movie, it displays at 2" by 2".

Placement Formatting is Lost When You Copy and Paste Text from a PDF into Another Application

ISSUE

When you copy text from a PDF file in Acrobat Exchange or Reader 3.0, and paste it into another application, the placement formatting (e.g., center, right justify, tabs, and multiple spaces between text) is not retained.

SOLUTION

Reformat the text after pasting it.

OR: Use the Select Graphics command to select the text you want to copy:

1. Choose Tools > Select Graphics.
2. Draw a box around the entire text region you want to copy, then choose Edit > Copy.
3. Paste the graphic (text region) into another application.

NOTE: When you use the Select Graphics command to copy text, Acrobat copies the text to the Clipboard as a graphic. You cannot edit text copied as a graphic.

ADDITIONAL INFORMATION

Acrobat does not format text as other applications do. When you copy text selected using the text selection tool or the Select All command, or use the Copy File to Clipboard command, the text's placement formatting is not retained when you paste it into another application. When you copy text using the Select Graphics command (Tools > Select Graphics), Acrobat copies the text as a graphic and formatting is retained.

MAC OS

Colors Display Poorly in Acrobat Exchange

ISSUE

Adobe Acrobat Exchange 2.x or Reader 2.x display colors in PDF files incorrectly (e.g., "splotchy," "washed out").

SOLUTIONS

Set the monitor to display more colors (e.g., 256, thousands, millions) in the Monitors control panel.

OR: Upgrade the video card or add more video RAM, depending on the model of Macintosh, to enable 256 colors.

OR: If the monitor can display only a maximum of four colors, change the system highlight color in the Color Control Panel to a color that is more desirable for viewing PDF files.

ADDITIONAL INFORMATION

Acrobat Exchange or Reader 2.x or earlier display colors in PDF files poorly (e.g., "splotchy," "washed out") when the Monitors control panel is set to display 16 or fewer colors.

When the Monitor control panel is set to display only four colors, Acrobat Exchange and Reader use the system's highlight color to help display the PDF file, which may result in unusually poor color display of images, depending on the selected system highlight color. To improve PDF display for Macintosh computers that display a maximum of four colors, change the system's highlight color in the Color control panel to a color that is more preferable for viewing PDF files.

Can't Copy Graphics from Exchange to Illustrator

ISSUE

You cannot paste an image copied from a PDF in Adobe Acrobat Exchange 3.0 into Adobe Illustrator (i.e., the Paste command is dimmed).

SOLUTION

Open the PDF file in Illustrator. Then, delete any elements you don't want, or copy and paste the elements you do want into a new Illustrator file.

ADDITIONAL INFORMATION

When you copy elements from a PDF, they are copied to the clipboard in bitmap format. Adobe Illustrator does not recognize bitmap information from the clipboard, and does not enable the Paste command when you copy a graphic from a PDF file in Acrobat Exchange.

Application Errors

MAC OS / WINDOWS

The Error "Unknown destination type 'FitW'" Occurs When Clicking a Link

ISSUE

When you click a link in a PDF file, Adobe Acrobat Exchange 2.x or Adobe Acrobat Reader 2.x returns the error, "Unknown destination type 'FitW'."

SYMPTOM
The PDF file was created with from a PostScript file that includes PDFMark operators.

SOLUTION
Replace the unsupported "FitW" destination type with the supported "FitBH" destination type:

1. Open the PostScript file in a word processor that saves as text-only (e.g., Microsoft Word)
2. Search for "[/FitW]."
3. Replace each occurrence of "[/FitW]" with "[/FitBH -32768]."
4. Save the PostScript file in text-only format and convert it to PDF format with Acrobat Distiller.

ADDITIONAL INFORMATION
Acrobat Distiller 2.x supports a programming language called PDFMark, which is very similar to PostScript. The PDFMark language is documented in a PDF file included with Acrobat Distiller named Pdfmark.pdf, which is located in the Acrobat Help folder (Macintosh) or the Acroread/Help directory (Windows). The PDFMark language can be used to automatically create bookmarks, links, annotations, and views during distillation that would otherwise be made manually in Acrobat Exchange. PDFMark comments can be added to PostScript files with text editing applications capable of saving or exporting in text-only format (e.g., Microsoft Word, Adobe PageMaker).

It is possible to define a link in Exchange or with PDFMark called "fit visible," that when clicked, jumps to the destination page and changes views so all elements on the destination page are visible except for margins and white space. The PDFMark documentation incorrectly states the way to request this view is with the "/FitW" keyword. The correct way to specify the fit visible destination is with the "/FitBH -32768" keyword. The error "Unknown destination type 'FitW'" is specific to Acrobat Distiller 2.x, as the PDFMark language for Distiller 1.0 does not support either the /FitW or /FitBH keywords.

Acrobat Exchange Returns Message "Highlights Will Not be Displayed" When Searching an Index

ISSUE
When you use Adobe Acrobat Search, it displays the message, "This document was changed since the index was last built, highlights will not be displayed."

SOLUTION
Rebuild the index.

ADDITIONAL INFORMATION
When you create an index of PDF files, Adobe Acrobat Catalog indexes each term by its location on the page. When you alter a page by removing or changing text, inserting or extracting pages, or adding notes, the location of terms on the page may change. So, when you search a PDF that has changed since the index was built, Search highlights the location of the term that is recorded in the index, and may highlight the wrong term. To ensure that Search highlights the correct terms, you should rebuild an index after changing any of the PDFs contained in that index.

If you know that the only alteration to a PDF was the addition of notes, click Highlight Anyway to the message, "This document was changed since the index was last built, highlights will not be displayed." Search will highlight terms as expected. If you know the document was altered by the removal or addition of pages, click OK in the message dialog box, and Search will not display any highlights in the indexed PDF files.

WINDOWS

Error "...maximum number of files are already open..." When Opening a PDF in Exchange 2.1

ISSUE
The error "There was an error opening this document. The maximum number of files are already open. No other files can be opened or printed until some are closed." occurs when you have the default limit of 10 PDF (Portable Document Format) files open in Adobe Acrobat Exchange or Reader 2.1 and you attempt to open another.

In Exchange or Reader 2.0, the error "There was an error opening this document. No more than ten documents can be opened at a time." appears when you attempt to open more PDFs than the default limit of 10.

SOLUTIONS
Close one or more open PDFs before opening another or activating a link to an unopened PDF.
OR: Install the AutoClose Plug-in. The AutoClose Plug-in automatically closes the least recently used document before Acrobat's limit of 10 is reached. For more information about the AutoClose Plug-in, see Related Records.
OR: When using Exchange or Reader for Windows, modify the ACROEXCH.INI or ACROREAD.INI file to limit the number of open documents to one under certain conditions. Adding the line "CloseAllOnOpen=1" to the [AdobeViewer] section of the ACROEXCH.INI or ACROREAD.INI file forces the open document to close when you open a new PDF via any of the following methods:

- A link created with the Open File link attribute.
- A DDE command
- Dragging and dropping PDF files on top of the Exchange or Reader executable files (i.e., ACROEXCH.EXE or ACROREAD.EXE) or program icons.
- Command line instructions
- Choosing Acrobat Reader Help or Acrobat Exchange Help from the Help menu in Reader or Exchange to open the Help PDF file.

To modify the ACROEXCH.INI or ACROREAD.INI file:

1. Open the ACROEXCH.INI or ACROREAD.INI file, located in the Windows directory, in a text-editor that saves in text-only format.
2. Add the following line to the [AdobeViewer] section:
   CloseAllOnOpen=1
3. Save the INI file in text-only format.

NOTE: Adding the "CloseAllOnOpen=1" line to the ACROEXCH.INI or ACROREAD.INI file will not close the open file when you open a new file via any of the following methods:

- The Open command on the File menu.
- Links created using the Go To View link attribute.

Error Importing GIF File in Adobe Acrobat Exchange 3.0

ISSUE

When you import a GIF file into Adobe Acrobat Exchange 3.0 using the Import Images command, Acrobat Exchange returns the error "Unknown Error reading (Path/filename) of file" or "Input file (Path/filename) is of an unknown or unsupported type."

SYMPTOM

The file is saved in GIF87a or GIF89a format, with interlacing, offsetting, or animation.

SOLUTION

Open the GIF file in an image editing application (e.g., Adobe Photoshop) and save it without interlacing, offsetting, or animation.

OR: Convert the GIF file to a PDF file. For instructions, see the Online Help in Acrobat Exchange.

ADDITIONAL INFORMATION

The GIF import filter included with Acrobat Exchange 3.0 does not support interlacing, offsetting, or animation in GIF87a or GIF89a files. When you import a GIF file saved with any of these features, Acrobat Exchange returns an error.

Error "Acrobat Exchange - TouchUp could not parse this page" in Exchange 3.0

ISSUE

When you use the touch-up tool to edit text in a PDF, Adobe Acrobat Exchange 3.0 returns the message, "Acrobat Exchange - TouchUp could not parse this page."

SYMPTOM

The PDF file contains security restrictions.

SOLUTION

Remove the Changing the Document and Selecting Text and Graphics security settings from the PDF file before using the touch-up tool:

1. Open the PDF file in Acrobat Exchange.
2. Choose File > Save As.
3. In the Save As dialog box, click Security.
4. If a Password dialog box appears, enter the Change Security Setting password in the Password text box.
5. In the Security dialog box, deselect Changing the Document and Selecting Text and Graphics, then click OK.
6. Save the file.

ADDITIONAL INFORMATION

Security options may be enabled in Acrobat Exchange to restrict users from performing any of the following operations on a PDF file: opening the document, printing the document, changing the document (e.g., editing text, extracting pages), selecting text and graphics, and adding or changing notes and forms fields.

The Changing the Document and Selecting Text and Graphics security options disallow the use of the touch-up tool, which is used to select and change text within a PDF file. When you attempt to use the touch-up tool on a PDF file that is secured with either or both of these security options, Acrobat Exchange returns the message, "Acrobat Exchange - TouchUp could not parse this page." You can change security options without entering a password if the author did not secure the file with a password. If the author used a password, you must have the password before changing the security settings.

Error "TouchUp cannot parse the page" When Using the Touch-up Tool on a PDF from Illustrator 6.01

ISSUE

Adobe Acrobat Exchange 3.0 returns the message, "TouchUp cannot parse the page" when you use the touch-up tool to edit text in a PDF created from Adobe Illustrator 6.01 using Acrobat PDF Writer.

SOLUTIONS

Open the original Illustrator 6.01 file and edit the text, then reconvert it to PDF using the PDF Writer.

OR: Open the original file in Adobe Illustrator 6.0 and convert it to PDF using the PDF Writer.

OR: Save the Illustrator 6.01 file as a PostScript file and then convert it to PDF using Acrobat Distiller 3.0.

ADDITIONAL INFORMATION

Exchange's touch-up tool enables you to edit text in a PDF file. However, when you use the PDF Writer to create a PDF from Illustrator 6.0, Illustrator sends all text information in the file to the printer as bitmap images rather than as actual text. When PDF Writer generates a PDF file, it interprets that bitmap information and creates a PDF file that does not contain text, but instead contains a bitmap image of the text. Therefore, you cannot edit that text with the touch-up tool.

Unlike Illustrator 6.01, Illustrator 6.0 sends text information to the PDF Writer printer driver as text, so when you open the resulting PDF in Acrobat Exchange, you can use the touch-up tool to edit the text as expected.

Acrobat Distiller interprets PostScript code from PostScript files, so text from the original file is converted to text in the PDF file. Saving files from either Illustrator 6.0 or 6.01 as PostScript files and then converting them PDF using Acrobat Distiller 3.0 creates PDF files that you can edit using the touch-up tool.

Acrobat Error "Files Not Available" When Using Index on Partitioned Macintosh Hard Disk

ISSUE

When you create an index using Adobe Acrobat Catalog 2.x for Windows, then transfer the index to a Macintosh hard disk partitioned with APS Utilities 3.06 and search it, Acrobat Exchange returns the error "Files Not Available."

SOLUTION

Move the index to a hard disk not partitioned with APS Utilities 3.06.

ADDITIONAL INFORMATION

APS Utilities 3.06 by Club Mac is a software partition application that recognizes both SCSI chains, 1 and 0. APS Utility changes the relative path structure for file locations, invalidating paths needed by the Acrobat Exchange Search plug-in to reference index files. When Acrobat cannot locate files in the index, it returns the error "Files Not Available." Moving the index to a hard disk not partitioned using APS Utilities 3.06 enables the Acrobat Search plug-in to recognize the path names and locate index files as expected.

MAC OS

Error "Adobe Type Manager cannot do font substitution..." When Launching Acrobat Reader or Exchange

ISSUE

When launching, Adobe Acrobat Reader or Exchange 2.0 or earlier return the error "Adobe Type Manager cannot do font substitution because a copy of ATM with your serial number is already in use by [User Name]." ATM 3.5.x or 3.6.x is installed.

SOLUTIONS

Upgrade to Reader or Exchange 2.1.

OR: Make sure the serial number used to personalize ATM is not being used for another copy of ATM installed on a different computer on the same network.

ADDITIONAL INFORMATION

ATM 3.5.x or 3.6.x have built-in network copy detection. If ATM detects another copy of ATM using a duplicate serial number on another Macintosh on the same network, it dims the Substitute for Missing Fonts option the ATM control panel and returns the message "Adobe Type Manager cannot do font substitution because a copy of ATM with your serial number is already in use by [User Name]." Adobe Acrobat Reader and Exchange require ATM to launch and will not launch unless the Substitute for Missing Fonts option is selected.

If you're installing more than one copy of ATM 3.5.x or 3.6.x, enter a different serial number in the Personalization dialog box for each copy.

Acrobat Reader 2.1 and Exchange 2.1 include ATM 3.8.3, which does not use network copy detection. ATM 3.8.x does not require a unique serial number for each copy of ATM running on different computers.

Error "Bad \BBox" When Opening PDF in Exchange

ISSUE

When you open a PDF file, Acrobat Exchange or Reader returns the error "The font 'xxx' contains a bad /BBox." and text displays as lines or does not display at all.

SYMPTOM

You created the PDF file with Adobe Acrobat Distiller 2.x.

SOLUTION

Use the PSPrinter driver 8.3 or later when creating PostScript files you'll process in Distiller. You may download the PSPrinter driver from the Adobe's Web site, or order it from Adobe Customer Services.

To install the PSPrinter driver:

1. Double-click the PSPrinter icon on the floppy disk.
2. Follow the on-screen instructions to complete the driver installation.

ADDITIONAL INFORMATION

Acrobat Exchange and Acrobat Reader read a character's bounding box information to determine its on-screen location. PSPrinter driver 8.3 and later include both the right and left sides of character bounding boxes when generating PostScript code. Macintosh PostScript printer drivers earlier than PSPrinter 8.3 include only the left side of a character's bounding box when generating PostScript code. When you open a file distilled from a PostScript file that does not contain information about the right side of a character's bounding box, Exchange or Reader returns the error "The font 'xxx' contains a bad /BBox," and displays the text as gray lines.

Printing Problems

MAC OS / WINDOWS/ UNIX

Printing to a PostScript Level 2 Versus PostScript Level 1 Printer From Exchange

Printing to a Level 2 PostScript printer rather than a Level 1 PostScript printer from Adobe Acrobat Exchange affords two major benefits: faster print times for photo-intense PDFs and greater network bandwidth when printing over a network.

When you print from Exchange to a Level 1 PostScript printer, Exchange must decompress images before sending them to the printer. Because of this, you'll need more free disk space when printing to a Level 1 PostScript printer. Adobe recommends that you have 10-20MB of free disk space when printing to a Level 1 PostScript printer.

When you print to a Level 2 PostScript RIP, decompression of graphics and images is done within the RIP, which can decrease print time on photo-heavy PDFs.

Finally, when printing over a network, network bandwidth is increased significantly when printing to a Level 2 PostScript printer because data is not decompressed until it reaches the RIP.

MAC OS / WINDOWS

Halftones Display and Print Incorrectly from Acrobat Exchange 2.1

ISSUE

Adobe Acrobat Exchange 2.1 and Acrobat Reader 2.1 display and print bitmap images with custom halftone functions differently from the application in which the bitmaps were created.

SOLUTION

Recreate the PDF file using Acrobat Distiller 3.0, then open and print the PDF file using Adobe Acrobat Exchange 3.0. OR: Resave the image with standard halftone functions.

ADDITIONAL INFORMATION

Acrobat Distiller 2.1 and earlier support standard halftone functions only, and convert application-defined halftones to standard halftone functions. Acrobat Distiller 3.0 preserves custom halftone functions (e.g., Adobe Photoshop images saved with customized dot shapes) in bitmap images and Acrobat Exchange 3.0 uses the custom halftone information when displaying a PDF and when printing it to a PostScript printer.

WINDOWS

Cannot Print Multiple PDF Files Using the Drag and Drop Feature in Windows 95

ISSUE

When you drag and drop multiple PDF files from Adobe Acrobat Exchange or Reader 3.0 to a printer shortcut in Windows 95, only one file prints. When you use the drag and drop method to print multiple files from other applications, they all print as expected.

SOLUTION

Use Exchange's or Reader's Print command to print each PDF individually.

ADDITIONAL INFORMATION

The Windows 95 Drag and Drop printing feature enables you to print one or more files by dragging and dropping the files' icons onto a printer shortcut. For each file you drop onto a printer shortcut, Windows starts a separate instance of the application (i.e., a partial launch of the application that takes place in memory) from which the file originated. While one instance begins printing the files, the other instances start a dynamic data exchange (DDE) conversation with the first instance requesting it to print the next file.

Acrobat Exchange and Reader 3.0 can only print one PDF file at a time. When you drag and drop more than one PDF file icon onto a printer shortcut, the first instance of Acrobat Exchange or Reader rejects all DDE conversations from other instances, and prints only the first file. The one file that does print is the one whose filename is first alphabetically.

MAC OS

PDF Files Do Not Print From Acrobat Exchange or Reader 2.0 or Later

ISSUE

When you print a PDF file from Adobe Acrobat Exchange or Reader 2.0 or later, it prints only partially, or doesn't print at all.

SOLUTIONS

Do one or more of the following:

A. Ensure your printer driver is the most current version available. A current version of Adobe's PSPrinter PostScript printer driver is located on Adobe's World Wide Web site (http//www.adobe.com).

B. Ensure you have enough free hard disk space available to create a duplicate temporary file while printing (i.e., at least two times the size of your file). To increase free hard disk space, delete unnecessary files and applications. Then, use a disk utility application to defragment the hard disk.

C. Disable non-System 7.5 extensions before printing. To disable extensions using the Extensions Manager control panel:
   1. In the Extensions Manager control panel, select the extensions you want to disable: Select System 7.5.x or System 7.5 Only from the Sets pop-up menu to disable all extensions except ATM and those included with your system software.
   OR: Selectively disable extensions by clicking to the left of an extension's name to remove the check mark.
   2. Close the Extensions Manager control panel.
   3. Restart your Macintosh.

D. Select either Sans or Serif, rather than Sans and Serif, in Acrobat's General Preferences dialog box:
   1. Choose File > Preferences > General (Acrobat 3.0) or Edit > Preferences > General (Acrobat 2.1).
   2. From the Substitution Fonts pop-up menu choose either Sans or Serif (Acrobat 3.0), or either Sans Only or Serif Only (Acrobat 2.1), then click OK.
   3. Close Acrobat and restart your Macintosh.

E. Recreate the Fonts folder in the System Folder:
   1. Move the Fonts folder from the System folder to the Desktop, then restart your Macintosh. A new Fonts folder appears in your System Folder.
   2. Copy the Adobe Sans MM and Adobe Serif MM font suitcases and PostScript fonts from the old Fonts folder to the new Fonts folder in the System Folder.
   3. Open your PDF file in Acrobat Reader or Acrobat Exchange and print.
   NOTE: If your file prints correctly after you recreate the Fonts folder, reintroduce your fonts by moving them from the old Fonts folder to the new Fonts folder. Move a few fonts at one time, then print. If an error occurs, the last group of fonts moved to the new Fonts folder includes the problem font.

F. Increase the size of your ATM font cache:
   1. Choose Control Panels from the Apple menu.
   2. Open the ATM control panel.
   3. Click the up arrow in the Font Cache box (ATM 3.0x) or the Character Cache Size box (ATM 4.0) to increase it (e.g., from 256K to 512K). 4. Exit ATM and restart your Macintosh.

ADDITIONAL INFORMATION

Third party extensions may conflict with Acrobat's ability to print PDF files. To determine if an extension is interfering with Acrobat, turn off all non-System extensions except ATM and print again. Acrobat will not start without ATM, so make sure to leave ATM enabled in the Extensions Manager dialog box.

When an Acrobat document contains fonts that are not installed on your system, Acrobat Exchange or Reader substitutes one of two multiple master fonts (i.e., AdobeSerifMM and AdobeSansXMM). You can reduce the amount of printer memory required to print a PDF file by selecting either Sans or Serif (Acrobat 3.0), or Sans Only or Serif Only (Acrobat 2.1) as the Substitution Fonts option in the General Preferences dialog box. When you select Sans or Sans Only, Exchange or Reader substitute AdobeSansXMM for all fonts used in the PDF, but not available on the computer. When you select Serif or Serif Only, Exchange or Reader substitute AdobeSerifMM for all fonts used in the PDF, but not available on the computer. AdobeSansXMM requires less printer memory than does AdobeSerifMM, but AdobeSerifMM is a better substitute for very thin, bold, narrow, or extended fonts.

If the Font folder in your system folder is damaged or contains damaged fonts, Acrobat Exchange or Reader may be unable to access the necessary font information to print your PDF document. When you remove the Fonts folder from the System folder, the System creates a new, undamaged, Fonts folder.

ATM's Font Cache is an allotment of memory that ATM uses to store the fonts it has rasterized. When the Font Cache is too small Acrobat may not be able to acquire all the information it needs to print a PDF file. ATM's default Font Cache size is 256K. You should increase the size of the Font Cache to 512K or more when your documents include a multiple master typeface (e.g., AdobeSerifMM), or you've used more than four typefaces on a page.

Installation Issues

WINDOWS

Removing Acrobat Exchange 2.1 in Windows

Adobe Acrobat Exchange 2.1 does not include an uninstall application for Windows 95 or Windows 3.1x. To remove Acrobat Exchange, remove the Acrobat Exchange files from the Acroexch directory and the Windows\System subdirectory, remove the PDF Writer 2.1 printer driver if you chose to install it, and then delete the lines Acrobat Exchange added in the Win.ini file.

For instruction on removing Adobe Type Manager (ATM), which you can also choose to install with Acrobat Exchange, see the document "Removing Adobe Type Manager 3.0x, 2.6, or 2.5."

To delete Acrobat Exchange 2.1 files:

1. Remove your personal files from the Acroexch directory and its subdirectories.
2. Delete the Acroexch directory, including its subdirectories.
3. Delete the following files from the Windows\System directory:

```
Pdfhlp.gid
Pdfhlp.hlp
Pdfwlib.dll
```

Pdfwritr.dll
Pdfwritr.drv

4. Delete the following files from the Window directory:
   Acroexch.ini
   Acrograf.ini
   Acrosrch.ini
   Acroweb.ini
   Weblink.ini
5. When running Windows 95, delete the Acrobat Exchange shortcut file from the Windows\Start Menu\-Programs\Adobe Acrobat directory.

To remove the Acrobat Exchange lines from the Win.ini file:

1. Make a backup copy of the Win.ini file in the Windows directory.
2. Open the original Win.ini file in a text editor that can save in text-only format (e.g., Notepad).
3. In the [Extensions] section, remove the line:
   `Pdfwriter =C:\Acroexch\Acroexch.exe^.pdf`
4. In the [Embedding] section, remove the line:
   `Acroexch.document=Adobe Acrobat Document,-Adobe Acrobat Document,C:\Acroexch\Acroexch.exe,picture`
5. In the [Devices] section, remove the line:
   `Acrobat PDFWriter=PDFWRITR,DISK:`
6. In the [Printer Ports] section, remove the line:
   `Acrobat PDFWriter=PDFWRITR,DISK:,15,45`
7. In the [Device] section, remove the line:
   `Acrobat PDFWriter=PDFWRITR,DISK:`
8. Remove the entire [Acrobat Pdfwriter] section.
9. Save the Win.ini file in text-only format.
10. Restart Windows.

No Acrobat Files on Hard Disk After Installing Acrobat Exchange 3.0

ISSUE
After you install Adobe Acrobat Exchange 3.0, no Acrobat program files appear on the hard disk.

SYMPTOM
When the installation was nearly complete, you closed the installer background window.

SOLUTION
Reinstall Acrobat Exchange and, instead of manually closing the background window, wait for the Installation Complete dialog box to appear, then click OK.

ADDITIONAL INFORMATION
If an error occurs when you install Adobe Acrobat 3.0, the Acrobat installer removes Acrobat from your hard disk. If you manually close the installer background window, the installer reacts as if an error has occurred and removes all Acrobat program files.

Error installing QuickTime for Windows from Acrobat Exchange

ISSUE
When you install QuickTime for Windows 2.04 using the Adobe Acrobat Exchange 2.1 install disks, the QuickTime installer returns the error "Error occurred when updating the System.ini." When you click OK, the message "Install incomplete, QuickTime for Windows installation is incomplete" appears.

SOLUTION
Update QuickTime for Windows to the most current version. To order QuickTime for Windows, contact Apple Computer.

ADDITIONAL INFORMATION
The QuickTime for Windows 2.04 installer, licensed by Adobe from Apple Computers, does not work as expected and returns the error "Error occurred when updating the system.INI." To install QuickTime for Windows, update QuickTime to the most current version. For help installing QuickTime for Windows, contact Apple Computer.

General Information

MAC OS / WINDOWS / UNIX

How Adobe Acrobat Exchange and Reader Programs Handle Fonts

This technical note is the second of two technical notes that describe how the Adobe Acrobat programs manage fonts. The technical note, "How the Adobe Acrobat Distiller and PDF Writer Programs Handle Fonts," as well as this technical note are available from the Adobe Fax Request Line. The information in these two technical notes is intended to help you troubleshoot font related problems with Acrobat documents and to help you better understand how the Acrobat software works.

This technical note tells you how the Acrobat Exchange and Reader programs display and print fonts contained in documents that have been converted to the Portable Document Format (PDF) by the Acrobat Distiller or PDF Writer programs.

Many of the terms used in this technical note are defined in the Glossary at the back of the technical note, "How the Adobe Acrobat Distiller and PDF Writer Programs Handle Fonts."

NOTE: The term "viewer" is used to refer to either the Acrobat Exchange or the Acrobat Reader program.

ABOUT ACROBAT SOFTWARE
The Acrobat Distiller and PDF Writer programs convert documents into the Portable Document Format (PDF). The

resulting PDF files can be viewed and printed with the Acrobat Exchange and Reader programs, which run on both Windows and Macintosh " computers.

ABOUT FONTS

The Distiller and PDF Writer programs must deal with every kind of font that can be used in a document. Documents created with Windows applications can contain PostScript Type1 and Type 3 fonts, Windows bitmapped and vector fonts, TrueType fonts, and PCL " fonts. Documents created with Macintosh applications can contain PostScript Type 1 and Type 3 fonts, Macintosh bitmapped fonts, and TrueType fonts. See the Glossary at the back of the previous tech note for descriptions of these font types.

In addition to font type, fonts are further classified by the set of characters included in the font. Character sets for Type 1 fonts, for example, include the ISO Latin 1, Expert, Small Capitals and Old Style Figures (SC & OSF), Symbolic, Cyrillic, and Kanji character sets. The ISO Latin 1 character set, the standard Type 1 character set, includes the standard English, French, Italian, and German alphabets; the Expert character set includes fraction and f ligature characters for the English alphabet; and the Cyrillic character set contains the Cyrillic alphabet used by Slavic languages such as Russian and Ukrainian. See the Glossary at the back of the previous tech note for descriptions.

When the Distiller and PDF Writer programs convert a document to a PDF file, they must deal with every kind of font used in the document. The technical note, "How the Adobe Acrobat Distiller and PDF Writer Programs Handle Fonts," describes in detail how the Distiller and PDF Writer programs handle the various kinds of fonts used in Windows and Macintosh documents. In general, however, each font is handled in one of the following ways:

A font descriptor is placed in the PDF file. This technique is used for Type 1 fonts that use the ISO Latin 1 character set (the standard character set). When the Type 1 font is not available on the viewing system, the Adobe Type Manager (ATM) program uses the information in the font descriptor to create a substitute font that looks like the original font. When the Type 1 font is available on the viewing system, it is used.

A font is embedded in the PDF file. This technique is used for Type 1 fonts that do not use the ISO Latin 1 character set (the standard character set), and for Type 3 fonts. When a Type 1 or Type 3 font is embedded in a PDF file, the font is always available for both viewing and printing.

A bitmapped font is converted to a bitmapped Type 3 font. This technique is used for Macintosh bitmapped fonts. The resulting bitmapped Type 3 font is embedded in the PDF file.

The characters of a bitmapped font are placed in a PDF file as bitmapped images. This technique is used, for example, by the Windows version of the PDF Writer for PCL bitmapped fonts when TrueType is inactive. When this technique is used, users cannot search for words that have been set in the font.

The characters of an outline font are placed in a PDF file as graphics. This technique is used by the PDF Writer programs for Type 1 and TrueType symbolic fonts and by both Distiller and PDF Writer programs for Windows vector fonts. When this technique is used, users cannot search for words that have been set in the font.

HOW THE ACROBAT EXCHANGE AND READER PROGRAMS DISPLAY AND PRINT FONTS

This section summarizes how the viewing programs handle fonts. Font characters represented as graphic objects or bitmapped images. The characters of fonts that are represented in a PDF file as graphic objects or bitmapped images require no special processing by the Acrobat viewers. These characters are displayed and printed just like any other graphic objects or bitmapped images.

Type 1 fonts The way the viewers handle a Type 1 font depends on whether the font is embedded in the PDF file, and, when the font is not embedded in the PDF file, whether the font is available on the viewing system.

When a Type 1 font is embedded in a PDF file or when a font is available on the viewing system:

- ATM uses the outlines of the characters to create bitmapped characters that are displayed on the screen
- The viewer uses the PostScript driver to download the font to PostScript printers
- ATM uses the outlines of the characters to create bitmapped characters that are printed to non PostScript printers; for PCL printers that accept downloaded fonts, ATM uses the PCL printer driver to create and download outline fonts to the printer
- When a Type 1 font is neither embedded in a PDF file nor available on the viewing system:
- ATM uses the font descriptor to create a substitute font that looks like the original
- ATM uses the outlines of the substitute characters to create bitmapped characters that are displayed on the screen
- The viewer uses the PostScript driver to download the substitute font to PostScript printers
- ATM uses the outlines of the substitute characters to create bitmapped characters that are printed to non PostScript printers; for PCL printers that accept downloaded fonts, ATM uses the PCL printer driver to create and download outline fonts to the printer

Type 3 fonts Type 3 fonts are always embedded in PDF files and so they are always available to the viewer programs. The viewer programs use the characters of Type 3 fonts to create bitmapped characters for the display. To print a Type 3 font on PostScript printer, the viewers use the PostScript driver to download the font to the printer. To print Type 3 font on a non PostScript printer, the viewers use the characters of the Type 3 font to create bitmapped characters that are then printed.

HOW TO TELL WHICH FONTS ARE USED IN A PDF FILE

You can use the Document Info command in the Acrobat Exchange and Reader programs to display a table that shows what fonts are present in a PDF file. To display the font table with Windows, press Ctrl+Shift when you choose Document Info from the File menu. To display the font table with the Macintosh, press Shift+Option when you choose the Document Info from the File menu.

Here is an example of the font table displayed by the Macintosh version of the Exchange program:

NOTE: When you first open an Acrobat document, not all of the fonts used in the document are necessarily listed in the font table. Only those fonts appearing on pages that have been processed by the viewer are shown. The easiest way to get the viewer to list all the fonts used in a document is to use the Find command to search for a fictitious word that does not exist in the document. Searching for a nonexistent word forces the viewer to process every page looking for the word.

Original Font This column lists the fonts used in the PDF document.

Used When the original font is not present on the viewing system, this column shows the font used to create a substitute font for the original font. (Typically, either AdobeSerifMM or AdobeSansXMM is used to create a substitute font.) When the font is embedded in the PDF file, this column shows "Embedded." When the original font is installed on the viewing system and is not embedded in the PDF file, this column is blank, which indicates that the font installed on the viewing system is being used.

Type For Windows, this column shows the type of the font that is being used for the original font (Type 1 or Type 3). For the Macintosh, this column shows the type of the original font (Type 1, Type 3, or TrueType).

Encoding This column shows internal engineering information that is used to develop and debug the Acrobat Exchange and Reader programs.

NOTE: See Help for the Exchange or Reader program for a description of the other fields in the Document Info document dialog box.

THE VIEWER FONT MANAGEMENT TABLES

The technical note "How the Acrobat Exchange and Reader Programs Handle FontsTables" contains tables that list the various kinds of fonts used in Windows and Macintosh documents. For each kind of font, the tables describe how the Windows and Macintosh viewer programs display and print fonts.

Acrobat Exchange Security Settings General Information

You can restrict access to a PDF document by saving it in Adobe Acrobat Exchange 2.0 or later with password security. You can set both a document password that restricts use of specific tools and menu items (e.g., printing, opening, text selection) and an owner password (i.e., Change Security Options) that restricts others from changing the security options you selected. When setting security options, also set an owner password that is different from the document password. If you do not set an owner password, anyone who opens the file can remove the restrictions. Both the open and owner passwords may be used to open a secured document, but security settings will be temporarily disabled if you use the owner password.

RC4 ENCODING

Adobe uses the RC4 encoding method by RSA Corporation to secure PDF documents. The RC4 method of encoding meets federal regulations, and federal officials can decode it on a need-to-know basis. If any legal issues are encountered as a result of the distribution of secured PDF files, the resolution of these issues are the responsibility of the author or distributor of the PDF files, not of Adobe Systems Incorporated.

SECURING A PDF FILE IN ACROBAT EXCHANGE

Security is a setting made from Within Acrobat Exchange's Save As dialog box. To set security from Acrobat Exchange:

1. Open you PDF and choose File > Save As.
2. Click Security in the Save As dialog box.
3. In the Security dialog box, enter a password in one or both of the password fields:
   - Open the Document password secures the PDF so readers must enter the password before they can open the PDF.
   - Change Security Options password secures the PDF so only the author, or anyone who has this password can set or change security settings.
4. Select security options from the Do Not Allow section, then click OK.
5. Enter a name and location for your file and click Save.

NOTE: You cannot open a secured file in Acrobat Exchange 1.0 or Acrobat Reader 1.0.

ADOBE ACROBAT CATALOG AND SECURED PDF FILES

Acrobat Catalog cannot index a PDF file to which you have applied password security. Before Catalog can index all the words in a PDF file, it must first open the file, and in some cases add a unique identifying code. Because Catalog cannot enter a password before opening a PDF file, it cannot perform the functions required to index the file. When you attempt to index a PDF file that has security applied, Catalog returns the error "[Filename] needs an open password. Password protected files cannot be indexed."

You can remove the password security from a PDF file if you are the author of the file or if you know the Change Security Options password. To remove the password security for indexing:

1. Open the PDF file in Acrobat Exchange 2.0 or later.
2. Choose File > Save As.
3. Click Security and enter your Change Security Options password in the Password dialog box.
4. In the Security dialog box, delete the passwords, then click OK.
5. Enter a new name for your file, then click Save.

WINDOWS

Acrobat Access View Plug-in for the Visually Impaired General Information

The Adobe Acrobat Access View plug-in helps visually-impaired users read PDF documents on-screen. It is available on the Adobe Web site for use with Acrobat Exchange 3.0 for Windows 3.x, Windows 95, and Windows NT.

The Access View plug-in displays PDF documents in a format useful for the visually impaired by presenting the textual content of a PDF file in a separate window from the graphically-rich PDF document. The window displays the text in an approximated reading order, presents multi-column text in a single column, and straightens non-horizontal text. Standard Acrobat features, such as hypertext links, notes, bookmarks, sounds, and movies, are available in Access View.

Acrobat Distiller®

Feature Techniques

MAC OS / WINDOWS / UNIX

Creating quality Adobe PDF files from TeX with DVIPS *by Kendall Whitehouse/EMERGE*

Documents converted from the TeX typesetting language into the Adobe PostScript language or Acrobat Portable Document format (PDF) files usually contain fixed-resolution bitmap fonts that do not print or display well on a variety of printer and computer screens.

This document explains how to configure Tomas Rokicki's DVIPS program to use device-inde-pendent, scalable fonts in a PostScript language file or PDF document to achieve optimal font quality on any output device.

BACKGROUND

The PostScript language can represent fonts in a number of different formats. PostScript Type 3 fonts can be described as either resolution-specific bitmaps or scalable outlines. PostScript Type 1 fonts are resolution-independent outline fonts that can be quickly rasterized by the font machinery in Adobe PostScript interpreters and software that uses the Adobe Type Manager (ATM) font rasterizer. Type 1 fonts can contain "hints" that tell the font machinery how to most effectively rasterize the font even at low resolutions or small font sizes.

The Computer Modern fonts, commonly used with Donald Knuth's TeX typesetting language, are typically rendered as fixed-resolution bitmaps (in TeX's PK format) even though they were derived from device-independent descriptions in Knuth's METAFONT language. A driver pro-gram translates TeX's DVI file and PK fonts to a printer-specific font format for printing.

The default behavior of DVIPS 1 is to convert the PK fonts into Type 3 bitmapped fonts when creating a PostScript language file. The resulting PostScript language file thus contains resolu-tion- specific Type 3 bitmapped fonts that are not device- and resolution-independent like scalable Type 1 fonts.

If the PostScript language file is sent to a specific printer, device dependence may not be a problem. If the file is sent to printers of varying resolutions, however, this may be a problem because the fonts will not print at the native resolution of the printer. Sending a file with 300 dot-per-inch (dpi) fonts to a 600 dpi printer produces output no better than that of a 300 dpi printer.

Similar problems occur when the PostScript language file is converted to Adobe Portable Doc-ument Format (PDF). Since a PDF file is designed to be viewed and printed on a wide range of devicesincluding both computer monitors and printers of varying resolutions, it works most effectively with scalable outline fonts.

Although Adobe Acrobat Distiller will convert a PostScript language file with bitmapped fonts into PDF, these fonts display slowly and do not render well on screen in the resulting PDF file. But, if you use Type 1 versions of the fonts you will get a compact file format that delivers the optimal font quality when used with any display screen, zoom mode, or printer resolution.

USING TYPE 1 FONTS WITH DVIPS

The default behavior of Rokicki's DVIPS is to embed Type 3 bitmapped fonts. You can configure DVIPS to not embed bitmapped fonts by performing two steps:

1. Create a font map file to identify the fonts you do not want to embed.

2. Tell DVIPS how to reference the font map file.

You can tell DVIPS to use Type 1 fonts automatically for all of your DVIPS jobs or manually on a per-job basis depending on how you reference the font map file. Your system administrator can also configure DVIPS to automatically use Type 1 fonts globally for all users.

In each case you have the option to replace the Type 3 bitmapped fonts with references to the Type 1 fonts or to actually embed the code for the Type 1 fonts. The former creates smaller files, but requires the fonts to be available when the PostScript language file is printed or dis-tilled. If the fonts are embedded in the PostScript language file, you don't need to worry about whether the fonts are present in the printer or available to Acrobat Distiller, but youll have a larger PostScript language file and you may encounter memory limitations in certain Post-Script implementations.

You need access to the Type 1 versions of the fonts you use in your documents in order to embed the font information. Type 1 versions of the Computer Modern fonts are available in the BaKoMa collection (see "References and Resources") and from commercial type vendors.

Before distributing files with embedded fonts, consult the license agreement for your font package. Some typeface vendors do not allow you to embed complete fonts into a PDF or Post-Script language file for public distribution. Contact the type vendor for more information. You may embed all fonts included in the Adobe Type library.

CREATING THE FONT MAP FILE

To tell DVIPS to use Type 1 fonts rather than Type 3 fonts, you first need to create a font substitution, or font map file, that lists the names of the fonts that DVIPS should not embed as bitmaps.

For example, to instruct DVIPS to not embed the standard Computer Modern fonts, the font map file would look as follows:

```
cmb10
cmbsy10
cmbsy6
cmbsy7
cmbsy8
cmbsy9
cmbx10
cmbx12
...
```

This example assumes that the PostScript language names of the fonts (as referenced by the PostScript language interpreter's findfont operator) are identical to the names of the TFM files used by TeX (as is the case with the BaKoMa fonts).

If the PostScript language name for the font differs from the name used by TeX, use the font map file to create aliases to map the TeX name to the PostScript language name of the font. For example, if the Type 1 version of the CM fonts use upper case names, the font map would look like this:

```
cmb10    CMB10
cmbsy10  CMBSY10
cmbsy6   CMBSY6
cmbsy7   CMBSY7
cmbsy8   CMBSY8
cmbsy9   CMBSY9
cmbx10   CMBX10
cmbx12   CMBX12
...
```

If you use other PostScript language fonts you can also use this alias feature to map the names of the PostScript language fonts to the names of the TeX font files, such as:

```
hlvr Helvetica
hlvo Helvetica-Oblique
hlvb Helvetica-Bold
hlvbo Helvetica-BoldOblique
...
```

Here the font file known to TeX as hlvr (the name of the TFM file) refers to the PostScript language font Helvetica, hlvo refers to Helvetica-Oblique, and so on.

In the previous three examples, only the names of the fonts are embedded in the PostScript language file, so the fonts must be available to the PostScript language interpreter when the file is printed or distilled.

To embed the code for the Type 1 font in the PostScript language file, add "<" followed by the path to the font file in either PFB or PFA format.

For example, if you have PFB versions of the CM fonts in the directory /usr/local/lib/tex/fonts/type1/, your font map file would look like:

```
cmb10 </usr/local/lib/tex/fonts/type1/
  cmb10.pfb
cmbsy10 </usr/local/lib/tex/fonts/type1/
  cmbsy10.pfb
cmbsy6 </usr/local/lib/tex/fonts/type1/
  cmbsy6.pfb
cmbsy7 </usr/local/lib/tex/fonts/type1/
  cmbsy7.pfb
cmbsy8 </usr/local/lib/tex/fonts/type1/
  cmbsy8.pfb
cmbsy9 </usr/local/lib/tex/fonts/type1/
  cmbsy9.pfb
cmbx10 </usr/local/lib/tex/fonts/type1/
  cmbx10.pfb
cmbx12 </usr/local/lib/tex/fonts/type1/
  cmbx12.pfb
...
```

How the font substitutions specified in your font map file affect your DVIPS jobs depends on how you reference the font map file, as described in the next section.

REFERENCING THE FONT MAP FILE

You can configure DVIPS to make these font substitutions automatically for all of your DVIPS jobs or manually on a per-job basis. Your system administrator can also configure DVIPS to automatically use Type 1 fonts globally for all users by placing the font map entries described above in the DVIPS system-wide psfonts.map file.

Using a Font Map File Automatically for All Jobs

To configure DVIPS to automatically perform the font substitutions for all jobs, create a font map file and then create a file in your home directory named .dvipsrc containing the line:

```
p +fontmap.map
```

where fontmap.map is the name of your font map file. (Make sure the p parameter is lowercase.)

With some implementations of DVIPS you may need to specify the full path to the font map file. For example, if your home directory is /users/kmw/ and your font map file is called embedCM.map, you would add the following line to your .dvipsrc file:

```
p +/users/kmw/embedCM.map
```

The plus sign (+) before the name of the font map file indicates that the font map file is refer-enced after the system-wide psfonts.map file and any assignments in your font map file are in addition to (and will override) those found in the psfonts.map file.

Now you can run DVIPS as usual:

```
dvips dvifilename
```

The font substitutions in your font map file will be used for all your DVIPS jobs.

Using a Font Map File On a Per-Job Basis

If you want to frequently switch between font map files, rather than editing your .dvipsrc file each time, you can create one or more printer-specificor, in this case, "output-specific" configuration files named config.printername that tell DVIPS to reference different font map files. You can then reference a specific configuration file by using the uppercase P parameter with the DVIPS command:

```
dvips -P printername dvifilename
```

For example, you can have a file CM.map like the first three examples that only places refer-ences to the fonts in the PostScript language file and another file embedCM.map that includes the font code as in the last example shown.

Then create a file named config.distiller containing a line with the lowercase p parameter that specifies the file CM.map:

```
p +CM.map
```

and a file named config.distillembed with the line that specifies the file embedCM.map:

```
p +embedCM.map
```

In some implementations of DVIPS you may need to give the complete path to the font map file.

The following command line would then create a PostScript language file containing only the names of the fonts:

```
dvips -P distiller dvifilename
```

The following command line would similarly create a PostScript language file with the actual font code embedded in the PostScript language file:

```
dvips -P distillembed dvifilename
```

Depending on how your implementation of DVIPS is configured, DVIPS may look for the config.printername file only in the current directory or in both the current directory and your home directory. If you want to change how DVIPS looks for configuration files, you can set the TEXCONFIG environment variable as described in the "Environment Variables" section of the DVIPS documentation.

CONVERTING A POSTSCRIPT LANGUAGE FILE TO PDF USING ACROBAT DISTILLER

Once you've created a PostScript language file, use Acrobat Distiller to convert the PostScript language file to a PDF file. For more detailed information, refer to the Acrobat Distiller Online Guide.

If you embedded the Type 1 font code in the PostScript language file created by DVIPS, you can simply distill the PostScript language file as usual. If you embedded only references to the Type 1 fonts, you need to make sure Acrobat Distiller has access to the PostScript language fonts. See "Giving Acrobat Distiller access to fonts" in the Acrobat Distiller Online Guide.

FORCING FONT SUBSETTING

Acrobat Distiller 2.1 provides configuration settings to enable both font embedding and font subsetting in a PDF file. For more information on these options see Embedding fonts in the Acrobat Distiller Online Guide.

Acrobat Distiller's default maximum subsetting threshold is 10%. In other words, if more than 10% of the characters in a font are included in the document, the entire font is embedded in the document.

You may want to change this setting to a higher value. This can produce a smaller PDF file and you may be required by the font vendor's license to subset the font if you plan to distribute the PDF file (contact the font vendor for details).

You can change the threshold for font embedding by adding a line to the Example.ps file in Acrobat Distiller's

TIP MAC OS / WINDOWS

Working with bitmap EPS graphics

Usually, the compression and downsampling features in Acrobat make it easy to get documents with bitmap graphics down to a small size. But every now and then you might run into a PDF file that doesn't seem to be compressing as much as it should. If this happens, check your document for bitmap EPS files—Acrobat cannot downsample or compress bitmap EPS graphics.

Use an image-editing application like Photoshop to save these graphics in another format, such as TIFF. If the image was saved as an EPS so it could include a clipping path, you're still in luck if you're using the graphic in a PageMaker publication—PageMaker will recognize a clipping path saved in a Photoshop 3.0.x TIFF.

startup directory. In UNIX, the file is called DStartup.ps and is located in <installdir>/custom.

For example, to change the embedding threshold to the maximum value of 99 percent, open Example.ps with a text editor and add the following line to the file:

```
<< /SubsetFonts true /MaxSubsetPct 99 >>
  setdistillerparams
```

Although it doesn't matter where in the file you put this line, it's a good idea to place it in the "FONT EMBEDDING" section.

Save this file, restart Acrobat Distiller, and create the PDF file as usual. In most cases, all of the embedded fonts will now be subsetted.

If you later want to restore the original default setting, simply comment out this line by preced-ing it with a percent sign (%) and restart Acrobat Distiller.

CHECKING THE PDF FILE

If you've been using Type 3 bitmapped fonts in your PDF files, you'll see the difference the Type 1 fonts make as soon as you open the file in Acrobat Reader or Exchange. With scalable Type 1 fonts the file displays more quickly and can be viewed in any zoom mode with no loss of font quality. Furthermore, you can print the PDF file on any printer and the fonts will be rendered at the maximum resolution of the printer.

If your document uses fonts that are not referenced in your font map file (but are available on your system in the standard TeX PK format) it may still include Type 3 fonts. The BaKoMa col-lection, for example, does not have the manfnt font typically used to typeset the METAFONT logo, and documents using this font will continue to include this as a bitmapped font.

Although the differences between the Type 3 bitmap fonts and the Type 1 fonts are usually apparent upon inspection, you can check which fonts are used in a PDF file by selecting File > Document Info > Fonts in Acrobat Reader or Exchange. From the Font Info window click List All Fonts.

The Type column will display whether the fonts are Type 1 or Type 3. If you're using DVIPS the Type 3 bitmapped fonts will also be named T1, T2, etc., while Type 1 fonts will display their correct names, such as cmr10, cmbx10, and so on. Fonts that have a six-character prefix added to the font name (such as KICOLA+cmr7) are Type 1 fonts that have been subsetted.

REFERENCES AND RESOURCES

Files The BaKoMa collection, containing Type 1 versions of the Computer Modern (CM) fonts (in PFB format), is available from the comprehensive TeX Archive Network (CTAN) at: http://jasper.ora.com/CTAN/tex-archive/fonts/postscript/bakoma/

Tomas Rokicki's DVIPS program is available from the comprehensive TeX Archive Network (CTAN) at: http://jasper.ora.com/CTAN/tex-archive/dviware/dvips/

Included with DVIPS is the TeX source for the DVIPS documentation, "DVIPS: A TeX Driver." This document contains detailed information on the features and configuration settings of DVIPS.

TeX is described in The TeXbook by Donald Knuth, published by Addison-Wesley Publishing Company.

The TeX program and related tools and information are available online from the comprehen-sive TeX Archive Network (CTAN) at: http://jasper.ora.com/CTAN/tex-archive/

TERMS AND CONCEPTS

BaKoMa fonts: The BaKoMa Fonts Collection from Basil K. Malyshev includes Type 1 versions of the basic Computer Modern fonts. The BaKoMa fonts are available from the comprehensive TeX Archive Network (CTAN) at: http://jasper.ora.com/CTAN/tex-archive/fonts/postscript/bakoma/

DVI: The "device-independent" file format used by TeX as an intermediate file between the TeX source code and a printer-specific output file. The TeX program converts TeX source code into a DVI file. A driver program then converts the DVI file into another format for viewing or printing. DVIPS, for example, converts a DVI file into a PostScript language file which can then be printed on a PostScript language printer or converted to PDF using Acrobat Distiller.

DVIPS: A DVI print driver written by Tomas Rokicki that converts a TeX DVI file into a Post-Script file. DVIPS is available from the comprehensive TeX Archive Network (CTAN) at: http://jasper.ora.com/CTAN/tex-archive/dviware/dvips/

PDF: The "Portable Document Format" (PDF) is the native file format of the Adobe Acrobat family of products. The goal of PDF is to enable users to easily and reliably exchange and view electronic documents independent of the environment in which they were created. The imag-ing model underlying PDF is based on Adobe PostScript language, but contains additional fea-tures to display, navigate, and annotate electronic documents.

The PDF file format is documented in the Portable Document Format Reference Manual by Tim Bienz and Richard Cohn, published by Addison-Wesley Publishing Company.

Adobe Systems' Technical Note 5156, "Updates to the Portable Document Format" contains additional information and is available on the Adobe web site at: http://www.adobe.com/Support/TechNotes.html

PFA: "Printer Font ASCII" — an ASCII (text-only) encoding of a PostScript Type 1 font.

PFB: "Printer Font Binary" — a binary encoding of a PostScript Type 1 font

PK Font: A bitmapped font in TeXs "packed" format. Although many PK fonts are derived from device-independent descriptions in the METAFONT language, a PK font is a device- and resolution-specific bitmap. When a driver program (such as DVIPS) converts a TeX DVI file to a printer-specific format, it typically converts the PK font into a printer-specific bitmapped font format (such as a PostScript Type 3 bitmapped font).

TeX: A typesetting language written by Donald Knuth.

TFM: A TeX font metric (TFM) file contains information

TIP MAC OS / WINDOWS

Watch it!

If you distill a lot of PDFs, you can make the task quicker and easier by using Acrobat Distiller's Watched Directories (PC) or Watched Folders (Mac) feature.

When you designate a watched directory or folder (using the "Watched Directory..." or "Watched Folder..." command on the Distiller menu), Distiller creates "In" and "Out" subfolders in the watched folder. You move or drag your PostScript files to that "In" folder. When Distiller is open, it will monitor a directory or folder at whatever time intervals you specify, detect the PostScript files you've put there, create PDFs, and send the completed PDFs (and PostScript files, if you like) to the "Out" folder. If you pile up PostScript files in the "In" folder and then open Distiller, it will see them all immediately. If you're using Windows, you can use the Distiller Assistant to automatically cause Distiller to open whenever PostScript files appear in the watched folder.

about a font's character widths, liga-tures, and kerning pairs (but not the actual shapes of the fonts, which are typically stored in a PK file). The TFM file is used by the TeX program to typeset the document and create a TeX DVI file.

(1) The information on DVIPS is based primarily on DVIPS version 5.55 for Unix. Other versions may differ — check the documentation provided with your version of DVIPS for more information.

Using the Example.ps File to Embed Fonts in a PDF With Distiller 1.0 and Later

To embed fonts in a PDF file using Adobe Acrobat Distiller 1.0, you must modify the font embedding commands and add the font names to the Example.ps file, which is located in the Startup directory or the Distiller directory. Acrobat Distiller 2.0 and later include an Embed All Fonts option, but you may also use the Example.ps file to embed fonts in a PDF created with these versions of the Distiller.

The Example.ps file runs automatically when you launch the Distiller and its commands are used by the Distiller until you exit the application. Among the many commands in the Example.ps file are some that initiate font embedding. By default, these commands are "remarked out" or inactive and are not used by the Distiller. To activate the font embedding commands, open the Example.ps file in a text editor that saves in text-only format and remove the percent sign at the beginning of the "%<</AlwaysEmbed" or "%<<NeverEmbed" lines. To tell Distiller which fonts to always embed or to never embed, include the font names in the "%<</AlwaysEmbed" or "%<<NeverEmbed" lines, respectively. Then, save the Example.ps file as text-only.

Default Font Embedding Commands in Example.ps File

```
%%% List specific fonts to always be embedded
% << /AlwaysEmbed [/Specific font name] >>
  setdistillerparams
%%% List specific fonts to never be embedded
% << /NeverEmbed [/Specific font name] >>
  setdistillerparams
%%% Specify that all fonts (other than those
  in the /NeverEmbed list) are to be embedded.
% Note that the core 14 fonts (Times,
  Helvetica, and Courier families, Symbol, and
% ITC Zapf Dingbats) are never embedded. THIS
  FEATURE SHOULD BE USED WITH CAUTION
% AS THE RESULTING PDF FILES MAY BECOME
  FAIRLY LARGE.
% << /EmbedAllFonts true >> setdistillerparams
```

SPECIFYING FONTS TO ALWAYS EMBED OR NEVER EMBED

When including a font name in either the "%<</AlwaysEmbed" or "%<<NeverEmbed" lines, make sure you use the font name listed in the PostScript file you're distilling; a font name in a PostScript file may not match the font's name as it appears in an application's font menu or in Adobe Type Manager (ATM).

To determine how fonts are listed in a PostScript file, make a test PostScript file using the fonts you want to embed in the PDF. Then, open that PostScript file in a text editor and look for the font name. If you have the Adobe Type on Call 4.x CD-ROM, you can check the font name in the Fntnames.pdf file, which is located in the Documentation folder (Macintosh) or the Document directory (Windows).

When typing the font name in either the "%<</AlwaysEmbed" or "%<<NeverEmbed" lines, make sure you enclose it in square brackets (i.e., [ ]).

When Distiller runs, it will first query ATM to see if fonts listed in the "%<</AlwaysEmbed" line are available. If a font is not available in ATM, Distiller will check its own font location lists to find a match for the specified font name. If a listed font can't be located, Distiller will substitute that font with Courier.

Adding Debugging Code to Postscript Files That Generate Errors in Distiller

If Adobe Acrobat Distiller generates an error when distilling a PostScript file, you may add debugging statements to the PostScript file to isolate the cause. When each page or EPS graphic in the PostScript file is preceded by a debugging statement, the Distiller's Message window indicates whether that element was processed successfully or caused a PostScript error.

The easiest way to determine where the error is occurring is to include a debugging statement for each page in the PostScript file. Once you've narrowed it down to a specific page or pages, you may then be able to isolate the error to a specific element (i.e., EPS graphic).

To add debugging statements for each page in a PostScript file:

1. Open the .PS file in a text editor that saves in text-only format (e.g., Windows Write, Teach Text),
2. Locate the first page, which is described in the PostScript file as follows:
   ```
   %%Page: 1 1
   ```
3. On a new line underneath the page number indicator, add "(Page 1) == flush." For example:
   ```
   %%Page: 1 1
   (Page 1) == flush
   ```
4. Locate each subsequent page and add the "(Page xx) == flush" debugging code for each.
5. Save the PostScript file as text-only, then process it through Distiller. As each page is successfully processed, "(Page xx)" will appear in Distiller's Message window. If Distiller cannot process a page because of a PostScript error, that page will not be displayed in the Message window.

NOTE: Once you've narrowed the error to a specific page, try adding the debugging code to the end of that page's section in the PostScript file as well. If the page process without error, "(Page xx)" should appear twice in the Message window. If "(Page xx)" appears only once in the Message window, the page was not processed completely.

If the page on which the error occurs contains an EPS graphic, you may use debugging statements to determine whether that graphic is responsible for the PostScript error.

To add debugging statements for an EPS graphic:

1. Open the .PS file in a text editor that saves in text-only format (e.g., Windows Write, Teach Text),
2. Locate the EPS graphic on the offending page. For example:
   ```
   %!PS-Adobe-3.0 EPSF-3.0
   ```
3. On a new line underneath the EPSF description, insert "(Beginning EPS Art) == flush". For example:
   ```
   %!PS-Adobe-3.0 EPSF-3.0
   (Beginning EPS Art) == Flush
   ```
4. Locate the end of the EPSF description, which is described in the PostScript file as follows:
   ```
   %%EndDocument
   ```
5. On a new line underneath "%%EndDocument," insert "(Ending EPS Art) == flush". For example:
   ```
   %%EndDocument
   (Ending EPS Art) == Flush
   ```
6. Save the PostScript file as text-only, then process it through Distiller. If the EPS graphic is processed successfully, "(Beginning EPS Art)" and "(Ending EPS Art)" will appear in Distiller's Message window. If Distiller cannot process a page because of a PostScript error, "(Ending EPS Art)" will not appear in Distiller's Message window.

Example.ps File for Distiller 2.x and 3.0 General Information

When Adobe Acrobat Distiller starts, it looks in the Startup folder for text files containing PostScript programs. If the Startup folder contains one or more text files, Acrobat Distiller assumes they are PostScript programs and uses them to initialize the virtual memory of its PostScript interpreter. The Startup folder in the Distiller folder includes an Example.ps file, which contains examples of the job options you can control in a Startup file (e.g., frequently used fonts, font embedding attributes).

When a PostScript file located in the Startup folder contains the "setdistillerparams" operator, the PostScript file affects all subsequently processed PostScript files. However, when the operator is used in PostScript files not located in the Startup folder, only the file that contains the operator is affected. The setdistillerparams operator controls a number of parameters Distiller uses when converting PostScript to PDF. Parameters that can be set and read using the setdistillerparams operator include controlling the compression of text and graphics, downsampling and encoding sampled images, and embedding Type 1 fonts and instances of Type 1 multiple master fonts. For more information on the PostScript language used in the Distiller 3.0 Example.ps file, see the Distparm.pdf file, which is located in the Acrobat3.0\Exchange\Help\ directory.

To activate a line in the Example.ps file so that Distiller uses that option when processing files, remove the semicolon at the beginning of the line and save the Example.ps file in text-only format.

Distiller 3.0 Example.ps File

NOTE: The Example.ps files included with Distiller 2.1 and 3.0 are not identical.

```
%
% File: Example.ps
%
% End-user startup PostScript job file.
  Include any permanent PostScript into
% this file.  This file will be executed as an
  "unencapsulated job"*
% each time the Acrobat Distiller applica-
  tion starts up.
%
% *See "PostScript(R) Language Reference
  Manual, Second Edition," Chapter 3.7.7
```

```
%
% note: This file will be overwritten each
  time you install Acrobat Distiller.
% We recommend you make a copy of this file
  to a different name and modify
% that copy.
%
% Each of the items below is presented as an
  example as is commented out. To
% actually use one of the examples,
  uncomment the line(s) of PostScript code by
% deleting the "%" character and modify to
  suit your needs.
%%% DEFAULT PAGE SIZE
%%% The Distiller recognizes most all
  PostScript page size operators. If you
%%% want to change the default page size
  used by Distiller, you may do so using
%%% the setpagedevice command. Page dimen-
  sions are in points (width x height).
% << /PageSize [612 792] >> setpagedevice
%%% MESSAGES
%%% Print a text string to the Messages
  window in the Status dialog
% (Your message here...) print flush
%%% JOB OPTION AND COMPRESSION SETTINGS
%%% To fine-tune the JPEG settings below, we
  suggest you only change the number
%%% directly following the /QFactor key. For
  QFactor > .50 use the Blend and
%%% Samples data in the .50 example; for
  QFactor < .50, use the Samples data in
%%% the .25 example and omit the Blend key.
  Please note the JPEG compression
%%% and downsampling is individually con-
  trollable for grayscale and color images.
%%% For reference, the default QFactor
  values for Acrobat Distiller 2.0 are:
%%%
%%%      High compression:      QFactor = 1.3
%%%      Medium-High compression:  QFactor =
  0.9
%%%      Medium compression:       QFactor =
  0.5
%%%      Medium-Low compression:   QFactor =
  0.25
%%%      Low compression:       QFactor = 0.1
% <</EncodeGrayImages  true
% /GrayImageFilter   /DCTEncode
% /GrayImageDict   << /QFactor 0.50 /Blend 1 /
  HSamples [2 1 1 2] /VSamples [2 1 1 2] >>
% /DownsampleGrayImages true
% /GrayImageResolution  72
%
% /EncodeColorImages  true
% /ColorImageFilter  /DCTEncode
% /ColorImageDict   << /QFactor 0.25 /HSamples
  [1 1 1 1] /VSamples [1 1 1 1] >>
% /DownsampleColorImages true
% /ColorImageResolution  72
%
% >> setdistillerparams
%%% CONVERT CMYK IMAGES TO RGB IMAGES
%%% Converting CMYK images to RGB can reduce
  file sizes and potentially improve the
%%% quality of some screen displays. Note
  that CMYK line art is NOT converted to RGB.
%%% The default setting for this option is
  true, but can be disabled via this file.
% << /ConvertCMYKImagesToRGB false >>
  setdistillerparams
%%% FONT EMBEDDING
%%% Specify that all fonts (other than those
  in the /NeverEmbed list) are to be embed-
  ded.
%%% as subsets. This is the recommended
  setting for Acrobat Distiller 2.0.
%%% Note that the core 14 fonts (Times,
  Helvetica, and Courier families, Symbol,
  and
%%% ITC Zapf Dingbats) are never embedded.
% << /EmbedAllFonts true /SubsetFonts true
  >> setdistillerparams
% List specific fonts to always be embedded
% << /AlwaysEmbed [/Carta] >>
  setdistillerparams
% List specific fonts to never be embedded
% << /NeverEmbed [/Carta] >>
  setdistillerparams
%%% PRE-LOADING FONTS INTO MEMORY
%%% Load a font into the FontDirectory
  dictionary (local VM)
% /Courier findfont pop
%%% AUTOMATIC IMAGE COMPRESSION FILTER
  SELECTION
%%% Automatic filter selection enables the
  proper handling of documents
%%% containing photographic and screen shot
  images. The Distiller examines
%%% samples in 8-bits-per-component images
  looking for sharp color changes.
%%% If it has sharp color changes, LZW
  compression is used; if it has smooth
%%% color changes, JPEG compression is used.
  The default setting for this
%%% option is true, but can be disabled via
  this file.
% <</AutoFilterColorImages false >>
  setdistillerparams
% <</AutoFilterGrayImages false >>
  setdistillerparams
%%EOF
```

Distiller 2.1 Example.ps File

```
%
```

```
% File: Example.ps
%
% End-user startup PostScript job file.
  Include any permanent PostScript into
% this file.  This file will be executed as an
  "unencapsulated job"*
% each time the Acrobat Distiller applica-
  tion starts up.
%
% *See "PostScript(R) Language Reference
  Manual, Second Edition," Chapter 3.7.7
%
% Each of the items below is presented as an
  example as is commented out. To
% actually use one of the examples,
  uncomment the line(s) of PostScript code by
% deleting the "%" character and modify to
  suit your needs.
%%% DEFAULT PAGE SIZE
%%% The Distiller recognizes most all
  PostScript page size operators. If you
%%% want to change the default page size
  used by Distiller, you may do so using
%%% the setpagedevice command. Page dimen-
  sions are in points (width x height).
% << /PageSize [612 792] >> setpagedevice
%%% MESSAGES
%%% Print a text string to the Messages
  window in the Status dialog
% (Your message here...) print flush
%%% JOB OPTION AND COMPRESSION SETTINGS
%%% Change or report the Distiller's Job
  Option settings
% << /DoThumbnails true >>
  setdistillerparams
%%% To fine-tune the JPEG settings below, we
  suggest you only change the number
%%% directly following the /QFactor key. For
  QFactor > .50 use the Blend and
%%% Samples data in the .50 example; for
  QFactor < .50, use the Samples data in
%%% the .25 example and omit the Blend key.
  Please note the JPEG compression
%%% and downsampling is individually con-
  trollable for grayscale and color images.
%%% For reference, the default QFactor
  values for Acrobat Distiller 2.0 are:
%%%
%%%     High compression:     QFactor = 1.3
%%%     Medium-High compression:  QFactor =
  0.9
%%%     Medium compression:       QFactor =
  0.5
%%%     Medium-Low compression:   QFactor =
  0.25
%%%     Low compression:      QFactor = 0.1
% << /EncodeGrayImages  true
% /GrayImageFilter  /DCTEncode
% /GrayImageDict  << /QFactor 0.50 /Blend 1 /
  HSamples [2 1 1 2] /VSamples [2 1 1 2] >>
% /DownsampleGrayImages true
% /GrayImageResolution  72
%
% /EncodeColorImages  true
% /ColorImageFilter  /DCTEncode
% /ColorImageDict  << /QFactor 0.25 /HSamples
  [1 1 1 1] /VSamples [1 1 1 1] >>
% /DownsampleColorImages true
% /ColorImageResolution  72
%
% >> setdistillerparams
%%% CONVERT CMYK IMAGES TO RGB IMAGES
%%% Converting CMYK images to RGB can reduce
  file sizes and potentially improve the
%%% quality of some screen displays. Note
  that CMYK line art is NOT converted to RGB.
%%% The default setting for this option is
  true, but can be disabled via this file.
% << /ConvertCMYKImagesToRGB false >>
  setdistillerparams
%%% FONT EMBEDDING
%%% Specify that all fonts (other than those
  in the /NeverEmbed list) are to be embed-
  ded.
%%% as subsets. This is the recommended
  setting for Acrobat Distiller 2.0.
%%% Note that the core 14 fonts (Times,
  Helvetica, and Courier families, Symbol,
  and
%%% ITC Zapf Dingbats) are never embedded.
% << /EmbedAllFonts true /SubsetFonts true
  >> setdistillerparams
% List specific fonts to always be embedded
% << /AlwaysEmbed [/Carta] >>
  setdistillerparams
% List specific fonts to never be embedded
% << /NeverEmbed [/Carta] >>
  setdistillerparams
%%% PRE-LOADING FONTS INTO MEMORY
%%% Load a font into the FontDirectory
  dictionary (local VM)
% /Courier findfont pop
%%EOF
```

Using Distiller's RunDir Procedure to Combine PostScript Files

You can use Adobe Acrobat Distiller's RunDir procedure to automatically combine multiple PostScript files into a single Portable Document Format (PDF) file. The RunDir procedure uses only one font subset for each embedded font.

There are two ways to use the RunDir procedure. One way is to open the premade Rundirex.txt file, located in the

Xtras folder in the Distiller folder, in a text editor that can save in text-only format (e.g., NotePad, TeachText) and edit the "PathName" line to reference the directory containing the PostScript files you want to combine into a PDF file. Complete directions on using the Rundirex.txt file are included in that file.

You can also create your own RunDir file instead of editing the premade Rundirex.txt file. To make your own RunDir file:

1. Open a text editor that can save in text only format (e.g., NotePad, TeachText).
2. Choose File > New, then enter the following information (where "PathName" is the name of the directory containing your *.PS files).

   When using Distiller for the Macintosh, enter the following:

```
%!
/PathName (Macintosh HD:Test:*.ps) def
/RunDir {{/mysave save def dup = flush
  RunFile clear cleardictstack mysave
  restore} 255 string file nameforall} def
PathName RunDir
```

   When using Distiller for Windows, enter the following:

```
%!
/PathName (c:\\\\mydir\\\\*.ps) def
/RunDir {{/mysave save def dup = flush
  RunFile clear cleardictstack mysave
  restore} 255 string file nameforall} def
PathName RunDir
```

   NOTE: Use pathnames that the computer running Acrobat Distiller will recognize (i.e., when you use Acrobat Distiller on a Macintosh, use the Macintosh pathname format, even if you create the RunDir file in Windows). When using Acrobat Distiller on a Network server, be sure to check with your system administrator and create a RunDir file with pathnames that reflect the correct platform.
3. Save the file as text-only and name it with a ".txt" extension (e.g., Mybook.txt).
4. Move all the PostScript files you want to distill using the RunDir procedure into the directory listed in the "PathName" line.

   NOTE: Files are distilled in alphabetical order and then numerical order, so name your files accordingly. For example:

```
Ac001.ps    Cover
Bt001.ps    Table of Contents
Ch001.ps    Chapter 1
Ch002.ps    Chapter 2
Ch003.ps    Chapter 3
In001.ps    Index
```

5. Launch Acrobat Distiller, choose File > Open, and select your RunDir file (e.g., Mybook.txt). Distiller opens the file, sequentially processes all PostScript files in the specified directory, and combines them into a single PDF file. The PDF file is given the same base name as the RunDir file, but is given a ".pdf" extension (e.g., Mybook.pdf).

   NOTE: The name of each PostScript file will appear in Distiller's log file and in Distiller's message window as it is processed. If you do not want Distiller to display the file names or if you want it to create a log file only when an error occurs, change the third line in step 2 to the following:

```
/RunDir {{/mysave save def RunFile clear
  cleardictstack mysave restore} 255 string
  file nameforall} def PathName RunDir
```

MAC OS / WINDOWS

Using the RunFile Procedure to Combine PostScript Files

The Acrobat Distiller and Acrobat Network Distiller applications support a predefined procedure called "RunFile" for processing multiple PostScript files into one PDF file. RunFile is a convenient alternative to combining multiple

TIP MAC OS / WINDOWS

Drag-and-drop Processing With the Acrobat Distiller

Drag-and-drop distilling with the Adobe Acrobat Distiller enables you to create one or more PDFs while bypassing Distiller's Save As PDF dialog box. To drag and drop distill, select a range of PostScript files in the File Manager (Windows), the Finder (Macintosh) or the desktop (Windows 95 or Macintosh) and drag them over the Distiller icon or alias to start the Distiller and process the files to PDF. As the PDF files are created, they are placed in the same folder or directory as the source PostScript files and named according to their original *.ps file names (the ".ps" extension is changed to ".pdf"). For example, Raygun.ps, Sunlight.ps, and Moonbeam.ps are named Raygun.pdf, Sunlight.pdf, and Moonbeam.pdf.

While the intent of drag-and-drop distilling is to bypass Acrobat Distiller's Save As PDF dialog box, you can force Acrobat Distiller to display the Save As PDF dialog box when using this distilling method by pressing the Command key (Macintosh) or Shift key (Windows) while you drag and drop the PostScript files. If you have more than one file selected and you want to see the Save As PDF dialog for each file, you must keep the Command key (Macintosh) or Shift key (Windows) depressed until the last file is processed.

PDF files into a single PDF file using Adobe Acrobat Exchange's Insert command.

USING THE RUNFILE PROCEDURE

NOTE: Use the exact syntax listed in the following procedure, including spaces and capital letters.

1. Using a text editor (Windows Write, Microsoft Word), type the following text in a new file:

```
%!
/prun {/mysave save def dup = flush RunFile
clear cleardictstack mysave restore} def
```

   The first line is a comment that identifies this file as a PostScript file. The next line defines a procedure to access the RunFile procedure.
2. On a new line, enter the location and name of a PostScript file you wish to process, in parentheses, followed by "prun." For example, when using Distiller for Windows:

```
(C:\\REPORTS\\JANUARY\\JANSALES.PS) prun
```

   OR: When using Distiller for Macintosh:

```
(Hard Disk 80:Reports:January:January
Sales.ps) prun
```

   This line instructs Distiller to process the jansales.ps file in the reports/january directory (or the January Sales.ps file in the January folder inside the Reports folder).

   NOTE: When using Distiller, pathnames are relative to the computer running the Distiller, which may not be the machine on which the file was created. This is especially important when using the Acrobat Network Distiller program, because the pathname to an In directory or folder used by the Network Distiller may be very different from the pathname to the same directory or folder used by a local workstation. This information can be obtained from your system administrator.
3. Add the location and name of each PostScript file you wish to process to the line created in step 2. Make sure there is one space between each entry.
4. Type the following on a new line to designate the end of the file:

```
%EOF
```

5. Save the file as text-only.
6. Place the file in the Distiller's In directory for processing. When you use the Distiller to process this file, it will read all specified PostScript files sequentially and combine them into a single PDF file. The PDF file will have the same name as the text-only file created in the steps above but will have a .pdf extension. The name of each PostScript file will appear in the Distiller's Messages window as it is being processed and will also appear in a log file.

   NOTE: If you do not want Distiller to display the PostScript file names or want it to create a log file only when an error has occurred, follow the steps above, substituting the following text for that listed in line 3 of step 1:

```
/prun {/mysave save def RunFile clear
cleardictstack mysave restore} def
```

Example:

The following RunFile procedure combines three PostScript files into one PDF file using the Distiller for Windows:

```
%! /prun {/mysave save def dup = flush
RunFile clear cleardictstack mysave
restore} def (C:\\WORK\\TITLEPG.PS) prun
(C:\\WORK\\BODY.PS) prun
(C:\\WORK\\INDEX.PS) prun %EOF
```

If this file is saved as final.ps and opened with Distiller, the three specified PostScript files in the directory called work on drive C: of the machine running Distiller would be processed and a file named final.pdf would be generated.

There are several example RunFile procedure files (runfile_. ps) in Distiller's Xtras directory.

USING THE RUNFILE PROCEDURE WITHOUT CLEARING THE DICTIONARY STACK

If you include PostScript files that are not completely self contained (i.e., they rely on a prolog having been run that leaves a procset dictionary on the stack), you must use a different procedure; otherwise errors may occur during the distilling process and the resulting PDF file may be incorrect. However, by not clearing the dictionary stack, you increase the probability that the Distiller will run out of memory and return with an error that would not have occurred had the PostScript files been distilled separately. Increasing the memory available to the Distiller may correct this problem.

To use the RunFile procedure without clearing the dictionary stack, follow the directions above, except in the second line of step 2 substitute the following:

```
/prun {dup = flush RunFile} def
```

If you also do not want a log file created unless an error has occurred, you can omit the second line of step 2 and access the RunFile procedure directly by substituting RunFile for prun in step 3. For example:

```
(C:\\REPORTS\\JANUARY\\JANSALES.PS) RunFile
```

Creating a PDF File from a FrameMaker 5 Document

To create a fully functional PDF (Portable Document Format) file from FrameMaker 5, create a PostScript file and then distill it using Adobe Acrobat Distiller. Do not print your document using PDF Writer; PDF Writer will create a PDF file that does not contain your original document's hypertext links.

When you print a book file to disk as a PostScript file, FrameMaker can create either a single PostScript file for the entire book, or separate PostScript files for each document in the book. If you choose to have FrameMaker create separate PostScript files, you can link the PostScript files, as well as external files, after you distill them with Acrobat Distiller.

SETTING UP DOCUMENTS WITH BOTH PORTRAIT AND LANDSCAPE PAGES

If your FrameMaker for the Macintosh documents contain both portrait and landscape pages, change the paper size in the Page Setup dialog box to a size that fits both orientations (e.g., tabloid). If the document's paper size is not large enough to fit both landscape and portrait orientation, landscape pages in the resulting PostScript and PDF files will be cropped.

If a larger paper size is not available in the Page Setup dialog box, set up your printer with the Acrobat Distiller PPD file:

1. Select the Chooser from the Apple menu.
2. Select the Apple LaserWriter or AdobePS printer driver in the left scrollbox, then select your printer in the right scrollbox.
3. Click Setup, then click the Select PPD button.
4. Select Acrobat Distiller (PPD) from the Select a PostScript Printer Description File scrollbox, then click Select.
5. Click OK in the Setup dialog box, then close the Chooser.

CREATING A POSTSCRIPT FILE FROM A FRAMEMAKER DOCUMENT

To print a document to disk as a PostScript file from FrameMaker:

1. Open your document in FrameMaker and choose File > Print. 2. In the Print dialog box, select Generate Acrobat Data, then click Acrobat Setup.
3. Move the paragraph tags for which you want to have a corresponding bookmark in the PDF file to the Include list.
4. To change the hierarchy of the paragraph tags (and their ensuing PDF bookmarks), select a paragraph tag in the Include Paragraphs list, then click on the left (<<) or right (>>) Bookmark Level buttons.
5. Click Set to save your settings.
6. Print the file to disk as a PostScript file. In FrameMaker for Windows, select Print Only to File, enter a path and filename in the text box, then click Print. In FrameMaker for the Macintosh, select File for Destination and then click Save.

NOTE: To ensure that links to other PDF files will work correctly from FrameMaker for the Macintosh, do not change the default filename of the PostScript file.

CREATING A POSTSCRIPT FILE FROM A FRAMEMAKER BOOK FILE TO PRINT A BOOK FILE TO DISK AS A POSTSCRIPT FILE FROM FRAMEMAKER:

1. Select the book (.bk) file from the bottom of the File menu.
2. When the book list appears, choose File > Print. 3. From the Print Files in Book dialog box, select the files you want to print, then click Print.
4. In the Print dialog box, select Generate Acrobat Data, then click Acrobat Setup.
5. Move the paragraph tags for which you want to have a corresponding bookmark in the PDF file to the Include list.
6. To change the hierarchy of the paragraph tags (and their ensuing PDF bookmarks), select a paragraph tag in the Include Paragraphs list, then click on the left (<<) or right (>>) Bookmark Level buttons.
7. Click Set to save your settings.
8. To create a single PostScript file in FrameMaker for Windows, select Print Only to File, enter a path and filename in the text box, then click Print. In FrameMaker for the Macintosh, select File for Destination and then click Save.
   NOTE: To ensure that links to other PDF files will work correctly from FrameMaker for the Macintosh, do not change the default filename of the PostScript file.
   To create a separate PostScript file for each document in the book, enter an asterisk in the filename text box instead typing a filename (Windows) or accepting the default filename (Macintosh).

DISTILLING THE FRAMEMAKER POSTSCRIPT FILE

To distill the FrameMaker PostScript file:

1. Launch Acrobat Distiller and choose File > Open.
2. Select the FrameMaker PostScript file and click OK (Windows) or Open (Macintosh).
3. Type a filename and choose a location for the file.
4. Click OK (Windows) or Save (Macintosh).

Acrobat Distiller automatically converts FrameMaker's text flow tags into PDF article threads and paragraph tags into PDF bookmarks.

Generating a PostScript File from QuarkXPress for the Macintosh for Use with Acrobat Distiller

This technical note describes how to print a QuarkXPress document to disk as a PostScript file so it can be distilled by Adobe Acrobat Distiller. Not following the steps below may cause an error to occur when you distill the PostScript file, or may cause unexpected results.

INSTALLING THE ACROBAT DISTILLER PPD FILE FOR QUARKXPRESS

QuarkXPress uses information in PPD (PostScript Printer Description) files when generating PostScript code. The Acrobat Distiller PPD file provides Quark with essential Acrobat Distiller information, such as built-in fonts, paper sizes, and resolution capabilities. Make sure you install the PPD file, even if you do not plan to use Acrobat Distiller on this computer.

To install the Acrobat Distiller PPD file, copy the XPress PDF-Acrobat Distiller PPD file from the Acrobat Distiller Xtras folder to the PPD folder in the QuarkXPress folder (QuarkXPress 3.3) or to the QuarkXPress folder (QuarkXPress 3.2 and earlier).

GENERATING A POSTSCRIPT FILE USING PSPRINTER 8.X OR LASERWRITER 8.3 AND EARLIER

To print a QuarkXPress document to disk as a PostScript file using the Adobe PSPrinter 8.x printer driver or the Apple LaserWriter 8.3 and earlier printer driver:

1. Open your document in QuarkXPress and choose File > Page Setup.
2. Select Adobe Acrobat Distiller from the Printer Type scroll box.

TIP MAC OS / WINDOWS

Using Keyboard Shortcuts with Distiller's Save as Dialog Box

By default, when you open a PostScript file in Adobe Acrobat Distiller, Distiller displays the Save as dialog box, enabling you to name the pending PDF file. There are several keyboard shortcuts you can use to bypass the Save as dialog box or force the PDF file to save to the last used directory or directory containing the source .PS file.

Bypassing the Save as Dialog Box:

To save a PDF in the same directory as the source .PS file without invoking the Save as dialog box, press the Shift key (Windows) or Option key (Macintosh) as you click on Open in Distiller's Open dialog box. Distiller will generate a PDF with the same name as the source PostScript file (the extension is changed to PDF) and save it in the same directory.

Forcing the PDF to Save in the Same Directory as the Source .PS File:

When you want to save a PDF in the same directory as the source .PS file but want to give it a different name, press the Control key (Windows) or Command key (Macintosh) while clicking Open in Distiller's Open dialog box. The Save as dialog box opens and the directory containing the source .PS file is selected as the target directory.

Forcing the Last Folder Used to Display as the Target Directory in the Save as Dialog Box When Drag-and-Drop Distilling:

To display the Save as dialog box with the last folder used set up as the default folder, press the Control key (Windows) or Option key (Macintosh) while dragging-and-dropping .PS files onto the Distiller. The Save as dialog box will display with the last folder used selected as the target directory.

3. Enter the document width and leave the Page Offset and Page Gap amounts at 0.
4. Set the orientation to Portrait, even if all or part of your document is landscape. When you open the resulting PDF file in Acrobat Exchange, the page will be in the proper orientation.
5. Click Options, then deselect the Smooth Graphics option. (When Smooth Graphics is selected, QuarkXPress adds thousands of Type 3 characters to your PostScript file in an attempt to smooth any bitmap graphics in your document, making your PostScript file much larger than it needs to be.)
6. Click OK to close the remaining dialog boxes.
7. Choose File > Print,.
8. Set the Destination option to File, then select your desired printer options and click Save.
9. Specify the name and destination for your PostScript file.
10. If you will be distilling the PostScript file on a different computer, select Font Inclusion, then select All or All But Standard 13 to ensure Acrobat Distiller has access to all of the fonts used in the document.
11. Click Save to generate the PostScript file.
12. Distill the PostScript file in the usual manner. If you normally drop your PostScript files into Acrobat Distillers In folder, consider saving the PostScript file directly into the In folder. Acrobat Distiller will automatically convert it to PDF format.

GENERATING A POSTSCRIPT FILE USING LASERWRITER 8.4

To print a QuarkXPress document to disk as a PostScript file using LaserWriter 8.4 or later:

1. Open your document in QuarkXPress and choose File > Page Setup.
2. Select your page size, then set the orientation to Portrait, even if all or part of your document is landscape. When you open the resulting PDF file in Acrobat Exchange, the page will be in the proper orientation.
4. Select QuarkXPress from the Page Attributes pop-up menu.
5. Select Adobe Acrobat Distiller from the Printer Type scroll box.
6. Specify a Paper Width and leave the Paper Offset and Paper Gap amounts at 0.
7. Select PostScript Options from the QuarkXPress pop-up menu, then deselect the Smooth Graphics option. (When Smooth Graphics is selected, QuarkXPress adds thousands of Type 3 characters to your PostScript file in an attempt to smooth any bitmap graphics in your document, making your PostScript file much larger than it needs to be.)
8. Click OK to close the Page Setup dialog box.
9. Choose File > Print,.
10. Select File from the Destination pop-up menu, then select your desired printer options and click Save.
11. Specify a name and destination for your PostScript file.
12. If you will be distilling the PostScript file on a different computer, click Font Inclusion, then select All or All But Standard 13 to ensure Acrobat Distiller has access to all of the fonts used in the document.
13. Click Save to generate the PostScript file.
14. Distill the PostScript file in the usual manner. If you normally drop your PostScript files into Acrobat Distillers In folder, consider saving the PostScript file directly into the In folder. Acrobat Distiller will automatically convert it to PDF format.

Creating a PostScript File from PageMaker for Use With Acrobat Distiller

This technical note describes how to print a PageMaker publication to disk as a PostScript file so it can be distilled by Adobe Acrobat Distiller 3.0.

The Create Adobe PDF Plug-in included with PageMaker 6.01 and earlier does not support Distiller 3.0; the plug-in included with PageMaker 6.5 does support Distiller 3.0. If you do not have access to PageMaker 6.5 or later, create a PostScript file in PageMaker and distill it manually using Acrobat Distiller 3.0.

CREATING A POSTSCRIPT FILE IN PAGEMAKER 6.X FOR USE WITH ACROBAT DISTILLER

To create a PostScript file from PageMaker 6.x (Macintosh and Windows) for distilling with Acrobat Distiller 3.0:

1. Open your publication in Adobe PageMaker 6.x.
2. Choose File > Print.
3. Select a PostScript printer from the Print To pop-up menu and the Acrobat Distiller PPD from the Type pop-up menu. The Acrobat Distiller PPD, which is automatically installed with Acrobat 3.0, provides PageMaker with Acrobat Distiller information, such as its built-in fonts, paper sizes, and color capabilities.
4. Click Paper. Select a paper size (e.g., Letter, Legal), or select Custom and enter the same width and height values you entered in the Page Setup dialog box, set the Page Orientation to Normal, then click OK.
5. Click Options to open the Print Options dialog box.
6. Select Write PostScript to File in the PostScript section. You can specify a new location and name by clicking Save As (Macintosh) or Browse (Windows). When using PageMaker on a Macintosh, click Save As to ensure the PostScript file is saved to the correct location.
7. Select Normal in the PostScript section.
8. Click Save to generate the PostScript file.

USING THE CREATE ADOBE PDF PLUG-IN TO CREATE A POSTSCRIPT FILE IN PAGEMAKER 6.5X

To create a PostScript file from PageMaker 6.5x (Macintosh and Windows) using the Create Adobe PDF Plug-in:

1. Open your publication in Adobe PageMaker 6.5x.
2. Choose File > Export > Adobe PDF.
3. Select the Prepare PostScript File for Distilling Separately option, which generates a PostScript file, but does not start Distiller.
4. Select the Use Distiller's Watched Folder option, then click Select to save the file to a watched folder.
   NOTE: If you do not select this option you can save the PostScript file to any location. However, if you don't save the file to a watched folder, Distiller will not process it automatically.
5. In the Watched Directories dialog box, select a watched folder. Select Auto-list From Distiller to list all watched folders monitored by Distiller.
6. Click View Options when you want to check or change the Distiller Job Options specified for the selected watched folder.
7. Click OK to return to the Create Adobe PDF dialog box, then click Export.
8. Name the file, then click Save.

Once you've created your PostScript file, you can distill it with Acrobat Distiller 3.0. If you save the PostScript file directly to a watched folder monitored by Acrobat Distiller, Distiller will automatically convert it to PDF.

WINDOWS

Generating a PostScript File from QuarkXPress Windows for Use with Acrobat Distiller

This technical note describes how to print a QuarkXPress document to disk as a PostScript file so it can be distilled by Adobe Acrobat Distiller. Not following the steps below may cause an error to occur when you distill the PostScript file, or may cause unexpected results.

INSTALLING THE ACROBAT DISTILLER PPD FILE FOR QUARKXPRESS

QuarkXPress uses information in PPD (PostScript Printer Description) files when generating PostScript code. The Acrobat Distiller PPD file provides Quark with essential Acrobat Distiller information, such as built-in fonts, paper sizes, and resolution capabilities. Make sure you install the PPD file, even if you do not plan to use Acrobat Distiller on this computer. To install the Acrobat Distiller PPD file for QuarkXPress, copy the Acrodist.ppd file from the Distiller\Xtras directory to the Quark\PDF directory.

GENERATING A POSTSCRIPT FILE FROM QUARKXPRESS

To print QuarkXPress document to disk as a PostScript file:

1. Configure your printer driver to print to a PostScript printer on FILE. For instructions, refer to the QuarkXPress Reference Manual.
2. Open your QuarkXPress document and choose File > Printer Setup.
3. Select PostScript Printer on FILE from the Specific Printer scroll box.
4. Select Acrobat Distiller from the Use PDF For scroll box.
5. Click OK close the Printer Setup dialog box.
6. Choose File > Print.
7. Select your desired printer options, then click OK.
8. Enter the name and destination for your PostScript file in the Print to File dialog box. (Add a ".ps" extension to the filename to distinguish it as a PostScript file.)
9. Click OK to generate the PostScript file.
10. Distill the PostScript file in the usual manner. If you normally drop your PostScript files into Acrobat Distiller's In directory name, consider saving the PostScript file directly into the In directory. Acrobat Distiller will automatically convert it to PDF format.

Running Acrobat Distiller Using Command Lines

You can run Adobe Acrobat Distiller 2.0x using command lines and command line switches that instruct Distiller to carry out specific functions. To enter command lines, choose File > Run in either Windows File Manager or Program Manager (Windows 3.x) or choosing Start > Run (Windows 95) and then enter command lines in the Run dialog box.

ACROBAT DISTILLER COMMAND LINES

The following examples assume Acrobat Distiller is on the current path. Entries between brackets ([ ]) are optional commands.

To process one or more PostScript files, use the following command line:

```
<Drive>:<DIR> SourceFile1[, SourceFile2...]
```

For example, to process a single file:

```
C:\acrodist sample.ps
```

For example, to process multiple files, type:

```
C:\acrodist myfile.ps, g:\my_dir\example.ps,
  d:\another.ps
```

To process a single PostScript file and then name the resulting PDF file, use the following command line and the "/o" switch:

```
<Drive>:<DIR> /o destFile sourceFile
```

For example:

```
C:\acrodist /o chap_1.pdf C:\draft.ps
```

NOTE: You cannot use the "/o" switch to distill multiple files using the command line. Distiller saves the resulting PDF file in the same directory as the source file, ignoring an output path included in the command line.

To quit Acrobat Distiller after it finishes distilling all PostScript files in watched directories and those specified using the command line (e.g., Distiller quits after reaching an idle state), use the following command line:

```
<Drive>:<DIR> /q [sourceFile1[,
  sourceFile2...]]
```

For example, to quit Distiller after it distiller all PostScript files in a watched directory:

```
C:\acrodist /q
```

For example, to quit Distiller after it distiller all PostScript files specified in the command line:

```
C:\acrodist /q myfile.ps, G:<DIR>\example.ps
```

Creating a PostScript File from QuarkXPress for Windows for Use With Acrobat Distiller

For best results when creating a PostScript file with QuarkXPress for conversion with Acrobat Distiller, use the Acrobat Distiller PPD file (Adistill.ppd), which provides Quark with essential Acrobat Distiller information (e.g., built-in fonts, custom paper sizes, and resolution capabilities). Acrobat 3.0 automatically installs the Acrobat Distiller PPD file into the Windows\System directory.

To create a PostScript file from QuarkXPress for distilling with Acrobat Distiller 3.0:

1. Configure your printer driver to print to a PostScript printer on FILE. For instructions, see the QuarkXPress Reference Manual.
2. Open your QuarkXPress document and choose File > Print.
3. In the Print dialog box, click Setup.
4. Select PostScript Printer on FILE from the Specific Printer pop-up menu.
5. Select Acrobat Distiller from the Use PDF For pop-up menu. The Paper Size option is dimmed after you select Acrobat Distiller because the Acrobat Distiller PPD accommodates custom page sizes. The minimum page size is 1-by-1", and the maximum page size is 45-by-45".
6. Enter the document's width in the Paper Width text box.
7. Click OK to close the Printer Setup dialog box and return to the Print dialog box.
8. Select your desired printer options, then click OK.
9. Enter the name and destination for your PostScript file in the Print to File dialog box. Add a ".ps" extension to the filename to distinguish it as a PostScript file.
10. Click OK to generate the PostScript file.

After you create the PostScript file, distill it with Acrobat Distiller 3.0. If you save the PostScript file directly to a watched folder monitored by Acrobat Distiller, Distiller will automatically convert it to PDF.

Creating a PostScript File from Corel Ventura Publisher 5.0 for Use With Acrobat Distiller

You can convert Corel Ventura Publisher files to PDF files using either the Adobe Acrobat PDFWriter or Acrobat Distiller. However, the PDF Writer will not convert Ventura file information to Acrobat notes, bookmarks, or hypertext links. To generate a PDF with these attributes intact, print the Ventura file to a PostScript file, then distill the PostScript file with Acrobat Distiller 3.0.

Before printing a Ventura Publisher publication, make sure you renumber the pages and generate the Index and Table of Contents twice. If you don't renumber twice, the Table of Contents, Index entries, and cross references may be incorrect in the resulting PDF file.

To create a PostScript file from Ventura Publisher for distilling with Acrobat Distiller 3.0:

1. Open your file (i.e., chapter or publication) in Ventura Publisher.
2. When printing a single chapter, Choose File > Print. When printing a multi-chapter publication, choose File > Print Publication.
3. In the Print dialog box, select a PostScript printer from the Printer pop-up menu. Make sure you select a PostScript printer that supports the color and page size requirements of your file.
4. In the Print dialog box, click Options.
5. In the Print Options dialog box, click the Options tab and then select the Acrobat (TM), Acrobat (TM) Notes, and Print Hidden Graphics options.

6. Click OK to close the Print Options dialog box and return to the Print dialog box.
7. Click Setup and select your page setup options: When you are printing pages that are in landscape orientation, click Landscape. You can then rotate the pages in Acrobat Exchange.
   OR: When you are printing custom page sizes, choose Custom from the Paper Size menu (custom paper sizes are not available for all printer drivers), then click Custom and enter the Width and Length values of your file.
8. Click OK to save your Setup options and return to the Print dialog box.
9. Select Print to File and then click OK.
10. Enter a name and destination for your PostScript file in the Print To File dialog box. Add a ".ps" extension to the filename to distinguish it as a PostScript file.
11. Click OK to generate the PostScript file.

After you create the PostScript file, distill it with Acrobat Distiller 3.0. If you save the PostScript file directly to a watched folder monitored by Acrobat Distiller, Distiller will automatically convert it to PDF.

MAC OS

Creating a PDF File From QuarkXPress for Macintosh

This technical note describes how to print a QuarkXPress document to disk as a PostScript file so it can be distilled by Adobe Acrobat Distiller 3.0.

INSTALLING THE ACROBAT PRINTER FILES

When writing PostScript code, QuarkXPress refers to the selected PPD (PostScript Printer Description) file or a (PDF) Printer Description File to get information about the output device (e.g., its built-in fonts, paper sizes, and resolution capabilities). When you are creating PostScript files for use with Acrobat Distiller, be sure you install the appropriate Distiller PPD or PDF file. If you are using QuarkXPress 3.3x, use the Acrobat Distiller (PPD) file; if you are using QuarkXPress 3.2x, use the XPress PDF - Acrobat Distiller file. You can distribute copies of either file to anyone creating PDF files from QuarkXPress 3.2x or 3.3x.

INSTALLING THE ACROBAT DISTILLER (PPD) FILE FOR QUARKXPRESS 3.3X

Acrobat 3.0 automatically installs the Acrobat Distiller (PPD) in the Printer Descriptions folder in the Extensions folder in the System Folder, as well as in the Xtras folder in the Adobe Acrobat 3.0 folder. If you have not installed Adobe Acrobat Distiller but have the Acrobat Distiller (PPD) file, copy the PPD file to either the Printer Descriptions folder or to the QuarkXPress 3.3x folder.

INSTALLING THE XPRESS PDF - ACROBAT DISTILLER FILE FOR QUARKXPRESS 3.2X

To install the XPress PDF -Acrobat Distiller file for QuarkXPress 3.2x, copy it from the Xtras folder in the Acrobat 3.0 folder to the folder containing the QuarkXPress application file.

GENERATING A POSTSCRIPT FILE USING PSPRINTER 8.X OR LASERWRITER 8.3 OR EARLIER

To create a PostScript file from QuarkXPress using the PSPrinter 8.x printer driver, or the LaserWriter 8.3 or earlier printer driver:

1. Open your document in QuarkXPress and choose File > Page Setup.
2. Select Acrobat Distiller (QuarkXPress 3.3x) or Adobe Acrobat Distiller (QuarkXPress 3.2x) from the Printer Type pop-up menu.
3. Set the orientation to Portrait, even if all or part of your document is landscape. When you open the resulting PDF file in Acrobat Exchange, the page will be in the proper orientation.
4. Enter the document width in the Paper Width text box.
5. Click Options, then deselect the Smooth Graphics option. When Smooth Graphics is selected, QuarkXPress adds thousands of Type 3 characters to your PostScript file in an attempt to smooth any bitmap graphics in your document, making your PostScript file much larger than it needs to be.
6. Click OK to close the remaining dialog boxes.
7. Choose File > Print.
8. Select File for Destination.
   NOTE: If Acrobat Distiller 3.0 is installed on your computer, you'll see a third Description option, PDF, in the Print dialog box. This option enables you to print to the Acrobat Distiller Assistant, which automatically creates a PostScript file, and then opens Acrobat Distiller and generates a PDF file. For more information on the Distiller Assistant, refer to the Acrobat Distiller online guide.
9. Select the desired printer options and click Save.
10. Specify the name and destination for your PostScript file.
11. Select PostScript Job from the Format pop-up menu.
12. Select the Level 2 Only option. This option enables Distiller to retain QuarkXPress color information so you see the same colors in your PDF as you see in your QuarkXPress document.
13. Select either ASCII or Binary. ASCII format creates a smaller file size but is not searchable outside of Acrobat (e.g., some Internet search engines do not support ASCII files). The binary format is searchable, but results in a larger file size.
14. If you will be distilling the PostScript file on a different computer, select All or All But Standard 13 from the Font Inclusion pop-up menu to ensure that all the font information is included in the PostScript file.
15. Click Save to generate the PostScript file.
    NOTE: If PSPrinter 8.3x and the QuarkXPress 3.32 Balloon Help file are both installed, QuarkXPress will re-

turn a system error when you print. To prevent the error, you may either remove the Balloon Help file from the QuarkXPress folder, or remove the PSPrinter 8.3x file from the Extensions folder in the System Folder. However, if you remove the PSPrinter file you cannot print to the PSPrinter driver.

GENERATING A POSTSCRIPT FILE USING LASERWRITER 8.4 OR LATER

To create a PostScript file from QuarkXPress using the LaserWriter 8.4 or later printer driver:

1. Open your document in QuarkXPress and choose File > Page Setup.
2. Select your page size from the Paper pop-up menu and set the Orientation option to Portrait, even if all or part of your document is landscape. When you open the resulting PDF file in Acrobat Exchange, the page will be in the proper orientation.
3. Select QuarkXPress from the Page Attributes pop-up menu.
4. Select Acrobat Distiller (QuarkXPress 3.3x) or Adobe Acrobat Distiller (QuarkXPress 3.2x) from the Printer Type pop-up menu.
5. Enter the document width in the Paper Width text box.
6. Select PostScript Options from the QuarkXPress pop-up menu, and deselect the Smooth Graphics option. When Smooth Graphics is selected, QuarkXPress adds thousands of Type 3 characters to your PostScript file in an attempt to smooth any bitmap graphics in your document, making your PostScript file much larger than necessary.
7. Click OK to close the Page Setup dialog box.
8. Choose File > Print.
9. Select File from the Destination pop-up menu.
10. Select Save As File from the General pop-up menu.
11. Select PostScript from the Format pop-up menu.
12. Select Level 2 Only for the PostScript Level option. When you use the Level 2 Only option, Distiller retains QuarkXPress color information so you see the same colors in Acrobat as you see in QuarkXPress.
13. Select either ASCII or Binary for the Data Format option. ASCII format creates a smaller file size, but is not searchable outside of Acrobat (e.g., some internet search engines do not support ASCII file types). The binary format is searchable but creates a larger file size.
14. If you will be distilling the PostScript file on a different computer, select All or All But Standard 13 from the Font Inclusion pop-up menu to ensure that all the font information is included in the PostScript file.
15. Click Save.
16. Specify a name and destination for your PostScript file.
17. Click Save to generate the PostScript file.

Once you've created your PostScript file, you can distill it with Acrobat Distiller 3.0. If you save the PostScript file directly to a watched folder monitored by Acrobat Distiller, Distiller will automatically convert it to PDF.

Unexpected Results

MAC OS / WINDOWS / UNIX

Pages are Cropped When Written to PDF by the Acrobat Distiller

ISSUE

Adobe Acrobat Distiller truncates pages with insufficient page size information (e.g., EPS files).

SOLUTION

Increase the default page size in the EXAMPLE.PS file so the complete document is included in the PDF's page area.

1. Open the EXAMPLE.PS file, located in the ACRODIST directory (Windows) or in the Startup folder of the Adobe Acrobat 2.0 folder (Macintosh), in a text editor that saves in text-only format (e.g., Windows Write, Teach Text).
2. Locate the following section in the EXAMPLE.PS file:
```
%%% DEFAULT PAGE SIZE
%%% The Distiller recognizes most all
  PostScript page size operators. If you
%%% want to change the default page size
  used by Distiller, you may do so using
%%% the setpagedevice command. Page dimen-
  sions are in points (width x height).
% << /PageSize [612 792] >> setpagedevice
```
3. Change the "/PageSize" dimensions to reflect a larger page size, up to 45" by 45". The "/PageSize" value is specified in points, so to determine the correct value for your page size, multiply each dimension by 72 (1 inch equals approximately 72 points).
   NOTE: When you know the page size in inches, you can let Distiller convert the measurements to points using the following syntax:
```
<< /PageSize [w 72 mul h 72 mul] >>
  setpagedevice
```
   where "w" is the width of the page in inches and "h" is the height of the page in inches. The height and width can be specified as floating point numbers (e.g. 6.654).
4. Remove the percent sign at the beginning of the line so Distiller uses the "/PageSize" value as the default. For example, to make the default page size 22" by 22", the line should read as follows:
```
<< /PageSize [1584 1584] >> setpagedevice
```
5. Save the EXAMPLE.PS file as text-only.

OR: Add the PostScript Level 2 command "<</PageSize [width height]>> setpagedevice" to the header of your PostScript file to change the page size.

NOTE: We recommend you only use this solution is you are familiar with and comfortable editing a PostScript file.

ADDITIONAL INFORMATION

Because EPS files don't contain page size information, Distiller uses its default page size, 8.5" by 11", when processing an EPS file. Using the "setpagedevice" operator in either the EXAMPLE.PS file or the PostScript file you're distilling, tells Distiller to create a PDF file with a specific page size.

When Acrobat Distiller starts, it looks in the Startup folder (Macintosh) or directory (Windows) for text files containing PostScript programs. If the Startup folder or directory contains one or more text files, Acrobat Distiller assumes they are PostScript programs and uses them to initialize the virtual memory of its PostScript interpreter. The Startup folder or directory created within the Distiller folder or directory when Acrobat Distiller is installed includes an EXAMPLE.PS file, containing examples of the job options it can affect.

When the "setdistillerparams" operator is used in a PostScript file located in the Startup folder or directory, it affects all subsequently processed PostScript files. However, when that operator is used in PostScript files not located in the Startup folder or directory, only the file that contains the operator is affected. If you're familiar with the PostScript language, you could use the "setdistillerparams" operator to specify different image-compression settings for every image in a document.

Text Copied from Interleaf PDF files Pastes as Unrecognizable Characters

Text copied from PDF files created in Acrobat Distiller 2.x or earlier from an Interleaf Publisher 5.0 or earlier PostScript file pastes into other applications as unrecognizable characters.

Interleaf Publisher is a DOS- or UNIX-based word processor that creates non-standard PostScript (*.ps) files. Interleaf *.ps files do not contain the ASCII information required by Acrobat Reader or Exchange 2.x or earlier to facilitate the Copy command, resulting in PDF files with text that can be highlighted, but not pasted correctly into other applications.

Correctly written PostScript includes a section of ASCII text, which Acrobat Exchange and Reader use for their Copy command, enabling copied text to be placed in the clipboard for export. Interleaf does not write ASCII text into *.ps files, but instead uses an encoding process where each character is replaced by a seven digit character code. When distilled, seven digit character codes allow text in PDF files to be rasterized for screen display, but does not allow that text to be copied and pasted.

The missing ASCII text from Interleaf PostScript files also makes text in PDF files unavailable for word searches or for indexing by Acrobat Catalog.

Bitmap Images Display Poorly in a PDF File Created with Distiller 2.x or Earlier

ISSUE

Bitmap images in PDF files created with Adobe Acrobat Distiller 2.x or earlier display and print distorted or with a quilted pattern.

SOLUTION

Reduce the amount of compression Distiller performs on the bitmap images:

1. Choose Distiller>Job Options.
2. In the Job Options dialog box, select the Compression pop-up menu in the appropriate image type section (i.e., Color Images, Grayscale Images, or Monochrome Images).
3. Select a lower level of compression (e.g., change JPEG High to JPEG medium), then click OK.

ADDITIONAL INFORMATION

To keep the size of PDF files to a minimum, Acrobat Distiller offers different compression schemes (i.e., JPEG, LZW) as well as different levels of compression for bitmap images. Compression reduces the amount of detail in a scanned image and the higher the compression setting, the more detail is lost. When the selected compression scheme is too high, images included in a PDF file may appear quilted or distorted. Reducing the amount of compression Distiller performs on images minimizes distortion, enabling images in a PDF to display and print as expected.

MAC OS / WINDOWS

Q When I distill a file containing graphics, some of the graphics look fine and some of them don't. Can you explain this inconsistency?

A We can take an educated guess based on your description. You probably have more than one kind of graphic in your file, and when you created the PDF, the Distiller may have handled each kind of graphic differently.

The Distiller contains controls for handling (that is, compressing) different kinds of bitmap graphics. When you export to PDF directly from an application such as PageMaker or Persuasion, you don't have the opportunity to check or change these Distiller options; the current settings are used (except in PageMaker 6.5, in which you can choose to override the Distiller's defaults when you use the export-to-PDF option). That's why your graphics don't all look equally good.

To rectify this, you can open the Distiller and change any options before you use an export-to-PDF function in another program. (Of course, you can change them whenever you use the Distiller on its own as well.)

The Distiller has separate downsampling defaults for color, grayscale, and monochrome bitmap images. A setting of 72 dpi is the default for color and grayscale images, and 300 is for monochrome, so it's more likely you're seeing unsatisfactory results with your color and grayscale images. (It's not likely that you're seeing unsatisfactory results with EPS or other vector images, since the Distiller cannot downsample those kinds of graphics.)

To improve the quality of your bitmap graphics for printing, change the Distiller's downsampling levels. The settings you choose will stay in place until you change them again. If you're toggling between creating PDFs for printout and creating them for the screen or online, remember to change your settings when you switch output formats, and maybe even jot them down once you've determined your optimal numbers. Here's how to change the settings in the Distiller.

1. Open the Acrobat Distiller.
2. Select "Job Options…" from the Distiller menu. In Distiller 3.0, click on the "Compression" tab to see compression options.
3. Increase the downsampling values. You may have to experiment a bit until you're satisfied with the results.

We've just described how to make changes in the Distiller, but you might have used PDFWriter to create the PDF file and experienced similar results—that is, inconsistencies in the quality of your graphics. To change the down-sampling settings in PDFWriter, follow these steps.

1. Open the PDFWriter setup dialog box. In Windows 3.1, double-click on "Printers" in the Windows Control Panel. Select Acrobat PDFWriter, then click "Setup…." In Windows 95, choose "Printers" from the Settings submenu of the Start menu. Right-click on the Acrobat PDFWriter icon, choose "Properties," select the "Details" tab, and then click "Setup…." On a Macintosh, if you're targeted for PDFWriter, just choose "Page Setup…" from the File menu in an application.
2. Select new compression values. Click "Compression…" to open the "Acrobat PDFWriter Compression" dialog box.
3. Print using PDFWriter as usual.

Page Widths Larger than 8.5 Inches Are Truncated when Using the Distiller PPD in Quark 3.31

ISSUE

The width of a PDF file created from a QuarkXPress 3.31 .PS using the Adobe Acrobat Distiller is truncated to 8.5 inches. For example, an 11-by-22 inch page in Quark is only 8.5-by-22 inches when printed to a .PS file, then distilled to PDF format.

SYMPTOM

The Paper Width option is dimmed in the Printer Setup dialog box (Windows) or Page Setup dialog box (Macintosh) in QuarkXPress.

SOLUTION

Create a custom printer file to remove the lines that cause the Paper Width option to be dimmed in QuarkXPress.

To create a custom printer file for the Distiller in Windows:

1. Exit to DOS and change to the windows\system directory.
2. Type "edit acrodist.ppd" to open the Distiller PPD file in MS-DOS Edit.
3. Locate the "*ModelName: 'Acrobat Distiller'" line and insert the word "Modified" before "Acrobat." For example:
   `*ModelName: "Modified Acrobat Distiller"`
4. Locate the "*NickName: 'Acrobat Distiller'" and insert the word "Modified" before "Acrobat." For example:
   `*NickName: "Modified Acrobat Distiller"`
5. Delete the following lines from the "*%Custom Page Sizes" section:

```
4 dict begin
pop     % pop /Orientation value off the
  stack to fix bug in PageMaker 5.0
2 array astore /Margins exch def
2 array astore /PageSize exch def
/ImagingBBox null def
currentdict end setpagedevice"
*End
```

6. Press the Alt key to highlight the File menu, use the Down Arrow key to select Save As, then press the Enter key.
7. Name the file modified.ppd and save it.
8. When creating a PostScript file in Quark, select the Modified Acrobat Distiller PPD from the Printer Type list in Quark's Printer Setup dialog box and enter the appropriate value in the Page Width box.

To create a custom Distiller printer description file for the Macintosh:

1. Open the Acrobat Distiller PPD in a text editor that saves in text-only format (e.g., TeachText, Simple Text). The Acrobat Distiller PPD file is located in the Printer descriptions folder in the Extensions folder in the System Folder.
2. Locate the "*ModelName: 'Acrobat Distiller'" line and insert the word "Modified" before "Acrobat." For example:
   `*ModelName: "Modified Acrobat Distiller"`
3. Locate "*NickName: 'Acrobat Distiller'" and insert the word "Modified" before "Acrobat." For example:
   `*NickName: "Modified Acrobat Distiller"`
4. Delete the following lines from the "*%Custom Page Sizes" section:

```
4 dict begin
pop     % pop /Orientation value off the
  stack to fix bug in PageMaker 5.0
2 array astore /Margins exch def
2 array astore /PageSize exch def
/ImagingBBox null def
currentdict end setpagedevice"
*End
```

5. Name the file modified.ppd and save it.
6. When creating a PostScript file in Quark, select the Modified Acrobat Distiller PPD from the Printer Type list in Quark's Page Setup dialog box and enter the appropriate value in the Paper Width dialog box.

ADDITIONAL INFORMATION

When creating a PostScript from a QuarkXPress document using the Acrobat Distiller PPD file, the Page Width option in the Printer Setup dialog box (Windows) or Page Setup dialog box (Macintosh) is dimmed. As a result, page widths greater than 8.5 inches are truncated. The Paper Width option is dimmed because of lines that were added to the Distiller PPD to make it compatible with Adobe PageMaker.

Using a custom printer file without those lines makes the Page Width option available and enables you to enter the correct page width when printing a page larger than 8.5 inches from QuarkXPress.

Wide PageMaker 5.0x Pages Display Tall in Acrobat 2.0

ISSUE

When you view a PageMaker 5.0x PDF file in Adobe Acrobat Reader or Adobe Acrobat Exchange, landscape (i.e., wide) pages appear rotated 90 degrees, so they display with a portrait (i.e., tall) orientation.

SOLUTIONS

In Acrobat Exchange, choose Edit > Pages > Rotate to correct the page orientation.

OR: Print the PageMaker publication to disk as a PostScript file using custom paper settings, then create the PDF with Adobe Acrobat Distiller:

1. Choose File > Print in PageMaker.
2. Select the Acrobat Distiller PPD file from the Type pop-up menu.
3. Change the page orientation to tall and click Paper.
5. Select Custom from the Size pop-up menu.
6. In the Custom Paper Size dialog box, reverse the numbers entered in the Size fields and select the Normal orientation. For example, if "8.5" and "11" appears in the Size fields, change the entries to "11" and "8.5."
7. Click OK to exit the Custom Paper Size dialog box, then click Options.
8. Select Write PostScript to File, then select Normal and Include Downloadable fonts, if desired. Name the PostScript file as desired and click Save to write the PostScript file to disk.
9. Launch Acrobat Distiller 2.0, choose File > Open, then select the PostScript file.

ADDITIONAL INFORMATION

To print landscape publications, PageMaker 5.0x prints pages as tall with objects rotated 90 degrees, which causes wide pages to appear tall when you print a PDF file from PageMaker using the Acrobat PDFWriter.

Distiller Converts Pattern Fills in Excel Files to Shades of Gray

ISSUE

The Adobe Acrobat Distiller converts pattern fills in *.PS files generated from Excel to shades of gray.

SOLUTIONS

Use the PDFWriter to create PDFs of Excel files containing pattern fills.

OR: Use different colors rather than pattern fills in Excel.

ADDITIONAL INFORMATION

Acrobat Distiller substitutes shades of gray for the fill patterns available with some drawing, painting, and charting applications. In most situations, this substitution produces acceptable results. However, if two bars of a bar chart are filled with left and right diagonal stripes, Acrobat Distiller fills both bars with the same shade of gray.

PDFs From QuarkXPress Display and Print Slowly, Cause Memory Errors, or Display Outline Fonts as White

ISSUE

Portable Document Format (PDF) files distilled from QuarkXPress documents using Adobe Acrobat Distiller display and print slowly from Adobe Acrobat Exchange and Acrobat Reader, cause Acrobat to run out of memory while opening or printing them, or, when they contain outline fonts, display the outline fonts as white characters.

SYMPTOM

Smooth Graphics is enabled in the QuarkXPress Page Setup dialog box.

SOLUTION

In QuarkXPress, disable Smooth Graphics in the Options dialog box in the Page Setup dialog box, then save the file as a PostScript file and convert to PDF using Acrobat Distiller:

1. Open your Quark document in QuarkXPress.
2. Choose File > Page Setup to open the Page Setup dialog box, then click Options.
3. Click the Smooth Graphics option under Printer Options to deselect it, then click OK.
4. Click OK to close the Page Setup dialog box.
5. Choose File > Print, select the File option under Destination, then click Save.
6. Enter a name for the PostScript file under Create File, then click Save.
7. Launch Acrobat Distiller, choose File > Open and select the PostScript file.

ADDITIONAL INFORMATION

When Smooth Graphics is enabled, QuarkXPress adds thousands of Type 3 fonts to the PostScript file in attempt to smooth any bitmap graphics in your document. A PDF file containing Type 3 fonts requires more memory for Acrobat Exchange and Acrobat Reader to display and more memory for your printer to print. PDF files containing Type 3 fonts may display slowly in Acrobat Exchange or Acrobat Reader, or cause your printer to run out of memory while printing. To ensure your document requires as little memory as possible to open and print, disable Smooth Graphics.

Smooth Graphics interprets outline fonts as graphics and adds Type 3 fonts to the text. Acrobat Distiller distills the Type 3 fonts in combination with the outline fonts and may convert them to white characters. To accurately convert outline fonts from QuarkXPress using Acrobat Distiller, disable Smooth Graphics.

Application Errors

MAC OS / WINDOWS/ UNIX

Error "invalidfont: OffendingCommand: findfont" When Distilling PostScript Files

ISSUE

When you distill a PostScript file containing text, Adobe Acrobat Distiller returns the PostScript error "invalidfont; OffendingCommand: findfont" followed by "Stack: /Font / [fontname]." The name of the font included in the error message is one of the base 13 Type 1 fonts required by Acrobat Distiller (i.e., Courier, Times, Helvetica, Symbol, or Zapf Dingbats).

SOLUTIONS

Do one or more of the following:

A. Make sure the folder or directory containing the base 13 Type 1 fonts appears in Distiller's Font Locations dialog:
   1. Choose Distiller > Font Locations.
   2. If the folder or directory containing the base 13 fonts does not appear in the Font Directories List, click Add Folder (Mac) or Add Directory (Windows).
   3. Select the folder or directory containing the base 13 fonts, then click OK.

B. If you are using Distiller for Windows, make sure the size of the Acrodist.ini file is smaller than 64K. If the size of the Acrodist.inii file is larger than 64K, reduce the size of the Acrodist.ini file by editing it:
   1. Make a backup copy of the Acrodist.ini file in the Windows directory.
   2. Open the original Acrodist.ini file in a text editor that can save in text-only format (e.g., WordPad).
   3. Remove unnecessary font lines (e.g., lines that reference fonts that are no longer installed).
   4. Save the file in text-only format.
   5. Restart Windows.

C. If you are using Distiller for the Macintosh, use the Distiller installer to install the base 13 Type 1 fonts:
   1. Start the Distiller installer.
   2. Select Custom Install from the pop-up menu in the upper left corner of the Installer dialog box, then click Install.
   3. Select the PostScript Fonts and the Font Database custom install options, then click Install.

ADDITIONAL INFORMATION

To distill PostScript files, Acrobat Distiller requires the 13 PostScript Type 1 fonts. If Distiller cannot find one or more of the base 13 Type 1 fonts when distilling a PostScript file containing text, it returns the PostScript error "invalidfont; OffendingCommand: findfont." Distiller cannot find a font when it is damaged, missing (i.e., not installed, in a network directory to which the Distiller has lost access), or located in a font directory not listed in Distiller's Font Locations dialog box.

Distiller for Windows may be unable to access one of the base 13 Type 1 fonts if the size of the Acrodist.ini file is close to or exceeds 64K. The Acrodist.ini file includes a listing of installed fonts, and may include fonts that are no longer installed.

Error "Limitcheck; Offending Command: pdfmark" When Distilling a Frame 5.x PS File

ISSUE

The error "%%[Error: limitcheck; OffendingCommand: pdfmark]%%" appears in the Adobe Acrobat Distiller 2.1 Message window when distilling a .PS file created in FrameMaker 5.x.

SOLUTIONS

When creating the .PS file in Frame, deselect the Generate Acrobat Data option in the Print dialog box. Then, manually create the PDF's links in Acrobat Exchange.

OR: Break the Frame document into several sections and distill each section separately.

ADDITIONAL INFORMATION

The maximum number of named destinations, or hypertext links, allowed by Acrobat Exchange and Reader is 4000. When you create a .PS file from Frame with the Generate Acrobat Data option selected in the Print dialog box, Frame includes hundreds or thousands of hypertext links in the output file. While many of these links are unusable by Reader and Exchange, they can easily push the number of links over the 4000 link limit.

When a PS file is processed by Distiller 2.1, Distiller monitors the number of links it encounters in the file. When it reaches the 4000 link limit, Distiller stops processing and returns the error "%%[Error: limitcheck; OffendingCommand: pdfmark]%%." Distiller 2.0 does not keep track of how many links are processed and will completely process a PS file with more than 4000 links. However, PDFs created with Distiller 2.0 are still subject to the 4000 link limitation of Exchange and Reader and may not view correctly.

WINDOWS

Q Sometimes when I use Acrobat Distiller, it won't process a PostScript file and gives the message "%%[Error:undefined; OffendingCommand: @PJL]%%." What's going on?

A Whenever you get an "undefined" PostScript error, it means that the Distiller encountered a command in your

PostScript file that it didn't understand—and whatever is listed as the "OffendingCommand" (in this case, "@PJL") is the command that caused the problem.

Fortunately, this problem has a simple cause and an easy solution. The "@PJL" command comes from a special driver for Hewlett-Packard printers that support automatic switching between PCL (printer control language) and PostScript modes. The driver inserts into its PostScript files special lines (which begin with "@PJL") that tell the printer to switch to its PostScript mode. Since Acrobat Distiller doesn't understand these codes, it gives you an error message.

The easiest way to fix this problem is to re-create your PostScript file using another PostScript driver—such as the regular Windows PostScript driver or the Adobe PostScript driver—that doesn't add these "@PJL" codes. Then the Distiller should be able to process the new PostScript file.

If you can't re-create the PostScript file (for instance, if you don't have the document or application from which it was created), there's another way you can fix the problem—you can use a text editor to remove the non-PostScript codes from your file. We do not recommend you try this unless you've edited PostScript code before and are comfortable doing so. Here's how.

1. First, make a backup copy of your PostScript file before editing it.
2. Open your PostScript file in an application that can save in the text-only format (Microsoft Windows Write or Microsoft WordPad will do).
3. Find the non-PostScript code in the file and delete it. You need to look in two places—at the top of the file and at the bottom. Here's an example of what you'd need to delete at the top of the file. (What code appears at the top of your PostScript file might look different from what's pictured below, but you'll probably need to delete everything that precedes the "% !PS-Adobe . . ." comment.)

   At the top of the next column is an example of what you'd need to delete at the bottom of the file. Again, the code you need to delete might be different from what we picture, but you'll probably need to delete everything that comes after the PostScript "%%EOF" comment (which indicates the end of the PostScript file).
4. When you're done, save the file in text-only format and try distilling it again. If the Distiller has a problem with it, note what error it gives you—if there's still some non-PostScript code in the file, it'll probably give you another "undefined" error. If so, make a note of what it listed as the "OffendingCommand," reopen your PostScript file, look for that command, remove it, resave in text-only, and try distilling once more.

Error "Offending Command: @PJL" When Distilling PS Files

ISSUE

Adobe Acrobat Distiller returns the following error when processing a .PS file:

```
%%[ Error: undefined; OffendingCommand: @PJL
 ]%%
%%[ Flushing: rest of job (to end-of-file)
 will be ignored ]%%
%%[ Warning: PostScript error. No PDF file
 produced. ] %%
```

SYMPTOM

The PostScript file was created while targeted to a Hewlett-Packard PostScript printer.

SOLUTION

Target a non-HP PostScript printer (e.g., Apple LaserWriter, generic Adobe PostScript driver) when creating a .PS file to process with the Acrobat Distiller.

ADDITIONAL INFORMATION

Hewlett-Packard Postscript devices insert PJL commands into the print stream, which indicate whether the print job is PostScript or PCL. Acrobat Distiller does not understand PJL commands and returns the error "...OffendingCommand: @ PJL..." when processing a .PS file containing these commands.

Error "Limitcheck, offending command: findfont" When Distilling .ps Files

ISSUE

Adobe Acrobat Distiller returns the error "Limitcheck, offending command: findfont" when processing a .ps file.

SOLUTION

Reduce the number of fonts available to Distiller by removing one or more of the directories listed in Distiller's Font locations dialog box.

NOTE: If only one directory is listed in the Font Locations dialog box, you must remove fonts from the system to decrease the size of the Acrodist.ini file.

OR: Remove all the directory entries in Distiller's Font Locations dialog box and begin adding them back one at a time until the problem recurs. Remove and reinstall the fonts in the directory listed when the error occurs.

It is not necessary to restart Distiller to update the Acrodist.ini file.

ADDITIONAL INFORMATION

Every font to which the Distiller has access is listed in the Acrodist.ini file, adding to the file size. Distiller may not be able to access fonts when the Acrodist.ini file is close to or exceeds 64K in size.

A damaged font can corrupt Distiller's internal font table, which is maintained while Distiller is running, and can prevent files from distilling.

Error "Cannot open interpreter. Invalid number..." When Launching Distiller

ISSUE
When you start Adobe Acrobat Distiller, it returns the error, "Cannot open interpreter. Invalid number. Failed to allocate raster buffers."

SOLUTIONS
Make sure the "Buffers=" line in the Config.sys file is set to 30 or higher. To change the "Buffers=" line:

1. Make a backup copy of the Config.sys file.
2. Open the original Config.sys file in a text editor that saves in text-only format (e.g., Notepad).
3. Change the "Buffers=" value to 30 or greater.
4. Save the Config.sys file in text-only format, then exit Windows and restart your computer.

OR: Open the System.ini file in an application that saves in text-only format and remark out (i.e., place a semicolon in front of) the following lines in the [386Enh] section:

```
SSVRDD.386
SSVCD311.386
PCCARD.386
```

Then, save the System.ini file in text-only format and restart Windows. The above lines are added when the Megahert PCI MCI card is installed and may cause the error, "Cannot open interpreter. invalid number. Failed to allocate raster buffers."

ADDITIONAL INFORMATION
Distiller requires that the "Buffers=" setting in the config.sys file be set to 30 or greater. If the "Buffers=" value is lower than 30, Distiller will return the error "Cannot open interpreter. Invalid number. Failed to allocate raster buffers" as it starts.

Error "Cannot find Cainlib.dll Occurs During Acrobat Distiller Installation

ISSUE
When installing, Adobe Acrobat Distiller 2.0 return the errors, "File Error: Cannot find file Cainlib.dll and "Error *** 0003 ****," and installation is halted.

SOLUTION
Change the Windows language in the International dialog box of the Windows Control Panel to English (American) before installing Acrobat:

1. Open the Windows Control Panel.
2. Double-click the International icon.
3. In the International dialog box, select English (American) from the Language pop-up menu and click OK.
4. Install Acrobat Distiller 2.0. After installing Acrobat Distiller 2.0, the language selection in the International dialog box may be returned to its original setting.

ADDITIONAL INFORMATION
The Acrobat 2.0 installer requires that the English (American)" language option be selected in the International dialog box of the Windows Control Panel.

Installation Issues

WINDOWS

Error "Invalid Page Fault" After Manually Removing and Reinstalling Acrobat Distiller

ISSUE
When you distill a PostScript file using Adobe Acrobat Distiller 3.0 in Windows 95, Distiller returns the error, "Illegal operation" or "Invalid page fault" and then closes.

SYMPTOM
You manually removed Distiller 3.0 (i.e., you did not use Windows' Add/Remove Programs command) and references to it in the Windows registry, then reinstalled it into a new directory.

SOLUTION
Remove Acrobat Distiller using Windows Add/Remove Programs feature, then reinstall Distiller into a directory whose name is 8 characters or fewer. To uninstall Distiller:

1. Choose Start > Settings > Control Panel, then double-click Add/Remove Programs.
2. Select Adobe Acrobat in the Add/Remove Programs Properties dialog box, and then click Add/Remove.
3. Reinstall Acrobat into a directory whose name consists of 8 characters or fewer.

ADDITIONAL INFORMATION
Manually removing an application and any references to it in the Windows 95 registry, then reinstalling the application can damage the Windows registry. When the registry is damaged, the operating system or your applications may not work as expected, or may return errors. Manually removing Distiller, editing the registry, and then reinstalling Distiller into a directory who name is longer than 8 characters, damages the registry and causes Distiller to return errors. The Add/Remove Programs feature in Windows enables you to remove Acrobat Distiller and make the necessary changes to the Windows registry without damaging it.

Removing Acrobat Distiller 2.1 in Windows

Adobe Acrobat Distiller 2.1 does not include an uninstall application for Windows 95 or Windows 3.1x. To remove Acrobat Distiller, you must remove its components and edit the Win.ini file manually.

REMOVING DISTILLER 2.1 COMPONENTS

To delete the Acrobat Distiller 2.1 components:

1. Remove your personal files from the Acrodist directory and its subdirectories.
2. Delete the Acrodist directory.
3. Delete the Acrodist.ppd and Acrodist.wpd files from the Windows\System directory.
4. Delete the Acrodist.ini and Acrodist.wpx files from the Windows directory.
5. When running Windows 3.1x, delete the Distiller Assistant icon from the Startup Group in Program Manager. OR: When running Windows 95, delete the Distiller Assistant application file from the Windows\Start Menu\Startup directory, and delete the Acrobat Distiller shortcut file from the \Programs\Adobe Acrobat directory.

REMOVING DISTILLER REFERENCES FROM THE WIN.INI FILE

To remove the Acrobat Distiller lines from the Win.ini file:

1. Make a backup copy of the Win.ini file, which is located in the Windows directory.
2. Open the original Win.ini file in a text editor that can save in text-only format (e.g., Notepad).
3. In the [Extensions] section, remove the following lines:
```
PS=C:\ACRODIST\ACRODIST.EXE ^.PS
EPS=C:\ACRODIST\ACRODIST.EXE ^.EPS
```
4. In the [Ports] section, remove the line:
```
\DISTASST.PS=
```
5. In the [Devices] section, remove the line:
```
Acrobat Distiller=pscript,\DISTASST.PS
```
6. In the [PrinterPorts] section, remove the line:
```
Acrobat Distiller=pscript,\DISTASST.PS,15,90
```
7. Remove the entire [PostScript,\DISTASST.PS] section.
8. Remove the entire [Acrobat Distiller,\DISTASST.PS] section.
9. Save the Win.ini file in text-only format.

MAC OS

Q I was trying to install the Acrobat Distiller 2.0 on my new Power Mac 9500, but I got a system error and the computer froze. What's going on?

A You've run into an incompatibility between the Acrobat Distiller 2.0 and the System software (version 7.5.2) used on the Power Mac 9500 and other Macs built around the 604 chip. Apple has released an update to this System software (7.5.2 version 2, available from Apple dealers) that doesn't have this problem. In addition, the most current version of Acrobat Distiller (2.1) installs fine under 7.5.2. You can get Distiller 2.1 by upgrading to Acrobat Pro 2.1—the upgrade costs $89 plus $7.50 for shipping and handling.

Removing Acrobat Distiller 2.1 and Earlier from a Macintosh.

Adobe Acrobat Distiller can be installed alone or with the other Acrobat applications (e.g., Acrobat Exchange, Acrobat Reader, Acrobat Catalog). When you install just Acrobat Distiller, its files are located in an Acrobat Distiller folder. When you install Distiller along with one or more of the other Acrobat components, the files for each application are located in a shared Acrobat folder.

Removing Acrobat Distiller 2.1 When No Other Acrobat Components are Installed To remove Acrobat Distiller 2.1 when you have it but no other Acrobat applications installed, you can simply remove any personal files from the Distiller folder, drag the entire folder to the Trash, and then drag the Acrobat Distiller (PPD) file from the Printer Descriptions folder in the Extensions folder in the System Folder to the Trash.

Removing Acrobat Distiller 2.1 When Other Acrobat Components are Installed If you have Acrobat Distiller 2.1 and one or more other Acrobat applications installed, the Distiller files are located in a shared Acrobat folder. To remove Acrobat Distiller from your Macintosh when its files are located in the shared Acrobat folder:

1. Move any personal files from the Acrobat or Acrobat 2.1 folder to the desktop or another location (e.g., a new folder, or on a floppy disk).
2. Drag the following files from the shared Acrobat folder to the Trash:
```
Acrobat Distiller application
Distiller Preferences file
Messages.log file
```
3. Drag the following files from Help folder in the shared Acrobat folder to the Trash:
```
Disthelp folder
Disthelp.pdx
Dst_Prm.pdf
Help-Distiller.pdf
ReadMe-Distiller.pdf
```
4. Drag the Fonts folder from the shared Acrobat folder to the Trash. 5. Drag the Distiller_private.ps file from the Tmp folder in the shared Acrobat folder to the Trash. 6. Drag the Xtras folder, located in the shared Acrobat folder to the Trash.
7. Drag the Acrobat Distiller (PPD) file, which is located in the Printer Descriptions Folder in the Extensions folder in the System Folder *,* to the Trash.
8. If you have installed QuarkXPress, drag the XPress PDF-Acrobat Distiller file to the Trash.

General Information

MAC OS / WINDOWS / UNIX

Minimum and Maximum Page Sizes Supported by Distiller 2.x and Exchange 2.x

Adobe Acrobat Distiller 2.x and Acrobat Exchange 2.x support a maximum page size of 45-by-45 inches. Distiller generates the error "%%[Error: configurationerror; OffendingCommand: setpageparams]%%" when you attempt to distill a page in which either dimension exceeds 45".

The minimum page size supported by Acrobat Exchange is 1-by-1 inch. Exchange doesn't allow you to crop a page to smaller than 1-by-1 inch.

Acrobat Distiller Menus General Information

JOB OPTIONS

Through this dialog box, the Distiller administrator sets compression options for text, graphics (vector line art), and all images. The dialog box also includes an option to have the Distiller program generate thumbnails.

The compression options available to Distiller are the same as those for PDF Writer. However, Distiller also can treat color and grayscale images differently. In addition, Distiller can perform image downsampling, which PDF Writer cannot. Current Job Option options are written into every DTIME.TXT file that Network Distiller maintains.

NOTE: If multiple Network Distillers are monitoring the same directory, the DTIME.TXT file will be overwritten be each Distiller. If each Distiller has different Job Options, there is no way for Distiller users to tell which Job Options were used on their file.

GENERAL JOB OPTIONS

The two General job options are "Compress (LZW) text and graphics," and "Generate thumbnails."

- Compress (LZW) text and graphics

  This option tells Distiller to use the LZW compression method on all text and vector line art components in the file. The LZW compression method does not lose information and helps reduce file size.
- Generate thumbnails

  This option tells the Distiller program to automatically generate thumbnails for every document it processes, and to display the thumbnails in the Page Box area of the program window. Thumbnails can increase the Distiller programs processing time and the size of the resulting PDF files. Therefore, carefully consider the trade-offs between generating thumbnails for all documents automatically and generating them on an as-needed basis with the Acrobat Exchange program. For documents with many illustrations and tables, such as newsletters, software manuals, and science textbooks, thumbnails are a powerful navigational tool. But for documents that contain few illustrations or tables, thumbnails are less useful because all the thumbnails look the same. The default does not have this option selected.

COLOR IMAGES JOB OPTIONS

The two Color Images job options are "Downsample to ___ dpi," and "Compression." See "Image Compression and Downsampling for more information.

- Downsample to ___ dpi

  Downsampling removes data from images (files containing bitmaps) to help create smaller file sizes for file distribution and quick display. For example, let's say an image has a resolution of 160 dpi. With this option selected and 72 as the entered value, the image is downsampled to 80 dpi. The ending resolution is determined by dividing the beginning resolution, 160, by the entered value, 72. That results in a ratio of just over 2 to 1. So the Distiller software divides the beginning resolution (160) by 2, and the ending resolution is 80. The default value is 72 because color images need to have a resolution that is approximately the same as that of the line screen resolution (the number of lines of dots per inch on a halftone screen) used by the output device. Most output devices are 300 dpi laser printers with a line screen resolution between 53 and 75. This default value also works well for monitor display (most monitors have a resolution between 72 and 100).
- Compression

  The JPEG compression settings here are the same as those for PDF Writer. However, with Distiller, you have the option of compressing using LZW as well as JPEG. JPEG compression removes data from the file, but LZW does not. Color images with a bit-depth resolution other than 24 or 16 bits per pixel are LZW compressed. You cannot change that setting through this dialog box.

  Grayscale Images Job Options

The two Grayscale Images job options are "Downsample to ___ dpi," and "Compression."

- Downsample to ___ dpi

  Downsampling on grayscale images works the same way as on color images.
- Compression

  The compression settings here are the same as those for color images. Grayscale images with a bit-depth resolution less than 8 bits per pixel are LZW compressed. You cannot change that setting through this dialog box. JPEG compression removes data from the file, but LZW does not. LZW compression is performed on all grayscale images with an image resolution less than 8 bits per pixel.

MONOCHROME IMAGES JOB OPTIONS

The two Monochrome Images job options are "Down-sample to ___ dpi," and "Compression."

- Downsample to ___ dpi

  The default setting for downsampling monochrome images is 300 dpi. To produce a good quality print, the monochrome image should be the same resolution as that of the output device. Generally, most people print to 300 dpi devices.
- Compression

  The choices for monochrome image compression are the same in Distiller as they are in PDF Writer.

MAC OS / WINDOWS

Acrobat Distiller 2.1 Job Options General Information

In the Job Options dialog box, the Distiller administrator sets compression options for text, graphics (vector line art), and images. This dialog box also includes an option for Distiller to generate thumbnails.

Distiller's compression options are the same as those for Acrobat PDF Writer 2.1. However, Distiller can process color and grayscale images differently and perform image downsampling, which PDF Writer cannot. Current Job Option options are written into every Dtime.txt file that the Network Distiller maintains.

If multiple Network Distillers are monitoring the same directory, each copy of Distiller overwrites the Dtime.txt file. If the copies of Distiller have different Job Options settings, it is not possible to determine which settings were used to process the file.

GENERAL JOB OPTIONS

The two General job options are Compress (LZW) Text and Graphics, and Generate Thumbnails:

- Compress (LZW) Text and Graphics

  This option instructs Distiller to use the LZW compression method on all text and vector line art components in the file. The LZW compression method does not lose information.

- Generate Thumbnails

  This option, which is deselected by default, instructs Distiller to automatically generate thumbnails for every document it processes, and to display the thumbnails in the Page Box area of the application window. Thumbnails can increase Distiller's processing time and the size of the resulting PDF file. You can also use Acrobat Exchange to generate thumbnails for individual PDF files. For documents containing many illustrations and tables, such as newsletters, software manuals, and science textbooks, thumbnails are a powerful navigational tool. But for documents that contain few illustrations or tables, thumbnails are less useful because all the thumbnails look the same.

COLOR IMAGES JOB OPTIONS

The two Color Images job options are Downsample to ___ dpi and Compression:

- Downsample to ___ dpi

  Downsampling removes data from images (bitmap files) to help create smaller file sizes. For example, if you have an image with a resolution of 160 dpi and you enter 72 dpi in the Downsample to option, Distiller downsamples the image to 80 dpi. To calculate the resulting downsampled resolution, divide the beginning resolution (160) by the value you enter (72) which equal a ratio of just over 2 to 1. Distiller rounds the ratio to the nearest whole number, and divides the beginning resolution by this number to determine the downsampled resolution (e.g., 160 / 2 = 80).

- Compression

  The JPEG compression settings here are the same as those for PDF Writer. Unlike PDF Writer, Distiller also gives you the option of using LZW compression. JPEG compression removes data from the file, but LZW compression does not. For 16- and 24-bit color images, you have the choice of LZW or JPEG compression, but for other images, Distiller uses LZW compression.

GRAYSCALE IMAGES JOB OPTIONS

The two Grayscale images job options are Downsample to ___ dpi, and Compression:

- Downsample to ___ dpi

  Downsampling grayscale images works the same way as with color images.

- Compression

  The compression settings for grayscale images are the same as those for color images. JPEG compression removes data from the file, but LZW compression does not. For images that have a bit depth less than 8 bits per pixel, Distiller uses LZW compression.

MONOCHROME IMAGES JOB OPTIONS

The two Monochrome Images job options are Downsample to ___ dpi, and Compression:

- Downsample to ___ dpi

  The default value for downsampling monochrome images is 300 dpi. To produce a good quality print, the monochrome image should be the same resolution as that of the output device.

- Compression

  The choices for monochrome image compression are the same in Distiller as they are in PDF Writer. None of the compression options results in loss of data. The compression options are CCITT Group 3 (used by many fax machines), CCITT Group 4 (works well with most images), LZW (best for images containing repeating patterns), and Run Length (best for images containing large areas of white or black).

WINDOWS

The Distiller Assistant for Windows General Information

The Distiller Assistant for Windows, included with Adobe Acrobat Pro 2.0 and later, enables you to "print" directly to the Acrobat Distiller so that you may create PDF files in one step. The Distiller Assistant generates a PostScript file, starts the Distiller, processes the PostScript file and creates a PDF. After the PDF is created the Distiller Assistant deletes the PostScript file.

The Distiller Assistant also monitors watched directories and starts the Distiller when a PostScript file is placed in any watched "In" directory. For more information about watched directories, refer to the online Help file included with the Distiller (Help_d.pdf).

The Distiller Assistant supports drag-and-drop processing in Windows 3.x (simply drag-and-drop a PostScript file onto the Distiller Assistant icon to create a PDF file). Drag-and-drop processing is not supported under Windows 95.

The Distiller Assistant is compatible with Windows NT 3.5.x, Windows 3.x, and Windows 95.

SETTING UP THE DISTILLER ASSISTANT

To perform its tasks, the Distiller Assistant program must be running in the background. To ensure that the Distiller Assistant is always running, copy the Distiller Assistant program item to the Windows Startup group so it initializes each time you start Windows.

The Acrobat Distiller installer adds "Acrobat Distiller" to the list of installed printers in Windows' Printer Control Panel. To print to the Distiller Assistant, you must configure it to the port "\DISTASST.PS." For information on configuring a printer port, refer to your Windows documentation. The Distiller Assistant requires Microsoft's PostScript printer driver version 3.56 or later.

DISTILLER ASSISTANT OPTIONS

The Distiller Assistant has no user interface. When running, it appears as an icon near the bottom of the screen (Windows NT, Windows 3.1) or on the Task Bar (Windows 95). To access its three options (i.e., View PDF File, Exit Distiller When Idle, Ask for PDF File Destination), click on the Distiller Assistant icon (Windows 3.1 and Windows NT) or right-click on the Distiller Assistant on the Task Bar (Windows 95). By default, all three options are selected.

- View PDF file—When this option is selected, the Distiller Assistant launches Acrobat Exchange and displays the PDF.
- Exit Distiller When Idle—When this option is selected, the Distiller Assistant launches Distiller using the /q switch so that Distiller closes when all queued files are processed and watched directories are empty.
- Ask for PDF File Destination—When this option is selected, a "Save as" dialog box appears for files printed to the Distiller Assistant. When "Ask for PDF File Destination" is not selected, files printed to the Distiller Assistant are named Distasst.pdf and are saved to the Acrobat Distiller directory.

USING THE DISTILLER ASSISTANT

To print to PDF using Acrobat Distiller, select the Acrobat Distiller printer as the target printer in the application from which you want to print. Distiller Assistant uses the Microsoft Windows PostScript printer driver (Pscript.drv) and routes the PostScript file to the C:\Acrodist directory and names it "Distasst.ps." The Distiller Assistant then attempts to extract the filename from the "%%Title" comment in the PostScript file, launch Acrobat Distiller, and request that it distill the file to the desired output name. When receiving a reply from Acrobat Distiller that distillation is complete, Distiller Assistant deletes the source PostScript file, and if the View PDF file option is selected, it opens the PDF document in Acrobat Exchange.

Acrobat Catalog®

Unexpected Results

MAC OS / WINDOWS / UNIX

Catalog's Schedule Build Time Setting Arrows Don't Work as Expected

ISSUE

The time setting in the Starting At text box of Adobe Acrobat Catalog 2.x's Schedule Builds dialog box doesn't change when you click the up or down arrow.

SOLUTION

Manually enter the time in the Starting At text box of the Schedule Builds dialog box.

ADDITIONAL INFORMATION

The up and down arrows in the Schedule Builds dialog box in Acrobat Catalog 2.x do not increase or decrease the time setting as expected.

MAC OS / WINDOWS

Q Why isn't my index working when I transfer it to another computer or to a CD-ROM?

A Your index is probably suffering from what we might call the "transfer disorientation" that occurs when the structural relationship of the index and its supporting files is changed or broken. Fortunately, this kind of disorientation is easier to fix than the kind you get coming home from your Far Eastern vacation.

When Catalog creates an index (which will be given a ".pdx" extension), it also creates a folder with the same name as the index, containing nine subfolders (see illustration below). The index and the support files contained in these subfolders are, in essence, a list of words found in a designated group of PDFs, and a map noting the locations of those PDFs. As long as all the index files and folders retain the relative hierarchy they had when you created the index, the index can be used on a Macintosh, in Windows, on a UNIX machine, or on a CD. But if the index is moved from its folder, the contents of the index folder or its subfolders are rearranged, or the indexed PDFs are moved to different folders, the index will not be able to function properly. You'll be able to tell it's not functioning properly when you use the "Search" command in Acrobat Exchange or Reader, and your index name is grayed out.

Here's an example. Say your "index.pdx" file is in a folder called "index," and all your indexed PDFs are in subfolders of "index." Your manager decides she wants all indexes in a single folder for easier access, so you move "index.pdx" into an "allindex" folder, but you don't move the "index" folder and its subfolders along with it. Regardless of the "allindex" folder's location, moving your "index.pdx" file without also moving the "index" folder and its subfolders renders your index useless (unless you regenerate the index in its new location). The "index" directory and its contents must stay intact when they're transferred or moved.

Here are a few more tips that'll help you make sure your indexes work correctly if you have to port them to another platform or to a CD that'll be used on various platforms. First, name all your PDFs using the DOS "8.3" file-naming convention (for example, "atozindx.pdx" instead of "alphabetical index"), make all folder names eight characters or less, and avoid punctuation and extended characters in your file and folder names. On a Mac, choose "Preferences…" from the Edit menu, click "Index," and check the "Make include/exclude folders DOS compatible" check box. Following these conventions is important even if your index and PDFs will be used in Windows 95—although it supports long file names, the current Windows versions of Acrobat Exchange and the Search Plug-in do not.

WINDOWS

Acrobat Catalog 2.0 Doesn't Process Indices at Scheduled Times

ISSUE

When you select the option to build indices at specific intervals (e.g. every 20 minutes) in the Schedule Builds dialog box, Adobe Acrobat Catalog 2.0 processes one index, then stops.

SOLUTION

In the Schedule Builds dialog box, specify a time that is later than the current time (i.e., current time according to your computer's clock) for the Starting At option.

ADDITIONAL INFORMATION

When you set your index schedule to start at your computer's current time, Acrobat Catalog has only enough time to process the first index in the build list. When you set your index schedule to start at time that is later than your computer's current time, Acrobat Catalog processes all scheduled indices, as expected.

Time Interval Setting Not Maintained in Acrobat Catalog

ISSUE

After you click Save in the Schedule Builds dialog box in Adobe Acrobat Catalog 3.0 or earlier, the value you select from the time interval pop-up menu disappears.

SOLUTION

Reselect the time interval and then click Start.

ADDITIONAL INFORMATION

Acrobat Catalog does not save the time interval settings in the Schedule Build dialog box. When you want to set a

TIP MAC OS / WINDOWS

Static or dynamic?

Acrobat Catalog creates either a static or a dynamic index. A static index is best used for "archival" documents—that is, a collection of PDFs that don't change often, or can't change (for example, PDFs burned onto a CD-ROM). To make an index static, click the "Options" button in the "Index Definition" dialog box and select "Optimize for CD-ROM."

Leave it unchecked if you want a dynamic index—the better choice for documents that are updated often, such as reports or forms kept on a server; you can set a dynamic index to update as often as you like. To select scheduling options for your dynamic index, go to the Index menu and select "Schedule…." In the "Schedule Builds" dialog box, choose a time scheme: "Continuously," "Once," or "Every (starting at a given time)."

specific interval for building your index, make sure you reselect the interval just before clicking Start to start the build. If you don't reselect the time interval before you click Start, Catalog may not process the index according to the desired schedule.

Application Errors

WINDOWS

Error "Could not create directory [directory name]" in Acrobat Catalog

ISSUE
When you attempt to create an index (*.PDX file) in Adobe Acrobat Catalog 2.0, Catalog returns the error "Could not create directory [directory name]."

SOLUTION
Make sure you have create rights to the network volume on which the .PDX is being generated. To change network rights, contact your network administrator.

ADDITIONAL INFORMATION
Acrobat Catalog 2.0 creates a new directory for every .PDX file generated. When you don't have create rights to the network volume on which the .PDX file is being created, Acrobat Catalog 2.0 is unable to create the directory and .PDX file.

Error "The index is currently unavailable..." Attaching to or Searching Index in Acrobat Exchange or Reader

ISSUE
When you attempt to attach to or search an index in Adobe Acrobat Reader or Acrobat Exchange, Acrobat returns the error "The index is currently unavailable. You will not be able to search its contents." The index is dimmed in the Acrobat Search window.

SOLUTIONS
Do one or more of the following:

A. Make sure your network server connection is valid.
B. Make sure the index has not been moved or deleted.
C. Make sure the index is not being purged and rebuilt when you attempt to access it.

ADDITIONAL INFORMATION
Acrobat returns an error when you try to attach or search an index if your connection to the network server where the index is stored is broken, the index has been moved or deleted, or the index is in the process of being purged and rebuilt.

When you purge and rebuild an index in Acrobat Catalog, the index, by default, becomes unavailable for 905 seconds (15 minutes). You can change this default in Acrobat Catalog so that the index is available sooner. To change the setting on the Macintosh, choose Edit > Preferences > Catalog Preferences and enter a value in seconds (from 30-905) in the Time Before Purge text box. To change the setting in Windows, open the Acrocat.ini file (located in the Windows directory) in a text-editor (e.g., NotePad) and change the value in the line "PurgeTime=905" to a value in seconds from 0-905, then save and close the file.

Error "Error in writing to log file - please check disk space" in Catalog

ISSUE
When you create, update, or rebuild an index in Adobe Acrobat Catalog 2.0, Catalog returns the error, "Error in writing to log file - please check disk space."

SOLUTIONS
Create more free disk space on the volume on which you're creating the index.
OR: If updating an index that has been updated previously, purge and rebuild it first to reduce the amount of disk space required to generate the index:

1. Choose Index > Purge.
2. In the Purge dialog box, select the index to purge, click OK.
   NOTE: Purging an index takes roughly the same amount of time as building it.
3. Choose Index > Open.
4. In the Open dialog box, select the index to rebuild and click OK.
   NOTE: To reduce the amount of disk space needed to rebuild the index, disable the Sounds Like, Word Stemming and Case Sensitive options, and add stopwords in the Open dialog box prior to rebuilding the index.

ADDITIONAL INFORMATION
The amount of free disk space Acrobat Catalog 2.0 needs to create or rebuild an index is equivalent to 10-30% of the of disk space consumed by the Acrobat Portable Document Format (PDF) files being indexed. For example, to generate an index for 100 MB worth of PDF files, Acrobat Catalog 2.0 needs 10-30 MB of available disk space. Updating an index multiple times requires more disk space than creating or rebuilding an index.

Error "The index is currently unavailable..." When Adding an Index to Search List in Windows NT

ISSUE
The error "The index is currently unavailable. You will not be able to search its contents" appears when you attempt to

add an index to Adobe Acrobat Search's "Available Indexes" list in Adobe Acrobat Exchange 2.0 or later running under Windows NT 3.5x. After clicking "OK" to the error message, all indexes are unavailable (i.e., grayed out) in the "Index Selection" dialog box.

SOLUTION
Install Windows NT Service Pack #2.

ADDITIONAL INFORMATION
Adobe Acrobat Catalog is not compatible with Windows NT 3.5x unless the NT Service Pack #2 is installed.

Acrobat Catalog Returns an Error When Building an Index

ISSUE
When you build an index using Adobe Acrobat Catalog 3.0 in Windows 95, Catalog returns an error message (e.g., "an error has occurred while processing"). When you click OK in the error message dialog box, nothing happens.

SYMPTOM
The hard disk you are using to build the index is low on free disk space (e.g., 10 MB free disk space or less).

SOLUTION
Restart the computer and increase the amount of free hard disk space. To increase free disk space, delete unnecessary files and applications.

ADDITIONAL INFORMATION
Acrobat Catalog creates temporary files when building indexes. When you build an index on a hard disk that has insufficient free disk space to create those temporary files, Catalog returns an error or a system error (e.g., freeze) occurs. The amount of free disk space that Catalog requires when building an index is dependent on the amount and size of the PDF files included in the index. When you use Catalog, your computer should have free disk space equal to or greater than 1.5 times the combined size of the PDF files to be indexed.

Catalog Errors Purging Index Optimized for CD-ROM

ISSUE
When you purge an index optimized for CD-ROM, Adobe Acrobat Catalog generates the following warning messages:

"Purging index."
"Search Engine Message: (0) Error E0-0849 (Vdb): Vdb 00000000.ddd, table '$$f' is corrupt (missing records)"
"Search Engine Message: (0) Error E0-0837 (Vdb): Error initializing 00000000.ddd"
"Search Engine Message: (0) Error E2-0106 (Partitions): Error creating document dataset for partition C:\1-TESTD~1\TESTIN~1\INDEX\parts\0000000"
"Attempting to fix broken collection"

SOLUTION
Ignore the messages, Catalog will purge the index successfully.

ADDITIONAL INFORMATION
Acrobat Catalog writes a file called "00000000.ddd" when generating a new index. When you create an index optimized for CD-ROM, Catalog writes the 00000000.ddd file differently than it would when creating an index not optimized for CD-ROM, as it assumes you will never purge or update the index. When Catalog purges an index optimized for CD-ROM and encounters the 000 00000.ddd file, it considers the file corrupt, when in fact it's not, and generates the error messages listed above. Catalog continues to purge the index as expected.

You can optimize an index for CD-ROM, by choosing Index > New, selecting the Options button, then selecting Optimize for CD-ROM.

Catalog Returns Message "'Filename' is Protected, Catalog Cannot Index File"

ISSUE
When you create an index, Adobe Acrobat Catalog returns the message, "'Filename' is protected, Catalog cannot index file."

SOLUTION
Open the PDF file in Acrobat Exchange and remove the Open File security setting.

ADDITIONAL INFORMATION
When Acrobat Catalog creates an index, it scans each PDF file to verify it is not damaged. If Catalog scans a PDF file that is secured with an Open password, it cannot scan the file and returns the error, "'Filename' is protected, Catalog cannot index file." Before using Catalog, make sure PDF files you're going to index do not have an Open password.

To remove the Open password from a PDF file in Acrobat Exchange:

1. Open the PDF file in Exchange and enter the password in the Password dialog box.
2. Choose File > Save As.
3. In the Save As dialog box, click Security.
4. In the Security dialog box, delete the password from the Open the Document text box, then click OK.
5. Save the file.

Error "General Protection Fault in module Compcore.dll at 0001.03DF" Building Index in Acrobat Catalog

ISSUE

When you build an index in Adobe Acrobat Catalog 3.0, Windows returns the error, "General Protection Fault in module Compcore.dll at 0001.03DF."

SYMPTOM

You removed the .pdx extension from the Index Definition.

SOLUTION

Rename the Index Definition file with the .pdx extension.

ADDITIONAL INFORMATION

The Index Definition file (*.pdx) is the main file in Acrobat Catalog's index structure. For Catalog to generate an index, the index definition file must have a .pdx extension. If the file does not have a .pdx extension, Catalog will not recognize it and cannot extract the information necessary to build the index.

Error "Internal Error has Occurred. Can't Retrieve Results. Sorry." When Searching Index With Exchange

ISSUE

When you search an index in Adobe Acrobat Exchange, Exchange returns the error "Internal error has occurred. Can't retrieve results. Sorry."

SOLUTION

Do one or more of the following:

A. Limit the title, subject, author, and keyword fields of each indexed Portable Document Format (PDF) file to 255 characters, including spaces and punctuation, then recreate the index.

   To change the characters in the title, subject, author, and keyword fields:

   1. Open the indexed PDF file in Acrobat Exchange.
   2. Choose File > Document info > General.
   3. Make changes to the document fields, then click OK.
   4. Save the file and repeat steps for other PDF files in the index that exceed the limit, then recreate the index.

B. Make sure the first 64 characters of each title in the index are unique in some way to the first 64 characters of every other title in the index, then recreate the index. For example, An index containing these two files is not searchable because the first 64 characters in their titles are identical:

   Stories and Pictures From Mount Ranier's Camp Muir On A Clear Sunny Day in Washington State Day 1

   Stories and Pictures From Mount Ranier's Camp Muir On A Clear Sunny Day in Washington State Day 2

   An index containing these two files is searchable because one character within the first 64 characters is unique to each title:

   Stories and Pictures From Mount Ranier's Camp Muir Day 1

   Stories and Pictures From Mount Ranier's Camp Muir Day 2

   To change the title of a PDF file:

   1. Open the indexed PDF file in Acrobat Exchange.
   2. Choose File > Document info > General.
   3. Change the title field so the first 64 characters are not exactly the same as other PDF titles in the index, then click OK.
   4. Save the file and repeat the steps above for other PDF files in the index with identical names, then recreate the index.

ADDITIONAL INFORMATION

Acrobat Catalog cannot create a searchable index for PDF files whose title, subject, author, and keywords document fields exceed 255 characters. Catalog also cannot create a searchable index for two or more PDF files with identical titles or with titles in which the first 64 characters are exactly the same, character for character. When your PDF files exceed Catalog's limits or have identical titles and you attempt to search an index containing the PDF files using Acrobat Exchange, Exchange returns the error "Internal error has occurred. Can't retrieve results. Sorry." To ensure your PDF files will be searchable in Acrobat Exchange, create them with titles, subjects, authors, and keywords that are under 255 characters long, and make sure your titles have a unique character within the first 64 characters.

Acrobat Catalog Returns Errors When Creating Index With Windows NT 3.51

ISSUE

When you create an index using Adobe Acrobat Catalog in Windows NT 3.51, Acrobat Catalog returns one or more of the following errors:

"Couldn't create directory C:/..."
"mkdir error"
"Index Build Failed"
"Permission Denied"

SOLUTION

When using Acrobat Catalog in Windows NT 3.51, install NT 3.51 Service Pack #2. To check whether you have an NT Service Pack installed, choose Help > About Program Manager in Windows Program Manager.

ADDITIONAL INFORMATION

Acrobat Catalog 2.x is compatible with Windows NT 3.51 when Service Pack # 2 is installed. When you create an index using Acrobat Catalog 2.x with any other version of Windows NT or NT Service Pack installed, Acrobat Capture will return an error message. To ensure that Acrobat Capture will successfully create an index, use Windows NT 3.51 with Service Pack #2.

Acrobat Capture®

Feature Techniques

WINDOWS

Q I hear that Acrobat 3.0 will include a Capture Plug-in. How will this differ from the stand-alone version of Capture that's already out there?

A The two "flavors" of Acrobat Capture are functionally very similar. The primary difference is that the full version supports batch processing; the Plug-in can process only one image at a time. The full version of Capture will continue to be an essential tool for organizations with a large legacy of hard-copy documents that need to be scanned and processed into PDF files.

Individuals or small organizations that aren't quite awash in documents may not need such a workhorse—the Plug-in will do the job nicely.

There are a few other differences as well. The stand-alone version of Capture has a full-featured PDF editor, the Capture Reviewer. Reviewer lets you fine-tune your PDFs in various ways, such as by adding or deleting text, changing fonts, and drawing lines or rectangles. It also lets you substitute an original image file for a section of the page that didn't translate well to PDF. Reviewer can also export text in various word-processing formats.

Either form of Capture allows you to change "suspect" text (text that may not have been interpreted correctly by Capture); in the Capture Plug-in this is done with an additional Plug-in called Touchup. The new Capture Plug-in will also be able to process images with color graphics (this feature will be added to the next full version of Capture).

Q I've received a word list from a friend of mine and I'd like to add her list to my Capture dictionary. Am I going to have to type in all these words manually?

A No, don't worry—you can incorporate the contents of her word list into the CUSTDICT.SPL file, which is Capture's custom dictionary and resides in the same directory as the Capture application (which is, by default, C:\CAPTURE). Capture installs both an internal dictionary (for example, USENG.NDX, SWEDISH.NDX) and the aforementioned custom dictionary file. The custom dictionary includes the names of all Adobe products.

If your friend's list is a custom dictionary for a word processor, it may already be in text-only (ASCII) format; if not, open it in a word processor and save it as a text-only file. In either case, make sure it has a .TXT extension to its filename. Then you can import the contents of that text file directly into the CUSTDICT.SPL file. Here's how to do it.

1. Make a backup copy of your custom dictionary file for safekeeping (for example, CUSTDICT.BAK).
2. In Capture, choose "Edit Custom Dictionary…" from the File menu, and then click "Import…."
3. From the "Files of Type" list, select "Text File (*.txt)."
4. Enter the path name and filename of the text file containing the words to import, or navigate to the appropriate directory and select the text file. Click "OK."
5. Capture will report how many words have been added to the custom dictionary. Click "OK."

To add a small number of words to Capture's current custom dictionary, open the CUSTDICT.SPL file in a text editor (after making a backup of the file). Scroll to the bottom and manually enter your new words, each on a line of its own (i.e., separated by carriage returns). When you are done, save the file with the same name.

If your friend's custom dictionary was created in Acrobat Capture, you can swap this dictionary with the one on your system. In fact, although it's not a built-in feature, you can use different Acrobat Capture dictionaries to accommodate different categories of documents. For example, you can have a custom dictionary for medical terms and another for musical terms. To use two or more custom dictionaries, follow the steps below.

1. Make a copy of your CUSTDICT.SPL file—for example, you might call it CUSTDICT.ONE.
2. In Capture, select "Edit Custom Dictionary…" from the File menu.
3. Add and delete entries to create the second dictionary. (See the tip at bottom left.)
4. Repeat these steps as necessary to create more custom dictionary files.

The active dictionary will always be the one with the name CUSTDICT.SPL. You can switch dictionaries at any time by swapping the names of the files. You don't need to restart Capture to do this.

If another Capture user has sent you their dictionary, you need only rename your own dictionary file, ensure that the name of your friend's dictionary is CUSTDICT.SPL, and put that file in the Capture directory.

TIP WINDOWS

Collation Limit in Acrobat Capture 1.0x

Adobe Acrobat Capture 1.0x allows you to collate two or more scanned images into a single output file. Although Capture can technically collate more than 100 images into a single file, Adobe Technical Support recommends that you limit collation to no more than 100 pages. PDFs containing more than 100 collated pages may not be stable (e.g., PDFs generate errors, links don't activate when clicked).

Smaller PDFs can be combined using the Insert Pages command in Acrobat Exchange. For more information on combining PDFs, refer to Acrobat Exchange's online Help.

File Formats for Saving Scanned Images in Capture 1.0

Adobe Acrobat Capture can save scanned images in the following formats:

- PCX
  This option saves the image as an uncompressed PCX.
- TIFF Compressed [Most Compatible]
  This option saves the scanned image as a CCITT Group 3 compressed TIFF file. It is considered "most compatible" because it is supported by a majority of the available graphics applications.
- TIFF Compressed [smallest]
  This option saves the image as a CCITT Group 4 compressed TIFF image.
- TIFF Uncompressed
  Saves the scanned image as an uncompressed TIFF image.

Any of these four options may be selected from the "File Format" drop-down list in the "Scan Images to Input Folder" dialog box that appears when you click on the "Scan" button in Capture.

Using the Visioneer PaperPort Scanner with Capture

The Visioneer PaperPort is a sheet fed desktop scanner, available in two models: PaperPort and PaperPort VX. The original PaperPort model supports 16 levels of gray and uses the Visioneer Desktop version 2.0 or 3.5. The PaperPort VX model supports 256 levels of gray and uses Visioneer Desktop version 3.5. Adobe Acrobat Capture 1.01 does not support the PaperPort scanner directly, but does support both models of the scanner when used with the Visioneer Desktop version 3.5. or later.

VISIONEER DESKTOP

The Visioneer Desktop software provides access to the Visioneer PaperPort scanner. Visioneer Desktop displays the icons of applications that are compatible with the PaperPort scanner and have a *.glk file in the PaperPort directory.

The *.glk file for Acrobat Capture (Caplink.glk) is available from Adobe's World Wide Web site (http://www.adobe.com/acrobat/products/captvisioneer.html). To install the Caplink.glk file, make sure it's 28,624 bytes and place it in the Paprport directory. If the Caplink.glk file is not 28,624 bytes, it didn't download correctly and you'll need to download it again.

ACROBAT CAPTURE SETUP OPTIONS

To access the Acrobat Capture setup options from the Visioneer Desktop, click the Settings icon (i.e., the picture of the PaperPort scanner) on the Desktop. In the PaperPort Scan Settings dialog box, scroll through the Category list and select the Capture icon to open the (Acrobat Capture) PaperPort Preferences dialog box. Choose from the following settings:

Default Output File Format
Select the output file format for your scanned TIFF images. The formats available in Visioneer Desktop are the same formats available in Acrobat Capture Output directory setup.

Default Output Path
Select the directory to which output files will be written.

Confidence Threshold for Suspect Words
Select the amount of time and resources Acrobat Capture spends deciphering unrecognized words and words not included in Capture's dictionary.

Save ACD File for Reviewing
When selected, Capture creates an editable Acrobat Capture Document (ACD).

Detect Non-Portrait Orientations
When selected, Capture recognizes and processes TIFF images that are not in portrait orientation: landscape CW, landscape CCW, and Inverted 180 degrees. See the Capture Help PDF (Help_cap.pdf) for more information about processing non-portrait TIFF images.

Display Link Icon
When selected, the Capture icon displays at the bottom of the Visioneer Desktop.

SCANNING WITH VISIONEER PAPERPORT

To scan using the Visioneer PaperPort scanner, open the Visioneer Desktop by either feeding paper into the scanner, which automatically

launches the Desktop, or launch the Visioneer Desktop by choosing Start > Programs > PaperPort > PaperPort (Windows 95), or by double-clicking on the Paprport.exe file located in the PaperPort directory (Windows 3.x).

TIFF images scanned with the PaperPort appear as thumbnails on the Visioneer Desktop. To process the TIFF image using Acrobat Capture, drag the thumbnail onto the Capture icon at the bottom of the Visioneer Desktop. Acrobat Capture launches and processes the TIFF according to the options selected in the PaperPort Preferences window. When Acrobat Capture processes TIFF images, it runs in the background behind the Visioneer Desktop.

To check Capture's progress, move your cursor to the portion of the Capture window visible behind the Visioneer Desktop. When you cursor displays as a spinning Acrobat symbol, Capture is still processing the TIFF. When your cursor displays as an arrow, Capture has finished processing the TIFF. To watch Acrobat Capture process your file, click on the Capture window to bring it to the front. To close Acrobat Capture, bring it to the front and choose File > Exit.

RECOMMENDED SCANNER SETTINGS USING ACROBAT CAPTURE
To access the PaperPort scanner settings from the Visioneer Desktop, click the Settings icon (i.e., picture of the PaperPort scanner) on the Desktop. The setting options are listed under Scan Mode in the PaperPort Scan Settings dialog box. When using Acrobat Capture with Visioneer Desktop, Adobe recommends selecting the Letter option. The Letter option sets the TIFF bit depth to 1, the resolution to 300 dpi, and the Image Mode to SharpPage. Acrobat Capture will only process 1 or 8 bit TIFF images with a resolution between 200 dpi and 600 dpi. When you select settings outside these limits, Capture will return the following error when you process the TIFF: "Images resolution outside supported range: 200-600 dpi."

To customize the PaperPort scanner settings, select Custom under Scan Mode, then click Edit Settings.

Unexpected Results

WINDOWS

Q In Capture, sometimes my Landscape pages don't get rotated, and are instead processed in Portrait. What can I do about this?

A Update to Capture 1.01. This new release of Capture includes a feature that allows you to select, or limit, what rotation options Capture will consider for your page, according to your specifications.

You can force Capture 1.01 to use a specific orientation by making only that option available. To make your selection, choose "Setup Processing Options…" from the Process menu (or click on the button with the dial on it at the bottom of the Capture window, or press Ctrl + O), and check the desired option(s). Your choices include:

Capture samples four portions of the image and selects what it considers the correct orientation from the checked rotation options based on the information it collects from its samples. Capture will then rotate the image accordingly. The orientations selected by default are Portrait and Landscape CW (clockwise). You can change these defaults to fit your needs.

NOTE: The more options you check, the longer the processing will take; Capture evaluates each page and considers each rotation option that's checked. If you're processing large batches of images, you'll save time by grouping them by orientation and selecting the one appropriate orientation for any given batch.

Also, remember that scanners don't all begin scanning in the same corner of the page; test the orientations listed above before you begin a large job.

Captured Text in a Text or Word-processor File is in the Wrong Order

ISSUE
The text blocks in a text or word-processor (e.g., Word, Word Perfect) file created in Adobe Acrobat Capture are in the wrong order.

SOLUTION
Reorder the text blocks in Capture Reviewer:

1. Open the ACD file in Capture Reviewer.
2. Choose View > Show Text Block Order. Numbered squares appear in each text block to show the order of text blocks on the page.
3. To move a block up in the order, Ctrl + click the border of the block and choose Edit > Swap Text Block with Previous. To move a block down in the order, select the block and choose Edit > Swap Text Block with Next. When a single text block is selected, pressing the Up Arrow key selects the previous block, and pressing the Down Arrow key selects the next block.
4. Continue to swap until they are in the correct order.

ADDITIONAL INFORMATION
When you choose a word-processing format (e.g., Word, Word Perfect) as an output file type in Acrobat Capture, text blocks are arranged in the same order in which Capture recognizes them. Capture's OCR (Optical Character Recognition) engine may not recognize text blocks in the same order in which they appear in the original scanned document.

Only First Page of Multiple-page TIFF File is Processed in Capture 1.0

ISSUE
Adobe Acrobat Capture 1.0 processes only the first page of a multiple-page TIFF file.

SOLUTION
Upgrade to Capture 1.01.

ADDITIONAL INFORMATION
The Acrobat Capture 1.0 documentation incorrectly lists multiple-page TIFF files as a supported file format. Capture 1.01 does support multiple-page TIFF files.

Double-clicking on an Image or Word-processing Icon in Capture Doesn't Start an Application

ISSUE
An image-editing or word-processing application does not launch as expected when you double-click on an image or word-processor document icon in Adobe Acrobat Capture 1.0x.

SOLUTION
Use the Windows File Manager to create an association between the image filename extension and the image-editing application or between the document filename and the word-processor application. To create an association:

1. Open the Windows File Manager.
2. Choose File > Associate.
3. Type the appropriate extension in the Files with Extension box, choose the application you want to associate with that extension from the Associate With pop-up menu, then click OK.

ADDITIONAL INFORMATION
To launch an image-editing or word-processing application by double-clicking on an icon in Capture, there must be an association between the image or document file's extension and the image-editing or word-processing application.

Suspect Words in an ACD File Aren't Saved as Bitmap Images in a PDF File

ISSUE
Suspect words in an Adobe Acrobat Capture 1.0 ACD file are not saved as bitmap images in the associated PDF file.

SOLUTION
Select the Suspect-Word options to save bitmap images for uncorrected and unverified suspects:

1. Open the ACD file in Reviewer.
2. Choose Tools > Setup Suspect-Word Options.
3. Select one or more of the Image options, then click OK.

ADDITIONAL INFORMATION
When none of the Image (PDF) options are selected in the Setup Suspect-Word Options dialog box, Capture does not save suspect words in an ACD file as bitmap images in the associated PDF file.

Unable to Place TIFF Images From Capture into Other Applications

ISSUE
An error message appears (e.g., "Unsupported compression type") or only a gray box displays when you try to place a TIFF image created in Adobe Acrobat Capture into another application (e.g., Adobe PageMaker).

SOLUTIONS
When scanning in Capture, select the "TIFF Uncompressed" option from the "File Format:" drop-down list in the "Scan Images to Input Folder" dialog box.
OR: Open and save the TIFF image in an image-editing application (e.g., Adobe Photoshop).

ADDITIONAL INFORMATION
TIFF images created in Acrobat Capture are not intended for use in other applications. When the "TIFF Compressed {Most Compatible]" option is selected in the "Scan Images to Input Folder" dialog box, TIFF images created in Capture will import very slowly into other applications and will only display as a gray box.

Pages are Converted to White-text-on-black Full-page Bitmap Images or No Text is Produced in Capture

ISSUE
Pages are converted to white-text-on-black full-page bitmap images or no text is produced for text and word-processor documents when you process them in Adobe Acrobat Capture 1.0.

SOLUTION
Rescan the page with the Invert or Reverse option selected (or deselected if it was already selected).
OR: Use an image-editing application (e.g., Adobe Photoshop) to reverse the page images.

ADDITIONAL INFORMATION
When scanner control software produces a negative image of a scanned page, that page will be converted to a white-text-on-black full-page bitmap image or no text will be produced when that page is processed in Capture.

Application Errors

WINDOWS

Error "0002 Not Enough Memory to Configure the PDF Writer" When Processing In Capture 1.0x

ISSUE
The error "0002 Not Enough Memory to Configure the PDF Writer" appears when you process scanned images in Adobe Acrobat Capture 1.0x.

SYMPTOM
Adobe Acrobat Exchange 2.0 or 2.1 was installed after Capture.

SOLUTION

Remove the PDF Writer files dated 10/14/94 (Exchange 2.0) or 8/18/95 (Exchange 2.1) from the windows\system directory and reinstall the PDF Writer driver from the Acrobat Capture Disks. The PDF Writer files are: pdfwritr.drv, pdfwlib.dll, and pdfhlp.hlp.

To reinstall the PDF Writer, launch the Capture installer and deselect all install options but the PDF Writer when prompted.

ADDITIONAL INFORMATION

Acrobat Capture ships with its own PDF Writer driver, version 2.01 (3/1/95). If Acrobat Exchange 2.0 or 2.1 is installed after installing Acrobat Capture, Capture's PDF Writer driver is updated with a different PDF Writer driver, which has the same version number. The PDF Writer drivers included with Exchange 2.0 and 2.1 are incompatible with Acrobat Capture.

Error "Another application is using the file MSVCRT20.DLL..." When installing Capture 1.01

ISSUE

The error "Another application is using the file MSVCRT-20.DLL, which the installer is attempting to update. Please shut down all other applications and then retry." appears when you are installing Adobe Acrobat Capture 1.01 in Windows 95.

SOLUTIONS

Restart Windows 95 in Safe mode before installing Capture 1.01. To start Windows 95 in Safe mode:

1. Choose Start > Shut Down.
2. Choose Restart the Computer.
3. Press the F8 key when "Loading Windows 95" appears on the screen.
4. Press 3 to select the Safe mode option, then press Enter.
5. Install Capture, then restart Windows.

OR: Rename the Startup directory and restart the computer before installing Capture 1.01. When Capture is installed, return the Startup directory to its original name.

OR: Restart the computer is MS-DOS mode and rename the MSVCRT20.DLL file to MSVCRT20.OLD. Then, start Windows 95 and install Capture.

NOTE: Make sure there's only one MSVCRT20.DLL file on the system. To check the entire system for the MSVCRT-20.DLL file, use the DOS ATTRIB command. For example:

```
attrib msvcrt20.dll /s
```

OR: Delete the MSVCRT20.DLL file before installing.

ADDITIONAL INFORMATION

The MSVCRT20.DLL file is installed with Microsoft Office and is initialized when you start Windows. The Capture installer attempts to update the MSVCRT20.DLL file but can't because it's in use by Windows. Restarting Windows in Safe mode, renaming the Startup folder, or renaming or deleting the MSVCRT20.DLL file prevents it from initializing when Windows starts, so that the Capture installer can update it successfully.

Error "Insufficient room on Drive C for temporary file, job canceled" in Capture or Reviewer

ISSUE

Adobe Acrobat Capture 1.0x returns the error "Acrobat PDF Writer Error. Insufficient room on Drive C for temporary file, job canceled" when attempting to save a processed image to PDF format.

SOLUTION

Remove the PDF Writer files dated 10/14/94 or 8/18/95 from the windows\system directory and reinstall the PDF Writer driver from the Acrobat Capture Disks. The PDF Writer files are: pdfwritr.drv, pdfwblib.dll, and pdfhlp.hlp.

To reinstall the PDF Writer, launch the Capture installer and deselect all install options but the PDF Writer when prompted.

ADDITIONAL INFORMATION

Acrobat Capture 1.0x has its own PDF Writer driver, version 2.01 (3/1/95). If Acrobat Exchange 2.0 or 2.1 is installed after installing Acrobat Capture, Capture's PDF Writer driver is replaced with Exchange's PDF Writer driver. The PDF Writer drivers included with Exchange 2.0 and 2.1 are incompatible with Acrobat Capture.

Error "Font needed by Capture cannot be found or system resources are too low..." Converting TIFF Image

ISSUE

When you convert a TIFF image to PDF format using Adobe Acrobat Capture, Capture returns the error "A font needed by Capture cannot be found or system resources are too low to access the font." Acrobat Capture does not return the error when converting TIFF images to other file formats.

SOLUTIONS

Do one or more of the following:

A. Increase the size of the font cache in Adobe Type Manager (ATM) to 512K or more by clicking the up arrow next to the Font Cache scroll box in the ATM 3.0x Control Panel, or in the Settings pane of ATM Deluxe 4.0 or ATM 4.0.

B. Remove all the installed fonts from ATM, remove all font references from the Win.ini file and the Atm.ini file, delete all Atmfonts.qlc files, restart Windows, then re-add your fonts.

ADDITIONAL INFORMATION

ATM's font cache is an allotment of memory that ATM uses to store the fonts it has displayed on screen. If the ATM font cache is set too low, ATM cannot store all the fonts needed by Acrobat Capture and Acrobat PDF Writer to convert a TIFF image to a PDF file. Increasing the font cache to 512K or more enables ATM to store a larger number of fonts in memory, making them available to Acrobat Capture and Acrobat PDF Writer during the TIFF to PDF conversion process.

When troubleshooting a font problem with ATM, remove all your fonts from ATM, then remove all font references from the Win.ini file and the Atm.ini file. Once you've cleaned up the Win.ini file and the Atm.ini file, you can re-add your fonts. Acrobat Capture installs the Base 13 fonts (Courier, Courier Bold, Courier Italic, Courier Bold Italic, Helvetica, Helvetica Bold, Helvetica Oblique, Helvetica Bold Oblique, Times, Times Bold, Times Italic, Times Bold Italic, and Symbol). Make sure you re-add these fonts before using Acrobat Capture.

The Atmfonts.qlc file contains display information for the last several fonts used, enabling ATM to display the fonts more quickly. Acrobat Capture and PDF Writer access ATM and the Atmfonts.qlc file when converting TIFF images to PDF files. If multiple copies of the Atmfonts.qlc file are installed or if the Atmfonts.qlc file is damaged, Acrobat Capture returns the error "A font needed by capture cannot be found or system resources are too low to access the font." ATM creates a new Atmfonts.qlc file when it cannot locate an existing Atmfonts.qlc file.

Error "Temp directory is full" When Processing a File in Capture

ISSUE

The error "Capture can't write to the temp directory. The temp directory is full." appears when you are processing an image in Adobe Acrobat Capture 1.0.

SOLUTIONS

Make sure there's a valid temp directory with adequate free disk space for Capture:

1. Choose "Preferences..." from the File menu.
2. Make sure the directory listed in the "Temporary Files" box at the bottom of the "Preferences" dialog box is a valid directory and that it's located on a drive with adequate free disk space for the file you're processing in Capture.

NOTE: The drive containing Capture's temp directory should have free disk space equal to two to three times the size of the file you're processing.

OR: If Exchange 2.0 or 2.1 was installed after Capture, remove the PDFWriter files dated 10/14/94 (Exchange 2.0) or 8/18/95 (Exchange 2.1) from the WINDOWS\SYSTEM directory and reinstall the PDFWriter driver from the Acrobat Capture Disks. The PDFWriter files are: PDFWRITR.DRV, PDFWLIB.DLL, and PDFHLP.HLP.

To reinstall the PDFWriter, launch the Capture installer and deselect all install options but the PDFWriter.

ADDITIONAL INFORMATION

Acrobat Capture ships with its own PDFWriter driver, version 2.01 (3/1/95). If Acrobat Exchange 2.0 or 2.1 is installed after installing Acrobat Capture, Capture's PDFWriter driver is updated with a different PDFWriter driver, which has the same version number. The PDFWriter drivers that ship with Exchange 2.0 and 2.1 are incompatible with Acrobat Capture.

Error "Growstub caused a GPF in module Pointer.dll" in Capture 1.0x

ISSUE

When you start Adobe Acrobat Capture 1.0x, the system returns the error, "Growstub caused a General Protection Fault in module Pointer.dll."

SOLUTIONS

Do one or more of the following:

A. Update to a version of the Microsoft mouse driver more current than version 9.02.
B. Change the mouse driver to "Microsoft, or IBM PS/2," and remove the reference to "pointer.exe" from the Win.ini file:
   1. Exit all Windows applications.
   2. Make backup copies of the Win.ini and System.ini files, which are located in the Windows directory.
   3. Double-click on the Windows Setup icon in the Main group of the Program Manager.
   4. Choose Options > Change System Settings.
   5. Select Microsoft, or IBM PS/2 from the Mouse pop-up menu.
   6. Click OK and follow the prompts to install the mouse driver. You may receive a prompt asking if you want to use the currently installed driver or install a new one. Select the currently installed driver option before installing a new one. If you choose to install a new driver, you will need your Windows installation disk set. Do not restart Windows when prompted.
   7. Exit Windows Setup.
   8. Open the original Win.ini file in a text editor that saves in text-only format (e.g., Windows Write, Notepad).
   9. Locate the "Load=" line in the [Windows] section and delete the reference to "pointer.exe," including its path (e.g., C:\windows\pointer.exe). After deleting the reference to "pointer.exe," there should be one space before any references remaining on the line.
   10. Save the Win.ini file in text-only format and restart Windows.
C. Ensure the "mouse.drv=" line in the [boot] section of the System.ini file points to the correct location of the Mouse.drv file (e.g., mouse.drv=C:\windows\mouse-.drv). When the "mouse.drv=" line does not point to the correct location of the Mouse.drv file, open the System.ini file in a text editor that saves in text-only for-

mat (e.g., Notepad, Windows Write) and edit the line so that it points to the correct location. When the "mouse.drv=" line reads "mouse.drv=mouse.drv," the Mouse.drv being accessed is most likely located in the Windows\System directory. By default, Windows installs the mouse driver in the Windows\System directory.

D. Make sure there's only one Mouse.drv file on the system and that it is the correct file size. The Mouse.drv file should be located in directory listed in the "mouse-.drv=" line in the [boot] section of the System.ini file. The Mouse.drv file for the "Microsoft, or IBM PS/2" should be either 10672 or 10144 bytes. Rename Mouse-.drv files whose size is not 10672 or 10144 bytes, as well as Mouse.drv files in directories other than those listed in the "mouse.drv=" line.

E. Reinstall the Mouse.drv file. When you install a new mouse driver, Windows may not overwrite the current mouse driver, requiring a "hard reset" (i.e., installing a different mouse driver, then reinstalling the desired mouse driver, thereby forcing an overwrite):

1. Ensure you have your Windows installation disk set or CD-ROM, then exit Windows.
2. From a DOS prompt, type "cd windows" to change to the Windows directory.
3. Type "setup" then press Enter to open the DOS version of Windows Setup.
   NOTE: You may press the F3 key to quit without saving changes.
4. Arrow up to the mouse line.
5. Press Enter or Return to open the list of pointing device choices.
6. Select "No mouse or other pointing device" then press Enter to select it.
6. Press Enter again to accept the configuration.
7. At the C:\Windows prompt, type "Setup."
8. Arrow up to the mouse line.
9. Press Enter to open the list of pointing device choices.
10. Arrow to "Microsoft, or IBM PS/2," then press Enter to select it.
11. Press Enter again to accept the configuration.
12. If Windows Setup displays the message "This driver for mouse is already installed on your system... Press Enter to use current, or Esc to install new.," press the Escape key to force an overwrite of the currently installed driver.
13. Setup may ask for an installation disk. Change the designated drive and directory to find the appropriate files.
14. Windows Setup automatically returns to DOS after finding and copying the necessary files.
15. Restart Windows.
16. Verify the Mouse.drv file size is either 10672 or 10144 bytes. By default, Windows Setup installs the Mouse-.drv file in the Windows\System directory.

F. Use the Windows File Manager to search all drives and directories for multiple Win.ini and System.ini files. The Win.ini and System.ini files should be located in the Windows directory; rename any other Win.ini and System.ini files.

ADDITIONAL INFORMATION

Information about your mouse is stored in the Win.ini and System.ini files. When there are multiple copies of these files, the mouse information in each file may differ, causing mouse conflicts in Capture and other applications.

To make backup copies of your System.ini or Win.ini files:

1. In the Windows File Manager, locate either the System-.ini or Win.ini file in the Windows directory, then click once to select it.
2. Choose File > Copy.
3. Insert a blank formatted disk into the disk drive.
4. In the To: box of the Copy dialog box, enter the appropriate disk drive letter (e.g., "A:\," 'B:\").
5. Click OK.

You can copy the backup Win.ini and System.ini files back into the Windows directory to restore original settings.

Error "Height or width of image beyond maximum (27 in)" When Processing an Image in Capture 1.0x

ISSUE

When you process an image in Adobe Acrobat Capture 1.0x, Capture returns the error "Height or width of image beyond maximum (27in)."

SOLUTIONS

Rescan the image at a size supported by Capture. The maximum image height & width supported by Capture is 27 inches. OR: Crop the image in an image-editing application (e.g., Adobe Photoshop) before processing it in Capture.

ADDITIONAL INFORMATION

Capture cannot process images whose width or height dimensions are greater than 27 inches. When you process an image whose height or width is greater than 27 inches, Capture returns the error "Height or width or image beyond maximum (27 in)."

Error "Problem Selecting Font. Adobe Type Manager May Not be Installed Properly" in Acrobat Reviewer

ISSUE

When you open an ACD file in Adobe Acrobat Reviewer 1.01, Reviewer returns the error "Problem Selecting Font. Adobe Type Manager May Not be Installed Properly." Nothing happens when you click OK in the error message dialog box.

SOLUTION

Use Adobe Type Manager (ATM) to delete the fonts required by Acrobat Capture. Then, reinstall the fonts by reinstalling Capture.

OR: Copy the contents of the Capture installation disks 3 and 4 to a new directory on your hard disk, then install the fonts from the new directory.

1. Create a new directory on your hard disk (e.g., C:\Install).
2. Copy the contents of Capture disks 3 and 4 to the new directory.
3. Open the ATM Control Panel and add the fonts. For instructions, see Additional Information.
4. Exit the ATM Control Panel.
5. Restart Windows.

ADDITIONAL INFORMATION

Acrobat Capture requires that the fonts on Capture installation disks 3 and 4 are installed in ATM. If the fonts are missing or damaged, Acrobat Reviewer will return the error "Problem Selecting Font. Adobe Type Manager May Not be Installed Properly." Deleting and reinstalling the fonts ensures they are not damaged and are available to Acrobat Capture and Acrobat Reviewer.

Acrobat Capture requires the following 41 Adobe PostScript Type 1 fonts:

Font, Menu Name(Style Link), Font File Name (*.pfm, *.pfb)
AvantGarde-Book, AvantGarde, Agw_____.*
AvantGarde-Demi, AvantGarde(Bold), Agd_____.*
AvantGarde-BookOblique, AvantGarde(Italic), Agwo_____.*
Bookman-Demi, Bookman(Bold), Bkd_____.*
Bookman-LightItalic, Bookman(Italic), Bkli_____.*
Courier, Courier, Com_____.*
Courier-Bold, Courier(Bold), Cob_____.*
Courier-BoldOblique, Courier(BoldItalic), Cobo_____.*
Courier-Oblique, Courier(Italic), Coo_____.*
Helvetica, Helvetica, Hv_____.*
Helvetica-Black, Helvetica-Black, Hvbl_____.*
Helvetica-BlackOblique, Helvetica-Black(Italic), Hvblo___.*
Helvetica-Bold, Helvetica(Bold), Hvb_____.*
Helvetica-BoldOblique, Helvetica(BoldItalic), Hvbo_____.*
Helvetica-Condensed-Black, Helvetica(CondensedBlack), Hvcbl___.*
Helvetica-Condensed-BlackObl, Helvetica(CondensedBlack),Italic, Hvco_____.*
Helvetica-Narrow, Helvetica-Narrow, Hvn_____.*
Helvetica-Narrow-Bold, Helvetica-Narrow(Bold), Hvnb_____.*
Helvetica-Narrow-BoldOblique, Helvetica-Narrow(BoldItalic), Hvnbo___.*
Helvetica-Narrow-Oblique, Helvetica-Narrow(Italic), Hvno_____.*
Helvetica-Oblique, Helvetica(Italic), Hvo_____.*
LetterGothic, LetterGothic, Lg_____.*
LetterGothic-Bold, LetterGothic(Bold), Lgb_____.*
LetterGothic-BoldSlanted, LetterGothic(BoldItalic), Lgbsl___.*
LetterGothic-Slanted, LetterGothic(Italic), Lgsl_____.*
NewCenturySchlbk-Roman, NewCenturySchlbk, Ncr_____.*
NewCenturySchlbk-Bold, NewCenturySchlbk(Bold), Ncb_____.*
NewCenturySchlbk-Italic, NewCenturySchlbk(Italic), Nci_____.*
NewCenturySchlbk-BoldItalic, NewCenturySchlbk(BoldItalic), Ncbi_____.*
Palatino-Roman, Palatino, Por_____.*
Palatino-Bold, Palatino(Bold), Pob_____.*
Palatino-Italic, Palatino(Italic), Poi_____.*
Palatino-BoldItalic, Palatino(BoldItalic), Pobi_____.*
Symbol, Symbol, Sy_____.*
Times-Roman, Times, Tir_____.*
Times-Bold, Times(Bold), Tib_____.*
Times-Italic, Times(Italic), Tii_____.*
Times-BoldItalic, Times(BoldItalic), Tibi_____.*
ZapfDingbats, ZapfDingbats, Zd_____.*

Error "Can't open system level scanner driver...[-4428]" When Scanning Using Adobe Acrobat Capture

ISSUE

Adobe Acrobat Capture generates the error "Can't open system level scanner driver, check installation [-4428]" when you scan a document.

SOLUTIONS

Do one or more of the following:

A. Remove and reinstall the scanner driver to make sure it is not damaged or has not been overwritten. For information on removing and reinstalling your scanner driver, refer to your scanner documentation.
B. Update the scanner driver.
C. When using Windows 95, make sure your system level scanner driver is loading successfully:
   1. Restart your computer and press F8 when the "Starting Windows 95" message displays.
   2. Select Step-by-Step Confirmation (option 5). This enables you to process each startup file (e.g., the Autoexec.bat file, Config.sys) line by line.
   3. Choose Yes to accept each startup file and confirm each line of the Autoexec.bat and Config.sys files. If the scanner device driver file fails to load and returns an error message, contact your scanner manufacturer for further assistance.
D. Contact your scanner manufacturer and request a diagnostic test of the scanner and the scanner drivers.
E. Use another TWAIN-compliant application (e.g., Adobe Photoshop) to acquire an image using the TWAIN driver for your scanner. If your scanner successfully acquires an image, try using the TWAIN driver with Acrobat Capture.
   NOTE: Acrobat Capture does not support all scanners using the TWAIN driver. It is possible TWAIN will acquire images in other applications but not acquire images in Capture.

ADDITIONAL INFORMATION

When you scan a document in Acrobat Capture and the system level driver for your scanner is damaged, outdated, or has been overwritten by another application, the ISIS scanner driver Adobe supplies cannot work as expected and Acrobat Capture returns the error "Can't open system level scanner driver, check installation [-4428]" occurs. To ensure your driver is not damaged or has not been overwritten by another application, remove and reinstall the scanner driver from your original scanner disks. To ensure you have the latest version of the scanner driver, contact the scanner manufacturer.

If you continue to get the error after updating and reinstalling your scanner driver, contact your scanner manufacturer and request a diagnostic testing utility. Many scanner manufacturers provide diagnostic utilities for customers.

Acrobat Capture supports some versions of TWAIN and some scanners using the TWAIN interface. Because of the limited support of TWAIN in Acrobat Capture, and because TWAIN scanner drivers do not process stack scans (multiple pages) as expected, Adobe recommends you use the ISIS drivers from Pixel Translation.

The TWAIN interface requires a TWAIN-supported scanner and plug-in software from the scanner manufacturer. To use TWAIN, follow the install instructions provided by your TWAIN scanner manufacturer. If the manufacturer does not provide a Source Manager and TWAIN Data Source (*.ds) file for your scanner, the TWAIN plug-in will not function. Adobe does not provide these software modules. Contact your scanner manufacturer for more information on using TWAIN with your scanner.

Acrobat PDF Writer®

Unexpected Results

MAC OS / WINDOWS / UNIX

Multiple Master Fonts Aren't Embedded

ISSUE
Multiple master fonts in a PDF file substitute to Adobe Sans MM or Adobe Serif MM when you open the PDF file on a computer that doesn't have the original multiple master fonts installed.

SYMPTOM
The PDF was created with the PDF Writer, and the Embed All Fonts option was selected in the Acrobat PDF Writer Font Embedding dialog box.

SOLUTIONS
Create the PDF file using Adobe Acrobat Distiller, which embeds multiple master fonts.
OR: When using PDF Writer, don't use multiple master fonts.

ADDITIONAL INFORMATION
Multiple master fonts aren't embedded by PDF Writer 2.0 and later for Windows or PDF Writer 1.0 and later for the Macintosh. As a result, multiple master fonts substitute to Adobe Sans MM or Adobe Serif MM when you open the PDF file on a computer that doesn't have the multiple master fonts installed.

Adobe Acrobat uses Adobe Sans MM and Adobe Serif MM to simulate unavailable fonts in a PDF file.

PDF Files Display and Print Slower than Expected

ISSUE
Adobe Acrobat PDF files created with Adobe Acrobat PDF Writer 2.0 or earlier display and print slower than expected.

SOLUTIONS
Use Adobe Acrobat Distiller 2.0 or earlier to create PDF files.
OR: Downsample images to simplify them before creating the PDF file using an image editing application (e.g., Adobe Photoshop 3.0 or earlier).

ADDITIONAL INFORMATION
Adobe Acrobat PDF Writer 2.0 and earlier are unable to downsample or decrease the resolution of bitmap images. Downsampling bitmap images prior to generating PDF files using the PDF Writer decreases PDF file size and improves screen display. Fastest display of PDF files containing bitmap images occurs when images are downsampled to 72 dpi prior to generating PDF files. PDF Writer 2.0 and earlier don't alter the resolution of bitmap images when the image is converted to PDF. Acrobat Distiller does support altering the resolution of bitmap images and provides options for downsampling bitmap images when creating PDF files.

Patterns Fills Become Solid Tints in Acrobat

ISSUE
Patterns fills and lines become solid tints when converted to PDF format.

SOLUTIONS
Use solid fills instead of pattern fills, and dashed lines instead of pattern lines, in documents you will convert into PDF files.
OR: If you are converting a document created in an application that supports custom PostScript patterns (e.g., MacroMedia FreeHand), use PostScript fills and lines.

ADDITIONAL INFORMATION
PDFWriter 2.0 and Distiller 2.0 or earlier substitute solid tints of gray or color for bitmap pattern fills and lines. The density of the tint substituted for the pattern fills corresponds to the relative density of the bitmap pattern (e.g., a pattern fill with 50% black pixels will be converted to a 50% tint of gray).

WINDOWS

PDFWriter Creates Bitmap Images of Illustrator 4.x for Windows Files

ISSUE
Adobe Acrobat PDF Writer 2.0 or earlier Portable Document Format (PDF) files created from Adobe Illustrator 4.x for Windows display and print as bitmap images.

SOLUTION
Print the Illustrator 4.x file to disk as a PostScript file and use Adobe Acrobat Distiller 2.0 or earlier to create the PDF file. For instructions, refer to the Adobe Acrobat Exchange 2.0 Getting Started manual.

ADDITIONAL INFORMATION
Acrobat PDF Writer 2.0 or earlier PDF files created from Illustrator 4.x for Windows display and print as bitmap images. Illustrator 4.x for Windows recognizes the Acrobat PDF Writer as a raster device (i.e., a device that accepts bitmap information only) and prints a bitmap description of the page rather than an object-oriented description. Acrobat Distiller interprets object-oriented PostScript information when converting Illustrator 4.x for Windows files to PDF files.

Line Endings in a Document Change When Written to PDF

ISSUE
The line endings in a PDF (Portable Document Format) file and in the document from which the PDF file was created aren't the same.

SOLUTIONS
Make sure you compose your document to the same printer driver you'll use to print. For example, if you're printing to the PDF Writer, select the PDF Writer in your application's printer setup dialog box. If you're creating a .PS file to use with the Distiller, make sure you choose the same PostScript driver in your application's printer setup and print dialog boxes.

ADDITIONAL INFORMATION
Most applications use information from the printer driver to establish line endings for printout and display. Line endings may change when the selected printer changes.

Because the textual information in a PDF is "locked," it cannot be reformatted. Changing the printing device in Acrobat Exchange or Reader after the PDF has been created will not affect its line endings.

MAC OS

Graphics in Quark 3.3 Documents Converted to PDF Display & Print as Boxes with Xs in Them

ISSUE
Quark-generated or imported graphics in QuarkXPress 3.3x documents converted to PDF using the PDF Writer or Acrobat Distiller display and print as boxes with Xs through them.

SOLUTIONS
Make sure Normal is selected as the Output option in Quark's Print dialog box when creating the *.ps file to be distilled through the Acrobat Distiller.
OR: When using the PDF Writer from Quark 3.3, set the Output option to Normal in the LaserWriter driver (or the PostScript driver you're using) before printing to the PDF Writer:

1. Select the LaserWriter driver (or the PostScript driver you're using) from the Chooser.
2. Open your file in Quark and choose File > Print.
3. Select Normal as the Output option in the Print dialog box.
4. Click on Print, then immediately cancel the print job using the Command + . (period) key combination to save the Normal setting. If you don't print and cancel the print job, Quark will revert to the previous Output setting.
5. Open the Chooser and reselect the PDF Writer, then return to Quark and print your file to PDF format.

NOTE: When printing to the PDF Writer from Quark 3.3.1, you can access the Output option directly using the PDF Writer and do not need to switch back and forth between it and the LaserWriter driver.
OR: Make sure the graphics are not being suppressed:

1. Select the graphic in QuarkXPress.
2. Choose Item > Modify.

3. Deselect Suppress Picture Printout or Suppress Printout.
4. Repeat steps 1-3 for all graphics that aren't imaging correctly.

ADDITIONAL INFORMATION

Graphics in QuarkXPress documents do not convert to PDF format correctly unless Normal is selected as the Output option in Quark's Print dialog box.

Acrobat PDF Writer Doesn't Appear in Chooser

ISSUE

After you install the Adobe Acrobat PDF Writer printer driver, it does not appear in the Chooser.

SYMPTOM

The QuickDraw GX extension is installed in the Extensions folder.

SOLUTION

Remove the QuickDraw GX extension from the Extensions folder in the System Folder and reinstall the PDF Writer.
OR: Use Extensions Manager to disable QuickDraw GX and reinstall the Acrobat PDF Writer.
NOTE: If you reenable QuickDraw GX, the Acrobat PDF Writer will disappear from the Chooser.

ADDITIONAL INFORMATION

The Acrobat PDF Writer printer driver is not QuickDraw GX compatible. When the QuickDraw GX extension is installed in the Extensions folder in the System Folder, the Acrobat PDF Writer does not appear in the list of available printers in the Chooser. Turning off QuickDraw GX through the Extensions Manager or moving the QuickDraw GX extension out of the Extensions folder enables you to successfully install and use the Acrobat PDF Writer.

Cannot Select Text in PDF Created From FreeHand 4.x or 5.x Using the PDF Writer

ISSUE

Text is not searchable or selectable in Portable Document Format (PDF) files created from MacroMedia FreeHand 4.x or later using the Adobe Acrobat PDF Writer.

SOLUTIONS

Create the PDF file using PDF Writer and FreeHand 3.x. Saving the file from FreeHand 4.x or later in FreeHand 3.x format will not create a PDF file with searchable text.
OR: Save the FreeHand 4.x or 5.x file as a PostScript file, then distill it using Adobe Acrobat Distiller.

ADDITIONAL INFORMATION

When you print from FreeHand 4.x or 5.x to a non-PostScript printer, FreeHand converts all information on the page to a single bitmap, making individual pieces of text unselectable. The Acrobat PDF Writer is a non-PostScript printer, so when you create PDF files from FreeHand 4.x or 5.x using the PDF Writer, all text is converted to a bitmap. When you open the resulting PDF file in Acrobat Exchange or Reader, the text is not selectable or searchable. FreeHand 3.x sends line art and text attribute information to non-PostScript printers, so when you print from FreeHand 3.x to the PDF Writer, text in the resulting PDF is both searchable and selectable in Acrobat Exchange and Reader.

Acrobat Distiller creates PDF files with searchable and selectable text from all versions of FreeHand.

PDF Writer Creates More Than One PDF File From Excel Workbook

ISSUE

When you print a Microsoft Excel workbook using the Adobe Acrobat PDF Writer and select the Print Entire Workbook option in Excel's Print dialog box, the PDF Writer creates an unpredictable number of Portable Document Format (PDF) files (e.g., Untitled 1, Untitled 2, Untitled 3...).

SOLUTIONS

Select the Selected Sheets option in Excel's Print dialog box, print the worksheets using the PDF Writer, then collate the resulting PDF files (i.e., insert pages from one PDF to another PDF) in Adobe Acrobat Exchange.
OR: Print the workbook to a PostScript file using the PSPrinter driver, then use Adobe Acrobat Distiller to convert the PostScript file to PDF format.

ADDITIONAL INFORMATION

When you select the Entire Workbook option in Excel's Print dialog box, the Acrobat PDF Writer generates an unpredictable number of PDF files. All the worksheets in the workbook are included in the resulting PDF files, but the order is random (e.g., a workbook containing three worksheets may result in one three-page PDF file, one one-page and one two-page PDF file, or three one-page PDF files). When you select the Selected Sheets option in the Excel print dialog box, the PDF Writer creates individual PDF files for each worksheet, which you can then collate into one PDF file using Acrobat Exchange. Acrobat Distiller creates one, all inclusive, PDF file from an Excel workbook PostScript file.

Word 6.0 Document Pages Are Wrong Orientation in PDF File Created by PDF Writer or Distiller

ISSUE

After you convert a Microsoft Word 6.0 document that contains both portrait and landscape pages to a PDF file using Adobe Acrobat PDF Writer or Adobe Acrobat Distiller, the resulting PDF file contains only portrait or only landscape pages. Some items on re-oriented pages may be cropped.

SOLUTION

Change the orientation of the pages in the Microsoft Word 6.0 document so they are all the same orientation, then create the PDF file.

OR: Create two different Word 6.0 documents for distilling where one document contains only landscape pages and the other only portrait pages, then convert the documents to PDF files using Acrobat PDF Writer or Acrobat Distiller. In Acrobat Exchange, combine the two PDF files using the Insert Pages command and use the Rotate Pages command to display the landscape pages in their appropriate orientation.

ADDITIONAL INFORMATION

Microsoft Word 6.0 enables you to include both portrait and landscape pages in a single document. When printing a document that contains both portrait and landscape pages, Microsoft Word describes landscape pages differently than those in a document that contains only landscape pages. This difference causes Acrobat PDF Writer or Acrobat Distiller to convert Microsoft Word documents that contain both portrait and landscape pages into PDF files that contain only portrait or landscape pages, causing objects outside of the page area of a re-oriented page to be cropped.

Acrobat PDF Writer and Acrobat Distiller convert Word 6.0 documents containing only portrait or only landscape pages to PDF files as expected.

Application Errors

WINDOWS

Errors Printing to the PDF Writer from WordPerfect 6.0

ISSUE

When you attempt to create a PDF (Portable Document Format) file from WordPerfect 6.0 using the PDF Writer, WordPerfect returns the error "Cannot create print file (directory/file may be write protected). Try another name?" and no PDF file is generated.

SOLUTION

Change the PDF Writer's connection from Disk to File in the Windows Control Panel:

1. Open the Windows Control Panel, located in the Main group of Windows, then double-click the Printers icon.
2. Select Adobe PDFWriter on Disk from the Installed printers list box, then click Connect.
3. Select File from the Ports pop-up menu in the Connect dialog box, click OK to close the Printers Control Panel.

ADDITIONAL INFORMATION

Word Perfect 6.0 only recognizes standard ports (e.g., "File," LPTx). When the PDF Writer is connected to the non-standard port "Disk," WordPerfect does not recognize it and generates the error "Cannot create print file (directory/file may be write protected). Try another name?" The PDF engine is not engaged, and no PDF file is generated.

Microsoft Works 3.0 Returns GPF When Printing to Acrobat PDF Writer

ISSUE

When you print to the Adobe Acrobat PDF Writer 2.0 printer driver from Microsoft Works 3.0, Microsoft Works returns the General Protection Fault (GPF) error "Application error, integer divide by zero."

SOLUTION

Print the Microsoft Works 3.0 file to disk as a PostScript file and use Adobe Acrobat Distiller to convert the PostScript file to PDF (Portable Document Format) format. For instructions, refer to the Adobe Acrobat Exchange 2.x Help file.

ADDITIONAL INFORMATION

When you print a Microsoft Works 3.0 document to PDF format using the PDF Writer, Microsoft Works returns a GPF error and does not create a PDF file. To create a PDF from a Microsoft Works 3.0 document, print the document to disk as a PostScript file and use Acrobat Distiller to convert the PostScript file to PDF format.

Printing Problems

MAC OS

Background Printing Disabled for PDF Writer 3.0

The Adobe Acrobat PDF Writer 3.0 does not support Background Printing and automatically disables the option in the Chooser. The Acrobat PDF Writer 3.0 ReadMe file inaccurately states that the PDF Writer 3.0 supports Background Printing.

When Background Printing is enabled, the application from which you are printing first spools the print file to the hard disk, then Print Monitor sends the file to the printer. Spooling the print file to the hard disk enables the printing application to process your print file in the background and the system to return primary control of the computer to you.

When Background Printing is disabled, the print job takes primary control of the computer, leaving your system unavailable for the duration of the print process. You can use Acrobat Distiller and the Distiller Assistant to create PDF files if you cannot leave your system unavailable during the PDF Writer printing process.

To create a PDF file using Acrobat Distiller Assistant:

1. Install the Adobe PS Printer version 8.3.1, which is located on the Acrobat 3.0 CD-ROM. See the instructions on the CD-ROM for more information.
2. In the Chooser, select the PSPrinter printer driver, select a PostScript printer from the list of printers, and then close the Chooser.
3. Open the original document in the application in which it was created.
4. Choose File > Print.
5. In the Print dialog box, select PDF for Destination, and then click Distill.
6. Enter a name and location for the PDF file.
7. If desired, select the View PDF File and Save PostScript File options.
8. Click Save.

NOTE: The LaserWriter 8.x printer driver does not support Acrobat Distiller Assistant. To use Distiller Assistant, use the Adobe PSPrinter 8.3.1 or later printer driver.

General Information

MAC OS / WINDOWS

How the PDF Writer Embeds Fonts General Information

Whether a font will be embedded or converted to outlines in a PDF file by Adobe Acrobat PDF Writer depends on the type of font used and on which platform the PDF file was created (i.e., Windows or Macintosh).

When Macintosh PDF Writer embeds a Type 1 font, all information within the screen font needed for screen display, except for bitmap information, is embedded in the PDF file along with font outlines. PDF Writer for Windows embeds the AFM (Adobe Font Metrics) and PFM (Printer Font Metrics) files, the outline font and the non-bitmap portion of the screen font. Embedding font information and converting characters to outlines enables Adobe Acrobat Exchange and Adobe Acrobat Reader to display and print fonts in PDF files from computers that do not have the fonts installed.

NOTE: From the Adobe Type Library, only Adobe Originals, fonts owned by Linotype-Hell AG or International Typeface Corporation, may be legally embedded in a PDF file with Acrobat PDF Writer. If you're embedding other fonts from the Adobe Type Library or fonts from other font vendors, permission from the vendor may be required for legal distribution of PDF files.

Fonts embedded by Acrobat PDF Writer for Windows:

- Type 3
- Type 1 symbolic (e.g., Zapf Dingbats)
- Type 1 Expert Fonts (e.g., AGaramond Expert)

Fonts embedded by Acrobat PDF Writer for Macintosh:

- Type 3
- Type 1 expert

Some fonts must be converted to character outlines to be included in a PDF file. Fonts converted to outlines cannot be selected using the Text Selection tool.

Fonts converted to character outlines by PDF Writer for Windows:

- TrueType symbolic
- Windows vector fonts
- PCL outline fonts

Fonts converted to character outlines by PDF Writer for Macintosh:

- Type 1 symbolic
- TrueType symbolic

Chapter Two

Adobe After Effects®

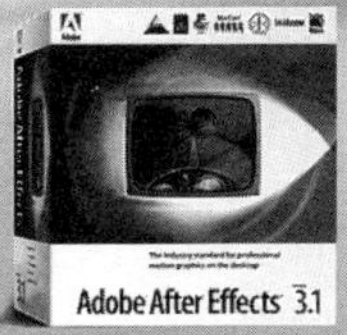

Adobe After Effects began in Aldus Corporation's College of Arts & Sciences (CoSA) division. Released in April 1997 as version 3.1, it is now available for both Mac OS and Windows 95 & NT. Described in the press as a "Photoshop on rollerblades," After Effects enables professional-quality composites, smooth 2D animations, and elaborate special effects. The interface gives the user total control and flexibility, along with superior quality output. With After Effects 3.1 you can produce on-air promos, multimedia CDs, music videos, and more—all from the desktop, at a fraction of the cost of dedicated systems.

Contents

Adobe After Effects®

Feature Techniques

MAC OS / WINDOWS

Creating and Editing After Effects Keyframe Data in Microsoft Excel General Information

You can use Microsoft Excel to create or edit keyframe data for your Adobe After Effects 3.x project. Doing so enables you to use Excel's numerical functions (e.g., linear series, growth series) to quickly generate a large number of keyframes, and also allows you to view all keyframe values simultaneously.

You can edit seven layer properties in Excel: Time Remap, Mask Feather, Anchor Point, Position, Scale, Rotation, and Opacity.

NOTE: In order for After Effects to correctly interpret keyframe data from Excel, you must strictly adhere to the following procedures.

EDITING KEYFRAME DATA IN EXCEL

To edit your existing keyframe data in Excel:

1. Open your project in After Effects 3.x.
2. In the Time Layout window, select all the keyframes for the layer you want to edit. You may select keyframes in more than one of the seven alterable layer properties, but you should not select keyframes from more than one layer.
3. Move the current-time marker to the earliest keyframe you selected (i.e., the selected keyframe that occurs first in chronological order), then note the current time displayed in the Time Layout window. (You will need to know this value when you paste your edited keyframe data back into After Effects.)
4. Choose Edit > Copy.
5. Start Excel and open a new spreadsheet.
6. Select cell A1, then choose Edit > Paste. Your After Effects keyframe data appears in the spreadsheet. Column A includes the name of each layer property; column B includes the frame number; and columns C, D, and E contain keyframe data. (Columns D and E may be blank if the layer property requires fewer than three variables [e.g., Rotation].)
7. Edit the numerical keyframe data as desired, but do not change any text.
8. Select the cells that contain your keyframe data. The upper-left cell should be A1, the lower-right cell should be in column E, and the last cell in column A should contain the words "End of Keyframe Data".
9. Choose Edit > Copy.
10. Open your After Effects project.
11. Move the current-time marker to the time you noted in step 3.
12. In the Time Layout window, select the layer whose properties you have edited, then choose Edit > Paste. After Effects replaces the keyframe data you copied in step 4 with the new data you edited in Excel.

CREATING KEYFRAME DATA IN EXCEL

To create keyframe data in Excel:

1. Open your project in After Effects 3.x.
2. Create at least one keyframe for each layer property you will edit in Excel. For example, if you will use Excel to generate a series of Position keyframes for your first layer, create the first keyframe in the series in your After Effects project.
3. In the Time Layout window, select all the keyframes for the layer you want to edit. You may select keyframes in more than one of the seven alterable layer properties, but you should not select keyframes from more than one layer.
4. Move the current-time marker to the earliest keyframe you selected (i.e., the selected keyframe that occurs first in chronological order), then note the current time displayed in the Time Layout window. (You will need to know this value when you paste your edited keyframe data back into After Effects.)
5. Choose Edit > Copy.
6. Start Excel and open a new spreadsheet.
7. Select cell A1, then choose Edit > Paste. Your After Effects keyframe data appears in the spreadsheet. Column A includes the name of each layer property; column B includes the frame number; and columns C, D, and E contain keyframe data. (Columns D and E may be blank if the layer property requires fewer than three variables [e.g., Rotation].)
8. Insert as many rows as needed for each layer property (e.g., if you wish to create an additional 100 keyframes

TIP MAC OS

Creating Plug-In Version List in After Effects 3.x General Information

To view a list of all installed After Effects 3.x plug-ins and their version numbers:

1. In After Effects 3.x, press Command + Shift + Option + Help. After Effects creates a text-only file, named AE Version Info, and saves this file in the same folder as the After Effects application.
2. Open the AE Version Info file in a text-editor (e.g., SimpleText).

for the Anchor Point layer property, insert 100 rows after the last row of keyframe data for the Anchor Point layer). Do not add or remove blank rows.

9. Add numerical keyframe data for each keyframe row as desired, but do not change the text.
10. Select the cells that contain your keyframe data. The upper-left cell should be A1, the lower-right cell should be in column E, and the last cell in column A should contain the words "End of Keyframe Data".
11. Choose Edit > Copy.
12. Open your After Effects project.
13. Move the current-time marker to the time noted in step 3.
14. In the Time Layout window, select the layer whose properties you have edited, then choose Edit > Paste. After Effects adds the keyframe data you created in Excel.

MAC OS

Q I'm considering buying a dual processor or multiprocessor to speed performance on my system. What kind of performance enhancements can I expect in After Effects?

A The level of performance enhancement you can expect varies depending on the type of processor you buy and what you are doing in After Effects. For example, a dual processor such as the nPOWER-equipped Mac 9500 Multiprocessor may apply effects or render movies 1.5 times faster than a single processor of the same speed. A quad processor such as the DayStar Genesis MP may work at 2.5 times the speed of a comparable single processor. As for other hardware brands, all multiprocessing machines use the same architecture developed by DayStar, so you shouldn't see any difference using a clone than you would using a DayStar.

There's a technique within After Effects that you can use to evaluate performance improvements on dual processor or multiprocessor systems. Try performing a series of tasks in After Effects on a multiprocessor system. Then press the Command key to direct After Effects to use the main processor only. With the Command key depressed, perform the same series of tasks to experience them without the speed enhancements.

Many tasks in After Effects benefit directly from the speed enhancements of a dual or multiprocessor. These include scaling, rotation, subpixel positioning, motion blur, blending, compositing, and applying many plug-in effects (including Alpha Levels, Basic 3D, Blend, Channel Blur, Emboss, Invert, and Twirl). Some third-party plug-in effects, such as Ultimatte and MetaTools Studio Effects, also take advantage of multiprocessing power.

Using Photoshop Plug-ins with After Effects General Information

Adobe After Effects enables you to use third-party plug-ins, such as Adobe Photoshop-compatible plug-ins, within After Effects. To use a third-party plug-in within After Effects, install the plug-in, or an alias to it, into the After Effects Plug-ins folder.

USING PHOTOSHOP 4.0 PLUG-INS WITH AFTER EFFECTS 3.X

Photoshop 4.0 plug-ins, including the Adobe Gallery Effects plug-ins, are not compatible with After Effects 3.x. If you install a Photoshop 4.0 plug-in (e.g., CompuServe GIF, Gallery Effects' Film Grain) into the After Effects Plug-ins folder, the plug-in may not appear as an output choice (e.g., Filmstrip), or it may cause a parameter or system error when you choose it in After Effects.

USING PHOTOSHOP 3.0X PLUG-INS WITH AFTER EFFECTS 3.X

You can use Photoshop 3.0x plug-ins in After Effects 3.x, although these plug-ins are designed for use with still images, and their effects cannot be animated over time. Third-party plug-ins designed for use with Photoshop 3.0x may be incompatible with After Effects 3.x.

After Effects 3.x installs Photoshop plug-ins that have been redesigned for use in After Effects. The names of these plug-ins appear in the Effect menu preceded by the text "PS+" (e.g., PS+ Wave), and their effects can be animated over time.

You can import additional file types in After Effects (e.g., BMP) by installing Photoshop's File Format plug-ins into the Input/Output folder in the Standard folder in the After Effects Plug-ins folder. When both applications include the same plug-in, use the import plug-in included with After Effects (e.g., use the After Effects Filmstrip plug-in, not the Photoshop Filmstrip plug-in).

The Gallery Effects 1.5.x plug-ins, included with Photoshop 3.x, are compatible with After Effects 3.x, and their effects can be animated over time.

USING PHOTOSHOP 2.5 PLUG-INS WITH AFTER EFFECTS 3.X

Photoshop 2.5 plug-ins are incompatible with After Effects 3.x. If you install Photoshop 2.5 plug-ins into the After Effects 3.x Plug-ins folder, a system error may occur, or After Effects may return an application error or damage files when you render movies.

USING PHOTOSHOP 3.0X PLUG-INS WITH AFTER EFFECTS 2.X

Photoshop 3.0x plug-ins are incompatible with After Effects 2.x. If you install Photoshop 3.0x plug-ins into the After Effects 2.x Plug-ins folder, a system error may occur, or After Effects may return an application error or damage files when you render movies.

USING PHOTOSHOP 2.5 PLUG-INS WITH AFTER EFFECTS 2.X

You can use all Displacement Map Photoshop 2.5 plug-ins and all File Format Photoshop 2.5 plug-ins, except for the Filmstrip, JPEG, and TIFF File Format plug-ins, within After Effects 2.x. You can use the Kodak CMS PhotoCD plug-in to import PhotoCD images, and you can use the Targa plug-in to import Targa files and sequences in 24-bit color (i.e., millions of colors). You cannot use any Photoshop 2.5 Acquire/Export plug-ins in After Effects 2.x.

Scanning Images for Use in After Effects General Information

Before scanning images for use in Adobe After Effects, you should carefully consider how they will be used in your final composition. When you scan an image at a higher resolution than necessary, your files occupy more disk space and take longer to render, and After Effects requires more Random Access Memory (RAM) to display the image. When you scan an image at a lower resolution than necessary, your image appears blocky or jagged.

DETERMINING OPTIMAL SCAN RESOLUTION

To determine the proper scan resolution, you need to determine the smallest portion of the image that will fill a frame of your After Effects composition. Once you have identified this portion, measure its height and width, then note the larger of these two dimensions. For example, consider a photograph that is 5-by-4 inches. You would like to display a portion of the image that is 4-by-3 inches, and zoom into an area that measures 2-by-1.5 inches. The smallest portion of the image that will fill a frame of your composition is 2-by-1.5 inches, so you note the larger of these two dimensions, which is 2 inches. Refer to this value as the source dimension.

Next, note the dimensions of your composition in pixels, then choose the larger of the two values as your composition dimension. For example, if your composition is 640-by-480 pixels, your composition dimension is 640 pixels.

Now you are ready to calculate the appropriate scan resolution using the following formula:

```
(composition dimension) / (source dimension)
  x (1 sample/pixel) = scan resolution
```

For example, if your composition dimension is 640 pixels and your source dimension is 2 inches, you should scan your photograph at (640 pixels / 2 inches) x (1 sample/pixel) = 320 samples per inch (spi). Note that your scanning software may refer to the scan resolution in pixels per inch (ppi) or dots per inch (dpi), but the results are the same.

CROPPING YOUR SCANNED IMAGES

Once you've scanned your image, you may want to remove (crop) the portions that won't be used in your final composition. For example, if you are only using a 4-by-3 inch portion of a 5-by-4 inch scanned photograph, you can crop an inch from the height and width so the image is reduced to 4-by-3 inches. Cropping unused image data is a useful way to reduce file size, rendering time, and RAM requirements.

While most scanning and image editing applications (e.g., Adobe Photoshop) allow you to crop scanned images, you can also use After Effects to crop an image before importing it into your final composition.

To crop an image in After Effects, determine the largest portion of the image that you will use in your composition, then create a new composition with the same dimensions. For example, if you have an image that is 720-by-648 pixels, and you will only use a portion of the image that is 288-by-216 pixels, create a new composition that is 288-by-216 pixels. Import the image into the composition, then position it so that the portion you want to retain is visible. When you save this frame, the new file contains only the image data that you need.

To save the cropped image in After Effects 2.x:

1. Choose File > Save Frame As > PICT.
2. In the Depth dialog box, choose a color depth from the Color Depth pop-up menu, then click OK.
3. Name the file, specify a target location, then click OK.

To save the cropped image in After Effects 3.x:

1. Choose Composition > Save Frame As > File.
2. Name the file, specify a target location, then click Save.
3. In the project's Render Queue, make the appropriate selections, then click Render.

After Effects 2.0 Network Rendering

If you have multiple Macintoshes connected over an Ethernet network, and multiple copies of After Effects and/or AE Rendering Engine, you can render one composition on multiple machines simultaneously, writing to a single destination folder on your network. This can dramatically decrease the amount of time it takes to render a composition.

Note that the network distribution is not automatic — you must set up each machine individually. A more convenient interface will be developed in the future.

Network rendering works for outputting sequences of single-frame files only (e.g. Sequence of PICT, Sequence of Photoshop, etc.), but not QuickTime movies. Your source footage may be of any supported type.

PROCEDURES

Before starting, you may wish to copy the project file and all its source footage onto each machine that will be rendering. This takes up more disk space, but the rendering will go faster. If you do this, you can avoid having "missing footage" by maintaining the same relative position between the project file and the footage. A simple example of this is to have the source footage in a folder that is in a folder with the project. If you have to move any files to get them into this arrangement, make sure you open and save the project before copying it and related footage to each machine, so the project "remembers" the new relative positions.

If you do end up with missing footage, just double-click on the missing item and find the moved file.

Follow the procedure below for each machine on which you wish to render. Each machine can be started at any time. The directions are the same for either After Effects or the After Effects Rendering Engine. You can have any combination of After Effects and Rendering Engines, both Power Macintosh and Macintosh versions. There is no limit to the number of machines that can be rendering simultaneously. In general, the more machines you have rendering, the faster the movie will be completed, but the overhead of network traffic will eventually slow things to a crawl when running with too many computers simultaneously. Test your setup with different numbers of machines rendering to see when adding another is not worth it. Network slowdowns can be detected by watching the time spent in the "Compressing & Writing" stage in the Show Details section of the Rendering dialog box.

The main danger with network rendering is making sure each machine is doing exactly the same thing. This means rendering the same project, same comp, with the same source footage, same times, same fonts, same effects, same preferences, and the same make-movie settings! Be very careful. We will make this more automatic in the future.

1. Open the project, either a local copy (as described above), or over the network.
2. Check your Preferences/General settings, making sure Extra Color Precision and Shutter Angle (if you are using motion blur) are set as you desire. If you are making a Millions+ movie, also check that Preferences/Output is set to write out the type of alpha channel (Straight or Premultiplied) that you desire.
3. Open the composition that you wish to render. Choose Make Movie from the Composition menu. Pick your desired settings in the Make Movie dialog box. You MUST turn on the "Skip Existing Files" option — this is VERY important. This option ensures that each machine will work on different frames!
4. WARNING: write down all your settings from the Make Movie dialog box (or do a screen dump) before clicking OK. Your settings on every machine must be identical, including the preferences mentioned above. Watch out that the starting frame number is the same too. Note that the time-span being rendered needs to be identical, and that the display of those times is affected by the Preferences/Time settings on each machine. After clicking OK, specify the name for the movie, and select a folder that is available on the network for all machines to render into. Note that the name of the movie must also be identical on all machines, and the same exact output folder must be targeted.
5. Your composition should now be rendering along happily. Go back to step 1 for each machine. You will see your folder begin to fill with frames. As each machine finishes a frame, it looks in the directory for the next file that is missing (i.e. skipping existing files) and begins to work on that frame. You can visually compare "Show Details" in each render progress dialog box to double-check that your settings are the same on each machine.

You can stop and start each machine independently at any time. However, if you have stopped a machine without starting it (or another) again, the frame that it was rendering may not be finished. Every time you start a machine, it checks for missing files from the beginning, so all missing frames will be filled in by starting just one machine again.

If you are using Apple's File Sharing to serve a network volume, we do NOT recommend using that machine to also render. Rendering on the server slows down all the clients' disk access, and can drastically reduce performance. We have had reports of conflicts with some control panels/extensions. If you absolutely must render from your server, please disable all non-Apple control panels and extensions. In fact, running any program on the server could put you at risk of conflicts.

We do not recommend using network rendering over LocalTalk because of its slowness. There should be no other problems, however.

WARNING: Do not share your plug-ins between machines. Make sure that you have a copy of the plug-ins folder on each machine that is running AE/Rendering Engine. The same rule holds for your modules in the "CAE Modules" folder.

MAYBE YOU DON'T WANT TO NETWORK RENDER

Note that if you don't want to network render, you can proceed as if the machines aren't networked and have multiple machines each render to their own local drives. This works for any output type, but has the disadvantage of forcing you to artificially break the composition up into different time-spans. Also, you can't take full advantage of all machines because each machine will finish at a different time. By network rendering you can be sure that all machines will be working together until rendering is completed. The disadvantage of network rendering is that you have to factor network overhead into the rendering time. This is of course not a problem if you render locally on each machine.

The procedures above assume that you are network rendering, but the process for rendering locally on each machine is basically the same. The differences are 1) your target output folder is different for each machine, 2) you must make sure that every machine is rendering a different work-area time-span, and 3) you do NOT need to turn on "Skip Existing Files".

After Effects Find Edges

STYLIZE & FIND EDGES
The Find Edges effect identifies the areas of the image that have significant transitions and emphasizes the edges. Edges can appear as dark lines against a white background or colored lines against a black background.

Find Edges works just like Adobe Photoshop's Find Edges filter, except that the image can be inverted and blended without applying another effect.

EFFECT CONTROLS
Invert
Inverts the image after the edges are found. When "Invert" is not checked, edges appear as dark lines on a white background. When Invert is checked, edges appear as bright lines on a black background.
Blend With Original
Blends the effect with the original source. Intermediate values give the layer an interesting "neon" look.

After Effects Bulge

This effect distorts an image around a given point. The horizontal and vertical extents of the bulge, the apparent height of the bulge, and the tapering of the bulge can all be adjusted. In addition, the edges of an image can be excluded from the distortion. In Best Quality, the distortion is antialiased.

HORIZONTAL RADIUS
Specifies, in pixels, the maximum horizontal extent of the bulge from the Bulge Center. As this value is increased, the width of the distortion increases.

VERTICAL RADIUS
Specifies, in pixels, the maximum vertical extent of the bulge from the Bulge Center. As this value is increased, the height of the distortion increases.

BULGE CENTER
Specifies the center of the distortion in the layer.

BULGE HEIGHT
Specifies the apparent height of the distortion. As the value is increased, the amount of distortion increases. Positive values make the bulge appear as if it is coming towards you; negative values make the bulge appear to recede. At 0, there is no distortion.

TAPER RADIUS
Specifies, in pixels, a radius for tapering the edge of the distortion. At 0, the bulge will appear similar to a sphere; as the Taper Radius increases, the boundary between the bulge and the undistorted areas of the layer will become smoother.

ANTIALIASING (BEST QUALITY ONLY)
Specifies an antialiasing factor when rendering in Best Quality. At High, rendering will take slightly longer but will look better.

PINNING
Pin All Edges specifies whether or not to exclude the edges of the layer from the distortion.

After Effects 3.0 Network Rendering

If you have multiple Macintoshes connected over an Ethernet (or faster) network, and multiple copies of After Effects, you can render one composition on multiple machines simultaneously, writing to a single destination folder on your network. This can dramatically decrease the amount of time it takes to render a composition.

Network rendering works by starting multiple machines simultaneously rendering the same project. As frames are generated, they are placed in a single destination folder. Each copy of the application can tell which frames to skip by examining the contents of the destination folder to see which frames are already rendered, or are in progress. The renders stop when they see that every frame has been created in the destination folder.

Note that the network distribution is not automatic - you must start each machine individually. A more convenient interface will be developed in the future.

Network rendering works for outputting sequences of single-frame files only (e.g. Sequence of PICT, Sequence of Photoshop, etc.), but not QuickTime movies. Your source footage may be of any supported type.

PROCEDURES
Before starting, you may wish to copy the project file and all its source footage onto each machine that will be rendering. This takes up more disk space, but the rendering will go faster. If you do this, you can avoid having "missing footage" by maintaining the same relative directory path between the project file and the footage. A simple example of this is to have the source footage in a folder that is in a folder with the project. If you have to move any files to get them into this arrangement, make sure you open and save the project before copying it and related footage to each machine, so the project "remembers" the new relative positions.

If you do end up with missing footage, just double-click on the missing item and find the moved file.

Follow the procedure below for each machine on which you wish to render. Each machine can be started at any time. You can have any combination of Power Macintosh and Macintosh versions. There is no limit to the number of machines that can be rendering simultaneously. In general, the more machines you have rendering, the faster the movie will be completed, but the overhead of network traffic will eventually slow things to a crawl when running with too many computers simultaneously. This is because the computers start to spend more time transferring files rather than rendering frames. Test your setup with different numbers of machines rendering to see when adding another is not worth it. Network slowdowns can be detected by watching the time spent in the "Compressing & Writing" stage in the Show Details section of the Rendering dialog box.

The main danger with network rendering is making sure each machine is doing exactly the same thing. This means rendering the same project, same comp, with the same source footage, same times, same fonts, same effects, same preferences, and the same render settings! By setting up the render queue before you open the project on all the machines, you are guaranteed that almost all of these settings are identical. It is your responsibility, however, to make sure that any required fonts are available on all the machines.

1. First you must set up your project's render queue to contain only the compositions that you wish to network render. Pick your desired render settings, but you MUST turn on the "Skip Existing Files" option - this is VERY important. This option ensures that each machine will work on different frames! Since the Skip Existing Files option doesn't work with overflow volumes nor multiple output modules, you will not be able to use these features with network rendering.
2. Specify the destination name for the output sequence, and select a folder that is available on the network for all machines to render into.
3. Save the project. On each machine, open the project, either a local copy (as described above), or over the network. If you are opening the project over a network, first lock the project in the Finder (Get Info, then check Locked). This will allow multiple machines to open the file simultaneously. Click Render. You can start each machine at any time.
4. Your composition(s) should now be rendering along happily. You will see your folder begin to fill with frames. As each machine finishes a frame, it looks in the directory for the next file that is missing (i.e. skipping existing files) and begins to work on that frame.

You can stop and start each machine independently at any time. However, if you have stopped a machine without starting it (or another) again, the frame that it was rendering may not be finished. Every time you start a machine, it checks for missing files from the beginning, so all missing frames will be filled in by starting just one machine again.

If you are using Apple's File Sharing to serve a network volume, we do NOT recommend using that machine to also render. Rendering on the server slows down all the clients' disk access, and can drastically reduce performance. We have had reports of conflicts with some control panels/extensions. If you absolutely must render from your server, please disable all non-Apple control panels and extensions. In fact, running any program on the server could put you at risk of conflicts.

We do not recommend using network rendering over LocalTalk because of its slowness. There should be no other problems, however.

WARNING: Do not share your plug-ins between machines. Make sure that you have a copy of the plug-ins folder on each machine that is running After Effects.

MAYBE YOU DON'T WANT TO NETWORK RENDER

Note that if you don't want to network render, you can proceed as if the machines aren't networked and have multiple machines each render to their own local drives. This works for any output type, but has the disadvantage of forcing you to artificially break the composition up into different time-spans. Also, you can't take full advantage of all machines because each machine will finish at a different time. By network rendering you can be sure that all machines will be working together until rendering is completed. The disadvantage of network rendering is that you have to factor network overhead into the rendering time. This is of course not a problem if you render locally on each machine.

The procedures above assume that you are network rendering, but the process for rendering locally on each machine is basically the same. The differences are 1) your target output folder is different for each machine, 2) you must make sure that every machine is rendering a different work-area time-span, and 3) you do NOT need to turn on "Skip Existing Files".

After Effects Median

This effect replaces each pixel with the median pixel value of its neighbors within a given radius. At low values, this effect is useful for reducing noise. At higher values, this effect gives an interesting painterly effect to a layer. This effect operates the same in Draft and Best Quality.

RADIUS

Specifies how many pixels to examine in the median operation. For instance, when this is set to 1 the Median will be performed on the eight neighboring pixels which are within one pixel of the center pixel.

OPERATE ON ALPHA CHANNEL

If checked, the median will be performed on the alpha channel as well. Otherwise, the Median effect only operates on the color channels.

After Effects Corner Pin

This effect distorts a layer by repositioning its four corners to simulate a perspective view. The new corners of the layer can be placed anywhere in the composition the effected layer will expand to fit. Corner Pin is especially useful for aligning layers with elements in other layers. For example, you can use Corner Pin to replace the video on a television screen, or to replace an image on a billboard. In Best Quality the distortion is antialiased.

IMPORTANT NOTE

There are instances where Corner Pin cannot create a valid perspective distortion from the locations of the four corners. The perspective map is not defined when the four corners define a concave or self-intersecting polygon. To conceptualize this, imagine that there are two line segments connecting the opposite corners of the layer. For the perspective map to be valid, these two line segments must intersect. If they do not, there is no proper perspective projection onto the quadrilateral described.

Rather than display a warning dialog box (and possibly halt your unattended rendering) the Corner Pin effect will render an invalid distortion. In most cases the effect is obvious the layer will become split into two or more pieces. Be careful when animating the corner controls do not let them interpolate in such a way as to cause the polygon to be concave or self-intersecting.

EFFECT CONTROLS

Upper Left

This point defines the point to which the upper left corner of the layer will be mapped in the distortion. You can move this point anywhere in your composition and the effect will grow the layer to fit. Please see the section IMPORTANT NOTE for more information about repositioning the corners of a layer.

Upper Right

This point defines the point to which the upper right corner of the layer will be mapped in the distortion.

Lower Left

This point defines the point to which the lower left corner of the layer will be mapped in the distortion.

Lower Right

This point defines the point to which the lower right corner of the layer will be mapped in the distortion.

Diaquest DDR (After Effects 3.0)

NEW FEATURES

There are two new features since the manual went to the printer. Both features are in the main DDR control screen:

1. Loop button:
   You can now loop your DDR between the inpoint and outpoint frames.
   Loop means playing from the inpoint frame to the outpoint frame, then again from the inpoint to the outpoint, etc. always going in a forward direction.
2. Ping-Pong: (Option click the Loop button)
   You can now ping-pong your DDR between the inpoint and outpoint frames.
   Ping-pong means playing from the inpoint frame to the outpoint frame, then going backwards to the inpoint, then forward again, etc.
   NOTE: While DDR is looping or ping-ponging, you can change the speed it plays at by using the step, option-step, play, and fast play buttons.

ATTENTION OPEN TRANSPORT USERS

1. Use System 7.5.2 version 1.1 (or later)
   It is strongly recommended that you obtain the latest Mac OS system updates. At the time of this writing, this means System 7.5.2 version 1.1. This includes the TCP/IP control panel version 1.0.6. To determine what version you have, go to the Apple menu and choose "About this Macintosh (". If it doesn't say "System Enabler 1.1" you should get the latest System 7.5.2 CD from Apple. It is available for free by calling (800) 769-2775 x5617.
2. Open Transport System 7.5.2 version 1.1 Problems
   There are at least two problems with Open Transport for After Effects DDR users:
   1. Open Transport has a default timeout of 5 minutes. This may cause problems for DDR users where After Effects is looking for a DDR that is not on-line. Normally, if a machine is missing, we time out in a few seconds and give an error. At the moment, we are not able to do this, except by waiting the 5 minutes.
   2. After Effects reports intermittent TCP errors with Open Transport.
      After Effects reports intermittent TCP time outs or other errors in reading and writing DDR frames.

   There is a work around!
   It addresses both problems.
3. The work around:
   - Remove the TCP/IP control panel (keep for future use).
   - Remove the two Open Transport Internet Libraries from the Extensions folder: (Open Tpt Internet Library and OpenTptInternetLib) Keep these for future use.
   - Place a copy of MacTCP 2.0.6 in your Control Panels folder
   - Place a copy of MacTCP Prep in your Preferences folder (if you have no MacTCP Prep, then ignore this step)
   - Restart
   - Verify that MacTCP is configured correctly.

   We are working with Apple to address this issue.

After Effects Numbers

This effect generates random and sequential numbers in different formats. You can use it to display random times and dates, timecode in any font, or to print the current date and time on a layer whenever its rendered, among other things.

USAGE NOTES

Use the Options dialog to choose the font, style, and alignment of the numbers.

Several of the types (Time, Numerical Date, Short Date, and Long Date) use the formats specified in the Date & Time control panel, which is in System 7.1 and higher. Date & Time provides a good deal of control over the formats. If you use more than one Macintosh to render a composition that uses the date or time types you must make sure the format specified in the Date & Time control panel is the same on all machines!

To make a new layer of numbers, follow these steps: make a new solid (Layer menu) that is large enough to contain the numbers. Invert the mask by choosing Mask/Invert in the Layer menu. Apply the Numbers effect. Adjust the controls to display the desired numbers but do not change the Channels or Invert Text controls.

The Size, Position, Text Color, Invert Text, and Channels controls are the same as those in the Basic Text effect. See pages 119 - 127 and pages 329 - 330 in the After Effects User Manual for example images and detailed explanations of these controls.

EFFECT CONTROLS

Type

Pop-up which specifies what type of number to generate. Note that the meaning of the Random Numbers, Value/Offset/Random Max, and Decimal Places controls (described below) varies based on what type is chosen. Number is a decimal number. Number Leading Zeros is a decimal number with 5 digits to the left of the decimal place at all times. Timecode 30, Timecode 25, and Timecode 24 are standard timecode formats (XX:XX:XX:XX) using the stated framerate. The timecode types use the layers current time. Time is a time value that uses the format specified in the Date & Time control panel. Numerical Date, Short Date, and Long Date are date displays that use the formats specified in the Date & Time control panel. Hexadecimal is a base 16 value (i.e. digits run from 0 to f).

Random Values

If checked, the values generated will be random, bounded as described below under Value/Offset/Random Max. If Value/Offset/Random Max is zero, values will be unbounded (they will be random across their maximum possible ranges).

Value/Offset/Random Max

This control varies based on the chosen type, and whether or not Random Values is checked. Note that you can click on the underlined value to the right of the Value/Offset/Random Max slider in the Effect Controls floater to set the value numerically. See the following list for details.

Number Value/Offset/Random Max determines the number that is displayed. If Random is checked, the number is bounded by zero and the slider value.

Timecode Value/Offset/Random Max is an offset for the timecode. Timecode is always displayed based on the layers current time. The slider value specifies a number of frames to add to the current time. Note that the absolute value of the slider is used as the offset negative timecodes are not displayed. If Random is checked, Value/Offset/Random Max is not used.

Time Value/Offset/Random Max is the number of minutes since midnight. If Current Time/Date is checked, Value/Offset/Random Max is ignored. If Random is checked, the time is bounded by 0 (12:00 AM) and the slider value.

Date If Current Time/Date is unchecked, Value/Offset/Random Max is the number of days since January 1, 1995 (zero on the slider corresponds to January 1, 1995). If Current Time/Date is checked, Value/Offset/Random Max is the number of days since the current date (zero on the slider corresponds to the current date). If Random is checked, the date is bounded by zero (either the current date or January 1, 1995) and the slider value.

Leap years are taken into consideration (e.g. 1996 has 366 days). Unfortunately the Macintosh clock starts on January 1, 1904 and does not go beyond February 6, 2040 (16472 days from January 1, 1995 send us mail if youre using the effect on that day!) so values greater than 16472 will be reborn at the start of time (i.e. 16473 will be January 1, 1904).

Hexadecimal Value/Offset/Random Max corresponds to the value displayed it will increment by 0x1 for every 0.0000125 that the slider increases, and it will increment by 0x10000 for every 1.0 that the slider increases. If Random is checked, the number is bounded by 0 and the slider value.

Decimal Places

Specifies the digits after the decimal point when Type is set to Number or Number Leading Zeros.

Current Time/Date

If Current Time/Date is checked and Type is set to Time, Numbers will display the current time. When in this current time/date mode other controls that affect the time value are ignored.

If Current Time/Date is checked and Type is set to one of the date options, Value/Offset/Random Max is the number of days since the current date (rather than January 1, 1995). For example, you can use this feature to make random dates from a specific month appear: set your Macs current date to the first of the month, check Current Time/Date and Random, and set the Value/Offset/Random Max slider to the number of days in the month. Dont forget to reset your Macs date! All types other than Time and the dates ignore this control.

Note that when Current Time/Date is checked the time or date displayed may vary every time a frame is rendered and may vary if you move from one Macintosh to another.

Size

Specifies the point size of the number displayed. We do not recommend animating the text size by changing the Size slider over time. There are slight variations in the appearance of characters at different point sizes and these variations may produce undesirable results when animated. If you want to animate the size of the text, apply Numbers to a solid, set Size to the largest point size you need and scale the solid over time (using scale keyframes).

Position

Specifies the position of the number within the layer. The behavior of this control is affected by the Alignment setting in the Options (dialog box. Position always positions the vertical center of the number relative to the layer. However, if the number is left-aligned, the point control positions the left edge; if right-aligned it positions the right edge; and if center-aligned it positions the center.

Text Color

Specifies the color of the number.

Invert Text

Inverts the area of the layer affected by Numbers.

Channels

Specifies how the number is placed into the four channels of the image. Used in conjunction with the Invert Text checkbox, this menu gives you six possibilities for matting the number into the layer.

Affect All Channels draws solid color text into the layer. It also sets the alpha channel of the area inside the text to be fully opaque, while not affecting the alpha of the area outside the bounds of the text.

If the Invert Text checkbox is checked, the opposite happens i.e., the area outside the text is filled with the specified color and made fully opaque, and the area inside the text remains untouched.

Affect Color Channels Only causes the text to be drawn into the color channels of the layer. In other words, the text is the same color as that specified by the Text Color control, and the area outside the text is unchanged.

Checking the Invert Text checkbox reverses this; the text has the source video within it and the area outside of the text is filled with the specified color. In both cases, the alpha channel of the video is entirely unaffected transparent parts of the source image remain transparent. This is useful if you want the text to be contained within the mask or existing alpha channel.

Affect Alpha Channel Only manipulates only the transparency of certain areas of the layer. With this item selected, the color and alpha channels remain untouched outside the text (showing the video of the source footage), and the areas inside the text are fully transparent, resulting in a punched-out stencil look.

If the Invert Text checkbox is checked, the layer remains untouched within the bounds of the text and fully transparent outside of it, resulting in a cookie-cutter effect.

After Effects Echo

This effect combines frames from many different times in a layer. It has a variety of uses, from a simple visual echo to streaking and smearing effects.

To incorporate a layers motion into the echo effect, follow these steps: Set up your motion before applying the effect. When you are satisfied with the motion, Compify the layer with the Mask, Effect and Geometrics option. This creates a new composition containing only that layer and its motion keyframes. Now apply the Echo effect. Each time Echo needs to retrieve a frame, it will get it from the nested composition which contains the motion. Try this with a large Number of Echoes and a short Echo Time to get smooth streaking and trail effects.

Note that a layers mask is ignored when the Echo effect is applied. To get around this, Compify the layer with the Mask and Effect option. This creates a new composition with the mask already applied; whenever Echo needs to retrieve a frame, it can do so from the composition with the mask already applied.

Echo Time (seconds)

Specifies the time, in seconds, between echoes. Negative values seek backwards in time; positive values echo forward in time.

Number of Echoes

Specifies the number of frames to combine for the echo effect. For example, if two echoes are specified, Echo will make a new image out of (current time), (current time + Echo Time) , and (current time + 2 * Echo Time.)

Starting Intensity

Specifies the intensity of the starting frame in the echo sequence. If this is set to 1, the first frame will be combined at its full intensity. If this is set to 0.5, the first frame is combined at half intensity, etc.

Decay

Specifies the ratio of intensities of subsequent echoes. For example, if the decay is set to 0.5, the first echo will be half the strength of the Starting Intensity. The second echo will then be half that or 0.25 times the Starting Intensity, and so on. Note that you can set this value larger than 1.0.

Echo Operator

Specifies the operation to perform between the echoes.

"Add" combines the echoes by adding their pixel values. If the starting intensity is too high, this mode can quickly overload and give you streaks of white. Set the Starting Intensity to 1.0/number of echoes and the Decay to 1.0 to blend the echoes equally.

"Maximum" combines the echoes by taking the maximum pixel value from all the echoes.

"Minimum" combines the echoes by taking the minimum pixel value from all the echoes.

"Screen" emulates combining the echoes by sandwiching them optically. This is similar to Add, but it will not overload as quickly.

"Composite In Front" uses the echoes alpha channels to composite them front to back.

"Composite In Back" uses the echoes alpha channels to composite them back to front.

After Effects Channel Blur

This effect blurs a layers red, green, blue, and alpha channels individually. In Best Quality, the blur is smoother. Use this effect for interesting glow type special effects, or if you want a blur which does not become transparent near the edges of the layer.

Red Blurriness

Specifies, in pixels, how much to blur the red channel of the layer. Larger values blur the red channel more, reducing noise and softening details.

Green Blurriness
Specifies, in pixels, how much to blur the green channel of the layer.
Blue Blurriness
Specifies, in pixels, how much to blur the blue channel of the layer.
Alpha Blurriness
Specifies, in pixels, how much to blur the alpha channel of the layer.
Edge Behavior
Describes how to treat the edges of the image when blurring. If unchecked, pixels outside of the image are considered black and transparent, which will make the edges of the blur semi-transparent and/or darker. If checked, Repeat Edge Pixels will repeat the pixels around the edges in the blurring operation, preventing the edges from darkening and/or becoming more transparent.

After Effects Change Color

This effect adjusts the hue, saturation, and lightness of a range of colors. You choose the range by specifying a base color and similarity values. The similarity can be an RGB similarity, a hue similarity, or a chroma similarity.

EFFECT CONTROLS
View
Pop-up which specifies what to view in the composition. Corrected Layer shows the results of the Change Color effect. Color Correction Mask shows which areas of the layer will be changed. White areas in the color correction mask will be transformed the most, dark areas the least.
Hue Transform
Specifies the amount, in degrees, to adjust the hue of the selected colors.
Lightness Transform
Specifies the amount to increase or decrease the lightness of the selected colors. Positive values will brighten the selected regions; negative values darken them.
Saturation Transform
Specifies the amount to increase or decrease the saturation of the selected colors. Positive values will saturate (move towards pure color) the selected regions; negative values desaturate (move towards gray) the selected regions.
Color To Change
Specifies the color youd like to change. Matching Tolerance and Matching Softness both use this color as a target for building the color correction mask.
Matching Tolerance
Specifies how strictly to match colors before they are affected by the color correction. With low tolerances, only colors very similar to the change color will be added to the color correction mask. Larger tolerances add more and more of the image to the color correction mask.
Matching Softness
Specifies the softness of the color correction in the chosen color space. Note that this does not necessarily soften the color correction mask geometrically, but affects the severity of the color correction for regions similar to the base color.
Match Colors
Specifies the criterion for determining similarity of two colors.

RGB means that the colors are examined using their red, green, and blue components. This is useful for a wide variety of applications, and is the fastest. Similarity in RGB space does not necessarily match a human beings perception of what color similarity is, however.

Hue matches colors based on their hue angle. Hue is a one-dimensional characteristic of color which is based on human perception. For example, a bright red, a light pink and a burgundy color may have very similar hue value (a hue of red, but differing values of saturation and lightness).

Chroma matching uses the two chromatic components to determine similarity, ignoring brightness. Chroma matching would therefore be sensitive to saturation and hue differences, but not to lightness differences. This is the slowest of the three options.
Invert Color Correction Mask
Inverts the mask that determines which colors to affect. If checked, all colors other than those selected by the Color To Change and matching behavior controls will be color corrected.

After Effects 3.1 Network Rendering

If you have multiple Macintoshes connected over an Ethernet (or faster) network, and multiple copies of After Effects, you can render one composition on multiple machines simultaneously, writing to a single destination folder on your network. This can dramatically decrease the amount of time it takes to render a composition.

Network rendering works by starting multiple machines simultaneously rendering the same project. As frames are generated, they are placed in a single destination folder. Each copy of the application can tell which frames to skip by examining the contents of the destination folder to see which frames are already rendered, or are in progress. The renders stop when they see that every frame has been created in the destination folder.

Note that the network distribution is not automatic - you must start each machine individually. A more convenient interface will be developed in the future.

Network rendering works for outputting sequences of single-frame files only (e.g. Sequence of PICT, Sequence of Adobe Photoshop, etc.), but not QuickTime movies. Your source footage may be of any supported type.

PROCEDURES
Before starting, you may wish to copy the project file and all its source footage onto each machine that will be rendering. This takes up more disk space, but the rendering will go faster. If you do this, you can avoid having “missing footage” by

maintaining the same relative directory path between the project file and the footage. A simple example of this is to have the source footage in a folder that is in a folder with the project. If you have to move any files to get them into this arrangement, make sure you open and save the project before copying it and related footage to each machine, so the project "remembers" the new relative positions.

If you do end up with missing footage, just double-click on the missing item and find the moved file.

Follow the procedure below for each machine on which you wish to render. Each machine can be started at any time. You can have any combination of Power Macintosh and Macintosh versions. There is no limit to the number of machines that can be rendering simultaneously. In general, the more machines you have rendering, the faster the movie will be completed, but the overhead of network traffic will eventually slow things to a crawl when running with too many computers simultaneously. This is because the computers start to spend more time transferring files rather than rendering frames. Test your setup with different numbers of machines rendering to see when adding another is not worth it. Network slowdowns can be detected by watching the time spent in the "Compressing & Writing" stage in the Show Details section of the Rendering dialog box.

The main danger with network rendering is making sure each machine is doing exactly the same thing. This means rendering the same project, same comp, with the same source footage, same times, same fonts, same effects, same preferences, and the same render settings! By setting up the render queue before you open the project on all the machines, you are guaranteed that almost all of these settings are identical. It is your responsibility, however, to make sure that any required fonts are available on all the machines.

1. First you must set up your project's render queue to contain only the compositions that you wish to network render. Pick your desired render settings, but you MUST turn on the "Skip Existing Files" option - this is VERY important. This option ensures that each machine will work on different frames! Since the Skip Existing Files option doesn't work with overflow volumes nor multiple output modules, you will not be able to use these features with network rendering.
2. Specify the destination name for the output sequence, and select a folder that is available on the network for all machines to render into.
3. Save the project. On each machine, open the project, either a local copy (as described above), or over the network. If you are opening the project over a network, first lock the project in the Finder (Get Info, then check Locked). This will allow multiple machines to open the file simultaneously. Click Render. You can start each machine at any time.
4. Your composition(s) should now be rendering along happily. You will see your folder begin to fill with frames. As each machine finishes a frame, it looks in the directory for the next file that is missing (i.e. skipping existing files) and begins to work on that frame.

You can stop and start each machine independently at any time. However, if you have stopped a machine without starting it (or another) again, the frame that it was rendering may not be finished. Every time you start a machine, it checks for missing files from the beginning, so all missing frames will be filled in by starting just one machine again.

If you are using Apple's File Sharing to serve a network volume, we do NOT recommend using that machine to also render. Rendering on the server slows down all the clients' disk access, and can drastically reduce performance. We have had reports of conflicts with some control panels/extensions. If you absolutely must render from your server, please disable all non-Apple control panels and extensions. In fact, running any program on the server could put you at risk of conflicts.

We do not recommend using network rendering over LocalTalk because of its slowness. There should be no other problems, however.

WARNING: Do not share your plug-ins between machines. Make sure that you have a copy of the plug-ins folder on each machine that is running After Effects.

MAYBE YOU DON T WANT TO NETWORK RENDER

Note that if you don't want to network render, you can proceed as if the machines aren't networked and have multiple machines each render to their own local drives. This works for any output type, but has the disadvantage of forcing you to artificially break the composition up into different time-spans. Also, you can't take full advantage of all machines because each machine will finish at a different time. By network rendering you can be sure that all machines will be working together until rendering is completed. The disadvantage of network rendering is that you have to factor network overhead into the rendering time. This is of course not a problem if you render locally on each machine.

The procedures above assume that you are network rendering, but the process for rendering locally on each machine is basically the same. The differences are 1) your target output folder is different for each machine, 2) you must make sure that every machine is rendering a different work-area time-span, and 3) you do NOT need to turn on "Skip Existing Files".

Motion Blur General Information

The Adobe After Effects Motion Blur effect creates smoother, more realistic movement in animations and reduces the strobe-like effects that occur when animating stills.

APPLYING MOTION BLUR

To apply motion blur, select the M switch for each layer you want to blur, then select Enable Motion Blur in the Time Layout window containing the layer(s) you want to blur.

SHUTTER ANGLE

The Shutter Angle setting (File > Preferences > General) controls the degree of Motion Blur used in a layer. The shutter opens at the time the original frame displays (i.e., each frame displays on the screen at the exact moment it would have appeared if motion blur was not applied), then the pixels are blurred according to the predicted positions of the pixels going forward from that moment in time. Pixel position predictions are made at shorter time intervals than the time interval between frames, and are based on the Anchor Point, Position, Rotation, and Scale settings of the layer. The opacity of the blurred pixels is based on the interval of the position prediction and the alpha channel of the image.

EXAMPLES OF DIFFERENT SHUTTER ANGLE SETTINGS

A composition with motion blur set to the default shutter angle of 180° and rendered at 30 frames per second will leave the shutter open for 1/60 of a second or half the duration of the frame.

A composition with motion blur set to a shutter angle of 0° and rendered at 30 frame per second will leave the shutter open for an infinitesimally short time (no motion blur).

A composition with motion blur set to a shutter angle of 360° and rendered at 30 frames per second will leave the shutter open for the full duration of the frame (extreme motion blur).

CALCULATIONS FOR MOTION BLUR

Motion blur is calculated using the final render frame rate. For example, a layer in a 60 frames per second composition nested in a 10 frames per second composition will be blurred with the 10 frames per second frame rate (i.e., only every sixth frame of the original layer will be used in the motion blur calculation).

After Effects Glow

This effect creates glows based on the alpha channel boundaries or the bright regions of an image. Glows can be rendered alone, or composited in front of or behind the layer with a variety of blending modes. The glows colors can be specified as a gradient of two colors, or of any number of colors using a Color Table or Arbitrary Map file from Photoshop.

In Best Quality the glow is smoother. Note that the smoother glow can change the appearance of the layer somewhat, especially if you are using arbitrary maps to color your glows. Be sure to preview the layer at Best Quality before rendering.

SAMPLE USAGE

Creating glows around bright parts of a layer

Apply the glow effect. Set Glow Based On to Color Channels, and choose a relatively high Glow Threshold. Increase Glow Radius to make the glow more diffuse; the default value produces a fairly tight glow. Use the Add or Screen Glow Operation. Add tends to brighten the image. If you want the glows to be a specific color, choose A & B Colors from the Glow Colors popup. You can then use Color A and Color B to specify a gradient for the glow. For example, you may want Color A (the areas near the glowing objects) to be a warmer color, while Color B (the more distant regions of the glow) is a cooler color.

Creating glows around the alpha channel of a layer

Choose Alpha Channel from the Glow Based On popup. You will likely get a warning explaining that this option does not work when Original Colors is chosen from the Glow Colors popup, so choose A & B Colors from the Glow Colors popup. Set new values for Color A and Color B. If you want the glow to appear behind the layer, choose Normal from the Glow Operation popup and Behind from the Composite popup. If you want the glow to appear on top of the layer, choose On Top from the Composite popup. Increase the Glow Radius to make the glow more diffuse.

For more interesting (and possibly less useful) effects, increase the number of Color Loops to create colorful ringing effects around the alpha edges.

EFFECT CONTROLS

Glow Based On

The glow can be performed by picking out the bright parts of the color channels or by using the solid parts of the alpha channel. Choose your preference here. (Note, though, that you cannot perform a glow based on the alpha channel and use the Original Colors option for the Glow Colors popup.) If your image is completely opaque, then you should make sure this control is set to Color Channels.

Glow Threshold

Specifies the brightness threshold around which to glow. Pixel values less than this will ignored for the glow operation. (As you lower this value, the glow is applied to more and more of the image.)

Glow Radius

Specifies the maximum distance of the glow. Large values give diffuse glows, small values give sharper glows.

Glow Intensity

Specifies the intensity of the glow. Increasing this slider generally increases the intensity of the glow, though the visual effect may or may not be intensification because of the Glow Operation.

Composite

Specifies the relative order of the glow and the original layer. On Top composites the glow over the original image with the Glow Operation transfer function. Behind composites the glow behind the original image. (Note that your image must have transparent regions for this option to be visible.) None shows the raw result of the Glow Operation before the glow is recombined with the original image. This is a useful option if you want to combine multiple glows.

Glow Operation

Specifies the method for recombining the glow with the original image. For glows based on the alpha channel, the

Normal operation gives the most intuitive behavior. For glows based on the color channels, Screen simulates combining the glows optically, while Add gives similar results but tends to oversaturate more quickly.

Glow Colors

Specifies which colors to use in the creation of the glow. Original Colors diffuses the original colors of the bright areas and recombines them with the original layer. A & B Colors use the colors specified by Color A and Color B as the colors in the glow. Arbitrary Map allows you to load colors from a Photoshop arbitrary map file to use as your glow. The Options button in the effect floater will bring up a standard Open dialog box to choose the arbitrary map file. (You can save these from the Curves dialog in Photoshop. If youre having trouble reading the files, make sure the pencil tool inside of the Curves dialog is chosen when you save from Photoshop.)

Color Looping

Specifies how the Color A and Color B values are used to create the glow. Sawtooth A->B simply creates a ramp between Color A and Color B. Likewise, Sawtooth B->A creates a ramp between Color B and Color A. Triangle A->B->A creates a ramp from A to B and then back to A. Likewise, Triangle B->A->B creates a ramp from B to A and then back to B.

Color Loops

Specifies the number of times to repeat the glow color gradient. Increasing this value creates ringing effects in your glow. This slider is only valid when the Glow Colors popup is set to A & B Colors or Arbitrary Map.

Color Phase

Use this angle to cycle through your color gradient. This angle control is only valid when the Glow Colors popup is set to A & B Colors or Arbitrary Map. Animate this value to create pulsating glows (especially effective when Color Loops is set to a value other than 1.)

A & B Midpoint

Specifies the midpoint of the color gradient created by Color A and Color B. As this value is lowered, the overall balance of colors shifts to Color B. As this value is increased, Color A has more influence over the gradient.

Color A, Color B

The two colors used in creating a glow gradient when A & B Colors is chosen for Glow Colors. Ignored in any other case.

After Effects Bevel Alpha

This effect gives a chiseled and lighted appearance to the alpha boundaries of an image, often giving 2-D elements a 3-D appearance. This effect works especially well for elements with text in the alpha channel. At Best Quality, the bevel is performed with subpixel accuracy.

EDGE THICKNESS

Specifies, in pixels, the thickness of the beveled edges. A minimum value of zero indicates no bevel at all.

LIGHT ANGLE

Specifies the direction from which light hits the bevels. Edges facing the light are made brighter; edges away from the light are in shadow and are made darker.

LIGHT COLOR

Specifies the color of the light, giving the effect of tinting the bevel. In general, lighter values are most effective for this parameter.

LIGHT INTENSITY

Specifies the contrast between dark and light edges and the rest of the image. Low intensity indicates that the shadowed edges only be darkened slightly and the highlighted edges brightened slightly. High intensity causes stronger darkening and brightening.

After Effects Gradient Wipe

This effect creates transitions based on the luminance values of another layer, called the gradient layer. The luminance of a pixel in the gradient determines the time at which the corresponding pixel in the original layer will become transparent. Dark areas of the gradient layer represent those areas which will become transparent first, followed by lighter areas.

For example, a simple grayscale gradient from left to right will produce a left to right wipe. The gradient layer need not be a still image; any layer in After Effects can be used as a gradient for unusual wipe effects. More interesting wipes can be created in a variety of ways. After Effects Ramp effect is a good starting point it can generate a variety of grayscale gradients.

For completely custom gradients, you can paint them in a program such as Adobe Photoshop or draw them in a program such as Adobe Illustrator. (The blend tool is especially useful here.)

EFFECT CONTROLS

Transition Completion

Specifies the completeness of the wipe. At 0%, the layer remains unchanged. At 100%, the layer is completely transparent, and at 50% the wipe is halfway done.

Transition Softness

Specifies the softness of the transition.

Gradient Layer

Specifies the layer to use as the transition gradient.

Gradient Placement

Describes how gradient layers are positioned. Tile Gradient tiles the gradient repeatedly over the image, starting at the upper left corner. Tiling works best with small gradient layers. Center Gradient places the gradient in the middle of the layer, cropping as necessary. Stretch Gradient stretches (or squashes) the gradient to the full size of the original layer.

Invert Gradient

Inverts the interpretation of the gradient layer. If checked, the transition will proceed from the light areas to the dark areas.

After Effects Mosaic

This effect fills a layer with rectangular regions of solid color. It is useful for simulating low resolution displays and for obscuring identities in the fashion of reality-based television shows. You can also animate it for a neat transition. At Best Quality, the edges of the mosaic are antialiased.

Horizontal Blocks
Specifies the number of mosaic divisions in the horizontal direction.

Vertical Blocks
Specifies the number of mosaic divisions in the vertical direction.

Sharp Colors
If checked, each tile gets the color of the pixel in its center in the unaffected layer. Otherwise, the tiles are colored with the average color of the corresponding region in the unaffected layer.

Previewing Audio in After Effects 2.x and Later

To preview audio by dragging the current-time marker in Adobe After Effects 3.1:

1. In the Time Layout window, select the Audio switch for each layer you want to preview.
2. Press Control while dragging the current-time marker in the Time Layout window.

To preview audio in After Effects 3.x:

1. Choose File > Preferences > General.
2. In the General Preferences dialog box, enter the duration of your audio preview in the Duration text box, then click OK.
3. Choose Composition > Preview > Audio (Here Forward).

To preview audio in After Effects 2.x:

1. Choose Edit > Preferences > General.
2. In the General Preferences dialog box, enter the duration of your audio preview in the Duration For Audio Preview text box, then click OK.
3. Choose Composition > Preview > Audio (Here Forward).

Unexpected Results

MAC OS / WINDOWS

Animation Files with Alpha Channels Are Black in After Effects 3.x

ISSUE

An imported animation file containing alpha channels appears as solid black frames in an Adobe After Effects 3.x composition.

SOLUTIONS

Reverse the animation file's interpretation method in After Effects:

1. Select the animation file in the Project window, then choose File > Interpret Footage > Main.
2. In the Alpha section of the Interpret Footage dialog box, select Inverted, then click OK.

OR: Save the animation file with an inverted alpha channel, then reimport it into the After Effects composition.

ADDITIONAL INFORMATION

After Effects interprets the black pixels of an alpha channel as transparent and the white pixels as opaque. If you import an animation file with an inverted alpha channel (i.e., white pixels defined as transparent and black pixels defined as opaque), the animation file appears black in your composition. After you select Inverted in the Interpret Footage dialog box, After Effects interprets the white pixels of an alpha channel as transparent and the black pixels as opaque.

While many applications, including After Effects, interpret the black pixels of an alpha channel as transparent, other applications (e.g., ElectricImage, Avid VideoShop) save files with inverted alpha channels by default.

Movies Drift In and Out of Focus During Playback in After Effects 3.x

ISSUE

Movies rendered in Adobe After Effects 3.x appear to drift in and out of focus when you play them back.

SOLUTIONS

Make sure the frame rate of your footage files matches the frame rate of your composition:

1. Select a QuickTime movie in your Project window, then choose File > Interpret Footage > Main.
2. In the Interpret Footage dialog box, select Conform To Frame Rate, then enter the composition's frame rate in the adjacent text box.
3. Repeat steps 1-2 for each QuickTime movie in your composition.

OR: Adjust the frame rate of your composition to match the frame rate of your footage files:

1. Select your composition in the Project window, then choose Composition > Composition Settings.
2. Enter a frame rate in the Frame Rate text box, then click OK.

OR: Disable frame blending:

1. In the Time Layout window, deselect the Frame Blending option for each layer in your composition. 2. Deselect Enable Frame Blending for each composition.

OR: Disable frame blending when you render your composition:

1. In the Render Queue window, select Custom from the Render Settings pop-up menu.
2. In the Render Settings dialog box, select Off For All Lay-

ers from the Frame Blending pop-up menu, select other options you want, then click OK.
3. In the Render Queue dialog box, click Render.

ADDITIONAL INFORMATION

If the frame rate of your footage files is different from the frame rate of your composition when frame blending is enabled, After Effects 3.x creates new frames to adjust for the difference in frame rates. It creates new frames by interpolation, causing them to appear less clear than the original source frames. When you play movies with interpolated frames interspersed between original frames, the movie appears to drift in and out of focus.

When frame blending is disabled, After Effects fills in missing frames by duplicating the original source frames.

MAC OS

Q When I use my DayStar Genesis MP machine to build and render animation-compressed QuickTime movies in After Effects or Premiere, I get a lot of bad frames that contain nothing but video "noise." Am I doing something wrong?

A Not at all. It sounds as if you're creating projects that contain track mattes and you're using the Adobe MP Accelerator 1.4 plug-in to accelerate rendering in After Effects (or the Premiere MP 1.0 plug-in to accelerate rendering in Premiere). These plug-ins don't process track mattes correctly and often generate frames full of video noise—called garbage frames—instead.

A track-matte effect allows the contents of one layer to show through another by using a property of the first layer to create transparency. Most often, the alpha channel of a layer is used as a matte, but you can also use other layer properties for partial transparency. For instance, a luma track matte uses the luminance values of a layer to create transparent areas; the greater the luminance value of a pixel, the more transparent it will be.

In After Effects, you set track mattes in the Time Layout window by positioning the matte layer on top of the fill layer. Then change from "Switches" to "Transfer Controls" in the pop-up menu and choose the desired matte effect for the fill layer from the TrkMat pop-up menu. The problem occurs when you choose "Luma Matte," "Luma Inverted Matte," or "Alpha Inverted Matte."

You can fix the problem by updating your version of the Adobe MP Accelerator plug-in to version 1.7. If you use Premiere on a multiprocessor, you should also update the Premiere MP plug-in 1.0 to version 1.0.1—the same problem occurs when you use the "Track Matte" transparency key (from the "Transparency Settings" dialog box in Premiere).

You can find the latest MP accelerator plug-ins in several places: on the Adobe Web site (www.adobe.com/supportservice/custsupport/tsfilelib.html), the Adobe BBS (206-623-6984), the Adobe FTP site (ftp://ftp.adobe.com), AOL, and CompuServe. You can also locate the latest plug-ins on DayStar's Web site (www. daystar.com/FTP/FTP.GnsMP.html) or in their MP Floppy Release 2.4, which contains the latest versions of the MacO/S Multiprocessing components.

Stuttered, Jerky, or Strobe-Like Playback in After Effects Movie Troubleshooting Guide

ISSUE

Movies rendered in Adobe After Effects 2.x or later strobe or stutter during playback.

SOLUTIONS

Do one or more of the following:

A. If the composition contains video clips with field information (e.g. digitized NTSC or PAL video), separate the fields using the correct field order for each video clip used in the composition before rendering the movie:
   1. Select a video clip that contains field information in the Project window.
   2. Choose File > Interpret Footage > Main.
   3. In the Interpret Footage dialog box, select the correct field order from the Separate Fields pop-up menu (After Effects 3.x) or Deinterlace pop-up menu (After Effects 2.x). The field order you select should match the field order of the video capture card that captured the video clip: choose Upper Field First for capture cards that are Field 1 dominant [Odd], or Lower Field First for capture cards that are Field 2 dominant [Even].
   NOTE: If your source clips are QuickTime movies precompiled at 60 fields per second (fps), select the same field order that was used to render the movie.
   4. Click OK.
   NOTE: To verify you have selected the correct field order for your video clip, press Option and double-click on the video clip in the Project window. Advance through the movie frame by frame by pressing the right arrow key on your keyboard. If the movie seems to stutter back and forth (e.g., it moves forward two frames, then backward one frame, etc.), then the field rendering order is set incorrectly. Repeat steps 1-4 and choose the opposite field order.
   5. Re-render the composition. The Field Render selection in the Render Settings dialog box should match the field order of the digitizing card that you use to record your movie to video tape. If the final movie will be played on a computer monitor only, choose Off from the Field Render pop-up menu.

B. If you're changing Scale values in addition to Position values over time for a particular layer, move the layer by altering its Anchor Point instead of its Position.

C. Make sure each layer's quality setting is set to Best quality in the Time Layout window by clicking the Quality switch until a solid forward slash (/) appears. If you have nested compositions, open each composition separately to set the layers to Best quality.

D. If the movie appears to drop frames (i.e., stutter) during playback, step through the movie frame by frame to verify that all frames are present. If all frames are present but the movie appears to drop frames during playback, render the movie with reduced settings, such as a lower frame rate, smaller frame size, or higher compression ratio. For more information refer to document 143314, available from Adobe FaxYI, the Adobe BBS, Adobe Techdocs e-mail, and Adobe's Technical Solutions database on the World Wide Web.

E. If the movie stutters during playback on an NTSC or PAL monitor, but plays smoothly on a computer monitor, make sure field rendering is turned on (i.e., Upper Field First or Lower Field First) in the Render Settings dialog box, and that the frame rate is high enough to ensure smooth playback (e.g., 29.97 fps or 30 fps for NTSC output).

ADDITIONAL INFORMATION

Each frame of NTSC or PAL video consists of two alternating fields of video data. One field contains the odd-numbered lines, while the other contains the even-numbered lines. Your hardware compressor's field rendering order (i.e., field dominance) determines whether the odd or even field plays first. When you play a movie whose field rendering order is opposite that of the playback system, the movie appears to strobe or stutter.

Separating fields with the correct field order before rendering movies ensures After Effects will apply effects and geometrics to each field separately, eliminating a cause of stuttered playback.

Because scaling is centered around the Anchor Point, pixels lying in a direction opposite the Anchor Point's direction of motion shift at a different rate than pixels lying in the same direction. This produces stuttered playback when the Anchor Point is not centered within the Composition. Moving a layer by altering its Anchor Point instead of its Position eliminates this cause of stuttered playback.

When a layer's Quality switch is not set to Best quality, After Effects does not use subpixel positioning to render that layer, causing the motion to appear stuttered or jerky.

When a movie's data rate exceeds the capabilities of the playback system, the playback application drops (i.e., skips) frames, causing the video to display stuttered or jerky. You can lower the movie's data rate to meet the capabilities of the playback system by reducing the render settings (e.g., frame size, frame rate, quality, etc.).

Movies created as a sequence of frames (i.e., without separate fields) play stuttered or jerky on NTSC and PAL monitors.

Unable to Open Movies Created in After Effects 2.x and Later

ISSUE

An error occurs when you double-click on a movie file created in Adobe After Effects 2.0 or later. The movie's icon displays as a generic document rather than a movie strip.

SYMPTOMS

The Finder returns one of the following errors:

"The document "filename" could not be opened, because the application program that created it could not be found. Do you want to open it using 'SimpleText'?"

"Cannot open file, application that created it cannot be found."

SOLUTIONS

Install Apple's MoviePlayer before opening the movie:

When using After Effects 3.x:

1. Insert the After Effects CD-ROM, then open the Third Party Goodies folder.
2. Drag the MoviePlayer folder to your desktop.

When using After Effects 2.x:

1. Insert the QuickTime and Utilities installation disk.
2. Drag the MoviePlayer folder from the root level of the disk to your desktop.

OR: When using After Effects 3.x, import the movie into an After Effects project, then double-click on the movie in the Project window. The movie opens in a QuickTime Footage window. Click the Play button to play the movie.

ADDITIONAL INFORMATION

When After Effects renders movies, it designates MoviePlayer as the creator application. The Finder attempts to locate MoviePlayer when you double-click on the movie, and returns an error if MoviePlayer is not installed.

Unable to Change Motion Window Magnification in After Effects Production Bundle 3.x

ISSUE

The magnification pop-up menu does not pop up when clicked in the Motion Tracking or Motion Stabilization windows in Adobe After Effects Production Bundle 3.x.

SOLUTION

Change the magnification using keyboard shortcuts (i.e., press, [comma] to zoom out, or press . [period] to zoom in).

ADDITIONAL INFORMATION

The magnification pop-up menu does not pop up in the Motion Tracking and Motion Stabilization windows in After Effects Production Bundle 3.x. The magnification pop-up menu pops up as expected in other After Effects windows.

Unable to Select CODEC in After Effects 2.0 or Later

ISSUE
In Adobe After Effects 2.0 or later, QuickTime compression/decompression algorithms (CODECs) do not list in the Compression Settings dialog box or display the controls for a different CODEC when selected.

SOLUTION
Force After Effects to recreate its preferences file:

1. Quit After Effects.
2. Delete the CoSA After Effects Prefs file (After Effects 2.0x) or the After Effects 3.0 Prefs file (After Effects 3.0).
3. Restart After Effects.
4. Choose Edit > Preferences (After Effects 2.0x) or File > Preferences (After Effects 3.0) to reset custom preference settings.

ADDITIONAL INFORMATION
The After Effects preferences file includes information on the available CODECs and how to access them. After installing a new CODEC, or when After Effect's preferences file is damaged, forcing After Effects to recreate its preferences file results in After Effects correcting or updating the information required to list or access CODECs.

Unable to Drag Footage Item to Root Level of Project in After Effects 3.0

ISSUE
When you drag a footage item from a project folder to the root level of the Project window in Adobe After Effects 3.0, the footage item remains within the project folder.

SOLUTION
Drag the footage item to the top of the Project window where footage thumbnails are displayed, then release the mouse button.

ADDITIONAL INFORMATION
Because footage items cannot be dragged from a project folder to the root level of the Project window, the footage item must be dragged to the top of the Project window, which displays footage thumbnails, to move the footage item to the root level of the Project window.

Basic Text is Cropped in After Effects 2.x

ISSUE
After Effects 2.x crops the right side of text created with the Basic Text effect.

SOLUTIONS
Use After Effects 3.0 or later.

OR: Type a space at the end of the line. To center the text after typing the space, type another space at the beginning of the line.

ADDITIONAL INFORMATION
After applying some fonts (e.g., italic PostScript font) to text, the Basic Text effect causes Adobe After Effects 2.x to crop the right side of the text. After Effects 3.0's Basic Text effect creates text that displays as expected.

Apple Color Picker Doesn't Display in After Effects

ISSUE
After selecting a color swatch in Adobe After Effects, the Apple HSL and Apple RGB color palettes do not display. Two or more monitors list in the Monitors control panel, and the monitor set to display the most colors is either turned off or disconnected from the Macintosh.

SOLUTIONS
In the Monitors control panel, decrease the color depth (i.e., select 256 or Thousands for the Colors setting) of the disconnected or turned off monitor so that it displays fewer colors than the other monitors.
OR: Connect and turn on the monitor set to display the most colors, then view the Apple Color Picker on that monitor.

ADDITIONAL INFORMATION
After connecting another monitor to your Macintosh, the Apple Color Picker displays on the monitor set to display the most colors, even when that monitor is turned off or disconnected. To display the Color Picker on the active monitor (i.e., the one that displays the menu bar in the Monitors control panel), set this monitor's color depth higher than the other listed monitors.

After adding an NTSC monitor and setting both connected monitors to millions of colors, the Apple Color Picker displays on the NTSC monitor by default. Because the Color Picker displays on the NTSC monitor by default, the Color Picker appears to be missing when the NTSC monitor is turned off.

Unable to Select Sequence Option in Import Dialog Box in After Effects

ISSUE
The Import Footage dialog box is truncated and the Sequence checkbox is hidden from view in Adobe After Effects.

SOLUTIONS
Click the Show Preview checkbox in the Import Footage dialog box, click Cancel or Done, then reselect the Import Footage command.
OR: When using After Effects 3.0, drag the folder contain-

ing your sequence from the Finder to the Project window. The sequence items are imported automatically.

ADDITIONAL INFORMATION
QuickTime controls the size of the Import Footage dialog box and resizes the dialog box when Show Preview is not checked, causing the Sequence checkbox to be hidden from view. After checking the Show Preview option, the Import Footage dialog box must be closed and reopened before it expands to its full size.

When the Show Preview option is deselected in another application that uses this standard QuickTime dialog box, it is deselected for all applications that use the dialog box.

Movies Contain White Frames in After Effects

ISSUE
QuickTime movies rendered in After Effects contain blank or white frames.

SOLUTION
Close other applications, or decrease the memory allocated to other open applications, until the largest unused block of RAM is 3 MB or higher.

ADDITIONAL INFORMATION
QuickTime requires additional RAM when rendering movies. When there is insufficient RAM, QuickTime is unable to render movies, resulting in After Effects-rendered movies that contain blank or white frames. When there is at least 3 MB of RAM available to QuickTime ensures it has the additional RAM it needs to render movies.

Unable to Start After Effects 2.0.2 Updater on Power Macintosh

ISSUE
When you double-click on the Adobe After Effects 2.0.2 Updater on a Power Macintosh with a 604 microprocessor (e.g., a Power Macintosh 7500, 8500, or 9500), the Updater quits without displaying an error message.

SOLUTIONS
Upgrade to After Effects 3.0.
OR: Install After Effects 2.0.2 from the full installation disk set, instead of from the Adobe After Effects 2.0.2 Updater.

ADDITIONAL INFORMATION
The After Effects 2.0.2 Updater checks for a resource present on 601-processor Power Macintosh computers (i.e., Power Macintosh 6100, 7100, or 8100). When the Updater does not locate this resource, the Updater is unable to start.

Bezier Handles Disappear Outside of Composition Window in After Effects 2.0.x

ISSUE
When you adjust position keyframes using bezier interpolation in Adobe After Effects 2.0.x, the bezier handles disappear outside of the Composition window and cannot be accessed.

SOLUTION
Upgrade to After Effects 3.0 or later.
OR: Press the Command key while clicking on a visible bezier handle to move all bezier handles into the Composition window.
OR: Zoom out with the Magnifier tool until the entire pasteboard and the bezier handles are visible, then drag them inside the Composition window.

ADDITIONAL INFORMATION
When you press the Command key while clicking on a bezier handle, After Effects moves all the bezier handles in the Composition window to an equal distance from their respective keyframes. For example, when you press the Command key and click on a bezier handle that is 10 pixels away from its keyframe, After Effects moves all other bezier handles to within 10 pixels from their respective keyframes. Bezier handles in After Effects 3.0 and later remain visible in the Composition window at all times.

The After Effects 2.0.2 Updater ReadMe incorrectly states that bezier handles don't disappear outside of the Composition window when using bezier interpolation in After Effects 2.0.2.

Layer Masks and Geometrics Ignored by Effects in After Effects

ISSUE
When you apply an effect to a layer in Adobe After Effects and use another layer (i.e., target layer) as a parameter, the masks and geometrics of the target layer are ignored by the effect.

SOLUTIONS
When using After Effects 3.x, pre-compose the target layer:
1. Select the target layer in the Time Layout window.
2. Choose Layer > Pre-compose.
3. In the Pre-compose dialog box, select the Move All Attributes into the New Composition option, which replaces the target layer with a composition containing the layer and all of the motion settings.
4. Use this new composition layer for the target of the effect instead of the original target layer.

OR: When using After Effects 2.0x, compify the target layer:
1. Select the target layer in the Time Layout window.
2. Choose Layer > Compify.
3. In the Compify dialog box, select the Mask, Effect, and

Geometrics option, which replaces the target layer with a composition containing the layer and all of the motion settings.

4. Use this new composition layer for the target of the effect instead of the original target layer.

ADDITIONAL INFORMATION

After Effects processes layer masks, geometrics, and effects in the order they are listed in the Time Layout window. When an effect targets another layer as a parameter (e.g., Set Matte option to Take Matte From [name of other layer]), After Effects does not process the target layer's mask and geometric information before processing the effect. When you Pre-compose or Compify the target layer, After Effects processes the masks and geometrics of the layer and includes all the processed information in a new composition. When you use this new composition as the target layer, all of the layers masks and geometrics apply to the effect because After Effects has already processed them.

Effects that use other layers as parameters include: Set Matte, Set Matte/Levels, Compound Arithmetic, Time Displacement, and Compound Blur.

In After Effects 3.x, you can use Transfer Controls and Track Matte instead of Compound Arithmetic, Set Matte, and Set Matte/Levels to control interactions between layers.

Motion Blur Not Applied to Layers in After Effects 3.x

ISSUE

Motion blur is not applied to layers as expected in Adobe After Effects 3.x, causing animated stills to display strobe-like, stuttered, or jerky.

SOLUTIONS

Do one or more of the following:

A. Apply Motion Blur to each layer you want blurred by selecting its Motion Blur switch in the Time Layout window. NOTE: If you have nested compositions, open each composition separately to enable Motion Blur.

B. Enable After Effect's Recursive Switches preference by choosing File > Preferences > General, selecting Recursive Switches in the General Preferences dialog box, then clicking OK.

C. Before rendering your composition, check Enable Motion Blur in the composition's Time Layout window.

ADDITIONAL INFORMATION

After Effects provides several ways to apply Motion Blur, allowing the user to control it globally or layer by layer. If Motion Blur is not enabled at all relevant levels, it is not applied when the composition is rendered.

When Recursive Switches is selected in the General Preferences dialog box, selecting the Motion Blur switch for one composition applies Motion Blur to all compositions nested within it. However, Motion Blur only affects the layers in the nested composition that have been marked for Motion Blur.

Because Motion Blur slows rendering and display, After Effects allows you to turn it off for the entire composition.

Last Frame is Missing in Reversed Layer in After Effects 3.0 and Earlier

ISSUE

After you reverse a layer's playback direction by pressing Command + Option + R in Adobe After Effects 3.0 and earlier, the last frame of the reversed layer (i.e., the first frame of the original footage file) is replaced by an additional copy of the preceding frame.

SOLUTION

Upgrade to After Effects 3.1.

ADDITIONAL INFORMATION

After Effects 3.0 and earlier incorrectly removes the last frame of a reversed layer and replaces it with a copy of the preceding frame. The problem is corrected in After Effects 3.1.

QuickTime Movies Play with Red Tint in After Effects 2.0.x

ISSUE

Movies rendered in Adobe After Effects 2.0.x play with a red tint when QuickTime 2.0x is installed. QuickTime compression is set to None, and the color depth is set to Thousands (i.e., 16-bit color).

SOLUTIONS

Upgrade to QuickTime 2.1 or later before rendering the movie.

OR: Render the movie with 24-bit color (i.e., millions of colors) or 8-bit color (i.e., 256 colors).

OR: Render the movie using a different compressor (e.g., Animation).

ADDITIONAL INFORMATION

QuickTime 2.0.x renders movies with 16-bit color incorrectly when the compression is set to None, causing the movie's frames to appear with a red tint. The problem is corrected in QuickTime 2.1 and later.

No Effects Appear in Effect Menu in After Effects 3.x

ISSUE

No effects appear in the Effect menu in After Effects 3.x.

SYMPTOM

The Remove All command is dimmed in the Effects menu.

SOLUTION
Move either the After Effects application or the Plug-ins folder so that they are in the same folder.

ADDITIONAL INFORMATION
When you start After Effects 3.x, it checks the folder containing the After Effects application and all folders nested in the application folder for plug-in effects. If After Effects does not find its Plug-ins folder or any other plug-in effects, it does not display any effects in the Effect menu.

Application Errors

MAC OS

Q When I start After Effects, I get the error message "After Effects Error: The Multi-processor acceleration module did not load correctly (37 § 0)." Will this affect performance?

A That depends on whether your Macintosh has a single processor or a dual processor or multiprocessor. The Adobe MP Accelerator plug-in doesn't work on a single-processor computer. If you've got one, and received this message, you probably moved the plug-in into the "Plug-ins" folder in the After Effects folder. Close After Effects and move the Adobe MP Accelerator plug-in back to the "¬Optional Plug-ins" folder in the After Effects folder. If you've renamed the folder or removed the "¬" symbol, change the name back to its original name, then restart After Effects. Press Option + L to create the "¬" symbol. (The "¬"symbol prevents After Effects from trying to load any of the plug-ins in this folder.)

If you see this message on a system with a dual processor or multiprocessor, your System Folder may not have all of the current system extensions required to run your multiprocessor. You can update your system extensions by downloading the DayStar Floppy Release 2.4 from their Web site (www.daystar.com).

Following is a list of the multiprocessor components that you should have in your "Extensions" folder:

```
MP Startup 1.0.8
Multiprocessing folder
  Multiprocessing API Library
  DayStar Dual Processor HAL 1.4.8
  DayStar Quad Processor HAL 1.4.8
```

This release includes other files as well, but only those that affect your system's multiprocessing capabilities are listed here. If the file names and version numbers in your "Extensions" folder are differentm from these, you may have an older version of the files, and you should update them. (NOTE: The "HAL" processors may also be called the Apple Dual Processor HAL and the Apple Quad Processor HAL. Apple and Daystar co-developed the Mac-O/S MP Library software, or Apple Multiprocessing API.)

Finally, make sure that the "Plug-ins" folder in the After Effects folder contains version 1.7 of the Adobe MP Accelerator plug-in. See the third question (to the left on this page) for details on how to obtain this plug-in at no charge.

Error "Effect could not be found..." Opening Project in After Effects 3.x

ISSUE
When you open a project in Adobe After Effects 3.x, After Effects returns the error "Effect [name] could not be found. It will no longer be applied to any layers."

SOLUTIONS
Do one or more of the following:

A. Make sure the plug-in effect referenced in the error message is installed in the After Effects Plug-ins folder before launching After Effects.
B. If the project was created using the After Effects Production Bundle, install the hardware key used to serialize the Production Bundle plug-in effects before launching After Effects.
C. If the project was created in After Effects 2.0.x and the missing effect has been renamed, updated, or excluded from After Effects 3.x, apply a new effect in After Effects 3.x and save the project.

ADDITIONAL INFORMATION
When opening a project, After Effects searches for all plug-in effects used in the project. If one of these plug-in effects is not available, After Effects returns an error message.

When you launch the After Effects Production Bundle for the first time, After Effects serializes the Production Bundle plug-in effects (i.e., encodes the hardware key's serial number into the Production Bundle plug-in effects). The hardware key used to serialize the plug-in effects must be installed whenever the effects are used, otherwise After Effects returns an error message when launched.

Some After Effects 2.0.x effects have been renamed, updated, or excluded from After Effects 3.x. Applying a new effect in After Effects 3.x and saving the project prevents After Effects from returning an error message when you open the project.

To generate a list of installed effects, press Command + Shift + Option + Help in After Effects 3.x. After Effects creates a text-only file, named AE Version Info, and saves this file in the same folder as the After Effects application. Open the file in a text editor to display the installed effects.

Error "Floating Point Unit not installed" When Launching After Effects 2.0.x

ISSUE
When you start Adobe After Effects on a Power Macintosh, the system returns the error, "Floating Point Unit not installed."

SOLUTION

Remove all effect plug-ins not engineered for use with After Effects for Power Macintosh, then restart After Effects. To determine whether a plug-in is compatible with After Effects for Power Macintosh, select the plug-in from the Finder, then choose File > Get Info. When "Mac & PowerMac" appears next to Version, the effect plug-in is compatible with After Effects for Power Macintosh. The effect plug-ins Basic Text 2.4, Fast Blur 1.7, Photoshop (4 channel) 2.0, Photoshop Filter 2.0, and Timecode 1.6 can be used with After Effects for Power Macintosh and After Effects for 68000-series Macintosh.

ADDITIONAL INFORMATION

The system returns the error, "Floating Point Unit not installed" when you start After Effects 2.0.x on a Power Macintosh with effect plug-ins engineered for use with 68000-series Macintosh. After Effects for Power Macintosh cannot use effect plug-ins that are engineered solely for use with After Effects for 68000-series Macintosh.

The effect plug-ins Basic Text 2.4, Fast Blur 1.7, Photoshop (4 channel) 2.0, Photoshop Filter 2.0, and Timecode 1.6 can be used with After Effects for Power Macintosh, but do not display "Mac & PowerMac" next to Version in the Get Info dialog box.

Error "Invalid Serial Number" When Starting After Effects 3.0

ISSUE

After you enter your product serial number while starting Adobe After Effects 3.0, the error "Invalid Serial Number" appears.

SOLUTIONS

Do one or more of the following:

A. Press the tab key to move to the serial number field to ensure previously entered characters are replaced, then reenter the serial number exactly as it appears on the inside cover of the After Effects User Guide.

B. Reenter numerals using another set of numeric keys (i.e., numeric keys above the alpha characters, numeric keys on the keypad).

C. If you upgraded to After Effects 3.0 from After Effects 2.0x, use the After Effects 3.0 serial number instead of using the After Effects 2.0x serial number.

ADDITIONAL INFORMATION

After Effects 3.0 requires a valid serial number to start. If you enter an invalid or unrecognized serial number, After Effects returns the error, "Invalid Serial Number."

After Effects 3.0 uses a format for its serial number that is different from the one After Effects 2.0x uses, and it requires you to enter your serial number the first time you start it after installation. After Effects 3.0 serial numbers have 17 characters, where the first three characters are the letters "EMW," the seventh character is a letter, all other characters are numerals, and the last three characters are preceded by a hyphen (e.g., "EMW111111AAA-111").

If software utilities, system extensions, or control panels affect the function of numeric keys on the keyboard, you may be able to enter the expected numbers using another set of numeric keys (e.g., numeric keys above the alpha characters).

Error -2048 Importing AIFF Sound Files in After Effects 2.0.2

ISSUE

The error "After Effects error: retrieving movie from file '[filename]' (-2048)" appears when importing Audio Interchange File Format (AIFF) files in After Effects 2.0.2. After clicking OK, the error "After Effects error: setting up movie" or "After Effects: file '[filename]' cannot be imported—files of type 'AIFF' are not supported" appears.

SOLUTIONS

Do one or more of the following:

A. Upgrade to After Effects 3.0.

B. Upgrade to QuickTime 2.1.

C. Convert the AIFF file to a QuickTime movie, then reimport the file.

ADDITIONAL INFORMATION

After Effects 2.0.2 plays and renders audio files as expected using QuickTime 2.0, but returns errors when importing AIFF files. After Effects 3.0 imports AIFF files as expected. After Effects cannot import compressed AIFF (AIFC) files, or audio files saved with 1:3 and 1:6 MACE compression.

Apple's MoviePlayer 2.0 and later can convert AIFF files to QuickTime movies.

Error "Reading resource error..." Launching After Effects 3.x

ISSUE

When launching Adobe After Effects 3.x on a computer with no Macintosh name, the following error appears: "Reading resource error. Resource is missing or damaged."

SOLUTION

Name the Macintosh in the Sharing Setup Control Panel before launching After Effects:

1. Open the Sharing Setup Control Panel.
2. Enter a name in the Macintosh Name text box.
3. Close the Sharing Setup Control Panel, then restart the computer.

ADDITIONAL INFORMATION

After Effects uses the Macintosh Name as the default user identity when personalizing the application. If there is no

Macintosh name, After Effects returns an error message when launched.

Insufficient Memory Errors in After Effects

ISSUE

The error "Not enough RAM. Increase memory allocation by [amount]." or "After Effects error: insufficient memory for [horizontal dimension] x [vertical dimension] image buffer. Use Get Info in the Finder to increase the application's memory size by at least [amount] K." appears in Adobe After Effects.

SOLUTIONS

Increase the amount of memory available to After Effects by doing one or more of the following:

A. Increase the amount of memory allocated to After Effects.
   NOTE: Ensure that the largest unused block of RAM is 3 MB or greater before rendering movies in After Effects.
B. Defragment the System heap:
   Choose "About After Effects" from the Apple menu when the application is active.
   OR: Restart the computer.
   OR: Use a third-party utility (e.g., Swatch 1.9, Zone Ranger 1.2).
C. Disable all Extensions, Control Panels, and fonts that are not needed when running After Effects to free up more memory, then restart the computer.
D. Reduce the amount of memory reserved for previous actions by doing one or more of the following:
   A. Choose Edit > Preferences > General (After Effects 2.0.2) or File > Preferences > General (After Effects 3.0). In the General Preferences dialog box, enter 5 next to Undo-able Actions, then click OK.
   B. Press Control + Clear to flush previous actions currently stored in memory.
   C. Choose Composition > Composition Settings, make no changes in the Composition Settings dialog box, then click OK to remove previous actions currently stored in memory.
E. Install additional RAM.
   OR: Reduce the complexity of the composition before rendering movies by doing one or more of the following:
   A. When working with nested compositions, render individual compositions as QuickTime movies, then reimport the movies into the project.
   B. When working with nested compositions in After Effects 3.0, collapse geometrics before rendering the movie:
      1. In the Time Layout window, select the layer for which you want to collapse nested graphics.
      2. In the layer info panel, select the Collapse Geometrics switch.

      NOTE: You cannot collapse a layer's geometrics when a mask or effect is applied to it.

ADDITIONAL INFORMATION

After Effects renders each frame of a composition one layer at a time. The memory required to render each frame varies depending on the complexity of the frame.

The memory required to render a movie is equal to the amount of memory required to render the most complex frame in the composition. To determine whether there is enough memory to render a movie from an After Effects 3.0 composition, choose Layer > Quality > Best and Composition > Resolution > Full before previewing the composition. When the entire composition previews correctly, there is enough memory to render the movie.

Memory requirements increase when After Effect's resolution is high, when using masks, applying effects, using 3:2 pulldown, cropping, stretching, and nesting compositions. The Drop Shadow, Track Matte, and Set Channels effects require more memory than other effects.

To estimate the memory required for a composition, see Further Reading.

When you are unable to close windows or exit from After Effects after receiving a low memory error, press Caps Lock, then click OK.

Error -50 Rendering Filmstrip File in After Effects 3.0

ISSUE

Adobe After Effects 3.0 returns the error "After Effects error -50. [49 1 36]" when rendering a filmstrip file that is 640-by-480 pixels or larger on a 680X0-based Macintosh computer.

SOLUTIONS

Upgrade to After Effects 3.1.

OR: Render the filmstrip file at a size smaller than 640-by-480 pixels.

OR: Render the filmstrip file using After Effects 3.0 on a Power Macintosh computer.

ADDITIONAL INFORMATION

After Effects 3.0 is unable to render filmstrip files at 640-by-480 pixels or larger on a 680X0-based Macintosh computer. After Effects 3.1 is able to render filmstrip files at 640-by-480 pixels or larger on a 680X0-based Macintosh computer.

Error "Error. Confounded Dongle" in After Effects

ISSUE

The error "Error. Confounded Dongle" or "Dongle nowhere to be found" appears when launching, importing, or opening files in Adobe After Effects.

SOLUTIONS

Do one or more of the following:

A. Make sure the connections between the keyboard, hardware key, and ADB port are secure.
B. When using After Effects on a Power Macintosh and the After Effects Rendering Engine is installed, make sure that the Rendering Engine application is not in the folder containing the After Effects application, or in a folder within the After Effects application folder.
NOTE: You can create an alias of the "Effects Plug-ins" folder, and locate this alias in the same folder that contains the Rendering Engine application.

ADDITIONAL INFORMATION

After Effects requires a hardware key, or dongle, to launch and perform basic operations. When the hardware key is not installed properly, After Effects returns the error "Error. Confounded Dongle" or "Dongle nowhere to be found."

When launching After Effects on a Power Macintosh, the application searches for the "CAE PowerPlug" file and the hardware key. When After Effects does not locate the "CAE PowerPlug" file in the same folder as the After Effects application, After Effects searches all folders within the After Effects application folder for the "CAE PowerPlug" file. When After Effects locates the "AERE PowerPlug" file before locating the "CAE PowerPlug" file, After Effects returns the error "Error. Confounded Dongle" or "Dongle nowhere to be found."

When launching the After Effects Rendering Engine on a Power Macintosh, the application searches for the "AERE PowerPlug" file and the hardware key. When the After Effects Rendering Engine does not locate the "AERE PowerPlug" file in the same folder as the After Effects Rendering Engine, the After Effects Rendering Engine searches all folders within the After Effects Rendering Engine folder for the "AERE PowerPlug" file. When the After Effects Rendering Engine locates the "CAE PowerPlug" file before locating the "AERE PowerPlug" file, the After Effects Rendering Engine returns the error "Error. Confounded Dongle" or "Dongle nowhere to be found."

After Effects and the After Effects Rendering Engine do not search for a PowerPlug file when running on a 68K Macintosh.

Font Error Importing or Dragging Illustrator File in After Effects 3.x

ISSUE

When you import or drag Adobe Illustrator files that contain GX-enabled TrueType fonts or stroked text in Adobe After Effects 3.x, After Effects returns one of the following error messages:

"[Filename] uses one or more fonts which are unavailable on this machine. (50 1 15)."

"Stroked text is unsupported by this version."

"[Filename] contains stroked text and uses fonts which are unavailable on this machine. (50 1 15)."

SOLUTIONS

Convert text to outlines in Illustrator 5.x and later before saving and importing the file into After Effects:

1. Select the text block with the Selection (pointer) tool, instead of the Type tool, then choose Type > Create Outlines.
2. Choose File > Save, then reimport the file into After Effects.

OR: Disregard the error message and click OK when it appears. The Illustrator file functions correctly in After Effects.

ADDITIONAL INFORMATION

When rasterizing (i.e., importing or dragging) Illustrator files containing GX-enabled TrueType fonts or stroked text, After Effects 3.x incorrectly identifies the fonts as improperly installed, and generates error messages.

Converting text to outlines in Illustrator preserves the shape of a font's characters without referencing the font itself, preventing After Effects from searching for the fonts used in the Illustrator file.

Although After Effects 3.x returns error messages when rasterizing Illustrator files containing GX-enabled TrueType fonts or stroked text, the Illustrator files function correctly in After Effects.

Error -2050 When Rendering Movies with Audio in After Effects 2.0.1 and Earlier

ISSUE

When rendering movies containing audio files in Adobe After Effects 2.0.1 and earlier, After Effects returns the error "CoSA After Effects error: adding to movie (-2050). (44141)."

SOLUTIONS

Use After Effects 2.0.2 or later. After Effects 2.x to 2.02 updaters are available from Adobe Systems, Incorporated and American Online.

OR: Make the movie without audio by selecting Output Audio: None in the Make Movie dialog box.

OR: Downgrade to QuickTime 1.6.x then recreate the movie:

1. Remove the following files from the Extensions folder in the System Folder:
   QuickTime 2.0
   QuickTime PowerPlug 2.0, when present
   QuickTime Musical Instruments 2.0
   Apple Multimedia Tuner, when present
2. Install QuickTime 1.6.1 (68000-series Macintosh) or QuickTime 1.6.2 (Power Macintosh).
3. Recreate the movie.

ADDITIONAL INFORMATION

Because After Effects 2.0.1 and earlier were developed for use with QuickTime 1.x, After Effects 2.0.1 and earlier return an error when processing audio files using QuickTime 2.0.

Error "Media100 codec timed out" When Rendering Movie in After Effects 2.x and Later

ISSUE
The error "Media100 codec timed out" appears when rendering a movie with Media100 compression in Adobe After Effects 2.x and later.

SOLUTION
Do one or more of the following:

A. Reinstall the Media100 compressor/decompressor (codec).
B. Reinstall your system software.
C. Make sure your hardware is functioning correctly by running the Media100 hardware test.

ADDITIONAL INFORMATION
If the Media100 codec is damaged, an error occurs when you render movies with Media100 compression in After Effects 2.x and later.

The Media100 codec may become damaged when accessed simultaneously by more than one application, especially when QuickTime 2.1 is installed. System and hardware problems may also damage the Media100 codec.

Media100 software includes a utility that diagnoses hardware problems.

Row Size Too Large Error in After Effects 3.x

ISSUE
When you work with a large layer in Adobe After Effects 3.x, After Effects returns error "After Effects error: row size too large. 17996." The layer or the layer's frame buffer exceeds 4000 pixels in height or width.

SOLUTIONS
Do one or more of the following:

A. Make sure the layer does not exceed 4000 pixels in height or width.
B. Remove any effects applied to the layer that increase the layer's frame buffer (e.g., Basic 3D, Drop Shadow, Wave Warp).
C. Reduce the layer's dimensions until the error message does not appear.
D. Apply effects to the layer in another application (e.g., apply a drop shadow in Adobe Photoshop) before importing the layer into After Effects.

ADDITIONAL INFORMATION
Although After Effects can import a file that exceeds 4000 pixels in height or width, After Effects is limited by QuickDraw's maximum display size of 4000-by-4000 pixels. When you are working with files that exceed 4000 pixels in height or width, After Effects returns an error message.

In addition, After Effects creates a frame buffer for every image in your composition, and the frame buffer should not exceed 4000-by-4000 pixels. Some effects increase the size of an image's frame buffer beyond its original dimensions (e.g., Basic 3D, Drop Shadow, Wave Warp), causing an error to appear when the frame buffer exceeds 4000-by-4000 pixels.

After Effects Hardware Key Troubleshooting Guide

ISSUE
After you install Adobe After Effects, the keyboard, mouse, or monitor do not function properly, or After Effects beeps or returns an error message when launched.

SYMPTOMS
The monitor displays black.

When you move the mouse, the pointer does not move on screen.

Nothing happens when you type on the keyboard.

After Effects returns one of the following error messages when launched:

"After Effects warning: [number] After Effects plug-ins couldn't be loaded because the hardware key couldn't be found [list of effects]."

"Hardware key could not be found."

"Error. Confounded Dongle."

"Dongle nowhere to be found."

SOLUTIONS

A. Make sure your hardware key is functioning properly by doing one or more of the following:
   1. If After Effects beeps five times when you launch, your hardware key is damaged. Contact Adobe Technical Support at 206-628-4526 for a hardware key replacement.
   2. Restart your computer after installing the hardware key.
   3. Make sure all ADB pins in the hardware key's connection are straight and intact.
   4. Make sure the connections between the keyboard, hardware key, and ADB port are secure.
B. Make sure the hardware key is compatible with your system and hardware configuration by doing one or more of the following:
   1. If you're using the After Effects 3.x Production Bundle, make sure the same hardware key that was used to serialize the Production Bundle plug-in effects is installed. If you do not have the Production Bundle hardware key, remove the Production Bundle plug-in effects from the After Effects Plug-ins folder, then reinstall the Production Bundle plug-in effects before starting After Effects.
   2. If you're using After Effects 2.0.2 on a Power Macintosh, make sure only one copy of the CAE PowerPlug is on your hard disk, and is installed in the same folder as the After Effects application.

3. If you're using After Effects 2.0.x on a Power Macintosh and the After Effects Rendering Engine is installed, make sure the Rendering Engine application is not in the folder containing the After Effects application, or in a folder within the After Effects application folder.
4. If you're using an AppleVision AV monitor, connect the hardware key directly to the ADB port on the Macintosh, rather than the ADB port on the monitor. If you need to connect the hardware key to the monitor, increase the amount of video RAM (VRAM) in the computer to 4 MB or more.
5. If you're using a Daystar Genesis MP workstation, upgrade to After Effects 3.0 or later. If errors occur in After Effects 3.0 or later, contact Daystar to verify that your power supply is compatible with the hardware key.
6. If hardware keys for other applications are installed (e.g., ImMIX MFE Turbo Cube), shut down your computer, remove all hardware keys except the After Effects hardware key, then restart your Macintosh.

ADDITIONAL INFORMATION

After Effects 2.0.x and the After Effects 3.x Production Bundle require a hardware key to launch and perform basic operations. If the hardware key is damaged or incompatible with your system and hardware configuration, After Effects and your computer's peripheral devices may not function properly.

When you start the After Effects Production Bundle for the first time, After Effects serializes the Production Bundle plug-in effects (i.e., it encodes the hardware key's serial number into the Production Bundle plug-in effects). The hardware key used to serialize the plug-in effects must be installed whenever the effects are used, otherwise After Effects returns an error message when started.

When you launch After Effects on a Power Macintosh, After Effects searches for the CAE PowerPlug file and the hardware key. If After Effects does not locate the CAE PowerPlug file in the same folder as the After Effects application, it searches all folders within the After Effects application folder for the CAE PowerPlug file. If After Effects locates the AERE PowerPlug file before locating the CAE PowerPlug file, After Effects returns an error message.

After Effects 2.0.x for the Power Macintosh cannot use 68K plug-in effects (i.e., plug-ins that are created for use on a 68000-series Macintosh).

When you launch the After Effects 2.0.x Rendering Engine on a Power Macintosh, the Rendering Engine searches for the AERE PowerPlug file and the hardware key. If the After Effects Rendering Engine does not locate the AERE PowerPlug file in the same folder as the After Effects Rendering Engine, it searches all folders within the After Effects Rendering Engine folder for the AERE PowerPlug file. If it locates the CAE PowerPlug file before locating the AERE PowerPlug file, it returns an error message.

The After Effects hardware key does not support a direct connection to the AppleVision AV monitor's ADB port when less than 4 MB of VRAM is installed.

The Daystar Genesis MP plug-in is designed for use with After Effects 3.0 and later, and is not compatible with After Effects 2.0.x. Some Daystar Genesis workstations have faulty power supplies that cause After Effects to return the error message "Hardware key could not be found." Daystar is replacing the faulty power supplies at no charge.

The After Effects hardware key may be incompatible with other hardware keys.

Error Starting After Effects 3.x When Production Bundle Effects are Installed

ISSUE

When you start After Effects 3.x while Production Bundle plug-in effects are installed, After Effects returns the error "After Effects warning: [number] After Effects plug-ins couldn't be loaded because the hardware key couldn't be found [list of effects]."

SOLUTIONS

If the project was created using the After Effects Production Bundle, install the hardware key used to serialize the Production Bundle plug-in effects before starting After Effects.

OR: Remove the Production Bundle plug-in effects from the After Effects Plug-ins folder, then reinstall the Production Bundle plug-in effects before starting After Effects.

ADDITIONAL INFORMATION

When you start the After Effects Production Bundle for the first time, After Effects serializes the Production Bundle plug-in effects (i.e., it encodes the hardware key's serial number into the Production Bundle plug-in effects). The hardware key used to serialize the plug-in effects must be installed whenever the effects are used, otherwise After Effects returns an error message when started.

Error When Starting After Effects by Double-Clicking an Effect Plug-in

ISSUE

When you double-click one of the effect plug-ins to start Adobe After Effects 3.x, the system freezes or one of the following error messages appear:

"After Effects error: retrieving movie from file "[effect filename]" - no QuickTime movie found (-2048). (10 ß 21)"

"After Effects error: file "[effect filename]" cannot be imported - files of type "eFKT" are not supported."

SOLUTION

Start After Effects by double-clicking its application icon.

ADDITIONAL INFORMATION

When you double-click one of the effect plug-ins to start

After Effects, After Effects attempts to open the plug-in. Because After Effects is unable to open its effect plug-ins, an error message appears.

Error "Error attempting to draw into world at wrong size [39 ß 84]" in After Effects 2.x & Later

ISSUE

When importing, rendering, selecting footage items, or scrolling through the Time Layout window in Adobe After Effects 2.x and later, After Effects returns the error "Error attempting to draw into world at wrong size [39 ß 84]."

SOLUTIONS

Choose File > Save, then close and reopen your project.

OR: Reimport the file that is causing the error:

1. Locate the file that is causing the error by selecting each item in the Project window until the error appears.
2. Resave the file in the application that created it.
3. Select the file in the After Effects Project window, then choose File > Replace Footage > File.
4. In the dialog box that appears, select the newly saved copy of the file, then click Open.

ADDITIONAL INFORMATION

After Effects returns an error when attempting to access a file whose dimensions have changed since the project was first opened.

Error "Missing QuickTime codec (-8961)" in After Effects 3.x

ISSUE

When you import a QuickTime movie, Adobe After Effects 3.x returns the error, "After Effects error: Retrieving movie from file [filename]. Missing QuickTime codec (-8961) (10ß21)."

SOLUTIONS

Install the compressor/decompressor (codec) used to compress the movie and then import it in After Effects.

OR: Compress the movie using one of the codecs installed on your computer and then import it in After Effects.

ADDITIONAL INFORMATION

To play QuickTime movies, the codec used to compress the movie must be installed on the playback computer. If you import a QuickTime movie in After Effects 3.x when the movie's codec is not installed, After Effects cannot import the movie and returns the error, "After Effects error: Retrieving movie from file [filename]. Missing QuickTime codec (-8961) (10ß21)."

You can use a software codec to recompress movies that were captured (i.e., digitized) and compressed with a hardware codec. You can open and play movies that were compressed with one of the standard QuickTime codecs (e.g., Cinepak, Animation) on any computer that has QuickTime installed.

Error "No QuickTime movie found (-2048)" in After Effects 3.x

ISSUE

When you import footage files, Adobe After Effects 3.x returns the error, "

After Effects error: Retrieving movie from file [filename]. No QuickTime movie found (-2048) (10ß21)."

SOLUTIONS

Do one or more of the following:

A. Select the appropriate file type when you import the file:
   1. Choose File > Import > Footage As.
   2. In the dialog box that appears, select your file's type from the File Type pop-up menu.
   3. Select the file you want to import, then click Open.
B. If the correct file type does not appear in the File Type pop-up menu, install the appropriate file format plug-in in the After Effects Plug-ins folder:
   1. Quit After Effects.
   2. Move the file format plug-in for the file type you want to import into the After Effects plug-ins folder. 3. Open your After Effects project, then choose File > Import > Footage As.
   4. In the dialog box that appears, select your file's type from the File Type pop-up menu.
   5. Select the file you want to import, then click Open.
C. Using another application (e.g., Adobe Photoshop, Equilibrium DeBabelizer), convert the file to one of the formats After Effects can import.

ADDITIONAL INFORMATION

When you import a file that does not contain file type information (e.g., files created on a computer running Microsoft Windows), After Effects 3.x imports the file as a QuickTime movie. If the file is not a QuickTime movie, After Effects cannot import the file and returns the error, "After Effects error: Retrieving movie from file [filename]. No QuickTime movie found (-2048) (10ß21)."

The file formats that appear in the File Type pop-up menu in After Effects depend on which file format plug-ins are installed in the After Effects Plug-ins folder. When you import a file in After Effects 3.x by choosing File > Import > Footage As, After Effects imports the file using an installed file format plug-in, where the file format plug-in it uses corresponds to the file type you select from the File Type pop-up menu.

You can import additional file types in After Effects (e.g., BMP) by installing the Photoshop 3.0x File Format plug-ins into the After Effects Plug-ins folder; however, Photoshop 4.0 plug-ins are incompatible with After Effects 3.x.

Error "The file format module could not parse the file" in After Effects 3.x

ISSUE
When you import a file by choosing File > Import > Footage As, Adobe After Effects 3.x returns the error, "After Effects error: The file format module could not parse the file. (45ß35)."

SOLUTIONS
Do one or more of the following:
A. Select the appropriate file type when you import the file:
  1. Choose File > Import > Footage As.
  2. In the dialog box that appears, select your file's type from the File Type pop-up menu.
  3. Select the file you want to import, then click Open.
B. If the correct file type does not appear in the File Type pop-up menu, install the appropriate file format plug-in in the After Effects Plug-ins folder:
  1. Quit After Effects.
  2. Move the file format plug-in for the file type you want to import into the After Effects plug-ins folder.
  3. Open your After Effects project, then choose File > Import > Footage As.
  4. In the dialog box that appears, select your file's type from the File Type pop-up menu.
  5. Select the file you want to import, then click Open.

ADDITIONAL INFORMATION
If you import a file in After Effects 3.x by choosing File > Import > Footage As, and the file format you select does not match the format of the file being imported, After Effects returns the error, "After Effects error: The file format module could not parse the file. (45ß35)."

The file formats that appear in the File Type pop-up menu in After Effects depend on which file format plug-ins are installed in the After Effects Plug-ins folder. You can import additional file types in After Effects (e.g., BMP) by installing Photoshop 3.0x File Format plug-ins into the After Effects Plug-ins folder; however, Photoshop 4.0 plug-ins are incompatible with After Effects 3.x.

Hardware Key Error Launching After Effects on DayStar Genesis Workstation

ISSUE
When you start Adobe After Effects on a DayStar Genesis computer, After Effects returns the error, "The hardware key cannot be found."

SOLUTIONS
Do one or more of the following:
A. Use After Effects 3.x.
B. Make sure the hardware key is not damaged or incompatible with other components of your system. For more information, see document 205002.
C. If you are starting After Effects 3.x, contact DayStar to verify that your power supply is compatible with the hardware key.
D. If you are using After Effects 2.x, remove the multiprocessor (e.g., Adobe MP Accelerator) plug-in from the After Effects Plug-ins folder.

ADDITIONAL INFORMATION
The Adobe MP Accelerator plug-in is designed to work with After Effects 3.0 and later, and is not compatible with After Effects 2.0.x. If the Adobe MP Accelerator plug-in is installed with After Effects 2.0.x on a DayStar Genesis multiprocessor computer, After Effects returns an error message when it starts.

If your hardware key is damaged or incompatible with your system and hardware configuration, After Effects returns an error message when it starts.

A faulty power supply in a DayStar Genesis workstation can cause After Effects to return an error message when it starts. Contact DayStar to determine whether you have a faulty power supply.

System Errors

MAC OS

System Freezes or Large Frames Render Slowly on Power Macintosh in After Effects

ISSUE
When rendering large frames on a Power Macintosh using Adobe After Effects 2.x and later, the system freezes or the frames render slowly.

SOLUTION
Turn on the Modern Memory Manager in the Memory control panel.

ADDITIONAL INFORMATION
The system freezes or large frames render slowly in After Effects 2.x and later when there is insufficient random-access memory (RAM) available to After Effects. The Modern Memory Manager removes unused information stored in RAM, making more memory available to After Effects when rendering large frames.

System Error (e.g. Freeze) When Rendering Movie in After Effects 2.0.x

ISSUE
Adobe After Effects 2.0.x returns a system error (e.g., freeze) when rendering movies.

SOLUTIONS

Upgrade to After Effects 3.0.

OR: Do one or more of the following:

A. Before rendering a movie, disable the Apple Multimedia Tuner by moving it out of the System Folder.
   NOTE: The Apple Multimedia Tuner cannot be disabled using Extensions Manager.
B. Restart the computer, then render the movie before launching other applications that use QuickTime (e.g., Adobe Premiere).
C. When Now Software's CE Toolbox is installed, disable it using Extensions Manager or move it out of the System Folder, then restart the computer before rendering a movie.

ADDITIONAL INFORMATION

The Apple Multimedia Tuner fragments the memory allocated to After Effects, causing After Effects to return a system error (e.g., freeze) when rendering large movies and movies with nested compositions. QuickTime 2.1 contains the code from the Apple Multimedia Tuner, and also fragments the memory allocated to After Effects, causing After Effects to return a system error (e.g., freeze) when rendering large movies and movies with nested compositions.

The Apple Multimedia Tuner can be moved from the Extensions folder to the Adobe Premiere Plug-Ins folder so that it can be used by Adobe Premiere, but not by After Effects. Premiere loads the Apple Multimedia Tuner into the System heap when starting. When the Apple Multimedia Tuner is loaded in the System, restarting the computer to remove Apple Multimedia Turner from the System prevents After Effects 2.0.x from slowing down and returning a system error while rending movies.

After Effects 3.0 prevents the Apple Multimedia Tuner and QuickTime 2.1 from fragmenting the memory allocated to After Effects.

General Information

MAC OS

Adobe MP Accelerator 1.7 Plug-in for After Effects 3.x General Information

The Adobe MP Accelerator plug-in for Adobe After Effects 3.x accelerates After Effects on multiprocessor computers (e.g., Power Macintosh 9500 MP, DayStar Genesis MP). When the multiprocessor plug-in installed, After Effects accelerates scaling, rotation, subpixel positioning, motion blur, blending, compositing, and other plug-in effects designed for use on multiprocessor systems. After Effects renders movies 1.5 times faster on dual-processor computers, and 2.5 times faster on quad-processor computers.

For a detailed list of changes in the Adobe MP Accelerator plug-in, refer to the Adobe MP Accelerator ReadMe file.

OBTAINING THE ADOBE MP ACCELERATOR 1.7 PLUG-IN

The Adobe MP Accelerator 1.7 plug-in is available in compressed form (Adobemp.sea.hqx) on Adobe's World Wide Web site (http://www.adobe.com/supportservice/custsupport/LIBRARY/aemac.htm), the Adobe FTP site, and the Adobe BBS. The plug-in is not available on disk.

The Adobe MP Accelerator plug-in, developed in cooperation with DayStar Digital, is also available in the DayStar MP Floppy v2.4, available from DayStar's World Wide Web site (http://www.daystar.com/FTP/FTP.GnsMP.html). The DayStar MP Floppy v2.4 also includes the Premiere MP 1.0.1 plug-in for use with Adobe Premiere 4.x on multiprocessor computers.

ADDITIONAL MULTIPROCESSOR ACCELERATION IN AFTER EFFECTS 3.X

To increase the number of accelerated functions in After Effects 3.x, install the MP Movie Pack control panel with QuickTime 2.5 or later. The MP Movie Pack, available from DayStar's World Wide Web site (http://www.daystar.com/FTP/FTP.GnsMP.html), adds multiprocessing capability to QuickTime 2.5 and later.

QuickTime Requirements for After Effects General Information

QUICKTIME REQUIREMENTS FOR AFTER EFFECTS 2.X

Use QuickTime 1.6.x or 2.0 with Adobe After Effects 2.x. The version of QuickTime you choose partly depends on the computer you are using:

- QuickTime 1.6.1 is designed for 68000-series Macintosh computers and consists of the QuickTime 1.6.1 extension only.
- QuickTime 1.6.2 is designed for Power Macintosh computers and consists of QuickTime 1.6.2 and the QuickTime PowerPlug 1.0.
- QuickTime 2.0 is designed for both 68000-series Macintosh computers and Power Macintosh computers. QuickTime 2.0 consists of the QuickTime 2.0 extension, QuickTime Musical Instruments 2.0, and, when installed on a Power Macintosh, QuickTime PowerPlug 2.0.
  NOTE: Do not use the Apple Multimedia Tuner 2.0.1 or QuickTime 2.1 with After Effects 2.x, as they will cause memory-related errors.

QUICKTIME REQUIREMENTS FOR AFTER EFFECTS 3.0

Use QuickTime 1.6.1 or later with After Effects 3.0. The version of QuickTime you choose partly depends on the computer you are using, as noted above. QuickTime 2.1 is installed by default with After Effects 3.0.

You can use After Effects 3.0 without having QuickTime installed, but you will not be able to read or write QuickTime files.

Adobe FrameMaker®

Chapter Three

Adobe FrameMaker's long and successful history continues as the world's most powerful tool for creating, maintaining, and distributing documents on MacOS, Windows, and UNIX systems. Acquired by Adobe in 1995 in a merger with Frame Technologies, version 5.1 combines word processing, page layout, graphics, and color features, and perhaps the finest on-line conversion capabilities into HTML, SGML, and PDF formats. It's ideal for publishers, corporate workgroups, and technical publications departments that produce books, catalogs, manuals, or on-line product information.

Contents

Adobe FrameMaker®

Feature Techniques

MAC OS / WINDOWS / UNIX

Q Is it possible to associate a condition tag with a particular paragraph format?

A Yes and no. Although it's not possible to build a condition tag into a paragraph format via the "Paragraph Designer" dialog box, you can use the "Find/Change" dialog box to search for paragraphs that use a certain paragraph tag and apply a condition tag to them. Here's how.

1. Copy the condition tag to the Clipboard. To do so, Apply the desired condition tag to a paragraph that's already assigned the paragraph tag you'll be "associating" with the condition tag. Then, with your insertion point in this paragraph, select "Conditional Text Settings" from the Copy Special submenu of the Edit menu.
2. Set the "Find" feature to find your paragraph tag. Select "Find/Change..." from the Edit menu. In the "Find/Change" dialog box, select "Paragraph Tag" from the "Find" pop-up menu. Make sure the name of the paragraph tag you want to search for is listed at the top right of the dialog box. If not, type in the name of that paragraph tag.
3. Set the "Change" feature to add your condition tag to found paragraphs. From the "Change" pop-up menu in the same dialog box, select "By Pasting."
4. Find and change. Click on the "Find" and then the "Change" button, and check to see that FrameMaker correctly applied the condition tag to the next instance of the paragraph tag. To make the change to all paragraphs with that particular paragraph tag, select the "Document" option to the right of the "Change All In" button, and then press "Change All In."

To ensure that you don't miss any paragraphs, you may want to hold off running this find-and-change operation until you're done adding paragraphs and assigning paragraph tags.

Does FrameMaker release 5 support trapping?

ISSUE

Does FrameMaker releasc 5 support trapping?

SOLUTION

FrameMaker release 5 does not support trapping on the Windows and UNIX platforms. There is a manual trapping technique discussed in Chapter 17 of the Using FrameMaker manual.

On the Macintosh, release 5 will correctly print EPSF files which have been trapped using Adobe Illustrator, Trapwise, Island Trapper, or any application that creates trapped EPSF.

For additional information concerning trapping and Trapwise on the Macintosh platform, see Related Records.

Is it possible to open a FrameMaker release 5 doc in FrameMaker 4?

ISSUE

I have a FrameMaker release 5 document that I must open in FrameMaker 4. Can this be done?

SOLUTION

If you save your files to MIF (Maker Interchange Format), they can be opened in earlier versions. However, any features that are new to a version will be ignored in earlier versions.

One of the major differences between FrameMaker 4 and FrameMaker 5 is the page layout. FrameMaker 5 has a new feature called a text frame. Text frames contain 1 or more text columns of the same size. The feature was added to FrameMaker 5 to allow for text, tables, and anchored frames to straddle text columns. If you have a text frame with multiple columns in FrameMaker 5, it will be converted to a single text column in FrameMaker 4. So, FrameMaker MIF files are backward compatible, but if you use new features you may have to touch up the file in the earlier version.

Also, when opening the MIF files in the earlier version, you will recieve MIF errors messages in the console window. For example:

```
maker: MIF: "/usr/people/foo.mif" (2206):
  Invalid opcode: FLocked.
maker: – Skipping these chars: maker: No >
maker: ——— Done skipping.
```

This is expected behavior when opening more recent MIF files in an earlier version. The error messages can be ignored.

Can a document have both landscape and portrait pages?

ISSUE

I want to have both in landscape and portrait pages in the same document. How do I do that?

SOLUTION

It is possible to have mixed orientation in the same document. Follow these steps to create a Landscape page:

1. Switch to your Master Pages - View/Master Pages.
2. Add a new Master Page - Special/Add Master Page.
3. Name the Master Page, Landscape for example, select the Empty button for Page Layout and click Add.
4. Rotate the new, blank master page - Format/Pages/Layout Commands/Rotate Page/Clockwise.
5. Open the graphic tool palette, select the text column icon and draw a text column on the landscape page. Select "Template for Body Page" and click Add.
6. You now have a Landscape Master Page which you can apply to your Body Pages.

This information is found on page 19-18 of the Using FrameMaker manual.

How does FrameMaker support and print color separations?

Q What input is required for color separations? How can we check to see if the input file meets the spec?

A Mac and Windows FrameMaker support EPSF for process and spot separation and CMYK TIFF for process separation only. You can tell on Mac that a TIFF is CMYK TIFF (as opposed to RGB or grayscale TIFF) by looking at the facet name in the object properties dialog for that particular image. Unix separates EPSF but not CMYK TIFF.

All versions of FrameMaker support both DCS (Desktop Color Separations) and "Pre-separated CMYK image" EPSF. This latter type is generated by some image manipulation programs such as Adobe Photoshop and EFI Cachet. In order to generate such an EPSF image, Photoshop must be in "CMYK" mode as opposed to "RGB" mode. In general, anything that Adobe Separator can separate, we can too. The only exception is EPSF files with referenced im-beded images. We don't support the EPSF "Include file" facility.

Q What does FrameMaker generate in its color output? What graphics can be fully separated? What can't be separated? What problems might be considered "common"? A bit of discussion of process vs. spot color would be helpful as well.

A In "Process color" you use different levels of four colors—Cyan, Magenta, Yellow, and Black—in order to produce any color that is printable on the page. For example, Cyan + Magenta gives dark blue. Magenta + Yellow gives red, Cyan + Yellow gives green. Cyan+Magenta+Yellow gives a dark color, which is almost black, and is usually replaced by black. (This is called Black Generation and Under Color Removal). No ink gives the color of the paper—usually white.

Other colors besides these eight are created using halftoning—that is—rendering the image as a "haltone screen" with many small cells, typically 60-300 cells or lines per inch (LPI). The higher the LPI, the more well defined the image details, but the fewer levels of gray (or color) which can be described. Lowering the LPI increases color choices while limiting detail. LPI should not be confused with the resolution of the device, measured in dots per inch (DPI) which on typesetters can range from 1200-3000. To get lots of colors and fine detail, you need to increase the resolution of the device, or DPI. This usually means running it in slower, hi-resolution mode.

As the image in an area gets darker, the spots, or halftone cells, get larger. Light colors have small dots. Dark colors have large dots which overlap each other up to the point that the page is fully saturated with a particular color. The actual shape of the dot can be tweeked in Mac Frame-Maker from the custom screens dialog, or by changing the ps_prolog in Unix FrameMaker. Typical dot shapes are round, line, and diamond. This is really a power-user feature, however.

Cells are arranged in a rectangular grid. There are (LPI) cells per inch on both dimensions of the grid. However, the grid is not always horizontal and vertical. Instead, it is rotated at a "screen angle." Cyan and Magenta are usually at 15° and 75°, Yellow at 0° (horizontal/vertical) and black at 45°. These angles are only approximate. Different imagesetters have specific settings for these angles, which are sometimes calculated to four decimal places, and are defined in the PostScript Printer Description (PPD) files. In Mac FrameMaker, you can specify a "screen set" from among the ones specified in the PPD file which allows you to choose an appropriate screen for the desired line frequency (LPI) and printer resolution (DPI).

There is a new screening technology called "stochastic screening" which does away with the concepts of grids, halftone cells, screens and angles. In this method. Colors are produced by a semi-random or "stochastic" arrangement of dots in no set pattern, but in a way that they are well distributed. Newer imagesetters use this method.

Spot color is a completely different approach to getting color on a page. Rather than trying to combine four colors, you simply use an ink with the desired color you want to use. You can still use halftoning to get different tints of that color between the pure color and white, but you are generally not combining spot colors to create new ones. There can be any number of spot colors on the page, but 6 is a practical maximum because this is the maximum number of rolers on any one printing press at most printing shops. With spot color, you can also use special inks, such as metalic reflective in, or varnishes, which give special effects to the finished piece.

Sometimes you combine spot and process color. For example, a 6 roll press can support four process colors (C, M,

Y, and K) and two aditional spot colors. In this way, for example, you can get a spot color, for, let's say your company "corporate" color which is known and measured very carefully, but still have color photographs using process color. FrameMaker supports combined process and spot color.

How do hypertext links behave when a file is converted to HTML?

FEATURE

How the HTML Lite filter converts the various types of hypertext links. How the converted links behave in a browser.

DETAIL

The links that convert are set apart from the rest of the doc by the fact that they are underlined and a different color than the rest of the text.

Here's a list of the FrameMaker links and a description of how they convert.

gotolink	- converts and behaves just like gotolink in FrameMaker
openlink	- converts and behaves like gotolink
gotoObjectId	- converts and behaves like Frame's gotoObjectId
openObjectId	- converts and behaves like gotoObjectId
nextpage	- converts and will jump you to first "page" of html doc
previouspage	- converts and will jump you to first "page" of html doc
alert	- does not convert
popup	- does not convert
matrix	- does not convert
gotopage	- does not convert links on
graphics	- do not convert
gotoObjectidFitWin	- does not convert
openobjectidFitWin	- does not convert

To summarize, the links that will convert and maintain their FrameMaker behavior are gotolink and gotoObjectId. The openlink and openObjectId convert but exhibit the goto behavior; that is, they do not open a new window. The next and previous page links are not useful as HTML documents have no concept of pages; they are a continuous scrollable stream of data. The links convert and will jump to the first "page" or screenful of data. Links on graphics do not convert as the HTML filter can only deal with information in the main text frame.

What file formats can FrameMaker release 5 import and export?

ISSUE

What file formats can FrameMaker release 5 import and export?

SOLUTION

Here is a list of the import and export formats FrameMaker release 5 supports

Text Import filters

Text Import Filters - All platforms:
ASCII
MS Word Windows 1.x, 2.x, 6.0
MS Word Macintosh 3.0, 4.0, 5.0, 5.1, 6.0
WordPerfect DOS 4.2, 5.0, 5.1
WordPerfect Windows 5.0, 5.1, 6.0
WordPerfect Macintosh 2.0
RTF 1.3
MIF
MML
Additional filters for Macintosh:
MacWrite 5.0
MacWrite II
Additional for UNIX:
IBM DCA
troff
Interleaf (IAF) 6.4, 8.0
Additional for MS Windows:
Ventura Publisher 3.0, 4.0

Text Export Filters

Text Export Filters - All platforms:
ASCII
MIF
RTF 1.2
HTML
Additional for Macintosh:
MacWrite 5.0
MacWrite II
Additional for UNIX:
Interleaf (IAF) 6.4
WordPerfect 5.1

Graphics Import Filters

Graphics Import Filters - All platforms:
AutoCAD DXF 10, 11, 12
CGM
CorelDRAW CDR 3
GEM 3
EPSI
EPSF
EPS
GIF
HPGL 2

TIP MAC OS / WINDOWS / UNIX

Creating drop caps in FrameMaker 5

To create a drop cap using FrameMaker 5, follow these steps:

1. Click at the beginning of the paragraph to which you want to add the drop cap.
2. Create an anchored frame for your drop cap. Select "Anchored Frame" from the Special menu, and in the "Anchored Frame" dialog box, select "Run into Paragraph" from the "Anchoring Position" pop-up menu. Set a width and height for your frame, too (if necessary, you can resize it later by selecting the anchored frame and dragging the handles to the desired width and height).
3. Create a text frame. Draw a text frame within the anchored frame using the text-frame tool (left) from the tools palette.
4. Create your drop-cap character. In the text frame, type the character you want for your drop cap and apply the appropriate formatting. Since the drop cap is created within an anchored frame, it'll flow with the text it's anchored to when you edit the document.

IGES
QuickDraw PICT
MacPaint
Micrographx DRW
Sun rasterfile (rf)
TIFF
WordPerfect WPG
Windows Metafile WMF
XWD
PCX
Additional for UNIX:
CCITT G4
RGB-SGI
Additional for MS Windows:
BMP 3.0, 3.1
Enhanced Metafile EMF

Can I get crop marks to show and print in PDF files?

ISSUE

I am printing a FrameMaker 5 document to a file with the Generate Acrobat Data option turned on so that I can create a PDF file. I also have Registration Marks turned on in the Print dialog. When I print the document, these marks are printed. Is it possible to see them in Acrobat Reader or Exchange as well?

SOLUTION

Registration or crop marks are not displayed by default when the Generate Acrobat Data option is turned on. If you turn this option off when printing to a file and then distill the resulting PostScript file, you will see the crop marks in Exchange. Of course, your hypertext links and cross-references will no longer work.

You can adjust the margins in Acrobat in order to see the crop marks. To do so, go to Edit->Pages->Crop and change the margins to all be 0. You may then save the file with these new margins if you want to make the crop marks show at all times for a particular file.

How can I create a drop cap in FrameMaker release 5?

ISSUE

I want to create a drop cap in FrameMaker release 5. How can I do this?

SOLUTION

"Using FrameMaker" manual Chapter 15 reviews anchored frame usage, which is one way to create a drop cap. This technical note offers an additional method for creating drop caps.

You can use the new Runaround feature of FrameMaker Release 5 to to accomplish this. First create a large letter (in this case a T) with the Text Line Tool (A Tool) and place it behind the Main Flowed Text Frame - more than likely this T will be under the upper left corner of the text frame. You then draw a polygon from the graphics tool pallet and place it over the T AND the Text Frame where the initial cap will be placed. With the polygon selected (handles showing on polygon edges) select Runaround Properties from the Graphics menu. This will bring up the Runaround Properties dialog box. Select the "Run around Contour" option and click on Set. If you have text in the text column, you will see it move to the edge of the polygon where before it was running over the polygon. You may need to reshape the polygon until the text wraps just right. Then give the polygon a fill of none and a pen of none. If View-Borders are on, then you will see a dashed line where the polygon is, but this will not print.

This method can be used for initial caps as well as for bitmap graphics in which auto wrap around will not work (no bounding box info). The two problems that you run into with wrap around is that it will not work with the Text Line Tool or with bitmap graphics which do not have white space on the edges. With Drop Caps, you can use the new

Anchored Frame feauture of "Run into Paragraph", but since it is an Anchored Frame, you cannot get the small text to go under the overlap of the large letter.

Tricky way to use autonumber formats to achieve a certain effect

ISSUE

Tricky way to use autonumber formats to achieve a certain effect.

SOLUTION

If a user has no figures in text, this will work for numbering equations:

```
Chapter <n+ >< =0>< =0>< =0>
     note: that's <[space]=0>
Section   .<n+ >< =0>
Subsection  . .<n+ >
Equation   -<n+ >
```

If the user has both figures and equations, use these formats:

```
Chapter <n+ >< =0>< =0>< =0>< =0>
     note: that's <[space]=0>
Section   .<n+ >< =0>
Subsection  . .<n+ >
Figure   -<A+>
Equation   -<n+ >
```

One nit: Unfortunately, there's a small update bug, so when you apply this new format, following subsections don't renumber. To force the renumber, you should add a *new* Section paragraph ahead of the first subsection paragraph, and then delete it again. After doing that, things seem to work fine.

AN EXAMPLE:

Please solve the following problem: I am creating a template to be used by writers of our technical manuals. Every paragraph must be numbered and within each chapter, figures must be numbered. I have set up paragraph formats as detailed below:

Paragraph tag	Autonumber field	Type of paragraph
Heading-1st	<n+ >.\t	Chapter
Heading-2nd	.<n+ >\t	Section
Heading-3rd	. .<n+ >\t	Suction
Seq-a	<a>)\t	List
Seq-i	*)\t*	*Sub-List*

This works as required BUT I must also have a paragraph format for the title which must be put under each figure. The figure title has the format "Figure x-y name of figure" where x = current chapter number and y = number of each figure in that chapter (incrementing by 1). Therefore, in Chapter1, there may be Figure1-1, Figure1-2, then in Chapter2, Figure2-1, Figure2-2, Figure2-3 and so on.

Here is the Solution:

Paragraph tag	Content of autonumber field
Heading-1st	<n+ >.< =0>< =0>< =0>< =0>< =0>< =0>\t
Heading-2nd	.<n+ >< =0>\t
Heading-3rd	. .<n+ >\t
Figure	Figure -.<n+ >\t
Table	Table -.<n+ >\t
Seq-a	<a=1>)\t
Seq-i	)\t

One nit: Unfortunately, sometimes when you apply new Heading-1st tags, following Heading* subsections don't renumber. To force the renumber, you should add a *new* Heading-1st paragraph ahead of the first subsection paragraph, and then delete it again by reapplying the previous tag again (If it was a Seq-a tag before you applied the new Heading-1st to it, then reapply Seq-a again). After doing this, numbering seems to work fine. It is possible that you won't run into renumbering problems though.

What is the limit for page size in a New Custom Document?

ISSUE

What are the width and height limits for a New Custom Document?

SOLUTION

Width limit is 216 inches. Height limit is 216 inches. If you attempt to create a larger page size, you will get the alert: Page size is too large.

Can Bitstream Fonts be used with FrameMaker 5.0?

ISSUE

Can Bitstream Fonts be used with FrameMaker 5.0?

SOLUTION

On the Macintosh and MS Windows platforms, we support anything you can install. On MS Windows, we support the Adobe Font installer.

For Adobe compatible fonts on the UNIX platform, the online manual Managing Frame Products describes how to convert the fonts and how to modify the fontlist file.

How do I name a table format in a file that was filtered from Word?

ISSUE

Why am I getting a message "Not all settings are specified. Fill in all settings and try again." when I try to create a New Format from an existing table?

SOLUTION

This message is put up when the existing table does not have a table tag. This can occur when a Word document, with a table, is filtered into FrameMaker. To create a table tag based on the existing table:

1. Put the insertion point in the table and open the Table Designer.
2. Click Commands->New Format and type in the name of the new tag. Check "Apply to Selection" and uncheck "Store in Catalog". Click on Create to create a table tag for this table.
3. Again click Commands->New Format and check "Store in Catalog". Click Create. The entry will now be accepted in the table catalog.

How do I remove the page numbers from every entry in my index?

ISSUE

I would like to remove the page number from each entry in my index. If I remove the <$pagenum> building block from the reference page, my automatic hypertext links are no longer generated. How can I easily remove all the page numbers (without having to edit each index marker) and still have my automatic hypertext links be generated?

SOLUTION

You can accomplish this by replacing the <$pagenum> building block on the reference page of the index with the <$nopage> building block and regenerate the index. Your automatically generated hypertext links will work fine unless you have more than one page number to go to (in this case it would go to the first page number for the entry).

WINDOWS

What does the TEMP space of MS Windows do? How does it effect FM?

ISSUE

I was told that I needed sufficient space in my TEMP directory for FrameMaker for MS Windows to run efficiently. How is the TEMP environment variable used?

SOLUTION

The TEMP directory is setup within your autoexec.bat file. You should have a SET TEMP statement.

MS Windows is writing TEMP files everytime you run MS Windows, start an application, filter, print, and other "housekeeping" functions.

By the time FrameMaker is launched, MS Windows has already written some TEMP files. When you start FrameMaker and open a file, only a few files have been added.

If the file you open has many graphics as you page past the graphics, TEMP files are being created, which means the drive where TEMP is set has less and less free disk space.

If you save the file, the graphics and other parts of the document which MS Windows wrote to TEMP get "used" in the doc. This *can* create more TEMP files.

You may need 5 to 10 times the file size only when you filter, not when you save. Remember that graphics imported by reference are filtered when you open the document.

TEMP files can be created when:

- Windows is running
- Other applications are running
- FrameMaker is running
- Graphics are displayed in FrameMaker
- Graphics are imported by reference. FrameMaker filters graphics imported by reference when the document is opened, and the graphics are displayed. In this case 5-10 times the size of the graphic may be written out in TEMP files.

If you go to save, MS Windows may not have enough room for TEMP files. FrameMaker is not creating these TEMP files - MS Windows creates these TEMP files as a part of normal Windows housekeeping.

*The number of TEMP files from the time after you have an opened document to the time you save *barely* changes. You can actually watch this happen:*

- Open a DOS window & do a DIR of the TEMP directory.
- Start FrameMaker and look at it again.
- Open a file (File/Open)
- Continue this scenario as you wish.

As you keep doing this, you will see that the FILE/OPEN command causes more TEMP files than other commands. The more graphics you have, the more TEMP files you get. If the graphics are imported by reference, you get even more files. When you save, the number of files changes slightly.

If files are opened in MIF format, you can get MANY TEMP files as FrameMaker converts the file to binary.

What does the "Use Postscript=On" setting in maker.ini do?

ISSUE

I see the setting "UsePostscript=On" in maker.ini. What does this setting do?

SOLUTION

This answer provides additional details to the description of this setting in the online manual, Customizing FrameMaker (section on Changing Initialization Files).

"UsePostscript=On" appends code to a printed PostScript file. This code essentially enables certain optimizations and other features which only make sense for PostScript printers:

1. Direct PostScript path-based clipping
2. PostScript scaling and rotation of metafiles and bitmap images.
3. Enables accurate CMYK composite color (bypassing GDI for certain color functions).

4. Enables process color separation (EPSF, etc.) features specific to PostScript printers. If the setting is "off", FrameMaker uses the Windows methods for printing only.

How do I integrate the MIF and/or MML manuals Help System?

ISSUE

How can I make the MIF and MML manuals a part of the FrameMaker 4 for Windows Online Manuals popup list in Help?

SOLUTION

Following is a description of how to add the MIF manual to the OnLine Manuals popup list. The MML manual would be handled similarly.

Make a MIF subdirectory of the manuals directory and place the MIF docs in this directory. Make a copy of maker4/help/maker/mainmenu.hlp to another directory. Open this copy in FM and unlock the doc. Go to View/ReferencePages and look for the line Release Notes. Under this line type a string for the entry in the dialog box, ex. MIF Manual. Create a new hypertext marker with the following:

```
openlink
<$path[onlinemanuals]>\mif\miftoc.doc:firstpage
```

Go to View/BodyPages and lock the document. Exit by clicking done and say yes when asked if you want to save. Test by clicking online manuals and then clicking the MIF Manual string. This should open the table of contents for the MIF manual. Copy this amended mainmenu.hlp over the maker4/help/maker/mainmenu.hlp file. Now when you open Help/Contents/OnlineManuals, you should be able to click on the new line, "MIF Manual", and open the table of contents. From the table of contents you can browse through the manual.

What configuration is needed to have Adobe's PS driver work with FM?

ISSUE

I am trying to use the Adobe PostScript driver with FrameMaker 3 or FrameMaker 4 for Windows. What configuration is needed?

SOLUTION

To use the Adobe PostScript driver with FrameMaker for Windows you need to do the following:

1. Make sure you have version 2.1.1 or 2.1.2 of the PS driver.
2. In the MAKER.INI file change the setting:
```
Use PostScript=On
        to
Use PostScript=Off
```
3. In the Adobe Postscript driver change the setting:
```
Optimize for Speed
   to
Optimize for Compatibility
```

This will resolve any problems you may incur.

NOTE: For LaserJet 4 printers, Microsoft recommends that you use the PCL driver 31.V1.18 or later. This driver is faster and will print as well as when it is in PostScript emulation.

The driver is available free of charge from any of the Microsoft online services. See the FrameMaker4 release notes, RELNOTES.DOC for more information about printing in Windows.

MAC OS

What is OPI and does FrameMaker support it?

ISSUE

What is OPI and does FrameMaker support it?

SOLUTION

OPI stands for Open Prepress Interface, and is a standard for handling large images. An opi server takes a large image and generates a "for placement only image" that is much smaller and easily worked with. There are two types of OPI images - TIFF OPI and EPSF OPI. The original Aldus specification and its updates specify only TIFF OPI, but many pre-press systems that support OPI also support EPSF OPI. The general idea behind OPI is that the pre-press house scans an image and generates both its own high-resolution image that stays with the scanner, and a low resolution TIFF (or EPSF) image which goes to the composition workstation, which is where FrameMaker is running. FrameMaker imports the low resolution image, and when it is printed, the PostScript RIP detects the OPI image at a particular position and orientation and substitutes the full resolution image. Every pre-press system has its own convention for creating and handling opi images, but at the base level, the link to the scan is held as an OPI comment in the postscript code.

Does FrameMaker support OPI?

Any application that supports importing and printing EPSF images supports EPSF OPI. FrameMaker fully supports this type of OPI image on all platforms. There is some support for TIFF OPI in the Macintosh version since FrameMaker 3, but it is untested and is probably buggy. We highly reccomend using EPSF OPI if at all possible.

Can you edit OPI images?

This depends on which pre-press system was used to create the image. While the opi image can be imported into FrameMaker, rotated, scaled and cropped, and the changes will be noted into the OPI comment in the Postscript, so that the scan will be rotated, scaled, and cropped just as the preview immage was. Changes to the opi image itselfvia changes to the postscript code, will NOT carry over to the scanned image.

Does Frame support OPI 1.3? In particular, do you support all the OPI 1.3 comments around images to be printed?
This is an untested feature. We think we've done all the right things, but can't say that we guarantee it. So it's not documented or advertised.
When printing an imported TIFF file, do you take Tag #32781 90x800D) and put that data into the %ALDImageID OPI comment?
No. That is an Aldus-specific, non-TIFF-standard tag. It is not documented in the TIFF 6.0 standard.

How can I create a list of paragraph tags and properties on the Mac?

ISSUE
How can I make a list of all paragraph tags and their properties in a document using FrameMaker release 5 on the Macintosh?

SOLUTION
FrameMaker 5 on the Macintosh is now scriptable using AppleScript. Using the sample AppleScript included with FrameMaker, "ListProps," this previously tedious process has become greatly simplified. This sample script creates a report for a document that contains the following information: the name of every paragraph format in the Paragraph Catalog and its properties, the paragraph formats used in the document, and the character formats used in the document.

You run this script by double clicking on the icon (in the Samples:Applescripts folder) or loading it into FrameMaker's temporary Script menu and accessing it, then clicking "Run" in the Script Editor.

Is Lucida Math (by Adobe) a font that can be used in equations?

ISSUE
Is Lucida Math (by Adobe) a font that can be used in equations? Is Lucida Math the same as Lucida New Math?

SOLUTION
The online document Customizing Frame Products (pg. 17) and Using FrameMaker Manual (pg. 29-15) refer to "Lucida New Math" as a possible font to use other than symbol in equations. They say: "If you want to use a font other than Symbol, Mathematical Pi, or LucidaNewMath, you must install the font and process it for use with the Frame product."

Lucida New Math (by Y&Y) and Lucida Math (by Adobe) are two different fonts. In order for Lucida Math to be used by the equation editor a math character font mapping file needs to be created. This is detailed in the customizing FrameMaker portion of the online manuals.

UNIX

What to do with email message containing compressed/uu-encoded FrameMaker file

ISSUE
What to do with email message containing compressed/uuencoded FrameMaker file

SOLUTION
A uuencoded and compressed file looks like:

```
begin 666 fsm.chapter1.enc
  M'YVO/)HD,6(D#9LR(&2X@ '#!X@1((Z4<5-
  &3A@Z9<B $),'A!&+;<HT";.F
  M8L*%"B
  ^@4,GS1LW<W2  D!$$3!)OP%L]8A(,&!)4R>.C,K'DSY\Z>5,*<F3.4
  M9E&E1SV^D=/F(E.(-8V\I ,BB1LS4ZNV?-
  D4Q$@Y)>5<KODBB)LQ:*9F] BR MS-
  J:1XZF&3,'1!@W&G\&E5)F#%<F8?*\J2,4*\V1<S#*L:D481*,;>[2U.J&
  MZY"+8=B\.5/VJ<XP/$%\IA-Z=%DB;\;4"=G99YDV<-
  A<+)-2 8\J;M+OZ5N%
  M)O@?OJ&<,;.Z]1DO"D#P4&X&.LWIRY,^!Q/
  &L,NO:=32.8'\.O4J<\HXH 4I'
  M.P@G;XY'ETY]?5#W8,C/
  QVXF")LT9[A!VV%EF,%5>?OM9X179$S$%O@QT$##
... [Lots of lines deleted] ...
```

Here's how to turn this into a FrameMaker file:

1. Save the email message to a file in your /tmp directory using the filename specified in the begin line: /tmp/fsm.chapter1.enc
2. Edit the file and remove the email header line so that the first line in the file is "begin ..."
3. At the UNIX prompt type
   `uudecode fsm.chapter1.enc`
4. This will create a file named fsm.chapter1.Z
5. At the UNIX prompt type
   `uncompress fsm.chapter1.Z`
6. Now you have your FrameMaker file fsm.chapter1
   NOTE: You must follow this order and uudecode before you uncompress the file. Likewise, when wanting to send a file (or instruct a user on how to send a file), it must be compressed and then uuencoded

To send file:

1. Compress the file
   `compress filename`
2. This will create filename.Z
3. Now uuencode this file
   `uuencode filename.Z filename.Z > filename.enc`
   where the first filename.Z is the current compressed file ane the second filename.Z is the name of the file when it is uudecoded and filename.enc is the name of the file after is it uuencoded.

As a courtesy to others on the internet, we discourage the use of email to transfer files over 50K.

Corrupted files; soft versus hard mounts

ISSUE

How do my FrameMaker documents become corrupted/ truncated?

SOLUTION

We recommend customers use "Hard" NFS mounts.

Corrupted or truncated files can be due to soft-mounting filesystems. Hard and Soft NFS mounts were invented by Sun Microsystems. By the very definition of Soft mounts, there are no guarantees that any file that any application writes will actually make it all the way to a soft-mounted disk because network interruption during a save can corrupt the writing-to-disk action.. This is a "feature" of how Sun designed Soft mounts. If this behavior is not acceptable for your files, then you should choose Hard mounts. FrameMaker tries to warn you if a document file that you think you wrote onto a soft-mounted disk didn't really all get put there by NFS, so you're still pretty safe with soft-mounts and FrameMaker if you pay attention to any alerts that FrameMaker puts up after you issue the Save command. Other programs (like vi, mail, etc.) may not have this sort of protection, so it's best to be very careful when using them on soft-mounted disks. If you've got a flakey network, or flakey workstations or hard drives, or if you run experimental versions of SunOS, it's safer to use hard-mounts, since the failure mode will occur much more often.

How do I configure FrameMaker to use Floating Accent keys?

ISSUE

I type a lot of accented characters. Can I change my keyboard so that certain characters become silent accent keys?

SOLUTION

To make FrameMaker 4 for X/Motif understand these silent accent keys, add the following to the file:

`$FMHOME/fminit/usenglish/display/XCommands.ow`

then restart FrameMaker or !ftk, choose ClearCurrentMacros, then click Begin.

```
———begin here———
SunFA_Acute      :1005FF03
**** acute aeiou
<Mo  dify Acutea
        <KeySeqNoLabel  \x1005FF03 a  >>
<Mo  dify Acutee
        <KeySeqNoLabel  \x1005FF03 e  >>
<Mo  dify Acutei
        <KeySeqNoLabel  \x1005FF03 i  >>
<Mo  dify Acuteo
        <KeySeqNoLabel  \x1005FF03 o  >>
<Mo  dify Acuteu
        <KeySeqNoLabel  \x1005FF03 u  >>
<Mo  dify AcuteA
        <KeySeqNoLabel  \x1005FF03 A  >>
<Mo  dify AcuteE
        <KeySeqNoLabel  \x1005FF03 E  >>
<Mo  dify AcuteI
        <KeySeqNoLabel  \x1005FF03 I  >>
<Mo  dify AcuteO
        <KeySeqNoLabel  \x1005FF03 O  >>
<Mo  dify AcuteU
        <KeySeqNoLabel  \x1005FF03 U  >>
SunFA_Tilde      :1005FF02
**** asciitilde ano
<Mo  dify Tildea
        <KeySeqNoLabel  \x1005FF02 a >>
<Mo  dify Tilden
        <KeySeqNoLabel  \x1005FF02 n >>
<Mo  dify Tildeo
        <KeySeqNoLabel  \x1005FF02 o >>
<Mo  dify TildeA
        <KeySeqNoLabel  \x1005FF02 A >>
<Mo  dify TildeN
        <KeySeqNoLabel  \x1005FF02 N >>
<Mo  dify TildeO
        <KeySeqNoLabel  \x1005FF02 O >>
SunFA_Grave      :1005FF00
**** grave aeiou
<Mo  dify Gravea
        <KeySeqNoLabel  \x1005FF00 a >>
<Mo  dify Gravee
        <KeySeqNoLabel  \x1005FF00 e >>
<Mo  dify Gravei
        <KeySeqNoLabel  \x1005FF00 i >>
<Mo  dify Graveo
        <KeySeqNoLabel  \x1005FF00 o >>
<Mo  dify Graveu
        <KeySeqNoLabel  \x1005FF00 u >>
<Mo  dify GraveA
        <KeySeqNoLabel  \x1005FF00 A >>
<Mo  dify GraveE
        <KeySeqNoLabel  \x1005FF00 E >>
<Mo  dify GraveI
        <KeySeqNoLabel  \x1005FF00 I >>
<Mo  dify GraveO
        <KeySeqNoLabel  \x1005FF00 O >>
<Mo  dify GraveU
        <KeySeqNoLabel  \x1005FF00 U >>
SunFA_Diaeresis      :1005FF04
**** dieresis aeiouy
<Mo  dify Diaeresisa
   <KeySeqNoLabel  \x1005FF04 a >>
<Mo  dify Diaeresise
   <KeySeqNoLabel  \x1005FF04 e >>
<Mo  dify Diaeresisi
   <KeySeqNoLabel  \x1005FF04 i >>
<Mo  dify Diaeresiso
   <KeySeqNoLabel  \x1005FF04 o >>
<Mo  dify Diaeresisu
```

```
   <KeySeqNoLabel  \x1005FF04 u >>
<Mo dify Diaeresisy
   <KeySeqNoLabel  \x1005FF04 y >>
<Mo dify DiaeresisA
   <KeySeqNoLabel  \x1005FF04 A >>
<Mo dify DiaeresisE
   <KeySeqNoLabel  \x1005FF04 E >>
<Mo dify DiaeresisI
   <KeySeqNoLabel  \x1005FF04 I >>
<Mo dify DiaeresisO
   <KeySeqNoLabel  \x1005FF04 O >>
<Mo dify DiaeresisU
   <KeySeqNoLabel  \x1005FF04 U >>
<Mo dify DiaeresisY
   <KeySeqNoLabel  \x1005FF04 Y >>
SunFA_Circum    :1005FF01
**** circumflex aeiou
<Mo dify Circuma
      <KeySeqNoLabel  \x1005FF01 a >>
<Mo dify Circume
      <KeySeqNoLabel  \x1005FF01 e >>
<Mo dify Circumi
      <KeySeqNoLabel  \x1005FF01 i >>
<Mo dify Circumo
      <KeySeqNoLabel  \x1005FF01 o >>
<Mo dify Circumu
      <KeySeqNoLabel  \x1005FF01 u >>
<Mo dify CircumA
      <KeySeqNoLabel  \x1005FF01 A >>
<Mo dify CircumE
      <KeySeqNoLabel  \x1005FF01 E >>
<Mo dify CircumI
      <KeySeqNoLabel  \x1005FF01 I >>
<Mo dify CircumO
      <KeySeqNoLabel  \x1005FF01 O >>
<Mo dify CircumU
      <KeySeqNoLabel  \x1005FF01 U >>
SunFA_Cedilla          :1005FF05
**** cedilla=comma c
<Mo dify CedillaC
     <KeySeqNoLabel  \x1005FF05 C  >>
<Mo dify Cedillac
     <KeySeqNoLabel  \x1005FF05 c  >>
————end here————
```

How do I create a macro which does a find/change?

ISSUE

Appendix C of the Using FrameMaker manual has an example of how to create a macro that searches. However, I would like to know how to create a macro which does a find and a change all in one. What steps would I follow?

SOLUTION

To create a macro which does a find and a change:

1. Type !fis to display the Find/Change Parameters dialog box
2. Enter the needed keystrokes to set up the Find and Change values
3. Press Return to activate the Set button when you have completed the setup
4. Type !fin to actually start the find
5. Use one of the following Replace sequences, depending on the required scope of the macro:

```
>From $FMHOME/fminit/usenglish/Commands–
<Command ReplaceOnce
    <Label Replace>
    <KeySequence \!ro>
    <Definition \x232>>
<Command ReplaceAll
    <Label Replace All>
    <KeySequence \!rg>
    <Definition \x233>>
<Command ReplaceAndFindAgain
    <Label Replace and Find Again>
    <KeySequence \!ra>
    <Definition \x234>>
```

So, to replace all you can use !rg, and this will warn you cannot be undone. To clear this alert in a macro, you will need to hit return once more.

Here is a sample which replaces all instances of 'blue' with 'red':

```
<Macro Macro1
<Label Macro1>
<Tr igger ^&>
<Tr iggerLabel ^&>
<Definition \!fis/START_DIALOG ^/Tab +/Tab
\s0/Return /Tab ^ublue/Tab  /Tab /Tab /Tab
/Tab \s0/Return /Tab ^ured/Tab /Tab 1/Tab /
Tab /Return /END_DIALOG \!fin\!rg/
START_DIALOG /Return /END_DIALOG>
<Mo  de NonMath>>
```

Unexpected Results

MAC OS / WINDOWS / UNIX

Q Why doesn't the character formatting in my cross-reference match the source text?

A This problem can have any of several causes. You may be using a version of FrameMaker that predates FrameMaker 5, you may not be using character tags to assign character formatting to your source text, or your source text may use a kind of character formatting that FrameMaker can't carry over to a cross-reference.

In versions of FrameMaker prior to 5, any character formatting applied to the source of a cross-reference doesn't appear in the cross-reference itself. For example, if you were cross-referencing a chapter title called "The ABCs of H2O," the cross-reference to it would read something like "See 'The ABCs of H2O' on page 5."

In FrameMaker 5, it's possible to preserve certain character formatting in your cross-references. Specifically, you can preserve superscripting, subscripting, and font family. There's just one trick: you must apply the character formatting as a character tag. In other words, select the character(s) to which you want to apply character formatting and apply an appropriate character format from the Character Catalog—don't select the formatting characteristics you want from the Format menu.

Why can't I turn off cropped for an anchored frame?

ISSUE

I am trying to turn off cropped for my anchored frame in FrameMaker release 5. Nothing seems to change, and when I go back into Special—Anchored Frame, it is still turned on. How can I turn off cropped?

SOLUTION

This is a bug in FrameMaker release 5. In all cases that we've seen, closing and re-opening the document, restarting FrameMaker and re-opening the document, or saving the file to MIF (use this as a last resort), will allow you to turn off the cropped option.

Why aren't the empty pages in my document being deleted?

ISSUE

I have Delete Empty Pages Before Saving & Printing set in my document. However, when I try to delete pages, the text is deleted but the empty pages are not. Why is this and is there a workaround?

SOLUTION

This information is available in the Using FrameMaker manual: FrameMaker deletes a blank page only if it uses the left or right master page, doesn't contain the start of a flow, and has no layout overrides; otherwise, FrameMaker assumes it's a page you want to keep and does not delete it.

In order to have the blank pages deleted, you will need to apply the left and/or right default master pages to the empty body pages and make sure you do not retain any layout overrides.

How can I get landscape pages to stay landscape when distilling to pdf?

ISSUE

I have a FrameMaker document that has landscape pages in it. When I save it to a PostScript file and distill it using Acrobat v2.0, the landscape pages come out as if they are portrait. I have to turn my head 90 degrees to read the information on the page. How can I fix this?

SOLUTION

This behavior can be seen when attempting to distill a landscape document created in ANY application.

MS Windows platform

On the Windows platform, this behavior has been logged as bug #84760 and there is currently no workaround.

After you have processed the .ps file through the Distiller, you can open the PDF file in Acrobat Exchange and Rotate the landscape pages.

Macintosh platform

On the Macintosh platform, choose Page Set Up from the File Menu Select a Paper Size of 11x17 or Tabloid. (If this is not available, switch PPD's to the HP4V or the Linotronic 330)

Now, when you choose Generate Acrobat Data, and save to a PostScript file, your distilled file will show on screen in the correct orientation.

In addition, a document with mixed landscape and portrait pages will print distill properly when this method is followed.

Why do cross references update even when auto updating is suppressed?

ISSUE

On page 10-19 (Unix) and page 10-18 (Mac/Win) the Using FrameMaker manual states: "If a document contains many cross-references, you can improve its opening and printing times by supressing automatic updating ..."

I have set Automatic Updating of Cross References to be suppressed, but when I print the file the cross references are updated and the document shows that changes have been made to it that need to be saved. Why?

SOLUTION

This is a bug in the FrameMaker release 5 documentation. Suppression of automatic updating applies only when a file is opened.

Why does the color in some CMYK TIFF images appear distorted?

ISSUE

Why does the color in some CMYK TIFF images display and print differently in Photoshop than they do in FrameMaker? For example, in Photoshop, a graphic appears grey and prints grey. In FrameMaker, it displays and prints green.

SOLUTION

When the CMYK TIFF image is viewed onscreen, we have to convert the CMYK channels to RGB. Our algorithm for doing this is pretty simple, especially when compared to Photoshop. We use standard conversion formulas for doing this, while PhotoShop uses a more sophisticated technique.

If the image is printed as a composite image (single page) to a color non-PostScript printer, the image is converted from CMYK to RGB (just like it was to the screen) and the image degradation happens on the printout.

If printed as a composite image to a PostScript printer, we send all of the CMYK image information without conversion. The printer takes over the interpretation of the raw CMYK data. So when the image is printing as a single color page from both FrameMaker and PhotoShop, they look the same.

If printed as process colors, with each of the CMYK layers coming out on a separate plate, then we match Photoshop's results exactly. Since this is the primary benefit of CMYK TIFF, and this is why we support it, we would expect this to work correctly and it does.

This is not considered to be a bug.

Why is the text cut off on my sideheads with a Frame Above?

ISSUE

I have applied a Frame Above to my sideheads and noticed that the tops of certain letters are cut off, even when I print my document. Why is this happening?

SOLUTION

This has been logged as bug #104297. Certain Frame Above's applied to the sidehead area will cut off the tops of some capital letters. The problem is the most evident with the fonts New Century Schoolbook and Helvetica. Also, Times 14 causes the problem upon printing, but it displays correctly. The problem is more obvious with larger fonts, or when text is bolded.

While you may see the problem in an 'in column' paragraph with a Frame Above as well, this is most likely resolved by refreshing the screen.

The workaround is to apply a fill of None to the reference frame on the Reference Page.

Why do some windows go off the screen when I use gotolinkfitwin?

ISSUE

I'm using the gotolinkfitwin and previouslinkfitwin hypertext commands. In some cases when the document is opened, the window goes off the bottom of the screen. How can I prevent this?

SOLUTION

The gotolinkfitwin executes a gotolink, which displays the document page in the current window and then resizes the window to fit the page. FrameMaker maintains the top and left positions of the window and expands down and right to accommodate the larger page. If you are executing a gotolinkfitwin from a smaller sized document, to a larger one, it is possible that the window will go off the bottom of the screen. The workaround is to position smaller documents toward the top and left of the screen to leave room for the window to expand. Enhancement request #105830 has been logged to have the gotolinkfitwin/previous-link-fitwin hypertext commands reposition the window in these cases.

Why can't I align multiline equations along the equal sign?

ISSUE

According to the documentation on page 29-9, I can align items in a vertical list and lines in a multiline equation along the left or right sides, the centers, or the equal signs.

This works for me in a vertical list, but not in a multiline equation. How can I get around this?

SOLUTION

Athough the alignments of Left, Right, and Center work for a multiline equation, Left of = and Right of = do not. There are two work-arounds:

1. Use a vertical list instead. For subsequent lines, you may want to use the Uequal Operator (labelled '=?').
2. Use manual alignment points., accomplished as follows:
   A. Type in the first line, up to where you would like the second to start.
      `EX:          x = a + b + c`
   B. Choose Line Breaking—Set Manual from the Positioning page.
   C. Start typing in the next line.
      `EX:          = c + b + a`
   D. If more lines are required, continue as above, inserting the manual line break and then typing the next line.
   E. Put your insertion point before the equal sign in the first line.
   F. Choose Alignment—Set Manual.

Why don't text insets update on open or with Edit-Update References?

ISSUE

I have imported a text file by reference in a document. I have made a change to the text file, but it is not updated when I re-open my document even though my text inset is marked for Automatic Update. I am also unable to update the reference by choosing Edit-Update References. Why is this happening?

SOLUTION

This behavior can occur when the machine running FrameMaker and the machine which owns the file system don't agree as to what time it is.

Text Insets are only updated if they are "stale". If you double click on the inset you will see when the text file was last modified (Source Last Modified:) and when the reference in the document was last updated (Last Update:). The reference will only be updated if Last Update is older than Source Last Modified. Source Last Modified gets its date from the machine where the file is located. Last Update gets its date from the machine running FrameMaker.

Example (UNIX):

FrameMaker is running on my machine, maxwell, but my text files are located on another machine, dune. If I check the time on these machines (at the same instance), I get the following:

```
maxwell= date  Wed Jul 19 09:34:55 PDT 1995
dune= date  Wed Jul 19 09:34:21 PDT 1995
```

dune's time is 34 seconds slower than maxwell's.

This means that I must modify my text file 35 or more seconds after the time of Last Update in order for the text inset to update when opening my document or when choosing Edit-Update References. Note that the time of Last Update only changes when an actual update occurs.

Double-clicking on an inset and choosing Update Now will update the reference regardless of time differences.

Why can't the symbol font be made bold in FrameMaker?

ISSUE

Why can't the symbol font be made bold? MS Word on the Macintosh allows the symbol font to be made bold. How does MS Word accomplish this?

SOLUTION

There is no bold symbol in PostScript, and FrameMaker does not "synthetically" bold the symbol font.

MS Word uses a custom font, called MTExt that enables this capability.

Why do I get a Compare Document when the documents are identical?

ISSUE

Why do I get a Compare Document when the documents I compared are identical?

SOLUTION

This will happen if one or both of the documents being compared have graphics which can not be displayed due to insufficient memory allocated to FrameMaker. The Document Compare utility is comparing the data or insets in both files. If a graphic is not displaying in one of the files but the corresponding graphic *is* displaying in the other document then FrameMaker detects a change because the information regarding the inset of the graphic is different.

With tables, why are flows selected differently in FrameMaker release 5?

ISSUE

Using FrameMaker Release 5, I have placed my insertion point in a table cell and selected Edit -> Select All in Flow. The complete flow is highlighted. In previous versions of FrameMaker only the table cell is highlighted. Why did this change? How can I select only the text in the table?

SOLUTION

In previous releases, the complete flow should have been selected when choosing Select All in Flow from a table cell. Engineering fixed the problem in FrameMaker release 5.

A flow is the text that streams through a series of connected columns. A table cell content is considered part of the text flow in which the cell is contained. This is why autonumbering advances through a table.

What should the Open Source button in Text Inset Properties do?

ISSUE

What is the expected behavior for the Open Source button in the Text Inset Properties dialog? Why doesn't the Open Source button open the file in the application that created it?

SOLUTION

The Open Source button in the Text Inset Properties dialog is designed to open the source as a FrameMaker document. There are a two things to mention in this regard. First, Chapter 3 of the Using FrameMaker Manual states that "You can open the source of a text inset from the document by clicking Open Source in the Text Inset Properties dialog box." This is not clear as to which application is opening it, but FrameMaker is intended. Second, this behavior is different than the "Open" button in the Object Properties dialog when dealing with graphics imported by reference (this will open the graphic in the original application).

Using Publish and Subscribe is a possible workaround for Macintosh users.

Why does text disappear behind an anchored frame?

ISSUE

I have an anchored frame with it's anchor position set to Run into Paragraph. The anchored frame spans an entire text column. Why does a portion of my text disappear beneath the anchored Frame?

SOLUTION

It is possible for the text to run beneath an anchored frame when the anchored frame is set to Run into Paragraph and the frame spans the entire text column. This occurs because the text is trying to run into the anchored frame either on the left or right side (depending on the alignment of the anchored frame). Thus, when there is no room for the text to run into the anchored frame due to the frame's width, the run into paragraph feature still tries to wrap text around the frame. Thus causing the text to disappear beneath the frame. If you set the anchored frame to Below Current Line, the text should reappear.

The Run into Paragraph setting is behaving according to design. You should not set an anchored frame to Run into Paragraph when it spans the entire text column.

Why are my character tags not showing in my TOC?

ISSUE

In previous releases of FrameMaker, if I applied a character tag rather than ad hoc formatting to certain words in a file, and then generated a TOC from this file, my character tags would remain. In FrameMaker release 5, none of my character tags are coming across. Why is this?

SOLUTION

Unfortunately the only workaround at this time it to retag the characters after generating the file.

This bug has been fixed in FrameMaker release 5.0.1.

Why are some paragraphs in the Composite Document incorrect?

ISSUE

I ran the Document Compare Utility on two documents and there are words in my composite document that are out of order and the condition tags that get applied to deleted and inserted text are applied to the wrong text. Why is this happening?

SOLUTION

Unfortunately, this bug was introduced in FrameMaker release 5. The bug number is 96242. For each paragraph that has a variable, cross-reference, or conditional text range, any differences that follow them (in the same paragraph) will cause the Composite Document to be built incorrectly.

The Composite Document can end up being only slightly off to really unreadable. Words end up out of order, and the delete/insert condition tags get applied to the wrong text.

This bug happens on a paragraph basis, so the next paragraph will be correct until the problem is encountered again.

There is no known workaround at this time.

Why don't paths specified in MIF resolve correctly?

ISSUE

Why don't paths specified in MIF resolve correctly?

SOLUTION

The MIF parser does not handle include statements correctly. If you have an include statement before other statements that specify paths then these other statements are not interpreted correctly. This is true for any MIF statement that contains a path such as external cross-references, referenced graphics, and book components.

For external cross-references and imported graphics you will get errors reporting BadFileName. For a book there are no errors but the book window will be empty.

For example, when the following MIF book file is opened there would be no book components listed in the book window:

```
<Book 4.0>
include (formats.mif)
<BookComponent
    <FileName '<c\>Newfile'>
    <StartPageSide ReadFromFile >
    <PageNumbering Continue >
  <PgfNumbering Continue >
    <PageNumPrefix ''>
   <PageNumSuffix ''>
    <DefaultPrint Yes >
    <DefaultApply Yes >
 > # end of BookComponent
 # End of Book
```

This is because the MIF parser incorrectly parses the statement because of the previous "include".

Workarounds:

1. put the include after any MIF statements that have pathnames
2. create a separate file that contains the MIF statements which have pathnames. For example,

```
     <Book 4.0>
include (formats.mif)
include (components.mif)
 # End of Book
 where componenets.mif contains the
following:
<BookComponent
    <FileName '<c\>Newfile'>
    <StartPageSide ReadFromFile >
    <PageNumbering Continue >
   <PgfNumbering Continue >
    <PageNumPrefix ''>
   <PageNumSuffix ''>
    <DefaultPrint Yes >
    <DefaultApply Yes >
 > # end of BookComponent
```

Where is the composite document when comparing 2 book files?

ISSUE

The manual says that I can compare 2 book files and get both a Summary and a Composite (CMP) document. When

I do this, only a Summary document opens. Is there a CMP document?

SOLUTION

A composite document is created for each file of the book that has changes. The CMP files are generated and saved into the directory of the newer book. The CMP files are not opened automatically, so it appears as though they have not been generated.

Why do table/figure titles wrap before the edge of the table/figure?

ISSUE

I have a table title (or a figure title) that left aligned and is wrapping before the text reaches the edge of the column or even before the text spans all the way across the table. Why?

SOLUTION

This can occur if you are going from a page with multiple text columns to a page with one text column. If you have a page has mutiple columns and you insert table, the table title extends only as far as the column width. If the table continues onto another page that has a single text column of greater width, then the title will wrap as if it were in the narrow column on the previous page.

Similarly, this can occur if the table anchor is in the multiple text column page but the table is in the one text column page, i.e. the table was set to start at Top of Page.

To work around this, insert the table title in a header row which is set up to straddle all of the columns in the table. If this is a figure title in an anchored frame, insert the anchor in a paragraph of its own which is tagged to start at top of column (or page).

Why is my anchored frame on the next page in FrameMaker release 5?

ISSUE

In FrameMaker 4, I created an anchored frame that was longer than the text column but had cropped turned on. It was on the same page as the anchor symbol itself. When I open this document in FrameMaker release 5, the anchor symbol is on one page but the anchored frame is on the next page. Why is this happening?

SOLUTION

The behavior in FrameMaker release 5 is correct. Since the anchored frame does not really fit within the text frame, FrameMaker release 5 places the anchored frame on the next page hoping to gain more room. However, there may still not be enough space to display the entire frame. If this is happening to you, change the anchored frame height so that it can fit within the text frame with no problem. The anchored frame should not be taller than the text frame.

Why is my anchored frame jumping to the next page in FM release 5?

ISSUE

I have an anchored frame that extends to the bottom of my text frame. When I save the file to MIF and reopen it, the anchored frame jumps to the next page.

Additionally, if I change the anchored frame to floating, it will also jump to the next page. If I then turn off floating, the anchored frame does not jump back to its original position. Why is this happening?

SOLUTION

These situations are both related to a round off error in FrameMaker release 5.

A similar bug also exists in earlier versions of FrameMaker, namely, if you turn on floating in FrameMaker 4, the anchored frame will also jump to the next page. However, if you turn floating off, it will jump back to its original position.

WORKAROUND

Before saving your document to MIF, change the Units under View-Options to Picas, and the anchored frame will not jump to the next page.

To get the anchored frame back to its original location after turning floating off, decrease the height of the anchored frame until it jumps back to the previous page. Then you can resize it back to the bottom edge of the text frame.

Why does the WordPerfect filter fail to filter a Master document?

ISSUE

Why doesn't FrameMaker release 5 filter my WordPerfect 6.0 master document? On the UNIX platfrom, I get a core dump. On the MS Windows platform, I get Fatal Error 00532965. On the Macintosh platform I get the message "Filter encountered an error..." and the conversion fails.

SOLUTION

Check to see if you have used the Import Text by Reference feature of WordPerfect. The WordPerfect filter can not handle this; bug # 98813 has been logged against the filter.

The workaround is to edit the WordPerfect document and remove the Import Text by Reference links.

Why does micropositioning of diacriticals disappear?

ISSUE

I have used micropositioning and spacing to position certain diacriticals in my equation. Now, when I open the file, all of my micropositioning and spacing is gone. What has happened?

SOLUTION

This is a very unfortunate bug in FrameMaker 4. If you do the following after positioning a diacritical using micropositioning or spacing:

- save/quit/open the file
- make a change to the file
- save and quit the file

Then all of the positioning will be lost when you open the file again.

The only workaround is to add your micropositioning and spacing after you are through making changes to the file.

Why does conditional text loose its condition after I Generate/Update?

ISSUE

I have a document that uses conditional text. In some of text that is conditional, I have cross-references which use a <Default Para Font> character tag. When I Generate/Update the the book or file, why does the conditional text that contains the cross-references lose the condition?

SOLUTION

The problem of conditional text "jumping" out of the condition when the <Default Para Font> is used in a cross-reference has been logged as bug #91073. The problem only appears to happen when the file is Generated/Updated.

WINDOWS

Q Why am I unable to save documents to a network drive? I get the warning: "Can't open <path><filename> for writing. Change the write permission for the file or directory, or use the Save As command to specify a directory and file to which you have write access. Then try again."

A By default FrameMaker won't save files to a network that doesn't support long file names, even when the name you've specified follows the "8.3" DOS file-naming conventions (eight or fewer characters followed by a period and a three-character extension). That's because subsequent files it might need to save along with your main document file (lock files, backup files, and so forth) would have names longer than 8.3 characters once FrameMaker added its usual extensions to those file names. Networks that don't support long file names include Novell Netware 3.x and earlier networks.

To solve this, select "Preferences..." from the File menu. In the "Preferences" dialog box, select the "Windows 3.1" cross-platform file-naming option and click the "Set" button. This will ensure that all files written by FrameMaker will be 8.3 or fewer characters.

NOTE: We recommend caution when saving your only version of any document (from FrameMaker or another application) directly to a network server, especially if that server has a history of instability. We recommend you keep a backup copy of such files whenever possible.

Q I've noticed that scrolling slows way down in documents that contain equations. What's going on?

A Chances are that you've selected a PostScript printer driver as your default Windows printer driver, and because FrameMaker makes a faulty system call to ATM and the TrueType font manager (and it makes a relatively large number of these calls when you're using a PostScript printer driver), your screen redraw can become very slow under these circumstances.

To work around this problem, select a PCL printer driver in FrameMaker. Choose "Print Setup..." from the File menu and choose a PCL printer driver (if a PCL printer driver is not installed, please consult your Windows users' guide for information on how to install one). Then, when you're ready to print your document, select "Print Setup..." from the File menu again and set your printer to the PostScript device you want to print to.

Note that switching between a PCL and PostScript driver may cause formatting changes in your document if you're using any fonts that are built into those devices. (For example, Zapf Dingbats is built into PostScript printers and is therefore available when you have a PostScript printer selected. Unless you also have a version of Zapf Dingbats installed in Windows with ATM, Zapf Dingbats won't be available when you've selected a PCL printer.) If you do need to switch between a PCL and a PostScript printer driver, make sure that all fonts in your document are ones installed via ATM or the TrueType font manager—such fonts will print on either PostScript or PCL printers.

Why do documents appear to have shrunk?

ISSUE

When I open files created with FrameMaker 3 or FrameMaker 4 in FrameMaker release 5, they appear to have shrunk. I have to zoom to a high zoom level (140%) to even read the documents. Why is this happening?

SOLUTION

When you install FrameMaker 5, the installation will detect the diagonal size of your monitor and display the information. This value is written to 'maker.ini' as the MonitorSize parameter.

During the installation of FrameMaker 3 and FrameMaker 4 for Windows, the value written to MonitorSize was '0in'. It was necessary for the user to edit 'maker.ini' to properly set this value.

If your documents were created in FrameMaker 3 or 4 with MonitorSize set to '0in' when the files are opened in FrameMaker Release 5, they will appear to have shrunk (display at a much lower zoom level).

To resolve the problem:

- Close FrameMaker release 5.
- Open 'maker.ini' in a text editor; this file resides in your FrameMaker home directory.
- Under the [Preferences] section there is a line that reads: MonitorSize=
- Set MonitorSize to whatever the setting was when the documents were created (probably '0in').
- Save 'maker.ini' as a text file.
- Reopen FrameMaker Release 5. Your documents will display as they did in previous versions of the product.

Why do I get a gray box when pasting an OLE object into FrameMaker?

ISSUE

I am pasting an OLE object into FrameMaker version 5.1. Why do I get a gray box with no facets on the object?

SOLUTION

The workaround is to save the file. When you reopen the file, the graphic does display properly retaining the OLE link.

How to Paste Text from Word Into FrameMaker so the Text Is Editable

ISSUE

When you paste text from Microsoft Word into FrameMaker 5 for Windows, the text is not editable.

SOLUTIONS

Use the Paste Special command to paste the text into FrameMaker in RTF format:

1. In Word, copy the text to the clipboard.
2. In FrameMaker, paste the text by choosing Edit > Paste Special.
3. Select Rich Text Format, then click OK.

OR: Modify the Maker.ini file so that "RTF" is at the beginning of the ClipboardFormatsPriorities list, then restart FrameMaker and paste the text using the Paste command:

1. Make a backup copy of the Maker.ini file.
2. Open the original Maker.ini file, located in the Maker5 directory, in a text editor that can save in text-only format.
3. Find the following line:
   ```
   ClipboardFormatsPriorities=OLE, EMF, META,
   DIB, BMP, MIF, RTF, TEXT
   ```
4. Move "RTF" to the beginning of the list, so the line reads:
   ```
   ClipboardFormatsPriorities=RTF, OLE, EMF,
   META, DIB, BMP, MIF, TEXT
   ```
   NOTE: Entries in the list must be separated by commas.
5. Save the Maker.ini file in text-only format.
6. Restart FrameMaker.
7. Copy the text in Word, then paste it in FrameMaker using the Paste command.

ADDITIONAL INFORMATION

When you paste text into FrameMaker, FrameMaker looks at the first item in the ClipboardFormatsPriorities line of the Maker.ini file for information on how to treat the text. Text pasted in the default format, OLE, is not editable in FrameMaker. RTF text is editable in FrameMaker, and retains its original formatting.

You can paste individual selections of text in RTF format using the Paste Special command. You can also make RTF the default format for pasted text by modifying the Maker.ini file, so it lists the RTF format first in the ClipboardFormatsPriorities line.

OLE (Object Linking and Embedding) enables one application to link or embed objects from another application. In order to edit an OLE object, you must double-click on it to launch the application that created the object, and then edit the object in that application.

MAC OS

Why are color EPSF images displayed as grayscale in FrameMaker 5.1?

ISSUE

I have a FrameMaker 5.1 file which contains imported color EPSF graphics. Why do these graphics display as grayscale?

SOLUTION

This is a bug in FrameMaker 5.1. Bug number 105335 has been logged.

Any EPSF graphic which contains black and spot colors, but no process colors, will display as grayscale in FrameMaker version 5.1. There is currently no workaround to this problem.

Why does FM use the symbol font when printing a registered trademark?

ISSUE

FrameMaker for the Macintosh version 4.x displays the registered trademark symbol correctly in all fonts. Upon printing, however, FrameMaker switches to the Symbol font, printing the Symbol font's similar serif glyph which is a different character code, and which is accessible from the keyboard with "option-[".

SOLUTION

FrameMaker is switching characters from the standard Apple encoding to the Symbol encoding according to the original LaserWriter encoding table, which is compatible with the earliest PostScript printers. With the advent of the LaserWriter Plus, Adobe expanded their standard character sets to allow fonts to have their own versions of glyphs such as Registered Trademark.

Using a more modern "symbol switch" table will allow use of those glyphs in all modern fonts and printers, but will make them print as blank on very old printers. Since most such printers will probably be out of service after the release of FrameMaker 4, it seems reasonable to go with the new tables in a future release of FrameMaker.
FrameMaker release 5 does resolve this issue.
For users with verisons earlier than FrameMaker release 5, there is a a user patch for people who don't mind getting their hands dirty with ResEdit and character translation tables:

Open the FrameMaker application with ResEdit and find resource CMAP 1000. This is a 256 byte table which translates symbol switch characters only from Apple standard encoding to Adobe Symbol encoding. If an entry is 0, this marks it as NOT being a symbol switch character, so you can set the entries for characters which you need from a particular font to 0.

Why can't I double click to open FM 4 files in FrameMaker release 5?

ISSUE
I upgraded to FrameMaker release 5. When I double click on FrameMaker 4 files, I get a message that the application which created the files could not be found. Why?

SOLUTION
Prior to FrameMaker release 5, all Frame products had the same creator, Fram. We kept the same creator because this provided the desired double-click behavior for users as they migrated to newer releases of FrameMaker. However, when upgrading from FrameMaker 3 to FrameMaker 4 there was some confusion over which version of FrameMaker would get launched when both versions were installed on a system . Users reported that FrameMaker was launch when they wanted FrameViewer and requested changes to this behavior.

Based on customer feedback, the creator for FrameMaker release 5 was changed from Fram to Fra5. Therefore, FrameMaker release 5 is not recognized as the creator of FrameMaker 4 files. FrameMaker 4 files need to be opened in FrameMaker release 5 via the Open dialog box or by dragging the FrameMaker 4 file on top of the FrameMaker release 5 icon (or an alias of it).

An option if you have System 7.5 is to use the Macintosh Easy Open Control Panel. If you double click a FrameMaker 4 file and the FrameMaker 4 application is not found, Easy Open displays a dialog box which suggests other applications for opening the file. Choose to open the FrameMaker 4 file in FrameMaker release 5 and Easy Open will store this selection and automatically select the same application in it's dialog box the next time a FrameMaker 4 file is double clicked. If you do not want the Easy Open dialog box to come up each time you wish to open a FrameMaker 4 file in FrameMaker release 5, turn off the Always show dialog box option in the Macintosh Easy Open Control panel (by accesssing it under the Apple menu). Easy Open is provided with System 7.5 but does work with System 7.0.1 and later.

Please note that Frv5 is the the creator for FrameViewer, FrameReader, and FrameMaker release 5 files saved as View Only. These changes to the creator for the FrameMaker release 5 family prevent the wrong application from being launched when different versions and different Frame products are installed on a system. Additionally, these changes to the creator allow users to distinguish between files of different FrameMaker versions when viewed by Name in the Finder.

Why are MM fonts in FM3 docs reformatted when opened in FM4?

ISSUE
I created a file in FrameMaker 3 and used Adobe Multiple Master fonts. Now when I open the file in Framemaker 4 I get a message that the fonts cannot be found and will be substituted. The exact same Multiple Master fonts are installed on my Mac. Why are the fonts not being found?

SOLUTION
FrameMaker 3 was not designed with Adobe Multiple Master fonts in mind. For this reason, although they barely work, the names that FrameMaker 3 gives them are incorrect. FrameMaker 4 fully supports Multiple Master fonts. However, it cannot support the old FrameMaker 3.0 names. For this reason, you will experience font errors and will have to reassign fonts when upgrading a 3.0 document which uses Multiple Master fonts. Fortunately, we have taken steps, starting in FrameMaker 4.0, to avoid this problem in the future by storing more information in the FrameMaker file format (both binary and MIF).

UNIX

Q I've noticed that after exiting FrameMaker 5, the colors it posted to the colormap are not released. Is there any way to force FrameMaker to release the colors it uses when I exit?

A Yes. One way to do so, of course, is to restart your window manager. But there's a much better solution and it's not very difficult. Essentially all you have to do is make some simple edits to two X resources so that FrameMaker won't permanently post data to the standard colormap. But before we go into the details, here's some background information.

Created by the X Window System, a standard colormap allows multiple applications to share the system colormap. When FrameMaker 5 starts, it looks for two X resources ("Maker.standardColorCubeName" and "Maker.standardGrayRampName") to determine if it should use a standard colormap that already exists.

If FrameMaker locates these resources and they aren't blank, FrameMaker checks to see if there are properties on the root window with matching names. If it successfully finds the properties, it uses that standard colormap—probably posted by another application—and then starts.

On the other hand, if FrameMaker locates these X resources, they aren't blank, and FrameMaker can't locate matching names from the root window, FrameMaker creates a standard colormap using the information specified in the "Maker.targetColorCube" and "Maker.targetGrayRamp" resources to determine what the color cube and gray ramp will look like. It then posts this standard colormap to the root window so other applications can use it.

The problem is that once a standard property has been posted, the only way to remove it is to restart the X Server. This is why the colors are not released when FrameMaker exits and why you've been experiencing this problem. If you want to prevent the permanent posting of the standard colormap properties, set the following X resources in your $HOME/.Xdefaults file:

```
Maker.standardColorCubeName:
Maker.standardGrayRampName:
```

There should be nothing, not even a space, after the colons shown above. These empty strings tell FrameMaker not to post the standard colormap distributions, and to delete the color allocations upon application exit.

Why doesn't FrameMaker release the colors it uses when I exit?

ISSUE

I've found that after exiting FrameMaker release 5, the colormap is not restored so sometimes my other applications don't start. What can I do to control this?

SOLUTION

A standard colormap is a creation of the X Window System that allows multiple applications to share the system colormap. When FrameMaker release 5 starts, it looks for 2 resources (Maker.standardColorCubeName and Maker.-standardGrayRampName) to determine if it should use a standard colormap that is already existing.

If FrameMaker locates these resources and they are non-blank, FrameMaker checks to see if there are properties on the root window with matching names. If it successfully finds the properties it uses that standard colormap, and then starts.

If FrameMaker locates these X resources and they are non-blank but FrameMaker can't locate matching names from the root window, then FrameMaker will create a standard colormap using the inforamtion specified in the targetColorCube and targetGrayRamp resources to determine what the color cube and gray ramp will look like. It then posts this standard colormap to the root window so other applications can use it.

The problem is once a standard property has been posted, the only way to remove it is to restart the X Server. This is why the colors are not released when FrameMaker exits. If you want to prevent the permanent posting of the standard colormap properties, set the following X resources in your $HOME/.Xdefaults file:

```
Maker.standardColorCubeName:
Maker.standardGrayRampName:
```

There should be nothing, not even a space, after the colons shown above. These empty strings tell FrameMaker to not post the standard colormap distributions, and to delete the color allocations upon application exit.

Why is FrameMaker release 5 slower than FrameMaker 4?

ISSUE

FrameMaker release 5 seems to take longer to load and is overall slower than FrameMaker 4. What are the reasons for this?

SOLUTION

FrameMaker release 5 will take longer to load compared to FrameMaker 4 because:

- It is a larger application with additional features.
- There are more api clients to initialize. The api clients are:
  wordcount
  clickprint (enables you to print online manuals)
  tutorialclient (allows you to run the online tutorial)
  miftortf (filter to save FrameMaker documents to RTF)
  htmllite (filter to save FrameMaker documents to HTML)
  If you don't plan to use any of these clients you can start maker with the option -noapi.
- It will take longer to load a FrameMaker 4 documents because it has to convert it to FrameMaker release 5 format.

FrameMaker release 5 is slower when opening and working in documents because:

- Many things such as cross-references are updated upon opening. You can suppress this. See Related Records for more information.
- The X resource Maker.clientBitmapSize is set to 5000000 by default; in FrameMaker 4 it was set to only 600000. This means that more memory is being allocated for the display of bitmaps and fonts.
- There is a new resource, Maker.colorDither. Refer to Relatd Records for information that explains this resource as well as the Maker.clientBitmapSize resource.
- The algorithms for displaying graphics have been changed to incorporate straddles, runaround graphics and the new text frames. Given the number of windows available at any given time, no matter what course we take, we're looking at one of two evils: 1) over-refreshing or 2) lack of refreshing which results in screen garbage and inaccurate displays.

It is important to know that FrameMaker, like most X applications (including the X server) does not release the swap space it has used until the application is exited. Refer to Related Records for more details. We suggest that you restart FrameMaker every 1 to 2 days depending on how much you use it. Keep an eye on the amount of available swap space you have with the command pstat -s:

sunos 4.1.x

```
% pstat -s  17996k allocated + 2376k re-
  served = 20372k used, 54468k available
```

solaris 2.x

```
% swap -s  total: 42044k bytes allocated +
  6992k reserved = 49036k used, 21796k
  available
```

FrameMaker release 5 requires a minimum of 40MB of available swap. You'll need more if you are running other applications (like FrameMaker 4) or if you are working with large graphics, tables, and book files.

Additionally,

- You may get many keysym errors at start up if you are not running X11R5. See Related Records for more details.
- You can suppress start up messages and the splash screen using X resources and/or command line options. See Related Records for more details.

Why are some of my colored equations printing as black?

ISSUE

I have applied the color Red to my equations via the Character Designer. When I print them, about every other equation prints as black. Sometimes the equation will be all black except for one symbol. How can I avoid this?

SOLUTION

We have seen this a few times, and the workaround is to change the color via the tools palette. For example:

1. Remove all character formatting by selecting the text in the equation and choosing 'default para font' from the Character Catalog.
2. Select the equation as an object, and change the color via the tools palette, either from the Color popup, or under Properties.

When the color is set in this manner equations print in color.

Application Errors

MAC OS / WINDOWS / UNIX

What does "invalid action object" mean in Adobe Acrobat?

ISSUE

I've got a very large book file. When I print to PostScript and generate a PDF file, all the hyperlinks are there. However, when you click on them, you get the error message "invalid action object". Why is this happening?

SOLUTION

You have encountered the "4K named reference limit" in Adobe Acrobat. This is an internal limitation of Acrobat Exchange and Acrobat Reader 2.0.

In order for FrameMaker to create hyperlinks in a book consisting of several documents, it generates "named references" to places that you might hyperlink to. A hyperlink can then point to a named reference rather than a specific page number and geometric position within that page. Unfortunately, there is a limit of about 4000 of these in Acrobat's own database even though the PostScript files created by FrameMaker and the PDF files created by the Acrobat distiller are OK.

The best workaround for now is to print the book as separate files. Select the book and print as normal, but when you get the save file dialog for saving the PostScript file, navigate to a destination directory and use a * as the file name. This will create a separate file for each document in your book, but it will limit the named references in each generated PS file to those that are needed to hyperlink within the book. This is different from printing each document in the book individually where potentially many more references may be generated because FrameMaker isn't sure what other documents may link into the one you are printing.

One final note, the files need to stay as separate, interlinked pdf files. Cross-file hyperlinks do work, so the result is pretty much the same except you get multiple windows in Exchange/Reader.

Why am I getting Internal Error 22E108 (150996206, 23121856 on Mac)?

ISSUE

When opening a FrameMaker release 5 document which contains some text insets, FrameMaker crashes. On my Mac, I get the error 150996206, 23121856 when opening the file. On my SunOS machine I see Internal Error 18F160 and on my Solaris 2 machine I see 22E108. Why is FrameMaker crashing?

SOLUTION

This is a bug in FrameMaker release 5.0 (bug #97305). It occurs when a FrameMaker document imports a text inset more than once (or on the Mac, when you have the same edition subscribed to more than once in a document).

To verify if this is the case in your file, generate a List of References and include text insets. You should see the same file listed twice.

The current workaround on the Mac is to publish the edition more than once. So if you need to refer to the information 3 times in your document, create three seperate editions. On the UNIX platforms you would need to import the file by copy instead of by reference.

Fortunately this bug was fixed in FrameMaker 5.0.1.

Why does FrameMaker release 5 crash or report errors with Word 6 files?

ISSUE

When I try to import Word 6 files into FrameMaker release 5, I get the error:

UNIX

The filter encountered an error and could not complete the translation.

OR: running word2mif from the command line: Input file not a MSWord file.

Macintosh

Unable to read filter output file. 30113:0 and in the API CLient Console Window it says: Input file not a MSWord file.

Windows

The filter encountered an error and could not complete the translation.

Why do I get this error, and how can I import my Word 6 files?

SOLUTION

There is a bug in the MS Word filter that shipped with FrameMaker release 5 for all platforms. This filter will fail with most, but not all Word 6 files.

This bug has been fixed in the maintenance release of FrameMaker release 5, version 5.0.1. Refer to Related Records for information on this release.

The error message you've encountered may occur for reasons other than this bug. If the problem persists with version 5.0.1, please contact Technical Support to troubleshoot the problem further.

Before the release of version 5.0.1 we released an updated filter for Windows FrameMaker release 5.0 only. This filter is now included in version 5.0.1, however it is still available on our online services.

What does "File is not 1K size" mean?

ISSUE

When I try to open a File, I get the error "File is not 1K size" and FrameMaker does not open the file. What does this error mean?

SOLUTION

FrameMaker adds bytes to binary (FASL) files at save time to round off their size to 1K chunks. This error message appears when a document's size, in bytes, is not a multiple of 1024.

On the UNIX platform, you can check a given file by using the command:

```
ls -l filename | awk '{print $4 / 1024 " x
  1024 bytes."}'
```

For example, using one of the FrameMaker release 5 demo files:

```
ls -l chapter1 | awk '{print $4 / 1024 " x
  1024 bytes."}'
```

will return

```
69 x 1024 bytes.
```

This would indicate that a file is ok.

If the byte count is not evenly divisible by 1024, then the bytes in the file are not the same as when FrameMaker saved the file (typically this occurs because the file has been truncated). If this occurs, we would recommend using a backup of the file; either one made by FrameMaker (a .backup file) if it exists or a backup you've made.

WINDOWS

With FM for MS Windows, what does the unavailable fonts error msg mean?

ISSUE

Why do I get the message "Unavailable Fonts" when I open FrameMaker documents, and how can I fix this?

SOLUTION

This message appears when a document is opened which uses fonts that are not available to it from the current system. For example, the FrameMaker Help documents and Sample documents use Adobe PS fonts. If these fonts and the Adobe Type Manager (ATM) have not been installed on the system, then FrameMaker is unable to access the fonts for display in the document. The Alert box is to notify the user that these fonts will be remapped to similar, available fonts.

Troubleshoot your "unavailable fonts" message one step at a time as follows:

1. In FrameMaker go to File/Preferences and check "Show File Translation Errors". Open a document with unavailable fonts and click OK to remap fonts. Use the ALT-TAB keyboard shortcut to get to the Frame Console. (Press the ALT key and hold it while tabbing through the selection of programs currently running in Windows. When Frame Console appears in the selection window, release the ALT key and TAB. The focus will be transferred to the Frame Console program. You can use this feature to return to FrameMaker or any other running program in Windows.) The Frame Console will contain a list of the unavailable fonts and the fonts to which they have been remapped.
2. If a TrueType font is missing, go to Program Manager/Main/Control Panel/Fonts and make sure that the TT font is on the list. If not, add it. If it is on the list, then click the TrueType button. Make sure the "Enable TrueType Fonts" option is selected.
3. While in this dialog box, if an Adobe font is missing, make sure that "Show Only TrueType Fonts in Applications" is NOT checked. This will block any non- TrueType font.

   Next go to Program Manager/ Main/ATM Control Panel and make sure the ATM is turned on. Check to see if the font is in the ATM control panel. If the font is in ATM and is not available in or any other Windows applications, then go to ATM and choose the ADD button. Select the directory in which the fonts are installed on your hard drive. Once you are in the right directory, you will see the fonts show up in the dialog box. ADD ALL OF THE FONTS.

4. What type of a printer do you have installed? Because FrameMaker is WYSIWYG it looks to Windows for the list of fonts for the default printer. You must have either a PostScript or PCL printer set as a default in Windows. Go to Program Manager/Main/Control Panel/ Printers to check the default printer. If a postscript or PCL driver is not set as default, set one of these drivers as default.

   There have been cases when the printer driver has been corrupted. From the Printers dialog box, click Setup and then About. If you get an alert at this point, then copy new printer driver files over the old ones in the Windows/System subdirectory.

5. If it is necessary to change the printer driver, then it may be necessary to add the Adobe fonts again. With ATM 2.02 and later, an installation of the fonts and the font manager affects the default printer ONLY! This was not documented by Adobe until version 2.5. Thus, many times the fonts do not show up in FrameMaker because the default printer has been changed since ATM was installed. This is in no way specific to FrameMaker. With the exception of Word2 and WordPerfect6, if the font is not available in FrameMaker, it will not be available in any Windows application. The card that comes with ATM states that if the printer is changed, the fonts must be added one time. This builds a list for the print device in the WIN.INI file. Windows applications are told about the fonts *from* Windows, usually at start-up. FrameMaker checks the print device to see what the printer is. The font list is acquired as part of what is asked for at the start up of FrameMaker.

What happens when I change the default printer in Windows?

ISSUE

I changed the default printer while FrameMaker was running. Now when I go back to FrameMaker I get a message that: "Printer information has changed. This may effect the formatting of your document."

What does this mean, and why is it happening?

SOLUTION

NOTE: The information below pertains to Windows 3.1 applications and does not pertain to Word 2, Notepad, or Windows Write.

What is Windows doing: When you make a printer the default in Windows the rules of the printer have to be resolved against the environment and the installed fonts.

Some print drivers do not support certain font weights, or "angles". A good example of this is the Adobe Symbol font. Based on the default printer you will only sometimes be able to use BOLD and ITALIC. By default, the Adobe Symbol does allow you to use BOLD and ITALIC. If the printer has a Symbol font built in, and/or it can do BOLD, then as soon as you make that printer the default in Windows all your Windows applications can use BOLD or ITALIC with the Symbol font. For an example of this, change your default printer from an HP LaserJet 2 to an Apple LaserWriter. You will see that you can now use the ITALIC and BOLD variations of Symbol. Change back to the HPLJ2, and you cannot BOLD or ITALIC with the Symbol font.

Another example relates to the typefaces themselves. If the PS printer has the "standard LaserWriter" 17 typefaces, and you do not have the Adobe Type Manager installed, then when you make the PS driver the default you will notice that all your Windows applications will have the 17 fonts even though you did not "add" anything. As an example, if you have ATM installed and you do not have the Zaph Dingbats font installed you will still be able to use the Zaph Dingbats font if the default print device is PostScript. Change the default printer to HP LaserJet and you will see the Zaph Dingbats go away. The difference is in what fonts the print driver *expects* will be in the printer. The driver expects that the PostScript device has the Zaph Dingbats font resident so it allows you to use it although not installed.

The last example is the metrics of the fonts. These are the things like the line spacing, character spacing, and the font type: symbol or text. In some cases you can switch to a print driver which is not completely setup to handle all of the metrics of the various fonts. One example of this is the early releases of the FAX drivers for Windows. Even though they are for faxing, you install them as a print driver so they are really print drivers. In the early releases of these drivers the "inter-character" spacing was not specified for TrueType fonts. The FAX drivers thought that this would come from the video driver (yes, the video driver. Video drivers have a lot to do with printing!). The spacing info from the video drivers was wrong in many cases. Since the FAX driver did not bother to calculate the widths, you would change from a regular print driver to a fax driver and all the characters with TT fonts would loose all the inter-character spacing. The words would be scrunched together in FrameMaker. At first the only workaround was to use Adobe fonts as they have their own "spacing" metrics built in. Today, TT fonts still do not have the spacing information so the print drivers have to have methods to deal with that. Sometimes when you change print drivers you will see the space between lines or characters change. This is because the different print driver has different metrics for handling TT fonts.

Again, the Adobe fonts have the spacing info "built-in". This keeps cross-platform better, and the result is consistency in the way a specific typeface works.

What FrameMaker is doing: When you change the default printer in Windows, FrameMaker has a way to check for this. If we know that the default printer has changed at all (even if you change it and then change it back), we then ask Windows for the new information. This process is the same one we use when you start the FrameMaker application. Once we have the new information about what has changed we assume it will effect the document and then we give you the message to reformat the doc. Remember the new info we get is more than the printer type, we get all the info about the fonts again. Most of the time, the new info we get about the fonts does not effect the document. Since we would have to parse the document to see the impact (this is a bit of unnecessary overhead), we know something has changed so we tell you this and give you the option to deal with it.

Some examples:

1. I had a PostScript printer driver and when I changed to the LaserJet 2 driver I lost the Bookman font: This indicates that the Bookman font was not installed into Windows. The Bookman font was made available by Windows because the PostScript print driver dictated it was available. You have bookman text in your FrameMaker document, so when you go back to FrameMaker and reformat the doc, all the Bookman will change to something else as it is no longer available.
2. I authored my document with TrueType fonts with the Default printer set as a FAX driver. Now that I change to a PostScript printer all the line spacing has changed: In this case the TT fonts were defined with one set of spacing metrics that are different than the ones in the PS driver. If you change back to the FAX driver, then the spacing will change back too.
3. I was using Courier in my document. When I changed to the "Foo" driver all the lines that use Courier went to fixed spacing: This can occur if the "foo" driver is setup for courier as a fixed-pitch font. If the driver tells Windows that a font is fixed-pitch and there is a way to print/display this, then it can change based solely on the print driver.

Printer resolution does not effect fonts in Windows. If you have a 300DPI, 800DPI, and 2400 DPI print driver with the same spacing metrics, the document and the spacing should not change. Windows does not know what the resolution of the print driver is.

What is "Setup Program files have been modified or corrupted"?

ISSUE

What does the error message "Setup Program files have been modified or corrupted" mean?

SOLUTION

You have installed a Network Server version of FrameMaker 4.02 on your network server. You now go to a different workstation and try to run Netsetup.

If you receive this error message, it is an indication that the workstations have a different mount point (drive letter). You have to edit the \maker4\netsetup\netsetup.ini file to reflect the correct drive letter and path.

If you look in the file \maker\netsetup\netsetup.ini, the NetPath statement is giving the drive letter and path from how the original installation took place. The NetPath statement needs to reflect how that particular workstation has mounted that area of the network server.

Example:

The workstation that originally installed FrameMakeron the server, mounts that area of the server as: e:\maker4. You go to a different workstation that is mounting that area as: f:\maker4. When you try to run Netsetup, you will receive the error message. To fix the problem, you need to edit the NetPath statement in \maker4\netsetup\netsetup.ini to reflect the correct drive and path for that particular workstation. Or, remount that area of the network server with the same drive letter.

MAC OS

Why do I get a "Cannot lock file for your use" message on the Mac?

ISSUE

I have changed my Cross Platform Compatibility Preference from Macintosh to Windows. Now when I open a file from the network I get the message, "Cannot lock this file for your use. Your changes to it may conflict with the work of others."

If I change the Cross Platform Compatibility Preference back to Macintosh I have no problems opening the file. Why does changing the Cross Platform Compatibility Preference from Macintosh to Windows cause the file locking error message to come up when opening files on the network?

SOLUTION

After the preference is changed, FrameMaker tries to create or modify an appropriately named ".lck" file in the same directory as the document being opened. If FrameMaker is trying to create a .lck file in a directory where you don't have write permissions, that could cause the error message. Additionally, the error message may be casued by the inability to create a legitimate ".lck" file name.

Why do I get an internal error when pasting a table or anchored frame?

ISSUE

Why do I get internal error 1377036,1369632 or 5012,139-7468,1390060 when I copy a table or anchored frame from a FrameMaker 4 file and paste it into a FrameMaker 5 file?

SOLUTION

This is a known problem in FrameMaker version 5.0 and 5.0.1. Bug number 99176 has been logged.

This internal error will occur if a table is selected in the Framemaker 4 file by Option-triple clicking or if an anchored frame is selected by clicking on the frame. The workaround is to select the table or anchored frame by highlighting the anchor and at least one character following the anchor in the FrameMaker 4 file. (If the anchor is at the end of a paragraph, select the paragraph symbol or end of flow symbol along with the anchor).

What does "Can't Initialize Font Array" mean?

ISSUE

When I try to launch FrameMaker, I see the message "Can't Initialize Font Array" and it fails. Why is this happening?

SOLUTION

This problem appears to be a conflict with the shareware control panel "Greg's Buttons". An update, version 3.1.3, to "Greg's Buttons" seems to resolve the problem.

UNIX

What causes the "This file has been corrupted...." error?

ISSUE

I opened some files stored on an NFS volume and I got the error message "This file has been corrupted. Please check your file system, disk and network." What does this mean? Can I get my file back? How did the file become corrupted?

SOLUTION

The error comes from a checksum violation. On opening a stored file, FrameMaker reads the total of data bits in the file into a code related to the length and content of the file. Then FrameMaker compares this "checksum" value with the previous checksum stored when the file was saved. When they don't match, there is a checksum violation. FrameMaker will not open a file with a checksum violation.

This is done to ensure document integrity, but more to assure that FrameMaker won't crash from opening a bad file—which may damage other open files or cause loss of work.

There are a few known causes for this corruption, but many possibilities. Basically, the file is either not written correctly, or has been changed after writing and reporting back to FrameMaker that it is correctly written.

Per engineering, there is a potential problem with soft mounted NFS file systems correctly writing FrameMaker files. This is not a problem with FrameMaker, it is part of the design of the NFS soft mount.

When Sun designed the soft mount, they were addressing the need for fast file saves. With a hard-mounted system, the file system reports back after a file is saved completely and correctly. With a soft mount, the system is designed to report back immediately that the file is finished writing, even if this is not true. This results in fast "saves", but with long files (such as those FrameMaker writes), binary files (as FrameMaker writes), on a busy network (typical of a UNIX FrameMaker installation), there is a possibility that the file will not be correctly written.

Adobe strongly recommends you use a hard-mounted file system for your FrameMaker document storage.

Other potential problems could be due to UNIX file system corruption (refer to your UNIX documentation on the fsck utility to check and how to repair UNIX file systems), disk errors (refer to your media initialization and formatting software), and network translation errors—especially in a mixed-platform environment. If a file has come from another platform and the originator can open the file, then move the file on a floppy to test network integrity, or over a serial connection to test floppy integrity.

As for file recovery, there is no circumvention to the checksum protection. Adobe designed in this mechanism and the potential risks in bypassing the checksum would make the file unstable. You can run the "strings" program against the file to recover some of the textual data, but reverting to a backup of the file is highly recommended. Using the "sum" utility on two files which are presumed identical but of which one will not open is a way to see the checksum differences.

Why does miftortf return Arithmetic exception (core dumped)?

ISSUE

When I run miftortf on my MIF file, I get the following error: "Arithmetic exception (core dumped)" Why is this?

SOLUTION

This a bug with the miftortf filter. The problem is that the file contains the MIF statement TblRulingPeriod and it is set to zero.

WORKAROUND

In a text editor you will need to change all the lines in your MIF file that look like this:

```
<Tb lRulingPeriod 0>
```

to this:

```
<Tb lRulingPeriod 1>
```

This can be done a variety of ways. Here are a couple suggestions:

1. open the MIF file in the vi editor and type the following: :1,$ s/TblRulingPeriod\ 0/TblRulingPeriod\ 1/g
2. Hold down the Shift key while opening the MIF file in FrameMaker so that the actual MIF text appears in a document. Use Edit-Find/Change to Find Text: <Tb lRulingPeriod 0> and Change To Text: <Tb lRuling-Period 1>. Turn on Change All in Document. Choose File-SaveAs and select Text Only as the Format.

After making your changes to the MIF file, rerun miftortf.

What does "Cannot read the file named filename" mean?

ISSUE

What does the message "Cannot read the file named filename" mean when opening a file?

SOLUTION

This message means your file has been corrupted. The message you should have received is "This file has been corrupted. Please check your file system, disk and network." See Related Records for further information on this message.

What does 'cannot allocate bitmap pool' mean and why doesn't FM start?

ISSUE

If I set the Maker.clientBitmapSize X resource to 100 million bytes, FrameMaker 5 won't start and I get the following error: "maker: cannot allocate bitmap pool. There is insufficient swap memory for FrameMaker to run. You need to exit some other processes in order to start FrameMaker."

I have plenty of SWAP and RAM on this machine. Is there a limit to Maker.clientBitmapSize?

SOLUTION

We limit bitmap allocations to 100 million bytes. We set the limit where we do because a few years ago we thought this to be a *really* big number, but now we know it is not. This has been logged bug #104289 with engineering. As a workaround, you can try setting the following X resource:

```
Maker.colorDither: False
```

This will not affect the bitmap allocation, but it will reduce the size of the images, and perhaps prevent the grey boxes

System Errors

MAC OS / WINDOWS / UNIX

Why does FrameMaker crash with Internal Error FE9D4?

ISSUE

What causes Internal Error FE9D4? Is there a workaround for this problem?

SOLUTION

This can occur if you use FrameMaker release 5 to open a FrameMaker 4 book, add some components (files) to the book and save it. Now some of the new components might have the same "Unique" field as some of the old ones. This can lead to crashes in two different FrameMaker release 5 operations: Generate and Rearrange.

This bug was fixed such that FrameMaker version 5.0.1 will not corrupt books in this manner. So, if you never used FrameMaker release 5 to add any components to any books originally generated in FrameMaker 4, you will be ok once you upgrade to version 5.0.1. If you upgraded from FrameMaker 4 to FrameMaker release 5, added a component to the book in release 5, and then upgrade to 5.0.1, you might still have a corrupted book. Version 5.0.1 can Rearrange book files without crashing even if the book is corrupted. However, given a corrupted book, version 5.0.1 may still crash when Generating.

The problem may be circumvented by writing out the book in MIF, removing the <Unique> statements, saving and rereading the MIF. FrameMaker will re-assign Unique values to the book components, and the book file will properly perform all book functions.

Opening all files in FrameMaker release 5 and saving them *before* adding any files to the book may also prevent the crash.

FrameMaker 5 Crashes Using Undo or Redo Command with Tables or Grouped Objects

ISSUE

An Internal Error or Fatal Error occurs when you use the Undo or Redo command while working with tables or grouped objects in FrameMaker 5.

SOLUTION

Do not use the Undo or Redo command when working with tables or grouped objects.

ADDITIONAL INFORMATION

FrameMaker 5 may crash when you use the Undo or Redo command while working with tables or grouped objects. For example, the error occurs when you do the following:

- convert text to a table so that the table spans two or more text columns or pages, then undo the conversion.
- group two or more FrameMaker-drawn objects, cut the objects, undo the cut, then redo the cut.

  In FrameMaker+SGML 5.1.1, the error occurs when working with grouped objects only.

In FrameMaker 5.0, the following error messages occur:

Platform	Error Message
SunOS 4.x	Internal Error A7FBC
Solaris 2.x (SunOS 5.x)	Internal Error 13FC28
Macintosh	Internal Error 1262972,1301056
Windows 3.1	Fatal Error 0047699c

In FrameMaker 5.1x, the following error messages occur:

Version and Platform	Error Message
5.1 and 5.1.1 for SunOS 4.x	Internal Error A9760
5.1 for Solaris 2.x (SunOS 5.x)	Internal Error 13B3D8

5.1.1 for Solaris 2.x (SunOS 5.x)	Internal Error 13ACD8
5.1 for HPUX	Internal Error 16840C
5.1.1 for HPUX	Internal Error 16843C
5.1 and 5.1.1 for AIX	Internal Error 101303E4
5.1 for IRIX	Internal Error 5AF0C4
5.1.1 for IRIX	Internal Error 5AB250
5.1 for Digital UNIX	Internal Error 207ACFBC
5.1.1 for Digital UNIX	Internal Error 2060B2DC
5.1 for Macintosh (68K)	Internal Error 511,1154068,7387152 (table) or 511,1154068,108009160 (grouped objects)
5.1.1 for Macintosh (68K)	Internal Error 511,1154072,7387152 (table) or 5111,1154072,108009160 (grouped objects)
5.1 for Power Macintosh	Internal Error 512,1277640,2153312 (table) or 512,1277640,1548456 (grouped objects)
5.1.1 for Power Macintosh	Internal Error 5112,1277324,2153184 (table) or 5112,1277324,1548140 (grouped objects)
5.1 for Windows 3.1	Fatal Error 0065aba6 (table) or 0051b595 (grouped objects)
5.1.1 for Windows 3.1	Fatal Error 0065aae6 (table) or 0051b595 (grouped objects)
5.1.1 for Windows 95 and NT	Fatal Error 0070daa6 (table) or 0057b115 (grouped objects)

FrameMaker 5.1x Crashes After Clicking Set in Show/Hide Conditional Text Dialog Box

ISSUE

An Internal Error or Fatal Error occurs in FrameMaker 5.1x after you click Set in the Show/Hide Conditional Text dialog box. You changed the display option for more than one condition tag before clicking Set.

SOLUTIONS

Do one or more of the following:

A. Save the document in MIF format, then open the MIF file in FrameMaker and change the display settings of the condition tags in the Show/Hide Conditional Text dialog box.

B. Change the display option for one condition tag at a time in the Show/Hide Conditional Text dialog box.

ADDITIONAL INFORMATION

If you change the display option for multiple condition tags in the Show/Hide Conditional Text dialog box, FrameMaker 5.1x returns one of the following errors after you click Set:

Version and Platform	Error Message
5.1 and 5.1.1 for SunOS 4.x	Internal Error A9760
5.1 for Solaris 2.x (SunOS 5.x)	Internal Error 13B3D8
5.1.1 for Solaris 2.x (SunOS 5.x)	Internal Error 13ACD8
5.1 for HP-UX	Internal Error 16840C
5.1.1 for HP-UX	Internal Error 16843C
5.1 and 5.1.1 for AIX	Internal Error 101303E4
5.1 for IRIX	Internal Error 5AF0C4
5.1.1 for IRIX	Internal Error 5AB250
5.1 for Digital UNIX	Internal Error 207ACFBC
5.1.1 for Digital UNIX	Internal Error 2060B2DC
5.1 for Macintosh	Internal Error 511,1154068,7387152
5.1.1 for Macintosh	Internal Error 5111,1154072,7387152
5.1 for PowerMac	Internal Error 512,1277640, 2153312
5.1.1 for PowerMac	Internal Error 5112, 1277324,2153184
5.1 for Windows 3.1	Fatal Error 00702086
5.1.1 for Windows 3.1	Fatal Error 0065aaa6
5.1.1 for Windows 95/NT	Fatal Error 0070Daa6

FrameMaker 5 Crashes When Opening Document Containing Text Inset

ISSUE

An Internal Error or Fatal Error occurs when you open a document that contains a text inset (i.e., a file imported by reference) in FrameMaker 5.

SOLUTION

Rename the source file, delete the unresolved text inset from the FrameMaker document, then reimport the source file:

1. Move or rename the source file.
2. Open the FrameMaker document.
3. When you receive an alert indicating the document contains unresolved text insets, click Continue.
4. Choose Edit > Find/Change.
5. Select Unresolved Text Inset from the Find pop-up menu, then click Find.
6. When the unresolved text inset is found and highlighted, delete it.
7. Rename the source file with its original name and reimport it.

ADDITIONAL INFORMATION

FrameMaker 5 stores link information for text insets in an internal context table, which it uses to automatically update text insets when you open a document. If items in the context table are incorrect or missing, an Internal Error or Fatal Error occurs as FrameMaker tries to update the text insets.

If you rename the source file, FrameMaker cannot locate it or update it, which prevents the Internal Error or Fatal Error from occurring. You can then delete the unresolved text inset and reimport the source file, which recreates the link.

In FrameMaker 5.1x, the following error messages occur:

Version and Platform	Error Message
5.1 and 5.1.1 for SunOS 4.x	Internal Error A9760
5.1 for SunOS 5.x (Solaris)	Internal Error 13B3D8
5.1.1 for SunOS 5.x (Solaris)	Internal Error 13ACD8
5.1 for HPUX	Internal Error 18640C
5.1.1 for HPUX	Internal Error 16843C
5.1 and 5.1.1 for AIX	Internal Error 101303E4
5.1 for IRIX	Internal Error 5AF0C4
5.1.1 for IRIX	Internal Error 5AB250
5.1 for Digital UNIX	Internal Error 207ACFBC
5.1.1 for Digital UNIX	Internal Error 2060B2DC
5.1 for Mac68k	Internal Error 511,1154068,7387152
5.1.1 for Mac68k	Internal Error 5111,1154072,7387152
5.1 for PMac	Internal Error 512,1277640,2153312
5.1.1 for PMac	Internal Error 5112,1277324,2153184
5.1 for Win31	Fatal Error 00702086
5.1.1P1c for Win31	Fatal Error 0065aae6
5.1.1P2c for Win95/NT 3.51	Fatal Error 0070daa6

WINDOWS / UNIX

Why am I crashing or getting no results when applying a master page?

ISSUE

When applying a master page to a body page, FrameMaker release 5 for UNIX crashes with no Internal Error or any sort of message while FrameMaker release 5 for Windows simply doesn't apply the master page (no alert message). The same thing happens if I am on the Master Page, go to the Body Page, and choose to Remove Overrides. Why is this happening?

SOLUTION

Check to see if the text frame(s) on the Body Page have autoconnect turned on. They may have a flow tag, but if autoconnect is not on, FrameMaker is paying attention only to the autoconnected flows, while the other text frames are returning NULL and crashing FrameMaker or causing the apply master page operation to fail without an alert. This has been logged as bug 97492.

The workaround is to turn on autoconnect in the text frame(s) on the Body Page, and then apply the Master Page. NOTE: This bug has been fixed in version 5.0.1, the maintenance release of FrameMaker release 5. Refer to Related Records for more information on version 5.0.1.

Why does FM crash when editing a file with table in an anchored frame?

ISSUE

I've added an anchored frame which contains a text column with a table that has a table title set to the bottom. Now when I try to edit text in the main flow, FrameMaker release 5 crashes. Why?

SOLUTION

Having the title at the bottom of a table in a text frame that's in an anchored frame that's in the flow will cause FrameMaker to crash when the text in the flow is subsequently edited. The workaround is to remove the title or place it above the table.

FrameMaker 5.0x Crashes When Viewing or Printing Page Containing Polyline

ISSUE

An Internal Error or Fatal Error occurs when you view or print a document page in FrameMaker 5.0x for UNIX or Windows. The page contains a polyline with overlapping line segments.

SOLUTIONS

Upgrade to Adobe FrameMaker 5.1.1

OR: Save the document as an MIF file, then remove the overlapping line segments from the MIF file by deleting duplicate Point statements and setting the NumPoints remark to the appropriate value:

1. Open the document.
2. Choose File > Save As.
3. Select Interchange (MIF) from the Format pop-up menu.
4. Name the file with an ".mif" extension, then click Save.
5. At the UNIX prompt, use the more command to search the MIF file for Point statements by typing:
   ```
   more filename.mif | grep "<Point"
   ```
   where "filename.mif" is the name of the MIF file.
6. Search the output of the more command for duplicate Point statements. For example, the final two Point statements below are duplicates:
   ```
   <Point  5.1875" 5.375">
   <Point  5.1875" 5.625">
   <Point  3.3125" 5.625">
   <Point  3.3125" 5.375">
   ```

```
<Point  3.3125" 5.375">
<Point  5.15972" 3.52778">
<Point  5.15972" 3.77778">
<Point  3.28472" 3.77778">
<Point  3.3125" 5.375">
<Point  3.3125" 5.375">
```

7. Open the MIF file in a text editor that can save in text-only format.
8. Locate the duplicate Point statements that you noted in step 6. For example:

```
<Nu mPoints 5>
<Point  5.1875" 5.375">
<Point  5.1875" 5.625">
<Point  3.3125" 5.625">
<Point  3.3125" 5.375">
<Point  3.3125" 5.375">
```

9. Remove the duplicate Point statements, then edit the NumPoints value so it equals the number of Points statements. For example:

```
<Nu mPoints 4>
<Point  5.1875" 5.375">
<Point  5.1875" 5.625">
<Point  3.3125" 5.625">
<Point  3.3125" 5.375">
```

10. Repeat steps 8 and 9 for all other duplicate Point statements.
11. Save the MIF file in a text-only format.

ADDITIONAL INFORMATION

An Internal Error or Fatal Error occurs in FrameMaker 5.0x for UNIX or Windows if you view or print a page that has a polyline with overlapping line segments. The errors returned by FrameMaker include:

Version and Platform	Error Message
5.0 for SunOS 4.x	Internal Error 152240
5.0.1 for SunOS 4.x	Internal Error 154B80
5.0 for Solaris 2.x (SunOS 5.x)	Internal Error 1EDB90
5.0x for Windows	Fatal Error 00523c29
5.0.1 for Solaris 2.x (SunOS 5.x)	Internal Error 1F119C
5.0 for HP-UX 9.X	Internal Error 220BF4
5.0.1 for HP-UX 9.x	Internal Error 166910

You can remove the overlapping line segments by saving the document in MIF format and deleting duplicate Points statements from the MIF file.

Why does FrameMaker crash when resizing a rotated text frame?

ISSUE

I have a text frame that includes a table. I have rotated the text frame and when I attempt to resize it, FrameMaker crashes with Internal Error 2ECD80 or 38F6E0. What is causing this crash?

SOLUTION

This is a bug in FrameMaker release 5. It will occur if you attempt to resize a rotated text frame that includes a table with the following format:

- Table Title is positioned Above or Below the table
- Table Alignment is Center

Workaround:

- resize the text frame by selecting it and going to Graphics-Object Properties and choosing the desired dimensions
- change Table Title Position to No Title
- change Table Alignment to Left, Right, Side Closer to Binding or Side Farther From Binding

NOTE: This bug has been fixed in version 5.0.1, the maintenance release of FrameMaker release 5.

Why does FM crash when changing a graphic's Object Property?

ISSUE

When I select an object and try to change it's properties via the Graphics- Object Properties dialog box, why does FrameMaker 4 crash with Internal Error 1B7240 or 1B72F8 (or 35E3B4 under Solaris 2.x) on the UNIX platform or "Fatal Error [10000001] occurred. An Internal Error has Occurred." on the MS Windows platform?

SOLUTION

These Internal Errors will occur if you have grouped a rotated and an unrotated text column or a rotated text column and another graphic and then tried to change the size in the Graphics-Objects Properties dialog box. The workaround is to ungroup and resized them individually.

WINDOWS

Why does FM hang while to importing a Ventura Publisher document?

ISSUE

When importing a Ventura Publisher file into FrameMaker for MS Windows, the import filter hangs. Why?

SOLUTION

There are several reasons why the Ventura Publisher import filter may hang during import into FrameMaker for MS Windows.

1. The Ventura Publisher file being imported may reside on a network drive, as opposed to the hard drive. The Ventura Publisher import filter was written to convert files in sections. The network may have difficultly with the size of the data. Move the file to the user's hard drive (if available), and try importing the file from the hard drive.
2. Windows may be low on TEMP space. MS Windows writes temporary files to the TEMP subdirectory speci-

fied in the user's autoexec.bat file. Temporary files are written when running Windows, starting an application, filtering, printing, etc. The user may need up to 5 to 10 times the imported file size in free disk space during filtering.

Check the setting in autoexec.bat:

```
SET TEMP= c:\temp
```

This path should point to a unique subdirectory, used only for Windows TEMP files. Next, go to the drive where the TEMP subdirectory resides (in this example, c:\) and check the space available on this drive using CHKDSK or equivalent DOS command. Make sure that the space available is at least 5 to 10 times the size of the Ventura Publisher file.

Please refer to Related Records for more information on the TEMP subdirectory.

3. The Ventura Publisher file may contain caption text that is greater than 48 characters. The filter currently stores up to 48 characters of caption information in a buffer during the import process. If more than 48 characters are contained in a Ventura Publisher caption, the filter will hang when it attempts to import the information.

   The workaround is to limit caption text in Ventura Publisher documents to 48 characters or less. To be safe, use 35 characters or less, to leave enough room for any possible formatting information surrounding the caption.

Why do I sometimes get SHARE violation messages?

ISSUE

Why do I sometimes get SHARE violation messages when running FrameMaker for MS Windows?

SOLUTION

DOS and MS Windows can only do one thing at a time. The SHARE utility is a program that tries to keep track of "what files are being opened on the local drive". This is necessary if two people are working on the same file. When the second user opens a file, he/she gets a message that the file is in "use". This is a way to notify the user that they may write over another user's work. Nonetheless, the user can open the file if necessary.

In a networking environment, SHARE only effects the local system. The file sharing on the network drive is handled by the network server. The real problems lie in the different ways that DOS SHARE and the networking sharing mechanisms operate.

Many things can go wrong with SHARE. One big problem arises if two users have the same file open and one of them exhibits a crash in MS Windows. This can cause SHARE to think that the file is still in use when it really is not in use. Subsequent uses of the file could result in a SHARE violation. SHARE problems and network problems are known by Microsoft, and are documented in Microsoft's \windows\networks.wri file.

SHARE violations can usually be worked-around by setting the file in question to "read only" in File Manager, File, Properties. If the SHARE violation persists after setting the file to read-only, there may be system configuration problems with SMARTDRV or other disk-caching software, compressed drives, RAM drivers, non-DOS files (Unix, Mac, etc.) or mismatched DOS versions.

There is only one known FrameMaker cause of a SHARE violation. If vector graphics are imported into FrameMaker 4.01P1h, a SHARE violation will be triggered on import, due to an incorrect flag set in the vector graphic import filters. FrameMaker 4.02 resolves this cause of the SHARE violation message.

If the SHARE violation occurs outside of importing vector graphics in FrameMaker 4.01P1h, or the error persists after installing FrameMaker 4.02P2b, check to see if the error occurs only when working on a network drive, or only when working on the hard drive.

If the problem only occurs when working on the hard drive, Microsoft has written a new version of the SHARE utility that should resolve the problem. This new version of SHARE is called VSHARE. It ships with Windows for Workgroups v. 3.11, but can be run with any version of Windows 3.1, and can be downloaded from Microsoft's on-line services. It will only resolve SHARE problems on the hard drive that occur in Windows. It will not resolve SHARE problems on any other drive, or SHARE problems outside of Windows. To see if VSHARE is running, view the \windows\system.ini file, [386enh] section. If VSHARE is running, you will see a line that reads:

```
VSHARE.386
```

If the problem still persists in Windows on the hard drive, contact Microsoft to troubleshoot further.

If the SHARE violation only occurs on a network drive, contact the network manufacturer to troubleshoot further.

Why is FM crashing with a general protection fault at 0004:7A2F?

ISSUE

When I try to invoke FrameMaker, it crashes with a General Protection Fault at 0004:7A2F. I can't start FrameMaker?

SOLUTION

The address 0004:7A2F points to the function SetCreationDate. If you look at the date under DOS, you will see that either the date is not set or it is set incorrectly. In any case, correcting the date to reflect the current date will allow FrameMaker to initialize.

This often happens with Toshiba Laptops.

Are there any problems with Win32s and S3 Windows video drivers?

ISSUE

Are there any problems with Win32s and S3 video drivers?

SOLUTION
There are some known problems with Win32s and S3 video drivers. These problems stem from bugs in MS Windows. When an application asks MS Windows to do a bit-block transfer (BitBlt) Windows will usually generate a few "faults" or errors. This happens whether or not Win32s is running. However, when Win32s is not running, MS Windows recovers from the faults. When a Win32-based application is running, Win32s catches all exceptions and transfers control to the nearest try/except frame. As a result, the BitBlt is interrupted.
This affects FrameMaker release 5 because it uses Win32s.
To troubleshoot this, verify that you have an S3 video card. If you do not, then you should immediately contact the card manufacturer and get the latest driver for your card. Most drivers are updated as often as once a month, and there is almost always a newer driver than the one shipped with the card.

If you do have an S3 video card, then you should also get the latest driver for the card, but you *may* also need to make the changes outlined below:

Certain (not all) S3 drivers which exhibit these problems can be made to work with Win32s by making the following edit to your SYSTEM.INI file before running any Win32-based applications:
This information is from the Microsoft Download service. Document #Q117153:
In the SYSTEM.INI file, you may find an entry in the [display] section

```
aperture-base=100
```

Change this entry to

```
aperture-base=0
```

Restart Windows and the display problems will no longer occur.

If this does not help, obtain the latest S3 drivers.
To get this, and more information, contact Microsoft on any of it's on-line services. The services are listed in any Microsoft documentation or inside your MS Windows manual.

MAC OS

How can I clear up floating point coprocessor errors with System 7.5?

ISSUE
Every now and then FrameMaker crashes and I get the message "Floating point coprocessor not installed" How can I clear this up?

SOLUTION
Installing the System 7.5 Update 1.0 can clear up the "floating point coprocessor not found" crashes that can occur randomly while running FrameMaker or any other application under System 7.5.

More information about the Update is available from the MacInTouch column offerd by MacWeek. The information available includes a brief description of the Update, excerpts from the release notes, and some know problmes with the Update. To access this nformation go to this URL http://www.macintouch.com/~ricford/sys751.html or choose MacInTouch from the MacWeek Home Page at http://zcias3.ziff.com/%7Emacweek/

The System 7.5 Update 1.0 is available at no charge from Apple. You must already have System 7.5 to use this patch. Apple has two ftp servers On their main server ftp.support.apple.com (130.43.6.3) the upgrade can be found in the directory /pub/apple_sw_updates/US/Macintosh/System Software

Apple also has a supplemental ftp server that only houses their product updates. The address of that server is ftptoo.-support.apple.com(130.43.6.4).

On both servers, the login is anonymous, and the password is your email address.

You may also get the update from the WWW by going to this URL http://www.info.apple.com and choosing Software Updates

The Release Notes are available at the URL http://www.info.apple.com/cgi-bin/read.wais.doc.pl?/wais/TIL/Macintosh!Software/System!7.5/Mac!S7.5!Update!1.0!-ReadMe

Why do I get a Type 4 error when printing?

ISSUE
I have a document with a page size of 1.75" x 11" that I am printing to 11" x 17" papersize. When I print composites, it prints fine, but if I try to print separations, FrameMaker crashes with a Type 4 error. Why?

SOLUTION
This is a divide by zero error, and is caused by the narrow page size. This is a bug in FrameMaker 4. The workaround is to create a larger page size, and draw on registration and crop marks by hand.

Why does RTF Export Utiltiy crash with Type 25 error?

ISSUE
The RTF Export Utiltiy is crashing with a type 25 error. What is happening?

SOLUTION
The Type 25 error message is an "Out of Memory" error. Usually this can be remedied by allocating more memory to the RTF Export Utility. Change the preferred size in the the Get Info dialog for the utiltiy to 2000k instead of the default of 1000k. If this does not solve the problem you can try the following:

1. Turn off extensions.
2. Convert tables to text in FrameMaker before filtering.
3. Cut the file into smaller documents and try converting the smaller files.

Why does FM/PowerMac crash when attempting to use filters with VM on?

ISSUE

FrameMaker crashes, often with a Type 11 error, when attempting to use the filters on the PowerMac.

SOLUTION

This is a bug which occurs only on the Power Macintosh when Virtual Memory is turned on. This bug involves the Progress Meter Bar that appears when filtering a file. This bug has been fixed in FrameMaker release 5.

Specific Details: This bug is caused by an attempt to convert a hard-coded C string to a Pascal string, call a Mac toolbox call, then convert back to a C string. Since the string is hard coded, and not a resource, it is a compiled part of the executable Code. On 68K machines, code resources always get loaded into RAM, and so converting C to pascal strings and back in place was not normally a problem. On the Power Macintosh with Virtual memory off, this is also true. On the Power Macintosh with VM *on*, however, the FrameMaker executable code is paged in from disk as needed by the VM system, and the VM system protects the code with hardware protection. When we try and do our string conversion (in place) from C to Pascal and back, it triggers the VM protection error, and FrameMaker crashes.

There are two workarounds to this problem:

1. Turn Virtual Memory off when filtering files in FrameMaker for Power Macintosh.
2. Use a Disk File Editor (such as found in Norton Utilities):
   1. Open the Data Fork of the Application file
   2. Search for the hex pattern:
      `'307E001480BF002080DF0024'`
   3. replace it with:
      `'307E00143860000080DF0024'`

   (note that only the middle 4 bytes change)

   NOTE: Workaround #2 has not been approved by Adobe Quality Assurance and is not supported by Technical Support.

UNIX

What does "Could not load library libsvld.a[dl.so]" in FM 5.1/IBM mean?

ISSUE

When I try starting FrameMaker version 5.1 on AIX 4.1.3, I get the following error: "Could not load library libsvld.a-[dl.so], Error was: No such file or directory" What does this mean?

SOLUTION

Your installation of AIX 4.1.3 is missing some dynamically linked libraries that were used to compile FrameMaker version 5.1. We have included these libraries on the 5.1 UNIX CD-ROM. To retrieve these libraries:

1. Mount the CD-ROM drive according to the instructions in the Installing Frame Products manual or Installation Notes.
2. cd /cdrom/extra.aix
3. Copy the two files in /cdrom/extra.aix (README and sysinst.tar) to your /tmp directory (or other temporary location) and follow the instructions in the README to install these libraries.

Why is FrameMaker hanging after displaying the splash screen?

ISSUE

FrameMaker 5 appears to be hanging. The splash screen comes up and the hourglass displays, but the FrameMaker opening window never appears. Why is this and how can I fix it?

SOLUTION

FrameMaker release 5 for UNIX has a new feature wherein it will list the names of the last five files you opened or saved with the Save As command under the File menu. This list is maintained in the fmfilesvisited file. It is possible that there is a file in your fmfilesvisited (Files Recently Visited) file that is mounted from a server that is currently down or unreachable. FrameMaker checks to see that the files in fmfilesvisited exist before it puts them under the File menu. Bug #96166 has been logged against this behavior. To work around the problem, check for a fmfilesvisited file in the following directories:

```
$HOME/fminit/UILanguage/configui
$HOME/fminit/UILanguage
$HOME/fminit
$HOME
```

or check if you have the following X resource set (xrdb -q | grep filesRecentlyVisitedPath):

```
Maker.filesRecentlyVisitedPath:
path_to_fmfilesvisited
```

First, kill the FrameMaker process, maker. Check for the maker process ID and use kill -9 to kill it. Then either remove the offending file from fmfilesvisited or remove fmfilesvisited altogether and try restarting FrameMaker.

Another symptom of this problem is that FrameMaker may appear to hang if you try to open a recently visited file listed under the File menu. This can be caused by the unavailability of that file because the server that holds the file is currently down.

If the system is hung, how can I force a core dump of FrameMaker?

ISSUE

If the system is hung, how can I force a core dump of maker?

SOLUTION

Go to another machine, rsh over to your machine, do a "ps" to find out the maker process number, then "kill -SEGV 12345" (where 12345 is the process number). That forces a core dump, and gives Frame a chance to debug a hard-to-reproduce problem.

Printing Problems

MAC OS / WINDOWS / UNIX

Why is FM reading closed files when I print a document with xrefs?

ISSUE

The documentation says that only cross-references to open files will be updated when you print a document. When I print a document containing external cross-references and all other documents are closed, I still see a message at the bottom of the print dialog box that says "Reading [filename]". Why is FrameMaker reading closed files?

SOLUTION

The documentation is correct, only internal cross-references and cross-reference to open documents are updated when you print.

The status bar says "Reading filename" because we did not come up with a more descriptive message that also fit in the status bar area. What is really happening is "Processing cross-references to filename and updating them IF filename is open".

MAC OS / WINDOWS

FrameMaker Does Not Delete Empty Pages When Saving or Printing Document

ISSUE

When you save or print a document with the Before Saving & Printing property set to Delete Empty Pages, FrameMaker does not remove empty pages at the end of the document.

SOLUTIONS

Apply the left or right master pages to the empty pages, then save the document.

To apply the left or right master pages to empty pages in FrameMaker 5:

1. Choose View > Body Pages.
2. Choose Format > Page Layout > Master Page Layout.
3. In the Use Master Page section, select the Right option if the document is single-sided, or the Right/Left option if the document is double-sided.
4. In the Apply To section, select the Pages option and enter the page range of the blank pages in the Pages and To fields, then click Apply.

To apply the left or right master pages to empty pages in FrameMaker 4:

1. Choose View > Body Pages.
2. Choose Format > Pages > Master Page Usage. 3. In the Use section, select the Normal Page Layout option.
4. In the On section, select the Pages option and enter the page range of the blank pages in the Pages and To fields, then click Set.

ADDITIONAL INFORMATION

You can specify that FrameMaker delete blank pages from the end of a document whenever you save and print the document by selecting Delete Empty Pages in the Numbering Properties dialog box. FrameMaker deletes a blank page at the end of the document only if it uses the left or right master page and contains no layout overrides. If you override the master page layout or apply a custom master page to a blank page, FrameMaker assumes you want to keep the page and does not delete it.

MAC OS / UNIX

Why are some of my fill patterns printing out backwards?

ISSUE

Two of the diagonal fill patterns and the horizontal fill pattern available in the FrameMaker Tools Palette print opposite of how they display. This only happens when I print to a PostScript Level 1 printer. Why is this happening?

SOLUTION

If you look at the expanded tools palette in the fill section, the three fills that cause a problem are the first and third fill patterns in the 4th row and the third fill pattern in the 5th row. These fill patterns display correctly and print correctly to PostScript Level 2 printers. These fill patterns print opposite of how they should to some (but not all) PostScript Level 1 printers (i.e., the horizontal fill pattern in the 4th row prints vertically).

WINDOWS / UNIX

Why don't spot separations work on tints that are less than 100%?

ISSUE

I have a couple of imported graphics in my document. One graphic includes 100% tint of a color and the other graphic includes 50% tint of a color. I also have a custom color that is a mixture of CMY and K and I have applied it to some artwork I drew in my document. I have placed these colors in the Print as Spot list in the Set Print Separations dialog. When I print this file, only the color that has a 100% tint prints on a spot plate. The others do not print. What is happening?

SOLUTION

FrameMaker 4 and FrameMaker release 5 for UNIX and MS Windows do not support spot color separation of tints less than 100%. This includes tints in custom colors applied to FrameMaker artwork and tints in imported graphics. This is an implementation limitation and there is really no workaround other than to print using the Macintosh version which does support tints as well as the Illustrator Overprint feature.

Multi-line Cross-Reference in Book Prints Overlapped from FrameMaker 5 for UNIX or Windows

ISSUE

When you print a book from FrameMaker 5 for UNIX or Windows, a cross-reference to a multi-line paragraph overprints on one line instead of printing on multiple lines.

SOLUTION

Open all the files in the book, generate and update the book, then print the book:

1. Press Shift and choose File > Open All Files in Book.
2. Choose File > Generate/Update.
3. Make sure the files you want to generate are listed in the Generate scroll box, then click Update.
4. Print the book.

ADDITIONAL INFORMATION

When you print a book from FrameMaker 5 for UNIX or Windows, multi-line cross-references overprint on one line if the book was generated and updated while the files in the book were closed. To print multi-line cross-references as expected, you must open all the files in the book before generating and updating the book.

WINDOWS

Why do equation divisor line display ok, but print strangely?

ISSUE

Why do my FrameMaker equation divisor lines look fine on screen, but print as multiple slashed lines compressed together?

SOLUTION

In FrameMaker 3.0, the equation divisor line was drawn with the graphics tool. In FrameMaker 4, the minus character is used to improve scaling of the divisor line in FrameMaker equations.

The minus character comes from the default font of the paragraph used with the equation. If a Character format is applied in the Functions section of the Equation Fonts, then this font is used to create the divisor (minus character) rather than the default paragraph font.

FrameMaker 3 files that use fonts in equations that have a slanted minus sign (such as AGaramond) will result in a "broken" divisor line when opened and printed from FrameMaker 4 (divisor line that appears as slashes compressed together "////").

Why don't spot color separations in imported graphics print?

ISSUE

I have imported a CMYK TIFF graphic that uses the colors black, white and magenta. I also have magenta text in my document. When I print spot color separations such that all colors are set to "don't print" except magenta, only the magenta text prints. The magenta portion of the imported graphic does not print. Why?

SOLUTION

FrameMaker 4/4.02 for MS Windows is capable of separating color in the following imported graphic formats:

DCS (Desktop Color Separation) CMYK TIFF Line art in Encapsulated PostScript (EPSF, EPSI and EPS binary) Bitmapped images in Encapsulated PostScript (if they can be separated in Adobe Separator)

FrameMaker 4/4.02 for Windows should be able to print both spot color and process separations for these imported graphic formats. However, only process color separations will print correctly. FrameMaker should be allocating a 24-bit image for both spot color and composite (no separation) printing, but currently the 24-bit image is created only for composite printing.

MAC OS

Can FM create a single PostScript file when printing a book?

ISSUE

Can FrameMaker on the Macintosh create a single PostScript file when printing a book. If not, can I concatenated the PostScript files into one?

SOLUTION

FrameMaker's PostScript files were designed to be printed as separate jobs. The PostScript generated by FrameMaker is encapsulated within the PostScript generated by either the Apple or the Adobe print driver. Neither supports both portrait and landscape pages in the same job or pages with different sizes, things which are possible with FrameMaker 4, the latter when printing a book. For this reason, FrameMaker needs to break-up the job. The PostScript interpreter frees all memory used by each job at the end, and the jobs count on this.

For the time being, this means that each job must be sent separately, and cannot be concatenated together.

New drivers are being developed which will allow us to avoid having to break-up jobs, but for now, there's nothing that can be done.

Why does rotated text print incorrectly from FrameMaker EPS?

ISSUE

When I create an EPS file from a FrameMaker document that has rotated text, the rotated text does not print correctly, why?

SOLUTION

There is a bug in FrameMaker or the print driver.

When printing/saving an EPS file via the print driver from FrameMaker on the Macintosh, rotated text becomes unrotated. The preview on the screen looks fine and the text is rotated. Upon printing the text unrotates. The output can result in unrotated text or text printing on various lines.

There is no workaround. The best option is to unrotate the text before printing to an EPS file, this insures that the result is at least by design.

Does FrameMaker support QuickDraw GX?

ISSUE

Does FrameMaker support QuickDraw GX?

SOLUTION

Frame recomends that QuickDraw GX not be installed on any Macintosh running FrameMaker 4.X. FrameMaker 4.X was designed to work with LaserWriter 8 and the older versions of Apple's print driver.

In order for FrameMaker 4.X to print at all under QuickDraw GX, all high-end PostScript printing features must be disabled. Printing happens as if it were a 72 dpi QuickDraw device, except that individual graphic elements (characters, graphic elements, etc.) draw at full resolution, but positioned on a 72 dpi "grid."

FrameMaker release 5 has no features to specifically support QuickDraw GX, but some work has been done to make it GX friendly.

FrameMaker release 5 was designed around, and best supports, Apple LaserWriter 8 and Adobe PsPrinter 8. Neither of these printer drivers supports QuickDraw GX and they will not be available in the Chooser if GX is installed. In order to do process separations or display images at full resolution on PostScript printers, we recommend using LaserWriter/ PsPrinter 8 print driver. FrameMaker treats all QuickDraw GX printers as non-PostScript printers whether they are PostScript or not. This means that features such as Adobe Acrobat support are disabled.

If you want to use the advanced PostScript printing capabilities of FrameMaker release 5 while using QuickDraw GX for other applications, then we suggest using the "QuickDraw GX Helper" extension that comes with GX. Here are the steps to use it:

1. Install QuickDraw GX using Custom Install to ensure that QuickDraw GX helper is installed. The GX helper extension is listed in the "QuickDraw GX Utilities" section.
2. Remove all old "LaserWriter" print drivers from your extensions folder except a single copy of either LaserWriter 8 or PsPrinter 8. Other non-PostScript traditional drivers, such as "ImageWriter" can stay.
3. Temporarily disable the QuickDraw GX extension by either moving it out of the Extensions Folder or using the Extensions Manager or a similar utility.
4. Drag all type 1 outline fonts back into the Fonts folder from the *Archived Type 1 Fonts* folder that may have been created in the System Folder as part of the QuickDraw GX installation process. The screen fonts which have been "Enabled" by GX will work correctly under both environments.
5. Restart your computer. QuickDraw GX should be disabled and any desktop printers should have generic icons.
6. Open the Chooser, and select LaserWriter/PsPrinter 8 and the printer that you wish to print to. You might try printing a sample page to make sure that everything is working correctly.
7. Reenable QuickDraw GX by undoing the actions taken in step 3 (move the QuickDraw GX extension back into the Extensions folder or use the Extensions Manager or similar utility to enable it).
8. Restart your computer. QuickDraw GX should be reenabled and desktop printer icons should reappear.
9. Open the Chooser and make sure that the LaserWriter

GX printer is selected and has been correctly configured for the printer you wish to print to.

10. Launch FrameMaker. A new item should appear in the Apple menu - courtesy of the QuickDraw GX helper - Turn Desktop Printing Off. Select this item. QuickDraw GX helper should automatically select the LaserWriter or PsPrinter 8 print driver that you had in the non-GX world.

At this point, you should be able to use the LaserWriter/PSPrinter 8 driver with FrameMaker release 5, and automatically switch to using the GX driver for other applications. Unfortunatly, changing printers requires temporarily disabling GX because the QuickDraw GX helper does not reenable all chooser features. On the other hand, some other GX features such as dragging document icons to desktop printer icons will work in a reasonable way.

If you are primarily interested in the desktop printing facilities of QuickDraw GX, we reccomend using the latest LaserWriter 8.3 driver which was released by Apple in the spring of 1995. This driver includes "Desktop PrintMonitor" which replaces the old PrintMonitor with a new Finder print queue facility similar to the one in GX.

NOTE: As usual, LaserWriter 8 and PsPrinter 8 are referred to as equals without regard to version number. These drivers have always been identical except for cosmetic differences. Always use the latest version available.

UNIX

What does "The requested paper size is not available..." mean?

ISSUE

When I print my FrameMaker release 5 document that I received from Europe, I get a single sheet of paper with the following message:

The requested paper size is not available in any currently-installed tray. Edit the PS file to "FMAllowPaperSizeMismatch true" to use default tray.

What does this mean?

SOLUTION

In FrameMaker 4, we added a check to ensure that the Paper Size dimensions in the Print dialog box matched the paper size of one of the installed trays. Users who wanted to remove this check could do so (see technical note 1238). In FrameMaker release 5, we have made it easier to force FrameMaker to print to the default tray, despite the mismatch.

From the beginning of the FrameMaker release 5 $FMHOME/fminit/ps_prolog:

```
% FrameMaker users specify the proper paper
  size for each print job in the
% "Print" dialog's "Printer Paper Size"
  "Width" and "Height~ fields.  If the
% printer that the PS file is sent to does
  not support the requested paper
% size, or if there is no paper tray of the
  proper size currently installed,
% then the job will not be printed.  The
  following flag, if set to true, will
% cause the job to print on the default
  paper in such cases.
/FMAllowPaperSizeMismatch          false def
```

You can change this in the $FMHOME/fminit/ps_prolog file to affect all files, create a $HOME/fminit/ps_prolog for certain users, or print individual FrameMaker documents to a file, and edit the FrameMaker PostScript file (for example, for those documents that will be sent to Europe).

How has the print process changed in FrameMaker release 5?

ISSUE

How has the print process changed in FrameMaker 5?

SOLUTION

FrameMaker release 5 has changed the printing process as compared to previous versions of FrameMaker.

In particular, all temporary files are put into $TMPDIR if it's set in your environment, or /tmp if $TMPDIR is not defined. In previous releases of FrameMaker, the process of building the PostScript output was continued in $HOME once it reached a 1MB size.

PRINTING TO A PRINTER

If you print-to-printer, FrameMaker release 5:

1. Writes out a temporary Intermediate Print Language (IPL) file
2. Fires up fmprintdr.ps (which reads and deletes the IPL file and writes a temporary PostScript file)
3. Fires up FMlpr (which spools the temporary PostScript file).

PRINTING TO A POSTSCRIPT FILE

For print-to-file, FrameMaker release 5 will no longer change the PostScript file name you specify. The reason it used to do that was to try to help you avoid printing over top of your document files accidently. Now we accomplish this goal by not allowing you to specify a file that already exists and has anything but PostScript in it.

If you print-to-file, FrameMaker release 5 first checks that if the file already exists. If the file exists and it's a PostScript file, then the file is removed. FrameMaker release 5 again writes out a temporary IPL file, and calls fmprintdr.ps which reads and deletes the IPL file and writes a PostScript file. The PostScript file has a temporary name until it has been completely written, and then it gets renamed to have the name you specified.

The net result of putting the IPL into a different temporary file, removing the old PostScript file, and renaming the new PostScript file at the last minute, is that it's now impossible for you to pick up the PostScript file at the wrong time or with the wrong contents.

Why do I get "ERROR: rangecheck" when printing docs w/graphics?

ISSUE

When I print a document that contains graphics to an Hewlett Packard LaserJet 4 printer, the following errors appear on a printed page: "ERROR: rangecheck OFFENDING COMMAND: getinterval" What is causing these errors?

SOLUTION

The current print configuration file is set for regular text. To resolve this problem you will need to load the correct HP interface file (/user/spool/lp) that supports graphics. For additional information on this configuration file, please consult your HP printer documentation.

Installation Issues

MAC OS / WINDOWS / UNIX

How do I install the FrameMaker release 5 HTML Lite filter?

ISSUE

I have installed FrameMaker release 5 but I cannot find the HTML export filter. How do I install it?

SOLUTION

You should find a card in the FrameMaker release 5 box detailing the HTML export filter installation procedure as follows:

All Platforms

Install FrameMaker release 5 or FrameMaker+SGML before installing WebWorks HTML Lite. After installing WebWorks HTML Lite, restart any Frame products that are running.

Macintosh

CD-ROM:

1. Insert the Frame Products CD-ROM and open the Extras folder.
2. Follow the instructions in the README file in the HTML Lite Installer folder.

Disk:

1. Insert the WebWorks HTML Lite disk.
2. Follow the instructions in the README file on the disk.

UNIX

CD-ROM:

Change to the html directory on the FrameMaker Products CD-ROM. Run the installation command and answer questions prompted by the script:

```
SGI, Sun               ./install.sh
IBM, Digital, HP       ./"INSTALL.SH;1"
```

Tape:

Change to the $FMHOME directory.
Run readtape.html

Windows

CD-ROM:

Insert the Frame Products CD-ROM
Run d:\extras\html\setup

Disk:

Insert the WebWorks HTML Lite disk.
Run a:\setup (where a:\ is your floppy disk drive)

MAC OS / WINDOWS

Installing WebWorks HTML Lite

WebWorks HTML Lite, an HTML filter included with FrameMaker 5, does not install automatically with FrameMaker 5 for the Macintosh, Windows 3.1x, or UNIX. It does install automatically with FrameMaker 5 for Windows 95 and Windows NT. You can manually install WebWorks HTML Lite by running its installer.

To install WebWorks HTML Lite on the Macintosh, follow the installation instructions in the ReadMe file on the WebWorks HTML Lite floppy disk, and on the FrameMaker 5 CD-ROM in the HTML Lite Installer folder in the Extras folder.

To install WebWorks HTML Lite in Windows from the FrameMaker 5 CD-ROM, insert the CD-ROM, choose File > Run in Program Manager, then type "d:\extras\html\-setup", where "d" is the CD-ROM drive indicator. To install from the WebWorks HTML Lite floppy disk, insert the disk, choose File > Run in Program Manager, then type "a:\setup," where "a" is the floppy drive indicator. After the installer starts, follow the instructions on screen.

To install WebWorks HTML Lite in UNIX, open the html directory on the Frame products CD-ROM and run the installation script for your UNIX platform:

```
Platform               Command
SGI, SunOS, Solaris    ./install.sh
IBM, Digital, HP       ./"INSTALL.SH;1"
```

NOTE: After installing WebWorks HTML Lite, restart any Frame products that are running.

For technical support on WebWorks HTML Lite, call Quadralay Technical Support at 512-305-0240.

WINDOWS

Why do I get an error on disk 3 when installing onto an NT server?

ISSUE

I am getting an error on disk 3 when I try to install FrameMaker 4 or 5 for Windows onto an NT Server. The disk does not appear to be bad. Why is this happening?

SOLUTION

The solution to the problem is to login to the NT Server as administrator and install FrameMaker.

Disk 2 and disk 3 contain the parts of 'frame.exe'. This 3MB file is loaded in two parts and then verified after it has been loaded. With NT Server, the first part of 'frame.exe' is sucessfully written to the destination from disk 2. When you get to disk 3, it will continute to add to the 'frame.exe' file. At the end of this operation the installer will check to see of all of 'frame.exe' was written intact. For some reason (either network traffic or security) the second part of 'frame.exe' does not install completely, and when the installer checks the file it sees that it is not all written (the file size is checked) so the installer gives you an error. This does not happen on all systems running NT Server. If the problem does not appear during install, then you will have no problems with any of the Frame products.

If the problem is encountered, you only need to be logged in as an administrator to install the product. Once installed, anyone with the proper permissions can use FrameMaker.

Does FrameMaker release 5 for MS Windows use Win32s?

ISSUE

Does FrameMaker release 5 for MS Windows use Win32s?

SOLUTION

FrameMaker release 5 requires version 1.2 or later of the Win32s components. If your system does not contain these components, they will be added during the FrameMaker release 5 installation. If your system contains an older version of the Win32s components, you will given the option to update these components during the FrameMaker release 5 installation. The Win32s components provided with FrameMaker install into the \windows and the \windows\-win32s directories.

The Win32s components, provided and maintained by Microsoft, add internal functionality to MS Windows. Win32s allows you to run 32-bit applications in the Windows 16-bit environment. For more information on Win32s, download technical article #Q95804 from Microsoft via one of their online services as listed in the MS Windows manual.

The following technical article from Microsoft gives an introduction to Win32s.

From: Microsoft Download Service
Doc# Q95804
The information in this article applies to:
- Microsoft Win32s versions 1.1 and 1.2

SUMMARY

The following is intended as a general introduction to Win32s. More information can be found in the "Win32s Programmer's Reference" and by querying for Knowledge Base articles on "Win32s".

MORE INFORMATION

General Information

The Win32 API consists of the Window 3.1 (Win16) API, with types stretched to 32 bits, plus the addition of APIs which offer new functionality, like threads, security, services, and virtual memory. Applications developed using the Win32 API are called "Win32-based applications". Win32s is a set of DLLs and a VxD which allow Win32-based applications to run on top of Windows or Windows for Workgroups version 3.1. Win32s supports a subset of the Win32 API, some directly (like memory management) and some through thunks to the 16-bit systems (particularly GDI and User). Win32s contains function stubs for the APIs that are not supported, which return ERROR_NOT_IMPLEMENTED. Win32s also includes 4 new APIs which support the Universal Thunk (UT). For details on which API are supported under Win32s, refer to the individual API entries in the help file "Win32 API Reference." Among the new features gained from Win32 are structured exception handling (SEH), FP emulation, memory-mapped files, named shared memory, and sparse memory.

Programming issues

Win32-based applications cannot use MS-DOS and BIOS interrupts; therefore, the Win32s VxD has Win32 entries for each Interrupt 21 and the BIOS calls. The Win32s DLLs may thunk to Win16 when a Win32 application makes a call. The 32-bit parameters are copied from the 32-bit stack to a 16-bit stack and the 16-bit entry point is called. The Win32 application has a 128K stack. When switching to the 16-bit side via UT, the same stack is used, and a 16:16 stack pointer is created which points to the top of the stack. The selector base is set so that there is at least an 8K stack for the 16-bit code. There are other semantic difference between Windows 3.1 and Win32. Windows 3.1 will run applications for Win32 nonpreemptively in a single, shared address space, while Windows NT runs them preemptively in separate address spaces. It is therefore important that you test your Win32-based application on both Windows 3.1 and Windows NT. If you need to call routines that reside in a 16-bit DLL or Windows from 32-bit code, you can do this using the Win32s Universal Thunk, RPC, or other client-server techniques. For a description of UT, please see the "Win32s Programmer's Reference" and the sample UTSAMPLE. DDE, OLE, WM_COPYDATA, the clipboard,

metafiles, and bitmaps can be used between 16-bit Windows-based and Win32-based applications on both Windows 3.1 and Windows NT.
Additional reference words: 1.10 1.20
KBCategory: kbprg
KBSubcategory: W32s
COPYRIGHT Microsoft Corporation, 1995.
Title: Win32 Software Development Kit Buglist
Document Number: Q95804 Publ Date: 05-JAN-1995
Product Name: Microsoft Win32 Software Development Kit
Product Version: 3.50

To get this, and more information, contact Microsoft on any of it's on-line services. The services are listed in any Microsoft documentation or inside your MS Windows manual.

How do I test a Win32s installation for problems?

ISSUE

I was asked to test my installation of Win32s. How do I do this?

SOLUTION

To test your installation of Win32s, you can use a program called Freecell. Sometimes you will have problems installing an application, or you may have intermittant crashes with an Win32 application if your Win32s installation has been messed up.

Below is a technical note from Microsoft about Freecell, where to get it, what it will test, and how to solve any problems you find.

From: Microsoft Download service Doc# Q121092
The information in this article applies to:
- Microsoft Windows operating system versions 3.1, 3.11
- Microsoft Windows for Workgroups versions 3.1, 3.11
- Microsoft Win32s, versions 1.0, 1.1, 1.15, 1.2

SUMMARY

Win32s is a set of DLLs and a virtual device driver (VD) that allow Win32-based applications to run on top of Windows or Windows for Workgroups. If you receive the following error message when you run or install a Win32s-based application This program cannot be run in DOS mode Win32s is either not installed or not installed properly. You can use Freecell to test your installation of Win32s.

MORE INFORMATION

Win32s Problems

Freecell is an application available with Win32s in the above locations. To test your installation of Win32s, run Freecell. If you are experiencing problems but Freecell runs properly, contact the manufacturer of the product you are attempting to run or install for further information. If Freecell generates an error, continue reading the following information.

One of the following error messages occurs when you run Freecell and Win32s is not installed properly:

- File Error: Cannot find OLECLI.DLL
- Win32s - Error: Improper installation. Win32s requires WIN32S.EXE and WIN32S16.DLL to run. Reinstall Win32s.
- Win32s - Error: Improper installation. Windows requires w32s.386 in order to run. Reinstall Win32s.
- Error: Cannot find file freecell.exe (or one of its components)...

Also, if Win32s is not installed properly, the display may be corrupted as soon as you run Freecell.

Resolutions

If Win32s is not installed correctly, check the following:

- If you are having video problems, check to see if you have an S3 video card. Certain S3 drivers do not work with Win32s. Either use the generic drivers shipped with Windows, or contact your video card manufacturer for an updated driver.
- Make sure that the following line is in your SYSTEM.INI file:
  `device=*vmcpd`
- If you have a printer driver by LaserMaster, remove it or comment it out. (It interferes with installing Win32s.) Reboot the computer so that the changes you made take effect. After you successfully reinstall Win32s, reinstall the driver or remove the comment characters.

  The driver interferes with installing Win32s because the LaserMaster drivers create a WINSPOOL device. The extension is ignored when the filename portion of a path matches a device name. As a result, when Setup tries to write to WINSPOOL.DRV, it fails because it attempts to write to WINSPOOL. In fact, any Win32-based application that tries to link to WINSPOOL.DRV also fails; however, most Win32-based applications that print under Win32s do not use the WINSPOOL application programming interfaces (APIs) because they are not supported in Win32s. As a result, you can usually disable this driver while installing Win32s and then re-enable it afterwards.
- Delete the WIN32S directory, the WIN32APP directory, and the W32SYS.DLL, W32S16.DLL, and WIN32S.EXE files from your hard disk.

  Edit the WIN32S.INI file on your hard disk. Change the line(s) SETUP=1 to read SETUP=0. Reboot your computer and reinstall Win32s.

  Although it is possible to install Win32s over an old installation of Win32s, it is recommended that you remove the old files before installing the new ones.
- Make sure that paging is enabled. From the Control Panel, choose the 386 Enhanced icon, choose Virtual Memory, then choose Change. Verify that the drive type is not set to None.
- Make sure that SHARE is enabled. Edit the AUTOEXEC.BAT file and add the following line if it is not already there:
  `C:\DOS\SHARE.EXE`

If you are running Windows for Workgroups or you have a file by the name VSHARE.386 on your system, you do not need to load SHARE in the AUTOEXEC.BAT file. If you have this file, edit the SYSTEM.INI file and add the following line to the [386Enh] section:

```
Device=VSHARE.386
KBCategory: kbpolicy kbdisplay kbinterop
  kberrmsg
KBSubcategory: win31 wfw wfwg
```

To get this, and more information, contact Microsoft on any of it's on-line services. The services are listed in any Microsoft documentation or inside your MS Windows manual.

MAC OS

What is the ASLM and do I need to install it?

ISSUE
What is the ASLM and do I need to install it?

SOLUTION
The Apple Shared Library Manager is a piece of system software written by Apple. It has it's own installer and is not part of the full install of FrameMaker release 5.

The ASLM is not required on PowerMacs.

The ASLM is needed to run the ImageMark graphic filters on 680x0 Macs. The following filters are provided by ImageMark:

- AutoCAD
- CGM
- Corel Draw
- GEM
- HPGL
- IGES
- MicroGrafx
- Windows Metafile
- WordPerfect Graphics

If the ImageMark graphic filters are not needed, FrameMaker will run just fine on 680x0 Macs without ASLM installed.

Why doesn't the tutorial work properly and/or give installation errors?

ISSUE
When I double click the FrameMaker tutorial to start it up, the hypertext links either fail to work or I get an error message telling me the tutorial was not installed correctly. Why?

SOLUTION
The FrameMaker tutorial must be accessed through Help, rather than double clicking it open. Go to FrameMaker Help and click on Tutorial to start it up so that all hypertext links work properly.

UNIX

Can a single machine license FrameMaker 4 and FrameMaker release 5?

ISSUE
Can I run multiple license processes, fm_fls, on the same machine? That is, can I have the same machine be the license server for both FrameMaker 4 and FrameMaker release 5?

SOLUTION
You can only have one license process run on a machine. The options are:

1. Designate another machine as the FrameMaker release 5 license server.
2. Add your FrameMaker release 5 licenses to your FrameMaker 4 licenses file by re-running fmsetupfls. We would recommend running fmsetupfls from the FrameMaker release 5 installation as it contains some bug fixes.
   To do this:
   A. Make a backup of your FrameMaker 4 licenses file called licenses.orig. By default, this is located in install_dir_4/fminit/licenses, where install_dir_4 is the directory in which FrameMaker 4 is installed.
   B. Copy the FrameMaker 4 licenses file over to the FrameMaker release 5 install_dir_5/fminit directory (install_dir_5 is the directory in which FrameMaker release 5 is installed).
   C. Run fmsetupfls from the FrameMaker release 5 directory:
   `install_dir_5/bin/fmsetupfls`
   When asked if you would like to start the license server process, answer Yes.
   D. When this has finished, copy or link the following 4 files back to install_dir_4/fminit directory (or wherever you have placed these files): licenses, env.csh, env.sh, fm_fls_auto.

NOTE: Legally, you are allowed to use only as many copies of FrameMaker as you have licenses for one version. That is, is you had originally purchased 10 FrameMaker 4 licenses but only upgraded 7 licenses to FrameMaker release 5, you can only run a total of 10 copies of FrameMaker 4 and release 5 at any one time.

Are imiges9.ini and imcgm9.ini missing from the installation?

ISSUE
Chapter 11 of the online manual Using Frame Filters discusses customizing graphics filters. It lists imiges9.ini and

imcgm9.ini in the "Customizing grahpics filters" section. However, these file s aren't in the $FMHOME/fminit/filters directory. Are these files available?

SOLUTION
The imiges9.ini is not in the installation because there are no user configurable parameters for the IGES filter.

The imcgm9.ini file is available to configure the CGM filter but is missing from the installation directory. Adobe Technical Support has made the imcgm.9.ini file available via our online services.

General Information

MAC OS / WINDOWS / UNIX

FrameMaker, FrameViewer, and Frame Developer's Kit (FDK) 5 Feature Summary

The new versions of FrameMaker and FrameViewer for Macintosh, UNIX, and Windows platforms include powerful new features and enhancements that dramatically increase users' productivity for authoring and distributing documents on multiple computing platforms. The products provide a complete solution for organizations that need the flexibility to publish and distribute documents on paper, over the Internet, or via other electronic distribution media.

U.S. and International English versions of FrameMaker, release 5 is available on Macintosh, Power Macintosh, Sun OS, Solaris, HP-UX and Windows computing platforms.

New Features FrameMaker 5's new features add more flexibility, power, and ease-of-use in several key categories including authoring efficiency, compound document support and cross-platform architecture, and online publishing capabilities. Some of the new features include:

Authoring Efficiency Automatic text runarounds allow users to quickly and easily flow text around graphics as a rectangular boundary, an arbitrary polygon, or following the contour of an irregular image. Runarounds can use the "page-location-based" approach commonly found in desktop publishing packages, or be included in an anchored frame that flows with the text.

Straddles allow headlines, tables, graphics, or footnotes to span multiple columns and side heads. Straddles can be defined at the paragraph level, allowing improved consistency. Automatic column balancing can even cross page boundaries, making FrameMaker's automatic composition capabilities the most powerful available on the desktop today.

An online tutorial enables users to learn FrameMaker, release 5 with an interactive lessons that can be easily referred to any time in the document creation process. FrameMaker's online help and reference documentation has also been upgraded in 5.

Compound Document Support & Cross-Platform Architecture Import text by reference. Regardless of computer platform, text can now be imported by reference into FrameMaker documents. Imported text can come from other FrameMaker documents, ASCII text, or word processing formats supported by FrameMaker's import filters. The imported text can retain its original format or pick up the new format from the destination FrameMaker document. This feature is very useful with documents that will be shared across platforms and contain boilerplate information.

Filter enhancements. The FrameMaker filter architecture has been totally re-engineered to provide consistent text and graphics import and export capabilities across all platforms. FrameMaker can import and export common text and graphic formats, allowing users to share information in existing documents.

Adobe Type Manage(TM) (ATM(TM)) and support for Type 1 fonts. ATM is included with the UNIX and Windows products. Support for Adobe Type 1 fonts is now available across all platforms making cross-platform movement of documents completely seamless.

Frame Developer's Kit. The Frame Developer's Kit(TM), or FDK, for Macintosh, UNIX and Windows platforms, is targeted at end-users, ISV developers, value-added resellers, and systems integrators who want to develop portable, value-added applications for FrameMaker, FrameViewer, and FrameMaker+SGML. The Frame Developer's Kit consists of a set of cross-platform development tools including Frame's Application Program Interface (API) and the Frame Development Environment (FDE).

The newly enhanced Frame API contains a set of function calls that allows users to write C-based applications to take more control of Frame product behavior, as well as communicate interactively with the user. With Frame's API, users can develop applications as simple as adding a new menu item, or as complex as building a complete document assembly system around Frame's products.

The FDE has been enhanced to help users make API applications portable to all platforms supported by Frame products.

Online Publishing More and more documents are being published electronically, across enterprise networks or over the Internet. FrameMaker is cementing its position as the authoring tool of choice for documents that will be distributed electronically. FrameMaker supports the four leading online distribution options with automatic hypertext link generation and standard output options to FrameViewer, the Internet/World Wide Web, Adobe Acrobat 2.0, and RTF export for WinHelp.

FrameViewer. FrameViewer, release 5 users can take advantage of the following new features for electronic document creation and distribution:

Custom titles in alert boxes enable document authors to easily create alert boxes that display messages with their own customized titles.

Pull-right pop-up menus can now have a submenu for another layer of linked commands.

Document by document hypertext preferences give users the ability to control window placement from the table of contents, indexes, or any other automatically generated information.

Internet/WWW publishing. FrameMaker, release 5 will include an integrated HyperText Markup Language (HTML) document conversion tool that automates the task of preparing documents for the World Wide Web. The HTML export option allows the user to define mappings from FrameMaker paragraph styles to HTML, and hypertext links to intra- and inter-document Uniform Resource Locators -even to other web sites.

Adobe(TM) Acrobat(TM) 2.0 Support. FrameMaker now generates enhanced PostScript files which can be used by the Acrobat Distiller to generate PDF Mark 2.0 compatible files. FrameMaker PostScript takes advantage of Acrobat features like bookmarks, article threads, cross-document hypertext links, annotations, and thumbnails.

RTF WinHelp. The RTF export filter has been enhanced to simplify the creation of WinHelp files.

Robust Features Building on previous versions, FrameMaker, release 5 incorporates features such as intelligent tables; FrameMath(TM); conditional text; a QuickAccess bar; object-oriented drawing tools; process, spot, Pantone and custom color; and automatic updating and generation of cross-references, tables of contents, and indexes. Also, with Instant View(TM), FrameMaker files can be immediately distributed by FrameViewer without post processing. This gives users the ability to eliminate time-to-market delays.

FrameViewer continues to provide high-quality online viewing of documents, hypertext navigation within and among documents, support for on-demand printing, support for platform-based multimedia, as well as graphics and text imported by reference.

PRICING AND UPGRADE INFORMATION

Pricing and Upgrade Information FrameMaker pricing is unchanged for the new releases. Contact your Frame representative or the appropriate reseller/distributor for Frame 4 to Frame 5 upgrade pricing.

FrameMaker 4 customers with an active FrameMaker Support Subscription (FSS) will automatically receive upgrades at no cost. Customers who purchase FrameMaker 4 after March 27, 1995 are eligible to receive a no-cost upgrade for a limited time.

Pricing for FrameViewer, release 5 is dependent on quantity. Please contact your Frame representative or reseller for more information.

International FrameMaker French, German, Swedish, Spanish, Italian, and Portuguese versions of FrameMaker, release 5 will also be available. For pricing and availability of international versions, please contact Martin Doettling, Frame's director of international product marketing, at 408/975-6141 or mxd@frame.com

What enhancements and bug fixes are included in FrameMaker 5.0.1?

FEATURE ENHANCEMENTS IN FRAMEMAKER 5.0.1

The FrameMaker 5.0.1 feature enhancements include:

Two new hypertext commands (gotoObjectIdFitWin and openObjectIdFitWin)
Enhanced TIFF import performance/cache
WorldScript support re-enabled (Macintosh only)

BUG FIXES IN FRAMEMAKER 5.0.1

Listed below are some specific fixes that are included in the 5.0.1 version. The list is not comprehensive but it captures many of the bugs which were reported by a large portion of the customer base. There are categories listed by platform as well as a final category of bugs which were core bugs (found in all platforms and fixed in all platforms).

There were a number of random crashes fixed in this release (for all platforms). Due in large part to the cryptic nature of those bug descriptions, many of them are not listed below.

MS-Windows specific items fixed in 5.0.1:

Bug	Description
98242	Pair Kerning broken.
97409	Resource leak when importing many Imagemark supported graphics.
97264	OLE support broken.
97327	Thumbnails of landscape documents won't print.
98696	Filename prefix changes after generating PDF file.

Mac specific items fixed in 5.0.1:

Bug	Description
96710	The Open button in the Object Properties dialog box and the Open Pulbisher button in the Subscriber Option dialog box failed to go to the source.
98207	Internal error 547016,484316 (PowerMac) and 4210980,52433296 when attempting to print from a book file with the Graphic tool palette open.
96972	The entire file prints when attempting to print a page range with incorrect page numbers specified.
97007& 98648	Various Internal errors which resulted when attempting to rearrange files in a book.
97993	Negative pages numbers fail to print unless individually specified.

UNIX Specific items fixed in 5.0.1:

Bug	Description
96766	fmbatch (HP) can't print book file without opening documents.

99332& 98501	Document Compare file and book crashes.
97496	Bus Error conflict of fmbatch with Solaris 2.5.
96283	Problem with run-in paragraphs and anchored frames.
97492	FrameMaker crashes when applying a master page to a body page when autoconnect is not turned on.
96436	Install program reports that installation was successful when actually, the install failed due to "file system full" problem.
96586	Problems importing MIF files containing EPSI graphics.

Multiple Platform (fixed in all platforms):

Bug	Description
	Various crashes which result with a table title set to below.
96817	Character formats are not brought over to the TOC.
89540& 93208	Anchored Frame dialog doesn't retain last settings.
96902	Index doesn't work from Book fie via Acrobat.
96944	Various problems with positioning of change bars.
98022	Crash resulting from the application of a hidden condition tag being applied to an achored frame.
97923	Random crashes when deleting spaces in a file with Smart Spaces enabled.
97618	Text in Body column doesn't repack after paragraphs in a sidehead are deleted.
97924	Text insets cause RTF export to fail.

UPDATE INFORMATION

NOTE: the 5.0.1 updates are a full FrameMaker installation. FSS Customers: Customers with active FSS as of 9/1/95 will automatically receive a free FrameMaker 5.0.1 update. We will send one update per platform per FSS contract. FSS Customers may request additional updates. The FSS updates will begin shipping the week of 10/16/95.

Non-FSS Customers: Customers who purchase FrameMaker version 5.0 between 9/1/95 and 11/1/95 will receive a 5.0.1 update free of charge. They are required to provide proof of purchase to Order Administration. You can FAX your proof of purchase to 408-975-6616.

FrameMaker Release 5 customers who are not on FSS (and purchased FrameMaker before 9/1/95) may purchase the 5.0.1 update from Frame Technology for $25. For U.S. and Canada, please call our Order Administration department: 408-975-6161 (7am-5pm Pacific) to order your update. The default media will be CD-ROM. If you need diskette media, please indicate that when you order.

The Macintosh and Windows 5.0.1 updates will also available via ftp and WWW.

FrameMaker 5.1.x Program Corrections

FrameMaker 5.1 corrects several problems that occurred in FrameMaker 5.0.x, which are listed below. The latest version of FrameMaker, Adobe FrameMaker 5.1.1, is a re-branding of FrameMaker 5.1 as an Adobe product only, and does not include any additional corrections or features.

You can upgrade to Adobe FrameMaker 5.1.1 by ordering the installation disks from Adobe Customer Services at 800-843-7263 (disks include a $19.95 shipping and handling fee). You can also download Adobe FrameMaker for the Macintosh and Windows from the Adobe FTP site at ftp.frame.com (FrameMaker for UNIX is not available online due to its size).

A single, compressed file of the FrameMaker for Windows installation disks (approximately 15 MB in size) is located on the FTP site in /pub/techsup/product_updates/dos/. If you have a slower Internet connection, you can also download separate compressed files for each installation disk from the maker511 directory inside the dos directory.

A single, compressed file of the FrameMaker for Macintosh installation disks (approximately 20 MB in size) is located in /pub/techsup/product_updates/mac/. If you have a slower Internet connection, you can also download separate files for each installation disk from the maker511 directory inside the mac directory.

CORRECTIONS IN FRAMEMAKER 5.1.X

Listed below are some specific corrections in FrameMaker 5.1.x. The list is not comprehensive, but it includes many of the problems reported by customers. The corrections are arranged by platform, followed with corrections that affect all platforms.

Problems fixed in FrameMaker 5.1.x for Windows:

Bug	Description
98242	Pair Kerning not working properly.
99357	MS Word import filter adds comma to index entries.
99832	Character display does not match character print.
100419	Crash when opening file with missing referenced graphics.
101610	Some WMF graphics displaying as a gray box.

Problems fixed in FrameMaker 5.1.x for the Macintosh:

Bug	Description
99337	Photoshop TIFF saved with Thumbnail preview displays distorted when imported into FrameMaker.
100418	Book files which contain all landscape pages print the first file properly, but all other files print in portrait orientation.
100956	Grayscale EPSF graphics which contain black and no other colors display in cyan.
101311	WordCount is grayed out (unavailable) even when the WordCount Module is properly installed.

104031 Imported TIFF images that are rotated in FrameMaker will display distorted and/or in the wrong orientation when the screen is refreshed.

Problems fixed in FrameMaker 5.1.x for UNIX:

Bug	Description
98731	Crash when updating character formats used in paragraph autonumbering.
99692	Crash when viewing or printing a page with a polyline.
100765	Can't use middle mouse button to add a reshape handle to a graphics line.

Problems fixed in FrameMaker 5.1.x on multiple platforms:

Bug	Description
98754	MS Word import filter doesn't bring over all index markers.
99107	Opening MIF file creates extra blank pages.
99520	FrameMaker crashing when generating a book file.
100173	Grayscale TIFFs embedded in EPS with other CMYK objects not separating properly upon print.
102807	Unable to select graphics inside anchored frame set to top of column when sideheads turned on.

WINDOWS

Q What fixes are included in the 5.1.2 update to FrameMaker for Windows 95/NT?

A The FrameMaker 5.1.2 update for Windows 95/NT only, which Adobe recently released, offers several fixes. Here are a few of the highlights.

- FrameMaker 5.1.2 doesn't crash under Windows NT 4.0 when you select an option from the "Properties" pop-up menu in the "Paragraph Designer" dialog box.
- Links will work correctly in PDF files distilled in Acrobat 2.x from FrameMaker 5.1.2–generated PostScript files.
- Using "Paste Special" to paste linked OLE2 graphics or text correctly creates a link in FrameMaker 5.1.2.

UNIX

Will Frame Products be affected in the year 2000 and beyond?

ISSUE

Will Frame Products be affected by the date change in the year 2000?

SOLUTION

Enhancement Request #105905 has been logged requesting we ensure that future versions of Frame Products work properly in the year 2000 and beyond. Whatever the current versions of Frame Products are in the year 2000, they will work correctly on the supported Operating Systems.

With regard to the current version of Frame Products (version 5) and as licensing seems to be a primary concern, we actually tried changing the system date on one of our SunOS machines to see if FrameMaker would be able to obtain a license. Unfortunately, we were unable to change the date on the machine as it wouldn't take anything greater than the year 1999. We were successful in changing the date on a Solaris machine to the year 2000 and had no problem running FrameMaker release 5 and getting a shared license.

Therefore, you may want to try changing the system date on one of your machines and try to run FrameMaker (you may find that older operating systems won't allow a date past 1999, as we did with SunOS). Other things to consider in addition to licensing may be system variables (such as current date and modification date), text imported by reference, and the document compare utility.

What UNIX platforms are supported with FrameMaker/FrameViewer?

ISSUE

Which UNIX platforms are supported with FrameMaker/Viewer 4 and FrameMaker/Reader/Viewer release 5?

SOLUTION

FrameMaker/FrameViewer 4 are supported on the following UNIX platforms:

HP: HP9000 Series 300, 400, 700 or 800, HP-UX 8.0 or 9.0
IBM: RISC System/6000, AIX 3.2.3 or 3.2.4
Motorola: Series 900 or 8000, SVr4/V88 version 4 or 4.1
SGI: Indigo or Indy, IRIX 5.1 or 5.2
Sun: SPARC, SunOS 4.1.3 and Solaris 2.1 or 2.2
SCO: 486 or Pentium-based systems, SCO ODT 3.0
DEC Alpha: Digital Alpha Station, Digital UNIX 3.0

FrameMaker/FrameReader/FrameViewer release 5 are supported on the following UNIX platforms:

HP: HP9000 Series 700 or 800, HP-UX 9.0
IBM: RISC System/6000 or PowerPC, AIX 4.1.3
SGI: Indigo or Indy, IRIX 5.1.1, 5.2 or 5.3
Sun: SPARC, SunOS 4.1.3 and Solaris 2.3 or 2.4
DEC Alpha: Digital Alpha Station, Digital UNIX 3.0 or 3.2

Adobe Illustrator®

The first Adobe application, Adobe Illustrator harks back to the mid-1980s. It has just been released in April 1997 as version 7.0 for both Windows and MacOS platforms. More than just an illustration program, now graphic artists, technical illustrators, desktop publishers, and on-line designers can work in a truly seamless workflow across platforms and between other graphics applications, like PageMaker and Photoshop. A decade of refinement, CMYK *and* RGB *color control, and direct-to-GIF is a small sampling of Adobe Illustrator 7.*

Contents

Adobe Illustrator®

Feature Techniques

MAC OS / WINDOWS

Q The "Lock" and "Hide" commands in the Arrange menu allow me to lock and hide selected objects in Illustrator. Is there a way to lock and hide the objects that aren't selected?

A Yes. Hold down the Alt key (Windows) or the Option key (Macintosh) while selecting "Lock" or "Hide" from the Arrange menu, and Illustrator will lock or hide all objects you do not have selected.

Q I use the PANTONE color palette all the time, so I'd love it if those colors would show up in the "Paint Styles" palette whenever I start a new illustration. Is there a way to make Illustrator do that?

A Yes. You can set several application-wide defaults by modifying a special file Illustrator refers to whenever you start a new illustration. This file is called STARTUP.AI in the Windows version 4.0x of Illustrator; in Illustrator 5.x for the Macintosh, the file is called "Adobe Illustrator Startup." It's located in the AI4 directory (Windows) or the "Plug-Ins" folder (Macintosh).

By modifying the Windows version of the file, you can change Illustrator's default patterns, graph designs, and custom colors. On the Macintosh, you can also define default gradients and window dimensions (what the size and position of your illustration window will be when you open new illustrations). To set other defaults, use the options listed on the Preferences submenu of the File menu.

Before altering the Illustrator startup file, make a backup copy of it. Then, open it just as you'd open any Illustrator document and modify it by adding, deleting, or modifying colors and other attributes. Or, if you have a document that already contains all the color definitions and other attributes you want to be your defaults, make it your startup file by saving it as STARTUP.AI in your AI4 directory (Windows) or as "Adobe Illustrator Startup" in your "Plug-Ins" folder within your Illustrator folder.

If you're adding new colors, patterns, or gradients to your startup file, make sure you not only define the new colors, patterns, and so forth, but also create a sample of each and place that sample on the page. If your new color, pattern, or gradient isn't used in your startup document, Illustrator will automatically delete it from your file when you reopen it later. If you want all the PANTONE colors or all the colors from one of the other color-library files to be in your startup document, but you don't want to have to create samples of each color, here's a shortcut: Instead of importing those colors into your startup document by using the "Import Styles" dialog box, make the color-library file your startup document. Although each color in the color-library files hasn't been assigned to objects in those files, Illustrator won't delete them automatically (these files have been specially created to prevent this).

Q I like to use my arrow keys to "nudge" objects. But is there a way to make a nudge bigger or smaller?

A Yes, you can adjust Illustrator's nudge value (the amount of distance an element will move when you press one of the arrow keys while that object is selected). In Windows, select "Preferences..." from the Edit menu, and enter a new value under "Arrow key distance" in the "Preferences" dialog box. On the Mac, select "General..." from the Preferences submenu of the File menu, and in the "General Preferences" dialog box, enter a new value under "Cursor keys."

Q I often bring artwork from Illustrator into Persuasion, and it's coming in with a white box around it. Is there a way to get rid of that white box?

A Yes, but you might not have to. That white box is a characteristic of the screen preview Illustrator saves with its EPS files under certain circumstances. It's visible only on screen and when you print to non-PostScript devices. So, if you'll be printing to a PostScript device from Persuasion and won't need to run your presentation on screen, you can just ignore it. But if you do need to do an on-screen presentation or print to a non-PostScript device, here's what you can do to get rid of it (the exact steps you need to take depend on what version of Illustrator you're using).

Illustrator 4.x. If you use Illustrator 4.x for Windows, the easiest way for you to get rid of the white box is to save your artwork in the Windows metafile (WMF) format instead of as an EPS. To do so, select "Export Art..." from Illustrator's File menu. In the "Export Art" dialog box, select "WMF - Microsoft Windows Metafile" from the "Export type" list, and click on the "Options..." button. Then, in the "WMF Output Filter Setup" dialog box, deselect the "Background Rectangle" option. Click "OK" to close that dialog box, and then click the "Export" button in the "Export Art" dialog box to save your artwork in WMF format.

Illustrator 5.x. If you've saved your EPS from Illustrator 5.x you shouldn't have a problem with a "white box" displaying around it in Persuasion—Illustrator 5.x automatically saves its EPS files without this characteristic.

Illustrator 6.0. To save your EPS from Illustrator 6.0 so it'll display without a white box in Persuasion, follow these steps. First, select "Save As..." from the File menu. In the save-as dialog box enter a name for your EPS, select "Illustrator EPS" from the "Format" list, and click "OK." Illustrator will display the "EPS Format" dialog box. Select "8-bit Macintosh" from the list of "Preview" options, and then deselect the "Include Document Thumbnails" option (that's the key to turning off the "white box" screen-preview effect). Click "OK" to save your EPS.

Q I've been making bar graphs, but the bars are awfully boring. Is there any way to customize the column bars?

A Sure. All you need to do is create a "graph design" (which is similar to a pattern tile) that you then apply to various columns in your graph. Here's how.

1. Start by creating a basic bar graph. Then, using the group-selection tool, select the smallest column (shortest bar) in the graph. Make a copy of it by selecting "Copy" and then "Paste" from the Edit menu.
2. Move the copy of your column bar out of the way of your graph, then alter it as you wish—for instance, you might change its fill or stroke color. Or, if you want to replace the bar with one or more graphic objects, you can place some other element in front of the column (it must not exceed the boundaries of the column), and then select the column and apply a fill and stroke of "None" so it's invisible. (Make sure the rectangle is behind the other art, or this won't work.)
3. Using the selection tool, select all the elements you assembled in step 2.
4. If you're using Illustrator 4.x for Windows, select "Define Graph Design..." from the Graph menu. If you're using Illustrator 5.x or 6.0 for the Mac, select "Design..." from the Graphs submenu of the Object menu.

TIP MAC OS / WINDOWS

An easy technique for a complex effect

Drawing complex geometric patterns is almost always easier on a computer than on paper, even when it doesn't look easy. For instance, the "warped" checkerboards shown here look difficult to draw, but they're not. Here's how to do it.

1. In a blank Illustrator document, draw a large square by holding down the Shift key while you drag the rectangle tool across your screen. While the square is still selected, turn off its center point. In Windows, do this by selecting just its center point with the direct-selection tool, and pressing Delete. On the Mac, choose "Attributes..." from the Object menu and deselect the "Show center point" option in the "Attributes" dialog box.

2. Use the direct-selection (hollow pointer) tool to select the top and bottom segments, and press the Delete key so you're left with just the left and right segments.
3. With the side segments selected, choose the blend tool and click on the top ends of both the segments. When Illustrator displays the "Blend" dialog box, enter an odd number in the "Steps" field (in our sample illustrations, we used 11 steps) and click "OK."
4. If you're in Windows, ungroup your blend steps.
5. Use the direct-selection tool to select just the top points of the two leftmost segments and press Ctrl + J (Windows) or Command + J (Macintosh) to join the points. Next, do the same to the third and fourth segments, the fifth and sixth segments, and so on until there's just one segment left over.

6. Join the bottom segments in a similar way, working from right to left instead: First, select the bottom endpoints of the two rightmost segments and join them. Then, join the next two segments, and so on.
7. Using the direct-selection tool, select just the top endpoints of all the line segments. Your artwork should look something like the illustration at top right.
8. After selecting the rotation tool, click on the top endpoint of the leftmost segment (this sets the point around which rotation occurs), then click on one of the top endpoints to the right, and drag them downward until they're vertical (holding down the Shift key while you rotate will help—doing so constrains your rotation to increments of 45 degrees.) Your illustration should look something like the example above.

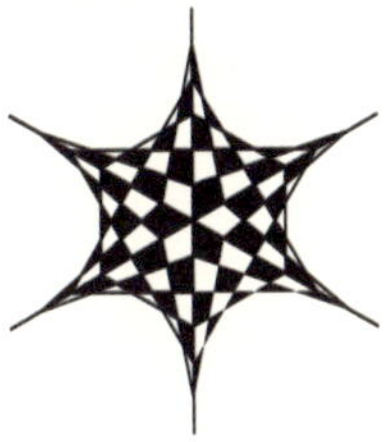

Use the rotation, skew, and other tools to alter your "warped" checkerboard for a variety of effects. The object at right consists of six checkerboards.

TIP MAC OS / WINDOWS

Stay in the middle of the road

A corollary to Murphy's Law is that your design demands expand to fit the abilities of the software. Now that creating text on flexible paths is a standard part of your repertoire, you may be looking for extra tricks to further refine that process. Here's a tip on aligning the type half above and half below the path.

Highlight text already on a path by either selecting it with the selection tool or highlighting it with the text tool. In Illustrator for Windows, choose "Type Style" from the Type menu and enter a negative value in the "Vertical Shift" text box that is one-fourth to one-third of the point size of the selected text. Click "OK" in the "Type Style" dialog box to apply the vertical shift to the text.

In Illustrator for the Macintosh, choose "Character" from the Type menu. Click on the lever in the lower-right corner of the palette to display the bottom half of the Character palette. Enter a negative baseline-shift value that is approximately one-fourth to one-third of the point size of the selected text, and then press Return or Tab to apply the option to the text.

Once you've set a negative baseline for your text, that value will remain the default for subsequent text you create. This is useful if you have many text-path combinations to set, but remember to change the baseline-shift value back to zero when you need unshifted text.

5. In the "Design" dialog box, click "New." Name the design and click "OK."
6. To add the design to a bar graph, use the group-selection tool to select the column(s) and any legend items you want to fill with the design. Then, if you're in Windows, select "Use Column Design…" from the Graph menu. If you're on a Mac, choose "Column…" from the Graphs submenu of the Object menu.
7. In the "Graph Column Design" dialog box, select a column design type. (In this example, we've selected "Repeating" because we want each column to be composed of several graph-design objects. If you select this design type, be sure to enter a value in the "Each design represents" field.) Select the design you want to use and any other attributes, and then click "OK" to apply the design to the selected column(s).
8. Repeat these steps to create and apply designs to your remaining columns.

For more information on custom graphs, see the Adobe Illustrator User Guide, "Using graph designs" on page 246 (Windows) or "About graph designs" on page 196 (Macintosh).

Q How can I trap a dashed line?

A It's not too hard to trap a dashed line in Illustrator—you can use one of the two following methods, depending on the colors of the line and its background. However, before you do any trapping in your document, be sure to talk to your print-production service providers (commercial printer, color house, and so forth) about how best to trap your publication. Depending on how complex your trapping needs are, they may recommend that you not do any of the trapping by yourself, and that you let them use Luminous TrapWise or some other dedicated trapping program for the job.

If your service providers suggest you trap your illustration yourself, here's a synopsis of what you should know. In general, you want to bleed the lighter color into the darker color. So, when the top object is a lighter hue than the one beneath it, use a spread trap. In a spread trap the lighter-colored, topmost object is enlarged by stroking its boundaries with the same color as its fill. When the top object is a darker hue than the one beneath it, use a choke trap. With a choke trap, the lighter background color is extended into the area of the top, relatively dark-colored object.

To create a spread trap for a dashed line that's lighter than its background color, do the following:

1. Create a light-colored dashed line on top of a relatively dark background. Make its line weight whatever you ultimately want it to look like (in our example, we drew a light green, 4-point dashed line). Be sure to select the round-cap or projecting-cap option in the Paint Styles palette (they're the two cap options on the right). If you select the butt-cap option, you'll end up with dashes that are trapped only on their outer sides. Do not set your line to overprint.
2. Copy the dashed line, then paste it in front.
3. Change the line weight of the top copy of your dashed line. You want to increase it by twice the trap width recommended by your service providers. For instance, our line was originally 4 points, so if we wanted a trap width of half a point, we'd increase the top line's weight to 5.
4. Set the top line to overprint. On screen, your dashed line will look thicker than you want it to be, but that extra weight is your trap, and it'll give you the printed results you're after. If you want to make sure you've set it up correctly, you can print test separations to a desktop printer.

NOTE: This spread method creates a trap for the entire dashed line, so it will look right only if you use it on dashed lines that are enclosed entirely within a background of the color you're using to trap them.

To create a choke trap for a dashed line that's darker than its background color, follow these steps.

1. Create your dark-colored dashed line against a light background, making sure you select the round-cap or projecting-cap option. Set the line width to its ultimate desired weight, minus twice the trap width recommended by your service provider (in this example, we chose to print a 4-point dashed line with the same suggested trap width of half a point, so we set the top dashed line to be 3 points). Do not set it to overprint.
2. Copy the line and paste the copy in front of the original.
3. Set the topmost line's width back to the desired stroke weight (in this case, 4 points). Set this line to overprint.

This technique knocks out the width of the line less the trap on the background color. Then, the darker line at full width overprints to lighter background and produces the desired result of the lighter background color bleeding into the darker dashed line color.

Q When I use a custom design for markers on a line or scatter graph, I can't seem to control the size of the markers. Is there any way to adjust them without using the scale tool?

A Yes. One way to do that is to make sure you're creating the markers to be just the size you want them to be on the graph. Here's how.

Whenever you create a custom design for a graph marker, you need to place a rectangle behind it. Illustrator uses this rectangle to determine the size of the marker design—it will always resize the design so that its backmost rectangle is exactly 6 by 6 points. So, to create a custom design that won't resize when you use it as a marker, follow these steps.

1. Create the artwork for the design at whatever size you want it to be on the graph. Then, select the rectangle tool and click it once. When the "Rectangle" dialog box appears, enter "6 pt" for both the width and height of the rectangle, and click "OK."
2. If you don't want the rectangle to be visible, assign it a fill and stroke of "None."
3. While the rectangle is still selected, send it to the backmost layer by pressing Ctrl + Shift + B (Windows) or Command + - (Mac), or select "Send to Back" from the Edit menu (Windows) or the Arrange menu (Mac).
4. Select both the rectangle and the design, and turn them into a custom graph design by selecting "Define Graphic Design..." from the Graph menu (Windows) or "Design..." from the Graphs submenu of the Object menu (Mac).
5. In the "Define Graph Design" (Windows) or "Design" (Mac) dialog box, click "New," enter a name for your graph design, and click "OK."

When you apply this design to your graph markers, it'll retain its original size and proportions. (To assign a custom design to graph markers, select one or more markers, then choose "Use Marker Design..." from the Graph menu in Windows, or use the direct-selection tool to choose "Markers..." from the Graphs submenu of the Object menu on the Mac. In the "Use Marker Design" or "Graph Marker Design" dialog box, select your design and click "OK.")

Q Is there some way I can get access to the hand tool while the type tool is still selected? Hitting the usual shortcut key, the spacebar, just inserts spaces in my text. This has been driving me crazy!

A Try this for quick sanity restoration. With the text tool selected, hold down the Ctrl (Windows) or Command (Macintosh) key; then, while continuing to hold it down, press the spacebar. This will display the zoom tool. Release the Ctrl or Command key, and you'll have the grabber hand. In Windows, release the spacebar as soon as you see the hand tool, and hold the mouse button down until you're done dragging—otherwise, you'll be back to getting spaces.

Q I scanned some artwork, then converted it from bitmap to vector artwork with Streamline and opened the file in Illustrator. How can I make the nonfilled areas of the artwork transparent so that I can see the background behind them?

A To get the result you want, you need to create a compound path out of the filled and nonfilled areas in your image.

The letter O is a good example of this, so we'll use it to explain how Streamline created what you're seeing. In the process of converting the letter O to an editable path, Streamline creates a solid white oval on top of a solid black oval. On a white background, this white oval will appear transparent, but of course that's an optical illusion—it's really opaque.

Once you've opened the file in Illustrator, select both circles that comprise the O and create a compound path: choose "Make Compound" from the Paint menu (or Ctrl + Alt + G) in Windows or "Make" from the Compound Path submenu of the Object menu (Command + 8) on a Macintosh. Voilà—your object is now transparent.

Q I've used other programs to plot graph points by entering x and y values for each point. Is this type of graphing possible in Illustrator, and if so, how do I do it?

A Yes, it's possible. The type of graph you describe is called a scatter graph, and here's how you can do it. Select "Graph

MICRO TIP MAC OS / WINDOWS

Say you're creating an illustration you're going to export as an EPS and use in a program like PageMaker, and you always want that illustration to be positioned at a certain spot on your page—for instance, if you're creating a logo that should always print in the upper-left corner of a letter-size page. Create the logo on a letter-size page, in the correct position, and export it with a bounding box the size of the entire page. Then, in PageMaker, position the EPS directly over your entire page and place other items on top of it.

Style" from the Graph menu on the PC or "Style..." from the Graphs submenu of the Object menu on the Mac. In the "Graph Style" dialog box, select "Scatter" and deselect "Connect data points." If you want to choose how axes are numbered, in the "Axis" area click "Left" to open the "Graph Axis Style" dialog box. Select "Use manual axis values" and enter values for your left axis. For example, enter a "Minimum label value" of 0, a "Maximum label value" of 5, and a "Value between labels" of 1. This will produce a graph with a range of numbers on the left axis from 0 to 5 in increments of 1. Do the same for the bottom axis if desired (click "OK," then click the "Bottom" button to make the "Graph Axis Style" dialog box reappear). If you want Illustrator to enter the values for you, select "Calculate axis values from data."

Select the graph tool (on the PC, drag out to select the scatter graph tool) and click and drag to create the graph, or click once on the artboard and enter the desired dimensions in points in the "Graph" dialog box. In the "Graph Data" dialog box, enter the y values in the first column and the x values in the second column, and then click "OK."

Q I see that I can now export to PDF and use Acrobat Reader to display my slide show. In the past I've always used Player. Now that I have a choice I'm not sure which one to use. What advice can you give me?

A Persuasion Player and Acrobat Reader each have their advantages; which one you choose will depend on which features are most important in a given presentation. You may even want to consider making both a Persuasion Player and an Acrobat Reader version of some presentations to use under different circumstances or with different audiences.

Here are some of the differences that you should keep in mind.

Color and resolution. Player is limited to a resolution of 640 by 480 pixels and to a color "depth" of 256 colors per slide. With Acrobat, the resolution and color depth at which your presentation displays will be limited only by the capabilities of the display system you're using.

- Animations. Player can display animated objects. Reader does not support animation.
- Movies and sounds. Both Player and Reader can play movies and sounds. Playback can be either manual or automatic in Player; in Reader it is manual only.
- Printing. You can't print Player presentations, but you can print PDFs from Reader.
- Consecutive play. In Player you can create a Show List that will play a series of Player files in order without further input from the presenter. Reader does not have a similar feature.

If you have Adobe Acrobat Exchange, you'll also be able to merge full or partial PDFs and add or rearrange PDF pages. Remember, however, that Acrobat Exchange is not included with Persuasion, although Persuasion Player and Acrobat Reader are.

Transferring Files Between Illustrator for Macintosh and Windows

To transfer files between an IBM-compatible computer and a Macintosh, either connect the two computers and use communications software to transfer the files, or use a disk drive specifically designed, or adapted, for this purpose. You

TIP MAC OS / WINDOWS

Changing colors automatically

Ever decide you want to change your colors after you've applied them to objects in your illustration? This can be time-consuming if the colors you want to change are process-color mixes and you've applied those colors to many objects. Fortunately, there's a great way to automate color changes in Illustrator—try using custom colors instead. This lets you easily redefine your colors and repaint objects by changing the CMYK values for the custom colors. For the best results, follow these steps:

1. Create your custom colors and apply them to your artwork.
2. Before redefining any colors, select "Save As..." from the File menu and save your file with a new name.
3. With only the second file open, use the "Custom Color" dialog box to change the CMYK values for your custom colors. It's a good idea to rename the colors—for instance, by adding a "2" at the end of the custom color name. This will help you keep track of the different color versions and will ensure your color definitions don't change unexpectedly if you have more than one illustration open at the same time. (If you have open two illustration files that contain custom colors with the same names but different CMYK percentages, the color definitions in the file most recently opened will override the color definitions in the other file.)

If you want to color-separate your custom colors as process colors, use the Separator utility to convert them to process. Or, if you print your separations from PageMaker, redefine those custom colors as process colors in PageMaker's Colors palette—hold down the Ctrl + Alt + Shift keys (Windows) or Command + Option + Shift keys (Macintosh) while clicking on your custom colors in the Colors palette. Doing so will toggle colors from spot (custom) to process, or vice versa. You'll know your custom colors have been redefined as process when they appear italicized in the Colors palette.

can connect IBM-compatible and Macintosh computers directly using a network, a null modem cable, or a modem at each computer, with or without a phone connection.

Check the size in bytes after you transfer files. The size in bytes of the original file and the transferred file should be identical. When the sizes differ by one or more bytes, the transfer was unsuccessful. Retransfer the file or transfer the file back to the computer from which it came and open the file. When the transfer is successful, the file opens on the computer on which the file was created. When the file sizes are identical, the file may not open on the IBM-compatible computer when a memory intensive network (e.g., TOPS) is loaded, causing low conventional memory. Reopen the file without the network loaded.

Opening Transferred Publications

Because the Macintosh and Windows operating systems use different methods for determining the creator application for documents, Adobe Illustrator uses file extensions and the MS-DOS file naming convention to recognize documents. DOS legal filenames contain up to eight characters, and may be followed by a period and a three-character filename extension that identifies the file type. For example:

Filename Extension	File Type
.ai	Adobe Illustrator document
.pdf	Portable Document Format file
.tif	TIFF image file
.eps	EPS file

MacLink Plus adds a space and "(bin)" to the file name when transferring files from an IBM-compatible computer to a Macintosh using the binary transfer option. Remove the extra space and the "(bin)" before opening the file on the Macintosh computer.

To open transferred Illustrator documents, choose File > Open in Illustrator. To open a file after opening and saving a transferred Illustrator file, you can either double-click on the file's icon or choose File > Open in Illustrator.

TRANSFERRING ILLUSTRATOR FOR THE MACINTOSH DOCUMENT TO ILLUSTRATOR FOR WINDOWS

When you save an Illustrator 5.0 or later document in Illustrator 4 or earlier format, Illustrator combines objects in the document on a single layer, converts gradient fills to masked blends, converts custom colors to process, converts tabs in point text to spaces, and converts tabs in area text to returns. When you save an Illustrator 5.0 or later document in an earlier format and then open the document in Illustrator 5.0 or later, Illustrator converts tab information back from spaces to tabs, but does not restore gradient objects and layer information.

When you save an Illustrator 5.x or 6.0 document in Illustrator 88 or 1.1 format, Illustrator releases compound paths contained in the document. When you save an Illustrator 5.x or 6.0 document in Illustrator 1.1 format, Illustrator releases masks.

When you save an Illustrator 6.0 document in Illustrator 5.x or earlier format, Illustrator ignores placed or opened image and raster data, and does not includes these in the saved Illustrator 5.x or earlier format document. When you save an Illustrator 6.0 document in Illustrator 5 or earlier format, Illustrator removes bitmap images (e.g., TIFF, PICT, Adobe Photoshop 2.5 files, rasterized Illustrator objects) from the document, but includes the masking object for masked bitmap images in the document.

After you save an Illustrator document in an earlier Illustrator format, select the desired format when you resave the document in another format. Illustrator 5.5 and later defaults to the last selected format when saving.

To transfer an Illustrator 5.5 and later for the Macintosh document to Illustrator 4.x for Windows, save the Illustrator document in Illustrator 4 or earlier format with a DOS legal filename using the .ai extension. To transfer an Illustrator 5.0.x and earlier for the Macintosh document to Illustrator 4.x for Windows, save the Illustrator document with the None (Omit EPSF Header) Preview option and the Adobe Illustrator 3 Compatibility option selected, and with a DOS legal filename using the .ai extension.

TRANSFERRING A MACINTOSH ILLUSTRATOR EPS FILE TO WINDOWS

To transfer an Illustrator 6.0 for Macintosh EPS file to Windows, save the Illustrator document in Illustrator EPS format with a DOS legal filename and the .eps extension. In the EPS Format dialog box, select the 1-bit IBM PC Preview option and the 6.0 or 5.0/5.5 Compatibility option.

To transfer an Illustrator 5.5 for the Macintosh EPS file to Windows, save the Illustrator document in EPS format with a DOS legal filename and the .eps extension. In the EPS Format dialog box, select the 1-bit IBM PC Preview option and the Illustrator 5 Compatibility option.

To transfer an Illustrator 5.0.x and earlier for the Macintosh EPS file to Windows, save the Illustrator document with the IBM PC Preview option and the Adobe Illustrator 3 Compatibility option selected, and with a DOS legal filename using the .eps extension.

Because Illustrator 5.0 creates an improperly formatted TIFF image screen preview (header) when saving EPS files with an IBM PC preview, Illustrator 5.0 EPS files saved with the IBM PC option selected for Preview displays as a gray box. Illustrator 5.01 and later create properly formatted IBM PC TIFF image screen previews.

TRANSFERRING ILLUSTRATOR FOR WINDOWS DOCUMENT TO ILLUSTRATOR FOR MACINTOSH

To transfer an Illustrator 4.x for Windows document to Illustrator 5.x or later for the Macintosh, save the Illustrator 4.x document with the Standard (No Preview) Preview option and the Adobe Illustrator 3 Compatibility option selected. When saving, Illustrator automatically adds the .ai extension to the Illustrator document's filename.

IMPORTING ILLUSTRATOR DOCUMENTS IN WINDOWS

To import (i.e., convert) an Illustrator document into a Windows application that supports importing or opening Illustrator 88 format files, save the Illustrator file with the

TIP MAC OS / WINDOWS

Transferring files across platforms

Illustrator creates files that can be opened, edited, or imported into almost any graphics or word-processing application on the Macintosh, in Windows, and on other platforms as well. Here are some pointers to help you transfer Illustrator files between the Macintosh and Windows.

WINDOWS TO MACINTOSH

If you create Illustrator files in Windows and need to bring them to the Macintosh, follow these guidelines:

- If you want to use your Illustrator file in a Macintosh application that can directly open or edit Illustrator files, such as Illustrator or Photoshop, save your Illustrator file by selecting the "Standard (No Preview)" preview option and the "Adobe Illustrator 3" compatibility option in the "Save As" dialog box.
- If you want to use your Illustrator file in a Macintosh application that can import EPS files as noneditable graphics, such as PageMaker, save your Illustrator file by selecting the "Black and White" or "Color" preview option and the "Adobe Illustrator 3" compatibility option in the "Save As" dialog box. Illustrator will produce an EPS with either a black-and-white or color TIFF screen preview, which should look fine on a standard 72-dpi Macintosh display (the black-and-white screen preview will give you a much smaller EPS file). Please also note that PICT previews are standard for EPS files on the Macintosh, so some applications may not display these TIFF previews correctly. Nevertheless, your EPS files should print correctly to any PostScript printer.

MACINTOSH TO WINDOWS

Whenever you take a Macintosh file to the DOS or Windows platform, be sure to name your file appropriately. Use eight characters or less for the main body of the name (don't use any spaces or punctuation) followed by a period and a three-character extension that indicates the file's format (for example, .EPS for Encapsulated PostScript files). Follow these additional guidelines for Illustrator files:

- If you need to use your Illustrator file in a Windows application that supports directly opening or editing EPS files, such as Illustrator 4.x or Photoshop 3.0, save your Illustrator file by selecting "EPS" from the Format pop-up menu in the "Save As" dialog box and click "OK." When the "EPS Format" dialog box appears, select the "None" preview option. If you'll be using the file in Illustrator 4.x in Windows, be sure to set the compatibility option to "Illustrator 3" and name your file with an .AI extension.
- If you want to use your Illustrator file in a Windows application that can import EPS files as noneditable graphics, such as PageMaker, save your Illustrator file by selecting the "EPS" format option in the "Save As" dialog box and clicking "OK." When the "EPS Format" dialog box appears, select the "1-bit IBM PC" preview option. Leave the compatibility setting at "Illustrator 5" and click "OK." If you have trouble printing an Illustrator 5 EPS from a Windows application, try saving it with a compatibility option of "Illustrator 3" instead.

Standard (No Preview) Preview option and Adobe Illustrator 88 Compatibility option.

To open an Illustrator document in CorelDRAW 5.x or later, save the Illustrator file with the Standard (No Preview) Preview option and Illustrator 3.0 Compatibility option selected. CorelDRAW 5.x and later converts Illustrator 3.x or earlier format.

To import an Illustrator document into a Windows application that does not import or open Illustrator EPS files, save from Illustrator 5.5 or later as a PDF (Portable Document Format) file, or save the document from Illustrator 4.x for Windows in BMP, CGM, DRW, DXF, PCT, PCX, SCD, TIF, WMF, or WPG format. When exporting from Illustrator 4.x for Windows in a bitmap format (e.g., BMP, TIF), Illustrator removes tracking and kerning in text.

When you save an Illustrator 6.0 document in Acrobat (PDF 1.1) or an Illustrator 5.5 document in Acrobat (PDF) file formats, Illustrator does not embedded fonts used in the document into the PDF file. To embed fonts in the PDF file, save the Illustrator Document in EPS file format, then convert the Illustrator EPS file to a PDF file using Adobe Acrobat Distiller.

FONTS

When you open or place an Illustrator file, Illustrator requires the fonts used in the Illustrator file to display text and to print the document as expected. If you open an Illustrator document containing unavailable fonts, Illustrator 4.x for Windows returns the error "The following typefaces cannot be found in the system and will display and print incorrectly. ['font name']." After you click OK, Illustrator returns the error "The artwork contains a character in a text object that may display or print incorrectly." After clicking OK again, Illustrator opens the document and substitutes Helvetica for unavailable fonts. To prevent Illustrator 4.x for Windows from substituting Helvetica for unavailable fonts, install the fonts used in the Illustrator document before opening, or reapply an available font to the text and save the Illustrator document. Illustrator 4.x for Windows does not support TrueType fonts.

When you open an Illustrator document containing unavailable fonts, Illustrator 5.x or later for the Macintosh returns the error "The document ["file name"] contains fonts which are unavailable or in a different format than originally specified: [font name, font name, font name]," which includes a list of the missing fonts.

TRANSFERRING GRAPHICS IN DOCUMENTS

EPS is the only graphic format supported by both Illustrator for the Macintosh and for Windows. If the EPS files contained in an Illustrator document are linked externally, transfer EPS graphics separately, then relink the EPS file after you transfer the Illustrator document. When you open an Illustrator EPS file saved with or without Include Placed Images selected, Illustrator requires an external link to the original EPS file.

After you open an Illustrator document containing an EPS file with an unsupported screen preview, Illustrator displays the EPS graphic as a box with an "X" in Artwork view, but prints it as expected to a PostScript printer. Illustrator for the Macintosh supports EPS files containing PICT screen previews. Illustrator for Windows supports EPS files containing TIFF image screen previews.

EPS files saved on the Macintosh usually include a PICT screen preview, where the PICT screen preview may either be a bitmap or vector (object-oriented) PICT graphic. EPS files saved in Windows contain a TIFF screen preview, as Windows does not support the PICT graphic format.

PLACING AND CONVERTING GRAPHICS

Illustrator 6.0 for the Macintosh opens PostScript Level 1, TIFF, EPS, PDF, PICT, and Photoshop 3.x format files. Illustrator 6.0 for the Macintosh places TIFF, EPS, and Photoshop 3.x format files. When you open a PostScript Level 1 file, vector EPS, PDF, or PICT file, Illustrator converts the file into Illustrator objects. After you open a bitmap EPS file in Illustrator 6.0, Illustrator includes the EPS file in the Illustrator document, since it cannot convert the EPS file into Illustrator objects. When you place a bitmap EPS file, Illustrator 6.0 places the EPS file's 72 dpi screen preview into the document and links the external bitmap EPS file to the Illustrator document. When you open or place a TIFF, PICT, or Photoshop 3.0 graphic file, Illustrator 6.0 includes the graphic within the Illustrator file and does not link to the external graphic file. When you save an Illustrator 6.0 file in Illustrator 5.0/5.5 and earlier format, Illustrator removes embedded bitmap graphics (e.g., TIFF, rasterized Illustrator artwork) from the Illustrator document.

When you open a PDF file or object-oriented PICT file by choosing the Open command, Illustrator 5.5 and later for the Macintosh convert the PDF file or object-oriented PICT file. The Open dialog box includes the Open This Document as Option that enables you to open the PICT graphic as either an Illustrator Template PICT or PICT. If you select the PICT open, Illustrator converts the vector PICT graphic into Illustrator objects. If you select the Illustrator Template PICT option, Illustrator converts bitmap and vector PICT graphics into an Illustrator template. After you open and then save a Macintosh Illustrator document in Illustrator 4.x for Windows, it removes template information in the Illustrator document.

When you import vector objects by choosing the Import Art command, Illustrator 4.x for Windows converts vector graphics to Illustrator objects. Illustrator for Windows converts the following formats to Illustrator objects: CGM (Computer Graphics Metafile), CHT (Harvard Graphics 2.x), CH3 (Harvard Graphics 3.0), DRW (Micrografx Drawing), DXF (AutoCAD Drawing Interchange), PCT (Macintosh Object Oriented PICT), PIC (Lotus 123 Picture), RND (AutoShade Rendering), WMF (Windows Metafile), and WPG (WordPerfect Graphic).

You can place Bitmap (.bmp), Windows PaintBrush (.pcx), and TIFF (.tif) graphics by choosing the Place Art command in Illustrator 4.x for Windows. When placing, Illustrator converts .bmp, .pcx, and .tif bitmap graphic file formats to bitmap EPS files, then saves the bitmap EPS file into the directory containing the original bitmap file. Illustrator links to the bitmap EPS files externally.

Illustrator for the Macintosh supports importing bitmap EPS files when you choose the Place Art command, and importd bitmap PICT graphics as an Illustrator Template when you choose the the Open command.

Stroking the Inside or Outside of a Path in Illustrator

Adobe Illustrator's "Stroke" feature paints a line on the path outlining it. Illustrator centers the stroke on the path: half of the stroke appears on one side of the path and half appears on the other side of the path. For example, when a circle is painted with a 4-point stroke, 2 points of the stroke appear on the inside of the circle and 2 points appear outside the circle.

You can make objects appear to have a stroke on only the inside or outside of the path by layering paths with different stroke weights or by masking half of the stroke.

STROKING THE OUTSIDE OF A PATH

To stroke the outside of a filled object in Illustrator 5.x for Macintosh:

1. Select the filled object.
2. In the Paint Style palette, select the Stroke box, then select a stroke color.
3. In the Stroke Weight text box, enter a stroke weight twice the size of the desired stroke. For example, enter "8" to create a 4-point stroke outside the object.
4. Copy the object, then choose Edit > Paste in Front.
5. With the copied object selected, select the Stroke box in the Paint Style palette, then apply a stroke color of None.

MICRO TIP MAC OS / WINDOWS

If you need to adjust the saturation of a process color (to create a lighter version of it for trapping or for any other reason) hold down the Shift key while dragging any one of the CMYK sliders. The rest of the sliders will move a relative amount, so you maintain the same balance between the CMYK components even though you're increasing or decreasing the color's overall saturation.

6. Select the original and copied objects, then choose Arrange > Group.

To stoke the outside of an unfilled object in Illustrator 5.x for Macintosh:

1. Select the unfilled object.
2. In the Paint Style palette, select the Stroke box then select a stroke color.
3. In the Stroke Weight text box, enter a stroke weight twice the size of the desired stroke. For example, enter "8" to create a 4-point stroke outside the object.
4. Copy the object, then choose Filters > Objects > Outline Path.
5. Choose Edit > Paste In Front.
6. With the copied object selected, click on the Stroke box in the Paint Style palette, then apply a stroke color of None.
7. Select the original and copied objects, then choose Filter > Pathfinder > Minus Front.

To stroke the outside of a path in Illustrator 4.x for Windows:

1. Select the object.
2. Choose Paint > Paint Style, then select a stroke color in the Paint Style dialog box.
3. In the Weight text box, enter a stroke weight twice the size of the desired stroke then click OK. For example, enter "8" to create a 4-point stroke outside the object.
4. Copy the object, then choose Edit > Paste In Front.
5. With the copied object selected, choose Paint > Paint Style.
6. In the Paint Style dialog box, paint the object with the desired fill and a stroke of None, then click OK.
   NOTE: When the object is not filled with a color or pattern, paint the object with a White fill.
7. Select the original and copied objects, then choose Arrange >Group.

STROKING THE INSIDE OF A PATH

To stroke the inside of a path in Illustrator 5.x for Macintosh:

1. Select the object.
2. In the Paint Style palette, select the Stroke box, then select a stroke color.
3. In the Stroke Weight text box, enter a stroke weight twice the size of the desired stroke. For example, enter "8" to create a 4-point stroke outside the object.
4. Copy the object then choose Edit > Paste In Front.
5. With the copied object selected, select the Stroke box in the Paint Style palette, then apply a stroke color of None.
6. Select the original and copied objects, then choose Object > Mask > Make.

To stroke the inside of a path in Illustrator 4.x for Windows:

1. Select the object.
2. Choose Arrange > Ungroup to ensure the object is a single, ungrouped path.
   NOTE: Objects drawn with the Rectangle and Oval tools are automatically grouped; ungroup the rectangle or oval, then delete the object's center point.
3. Choose Paint > Paint Style, then select a stroke color in the Paint Style dialog box.
4. In the Weight text box, enter a stroke weight twice the size of the desired stroke then click OK. For example, enter "8" to create a 4-point stroke outside the object.
5. Copy the object, then choose Edit > Paste In Back.
6. With the copied object selected, choose Paint > Paint Style.
7. In the Paint Style dialog box, paint the object with the desired fill and a stroke of None, select Mask, then click OK.
8. Select the original and copied objects, then choose Arrange > Group.

No Registration Color in Adobe Illustrator 7.0

ISSUE

A registration color (i.e., a color that prints on all separations) is not available anywhere in Adobe Illustrator 7.0.

SOLUTIONS

Create a registration color for the document in Illustrator by doing one or more of the following:

NOTE: After you create the registration color, you can add it to the Swatches palette to use until you close the document, or you can add it permanently to Illustrator's startup file so you can use it in any Illustrator document. For instructions on how to add the color to the startup file, see Additional Information.

A. Print an object on all process separations:
   1. Create an object that will appear on all plates.
   2. Create a new process color that is defined as 100% Cyan, 100% Magenta, 100% Yellow, and 100% Black.
   3. Apply the color to the object.
B. Print an object on all custom-colored separations:
   1. Create or select an object you want to print on all separations.
   2. Apply a fill or stroke with a custom color you have used elsewhere in the document to the object.
   3. Copy the object, then choose Edit > Paste In Front.
   4. Apply a second custom color you have used elsewhere in the document to the pasted object.
   5. Select Overprint Fill or Overprint Stroke in the At-

tributes palette, then press Return (Macintosh) or Enter (Windows).

6. Repeat steps 2 through 5 for each custom color you want to print as a registration color.

ADDITIONAL INFORMATION

Unlike some applications (e.g., Adobe PageMaker, QuarkXPress), Illustrator does not include a default color that prints on all separations (i.e., a registration color).

The Illustrator startup file (i.e., Adobe Illustrator Startup file on the Macintosh or the Startup.ai file in Windows) is an document that Illustrator loads when it is started. The startup file specifies a variety of settings (e.g., colors, gradients, fill patterns, path patterns, imageable area, size of default window).

To add a registration color to the Illustrator startup file:

1. Make a backup of the Adobe Illustrator Startup file (Macintosh) or the Startup.ai file (Windows), which is located in the Plug-Ins folder in the Illustrator folder.
2. In Illustrator, open the original Adobe Illustrator Startup file (Macintosh) or the Startup.ai file (Windows).
3. Create a process color defined as 100% cyan, 100% magenta, 100% yellow, and 100% black.
4. Drag the new color from the Fill or Stroke box in either the Toolbox or the Color palette to the Swatches palette, or select New Swatch in the Swatches palette pop-up menu.
5. Double-click the new swatch, or select it and select Swatch Options from the Swatch palette pop-up menu.
6. In the Swatch Options dialog box, specify a name for the swatch if desired, then click OK. Make sure the Color Mode is Process Color.
7. Save the Illustrator startup file without changing the name, then restart Illustrator.

Creating Efficient Illustrator Files and Improving Print Performance

CREATING EFFICIENT ADOBE ILLUSTRATOR FILES

To create efficient Adobe Illustrator files, do one or more of the following:

A. Scan imported bitmap EPS files at a resolution optimized for print resolution (e.g., lpi x 2 = ppi or spi).

B. Use low (e.g., 3) or high (e.g., 200) screen rulings sparingly.

C. Avoid or minimize multiple screen rulings within a single document.

D. Limit the number of text transformations, type along a path, and typeface changes.

E. Delete or move objects hidden behind other elements to a non-printing layer elements.

F. Copy and paste Illustrator elements between documents

TIP MAC OS / WINDOWS

Creating circulating blends

If you ever need to create a circular blend (a blend that rotates around a point), here's a good technique. In the following example, we'll show you how to create a circular rainbow blend.

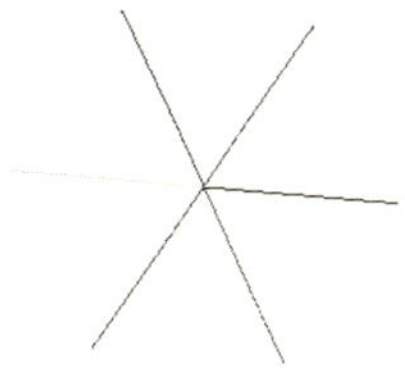

1. Draw a line that's roughly the radius of the blend you want to create.
2. Select the line, and then select the rotation tool. Click on the end of the line you want to act as the center of your blend (on the PC, hold down the Alt key while doing so; on the Mac, hold down the Option key).
3. When the "Rotate" dialog box appears, enter a value of 60 degrees and click the "Copy" button. Illustrator will make a copy of your line that's rotated 60 degrees around the center point of your soon-to-be-circular blend.
4. Repeat step 3 four times by pressing Ctrl + D (Windows) or Command + D (Mac), which is equivalent to selecting the "Repeat Transformation" option four times—you should end up with six lines rotated evenly around your center point.

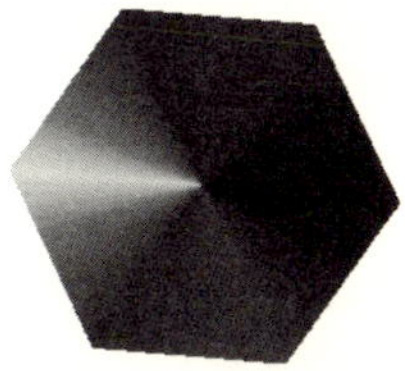

5. Assign a weight of one point to the lines, and assign the colors you want to them as well. In our example, we used red, yellow, green, cyan, blue, and magenta.
6. Select the first two lines only. With the blend tool, click on their outer points. When the "Blend" dialog box appears, enter an appropriate number of blend steps (for information on how to determine what's appropriate, see your Illustrator User Guide), and click "OK." Illustrator will group the intermediate steps of the blend and leave them selected—we recommend that you hide them by pressing Ctrl (Windows) or Command (Mac) + 3. This will make the next step easier.
7. Repeat step 6 with the remaining pairs of lines.

When you're done, you can press Ctrl (Windows) or Command (Mac) + 4 to show all the components of your blend. Then you can fine-tune the artwork by masking it with another shape—refer to your User Guide for more information on masking.

instead of placing them as EPS files.

G. Use gradient fills instead of blends when printing from Illustrator 5.5 to a PostScript Level 2 device.

H. Use the minimum number of steps when creating a blend.

I. Ungroup elements and nested groups.

J. Split nested composite paths.

K. Simplify paths by using the minimum number of points needed to draw the path.

L. Split long complex paths into shorter line segments using the Split Long Paths option or the scissors tool.

M. Transform or crop bitmap EPS files in an image editing application (e.g., Adobe Photoshop) before importing them.

N. Use filled paths in place of clipping paths (i.e., masks) or composite paths.

O. Use duplicated elements instead of pattern fills.

P. Eliminate any unused patterns, custom colors, and gradients.

Q. Limit the number of complex elements in the document. For information, see Complex Elements below.

DECREASING PRINT TIMES WHEN PRINTING ADOBE ILLUSTRATOR FILES

To decrease print times, do one or more of the following:

A. Save DCS and EPS images in binary format instead of ASCII (hex) format.

B. Increase the flatness value by setting a flatness value at the printer or by using a Riders file.

C. Use fonts that are available at the printer (e.g., resident in the printer's hard disk or ROM).

D. Remove any unused gradients, patterns, and custom colors.

E. Deselect the Unlimited Downloadable Fonts option in the Page Setup Options dialog box (Macintosh only).

F. Specify the smallest paper size needed in the Document Setup dialog box.

G. Print through Ethernet connections.

COMPLEX ELEMENTS IN AN ILLUSTRATOR DOCUMENT

The greater the number or combination of elements listed below, the more memory-intensive the Illustrator document will be.

Effects and elements that have the potential to be memory intensive or complex include:

- Compound paths (e.g., text converted to paths)
- Pattern fills
- Gradient fills
- Bitmap EPS files
- Vector EPS files
- EPS files containing clipping paths
- Masks
- Paths with many points or curves
- Transformations
- Text on a path
- Screen ruling changes
- Stroked text
- Text with horizontal scaling, tracking, or kerning applied
- Large page sizes
- Downloadable fonts
- High or low screen rulings
- High resolution

Specifying Document-Specific Screen Frequency (lpi) in Illustrator

By default, Adobe Illustrator documents do not contain screen frequency (lpi) information, and print using the default lpi value set at the printer. You can customize the global screen frequency, angle, spot function, and flatness values in Illustrator 5.x and later, however, by editing the PostScript code in a Riders file. Illustrator loads the Riders file, named "Adobe Illustrator EPSF Riders," from the Plug-ins folder.

The Riders or RidersMaker plug-in filter creates Riders files. Riders file settings are included when you print an Illustrator document or save it in EPS format, but not when you save it in Illustrator format. Riders file settings an Illustrator EPS file are used when you print the EPS file from a separation or layout application (e.g., QuarkXPress, Adobe PageMaker, Adobe Separator, Adobe PrePrint). The settings print on every separation plate, and custom screen angles are applied to all inks within the EPS file. The settings remain in the EPS file until you open and resave it in Illustrator with new values specified in the Riders file. If you save the EPS file without an installed Riders file, the settings are removed or not included in the EPS file.

To specify a custom lpi value in Illustrator 6.0.x or later:

1. Install the Rider plug-in filter by moving the Riders file from the Riders Folder in the Utilities folder to the Filters folder in the Plug-Ins folder. The Riders plug-in filter adds an Other submenu to the Filters menu.
2. Start Illustrator and Choose Filter > Other > Make Riders to create a Riders file.
3. In the Make Riders dialog box, choose one of the preset screen frequency values from the Screen Frequency pop-up menu or select Other to specify a custom screen frequency from 1.0000 and 999.0000 lines per inch (lpi).
4. Click Make to save the Riders file named Adobe Illustrator EPSF Riders in the Plug-ins folder.

To specify a custom lpi value in Illustrator 5.5:

1. Install the Rider plug-in filter by moving the Riders file from the Riders Folder in the Separator & Utilities folder to the Plug-Ins folder. The Riders plug-in filter adds an Other submenu to the Filters menu.
2. Start Illustrator and Choose Filter > Other > Make Riders to create a Riders file.
3. In the Make Riders dialog box, choose one of the preset screen frequency values from the Screen Frequency pop-up menu or select Other to specify a custom screen frequency from 1.0000 and 999.0000 lines per inch (lpi).
4. Click Make to save the Riders file named Adobe Illus-

trator EPSF Riders in the Plug-ins folder.

To specify a custom lpi value in Illustrator 5.0.x:

1. Install the Riders plug-in included with Illustrator 5.0.x by moving the RidersMaker file from the 3rd Party Utility folder in the Separator & Utilities folder to the Plug-Ins folder. The RidersMaker plug-in adds a Riders submenu to the Filters menu.
2. Create a Riders file with the RidersMaker plug-in filter by choosing Filters > Riders > Make Custom Riders.
3. Check Screen Frequency and click Setup to set a custom screen frequency from 1.0000 and 999.0000 lines per inch (lpi).
4. Click Make to save the Riders file as Adobe Illustrator EPSF Riders in the Plug-ins folder.

To remove Riders file settings, move the Adobe Illustrator EPSF Riders file from the Illustrator Plug-Ins folder, open the EPS file in Illustrator, then save in the desired format. Illustrator can remain open while the Riders file is created or deleted.

Illustrator 7.0 Riders File and Filters

The Riders plug-in filter creates a Riders file (i.e., "Adobe Illustrator EPSF Riders" PostScript file). Adobe Illustrator 7.0 uses the Riders file to specify a global screen frequency, angle, spot function, and flatness value for Illustrator documents. The Riders file is also able to add annotations and an error handler to Illustrator documents. Riders file's information and settings are included when you print or save in EPS format from Illustrator 7.0. Rider file settings are not saved in Illustrator 7.0 documents.

To install the Riders plug-in included with Illustrator 7.0, move the Riders plug-in, which is installed in the Riders folder in the Utilities folder, into the Plug-ins folder. The Riders plug-in adds an Other submenu to Illustrator's Filter menu. To create a Riders file using the Riders plug-in, choose Filter > Other > Make Riders, select the desired Riders options, then click Make to save the Riders file named "Adobe Illustrator EPSF Riders" in Illustrator 7.0's Plug-ins folder. To specify a custom screen frequency, angle, spot function, flatness, or to add an annotation, select the desired settings from the list of available options in the pop-up menus in the Make Riders dialog box.

To remove the Riders file settings from an Illustrator EPS file, remove the "Adobe Illustrator EPSF Riders" file from the Illustrator 7.0 Plug-ins folder, open the EPS file in Illustrator, then save in the desired format. The Adobe Illustrator EPSF Riders file can be removed from the Plug-ins folder in Illustrator by choosing Filter > Other > Delete Riders, selecting the Adobe Illustrator EPSF Riders file and clicking Delete. Illustrator does not need to be restarted after changing or deleting the Riders file.

RIDERS OPTIONS

The Riders plug-in adds Other > Make Riders and Other > Delete Riders to the Filter menu. Riders file options saved in an Illustrator EPS file are not overridden when you print from a separation or layout application (e.g. QuarkXPress, PageMaker, Adobe Separator, PrePrint). Riders file options (e.g., screen frequency, angle, spot function, annotations) print on every separation plate.

Make Riders Command

The Make Riders command enables you to select the following options in the Make Riders dialog box for creating a Riders file ("Adobe Illustrator EPSF Riders" PostScript file).

- Screen Frequency
  Select a preset screen frequency value from the Screen Frequency pop-up menu or select Other to specify a custom screen frequency from 1.0000 and 999.0000 lines per inch (lpi).
- Screen Angle
  Select a preset angle from the Screen Angle pop-up menu or select Other to specify a custom screen angle from 0 and 360.0000 degrees.
- Spot Function
  Seven spot functions are included with the Riders plug-in: Simple Round, Inverted Round, Euclidean Composite, Rhomboid, Line, Diamond, and Inverted Elliptical. Custom spot functions can be imported through the Riders plug-in. Illustrator includes "Spot Function Template" as an example of the required spot function file format. For instructions on importing custom spot functions, see Adding Custom Spot Functions.
- Flatness
  Select a preset screen frequency value from the Screen Frequency pop-up menu or Other to specify a custom screen frequency from 1.0000 and 999.0000 lines per inch (lpi).
- Annotation
  Select Setup from the Annotation pop-up menu, type an annotation of up to 254 characters, then click Done. You can format the annotation text in one of the standard 13 fonts (Courier, Helvetica, Times, and Symbol), and use any size between 6 to 24 points. The Riders file annotation prints on the bottom left corner of the Illustrator document. Text automatically wraps in the Annotation Setup dialog box. On the Macintosh, press-

MICRO TIP MAC OS / WINDOWS

Want to see more, or less, of your Paint Styles palette or dialog box? On the PC, you can change the dialog box's view by clicking on the "Options" button. On the Mac, you can click on the downward-pointing triangle at the upper right corner of the palette, and select one of the display options on the pop-up menu that appears. Or, to bypass that pop-up menu, just click on different portions of the thumbnail of the Paint Style palette just to the left of that menu to change which portions of the palette display.

ing Return in the Annotation Setup dialog box saves the annotation and returns you to the Make Riders dialog box.

- Error Handler
  Selecting Include from the Error Handler pop-up menu includes a PostScript error handler with Illustrator print and EPS files. When a PostScript error occurs, the Riders file error handler prints the PostScript error message on the Illustrator document.

DELETE RIDERS COMMAND

The Delete Riders command enables you to remove selected Riders file from the hard disk.

ADDING CUSTOM SPOT FUNCTIONS

You can import custom spot functions through the Riders plug-in. The "Spot Function Template," included with Illustrator 7.0, is an example of the required spot function file format. Illustrator 7.0 installs the "Spot Function Template" in the Utilities folder in the Illustrator 7.0 application folder.

disclaimer: The creation of custom spot functions is not supported by Adobe Systems Incorporated. The Spot Function Template is provided as a guideline. Experience with PostScript is highly recommended. Importing an incorrectly formatted spot function could prevent Illustrator from printing.

To import custom spot functions into Illustrator 7.0:

1. Choose Filters > Riders > Make Riders.
2. Select Import from the Spot Function pop-up menu in the Make Riders dialog box.
3. Click OK in the warning dialog box.
   Select the spot function text-only file and click Import.

MAC OS

Q *(5.5 only)* **How do I get a soft return in Illustrator?**

A To type a soft return, which starts a new line without starting a new paragraph, press the Enter key (on the numeric keypad) instead of the Return key. Starting a new line without starting a new paragraph will ensure that the new line isn't affected by certain paragraph settings such as first-line indents and the "Leading before ¶" feature.

Q *(5.5 only)* **My service bureau wants me to take a list of file details, such as the fonts and custom colors I used, when I take my Illustrator files in for output. Is there an easy way to get a listing of this information?**

A Yes. Use the "Document Info" filter to save a text file listing the custom colors, patterns, gradients, fonts, and placed art in your illustration. To do so, deselect everything in the file, then choose "Document Info..." from the Other submenu of the Filters menu. In the "Document Info" dialog box, click "Save," and the filter will save a text file with all the above-listed information. Remember to take the text file along with your Illustrator file to your service bureau.

Q Is there any way to slice through a path without having to use the scissors tool?

A Yes. Several of the Pathfinder filters allow you to "cut" objects using other paths. Some of the Pathfinder filters most useful for cutting are the "Minus Front," "Minus Back," "Divide," and "Crop" filters. To use them, select both the path you want to cut and the path with which you want to cut it, then select the appropriate filter from the Pathfinder submenu of the Filters menu.

Here are some examples that show how the filters work. Note that the paths that the Pathfinder filters create are grouped. If you want to edit parts of your paths after running a Pathfinder filter on them, you'll need to either ungroup them or select individual elements in the grouped paths using the direct-selection (hollow) tool.

- The "Minus Front" and "Minus Back" filters do essentially the same thing: they subtract either the foremost path selected ("Minus Front") or the hindmost object ("Minus Back") from whatever other path(s) you have selected. When you use the "Minus Front" filter, the resulting path uses the path attributes (fill, stroke, and so forth) of the original elements' hindmost object. When you use the "Minus Back" filter, the resulting path takes on the attributes of the original elements' foremost object.
- The "Crop" filter works exceptionally well when you want to crop an object without loosing its fill characteristics. Make sure the object you're cutting is in back of the object you're using to crop it—the resulting path will take on the attributes of the original elements' hindmost object. In order for the "Crop" filter to work, the hindmost element must be assigned a fill.
- The "Divide" filter is great when you want to split a path along another path, but you don't want to lose parts of your filled object or have its path attributes altered. (Make sure the path you use to "cut" doesn't have a fill assigned.)

Q What's the best way to trap a solid object against a blend or gradient?

A What works best depends on which object is darker. Here are some guidelines to help you determine the best method.

If your gradient is darker than the solid object, trapping should be a snap. Select both of the objects and choose "Trap" from the Pathfinder submenu of the Filters menu. In the "Pathfinder Trap" dialog box, adjust the trap settings as you wish, and click "OK." The filter will spread the solid light-colored object into the gradient.

If your gradient is lighter than the solid object, you'll need to go through a few more steps for the best trapping results. If you just select your objects and run the "Trap" Pathfinder filter on them, the filter will spread your gradient into your darker solid-colored object. However, the filter won't create a trap with a gradient color—it'll use a solid

TIP MAC OS

Easy grids in Illustrator 5.5

In Illustrator 5.5, you can use the "Rows & Columns" filter to create an evenly proportioned, rectangular grid. For example, if you want to make a 10 x10 grid, draw a rectangle the size of the page (or covering the area for which you want a grid), select "Rows & Columns..." from the Text submenu of the Filter menu, and enter 10 in the "Columns" field, 10 in the "Rows" field, and 0 in the "Gutters" field. The "Rows & Columns" filter will fill your page with equally sized rectangles in 10 rows and 10 columns. Then select all the rectangles and turn them into guides by selecting "Make" from the Guides submenu in the Object menu.

If you need a grid based on squares (one in which the row height is the same as the column width), begin this process by drawing a square instead of a rectangle. To draw a square, hold down the Shift key while drawing a box with the box tool.

color instead (a solid CMYK color if your gradient is made of process colors, or a non-gradient combination of your spot colors if your gradient consists of spot colors). If there's little contrast between the two end colors of your gradient, this may be an acceptable trapping method. However, if there is a lot of contrast between your gradient colors, any misregistration on press could leave some inappropriately colored gaps between your objects. To prevent this, try this method for trapping a light gradient and a dark solid color:

1. Change your gradient-filled object to a light, solid color. (Don't worry—this is a temporary change.)
2. Select that object and the dark-colored solid object it abuts or overlaps, and select "Trap" from the Pathfinder submenu of the Filters menu. When the "Pathfinder Trap" dialog box appears, make any adjustments you want to the trap settings.
3. Once the filter creates the trapping object, select the object that's supposed to be filled with the gradient and reassign the gradient.
4. Open the Gradient palette by selecting "Gradient..." from the Object menu. Select the gradient you're using in the object you're trapping, and click on the "Duplicate" button. Illustrator will create a new gradient based on the gradient you had selected.
5. Reduce the saturation of your new gradient. If you're using spot colors, select one of the endpoints and set its "Tint" level (the option is located at the bottom left of the dialog box) to about 40% of its original tint level. If you're using process colors, hold down the Shift key while you adjust one of the CMYK sliders (this will make the other sliders adjust a relative amount). Do the same with the other endpoint colors, then name the new tint something that will help you remember its function.
6. Assign the new gradient to the trap object, and use the Paint Style palette to make sure the gradient uses the same angle as the gradient in the trapped object. Also, make sure the trapping object's fill is set to overprint (that option is also located in the Paint Style palette).

The gradient trap you created will give you excellent trapping results in almost any situation. If, however, you have a gradient that goes from a very dark color to a light color and it abuts a medium-colored object (so part of it should spread and part of it should be choked for the best possible trap), you may want to have your color house or other service provider do your trapping for you with a product such as Adobe TrapWise, which can handle such complex trapping situations.

Q I've noticed that text extruded in Dimensions has an angled baseline. But when I rotate it back to a horizontal position it's incorrectly skewed. Is there an easy way to fix this?

A Sure. One way is to rotate your text back to a horizontal-baseline position in Dimensions. Then use Illustrator to skew the text back to a vertical axis. Here's how:

1. First, create your extruded text in Dimensions: Select "New Artwork" from the Artwork menu, and in the new window use the text tool to type your text. Adjust the font, size, and kerning as you wish, click "Apply" and close the window.
2. With your text still selected, double-click the rotation tool to open the Rotate palette. Enter a rotation value of -11.3 degrees for the Z axis and click the Rotate palette's "Apply" button.
3. Select "Extrude..." from the Operations menu. In the Extrude palette, make sure the default Caps option (the bottom option) is selected, set a depth value, and click "Apply" to extrude your text. Then, with the text still selected, set its colors in the "Surface Properties" dialog box (to open this dialog box, select "Surface Properties..." from the Appearance menu). Render your text by selecting "Draft Render," "Shaded Render," or "Wireframe Render" from the View menu.
4. Export your extruded text to Illustrator. You can do this by selecting the text, copying to the Clipboard, and then pasting it into Illustrator; or you can select "Export..." from Dimension's File menu, export your image, and open it in Illustrator. Once it's in Illustrator, each of the letters in the text will be selectable as an individual element, so you may want to group the letters to prevent accidentally moving or transforming just part of the text.
5. With all the text selected, double-click on the shear tool in Illustrator's toolbox. In the "Shear" dialog box, enter a shearing angle value of -10.75 degrees for the horizontal axis only and click "OK."

Q *(5.5 only)* **On page 14 of the Adobe Illustrator 5.5 Beyond the Basics book there's some type that has a curved baseline, but the tops of the letters aren't curved. How can I get that effect?**

A Use Illustrator's "Free Distort" filter. Here's how.

1. Type your text (in this example we use the word BANTAM), adjust and kern it as you like, then select the text block and choose "Create Outlines" from the Type menu.
2. Select the letters BAN, and choose "Free Distort..." from the Distort submenu of the Filters menu.
3. In the "Free Distort" dialog box, move the bottom-left corner point down about 1/4 of the height of the letters, or however much you like.
4. Click "OK."
5. Now select just the first BA and run the filter again, either by pressing Command + Shift + E or by selecting "Free Distort" from the Filter menu again (this will distort your letters by the same amount you used in step 3).

6. Repeat step 5, but this time do it only for the first letter, B.
7. Next, select the last three letters, TAM.
8. Select "Free Distort..." from the Distort submenu of the Filters menu. In the "Free Distort" dialog box, adjust the bottom-right point downward by the same amount as you adjusted the bottom-left point in step 3. Return the bottom-left point to its original baseline position, and click "OK."
9. Now run the filter on just the letters "AM" as in step 5, and then run it on just the last letter "M."

MICRO TIP MAC OS

Need to run a filter with the same settings more than once? Once you run it the first time, you don't need to navigate through the Filters menu to get to it again. Just press Command + Shift + E, and Illustrator will run the last filter you used with the settings you specified. This will work until you shut down and restart Illustrator (when you do so, Illustrator "forgets" what filter you used last).

Q Is there a quick way to convert a process color to a custom color?

A Yes. Instead of retyping the process values in the "Custom Color" dialog box, just drag a swatch of the process color (from the "Fill" icon, the "Stroke" icon, or one of the color swatches on the left side of the "Paint Styles" palette) onto the custom-color icon, which is the medium-green icon on the right side of the Paint Styles palette. When you do so, Illustrator will display the "Custom Color" dialog box, with your color defined and named according to its process components. Change any of the settings if you want, and click "OK."

Q *(5.5 only)* **I want to change the color of some Dimensions artwork in one of my Illustrator files, but when I try to assign a different color, Illustrator changes the entire object to that color—destroying all the shading. Do I have to use Dimensions to edit the object's color?**

A No. Fortunately, Illustrator 5.5 has a number of filters that'll do the trick.

The reason it's hard to use Illustrator to edit colors of Dimensions-created art is that Dimensions artwork comes into Illustrator as a collection of "mini-objects," each with its own solid color. Collectively, these objects create the illusion of graduated color and shading. To adjust the color of the grouped objects without compromising the shading effect, try the following.

First, select all the objects that comprise the Dimensions artwork whose colors you want to adjust. Next, select "Adjust Colors..." from the Colors submenu of the Filter menu. In the "Adjust Colors" dialog box, increase the percentage of any of the process-color components (cyan, magenta, yellow, and black) in the objects, or decrease those percentages. (NOTE: You can't increase some color components and decrease others at the same time—to accomplish both, you'll need to run the filter twice.) Other filters that can come in handy for adjusting the color of Dimensions artwork are the "Desaturate," "Desaturate More," "Invert Colors," "Saturate," and "Saturate More" filters, all of which are located on the Colors submenu of the Filters menu.

Q *(5.5 only)* **I have some artwork that has too many anchor points and needs to be simplified. I've used the delete-anchor-point tool, but this is rather time-consuming. Is there an easier way?**

A Yes. BeInfinite, Inc., makes a freeware Plug-in called "Smart Remove Points" that will automatically remove extra anchor points without changing the artwork's appearance. The Plug-in is available in the "Illustrator Tools Library" section of the Illustrator SIG (special interest group) area in the Adobe forum on America Online (keyword "Adobe"). Download the file labeled "Smart Remove Points revised"—it's a self-extracting file that'll expand into the Plug-in and a demonstration file with instructions on how to use it.

If you want additional information, you can reach BeInfinite by phone at (800) 554-6624, by fax at (404) 339-

TIP MAC OS

Cool effects with layered lines

You can generate a variety of useful and decorative effects by varying the dash patterns of your lines and then layering the lines. The chart below provides recipes for just a few examples.

To create the layered-line effects, hold down the Option key while selecting the line (this ensures that the entire line is selected) and use the Paint Style palette to paint it using the values shown in the first row of the recipe. (You'll need to expand your Paint Style palette to view all the line options—click on the down arrow in the upper-right corner of the palette to view a pop-up menu of the palette's display options.) Then copy the line, choose "Paste in Front" from the Edit menu, and paint the copy using the values in the next row of the recipe. Repeat this procedure until you've created and painted all the layers. When you've achieved the effect you want, group the lines by selecting "Group" from the Arrange menu. Experiment with your own dash patterns to create other effects.

Line Effect Settings

	Stroke color	Stroke weight (in points)	Line cap style	Dash pattern
Checkered effect				
	100%	21	Butt	3, 3
	100%	15	Butt	Solid
	White	15	Butt	3, 3
	White	9	Butt	Solid
	100%	9	Butt	3, 3
	100%	3	Butt	Solid
	White	3	Butt	3, 3
Hollow balls				
	100%	10	Round	0, 10
	White	5	Round	0,10
Railroad tracks				
	100%	12	Butt	2, 4
	100%	7	Butt	Solid
	White	6	Butt	Solid
	100%	5	Butt	Solid
	White	4	Butt	Solid
	100%	4	Butt	2, 4

3864, or via E-mail at BeInfinite@aol.com. You can also write to them at 4651 Woodstock Road, Suite 203 #210, Roswell, GA 30075-1686.

Q *(5.5 only)* **I have some text that was converted to outlines and then placed over another object. I'd like to create a compound path of the text and object, but when I do, the type outlines that extend beyond the object take on the object's color. Is there any way to have a compound path that contains multiple colors?**

A Yes. Start by creating the compound path as you normally would. If you're working with text, you'll first need to convert the text to paths by selecting it with the selection tool and choosing "Create Outlines" from the Type menu. Then select all the objects you want to turn into a compound path, and choose "Make" from the Compound Paths submenu of the Object menu.

After you've created the compound path, select it and then choose "Divide" from the Pathfinder submenu of the Filters menu. That'll divide the compound path into a group of separate objects (so make sure you're finished arranging your elements before running the "Divide" filter). Next, with the direct-selection tool, select the objects you want to color, and use the Paint Style palette to color the objects however you like.

Q I recently upgraded from Illustrator 5.5 to 6.0, but several people in my office still have 5.5. Will they be able to open my 6.0 documents in 5.5?

A Yes. Illustrator 6.0 can save in various formats, including Illustrator 5, Illustrator 4, Illustrator 3, Illustrator 88, Illustrator 1.1, and—of course—Illustrator EPS format. But saving your artwork in an older file format may mean Illustrator will have to alter or omit certain elements in your artwork if they're not supported by that format. For instance, if you save an Illustrator 6.0 document in Illustrator 5 format, Illustrator will remove any bitmap elements not supported by Illustrator 5.x (such as TIFFs, bitmap PICTs, rasterized Illustrator elements, and files from Adobe Photoshop 2.5 or later), although it will retain any elements you've used to mask those bitmap objects. Therefore, if you know you'll need to swap Illustrator files with colleagues working in Illustrator 5.x, you may want to refrain from using such bitmap elements in your artwork (instead, try saving your bitmap element as an EPS from Photoshop—both Illustrator 5.x and 6.0 support bitmap EPS files) until your colleagues can upgrade to Illustrator 6.0, too.

To allow Illustrator 5.x users to open your Illustrator 6.0 artwork, select "Save As…" from Illustrator 6.0's File menu. In the save-as dialog box, select "Illustrator 5" from the "Format" list, and click "OK." Illustrator will display a dialog box to remind you that saving your file in an older format may change some of its elements—click "OK" to close that dialog box.

Q When I run the "Smart Punctuation" filter, it doesn't convert numbers separated with a slash into nicely formatted fractions. What am I doing wrong?

A You're probably working with a typeface family that doesn't provide the fraction characters that the "Smart Punctuation" filter requires. In order for the filter to replace fractions, you must have the expert version of the font you're using installed—for example, if you're using Adobe Garamond, you'd also need the Adobe Garamond Expert font. But not all typeface families offer expert fonts, so if your font doesn't have an "expert" counterpart, you won't be able to get these special fraction characters. Also, for this automatic replacement to work, the "Smart Punctuation" filter needs to know which expert fonts correspond to which regular typefaces—it does this by looking in the "Expert Font Table" text file located in Illustrator's "Plug-Ins" folder. To see which expert fonts the "Smart Punctuation" filter recognizes, you can open this file in any text editor. You can even add fonts to it by following the directions at the top of the file (just be sure to make a backup copy of it first, and save it in the text-only format when you're done editing).

When you're working with fractions, you should also bear in mind that expert fonts come with only a limited number of fraction characters—generally just H, N, O, G, I, J, K, L, and M—so these are the fractions that the "Smart Punctuation" filter can replace. If you have an expert font but want to use a fraction not included as a character in that font, there's probably an easy way to create a similar-looking fraction. Most expert fonts include a set of old-style figures reduced in size to match the denominator (lower number) of the fraction character, plus a set of old-style figures reduced in size and superscripted to use for the fraction numerator (the top half of the fraction). To create your fraction, combine these characters with a virgule "fraction bar" character (in most expert fonts you can type this character by pressing the forward-slash key; in a standard typeface press Option + Shift + 1) and kern your nominator and denominator toward or away from the virgule if necessary. (To find out what characters your expert font contains and what keyboard shortcuts to use to type them, use the "Key Caps" utility available on the Apple menu.)

To make fractions when you don't have an expert font, try using regular numbers (you'll need to shrink them down and add a baseline shift to the top number) and combine them with the virgule character (Option + Shift + 1).

Q *(6.0 only)* **I'm trying to create a pattern from an object that's filled with a gradient, but I get a message saying patterns can't be created from objects that are painted with gradients or patterns. Is there any way around this?**

A Yes. All you have to do is convert your gradients and patterns to a series of individual elements. Fortunately, that's a lot easier than it sounds—in Illustrator 6.0, it takes only about two steps.

First, select any gradient- or pattern-filled objects you want to use in a new pattern and choose "Expand..." from the Object menu (the new "Expand" feature converts gradients and patterns to individual objects). Illustrator will display a dialog box that allows you to enter a value for the number of blends it will use to simulate gradients (this setting has no effect on patterns). If your final output will be to an imagesetter or another high-resolution device, be sure you enter the maximum value, 255 steps, to prevent banding. If you're printing to a lower-resolution device like a 300- or 600-dpi printer, a value of 30 to 50 blend steps should be adequate. Click "OK" to close that dialog box. The Expand feature will convert your gradients and patterns to individual objects masked by a path based on your original object.

Next, make sure all your expanded elements and their masks are selected, and then choose "Divide" from the Pathfinder submenu of the Filters menu—this will "crop" your expanded elements based on the masking objects and eliminate the masks (which is necessary because you can't use masks in a pattern).

Now you're ready to create your pattern. Select all the pattern elements and choose "Pattern..." from the Objects menu. In the "Patterns" dialog box, click the "New" button, enter a name for your pattern, and click "OK."

Note that converting custom-color gradients to blends (which is what Expand does) will give you process-color blend steps.

Q *(6.0 only)* **Sometimes my Gallery Effects filters are grayed out. I thought they were supposed to work on all images in Illustrator. Am I missing something?**

A Yes, but something that's easy to fix. You're trying to run one of the Gallery Effects filters on a vector element instead of a raster element, which won't work. The GE filter set (volumes 1, 2, and 3) works with rasterized Illustrator artwork, RGB or grayscale Photoshop images, or other parsed bitmap RGB or grayscale images. If you've selected a vector image, you'll see the "Gallery Effects: Classic Art" choices on Illustrator's Filter menu, but the specific filter names will be grayed out.

Therefore, before you apply a Gallery Effects filter to an object in Illustrator, make sure it's an RGB or grayscale raster image. To rasterize an image, select the Illustrator artwork, choose "Rasterize..." from the Object menu, and, in the "Rasterize" dialog box, select either RGB or Grayscale from the "Color Model" drop-down list. If you want to run Gallery Effects filters on CMYK bitmap images in Illustrator, you'll need to take them into Photoshop, resave them in RGB or grayscale mode, and reimport them into Illustrator.

Q *(6.0 only)* **I created some artwork in an Illustrator file, and then I dragged and dropped it into Photoshop 3.0.5. But when it got there, some of the elements were missing. What happened to them?**

A They've "disappeared" either because they were on a nonprinting layer in Illustrator or because they aren't supported by Photoshop. If the former is true, they're easy to get back. If the latter, you may have to revamp your design or your strategy a bit.

If the elements that are missing are Illustrator-drawn vector objects—which should import correctly—make sure that the layer the objects are on is set to print before you drag and drop your artwork into Photoshop.

To do this, open the Illustrator file, double-click on a layer name in the Layers palette to display the "Layer Options" dialog box, and make sure the "Print" option is checked. Repeat for each layer that contains elements that you plan to take into Photoshop.

Photoshop does not support certain objects and effects coming from Illustrator, including placed EPS files, bitmap images (e.g., TIFF, PICT, and rasterized Illustrator artwork), pattern fills and strokes, and stroked text. When you open, paste, or drag and drop an Illustrator 6.0 document containing bitmap images or placed EPS files into Photoshop, or any of these elements individually, Photoshop omits them and converts all other elements into a composite bitmap image. Photoshop converts unsupported fills such as Illustrator patterns to a solid gray or black fill, and stroked text to unstroked text. (Photoshop 3.0.x supports Illustrator gradients, but Photoshop 2.5 doesn't; it will convert gradients to solid gray or black fills.) When you attempt to drag, open, or copy these unsupported formats or effects into Photoshop, you will receive an alert message that lets you know elements may not import correctly.

In Illustrator 6.0, you can run the "Expand" command on patterns and convert stroked text to outline paths to convert them into formats Photoshop supports.

Q *(6.0 only)* **The User Guide says to use the "Place" command to import text and graphics into Illustrator 6.0. But when I try to place some text, it doesn't work and I get a message that the format is incorrect. When**

TIP MAC OS

Creating custom line screens in Illustrator

If you need to create a custom halftone screen from Illustrator, you have a couple of options—which one works best will depend on what sort of illustration you've created, whether you'll print it from Illustrator or another application, and which halftone screen settings you want to customize. Here's a brief overview of these options. Before selecting halftone screen settings, be sure to ask your imagesetting service provider and commercial printer what settings will work best on their imagesetting and printing equipment.

Use the Adobe Separator Utility 5.0.1 to set custom line screens. If you'll be producing your color separations using the Adobe Separator Utility 5.0.1, which comes with Adobe Illustrator 5.5, you can use it to specify custom screen rulings and angles for each of your ink colors.

Set your halfone screen options from a page-layout application. If you'll be saving your illustration as an EPS and importing it into PageMaker or another page-layout application for final output, you can set your halftone screens there (if your page-layout application gives you that option). In PageMaker, there are two ways to do this. First, you can set custom screen rulings and angles for each ink in the "Colors" print dialog box. You can also change frequency, angle, and other halftone-screen settings by editing your PPD or custom printer file. See the next paragraph for more information.

Edit a PPD file. Whether you're producing color separations from the Adobe Separator utility, from PageMaker, or from another application that uses PPD files, you can use custom halftone screen settings you've written into a PPD or custom printer file. To edit a PPD or custom printer file in this manner, you'll need a rudimentary understanding of PostScript. For more information, see FaxYI document 4002, "Editing line screens in a PPD file."

Use the "Riders" Plug-in filter. Illustrator 5.5 includes a Plug-in filter called "Riders" (or "Riders Maker" in Illustrator 5.0) that lets you set custom screen rulings, angles, and halftone dot shapes for particular EPS files ("Riders" isn't installed automatically—you'll need to move it from the Riders Folder in the "Separator & Utilities" folder to your "Plug-Ins" folder). Using the "Riders" Plug-in filter is convenient and easy, but it has some limitations—for instance, the screen ruling, angle, and dot shape you set in "Riders" is used for all your inks, which can cause moiré patterns if your inks overlap and you're printing on a traditional press using traditional screening technology. However, if you're using a continuous-tone printing process like silkscreening or you're after a special effect, "Riders" can be extremely useful. Note that if you create an EPS with custom screen settings, you won't be able to override these settings using the other methods listed in this tip. For more information on the "Riders" Plug-in, see the Adobe Illustrator User Guide and FaxYI document 4021, "Illustrator Riders filter: General information."

I try it with graphics, sometimes Illustrator asks if I want to place or parse the file. I'm a little confused.

A You won't be confused for long—it's just a matter of being in the right place with the right tool.

When you're importing text into Illustrator, select the text tool. Drag a text box on the page, then select "Import Text..." from the File menu and select the text file you want to import. Click "Import" to bring the text into your Illustrator file.

The "place or parse" message you're referring to appears only when you're importing a bitmapped EPS file. When you choose "Placed EPS," the bitmap image will import as a linked graphic and will display with an "X" through the center of its screen preview when the graphic is selected and you're in Preview mode. (Of course, the graphic will print to any PostScript device without the "X.") When you choose "Parsed EPS," the image will be embedded in the Illustrator file, and the screen preview won't have an "X" in it.

Placed EPS files, since they are linked, are not modified when you bring them into Illustrator. Illustrator has always handled placing EPS files in this manner. The parsed-EPS format, however, is new: when you parse a file, it becomes embedded in the Illustrator document, retaining its original resolution. The size of the parsed bitmap image may increase when you save it in Illustrator.

Which method should you choose, and how can you distinguish between them? Once the image has been imported, the only difference you'll see on screen is the "X" through the screen preview in the placed EPS when it's selected. Choose either the "Parsed" or the "Placed" option if you're planning to print composites. Use "Parsed" when your artwork will be used in online publishing or other documents to be viewed on screen only. Use "Placed" to import images that are to be printed at high resolution or color-separated for print-publishing purposes. And remember that you can't use Photoshop and Gallery Effects filters on placed bitmaps, only on parsed bitmaps.

Q (6.0 only) When I try to access one of the help topics in Illustrator, I get a message that says, "Please insert the disk: Adobe Illustrator Deluxe." Why does it want the CD?

A Illustrator's prompting you to insert the CD because it's looking for the "User Guide.pdf" file that's located on the CD (that file contains all the help information). You can get this message whether or not you have the CD inserted—and you'll continue to get it whenever you select a help topic until you help Illustrator find this PDF file. To close the dialog box, press its "Cancel" button. You'll then see the dialog box with the long alert message shown below.

Insert the Deluxe CD if you haven't already, press the "Find" button, and navigate to the "Online Documentation" folder on the CD—that's where the "User Guide.pdf" file is located. If you've copied the "User Guide.pdf" file from the CD to your hard drive, navigate to that location on your hard drive instead. (If you want to use the help feature frequently, don't want to have to insert your Illustrator CD every time you use help, and have plenty of hard disk space available—the "User Guide.pdf" file takes up about 7.5 MB—copying the "User Guide.pdf" file to your hard drive might be a good idea.) You should have to go through the process of "finding" the User Guide file only once; thereafter, Illustrator should remember the location of the help file.

NOTE: There's one more thing that can cause the long alert message to appear—not having Acrobat Reader or Exchange installed before you select one of Illustrator's help topics. Before you use the help feature, make sure one of these applications is installed. Acrobat Reader comes on the Illustrator Deluxe CD—look in the "Acrobat Reader - Install" folder inside the "Adobe Products" folder, and double-click on the "AcroRead.mac" icon to install it.

TIP MAC OS

Inner transformations

Here's an easy way to transform (move, rotate, resize, or skew) the elements in a pattern-filled object instead of transforming the path that contains the pattern. First, select the pattern-filled path with the selection tool. Then, click on the transformation tool you want to use on it. While holding down the P key, use the transformation tool on the object. As you drag the transformation tool, the preview that Illustrator shows on screen might make it look as though it's transforming the path, not the pattern. But when you let go of the tool, Illustrator will transform the pattern elements, not the path.

Q (5.0 and later) I want to change the font used in several documents, so I've been manually selecting all the text and reassigning the font from the Type menu. Is there a quicker way to do this?

A Yes, there is a quicker way, and it gives you an additional bonus prize. Illustrator has a little-known "Find Font" command that creates a list of all the fonts used in a document and allows you to search for and replace them. You can also change the font's type style, color, and kerning. The bonus feature is that you can save and print this font list as a separate file that you can then keep as a handy reference or give to a service provider, for instance.

To use the "Find Font" command, choose "Find Font..." from the Type menu in Illustrator 6.0. (In Illustrator 5.x, select "Find Font..." from the Text submenu on the Filter menu.) Select a font name from the "Find Fonts in Document" list. Illustrator selects the most recently entered instance of the selected font in your document.

To move ahead, you can choose either the "Find Next" option to find the next instance of that font, or you can click the "Skip" button to go to the next name in the font list and search for that font.

Next, select your desired replacement font from the "Replace Fonts" list. Click either "Change" to change only that instance of the selected font, or "Change All" to change all instances of the selected font. When there are no more instances of that font in your document, the font name is removed from the "Find Fonts in Document" list.

What kinds of fonts do you want to see? In the "Find Font" dialog box, you can select any combination of multiple-master, Type 1, TrueType, or "standard" (that is, Courier, Helvetica, Symbol, and Times) fonts that you'd like to see displayed. They're all selected by default. (NOTE: In order to display multiple-master fonts, you have to check both the "Multiple Master" and "Type 1" options.)

How many fonts do you want to see? Choose between "System List" and "Document List" for your available replacement-font options. "System List," of course, gives you more choices but will take longer to appear, since it has to parse all your installed fonts. "Document List" opens relatively quickly but limits your replacement choices to the fonts that are already in the document.

And where do you want to see them? And now the moment you've all been waiting for—the printable list of fonts. To save a list of all fonts found in the document (plus dimensions and resolution), click the "Save" button in the "Find Font" dialog box, then enter a name and a location for your file, and click "Save" again. Illustrator creates a SimpleText document that will be welcome in any service bureau.

TIP MAC OS

Creating a four-way blend *(5.5 only)*

Using the Pathfinder Hard or Soft filter, you can create a four-way blend. Try it out by following the steps listed below.

1. Draw a rectangle 10 points wide and 140 points tall: click once on your page with the rectangle tool and when the "Rectangle" dialog box appears, enter the correct measurements.
2. Copy the rectangle (press Command + C) and paste a copy on top of the original object (press Com-mand + F). Then move the copy 100 points to the right (select "Move..." from the Arrange menu, and enter a value of 100 points under "Horizontal," and 0 points under "Vertical").
3. Select both rectangles, press Command + C to copy them, then press Command + F to paste a copy on top of the originals. Double-click on the rotate tool, and when the "Rotate" dialog box appears, enter a rotation value of 90 degrees.
4. Color both the top and right rectangles 100% process yellow.
5. Color the bottom and left rectangles 100% process cyan and 100% process magenta, respectively.
6. Blend the top rectangle into the bottom rectangle using 20 steps.
7. Blend the left rectangle into the right rectangle using 20 steps.
8. Select all the rectangles blending from the top to the bottom (make sure you select the very top and very bottom rectangles) and select "Merge" from the Pathfinder submenu of the Filters menu (this removes any overlap in the blend steps). Repeat for all the rectangles blending from left to right.
9. Select all the elements and choose "Hard..." from the Pathfinder submenu of the Filters menu. In the "Pathfinder Hard" dialog box, click "OK." Or try the "Pathfinder Soft" filter for a different effect.

Pathfinder Hard

Pathfinder Soft 25%

Pathfinder Soft 50%

Pathfinder Soft 75%

Pathfinder Soft 100%

Pathfinder Soft 500%

Q Something that I've been trying to work around for a while is that the Same Fill Color filter doesn't select type. This can become somewhat time consuming when I work in files with several different text blocks. Do you have any suggestions?

A You're right—you can't select text using a filter from the Select submenu of the Filter menu (e.g., Same Fill Color, Same Paint Style) in Adobe Illustrator 5.5 or later. For example, when you use Same Fill Color, Illustrator selects all drawn objects with the same fill color, but doesn't select any text. The Select filters included with Illustrator 5.5 and later select only objects drawn in Illustrator. They don't select bitmap images, imported EPS files, or text. Here are a few ideas for achieving the results you want.

After you've run the appropriate Select filter(s) on your objects, hold down the Shift key and click on the text to add it to your selection. Make the desired changes. You can then group the text and objects so you can make future changes easily by selecting any object in the group with the selection tool. Or you can convert the text to outlines before you apply a Select filter. We probably don't have to remind you that once you convert the text to outlines, you won't be able to modify the objects as text anymore.

If you'd rather not convert your text to paths, here's another option. Use the Cytopia Software Incorporated (CSI) Select Text Plug-in filter to select text based on font, size, or text type (e.g., point type, path type, area type). The CSI Select Colors filter will select objects and text based on fill and stroke color. Cytopia Software Socket Set Volumes One and Two for Illustrator 5.5 or later enhance functionality and workflow. (SelectText is in Volume One.) The Plug-ins are installed in Illustrator's "Plug-ins" folder and appear on the Filter menu in the Colors, Objects, Other, and Select filter submenus. The Socket Set Plug-ins allow you to apply, preview, repeat, and undo the filter function within each of the Plug-ins' dialog boxes. If you want additional information, you can reach Cytopia Software Incorporated by phone at (800) 588-0274, by fax at (415) 364-4592, or on the Web at www.cytopia.com. Socket Set was reviewed in "Get Set to be more productive" by Ted Alspach, Adobe Magazine, September/October 1996, page 32.

Q I've started using the eyedropper and paint-bucket tools more often to sample and apply colors to my artwork. I want to be able to sample just the fill of an object, not the stroke. When I use the Eyedropper tool, it picks up both the fill and stroke. Can I change this?

A Yes. Many of the eyedropper and paint-bucket attributes can be customized by double-clicking on the tool in the toolbox and selecting the desired options. For the effect you want, you would leave the "Fill" option selected in the "Eyedropper picks up" section, but deselect the "Stroke" option. After that, any artwork you sample with the eyedropper tool will pick up only the Fill attributes.

Q How do I get rid of those little triangles after using the Offset Path filter with a negative number?

A The trick is to divide and conquer—that is, use the Divide filter (select "Divide" from the Pathfinder submenu of the Filter menu) on the element that now sports the triangles. The Divide filter splits an object up into its component shapes. If your element doesn't have too many points, you can do this right in your original Illustrator document. Select and delete the extraneous triangles with the direct-selection tool.

TIP MAC OS

Multiple files in one—and other tips for layers

If you need to make multiple versions of one file, with each version sharing certain elements—for instance, the same artwork but different text—there's a great way to "combine" those files using layers. Just assign all the elements that would normally be in a separate file to a separate layer, and turn layers on and off to view and print the different "versions" of the file. Clark Daily of Maitland, Florida, sent us this tip—he uses this technique to create files in several different languages. The artwork goes on one layer, the English text goes on another, the Spanish text on another, and so on. When he wants to view, edit, or print the Spanish version, for instance, he turns off all but the artwork and Spanish-text layers. This technique allows him to use his storage space more efficiently, and also helps him avoid version-control problems (if he wants to change the artwork, he doesn't have to change it in the Spanish version of the file, the English version of the file, and so on).

Here are a few more of our favorite layers tips.

- To move an element from one layer to another, first select the element, then in the Layers palette, click on the little blue dot at the far right of the layer name. Drag the blue dot to the layer to which you'd like to move your element (for this to work, the layer to which you're moving the object must be unlocked).
- You can help yourself keep track of which elements go on which layers by color-coding them. To do so, select a layer, and in the Layers palette's pop-up menu, choose "Layer Options for [the layer you selected]…." Illustrator will display the "Layers Options" dialog box, in which you can choose a color from the "Selection Color" pop-up menu. Click "OK" to exit the dialog box. Illustrator will display a swatch of that color next to that layer's name in the Layers palette, and when you select an element on that layer, Illustrator will outline that element with the color you've associated with that layer.

TIP MAC OS

Ornate constructions

(6.0 only) You can use the "Repeat Transform" function to take the repetition out of creating a complex image. Any adjustments you make in the "Transform Each" dialog box will be treated as a single, repeatable action. Here's an example.

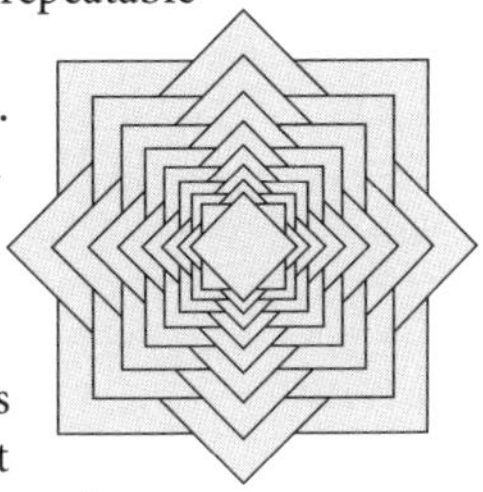

To create the image shown at left, draw a square and give it a fill and 2-point stroke. Choose "Transform Each..." from the Arrange menu, then set both the horizontal- and vertical-scale options to 90 percent and the rotate angle to 45 degrees. When you're done, click "Copy." Then select "Repeat Transform" (Command + D) 14 more times.

You can vary this technique in an infinite number of ways using any of the settings in the "Transform Each" dialog box. Note that this technique does not scale the line weights (even when "Scale line weight" is set as the default in "Preferences"). Also, be aware that when you rotate irregularly shaped objects (that is, not a rectangle or an oval), they will not always revolve around the true center point.

If your design element has many points or corners, it might be easier to copy and paste the artwork into a new file to get rid of the triangles. Once you're there, run the Divide filter as described above. Deselect the art you want to keep, and delete the rest. Or select the desired portion of your artwork with the direct-selection tool, and then copy just the newly offset shape back into your original file, leaving the triangles behind.

Q I'd like to mix different percentages of two custom colors. Is this possible?

A Yes. There are a few ways to do this depending on the type of effect you're trying to achieve. If your artwork is limited to two colors, what you can do is set one color to overprint by selecting the "Overprint" option in the Paint Style palette. Keep in mind that you won't be able to see the effect of overprinting on screen. See pages 242–44 in your Adobe Illustrator User Guide for more information and examples of overprinting.

If you don't need to limit your number of custom colors (or if you'll be converting the colors to process at print time), you can overlap your colors and run either the Hard or Soft filter (from the Pathfinder submenu). The Hard filter gives the impression of overprinting. The resulting color is created by combining the highest CMYK values for each object. The Soft filter gives the impression of transparency. You can enter a "Mixing rate" value of 1 to 100 percent. The higher the value, the higher the level of transparency.

Illustrator converts custom colors to process equivalents in order to run these filters. If you want, you can change them back to custom colors after you've run the filters.

If you'd like to change your newly combined color to a custom color, use the eyedropper tool to sample it. Then drag a swatch of the process color from the fill icon on the left side of the Paint Style palette onto the custom-color icon (the green icon on the right side of the palette). Illustrator will display the "Custom Color" dialog box. Make any changes you'd like, then click "OK."

Q Is there any way to turn off drag and drop? I sometimes want the window to scroll when I drag objects, but they keep ending up on my desktop!

A Drag and drop doesn't come with an "off" button. However, you can work around it when you want to make your window scroll. Select the object you want to move. Then drag the cursor over the title bar or the bottom scroll bar and hold it there to scroll the window up or down. Dragging the object over the right scroll bar causes the window to scroll to the right horizontally. When you've scrolled to the correct location, move your cursor away from the scrolling position (without releasing the mouse button) and arrange your object where you want it.

Adding Custom and PANTONE Colors to Illustrator 5.x Startup File

While starting, Adobe Illustrator 5.x reads the Adobe Illustrator Startup file in the Plug-Ins folder. It then adds custom colors, gradients, graph designs, and patterns included in the Startup file to the Paint Style palette, and adopts the Startup file's magnification size, window size, viewing preferences (e.g., Preview, Artwork, Show Rulers, Views), scroll position, Document Setup settings, and Page Setup settings.

You can customize Illustrator's default settings by adding new custom colors, gradients, or designs to the Startup file or by changing the settings it contains. You cannot, however, copy the contents of a custom color library file (e.g., PANTONE, TRUMATCH) into the Adobe Illustrator Startup file. To permanently add a custom color library to the Illustrator Paint Style palette, create a copy of the custom color library file and rename the copy "Adobe Illustrator Startup," then copy the contents of the original Adobe Illustrator Startup file into the renamed copy of the custom color library file.

To add a custom color library to the Adobe Illustrator Startup file:

1. Create a backup copy of the Adobe Illustrator Startup

TIP MAC OS

Power blending

You're probably already familiar with blending between two objects, but did you know you can blend just the fill color of three or more objects? Illustrator's blending filters make this possible. To try them out, create a series of differently colored objects, select them, then choose "Blend Horizontally," "Blend Vertically," or "Blend Front to Back" from the Colors submenu of the Filters menu.

When you use the "Blend Horizontally" filter, it looks at the leftmost and rightmost selected objects' fill colors and changes the colors of all the middle objects to various mixes of those colors, creating a gradated color effect. The "Blend Vertically" filter has a similar effect, but it bases the colors on the fills of the top and bottom selected objects. The "Blend Front to Back" filter assigns colors based on your objects' stacking order, with the foremost and hindmost objects determining the blend. Note: The blending filters change just the colors of your objects, not their layering order.

file in the Plug-Ins folder and name the backup copy using a different name (e.g., name the backup copy " the extension "Adobe Illustrator Startup.old").

2. Duplicate the desired color library file. Illustrator 5.x includes the FOCOLTONE, PANTONE, TRUMATCH, and TOYO color libraries, which it installs in the Color Systems folder.
3. Rename the duplicated color library file to "Adobe Illustrator Startup" and move it into the Plug-Ins folder.
4. In Illustrator 5.x, open the copy of the Adobe Illustrator Startup file (e.g., Adobe Illustrator Startup.old file).
5. Copy all elements in the file by choosing Edit > Select All and then Edit > Copy.
6. Open the original Adobe Illustrator Startup file, then choose Edit > Paste.
7. Save the Adobe Illustrator Startup file, then quit Illustrator. When you restart Illustrator, it will read the customized Adobe Illustrator Startup file and add the custom color library to the Paint Style palette.

Working With Illustrator 6.0 Files in Illustrator 5.x

Adobe Illustrator 5.x can place Illustrator 6.0 EPS files, open Illustrator 6.0 PDF files, and open Illustrator 6.0 files saved in an Illustrator file format prior to Illustrator 6.0 (e.g., Illustrator 5.0/5.5). Adobe Illustrator 5.x cannot open Illustrator 6.0 files (i.e., Illustrator EPS file or Illustrator document) containing bitmap image data (e.g., TIFF images). When opening an Illustrator 6.0 file containing image data, Illustrator 5.x returns the error "Can't open the illustration. The illustration contains an incomplete or garbled object description."

When saving an Illustrator 6.0 file in Illustrator 5.5 or earlier format, Illustrator 6.0 displays the alert "You are saving this document in [various] format. Saving this document in an older format may disable some editing features when the document is read back in." Illustrator 6.0 then removes the image data when saving the file.

Illustrator 5.5 and later can open Illustrator 6.0 PDF files containing image data. When Illustrator 5.5 opens the PDF file, it extracts the image data then saves it as an EPS file. While opening the PDF file, Illustrator 5.5 displays the alert "Select a folder for placed images. These files will be extracted as EPS files and placed in this folder." followed by the prompt to select a location for the saved extracted image data EPS files. When saving an Illustrator 6.0 file in PDF format, Illustrator converts gradient fills into blends, pattern fills into masked objects, patterned lines into a lines stroked with 50% Black, and text blocks into individual lines of path text.

Illustrator 6.0 includes image data in documents when you:

- Open a bitmap EPS, PICT, Photoshop, or TIFF file
- Place a bitmap PICT, Photoshop, or TIFF file
- Parse a bitmap EPS file
- Rasterize Illustrator artwork
- Import objects using the drag-and-drop method

When you place a bitmap EPS file in an Illustrator 6.0 document, Illustrator creates a link to the original EPS file instead of embedding the image data. Illustrator 5.x can open Illustrator 6.0 files containing placed bitmap EPS files.

The Document Info command enables you to view general document information and the characteristics of the objects in the Illustrator file. The Selection Info command enables you to view the characteristics of a selected object in the Illustrator file.

To determine if an Illustrator 6.0 contains embedded image data, deselect all elements, choose File > Document

MICRO TIP MAC OS

Need to copy something from one layer to another quickly? Try this. Use the selection tool to select the item(s) you want to copy. Next, find the colored dot that appears to the right of the object's current layer in the Layers palette. With your Option key held down, drag the dot (your cursor will turn into a hand icon with a red plus sign) to the layer to which you want to copy the object.

Info, then select the Raster Art option in the Document Info dialog box. When a file does not include embedded image data, the word "NONE" appears next to Raster Art. When the Illustrator file contains embedded image data, the image's color type (e.g., RGB), bits per pixel (e.g, 24), number of channels, size in K and pixels, dimensions in points, and resolution in pixels per inch list in the Raster Art section of the Document Info dialog box.

To determine if a specific object contains image data, select the object and choose File > Selection Info.

Adding Library Colors to Illustrator 6.0's Startup File

When starting, Adobe Illustrator 6.0 reads the Adobe Illustrator Startup file in the Plug-Ins folder. It adds any custom colors, gradients, graph designs, or patterns in the Startup file to the Paint Style palette, and adopts the Startup file's magnification size, window size, viewing preferences (e.g., Preview, Artwork, Show Rulers, Views), scroll position, Document Setup settings, and Page Setup settings.

You can customize Illustrator's default settings by adding new custom colors, gradients, or designs to the file, or by changing its settings. However, you cannot copy the contents of a custom color library file (e.g., PANTONE, TRUMATCH) into the Adobe Illustrator Startup file. To permanently add a custom color library to the Illustrator Paint Style palette, rename a copy of the custom color library file "Adobe Illustrator Startup," then copy the contents of the original Adobe Illustrator Startup file into the renamed copy of the custom color library file.

Illustrator 6.0 includes 10 path patterns in the Adobe Illustrator Startup file: Arrow1.2.out/in, Arrow1.2.side, Dblline1.2side, Dblline1.2outer, Laurel.inner, Laurel.outer, Laurel.side, Robe.side, Tribevel.side, and Tribevel.outer. The patterns are not applied to objects, so after you copy the contents of the original Adobe Illustrator Startup file into the renamed custom color library file, apply the patterns to objects to ensure Illustrator loads them when launching.

To add a custom color library to the Adobe Illustrator Startup file:

1. Create a backup copy of the existing Adobe Illustrator Startup file by changing its name (e.g., add the extension ".old" to the Adobe Illustrator Startup file name).
2. Duplicate the desired color library file. Illustrator 6.0 includes the FOCOLTONE, PANTONE, TRUMATCH, and TOYO color libraries, which are installed in the Color Systems folder.
3. Rename the duplicated color library file "Adobe Illustrator Startup" and move it into the Plug-Ins folder.
4. Open the Adobe Illustrator Startup.old file in Illustrator 6.0.
5. Copy the contents of the Adobe Illustrator Startup.old file by choosing Edit > Select All, then Edit > Copy.
6. Open the Adobe Illustrator Startup file, then choose Edit > Paste.
7. Draw 10 paths in the Adobe Illustrator Startup file.
8. Apply a path pattern to each path.
9. Save the "Adobe Illustrator Startup" file, then quit Illustrator. When relaunched, Illustrator will read the new Adobe Illustrator Startup file and add the custom color library to the Paint Style palette.

TIP MAC OS

Seeing stars

(6.0 only) Illustrator 6.0 offers a great way to create interesting effects with the objects you can draw using tools on the Plug-in tools palette (stars, polygons, and spirals). By holding down the "W" key when you use these tools, you can create multiple objects at once. Try the following exercise to see what we're talking about.

First, click on one of the object-drawing tools on the Plug-ins tools palette. Click and drag the tool across your page to draw an object. Then, before letting go of your mouse, hold down the "W" key and start dragging toward the center of your object—Illustrator will start creating multiple objects (how many it creates will depend on how fast you drag). For an even more interesting effect, don't drag in a straight line—drag in an arc toward the center to create a "rotating" effect with the objects. Let go of the mouse to see the results.

And here are some other things you can try with the object tools on the Plug-in tools palette: press the up or down arrow key to increase or decrease the number of spikes on a star, sides on a polygon, or segments on a spiral; hold down the Shift key while you're drawing to constrain a polygon or star to a vertical axis, or a spiral to a vertical, horizontal, or 45-degree axis; hold down the Control key to adjust the decay of a spiral or the pointiness of a star; hold down the spacebar to move any of these objects around your page while you're drawing; or hold down the Option key to constrain a star's angles in such a way that each segment runs parallel with another segment.

To get the blended effect in the objects below, we selected all the stars, assigned them a fill, deselected all but the top star, assigned it a contrasting color, reselected all the stars we'd drawn, and then chose "Blend Front to Back" from the Colors submenu of the Filters menu.

New Save and Save As Dialog Box Options in Illustrator 5.5

The Save and Save As dialog box options for selecting a file format and choosing a EPS screen preview in Adobe Illustrator 5.5 are different from those in Illustrator 5.0.x and earlier.

ILLUSTRATOR 5.5

In Illustrator 5.5, selecting Illustrator 1.1, Illustrator 88, Illustrator 3, Illustrator 4, or Illustrator 5 from the Format pop-up menu in the Save or Save As dialog box saves the file in Illustrator document format.

Choosing the Acrobat (PDF) format saves the Illustrator 5.5 document as a Portable Document Format (PDF) file.

Selecting EPS in the Illustrator 5.5 Save or Save As dialog box saves the Illustrator document with an Encapsulated PostScript Format (EPSF) header. When EPS is selected from the Format pop-up menu in the Illustrator 5.5 Save or Save As dialog box, the EPS Format dialog box appears with the option to select the compatibility format and screen preview of the EPS.

The Compatibility option in the Illustrator 5.5 EPS Format dialog box, (e.g., Illustrator 5, Illustrator 3) specify the format of Illustrator with which the EPS file is compatible.

The Preview options in the EPS Format dialog box specifies the screen preview of the EPS file. Illustrator 5.5 has four EPS screen preview options: None, 1-bit IBM PC, 1-bit Macintosh, and 8-bit Macintosh. Saving an Illustrator 5.5 document with a 1-bit Macintosh preview creates an EPS file with a black-and-white bitmap PICT preview. Illustrator 5.5 documents saved with an 8-bit Macintosh contain a 256-color or 256-shades of gray bitmap PICT preview. Selecting the 1-bit IBM PC Preview option in Illustrator 5.5 creates a EPS file with a black-and-white TIFF preview.

Illustrator Preview Options

5.5 Preview Options	5.0.x and earlier Preview Options
None	None (Include EPSF Header)
1-bit IBM PC	IBM PC
1-bit Macintosh	Black & White Macintosh
8-bit Macintosh	Color Macintosh

To create an EPS file in Illustrator 5.5:

1. Choose File > Save or File > Save As.
2. Select EPS from the Format, then click Save.
3. In the EPS Format dialog box, select EPS file Preview and Compatibility options, then click OK.

In Illustrator 5.0.x and earlier, selecting the Preview options of None (Include EPSF Header), Black & White Macintosh, Color Macintosh, and IBM PC saves the Illustrator document in EPS format. Selecting the None (Omit EPSF Header) Preview option in the Illustrator 5.0.x and earlier saves the file as an Illustrator document. The Compatibility option (e.g., Illustrator 5, Illustrator 3) selected in the Save or Save As dialog box specifies the version of Illustrator with which the Illustrator document or EPS file is compatible.

Tabs in Illustrator 5.5 Feature Summary

FEATURE

Adobe Illustrator 5.5 includes both character tabs and graphical tabs.

The Tab Ruler palette in Adobe Illustrator 5.5 enables you to set a character tab's position and tab style (left-justified, center-justified, right-justified, decimal-justified). Left-justified tabs aligns the first character following the tab to the tab stop on the Tab Ruler. Center-justified tabs align the center of the first word following the tab to the tab stop on the Tab Ruler. Right-justified tabs align the right-most character following the tab to the left side of the tab stop on the Tab Ruler. Decimal-justified tabs align the decimal point or right-most character following the tab to the tab stop on the Tab Ruler.

Graphical tabs are paths that define left-justified tab stops in area text.

IMPLEMENTATION

To access the Tab Ruler palette:

Choose Window > Show Tab Ruler, or press Command + Shift + T.

To set a character tab:

1. Select the text object with the Text tool or one of the selection tools.
2. Choose Windows > Show Tab Ruler (Command + Shift + T).
3. Select Alignment in the upper right-hand corner of the Tab Ruler palette.
4. Select the desired tab style (i.e., left-justified, center-justified, right-justified, or decimal-justified), then click on the Tab Ruler to position the tab stop; click and drag the tab stop on the Tab Ruler to change its position.

To change a tab style:

1. Select the text object with Text tool or one of the selection tools.
2. Choose Windows > Show Tab Ruler (Command + Shift + T).
3. Click on the tab stop in the Tab Ruler, then select the desired tab style (i.e., left-justified, center-justified, right-justified, or decimal-justified). To deselect the tab, click on the Tab Ruler palette to the right of the tab position.

To remove a tab stop:

1. Select the text object with Text tool or one of the selection tools.
2. Choose Windows > Show Tab Ruler (Command + Shift + T).
3. Select a tab stop on the Tab Ruler palette and drag it to the top or left of the ruler. When delete appears in the

Tab Position box, release the tab. Tabs can not be removed by dragging them to the right or to the bottom of the palette.

To create a graphical tab:

1. Create an area text block containing tabs.
2. Create a path by drawing a line using the Pen, tool then apply a fill and stroke paint style of None to the line.
3. Position the path over the area text block containing tabs.
4. Select the line and the area text, then choose Type > Make Wrap.
5. Select and move the line with the direct-selection tool to position the graphical tab.

DETAIL

Opening the Tab Ruler palette while a text block is selected automatically expands the Tab Ruler to the size of the text block, and aligns it to the top of the text block. To change the width of the Tab Ruler palette, click and drag on the extended Tab Ruler button in the lower right hand corner of the palette. Clicking on the Alignment box in the upper right hand corner of the palette resizes the Tab Ruler to the size of the type area. The height of the Tab Ruler palette cannot be adjusted.

Illustrator positions default left-aligned auto tabs on the Tab Ruler every half inch. Once a tab is set on the Tab Ruler, the Auto Tabs to the left of the new tab become inactive. Changes made in the Tab Ruler palette apply to the next text object selected. Tabs can only be placed at whole point increments. When measuring in inches or millimeters, the tab aligns to the nearest whole point equivalent. Select Snap to constrain the tabs to tick marks on the Tab Ruler. Pressing Control while positioning a tab temporarily enables or disables the Snap option. Pressing Shift while dragging a tab stop moves all tab stops to the right of the selected tab.

The Tab Ruler's measurement system is determined by the unit of measure selected in the Document Setup dialog box. Clicking on the tab position indicator in the Tab Ruler palette changes the measurement system. The Ruler Unit setting in the General Preferences dialog box changes the unit of measure for all new Illustrator documents.

Graphical tabs cannot be used with path text or point text. Graphical tabs can be used in conjunction with tab stops on the Tab Ruler palette. When creating a graphic tab, the Make Wrap command is dimmed when the text selected is path text or point text.

Converting a Text Path to an Object Path in Illustrator 5.x or Later

When you click on a path with the Type or Type Path tool In Adobe Illustrator 5.x or later, Illustrator converts the path to a text path. Once a path is converted to a text path, the text and path become a single object. When you place text on a path, the path can not be manipulated or transformed (e.g., scaled, sheared, reflected) separately from the text. If you create a text block over or near a path, Illustrator may accidentally convert the path to a text path.

To convert a text path to an object path:

Use the Revert Text Path filter in Illustrator 5.x to convert the text path to a path object:

1. Quit Illustrator.
2. Move the Revert Text Path plug-in filter from the Optional Plug-Ins folder into the Illustrator Plug-Ins folder.
3. Restart Illustrator and open the document containing the text path.
4. Click on the path with the Text tool, then choose Edit > Select All (Command + A).
5. With the selected text from the path selected, choose Edit > Cut (Command + X).
6. Deselect the path (Command + Shift + A).
7. Paste the text block on the artboard (Command + V).
8. Choose View > Artwork and select the text path with the pointer tool.
9. With the text path selected, choose Filters > Text > Revert Text Path.
10. Select or deselect Delete Text Path in the Revert Text Path dialog box and click OK.

NOTE: When you select Delete Text Path, Illustrator converts the text path to a path object. When Delete Text Path is not selected in the Revert Text Path dialog box, the origi-

TIP MAC OS

Cut it out

Illustrator 6.0 offers a handy way to cut objects—it's the knife tool, and it's located on the Plug-in tools palette. Here are two ways to use it.

To slice through an object or group of objects just as though you're using a razor blade, click on the knife tool and drag it wherever you want to make a cut. It'll slice through any Illustrator-drawn objects (whether or not they're selected), but won't work on placed images. Hold down the Shift key if you want to constrain your cutting to vertical, horizontal, or 45-degree straight lines.

You can also use the knife tool to turn any Illustrator-drawn object into a cookie-cutter-like tool. Just select the object you want to turn into your "cookie cutter," and select "Apply Knife" from the Object menu. Watch out, though—this cookie cutter is sharp. It'll cut through any selected or unselected object (except a placed image) that lies across its path—either on top of it or beneath it in the stacking order. You should also bear in mind that the knife tool will remove the stroke on any path it cuts.

nal text path remains and a duplicate in the same position is converted to an object path.

OR: In Illustrator 5.0.x, copy and paste the text path with the Group Selection tool (i.e., the white selection arrow with a plus sign).

Unable to Specify Object-Specific Screen Frequency (lpi) in Illustrator

ISSUE

You cannot assign an object-specific screen frequency (lpi) to a drawn object or text object in Adobe Illustrator 5.x and later.

SOLUTION

Set the desired lpi in a Riders file, then save the object in an EPS file and import it as an EPS graphic:

1. Create a Riders file to specify the desired lpi. For instructions, see Additional Information.
2. Copy the objects you want to print with the custom lpi value into a new Illustrator document, then save it in EPS format.
3. Remove the Adobe Illustrator EPSF Riders file from the Plug-Ins folder.
4. Place the EPS file into the original Illustrator document.
5. Repeat steps for 1-4 for each object or group of objects requiring a different element-specific lpi value.

NOTE: Documents containing multiple lpi settings may print slowly or generate PostScript memory errors (e.g., "limitcheck; OffendingCommand: setscreen").

ADDITIONAL INFORMATION

By default, Adobe Illustrator documents do not contain screen frequency (lpi) information, and print using the default lpi value set at the printer. You can customize the global screen frequency, angle, spot function, and flatness values in Illustrator 5.x and later, however, by editing the PostScript code in a Riders file. Illustrator loads the Riders file, named "Adobe Illustrator EPSF Riders," from the Plug-ins folder.

Riders file settings are included when you print an Illustrator document or save it in EPS format, but not when you save it in Illustrator format. Riders file settings an Illustrator EPS file are used when you print the EPS file from a separation or layout application (e.g., QuarkXPress, Adobe PageMaker, Adobe Separator, Adobe PrePrint). The settings print on every separation plate, and custom screen angles are applied to all inks within the EPS file. The settings remain in the EPS file until you open and resave it in Illustrator with new values specified in the Riders file. If you save the EPS file without an installed Riders file, the settings are removed or not included in the EPS file.

To specify a custom lpi value in Illustrator 6.0:

1. Install the Rider plug-in filter by moving the Riders file, located in the Riders Folder in the Utilities folder, into the Filters folder in the Plug-Ins folder. The Riders plug-in filter adds an Other submenu to the Filters menu.
2. Launch Illustrator and choose Filter > Other > Make Riders.
3. In the Make Riders dialog box, choose one of the preset screen frequency values from the Screen Frequency pop-up menu, or select Other to specify a custom screen frequency from 1.0000 to 999.0000 lines per inch (lpi).
4. Click Make to save the file, named Adobe Illustrator EPSF Riders, in the Plug-ins folder.

To specify a custom lpi value in Illustrator 5.5:

1. Install the Rider plug-in filter by moving the Riders file, located in the Riders folder in the Separator & Utilities folder, into the Plug-Ins folder. The Riders plug-in filter adds an Other submenu to the Filters menu.
2. Launch Illustrator and choose Filter > Other > Make Riders.
3. In the Make Riders dialog box, choose one of the preset screen frequency values from the Screen Frequency pop-up menu, or select Other to specify a custom screen frequency from 1.0000 to 999.0000 lines per inch (lpi).
4. Click Make to save the Riders file, named Adobe Illustrator EPSF Riders, in the Plug-ins folder.

To specify a custom lpi value in Illustrator 5.0.x:

1. Install the Riders plug-in included with Illustrator 5.0.x by moving the RidersMaker file, located in the 3rd Party Utility folder in the Separator & Utilities folder, into the Plug-Ins folder. The RidersMaker plug-in adds a Riders submenu to the Filters menu.
2. Launch Illustrator and choose Filter > Riders > Make Custom Riders.
3. Select the Screen Frequency option and click Setup to set a custom screen frequency from 1.0000 to 999.0000 lines per inch (lpi).
4. Click Make to save the Riders file, named Adobe Illustrator EPSF Riders, in the Plug-ins folder.

To remove Riders file settings:

1. Remove the Adobe Illustrator EPSF Riders file from the Illustrator 5.x or 6.0 Plug-Ins folder.
2. Open the EPS file in Illustrator.
3. Save the illustrator document in the desired format. Illustrator can remain open while the Riders file is created or deleted.

TIP MAC OS

Layer control

By default, Illustrator adds new layers to the top of the list. To add a layer in a particular place, select the layer you want to be below the new layer. Hold down the option key as you go to the Layer pop-up menu. Now, instead of saying "New Layer...," it will say "New Layer Above Layer X...."

Placing or Opening Bitmap Images in Illustrator 5.x

Adobe Illustrator 5.x can import bitmap images two ways: it can open PICT and MacPaint images as templates, and it can place DCS and EPS images. Illustrator 5.x and earlier cannot open or place images saved in TIFF format.

When opening a PICT or MacPaint file as a template, Illustrator 5.x converts the file into a 1-bit image in the background of the Illustrator document. A template is an uneditable and non-printing graphic, which can be traced to create artwork in an Illustrator document. To display or hide a template, choose "Show Template" or "Hide Template" in the View menu.

When creating an Illustrator document that will be printed as separations from a layout application (e.g., Adobe PageMaker, QuarkXPress), place color images in the Illustrator document as either Duotone or CMYK EPS format, then save the Illustrator document as an EPS file with "Include Placed Images" selected. Do not use DCS files in an Illustrator EPS that will be separated in a layout application (e.g., PageMaker, QuarkXPress).

Desktop Color Separation (DCS) is an enhancement to the Encapsulated PostScript (EPS) graphic format used to produce color separations. DCS files formatted in DCS specification 1.x include five files, the main file containing a low resolution preview and the four process color files (Cyan, Magenta, Yellow, Black) containing the high resolution color information. In DCS specification 2.0, all the color separation information is contained in a single file (i.e., the "main" file).

TIP MAC OS

Build your own pyramid

It's late in the day, you're out of coffee, and your client didn't like your latest design. It's a good time to know how to go beyond the preformatted shapes in Dimensions and break the cube/cylinder mold. Introduce yourself to new shapes and structures by creating this simple pyramid. (If only it had been this easy the first time they made these.)

1. Choose "New Artwork" from the Artwork menu to open a two-dimensional (2-D) window.
2. Click on the rectangle tool in the toolbox and draw a square while holding down the Shift key. Note the size of the box, which appears in the status bar (e.g., 3 inches).
3. Click "Apply" to apply the 2-D artwork into the 3-D application window. Close the 2-D window.
4. Choose "Extrude…" from the Operations menu to open the Extrude palette. Enter 1⁄2 the size of a side of your square (e.g., 1.5 inches for a 3-inch square) in the "Depth" field, then click "Apply."
5. With the square (which is now a cube) selected, choose "New Bevel" in the Extrude palette. Click "New" in the dialog box that appears.
6. Select the pen tool in the toolbox. In the "Untitled" Art:Bevel window, draw a 45-degree line by holding down the Shift key while you click two points with the pen tool. (Note: Do not click and drag with the pen tool; this will create a curved path.)
7. Click "Apply" to apply the new bevel to the square. Close the "Extrude" dialog box.
8. To change the proportions of the pyramid, select "Scale" from the Operations menu to bring up the Scale palette. Select "Non uniform" and "Local," then increase or decrease the Z-axis value.

To create a template:

1. Create and save an image in PICT or MacPaint format.
2. Launch Illustrator, then press Option while choosing File > New.
3. In the "Template" dialog box, select the PICT or MacPaint file and click "Open."

After placing an EPS and DCS graphic, you cannot edit or modify the imported graphic (e.g., change the color or resolution), but you can manipulate the imported graphic using the transform tools (i.e., Scale, Rotate, Shear).

One-bit, grayscale, Duotone, RGB, or CMYK bitmap information can be saved in EPS format. Use preseparated EPS formats (e.g., CMYK EPS, DCS file, Duotone) when printing separations. Adobe Separator, QuarkXPress, and Adobe PageMaker are unable to separate bitmap RGB EPS files contained in Illustrator EPS files. Bitmap RGB EPS files print as composite from Illustrator.

When separating an Illustrator EPS file containing a DCS file in Adobe Separator, save the Illustrator EPS file without selecting "Include Placed Images" and store the DCS files and Illustrator EPS file in the same location.

To create an Illustrator EPS file containing a DCS file for color separation:

1. In Illustrator, choose File > Place Art.
2. In the "Place Art" dialog box, select the DCS main file and click "Place."
3. When the Illustrator artwork is complete, choose File > Save.
4. Save the Illustrator document in EPS format with "Include Placed Images" deselected.
5. When the message "Make sure you have selected the

include placed image option if you plan to open or print your file using another application" appears, click "Save without placed image."

6. Quit Illustrator.
7. Move the Illustrator EPS file and the five DCS files to the same location.
8. Open the Illustrator EPS in Separator.

Adding Custom and PANTONE Colors to Illustrator 5.x and later Startup File

While starting, Adobe Illustrator 5.x and later read the Adobe Illustrator Startup file, which is in the Plug-Ins folder. Illustrator then adds custom colors, gradients, graph designs, and patterns included in the Startup file to the Paint Style palette, and adopts the Startup file's magnification size, window size, viewing preferences (e.g., Preview, Artwork, Show Rulers, Views), scroll position, Document Setup dialog box settings, and Page Setup dialog box settings.

You can customize Illustrator's default settings by adding new custom colors, gradients, or designs to the Startup file or by changing the settings it contains. You cannot, however, copy the contents of a custom color library file (e.g., PANTONE, TRUMATCH) into the Adobe Illustrator Startup file. To permanently add a custom color library to the Illustrator Paint Style palette, create a copy of the custom color library file, rename it "Adobe Illustrator Startup," then copy the contents of the original Adobe Illustrator Startup file into the renamed copy of the custom color library file.

To add a custom color library to the Adobe Illustrator Startup file:

1. Create a copy of the Adobe Illustrator Startup file, which is in the Plug-Ins folder, and then rename it (e.g., name the copy "Adobe Illustrator Startup.old").
2. Create a copy of the color library file that contains the colors you want to include in your Startup file. Illustrator 5.x includes the FOCOLTONE, PANTONE, TRUMATCH, and TOYO color library files, which it installs in the Color Systems folder.
3. Rename the copy of the color library file to "Adobe Illustrator Startup" and then move it into the Plug-Ins folder.
4. Open the copy of the Adobe Illustrator Startup file (e.g., Adobe Illustrator Startup.old).
5. Copy all elements in the file by choosing Edit > Select All and then Edit > Copy.
6. Open the Adobe Illustrator Startup file located in the Plug-Ins folder, then choose Edit > Paste.
7. Save the Adobe Illustrator Startup file, then quit Illustrator. When you restart Illustrator, it will read the customized Adobe Illustrator Startup file and add the custom color library to the Paint Style palette.

MICRO TIP MAC OS

Oops—you entered text in all caps, and now you wish you could automatically change it to mixed case for your newsletter headline. It's "Change Case" to the rescue! Select the text and choose "Change Case..." from the Type menu, then select the "Mixed Case" option. (But remember, even "Change Case" can't make lowercase letters out of a typeface that includes only uppercase letters.)

Artwork View Speedup Filter

The Artwork View Speedup plug-in for Adobe Illustrator accelerates screen display in Illustrator 5.x when all layers are set to Artwork view. The plug-in does not accelerate screen display in Illustrator 6.0.x.

The Artwork View Speedup plug-in is automatically installed in the Optional Plug-Ins folder (Illustrator 5.5 and later) or the Separator & Utilities folder (Illustrator 5.0.1 and earlier) in the Illustrator application folder. To activate the plug-in in Illustrator 5.x, move it into Illustrator's plug-ins folder and then relaunch Illustrator. When the plug-in is installed, Illustrator 5.x displays all selection handles in black instead of the layer's selection color.

FreeHand Format Plug-in for Adobe Illustrator 6.0.x

The FreeHand Format plug-in enables Adobe Illustrator 6.0.x to open files created in Macromedia FreeHand 5.01 and earlier for the Macintosh, and FreeHand 5.0 and earlier for Windows. When the FreeHand Format plug-in is installed, files with a FHD3 or AGD1 file type list in Illustrator's Open dialog box, and Illustrator can convert the FreeHand artwork to the closest Illustrator equivalent.

The FreeHand Format plug-in is included with Illustrator 6.0.1. The plug-in is also available from Adobe Customer Services, and is posted on the Adobe World Wide Web site, the Adobe FTP site, and the Adobe BBS. The FreeHand Format plug-in does not support FreeHand 5.5 files.

PREPARING FREEHAND FOR WINDOWS FILES

FreeHand for Windows files do not have a FHD3 or AGD1 file type. To open them in Illustrator, you must first alter their file type to FHD3 (FreeHand 3.0) or AGD1 (FreeHand 4.0 or 5.0) using a resource editor such as ResEdit, Disktop, or File Fanatic.

disclaimer: This procedure is not supported by Adobe Systems and is only provided as a guideline. Experience using ResEdit is highly recommended, since it can change or remove any resource from any file. Always modify a copy of the file to be edited. Never modify an open file. If the wrong resource is modified or alterations are incorrectly performed, the application can be damaged. In the event of problems, revert to the original copy.

TIP MAC OS

Creating a marbled texture

(6.0 only) With a combination of Photoshop filters and creativity, you can create many interesting effects on rasterized objects. Here's one way to generate marblelike textures.

1. Create an object, fill it with a solid color, and select "Rasterize..." from the Object menu. In the "Rasterize" dialog box, choose "RGB" for your color model and select a resolution—medium will work just fine in this case. (You must use the RGB color model because some Plug-ins, including the Gallery Effects filters, work only in this color mode.) If your object is not rectangular, select "Create Mask." You probably don't want to choose "Anti-Alias" unless you're sure you'll be using a white background. When you've made your selections, click "OK."
2. With the object still selected, choose "GE Mosaic..." from the "Gallery Effects: Classic Art 1" submenu of the Filter menu.
3. In the "Adobe Gallery Effects Mosaic" dialog box, set the "Lighten Grout" option from the default of 9 down to about 5–7 (click the "Preview" button to see what the results will look like), then click "Apply."
4. With the artwork still selected, select "GE Glass..." from the "Gallery Effects: Classic Art 3" submenu of the Filter menu. In the "Adobe Gallery Effects Glass" dialog box, experiment with the "Distortion" and "Smoothness" settings, clicking on the "Preview" button frequently to see the results of various combinations. When you're satisfied with the results, click "Apply."

You can vary this technique using a variety of filters and settings. For instance, try the "GE Sponge," "GE Rough Pastels," or "GE Ripple" filter, and experiment for the best results. (Note: Some of these Plug-ins aren't installed automatically with Illustrator. You can install these optional Plug-ins from the "Adobe Gallery Effects" folder in the "Adobe Products" folder on your Illustrator 6.0 Deluxe CD. If Illustrator is open when you add or install these filters, remember that you have to close and relaunch it before you can use these Plug-ins.) You should also bear in mind that when you rasterize an object in Illustrator, the color definitions change. If you color-separate this object, you may get slightly different CMYK results than you would have had you not rasterized it.

Finally, if you want to save your texture as an EPS graphic, you may want to re-rasterize it as CMYK before saving.

To change the FreeHand file's type in ResEdit:

1. In ResEdit choose File > Get File/Folder Info
2. Select the FreeHand file in the Get File/Folder Info dialog box, then click Get Info.
3. In the Info dialog box, change the Type field to "FHD3" (FreeHand 3.x) or to "AGD1" (FreeHand 4.0 or 5.0).
4. Save the FreeHand file and quit ResEdit.

INSTALLING THE FREEHAND FORMAT PLUG-IN

To install the FreeHand Format plug-in, quit Illustrator, move the decompressed FreeHand Format file to the File Formats folder in Illustrator's plug-ins folder, and restart Illustrator.

If FreeHand files with a FHD3 and AGD1 file type do not list in the Open dialog box after you install the plug-in, reset the Illustrator plug-ins preference. To reselect the Plug-ins preference: 1. Choose File > Preferences > Plug-ins in Illustrator.

2. Locate Illustrator's Plug-ins folder, then click once to select it.
3. Click the Select 'Plug-ins' button, located under the scrollbox at the bottom of the Plug-ins Preferences dialog box.
4. Click OK to the message "Plug-ins in the folder 'Plug-Ins' won't be available until you restart Illustrator."
5. Restart Illustrator.

CONVERTING FREEHAND FILES

When Illustrator opens a FreeHand file, it converts the FreeHand objects to the closest Illustrator equivalent objects. If Illustrator is unable to convert a FreeHand object to its Illustrator equivalent, it removes the object from the converted file.

Document Setup

Illustrator does not preserve the page size and orientation set in the original FreeHand file. Instead, it converts the FreeHand page boundaries into guides, then uses the page size and orientation set in the Adobe Illustrator Startup file.

FreeHand 5.0.x can create a larger artboard than Illustrator 6.0x: FreeHand 5.0x supports an artboard of 222 inches (15984 points), while Illustrator supports an artboard size of 120 inches (8640 points). FreeHand 4.x supports an artboard size of 54 inches (3888 points).

FreeHand 5.x's default page is a tall, letter-size page positioned in the lower-left corner of the pasteboard, 1618 points from the bottom of the pasteboard and 1725 points from the left side of the pasteboard. When Illustrator opens a FreeHand 5.0.x file, it converts approximately a 6350-by-6315 point area beginning from the lower-left corner of the FreeHand pasteboard. Illustrator clips any artwork that extends beyond the 6350-by-6315 area.

Illustrator and FreeHand measure objects differently. When you measure and object with the Info or Control palette in Illustrator 6.x, Illustrator includes the stroke

MICRO TIP MAC OS

To make it easier to work with guides, create a separate Guides layer and position the guides on it. You can then show, hide, lock, or unlock guides with a quick click in the Layers palette, rather than by choosing different menu commands.

weight in the measurement. For example, a 200-point square painted with a 12-point stroke measures 212 points in Illustrator's Info palette. When FreeHand measures an object in the Inspector palette, it reports a dimension that does not include the stroke weight. For example, a 200-point square painted with a 12-point stroke displays a 200-point width and height in FreeHand.

Paint Style

FreeHand can create named tints as well as named and unnamed process and spot colors. Illustrator can create named spot colors (i.e., custom colors) but does not support naming tints or process colors. When Illustrator opens a FreeHand file, it converts named process colors, and tints of unnamed process colors, to custom colors. For example, when Illustrator opens a FreeHand file containing a process PANTONE color, Illustrator converts the process PANTONE color to a custom color (i.e., spot color).

Illustrator does not support object-level spot function, angle, or frequency settings. When Illustrator converts a FreeHand file, it removes these object-level settings.

FreeHand can create eight fill paint styles: basic, custom, graduated, pattern, Postscript, radial, textured, and tiled. Illustrator supports only three of these styles: basic, graduated, and tiled. When Illustrator opens a FreeHand file, it converts graduated and radial fills to gradient fills, tiled fills to pattern fills, and pattern, PostScript, or textured fills and strokes to a fill and stroke of None.

Imported Graphics

Illustrator can convert linked EPS files and embedded, uncompressed, 72-ppi TIFF and PICT files. When Illustrator opens a FreeHand file containing an unsupported graphic, it converts it into a rectangle with a fill and stroke of None, scales the graphic, changes its position, or deletes it from the converted file.

EPS

Illustrator cannot open FreeHand files containing embedded EPS files. When Illustrator opens a file containing an embedded EPS file, it returns the error "Error converting file. The file contains elements not supported by the converter."

When Illustrator opens a FreeHand file containing a linked EPS file, Illustrator retains the link between the converted file and the external EPS file. If the FreeHand file's link to the EPS file is broken, Illustrator replaces the EPS graphic with a rectangle filled and stroked with None.

TIFF

Illustrator cannot convert linked TIFF images in FreeHand files. When Illustrator opens a file containing a linked TIFF image, it replaces the image with a rectangle filled and stroked with None.

When Illustrator opens a FreeHand file containing embedded TIFF image that is not compressed, Illustrator converts the TIFF to a 72-ppi image, then resizes the image to distribute the pixels at 72 pixels per inch (ppi/72 x original image dimensions = imported image dimensions). Images with a resolution greater than 72 ppi increase in size, and those with a resolution less than 72 ppi to decrease in size. For example, when Illustrator opens a FreeHand file containing a 146-by-146 point, 150-ppi TIFF file, Illustrator increases the size of the TIFF to 300-by-300 points.

When Illustrator opens a FreeHand file containing an embedded, LZW-compressed TIFF file, Illustrator resizes the image to distribute the pixels at 72 pixels per inch, then converts the TIFF to a rectangle with a fill and stoke of None. Illustrator positions the rectangle above its original location. For example, Illustrator converts a 150-ppi, 146-by-146 point TIFF file to a 300-by-300 rectangle with a fill of None, and positions the bottom of the rectangle 300 points above the TIFF's original location.

PICT

When Illustrator opens a FreeHand file containing a 72-ppi PICT file that is not compressed, Illustrator converts the PICT and keeps it in its original location.

Illustrator changes the position of PICT files with a resolution other than 72 ppi: if the PICT file's resolution is greater than 72 ppi, Illustrator moves it up and to the right of its original position; if the PICT file's resolution is less than 72 ppi, Illustrator moves it down and to the left of its original position.

When Illustrator converts a FreeHand file containing a JPEG-compressed PICT file, Illustrator retains the QuickTime PICT icon and then repositions the PICT image based on its resolution, as described above.

Publish and Subscribe

Illustrator does not support Publish and Subscribe commands in FreeHand files. When Illustrator opens a FreeHand publisher file, it removes the file's publish command and the converted file does not link to the edition file published in FreeHand. When Illustrator opens a FreeHand subscriber file, it deletes any subscribed edition from the converted file. Illustrator can not open FreeHand edition files; when doing so it returns the error "The file "[File Name]" is in unknown format and cannot be opened."

Text

You can format text in FreeHand by applying a stylized font to it (e.g., B Helvetica Bold) or by choosing a plain font (e.g., Helvetica) and then applying a type style to the font (e.g., Bold, Italic). Illustrator does not support FreeHand type styles, and converts type-styled text to a plain font. When Illustrator converts text formatted in a stylized font, Illustrator retains the font applied in FreeHand (e.g., B Helvetica Bold.)

Because FreeHand and Illustrator specify the layout of text in different ways, the position and layout of text in a FreeHand file may change when you open the file in Illustrator.

When Illustrator converts a FreeHand file containing linked text blocks, Illustrator breaks the link between the text blocks places all the text in the first text object. For example, after converting a FreeHand file containing text on three linked paths, Illustrator breaks the link between the three paths and placcs all the text on the first path.

When Illustrator converts a FreeHand file containing text blocks formatted in rows and columns, Illustrator converts each row and column into separate, linked area-type text blocks.

When Illustrator converts skewed text on a path in a FreeHand file, it removes the skewed attribute from the text.

Illustrator can not convert FreeHand 3.x text formatted with a stroke text attribute. When Illustrator opens a FreeHand 3.x file containing stroked text, Illustrator paints the text with a stroked of None.

Illustrator cannot convert all text characters in FreeHand files created in a non-English version of FreeHand (e.g., Japanese FreeHand). When Illustrator opens a file created in a localized FreeHand, Illustrator returns an error message, or maps the text character to the current keyboard layout and replaces any international characters with bullets.

Unexpected Results

MAC OS / WINDOWS

Q I opened an Illustrator file in Photoshop, and my gradients turned into solid fills. What happened?

A Versions of Photoshop prior to 3.0 don't recognize gradient fills and can't rasterize them. However, Photoshop 3.0 can rasterize gradient fills, so you may want to upgrade to that version.

If you have an object with a gradient fill and need to open it in a version of Photoshop prior to version 3.0, save your Illustrator file in the Illustrator 3.0 format—that will convert your gradients to step blends and masks, which Photoshop version 2.x will be able to rasterize.

Q I have two art objects in Illustrator and I selected "Make" from the Compound Paths submenu of the Object menu, but nothing happened. Why?

A Usually, when you make two or more paths into a compound path, the parts of the objects that overlap become transparent. Sometimes, however, the objects remain filled if their paths are drawn in the same direction—which is probably what happened to you.

When this occurs, you can make the overlapping portions of the objects transparent by reversing the direction of one of the paths. Start by using the direct-selection tool to select one of the objects. Next, if you're using Illustrator 5.x, select "Attributes..." from the Object menu, and in the "Attributes" dialog box, select "Reverse path direction" if it's not already selected (or, if it is selected, deselect it). Click "OK"—the overlapping parts of your objects should now appear transparent.

If you're using an earlier version of Illustrator, the "Reverse path direction" option is located in the "Paint Style" dialog box, which you can open by selecting "Paint Style..." from the Paint menu.

Q I've noticed that if I export a drawing as an EPS from different versions of Illustrator, I end up with different bounding boxes. What's going on, and how can I control the size of the bounding box Illustrator creates?

A You've probably noticed differences among your bounding boxes because different versions of Illustrator include different kinds of elements in exported EPS files, and which elements Illustrator exports determines what the dimensions of your bounding boxes are.

When Illustrator 5.0.x exports an EPS, it does not include any paths with a fill and stroke attribute of "None." If you have disconnected anchor points with a fill attribute of any color, Illustrator 5.0.x will include them in your EPS even though they're not visible on screen.

On the other hand, Illustrator 4.0x for Windows, Illustrator 5.5 for the Macintosh, and Illustrator 3.x and earlier for the Macintosh include all your document's elements, including paths with fill and stroke attributes of "None," in exported EPS files.

If you want to create an EPS with specific bounding-box dimensions, try this. Draw a rectangle with a fill attribute of any color where you want your bounding box to be, and delete any two of its opposite corner points. Unless there's an element on your page that falls outside the rectangle's area, its anchor points will define your bounding box. (To see if any other objects are on your page, switch to the pointer tool, zoom out so you can see the whole page, and press Ctrl + A in Windows or Command + A on the Macintosh to select everything on the page.)

Q I've used both Illustrator and Streamline to convert text to paths, and Illustrator seems to do it better. Streamline is a tracing program, so what gives?

A The reason Illustrator and Streamline seem to "trace" text differently is because they both don't actually trace text. Illustrator can convert text to paths (when you use the "Create Outlines" command on the Type menu). When it does so, it isn't just tracing the text: it works via ATM (Adobe Type Manager) to access the outline files for the fonts and draw those outlines just as your PostScript printer would.

Streamline, on the other hand, has a slightly tougher job to do when it traces text. Since Streamline works with bitmap graphics that don't contain any actual font information, it must literally trace any text in your bitmap files: it looks at each pixel in the graphic, determining what color it is, and attempts to join pixels of similar colors together by drawing a path along their boundary. With text—especially any text that has been rendered with anti-aliasing—the boundary isn't always easy to define.

If you need to trace text in Streamline, you'll get the best results with text in very large point sizes (try 100 points or higher), saved at a high resolution without anti-aliasing, in a solid color with a highly contrasting background color—black and white is ideal.

Q I wanted to create a special zoom effect with some letters, so I converted them to paths, copied them, offset the copies, and then blended each letter. But it looked awful on the letters that contain holes—the holes just disappeared! What happened?

A The holes in your letters disappeared because those letters are compound paths, and when you blend compound paths the effect only works on the outside path—hence, no more holes (the "hole" is actually a path inside another path). See Figure 1 for an example.

Fig. 1

If you need to blend any kind of compound path, including a letter that contains a hole (also called a counter), you'll need to convert that element to a single path. Here's one way to do that. (NOTE: This technique only works for paths that contain a fill with no stroke.)

Fig. 2

1. Create your compound path. If you're working with a letter, type the letter, select the text block, and choose "Create Outlines" from the Type menu. Then make a copy of the resulting compound path and set it aside (you'll use it later if you want to add a stroke).
2. Select "Artwork" from the View menu (looking at your art this way will make the following steps much easier).

Fig. 3

3. Select your compound path and choose "Release" from the Compound Paths submenu of the Object menu.
4. Using the scissors tool, make one cut in the inside path and one in the outside path.

Fig. 4

5. Make sure your paths are deselected (press Ctrl + Shift + A in Windows or Command + Shift + A on the Mac), then use the direct-selection tool to select a path endpoint on the outside path where you just made a cut, and move that endpoint away from the other outside-path endpoint. (One easy way to do this is to use your arrow tools to "nudge" your endpoints a certain distance.) Repeat on one of the endpoints you created on the inside path. Your object should look something like Figure 2.

Fig. 5

6. Press Ctrl + Shift + A (Windows) or Command + Shift + A (Mac) to make sure nothing is selected, then use the direct-selection tool to select an endpoint from your inside path and one from your outside path. (Be careful which two endpoints you select: think of your four endpoints as corners of a square—you should select two endpoints on the same side of the "square," not two endpoints on opposite corners of the square.) Join the endpoints by pressing Ctrl + J (Windows) or Command + J (Mac). Repeat for the other two endpoints. Your object should look something like Figure 3.
7. Using the direct-selection tool, return the endpoints you moved in step 5 to their original positions. Your object should look something like Figure 4.
8. If your object has any additional "inside" paths (for instance, the bottom "hole" in the B), repeat steps 4–7 on them. When you're done, you'll have a single path that you can blend without losing its holes, as in Figure 5.

If you want to add a stroke to your path, use the extra copy of the original compound path that you set aside in step 1. Apply the stroke to that object and layer it over your single-path object.

Q Why are some of the corners on my paths squared off instead of pointed?

A Your corners (joins) might look "squared off" because Illustrator is using beveled caps for those joins, and there could be two reasons for this. First, you may not have set that path to use angled joins in the "Paint Style" dialog box (Windows) or palette (Mac)—to check, select the path and see which "Join" option is selected in the "Paint Style" dialog box or palette. If the pointed "Join" option is highlighted, but your join still appears beveled, you probably need to increase the "Miter limit" setting.

The "Miter limit" setting controls how "pointy" your pointed joins can get before Illustrator bevels them instead. Why is there a miter limit setting? With very acute angles—especially with thick lines—pointed joins can start to bump into other objects or just look ridiculously long if no miter limit is set.

Here's how the miter-limit setting works. When the ratio of the miter length (illustrated above) to the line width exceeds the miter limit, you get a beveled join instead of a point. Since the miter length changes in direct proportion to the line width, the ratio of the miter length to line width (and therefore the miter limit) is affected exclusively by the angle of the join. Illustrator's miter-limit default setting, which is 4, will cause joins to bevel if the join's angle is less than about 29 degrees.

To increase the allowable "pointiness" of your joins, increase your miter limit. You can set the miter limit to anything between 1 (which will bevel all your joins) to 500, which will not bevel anything but the most acute of angles. No matter how high you set your miter limit, however, Illustrator will bevel your join if the miter limit times the stroke (line) width is greater than 1800 points.

Q Why aren't the gray lines on my artboard centered?
A The gray dotted lines you see on your page represent the imageable area for that page—in other words, that part of the page on which your printer can actually print things. There's a certain area near the outside of your page that a printer cannot print on (often because this is the part it grips while it moves the paper through its system) and therefore Illustrator marks off this area with the gray dotted lines you see on your artboard. Not all printers' imageable areas are centered on the page—for instance, a printer might need to grip more paper at the top of a page, and therefore its imageable area's center will be slightly below the real center of the paper (as in the illustration shown above). The page size and the information on where this imageable area lies on the page for your model of printer comes from the printer driver or PPD you're using.

If you want to make sure you don't place anything on your page that will fall outside your printer's imageable area, be sure you use the right printer driver and/or PPD for your printer, and keep your elements within the dotted lines on your artboard. To move the dotted lines around your artboard, use the page-tiling tool located on your Tools palette (see the illustrations at right). If all your artwork doesn't fit within those dotted lines, use Illustrator's tiling feature to print parts of your artwork on separate sheets of paper—see your Adobe Illustrator User Guide for more information.

Q When I use several elements as a mask, I find that all but one of the elements disappears. What's wrong?
A Nothing is wrong—that's how Illustrator's masking feature is supposed to work. Whenever you create masks in Illustrator, the effect you get will depend heavily on the order in which you drew your elements (which determines the elements' position in the layer stacking order)—only elements in certain layer-stacking positions will act as a masking or a masked element. To use more than one element as a mask, you'll need to take an extra step or two to manipulate your layer-stacking order and therefore get the effect you're after. The exact steps you need to follow depends on whether you're using Illustrator for Windows or for the Macintosh.

In Illustrator for Windows, you can create a mask by placing the element(s) you want to use as a mask in the bottom of the stacking order (you can do this either by drawing these elements first or by selecting them and choosing "Send to Back" from the Arrange menu). Next, make sure the elements are ungrouped, and if any are rectangles or ovals, delete their center points. Now—and here's the catch if you want to use more than one element as a masking object—select the elements and choose "Make Compound" from the Paint menu (this will make Illustrator treat those elements as a single element). Select the element and choose the "Mask" option in the Paint Styles dialog box. Your element will then mask all objects that are on top of it in the stacking order, and any objects that aren't positioned within the masking object's area will disappear. To make those objects reappear, choose "Artwork Only" from the View menu, select your masking object and the object(s) you want it to mask, and then choose "Group" from the Arrange menu.

In Illustrator 5.5 for the Macintosh, you can create a mask by placing the element(s) you want to use as a mask at the top of the stacking order, either by drawing those elements last or by selecting them and choosing "Bring to Front" from the Arrange menu. If you want to use more than one element as a mask, select those elements and choose "Make" from the Compound Path submenu of the Object menu. Finally, select both your masking element and the element(s) you want it to mask, and choose "Make" from the Masks submenu of the Object menu.

Text in an Illustrator 5.5 File Reflows When Opened in Illustrator 6.0 or Later

ISSUE

Text in an Adobe Illustrator 5.5 file reflows when you open the file in Illustrator 6.0 or later.

SOLUTIONS

Reformat the text in Illustrator 6.0 or later.
OR: Reformat the text in Illustrator 5.0.x , then open the Illustrator 5.0.x file in Illustrator 6.0 or later.
OR: Convert text to outlines in Illustrator 5.5, before opening the Illustrator 5.5 file in Illustrator 6.0 or later.
NOTE: Apply a zero-point white stroke to small text (i.e., 24 points or less) to prevent the line weight of the stroke from distorting the shape of small characters when converted to outlines.

ADDITIONAL INFORMATION

Illustrator 6.0 and later compose text differently than does Illustrator 5.5. When you open an Illustrator 5.5 file in Illustrator 6.0, Illustrator reflows text that includes tab characters or text that is horizontally scaled. For example, after you open an Illustrator 5.5 file in Illustrator 6.0 or later, the line ending and tab position of text formatted with tabs or horizontal scaling changes.

Illustrator 5.5 incorrectly displays and prints horizontally scaled text formatted with Right, Center, Justified, or Justify Last Line alignment. For example, horizontally scaled, justified text appears justified on screen, but does not print justified.

Illustrator 6.0 and later do not reflow text when opening an Illustrator 5.0.x file.

Illustrator EPS File Dimensions Larger Than Expected

ISSUE

When you import an Adobe Illustrator EPS file into a page layout application (e.g., Adobe PageMaker, QuarkXPress), the Illustrator EPS file's dimensions are larger than expected (i.e., the bounding box is larger than necessary to contain the EPS file's objects). Objects within the EPS file are not visible or only appear in close magnification (e.g., 400%).

SOLUTION

Resave the Illustrator artwork with only the desired objects included in the EPS file:

1. Open the EPS file in Illustrator.
2. Use the direct-selection tool to drag a selection marquee around the objects to be included in the EPS file. NOTE: Only object segments touching or within the selection marquee will be selected.
3. Copy and paste the selected objects into a new Illustrator document.
4. Delete any guides pasted into the new Illustrator document, then save the document as an EPS file.

ADDITIONAL INFORMATION

When you save a document as an EPS file, Illustrator creates a bounding box that includes all objects in the document, including objects and anchor points located on the Artboard outside the Page boundary, or objects on hidden layers. When you view an imported EPS file that has a large bounding box, the Illustrator EPS file's artwork may preview at a reduced size or may not be visible. Selecting and copying specific objects into a new Illustrator document with the direct-selection tool ensures disconnected anchor points and unwanted objects are not included when Illustrator creates the EPS file.

When a guide is released in Illustrator, it becomes a path. Paths, like points and other elements in the document, are included when Illustrator calculates the size of an EPS file's bounding box. Selecting a released guide with the direct-selection tool and pressing Delete removes the released guide's path, but does not remove its anchor points.

When creating EPS files, Illustrator 5.0.x incorrectly includes Direction handles, masked objects outside the mask, and guides painted with a fill or stroke attribute, resulting in EPS files with larger than expected bounding boxes. Illustrator 5.5 and later does not include Direction handles, masked objects outside the mask, or guides when creating the EPS file.

Can't Copy and Paste from Illustrator into Another Application

ISSUE

When you copy an object in an Adobe Illustrator 5.x file and paste the object into another application (e.g., Microsoft Word), the object does not display as expected or displays as a PostScript icon. For example, when you copy a circle you created in Illustrator 5.5 and paste it into a Microsoft Word 5.x file, the circle appears as a PostScript icon with the words "Adobe Illustrator artwork" beneath the icon.

SOLUTIONS

Save the Illustrator artwork as a EPS file and place the EPS file into destination file.

OR: Publish the Illustrator objects and then subscribe to the Edition in the destination file:

1. Select the objects you want to import into the destination file.
2. Copy the selected objects and then paste them into a new Illustrator document.
3. Save the new Illustrator document.
4. Select the objects in the new Illustrator document and then choose Edit > Publishing > Create Publisher.
5. In the Publish dialog box, select a format for the Edition (i.e., PICT Only or PICT and EPS), then click Publish.
6. Save the Illustrator document.
7. Subscribe to the Illustrator Edition file in the destination file.

OR: Copy the Illustrator object to the System clipboard as a PICT image with embedded PostScript comments:

1. Select the objects in Illustrator.
2. Press the Option key and choose Edit > Copy.
3. Choose Edit > Paste in the destination file.

ADDITIONAL INFORMATION

Illustrator 5.x, Adobe Streamline 3.x, Adobe Dimensions 2.x, and Adobe Photoshop 2.5.x and later use a proprietary internal clipboard. When you copy and paste an object in these Adobe applications, they copy and paste the object to their proprietary internal clipboard. When you quit Illustrator or switch to another application, these Adobe applications convert the objects on their internal clipboard to an AICB formatted PostScript language file. You can copy and paste AICB format clipboard objects between Adobe applications (i.e., Illustrator 5.x, Streamline 3.x, Dimensions 2.x, and Photoshop 2.5.x and later), but when you paste an Illustrator 5.x object in AICB format in an application that does not support the AICB format (e.g., Microsoft Word, Adobe PageMaker 5.x), the object does not appear as expected or appears as a PostScript icon.

When you copy or cut an object while pressing the Option key in an Illustrator 5.x document, Illustrator copies the selected object to the system clipboard as a bitmap PICT image with embedded PostScript comments. PICT graphics describe objects using the QuickDraw language and Illustrator describes objects using the PostScript language. Illustrator drawing features that are supported by PostScript may not be supported by the QuickDraw language. When you paste an Option-copied graphic in another application, the bitmap PICT graphic may display and print differently than the object displays and prints in Illustrator.

Illustrator 5.x and Later Uses Symbol for Special Characters on 68K Macintosh and 604 Power Macintosh Computers

ISSUE

When opening a file, Adobe Illustrator 5.x and later returns the error "The document [filename] contains fonts which are unavailable or in a different format than originally specified." The Symbol typeface appears in the missing font list, but the document does not contain text formatted in Symbol.

SOLUTIONS

Convert special or option characters in the document to outlines:

1. Remove the Option characters from the text object.
2. Create a separate text object for each special or option character.
3. Select the text object with the selection tool, then choose Type > Create Outlines.

OR: Install the Symbol font.

ADDITIONAL INFORMATION

Illustrator 5.x and later returns the error "The document [filename] contains fonts which are unavailable or in a different format than originally specified." while opening a file containing special or option characters when the Symbol font is not installed on a Macintosh computer (68000-series processor) or a Power Macintosh with an PowerPC 604 processor.

The extended, option, or special characters standard to most fonts can be included in a PostScript screen (bitmap) font, but are not included in the printer (outline) font.

When printing to a PostScript device, Illustrator 5.0.1 and earlier reads the font's printer font. When these extended characters are not included in the printer font, the missing character prints as a blank space. Characters not included in the printer font display on screen using the screen font, the Symbol printer font, or the Symbol TrueType font.

Illustrator 5.5 prints these standard extended characters by substituting their Symbol font equivalent. Because Symbol font is installed in the ROM of PostScript devices, the Symbol font does not need to be installed on your computer to print these Option characters from Illustrator 5.5.

Illustrator EPS File Dimensions Larger Than Expected

ISSUE

When you import an Adobe Illustrator EPS file into a page layout application (e.g., Adobe PageMaker, QuarkXPress), the Illustrator EPS file's dimensions are larger than expected (i.e., the bounding box is larger than necessary to contain the EPS file's objects). Objects within the EPS file are not visible or only appear in close magnification (e.g., 400%).

SOLUTION

Resave the Illustrator artwork with only the desired objects included in the EPS file:

1. Open the EPS file in Illustrator.
2. Use the direct-selection tool to drag a selection marquee around the objects to be included in the EPS file.
   NOTE: Only object segments touching or within the selection marquee will be selected.
3. Copy and paste the selected objects into a new Illustrator document.
4. Delete any guides or guide anchor points pasted into the new Illustrator document, then save the document as an EPS file.

ADDITIONAL INFORMATION

When you save a document as an EPS file, Illustrator creates a bounding box that includes all objects in the document, including objects and anchor points located on the Artboard outside the Page boundary. When you view an imported EPS file that has a large bounding box because of included elements on the Artboard outside the Page boundary, the Illustrator EPS file's artwork may preview at a reduced size or may not be visible. Selecting and copying specific objects into a new Illustrator document with the direct-selection tool ensures disconnected anchor points and unwanted objects are not included when Illustrator creates the EPS file.

When a guide is released in Illustrator, it becomes a path. Paths, like points and other elements in the document, are included when Illustrator calculates the size of an EPS file's bounding box. Selecting a released guide with the direct-selection tool and pressing Delete removes the released guide's path, but does not remove its anchor points.

When creating EPS files, Illustrator 5.0x incorrectly include Direction handles, masked objects outside the mask, and guides painted with a fill or stroke attribute, resulting in EPS files with larger than expected bounding boxes. Illustrator 5.5 and later does not include Direction handles, masked objects outside the mask, or guides when creating the EPS file.

Changes to Graph Data and Style Don't Affect Illustrator Graphs

ISSUE

Graphs ungrouped in Adobe Illustrator 5.x or later are not affected by changes you make in the Graph Data and Graph Style dialog boxes.

SOLUTIONS

Import the grouped graph from an earlier version of the Illustrator document.

OR: Recreate the graph.

OR: Instead of ungrouping graphs to change elements in it, use the direct-selection or group-selection tools.

ADDITIONAL INFORMATION

Graphs are special grouped objects in Illustrator that you can customize using options in the Graph Style and Data Style dialog boxes. When you ungroup a path, Illustrator converts it to paths and fill objects. Graph commands (e.g., changes to graph data or style) do not affect these non-graph objects.

When you ungroup a graph in Illustrator 5.x, Illustrator returns the error, "The selection contains a graph. After a graph is ungrouped you will no longer be able to access its graph style, its data or change its graph designs."

Fill Overprint Option Dimmed for Pattern Fills in Illustrator 5.x or Later

ISSUE

After you select an object painted with a pattern fill in Adobe Illustrator 5.x or later, the Fill Overprint option in the Paint Style palette is dimmed.

SOLUTIONS

Overprint the color applied to the pattern fill when printing color separations of the Illustrator EPS graphic in a separations application (e.g., Adobe Separator).

OR: Paint the objects in the pattern fill with an overprinting fill or stroke:

1. In Illustrator, choose Object > Pattern.
2. In the Pattern dialog box, select the pattern you want to overprint, click Paste, then click OK. Illustrator pastes the pattern into the Illustrator document.
3. Select the pattern objects you want to overprint, then select the Overprint option in the Paint Style palette.
4. Select the entire pattern, then choose Object > Pattern.
5. In the Pattern dialog box, click New, name the new pattern, then click OK.
6. Apply the overprinting pattern fill to objects.

ADDITIONAL INFORMATION

Illustrator 5.x and later dims the Fill Overprint option in the Paint Style palette after you select an object painted with a pattern fill. Pattern fills overprint when the color applied to the pattern is set to overprint in the application separating the Illustrator EPS graphic (e.g., Separator), or when elements used to create the pattern fill are painted with an overprinting fill or stroke.

Unable to Object Link and Embed (OLE) in Illustrator

ISSUE

Unable to use Object Linking and Embedding (OLE) in Adobe Illustrator 4.x for Windows or in Illustrator 5.x or 6.0.x for the Macintosh.

SYMPTOMS

Unable to select Illustrator as an OLE server application.
Cannot create a OLE link to an existing Illustrator file.
Cannot paste link files into Illustrator or from Illustrator.

SOLUTION

Save or export the Illustrator document in a graphic format (e.g., EPS, WMF), then import the graphic file in the destination application without an OLE link.

ADDITIONAL INFORMATION

Illustrator 4.x for Windows and Illustrator 5.x and 6.0.x for the Macintosh are neither OLE Server applications nor OLE Client applications and, therefore, do not support OLE events.

WINDOWS

Vertical Text Changes to Horizontal After Reopening in Illustrator 4.1

ISSUE

Vertical text blocks created in an Illustrator 4.x document change to horizontal text blocks when you open the document in Adobe Illustrator 4.1. The text blocks were created by pressing Shift while clicking the Type tool.

SOLUTIONS

Recreate the vertical text block, then convert the text to outlines before closing the document.

OR: Create the vertical text block by typing a paragraph return after each letter and applying Center alignment to the text block.

ADDITIONAL INFORMATION

By default, clicking on the page with the Type tool in Illustrator 4.x creates a horizontal text block. In Illustrator 4.0x, pressing Shift while clicking the page with the Type tool creates a vertical text block.

Illustrator 4.1 does not support vertical text blocks, and incorrectly displays a vertical I-beam when you press Shift with the Type tool selected. Closing then re-opening an Illustrator 4.1 document, or opening an Illustrator 4.0x document in Illustrator 4.1, causes vertical text blocks to change to horizontal text blocks.

The vertical text block feature is implemented Kanji Illustrator 4.x, but is unavailable in International English Illustrator 4.1.

To create columns of vertical text:

1. Click and drag the Type tool to create an area text block one character wide.
2. Select the text block with the Direct select tool, then press Option and drag to create an additional text block.
3. Repeat step 2 to create the desired number of text columns.

TIP WINDOWS

Fixing Paint Styles problems in 4.1

If Illustrator freezes when you use the "Paint Styles" dialog box in Illustrator 4.1, chances are you ran the 4.1 patch application on a version of Illustrator prior to 4.03. Unfortunately, the 4.1 patch application doesn't work correctly in this situation, so you'll need to do one of the following:

- Call Adobe Customer Services at (800) 521-1976 and request a disk set for Illustrator 4.1. When you get the disk set, reinstall Illustrator from it.
- Reinstall Illustrator 4.0, then run the 4.03 patch application on it (this patch application is available on Adobe's free bulletin-board system, and on CompuServe, AOL, and the Microsoft Network—for information on these services, see pages 98–99). Next, use the 4.1 patch application to upgrade Illustrator 4.03 to 4.1.

4. Select the text containers, then choose Type > Link Blocks.
5. Select the Type tool and click in the first text column.
6. Type the desired text, pressing Return after each character. Use leading to control the space between each character in the vertical text block.

Unable to Create Artwork Larger Than 18"-by-18" in Illustrator 4.x

ISSUE

You cannot create artwork larger than 18-by-18 inches in Adobe Illustrator 4.x.

SOLUTIONS

Create the artwork at a reduced size, then scale it to the desired size when printing. For example, when the final artwork size is 24-by-18 inches, create the artwork at 50% of the desired size (i.e., 12-by-9 inches), then print with the Scaling (%) option, which is located in the Options dialog box in the Print Setup dialog box, set to 200%.

OR: Create the artwork at a reduced size, save the Illustrator document as an EPS file, then place and scale the EPS file in a page layout application that supports dimensions larger than 18-by-18 inches (e.g., Adobe PageMaker, QuarkXPress).

OR: Save the artwork at the desired size from Illustrator and print from an application that displays EPS file larger than 18-by-18 inches (e.g., Adobe PageMaker, QuarkXPress):

1. Create the artwork at a reduced size.
2. Center the artwork on the Artboard and scale it from center to the desired size with the Scale tool.
3. Save the Illustrator document as an EPS file.
4. Place the EPS file in an application that displays EPS file larger than 18-by-18 inches (e.g., Adobe PageMaker, QuarkXPress).

ADDITIONAL INFORMATION

The maximum Artboard size in Illustrator 4.x is 18-by-18 inches. When an object in Illustrator 4.x is scaled lager than 18-by-18 inches with the Scale tool, the portion of the object positioned outside the Artboard is not visible on screen, but the entire object is included when saving in EPS format or when printing to a PostScript printer.

Artwork smaller than 18-by-18 inches can be printed at a larger size from Illustrator by increasing Scaling (%) value in the Options dialog box in the Print Setup dialog box.

Because Illustrator describes objects using the PostScript page description language, which is resolution independent, scaling does not affect the printing resolution of Illustrator-drawn objects. Scaling does affect the printing resolution of bitmap objects (e.g., EPS graphic containing image information) imported into Illustrator. Bitmap images are not resolution independent as the scaled bitmap image's printing resolution is determined by the image's original size and resolution.

Running Illustrator 4.0x in Windows 95

Adobe Illustrator 4.0x is incompatible with Windows 95. Illustrator 4.1 is compatible with Windows 95, but it is not Windows 95 logo-compliant. Windows 95 logo-compliant applications meet the required Windows 95 Logo criteria, which includes support of system level features (e.g., long filenames, 32-bit addressing, new user interface shell) and additional functionality (e.g., OLE 2.0).

When running Adobe Illustrator 4.0x on Windows 95, a system error (e.g., General Protection Fault error, freeze) may occur when performing Illustrator operations (e.g., launching, saving an EPS file, working in Preview mode).

To run Illustrator 4.0x on a computer running Windows 95, set up the computer to run either Windows 95 or Windows 3.x (i.e., dual boot), then run Illustrator in Windows 3.x. Illustrator 4.0x EPS graphics created in Windows 3.x can be imported and previewed in apps running in Windows 95.

To create an Illustrator EPS graphic in Windows 3.x and import it into a Windows 95 application:

1. Restart the computer.
2. When the Starting Windows 95 screen appears, press F4 to prevent Windows 95 from starting. The system returns the message "Now loading your previous version of MS-DOS."
3. At the C: prompt, type "WIN" and then press Enter to launch Windows 3.x.

4. Start Illustrator 4.0x and then create your artwork.
5. Save the artwork as an EPS graphic, then exit Illustrator and Windows.
6. Restart your computer in Windows 95.
7. Launch the desired Windows 95 application and then import the Illustrator EPS graphic.

Unable to Join Anchor Points in Illustrator 4.x

ISSUE
When joining two anchor points, Illustrator 4.x returns the error "To join paths, please select two endpoints of open paths that are the same group and that are not text paths."

SOLUTION
Ungroup the paths before joining them by choosing Arrange > Ungroup.
NOTE: After ungrouping a rectangle or oval, delete the object's center point. Objects drawn with the Rectangle and Oval tools are automatically grouped objects.

ADDITIONAL INFORMATION
Illustrator 4.x's Join command cannot connect the endpoints of grouped paths. Choosing Arrange > Join when a grouped path is selected causes Illustrator to return the error "To join paths, please select two endpoints of open paths that are the same group and that are not text paths."

Clicking on a grouped path with the selection tool in Illustrator 4.x selects all the anchor points on the path (i.e., the points appear as solid squares). Clicking on a ungrouped path with the selection tool does not select the path's anchor points (i.e., the points appear as empty squares).

To close a single open path or to join two paths, select the endpoints to be joined with the direct-selection tool, then choose Arrange > Join.

Placed Templates Do Not Display at 100% in Illustrator 4.x

ISSUE
After placing a BMP or PCX file as template in Adobe Illustrator 4.x, the dimensions of the template are larger or smaller than the dimensions of the original BMP or PCX file. For example, after placing a 2-by-2-inch BMP file as a template in Illustrator 4.x, the placed template is 4-by-4 inches.

SOLUTIONS
Before importing the bitmap into Illustrator 4.x, reduce the dimensions of the BMP or PCX file to 18-by-18 inches or smaller, then resave it at a resolution of 96 pixels per inch (ppi).

ADDITIONAL INFORMATION
When Illustrator 4.x places a BMP or PCX file with a resolution other than 96 ppi, Illustrator resizes the image to distribute the pixels at 96 ppi (i.e., ppi / 96 x original image dimensions = imported image dimensions). BMP or PCX files with a resolution greater than 96 ppi increase in size when imported into Illustrator; BMP and PCX files with a resolution less than 96 ppi decrease in size.

To resample a BMP file in Photoshop 3.0.x:
1. Open the image in Photoshop, then choose Image > Image Size.
2. Deselect the File Size Constrain option, enter the desired resolution (e.g., 96 ppi), then click OK.
3. Save the BMP file.

Custom Colors in Imported Illustrator 4.x EPS File Don't List

ISSUE
Custom colors included in an Illustrator 4.x EPS file do not list as expected after opening or importing the EPS file into another application. The custom colors that are not listed are contained in an EPS file contained in the Illustrator EPS file.

SOLUTIONS
Add the custom color to the Illustrator EPS file:
1. Open the EPS file in Illustrator 4.x and relink to the imported EPS file.
   NOTE: Because Illustrator always maintains an external link to imported or included EPS files, you must relink to the imported EPS file when opening an Illustrator EPS file containing an imported EPS, regardless of whether "Include Placed Images" was selected when the Illustrator EPS file was saved.
2. Choose Paint > Custom Color.
3. In the "Custom Color" dialog box, create the custom colors used in the included EPS file, then click "OK." Define the custom colors using the exact name and CMYK values used to create the custom colors in the included EPS file.
4. Select the pen tool and click once on the page to create an anchor point.
5. Apply the custom color to the anchor point.
6. Select the anchor point and choose Edit > Send to Back.
7. Repeat steps 4-6 for each custom color used in the included EPS file.
8. Save the Illustrator document as an EPS file with "Include Placed Images" selected.

OR: Create and apply the missing custom color to objects in the layout application:
1. In the layout application in which the Illustrator EPS file is imported, create the missing custom colors using the same name and process color definition (i.e., CMYK).
2. Create a small object and apply the new custom color.
3. Move the object off the page, or hide it by creating another element.
4. Repeat steps 2-3 for each new custom color.

OR: Open the Illustrator EPS file in a text editor and add

the custom color to the Illustrator EPS header. For instructions, see Additional Information.

ADDITIONAL INFORMATION

When Illustrator 4.0.x for Windows saves an Illustrator document containing a placed EPS file, the custom colors in the placed EPS file are not added to the header of the Illustrator 4.0.x EPS file. When the Illustrator EPS file is opened in Adobe Separator or imported into a layout application (e.g., PageMaker, QuarkXPress), only the custom colors listed in the header of the Illustrator EPS file appear. When an Illustrator 4.x EPS file containing a placed EPS file with custom colors is printed as separations, the objects with a custom color applied in the placed EPS file do not print on any separation.

Adding the custom colors to the "%%CMYKCustomColor:" and "%%DocumentCustomColors:" sections in the header of the Illustrator EPS file, or applying the custom color to objects in the Illustrator EPS file or to objects in the layout application, ensures the custom-colored objects in the included EPS file separate as expected.

Illustrator 5.x and 3.x for Macintosh EPS files includes the placed EPS file's custom colors in the header.

To open the Illustrator EPS file in a text editor and add the custom color to the Illustrator EPS header:

DISCLAIMER: Adobe Systems does not support modifying an Illustrator document with a text editor. Familiarity with opening EPS files in a text editor and saving in text-only (e.g., ASCII) format is required. Experience with PostScript language is highly recommended. Always modify a copy of the original Illustrator file. If alterations are incorrectly performed or the file is saved in the wrong format, the Illustrator file can be further damaged. Always modify a copy of the Illustrator document. In the event of problems, revert to the original copy.

1. Open a copy of the Illustrator 4.0.x EPS file in a text editor that can save in text-only format (e.g. Windows Write, Microsoft Word).
2. Remove any characters that appear in the first line of text before "%!PS". A valid EPS file begin with "%!PS." For example:
```
%!PS-Adobe-3.0 EPSF-3.0
```
3. Search for "%%BeginDocument:" to locate the included EPS file. The location and the appearance of the included EPS file varies with each Illustrator EPS file. This is a sample of an EPS file included in an Illustrator EPS file:
```
(C:\\AI4\\PLACE.EPS)
%%BeginDocument: C:\AI4\PLACE.EPS
%!PS-Adobe-3.0 EPSF-3.0
%%Creator: Adobe Illustrator(TM) for Win-
  dows, version 4.0
%%For: (John Doe        ) (Adobe Systems   )
%%Title: (PLACE.EPS)
%%CreationDate: (7/17/95) (2:43 PM)
%%BoundingBox: 174 310 450 530
%%DocumentProcessColors:
%%DocumentSuppliedResources: procset
  Adobe_packedarray 2.0 0
%%+ procset Adobe_cmykcolor 1.1 0
%%+ procset Adobe_cshow 1.1 0
%%+ procset Adobe_customcolor 1.0 0
%%+ procset Adobe_IllustratorA_AI3 1.0 0
%AI3_ColorUsage: Color
%%DocumentCustomColors: (cherry)
%%+ (ocean)
%%CMYKCustomColor: 0 1 0.5 0 (cherry)
%%+ 1 0.5 0 0 (ocean)
%AI3_TemplateBox: 306 396 306 396
%AI3_TileBox: 18 8 593 783
%AI3_DocumentPreview: PC_TIFF
%%Template:
%%PageOrigin:18 8
%%AI3_PaperRect:-18 784 594 -8
%%AI3_Margin:18 -9 -19 8
%%EndComments
%%BeginProlog
%%BeginResource: procset Adobe_packedarray
  2.0 0
%%Title: (Packed Array Operators)
%%Version: 2.0
%%CreationDate: (8/2/90) ()
%%Copyright: ((C) 1987-1990 Adobe Systems
  Incorporated All Rights Reserved)
```
4. Locate the line in the included EPS file that begins with "%%DocumentCustomColors." For example:
```
%%DocumentCustomColors: (cherry)
```
5. Select and copy the color name in parenthesis after "%%DocumentCustomColors:" and the lines beginning with "%%+". The first custom color name appears after "%%DocumentCustomColors:." Additional custom colors will appear bellow "%%DocumentCustomColors:" beginning with "%%+." For example:
```
%%DocumentCustomColors: (cherry)
%%+ (ocean)
```
6. Return to the beginning of the Illustrator EPS file's text to locate the first instance of "%%DocumentCustomColors." The custom colors used in the included EPS file do not appear after this "%%DocumentCustomColors" line. For example:
```
%%DocumentCustomColors: (red)
%%+ (blue)
```
7. Insert the cursor after the last color name in the "%%DocumentCustomColors" section then press return.
8. Type "%%+" followed by a space, then paste the color names copied from the included EPS "%%DocumentCustomColors" line. For example:
```
%%DocumentCustomColors: (red)
%%+ (blue)
%%+ (cherry)
%%+ (ocean)
```
9. Return to the included EPS file and locate the line that begins with "%%CMYKCustomColor." For example:
```
%%CMYKCustomColor: 0 1 0.5 0 (cherry)
```

10. Select and copy the numerical values and color name in parentheses following "%%CMYKCustomColor:" and "%%+." For example:
```
%%CMYKCustomColor: 0 1 0.5 0 (cherry)
%%+ 1 0.5 0 0 (ocean)
```
11. Return to the beginning of the EPS file then locate the first instance of "%%CMYKCustomColor." The custom colors used in the included EPS file do not appear after this "%%CMYKCustomColor" line. For example:
```
%%CMYKCustomColor: 0 1 0 0 (red)
%%+ 1 0 0 0 (blue)
```
12. Insert the text cursor after the last color name in the "%%CMYKCustomColor:" section and press return.
13. Type "%%+" followed by a space, then paste the color names copied from the included EPS "%%CMYK-CustomColor" line. For example:
```
%%CMYKCustomColor: 0 1 0 0 (red)
%%+ 1 0 0 0 (blue)
%%+ 0 1 0.5 0 (cherry)
%%+ 1 0.5 0 0 (ocean)
```
    NOTE: Add the custom colors to the "%%CMYKCustomColor:" section in the same order as they appear in the ""%%DocumentCustomColors:" section.
14. Save the Illustrator EPS file in text-only format. Saving the Illustrator EPS file in text-only format causes the EPS file's screen preview to be lost, and the EPS file appears as gray box in Separator or when placed in a layout application (e.g., PageMaker, QuarkXPress).

RTF Files Import with Unexpected Font in Illustrator 4.x

ISSUE

After importing a Rich Text Format (RTF) file into Adobe Illustrator 4.x, the imported text displays in a different font or typestyle (e.g., Bold, Italic) than expected.

When importing a RTF file, Illustrator returns the error "The following typefaces cannot be found in the system and will display and print incorrectly. [missing font names]." After click OK in the error dialog box, the imported text displays in a different font or typestyle (e.g., Bold, Italic) than expected.

SOLUTIONS

Resave in text-only format, import the text as a text-only file into Illustrator 4.x, then reformat the text in Illustrator.
OR: Import the RTF file into Illustrator 4.x, then reapply the desired font to the text in Illustrator. If the error "The following typefaces cannot be found in the system and will display and print incorrectly. ['font name']" appears when importing the RTF file into Illustrator 4.x, click OK in the error dialog box.

ADDITIONAL INFORMATION

Illustrator 4.x does not properly import Rich Text Format (RTF) files. When importing a RTF file, Illustrator 4.x applies the currently selected font, or the font Times-Roman, to the imported text. Importing a RTF file exported from PageMaker 5.0 or later into Adobe Illustrator 4.x causes Illustrator to return the error "The following typefaces cannot be found in the system and will display and print incorrectly. [missing font names]." After clicking OK in the error dialog box, Illustrator imports the RTF file and applies the font Times-Roman to the imported text, instead of the font originally applied.

When importing RTF files, Illustrator 4.x may import the names of the fonts used in the RTF file, and add these font names to the beginning of the text.

Unable to Open Illustrator 4.x File by Double-Clicking in Windows 95 Explorer

ISSUE

You cannot open an Illustrator file by double-clicking on the file in the Windows 95 Explorer while Adobe Illustrator 4.x is running.

SOLUTIONS

Use the Open command in Illustrator to open the file.
OR: Close the Illustrator application, then double-click on the Illustrator file.

ADDITIONAL INFORMATION

Because Illustrator 4.x is not a Windows 95 logo-compliant application, double-clicking on an Illustrator file in the Windows 95 Explorer activates the Illustrator application, but does not open the Illustrator file. When Illustrator is open, double-clicking on an Illustrator file causes Windows 95 to send the command "WM_SYSCOMMAND/SC_RESTORE" to Illustrator. The command "WM_SYSCOMMAND/SC_RESTORE" activates Illustrator, but does not open the Illustrator file. Double-clicking an Illustrator file when Illustrator 4.x is not open launches Illustrator and opens the Illustrator file.

Illustrator 4.0.x and earlier are not compatible with Windows 95. Illustrator 4.1 is compatible with Windows 95, but it is not Windows 95 logo-compliant.

Type Displays Incorrectly in Illustrator 4.0x

ISSUE

When you type text in Adobe Illustrator 4.x, the cursor is as large as the screen or the text displays upside-down or backwards. When you change the font applied to the text block, the text and cursor display correctly.

SOLUTION

Remove the font substitution information from the [Aliases] and [Synonyms] sections in the Atm.ini file.

1. Close all applications.
2. Make a backup of the Atm.ini file, which is located in the Windows directory

3. Open the original Atm.ini file in a text editor that saves in text-only format (e.g., Windows Write, Notepad).
4. Remove the any font substitution lines following the [Aliases] and [Synonyms] sections except for "Courier=Courier." For example:

   Change

   ```
   [Aliases]
   Times=TimesNewRomanPS
   Helvetica=Helv
   Helvetica=Arial
   Courier=Courier
   [Synonyms]
   Helv=Helvetica
   Tms Rmn=Times
   Courier=Courier
   ```

   To

   ```
   [Aliases]
   Courier=Courier
   [Synonyms]
   Courier=Courier
   ```
5. Save the Atm.ini file in text-only format and restart Windows.

ADDITIONAL INFORMATION

When the [Aliases] or [Synonyms] section in the Atm.ini file references an absent font or a font incompatible with Illustrator 4.x (e.g., TrueType), text formatted in that font displays upside-down or backwards or the text cursor expands to the size of the screen. This most frequently occurs with text formatted in Times or Helvetica.

The [Aliases] section in the Atm.ini indicates which PostScript outline font ATM displays in place of the resident Windows bitmapped font. In the [Aliases] section, the font name to the left of the equal sign is a bitmapped font. The font name to the right of the equal sign indicates the PostScript outline font used in place of the bitmapped font. In the [Synonyms] section, the font pairs are interchangeable. The ATM Installer defines aliases for the fonts Helv, Tms Rmn, Courier, Roman, and Modern.

When you select Use Pre-built or Resident Fonts in the ATM Control Panel, ATM uses the installed bitmapped font point sizes and rasterizes the PostScript outline font for any unavailable point sizes. When Use Pre-built or Resident Fonts is not selected, ATM uses the PostScript outline font to rasterize all sizes of the aliased bitmapped font.

The "courier=courier" line in the [Aliases] and [Synonyms] sections is used when an application requests the smallest available fixed-pitched font. When this line is not present, ATM provides some applications with a 1-point Courier font.

Text Cursor is Sideways in Illustrator 4.1

ISSUE

Pressing the Shift key while the Type tool is selected in Adobe Illustrator 4.1 causes the text cursor (I-beam) to be horizontal. Pressing Shift and clicking the Type tool creates a vertical text block instead of a horizontal text block.

SOLUTIONS

Create a text insertion point by clicking the Type tool on the page, then press the Shift key and drag to create a square text area.

OR: Close and reopen the file containing vertical text blocks.

OR: Create area type by drawing a rectangle, then clicking in it with the Type tool:

1. Select the Rectangle tool from the Toolbox.
2. Double-click on the page.
3. In the Rectangle dialog box, enter Width and Height values, then click OK.
4. Select the Type tool, then click in the rectangle.

ADDITIONAL INFORMATION

By default, clicking with the Type tool in Illustrator 4.x creates a horizontal text block. In Illustrator 4.1, pressing the Shift key while the Type tool is selected incorrectly changes the text cursor from a vertical I-beam to a horizontal I-beam. Pressing Shift and clicking with the Type tool creates a vertical text block instead of a horizontal text block. After closing then opening an Illustrator 4.1 file containing a vertical text block, vertical text blocks change to horizontal text blocks.

Fonts Substitute to Times Roman in PDF File Distilled from Illustrator 4.1 EPS File

ISSUE

When you use Adobe Acrobat Distiller to create a PDF file from an Adobe Illustrator 4.1 EPS file, text in the PDF file is formatted in Times Roman, instead of in the font applied in Illustrator.

SOLUTIONS

In Illustrator 4.1, resave the EPS file with the Include All Fonts As Type 3 option selected in the Save As dialog box, then redistill the file using Acrobat Distiller.

OR: Print the Illustrator 4.1 file to disk as a PostScript file, then distill the PostScript file using Acrobat Distiller.

NOTE: When printing to disk, make sure the fonts used in the Illustrator file are referenced in the [PostScript,FILE] section of the Win.ini file for the PostScript printer driver connected to the File port. For instructions, see Additional Information.

OR: Open the Illustrator 4.1 EPS file in Illustrator 4.03, save it in EPS format, then distill it using Acrobat Distiller.

OR: In Illustrator 4.x, convert the text to outlines, resave the file in EPS format, then distill it using Acrobat Distiller.

ADDITIONAL INFORMATION

When saving EPS files, Illustrator 4.1 does not include the font information that Acrobat Distiller requires to include specified fonts in PDF files. When you save an Illustrator

4.1 EPS file with the Include All Fonts As Type 3 option deselected, Acrobat Distiller substitutes the fonts in the Illustrator 4.1 EPS file with Times Roman when distilling the EPS file.

When you select the Include All Fonts As Type 3 option, Illustrator 4.1 includes PostScript Type 3 font information, instead of Type 1 font information, in EPS files. Unlike PostScript Type 1 fonts, PostScript Type 3 fonts do not include hinting information.

When Illustrator 4.1 creates PostScript files and when Illustrator 4.03 saves EPS files, Illustrator includes the font information Acrobat Distiller requires to include the specified fonts when distilling the PDF file.

To make sure your fonts are referenced in the [PostScript,FILE] section of the Win.ini file, add the fonts after connecting your printer to the File port.

To connect the PostScript printer to the File port in Windows 95:

1. Open the Printers Control Panel, right-click the printer to which you're printing in Illustrator, then select Properties from the pop-up menu.
2. In the Properties dialog box, click the Details tab, select File from the Print to the Following Port pop-up menu, then click OK.

To connect the PostScript printer to the File port in Windows 3.1x:

1. Open the Printers Control Panel, select the PostScript printer driver to which you're printing from the Installed Printers list, then click Connect.
2. In the Connect dialog box, select File from the Ports list box, then click OK. The PostScript printer driver appears in the Installed Printers list with the words "on FILE."
3. With the newly configured PostScript printer driver selected, click Set As Default Printer, then click Close.

Dashed Lines Export as Solid Lines from Illustrator 4.x

ISSUE

After exporting (i.e., File > Export Art) a file containing dashed lines from Adobe Illustrator 4.x, the dashed lines in the exported Illustrator file display and print solid.

SOLUTIONS

Open the Illustrator file in Adobe Photoshop 3.x, then save the file in the desired format (e.g., TIFF, BMP).

OR: Save the Illustrator file in EPS format and place the EPS file into an application that supports that format (e.g., PageMaker).

ADDITIONAL INFORMATION

When Illustrator 4.x exports artwork with the File > Export Art command, it converts any dashed lines in the artwork to solid lines. Dashed lines in Illustrator EPS files are not converted to solid lines. Photoshop 3.x is able to rasterize dashed lines in Illustrator documents and EPS files.

Dimensions of Artwork Change When Exported from Illustrator 4.x in DXF Format

ISSUE

After you export a file from Adobe Illustrator 4.x in DXF format, the dimensions of the artwork in the DXF file are larger or smaller than the dimensions of the Illustrator artwork.

SOLUTIONS

Open the DXF file in an application that accepts DXF formatted files and scale the artwork to its original size.

OR: Convert the Illustrator file to a DXF file using an application that converts Illustrator 4.x format files to DXF files (e.g., QuarterDeck Select Hijaak 95, Hijaak Graphics Suite 3.0).

ADDITIONAL INFORMATION

When Illustrator 4.x exports artwork in DXF file format, it incorrectly calculates the dimensions of the artwork and changes the dimensions of the artwork in the DXF file. For example Illustrator 4.x exports a 72-by-72 point rectangle Illustrator artwork to a 360-by-350.424 points DXF file.

Illustrator 4.1 Custom Color Swatches Missing in Custom Color or Paint Style Dialog Box

ISSUE

After you save a file in Adobe Illustrator 4.1 and then close and reopen the file, some of the custom colors list multiple times or appear without a color swatch in the Custom Colors and Paint Style dialog boxes.

SOLUTIONS

Remove the duplicate custom colors and then rename the remaining colors:

1. Select Paint > Custom Color.
2. In the Custom Color dialog box, click Select All Unused.
3. Rename the remaining colors until all color names display with a color swatch, then click OK.

OR: Work with the file in Illustrator 4.0.3:

1. Open the file in Illustrator 4.0.3.
2. Select Paint > Custom Color.
3. In the Custom Color dialog box, click Select All Unused, then click OK.

NOTE: If you reopen the Illustrator 4.0.3 file in Illustrator 4.1, Illustrator 4.1 will reduplicate the custom colors.

ADDITIONAL INFORMATION

Illustrator 4.1 may incorrectly create custom colors when the name contains the same word with different capitalization (e.g., Audio Red, Audio Pale Gray, audio gold, and Einstein gold). Illustrator displays the name of the incorrectly created custom colors, but does not display a color swatch for the these colors in the Custom Color and Paint Styles dialog boxes. When Illustrator 4.1 saves and then reopens a file that contains custom colors without a color swatch, it duplicates the colors and then lists the duplicate colors in the Custom Color and Paint Styles dialog boxes.

Illustrator 4.0.x correctly creates Custom Colors that contain similar names with varied capitalization.

MAC OS

Q *(5.5 only)* **Every now and then something happens to one of my paths, and all of a sudden I can't fill or stroke it anymore. What causes this?**

A Chances are you accidentally converted your path from an art path to a text path—probably by clicking on it with the text tool. Text paths can't be filled or stroked (if you try to apply one of these attributes to a text path, it will only affect any text you've placed on that path, not the path itself).

To change your path back to an art path, use the "Revert Text Path" filter, one of Illustrator's optional Plug-Ins. The "Revert Text Path" Plug-In converts text paths that contain no text back into art paths.

To install the "Revert Text Path" Plug-In, move it from the "Optional Plug-Ins" folder to the "Plug-Ins" folder, and restart Illustrator. Open your illustration, select the text path with the pointer tool, then choose "Revert Text Path..." from the Text submenu of the Filters menu.

If your text path contains any text (including spaces), Illustrator won't convert your text path. If this happens, click on the text path with the text tool, choose "Select All" from the Edit menu, press the Delete key to delete all characters on the path, then try running "Revert Text Path" again.

Q *(5.5 only)* **I created a blend using a custom color and a process color, and it looked great on screen but didn't separate right. What went wrong? Should I use a gradient instead?**

A Your blend didn't separate correctly because Illustrator doesn't fully support custom-to-process blends. If you create a blend like this, you'll be able to color-separate the two end objects in your blend (they'll print on the appropriate process and spot plates), but all the intermediate steps will print exclusively on process plates. Using a gradient fill instead may not get you the results you're after, either—spot-to-process gradients color-separate entirely or in part to process plates, depending on whether you use the gradient tool to start your gradient at a midpoint in your object.

If you need your blend to print with a spot color, try the following workaround—it involves creating two blends, one with your spot color and one with your process color, and overlaying and overprinting them to achieve a true spot-to-process blend.

1. Assign your spot color to the end object you want to print as that color (let's call this object object A).
2. Assign your spot color to the other end object (object B), but set that color's tint to 0% in the "Paint Style" palette.
3. Blend the two objects using the Blend tool.
4. Select just the end objects of your blend, not the intermediate steps. Press Command + C to copy them and press Command + F to paste the copy directly on top of the originals.
5. Select the copy of object B and assign your process color. Using the "Paint Style" palette, set the process color to overprint. Then, select the copy of object A and assign it a process color that consists of 0% cyan, magenta, yellow, and black.
6. Blend the two objects. Afterward, what you'll see on screen is just the top blend consisting of your process colors—you won't see the spot-color blend beneath it. Nevertheless, your blend will color-separate correctly. Just make sure your spot color is set to print at an angle recommended by your commercial printer or service bureau, or you could end up with a moiré pattern.

For more information on using different combinations of spot, process, and Illustrator's default black and white colors in blends and graduated fills, see the chart below.

Color-separation behavior of Illustrator blends and gradients

	Blends	Gradients
Spot color to spot color	Intermediate steps separate as process[1]	Separate correctly to spot-color plates
Spot color to process color	Intermediate steps separate as process[1]	Entire gradient separates as process colors[2]
Process color to process color	Separate correctly to process plates	Separate correctly to process plates
Default black to process color	Separate correctly to process plates	Separate correctly to process plates
Default black to spot color	Intermediate steps separate as process[1]	Separate correctly to process-black plate and spot-color plate
Default white to process color	Separate correctly to process plates	Separate correctly to process plates
Default white to spot color	Intermediate steps separate as process[3]	Separate correctly to spot-color plate

[1] *If you don't want the intermediate steps of your blend to print on process plates, create two blends and overlay them (this technique is explained in detail at left).*

[2] *If you want to create a gradient fill with a spot and a process color, try this: First, create a gradient that goes from your spot color to a 0% tint of the same color. Next, duplicate the object and fill it with a gradient that goes from process white to your process color. Overlay the objects and make sure the top object is set to overprint.*

[3] *To create a blend from a spot color to white, blend from the spot color to a 0% tint of the same color (not to Illustrator's default white, which is a process color).*

Q When I use Adobe Streamline to create a tracing file that's 25 square inches and then bring it into Illustrator, it becomes 18 square inches. What's up?

A What you're seeing is the result of a safeguard built into Steamline. To ensure Streamline would work well with Illustrator, Adobe designed Streamline so that the files it creates would never exceed the maximum size of Illustrator's artboard, which is 18 x 18 inches in Illustrator 3.x and 4.x (in Illustrator 5.5, your artboard can be a maximum of 120 x 120 inches). When you create a tracing that's larger than 18 x 18 inches, Streamline automatically reduces it when you save.

If you want to scale your Streamline file back to its original dimensions in Illustrator, select it with the pointer tool, double-click on the scaling tool, and in the "Scale" dialog box, enter the percentage by which you want to scale the object. For example, if your Streamline file was originally 25 x 25 inches and was scaled down to 18 x 18 inches, you'd divide 25 by 18 to get 1.3889, or 138.89%.

Q My type does not appear on screen even though the cursor moves with each letter I type and the paint style is set to black. What's wrong?

A You're probably seeing a symptom of a conflict between a PostScript font and a TrueType font that share the same name. And in most cases, the problem lies with dual versions of Courier, Helvetica, Times, or Symbol.

The System software installs TrueType versions of certain fonts—Courier, Helvetica, Symbol, and Times—that mimic and have the same names as the "Base 13" set of PostScript fonts (the set of PostScript fonts built into virtually all PostScript printers). Adobe Illustrator installs the PostScript versions of these fonts to ensure that ATM will be able to display these commonly used typefaces.

You should not have both TrueType and PostScript versions of the same font. Decide which kind you want to keep (if you print to PostScript printers or imagesetters, you may want to keep the PostScript versions) and remove the other kind. To remove the TrueType versions, close all your applications, and then open the Fonts folder within your System Folder. In the suitcases for Courier, Helvetica, Times, and Symbol, look for any TrueType fonts—you'll be able to spot them by their icons, which show three "A" letters (if all your icons look like generic gray pages, change your view to "Icon" or "Small Icon"). Drag these TrueType fonts out of your Fonts folder to the trash or to a folder that's not inside your System Folder.

If you continue to have this "invisible font" problem, you may have other fonts in both PostScript and TrueType versions. To find these conflicts you can either catalog all your fonts manually (by sifting through all your suitcases and font folders), or you can scan your system with Adobe CheckList or another utility that can identify this kind of font redundancy.

Q *(6.0 only)* **I created a pattern in Illustrator 6.0, and when I fill an object with this pattern, there's extra white space between the pattern tiles. What is wrong?**

A Chances are you just need to make sure that the backmost element of your pattern tile is a rectangle with a fill and stroke of "None." Here's why.

When you create a pattern in Illustrator 6.0, there are two ways you can define the boundary that defines the tile (we'll call this the bounding box). First, you can draw all the objects you want to be part of your tile, then draw a rectangle wherever you want the bounding box to be—and that bounding box does not have to completely enclose your objects, but its fill and stroke must be set to "None." The elements in figure 1 show an example of such a design.

If you created a pattern tile from those objects, each pattern tile would consist only of the parts of the elements that were enclosed by the rectangle with no fill or stroke. In this case, you'd get a seamless-tile effect, as shown in figure 2. (NOTE: To get this seamless effect, we carefully positioned the elements in figure 1 to align perfectly once tiled.)

The other way to define a pattern-tile bounding box is to let Illustrator do it for you—but you give up a lot of control that way. If you don't place a rectangle with a fill and stroke of "None" in back of your other pattern-tile elements, Illustrator will draw one for you—and it will fit snugly around all your pattern elements, as in figure 4.

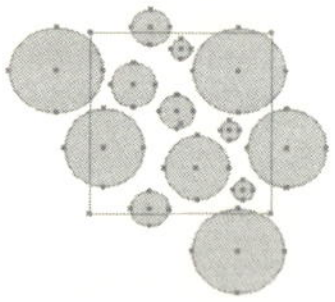

Fig. 1

Fig. 2

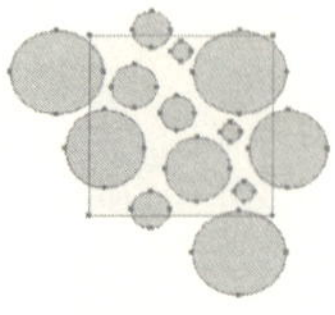

Fig. 3

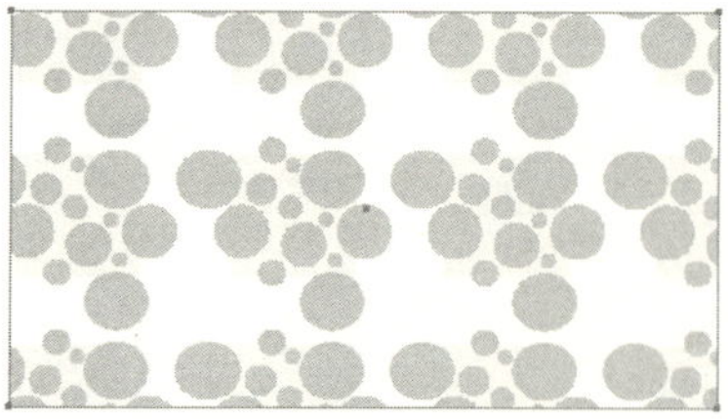

Fig. 5

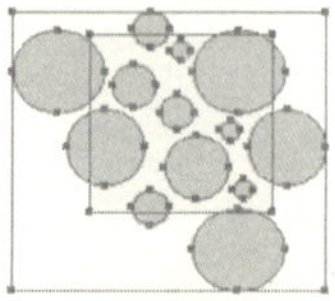

Fig. 4

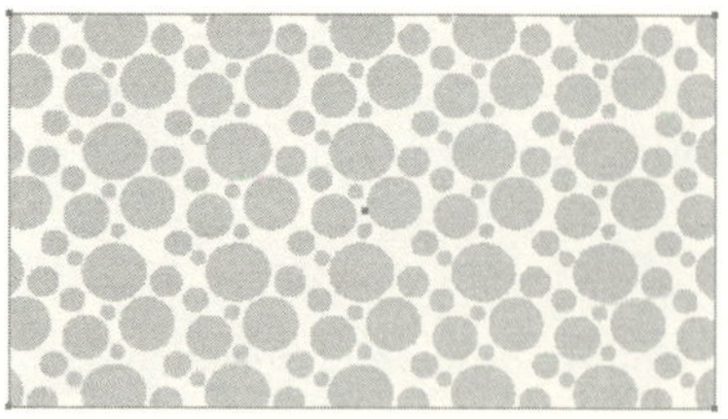

Fig. 7

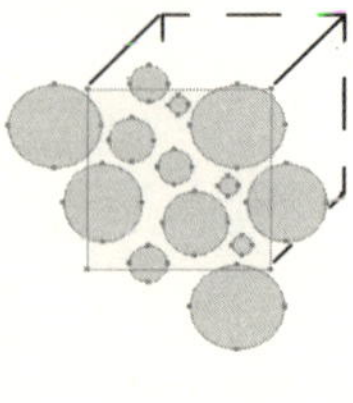

Fig. 6

TIP MAC OS

Quick fixes for common problems

If you're experiencing odd problems in Illustrator, you may be able to quickly and easily eliminate the cause. Try the following before calling technical support.

Delete, move, or rename Illustrator's preferences file. This file occasionally gets damaged, and can then cause problems such as missing palettes and missing menus, or a "Can't open the hyphenation file 'US English Hyphenation.' Text will not be hyphenated" error when Illustrator launches. Here's how to eliminate the preferences file.

1. Quit Illustrator 5.x.
2. Delete the "Adobe Illustrator 5.5 Prefs" or "Adobe Illustrator Prefs" file, located in the "Preferences" folder in the System Folder.
3. Restart Illustrator.

Illustrator will create a new preferences file the next time you quit the program.

Respecify your Plug-ins folder. If any of your Plug-ins are missing or not working properly, respecify the Illustrator Plug-ins folder. Here's how.

1. In Illustrator, select "Plug-ins..." from the Preferences submenu of the File menu.
2. In the "Plug-ins Preferences" dialog box, locate your Plug-ins folder (by default it's called "Plug-Ins" and is located within your "Adobe Illustrator" folder), then click once to select it.
3. With the "Plug-Ins" folder selected, click the "Select 'Plug-Ins'" button, located at the bottom of the "Plug-ins Preferences" dialog box.
4. When Illustrator displays the alert, "Plug-in filters in the folder 'Plug-Ins' won't be available until you restart Illustrator," click "OK."
5. Quit and relaunch Illustrator.

Here's an example. Say you create the elements shown in figure 3. If you make them into a pattern tile, the pattern would have white "rivers" of space between each set of tiles, as in figure 5. Fortunately, it's easy to work around this problem. Follow these steps.

1. Select "Pattern..." from the Objects menu. In the "Patterns" dialog box, select the pattern you're having trouble with, and click "Paste." Click "OK."
2. Find the copy of the pattern tile that Illustrator copied onto your page in the previous step—it should still be selected. You'll notice that the bounding box Illustrator drew for it will be selected, too, as in figure 4.
3. Select only the outside rectangle and delete it.
4. Draw your own bounding box, assign it a fill and stroke of "None," and select "Send to Back" from the Arrange menu to ensure it'll be the backmost element in your pattern tile. If you want to base your bounding box on a rectangle that's already part of the pattern tile (for instance, a rectangle with a fill or stroke color, like the pale yellow one shown in our example), select that rectangle, press Command + C to copy it, and then press Command + B to paste a copy of it in back of the other elements. While it's still selected, assign it a fill and stroke of "None." That should give you a proper bounding box, as in figure 6.
5. Select all the elements in your pattern tile, including the rectangle with the fill and stroke of "None," and choose "Pattern..." from the Objects menu. In the "Patterns" dialog box, click "New," give your pattern a name, and click "OK" to close the dialog box.

Your new pattern should lack extra white space between the tiles, as in the example shown in figure 7.

Q *(6.0 only)* **Using the "Select All Unused" option in the "Custom Color" dialog box leaves some colors unsel-ected, such as "Saturn Red," which I know I have not used. Why?**

A Actually, those colors are being used, in a sense. They're part of your default patterns, which are defined in the "Adobe Illustrator Startup" file. Illustrator considers those colors "used" until the default patterns are deleted from your illustration file.

You can remove any colors from the "Custom Color" dialog box—even if the colors are being used—by selecting them (hold down the Shift key to choose more than one) and clicking the "Delete" button. Click "OK" to the message "Some objects in an open file or the clipboard are painted with the selected custom color. Deleting it will cause them to be painted black."

If you want to be able to use the "Select All Unused" option in the "Custom Color" dialog box to delete colors defined in patterns you're not using, try this. Select "Pattern..." from the Object menu, and in the "Pattern" dialog box, press the "Select All Unused" button, then press "Delete." When you reopen the "Custom Color" dialog box, press "Select All Unused" and "Delete" again. This will delete the patterns and their colors from all currently opened documents, but not from the "Adobe Illustrator Startup" file. Once you close and relaunch Illustrator, any new illustrations you create will contain definitions for the patterns and colors defined in the "Adobe Illustrator Startup" file.

If you don't want the illustrations you create to have these patterns and custom colors in them, there are two things you can do. First, you can delete those patterns and colors from the "Adobe Illustrator Startup" file. Here's how.

1. After making a backup copy of it, open the "Adobe Illustrator Startup" file, which is located in Illustrator's "Plug-ins" folder.
2. Use the "Pattern" and "Custom Color" dialog boxes to delete any colors you don't want to appear in new illustrations you create. If you want to delete all the custom colors and patterns, you can make this task easier by first deleting the examples of those patterns and colors directly from the startup file page (see the illustration above). Once you've done that, you can use the "Select All Unused" option in the "Pattern" and "Custom Color" dialog boxes to select those patterns and colors en masse, and then delete them.
3. Save the "Adobe Illustrator Startup" file.

Another way to eliminate the superfluous custom-color definitions from these patterns is to update your "Adobe Illustrator Startup" file. A revised version of the file, which does not use custom colors in its patterns, is available to download free of charge from the Adobe BBS (206-623-6984) or the Adobe Web site (http://www.adobe.com/supportservice/custsupport/tsfilelib.html).

Q *(6.0 only)* **Whenever I rasterize artwork in Illustrator 6.0 as CMYK, the color values seem to change. Why does this happen?**

A When Illustrator converts artwork into a bitmap image, the process components of colors in the artwork increase. The larger the percentage of black in the color, the greater the change in the process components after Illustrator converts the artwork to a bitmap image. For example, rasterizing an 80-percent black object creates a 71.1-percent cyan, 57.3-percent magenta, 59.5-percent yellow, 32.9-percent black bitmap image. Here's why.

When rasterizing artwork, Illustrator uses a color-conversion table similar to Photoshop 3.x's "Medium Black Generation" preference (in the "Separation Setup" dialog box). The "Black Generation" setting in Photoshop controls how Photoshop generates black when converting Illustrator artwork or a bitmap image to CMYK color mode. The "Medium Black Generation" preference adds cyan, magenta, and yellow values to black areas for a darker, richer black. The "Maximum Black Generation" preference converts all black pixels to pure black (without cyan, magenta, or yellow).

If, when you rasterize your artwork, you'd rather have your black areas converted to pure black, you should use Photoshop for the rasterization. First, in Photoshop, select "Separation Setup..." from the Preferences submenu of the File menu. In the "Separation Setup" dialog box, select the "Maximum" setting from the "Black Generation" pop-up menu, and click "OK." Then select "Open" from Photoshop's File menu, locate and select your Illustrator artwork file, and click "Open." When the "Rasterize Adobe Illustrator Format" dialog box appears, set the "Mode" option to "CMYK Color," select the resolution you want, and click "OK." Finally, save the rasterized file in TIFF or EPS format, and place it back into Illustrator.

If you use the EPS format, we recommend that you select the "Placed EPS" option, not the "Parsed EPS" option, in the dialog box that appears while you're placing the bitmap EPS (selecting the "Placed EPS" option won't rerasterize, and thus change the color values of, the file you're importing using "Medium Black Generation").

Warning "Saving this file... may disable some editing features" When Saving an Illustrator File in Earlier Format

ISSUE

When you save an Adobe Illustrator 5.x or 6.0 document in an earlier format (e.g., Illustrator 5, Illustrator 3), Illustrator returns the error "Saving this document in older Adobe Illustrator file formats may disable some Adobe Illustrator 5.0 editing features within this document when it is read back in." or "You are saving this document in Adobe Illustrator [the select format version] format. Saving this document in an older format may disable some editing features when the document is read back in."

SOLUTIONS

Save a copy of the Illustrator document in its original format before saving in an earlier format:

1. Save a copy of the Illustrator document in the format version in which you are working. For example, when working in Illustrator 5.x save a copy of the document in Illustrator 5 format.
2. Chose File > Save As.
3. In the Save As dialog box change the file name, select the earlier Illustrator format and click Save.
4. When the warning "Saving this document in older Adobe Illustrator file formats may disable some Adobe Illustrator 5.0 editing features within this document when it is read back in." or "You are saving this document in Adobe Illustrator [the select format version] format. Saving this document in an older format may disable some editing features when the document is read back in." appears, click OK.

   note: Illustrator version specific features (e.g., tabs, layers, gradients, bitmap images) are lost or modified when the document is saved in an earlier format that does not support that feature.

OR: When the Illustrator document does not contain Illustrator 5.x or later features, save the Illustrator document in the desired format and click OK in the alert dialog box.

ADDITIONAL INFORMATION

When you save an Adobe Illustrator 5.x document in an earlier format, Illustrator returns the alert "Saving this document in older Adobe Illustrator file formats may disable some Adobe Illustrator 5.0 editing features within this document when it is read back in." When you save an Illustrator 6.0 document in an earlier format, Illustrator returns the alert "You are saving this document in Adobe Illustrator [the select format version] format. Saving this document in an older format may disable some editing features when the document is read back in." The alerts occur even when the document doesn't contain Illustrator 5.x or 6.0 specific features. Documents containing Illustrator 5.x or 6.0 specific features (e.g., tabs, layers, gradients, bitmap images) are modified when saved in an earlier format.

When you save an Illustrator 5.0 or later document in Illustrator 4 or earlier format, objects in the document are combined on a single layer, tabs in point text are converted to spaces, tabs in area text are converted to carriage returns. Gradient fills are converted to a masked blend, and custom-colored gradients are converted to process blends. Illustrator 3.x and earlier for the Macintosh and 4.x and earlier for Windows do not support gradients, instead using the Blend tool to create blends, a series of intermediary shapes and colors between two objects.

When you save and Illustrator 5.0 or later document in an earlier format and then reopen it in Illustrator 5.0 or later, tab information is converted back from spaces to tabs. Gradient objects and layer information are not restored.

Saving an Illustrator 6.0 document in Illustrator 5 or earlier format removes any bitmap images (e.g., TIFF, PICT, Adobe Photoshop 2.5 files, rasterized Illustrator objects) from the document. The masking object for masked bitmap images remains in the document.

Illustrator 5.5 and later defaults to the last selected format when saving. After saving an Illustrator document in a different format, Illustrator continues to save the document in that format until you specify otherwise.

Text Doesn't Appear or Appears as Lines in Illustrator 5.x or Later

ISSUE

When you type text in Adobe Illustrator 5.x or later, Illustrator does not display the text or displays vertical lines instead of characters.

SOLUTION

Make sure only one version of the font applied to the text (i.e., PostScript or TrueType) is installed. To determine the font's version, see Additional Information.

ADDITIONAL INFORMATION

Illustrator cannot display text when both the TrueType and PostScript version of the font applied to the text are installed.

Each PostScript font has two files: a bitmap (screen) font and a printer (outline) font. PostScript bitmap fonts list as "font" under the Kind field in System 7. Their icons display as a dog-eared page with an "A," and they include a point size in their name (e.g., Times 10, Geneva 14).

PostScript printer fonts list as "PostScript font" under the Kind field in the System 7.1 or later and as "system extension" in System 7.0.x. Their names are usually composed of the first five characters of the font name and the first three of the style (e.g., HelveBol, CouriObl, Symbo, TimesBollta), and do not include a point size. The icon for an Adobe Type 1 printer font displays as a white "A" on a page with horizontal lines. Type 1 fonts created by other vendors and Type 3 printer fonts have different icons.

TrueType fonts list as "font" under the Kind field in System 7.x. Their icons display as dog-eared pages with three letter "A"s in progressively larger sizes. They do not include a point size in their name.

To remove a TrueType or PostScript font in System 7.1 or later:

1. Quit all applications.
2. Open the Fonts folder in the System Folder.
3. Choose View > by Name.
4. Remove either the TrueType or PostScript bitmap font file if both versions are installed (e.g., delete the TrueType font "Helvetica" if the PostScript bitmap font "Helvetica 10" is installed).

To remove TrueType or PostScript fonts in System 7.0x:

1. Quit all applications.
2. Open the System Folder, then double-click on the System file.
3. Choose View > by Name.
4. Remove either the TrueType or PostScript bitmap font file if both versions are installed (e.g., delete the TrueType font "Helvetica" if the PostScript bitmap font "Helvetica 10" is installed).

Illustrator 5.x and Later Select Filters Don't Select Objects Painted with Tint of Process Color

ISSUE

After selecting an object painted with a process color in Adobe Illustrator 5.5 or later, choosing Filter > Select > Same Fill Color, Filter > Select > Same Stroke Color, or Filter > Select > Same Paint Style does not select objects painted with a tint of the selected process color.

SOLUTION

Use a custom color instead of a process color while creating your artwork then, using the Select Filters, convert the custom color to process before printing.

ADDITIONAL INFORMATION

In Illustrator 5.x and later, the Select Same Fill Color, Select Same Stroke Color, and Select Same Paint Style filters select objects painted with a custom color using the name of the custom color, and objects painted with a process color using the percentages of Cyan, Magenta, Yellow, and Black (CMYK) values that define the process color. After selecting an object painted with a process color and choosing Filter > Select > Same Fill Color, Filter > Select > Same Stroke Color, or Filter > Select > Same Paint Style, the Select Filters only select objects painted with process colors defined using the same CMYK percentages.

After selecting an object painted with a custom colored in Illustrator 5.5, then choosing Filter > Select > Same Fill Color, Filter > Select > Same Stroke Color, or Filter > Select > Same Paint Style, the Select Filters select objects painted with the same custom color and objects painted with a tint of the same custom color. For example, after selecting an object painted with 10% Blue then choosing Filter > Select > Same Fill Color, the Select Filter selects objects painted with Blue, 50% Blue, and 10% Blue.

To create a custom color in Illustrator 5.x and later:

1. Choose Object > Custom Color.
2. In the Custom Color dialog box, click New, then name the Custom Color.
3. Enter the Cyan, Magenta, Yellow, and Black (CMYK) values, then click OK.

To convert an existing process color to a custom color:

1. Select an object painted with a process color.
2. In the Paint Styles palette, drag the process color from the Fill or Stroke box to the custom color swatch.
3. In the Custom Color dialog box, click OK to create a custom color.
4. Apply the custom color to objects painted with the process color.

To convert custom colors to a process color in Illustrator 6.0:

1. Select any object painted with the custom color using the Filter > Select > Same Fill Color, Filter > Select > Same Stroke Color, or Filter > Select > Same Paint Style commands.
2. With the custom colored objects selected, choose Filter > Colors > Adjust Colors.
3. Select the desired option (i.e., Convert to Process, Fill, or Stroke) in the Convert section of the Adjust Colors dialog box, then click OK.

To convert custom colors to a process color in Illustrator 5.x:

1. Quit Illustrator.
2. Move the Custom to Process filter file, located in the Optional Plug-Ins folder in the Illustrator application folder, into the Plug-Ins folder.
3. Open the document containing a custom color in Illustrator.
4. Select an object painted with a custom color, then choose Filter > Select > Same Fill Color, Filter > Select > Same Stroke Color, or Filter > Select > Same Paint Style.
5. With the custom colored objects selected, choose Filter > Colors > Custom to Process.
6. In the Custom to Process dialog box, select Retain Tint, then click OK.

Pressing Shift While Using Knife Tool Creates Extra Line Segment in Illustrator 6.0.x

ISSUE

After you press the Shift key while cutting an object horizontally or vertically using the knife tool, Adobe Illustrator 6.0.x adds a short line at the end of the cutting path. The added line extends up and to the right at a 45 degree angle from the end of the cutting path.

SOLUTIONS

Click inside the object, then press the Shift key and drag the knife tool to the outside of the object. For example, to cut the left side of a rectangle, click in the center of the rectangle, then press the Shift key and drag the knife tool to the left of the left side of the rectangle.

OR: Cut the object from the outside of the object to the inside of the object using the knife tool, select the Delete Anchor Point tool, then click on the anchor point at the end of the added line segment to remove the additional line segment.

OR: To prevent the knife tool from creating an additional line, avoid pressing the Shift key while dragging the knife tool.

ADDITIONAL INFORMATION

Illustrator 6.0.x's knife tool cannot cut objects at a vertical or horizontal angle (i.e., 180, 90, or 0 degree path). Pressing the Shift key while dragging the knife tool constrains the cut to a 0, 90, or 180 degree angle. Illustrator 6.0.x adds an additional line segment to the end of the cutting path after you cut a line segment by pressing the Shift key while cutting using the knife tool. For example, pressing the Shift key and dragging the knife tool from the left side of a rectangle to the center of a rectangle adds an additional line segment to the cutting path that extents up and to the right at a 45 degree angle.

When you click the knife tool inside the object and then drag from the inside of the object to the outside the object, Illustrator creates a cutting path that ends outside of the object without creating a line segment at the end to the cutting path.

Objects Missing After Opening Illustrator 5.x or Later File in Photoshop 3.x

ISSUE

After opening or pasting an Adobe Illustrator 6.0 file into Adobe Photoshop 3.x, vector objects (e.g., Illustrator text, Illustrator-drawn objects) do not appear in the rasterized EPS file in Photoshop.

SOLUTION

Before opening or pasting the Illustrator 6.0 file into Photoshop, make the layers containing the missing objects printing layers, instead of nonprinting layers, in the Illustrator

6.0 document. To make a layer a printing layer in Illustrator 6.0:

1. In Illustrator 6.0, double-click on a layer name in the Layers palette.
2. In the Layer Option dialog, select the Print option, then click OK.

ADDITIONAL INFORMATION

When opening or pasting an Illustrator 6.0 file, Photoshop converts the Illustrator document into a bitmap image, ignoring objects on nonprinting layers, EPS files, and bitmap images. When opening pasting an Illustrator document containing an unsupported fill (i.e., pattern, gradient), Photoshop converts the object's fill to a solid gray or black fill. Photoshop converts stroked text into unstroked text.

Deselecting the Print option in the layer's Layer Options dialog box in Illustrator 6.0 makes the layer a nonprinting layer.

Photoshop 3.0.x is unable to convert the following elements in Illustrator 5.5 or later files:

- Placed EPS files
- Bitmap images (e.g., TIFF, PICT, rasterized Illustrator artwork)
- Pattern fills and strokes
- Stroked text
- Objects on nonprinting layers (Illustrator 6.0 files only)

Unable to Create Outlines in Illustrator 5.x or Later

ISSUE

After you select text in Adobe Illustrator 5.x and later, the Create Outlines command in the Type menu is dimmed, or an error occurs.

SYMPTOMS

Illustrator 5.x or later returns the error "Can't create type outlines. The selection must contain non-empty text objects, and outline files must be available for the fonts in the text." or "Can't create outline. The outline file for one or more of the fonts couldn't be found."

SOLUTIONS

Do one or more of the following to convert text to outlines:

A. Select the text block with the Selection (pointer) tool, instead of the Type tool, then choose Type > Create Outlines.
B. Ensure the PostScript printer (outline) font file or TrueType font file for the typeface applied to the selected text is installed.
C. Verify Adobe Type Manager (ATM) 2.03 or later is installed and enabled by selecting On in the ATM control panel.

NOTE: When extensions are disabled in System 7.x by pressing the Shift key while restarting, ATM is inactive, but On remains selected in the ATM control panel.

ADDITIONAL INFORMATION

The Create Outlines command in Illustrator 5.x and later's Type menu converts text selected with the pointer tool to editable paths. The Create Outlines command is dimmed when text is selected with the Type tool.

To create an outline of text formatted with a PostScript font, ATM and the PostScript outline font file must be installed. Text formatted with a TrueType font can be converted to outlines without ATM installed.

When a single TrueType font is installed, Illustrator 5.x and later displays the entire type family. When converting text formatted with a TrueType font to an outline, Illustrator 5.x and later requires the TrueType font file to be installed.

In Illustrator 5.x and later, the error "Can't create type outlines. The selection must contain non-empty text objects, and outline files must be available for the fonts in the text." appears if you choose Create Outlines when ATM is not installed, or the selected TrueType font is not available.

The error "You won't be able to print with [font name] or stroke its characters because the font's outline file is missing or ATM is turned off." appears if you select a font from the Font menu in Adobe Illustrator 5.5 and later when the text formatted in a PostScript font does not have a corresponding PostScript outline font file available.

Apply Knife Command Doesn't Work with Vertical or Horizontal Lines in Illustrator 6.0

ISSUE

When you use the Apply Knife command on an object in Adobe Illustrator 6.0 while an open vertical or horizontal path is selected, Illustrator does not cut the object.

SOLUTIONS

Cut the object with the knife tool. Pressing Shift while dragging the knife tool constrains the cut to 0 or 90 degrees.

OR: Add a 45 degree line segment to the end of the path you want to use as a cutter, then choose Object > Apply Knife.

OR: Select the object you want to use as a cutter and the object you want to cut, then choose Filter > Pathfinder > Divide.

NOTE: Illustrator 6.0 groups objects cut with the Divide filter and then moves the grouped object to the foreground. Ungroup the cut object after using the Divide filter.

ADDITIONAL INFORMATION

The Apply Knife command in Illustrator 6.0 cannot cut objects with open, straight, vertical or horizontal paths (i.e., a 180, 90, or 0 degree path). Applying the Object > Apply Knife command to an object while an open vertical or horizontal path is selected does not cut the object.

Rasterizing Artwork Changes Color Definitions in Illustrator 6.0

ISSUE

The process components (i.e., cyan, magenta, yellow, black) of colors in Adobe Illustrator 6.0 artwork increase after converting the artwork to a bitmap image using the Rasterize command.

SOLUTION

Rasterize the artwork in Adobe Photoshop 3.x, with the Photoshop Black Generations preference set to Maximum:

1. Launch Photoshop, then choose File > Preferences > Separation Setup.
2. Change the Black Generation setting to Maximum, then click OK.
3. Choose File > Open, select the Illustrator file, then click Open.
4. In the Rasterized Adobe Illustrator Format, set the Mode option to CMYK Color, select the desired resolution, then click OK.
5. Save the raserized file in TIFF or EPS format.
6. Place the TIFF or EPS file into Illustrator.

NOTE: When placing an EPS format graphic, the Open dialog box appears after selecting the EPS graphic in the Place dialog box. Choose Placed EPS, not Parsed EPS, for the Open this Document As option in the Open dialog box.

ADDITIONAL INFORMATION

When Illustrator converts artwork into a bitmap image, the process components of colors in the artwork increase. The larger the percentage of black in the color, the greater the change in the process components after Illustrator converts the artwork to a bitmap image. For example, rasterizing an 80% black object creates a 71.1% cyan, 57.3% magenta, 59.5% yellow, 32.9% black bitmap image.

When rasterizing artwork, Illustrator uses a color conversion table similar to Adobe Photoshop 3.0x's Medium Black Generation preference. The Black Generation setting in Adobe Photoshop controls how Photoshop generates black when converting Illustrator artwork or an image to CMYK color mode. The Medium Black Generation preference adds cyan, magenta, and yellow values to black areas for a darker, or richer, black. The Maximum Black Generation preference converts all black pixels to the Black channel, creating a simple, or pure, black.

Unable to Drag and Drop from Illustrator into Photoshop

ISSUE

After importing an image from Adobe Illustrator into Adobe Photoshop using drag and drop, the image does not appear in Illustrator.

SOLUTIONS

Do one or more of the following:

A. Drag and drop the image from Illustrator 6.0 or later.
B. Drag and drop into Photoshop 3.0.4 or later.
C. Use System 7.5 or later.

OR: When using the System 7 Pro (Finder 7.1.3), install the Macintosh Drag and Drop system extension.

OR: Open or place the Illustrator file in Photoshop.

ADDITIONAL INFORMATION

Illustrator 6.0 and later, and Photoshop 3.0.4 and later, supports the Macintosh drag-and-drop feature available in System 7.1.3 and later. When the Macintosh Drag and Drop extension included with System 7.1.3 is not installed, or when you use a version of Illustrator or Photoshop that does not support drag and drop, dragging an Illustrator image into Photoshop causes the image not to appear in Illustrator.

System 7.1.3 includes extensions and an updated Finder that supports drag and drop. System 7.5.1 and later integrates drag-and-drop support into the system software. System 7.1.1 and earlier does not support drag and drop.

When you drag and drop an image that contains a bitmap image, EPS file, pattern fill, pattern stroke, or stroked text from Illustrator 6.0 into Photoshop 3.0.4 or later, an error occurs.

Unable to Cut Compound Path With Knife Tool in Illustrator 6.0

ISSUE

Dragging the Knife tool over portion of a compound path or choosing Object > Apply Knife while the selected object is over a compound path does not cut the compound path in Adobe Illustrator 6.0.

SOLUTIONS

Release the compound path, then cut the path using the Knife tool or by choosing Object > Apply Knife.

OR: Cut the path by dragging the Knife tool across all paths in the compound path.

ADDITIONAL INFORMATION

The Illustrator 6.0 Knife tool is unable to cut individual objects within a compound path, resulting in objects not being cut after dragging the Knife tool over portion of a compound path or after choosing Object > Apply Knife while the selected object is over a compound path. Releasing the compound path enables Illustrator to cut the path with the Knife tool and the Apply Knife command.

Unable to Display EPS file in Illustrator 5.x in High Magnifications

ISSUE

After you switch to a high magnification (e.g., 1200%) view in Adobe Illustrator 5.x, Illustrator does not display EPS files or a system error (e.g., freeze, Type 1) occurs.

SOLUTIONS

Reduce the magnification view.
OR: Reduce the size of EPS file's screen preview by reducing the size of the artwork contained in the EPS file.

ADDITIONAL INFORMATION

Illustrator is unable to display an EPS file when the size of the EPS file's screen preview exceeds Illustrator 5.x's display size limit. The size of an EPS file's screen preview changes with the document's magnification view. For example, a 6-by-13" EPS file has a display size of 6-by-13"" when displayed at actual size (i.e., 100% magnification) and a 72-by-156" display size when viewed at 1200%. Illustrator 5.5's display size limit is approximately 145 inches (10368 pixels). Illustrator 5.0.x's display size limit is approximately 455 inches (32,768 pixels). When either the height or width of an EPS file exceeds Illustrator's display size limit, the EPS file does not display, or a system error (e.g., freeze, Type 1) occurs.

To determine the display size of an EPS file, multiply the EPS file's dimensions (i.e., the EPS file's bounding box size) by the document's magnification view percentage. For example, in Illustrator 5.5, the display size of a 6-by-13" EPS file at a 1200% magnification is 169 inches (13 inches multiplied by 1200%), which exceeds Illustrator 5.5's display size limit. To determine the display size in pixels, multiply the dimensions in inches by 72 (e.g., 13 inches = 936 pixels).

Elements Missing After Saving Illustrator 6.0 File

ISSUE

Elements in an Adobe Illustrator 6.0 file are missing after you save and reopen the file.

SYMPTOMS

The file was saved in Illustrator 6.0 after it was printed with the Selection Only option in the Print dialog box selected.

All layers are visible in the file.

SOLUTIONS

Open a copy of the file that was saved before it was printed with the Selection Only option.
OR: To prevent Illustrator from deleting elements from the file: Use the Selection Only option in Illustrator 6.01.
OR: Deselect the Selection Only option in Illustrator 6.0 Print dialog box before saving the file.
OR: Before saving the file with the Selection Only option selected in the Print dialog box, make all elements visible by choosing Arrange > Show All, make all layers visible and unlocked by selecting Show and deselecting Lock in the Layers Option dialog box, then choose Edit > Select All.

ADDITIONAL INFORMATION

After you print an Illustrator 6.0 file with the Selection Only option selected, then save the file, Illustrator removes unselected elements from the file.

Clicking the Pen Tool Deletes Previously Cut Objects in Illustrator 6.0

ISSUE

After you cut an object in Adobe Illustrator 6.0 using the Object > Apply Knife command and then click the pen tool, Illustrator displays only a portion of the object. After you force Illustrator to redraw the screen by changing views, the cut object is no longer in the document.

SOLUTIONS

Revert to a version of the document that contains the cut object, reapply the Object > Apply Knife command to the object, deselect the cut object (e.g. press Command + Shift + A), and then click the pen tool.
OR: To prevent Illustrator from deleting the cut object: Deselect the cut object (e.g. Command + Shift + A) and then click the pen tool.
OR: After cutting the object using the Object > Apply Knife command, select another tool (i.e., selection tool) and then click the pen tool.
OR: Click on the pen tool in the toolbox and then cut the object using the Object > Apply Knife command.

ADDITIONAL INFORMATION

When you use the pen tool to create an object with an open path in Illustrator 6.0, cut the object using the Object > Apply Knife command, and then click anywhere in the document using the pen tool, Illustrator deletes the cut object. Illustrator displays a portion of the deleted object the screen is redrawn.

Illustrator EPS Files Display Larger or Crop Marks Change Position in Separator 5.x

ISSUE

After opening an Adobe Illustrator 5.x or 3.x EPS file in Adobe Separator 5.0.x, Separator 5.0.x displays the bounding box size larger than expected, and displays and prints the document's crop marks in a position different than originally set in Illustrator. The Illustrator EPS file's width or height is smaller than 72 points.

SOLUTION

Use Illustrator's Trim Marks plug-in filter to create trim marks for each color separation:

1. In Illustrator 5.x, remove crop marks in the Illustrator document by choosing Object > Cropmarks > Release.
2. Draw a rectangle to define the trim size of your artwork.
3. Select the rectangle, then choose Filters > Create > Trim Marks.
4. Select the trim marks.
5. In the Paint Style palette, apply one of the colors used in the document to the stroke of the trim mark, then select the Stroke overprint option.
6. Copy the trim marks, then choose Edit > Paste in Front.
7. Repeat steps 4-6 for each color separation.
8. Resave the Illustrator document as an EPS file.

ADDITIONAL INFORMATION

The minimum bounding box size of an EPS file that Separator 5.0.x supports printing is 72 x 72 points (i.e., 1 inch square). When separating an Illustrator EPS file whose bounding box's width or height is smaller than 72 points, Separator 5.0.x creates a 72 by 72 point bounding box and crop marks.

Illustrator's Trim Marks filter creates trim marks based on the size of the selected objects. Separator prints trim marks as artwork. Trim marks included in EPS files do not affect crop marks included in an EPS file or the EPS file's bounding box size.

Rasterizing a Graph with Create Mask Option Doesn't Mask the Graph in Illustrator 6.0

ISSUE

After rasterizing a graph in Adobe Illustrator 6.0 with the Create Mask option selected in the Rasterize dialog box, Illustrator does not mask the background of the graph.

SOLUTION

Ungroup the graph, rasterize it, and then mask the rasterized graph with ungrouped graph objects:

1. Delete the rasterized graph, then select the original graph.
2. Choose Arrange > Ungroup, and then Click OK to the alert "The selection contains a graph. After a graph is ungrouped you will no longer be able to access its graph style, its data or change its graph design."
3. Choose Arrange > Ungroup until the Ungroup command is dimmed (i.e., grayed out).
4. Select all of the ungrouped graph except the text, then choose Edit > Copy.
5. With all of the ungrouped graph except the text selected, choose Object > Rasterize.
6. In the Rasterize dialog box, deselect the Create Mask option, set the desired resolution and color model setting, then click OK.
7. Choose Edit > Paste in Front to paste the ungrouped graph in front of the rasterized graph and then choose Object > Compound Paths > Make.
8. Select the compound path object and the rasterized graph and then choose Object > Mask > Make. Do not select the text.
9. Select the text, the mask, and the rasterized graph, and then choose Edit > Group.

ADDITIONAL INFORMATION

When Illustrator 6.0 rasterizes a graph, it creates an image with an opaque bounding box that includes all the elements in the graph. When Illustrator rasterizes a graph with the Create Mask option selected, Illustrator creates the raster image on top of the original graph and does not mask the image.

The Illustrator graph tool creates six different graph styles. Graphs are special grouped objects customizable with options in the Graph Style and Data Style dialog boxes. When a graph is ungrouped, it becomes paths and fill objects. Graph commands (e.g., changes to graph data or style) do not affect non-graph objects (i.e., ungrouped graphs).

Illustrator 5.5 Change Case Filter Changes Text Attributes

ISSUE

In Adobe Illustrator 5.5, when the "Change Case" filter is applied to a text block containing multiple paint styles or type attributes (e.g., typeface, size), the highlighted text changes to the type attributes and paint style of the character immediately preceding the selection.

SOLUTION

Reapply the paint style and type attributes to the text changed by the "Change Case" filter.

ADDITIONAL INFORMATION

When the "Change Case" filter (i.e., "Text/Change Case" plug-in) included with Illustrator 5.5 is applied to a text block containing multiple paint styles or type attributes (e.g., typeface, size), the highlighted text changes to the type attributes and paint style of the character in front of it.

The "Change Case" filter changes text from the current case setting to all uppercase, all uppercase or mixed case. When the "Mixed Case" option is selected in the "Change Case" filter, the first character of each word is changed to uppercase.

Objects in Illustrator 6.0 Patterns Not Clipped as Expected

ISSUE

After creating a pattern fill in Adobe Illustrator 6.0, a space appears between the pattern tiles, and the pattern objects outside the bounding rectangle aren't clipped. For example, after creating a pattern containing a red bounding rectangle and yellow circle that extends beyond the edge of the red bounding rectangle, a white area appears between the red pattern tiles and the yellow circle is not clipped by the red bounding rectangle when you paint an object with the pattern fill.

SOLUTION

Apply a fill and stroke of None to the pattern's bounding rectangle, then reapply the pattern:

1. Choose Object > Pattern.
2. In the Pattern dialog box, select the pattern, click Paste, then click OK to paste the pattern on the Illustrator page.
3. Delete the rectangle with a fill and stroke of None that surrounds the pasted pattern.
4. Select the bounding rectangle (i.e. the rectangle beneath the pattern), then choose Edit > Copy.
5. Choose Edit > Paste in Back, then apply a fill and stroke of None to the copy of the bounding rectangle.
6. Drag a selection marquee around the pattern with the selection tool, then choose Object > Pattern.
7. In the Pattern dialog box, click New, name the pattern, then click OK.
8. Apply the new pattern to the desired objects.

ADDITIONAL INFORMATION

When you create a pattern in Illustrator 6.0, Illustrator defines the bounding box of the pattern tile using the backmost rectangle painted with a fill and stroke of None (i.e., the bounding rectangle). When the backmost rectangle is painted with a color, Illustrator 6.0 creates a bounding rectangle with a fill and stroke of None surrounding all of the objects in the pattern. The bounding rectangle created by Illustrator 6.0 does not clip the objects in the pattern fill and a space appears between the pattern tiles.

Illustrator 5.5 defines the size of the pattern tile by the backmost rectangle in the pattern, regardless of the rectangle's Fill and Stroke paint style.

Application Errors

MAC OS / WINDOWS

Error "Offending Operator 'gsave'" Opening EPS Graphic in Illustrator

ISSUE

When opening a bitmap EPS graphic in Adobe Illustrator, the error "Offending Operator 'gsave'" appears.

SYMPTOMS

The error "Opened the artwork up to the following error conditions. The illustration contains an illegal or misplaced operator. Offending Operator 'gsave'" appears when opening a bitmap EPS graphic in Illustrator 5.x for Macintosh.

When opening a bitmap EPS graphic in Illustrator 3.x for Macintosh or Illustrator 4.x for Windows, the error "Can't open the illustration. The illustration contains an illegal or misplaced operator. Offending Operator 'gsave'" appears.

SOLUTION

Import the EPS graphic using the "Place Art..." command.

ADDITIONAL INFORMATION

Illustrator is an object-oriented drawing application and does not support opening EPS graphics containing bitmap information. When a bitmap EPS graphic (e.g., Adobe Photoshop EPS file) is opened in Illustrator, the error "Offending Operator 'gsave'" appears.

Illustrator 5.x for Macintosh opens object-oriented PICT graphics (e.g., Claris MacDraw), PDF (Portable Document Format) files, and Illustrator 5.x and earlier documents and EPS files.

NOTE: Illustrator 5.5 and later opens PDF files, versions 5.0.1 and earlier do not. Illustrator 3.x for Macintosh opens Illustrator 3.x and earlier documents and EPS files. Illustrator 4.x for Windows opens Illustrator 4.x and earlier documents and EPS files.

To import EPS graphics into Illustrator 5.x and earlier for Macintosh, use the "Place Art.." command.

To import EPS files, Bitmap (.BMP) graphics, PC PaintBrush (.PCX) graphics, and TIFF images into Illustrator 4.x and earlier for Windows, use the "Place Art..." command.

Error "File [filename] Has Been Placed Inside Itself..." Opening Illustrator Document

ISSUE

When opening an Adobe Illustrator 4.x for Windows or Illustrator 5.x for Macintosh document with a placed EPS graphic, Illustrator returns the error "The file [filename] has been placed inside itself. It has been removed from the artwork." After you click OK in the error dialog box, the Illustrator file opens without the EPS graphic.

SOLUTIONS

Recreate the EPS graphic, then replace it into the Illustrator document.

OR: Place the Illustrator EPS file that includes the placed EPS graphic into a new Illustrator document:

1. In Illustrator, choose File > New.
2. Select File > Place Art.
3. In the Place dialog box, select the Illustrator EPS file, then click Place.

ADDITIONAL INFORMATION

When you save an Illustrator EPS file or Illustrator document containing a placed EPS graphic with the same filename and location as the placed EPS graphic, the Illustrator file overwrites the original placed EPS file, causing Illustrator to return the error "The file [filename] has been placed inside itself. It has been removed from the artwork."

When you save an Illustrator EPS file with the Include Placed Images option selected, Illustrator includes the placed EPS graphic in the Illustrator EPS file. When Illustrator opens an EPS file, it requires an external link to the placed EPS graphic file contained in the Illustrator EPS file, even when the Illustrator EPS file was saved with Include Placed Images selected.

Error "The Document [filename] Contains Fonts Which are Unavailable..."

ISSUE

When opening an Adobe Illustrator 5.x file, Illustrator returns the error "The document [filename] contains fonts which are unavailable or in a different format than originally specified," or "The following fonts are either not available or are only available in a different format than originally specified in the document."

SOLUTIONS

Do one or more of the following:

A. Ensure Type 1 or TrueType font files are installed and accessible to Illustrator:
   1. Remove font management utilities (e.g., Suitcase, MasterJuggler) from the System Folder, then restart the Macintosh.
   2. Install the PostScript printer (outline) font file or TrueType font file for the selected typeface into the System Folder.

B. Ensure only one version of the selected font (i.e., PostScript or TrueType) is installed. To determine the font's version, double-click on the font file at the Finder. After you double-click, TrueType fonts display sample text in 3 sizes, PostScript screen fonts display sample text in one size, and PostScript outline fonts display the message "PostScript font. This is a file that your Macintosh uses to display characters."

C. In System 7.0.1 and later, reinstall fonts and recreate the Fonts folder to ensure both the font and Fonts folder are not damaged:
   1. Move the Fonts folder from the System Folder onto the desktop and restart the Macintosh. After the Macintosh restarts, a new, empty Fonts folder is created in the System Folder.
   2. Reinstall the PostScript screen (bitmap) and printer (outline) font files or TrueType font file from the font's installation disk into the new Fonts folder.
   3. Move the other font files from the Fonts folder located on the desktop into the new Fonts folder in the System Folder. Do not replace fonts that already exist in the new Fonts folder.

D. In System 7.0 and earlier, reinstall the fonts into the System Folder to ensure they are not damaged:
   1. Quit all applications.
   2. Remove the screen (bitmap) font suitcases and the printer (outline) font files or TrueType font files.
   3. Reinstall the fonts into the System Folder from the font's installation disk. For instructions on installing fonts, see Additional Information.

E. Reapply the font to the text in Illustrator.

ADDITIONAL INFORMATION

An error occurs when Illustrator 5.x opens a file containing text formatted in a font that is damaged, unavailable, or in a different format (i.e., PostScript instead of TrueType).

To determine if a TrueType or PostScript bitmap font is damaged, double-click on the font file at the Finder to display its sample text. If the font does not open or opens without displaying sample text, the font file may be damaged. Reinstalling TrueType or PostScript bitmap and outline font files ensures the fonts are not damaged.

To install fonts in System 7.0.1 and later:

1. Quit all applications.
2. Move the font files into the Fonts folder inside the System Folder, or drag the font files onto the System Folder icon to allow the system to automatically place the font files in the proper location.

To install fonts in System 7.0:

1. Quit all applications.
2. Select all screen (bitmap) font suitcases.
3. Move screen font suitcases into the System suitcase, located in the System Folder.
4. Select all the printer (outline) font files.
5. Drag printer font files into the Extensions folder, located in the System Folder.

   NOTE: Steps 2-5 can be combined by selecting both the font suitcases and printer font files together, then dragging them onto the System Folder icon to allow the system to automatically place the font files in the proper location.

To install fonts in System 6.07 and 6.08:

1. Launch the Font/DA Mover.
2. Ensure the System file contents are displayed on the left side of the Font/DA Mover.
3. On the right side of the Font/DA Mover, navigate to the font folder that contains the desired fonts.
4. Select a font you want to install and click "Install."
5. Repeat step 4 for each font to be installed.
6. Quit the Font/DA Mover.
7. Select all the printer (outline) fonts.
8. Drag the printer fonts into the System Folder.
9. Restart the computer.

WINDOWS

Q *(4.1 only)* **When I place a file from Photoshop into Illustrator, I sometimes get an alert that says, "Can't read the TIFF image inside the EPS file," and after I click "OK" in the alert box, the EPS file displays as a gray box. What happened to my graphic?**

A It's still there, but it's an EPS that contains a clipping path and an 8-bit screen preview, which are stored in a format Illustrator can't display (but will print just fine to a PostScript printer). Here's some information on why this happens and what you can do about it.

Photoshop for Windows saves clipping paths and 8-bit TIFF screen previews into an alpha channel. Illustrator can't display the alpha channel, so it returns the alert message and doesn't import the preview. If you don't need to see the details of the image while you work on layout, then there's no need to change anything—this graphic will print correctly to a PostScript device. If you save your EPS in Photoshop with a 1-bit screen image, you'll be able to see it on screen, but you still won't see the results of the clipping path. If you need a better preview of the graphic on screen, the following steps show you how to bring the EPS and its clipping path into Illustrator as separate files and then to combine them there, using the clipping path as a mask for the EPS image.

1. With the EPS file opened in Photoshop 2.5.x or later, choose "Export" from the File menu, then choose "Paths to Illustrator…."
2. Name the path in the "Export" dialog box and save the path as an .AI file.
3. Save the Photoshop EPS file without the clipping path.
4. In Illustrator, open the clipping path you saved in Photoshop in step 2. Change to Artwork view if necessary.
5. Select the path, choose "Paint Style" from the Paint menu, then select "Mask" and click "OK."
6. Choose "Place Art…" from the File menu, select the Photoshop EPS file, and click "Place."
7. Use the crop marks and guides to position the EPS file. When you've finished, choose "Release Cropmarks" from the Arrange menu. Delete the resulting square.
8. Choose "Select All" from the Edit menu, then choose "Group" from the Arrange menu. Copy and paste the masking group into the desired Illustrator document.

If you have multiple paths that you want to use as one mask in Illustrator, select them all and create a compound path before you create the mask.

Q *(4.x only)* **When I launch Illustrator 4.1 from my Windows 95 desktop icon, I get a message that says, "The ruler font could not be located," followed by a second message that says, "Adobedlg.dll could not be found." What's wrong?**

A It sounds like you moved your AI41.EXE file from your AI41 folder to the desktop, rather than creating a shortcut on the desktop. When Illustrator launches, it looks in the active folder (wherever AI41.EXE is) for the other necessary application files. If AI41.EXE is on the desktop, Illustrator can't locate the other files, which are still in the AI41 folder, and these messages will appear.

Move the AI41.EXE file from the desktop back to the AI41 folder. You can then double-click on AI41.EXE to launch Illustrator 4.x, or create a shortcut to launch it from the desktop. To create a shortcut, click on the AI41.EXE file in the AI41 folder with the right mouse button and drag it to the desktop. Then choose "Create Shortcut(s) Here" from the menu that appears when you release the mouse button.

Technically speaking, this could also happen with Illustrator 4.0x. You should be using Illustrator 4.1 in Windows 95, but if you're using 4.0x, you will still encounter the same problem and receive the same messages if you move the .EXE file out of the AI4 folder.

Q When I try to place a template in Illustrator 4.x, I get the message "Can't place a new template. Template size too big!" Is my template really too big?

A Yes—at least for the format you're using. Illustrator will give you this message whenever you try to place a very large BMP or PCX file as a template. Exactly what constitutes "too big" can vary depending on the exact dimensions and resolution of your image (more on that below), but you'll generally run into this message if you try to import a BMP or PCX that's greater than approximately 18 by 18 inches and 96 ppi (pixels per inch).

When you place into Illustrator 4.x a BMP or PCX file with a resolution other than 96 ppi, Illustrator automatically resizes the image to distribute the pixels at 96 ppi. If that makes the image larger than 18 inches wide or high (which are the dimensions of Illustrator's artboard), you'll get the "Template size too big!" message.

To prevent this message from appearing, you can do either of the following.

First, one easy way to get around the error message is to save your image as an uncompressed one-bit TIFF instead of a BMP or PCX file. Be aware, however, that although your template will appear to exceed the boundaries of Illustrator's 18-by-18-inch artboard, you still won't be able to place artwork outside the artboard. That may be fine if you intend to use only the portion of the template that falls within the artboard, but otherwise you should use the workaround described next.

Your other option is to reduce the resolution and/or dimensions of your image so that it won't exceed 18 inches in width or height once it's been resized to a resolution of 96 pixels per inch. If you're not sure how to do that, follow these steps.

1. Open the image in Photoshop, and select "Image Size" from the Image menu.
2. In the "Image Size" dialog box, select the "Proportions" constrain option. Change the measurement units for the "Width" and "Height" values to inches; change the units for resolution to pixels per inch.
3. Enter a value of 96 pixels per inch in the "Resolution" text box.
4. If step 3 did not resize the image to the proper size, deselect the "File Size" constrain option and enter the dimensions the template should be (making sure the largest dimension is 18 inches).
5. Click "OK" to close the "Image Size" dialog box.

When you're done, you should be able to resave your BMP or PCX and place it as a template in Illustrator without encountering the "Template size too big!" message.

Offending Command "Ar" When Opening Illustrator 5.x File in Illustrator 4.x for Windows

ISSUE
When you open an Adobe Illustrator 5.x for Macintosh file in Adobe Illustrator 4.x for Windows, Illustrator returns the error, "Can't open the illustration: The illustration contains an illegal or misplaced operator. Offending command 'Ar'."

SOLUTION
Open a copy of the file in Illustrator 5.x for Macintosh and save it in Illustrator 4.x or earlier format.
NOTE: Illustrator 5.x-specific features (e.g., tabs, layers, gradients) are lost or modified when the document is saved in Illustrator 4 or earlier format.

ADDITIONAL INFORMATION
Illustrator 4..x for Windows is unable to open files saved in Illustrator 5 format. When you open an Illustrator 5.x for Macintosh file in Illustrator 4.x for Windows, Illustrator returns the error, "Can't open the illustration: The illustration contains an illegal or misplaced operator. Offending command 'Ar'."

System Error When Running Illustrator 4.0.x in Windows 95

ISSUE
A system error occurs when you run Adobe Illustrator 4.0x in Windows 95.

SYMPTOMS
Illustrator return the error, "The font ruler file is damaged or missing." as it starts.

The increment numbers on the rulers display as letters when you view an Illustrator document in high magnification (e.g., 400%).

The system returns an error (e.g., General Protection Fault in Dibeng.dll) as Illustrator displays a document in Preview mode.

The system returns an error (e.g., "This program has performed an illegal operation and will be shut down.") when you save an Illustrator file as an EPS graphic.

SOLUTIONS
Use Illustrator 4.1.
OR: Set up the computer to run either Windows 95 or Windows 3.x (i.e., dual boot), then run Illustrator 4.0x in Windows 3.x.

ADDITIONAL INFORMATION
While Illustrator 4.1 is compatible with Windows 95, Illustrator 4.0x is not.

Illustrator EPS graphics created in Windows 3.x can be imported and previewed in applications running in Windows 95. To create an Illustrator EPS graphic in Illustrator 4.0x and import it into a Windows 95 application:

1. Restart your computer.
2. When the "Starting Windows 95" screen appears, press F4 to prevent Windows 95 from starting. The message "Now loading your previous version of MS-DOS" appears.
3. At the C: prompt , type "win" and press Enter to start Windows 3.x.
4. Start Illustrator 4.0x and create your artwork.
5. Save the artwork as an EPS graphic, then exit Illustrator and Windows.
6. Restart your computer in Windows 95.
7. Start the destination Windows 95 application and import the Illustrator EPS graphic.

Error Placing Photoshop EPS File Containing Clipping Path into Illustrator 4.0.x

ISSUE
When placing an Adobe Photoshop 2.5 or later EPS file that includes a clipping path and TIFF image with a 8-bit screen preview into Adobe Illustrator 4.0.x, Photoshop returns the error "Can't read the TIFF image inside the EPS file." After clicking OK in the error message, the EPS file displays without a screen preview (e.g., as a gray box).

SOLUTION
Save the EPS file without including a clipping path, then mask the EPS file in Illustrator 4.0.x:

1. Open the EPS file in Photoshop 2.5.x or later.
2. Choose File > Export > Paths to Illustrator.
3. Name the path in the Export dialog box and click Save.
4. Save the Photoshop EPS file without the clipping path, then quit Photoshop.
5. Launch Illustrator and open the clipping path exported from Photoshop.
6. Choose View > Preview Illustration.
7. Choose Edit > Select All, then choose Paint > Paint Style.
8. In the Paint Style dialog box, select Mask then click OK.
9. Choose File > Place Art.
10. In the Place Art dialog box, select Encapsulated PostScript (.EPS) from the format pop-up menu, then select the Photoshop EPS file and click Place.
11. Use the crop marks and guides to position the EPS file.
12. Choose Arrange > Release Cropmarks.
13. Choose Edit > Select All, then choose Arrange > Group.
14. Copy and paste the masking group to the desired Illustrator document.

ADDITIONAL INFORMATION

Illustrator 4.0.x is unable to display a Photoshop EPS file that contains a clipping path. Photoshop for Windows saves clipping paths and 8-bit TIFF screen previews into an alpha channel in the EPS file. When importing a Photoshop EPS file containing an alpha channel, Illustrator 4.0.x returns the "Can't read the TIFF image inside the EPS file." error and the EPS file imports without its screen preview.

Error "You must have at least one font installed" When Starting Illustrator 4.0x

ISSUE

When you start Adobe Illustrator 4.0x, it returns the error "You must have at least one font installed to run Illustrator."

SOLUTIONS

Do one or more of the following:

A. Install Adobe Type Manager (ATM) 2.02 or later.

B. In the ATM Control Panel, select On:
   1. Double-click on the ATM Control Panel icon in the Main group of Program Manager.
   2. In the ATM Control Panel, select On, then click Exit.
   3. When the message "You must restart Windows for your change to take effect. Restart Windows or Return to current Windows session" appears, click Restart Windows.

C. Ensure the ATM Control Panel is active. When ATM is not active, the word "Inactive" appears in the Version section of the ATM Control Panel.

D. Install at least one PostScript Type 1 font:
   1. Start the ATM Control Panel, then click Add.
   2. In the Directories section of the Add ATM Fonts dialog box, navigate to the Pfm subdirectory of the Psfonts directory.
   3. In the Available Fonts section of the Add ATM Fonts dialog box, select the font or fonts you want to install.
   4. Select Install Without Copying Files and Autodownload for PostScript Driver, then click Add.
      NOTE: When no PostScript printer driver is installed, the Install Without Copying Files and Autodownload for PostScript Driver options are dimmed.
   5. Click Exit to close the ATM Control Panel.

E. Delete the Ps_enum.ebf and Hostfont.ebf files from the Windows directory, then restart Windows.

F. Start Illustrator to determine the last font it reads before it returns the error, then remove that font:
   1. Start Illustrator and note the last font name that displays in the startup screen before it returns the error "You must have at least one font installed to run Illustrator."
   2. Start the ATM Control Panel, select the font noted in step 2, then click Remove.
   3. In the ATM Control Panel dialog box, select the Delete Font from Disk and No Confirmation to Remove Fonts options to delete the selected fonts from your hard disk, then click Yes.
   4. Delete the Ps_enum.ebf and Hostfont.ebf files from the Windows directory.
   5. Restart Windows.

G. Remove all fonts from ATM and then reinstall one PostScript font from the original font disk:
   1. Start the ATM Control Panel, select all fonts, then click Remove.
   2. In the ATM Control Panel dialog box, select the Delete Font from Disk and No Confirmation to Remove Fonts options to delete the selected fonts from your hard disk, then click Yes.
   3. Insert the font installation disk into the disk drive, then click Add.
   4. In the Directories section of the Add ATM Fonts dialog box, double-click the disk drive letter containing the font installation disk. Use the scroll bar to navigate to the desired font.
   5. In the Available Fonts section of the Add ATM Fonts dialog box, select the font you want to install.
   6. Deselect Install Without Copying Files and select Autodownload for PostScript Driver, then click Add.
   7. Close the ATM Control Panel.
   8. Delete the Ps_enum.ebf and Hostfont.ebf files from the Windows directory.
   9. Restart Windows.

H. Install Windows, ATM, at least one Postscript font, and Illustrator on the internal hard disk.

I. Ensure PostScript fonts are in the C:\Psfonts directory. If the fonts are in a nested subdirectory (e.g., C\Windows\Fonts\Pscpt\Psfonts\Pfm\), Illustrator may be unable to locate the PostScript fonts.

J. Ensure the size of the Win.ini file is 32K or smaller. If the Win.ini file exceeds 32K in size, make a backup copy of the Win.ini file and then decrease its size by removing entries, sections, or font lines (e.g., True Type fonts in the [fonts] section, ATM fonts in the [PostScript, LPTx] section) that you no longer need.

K. Delete the Atmfonts.qlc file from the Psfonts subdirectory, delete the Ps_enum.ebf and Hostfont.ebf files from the Windows directory, and then restart Windows.

ADDITIONAL INFORMATION

To start, Illustrator 4.0x requires ATM 2.02 or later and at least one PostScript font installed in ATM. If the Ps_-enum.ebf or Hostfont.ebf file is damaged, no PostScript fonts are installed in ATM, Illustrator is unable to locate a PostScript font, or an installed PostScript font is damaged, Illustrator 4.0x returns the error "You must have at least one font installed to run Illustrator" when starting.

Illustrator 4.0x installs the Ps_enum.dll, which is the Enumerator file. The Enumerator file collects a list of the installed fonts from the Atm.ini file, Win.ini file, and PPD files, and then creates a database known as an .Ebf file (e.g., Enum.ebf, Ps_enum.ebf, Hostfont.ebf) for each installed printer driver using PostScript Type 1 fonts. The Hostfont.ebf file is a database of installed Type 1 softfonts.

If the Ps_enum.ebf or Hostfont.ebf file is missing, the Enumerator recreates it when you start Windows.

Error Opening or Importing Initial Caps file

ISSUE

You cannot open or import an Adobe Initial Caps for Windows file in an application that does not support Adobe Illustrator 88 format.

SOLUTIONS

Obtain a new copy of Initial Caps for Windows saved as EPS files, rather than as Illustrator (.ai) documents.
OR: Open the Initial Caps file in a drawing application that supports Adobe Illustrator 88 format (e.g., Adobe Illustrator) and save it in another format (e.g., EPS).
OR: Open the Initial Caps file in Adobe Photoshop and save it in bitmap format (e.g., TIFF, EPS).
NOTE: Saving an Initial Caps file from Photoshop as a bitmap makes it resolution-dependent, which may compromise quality and increase file size.

ADDITIONAL INFORMATION

Initial Caps is a clip art collection of ornate capital letter characters. The files in the Windows Initial Caps collection are incorrectly formatted as Illustrator (.ai) documents instead of EPS graphics. Initial Caps for Macintosh are properly formatted as Illustrator 88 EPS files.

Error "Invalid File Type" When Importing a WPG File into Illustrator 4.x

ISSUE

When you import a WordPerfect 6.0 for Windows WPG (Word Perfect Graphic) file into Adobe Illustrator 4.x, Illustrator returns the error "Invalid file type."

SOLUTION

Import a similar WordPerfect 5.x WPG graphic.

ADDITIONAL INFORMATION

Illustrator does not support WPG version 2 graphics; the clipart included with WordPerfect for Windows 6.0 is saved in WPG version 2 format. The clipart included with WordPerfect for Windows 5.x is saved in WPG version 1.x format, which is supported by Illustrator 4.x.

WordPerfect 6.0 and earlier does not allow you to save graphics in WPG format.

MAC OS

Q *(5.5 only)* **When I try to open a PICT file from Photoshop in Illustrator 5.5, I get a "Bitmapped image objects (not supported)" error. Is there any way to import PICTs into Illustrator?**

A Yes, but Illustrator offers different levels of support to different kinds of PICTs. There are two kinds of PICT files: vector and bitmapped. Because Photoshop is an editing program for bitmap images, it creates bitmapped PICTs. Illustrator, on the other hand, is a vector-based program and can open vector PICTs, but does not fully support bitmap PICTs. If you have a bitmap PICT you want to use in Illustrator, you have a couple of options:

- You can use the bitmap PICT as an Illustrator template. To do so, select "Open" from Illustrator's File menu, choose your bitmap PICT as the file to open, and click "OK." When Illustrator gives you the option to open the PICT as an "Illustrator Template (PICT)" or as a "PICT," select the first option. Doing so will open a new illustration in which your bitmap PICT will appear as a nonprinting, black-and-white bitmapped image you can trace over.
- You can convert your bitmap PICT to a vector graphic using an application such as Adobe Streamline.
- You can use Photoshop to save your PICT as an EPS. Then you can import it into Illustrator using the "Place Art…" command from the File menu. You'll be able to print the EPS from Illustrator, but you won't be able to edit it.

Error Opening or Parsing EPS File in Illustrator 6.0

ISSUE

The error "EPS Parser has encountered a problem with this file" appears in Adobe Illustrator 6.0 when opening a JPEG-encoded EPS file or when placing a JPEG-encoded EPS file with the Parsed EPS option selected in the Place dialog box.

SOLUTIONS

When placing an EPS file, select Place EPS, instead of Parsed EPS, in the Place dialog box.
OR: Save the EPS file with binary or ASCII encoding, instead of with JPEG encoding.

ADDITIONAL INFORMATION

Illustrator 6.0 can open and parse PostScript Level 1 EPS files. Because JPEG encoding is a PostScript Level 2 feature, Illustrator 6.0 cannot open or parse JPEG-encoded EPS files. Opening a JPEG-encoded EPS file or placing a JPEG-encoded EPS file with the Parsed EPS option selected in the Place dialog box in Illustrator 6.0 causes Illustrator to return the error "EPS Parser has encountered a problem with this file."

Illustrator 6.0 can open EPS files saved with ASCII or binary encoding. Illustrator can place JPEG-encoded bitmap EPS files when the Place EPS option is selected in the Place dialog box.

The Fish.eps, Bike.eps, and Rider.eps Illustrator 6.0 tutorial files are JPEG-encoded bitmap EPS files. Illustrator installs the Fish.eps file in the Fundamental folder in the

Tutorial folder in the Illustrator 6.0 application folder. Illustrator installs the Bike.eps and Rider.eps files in the Columns folder in Fundamental folder in the Tutorial folder in the Illustrator 6.0 application folder.

Photoshop 3.0x can save EPS files with the following encoding options: binary, ASCII, JPEG (low quality), JPEG (medium quality), JPEG (high quality), and JPEG (maximum quality). Joint Photographic Experts Group (JPEG) is a compression algorithm that discards extra data not essential to displaying an image.

Out of Memory Error Saving an EPS File in Illustrator

ISSUE

When you save an EPS files in Adobe Illustrator, Illustrator returns the error, "Can't save preview, but all other information was saved successfully. Nearly out of memory. Please save your files immediately. Free up more memory to continue."

SOLUTIONS

Save the EPS file with a black-and-white preview (i.e., 1-bit Macintosh or Black and White Macintosh).

OR: Ensure Illustrator has enough memory to save the EPS file by doing one or more of the following:

A. Close all Illustrator documents except the one in which you are working.
B. Reduce the number of Undo levels in Illustrator 5.x:
   1. Choose File > Preferences > General.
   2. In the General Preferences dialog box, enter a smaller value in the Undo Levels edit box, then click OK.
C. Increase the amount of random-access memory (RAM) allocated to Illustrator:
   1. Quit all open applications and restart the system without Extensions. To disable Extensions, use the Extensions Manager control panel included with System 7.5 or later, or move the Extensions folder onto the Desktop and restart the Macintosh.
   2. Choose About This Macintosh from the Apple menu.
   3. Note the Largest Unused Block (i.e., available memory) value, then close the window.
   4. Select the Illustrator application icon, then choose File > Get Info.
   5. Increase the Current Size (System 6.x with MultiFinder, System 7.0.x) or Preferred Size (System 7.1 or later) value, not exceeding the Largest Unused Block value noted in step 3.
   6. Close the window, then restart Illustrator.

ADDITIONAL INFORMATION

When Illustrator does not have enough memory to save an EPS file with a preview, it returns the error, "Can't save preview, but all other information was saved successfully. Nearly out of memory. Please save your files immediately. Free up more memory to continue."

The amount of memory Illustrator requires to create a screen preview corresponds to the dimensions of the Illustrator file and the type of preview (i.e., 1-bit Macintosh or 8-bit Macintosh). Illustrator requires more memory to create an EPS with a color preview (e.g., 8-bit Macintosh or Color Macintosh) than it does to create one with a black-and-white preview or no preview.

Offending Operator Error Opening Illustrator File Troubleshooting Guide

ISSUE

The error "Opened the artwork up to the following error condition: The illustration contains an illegal or misplaced operator. Offending operator: [varies] Context: [varies]" or "Can't open the illustration. The illustration contains an incomplete or garbled object description. Offending operator: [varies] Context: [varies]" appears when opening a file in Adobe Illustrator 5.x

SOLUTION

To open the file in Illustrator, do one or more of the following:

A. For instructions on opening an Illustrator file returning one of the following Offending operator or Context errors, see Additional Information:
   - "Offending operator: '%%CMYKCustomColor:'" when opening an Illustrator 5.5 document.
   - "Offending operator: '%%CMYKCustomColor:'" when opening a FreeHand file which has been saved in Illustrator format.
   - "Offending operator: '%%DocumentCustomColor'" when open the Illustrator file that contains a PageMaker EPS file.
   - "Offending operator: 'TZ:'"
   - "%A13_note:" appears in the "Context:" text of the error message when opening an Adobe Illustrator 5.0 document containing objects with an annotation set in the "Attributes" dialog box.
B. When the "Offending operator: 'gsave:'" appears, create a new Illustrator file and use the "Place Art" command to import the bitmap EPS file.
C. Ensure Illustrator is able open other files by opening an Illustrator tutorial file, or by creating a new document in Illustrator, saving it to a local hard drive, then reopening it.
D. Open a backup copy of the file in Illustrator.
E. Move the file to a local volume that is not a floppy drive (e.g., your hard drive), restart with Extensions off by restarting the Macintosh with the Shift key held down, then open the file in Illustrator.
F. Open the file in Illustrator installed on another computer.
G. Break the link to all EPS file placed in the Illustrator file by moving or renaming the EPS files.
H. Reinstall all fonts used in the Illustrator file from their original source (e.g., font disk).

I. Distill the Illustrator EPS file in Acrobat Distiller 1.0, then open the PDF file in Illustrator 5.5. Distiller can not create a PDF file of an Illustrator file that does not contain an EPSF header (i.e., .AI file).
NOTE: Illustrator 5.5 does not open PDF files created in Distiller 2.0 or later.

J. Recreate the file in Illustrator after resaving or recreating graphics, templates, and custom colors used in the original Illustrator file. Recreate all elements copied in from other Illustrator files.

ADDITIONAL INFORMATION

When opening a file in Illustrator, Illustrator reads and interprets the PostScript code contained in the file. When the file contains incorrectly formatted PostScript code, the error "Opened the artwork up to the following error condition: The illustration contains an illegal or misplaced operator." or "Can't open the illustration. The illustration contains an incomplete or garbled object description." appears. The text following the "Offending operator:" and "Context:" section of the error message indicate the PostScript code that Illustrator is unable to interpret.

Illustrator is an object-oriented drawing application and does not support opening EPS graphics containing bitmap information. When a bitmap EPS graphic (e.g., Adobe Photoshop EPS file) is opened in Illustrator, the error "Offending operator 'gsave'" appears.

Saving an Illustrator 5.x file containing FreeHand 5.0.x guides, a process-colored PageMaker EPS files, globally changed graphs, or extended characters formatted in a font alphabetically below Symbol in the font menu causes Illustrator to write incorrectly formatted PostScript code in the Illustrator file.

Other system and hardware problems can cause the PostScript code in a file to become damaged. Incorrectly formatted PostScript code can be written when the application creating the file is damaged, the file contains damaged elements, or the application saves the file over the network or directly to a disk. Writing a file to a damaged volume, or compressing or encrypting a file may damage it. A damaged file may be associated with particular elements, links, font, custom colors, or template.

To avoid creating damaged Illustrator files, reinstall Illustrator and delete the Adobe Illustrator Preferences file from the Preferences folder in the System Folder. Rebuilding the Desktop file, reinstalling the system software, using virus protection software (e.g., Sam, Virex), and scanning and repairing the hard drive with a disk utility (e.g., DiskTools, Norton Disk Doctor) will help ensure the files you create are not damaged by your operating environment.

To repair the PostScript code of Illustrator files that return the error Offending operator: "%%CMYKCustomColor," "%%DocumentCustomColors," "%%+()," "TZ," or "%A13_NOTE:" using a text editor:

disclaimer: Adobe Systems does not support modifying an Illustrator file with a text editor. Familiarity with editing EPS files in a text editor and saving in text-only (e.g., ASCII) format is required. Experience with PostScript language is highly recommended. Always modify a copy of the original Illustrator file. If alterations are incorrectly performed or the file is saved in the wrong format, the Illustrator file can be further damaged. In the event of problems, revert to the original copy.

To repair the Illustrator file that opens with the error "Offending operator: '%%CMYKCustomColor:'", open the Illustrator file in Macromedia FreeHand 5.x or in a text editor and edit the name of the offending color.

To repair the Illustrator file that opens with the error "Offending operator: '%%DocumentCustomColors' or '%%+()'", open the Illustrator file in a text editor and remove the offending operator line [i.e., "%%DocumentCustomColors: ()" or "%%+()"] in the Illustrator document and the PageMaker EPS file in a text editor.

To repair the Illustrator file that opens with the error "Offending operartor: 'TZ'", open the Illustrator file in a text editor and add a "[" to the beginning of the "/_Symbol_/Symbol 0 0 0 TZ" line.

To repair the Illustrator 5.0 file that opens with "%A13_NOTE:" in the "Context:" text of the error message, open the Illustrator 5.0 document in a text editor and remove the end of paragraph (i.e., return) character in the annotation text.

Error When Dragging and Dropping From Illustrator 6.0 to Photoshop 3.0.4

ISSUE

An error occurs when using the drag-and-drop feature to import artwork from Adobe Illustrator 6.0 into Adobe Photoshop 3.0.4 or later.

SYMPTOMS

When you drag and drop artwork containing a placed EPS file or bitmap image, Photoshop returns the error "Could not complete your request because there were no filled or stroked objects on the clipboard."

When you drag and drop a pattern fill or stroke, Photoshop returns the error "The clipboard uses patterned strokes or fills. These are unsupported by the Adobe Illustrator parser. Paste anyway?"

When you drag and drop stroked text, Photoshop returns the error "The clipboard contains stroked text. This is unsupported by this version of Photoshop. Paste anyway?"

SOLUTIONS

Save a copy of the artwork in Illustrator 6.0 as a 72 dpi bitmap file, then open the bitmap file in Photoshop.
NOTE: Illustrator cannot convert bitmap files back into Illustrator artwork.
OR: Avoid dragging and dropping bitmap images, EPS files, stroked text, pattern fills, or pattern strokes into Photoshop by doing one or more of the following:

A. Open EPS files and bitmap images in Photoshop, instead of using the drag-and-drop feature to import placed EPS files or bitmap images from an Illustrator file into Photoshop.

B. Use the Expand command in Illustrator 6.0 to convert pattern fills and strokes into individual elements masked by a path:
   1. Select an object filled or stroked with a pattern, then choose Object > Expand.
   2. In the Expand Gradient/Pattern dialog box, enter 255 in the Number of Steps text box, then click OK.

C. Convert stroked text to outlines in Illustrator 6.0 by selecting the text and choosing Type > Create Outlines.

ADDITIONAL INFORMATION

Photoshop 3.0 and later cannot convert the following elements in Illustrator artwork: placed EPS files, bitmap images, stroked text, pattern fills, and pattern strokes. An error occurs when you open or import Illustrator artwork containing elements that Photoshop cannot convert.

Importing Illustrator artwork containing a placed EPS file or bitmap image causes Photoshop to return the error "Could not complete your request because there were no filled or stroked objects on the clipboard." After you click OK in the error dialog box, Photoshop converts the supported elements in the artwork and omits the EPS files and bitmap images.

Importing an Illustrator element painted with a pattern fill or stroke causes Photoshop to return the error "The clipboard uses patterned strokes or fills. These are unsupported by the Adobe Illustrator parser. Paste anyway?" After you click OK in the error dialog box, Photoshop converts the pattern fill and stroke to a solid gray or black fill and stroke.

Importing Illustrator text painted with a stroke causes Photoshop to return the error "The clipboard uses patterned strokes or fills. These are unsupported by the Adobe Illustrator parser. Paste anyway?" After you click OK in the error dialog box, Photoshop imports the stroked text as unstroked text.

Error "Illustrator requires 32-bit QuickDraw" When Starting Illustrator 5.x

ISSUE

When starting, Adobe Illustrator 5.x returns the error, "Illustrator requires 32-bit QuickDraw."

SOLUTIONS

To run Illustrator 5.x on a color Macintosh (i.e., Macintosh II or later) with System 6.x, install 32-bit QuickDraw:

1. Open the Printing Tools disk provided with the Macintosh System 6.x installation disks.
2. Open the Apple Color folder and move the 32-bit QuickDraw file into the System Folder.
3. Restart the Macintosh and start Illustrator.

OR: Use Illustrator 5.x on a color Macintosh (i.e., Macintosh II or later) running System 7.x.

OR: Use Illustrator 3.2.3 or earlier on a black-and-white QuickDraw Macintosh computer (e.g., Macintosh Plus, Macintosh SE, Portable).

ADDITIONAL INFORMATION

Illustrator 5.x requires color QuickDraw. When you start Illustrator 5.x on a color Macintosh (i.e., 68020, 68030, or 68040 processor) running system 6.x without 32-bit QuickDraw or on a black-and-white Macintosh (i.e., 68000 processor), it returns the error, "Illustrator requires 32-bit QuickDraw." Black-and-white QuickDraw Macintosh computers (e.g., Macintosh Plus, Macintosh SE, Portable) do not support 32-Bit QuickDraw. Black-and-white QuickDraw Macintosh computers with a 68020 or 68030 acceleration card (e.g., Macintosh SE with a Mobius 68020 accelerator) are not compatible with Illustrator 5.x.

Color QuickDraw is a library of extensions to standard QuickDraw that provides support for color displays (e.g., PixelMaps). The ability of a Macintosh to support Color QuickDraw is a function of the processor in use. Color QuickDraw is available in Macintosh computers that use the 68020, 68030, or 68040 processor. Macintosh computers that use the 68000 processor do not support Color QuickDraw and thus, do not support color monitors.

32-Bit QuickDraw is a library of extensions to the Color QuickDraw family providing support for drawing to 32-bit color monitors. With System 6.x, the 32-Bit QuickDraw Startup document (INIT) is necessary for Macintosh II computers with ROM (read-only memory) sets issued prior to the Macintosh IIci (i.e., Macintosh II, IIx, IIcx, SE/30) as these Macintosh models do not have 32-Bit QuickDraw in ROM. 32-Bit QuickDraw version 1.2 (issued with System software 6.0.5) corrected some known issues in the Macintosh IIci series ROM. System 7.x does not install the 32-Bit QuickDraw INIT (system extension) as it is built into the system software.

Error "Can't open the hyphenation file..." When Starting Illustrator 5.x

ISSUE

When you start Adobe Illustrator 5.x, Illustrator returns the error "Can't open the hyphenation file 'US English Hyphenation'. Text will not be hyphenated" appears. After you clicking OK in the error dialog box Illustrator 5.x starts, but loads only the built-in plug-in filters.

SOLUTIONS

To ensure the "US English Hyphenation" plug-in filter is installed and Illustrator 5.x is linked to the Plug-Ins folder, do one or more of the following:

A. Respecify the Illustrator Plug-Ins folder preference:
   1. In Illustrator, Choose File > Preferences > Plug-ins.
   2. In the Plug-ins Preferences dialog box, locate the Plug-Ins folder, then click once to select it.
   3. With the Plug-Ins folder selected, click the Select

Plug-Ins button, located at the bottom of the Plug-ins Preference dialog box.
4. Click OK to the warning dialog box that appears, then quit and restart Illustrator.

B. Install the "U.S. English Hyphenation" file in the Illustrator 5.0.x Plug-Ins folder.

C. Automatically relink Illustrator 5.x to the Plug-Ins folder by recreating the Illustrator preference file:
1. Quit Illustrator 5.x.
2. Delete the "Adobe Illustrator 5.5 Prefs" file or "Adobe Illustrator Prefs" file, located in the Preference folder in the System Folder.
3. Place the Plug-Ins folder in the Illustrator 5.x application folder and start Illustrator. Illustrator 5.x automatically creates a link to Plug-Ins folder when the Plug-Ins folder is located in the folder containing the Illustrator application.

ADDITIONAL INFORMATION

The Illustrator 5.x hyphenation language dictionaries (e.g., Danish, Dutch, Finnish, French, German, Hungarian, Italian, Norwegian, Spanish, Swedish, U.K. English, and U.S. English) are plug-in filter files, which are installed in the Plug-Ins folder. If the "U.S. English Hyphenation" file is not installed in the Plug-Ins folder or the Illustrator link to the Plug-ins folder is broken, Illustrator will return the error "Can't open the hyphenation file 'US English Hyphenation'. Text will not be hyphenated" as it starts. If you clicking OK in the error dialog box, Illustrator will start, but text formatted with the "US English" hyphenation dictionary will not hyphenate automatically.

When the Illustrator 5.x link to the Plug-ins folder is broken, only the built-in filters are available in the Filters menu (e.g., "Select Inverse"). The "Select Inverse" filter is part of the Illustrator 5.0.x application. The "Illustrator File Format...," "Illustrator Template Format...," "Place EPS 5.5," and "Select Inverse" filters are part of the Illustrator 5.5 application. In Illustrator 5.x, the "About Plug-in" submenu under the Apple menu lists currently installed plug-in filters.

To verify other plug-in filters in the Plug-Ins folder are loading, choose About Plug-in from the Apple menu in Illustrator. The currently installed plug-in filters list in the About Plug-in submenu. When only the built-in filters (i.e., "Select Inverse" in Illustrator 5.0.x or "Illustrator File Format...," "Illustrator Template Format...," "Place EPS 5.5," and "Select Inverse" in Illustrator 5.5) list in the About Plug-in submenu, Illustrator is not linked to Plug-Ins folder and external plug-in filters are not loaded.

Error "The filter failed...." When Applying the Outline Path Filter in Illustrator 6.0

ISSUE

The error "The filter failed to complete the requested command. (diagnosis: 1, ("Assert", b))" appears when you choose the Outline Path plug-in filter in Adobe Illustrator 6.0.

SOLUTION

Restart Illustrator 6.0, then apply the Outline Path filter to the desired object.

ADDITIONAL INFORMATION

If you cancel the Outline Path filter in Illustrator 6.0 by clicking Stop in the Outline Path Progress dialog box or by pressing Command + . (period), you cannot apply the Outline Path filter again during the current Illustrator session. Selecting Filter > Objects > Outline Path after canceling the Outline Path filter causes the error "The filter failed to complete the requested command. (diagnosis: 1, ("Assert", b))" to appear.

To prevent the error from occurring, do not cancel the Outline Paths filter. Wait until the Outline Path filter is complete, then use the Undo command to return the Illustrator file to its previous state.

Error "...file is encrypted and cannot be opened" When Opening PDF File in Illustrator 5.5 & Later

ISSUE

When you open a PDF file in Adobe Illustrator 5.5 and later, Illustrator returns the error "Acrobat PDF File Format is having difficulties. The file is encrypted and cannot be opened." You can open, modify, and print the same PDF file in Acrobat Exchange 2.x.

SOLUTION

Open the PDF file in Acrobat Exchange and remove its password and other security controls:
1. Open the PDF in Acrobat Exchange 2.x, enter the Open Document password if prompted, choose File > Save As.
2. In the Save As dialog box, click Security, enter the Change Security Options password if prompted, then click OK.
3. In the Specific Password section of the Security dialog box, delete the text in the Open the Document text box and the Change Security Options text box.
4. In the Do Not Allow section of the Security dialog box, deselect Printing, Changing the Document, Selecting Text and Graphics, and Adding or Changing Notes, then click OK.
5. Save the PDF file.

ADDITIONAL INFORMATION

Illustrator 5.5 and later cannot open PDF files containing a password or other security controls. Opening a PDF file containing a password in Illustrator 5.5 or later causes Illustrator to return the error "Acrobat PDF File Format is having difficulties. The file is encrypted and cannot be opened."

Error When Selecting Font in Illustrator 5.5 or Later

ISSUE

When you select a font in Adobe Illustrator 5.5 or later, Illustrator returns the error "You won't be able to print with [font name] or stroke its characters because the font's outline file is missing or ATM is turned off."

SOLUTIONS

Do one or more of the following:

A. Ensure the Type 1 or TrueType font files are installed and accessible to Illustrator.
   1. Disable font management utilities (e.g., Suitcase, MasterJuggler) by removing the font management extension from the System Folder and restarting the Macintosh.
   2. Install the PostScript printer (outline) font file or TrueType font file for the selected typeface into the System Folder.

B. Ensure only one version of the selected font (i.e., PostScript or TrueType) is installed. To determine the font's version, double-click on the font file at the Finder. When you double-click a TrueType font file, the sample text displays in three sizes. When you double-click a PostScript screen font file, the sample text displays in one size. After double-clicking a PostScript outline font file, the message "PostScript font. This is a file that your Macintosh uses to display characters." appears.

C. Enable Adobe Type Manager (ATM) 3.0 or later by selecting On in the ATM Control Panel.
   NOTE: When extensions are disabled under System 7.x, ATM is inactive but On remains selected in the ATM Control Panel.

D. Reinstall ATM 3.0 or later. ATM 3.6.1 is included with Adobe Illustrator 5.5. ATM 3.8 and later installs the "~ATM (TM)" Control Panel file in the Control Panels folder in the System Folder. ATM 3.6.1 and earlier installs the "~ATM (TM)" Control Panel file in the Control Panels folder and the ATM driver (i.e., "~ATM 68000" or "~ATM 68020/030/040") in the System Folder.

E. Reinstall fonts and recreate the Fonts folder (System 7.1 and later) to ensure they are not damaged:
   1. Move the Fonts folder from the System Folder onto the desktop then restart the Macintosh.
   2. After the Macintosh restarts, a new empty Fonts folder is created in the System Folder.
   3. Reinstall the PostScript (screen and outline) font files or TrueType font file from the font's installation disk into the new Fonts folder.
   4. Move the other font files from the Fonts folder located on the desktop into the new Fonts folder in the System Folder. Do not replace any fonts that already exists in the new Fonts folder.

ADDITIONAL INFORMATION

Illustrator 5.5 and later returns the error "You won't be able to print with [font name] or stroke its characters because the font's outline file is missing or ATM is turned off." when you select a typeface from the Font menu that does not have a corresponding PostScript outline or TrueType font file available, when ATM is disabled or damaged, or when a font management utility is not delivering font information accurately.

Error "...not enough memory..." When opening PDF File in Illustrator 5.5

ISSUE

When opening a Portable Document Format (PDF) file, Adobe Illustrator 5.5 returns the error "Acrobat PDF File Format is having difficulties. There is not enough memory to complete the operation." The PDF file can be viewed in Adobe Acrobat Exchange or Adobe Acrobat Reader.

SOLUTIONS

Recreate the PDF file using Acrobat Distiller.

OR: Ensure Illustrator has enough memory to convert the PDF file by doing one or more of the following:

A. Increase the memory allocated to Illustrator 5.5.

B. Increase the amount of available space on the startup volume.

C. Simplify the PDF file before opening it in Illustrator 5.5 by do one or more of the following:
   A. Reduce the number of objects in the PDF file.
   B. Reduce the resolution (dpi) of images in the PDF file.
   C. Remove placed images in the PDF file.
   D. Resave the PDF file in Acrobat Distiller without image compression.

ADDITIONAL INFORMATION

When the PDF file is damaged, when there is insufficient application memory, or when there is insufficient hard disk space for Illustrator to convert the PDF file, Illustrator returns the error "Acrobat PDF File Format is having difficulties. There is not enough memory to complete the operation." when opening a PDF 1.x file.

Adobe Illustrator uses the Acrobat PDF File Format plug-in filter to convert PDF files into Illustrator objects. When Illustrator 5.5 converts a PDF file containing images, Illustrator extracts the images from the PDF file and stores them as linked EPS file. PDF file that containing compressed images require more application memory and hard disk space to convert than PDF files with non-compressed images.

Error "%%CMYKCustomColor" Opening FreeHand 5.0 File in Illustrator 5.x

ISSUE

When opening a file in Adobe Illustrator 5.x, the error "Can't open the illustration. The illustration contains an incomplete or garbled object description. Offending Operator: '%%CMYKCustomColor'" appears.

SYMPTOMS

The file being opened is a Macromedia FreeHand 5.0 file exported in Illustrator 5, 3, or 88 format. The file contains guides.

SOLUTIONS

Open the file in Illustrator 6.0 and save it in Illustrator 6.0 or Illustrator 5.0/5.5 format.

OR: Open the file in FreeHand 5.0, name all unnamed colors, then re-export the file in Illustrator format.
OR: In Illustrator 5.x, open a copy of the exported FreeHand file that has not been opened and saved in Illustrator, name all unnamed custom colors, then save the file.
OR: Name the unnamed color using a text editor, then open the file in Illustrator 5.x or earlier. For instructions, see Additional Information.
OR: To prevent the error from occurring, ensure the FreeHand file does not contain guides and the Illustrator file does not contain unnamed colors. For instructions, see Additional Information.

ADDITIONAL INFORMATION

Illustrator 5.x is unable to open files that include custom colors that do not have a name (i.e., an unnamed color). When opening an Illustrator file containing an unnamed custom color, Illustrator returns the error "Can't open the illustration. The illustration contains an incomplete or garbled object description. Offending operator: '%%CMYKCustomColor'."

FreeHand 5.0 files that contain guides and are exported in Illustrator format include an unnamed color (i.e., "0 0 0 1 ()"). Illustrator is able to open the file because the unnamed color is not a custom color. When Illustrator 5.x saves the file, however, Illustrator defines the unnamed color using the "%%CMYKCustomColor: 0 0 0 1 ()" line. After saving the file, Illustrator 5.x is unable to reopen the file because it contains an unnamed custom color defined using the "%%CMYKCustomColor: 0 0 0 1 ()" line.

When Illustrator 6.0 opens a file containing an unnamed custom color, Illustrator 6.0 names the custom color (e.g., Untitled 1) and adds the color to the custom color list.

To name the unnamed color using a text editor, then open the file in Illustrator 5.x or earlier:
disclaimer: Adobe Systems does not support modifying an Illustrator file with a text editor. Familiarity with editing EPS files in a text editor and saving in text-only (e.g., ASCII) format is required. Experience with PostScript language is highly recommended. Always modify a copy of the original Illustrator file. If alterations are incorrectly performed or the file is saved in the wrong format, the Illustrator file can be further damaged. In the event of problems, revert to the original copy.

1. Open a copy of the file in a text editor that can save in text-only format (e.g., TeachText, Microsoft Word).
2. Locate the "CMYKCustomColor" color operator line. For example:
   %%CMYKCustomColor: 0 0 0 1 ()
3. Insert the text cursor between the open and close parentheses and type a word (e.g., "color"). For example:
   %%CMYKCustomColor: 0 0 0 1 (color)
4. Save the Illustrator file in text-only format.
5. In Illustrator, choose File > Open, locate the edited copy of the Illustrator file in the Open dialog box, and click Open.
6. Ensure Lock is selected in the Guides submenu in the Objects menu.
7. Select the objects in the Illustrator file with the Direct Selection tool and choose Edit > Copy.
8. Choose File > New to create a new illustrator file, then select Edit > Paste to import the objects from the original file.
9. Choose Object > Custom Color, select the color named in the text editor (e.g., Color), press Delete, then click OK.
10. Save the new Illustrator file.

To prevent the %%CMYKCustomColor error from occurring, do one or more of the following:

A. Remove the guides from the FreeHand 5.x file before exporting the file in Illustrator format.
B. Name all unnamed custom colors before saving a file in Illustrator.
C. Open the FreeHand file in a text editor and remove the unnamed color, then open the file in Illustrator 5.x or earlier:
   1. Open a copy of the file in a text editor that can save in text-only format (e.g., TeachText, Microsoft Word).
   2. Locate the "0 0 0 1 () 0 X" line. For example:
```
(Guides) Ln
300 Ar
0 0 0 1 () 0 X
0 189.8166 m
612 189.8166 L
(N) *
```
   3. Remove the "0 0 0 1 () 0 X" line. For example:
```
(Guides) Ln
300 Ar
0 189.8166 m
-612 189.8166 L
-(N) *
```
   4. Save the Illustrator file in text-only format.
   5. In Illustrator, choose File > Open, select the edited copy of the FreeHand file in the Open dialog box, then click Open.

To open an EPS graphic as a text file in Microsoft Word 6.x:

1. Quit Microsoft Word.
2. At the Finder, move the EPS-TIFF converter file from the folder containing the Microsoft Word application to another location (e.g., the Desktop), then relaunch Word.
3. Press Shift and choose File > Open to list all files in the Open dialog box.
4. Select an EPS file and click Open.

To open an EPS graphic as a text file in Microsoft Word 5.x:

1. Quit Microsoft Word.
2. At the Finder, move the EPS-TIFF-PICT converter file from the Word Commands folder to another location (e.g., the Desktop), then relaunch Word.
3. Press Shift and choose File > Open to list all files in the Open dialog box.
4. Select an EPS file and click Open.

To open an EPS graphic as a text file in Microsoft Word 4.x:
Press Shift and choose File > Open.

Error "Offending Operand: 'Tt'" When Opening Illustrator 6.0 Document

ISSUE
When opening a file, Adobe Illustrator 6.0 returns the error "Can't open the Illustration. The illustration contains an illegal operand. Offending operator: 'Tt'." Illustrator then opens the fil, but omits some text blocks in it.

SOLUTIONS
Modify the Illustrator file in text editor:
disclaimer: Adobe Systems does not support modifying an Illustrator document with a text editor. Familiarity with opening EPS files in a text editor and saving in text-only (e.g., ASCII) format is required. Experience with PostScript language is highly recommended. Always modify a copy of the original Illustrator file. If alterations are performed incorrectly or the file is saved in the wrong format, the Illustrator file can be further damaged. In the event of problems, revert to the original copy.

1. Open a copy of the file in a text editor that can save in text-only format (e.g., TeachText, Microsoft Word).
2. Locate the following line:
   `-10000 Tt`
3. Delete the hyphen at the beginning of the line so it reads:
   `10000 Tt`
4. Repeat steps 2 and 3 for each "-10000 Tt" line in the file.
5. Save the file in text-only format, then open it in Illustrator.

OR: To prevent the "Offending Operator: 'Tt'" error, use Illustrator 6.0 for the Power Macintosh or Illustrator 6.0 Universal to create and save documents containing text formatted with the Fit Headline command.

ADDITIONAL INFORMATION
When you save a file containing an empty line of area text formatted with the Fit Headline command in Illustrator 6.0 for the 68000-series Macintosh (68K), Illustrator writes incorrect PostScript comments for the empty line of text. When you then open the file in Illustrator 6.0 for the Macintosh, Power Macintosh, or Universal Macintosh, Illustrator returns the error: "Can't open the Illustration. The illustration contains an illegal operand. Offending operator: 'Tt'."

When you apply the Fit Headline command to an empty line of area text, Illustrator returns the error "One or more paragraphs could not be adjusted enough to fit. Please alter the point size and try again."

Illustrator 6.0 for the Power Macintosh and Universal Macintosh write correct PostScript comments for empty lines of text formatted with the Fit Headline command.

Error "This plug-in is incompatible ...." When Selecting Filter in Illustrator 6.0

ISSUE
After you select a plug-in filter from the Filter menu in Adobe Illustrator 6.0, the error "This plug-in is incompatible with this version of the host program." partially displays in the upper-left corner of the screen.

SOLUTION
Install a version of the plug-in compatible with Illustrator 6.0 or Adobe Photoshop 3.0.4 or later.

ADDITIONAL INFORMATION
Illustrator 6.0 supports Illustrator 6.0- and Adobe Photoshop 3.0.4-compatible plug-ins. When you select an incompatible plug-in from the Filter menu in Illustrator 6.0, Illustrator returns the error "This plug-in is incompatible with this version of the host program."

The plug-ins installed with the Adobe Photoshop 3.0.5 Tryout included on the Adobe Illustrator 6.0 Deluxe CD-ROM are compatible with Photoshop 3.0, not Illustrator 3.0.4 or later.

To install a plug-in, move the desired plug-in into the Illustrator plug-ins folder. To enable Illustrator 6.0 to share plug-ins with Photoshop, place an alias of the Photoshop Plug-ins folder or alias of a Photoshop plug-in file in the Illustrator Plug-ins folder.

Error "%%DocumentCustomColors" or "%%+()" Opening Illustrator 5.x Document

ISSUE
When you open a file in Adobe Illustrator 5.x or earlier, Illustrator returns the error "Can't open the illustration. The illustration contains an incomplete or garbled object description." The offending operator in the error message is "%%DocumentCustomColors" or "%%+()."

SYMPTOMS
The Illustrator file contains an Adobe PageMaker EPS file.

The PageMaker EPS file uses PageMaker's default black or process colors, and does not use spot colors.

SOLUTIONS
Open the Illustrator 5.x file in Illustrator 6.0.
OR: Remove the offending operator lines from the Illustrator document and the PageMaker EPS file in a text editor. For instructions, see Additional Information.
OR: Convert the Illustrator EPS file to Portable Document Format (PDF) using Acrobat Distiller 1.0, and open it in Illustrator 5.5:

1. Launch Acrobat Distiller 1.0 and choose File > Open. (Illustrator 5.5 installs Distiller 1.0 in the Acrobat folder inside Illustrator 5.5 folder.)
2. Select the Illustrator EPS file and click Open.
3. Name the PDF file and click Save.
4. After Distiller converts the file to PDF, choose File > Quit.
5. Open the PDF file in Illustrator 5.5.

OR: To prevent the error from occurring, do one or more of the following prior to placing the PageMaker EPS file in the Illustrator document:

A. Remove the "%%DocumentCustomColors: (atend)" and "%%DocumentCustomColors:" lines from the PageMaker EPS file in a text editor. For instructions, see Additional Information.

B. Include a spot color in the PageMaker EPS file. You can place a spot-colored object behind another element on the page or cover the object with a white box before printing the publication to disk as an EPS file.

C. Convert the PageMaker EPS file to PDF using Acrobat Distiller 1.0, then open the PDF in Illustrator 5.5:

1. Launch Acrobat Distiller 1.0 and choose File > Open. (Illustrator 5.5 installs Distiller 1.0 in the Acrobat folder inside Illustrator 5.5 folder.)
2. Select the PageMaker EPS file and click Open.
3. Name the PDF file and click Save.
4. After Distiller converts the file to a PDF file, choose File > Quit.
5. Open the PDF file in Illustrator 5.5.

OR: Save the Illustrator file in EPS format and place it into the PageMaker publication.

ADDITIONAL INFORMATION

Illustrator 5.x and earlier cannot open files that include unnamed custom colors. When you open an Illustrator file containing an unnamed custom color, Illustrator 5.x returns the error "Can't open the illustration. The illustration contains an incomplete or garbled object description. Offending Operator: %%DocumentCustomColors." Illustrator 6.0 can open files that include unnamed custom colors.

PageMaker adds the "%%DocumentCustomColors:" line to the end of its EPS files to denote the spot colors used in the EPS file. If the PageMaker file contains only process colors, the "%%DocumentCustomColors:" line is not followed by a spot color name. When Illustrator saves a file containing a PageMaker EPS file, Illustrator adds the line "%%DocumentCustomColors: ()" or "%%+()" to the Illustrator file. After saving the file, Illustrator cannot reopen the file because it contains an unnamed custom color defined using the "%%DocumentCustomColors: ()" or "%%+()" line.

PageMaker's default Black is a process color.

To remove the offending operator lines from the Illustrator file and the PageMaker EPS file:

disclaimer: Adobe Systems does not support modifying an Illustrator document with a text editor. Familiarity with opening EPS files in a text editor and saving in text-only (e.g., ASCII) format is required. Experience with PostScript language is highly recommended. Always modify a copy of the original Illustrator file. If alterations are incorrectly performed or the file is saved in the wrong format, the Illustrator file can be further damaged. Always modify a copy of the Illustrator document. In the event of problems, revert to the original copy.

1. Open a copy of the Illustrator file in a text editor that can save in text-only format (e.g., TeachText, Microsoft Word).
2. Locate the offending operator line (i.e., "%%DocumentCustomColors: ()" or "%%+()") and remove it from the header of the Illustrator file. For example:

```
%%DocumentCustomColors: ()
```

OR:

```
%%DocumentCustomColors: (Red)
%%+()
```

3. Save the file in text-only format, then close the file.
4. Open a copy of the PageMaker EPS file in a text editor that can save in text-only format.
5. Locate the "%%DocumentCustomColors: (atend)" operator line and remove it from the header of the EPS file. For example:

```
%!PS-Adobe-3.0 EPSF-3.0
%%Title: Untitled-1
%%Creator: PageMaker 6.0
%%CreationDate: 9-29-1995, 13:45:44
%%For: fred anderson
%%BoundingBox: 0 0 288 288
%%ALDBoundingBox: 0 0 288 288
%%DocumentNeededResources: (atend)
%%DocumentSuppliedResources: (atend)
```

%%CMYKCustomColor: (atend)
%%DocumentCustomColors: (atend)
%%DocumentProcessColors: (atend)
%ADBDocumentInks: (atend)

6. Locate and remove the "%%DocumentCustomColors:" operator line from the end of the PageMaker EPS file. For example:

%%DocumentProcessColors: Cyan Magenta Yellow
%%DocumentCustomColors:
%%CMYKCustomColor:
%ADBDocumentInks:
%ADBDocumentMultiInkColors:
%%EOF

8. Save the EPS file in text-only format, then quit the text editor. (Saving the PageMaker EPS file in text-only format may remove the EPS file's screen preview.)
9. Break the link between the Illustrator file and the imported PageMaker EPS file by changing the name of the original PageMaker EPS file.
10. Open the edited Illustrator file in Illustrator 5.x.
11. When the Link dialog box appears, locate the edited PageMaker EPS and click Place. If the Link dialog box does not appear, the link to the imported PageMaker EPS file was not broken.

To open an Illustrator file or EPS file as a text file in Microsoft Word 6.x:

1. Quit Microsoft Word.
2. At the Finder, move the EPS-TIFF converter file from the folder containing the Microsoft Word application to another location (e.g., the desktop), then relaunch Word.
3. Press Shift and choose File > Open.
4. Select an EPS file and click Open.

To open an Illustrator file or EPS file as a text file in Microsoft Word 5.x:

1. Quit Microsoft Word.

2. At the Finder, move the EPS-TIFF-PICT converter file from the Word Commands folder to another location (e.g., the desktop), then relaunch Word.
3. Press Shift and choose File > Open.
4. Select an EPS file and click Open.

To open an Illustrator file or EPS file as a text file in Microsoft Word 4.x, press Shift and choose File > Open.

Error "Disk Full" Opening or Importing Bitmap Image Into Illustrator 6.0

ISSUE

The error "Disk full" appears when placing or opening a bitmap image (e.g., TIFF, EPS, PICT) in Adobe Illustrator 6.0.

SOLUTIONS

Increase the amount of disk space available on the startup volume so that it equals two to three times the file size of the image.

OR: Save the image as an EPS file, then place it in Illustrator 6.0.

ADDITIONAL INFORMATION

When Illustrator 6.0 places a bitmap PICT, Photoshop, or TIFF file, or opens a bitmap EPS, PICT, Photoshop, or TIFF file, Illustrator temporarily stores the imported image on the startup disk. When there is insufficient disk space available on the startup disk to store the image, Illustrator 6.0 returns the error "Disk full."

Illustrator 6.0 imports bitmap data as ASCII code within the Illustrator document. Bitmap images saved with Binary encoding increase by at least twice their original size when converted to ASCII data in an Illustrator 6.0 document.

Illustrator 6.0 does not include bitmap data when placing EPS files, instead creating a link between the placed EPS file and the Illustrator document.

Illustrator 6.0 uses the startup disk as a temporary disk space for storing data and performing computations. The location of this scratch disk cannot be changed.

Error "Offending Operand: 'TZ'" When Opening Illustrator 5.5 Document

ISSUE

When you open an Adobe Illustrator 5.5 document, Illustrator returns the error "Opened the art work up to the following error condition: the illustration contains an illegal operand. Offending Operand: 'TZ.'"

SOLUTIONS

Open and the Illustrator 5.5 document in Illustrator 6.0.

OR: Modify the Illustrator file in text editor:

disclaimer: Adobe Systems does not support modifying an Illustrator document with a text editor. Familiarity with opening EPS files in a text editor and saving in text-only (e.g., ASCII) format is required. Experience with PostScript language is highly recommended. Always modify a copy of the original Illustrator file. If alterations are incorrectly performed or the file is saved in the wrong format, the Illustrator file can be further damaged. Always modify a copy of the Illustrator document. In the event of problems, revert to the original copy.

1. Open a copy of the Illustrator 5.5 document in a text editor that can save in text-only format (e.g., TeachText, Microsoft Word).
2. Locate the line:
   `/_Symbol_/Symbol 0 0 0 TZ`
3. Type a bracket at the beginning of the line so it reads:
   `[/_Symbol_/Symbol 0 0 0 TZ`
4. Save the file in text-only format, then open the file in Illustrator.
5. Type a character (e.g., space character, character with white fill applied) and apply the font Symbol or a font that lists alphabetically above Symbol in the font menu (e.g., Helvetica), then save the Illustrator document.

OR: To prevent Illustrator from returning the error, "Offending Operand: 'TZ'" opening documents, apply the font Symbol, or a font that lists alphabetically above Symbol in the font menu (e.g., Helvetica), to any character in the document.

ADDITIONAL INFORMATION

Illustrator 5.5 does not write font encoding and reencoding information correctly in documents that contains a special or extended character or contains only fonts that are listed alphabetically below Symbol (e.g., Times). Illustrator 5.5 cannot decipher the incorrect font encoding when opening the damaged file, resulting in the error "Opening the art work up to the following error condition: the illustration contains an illegal operand. Offending Operand: 'TZ' " to appear when opening the document in Illustrator 5.x.

Illustrator 6.0 writes correct font encoding when saving an Illustrator 6.0 document containing extended characters and contains only fonts that are listed alphabetically below Symbol in the font menu. Illustrator 6.0 opens Illustrator 5.5 files containing incorrect font encoding without returning the "Offending Operand: 'TZ'" error, but is unable to correctly rewrite the font encoding when saving the document.

Opening the Illustrator 5.5 document in a text editor and typing the bracket in front of the file's "/_Symbol_/Symbol 0 0 0 TZ" PostScript code enables Illustrator to open the file without returning the "Offending Operand: 'TZ'" error. The bracket character ("[") at the beginning of a line ending with the TZ operator indicates the start of a font encoding. The TZ operator creates a new font from an existing font by changing portions of the new font's encoding vector.

Saving the file with at least one character formatted with the font Symbol, or a font that lists alphabetically above Symbol in the font menu (e.g., Helvetica), prevents Illustrator 5.5 from damaging the document.

To open an EPS graphic as a text file in Microsoft Word 6.x:

1. Quit Microsoft Word.
2. At the Finder, move the "EPS-TIFF" converter file from the folder containing the Microsoft Word application to another location (e.g., the desktop), then restart Word.
3. Hold the Shift key while choosing File > Open to list All Files in the Open dialog box.
4. Select an EPS file, then click Open.

To open an EPS graphic as a text file in Microsoft Word 5.x:

1. Quit Microsoft Word.
2. At the Finder, move the "EPS-TIFF-PICT" converter file from the Word Commands folder to another location (e.g., the desktop), then restart Word.
3. Hold the Shift key while choosing File > Open to list All Files in the Open dialog box.
4. Select an EPS file, then click Open.

Error "...illustration contains an illegal or misplaced operator..." Opening Illustrator 5.0 Document

ISSUE

When you open an Adobe Illustrator 5.0 document containing objects with an annotation set in the Attributes dialog box, Illustrator returns the error, "Opened the artwork up to the following error condition: The illustration contains an illegal or misplaced operator. Offending operator: [varies] Context: [varies]" where "%A13_note:" appears in the "Context:" text.

SYMPTOMS

The error message's "Offending operator:" and ""%A13-_note:" in the Context:" text contains portions of annotation text applied to objects in the Illustrator document.

SOLUTION

Open the Illustrator 5.0 document in a text editor and remove the end of paragraph (i.e., return) character in the annotation text:

disclaimer: Adobe Systems does not support modifying an Illustrator document with a text editor. Familiarity with opening EPS files in a text editor and saving in text-only (e.g., ASCII) format is required. Experience with PostScript language is highly recommended. Always modify a copy of the original Illustrator file. If alterations are incorrectly performed or the file is saved in the wrong format, the Illustrator file can be further damaged. Always modify a copy of the Illustrator document. In the event of problems, revert to the original copy.

1. Open the Illustrator 5.0 document and note the error message's "Offending operator:" and "%A13_note:" text that contains portions of the annotation text.
2. Open a copy of the Illustrator 5.0 document in a text editor that can save in text-only format (e.g., TeachText, Microsoft Word).
3. Locate the last line in the "Context:" section of the error message proceeded by "%AI13_note:". For example:
   ```
   %AI3_note:Red circle
   purple 12pt line
   ```
4. Delete the end of paragraph (i.e., return) character between the two lines. For example:
   ```
   %AI3_note:Red circle purple 12pt line
   ```
5. Save the Illustrator document in text-only format.
6. In Illustrator, open the edited copy of the Illustrator file.

ADDITIONAL INFORMATION

When you open an Adobe Illustrator 5.0 document containing incorrectly formatted PostScript code, Illustrator returns the error, "Opened the artwork up to the following error condition: The illustration contains an illegal or misplaced operator."

When you press Return in Illustrator 5.0 to force a line break in the Attributes dialog box, Illustrator incorrectly formats the PostScript code describing the annotation. For example, in an Illustrator 5.0 document containing an annotation that reads:

```
Red circle
purple 12pt line
```

Illustrator 5.0 incorrectly formats annotation text in the PostScript code as:

```
%AI3_note:Red circle
purple 12pt line
```

When you open the Illustrator 5.0 document, Illustrator generates the following error:

"Opened the artwork up to the following error condition: The illustration contains an illegal or misplaced operator."

```
Offending operator: 'purple'
Context:
0 R
0 .85 1 0 0 (Purple) 0 X
800 Ar
0 J 0 j 12 w 4 M []0 d
%A13_note:Red circle
purple
```

Illustrator 5.0.1 and later correctly format annotation text in the PostScript code. For example:

```
%AI3_note:Red circle
%AI5_NoteMore:purple 12pt line
```

To open an EPS graphic as a text file in Microsoft Word 6.x:

1. Quit Microsoft Word.
2. At the Finder, move the "EPS-TIFF" converter file from the folder containing the Microsoft Word application to another location (e.g., the desktop), then restart Word.
3. Press Shift and choose File Open so that Illustrator lists All Files in the Open dialog box.
4. Select an EPS file and click Open.

To open an EPS graphic as a text file in Microsoft Word 5.x:

1. Quit Microsoft Word.
2. At the Finder, move the "EPS-TIFF-PICT" converter file from the Word Commands folder to another location (e.g., the desktop), then relaunch Word.
3. Press Shift and select "Open" from the file menu to list "All Files" in the "Open" dialog box.

4. Select an EPS file and click "Open."
To open an EPS graphic as a text file in Microsoft Word 4.x: Press Shift and select "Open" from the file menu.

Error "Artwork which contains placed objects..." When Saving in Illustrator 6.0.x

ISSUE
When you save an Adobe Illustrator 6.0.x file in Photoshop 3 or TIFF format, Illustrator returns the error, "Artwork which contains placed objects cannot be saved in TIFF [or Photoshop] format." The Illustrator file contains an imported vector (object-oriented) EPS file.

SOLUTION
Remove the vector EPS files, then replace them by choosing File > Place and selecting the Parsed EPS option, instead of the Place EPS option, in the Place dialog box.

ADDITIONAL INFORMATION
Illustrator uses the TIFF Format and Photoshop 3 Format plug-ins to convert Illustrator files into a bitmap image. The TIFF Format and Photoshop 3 Format plug-ins cannot convert vector EPS files (e.g., Illustrator EPS, PageMaker 6.0 EPS) that were imported with the Place EPS option.

System Errors

WINDOWS

Q I just upgraded to Illustrator 4.1 so I'd be compatible with Windows 95, but now my screen freezes or redraws incorrectly when I'm in "Preview Illustration" mode. What's wrong?

A What you're experiencing is a conflict between Illustrator and the driver for your video card (which probably uses an S3 chip set). Not to worry, though—you can easily fix this problem by changing a setting in your AI41.INI file. Follow these steps:

1. If you have Illustrator running, exit it completely.
2. Find the AI41.INI file, which is located in the Windows 95 directory (called "Windows" by default), and make a backup copy of it. You can call your backup copy something like AI41INI.BAK.
3. Open the file in a word-processing or text-editing program that can save in text-only format (the WordPad or Notepad applications will do).
4. Locate the PREVIEWMODE=0 line in the [Driver] section of the file.
5. Change the line PREVIEWMODE=0 so that it reads PREVIEWMODE=1.
6. Save the AI41.INI file in the text-only format, and then restart Illustrator.

Here's a little information on why this procedure fixes the problem. Illustrator, like any Windows program, must work with Windows system-level components to draw objects on screen. These components include GDI.EXE (graphical device interface—the part of Windows that oversees all screen display and non-PostScript printing operations) and your video card's driver. Most applications send screen-display information directly to GDI.EXE, which must then pass that information to a specific video driver. However, Illustrator is designed to send information directly to the video driver, bypassing GDI.EXE, which can significantly speed screen display. But certain video drivers, such as some of those for video cards with S3 chip sets, can't correctly interpret all of Illustrator's screen-display instructions, and when that happens you might see screen-redraw problems or your screen might freeze.

Changing the PreviewMode=0 line in the AI4.INI file to PreviewMode=1 makes Illustrator send those display instructions to GDI.EXE instead—and GDI.EXE doesn't have a problem interpreting Illustrator's screen-display instructions. Although this fixes the screen freezes and screen-redraw problems, it'll mean Illustrator's screen will redraw relatively slowly.

Keep in touch with the manufacturer of your S3-based video card. They might come out with new Windows 95 video drivers that will allow you to run Illustrator without the AI41.INI change explained above.

System Freezes Accessing Paint Style in Illustrator 4.1

ISSUE
A system error (e.g., freeze) occurs when you choose Paint > Paint Styles or press Control + I in Adobe Illustrator 4.1.

SYMPTOMS
Illustrator 4.02 or earlier was updated to Illustrator 4.1.

Illustrator 4.1 is running in Windows 95 Safe mode.

SOLUTIONS
Remove the AI4 directory, then install Illustrator 4.1 from a full (retail) Illustrator 4.1 disk set, available from Adobe Systems.

OR: Update Illustrator 4.02 or earlier to Illustrator 4.03, then update to Illustrator 4.1:

1. Remove the AI4 folder and the AI4.INI file from the Windows folder.
2. Install Illustrator 4.02 or earlier.
3. Update to Illustrator 4.03 using the Illustrator 4.03 Patch, then restart Windows. The Illustrator 4.03 Patch (e.g., AI403Ptc.zip) is available on America Online, CompuServe, and the Adobe BBS. For instructions on installing the Illustrator 4.03 Patch, see Additional Information.
4. Update Illustrator 4.03 to Illustrator 4.1, then restart Windows.

ADDITIONAL INFORMATION

The Illustrator 4.1 updater does not properly update Illustrator 4.02 or earlier, causing the system to freeze when you choose Paint > Paint Styles or press Control + I in Illustrator 4.1. The Adobe Illustrator 4.03 Patch updates Illustrator 4.02 and earlier to Illustrator 4.03.

Using the drawing tools or accessing the Paint Styles dialog box in Illustrator 4.1 while Windows 95 is running in Safe mode and Illustrator is set to communicate directly with the display mini-driver causes the error "General Protection Fault in ADOBEVUE.DLL" to occur.

To install the Illustrator 4.03 Patch:

1. Download the AI403Ptc.zip file and place it in the AI4 folder.
2. Exit Windows and, at the DOS prompt, change to the Illustrator directory (ai4). For example, at the DOS prompt, type:
   ```
   cd\ai4
   ```
3. Unzip the AI403Ptc.zip file using Pkunzip. For example:
   ```
   pkunzip ai403ptc.zip
   ```
4. Type "patch-ai" and press Enter.
5. Use the DOS move command to move the patchsys.bat file to the system subdirectory. For example, type:
   ```
   move c:\ai4\patchsys.bat
    c:\windows\system\patchsys.bat
   ```
6. Move the patch.exe file to the system subdirectory. For example, type:
   ```
   move c:\ai4\patch.exe
    c:\windows\system\patch.exe
   ```
7. Move the patchsys.rtp file to the system subdirectory. For example, type:
   ```
   move c:\ai4\patchsys.rtp
    c:\windows\system\patchsys.rtp
   ```
8. Switch to the System subdirectory. For example, type:
   ```
   cd\windows\system
   ```
9. Type "patchsys" at the DOS prompt and press Enter. The Illustrator 4.03 Patch updates Illustrator.
10. When the patch is completed, restart Windows.

Illustrator 4.1 Freezes When Previewing Artwork in Windows 95

ISSUE

Adobe Illustrator 4.1 freezes or redraws incompletely in Preview Illustration view when running in Windows 95. The computer's video display card is using the S3 chipset (e.g., Diamond Stealth).

SOLUTION

Disable Illustrator's ability to directly call S3 video mini-driver functions by changing the "PreviewMode=0" line to "PreviewMode=1" in the Ai41.ini file:

1. Exit Illustrator 4.1.
2. Open the Ai41.ini file, located in the Windows 95 directory, in a text editor that can save in text-only format (e.g., WordPad, Notepad).
3. Locate the "PREVIEWMODE=0" line in the [DRIVER] section.
4. Edit the "PREVIEWMODE=0" line by changing the number "0" to "1" so that it reads: PREVIEWMODE=1
5. Save the Ai41.ini file in text-only format.

ADDITIONAL INFORMATION

Illustrator 4.1 sends display commands directly to the Windows 95 display mini-drivers. Illustrator uses the S3 mini-driver to display artwork in Preview Illustration view on a computer using an S3 video chipset and running Windows 95. Illustrator 4.1 is not compatible with the Windows 95 S3 mini-driver. In Illustrator 4.1, magnifying or redrawing artwork in Preview Illustration view on a computer using a S3 video chipset and running Windows 95 causes Illustrator to freeze or the artwork to display incompletely.

After reading the "PreviewMode=1" line in the Ai41.ini file, Illustrator 4.1 uses the universal driver, instead of the S3 mini-driver, to display artwork. Illustrator 4.1 displays artwork more slowly when using the universal driver than when using of the S3 mini-driver.

Video cards that use the S3 chipset include Diamond Stealth cards, DEC display adapters, Hercules Graphite cards, Number Nine GXE cards, and the Orchid Fahrenheit cards.

Error "GPF in Commdlg.dllL" When Starting Illustrator 4.x

ISSUE

When you start Adobe Illustrator 4.x, the system returns the error "GPF in Commdlg.dll."

SOLUTIONS

Do one or more of the following:

A. Restart Windows, then start Illustrator.

B. Remove or rename all duplicate Commdlg.dll files, leaving one Commdlg.dll file located in the Windows\System directory.

C. Reinstall the Commdlg.dll file from the Windows installation disks:
   1. Restart Windows.
   2. Use the Windows File Manager to rename the Commdlg.dll file in the Windows\System directory to Commdlg.old.
   3. Copy the compressed Commdlg.dll file (i.e., Commdlg.dl_) from the Windows installation disks to the Windows\System directory.
   4. Copy the Expand.exe file from the Windows directory to the System directory.
   5. Exit Windows.
   6. At the DOS prompt, change to the Windows\System directory.
   7. Using the "Expand" command, decompress the Commdlg.dl_" file. For example:
      ```
      EXPAND COMMDLG.DL_ Commdlg.dll
      ```

8. Restart Windows.

D. Reinstall the Commdlg.dll from DOS:
   1. Exit Windows.
   2. At the DOS prompt, change to the Windows\System directory.
   3. Using the "REN" command, rename the Commdlg.dll file, then press Enter. For example:
      `REN Commdlg.dll COMMDLG.OLD`
   4. Copy the compressed Commdlg.dll file (Commdlg.dl_) from the original Windows installation disks to the Windows\System directory. For example:
      `COPY A:\COMMDLG.DL_ C:\WINDOWS\SYSTEM Commdlg.dll`
   5. Copy the Expand.exe file from the Windows directory to the System directory. For example:
      `COPY C:\WINDOWS\EXPAND.EXE C:\WINDOWS\SYSTEM EXPAND.EXE`
   6. Change to the System directory and use the "Expand" command to decompress the Commdlg.dl_ file. For example:
      `EXPAND COMMDLG.DL_ Commdlg.dll`
   7. Restart Windows.

ADDITIONAL INFORMATION

Illustrator 4.x installs a Commdlg.dll file into the Windows\System directory. When a Commdlg.dll file with a date other than 11/01/93 is located in the Windows\System directory, the Illustrator installer will return the message "The file c:\windows\system\Commdlg.dll already exists and has a different date than the file Adobe Illustrator is about to install. Do you wish to overwrite the current file on the system?" If the Commdlg.dll file is overwritten and you start Illustrator without first restarting Windows, the system will return the error "GPF in Commdlg.dll." The error occurs when Windows accesses a version of the Commdlg.dll file that is different from the Commdlg.dll already loaded by Windows.

The Commdlg.dll file governs dialog boxes common to all Windows applications. Only one Commdlg.dll file should be installed on the system and should be located in the Windows\System directory.

Error "GPF in AI41.EXE" When Saving Files in Illustrator 4.1

ISSUE

When you save a file in Adobe Illustrator 4.1 running in Windows 3.x or Windows 95, the system returns the error, "An error has occurred in your program. To keep working anyway, click Ignore and save your work in a few file. To quit this program, click Close. You will lose information entered since your last save." If you click Ignore in the error dialog box, the system returns the same error. If you click Close, you receive the error, "This program has performed an illegal operation and will be shut down. ILLUSTRA caused a general protection fault in module AI41.EXE at 001b:00004e7a."

SOLUTION

Set the system date to December 31, 2037 or earlier:

In Windows 95:

1. Select Start > Settings > Control Panel.
2. Double-click the Date/Time Control Panel.
3. Click the Date & Time tab, change the date, and click OK.

In Windows 3.x:

1. Double-click the Control Panel icon in the Main group.
2. In the Control panel window, double-click the Date/Time icon.
3. Change the date and then click OK.

ADDITIONAL INFORMATION

When Illustrator 4.1 saves a file, it sets the file's creation and modification date using the date provided by the operating system. Illustrator 4.1 does not support dates later than December 31, 2037, so if you save a file in Illustrator 4.1 when the date is set to January 1, 2038 or later, it causes a General Protection Fault error.

The General Protection Fault error may include the following addresses:

```
001b:00004e7a
001b:00004e84
001b:00004fe2
001b:00004fef
001b:00005089
```

Error "Run_enum caused a GPF in Ps_enum.dll" When Starting Illustrator 4.0.x in Windows 3.x

ISSUE

When you start Adobe Illustrator 4.0x in Windows 3.x, the system returns the error, "Run_enum caused a general protection fault in module Ps_enum.dll."

SOLUTIONS

Do one or more of the following:

A. Rename any files on your system that have an .ebf extension and restart Illustrator:
   1. In File Manager choose File > Search.
   2. In the Search dialog box, type " *.ebf" in the Search For text box and "c:\" in the Start From text box, then click OK.
   3. Rename the *.ebf files listed in the Search Results window (e.g., change Enum.ebf to Enum.old).
   4. Restart Illustrator 4.0x.

B. Remove all PostScript fonts then re-add them in Adobe Type Manager (ATM) 2.0.1 or later.

ADDITIONAL INFORMATION

The Enumerator (Ps_enum.dll) is a database that keeps a list of all PostScript fonts currently available to Windows applications by reading the Atm.ini, Win.ini, and *.ppd files. The *.ebf files (e.g., Enum.ebf, Ps_enum.ebf, Hostfont.ebf) are the preference files for the Enumerator. The Hostfont.ebf contains the list of installed Type 1 Soft fonts.

When starting, Illustrator 4.0.x accesses the *.ebf files (e.g., Enum.ebf, Hostfont.ebf) for a list of the installed PostScript fonts. When the *.ebf files are not available (e.g., they are missing or damaged), Illustrator accesses the Ps_enum.dll file, which creates new *.ebf files.

When you install a new version of the Ps_enum.dll and do not restart Windows, Windows may generate a GPF error as Illustrator accesses the Ps_enum.dll. For example, when you install Illustrator 4.03, then start it without restarting Windows, Windows returns the error, "Run_enum caused a general protection fault in module Ps_enum.dll."

If you start Illustrator 4.0x when one or more PostScript font or *.ebf file is a damaged, Illustrator will return the error, "Run_enum caused a general protection fault in module Ps_enum.dll"

MAC OS

Q Whenever I try to import an RTF file into Illustrator 6.0, I get the error that Illustrator "unexpectedly quit because an error of type 1 occurred." Same for exporting text. What's wrong?

A Chances are you're using a Macintosh with a PCI local bus (e.g., an Apple 7500, 8500, or 9500, or a 604-based Macintosh-compatible with a PCI local bus), and you're running into an incompatibility between that hardware and the filter Illustrator uses to import and export RTF—the Claris XTND for Illustrator filter, version 1.3 (this filter is located in the "Claris Translators" folder in the "Claris" folder within the System Folder). Illustrator 5.0 and later versions install these Claris filters by default.

Fortunately, it's not hard to work around this problem. Just copy and paste the text into or out of Illustrator instead of using the "Import Text" command. When you use the Clipboard to import or export your text, Illustrator will use the text-only filters, not the RTF filters, so you won't run into any of the system errors that can occur with RTF filters (type 1, type 3, or a system freeze). Or, when you're importing text, resave your incoming file in text-only format and use the "Import Text" command.

System Error When Starting Illustrator, Troubleshooting Guide

ISSUE

A system error (e.g., freeze) occurs while Illustrator is reading fonts during startup, as indicated in the Illustrator startup screen.

SOLUTIONS

Do one or more of the following:

A. Ensure fonts are loaded in the system:
   1. Restart the Macintosh computer without extensions and disable font management utilities (e.g., ALSoft MasterJuggler, Symantec Suitcase). To turn all extensions off upon startup in System 7, restart the computer holding the Shift key down until the message "Welcome to Macintosh. Extensions Off." appears.
   2. Install fonts previous installed using a font management utility into the System.

B. Verify installed fonts and the Fonts folder are not damaged by reinstalling fonts and recreating the Fonts folder in System 7.1 or later:
   1. Move the Fonts folder from the System Folder onto the desktop.
   2. Restart the Macintosh. After the Macintosh restarts, a new empty Fonts folder is created in the System Folder.
   3. Ensure Illustrator launches without any fonts located in the Fonts folder.
   4. Move fonts, one a time, from the old Fonts folder located on the desktop, into the new Fonts folder located in the System Folder.
   6. After moving a font into the new Fonts folder, then restart Illustrator.
   7. Repeat steps 3-4 until a font moved into the Fonts folder causes a system error when starting Illustrator.
   8. Ensure fonts preventing Illustrator from starting are not damaged by deleting and reinstalling both the bitmap (screen) and outline (printer) font file.

ADDITIONAL INFORMATION

When starting, Illustrator reads open fonts files. Illustrator 5.x and later displays the font name in the startup screen as it reads each font. When a damaged font is read or a conflict with a font management utility occurs, a system error appears when Illustrator is reading fonts while starting.

To determine if a TrueType or PostScript bitmap font is damaged, open the font suitcase then the font file to display the sample text. When a TrueType or bitmap font fails to open or opens without displaying sample text, the TrueType or bitmap font file may be damaged. Reinstalling TrueType or PostScript bitmap and outline font files from the font's installation disk or from the system installation disk set ensures the fonts are not damaged.

Installing fonts in System 7.01 and later:

1. Quit all applications.
2. Move the font files into the Fonts folder inside the System Folder, or drag onto the closed System Folder icon. When dragging the fonts on a closed System Folder, the system automatically places the fonts in the proper location.

Installing fonts in System 7.0

1. Quit all applications.
2. Manually move the font files into the System Folder:
   1. Select all screen (bitmap) font suitcases.
   2. Move screen font suitcases into the System suitcase, locate in the System Folder.
   3. Select all the printer (outline) font files.
   4. Drag printer font files into the Extensions folder, located in the System Folder.

OR: Have the system automatically move font files in the proper location by selecting both the font suitcases and printer font files together, then dragging them onto the closed System Folder icon.

Unable to Open or Print from Illustrator with QuickDraw GX Installed

ISSUE

A system error (e.g., "Application unknown has unexpectedly quit," freeze) appears after you launch Adobe Illustrator or after you choose File > Print in Illustrator when QuickDraw GX installed.

SOLUTION

Deinstall QuickDraw GX, then restore Macintosh printing and Type 1 PostScript fonts:

1. Deinstall QuickDraw GX. For instructions, see Additional Information.
2. Restore standard Macintosh printing for all applications:
   A. Launch the Apple Installer on the QuickDraw GX Install disk by double-clicking on the Install QuickDraw GX installer control file.
   B. Select Custom Remove from the pop-up menu in the installer dialog box.
   C. Select the following options for Custom Remove: Base QuickDraw GX Software for this Macintosh, Base QuickDraw GX Software for any Macintosh, QuickDraw GX Utilities, ATM for QuickDraw GX, and All QuickDraw GX Drivers for Apple Printers.
   D. Set the Destination Disk to the disk containing the system software; use the Switch Disk button to select another disk, if your System is on another attached hard disk.
   E. Click the Remove button. When complete, restart the Macintosh.
3. Restore Type 1 PostScript fonts:
   A. Move all enabled font suitcases, located in the Fonts folder in the System Folder by default, to a different location. Enabled suitcases contain converted TrueType versions of Type 1 PostScript fonts, in addition to the bitmap (screen) fonts.
   B. Move fonts contained in the Archived Type 1 Fonts folder, located in the System Folder, into the Fonts folder, and delete the empty Archived Type 1 Fonts folder.
   C. Move other fonts enabled using the Type 1 Enabler application to another folder not accessed by any font management utility (e.g., Suitcase). Move the original archived copy of the Type 1 font back to the desired folder to make it available to the management utility.
   D. Reinstall Adobe Type Manager versions other than ATM/GX 3.7.

ADDITIONAL INFORMATION

Adobe Illustrator 6.x and earlier do not support Apple QuickDraw GX. Apple's QuickDraw GX is an updated version of QuickDraw, the language that controls Macintosh display and printing. QuickDraw GX enhances printing and font handling, and supports Portable Digital Documents (PDDs) and color management software. QuickDraw GX is included with Apple Macintosh System 7.5.x and printing utilities (e.g., Pierce Print Tools).

To support QuickDraw GX printing, applications must recognize GX printer drivers and include QuickDraw GX options in the Print and Page Setup dialog boxes. To support QuickDraw GX TrueType fonts, applications must recognize their extended character set, which includes up to 65,000 characters per font, and their line layout capabilities for text composition. QuickDraw GX-compatible applications automatically handle kerning, justification, special characters (e.g., automatic ligature substitution), proper use of swash and standard characters, morphing for weight and width, and formation of fractions and ordinals (e.g., superscripting "nd" in "2nd," "3" in "2 to the 3rd power").

When you use the QuickDraw GX Easy Install option to install QuickDraw GX, the Apple Installer does not install the QuickDraw GX Helper extension. The QuickDraw GX Helper extension enables the bypassing of Desktop printing when you print from an application.

To disable Desktop Printing, launch an application and choose Turn Desktop Printing Off from the Apple menu, which causes the following alert to appear: "Click OK to use the '[driver name]' driver for printing from this application. To continue using Desktop printing from this application, click Cancel." The printer driver name included in the alert is the QuickDraw GX default printer driver created in the Chooser. For example, if you're printing to a PostScript printer the alert reads "Click OK to use the LaserWriter driver for printing...." For PostScript printers, QuickDraw GX Helper chooses the LaserWriter 7.2 PostScript printer driver if it is installed. If the LaserWriter 7.2 printer driver is unavailable, QuickDraw GX Helper chooses the LaserWriter 8.x printer driver. If the Helper cannot locate a QuickDraw GX-compatible printer driver, it displays the following alert: "The QuickDraw GX Helper was unable to find a driver compatible with your default desktop printer named '[Driver Name].' Make a different desktop printer your default printer, then choose 'Turn Desktop printing off' again."

To disable QuickDraw GX, remove it using the Apple Installer's Custom Remove option, use Extensions Manager to turn off the QuickDraw GX extensions, or use QuickDraw GX Helper extension to turn Desktop Printing off for specific applications. To restore PostScript Type 1 after disabling QuickDraw GX using the installer or QuickDraw GX Helper, remove the enabled fonts and reinstall the original Type 1 fonts located in the Archived Type 1 Fonts.

System Error When Saving PDF File on Power Macintosh with PCI Bus from Illustrator 5.5

ISSUE

A system error (e.g., "Application unexpectedly quit due to an error unknown.") appears when you save a Portable Document Format (PDF) file from Adobe Illustrator 5.5. Illustrator is running on a Macintosh with a Peripheral Component Interconnect (PCI) local bus (e.g., Apple Power Macintosh 9500, PowerComputing PowerCenter 120).

SOLUTIONS

Open the Illustrator file in Illustrator 6.0 and save it as a PDF file.

OR: Use the Adobe Acrobat PDF Writer driver to print the Illustrator document as a PDF file:

1. Select the PDF Writer printer driver in the Chooser. For instructions on installing the PDF Writer see Additional Information.
2. In Illustrator, open the document to be printed as a PDF.
3. Choose File > Print.
4. Click OK in the Print dialog box.
5. Name the PDF file, then click Save.

OR: Print the file to disk as a PostScript file from Illustrator, then distill the PostScript file using Adobe Acrobat Distiller 1.0.

OR: Save the document as a PDF file from Illustrator running on a Macintosh or Power Macintosh computer model that does not use a PCI local bus.

ADDITIONAL INFORMATION

Because the Acrobat PDF File Format plug-in module, which enables you to save an Illustrator document in PDF format, is not compatible with the Peripheral Component Interconnect (PCI) local bus, saving an Illustrator file in PDF format causes the system to return an error (e.g., "Application unexpectedly quit due to an error unknown.").

To install the PDF Writer included with the Illustrator 5.5:

1. Insert the Adobe Illustrator 5.5 Deluxe CD or Installer-Disk 1 installation disk.
2. Start the Adobe Illustrator 5.5 Installer.
3. In the Install Script window, choose Custom Install from the pop-up menu.
4. In the Check Features to be Installed list, select Adobe Acrobat Software, then click Install. The Adobe Acrobat Software custom install option installs the PDF Writer printer driver in the Extensions folder and an Adobe Illustrator 5.5 folder containing the Acrobat software.

Alert "...shut down your computer now?" After Pressing Any Key in Illustrator 5.5 or Later

ISSUE

When you press any key while running Adobe Illustrator 5.5 or later on a 68000-series (68K) Macintosh, the system returns the alert "Are you sure you want to shut down your computer now?" System 7.5.1 is installed.

SOLUTIONS

Restart your Macintosh.

OR: Update to System 7.5.3 or later.

OR: Do not press the Power key while running Illustrator 5.5 or later in System 7.5.1.

ADDITIONAL INFORMATION

If you press the Power key while running Illustrator 5.5 and later on a 68K Macintosh with System 7.5.1 installed, and then click Cancel in the shut down alert that appears, the system returns the shut down alert when you press any subsequent key.

The Power key can be used to shut down or restart a computer running System 7.5.1 and later. When you press the Power key, the system returns the alert "Are you sure you want to shut down your computer now?" with the option to Restart, Sleep, Cancel, or Shut Down.

If you click Cancel while running Illustrator 5.5 in System 7.5.1 or later on a Power Macintosh, or in System 7.5.3 or later on a 68K Macintosh, the system does not return the shut down alert when you press any subsequent key.

System Error Launching or Printing from Separator with QuickDraw GX Installed

ISSUE

When QuickDraw GX is installed, a system error occurs when you launch Adobe Separator 5.x or choose File > Print in Separator.

SOLUTION

Deinstall QuickDraw GX and restore PostScript Type 1 fonts.

To restore standard Macintosh printing for all applications:

1. Double-click on the Install QuickDraw GX icon on the QuickDraw GX disk.
2. Select Custom Remove from the pop-up menu in the Installer dialog box.
3. Select the following Custom Remove options: Base QuickDraw GX Software for this Macintosh, Base QuickDraw GX Software for any Macintosh, QuickDraw GX Utilities, ATM for QuickDraw GX, and All QuickDraw GX Drivers for Apple Printers.
4. Set the Destination Disk to the disk containing the system software; use the Switch Disk button to select another disk if your System is on another attached hard disk.
5. Click the Remove button. When complete, restart the Macintosh.

To restore PostScript Type 1 fonts:

1. Move all enabled font suitcases, located in the Fonts folder in the System Folder by default, to a different lo-

cation. Enabled suitcases contain converted TrueType versions of the PostScript Type 1 font in addition to the bitmap (screen) fonts.

2. Move fonts contained in the Archived Type 1 Fonts folder into the Fonts folder, and delete the empty Archived Type 1 Fonts folder.
3. Move other fonts enabled using the Type 1 Enabler application to another folder not accessed by any font management utility (e.g., Suitcase). Move the original archived copy of the Type 1 font back to the desired folder to make it available to the font management utility.
4. Reinstall a version of Adobe Type Manager other than ATM/GX 3.7.

ADDITIONAL INFORMATION

Adobe Separator 5.x does not support Apple QuickDraw GX.

Apple's QuickDraw GX is an updated version of QuickDraw, the language that controls Macintosh display and printing. QuickDraw GX enhances printing and font handling, and supports Portable Digital Documents (PDDs) and color management software. QuickDraw GX is included with System 7.5 and with printing utilities (e.g., Pierce Print Tools).

To support QuickDraw GX printing, applications must recognize GX printer drivers and include QuickDraw GX options in the Print and Page Setup dialog boxes. To support QuickDraw GX TrueType fonts, applications must recognize their extended character set, which includes up to 65,000 characters per font, and their "line layout" capabilities for text composition. QuickDraw GX-compatible applications automatically handle kerning, justification, special characters (e.g., automatic ligature substitution), proper use of swash and standard characters, morphing for weight and width, and formation of fractions and ordinals (e.g., superscripting "nd" in "2nd," "3" in "2 to the 3rd power").

System Error When Changing Drop Shadow Option for Pie Chart in Illustrator 5.0.x

ISSUE

When you select or deselect the Drop Shadow option in the Graph Style dialog box in Adobe Illustrator 5.0.x, a system error (e.g., Type 1) occurs.

SOLUTIONS

Use Illustrator 5.5 or later.

OR: In Adobe Illustrator 5.0.x, apply a solid fill to the pie chart and then change the Drop Shadow option:

1. Apply a solid fill (e.g., black) to pie chart areas where graduated fills are applied.
2. Select the entire pie chart with the Selection tool, then choose Object > Graph > Style.
3. Select or deselect Drop Shadow in the Graph Style dialog box, then click OK.
4. Reapply graduated fills to the pie chart.

ADDITIONAL INFORMATION

A system error (e.g., Type 1 error) occurs in Illustrator 5.0.x when you change the Drop Shadow option of a pie chart that has a graduated fill applied.

Filter or System Error When Launching Illustrator 6.0 on 12-Inch Monitor

ISSUE

When you launch Adobe Illustrator 6.0 on a Macintosh with a low-resolution startup monitor (e.g., Apple 12-inch, Macintosh Color Classic), Illustrator returns one of the following errors while loading a plug-in filter:

"A filter has occurred: PARM" appears when loading the Inkpen plug-in.

"The application 'unknown' has unexpectedly quit, because of an error type [varies] has occurred." when loading the Online Guide Access plug-in.

"Sorry a system error has occurred. 'Adobe Illustrator 6.0' unimplemented trap." when loading the Text Find plug-in.

"Upper/Lower Case filter could not allocate global storage record." when loading the Change Case plug-in.

SOLUTIONS

Update to Adobe Illustrator 6.0.1.

OR: Launch Illustrator 6.0 on a Macintosh with a high-resolution (i.e., 640 x 480 pixels or higher) startup monitor.

OR: Prevent Illustrator 6.0 from loading plug-in filters by moving the Plug-ins folder to another location (e.g., the desktop) before launching Illustrator.

ADDITIONAL INFORMATION

Illustrator 6.0 requires a startup monitor with a resolution of 640 x 480 pixels or greater to load its plug-in files. If you launch Illustrator 6.0 on a Macintosh with a startup monitor whose resolution is 512 x 384 pixel or less, and the Ink Pen, Online Guide Access, or Text Find plug-in is installed, a filter error or system error occurs. If the Ink Pen, Online Guide Access, or Text Find filters are not installed, Illustrator 6.0 launches without error, but the Filter menu will not display and some installed plug-ins will not be unavailable (e.g., Plug-in Tools).

Illustrator 6.0.1 does not require a startup monitor with a resolution of 640 x 480 pixels or greater to load its plug-in files.

System Error When Importing Text into Illustrator 5.x and Later on Macintosh with PCI Local Bus

ISSUE

After clicking Import in the Import Text dialog box in Adobe Illustrator 5.0 and later, a system error (e.g., freeze, Type 1) occurs. Illustrator is running on a Macintosh with a Peripheral Component Interconnect (PCI) local bus (e.g., Power Macintosh 9500, 8500, 7500, 7200).

SOLUTIONS

Copy and paste the text into Illustrator instead of importing the text using the Import Text command.

OR: Save the text file in text-only format before importing using the Import Text command.

OR: Import the RTF file into Illustrator running on a Macintosh without a PCI local bus .

ADDITIONAL INFORMATION

Illustrator 5.0 and later imports RTF files using the XTND for Illustrator 1.3 plug-in filter, which is not compatible with the PCI local bus. Importing an RTF file in Illustrator 5.0 or later on a Macintosh with a PCI local bus causes a system error (e.g., freeze, Type 1) to occur. Illustrator 5.0 and later installs the XTND for Illustrator 1.3 plug-in filter in the Claris Translators folder in the Claris folder in the System Folder.

Illustrator 5.0 and later uses the Text plug-in filter, which is compatible with the PCI local bus, to import text from the clipboard or import a text-only file.

Printing Problems

MAC OS / WINDOWS

Q I have a document that won't print—all I get is a "Limitcheck" error message. What's wrong?

A Whenever you get a limitcheck error, it means that something in your document exceeds some kind of PostScript limit—often because it's too complex. You can get a good idea what the cause is from the "Offending Command" that accompanies the limitcheck error. An offending command of "Fill" typically indicates that a blend, mask, or pattern is too complex; an offending command of "Curveto" usually means a path has too many points; and a "Clip" offending command generally means a mask is too complex.

To solve a limitcheck problem, you'll need to simplify the element or elements that are too complex. To do so, start by setting a higher flatness value.

The flatness setting determines the number of straight-line segments that are used to define a curve, and it affects how accurately a curve is drawn. Curves are made up of small line segments—the smaller the line segments, the more detailed and complex the curve. With higher flatness values, curves don't contain as many line segments and therefore don't retain as much detail and accuracy, but will be less complex and easier to print.

In Illustrator 5.0 and later, the only way you can set a flatness value is indirectly, by changing your "Output Resolution" setting. (For information on setting flatness values in versions of Illustrator prior to 5.0, see the Adobe Illustrator User Guide for that version.) To calculate a flatness value, Illustrator 5.0 or later takes the actual resolution of your output device and divides it by the "Output Resolution" value assigned that object. For example, if you print to a 2400-dpi imagesetter and an object's "Output Resolution" value is 800, its flatness value will be 3 ($2400 \div 800 = 3$).

There are two ways to set the "Output Resolution" setting (and therefore the flatness value) for objects in your illustrations. Whenever you draw an object, it automatically uses your illustration's default flatness value, which is determined by the "Output Resolution" setting in the "Document Setup" dialog box. If you want to change the default flatness setting for your illustration, select "Document Setup..." from the File menu, and in the "Document Setup" dialog box, change the "Output Resolution" value. The new value will take effect for objects you create thereafter (objects already drawn will retain their original flatness values).

To change the flatness values of any object you've already created, select the object, choose "Attributes..." from the Object menu, and alter the "Output Resolution" setting in the "Attributes" dialog box.

If you're not sure what flatness value to use, start with a value of 3. At that setting, curves will rarely look noticeably different from those with a lower setting, but your illustration will print far more quickly. To increase the flatness value (and therefore speed print times) for individual objects, select them and use the "Attributes" dialog box to decrease their "Output Resolution" setting.

If increasing your flatness value doesn't eliminate limitcheck errors, try splitting complex paths. The "Split Long Paths" option will do this automatically. To use this feature in Illustrator 5.0 and later, make a backup copy of your illustration, then choose "Document Setup..." from the File menu. In the "Document Setup" dialog box, select the "Split Long Paths" option. When you do so, Illustrator uses the "Output Resolution" setting in the same dialog box to determine how it must split paths to ensure they aren't too complex for your output device's resolution. For the maximum amount of path splitting, set your "Output Resolution" to 9600, and click "OK." (NOTE: In earlier versions of Illustrator, the "Split Long Paths" option is located in the "Preferences" dialog box.)

To see how choosing "Split Long Paths" affected your illustration, select "Artwork" from the View menu—you'll see a series of horizontal lines that represent where Illustrator split your paths. (These lines don't print.) Splitting paths may make editing them afterward more difficult. If you want to restore your paths, either revert to the backup copy you made of your illustration before using the "Split Long Paths" option, or rejoin your paths manually.

The "Split Long Paths" option does not affect text, masks, compound paths, or stroked paths. If you need to split such elements, cut them with the scissors tool.

Q I painted an object with a process color, set the object to overprint, and positioned it on top of another

object. But when I printed color separations, some of the inks appeared to knock out, not overprint. Why?

A You're right that some of the inks may not be overprinting. Here's a look at why. When you set an object to overprint, you're specifying that all of the inks used to print the object must overprint. However, you cannot overprint a screen of one ink on another screen of the same ink. You've probably applied to your top and bottom objects process colors that have one or more inks in common. When you printed your separations, the shared inks in the top object would have knocked out the shared inks in the background object where they overlapped, leaving you with only the screened amount of the top object printing.

An example may make this more clear: Let's say that you create an object and apply a color to it that is composed of 40% cyan, 60% magenta, and 20% yellow. This object is set to overprint. You move it on top of another object that has 70% cyan applied to it, and then print separations. The 40% cyan cannot overprint another cyan screen, so any area where the 40% cyan overlaps the 70% cyan, only the 40% cyan prints. However, the 60% magenta and the 20% yellow overprint as expected.

You have several options for fixing the problem. First, if you're overprinting the object to avoid misregistration on press, you can relax. The two objects contain common inks, so there will be no light gaps even if misregistration occurs. Simply turn overprinting off. (You may also want to talk to your commercial printer about other ways to account for misregistration on press.) Alternatively, you can analyze the color to see if you can do without the ink that's knocking out. In the example given, you could delete cyan from the top color and let the other inks overprint; or, on a Macintosh, you could delete cyan from the top color and use the Trap filter to trap the other colors (choose "Trap..." from the Pathfinder submenu on the Filter menu). Remember that overprinting one process color on another can result in unpredictable colors on press. For more information on overprinting, see the Adobe Illustrator Color Guide, pages 11–16 (Windows), or the Adobe Illustrator 6.0 User Guide, pages 242–4 and 248–9 (Macintosh).

Black-and-White (1-bit) TIFF Image Doesn't Separate from Illustrator 6.0 or Later

ISSUE

When you print separations from an Adobe Illustrator file that includes a 1-bit TIFF image, Illustrator 6.0 or later either does not print the TIFF image or prints it on the wrong color separation(s).

SOLUTION

Apply a fill color to the TIFF image & then print separations.

ADDITIONAL INFORMATION

When you import a 1-bit TIFF image into Illustrator 6.0 or later, Illustrator applies a fill and stroke of None to it. When printing separations of a file containing a 1-bit TIFF image with a fill and stroke of None, Illustrator either does not print the TIFF image, or prints the TIFF image on the same separation as another color in the Illustrator file. For example, when you print separations of an Illustrator 6.0 or later file containing a Yellow circle behind a 1-bit TIFF image with a fill and stroke of None, Illustrator prints the 1-bit TIFF image on the yellow separation instead of on the black separation.

If a 1-bit TIFF is the backmost object in the Illustrator file, it will print on all plates.

Error "The page size selected in Page Setup is smaller..." Printing Separations in Illustrator 6.0

ISSUE

When you print color separations from Adobe Illustrator 6.0 or later, Illustrator returns the error, "The page size selected in Page Setup is smaller than the page size specified in the Separation Setup dialog. Your output may be clipped or fail to print properly."

SOLUTIONS

Do one or more of the following to ensure the page size and imageable area selected in the Separation Setup and Page Setup dialog boxes are the same:

A. Select the same PPD file in the printer driver's setup dialog box in the Chooser and in Illustrator's Separation Setup dialog box.
B. Select the same page size in the Page Setup and Separation dialog box.
C. If you are using LaserWriter 8.3.x or earlier, click Options in the Page Setup dialog box and select the Larger Print Area (Fewer Downloadable Fonts) option before printing separations.

ADDITIONAL INFORMATION

Adobe Illustrator 6.0 and later use the specified PPD file, the page size selected in the Separation Setup dialog box, and the page size and options selected in the Page Setup dialog box to determine a printer's imageable area. When the page size and imageable area selected in the Page Setup dialog box and Separation Setup dialog box do not match, Illustrator will return an error.

Some PPD files contain page sizes with multiple imageable area dimensions. For example, the Apple LaserWriter 16/600 PS PPD file contains a US Letter (588-by-768) and US Letter Small (522-by-730) page size. In the Separation Setup dialog box, the dimensions following the page size name (e.g., 588-by-768) indicate the imageable area of the selected page size.

The Larger Print Area (Fewer Downloadable Fonts) option in the Page Setup dialog box adjusts a page's imageable area. When the PPD file specified for the printer driver contains a page size with multiple imageable area dimensions, the Page Setup dialog box usually defaults to the smallest imageable area. To print a page size with the largest imageable area, click Options in the Page Setup dialog box and select the Larger Print Area (Fewer Downloadable Fonts) option before printing. LaserWriter 8.4 and later do not include the Larger Print Area option.

The Use Page Setup option in the Document Setup dialog box does not affect the page size specified in Separation Setup dialog box.

Error "The PPD file for the current printer does not match..." when Printing from Illustrator 6.0 or Later

ISSUE

When you print separations from Adobe Illustrator 6.0.x or later, Illustrator returns the error "The PPD file for the current printer does not match the PPD file used by the Separation Setup dialog. Your output may be clipped or fail to print properly."

SOLUTION

Ensure the same PostScript Printer Description (PPD) file is selected in Illustrator's Separation Setup dialog box and in the printer driver in the Chooser (e.g., LaserWriter 8.x).

ADDITIONAL INFORMATION

Illustrator 6.0 and later use information from the PPD file specified in the printer driver and in the Separation Setup dialog box to determine the page size and imageable area available at the printer. If the PPD file specified in the printer driver does not match the one specified in Illustrator's Separation Setup dialog box, Illustrator 6.0 and later will return an error when you print separations.

Specifying the same PPD file in the printer driver and in Illustrator 6.0 and later ensures that Illustrator uses the identical page size and imageable area information.

Memory-related PostScript Error ("VMerror," "limitcheck") When Printing from Illustrator Troubleshooting Guide

ISSUE

When you print an Adobe Illustrator 5.x or later document to a PostScript printer, the PostScript error, "VMerror," "limitcheck," or "Fatal System Error; OffendingCommand: [varies]," occurs.

SYMPTOMS

The printer blinks or begins to print the document, then stops (i.e., the printer resets itself) before printing the document.

The printer takes a long time to print the document.

SOLUTIONS

Do one or more of the following:

A. Reset the printer's memory by turning the printer or the RIP off, waiting approximately 30 seconds, then turning it back on.

B. When the document includes downloadable fonts, download the outline (printer) fonts to the printer's RAM or hard disk, or decrease the number of downloadable fonts used in the document.

C. When printing to a desktop printer, print with a smaller paper size selected in the Page Setup dialog box (e.g., Letter instead of Legal).

D. When printing curved lines, increase the flatness value of the Illustrator objects. To increase the flatness value: Change the Output resolution in the Attributes tab (Illustrator 7.0) or the Attributes dialog box (Illustrator 5.x and 6.x):
   1. Choose Edit > Select All.
   2. Choose Window > Show Attributes (Illustrator 7.0) or Object > Attributes (Illustrator 5.x and 6.x).
   3. In the Attributes palette, enter a number in the Output text box smaller than the existing number, then press Enter.

NOTE: To determine the flatness at which an object prints, divide the printer resolution by the object's output resolution. For example, an object with an 800 dpi output resolution prints to a 2400 dpi printer with a flatness of 3.

OR: In Illustrator 5.5 and later, create a Riders file to increase the flatness of Illustrator objects. When printing to a 300 dpi printer, increase flatness to 3, when printing to a 1270 dpi printer increase flatness to 6, and when printing to a 2450 dpi printer increase flatness to 8.

E. Select Split Long Paths in the Document Setup dialog box:

   NOTE: Saving or printing with Split Long Paths selected alters the paths, but the altered paths are not saved until you save the document.
   1. Make a backup of the document.
   2. Choose File > Document Setup.
   3. In the Paths section of the Document Setup dialog box, select Split Long Paths, type "5080" in the Output resolution text box, then click OK. Specifying 5080 for the output resolution, which is the maximum setting, ensures that Illustrator splits as many paths as possible.

F. In Illustrator 6.0.x or later, convert gradient fills into masked blends using the Expand command (Illustrator 6.0.x) or the Expand Fill command (Illustrator 7.0):
   1. Make a backup of the document.
   2. Select the gradient object, then choose Object > Expand Fill (Illustrator 7.0) or Object > Expand (Illustrator 6.0.x).
   3. In the Expand Gradient/Patterns dialog box, type 255 in the Number of Steps text box, then click OK.

G. Reduce the number of steps used in blended objects.

H. Simplify the patterns used in the document (e.g., avoid using blends, gradient fills, or fonts in a pattern).

I. In Illustrator 6.0 or later, select an object with a pattern fill, then choose Object > Expand Fill (Illustrator 7.0) or Object > Expand (Illustrator 6.x).

J. Ungroup elements and nested groups.

K. Change the stacking order by moving complex elements to the back of the current layer or to a different layer.

L. Simplify drawn objects by decreasing the number of points on each path. Before drawing with the Freehand or Autotrace tool, increase the Freehand tolerance and Auto Trace gap value in the General Preferences dialog box to reduce the number of points created for each path.

M. Limit the number of complex elements or simplify complex elements. The offending command included in the PostScript error may indicate the type of element causing the PostScript error. To determine which elements are complex, see Additional Information.

N. Remove unused patterns, custom colors, and gradient fills:

In Illustrator 7.0:

1. Choose Window > Show Swatches to display the Swatches palette..
2. From the pop-up menu in the Swatches palette, select Select All Unused.
3. Click the trash can icon at the bottom of the Swatches palette.

In Illustrator 5.x and 6.x:

1. Choose Object > Patterns, Object > Custom Colors, or Object > Gradients.
2. In the Patterns, Custom Colors, or Gradients dialog box, click Select All Unused, then click Delete.
3. Click OK to close the dialog box, then save the document.

O. Print at a lower resolution.

P. Limit the number of exit server applications (e.g., calibration software, screening software, error handler software) at an imagesetter.

Q. When printing to a Linotronic imagesetter, perform a Disk Restore. When printing to any other imagesetter, delete the font cache.

R. Print to a device that has more printer memory.

ADDITIONAL INFORMATION

The PostScript errors, "VMerror" or "limitcheck" occur when you print a document whose complexity requires more memory than is available at the printer. The type of elements used in an Illustrator document, rather than the document's file size, affect how much memory the printer needs to process the document.

When the printer is unable to return an error because of low memory, printing stops. When the printer has a very small amount of memory available, instead of terminating the print job, the printer may attempt to print the document using the available memory. Elements are then imaged in smaller groups, using the limited memory, resulting in extremely long processing times. The job may not print at all, depending on the memory requirements of the remaining elements in the file.

In Illustrator 6.0 and later, the Expand command converts gradients and patterns into a series of masked objects, and converts gradient fills into a masked blend. To specify the number of steps in the blend, choose Object > Expand Fill (Illustrator 7.0) or Object > Expand (Illustrator 6.x). Specifying 255 steps in the Expand Gradient/Pattern dialog box enables Illustrator to use the maximum number of steps possible for the blend.

When printing, some applications download preparation files that occupy printer memory. Clearing the printer's memory after printing from an application that downloads a printer preparation file ensures that the maximum amount of memory is available for printing.

PostScript interpreters image elements from the back layer to the front layer, one layer at a time. When a "VM-error" or "limitcheck" error message occurs and only a portion of the document prints, the next element or layer that should have printed is most likely the element that exceeded the printer's available memory.

The greater the number or combination of complex effects and elements, the more memory the document will require to print. Complex effects and elements include masks, EPS files containing clipping paths, compound paths (e.g., text converted to paths), pattern fills, gradient fills, and bitmap EPS files.

Illustrator Custom Color Blends Separate as Process

ISSUE

After you separate an Adobe Illustrator EPS file containing blended objects painted with a custom color (i.e., spot color), the intermediate blend steps print on the process separations instead of on the custom color separation.

SOLUTIONS

Open the EPS file in Illustrator 5.x or later, then replace the blend object with a gradient fill.

OR: When the EPS file doesn't contain all four process colors, redefine each of the custom colors as 100% of one of the process colors (e.g., redefine Red as 100% magenta, or Blue as 100% cyan), then reblend the objects.

OR: Manually create a graduation between two custom colors by creating a blend of two objects:

NOTE: Illustrator cannot display both finished blended objects, but it will print them as expected on the custom color separation.

1. Create the beginning and end blend objects.
2. Select the objects and choose Edit > Copy.
3. Apply a custom color to one of the objects, and a 0% tint of the same custom color to the other.
4. Blend the objects.
5. Choose Edit > Paste In Front to paste a copy of the objects you copied in step 2 in front of the original objects.
6. Apply the second custom color to one of the pasted objects, and a 0% tint of the same custom color to the

other pasted object. Apply the second custom color in the opposite direction of the blend created in step 3 (e.g., if you applied the 100% tint of the first custom color to the beginning object in step 3, apply the 0% tint of the second custom color to the beginning object).

7. Apply an Overprint attribute (Illustrator 7.0) or paint style (Illustrator 5.x and 6.x) to the objects painted with the second custom color (i.e., the blend objects in the topmost blend).
8. Blend the objects painted with the second custom color.
9. Save the file as an EPS file.

NOTE: To prevent a moire pattern when printing separations, specify a different screen angle for each custom color (e.g., 45 degree Red, 0 degree Blue).

ADDITIONAL INFORMATION

Illustrator 5.x and later enable you to create custom color-to-custom color gradient fills, but not custom color-to-custom color blends. When creating a blend between objects painted with two different custom colors, Illustrator paints the intermediate steps of the blend with the process equivalent of the blended custom colors, causing the object to print on the process separations.

In Illustrator 5.x and 6.x, custom colors are named spot inks defined using the CMYK color model. Illustrator lists spot inks under the Custom Color option in the Paint Style palette. Process colors are unnamed colors defined by a percentage of cyan, magenta, yellow, and black using the Process color option in the Paint Style palette.

In Illustrator 7.0, spot colors (i.e., custom colors) are named spot inks defined using the CMYK, RGB, HSB or Grayscale color models. Spot inks have an icon with a dot in the Swatches palette, and you can double-click the swatch to view the Swatch Options dialog box, which lists the color mode (i.e., process or spot). Process colors can be either named or unnamed colors defined by a percentage of cyan, magenta, yellow, and black using the Color palette and selecting the CMYK model from the pop-up menu.

WINDOWS

Q (4.1 only) I've applied horizontal scaling to some text in Illustrator 4.1, and it looks fine on screen. However, it prints unscaled. Did I do something wrong?

A No—Illustrator did. When you print to a PostScript printer, Illustrator 4.1 does not send the horizontal-scale percentage specified in the "Type Style" dialog box to the PostScript printer driver, causing the type to print unscaled. However, there are several ways for you to get the horizontally scaled text to print correctly.

You can save the Illustrator file as an EPS, then place it into a target application, such as PageMaker—or even back into Illustrator. It will print correctly there.

If you're going to print directly from Illustrator, the easiest way to work around the problem and leave your text editable is to use the scale-dialog tool (—the one with the plus sign) to scale the text. Here's how.

1. Select the text, then select the scale-dialog tool.
2. Click once on the page. The point where you click determines the point from which the text will be scaled (i.e., the scaling origin point).
3. In the "Scale" dialog box, select "Non-Uniform Scale," then type the desired scaling percentage in the "Horizontal" text box.
4. Click "OK" to apply the horizontal scaling.

You have a few additional options for printing horizontally scaled text. For instance, you can convert the text to outlines using the "Create Outlines" command prior to printing the file. You can also open your Illustrator 4.1 file in Illustrator 4.0.3 or earlier (if you have it and Windows 3.x)—it will print correctly from there. Or, if you have access to Adobe Acrobat, you can use the Acrobat PDFWriter printer driver to create a PDF file of the horizontally scaled text, which will print correctly to your PostScript (or other) printer. Finally, you can print your 4.1 file to a non-PostScript printer if you have one; the horizontal scaling will print successfully there.

Creating a PostScript Print File from Illustrator 4.x for Windows

To create a PostScript print file from Adobe Illustrator 4.x, connect your PostScript printer to the File port, and name the PostScript file when printing from Illustrator.

To install a PostScript printer driver, install either the Microsoft Windows PostScript 3.5 or later printer driver or the Adobe PostScript printer driver 2.1 or later (Adobe PS):

1. Open the Windows Control Panel, then double-click on the Printers icon.
2. In the Printers dialog box, click Add.
3. Select Install Unlisted or Updated Printer from the List of Printers, then click Install.
4. Insert the printer driver disk and locate the printer driver by entering the path location or by clicking Browse.
5. Choose the appropriate model for your PostScript printer, then follow the prompts to install the printer driver. The driver you install appears in the list of Installed Printers in the Printers dialog box.

To connect the PostScript printer to the File port:

1. In the Printers Control Panel, select the PostScript printer driver from the Installed Printers list, then click Connect.
2. In the Connect dialog box, select File from the Ports list box, then click OK. The PostScript printer driver appears in the Installed Printers list with the words "on FILE" at the end of its name.
3. With the newly configured PostScript printer driver selected, click Set As Default Printer, then click Close.

To install PostScript fonts using Adobe Type Manager (ATM):

1. In the Printers Control Panel, select File as the default printer for the PostScript printer driver.

2. Open the ATM Control Panel by double-clicking its icon, which is located in the Main group of Windows Program Manager, by default.
3. Select all fonts in the Installed ATM Fonts list, then click Remove.
4. In the Remove [font name] window, select No Confirmation to Remove Fonts, deselect Delete Fonts from Disk, then click Add.
5. In the Add ATM Fonts dialog box, select Autodownload for PostScript Driver.
6. Click in the Directories list and navigate to the directory containing the font files. By default, ATM installs the font files in the Psfonts\Pfm directory.
7. Select the fonts you want to install from the Available Fonts list, then click Add.
8. If desired, change your default printer in the Windows Printer Control Panel.

To print to disk from Illustrator:

1. Open the Illustrator document you want to print to disk.
2. Choose File > Print Setup.
3. Select the PostScript printer driver on File from the Specific Printer pop-up menu, then click OK.
4. Choose File > Print, then click OK.
5. Type a filename, using the .Ps or .Prn filename extension if desired, and a path location in the Output File Name text box, then click OK.

Limitcheck PostScript Errors When Printing From Illustrator 4.x

ISSUE

When printing from Adobe Illustrator 4.x to a PostScript printer, a limitcheck PostScript error (e.g., "limitcheck; OffendingCommand: clip," ""limitcheck; OffendingCommand: imagemask,") appears or the Illustrator document processes at the printer but does not print.

SOLUTION

Do one or more of the following to simplify the Illustrator document:

A. Open a copy of the Illustrator document, select "Split long paths on Save/Print" in the "Preferences" dialog box and reprint:

   NOTE: Saving or printing with "Split long paths on Save/Print" alters the paths in your Illustrator document.

   1. Save the Illustrator document with a new name.
   2. Choose "Preferences..." from the Edit menu and select "Split long paths on Save/Print."
   3. Enter 5080 for the "Output resolution" and click "OK." 5080, which is the maximum dpi allowed in the "Output options box," ensures the most path splitting.

   NOTE: Settings in the Illustrator "Preferences" dialog box are application settings and affect all documents. Deselect "Split long paths on Save/Print" after printing.

B. Simplify drawn objects by decreasing the number of points per path. When drawing with the Freehand or Autotrace tool, increase the "Freehand tolerance" value and "Auto Trace gap" distance in the "Preferences" dialog box to reduce the number of points created per path.

C. Increase the Flatness value for the Illustrator drawn objects:

   1. Choose "Select All" from the Edit menu.
   2. Select "Paint Style..." from the Paint menu, enter the desired Flatness value and click "OK." When printing to a 300 dpi printer, increase the Flatness to 3, when printing to a 1270 dpi printer, increase the Flatness to 6 and for a 2450 dpi printer, increase the Flatness to 8.

   NOTE: The lower the resolution of the printer, the greater the effect the Flatness value has on drawn curves in an Illustrator document. When the Flatness setting is too high for the output resolution, flat segments appear along the curves in the path.

D. Create masks and patterns using a collection of simple shapes rather than a single complex object. This is especially important when masking shapes or using patterns.

E. Decrease the number of PostScript fonts download to the printer by changing the fonts applied in the Illustrator document to printer resident fonts or converting the type in the Illustrator document to outlines.

F. Limit the number of patterns, masks, and compound paths used.

G. Print the Illustrator document at a lower resolution. Complex illustrations are simpler to print to a 300 dpi desktop printer than to a 2540 dpi imagesetter.

ADDITIONAL INFORMATION

Limitcheck PostScript errors occur when a PostScript implementation limit has been exceeded. For example, when the printer memory requirements of file, or a limit as defined in PostScript has been reached. The offending command following the PostScript error indicates what was being process at the time the error occurred and can help in isolating the cause to the Limitcheck error.

Offending commands related to complexity of objects:

charpath Complex text or text effects.

clip, eoclip Graduated or radial fills, complex or compound paths, text effects, masks.

curveto Complex curve paths.

fill, eofill Complex or compound paths.

lineto, moveto Paths composed of many points (may include converted PICT graphics).

makefont Text effects (includes scaled, skewed, rotated, or reflected text).

stroke Complex paths, paths with complex fills and outline strokes, or converted PICT graphic.

image Bitmap or paint-type images.

imagemask 1-bit or paint-type bitmap image, bitmap fonts.

NOTE: A complex path can be described as one that contains many points; a path may be too complex for the current "flatness" settings of an element in your illustration application. Refer to your user manual for more information about flatness settings.

The number of times a path is split by the "Split long paths on Save/Print" option is determined by the "Output resolution" setting in the "Preferences" dialog box, the type of fill applied to the path and the path's Flatness setting. "Split long paths on Save/Print" has the greatest effect on paths filled with a pattern fill. "Split long paths on Save/Print" does not affect compound paths, masks or unfilled paths. Objects painted with both a stroke and a fill are split into two paths by "Split long paths on Save/Print," one path painted with a fill and no stroke and the second path painted with a stroke and no fill. When "Split long paths on Save/Print" is selected, paths with a low Flatness value applied in the "Paint Styles" dialog box split more than paths with a greater Flatness value.

Once an illustration is printed or saved with "Split long paths on Save/Print" selected, the split paths in the illustration cannot be automatically reassembled.

To rejoin sections of a split path:

1. Select "Artwork & Template" or "Artwork Only" from the View menu.
2. Position a horizontal ruler guide over the path segments dividing the paths created by saving or printing with "Split long paths on Save/Print" selected.
3. Open each segmented path section by selecting and deleting the horizontal path dividing them.
4. Select two of the overlapping end points where the horizontal guide touches the path and choose "Join" from the Arrange menu.
5. Repeat steps 3 - 4 until the split path is joined.

TIFF Exported From Illustrator 4.x Prints With Bounding Box

ISSUE

A TIFF file exported from Adobe Illustrator 4.x and placed into a layout application (e.g., Adobe PageMaker) displays and prints with a black border around part or all of its bounding box.

SOLUTIONS

Open the Illustrator file in Illustrator 4.x, then export it in 8 Color, 16 Color, or 256 Color format:

1. Open the Illustrator file and choose File > Export Art.
2. In the Export Art dialog box, select TIF -Tag Image File Format from the Export type pop-up menu, then click Options.
3. Select the 8 Color, 16 Color, or 256 Color option from the Format section of the TIFF Output Filter Setup dialog box, then click OK.
4. In the Export Art dialog box, name the file with a ".tif" extension, then click Export.

OR: Open the Illustrator file in Illustrator 4.x and export it as a 96 dpi Bi-Level, 16 Gray, 256 Gray, or 24 bit RGB Color format TIFF file:

1. Open the Illustrator file and choose File > Export Art.
2. In the Export Art dialog box, select TIF -Tag Image File Format from the Export type pop-up menu, then click Options.
3. Select the Bi-Level, 16 Gray, 256 Gray, or 24 bit RGB Color option from the Format section of the TIFF Output Filter Setup dialog box.
4. Select Screen option from the Resolution section of the TIFF Output Filter Setup dialog box, then click OK.
5. In the Export Art dialog box, name the file with a ".tif" extension, then click Export.

OR: Open the original Illustrator file in Adobe Photoshop 3.0x and save the rasterized Illustrator artwork in the desired TIFF format.

ADDITIONAL INFORMATION

TIFF files exported from Illustrator 4.x in any of the following formats display with a black border around all or part of their bouding boxes: Bi-Level, 16 Gray, 256 Gray, or 24 bit RGB Color format with the Printer Resolution option or a custom Resolution option selected in the TIFF Output Filter Setup dialog box.

TIFF files exported from Illustrator 4.x in any of the following formats don't display with a black border around all or part of their bounding boxes: 8 Color, 16 Color, or 256 Color format with any resolution setting and Bi-Level, 16 Gray, 256 Gray, or 24 bit RGB Color format with the Screen Resolution option selected in the TIFF Output Filter Setup dialog box.

PostScript Font Substitution When Printing from Illustrator 4.1 in Windows 3.x

ISSUE

When you print an Adobe Illustrator 4.1 file to a PostScript printer using the Adobe PSPrinter 2.1.1 or 3.0.x printer driver (PSPrinter), Illustrator returns the error "Can't download the font, Please re-install the Type 1 font." The Illustrator file prints, but text formatted with a PostScript font prints in the printer's default font (e.g., Courier, Times).

SYMPTOM

Text formatted with the same PostScript font prints correctly from other applications (e.g. Windows Write).

SOLUTIONS

Add a [PostScript, Printer] section and a "softfonts=1" line to the end of the Win.ini file before printing using the Adobe PSPrinter 2.1.1 or later:

1. Make a backup copy of the Win.ini file, located in the Windows directory.
2. Open the original Win.ini file in a text editor that can save in text-only format (e.g., Windows Write, Notepad).
3. Add the following two lines to the end of the Win.ini file:

```
[PostScript,<port>]
softfonts=1
```

where <port> is your active printer port (e.g., [PostScript, LPT2]).

4. Repeat step 3 for each active printer port. For example:

```
[PostScript,LPT2]
softfonts=1
[PostScript,FILE]
softfonts=1
```

5. Save the Win.ini file in text-only format, then restart Windows.

OR: Remove and re-add the fonts in Adobe Type Manager (ATM) 3.0x with the Microsoft PostScript 3.5x printer driver specified as the default printer:

1. Install the Microsoft PostScript 3.5x printer driver if it is not already installed. For instructions, see Additional Information.
2. Specify the Microsoft 3.5x printer driver as the default printer in the Printers Control Panel.
4. In the ATM 3.0x Control Panel, select all fonts in the Installed ATM Fonts list, then click Remove.
5. In the Remove dialog box, select the No Confirmation to Remove Fonts option, deselect the Delete Fonts From Disk option, then click Yes or Yes to All.
6. After removing the fonts, click Add in the ATM Control Panel.
7. In the Add ATM Fonts dialog box, select the Autodownload for PostScript Driver option.
   NOTE: When no Microsoft PostScript printer driver is installed, the Install Without Copying Files and Autodownload for PostScript Driver options are dimmed.
8. Navigate to the directory containing the font files to add. By default, ATM stores font files in the Psfonts\Pfm directory.
9. Select the fonts you want to install from the Available Fonts list, then click Add.
10. Exit the ATM Control Panel, then restart Windows.

ADDITIONAL INFORMATION

When you print a file containing text formatted with PostScript fonts, the printer driver downloads the outline (i.e., printer) font files for any PostScript fonts that are not resident at the printer. If the printer driver doesn't download a non-resident font, text formatted with it prints in the printer's default font (e.g., Courier, Times).

When Illustrator 4.1 prints, it reads the "softfonts=" line in the Win.ini file to determine if the print file contains downloadable fonts. If the softfonts line equals one or greater (e.g., "softfonts=1"), Illustrator instructs the printer driver to download the PostScript fonts used in the Illustrator file. If the softfonts line equals zero (e.g., "softfonts=0") or if there is no softfonts line in the Win.ini file, Illustrator 4.1 does not instruct the printer driver to download PostScript fonts and returns the error "Can't download the font, Please re-install the Type 1 font.

When you add fonts in ATM 3.0x while a PCL printer driver or PSPrinter 2.1.1 or 3.0.x is installed as the default printer, ATM lists the installed PostScript fonts only in the Atm.ini file. It does not add a [PostScript, <port>] section, softfont line, or font entries to the Win.ini file.

When you add fonts in ATM 3.0x with the Autodownload for PostScript Driver option selected in the Add ATM Fonts dialog box and the Microsoft 3.5x or later printer driver installed as the default printer driver, ATM adds a softfont line and font entries to each [PostScript,<port>] section of the Win.ini file that specifies a different port. For example:

```
[PostScript,LPT1]
ATM=placeholder
softfonts=4
softfont1=c:\psfonts\pfm\zjrg____.pfm,c:\psfonts\
  zjrg____.pfb
softfont2=c:\psfonts\pfm\zjrg____.pfm,c:\psfonts\
  zjrg____.pfb
softfont3=c:\psfonts\pfm\zjrg____.pfm,c:\psfonts\
  zjrg____.pfb
softfont4=c:\psfonts\pfm\zjrg____.pfm,c:\psfonts\
  zjrg____.pfb
[PostScript,FILE]
ATM=placeholder
softfonts=4
softfont1=c:\psfonts\pfm\zjrg____.pfm,c:\psfonts\
  zjrg____.pfb
softfont2=c:\psfonts\pfm\zjrg____.pfm,c:\psfonts\
  zjrg____.pfb
softfont3=c:\psfonts\pfm\zjrg____.pfm,c:\psfonts\
  zjrg____.pfb
softfont4=c:\psfonts\pfm\zjrg____.pfm,c:\psfonts\
  zjrg____.pfb
```

ATM does not add any font entries to the Win.ini file if the Autodownload for PostScript Driver option is not selected in the Add ATM Font dialog box.

To install the Microsoft 3.5x printer driver:

1. Insert the disk containing the PostScript printer driver (e.g., Windows installation disk).
2. Open the Printers Control Panel.
3. Click the Add button in the Printers dialog box.
4. Select the Install Unlisted or Updated Printer option from the List of Printers scrollbox, then click Install.
5. Locate the printer driver by entering its pathname or by clicking Browse.
6. Choose the appropriate model for your PostScript printer, then follow the prompts to install the printer driver. The PostScript printer driver you install will appear in the Installed Printers box in the Printers dialog box.

Horizontally Scaled Text Prints Unscaled to PostScript Printer from Illustrator 4.1

ISSUE

When you scale text horizontally by specifying a Horizontal Scale percentage in the Type Style dialog box in Adobe Illustrator 4.1, it prints unscaled to a PostScript printer.

SOLUTIONS

Save the Illustrator 4.1 file as an EPS file, then place the EPS file into Illustrator or a page layout application (e.g., Adobe PageMaker, QuarkXPress).

OR: Scale the text with the scale-dialog tool in Illustrator 4.1:

1. Select the text.
2. Press Alt while clicking in the document with the scale tool, or click in the document with the scale-dialog tool (i.e., the scale tool with a plus sign, available from the scale tool pop-up menu in the toolbox). The point where you click determines the point from which the text will be scaled (i.e., the scaling origin point).
3. In the Scale dialog box, select the Non-Uniform Scale option, then type the desired scaling percentage in the Horizontal text box.
4. Click OK to apply the horizontal scaling.
5. Use the direct-selection tool to resize the text rectangle to the desired width.

OR: Use the Create Outlines command to convert the horizontally-scaled text to outlines before printing.

OR: Open and print the Illustrator 4.1 file in Illustrator 4.0.3.

OR: Print to a non-PostScript (PCL) printer.

ADDITIONAL INFORMATION

When printing to a PostScript printer, Illustrator 4.1 does not send the Horizontal Scale percentage specified in the Type Style dialog box to the PostScript printer driver, causing the type to print unscaled. Type scaled horizontally with the scale tool prints scaled from Illustrator 4.1 to a PostScript printer.

When you print from Illustrator 4.1 to a PCL printer or when you print from Illustrator 4.0.3, type formatted with a Horizontal Scale percentage in the Type Style dialog box prints with the specified horizontal scaling.

PostScript Error "Undefined; OffendingCommand: Stack -mark-" Printing an Illustrator 4.1 EPS

ISSUE

When you print an imported Adobe Illustrator 4.1 EPS file to a PostScript printer, the printer returns the PostScript error "Undefined; OffendingCommand: Stack -mark-."

SOLUTIONS

Resave the EPS file in Illustrator 3 compatibility format with a Color or Black & White preview, then reimport the EPS file.

OR: Open the EPS file in Illustrator 4.0.3 , save the file in Illustrator 3 or Illustrator 88 format with a Black & White or Color preview, then reimport the EPS file.

OR: Open the EPS file in Illustrator 4.x, then print the EPS file.

OR: Open the Illustrator 4.1 EPS file in a text editor, remove the lines between the "%%PageTrailer" and "%%Trailer" comments, then reimport the EPS file.

NOTE: After modifying an EPS file in a text editor, the EPS file displays as a gray box.

ADDITIONAL INFORMATION

When Illustrator 4.1 saves a file in Illustrator 88 or Illustrator 1.1 format with a Color or Black & White preview, Illustrator inserts binary text and may include an alert message between the "%%PageTrailer" and "%%Trailer comments. When you print an Illustrator 4.1 Illustrator 88 or 1.1 formatted EPS file to a PostScript printer, the printer cannot interpret the lines between the "%%PageTrailer" and "%%Trailer" comments and returns the PostScript error "Undefined; Offending Command: Stack -mark-."

Illustrator 4.1 does not insert extra lines between the %%PageTrailer and %%Trailer comments when saving an EPS file in Illustrator 3 format. Illustrator 4.0.3 does not insert additional lines between the %%PageTrailer and %%Trailer comments.

To remove lines between the "%%PageTrailer" and "%%Trailer" comments in an Illustrator 4.1 EPS file: disclaimer: Adobe Systems does not support modifying an Illustrator file with a text editor. Familiarity with opening EPS files in a text editor and saving in text-only (e.g., ASCII) format is required. Experience with PostScript language is highly recommended. If alterations are incorrectly performed or the file is saved in the wrong format, the Illustrator file can be further damaged. Always modify a copy of the Illustrator EPS file. In the event of problems, revert to the original copy.

1. Open a copy of the Illustrator EPS file in a text editor that can save in text-only format (e.g., Windows Write, WordPad).
2. Remove the binary characters before the "!PS-Adobe-2.0 EPSF-1.2" comment in the first line.
   For example, change:
   ```
   –"  -u  i˘˘%!PS-Adobe-2.0 EPSF-1.2
   ```
   to:
   ```
   %!PS-Adobe-2.0 EPSF-1.2
   ```
3. Locate the "%%PageTrailer" and "%%Trailer" comments. For example:
   ```
   %%PageTrailer
   \£Ï'7ifl\–  GWZ»
   0Æ ¬ƒ>¯ø wB¯ø‡˘°ø  Saving this document in
     Adobe Illustrator 1.1 or Adobe Illustrator
     88 format may disable some Adobe Illustra-
     tor 3.0 editing features in this document
     when it is read ba
   %%Trailer
   ```
4. Remove the lines between the "%%PageTrailer" and "%%Trailer" comments so that it reads:
   ```
   %%PageTrailer
   %%Trailer
   ```
5. Remove the lines, which may be a thousand or more, that follow the "%%EOF" comment.
   NOTE: The Binary text before the "!PS-Adobe-2.0 EPSF-1.2" comment and following the "%%EOF" comment

describes the screen preview for the EPS file. After you remove the lines between the "%%PageTrailer" and "%%Trailer" comments, the screen preview is no longer useable. After you import the modified EPS file, the EPS file appears as a gray box. Opening an EPS file in Illustrator after you remove the lines between the "%%PageTrailer" and "%%Trailer" comments but do not remove the binary text before the "!PS-Adobe-2.0 EPSF-1.2" comment causes Illustrator to return the error "Can't open the illustration. The illustration doesn't start with the %!PS-Adobe- comment. Offending command: 'EPSF-1.2'."

6. Save the file in text-only format with the ".eps" filename extension.

MAC OS

Q *(5.5 only)* **Sometimes when I print gradient fills to an imagesetter, my job won't print. What should I do?**

A Some older, PostScript Level 1 and PostScript-clone RIPs (raster image processors) consistently have difficulty printing objects with linear gradient fills. Print jobs with such fills will process indefinitely or cause timeout errors on these RIPs. In addition, some PostScript Level 2 RIPs will print such gradients incorrectly, with small notches.

If you run into this problem, and you're using a version of Adobe Illustrator prior to 5.5, try saving your file in the Adobe Illustrator 3.0 format (this will convert your gradients to step blends and masks) or use a different type of imagesetter. Sometimes changing the orientation of your page (if your imagesetter can accommodate a different orientation) will also solve the problem.

If you're using Adobe Illustrator 5.5, there's an easier way to eliminate this problem. Select "Document Setup..." from the File menu, and in the "Document Setup" dialog box, select the "Compatible Gradients Printing" option. This will convert your gradients to step blends and masks.

We recommend you use this option to print gradients only on imagesetters that have problems with them—using this option in other situations may slow printing noticeably.

Q *(5.5 only)* **I use Illustrator to print to a plotter that cuts vinyl lettering for signage. I'm trying to create text that has only a stroke, with no fill, but it doesn't seem to be working. What am I doing wrong?**

A If you want your vinyl cutter to cut letters that look as if they have no fill, you'll need to follow a few extra steps. But before we go into the details, here's an overview of how the vinyl-cutting plotter works with Illustrator files.

Most plotters print just paths, not fills. So if you draw a line in Illustrator and apply a thick stroke to it, your vinyl cutter will cut along the center of the path (the line you'd see if you were looking at the stroked line in "Artwork" mode). For the plotter to cut around the perimeter of the stroke, you'd need to turn that perimeter into a path. Fortunately, there's an easy way to do that in Illustrator. Just select the path and then choose "Outline Path" from the Objects submenu of the Filters menu.

To create this sort of effect for text, type the text you want, select it with the pointer tool, and then choose "Create Outlines" from the Type menu. Next, with the text still selected, use the Paint Style palette to assign a fill of none and a stroke of whatever weight you want. To preview the results accurately, make sure "Preview" is selected from the View menu. When the text looks the way you want, run the "Outline Path" filter on it as explained above.

At this point—whether with objects or text—you're almost done. To view your results accurately, select "Artwork" from the View menu (this will show you just the paths of your artwork—not their strokes or fills). If you see any triangles at the corner points of your paths, be sure to select those objects and choose "Unite" from the Pathfinder submenu of the Filters menu—that'll get rid of the triangles, and your paths will be ready for the plotter.

Q Some custom-color artwork that I imported into Illustrator from Dimensions is separating as process colors rather than custom colors. Why does this happen and how can I fix it?

A Chances are that part of your Dimensions object is printing on the correct custom-color separation or separations, but the rest of it isn't because it's defined as process colors. Sound confusing? Here's a more detailed explanation.

When you shade an object in Dimensions to create a 3-D effect, Dimensions creates a series of blend steps (which are actually separate objects that give the illusion of graduated color). Dimensions calculates the colors of the blend steps based on your "Fill" color and "Shade" color (which you define in the Surface Properties palette). If those colors are different custom colors, or if one's a process color, all the intermediate steps in your rendered object will be defined as process colors and will separate accordingly. And if you leave the "Shade" color at its default (which is process black), your intermediate blend steps will certainly be defined as process colors.

If you need the intermediate steps in your blend to print on custom-color separations, you have to define your "Fill" and "Shade" color as tints of the same custom color—for instance, have the "Shade" color be 100% of your custom color, and your "Fill" color be a very light tint of the same custom color. This often gives good-looking results if your custom color is very dark; however, with light custom colors, there may not be enough contrast between your fill and shade colors to give you a convincing 3-D effect. If you find yourself in that situation, here's a good workaround.

Say you're using the custom color "Gold" for your "Fill" color, and want it to blend to process black, but you want the intermediate steps to print as a mix of black and your spot color—not as process colors. Try this.

1. First, select "Gold" for your "Fill" color, and define your "Shade" color as a 0% tint of Gold. After rendering, copy and paste your object into Illustrator.

2. Back in Dimensions, change your "Shade" color to black, and define your "Fill" color as a 0% tint of black. Render again, then copy and paste the object into Illustrator.
3. In Illustrator, the two objects should already be perfectly aligned. If they're not, group each one and then align them (which might be easier in "Preview" mode). Then, select the top object with the selection tool (), and set the fill color to overprint using the Paint Style palette.

Although you'll see only the top object on screen, they'll both print together to create the custom-to-process blend you're after.

Gradient Fills Don't Print or Print Incorrectly to PostScript Level 1 Devices from Illustrator 5.x or Later

ISSUE

When you print to a PostScript Level 1 device from Adobe Illustrator 5.0 or later, documents containing a gradient fill begin to process, but do not print. Gradient fills do not print or print incompletely.

SOLUTIONS

Open the document in Illustrator 5.5 or later and print with the Compatible Gradient Printing option selected in the Document Setup dialog box.

OR: Open the file in Illustrator 6.0 and use the Expand command to convert the gradient fill to a masked blend:

1. Select the gradient fill, then choose Object > Expand.
2. In the Expand Gradient/Pattern dialog box, type 255 in the Number of Steps text box, then click OK.

OR: Open the document in Illustrator 5.0.x and save in Illustrator 3 format.

NOTE: Objects in an Illustrator 5.x document may be lost when saving in Illustrator 3 compatible format. When saving an Illustrator 5.x document in Illustrator 3.x or earlier format, Illustrator combines objects in the document onto a single layer, converts gradients to blends, converts tabs in point text to spaces, and converts tabs in area text to returns.

ADDITIONAL INFORMATION

Some PostScript Level 1 devices cannot process the conditional PostScript routine used to define Illustrator 5.0 and later gradients. For example, a PostScript Level 1 imagesetter may print only a portion of a gradient fill object in an Illustrator 5.0 or later document, or it may begin to process the document, then stop.

When the Compatible Gradient Printing option is selected in the Document Setup dialog box, Illustrator 5.5 and later uses different PostScript code to define a gradient fill, which enables gradient fills to print to PostScript Level 1 devices. When the Compatible Gradient Printing option is selected, Illustrator describes gradient fills as blends (i.e., multiple objects each filled with a unique color) by adding the "/lv1Fix true def" PostScript code, Printing with the Compatible Gradient Printing option selected increases the time required to image gradient fills.

In Illustrator 6.0, the Expand feature converts gradient fills and patterns into a series of masked objects, gradient fills becoming a masked blend. You can specify the number of steps in the blend in the Expand Gradient/Pattern dialog box where 255 steps is the maximum number of steps possible in the blend.

Saving an Illustrator 5.x and later document in Illustrator 3.x format converts gradient fills to a masked blend. Illustrator 3.x and earlier does not support the Gradient option in the Paint Styles palette. Instead, Illustrator 3.x and earlier uses the Blend tool to create blends, a series of intermediary shapes and colors between two objects. Illustrator 3.x blends may take longer to image than Illustrator 5.x and later gradients, but print more reliably to PostScript Level 1 devices.

Curved Objects in Imported and Scaled Illustrator EPS Print Square or Beveled

ISSUE

After importing and scaling an Adobe Illustrator 5.x EPS file in a page layout application (e.g., Adobe PageMaker, QuarkXpress), curved objects in the EPS file print "squared" or "beveled" to a PostScript printer.

SOLUTIONS

Increase the Output Resolution applied to the Illustrator 5.x objects:

1. Open the EPS file in Illustrator 5.x.
2. Select all the objects in the Illustrator EPS file.
3. Choose Object > Attributes.
4. In the Attributes dialog box, increase the Output Resolution value to twice the current setting (e.g., 1600 dpi) then click OK. The default Output Resolution is 800 dpi.
5. Save and reimport original Illustrator EPS file.

OR: Resave the Illustrator 5.x EPS file in Illustrator 3.x format:

NOTE: When you save an Illustrator 5.x document in Illustrator 3.x or earlier format, all objects are moved to a single layer, gradients are converted to blends, custom colors are converted to process, and tabs are converted to spaces.

1. Open the EPS file in Illustrator 5.x.
2. Save the Illustrator EPS file in Illustrator 3 format.
3. Replace the Illustrator EPS file in the layout application.

OR: Use a Riders file to set the flatness value of objects in the Illustrator EPS file:

1. Open the EPS file in Illustrator 5.x.
2. Create a Riders file with the desired flatness setting (e.g., .2). For instructions on creating a Riders file, see Related Records.
3. Save then replace the Illustrator EPS file in the layout application.

OR: Scale the elements in Illustrator 5.x, then place the Illustrator EPS file in the layout application.

ADDITIONAL INFORMATION

When you scale an Illustrator EPS file the flatness value in the EPS file increases, which may cause curved elements to print "squared" or "beveled." The lower the resolution of the printer, the more beveled the curves of the object in the EPS file print.

Illustrator 5.x applies a flatness formula to all objects drawn in Illustrator. The amount of flatness applied to an Illustrator object is based on the Output Resolution setting in the Attributes dialog box. The Flatness value equals the printer's resolution divided by the object's Output Resolution. Illustrator 5.x automatically applies a 800 dpi Output Resolution setting to all drawn objects.

Saving an EPS file in Illustrator 3 format removes the flatness formula applied to the EPS files. Flatness in Illustrator 3.x is set by specifying a flatness value in the Paint Styles dialog box.

Flatness settings in the Adobe EPSF Riders file override the object's Output Resolution setting in the Attributes dialog box.

Illustrator 6.0 Files Print Without Riders File Settings

ISSUE

Adobe Illustrator 6.0 files print without the screen frequency, screen angle, or spot function set in the Adobe Illustrator EPSF Riders file.

SYMPTOM

The Use Printer's Default Screen option is deselected in the Document Setup dialog box.

SOLUTION

Select the Use Printer's Default Screen option in the Document Setup dialog box before printing the Illustrator 6.0 file.

ADDITIONAL INFORMATION

When you print an Illustrator 6.0 file or save it as an EPS file with the Use Printer's Default Screen option deselected, the file does not use the screen frequency, screen angle, or spot function set in the Riders file. For example, when you separate a file from Illustrator 6.0 with the Default Screen option deselected, Illustrator prints the file with the screen frequency selected in the Separation Setup dialog box instead of the Riders file.

Painting an object with a gradient fill in Illustrator 6.0 automatically deselects the Default Screen option in the Document Setup dialog box.

In Illustrator 5.x, the Use Printers Default Screen option does not override the screen frequency, screen angle or spot functions print set in a Riders file.

Curved Objects Print Square or Jagged from Illustrator 5.x

ISSUE

When printing to a PostScript printer, Adobe Illustrator 5.x prints curved objects squared or jagged. The scaling resolution specified in the printer driver's Page Setup dialog box is greater than 100%.

SOLUTIONS

Scale the objects in Illustrator 5.x, then print the document at 100% scale.

OR: Increase the Output Resolution setting for all objects in the document:

1. In Illustrator 5.x, choose Edit > Select All.
2. Choose Object > Attributes.
3. In the Attributes dialog box, increase the Output Resolution value and click OK. The default Output Resolution is 800 dpi.

ADDITIONAL INFORMATION

When you scale an Illustrator document while printing by increasing the scaling percentage in printer driver's Page Setup dialog box, the flatness value applied to the Illustrator objects increases, resulting in curved objects printing "squared" or "jagged."

Illustrator 5.x applies a flatness formula (i.e., flatness = printer's resolution / object's output resolution) to all objects drawn in Illustrator. The flatness value applied to an Illustrator object is based on the Output Resolution setting in the Attributes dialog box, where the flatness value equals printer's resolution divided by the object's Output Resolution setting. Illustrator 5.x automatically applies a 800 dpi Output Resolution setting to all Illustrator-drawn objects.

Illustrator 6.0 Separations Print Line Spot Function Instead of Dot Spot Function

ISSUE

When you print separations from Adobe Illustrator 6.0, the separations print with a line spot function instead of dot spot function. The Plug-ins folder does not contain an Adobe Illustrator EPSF Riders file.

SOLUTIONS

Reselect your PPD (PostScript Printer Description) file in the Separation Setup dialog box before printing:

1. Choose File > Separation Setup, then click Open PPD in the Separation Setup dialog box.
2. Reselect your PPD file in the Choose a PPD dialog box and click Open.
3. Click OK in the Separation Setup dialog box, then print the Illustrator file.

OR: Copy and paste the illustration into a new Illustrator document, then print.

OR: Save the Illustrator document in EPS format and then separate the EPS file in an another application (e.g., Adobe Separator 5.0.x).
OR: Use a Riders file to set the spot function to Simple Round in the Illustrator file:

1. Quit Illustrator.
2. Install the Rider plug-in filter by moving the Riders file, which is installed in the Riders Folder in the Utilities folder, into the Filters folder in the Plug-ins folder. The Riders plug-in filter adds an Other submenu to the Filters menu.
3. Launch Illustrator and Choose Filter > Other > Make Riders.
4. In the Make Riders dialog box, select None from the Screen Frequency, Flatness, Screen Angle, Annotation, and Error Handler pop-up menus.
5. Select the Simple Round Dot option from the Spot Function pop-up menu, then click Make. Illustrator saves a file named Adobe Illustrator EPSF Riders in the Plug-ins folder.
6. Choose File > Document Setup, select the Use Printer's Default Screen option, then click OK.

NOTE: The Riders file does not change the spot function applied to the color bars. Illustrator does not use the settings in the Riders file when Use Printer's Default Screen is not selected in the Document Setup dialog box.

ADDITIONAL INFORMATION

When you save an Illustrator 6.0 file after clicking OK in the Separation Setup dialog box, Illustrator includes the PPD information (e.g., page size, line screen) in the file. If you reopen and print an Illustrator file containing PPD information, Illustrator separates the file using a line spot function instead of the default spot function. Illustrator defines the spot function using "{ }" instead of "{ abs exch abs 2 copy add 1 gt { 1 sub dup mul exch 1 sub dup mul add 1 sub } { dup mul exch dup mul add 1 exch sub } ifelse }."

Reselecting the PPD file in the Separation Setup dialog box after reopening the file causes Illustrator to use the default spot function defined in the PPD file, instead of the "{ }" spot function defined in the Illustrator file.

To prevent Illustrator from saving the PPD information in the Illustrator file, save the file before opening the Separation Setup dialog box and do not save the file after clicking OK in the Separation Setup dialog box. If the file was saved after clicking OK, copying and pasting the artwork to a new file creates an Illustrator file without the PPD information.

Illustrator 6.0 uses the Adobe Illustrator EPSF Riders file to specify a global screen frequency, angle, spot function, and flatness value for Illustrator files. The Riders file can also add annotations and an error handler to Illustrator files. Riders file information and settings are included when you print an Illustrator file or save a document in EPS format from Illustrator 6.0. Rider file settings are not saved in Illustrator 6.0 documents.

Extra Blank Pages Print After Each Separation from Illustrator 6.0

ISSUE

When you print separations from Adobe Illustrator 6.0, the printer emits an extra blank page after each separation.

SOLUTIONS

Print the Illustrator document using the Apple LaserWriter 8.x or Adobe PSPrinter 8.x printer driver.
OR: Save the Illustrator document as an EPS file, then print separations of the EPS file from another application (e.g., Adobe Separator 5.01, Adobe PageMaker 6.0x).

ADDITIONAL INFORMATION

When you print separations from Illustrator 6.0 using the Apple LaserWriter 7.x printer driver, the printer emits a blank page after each separation. The LaserWriter 7.x printer driver adds an "(atend)" command to the header of print files, which directs it to use the page number definition created by Illustrator 6.0 in the "%%pagetrailer" section of the print file. Because Illustrator defines the number of pages in the "%%pagetrailer" section incorrectly, the printer driver adds an extra blank page after each separation.

The LaserWriter 8.x and PSPrinter 8.x printer drivers define the number of pages to be printed in the header of the print file, rather than using Illustrator's page number definition in the "%%pagetrailer" section of the print file.

Illustrator Custom Color Gradients Render as Process in TrapWise and PrePrintPro

ISSUE

Luminous TrapWise 2.1b or earlier traps custom-colored (i.e., spot-colored) gradients in an Illustrator 5.5 EPS file as process-colored objects. TrapWise and Luminous PrePrintPro 1.0 report the gradients have process component inks when measured with the densitometer tool.

SOLUTIONS

Open and then resave the EPS file in Illustrator 6.0.
OR: Update Illustrator 5.5 to Illustrator 5.5a, then open and resave the EPS file in Illustrator 5.5a. For instructions on updating to Illustrator 5.5a, see Additional Information.

ADDITIONAL INFORMATION

The internal raster image processor (RIP) that TrapWise and PrePrintPro use to analyze images is a composite color RIP. Because Illustrator 5.5 gradients render as process colors to a composite color RIP (e.g., QMS ColorScript), TrapWise traps the gradients as process-color objects, and both TrapWise and PrePrintPro report the gradients have process component inks when you measure them using the densitometer tool. When you print separations of Illustrator 5.5 gradients, the gradients print on the custom color separations and the traps print on the process separations.

TrapWise 2.1b or later and PrePrintPro 1.0 trap custom-colored gradients created by Illustrator 5.5a and later as spot colors. You can update Illustrator 5.5 to 5.5a using the Illustrator 5.5a patcher, available on America Online, CompuServe, the Adobe BBS, and the Adobe FTP site. Technical support for Illustrator 5.5a and the Illustrator 5.5a patcher is available from Luminous.

To update Illustrator 5.5 to Illustrator 5.5a:

1. Double-click the Illustrator 5.5a patcher.
2. Click the Patch button.
3. Select the Adobe Illustrator 5.5 application, then click Patch.
4. Select the folder in which you want to save the Illustrator 5.5a application, then click Save.
5. When the update is complete, click OK to close the Illustrator 5.5a patcher.

NOTE: The "5.5a" version number does not appear in the Illustrator startup screen, but does appear in the Illustrator Get Info window. To view the version of Illustrator, select the Illustrator 5.5 application icon at the Finder and then choose File > Get Info.

Error "The PPD file for the current printer does not match..." Printing From Illustrator 6.0

ISSUE

When you print separations from Adobe Illustrator 6.0x, Illustrator returns the error "The PPD file for the current printer does not match the PPD file used by the Separation Setup dialog. Your output may be clipped or fail to print properly."

SOLUTION

Ensure the same PostScript Printer Description (PPD) file is selected in the Illustrator 6.0 Separation Setup dialog box and in the printer driver in the Chooser (e.g., LaserWriter 8.x). The selected PPD file name and location must be the same in Illustrator 6.0 and in the printer driver.

ADDITIONAL INFORMATION

Illustrator 6.0 uses information from the PPD file specified in the printer driver and in the Separation Setup dialog box to determine the page size and imageable area available at the printer. When the PPD file specified in the printer driver does not match the one specified in the Illustrator 6.0 Separation Setup dialog box, printing separations from Illustrator 6.0 causes Illustrator to return the error "The PPD file for the current printer does not match the PPD file used by the Separation Setup dialog. Your output may be clipped or fail to print properly."

Specifying the same PPD file in the printer driver and in Illustrator 6.0 ensures that identical page size and imageable area information is being utilized by Illustrator.

Special Characters Print as Blank Space from Illustrator 5.0.1 or Earlier

ISSUE

When printing from Adobe Illustrator 5.0.1 or earlier, extended characters (i.e., option characters) that have a Symbol font equivalent appear on screen, but print as a blank space to a PostScript device.

SOLUTIONS

Print the document containing the extended characters from Illustrator 5.5 or later.

OR: Apply the font Symbol to the text, then retype the desired character for the Symbol font equivalent. For Symbol font equivalent keystrokes, see Additional Information.

OR: Convert the special character to a path using the Create Outlines command:

1. Install the Symbol printer (outline) font or Symbol TrueType font.
2. Select the text containing the extended character with the selection tool.
3. Choose Type > Create Outlines.

ADDITIONAL INFORMATION

The extended, option, or special characters standard to most fonts can be included in a PostScript screen (bitmap) font, but are not included in the printer (outline) font.

When printing to a PostScript device, Illustrator 5.0.1 and earlier reads the printer font file. When these extended characters are not included in the printer font file, the missing character prints as a blank space. Characters not included in the printer font display on screen using the screen font, the Symbol printer font, or the Symbol TrueType font.

Illustrator 5.5 prints these standard extended characters by substituting their Symbol font equivalent.

Symbol font equivalents for the extended characters:

	Non-Symbol Font Extended Character	Symbol Font Extended Character
Apple logo symbol	Option + Shift + K	Same
Approximation symbol	Option + X	Option + 9
Delta (lowercase, differation symbol)	Option + D	Option + D
Delta (uppercase)	Option + J	Shift + D
Diamond, lozenge symbol	Option + Shift + V	Option + Shift + 7
Greater-than-or-equal-to symbol	Option + period	Same
Infinity	Option + 5	Option + 8
Integral symbol	Option + B	Option + Shift + ;

Less-than-or-equal-to symbol	Option + comma	Option + 3
Not equal	Option + =	Option + p
Pi symbol (lowercase)	Option + P	P
Pi symbol (uppercase)	Option + Shift + P	Option + Shift +]
Root symbol	Option + V	Option + /
Summation-of symbol	Option + W	Option + Shift + M
Upper omega	Option + Z	Shift + W

Installation Issues

WINDOWS

Removing Illustrator 4.x from Windows 95

To manually remove Illustrator 4.x from Windows 95, delete the Illustrator 4.x directory, Illustrator 4.x shortcut file, and the Illustrator entries in the Win.ini file. Then, remove Illustrator entries from the [extensions] section in the Win.ini file using the System Configuration Editor.

You cannot uninstall Adobe Illustrator 4.x in Windows 95 using the Add/Remove Programs Control Panel because Adobe Illustrator 4.x is not Windows 95 logo-compliant.

To delete Illustrator's directory and files using Windows Explorer:

1. Choose Start > Programs > Windows Explorer.
2. In Windows Explorer, delete the Illustrator directory (e.g., AI4).
3. Delete the Adobevue.dll file from the Windows\System directory.
4. Delete the following files from the Windows directory:
   - Tapalett.ini
   - Enum.ebf
   - Hostfont.ebf
   - Ps_enum.ebf
   - Ai41.ini (Illustrator 4.1) or Ai4.ini (Illustrator 4.0.x)
   - Typealgn.ini
5. Delete the Setup.ai and Aiunpack.ini files from the Windows\Temp directory.
6. Delete the Illustrator 4.x shortcuts file from the Windows\Start Menu\Programs\Adobe directory.

To remove Illustrator entries from the [extensions] section in the Win.ini file:

1. Choose Start > Run.
2. Type "sysedit" in the Open text box, then click OK.
3. Select the Win.ini file, then delete the following lines from the [extensions] section:
   For Illustrator 4.0.x:
   ```
   AI=C:\AI4\AI4.EXE ^.AI
   TAL=c:\typealgn\TYPEALGN.EXE ^.TAL
   ```
   For Illustrator 4.1:
   ```
   AI=C:\AI4\AI41.EXE ^.AI
   TAL=c:\typealgn\TYPEALGN.EXE ^.TAL
   ```
4. Save the Win.ini file in text-only format, exit the System Configuration Editor, and then restart Windows 95.
   NOTE: When you open the Win.ini file in the System Configuration Editor, it automatically creates a backup copy of your Win.ini file named "Win.syd" in the Windows directory.

Removing Illustrator 7.x in Windows 95 or Windows NT 4.0

You can uninstall Adobe Illustrator 7.0 from Windows 95 or Windows NT 4.0 using the Add/Remove Programs utility, which will remove all files installed by Adobe Illustrator and Illustrator registry entries, or you can remove Illustrator manually. When you remove Illustrator manually, registry entries and shared files (e.g., color management file, *.ini files) are not automatically removed. Before uninstalling Illustrator, move any files you created to a location other than the Illustrator directory.

To remove Illustrator 7.0 using the Add/Remove Programs utility:

1. Exit all applications.
2. Restart Windows.
3. Choose Start > Settings > Control Panel.
4. Double-click Add/Remove Programs.
5. Select Adobe Illustrator 7.0 from the scroll box in the Install/Uninstall pane, then click Add/Remove.
6. Click Yes in the Confirm File Deletion dialog box.
7. Follow the on-screen instructions. The Add/Remove Programs utility will ask whether you want to remove files that may be shared by other programs. If you are not certain whether these are needed by other applications, click No.
8. Click OK after the uninstall is completed to close the Add/Remove Programs Control Panel.

Removing Illustrator 4.0x in Windows 95

To manually remove Illustrator 4.0x in Windows 95, delete the Illustrator 4.0x directory, Illustrator 4.0x shortcut file, and the Illustrator entries in the Win.ini file. Then, remove Illustrator entries from the [extensions] section in the Win.ini file using the System Configuration Editor.

You can uninstall Windows 95 logo-compliant applications using the Add/Remove Programs option in the Control Panel folder, but because Adobe Illustrator 4.0x is not Windows 95 logo-compliant, you cannot remove it using the Add/Remove Programs option.

To delete Illustrator's directory and files using the Explorer:

1. Choose Start > Explore.
2. In the Explorer, delete the Illustrator directory (e.g., AI) and its contents.
3. Delete the Adobevue.dll file from the Windows\System subdirectory.
4. Delete the following files from the Windows directory:
   ```
   Tapalett.ini
   Enum.ebf
   Hostfont.ebf
   Ps_enum.ebf
   Ai4.ini
   Typealgn.ini
   ```
5. Delete the Setup.ai and Aiunpack.ini files, if present, from the Windows\Temp subdirectory.
6. Delete the Illustrator 4.x file (Illustrator 4.0x shortcuts file), which Illustrator installs in the Windows\Start Menu\Programs\Adobe subdirectory.

To remove Illustrator entries from the [extensions] section in the Win.ini file:

1. Choose Start > Run.
2. In the Run dialog box, type "SYSEDIT" in the Open text box, then click OK.
3. Select the Win.ini file, then delete the following lines from the [extensions] section:
   ```
   AI=C:\AI4\AI4.EXE ^.AI
   TAL=c:\typealgn\TYPEALGN.EXE ^.TAL
   ```
4. Save the Win.ini file, exit the System Configuration Editor, and then restart Windows 95.

   NOTE: The System Configuration Editor automatically creates a backup copy of the original Win.ini file named "Win.syd" in the Windows directory.

MAC OS

Q *(5.5 only)* **The Illustrator Deluxe CD contains some spelling dictionaries. Can I install them?**

A Yes. The Illustrator 5.5 spelling dictionaries need to be located in Illustrator's "Plug-Ins" folder for Illustrator to recognize them. Since they're not compressed, all you need to do is copy (drag) them from the CD's "Spelling Dictionaries" folder within the "Illustrator Goodies" folder to your hard disk's "Plug-Ins" folder within your "Adobe Illustrator" folder.

Once the spelling dictionaries are installed, you can use them to spell-check by selecting "Check Spelling..." from the Text submenu of the Filters menu, and in the "Check Spelling" dialog box, clicking on the "Language..." button. Illustrator will prompt you to select one of the dictionaries installed in your Plug-ins folder.

Spelling dictionaries included on the CD are Brazilian Portuguese, Canadian French, Danish, Dutch, Finnish, French, German, Italian, Lisbon Portuguese, Mexican, Norwegian, Spanish, Swedish, Swiss German, and UK and US English.

Q *(6.0 only)* **Illustrator 6.0 doesn't install on my Mac running the French Canadian OS. It gives me an alert message—"Please insert the disk: 'Install - Disk 1'"—but the same CD installs fine onto my UK English Mac. What's up?**

A Nothing serious—just a minor language barrier. ATM has installed itself "speaking" French Canadian, but Illustrator's installer hasn't been told to speak French Canadian, and the request for Disk 1 is a sign of its confusion. Read on for details on how to fix this problem.

The International version of Illustrator 6.0 ships with the multilingual version of ATM 3.9, which is installed when you choose Illustrator's "Easy Install" option. The ATM installer detects the language of the Mac OS and installs the appropriate localized version of ATM. However, it doesn't switch back to English when it's done, leaving the Illustrator Installer stranded in another language without a dictionary. This is when the installer displays the alert message "Please insert the disk: 'Install - Disk 1.'"

Use the Illustrator Installer "Custom Install" option, or the ATM Installer, to install ATM 3.9 before installing Illustrator 6.0.

Installing Illustrator 6.0

Before installing Adobe Illustrator 6.0, read the ReadMe file, ensure your computer meets the system requirements listed in the Adobe Illustrator 6.0 Getting Started manual and has sufficient free hard disk space, and disable any unnecessary extensions.

README FILE

The Illustrator 6.0 ReadMe file is located on Install-Disk 1 and in the Install-Disk 1 folder in the Adobe Illustrator 6.0 folder on the Adobe Illustrator 6.0 Deluxe CD-ROM. The ReadMe file includes late-breaking information not available in Illustrator's manual or online documentation. Read this document before installing Illustrator, paying particular attention to sections related to installation and troubleshooting. After installation, the installer locates the ReadMe file in the Adobe Illustrator 6.0 folder on your hard disk.

DISABLING EXTENSIONS

Before installing Illustrator 6.0 from the installation disk set, disable all extensions by restarting computer with the Shift key held down until the message "Welcome to Macintosh. Extensions off." appears (System 7.x) or by using the Extension Managers control panel to enable the System 7.5 Only set of extensions. When installing from the Adobe Illustrator 6.0 Deluxe CD-ROM, disable all extensions except those required by your CD-ROM drive.

VALID SERIAL NUMBERS

The Adobe Illustrator serial number is located on the first page of the Illustrator 6.0 User Guide and on the registration card. Adobe Illustrator 6.0 serial numbers begin with

AAW5 and AAW6. When upgrading from Illustrator 5.x to Illustrator 6.0, use your Illustrator 5.x serial number. When upgrading from Illustrator 3.x or earlier to Illustrator 6.0, use your Illustrator 6.0 serial number. Illustrator 6.0 does not accept Illustrator 3.x and earlier serial numbers.

PLUG-INS

Illustrator 6.0 supports Illustrator 6.0- and Adobe Photoshop 3.0.4-compatible plug-ins. When you select the Easy Install option, the following plug-ins are installed in the Illustrator plug-ins folder: Extensions (e.g., Control Palette, Flatten Suite), File Format (e.g., BMP, Amiga IFF), Gallery Effects, Help, Text, Tools, Colors, Create, Distort, Ink Pen, Objects, and Stylize. When you select the Optional Plug-ins custom install option, the following plug-ins are installed in an Optional Plug-ins folder in the Illustrator folder: the Adobe Illustrator Parser, Artwork View Speedup, Offset Path - 68k FPU Only, and Outline Path - 68k FPU Only.

Additional plug-ins (e.g., Cytopia Socket Sets Demo, KPT Vector Effects Demo) are included in the Illustrator Plug-ins folder in the Third Party Products on the Adobe Illustrator 6.0 Deluxe CD-ROM. To install the optional and third party plug-ins, move the desired plug-in into the Illustrator plug-ins folder.

Illustrator 6.0 can share plug-ins with Photoshop. To share plug-ins with Photoshop, place an alias of the Photoshop plug-ins folder or plug-in file in the Illustrator plug-ins folder.

FONTS

The Adobe Illustrator 6.0 Deluxe CD-ROM includes 89 Type 1 PostScript fonts. The Adobe Type Library folder contains 53 Adobe fonts, and the Image Club folder in the Adobe Type Library folder contains 36 Image Club fonts. The Illustrator 6.0 Installer installs Courier, Helvetica, Symbol, and Times in the Adobe Type Folder in the Illustrator 6.0 application folder. Illustrator 6.0 does not install any fonts into the System Folder.

To install a font included with Illustrator 6.0 in System 7.1 or later:

1. Close all open applications.
2. Remove the TrueType version of the font you want to install from the Fonts folder in the System Folder.
3. Copy the printer (outline) font files and screen (bitmap) font files from the Adobe Illustrator 6.0 Deluxe CD-ROM or the Illustrator application folder into the Fonts folder in the System Folder. For example, to install the Rosewood font in System 7.1 or later, copy the Rosewood bitmap font file, the RosewFil printer font file, and the RosewReg printer font file from the Rosewood folder in the Adobe Type Library folder on the Adobe Illustrator Deluxe CD-ROM into the Fonts folder in the System Folder on your Macintosh.

NOTE: System 7.1 and later cannot locate font files installed in a folder within the Fonts folder (e.g., Rosewood font files in the Rosewood folder in the Fonts folder).

Disk 1 Doesn't Eject When Installing Illustrator 5.5

ISSUE

When you install Adobe Illustrator 5.5, the installer requests Disk 2 without ejecting Installer-Disk 1, preventing installation from continuing.

SOLUTIONS

Install Adobe Illustrator 5.5 from the CD-ROM.

OR: Copy each disk to a hard disk and then install Adobe Illustrator 5.5 from the hard disk:

1. Insert Disk 1, select the disk's icon, and then copy it onto the hard disk's icon. The system copies the contents of Disk 1 into a folder it names Installer-Disk 1 on the hard disk.
2. Repeat step 1 for the remaining installation disks.
3. Open the Installer-Disk 1 on the hard disk, and double-click the Installer application to begin installation.
4. Follow the on-screen instructions, then after a successful installation delete the installation disk folders.

OR: When installing on a Macintosh that has both a 800K and 1.44 MB disk drive, disconnect the 800K disk drive.

ADDITIONAL INFORMATION

Illustrator 5.5 use the Apple Installer 4.0, which cannot install on a Macintosh that has both an 800K and a 1.44 MB disk drive (e.g., upgraded Macintosh II) connected.

PDFWriter Shortcut Not Installed with Illustrator 5.5

ISSUE

Unable to locate the "PDFWriter Shortcut" control panel described in the "PDFWriter * ReadMe" installed with Adobe Illustrator 5.5.

SOLUTION

Download the "PDFWriter Shortcut" control panel file from the Adobe Technical Support BBS.

ADDITIONAL INFORMATION

The "PDFWriter * ReadMe" file installed with Illustrator 5.5 refers to a "PDFWriter Shortcut" control panel file. The "PDFWriter Shortcut" control panel is not included with Illustrator 5.5.

The "PDFWriter Shortcut" control panel sets a keyboard shortcut (e.g. Control) that when pressed while selecting "Print..." from the File menu in Illustrator temporarily switches the currently selected printer driver to the PDF Writer driver.

Reinstalling Illustrator for Macintosh

Adobe Illustrator can be installed from the Adobe Illustrator Deluxe CD-ROM or from Illustrator Installer disks. To ensure the installer does not overwrite any existing files, remove all the installed Illustrator components from your hard disk before reinstalling Illustrator.

Before installing Illustrator from the installation disk set, disable all extensions. To start with extensions off, restart the computer with the Shift key held down until the message "Welcome to Macintosh. Extensions off." appears (System 7.x). When installing from the Adobe Illustrator Deluxe CD-ROM, disable all extensions except those required by your CD-ROM drive. See Related Records for more information on how to properly enable Apple CD-ROM extensions.

REMOVING THE ILLUSTRATOR COMPONENTS

1. Remove the Adobe Illustrator application folder. The Adobe Illustrator application folder is installed onto the internal hard disk by default. If you cannot find the Illustrator application folder on the internal hard disk, use the Find command to locate the folder containing the Illustrator application folder. Move any personal files out of the Illustrator application folder, and then drag the Adobe Illustrator application folder to the trash.
2. Remove the Claris XTND System, Text, and XTND for Illustrator files. Illustrator installs the Claris XTND System file and a Claris Translators folder containing the Text and XTND for Illustrator files in a Claris folder inside the System folder. Use the Find command to locate any Claris files that have been moved from the Claris folder. If you have other applications that use the Claris filters (e.g., Claris FileMaker Pro), move the Claris folder to the desktop, then after you reinstall Illustrator, move the Claris files from the desktop to the Claris folder in the System folder. Do not replace any files that already exist in the new Claris folder.
3. Remove the Adobe Illustrator preferences file. The Adobe Illustrator preferences are located in the Preferences folder inside the System folder. The Illustrator 5.0.x preference file is named "Adobe Illustrator Prefs," the Illustrator 5.5 preference file is named "Adobe Illustrator 5.5 Prefs," and the Illustrator 6.x preference file is named "Adobe Illustrator 6.0 Prefs."

INSTALLING ILLUSTRATOR FROM CD-ROM

To install Illustrator from CD-ROM, restart the Macintosh, disable all extensions except those required by the CD-ROM drive, insert the Illustrator Deluxe CD into the CD-ROM drive, and run the Illustrator installer:

1. Double-click the Adobe Illustrator installer icon.
2. Click Continue when the Adobe Illustrator Installation screen appears.
3. Click Continue when the Read Me file appears.
4. In the Installer dialog box, choose either Easy Install or Custom Install, then click Install.
5. When the installation is complete, a message appears indicating the installation was successful. Click Quit to exit the installer and then restart the Macintosh.

INSTALLING ILLUSTRATOR FROM DISKS

To install Illustrator from disks, disable all extensions by restarting the Macintosh with the Shift key held down, insert Disk 1-Installer into the disk drive, and run the Illustrator installer:

1. Double-click the Adobe Illustrator installer icon.
2. Click Continue when the Adobe Illustrator Installation screen appears.
3. Click Continue when the Read Me file appears.
4. In the Installer dialog box, choose either Easy Install or Custom Install, then click Install.
5. When the installation is complete, a message appears indicating the installation was successful. Click Quit to exit the installer and then restart the Macintosh.

INSTALLING ILLUSTRATOR FROM DISKS IMAGES COPIED TO THE HARD DISK

To install Illustrator from disk images copied to the hard disk:

1. Copy the Adobe Illustrator [version #] folder from the Adobe Illustrator Deluxe CD-ROM or drag each installation disk to your hard disk. 2. Restart the Macintosh will the Shift key held down to disable all extensions. 3. Double-click the Adobe Illustrator installer icon in the Installer-Disk 1 folder.
4. Click Continue when the Adobe Illustrator Installation screen appears.
5. Click Continue when the Read Me file appears.
6. In the Installer dialog box, choose either Easy Install or Custom Install, the click Install.
7. When the installation is complete, a message appears indicating the installation was successful. Click Quit to exit the installer and then restart the Macintosh.

Error "There is a problem with the disk" When Installing Illustrator 5.5

ISSUE

When you install Adobe Illustrator 5.5 on a Macintosh running System 7.1 or later, the installer returns the error "There is a problem with the disk you are installing onto. No installation can take place. Try installing onto another disk." or "The Installer needs to create a folder named "System Folder" on the disk "[volume name]" but a file with this name already exists. Please rename this file or move it to another folder."

SOLUTION

Remove the Fonts folder from the System Folder, recreate a new Fonts folder by restarting your Macintosh, and then reinstall Illustrator 5.5:

1. Move the Fonts folder from the System Folder to a different location (e.g., desktop).
2. Disable extensions by restarting the Macintosh while holding down the Shift key until the system returns the message "Welcome to Macintosh. Extensions off."

3. Insert and open the installation disk named "Installer-Disk 1," double-click on the Installer, and then select Easy Install.
4. Follow the on-screen instructions to complete the installation and then restart the Macintosh. When restarting, the system creates a new Fonts folder in the System Folder and Illustrator installs the Adobe Sans, Adobe Serif, Courier, Helvetica, Symbol, Times, Zapf Dingbats fonts in the new Fonts folder.
5. Move fonts not installed by Illustrator 5.5 from the old Fonts folder to the new Fonts folder in the System Folder.
6. After moving your fonts into the new Fonts folder in the System Folder, delete the old Fonts folder.

ADDITIONAL INFORMATION

When you install Illustrator 5.5 by selecting the Easy Install installation option, it installs the Adobe Sans, Adobe Serif, Courier, Helvetica, Symbol, Times, and Zapf Dingbats fonts in the Fonts folder in the System Folder. If the Fonts folder is damaged, the installer cannot install fonts into the Fonts folder and returns the error "There is a problem with the disk you are installing onto. No installation can take place. Try installing onto another disk."

The Alert "Please insert the disk: 'Install - Disk 1'" Appears When Installing Illustrator 6.0

ISSUE

When installing from the Adobe Illustrator 6.0 Deluxe CD-ROM by selecting the Easy Install option on a Macintosh running a non-English system, Adobe Illustrator returns the alert "Please insert the disk: 'Install - Disk 1'."

SOLUTION

Install Adobe Type Manager (ATM) 3.9 using Illustrator's Custom Install option before installing Illustrator 6.0:

1. Launch the Adobe Illustrator 6.0 Installer.
2. In the Install Script window, choose Custom Install from the pop-up menu.
3. In the Check Features to be Installed list, select Adobe Type Manager then click Install.
4. When the alert "Installation was successful. If you are finished click Quite to leave the Installer. If you wish to perform additional installations, click Continue." click Continue.
5. In the Install Script window, deselect Adobe Type Manager, select the desired Adobe Illustrator 6.0 options (e.g., Adobe Illustrator 6.0 Universal), then click Install.
6. Follow the on-screen installation option, then restart the Macintosh when the installation is complete.

OR: Install Adobe Type Manager (ATM) 3.9 using the ATM Installer before installing Illustrator 6.0:

1. Install Adobe Type Manager (ATM) 3.9 using the ATM Installer located in the ATM Program Disk folder inside the Adobe Illustrator 6.0 folder on the Adobe Illustrator 6.0 Deluxe CD-ROM.
2. Launch the Adobe Illustrator 6.0 Installer.
3. In the Install Script window, choose Custom Install from the pop-up menu.
4. In the Check Features to be Installed list, select the desired Adobe Illustrator 6.0 options (e.g., Adobe Illustrator 6.0 Universal), then click Install.
5. Follow the on-screen installation option, then restart the Macintosh when the installation is complete.

ADDITIONAL INFORMATION

Installing Illustrator 6.0 by selecting Illustrator's Easy Install option installs ATM 3.9 and Illustrator 6.0. While ATM 3.9 installs it identifies the system's language (e.g., French, German) then installs the appropriate localized version of ATM (e.g., German ATM 3.9). When ATM 3.9 is installed with the Illustrator 6.0 Easy Install option on a non-English system, the ATM installer uses the system's language (e.g., French, German) instead of English, causing Illustrator's installer to return the alert "Please insert the disk: 'Install - Disk 1'."

Installing ATM 3.9 before installing Illustrator prevents the Illustrator installer from installing ATM 3.9 and Illustrator's installer from returning the alert "Please insert the disk: 'Install - Disk 1'" to appear.

Installing a Foreign Language Spelling Dictionary in Illustrator 5.5

The Text/Check Spelling plug-in filter for Adobe Illustrator 5.5 uses the language dictionaries installed in the Plug-Ins folder to compile a list of misspelled words in your document. When the Text/Check Spelling filter is installed in the Plug-Ins folder, the Check Spelling command appears in the Filters > Text menu.

The "UK English 7.5" and "US English 7.5" spelling dictionaries files are installed by default in the Plug-Ins folder. Additional spelling dictionaries are included with the Illustrator 5.5 Deluxe CD-ROM.

To install a spelling dictionary and open it in Illustrator:

1. Quit Illustrator.
2. Copy the desired spelling dictionary (e.g., Swedish 7.5) from the Spelling Dictionaries folder in the Illustrator Goodies folder on the Illustrator 5.5 Deluxe CD-ROM to the Illustrator 5.5 Plug-Ins folder.
3. Restart Illustrator.
4. Choose Filters > Text > Check Spelling.
5. In the Check Spelling dialog box, click Language.
6. Select a language dictionary and click Open.

The Adobe Illustrator 5.5 Deluxe CD contains the following spelling dictionaries:

Brazilian Portuguese 7.5
Canadian French 7.5
Danish 7.5
Dutch 7.5
Finnish 7.5
French 7.5

German 7.5
Italian 7.5
Lisbon Portuguese 7.5
Mexican 7.5
Norwegian 7.5
Spanish 7.5
Swedish 7.5
Swiss German 7.5
UK English 7.5
US English 7.5

General Information

MAC OS / WINDOWS

Creating Masks in Illustrator

Masking is a method of viewing and printing a selected part of a larger background design by blocking out unwanted areas. Adobe Illustrator masks elements by cropping or clipping them with a masking object. Mask objects can be single open, closed, or compound paths.

To use text as a masking object, convert the text into a single compound path using the Create Outlines command. To make the text a single compound path after converting it to outlines, use the Release Compounds command then the Make Compounds command.

To transform (e.g., move, scale) the masking object and artwork as a single element, group the masking object and artwork before transforming. Use the Direct-selection tool to move or edit the masked artwork, or to mask objects independently.

CREATING MASKS IN ILLUSTRATOR 5.0 AND LATER FOR THE MACINTOSH AND POWER MACINTOSH

In Illustrator 5.x, the topmost object (i.e., masking object) masks or crops the selected objects beneath it. After creating a mask in Illustrator 5.5 and later, Illustrator paints the masking objects with a fill and stroke of None. Use the Fill & Strokes for masks filter to apply a paint style to the masking object.

To create a mask in Illustrator 5.x and later:

1. Select the masking object.
2. Choose Arrange > Bring To Front to position the masking object directly in front (i.e., on top) of the objects to be masked. When the masking object and the artwork to be masked are on different layers, the masking object must be on the topmost layer.
3. Select both the masking object and the artwork you want to mask, then choose Object > Masks > Make.

CREATING MASKS IN ILLUSTRATOR 4.X FOR WINDOWS

In Illustrator 4.x, the bottom most ungrouped path with a mask paint style crops or masks the objects above. When creating a document with multiple masked objects, create the individual masked objects in separate documents then combine the masked objects into a single document by copying and pasting them into one document.

To create a mask in Illustrator 4.x for Windows:

1. Select the masking object.
2. Ensure the masking object is a single ungrouped path by choosing Arrange > Ungroup.
   NOTE: After ungrouping a rectangle or oval, delete the object's center point. Objects drawn with the Rectangle and Oval tools are automatically grouped objects.
3. With the masking object selected, choose Paint > Style, select Mask in the Paint Style dialog box, then click OK.
4. Position the masking object behind (i.e., below) the artwork you want to mask. Use the Send To Back or Bring To Front commands to ensure the correct placement order of the objects in the Illustrator document.
5. Group the masking object and the artwork to be masked.
   NOTE: When the artwork is not grouped with the masking object, the mask contains all elements in the Illustrator document that are in front of the masking object.
   When the masked object is not visible in Preview view, do one or more of the following:
   A. Change the stacking order by selecting the masking object then choosing Edit > Send to Back.
   B. Ensure the masking object is grouped to the artwork being masked.
   C. Ensure only one path in the Illustrator document has the Mask paint style applied.

Illustrator Anchor Points General Information

In Adobe Illustrator, a path is any line you create using the Illustrator drawing tools or by applying the Convert to Outline command to text. A path can consist of a single anchor point, a single segment, or two or more segments. The beginning and ending of each segment is defined by anchor points, which appear when the path is selected. The first and last anchor points on an open path are the endpoints.

When you select an anchor point it displays as a solid square. On curved path segments, a selected anchor point also displays one or two direction points at the ends of direction lines. A direction line is a straight line between an anchor point and its direction point. Direction points and lines define the shape of a curved path.

DIFFERENCE BETWEEN SMOOTH AND CORNER POINTS

Illustrator uses two types of anchor points: smooth anchor points and corner anchor points. A smooth anchor point consists of two direction lines that move together. When you move a direction point on a smooth point, both direction lines move simultaneously and the curved segments on each side of the anchor point adjust. For example, the anchor point between two curved line segments is a smooth anchor.

A corner anchor consists of zero to two direction lines that move independently. When you move the direction point on a corner point, only one direction line moves, adjusting the curve on one side of the anchor point. For example, the anchor point between a curve and straight line segment is a corner anchor.

CONVERTING SMOOTH POINTS TO CORNER POINTS

The convert-direction-point tool converts smooth points to corner points and corner points to smooth points by extending and retracting the directional lines and adjusting the position of directional points. The convert-direction-point tool, located with the additional tools under the Scissors tool on the toolbox, displays on the toolbox as a solid anchor point with extended direction lines. You can temporarily access the convert-direction-point tool when a selection tool is chosen by pressing the Control key. When you select the Convert-direction-point tool, the selection arrow changes to an upside down "V."

To convert a smooth point to a corner point without direction lines:

1. Use the direct-selection tool to select a single smooth point within a path.
2. Select the convert-direction-point tool, then click on the smooth point.

To convert a smooth point to a corner point with directional lines:

1. Select a single smooth anchor point with the direct-selection tool.
2. Select the convert-direction-point tool, then click and drag on one of the smooth point direction points.

To convert a corner point to a smooth point:

1. Select a single the corner point with the direct-selection tool.
2. Click on the corner point with the convert-direction-point tool, then drag to extend the direction lines.
3. After the corner point is converted to a smooth point, use the direct-selection tool to reposition the direction points and adjust the curves created by the smooth point.

JOINING AND AVERAGING ANCHOR POINTS

The Join command (Command + J) closes a path by joining the endpoints on a single path. It can also connect endpoints on two separate open paths to create a single path. The Join command appears under the Object menu in Illustrator 5.x and under the Arrange menu in Illustrator 3.x and earlier.

To close a single open path:

Select the path with the selection tool, then use the Join command (Command + J).

To join two paths:

1. Select an endpoint on each path with the direct-selection tool.
2. Use the Join command (Command + J).

The Average command (Command + L) moves two or more selected anchor points to a position that is the average of their current location. You can use the command to place selected points directly on top of one another and to line up a series of points either horizontally or vertically.

To average anchor points:

1. Select the anchor points with the direct-selection tool.
2. Choose Object > Average.
3. In the Average dialog box, select the desired averaging option and click OK. The Both option places the selected points on top of each other. The Horizontal option averages the position of the selected points and aligns them horizontally. The Vertical option averages the position of the selected points and aligns them vertically.

You can also combine the Join and Average commands (i.e., Command + Option + J) to place two endpoints in the same location and merge them into one point.

To combine the Join and Average commands to average and join two paths:

1. Select the endpoints to be joined with the direct-selection tool.
2. Press Command + Option + J.

WINDOWS

Contents of the Illustrator 4.x Ai4.ini File

The Adobe Illustrator 4.x Ai4.ini file contains the following sections and lines. After each section is a brief summary of its purpose.

```
[preferences]
version=28
snapToPoint=1
previewPatterns=1
showIllustrations=1
transformPatterns=0
scaleLineWeight=0
doSplitPath=0
tilingMethod=2
rulerType=2
cursorKeyLength=1
freehandTol=2
outlineTol=1
ovalRadius=12
printerResolution=300
```

The lines in the [preferences] section describe options selected in the Preferences dialog box. Valid options are 0=No and 1=Yes. In sections that have more than two choices, valid options are 0, 1, and 2.

```
[constrain]
angle=0
cos=16384
sin=0
```

The value for angle represents the value specified for the constrain angle in the Preferences dialog box.

```
[text]
```

```
units=2
sizeIncrement=2
riseIncrement=2
kernIncrement=20
```

The lines in the [text] section describe options selected in the Type Preferences dialog box. Valid options for Units are: 1=Centimeters, 2=Inches, and 3=Picas/Points. The "sizeIncrement," "riseIncrement," and "kernIncrement" lines refer to the Size/Leading, Vertical Shift, and Kerning/Tracking options, respectively.

```
[Graph Data]
Auto Labels=1
```

The "Auto Labels" line specifies whether the Options > Automatic Labels command in the Graph Data dialog box is selected. Valid options are 0=No (auto labels off) and 1=Yes (automatic labels on).

```
[Tools]
threeDDialogs=0
```

The "threeDDialogs" line specifies if your dialog boxes appear with a three dimensional look. Valid options are 1=Yes (display dialog boxes using three dimensional look) and 0=No (display standard dialog boxes).

```
[Status Bar]
visible=1
```

The "visible" line specifies whether the status bar at the bottom of the Adobe Illustrator window is enabled. The default value is 1=enabled. Changing this value to 0 disables the status bar (not recommended).

```
[Color Palette]
# 1=Hsl
2=Hsb
3=Rgb
4=Cmy
ColorModel=1
EnableModes=1
```

The value of the "ColorModel" line changes which color model option, in addition to the Red, Green, and Blue option, the Color Picker displays. Valid options are: 1=Color Picker also displays the Hue, Saturation, and Luminance option (default value), 2=Color Picker also displays the Hue, Saturation, and Brightness option, 3=Color Picker displays also the Cyan, Magenta, and Yellow option, and 4=Color Picker only displays the Red, Green, and Blue option. The "EnableModes" line determines whether the Color Picker includes a hidden box that enables you to select one of four different color modes from a pop-up menu. Valid options are 1=hidden box included and 0=hidden box disabled.

```
[Tool Palette]
rightButton=0,0,X,X,X,X,X,X,X,X,X,X,X,
middleButton=1,X,0,X,X,X,X,X,X,X,X,X,X,
template=toolbox
state=390
family=1
toolbox=0,1,0,0,0,0,0,0,0,0,0,0,0,0,
```

The [Tool Palette] section describes Toolbar options. Avoid changing these options since changing them can result in unpredictable behavior. Both the "rightButton" and "middleButton" lines refer to the buttons on the mouse and how they control different functions on the Toolbar. The "template=toolbox" lines refers to the current toolbox setting and the order of the tools in the toolbox (the "alttools" value orders the tools differently). The "state," "family," and "toolbox" lines indicate the status of the various tools and their placement in the toolbox.

```
[Driver]
IS8514=4
interlacedDisplay=0
```

Adobe Illustrator 4.0 the [Driver] section for referencing different video cards where the IS8514 value is either 4 or 5. Illustrator uses the default value of 4 for most video cards and the value of 5 for video cards such as the ATI VGAUltra, ATI Ultra Pro , VGA XL, Orchid Farenheit 1280 , and the Dimond Stealth video cards. When starting, Adobe Illustrator reads the System.ini file to determine the IS8514 value. If you change the IS8514 value, Adobe Illustrator may change it when starting. To force Adobe Illustrator to use and not change the IS8514 value, precede the 4 or 5 value with the number 10 (e.g., IS8514=105). Only change the IS8514 value when colors are not appearing properly onscreen.

```
[progressives]
DisableProgressives=0
```

RGB values used in the progressive colors dialog
for cmyk, uppercase letters indicate 100% color, lowercase 0%

```
/* CMYK */
values00=1 # R
values01=1 # G
values02=1 # B
/* CMYk */
values03=0 # R
values04=0 # G
values05=0 # B
/* CMyK */
values06=1 # R
values07=1 # G
values08=0 # B
/* CMyk */
values09=0 # R
values10=0 # G
values11=0 # B
/* CmYK2*/
values12=0.9375
values13=0.01622 # R
values14=0.496231 # G
/* CmYk */
values15=0 # B
values16=0 # R
values17=0 # G
/* CmyK */
values19=0.000015 # R
values18=1 # B
values20=0.000015 # G
/* Cmyk */
```

ILLUSTRATOR General Information

```
values21=0 # B
values22=0 # R
values23=0 # G
/* cMYK */
values24=0.007446 # B
values25=0.626358  # R
values26=0.7755 # G
/* cMYk */
values27=0 # B
values28=0 # R
values29=0 # G
/* cMyK */
values30=0.001983 # B
values31=0.53125 # R
values32=0.217147 # G
/* cMyk */
values33=0 # B
values34=0 # R
values35=0 # G
/* cmYK */
values36=0.075225 # B
values37=0.005874 # R
values38=0.488265 # G
/* cmYk */
values39=0 # B
values40=0 # R
values41=0 # G
/* cmyK */
values42=0 # B
values43=0 # R
values44=0 # G
/* cmyk */
values45=0 # B
values46=0 # R
values47=0 # G
values48=0 # B
```

The CMYK values listed in the [progressives] section correspond to the colors in the Progressive Colors dialog box.

Adobe Dimensions®

Feature Techniques

MAC OS

Q Whenever I try to wrap type around a cylinder, it never looks quite right. Is there a special trick I'm missing?

A There's no particular trick, but a few specific steps will help you master the basic process, and then you'll be able to expand on your techniques.

1. In Dimensions, create the cylinder. (You can also wrap text around a cone, although the text may become somewhat distorted.)
2. Choose "Map Artwork" from the Appearance menu (or press Command + Option + M). You'll see this message: "Multiple faces selected. Use the direct select tool or the TAB key to select a single face." Press Tab until you have selected the body of the cylinder (usually three times). Choose "Export" from the File menu. Export your file in Adobe Illustrator format.
3. Launch Illustrator and open the file you just exported. You will see the two-dimensional artwork guides of your cylinder from the "Mapped Artwork" window in Dimensions.
4. Select the text tool, drag a text box from the left side of the guides to the right, and type in your text.
5. Select the shear tool and click once at the left baseline point of the first line of text. Your cursor will become an arrowhead. Holding down the Shift key, click to the far right of the text box and drag downward until the right baseline of the first line of text is even with the baseline of the second. Release the mouse button. Or, instead of using the shear tool, you can rotate the type as described above, then select just the text box with the group selection tool. Double-click the rotate tool, remove the "-" sign before the number in the "Rotate" dialog box, then click "OK." This returns the text box to its original orientation.
6. Select "Create Outlines" from the Type menu. Apply the desired paint style to your objects (but be aware that you can't fill them with patterns or gradients). Save your file in Illustrator format or copy to the Clipboard.
7. In Dimensions, select the cylinder and choose "Map Artwork" from the Appearance menu. Import the saved Illustrator file or paste from the Clipboard.
8. If necessary, move the pasted elements within the guides (the left or shaded side of the "Mapped Artwork" window corresponds to the "back" or far side of the cylinder). Click the "Apply" button within the "Mapped Artwork" window, and then close the window.

Two notes for your text-wrapping files: First, it's easiest to see the results if you apply no fill, stroke, or shade (in the Surface Properties palette) to the cylinder. Second, if you're planning to create a shaded cylinder, you might want to select the "Shade Mapped Artwork" option in the Dimensions "Preferences" dialog box, to create corresponding shades in the lettering, keeping in mind that this will take longer to render and print, and will add complexity to the file.

Unexpected Results

MAC OS

Dimensions 2.0 EPS Displays with a White Bounding Box

ISSUE

The bounding box area (i.e., background) of an Adobe Dimensions 2.0 EPS graphic exported with a "Color Macintosh" or "Black & White Macintosh" preview and placed into other applications (e.g., Aldus PageMaker, Adobe Illustrator) displays as opaque white.

SOLUTION

Open the Dimensions 2.0 EPS graphic in Illustrator then save it as an EPS graphic with a Macintosh preview.

ADDITIONAL INFORMATION

Dimensions 2.0 incorrectly writes the screen preview of EPS graphics exported with the "Color Macintosh," "Black & White Macintosh" or "1-bit IBM PC" preview option. When a Dimensions 2.0 EPS graphic with a "Color Macintosh," "Black & White Macintosh" or "1-bit IBM PC" preview is placed into an application (e.g., PageMaker, Illustrator), the bounding box area surrounding the Dimensions artwork displays as opaque white. When the Dimensions EPS graph-ic is printed to a PostScript printer, the bounding box area does not print.

Font Missing in Font Menu in Dimensions 2.x

ISSUE

After you select the Font pop-up menu or type a font name in the Character dialog box, Adobe Dimensions 2.x does not list an expected font.

SOLUTIONS

Do one or more of the following:

A. Install either the PostScript Type 1 or TrueType font files and ensure they are accessible to Illustrator:
   1. Disable installed font management utilities (e.g., Suitcase, MasterJuggler) by removing the font management extension from the System Folder and restarting the Macintosh.
   2. Install the PostScript screen and printer (outline) or TrueType font file for the selected typeface.

B. When both the PostScript and the TrueType version of the font are installed, remove either the PostScript or the TrueType version of the font. To determine whether a font is a PostScript or TrueType font, double-click on the font file in the Finder. After double-clicking a TrueType font file, the sample text displays 3 sizes. After double-clicking a PostScript screen font file, the sample text displays in one size. After double-clicking a PostScript outline font file, the Finder returns the message "PostScript font. This is a file that your Macintosh uses to display characters."

C. Enable Adobe Type Manager (ATM) 3.0 or later by selecting On in the ATM control panel.
   NOTE: After disabling extensions in System 7.x, ATM is disabled but On is selected in the ATM control panel.

D. Reinstall ATM 3.0 or later.

E. Recreate the Fonts folder (System 7.1 and later) and reinstall fonts to ensure they are not damaged:
   1. Move the Fonts folder from the System Folder onto the desktop, then restart the Macintosh.
   2. After restarting the Macintosh, the system creates a new empty Fonts folder in the System Folder.
   3. Reinstall the PostScript screen and outline font files or the TrueType font file from the font's installation disk into the new Fonts folder.
   4. Move the other font files from the Fonts folder located on the desktop into the new Fonts folder in the System Folder. Avoid replacing fonts that already exist in the new Fonts folder.

ADDITIONAL INFORMATION

For a typeface to appear in Dimensions 2.x' font list, either the TrueType font file or the PostScript screen and printer font file must be installed. When the PostScript outline file or the TrueType font file is not installed, or when the font management utility loading the fonts conflicts with Dimensions, the font does not appear in Dimensions' font list.

Dimensions 2.x requires ATM to use PostScript fonts. When ATM is disabled or damaged, only TrueType fonts appear in Dimensions' font list.

ATM 3.6.1 is included with Adobe Illustrator 5.5. ATM 3.8 and later installs the ~ATM (TM) control panel in the Control Panels folder in the System Folder. ATM 3.6.1 and earlier installs the ~ATM (TM) control panel in the Control Panels folder and the ATM driver file (i.e., ~ATM 68000 or ~ATM 68020/030/040) in the System Folder.

Dimensions 2.x Sequences Missing Artwork When Opened in Photoshop 3.x or Premiere 4.x

ISSUE

When you open an Adobe Dimensions 2.x sequence in Adobe Photoshop 3.x or Adobe Premiere 4.x, the Dimensions artwork does not display or displays incompletely.

SYMPTOMS

When you open a sequence in Premiere 4.x, the first two frames of the filmstrip are blank, but subsequent frames contain the Dimensions artwork.

No artwork displays after opening a sequence in Photoshop 3.x.

When opened in Illustrator 5.x, the first and second sequence files do not contain the same page size in the Dimensions text box in the Document Setup dialog box as subsequent sequences files.

SOLUTION

Open the first two Dimensions 2.x sequences files in a text editor to change their bounding box coordinates:

DISCLAIMER: Adobe Systems does not support modifying a Dimensions file with a text editor. Familiarity with opening EPS files in a text editor and saving in text-only (e.g., ASCII) format is required. Experience with PostScript language is highly recommended. Always modify a copy of the original Dimensions file. If alterations are incorrectly performed or the file is saved in the wrong format, the Dimensions file can be further damaged. In the event of problems, revert to the original copy.

1. Open the third file in the sequence (i.e., the first one that previews properly in Premiere 4.x) in a text editor that can save in text-only format (e.g., TeachText, Micro-soft Word).
2. Locate and copy the lines beginning with "%%BoundingBox," "%%TemplateBox," and "%%HiResBoundingBox." For example:
```
%%BoundingBox: 49 60 530 685
%%TemplateBox: 49 60 530 685
%%HiResBoundingBox: 49.9937 60.7043
 529.9623 685.0072
```
3. Close the third sequence file, then open the first sequence.
4. Select the lines that begin with "%%BoundingBox," "%%TemplateBox," and "%%HiResBoundingBox," then paste the lines copied from third sequence file.
5. Save in text-only format, then close the file.
6. Open the second sequence file and repeat steps 4 -5.

ADDITIONAL INFORMATION

When creating a sequence, Dimensions 2.x writes incorrect bounding box coordinates in the "%%BoundingBox," "%%TemplateBox," and "%%HiResBoundingBox" lines in the first two sequences files. Photoshop and Premiere use the "%%HiResBoundingBox" lines in each sequence file to determine the bounding box of the Dimensions artwork. When opening a Dimensions sequence that does not contain the correct bounding box coordinates in Photoshop or Premiere, the Dimensions artwork doesn't appear because it is not rasterized.

When a Dimensions sequence is opened in Illustrator 5.x, Illustrator uses the "%%TemplateBox:" line to determine the document's page dimension.

Application Errors

MAC OS

Page Setup Error Opening a Dimensions File

ISSUE

When opening a document in Adobe Dimensions 2.0, the error "The document was saved with a different page setup. Please choose Page Setup from the File menu." appears.

SYMPTOM

Documents opened in Dimensions with this error display at the original page size until the "Page Setup" dialog box is opened.

SOLUTIONS

Reselect the paper size in the "Page Setup" dialog box:

1. In the Chooser, select a printer that supports the page size of the Dimensions document.
   note: The PPD selected in LaserWriter 8.x "Setup" dialog box affects the page sizes available for the chosen printer.
2. Open the document in Dimensions and choose "Page Setup..." from the File menu.
3. In the "Page Setup" dialog box, select the desired page size and click "OK."

OR: Continue to work on the document in Dimensions without accessing the "Page Setup" dialog box or printing.

ADDITIONAL INFORMATION

The page sizes available in the in Dimensions "Page Setup" dialog box are supplied by the printer and PPD selected in the Chooser. When opening a Dimensions document after selecting a printer or PPD that contains different page sizes and imageable area parameters, the error "The document was saved with a different page setup. Please choose Page Setup from the File menu." appears. After opening the Dimensions document and clicking "Cancel" in the "Page Setup" dialog box, the document page size changes to the default page size selected in the "Page Setup" dialog box.

Adobe Streamline®

Unexpected Results

MAC OS / WINDOWS

DXF File Saved from Streamline 3.x Contains Added Straight Lines

ISSUE

After you save a file in DXF format from Adobe Streamline 3.x and then place or open the DXF file in another application, the DXF file contains extra straight line that run through the artwork, or it contains straight lines instead of the converted artwork.

SOLUTIONS

In Streamline 3.x, reduce the size of the image to 34 inches or less and then resave the image in DXF format.

OR: Save the file in a format other than DXF (e.g., Adobe Illustrator 5 format).

ADDITIONAL INFORMATION

When Streamline 3.x converts a 34 inch or greater image into a DXF file, it distorts the converted artwork and adds extraneous straight lines to the file.

MAC OS

Unable to Acquire Scanning Device in Streamline 3.x

ISSUE

When you choose File > Acquire > TWAIN Acquire in Adobe Streamline 3.x, nothing happens (i.e., the scanner's Acquire dialog box does not appear and no error occurs). You can scan an image using your scanning software outside of Streamline.

SOLUTIONS

Do one or more of the following:

A. Install the scanner's import plug-in into the Streamline plug-ins folder, relaunch Streamline, choose File > Acquire, then select the plug-in for the scanner (e.g., ScanWizard, VistaScan).

B. Respecify the Streamline plug-ins folder:
   1. In Streamline, choose File > Preferences > Plug-ins.
   2. In the Plug-ins Preferences dialog box, locate the folder containing the scanner's plug-in file, then click once to select it.
   3. With the folder selected, click the Select 'Plug-ins' button, located at the bottom of the Plug-ins Preference dialog box.
   4. Quit and relaunch Streamline.

ADDITIONAL INFORMATION

When you choose File > Acquire > TWAIN Acquire in Streamline 3.x while attached to a scanner that does not support the TWAIN import filter, Streamline cannot acquire the scanner. Scanners that use a proprietary plug-in (e.g., Mictrotek, Umax) do not support the TWAIN import filter. Instead, you can acquire images from them using their proprietary plug-in by choosing File > Acquire and selecting the plug-in for the scanner.

Streamline 3.x includes the Anti-Aliased PICT, PICT Resource, and TWAIN plug-ins for acquiring images from a scanning device. Streamline's Acquire command loads the import plug-ins installed in the plug-ins folder and displays them in the Acquire submenu of the File menu. The Adobe Streamline Preferences file stores the location of Streamline's plug-ins folder.

When Streamline's link to the plug-ins folder is broken, or the plug-ins folder does not contain any import plug-ins, Streamline dims the Acquire command.

TIFF Image Doesn't List in Streamline 3.x's Open Dialog Box

ISSUE

Adobe Streamline 3.x for Macintosh does not list a TIFF image created in a Windows application in its Open dialog box.

SOLUTIONS

Change TIFF image's File Type to "TIFF" using a utility such as ResEdit, DiskTop, or DiskTools. For instructions on changing the file type using ResEdit, see Additional Information.

OR: Open the TIFF image in a Macintosh application and save it in TIFF format (e.g., Adobe Photoshop 3.x).

OR: Use Streamline 3.x for Windows to convert (i.e., trace) the TIFF file to line art.

ADDITIONAL INFORMATION

When opening a file, Streamline 3.x for Macintosh reads the File Type to identify the file's format. When a TIFF image has a File Type other than "TIFF," Streamline 3.x does not list the TIFF image in its Open dialog box. After you transfer a TIFF image from Windows to Macintosh, the TIFF image has a "TEXT" or "BINA" File Type instead of the expected "TIFF" File Type.

To change the File Type of a TIFF image using ResEdit:

DISCLAIMER: This procedure is not supported by Adobe Systems and is only provided as a guideline. Experience using ResEdit is highly recommended, since it can change or remove any resource from any file. Always modify a copy of the file to be edited. Never modify an open file. If the wrong resource is modified or alterations are incorrectly performed, the application can be damaged. In the event of problems, revert to the original copy.

1. Start ResEdit.
2. Choose File > Get File/Folder Info, then select the TIFF image in the Get File/Folder Info dialog box.
3. In the Info for [TIFF name] dialog box, change the Type to "TIFF."
4. Save and close the TIFF image.

Acquire Command is Dimmed in Streamline 3.x

ISSUE

The Acquire command is dimmed in Adobe Streamline 3.x's File menu.

SOLUTIONS

Do one or more of the following:

A. Make sure the plug-in files (e.g., Anti-Aliased PICT, PICT Resource, TWAIN) are located in a plug-ins folder in the Streamline application folder.
B. Respecify the Streamline plug-ins folder:
   1. In Streamline, choose File > Preferences > Plug-ins.
   2. In the Plug-ins Preferences dialog box, locate the folder containing the scanner's plug-in, then click once to select it.
   3. Restart Streamline.

ADDITIONAL INFORMATION

When Streamline 3.x's link to the plug-ins folder is broken, or when the plug-ins folder does not contain any import plug-ins, Streamline dims the Acquire command in the File menu.

Streamline 3.x installs the Anti-Aliased PICT, PICT Resource, and TWAIN plug-ins for acquiring images from a scanning device into the Plug-ins folder in the Streamline application folder. Streamline's Acquire command loads the plug-ins installed in the plug-ins folder. The import plug-ins appear under the File > Acquire submenu.

The Adobe Streamline Preferences file stores the location of Streamline's plug-ins folder.

Unable to Save in FreeHand Format from Streamline 3.1

ISSUE

You cannot save an Adobe Streamline 3.1 file in FreeHand 3 format.

SOLUTION

Save the image from Streamline 3.1 in Illustrator format (e.g., Illustrator 3):

1. After converting the image to a trace file in Streamline 3.x, choose File > Save Art.
2. In the Save As dialog box, select None (Omit EPSF Header) as the Preview option and Illustrator 1.1, Illustrator 88, Illustrator 3, or Illustrator 5 as the Compatibility option, then click Save.
3. Open the converted Streamline file in MacroMedia FreeHand 4.x or later.

ADDITIONAL INFORMATION

Streamline 3.1 saves in Illustrator 1.1, Illustrator 88, Illustrator 3, Illustrator 5, PICT, and DXF compatibility formats. Streamline 3.0 saves in Illustrator 1.1, Illustrator 88, Illustrator 3, Illustrator 5, PICT, DXF, and FreeHand 3 compatibility formats.

The Adobe Streamline 3.0 User guide describes Illustrator 1.1, Illustrator 88, Illustrator 3, Illustrator 5, PICT, DXF, and FreeHand 3 as available formats in Streamline 3.0's Save As dialog box. When you want to open a Streamline 3.1 graphic in FreeHand 4.0, the Addendum to the Adobe Streamline 3.0 User Guide suggests saving the graphic in Illustrator 3 format.

FreeHand 4.x supports opening Illustrator 3 and earlier formats. FreeHand 5.x opens Illustrator 5 and earlier formats.

Can't Copy and Paste Within Streamline 3.x

Adobe Streamline 3.x does not support copying and pasting Streamline objects within Streamline 3.x. If you copy and then paste a Streamline 3.x object into the same or different Streamline file, Streamline dims the Paste command. The Streamline 3.0 User Guide incorrectly states that you can copy and paste objects within Streamline.

You can copy a Streamline object and paste it into another application that recognizes PostScript files (e.g., Adobe Illustrator, Adobe Photoshop).

Adobe PageMaker®

Adobe PageMaker 6.5 is the world's most popular and powerful design and layout application. Since Aldus Corporation merged with Adobe Systems in 1995, PageMaker has become so versatile you can produce virtually any type of publication with its new features such as multiple master pages, document-wide layers, and text and graphic frames. The application that enabled the desktop publishing revolution to begin, is now about working smarter. Its scripting engine can automate your entire workflow process. Direct-to-PDF is saving lots of people lots of time. See for yourself: Adobe FAQ, crafted with PageMaker 6.5.

Contents

Adobe PageMaker®

Feature Techniques

MAC OS / WINDOWS

Q Is there a way to replace or remove a color that has been applied to multiple objects?

A Yes. You can either remove the color altogether—and have PageMaker assign black to the objects that had been assigned that color—or replace it with another existing color.

To remove a color, select "Define colors..." from the Element menu. In the "Define colors" dialog box, select the color you want to remove and click the "Remove" button. If that color is assigned to any objects, PageMaker will display a dialog box that gives you the option to change those objects to black or to cancel the color removal.

If you want to change one color (let's call it "Color1") to another color (which we'll call "Color2"), so that any objects assigned Color1 become Color2, follow these steps:

1. In the "Define colors" dialog box, select the color you want to replace (Color1) and click the "Edit..." button.
2. In the "Edit color" dialog box, change the name of Color1 to that of Color2. Be sure to spell it exactly the way the replacement color is spelled: use the same spacing, capitalization, and hyphenation. Otherwise, you'll simply change the name of your first color.
3. Click "OK." PageMaker will display a dialog box that says, "Change all Color1 items to Color2?" If you click "OK," PageMaker will return to the "Edit color" dialog box, where you can click "OK" again to complete the process. All the items that had been assigned your Color1 color will now be assigned the Color2 color, and your Color1 color will no longer appear on the Colors palette.

Note that you cannot remove or replace a color imported with an EPS file that you still have in your publication. Such colors are preceded by a "PS" icon on the Colors palette. You can, nevertheless, replace a non-EPS color with an EPS color.

Q The last issue of the magazine had a tip on making nonprinting text. Is there a way to make graphic elements nonprinting?

A Yes—you can use PageMaker's Scripting feature to make graphics as well as text blocks nonprinting. Nonprinting elements are handy to use as notes or visual signals to colleagues or service providers, or as guides to help you lay out your publication.

The following scripts take advantage of the scripting language's "suppressprint" command. This command allows you to determine whether a PageMaker object prints or not. For more information on the "suppressprint" and other scripting commands, see the Aldus PageMaker 5.0 Script Language Guide, available from Adobe Customer Services at (800) 628-2320. If you're not familiar with scripting or any type of macro language, don't worry—all you need for these steps is a little curiosity and some typing skills.

SCRIPT 1: TURNS A TEXT BLOCK INTO A NONPRINTING ELEMENT

To create the following script, open the Story Editor and select "New story" from the Story menu, then type the following text exactly as it appears below. Do not use any tabs. In addition, do not use typographer's quotes (you may need to temporarily turn off the "Use typographer's quotation marks" option in the "Preferences" dialog box). The following code contains the symbol ""—when you see this symbol, do not press the Return or Enter key to start a new line. Just press the spacebar once.

```
definecolor "non-repro blue",
   0, 0, 1, 40, 100, 100
printink "non-repro blue", 0,"",""
suppressprint 1
textedit
textselect +textblock
color "non-repro blue"
```

Next, select "Export" from the File menu, and select "Text-only" from the Format pop-up menu. Enter a name for your script—whatever name you choose will be what appears in the "Run script" dialog box, so use something easy to remember, like "off_text" (if you use PageMaker for Windows, your script name must be eight characters or less) or "nonprinting text block." Then, save your script in the SCRIPTS folder or directory—in Windows, it's a subdirectory of your PM5 directory; on the Mac, that folder is located within your "Aldus PageMaker 5.0" folder.

To use your script, select a text block with the pointer tool (if you select text with the text tool, the script won't work). Then, choose "Run script..." from the Additions submenu of the Utilities menu. In the "Run script" dialog box, select the script you named, and click "OK."

TIP MAC OS / WINDOWS

Creating nonprinting notes

Ever wish you could create a nonprinting note or comment in PageMaker? While there isn't a specific feature for this, you can create this effect in other ways. Here are two methods.

First, if your publication will be printed in a single color or your final output will be to color separations, create a special spot color for your notes. (Call it something like "nonprint notes.") Then, when you're ready to print your publication, select "Separations" in the "Color" print dialog box and select only the colors you do want to print. If a service bureau will be creating final output for you, make sure you let them know you've done this—otherwise, they might print separations for your notes, or worse, convert your notes color to a process color and print them that way.

If that method isn't practical—for instance, if you'll be printing final output or critical proofs to a composite color device—try this instead. Create a special style for your notes and assign it to any text you don't want to print during final output or certain proofs. Then, when you want to print everything in your document except the notes, edit your style so that the color of the text becomes "Paper." Just make sure none of the text is placed over colored backgrounds. Also, be sure to use a font that will be resident in your final output and proofing device, or that you're using elsewhere on the same page—that will ensure PageMaker doesn't end up downloading a font for your paper-colored text.

The script will do the following: First, it defines a color called "non-repro blue" and sets that color to be nonprinting (in other words, unchecks that ink in the ink list of the "Separations" section of the "Colors" print dialog box, so you won't get a "non-repro blue" plate if you print separations). Next, using the "suppressprint" command, it changes the entire text block into a nonprinting element. Then the script will select all the text in the text block and set its color to non-repro blue. Although the non-repro blue color doesn't cause the text to be nonprinting, it will help flag the text as a non-printing element.

SCRIPT 2: TURNS A TEXT BLOCK BACK INTO A PRINTING ITEM

To create this script, follow the directions in Script 1 to turn the following text into a script—name it something like "on_text" or "printing text block."

```
suppressprint 0
textedit
textselect +textblock
color "Black"
```

To use this script, select the pointer tool and click on a text block that's currently defined as a nonprinting element. Select "Run script..." from the Additions submenu of the Utilities menu, select your new script from the "Run script" dialog box, and click "OK." The script will change your text block back into a printing element and assign its color to black. (If you want your text to be some other color, you'll need to change it manually.)

SCRIPT 3: TURNS GRAPHIC ELEMENTS INTO NONPRINTING ITEMS

The following script turns graphic elements (PageMaker-drawn lines, boxes, and ovals, as well as imported graphics) into nonprinting elements. When you see the "" symbol, do not press the Return or Enter key to start a new line—just press the spacebar once.

```
definecolor "non-repro blue",
   0, 0, 1, 40, 100, 100
printink "non-repro blue", 0,"",""
suppressprint 1
color "non-repro blue"
```

Before running the script, use the pointer tool to select the graphic elements you want to make nonprinting. The script turns the object or objects you had selected into nonprinting elements and applies the "non-repro blue" color to them. (If you run this script on an imported color graphic, it won't change the object's on-screen colors.)

SCRIPT 4: TURNS GRAPHIC ELEMENTS INTO PRINTING ITEMS

To turn graphic elements back into printing items, select them with the pointer tool and run the following script.

```
suppressprint 0
color "Black"
```

This script will turn off the "suppressprint" command for the selected objects and assign them the color Black. If you want your object to be some other color, you'll need to change it manually. If your object is an imported color graphic that should not be assigned any color, select it and choose "Restore original color" from the Element menu.

Q I keep hearing about PPDs. They sound pretty important, but I don't quite understand why. What exactly are they?

A PPD (PostScript printer description) files are text-only files, written in the PostScript language, that describe the model-specific characteristics of PostScript devices (printers, imagesetters, and so forth). PageMaker and other applications that use PPDs rely on these files to give them the

MICRO TIP MAC OS / WINDOWS

If you want a word to hyphenate at a certain point and it isn't already doing so (perhaps because it's a word PageMaker's dictionary doesn't recognize), don't use a regular hyphen—if your text rewraps, that hyphen could end up in the middle of a line. Instead, use a discretionary hyphen (Ctrl + - in Windows; Command + - on the Mac). A discretionary hyphen is only visible when called into action—in other words, when the word in which it appears is at the end of a line and needs to break. At other times, the discretionary hyphen remains discreetly invisible.

information they need to print correctly and efficiently to PostScript devices.

When you print from PageMaker, you should select the right PPD file for your PostScript device from the "Type" pop-up menu in PageMaker's "Print document" dialog box. If you don't use the right PPD, chances are you won't be able to take advantage of all your printer's features, your jobs might print less quickly, and (in extreme cases) you could even receive PostScript errors.

Here's a partial list of the model-specific features described in a PPD file and why PageMaker needs that information when it prints:

- How much free virtual memory your PostScript device has. The free virtual memory setting in a PPD reflects how much RAM your PostScript device has available to produce the rasterized page descriptions of your files ("free virtual memory," in this case, is actual RAM and has nothing to do with your printer's hard disk). PageMaker uses this number to determine the most efficient way to download PostScript resources such as fonts. If you're using a PPD that says your printer has less free virtual memory than it really does have, PageMaker might download, flush, and redownload fonts more frequently than necessary, thereby needlessly increasing your print times. If your PPD file has a free virtual memory setting that's too high, you could experience PostScript errors.
- What fonts are built into your PostScript device. PageMaker uses the PPD's list of built-in fonts to determine which fonts it must download. Using the right PPD with the right font list will ensure PageMaker can download the correct fonts for the fastest possible output without font substitution.
- Your PostScript device's paper options. PPD files include information about what paper sizes and trays your PostScript device supports, and whether or not it offers custom paper sizes. Using the right PPD file ensures you can take advantage of all your PostScript device's paper features.

PageMaker 5.0 ships with dozens of PPD files—if you need to install one, just run the setup program "ALDSET-UP.-EXE" or PM5SETUP.EXE (Windows) or "Aldus Installer/Utility" (Macintosh) on the first PageMaker installation diskette. If PageMaker didn't come with a PPD file for your PostScript device, there are several places you can obtain one. First, try Adobe's free BBS at (206) 623-6984 and look in the "PPD files" folder in the "File Library" section. If you don't have a modem, try the nearest Adobe Authorized Service Provider, who may download the file for you. If those options don't pan out, try going directly to your PostScript device's manufacturer, who can supply you with a PPD file or recommend one that's a close match.

The information in PPD files reflects the model-specific characteristics of your PostScript device as it was manufactured. However, if you've changed your PostScript device—by adding fonts, memory, or other features—your PPD won't accurately describe your device anymore. If you want to take full advantage of the features you've added, you'll need to update the information about your printer. Fortunately, Adobe offers some utilities that make that easy.

If you use the Windows version of PageMaker, you can get a utility called "Update PPD"—the current version is 2.0 and it's available on Adobe's free BBS (call 206-623-6984 and download the "UPPPD2.ZIP" file from the section File Library: PM5: PC: UpdatePPD V2) and on Adobe's forums on CompuServe and America Online (see pages 114-15 for information on those forums). It's also included in the PageMaker 5.0 Enhancement Pack for Windows, available through Adobe Customer Services at (800) 628-2320 for a shipping and handling charge of $9.95.

If you use PageMaker 5.0 for the Macintosh, you can use the "Update PPD" Addition, which came with PageMaker. The most recent version of Update PPD is 1.7, and it's available on Adobe's free BBS (download "UPdp17.sea" from the section File Library:PM5:MAC:UpdatePPD) and on CompuServe and America Online. It's also in the Macintosh PageMaker 5.0 Enhancement Pack (see the previous paragraph for ordering information).

Both the Windows and Macintosh "Update PPD" utilities create a custom printer file, which is a special kind of PPD file that appends or overrides the information in the original PPD file. After creating a custom printer file with one of these utilities, be sure to use it when you print—select the new file instead of your original PPD from the "Type" pop-up menu in the "Print document" dialog box.

Q My office recently installed Adobe Acrobat Pro, and now we want to be able to create PDF files from our PageMaker publications. What's the best way?

A If you installed the "Pro" version of Adobe Acrobat, you have all four of the major components of Acrobat: the Acrobat Reader, the PDFWriter, Acrobat Exchange, and Acrobat Distiller. With these tools you have two options for creating PDF (Portable Document Format) files from PageMaker or most any application.

The easiest way is to use the PDFWriter, a special-purpose printer driver that lets you use the "Print" command to print directly to a PDF file. However, using the PDFWriter won't always give you the best results. The PDFWriter is a non-PostScript driver, and as such won't produce ideal results with documents from high-end layout programs, such as PageMaker, that are designed to produce their own PostScript code. If you use the PDFWriter to produce PDF files from PageMaker, you may notice color shifts in your documents, your transformed graphics may print untransformed, the screen previews of EPS files will print instead of the EPS files themselves, and your PDF files may be inconveniently large (larger than the PageMaker publication files from which they were created).

Despite these limitations, using the PDFWriter may be a good option if you want to quickly make a PDF file from a simple publication, if your PDF file will be viewed primarily on screen, or if your publication doesn't contain EPS files. Here's how to use the PDFWriter.

1. Select the Acrobat PDFWriter driver. In Windows, you can set that right in PageMaker—select "Acrobat PDFWriter" from the "Print to" drop-down menu in the "Print document" dialog box. On the Macintosh, select "Acrobat PDFWriter" in the Chooser.
2. Print your document as you normally would.
3. Enter a name for your PDF file when the Acrobat PDFWriter prompts you to. We recommend keeping the filename to eight characters or less and adding a ".PDF" extension to the end of the filename—that ensures your PDF file will be easy to identify and open on any platform (Macintosh, Windows, DOS, or UNIX).

Another way to create a PDF file from PageMaker is to print to a PostScript file, then process that file through the Acrobat Distiller. Using this method gives you more control over how your graphics will look and print in the PDF file, and, in many cases, will also give you higher-quality results (especially if your document contains EPS files). Also, if your publication contains high-resolution bitmap images that you want to downsample for on-screen viewing or relatively low resolution printing, you should use the Distiller.

To use the Distiller to create a PDF file from a PageMaker publication, follow these steps:

1. When your publication is ready to convert to PDF, save it and select "Print..." from PageMaker's File menu.
2. In PageMaker's "Print document" dialog box, make sure you're set to print to the right device. If you're using PageMaker for Windows, change your "Print to" printer to "Acrobat Distiller on \DISTASST.PS" (you can also select another PostScript printer driver, but if you do, you must select the "Write PostScript to file" option in step 4). If you're working on the Macintosh, make sure you've selected the "LaserWriter 8.1.1" or "PSPrinter 8.1.1" (or later) driver in the Chooser.
3. Select the Acrobat Distiller PPD from the "Type" pop-up menu in the "Print document" dialog box. If you're using PageMaker for Windows and the "Acrobat Distiller" PPD isn't available on this menu, you probably need to change its location on your hard disk. When you install the Distiller in Windows, it puts the Acrobat Distiller PPD (ACRODIST.PPD) in the ACRODIST\XTRAS directory. However, PageMaker won't see it there, so make a copy of that file and put it in the ALDUS\USENGLSH\PPD4 directory.
4. Make sure your publication will print to a PostScript file. On the PC, there are two ways to do this. One way is to select the "Acrobat Distiller C:\DISTASST.PS" device from the "Print to" drop-down menu. This will make your publication print to a PostScript file called DISTASST.PS, which will be located in your root directory. If you run the Acrobat Distiller Assistant, it will automatically distill this file for you. (The Distiller Assistant is available only on the PC; for more information, see its documentation.)

   The second way in Windows—and the only way on the Macintosh—that you can make PageMaker print your publication to a PostScript file is by selecting "Write PostScript to file" in the "Options" print dialog box and

TIP MAC OS / WINDOWS

Guides be gone

It's easy to get carried away with PageMaker's ruler guides during the design process—sometimes, before you know it, your screen is a maze of cyan lines obscuring your layout. Here are a few ways to eliminate this visual clutter:

- If you want to hide your ruler, column, and margin guides temporarily, press Ctrl + J (Windows) or Command + J (Macintosh). This keyboard shortcut deselects "Guides" from the "Guides and rulers" submenu of the Layout menu. (And, on a related note, pressing Ctrl + J or Command + J twice very quickly is a great way to force PageMaker to redraw your screen without zooming into a different portion of your page.)
- If you want to restore your ruler, column, and margin guides to the positions you defined on your master page, select "Copy master guides" from the Layout menu. (If this item is grayed out, deselect the "Lock guides" option on the "Guides and rulers" submenu of the Layout menu.)
- If you want to get rid of all your ruler guides, not just copy the ones from your master pages (especially if your master pages are where all the clutter is), hold down the Shift key while selecting "Guides" from the "Guides and rulers" submenu of the Layout menu—this will erase all the ruler guides from the current page. If this has no effect, make sure you deselect the "Lock guides" option from the same menu before trying it again.

entering a name for your file in the adjacent text field.

5. In the "PostScript" section of PageMaker's "Options" print dialog box, make sure the "Normal" option (not "EPS" or "For separations") is selected.
6. If you'll be distilling your PostScript file on the same computer on which you created it, or from some other computer that will have all the fonts you've used in your document installed, you can deselect the "Include downloadable fonts" option in PageMaker's "Options" print dialog box. Leaving that option selected would make your PostScript file unnecessarily large—if those fonts are installed when you process the file through the Distiller, it will be able to obtain all the font information it needs from your operating system.
7. If you're printing a file that contains bitmap graphics, we recommend you select the "Normal" (instead of "Optimized") graphics option.
8. Select any other printing options you want, and press "Save" (or "Print" if you're in Windows and did not select the "Write PostScript to file" option). PageMaker will print your document to a PostScript file.
9. Once you've created your PostScript file, you're ready to process it through the Distiller. (If you're in Windows and you're using the Distiller Assistant, you won't need to perform this step—Distiller Assistant will do it for you.) Refer to the Distiller documentation for information on how to control font embedding and graphic compression.

Q I create instructional language workbooks in PageMaker, and often need to create sentences that contain a fill-in line with descriptive words underneath it (see the bottom example below). I tried using drawn rules and a separate text block, but they stay behind if the text reflows. Any suggestions?

A There is a way to do it, although it's a little tricky. Essentially, you type the descriptive word after the line, and then use negative kerning, a small font size, and baseline shift to get the word underneath the line. Here's how we created the example below—you may want to adjust the measurements for your situation, but the basic technique should be adaptable.

See Billy__________ verb after the ball

See Billy__________ *verb* after the ball

See Billy__*verb*__ after the ball

See Billy__________ after the ball
verb

1. Type "See Billy __________ verb after the ball." Use 10 underscore characters for the line.
2. Select the space before the word "verb" and replace it with a nonbreaking space character (Ctrl + Shift + H in Windows, Option + spacebar on the Mac).
3. With the text tool, select the nonbreaking space character. Display the Control palette if it isn't already visible (Ctrl + ' in Windows, Command + ' on the Mac). In the text-size field, enter a point size of 100, and then press the Tab key to move to the leading field. There, enter the leading of your text (in our case, 24 points). Press Return or Tab to leave that field.
4. Back on your page, use the text tool to select the word verb. In the Control palette, change the word's size to 7 points, and click the "I" button to italicize it.
5. Click an insertion point immediately before the letter v in verb. (If you're not sure where you are, open the Story Editor and find the insertion point there, then close the Story Editor.) Use the left-hand kerning button in the Control palette to apply negative kerning until verb is centered over the underscores.
6. Select the word verb. The easiest way is to leave the cursor where it was, just preceding the word, and hold down Shift while pressing the right arrow key four times. Alternatively, open the Story Editor and select it there, then close the Story Editor.
7. In the lower-right corner of the Control palette, click the down arrow to lower the word's baseline until it's underneath the underscores. (Or you can enter a number in the text field—in our case, it was 8 points down, which you enter as –0p8).
8. With the word verb still selected, press the right arrow key once. This puts the cursor immediately before the a in after. Press the spacebar until the word after is aligned to the right of the underscore characters.

NOTE: PageMaker doesn't update its display of baseline-shifted text, so you may get some odd screen behavior—the shifted word may sometimes disappear, or get split in two. If that happens, just force a screen redraw, either by choosing any view from the Layout menu or by pressing Ctrl + J (Windows) or Command + J (Mac) twice. Also, if you need to edit the text at all, you'll find it's much easier in the Story Editor.

Q When I place certain graphics in my PageMaker documents, I get a message asking if I want to replace colors defined in the EPS. Why is this happening, and what should I do?

A PageMaker displays this alert message when it finds a color name in an EPS file that already exists in the PageMaker publication, but with a different definition—either it uses different CMYK values, or it is defined as a different color type (e.g., spot, process, tint). The message reads, "The color name '[colorname]' already exists in this publication with a different definition. Replace it with the color in the EPS?" You can choose "Yes" or "No"; on the Mac, you can also choose "Yes to all" or "No to all," which covers any additional colors with multiple definitions.

Choosing "Yes" (or "Yes to all") allows the EPS color's definition to override PageMaker's definition of that color. Any elements assigned that color in PageMaker will change to the imported EPS color's definition. Conversely, choosing "No" (or "No to all") lets PageMaker's definition of the color override the imported EPS's definition, so elements

TIP MAC OS / WINDOWS

Sharing styles among publications

If you've ever designed a series of publications that need a consistent graphic identity, you probably know it's important to use the same styles throughout those publications. That's easy enough to do if you create all the publications from the same template (and just define all your styles in that template before you start on the individual publications). But most of us update our styles as we work, experimenting with and changing our "draft" styles. Fortunately, there are a couple of ways to share styles among publications after you've begun work on them.

Use the "Copy" command in the "Define styles" dialog box to copy all the styles from one publication to your active publication. Select "Define styles..." from the Type menu and, in the "Define styles" dialog box, click on the "Copy" button. PageMaker will display the "Copy styles" dialog box, in which you can select the publication whose styles you want to copy into your active publication. Click "OK."

If you use the "Copy" command in the "Define styles" dialog box to copy a PageMaker style into a publication that already has a style by that name, the incoming style definition will replace the definition of the existing style (you'll receive the alert pictured at right). In addition, if some of the styles in your publication are based on a style that's overridden by an incoming style, some of those styles' attributes may change too, just as they would if you edited the original style on which they're based. If you want to prevent incoming styles from overriding or affecting existing styles, name your styles differently from publication to publication.

Use the Clipboard to copy one or a few styles from one publication to another. To do so, open the publication that contains the styles you want to copy elsewhere. Select text that contains paragraphs assigned each of the styles you want and copy it to the Clipboard (select "Copy" from the Edit menu, or press Ctrl + C in Windows or Command + C on the Mac).

Open the publication into which you want to copy the styles. Select "Paste" from the Edit menu or press Ctrl + V (Windows) or Command + V (Macintosh) to paste the text and copy the styles to that publication's Styles palette. If you use this method to copy a PageMaker style into a publication that already has a style by that name, the existing style in the active publication will not change to the incoming style's definition—and the incoming text assigned that style will take on the attributes of your existing style definition.

in the EPS file assigned that color will print using PageMaker's color definition. In either case, the color(s) in question will appear in the Colors palette preceded by a "PS" icon.

Combining color definitions can get pretty tricky, for several reasons.

- On-screen display. If you override the EPS's color definitions with those from PageMaker (by choosing "No" or "No to all"), the EPS colors won't change on screen—their appearance is determined by the EPS's screen preview, which PageMaker can't alter. If you do override the PageMaker definitions with the EPS ones, the PageMaker colors will shift on screen to reflect the new definition, but still may not match the way the EPS colors display. So be sure to keep track of your color definitions, especially if other people are going to be working on the document—it can be a surprise to find that two elements with different on-screen appearances are actually the same color when you print.
- Spot vs. process colors. PageMaker will display the alert message if anything about the colors' definitions is different—for instance, if one is a spot color and the other is a process color. So, unless you're careful, you can wind up converting from one color type to the other without meaning to. (Remember, process colors are italicized in PageMaker's Colors palette.) Also, of course, if you're working with spot-color separations, the colors' CMYK definitions don't matter—the important thing is applying the right color names to the right elements, so that everything winds up on the proper printing plate.
- Unplanned color-name overlap. Sometimes, you don't realize until you see the alert message that there are colors in the EPS file named the same as those in the PageMaker document. The alert message doesn't have a "Cancel" button—what if you want to keep the colors separate? Go ahead and choose "No" (or "No to all") in the alert box, place the graphic, and then delete it. Then choose "Define colors..." from the Element menu and rename the colors in question (or rename them in the application that created the EPS, and re-export the EPS). Also, see the following paragraph for another approach to this situation.
- The "Preserve EPS colors" option. If you've changed the definition of a color in an EPS—either by overriding the EPS definitions upon import, or by using PageMaker's "Edit colors..." command after importing—you can print the EPS colors as originally defined by checking "Preserve EPS colors" in PageMaker's "Color" print dialog box. The only thing this can't "undo" is if you've altered the color's type, such as from spot to process.
- Differences in case sensitivity. PageMaker ignores capitalization in color names, but PostScript does not—and

there's one scenario in which this can cause trouble. The problem arises when (a) the EPS graphic contains process colors whose names are identical to those in PageMaker except in how they're capitalized (such as "pea green" vs. "Pea Green"), and (b) you let the definitions in PageMaker override those in the EPS file—that is, you choose "No" (or "No to all") in the alert box. The Colors palette will contain only "Pea Green," but both the original color definitions (for "pea green" and "Pea Green") will be used when you print to a PostScript device.

Q I work with a service bureau that gives me a discount if I supply them with a PostScript file instead of my PageMaker publication. That's great, but I'm a nervous wreck when I do this with a color publication. Is there any way to check the PostScript files before I pay to have them run out on film?

A Yes, there are several things you can do to check your publication before imagesetting. Whether you give your service bureau a PageMaker publication file or a PostScript file that'll be color-separated, you should always print color separations to a PostScript device in-house. Often a desktop PostScript printer will work fine for this purpose, but if you don't have a PostScript printer in house you can run your PostScript file through Acrobat Distiller (which is a PostScript device), and then view your file in Acrobat Reader or Acrobat Exchange.

If you're new to imagesetting and aren't sure how to prepare files for a service bureau, talk to them about your job before your proceed. You might also want to consult the following FaxYI documents: 315120, "Writing Post-Script to File for Output at a Service Bureau from Page-Maker 5.0x (Windows)"; 315115, "Preparing a PostScript File in PageMaker 5.0x (Windows)"; and 215116, "Preparing a PageMaker Publication for a Service Bureau (Macntosh)."

Printing test separations to a desktop PostScript printer. If your publication will be color-separated, it's a good idea to try printing color separations in house to a PostScript desktop laser printer. If your publication and the necessary printer marks (registration marks, crop marks, and color-separation names) won't fit on your laser printer's paper, select the "Reduce to fit" option in the "Paper" print dialog box. Some things to look for on test separations include objects not printing on the right separation, objects printing on all the separations (such objects were probably assigned the color "Registration" instead of "Black"), and overprinting behavior. For a more comprehensive list of things to check, see "It Just Takes Two" (Aldus Magazine, November 1994, pages 42–47).

If you want to print test separations of your final PostScript files (the ones you'll actually give to your service provider), you may not be able to print them successfully on your desktop PostScript printer without a utility like Systems of Merritt's LaserCheck. LaserCheck is a PostScript program that you download to your desktop PostScript printer (which must have a true Adobe PostScript interpreter, not a "clone" interpreter). LaserCheck allows your desktop printer to simulate an imagesetter—it will automatically scale your publication down so it fits on whatever paper you have, and prints a variety of useful information about your print job (like what fonts it requires) in the margins of the paper. For more information, call Systems of Merritt at (334) 660-1240, or E-mail them at 70363.3724@compuserve.com.

Use Acrobat as a proofing tool. If you don't have a PostScript printer in house, another great way to print test separations is by using Adobe Acrobat. Adobe Acrobat software is primarily intended for creating and viewing electronically published documents (see "Beyond Paper with PageMaker 6.0" on page 64 for more information), but it also provides a great way to interpret and view PostScript files. Acrobat Distiller can read in a PostScript file you create from PageMaker or any other application, and convert it to a PDF (Portable Document Format) file that you can view in Acrobat Reader (which also comes with PageMaker 6.0) or Acrobat Exchange. For more information on Acrobat, see its documentation and Help files.

Q Can I open my old publications in PageMaker 6.0?

A Yes. PageMaker 6.0 can open and convert publications from PageMaker 4.x and PageMaker 5.0 as long as your older publications are from the same platform as the one on which you're converting them. In other words, the Mac or Power Mac versions of PageMaker 6.0 can convert Mac PageMaker 4.x and Mac or Power Mac 5.0 publications; the Windows version of PageMaker 6.0 can convert Windows PageMaker 4.0 and 5.0 publications. If you want to convert a 4.x or 5.0 publication to 6.0 format and translate it from the Mac/Power Mac platform to Windows (or vice versa), you'll need to convert that publication to 6.0 on its original platform and then translate it to the other platform, or you can translate it to the same PageMaker version on the other platform and then convert it to 6.0.

TIP MAC OS / WINDOWS

Send in the clones

Many drawing applications offer a "cloning" feature—a way to paste a copy of an object directly onto its original. There's no "Clone" command in PageMaker's menus, but you can get the same effect anyway. To clone an object in PageMaker, select it with the pointer tool, and press Ctrl + C (Windows) or Command + C (Mac) to copy it to the clipboard. Then press Ctrl + Shift + P (Windows) or Command + Option + V (Mac) to paste a copy of the object onto the original. One handy use of this is to get two identical objects lined up horizontally—clone the first one, then Shift-drag the clone (which keeps its motion horizontal).

To convert your old publications, all you need to do is select "Open..." from PageMaker 6.0's File menu, and in the "Open Publication" dialog box, select the PageMaker 4.x or 5.0 publication you want to convert. (If you're using PageMaker 6.0 for Windows, you'll first need to select "Older PageMaker Files" from the "Files of Type" list.) Click "OK." PageMaker 6.0 will convert your files and open untitled versions of them.

When you convert PageMaker 5.0 publications to 6.0 format, you shouldn't see any changes to your files—line endings, graphics, and so forth should remain the same unless, of course, you're missing fonts required by the publication or you no longer have graphics that were linked to the publication but not stored internally. It's also possible that some line endings could change if your PageMaker 5.0 user dictionary contains hyphenation information that your PageMaker 6.0 dictionary does not.

To prevent such changes, try the "Use PM5 Custom Settings" utility that comes with PageMaker 6.0. This utility allows you to copy dictionaries, custom dictionaries, custom color libraries, and tracking values from PageMaker 5.0 to PageMaker 6.0. See the Adobe PageMaker 6.0 Getting Started manual for more information.

You're more likely to see changes if you convert your PageMaker 4.x publications to PageMaker 6.0 format, mostly because there are differences between the way PageMaker 4.x and 5.0/6.0 track text (PageMaker 5.0 and 6.0 use the same tracking values, which are slightly looser than the tracking values PageMaker 4.x uses). If you used tracking in your 4.x publications and want to prevent them from changing when you convert them to 6.0, do the following:

1. Copy the PageMaker 4.x tracking-values file to the folder or directory that contains the publication(s) you want to convert (you'll need to keep that file there for the tracking values to remain in effect for publications in that folder). In Windows, this file is called KERNTRACK.BIN and is located in the PM4 directory. On the Mac, the file is called "Kern Tracks" and is located in the "Aldus" folder in your System Folder.
2. Rename that file to the name used by PageMaker 5.0 and 6.0. In Windows, that name is TRAKVALS.BIN. On the Mac, the name is "Tracking Values."
3. Convert your publication.

There's just one more thing you should be aware of if you're converting publications. In certain unusual cases, PageMaker 6.0 cannot open and convert PageMaker 4.x and 5.0 files that have damaged elements or file-structure anomalies, even though those files can be opened in PageMaker 4.x or 5.0. (PageMaker 4.x and 5.0 could ignore certain problems in files and open and print them anyway.) If you run into a file like this, open it in PageMaker 4.x or 5.0 and perform some troubleshooting steps on it. Try a diagnostic recompose while no objects are selected (in Windows, hold down Ctrl + Shift while selecting "Hyphenation..." from the Type menu; on the Macintosh, hold down Option + Shift while selecting "Hyphenation..."). Save the publication with the "Save as..." command, and try converting it again. If it still won't convert, open it in PageMaker 4.x or 5.0, copy the publication's elements into a new publication file, and try converting it once more.

MICRO TIP MAC OS / WINDOWS

> You can also use discretionary hyphens to prevent specific words from hyphenating. To do so, place the discretionary hyphen (Ctrl + - in Windows, Command + - on the Mac) immediately before the word's first character.

Q Can I have PageMaker 6.0 and 5.0 on one computer?
A Yes, you can run versions 5.0 and 6.0 on the same computer (Windows, Macintosh, or Power Macintosh). That's because PageMaker 5.0 and 6.0 don't share any files that are named the same and located in the same folders.

Although you won't run into any technical problems having both programs installed on the same machine or even running simultaneously, you shouldn't plan on doing it long-term if you've purchased an upgrade version of PageMaker 6.0. When you purchase an upgrade (not the full retail version of the product), you're not buying another copy of PageMaker, and therefore can't legally have an additional copy installed. However, the PageMaker 6.0 upgrade licensing agreement allows you to have both PageMaker 5.0 and 6.0 installed for a period of 90 days, so you have both at your disposal while you're converting publications and learning PageMaker 6.0's new features.

Q *(6.0 only)* **I'd like to take advantage of the color-management system in PageMaker, but I don't understand what source profiles I should select when I import images. Is there any easy way to decide which one is best to use?**
A Deciding what source profile to use shouldn't be too difficult—but before you can, you'll need to understand what those profiles do. Here's a very brief explanation.

A color-management source profile describes the color characteristics of the device a color image came from—what color model (RGB, CMYK, or LAB, for instance) that device uses and how it tends to describe color within that model. That information allows the color management system to translate the image into and out of a neutral color space so you get more consistent color output (to a monitor, printer, or other device). This explanation should help you visualize the process to some degree, but if you're new to color management you'll benefit from a more complete overview—try Bruce Fraser's "Color Under Control" article in the September/October issue of Adobe Magazine, pages 41–45. And if you haven't already, go through the color-management chapter in the Adobe PageMaker 6.0 User Guide, pages 241–54.

To assign a source profile to a bitmap image you're placing into PageMaker, you'll need to know where that bitmap image came from (a particular scanner or a Photo CD, for instance) and whether it's been edited or color-corrected on screen in an application like Photoshop. Then follow the guidelines below. NOTE: We don't recommend that you assign source profiles at the time you import an image (using the "CMS Source..." button in the "Place" dialog box). Instead, assign your source profile after you've imported an image by selecting it and choosing "CMS Source..." from the Image submenu of the Element menu. When PageMaker places the image, it parses it to determine what color model it uses (CMYK or RGB, for instance)—and that allows PageMaker to present you with a shorter, more appropriate list of profiles to choose from.

If your image was scanned and hasn't been edited on screen in an image-editing program like Photoshop, use the source profile for that scanner model. If PageMaker 6.0 did not include a source profile for that scanner, contact the manufacturer of your scanner to see if it can be purchased. If one isn't available, you can contact Kodak at (800) 235-6325 to purchase the Precision Input Color Characterization (PICC) software, which will enable you to create a custom profile for your scanner or other input device.

If the image was scanned and then color-corrected on screen in an image-editing application, you should select the source profile for the monitor the image was displaying on when it was color-corrected. But you should assign a source profile only if that monitor was calibrated at the time your image was color-corrected—if the monitor wasn't calibrated, do not assign a source profile. If you need a particular monitor source profile that didn't come with PageMaker, you can do one of three things. First, contact the monitor manufacturer to see if a source profile is available from them. Second, you can use the Kodak Monitor Installer Utility that came with PageMaker to create or edit a monitor profile. Third, you can contact Kodak to obtain the Precision Input Color Characterization software (see the previous paragraph for more information).

If the image you're working with is from a Kodak Photo CD, then choose the source profile that best matches the original film type (Ektachrome or Kodachrome, for instance)—this information will be accessible from the "Kodak Photo CD Import Filter" dialog box that displays automatically when you place a Photo CD image in PageMaker. In that dialog box, click on the "Image Info" button, note the string of numbers and letters next to "Product Type of Original" (as shown above), and click "OK."

MICRO TIP MAC OS / WINDOWS

> If you run into NCD errors because more users are running the same copy of PageMaker than is permitted by that license, you can use the "WINBUMPS" utility (located in the ALDUS\USENGLSH\UTILITY directory) to increase the number of users permitted to run that copy of PageMaker. But first you'll need to buy enough copies of PageMaker or PageMaker licenses to cover that increase, and you'll need to get a password from Adobe Customer Service. See FaxYI document 315404, "Running PageMaker 5.0 WINBUMPS Utility . . ." for more information.

When you're ready to assign a source profile to the image, you can find the right one by selecting the Photo CD profiles one at a time, paying attention to the string of numbers and letters that appears in the bottom section of the dialog box, until you find a profile with the same string that appeared in the "Image Info" dialog box when you placed the image into your publication.

Please note: If you don't have complete information on a particular image's source, you should not try to color-manage it (in other words, don't assign any source profile to it).

Q What exactly is the difference between using "Save" versus "Save As" when saving a file in PageMaker? Is one better than the other?

A You're not going to catch us opining that one feature is better than the other—too subjective. "Save" and "Save As" ultimately serve the same purpose, but differ in function and performance.

By default, "Save" is faster than "Save As." It's faster because when you select "Save," PageMaker is only appending your document by adding your latest changes and additions to the end of the file. When you choose "Save As," PageMaker rewrites your entire file to incorporate all the current information about the publication. Obviously, this process takes longer, because PageMaker is performing additional functions.

Here's a real-world example of the differences between "Save" and "Save As." Let's say you have an existing document that contains an embedded 429-K graphic, and that the total file size of your publication at this point is 545 K.

Then you decide to delete that graphic and import and embed a new 1-MB graphic in its place. At this point, if you did a regular "Save," both graphics (the deleted and the new) would still be a part of the document, even though you see only the new one. As a result, your file size will increase to reflect the additional graphic you've added to the publication. With our sample publication, the file size would be 1.6 MB after doing a regular "Save."

If you do a "Save As," on the other hand, PageMaker removes the 429-K graphic from the document, so the sample publication would now be about 1 MB in size.

Don't be fooled—or disappointed—because "Save As" has no keyboard shortcut. You can have it all—the functionality of making the file smaller and the easy access via keyboard shortcut—by specifying that the "Save" function have the same properties as the "Save As" function. Here's how:

1. Select "Preferences..." from the File menu.
2. Choose "Smaller" in the "Save options" area.
3. Click "OK."

When the "Save option" is set to "Smaller," selecting "Save" from the File menu or pressing Ctrl + S (Windows) or Command + S (Mac) is functionally the same as doing a "Save As."

(If you don't want to wait around for "Save As" every time you save, we still recommend using it at least once a day if you've been working a great deal on a document, to clean out excess data from your publication. When you do

TIP MAC OS / WINDOWS

Punctuation hang-ups

If you're centering text or setting a small amount of left-aligned or right-aligned text in a formal way, your work will look more finished if you "hang" your punctuation (in other words, rig your text so punctuation at the beginning or end of a line isn't taken into account for the text's centering or alignment).

It's easy to create this effect in PageMaker. For lines of centered text, make sure lines that begin or end with punctuation marks contain those marks at both ends of the line. Then, select the punctuation you don't want visible, and apply a color of "Paper" (or your background color) to it. In the example below, we've outlined our extra punctuation so you can better see what we've done:

.Furious, she slammed the door.
.There was a deathly pause.
"And don't ever let me catch you dangling"
.an elliptical phrase again!" she roared.

To hang text in small quantities of left-aligned text or right-aligned text, make sure all the lines contain the same punctuation along their aligned side. Select the punctuation you don't want visible, and apply the "Paper" color or your background color to it (shown below in outline).

"Furious, she slammed the door.
"There was a deathly pause.
"And don't ever let me catch you dangling
"an elliptical phrase again!" she roared.

Furious, she slammed the door.
There was a deathly pause.
"And don't ever let me catch you dangling.
an elliptical phrase again!" she roared.

Tip submitted by Peter Zelchenko, InfoComm Electronic Prepress, Chicago, Ill.

this, choose "Save As"; then, when prompted to replace the existing version of the file, click "Yes." Of course, it's also a good idea to choose "Save As" once in a while to really save your file to another name, as a backup.)

Having large publications is not inherently dangerous. However, it's a good idea to keep your documents as trim as possible; there's no reason to store unnecessary information. By using "Save As" frequently, you'll have happier, healthier, and smaller documents.

Q *(6.0 only)* **I thought clipping paths were importable only with an EPS graphic, yet I've heard it's possible to import TIFF graphics that have clipping paths into PageMaker 6.0. Is this true?**

A Yes. PageMaker 6.0x can read a TIFF with a clipping path from Adobe Photoshop 3.0 or later. Clipping-path information is stored in the alpha channel of a TIFF, and PageMaker 6.0 includes the ability to read channel and path information. Translated into English, PageMaker can now print using the transparent background created by the clipping path—and that means an end to (or at least a way to get around) those unforgivingly opaque rectangular boundaries.

One of the welcome benefits of this technology is that you can take advantage of clipping paths when you print to a non-PostScript printer. TIFFs can also be compressed, whereas EPS graphics cannot.

Of course, PageMaker still supports clipping paths in EPS graphics (although under Windows 3.11 they may not print to non-PostScript printers—see the second question on page 75 for more information).

Q I've created a table of contents, but the entries in it are displaying in a different order from how they appear in my publication. Is this feature broken, or am I doing something wrong?

A Neither. It's just a question of the order in which PageMaker reads the information on the page. Fortunately, your problem can be easily solved and avoided in the future once you understand how the feature works.

PageMaker orders the TOC entries based on the relative positioning of the text blocks on a page. When there are multiple text blocks on a page, even if those blocks are all part of a single threaded story, PageMaker lists entries from text blocks farthest to the left first, even if other text blocks begin higher on the page. If they are all equally aligned, PageMaker lists them in order down the page. The feature was designed this way to simplify the creation of a table of contents for multiple-column pages. Check your text blocks to ensure that the left sides of their windowshade handles are all precisely aligned vertically. If necessary, use the Control Palette (or a guide, making sure Snap to Guides is enabled) to verify the alignment of the text blocks . Then recreate the TOC using "Create TOC..." from the Utilities menu.

One way to ensure a correctly ordered table of contents is to use one long story for the main body of your work, with all heads (or, more specifically, TOC entries) identically aligned. But, since it's not always possible or desirable to use such a rigid layout, it's important to know what's going to happen when you use multiple, non-aligned text blocks. And remember, the TOC is an editable story; you can always correct the order manually, after your layout is complete.

Q When I'm importing a graphic, I often receive the message "The graphic in the document would occupy [size] Kbytes in the publication. Include complete copy in the publication anyway?" I usually just click "Yes," but I'm never sure if this is the right choice. What difference does it make?

A Clicking "Yes" could make a big difference if you plan to import many large graphics into a PageMaker publication; as is often the case, you have to consider the trade-offs inherent in your choices. The question you describe above really asks you: "Do you want to make your PageMaker publication much larger, but not have to keep track of your original graphic files, or would you prefer to keep your publication small but have to monitor the graphic files?" Links are at the core of this discussion, so we'll review them here.

Whenever you import something into PageMaker using the "Place..." command, it creates a link to the original file, regardless of what kind or size of text document or graphic you are importing. This link consists of a path that tells PageMaker where the file is located. To see the path, choose "Links..." from the File menu, click on one of the links, and then click the "Info..." button. Look at the "Location" information on the right side of the window. That's the path.

Links are created for two basic reasons. One is that links allow you to dynamically update information that has been placed into your publication. For instance, say you place a graphic into PageMaker on Tuesday, and then on Wednesday you open up that graphic in Photoshop, make some changes, and save it. The next time you open the PageMaker publication containing that graphic, PageMaker will notice that the graphic has been modified since the publication was last opened. You can set PageMaker to automatically update a graphic whenever changes are made to it so that you don't have to re-import the modified graphic into PageMaker. See "Managing linked text and graphics," which starts on page 304 of the Adobe PageMaker User Guide.

The second reason that PageMaker creates a link will address your original question. In order to help you maintain your publications at a manageable size, PageMaker provides you the option of not including the graphic as part of the publication. Every graphic that you store in the publication will add its own size to the total publication size. So if you have a graphic that is 500 K and you add it to a 150-K publication by clicking "Yes" to the question above, your total publication size would then become approximately 650 K. If you click "No" to the question above, the publication will include only a low-resolution bitmap or screen image as a placeholder, so the total publication size would increase only slightly—say, to approximately 200 K.

Smaller publications take up less RAM and less of your computer's resources, which adds up to better performance while you're working in that publication. Smaller publications also have less chance—even on a purely statistical basis—of becoming damaged or having read/write problems when being opened, closed, or moved, especially in a network environment.

Given this, the answer to your question seems obvious, right? Well, not exactly. You still have to weigh the advantages and disadvantages.

You've already seen some of the benefits of saying "No"—of not including a copy of graphics in your publication. The disadvantage is that PageMaker becomes completely dependent on that link to the original image. If that link is ever broken, the image may not print properly. (Links are broken when the original image is no longer at the location specified in the "Links" dialog box, because it has been moved, renamed, or—heaven forbid— deleted.) The good news is that PageMaker will warn of this danger automatically when you try to print a document containing broken links critical for printing, and will give you a choice of printing anyway or canceling the job. As a result, when you store graphics outside of your publication, you must

TIP MAC OS / WINDOWS

Screen redraws on command

There are lots of times when forcing PageMaker to redraw the screen can help you see things better. One obvious way to get PageMaker to do this is by switching views, but that can be a hassle if you've zoomed into a particular area of your page and don't want to move. When that's the case, try this: redraw your screen by quickly pressing Ctrl + J (Windows) or Command + J (Mac) twice. Those keyboard shortcuts turn PageMaker's ruler and margin guides either on or off, and they also force a screen redraw. Using the shortcut twice in quick succession doesn't change whether your guides are displaying, but it does force a screen redraw without changing your view.

manage your links carefully; moving or renaming files will cost you in time down the line if nothing else (although PageMaker has thoughtfully included an "All linked files" option in the "Save As" dialog box for just those occasions when you need to gather up your files for remote printing).

One of the primary advantages of clicking "Yes" to store images in the publication is the relative freedom of not having to manage your links (unless the graphics change). Because the image is included as part of the publication, PageMaker no longer depends on the link to print the image. The original can be moved, renamed, or deleted, and, in most cases, PageMaker will still be able to print the image properly. If your graphics seldom change, all the better.

In general, if you are working with a large number of graphics (say, around 20 or more per publication), or graphics larger than 1 MB, you should avoid including a copy of the graphics in the publication. If you have only a few graphics in your publication, and they're fairly small, they won't significantly increase the size of your publication. Under these circumstances, it might be to your advantage to embed the graphics. Another time to consider linking graphics is when including them would cause your file to be very large. "Very large" is a matter of personal preference and experience, perhaps influenced by how often you have to move your files to different locations. As a very general starting point, we suggest that 5 MB is a suitable threshold over which to consider linking.

Here are a few ways that PageMaker can help you customize the way that you handle storing graphics on a publication-specific or application-wide basis.

- Adjust the size threshold for automatically storing graphics (by default, 256 K). Select "Preferences..." from the File menu, then click "More..." and change the value in the "Alert when storing graphics over" box. To make this the default setting for any document you subsequently create in PageMaker, make the change without any PageMaker documents open.
- Tell PageMaker whether or not you'd like to automatically store everything in the publication by default. Choose "Link Options..." from the Element menu, making sure no element is selected. Leave "Store copy in publication" checked to automatically include copies of all graphics (remembering that PageMaker will still alert you when placing graphics larger than the size you designated under "Preferences") or unchecked to keep the full graphics outside the publication. By default, this option is checked for all new publications you create.
- In PageMaker 6.01, use the new Global Link Options Plug-in (from the Utilities menu) to further customize your graphics storage options on a page-by-page basis. The Global Link Options Plug-in also lets you change from internal to external (or vice versa) at any time. If you switch from internal storage to linking, remember to then use "Save As..." so PageMaker can purge the stored graphics from the publication.

Q I've heard that Adobe recommends that you should always save PageMaker publications directly to a fixed hard drive. Is this true? If so, why?

A Yes, this is true. Many removable hard drives and other removable media are fast, flexible, and inexpensive ways to expand your hard-drive capacity. They're also great for archiving and backing up your data (something we recommend vigorously!). But we don't recommend saving your publications directly to them. Instead, save to your hard drive and then copy it to your removable disk or cartridge. Here's why.

Although many types of removable media are very reliable, many aren't quite as reliable as fixed hard drives, because they get . . . well, removed and moved around quite a bit. This can expose them to all sorts of environmental hazards like magnetism, dust, and moisture, which can damage the disk and its contents. And some types of removable media aren't designed for constant reading, writing, and modification the way fixed hard drives are. If you're not sure how your type of removable media is intended to be used, check with its manufacturer. For comparative information on the reliability and other features of various removable media, look for reviews in hardware-oriented computer magazines.

When you save your publications directly to removable media instead of copying them there after you've saved them to a fixed hard drive, you miss out on copy verification. When an application (not just PageMaker) saves a file to disk, no copy verification occurs. As a result, if there is a problem with the part(s) of the media the file has been written to, that file will get damaged and you wouldn't necessarily know about it until the next time you try to open the file. However, when you copy a file from your local hard drive to another drive, copy verification does occur. This way, you're more likely to detect a problem with the media that the file is being written to, if one occurs.

Q Using PageMaker, I created a logo that consists of text with a few drawn elements. How can I export it from PageMaker so I can use it in other applications?

A Since PageMaker isn't a drawing application, it's not specifically designed to do this. Our recommendation is that you use a drawing application such as Illustrator for this sort of work. But if you're in a pinch and need to turn some PageMaker elements into a graphic, there are a few methods you can use. The one that will give you the highest-quality results is the EPS method (explained on the next page), but this will work only if you're printing to a PostScript device. The first three solutions below will work in other situations.

MICRO TIP MAC OS / WINDOWS

By holding down the Control + Shift keys (Windows) or the Control key (Macintosh) while redrawing your page, you can view graphics in high resolution when "Normal" is selected in the "Preferences" dialog box.

MICRO TIP MAC OS / WINDOWS

Have a PPD that's not showing up in your "Type" pop-up menu? Perhaps the PPD file is in the wrong folder or directory. In Windows, make sure your PPD file is the ALDUS/USENGLSH/PPD4 directory (or whatever your PPD4 directory is according to the "PPD4=. . ." line in the [Aldus] section of your WIN.INI file). On the Mac, make sure it's in the "Printer Descriptions" folder in your "Extensions" folder within the System Folder.

Turn your graphic into a PICT (Mac only). If you're using PageMaker on the Mac, you can select all the elements in your logo, choose "Copy" from the Edit menu, and then select "Paste Special..." from the Edit menu. In the "Paste Special" dialog box, select the PICT format and click "OK." PageMaker will paste a vector PICT version of your logo back in your document. You can also paste the PICT into an image-editing application such as Photoshop. But be aware that it won't come into Photoshop at a very high resolution (just 72 dpi), so to improve the results you can try enlarging your logo before copying it to the Clipboard.

Take a screen capture of your logo. Zoom into your logo so it's as big as you can get it while still fitting it on your screen. If you're using Windows, press the Print Screen key; if you're on a Mac, press Command + Shift + 3.

In Windows, this will cause the system to take a picture of your entire screen and place it on the Clipboard. Then you can paste the Clipboard's contents into Photoshop or another image-editing application where you can crop it and save it in whatever format you like. It's also possible to paste it into PageMaker as is, and crop it there.

On the Mac, pressing Command + Shift + 3 will cause the system to take a picture of your entire screen and save it as a PICT called "Picture 1" (or "Picture 2," "Picture 3," and so on if you've already taken some screen captures) on your startup drive. Open that PICT in an image-editing application such as Photoshop, crop it as you wish, and save it in any format. You can also place it into PageMaker and crop it there.

How successful you are with this method will depend on how large a screen capture you can take of your image—the larger it is, the finer its resolution will be. And your capture will be only as good as your elements' screen display is. If you're taking a screen capture of a bitmap object (e.g., a TIFF), you can maximize its display quality by entering 1024 in the "Define standard display by size" field in the "More Preferences" dialog box—but you must do this before you import the graphic into PageMaker.

Print and scan the image. It's a pretty low-tech solution, but it can work just fine under certain circumstances. Keep in mind that the scanned version will be only as good as the printed copy, and it'll be resolution-dependent. So if you need to print it large or to a high-resolution device, it may look unacceptably jagged. For guidelines on getting the best result from your scanning, check out the Print Publishing Guide (PageMaker 6.x) or Commercial Printing Guide (PageMaker 5.0).

Turn your graphic into an EPS. This can be a great choice if you'll need to print your logo only to PostScript printers. Before you do this, make sure you have a PostScript printer driver installed and selected as your "Printer" in the "Print Document" dialog box (Windows) or in the Chooser (Macintosh). Then follow these steps.

1. Copy and paste your logo to a new document. To do so, select the objects that comprise your logo, and choose "Copy" from the Edit menu. Choose "New" from the File menu to create a new publication, and in the new-publication dialog box, click "OK." Select "Paste" from the Edit menu to paste the object(s) on the page.
2. At this point, adjust the size of your page using the "Document Setup" dialog box so that it fits snugly around the logo—the dimensions of your page will determine the bounding box (outer dimensions) of the EPS.
3. To open the "Print Options" dialog box, select "Print..." from the File menu, and click the "Options..." button.
4. Check the box that says "Write PostScript to file," and then click the radio button that says "EPS."
5. Click the "Browse..." button (Windows) or the "Save As..." button (Macintosh) to specify a name and location for the EPS file you're about to create, and then click "OK."
6. Click "Save." PageMaker will save your page as an EPS graphic.

If you're using PageMaker 6.0 or earlier for Windows, your EPS won't have a screen preview (it'll appear as a gray box on screen), but you'll still be able to import it into any application that supports the EPS format, and it'll print fine to any PostScript device. When you import EPS images without screen previews into PageMaker 6.5 for Windows, PageMaker can generate a screen preview for it on the fly. If you're using PageMaker for the Macintosh, your EPS will have a PICT screen preview. If you print an EPS without a screen preview to a non-PostScript device, it'll print as a gray box; if you print a Macintosh PageMaker–generated EPS from a Macintosh application, it'll print as a screen-resolution PICT.

One last note: If you're using PageMaker 6.5, you may be wondering whether you can use the Export Graphic feature to turn your logo into a graphic. Unfortunately, you can't—the option will be grayed out if you try to choose it while you have anything but an imported graphic selected. This feature is designed to export graphics that have been placed into PageMaker, not graphics that have been created within PageMaker.

Q Is there a way to get an EPS graphic to overprint in my PageMaker publication?

A Yes. But what approach you should take depends on what kind of EPS you're dealing with—a bitmap EPS (an EPS that contains just raster data, such as an EPS saved from Photoshop or another image-editing program), a vector

TIP MAC OS / WINDOWS

"Coloring" portions of text using masks

With PageMaker 6.0's masking feature, you can create a variety of complex effects. For instance, you can color portions of text—here's how we created the example below.

1. First, we created the colored fork out of a PageMaker-drawn circle and several rectangles layered together, and then typed some black text over it.
2. Next, we selected the text with the pointer tool, copied it to the Clipboard, and sent it behind the fork (the shortcut command for that is Ctrl + B in Windows or Command + B on the Mac).
3. Using the power-paste command (hold down the Alt key in Windows or Option key on the Mac while selecting "Paste" from the Edit menu), we placed a copy of the text right on top of the original. Then we selected it with the text tool and applied our background color.
4. Finally, we selected the background-colored text and the circle portion of the fork and chose "Mask" from the Element menu. The illustration at right shows the result.

EPS (an EPS that consists of artwork composed as filled and stroked paths—this is the sort of EPS you create in drawing applications like Illustrator or Macromedia FreeHand), or a vector EPS that contains raster images.

First, a quick overview of your options. If you're using a vector EPS, you're in good shape—you can set all or some of the elements to overprint at the object level in your drawing application. Or, if you're dealing with a bitmap EPS, you can get them to overprint in PageMaker if they're grayscale or one-bit images. And finally, if you're dealing with a color bitmap EPS, there's a special workaround you can use. Here are more details.

Vector EPS files. The most flexible method for setting a vector EPS to overprint is to assign all or some of its elements to overprint within the drawing application before exporting it. For instance, if you use Illustrator, you can set elements to overprint by selecting them and choosing the "Overprint" option for their fill and/or stroke in the "Paint Styles" dialog box or palette.

If you don't have Illustrator or another drawing application in which you can set your EPS elements to overprint, you have another option. You can select the EPS in PageMaker and assign an overprinting color to it. (When we say "overprinting color," we mean a color for which you've selected the "Overprint" option in PageMaker's "Edit Color" dialog box—selecting this option will cause all objects assigned that color to overprint. If you want an overprinting and a nonoverprinting version of a color, make a 100% tint of that color and assign one to overprint and the other not to.) All the elements in your EPS will print as tints of the color you assigned it, and they'll overprint, too. (NOTE: The EPS may not change color on screen—it will do so only if the EPS screen preview is a one-bit raster image, which is common in Windows, but not common on the Mac.)

Bitmap EPS files. If you have a grayscale or one-bit (black-and-white) bitmap EPS graphic that you want to overprint, you're in luck if you're using PageMaker 6.5. All you need to do is select the graphic in PageMaker and assign an overprinting color to it.

If you're not using PageMaker 6.5, or if you want to overprint a bitmap EPS that isn't grayscale or one-bit (for instance, a CMYK or RGB bitmap EPS file), one option you have is to convert that element to grayscale or one-bit to get it to overprint. Then you'll be able to assign it an overprinting color in PageMaker (of course, you lose all the original color in your image this way). But here's another option: If you're trying to get your color image to overprint a background object that you can set to overprint (for instance, a PageMaker-drawn element), set the background element to overprint, and then select the color bitmap image and send it in back of the background image—that should give you the separation results you want. If that's not workable for any reason and your primary concern is trapping the image, consult your color house or other service providers for another solution.

Vector EPS files that contain bitmap elements. This situation is a bit trickier since there are several types of bitmap elements you can include in a EPS file, and they all behave somewhat differently depending on the drawing application and PageMaker version you're using. But here are some rough guidelines. First, if you're interested in getting a color bitmap element in a vector EPS to overprint, you're out of luck—you can't set it to overprint in Illustrator, and assigning it an overprinting color in PageMaker won't help, either.

Depending on what version of PageMaker you have and what kind of raster element you're dealing with, you may be able to set a one-bit or grayscale bitmap element to overprint in Illustrator or assign an overprinting color to it in PageMaker. But doing so may not be the best idea—if you're trying to overprint all or part of such a complex image for trapping purposes, you may be better off leaving this trapping job to your color house or other service provider. Ask them what they recommend. And if you need more information on this topic, you can consult Adobe's technical-solutions database, which will have specific information on what it takes to overprint raster elements within a vector EPS by the time you read this.

Q Is there any way to make a placed bitmap graphic's background transparent?

A Whether or not the background of a bitmap graphic is opaque or transparent is primarily determined by the graphic's file format. In the case of grayscale or color bitmap images, for instance, the background pixels—even if they're pure white—are always opaque. However, if you want a transparent background for your graphics, you've got a number of options.

Some of these options involve using EPS graphics. But remember—if you're printing to a nonPostScript printer, you'll only be able to print the EPS graphic's screen preview, which may not be as high-resolution and high-quality as the EPS, and may not behave the same way the EPS itself does in other ways (such as transparency). We recommend you stick with TIFFs whenever possible if you're printing to a non-PostScript printer.

Use a clipping path. You can create the appearance of transparency in opaque images by using a clipping path. A clipping path is a vector path that masks areas in an image—any pixels that fall outside the clipping path are treated as if they're invisible. PageMaker 5.0x and later support clipping paths saved with EPS images. PageMaker 6.x supports clipping paths saved with TIFF images as well. For more information on creating and using clipping paths, please see the Photoshop User Guide or the manual for your image-editing application.

Use a one-bit (black-and-white or "monotone") graphic format. One-bit graphics contain just a single bit of information per "dot" (image sample). This bit is a kind of switch that describes whether a pixel is "on" or "off." When it's "on" you get a colored (e.g., black) pixel. When it's "off" you'll get either a white or transparent pixel depending on the application you're working with and the graphic format the image is saved in. If the image is saved as a TIFF, whether or not this "off" pixel is transparent or opaque is dependent on the application that it's imported into. PageMaker treats the "off" pixel for TIFF images as transparent.

If the image is saved as an EPS, the creator application determines whether or not this image is opaque or transparent. To create a transparent one-bit EPS from Photoshop, be sure you've selected the "Bitmap" mode for your image ("Bitmap," in this case, is synonymous with one-bit). When you save in the EPS format, Photoshop will display the "EPS Format" dialog box, where you can make sure the "Transparent Whites" option is selected.

Color the background of the image to match the object in your layout. If you've got a color or grayscale image, there might be an alternative to using clipping paths, depending on how you're using the graphic in your layout. This technique involves coloring the "background" pixels in your image to match the color it'll sit on in PageMaker.

There are two common reasons for doing this. First, it can be handy if you're using an image-editing application that doesn't support clipping paths. Second, it can be a good option if you don't want the artificially sharp vector edge that a clipping path leaves around your image (which can look especially poor with "natural" or photographic-type images). Regardless of your reason for using this technique, you must place your image on a solid-color area in PageMaker for this to work. Here's how to do it.

1. Figure out and jot down the exact definition of your PageMaker background color. For instance, if you'll be placing your graphic over a PageMaker-drawn box assigned a purple color, you'd need to know its specific CMYK or RGB components. (Whether you should be using CMYK or RGB depends on how you'll output your document.)
2. In your image-editing application, create a color that matches your PageMaker background color. To do so, you'll first need to make sure your image is using the same color model (CMYK or RGB) as your PageMaker publication.
3. Apply that color to the "background" area of your image.
4. Save the image and import it into PageMaker. Since your goal here is to preserve the exact CMYK or RGB definition of your colors, we recommend not using color management on your imported image.

For more information on creating transparent images in Photoshop for use in PageMaker, see "Creating Transparent Images in Photoshop."

TIP MAC OS / WINDOWS

Getting tabs lined up

If you've ever unsuccessfully tried to lay out a list in which elements on the left align with the left side of your text block and elements on the right align with the right side of your text block, read on. You can do this quickly and easily without getting anywhere near the "Indents and Tabs" dialog box.

First, insert a tab character between the left element and right element on each line. Second, highlight the text and press Ctrl + Shift + R (Windows) or Command + Shift + R (Mac). This is the same thing as selecting "Right" from the Alignment submenu of the Type menu, and will give you the results you're after.

How PageMaker Layers Compare to Layers in Illustrator and Photoshop

USING LAYERS IN ADOBE PAGEMAKER 6.5

You can use layers in PageMaker to edit, hide, or lock selected objects. For example, you can put notes for your service provider on a layer separate from the rest of the publication. Or, you can use layers to create a brochure that you will distribute in several languages, using a different layer for the text and objects that are specific to each language.

PageMaker's Layers palette is similar to the Layers palettes in Adobe Illustrator and Adobe Photoshop. Like Illustrator and Photoshop, PageMaker places objects or text onto the layer that is selected in the Layers palette at that time. In all three applications, you access the Layers Options dialog box by double-clicking on the layer's name or by selecting the layer and choosing Layer Options from the Layers palette menu. To change the order of layers in each application, you drag a layer up or down to a new position in the Layers palette.

Some of the features in PageMaker's Layers palette are unique to PageMaker. For example, PageMaker's layers apply to the entire publication. A layer you create while page one is displayed is also available for all other pages in the publication. PageMaker's Layers palette menu also includes a Delete Unused Layers command, which enables you to delete all layers that do not any contain objects.

HOW PAGEMAKER'S LAYERS COMPARE WITH ILLUSTRATOR'S LAYERS

If you already use layers in Illustrator 5.x or later, you'll find PageMaker's Layers palette familiar. Following is a list of Illustrator layer functions as they compare with PageMaker's layer functions.

Accessing the Layers Palette

To display the Layers palette in PageMaker or Illustrator, choose Window > Show Layers. You can also press Control + 8 (Windows) or Command + 8 (Macintosh) in either application.

Creating New Layers

To create a new layer in PageMaker or Illustrator, choose New Layer from the Layers palette menu. In PageMaker, you can also click the New Layer icon in the palette (i.e., the icon with the blank sheet of paper to the left of the trash icon).

Displaying or Hiding Layers

To display or hide a layer in PageMaker, click on the eye symbol to the left of the layer's name. To display or hide a layer in Illustrator, you must click on the dot in the eye column to the left of the layer's name. You can also choose Layer Options from the Layer palette menu in either application, then select or deselect the Show Layer option.

To hide all but the selected layer in PageMaker, you hold down the Alt key (Windows) or the Option key (Macintosh) while clicking on the eye icon. To hide all but the selected layer in Illustrator, you click on the eye icon without holding down any modifying keys. You can also choose Hide Others from the Layers palette menu in either application.

Locking or Unlocking Layers

To lock or unlock a layer in PageMaker, click on the pencil symbol to the left of the layer name. To lock or unlock a layer in Illustrator, you click on the dot in the pencil column to the left of the layer's name. You can also choose Layer Options from the Layer palette menu in either application, then select or deselect the Lock option.

To lock all but the selected layer in PageMaker, hold down the Alt key (Windows) or the Option key (Macintosh) while clicking on the pencil icon. To lock all but the selected layer in Illustrator, you click on the pencil icon without holding down any modifying keys. You can also choose Lock Others from the Layers palette menu in either application.

Moving Objects to Another Layer

To move an object from one layer to another in either application, select the object and then drag the colored dot in the Layers palette from the original layer to the new layer.

Retaining Layers When Pasting

To retain layer assignments when pasting objects from one document to another, choose Paste Remembers Layering from the Layers palette in PageMaker or Paste Remembers Layers in Illustrator.

Identifying an Object's Layer

To identify the layer assignment for an object in PageMaker or Illustrator, select the object. The color of an object's handles correspond to the color of the layer to which it is assigned.

HOW PAGEMAKER'S LAYERS COMPARE WITH PHOTOSHOP'S LAYERS

If you already use layers in Photoshop 3.0.x or 4.0, you'll find PageMaker's Layers palette familiar. Following is a list of Photoshop layer functions as they compare with the same functionality in PageMaker's layers.

Accessing the Layers Palette

To display the Layers palette in PageMaker, choose Window > Show Layers. To display the Layers palette in Photoshop, you choose Window > Palettes > Show Layers. You can also display the palette by pressing Control + 8 (Windows) or Command + 8 (Macintosh) in either application.

Creating New Layers

To create a new layer in PageMaker or Photoshop, click the New Layer icon at the bottom of the palette (i.e., the button with the blank page). You can hold down the Alt key (Windows) or the Option key (Macintosh) while clicking the button to create a layer with the default settings rather than displaying the Layer Options dialog box. You can also choose New Layer from the Layers palette menu in either application.

Displaying or Hiding Layers

To show or hide a layer in PageMaker or Photoshop, click on the eye icon to the left of the layer's name in the Layers

MICRO TIP MAC OS / WINDOWS

> If you want to be able to edit EPS process colors in PageMaker, create them as CMYK spot colors in your drawing application (or "custom colors" in Illustrator). Then, in PageMaker, you can convert them to process colors through the "Define colors" dialog box. Or you can convert them to process when you print, by clicking "All to process" under "Separations" in the "Color" print dialog box.

MICRO TIP MAC OS / WINDOWS

If you forget to set your print orientation correctly when you're making a PDF file, and you end up with a sideways document, you might not have to start over. As long as your PDF pages didn't get cropped and you have Acrobat Exchange, you can rotate your pages back to where they should be. In Exchange, open the document, and from the Page submenu of the Edit menu, select "Rotate...." In the "Rotate Pages" dialog box, make the changes you wish and click "OK."

palette. You can also select or deselect Show Layer in the Layers Options dialog box in PageMaker.

Removing Layers

To remove a layer in PageMaker or Photoshop, drag the layer to the Trash icon at the bottom of the Layers palette, or select the layer and choose Delete Layer from the Layers palette menu.

Merging Layers

To merge layers in PageMaker, hold down the Shift key to select multiple layers, then choose Merge Layers from the Layers palette menu. To merge layers in Photoshop, you display the layers you want to merge, then choose Merge Layers from the Layers palette menu.

PageMaker 6.5 Frames General Information

Adobe PageMaker 6.5's frames are containers for text or graphics that enable you to define a publication's layout before you include content. A frame can contain text, a graphic, or text and inline graphics. Frames complement PageMaker's flexible open page format to enable you to create publications more efficiently.

CREATING FRAMES

You can create a frame by using any of the frame tools (i.e., any shape with an X in it) in the Toolbox. You can also convert an existing PageMaker-drawn object into a frame by selecting the object, then choosing Element > Frame > Change to Frame. Because frames are PageMaker-drawn objects, you can modify their shapes just as you modify ellipses, polygons, or boxes you draw in PageMaker.

PageMaker's frames are not defined as graphic frames or text frames until you attach content. Once you attach content to a frame, PageMaker groups the frame and its contents and you can move, resize, or edit them as one object.

To remove the object from a frame, choose Element > Frame > Separate Content.

USING FRAMES WITH TEXT

Frames enable you to shape text objects before you determine the publication's content, giving you greater control over the layout of the page. Working with text in frames, however, is much like working with other text in a PageMaker publication. You can format, thread, autoflow, edit, or use any of PageMaker's other text features with text in frames.

Attaching Text to a Frame

You can attach text to any frame in PageMaker, including custom-shaped polygon or ellipse frames. To attach text to a frame, type the text directly into a frame, or import it into a frame using the Place command. To add text to an empty frame or a frame that already contains text, use the text tool to click an insertion point in the frame, then type. To attach text to a frame as you import it, select the frame, choose File > Place, then select Within Frame in the Place dialog box before placing the text file.

You can also place, paste, paste special, drag, or subscribe (Macintosh only) text into the publication, then attach the text to the frame. To attach text to a frame, select the text block and the frame, then choose Element > Frame > Attach Content.

Editing Text in Frames

You can format text in frames just as you format other text in a PageMaker publication. To edit text in a frame, use the text tool to click an insertion point or highlight the text you want to modify. You can change the font, font size, type style, or any other character or paragraph specification to text within a frame. You can also apply styles to text in a frame just as you apply styles to text in a text block. To apply a style to text, select the paragraph or paragraphs with the text tool, then click on the style name in the Styles palette.

Threading Text Frames

When you thread text objects, PageMaker recognizes them as a single story, enabling you to edit and flow the text objects in relationship to each other. A story can contain multiple text frames or multiple text blocks, but it cannot contain both.

To thread text frames, select the first frame with the pointer tool and click on its bottom windowshade handle. When PageMaker displays the threading icon, which looks like a short chain, click on the next frame in the story. You can repeat these steps to thread as many frames as you like, in any order, including frames on other pages. To view the order of your threaded frames, select any threaded frame, then choose Element > Frame > Next Frame or Element > Frame > Previous Frame.

You can autoflow text through frames that you have already threaded by placing text into the first frame in the thread. PageMaker automatically flows the text through all the threaded frames.

To remove a frame from the thread, select the frame with the pointer tool and choose Element > Frame > Remove From Threads. When you choose this command, threaded text will skip the selected frame and flow into the next frame in the thread.

Accessing the Story Editor from a Text Frame

To access the Story editor from a text frame, select some of the text with the text tool, then choose Edit > Edit Story or triple-click the text frame with the pointer tool.

USING FRAMES WITH GRAPHICS

Frames enable you to specify the size and shape of graphics before you import them, giving you greater control over the layout of the page. A frame also acts as a keyline that is automatically grouped with the graphic. In addition to resizing, altering, and moving a graphic within a frame just as you would any other object, you can position a graphic within a frame.

Attaching a Frame to a Graphic

To attach a graphic to a frame as you import it, select the frame, choose File > Place, then select Within Frame in the Place dialog box before placing the graphic file. You can also place, insert, paste, paste special, drag, or subscribe (Macintosh only) the object into the publication, then attach the graphic to the frame. To attach a graphic to a frame, select both the frame and the graphic, then choose Element > Frame > Attach Content.

Specifying Frame Options for Graphics

You can position a graphic within a frame in three ways. You can choose to crop the graphic to the size and shape of the frame, resize the frame to fit the graphic, or resize the graphic to fit the frame. You can also adjust the vertical and horizontal alignment of the graphic within the frame.

By default, PageMaker attaches a graphic to the top left corner of the frame and crops the graphic to fit the frame. To specify a different position for the graphic, choose Element > Frame > Frame Options. When you select options in the Frame Options dialog box while you have a frame selected, the options you select apply only to that frame. When you select options in the Frame Options dialog box while a publication is open, the options you select become the defaults for that publication only. When you select options in the Frame Options dialog box while no publication is open, the options you select become PageMaker's defaults.

Attaching OLE Objects

To attach an OLE object to a frame, insert or paste the object into PageMaker, then select the object and the frame and choose Element > Frame > Attach Content.

To edit an OLE object that is attached to a frame, hold down the Control key (Windows) or the Command key (Macintosh) while selecting the frame to subselect the object. Then hold down the Alt key (Windows) or the Option key (Macintosh) while double-clicking the object or choose Edit > Edit < OLE

Server Application > Object. The OLE server application will start so that you may edit the object.

LIMITATIONS OF PAGEMAKER S FRAMES

PageMaker's frames enable you to lay out the page with greater control. Keep in mind the following limitations, however, when using frames:

- Text does not scale automatically when you resize a frame. To change the size of text when you resize a frame, you must select the text with the text tool and assign a new point size.
- You can thread frames together to create columns, but you cannot create multiple columns within a frame. To create columns on a page you can also use PageMaker's Column Guides command.
- You can attach objects to a frame after inserting, pasting, or dragging them into PageMaker, but you cannot insert, paste, or drag objects directly into a frame.
- You cannot rotate the contents of a frame independently of the frame. When you attach a rotated object to a frame, PageMaker removes its transformation.
- You cannot apply text wrap to a frame within a frame.
- To change the shape of a frame, you must separate the contents from the frame, then create a new frame. There is no command to change frame shapes in PageMaker.
- You cannot attach objects on a publication page to a frame that is located on the master page.
- You can specify an inset value for text in a frame, but not for a graphic in a frame.
- A single frame cannot contain both text and independent graphics.

TIP MAC OS / WINDOWS

Creating horizontal rules for HTML documents

(6.0 only) Horizontal rules on a Web page serve the important function of dividing up sections of information. They work much like paragraph rules in PageMaker, separating paragraphs or sections, moving with the text they're connected to, and providing visual breaks.

It's easy to create a horizontal rule for your Web page in PageMaker by making a line into an inline graphic.

1. Draw a horizontal line of any length using the line tool.
2. Using the pointer tool, select the line and choose "Cut" from the Edit menu.
3. With the text tool, position the cursor to where you would like the line to appear in the text, then choose "Paste." Your line will appear in the text block.

When the page or story containing the line is exported as HTML, the HTML Author Plug-in will create an "<HR>" tag for the line that, when read by a Web browser, will be interpreted as a horizontal rule in its own separate paragraph.

TIP MAC OS / WINDOWS

Wrap it to go

Use PageMaker's text wrap feature to create reusable wraps for text effects. You can create different shapes or lines either in PageMaker or in a graphics program, apply text wrap to them, and then adjust the boundary so that it conforms to the contour of the object. Click with the pointer tool on the dotted boundary line that defines a text wrap to create individual points that serve as anchors. Using an object as a kind of template, you can then drag these anchor points into position along the edge of the form or object. (For more detailed instructions on text wrap, see page 178 of the Adobe PageMaker User Guide.)

After you're done, apply the color "Paper" to the graphic or "None" to its line style to make it disappear, leaving just the dotted boundary line that you can use to shape text in your layout. Send the graphic to the back to avoid possible printing conflicts. When you're finished, add your new shapes to the Library palette for use in other publications.

If you're using an imported graphic as your template, make sure you save it as a black-and-white bitmap before you import it into PageMaker and create your customized text wrap—otherwise you may not be able to hide it by applying the color "Paper" to it.

References for PageMaker 6.5 Keyboard Shortcuts

The following sources include information about keyboard shortcuts in Adobe PageMaker 6.5.

Quick Reference Card

The Quick Reference Card included with PageMaker lists frequently used keyboard shortcuts in PageMaker 6.5.

Online Help

PageMaker's Help menu provides a comprehensive list of PageMaker 6.5 shortcuts, a list of those shortcuts that are different from PageMaker 6.0x, and a list of shortcuts that are new in PageMaker 6.5.

PageMaker 6.5 Getting Started Guide

The PageMaker 6.5 Getting Started guide includes information about shortcuts in the What's New section.

Diagnostic Recompose Feature Summary

FEATURE

The diagnostic recompose command is a group of functions that checks the integrity of some structures within a PageMaker publication and repairs specific types of inconsistencies.

IMPLEMENTATION

To perform a diagnostic recompose:

1. Make a backup copy of the publication.
2. In the backup copy, click on the pointer tool in the toolbox to ensure nothing on the page is selected.
3. Hold down Shift + Option (Macintosh) or Shift + Control (Windows) while choosing Type > Hyphenation. When the diagnostic recompose routines are finished, the computer beeps or the menus blink either once, twice, or three times to indicate diagnostic results.

To perform a global recomposition without the diagnostic routines:

1. Select the pointer tool so nothing on the page is selected.
2. Hold down the Option key (Macintosh) or Shift key (Windows) while choosing Type > Hyphenation. When the global recomposition routines are finished, the computer beeps or the menus blink once.

DETAIL

Diagnostic recompose checks for and repairs only a small number of inconsistencies. It is specifically designed to detect and repair inconsistencies that can cause "Bad Record Index" errors, but does not check for every possible cause. After the recomposition is finished, use the Save As command to save the file to the same or a different name to ensure PageMaker rewrites the publication with the changes made during the diagnostic recompose.

Before performing a diagnostic recompose, make sure the computer's sound is on. When the sound is off on a Macintosh when PageMaker performs a diagnostic recompose, you'll see the PageMaker menus blink, instead of hearing beeps. The number of beeps, or blinks, you receive when running a diagnostic recompose on an IBM-compatible computer may not accurately indicate the findings of the diagnostic recompose. Many IBM-compatible computers have speakers that have become disconnected, or that don't function quickly enough to differentiate between one or more beeps.

Diagnostic Recompose Beeps

One Beep: The recomposition was successful and PageMaker found no repairs to make.

Two Beeps: PageMaker repaired 1 or more minor problems.

Three Beeps: PageMaker found a severe problem it could not correct, or could not complete the diagnostics listed below due to insufficient memory.

The diagnostic recompose command performs the following operations:

1. *Style Sheet Cleanup*

   This routine performs a number of checks on the style sheet formatting and the interrelationships between styles in the style sheet, which include:

- Ensuring next styles refer to existing styles; invalid references are set to Same style.
- Ensuring parent styles refer to existing styles; invalid references are set to No style.
- Ensuring text color and rule colors are valid; invalid settings are reset to Black.

2. *Story Cleanup*
   Story cleanup scans through all the stories in the publication and checks that:
   - Paragraphs are assigned an existing style, or No style; invalid references are set to No style.
   - Text colors and rule colors are valid; invalid colors are set to Black.
   - Index entries are valid, making sure that the topic exists and that some internal fields are valid, as well as checking next style and paragraph range settings for index entries of those types. If story cleanup finds an index entry that refers to a topic that does not exist, it adds "**Bad Topic**" to the index and the entry is modified to refer to it. Because the bad topic starts with an asterisk, it appears in the Symbols section of the publication's index.
3. *Index Cleanup*
   In addition to the cleanup performed for each story, index cleanup scans PageMaker's table of cross reference entries. If an entry points to a nonexistent topic, "**Bad Topic**" is added to the index and the entry is modified to refer to it.
4. *Links Cleanup*
   Links cleanup scans through all the graphics and stories in the publication. If inconsistent link information is found, the problem link is removed. Links cleanup also checks internal values for consistency and repairs them.
5. *Global Recomposition*
   Composition is the portion of PageMaker responsible for determining where text belongs when in layout mode. Composition determines where line breaks occur, taking into account point size, type style, paragraph indents, Keep With settings, and other text attributes. Global recomposition forces PageMaker to recalculate the line breaks for all stories in the publication.

Limitations of PageMaker 6.5 HTML Export

FEATURE

The World Wide Web displays information in units called pages, which are built using a standard called the hypertext markup language (HTML) . In Adobe PageMaker 6.5, you can use the HTML export feature to create HTML pages that you can publish on the World Wide Web. PageMaker creates HTML pages that conform to the 3.2 version of the HTML specification. The following points describe how important aspects of your publication are exported:

Type

HTML uses a limited set of named text formats which are conceptually similar to paragraph styles. For example, there are HTML styles for headings, body text, and indented paragraphs. You can specify how to map paragraph styles applied on exported pages to HTML formats. Because HTML does not let you control typeface, leading, tracking, kerning, tab positions, and other type specifications, the line endings and depth of text columns on a PageMaker page are not preserved in HTML. The characters-level attributes Bold, Italic, Underline, and Reverse as well as the color of your type, are preserved on export.

Graphics

HTML supports the GIF and JPEG image formats. PageMaker automatically converts copies of imported graphics (whether inline or independent) to GIF or JPEG. Shapes drawn with PageMaker drawing tools are not exported, with the exception of horizontal lines which become horizontal rules in HTML.

Page Layout

Using HTML tables, PageMaker can approximate multi-column page design, including elements outside margins, text, and graphics that span columns, and text wrapping around graphics. You can also choose not to approximate page layout; the result is one column of contiguous text, with graphics occupying separate paragraphs and flowing along with the text.

Typographical Design Limitations

Remember that type settings that affect typographical density (such as line breaks, letter spacing, and word spacing) are completely determined by the fonts used by a particular browser. Other type attributes that are completely controlled by World Wide Web browsers, and won't be preserved if you specify them in PageMaker, include:

- font, type size, and leading
- horizontal scaling
- tracking and kerning
- Outline and Shadow type styles
- paragraph alignment (unless Preserve Approximate Page Layout is selected)
- indent and tab positions

PAGE LAYOUT LIMITATIONS

If you design a multi-column layout and want to preserve the layout in HTML, remember that the Export to HTML feature can only approximate your page layout. The limitations are due to the HTML language itself; for example, since most typographical characteristics are not preserved in HTML, the length of text columns is not preserved. The following are unsupported features in HTML and might

MICRO TIP MAC OS / WINDOWS

Don't like the way your leader dots look? Are they too small? Too far apart? Too bold? Because PageMaker bases their formatting on that of the character immediately preceding the tab, you can format the dots almost any way you want: just insert a thin space before the tab, and format it however you like.

require page layout changes in PageMaker to produce acceptable HTML:

- Objects transformed (rotated, skewed, or flipped) in PageMaker are untransformed in HTML. You can transform the object in an illustration or image-editing application and re-import into PageMaker if you want the object to remain transformed in HTML.
- Overlapping objects in PageMaker are separated in the exported HTML, with results that may not be satisfactory. Before exporting, revise your design so that objects do not overlap.
- Non-rectangular text wrap shapes are not approximated in HTML, and results in objects being moved. Be sure to apply the standard rectangular text wrap shape, or revise the design to avoid non-rectangular text wrap.
- The content of a frame is exported, but not the surrounding frame itself. Non-rectangular frames become rectangular. Images that extend beyond the visible frame area are cropped in the exported file to approximate the original layout. (If you export without preserving layout, the image in the frame is uncropped.)
- PageMaker-drawn graphics are not exported, with the exception of horizontal strokes, which are exported as HTML horizontal rules.
- A masked object is unmasked. Before exporting, unmask the elements and, if you masked an image, crop it with the cropping tool. If you masked text, recreate the effect in an illustration program and import it as a graphic.

HTML STYLES AVAILABLE IN HTML EXPORT DIALOG BOX

The simplest way to create a page for the Web is to use PageMaker paragraph styles that correspond to the HTML markup tags you want to use. This ensures that you are using styles supported by the HTML export feature. You can add the styles to your Styles palette directly, or import them along with the content of an HTML file, for example by using File > Place and selecting an HTML file to import. The following HTML styles are available in the HTML Export dialog box:

H1, H2, H3, H4, H5, H6 Six levels of subheads. H1 has the largest type size, H6 the smallest.

ADDRESS Sets an address or other short text apart from the body text.

BLOCKQUOTE Sets one or more paragraphs of text apart from the body text.

BODY Text Normal paragraphs of body text.

Definition List List format. The browser automatically indents each paragraph with this format.

Directory List List format. Usually, the browser automatically indents and adds a bullet before each paragraph with this format.

MENU List Similar to an ordered list, but more compact

OL List Ordered list. Use for a numbered list. Usually, the browser automatically adds the correct number before each item.

PREFORMATTED Prevents text from being reformatted when changes are made to a browser's styles definitions.

UL List Unordered bullet list. Usually, the browser automatically adds a bullet before each item.

Scripts Included with PageMaker 6.5

Scripts are text files that contain simple commands and queries which automate tasks in Adobe PageMaker 6.5x, such as setting up pages or importing a standard set of elements. You run scripts from the Scripts palette, which PageMaker displays when you choose Window > Plugin Palettes > Show Scripts.

PageMaker 6.5 includes scripts to automate processes, run plug-ins, and create templates. This document describes the function of each of these scripts, listing them according to the folders and subfolders that appear in the Scripts palette.

COLOR FOLDER

- *Add Rich Black* Adds a Rich Black color (100% black, 50% cyan, and 50% yellow) to the Colors palette. You can use the Rich Black color to give depth to black objects.
- *Add Varnish Plate* Adds a Varnish color (5% yellow) to the Colors palette. You can apply the Varnish color to objects you want to print with a varnish.
  Document Layout folder
- *New Object Layer* Moves all objects in the category or categories you select (EPS, Other Objects, PM Graphics, or Text) to a new layer. If you select Include Groups, the script moves all groups containing objects in the selected categories to the new layer. If you select Include Frames, the script moves all frames that contain objects in the selected categories to the new layer; if you do not select Include Frames, the script considers frames as PageMaker-drawn objects.
- *Object Guides* Adds ruler guides to the top, bottom, left, or right edges of all selected objects.

MASTER PAGES FOLDER

- *Combine Master Pages* Copies the objects from one master page onto another master page.
- *Remove Unused Masters* Removes any master pages that are not applied to any publication pages.

ELEMENT FOLDER

- *Button* Creates a three-dimensional button by drawing a polygon with a shaded border. You can use this button as a source for hyperlinks.

ATTACH TEXT FOLDER

- *Attach Caption* Creates a caption from text you enter, then groups it with the selected object.

TIP MAC OS / WINDOWS

Automatic reverse heads

If you've ever worked extensively with reverse type, you know it can be hard to handle—primarily because you need to keep track of both the text block and the background element from which it's reversed. Of course, grouping the text with the background element can help. But have you ever longed for something even easier? If so, here's a classic PageMaker tip for automating reverse-type headlines.

The key to this tip is paragraph rules—essentially, you set up a style for your reversecolor headline and add a paragraph rule that falls exactly behind the text. Start with the following steps.

1. First, start with one of your headlines or other single lines of text that you want reversed. Give it whatever font, size, leading, and other character attributes you want, including the "Reverse" setting or "Paper" color option if you're after a reverse-text effect.
2. Base a style on your sample text. With your text tool clicked inside it, hold down Ctrl (Windows) or Command (Mac) while clicking on "No Style" in the Styles palette. Name your style in the "Edit Style" dialog box which then appears.
3. Click on "Para...," and in the "Paragraph Specifications" dialog box, click "Rules..." to open the "Paragraph Rules" dialog box. Once there, select "Rule above paragraph," and within that section of the dialog box, select a line style for your paragraph rule (its size should probably be close to or a little bigger than your type size). You should also select a line color, and if necessary, a tint. Select "Width of text" for the line-width setting.
4. Click "Options..." to open the "Paragraph Rule Options" dialog box. Enter a value for the "Top" picas-above-baseline setting (the name for this setting varies depending on what measurement system you're using—for instance, it'll be called the inches-above-baseline setting if you're using inches). This setting will determine where the paragraph rule sits relative to the baseline of your text. If you set this value to the thickness of your rule, the bottom of your paragraph rule will sit right on the baseline, which can be a nice effect if you don't mind having your descenders fall below the rule. If you want the rule a bit lower, set the "Top" picas-above-baseline setting to be a bit less than your rule thickness. note: If your default measurement system is set to something other than picas, you'll need to be careful how you enter this setting. For instance, if your measurement system is set to inches, and you enter "12," your rule will be positioned 12 inches above the baseline. To enter 12 points for this setting, type "p12" (for 12 points) or "1p" (for 1 pica, which is equivalent to 12 points). To enter a value such as 1 pica, 2 points, enter "1p2."

To get just the right effect you may need to fiddle with some of the variables discussed above. And here's one more tip: If you don't want your rule to end abruptly after your last character, add a fixed space after it—we favor a thin space (a quarter em), which you can type by pressing Ctrl (Windows) or Command (Mac) + Shift + T, but an en or em space will work too. If you add the same space to the beginning of your line, both the beginning and end will have an equal amount of extra rule.

GROUP FOLDER

- *Nested Group* Groups two or more groups into a larger group. The nested groups are retained when you run the Nested Ungroup script.
- *Nested Ungroup* Ungroups a group you created using the Nested Group script, restoring the original groups.
- *Resize Group* Resizes all objects in a group, including text blocks. Adjusts font size and text block width.

POLYGONS FOLDER

- *Adjust Polygon Miter Limit* Adjusts a polygon's miter limit (i.e., the point at which a corner becomes beveled, or squared-off, rather than pointed). Individual polygon angles are more likely to be beveled with a smaller miter limit. You'll see the greatest difference when you run this script on inset polygons with sharp angles.
- *Reverse Polygon Line Hang* Reverses the direction of a polygon's stroke, known as "line hang." Polygons drawn clockwise are "inside-hung;" those drawn counter-clockwise are "outside-hung." Inside-hung polygons appear smaller than outside-hung polygons, but the difference is only noticeable on polygons with a large stroke applied. The line hang affects fills and text wrap boundaries.
- *Zigzag* Converts a straight line into a zigzag line, using the same stroke and color as the original line.

TRANSFORM FOLDER

- *Reflect Around Line* Reflects selected objects around a selected line. If you select more than one line, the script uses the uppermost line as the axis around which the other objects are reflected. If you haven't selected a line, the script doesn't reflect any objects.

MICRO TIP MAC OS / WINDOWS

PageMaker won't override certain kinds of local formatting when you apply a style to a paragraph. These are bold and italic attributes (applied as character formatting, not through the Font menu), most of the other attributes available on the Type Style submenu of the Type menu (underline, strikethrough, shadow, and outline), case attributes (all caps or small caps), and position attributes (subscript and superscript).

- *Transform Each Object* Transforms (i.e., reflects, rotates, or skews) each selected object, relative to the center of each object. This method differs from applying transformations to several objects at once through the Control palette, because the Control palette applies the transformations relative to one proxy for all the objects.

IMAGES FOLDER

Graphic Resolution folder

- *Gray Out Graphics* Changes the Graphics Display preference to Gray Out.
- *High Res Graphics* Changes the Graphics Display preference to High Resolution.
- *Normal Res Graphics* Changes the Graphics Display preference to Standard.

OUTLINE FOLDER

- *Apply Hyperlink Style* Defines and applies a style for hyperlink sources you have created in text, enabling you to identify text that is part of a hyperlink without switching into Browse mode. You select a color and text attribute (i.e., Bold, Italic, or Underline) for the style in the script dialog box. The script's style only applies to text you have already hyperlinked in the active publication. The script does not add a style to the Styles palette.

PRINTING FOLDER

Trapping folder

- *95pct Gray as Black* Changes the Black Limit in the Trapping Preferences dialog box to 95%.
- *Overprint all Black Objects* Sets all black objects, including text, strokes, and fills, to overprint.
- *Overprint Black Text* Sets black text to overprint.
- *Overprint Black Fill Stroke* Sets black fills and strokes to overprint.

RUN PLUG-INS FOLDER

The scripts in the Run Plug-ins folder enable you to run the following plug-ins without having to choose the Utilities > Plug-ins command: Add Cont'd Line, Balance Columns, Build Booklet, Bullets and Numbering, Drop Cap, Grid Manager, Keyline, and Running Headers and Footers.

TEMPLATE FOLDER

NOTE: The following templates require certain Type 1 fonts. To run the template scripts successfully, install the fonts included with PageMaker 6.5. On the Macintosh, the fonts are installed when you install PageMaker. In Windows, the fonts are located in the Pm65\extras\fonts directory on your system; they are installed when you install ATM 4.0 Lite, included with PageMaker.

- *Biz Cards* Creates a new 4-up publication with guides for 8 business cards per letter-sized page.
- *Brochure 1* Creates a 2-sided, 3-column, letter-sized landscape brochure.
- *Brochure 2* Creates a 2-sided, 6-column, letter-sized landscape brochure.
- *Brochure 3* In PageMaker for the Macintosh, this script creates a 2-sided, 4-column, letter-sized landscape brochure. In PageMaker for Windows, this script creates the same publication as the Brochure 2 script.
- *Brochure 4 (Windows only)* Creates a 2-sided, 4-column, letter-sized landscape brochure.
- *Calendar 1* Creates a one-page, letter-sized tall calendar for the month and year you specify.
- *Calendar 2* Creates a one-page, A4 wide calendar, not specific to month or year.
- *Calendar 3* Creates a one-page, A4 wide calendar, not specific to month or year, with a different design than Calendar 2.
- *CD Liner* Creates a one-page layout for a CD case liner, including guides and crop marks.
- *CD Notes* Creates a one-page layout for a CD case insert, including guides and crop marks.
- *Envelope* Creates a business-size (COM-10) envelope layout.
- *Fax Cover Sheet* Creates a tall, letter-sized fax cover sheet.
- *Invitation* Creates a folded invitation card, 5.25 inches wide by 8.25 inches tall.
- *Invoice* Creates guides and text for a standard, letter-sized invoice.
- *Letterhead* Creates the guides and layout for four standard business letterhead designs.
- *Manual* Creates an 8-page letterhalf (5.5" by 11") manual that includes styles and layout for a title page, content pages, Table of Contents, Index, and glossary.
- *Newsletter 1* Creates a 4-page, 3-column, letter-sized tall newsletter.
- *Newsletter 2* Creates a 4-page, 3-column, letter-sized tall newsletter with a complex layout that includes sidebars.
- *Newsletter 3* Creates a 4-page, 4-column, tabloid-sized tall newsletter.
- *Press Release* Creates a 2-page, letter-sized standard press release document.
- *Resume* Creates a 1-page letter-sized standard resume.
- *Sign* Creates tabloid-sized signs, one wide and one tall.
- *Spiral Notepad* Adds lines to an open publication with double-sided, facing pages to simulate a spiral notepad.

TEXT FOLDER

Frame and Story folder

- *Frame Story* Creates a frame around each text block in a story.
- *Merge Framed Stories* Merges two framed stories into a single, threaded story. Note that the script may move hyperlinks, sources, or anchors unexpectedly.
- *Merge Stories* Merges two stories into a threaded story. Note that the script may move hyperlinks, sources, or anchors unexpectedly.
- *Split Framed Story* Unthreads two threaded frames. Note that the script may move hyperlinks, sources, or anchors unexpectedly.
- *Split Story* Unthreads two threaded text blocks. Note that the script may move hyperlinks, sources, or anchors unexpectedly.

Other folder

- *Find Overset Text* Searches all text blocks in a publication to locate overset text (i.e., text that has not been placed.)
- *Hanging Character* Creates a hanging character, or a character to the left of a textblock's boundary.
- *Ligatures* Adds or removes ligatures.
  Styles folder
- *Remove Unused Styles* Removes paragraph styles that are not applied to any text in the publication.
- *Styles Info* Queries the publication for paragraph style information, then reports that information in a new publication.

Text Block folder

- *Column Breaker* Breaks a single text block into the number of columns you specify.
- *Scale Text Block* Resizes a text block, adjusting the font size and width proportionally.

Using Master Pages in PageMaker 6.5

The design of your PageMaker publication will be more cohesive if each page is built on a common master page. A master page typically contains basic design elements (e.g., headers, footers, page numbers) that you would like to appear on many or all pages in your publication. Master pages can also contain layout guides (e.g., column guides, ruler guides, margin guides). Adobe PageMaker 6.5 enables you to create as many master pages as you need in a publication, increasing layout flexibility and control. This document includes general suggestions for using master pages.

PLANNING

Planning is the key to using master pages successfully. Before you add any text or graphics, think about how the final publication will look. Identify which elements are common to multiple pages: Will some pages require the same logo, or will some pages use the same column guide format? Create master pages for those publication pages that share common design elements. Creating a separate master page for every publication page will make your publication unnecessarily complex, so remember your design plans when creating new master pages.

Do not add text or graphics to your publication pages until you've created and assigned all master pages. Assigning a master page to a publication page does not affect any objects already placed on the publication page, but objects placed on the publication page could overlap master page objects. So that you don't have to move objects to conform to new master guides or other master items, assign master pages to publication pages before placing text or graphics in the publication.

INSERTING OR REMOVING PAGES

You can create a one-page or two-page master. When you insert or remove an odd number of pages in a double-sided publication, the left pages become right-hand pages, and vice versa. If a left-hand pages was assigned the left side of a two-page master spread, PageMaker will assign the right side of the same two-page master spread. PageMaker cannot apply the left side of a master spread to a right-hand page, or the right side of a master spread to a left-hand page.

CREATING AND REMOVING MASTER PAGES

To create a new master page:

1. Choose Window > Show Master Pages.

TIP MAC OS / WINDOWS

Freeze your page numbers

Sometimes you might want to add a certain number of pages to your publication without disrupting the page numbers that have been assigned automatically. For instance, say you want to add front matter to your publication, and have the fourth or fifth page retain page-one status. Of course you can use PageMaker's Book feature to do this (see PageMaker's User Guide for more information). But here's another way.

Before adding pages, save your file and run the "Build Booklet" Plug-in on it. In the "Build Booklet" dialog box, set the "Layout" option to "None" and click "OK." The resulting publication should be an exact duplicate of the original publication with one important exception: the page-number markers (LM and RM) will no longer be on the master pages. Instead, you'll have static page numbers on each page. When you add pages to the publication, it won't disrupt the numbers on the existing pages.

2. In the Master Pages palette, choose New Master from the Master Pages palette Menu, or click the New Master icon.
3. In the New Master Page dialog box, choose whether you want a single-page or a two-page spread by selecting One Page or Two Page. 4. Specify the margins, number of columns, and space between the columns.
5. Type a name for the master page, then click Create.

To remove a master page and its objects:

1. Choose Window > Show Master Pages.
2. In the Master Pages palette, select the master page you wish to remove.
3. Choose Delete from the Master Pages palette Menu, or drag the selected master page onto the Trash icon.
4. When the message, "Delete master page "[xxxxx]" and all its contents?" appears, click Delete.

Using PageMaker 6.5 Scripts Effectively

Scripts are text-only files that contain simple commands and queries that automate Adobe PageMaker 6.5 tasks, such as setting up pages or importing a standard set of objects. PageMaker includes several scripts, which you can select in the Scripts palette. You can also create your own scripts.

To create and use scripts in PageMaker 6.5 more effectively:

- For a description of what a script included with PageMaker does, select it in PageMaker's Scripts palette and then choose Edit Script from the Scripts palette menu. The first few lines explain the purpose of the script.
- To group the scripts you use frequently into one script folder, move the script files into one folder inside the Scripts folder. The Scripts folder is in the Pm65\Rsrc\Usenglsh\Plugins folder (Windows) or in the Plugins folder in the RSRC folder in the Adobe PageMaker 6.5 folder (Macintosh).
- You can create a script in any text editor that can save in text-only format. After you create the script, save it in text-only format, then copy it into your Scripts folder to use it in the Scripts palette.
- To find out which commands were used to script a set of actions, select the script in the Scripts palette, then choose Edit Script from the Scripts palette menu. To use the same commands in a new script, select the section of the script you want to copy, then press Ctl + C (Windows) or Command + C (Macintosh). You can then paste the copied sections into a new script.
- In PageMaker for Windows, you can edit or trace a script quickly by right-clicking on the script name, then choosing Edit Script or Trace Script from the Scripts palette menu.
- See the Script Language Guide in PageMaker's on-line help for a complete listing of scripting commands and queries.

To read the Script Language Guide in PageMaker for Windows, choose Help > Help Topics, then double-click Script Language Guide at the bottom of the Contents section. If you select Quick Reference, you can browse an index of commands and queries. If you select Commands and Queries, you can find commands or queries by function.

To read the Script Language Guide in PageMaker for the Macintosh, choose Help > PageMaker Help Topics, then double-click Using Scripts. Double-click on Creating and Editing Scripts, then click Script Language Guide. You can browse an index of commands and queries in the Script Language Guide.

To see the parameters for using a command, as well as an example of its use, double-click on the command in the Script Language Guide.

- For in-depth information about PageMaker's scripting language, see PageMaker Scripting: A Guide to Desktop Automation by Hans Hansen, available from Adobe Press. This book and its companion CD-ROM contain explanations for PageMaker scripting commands, sample scripts, hints, and how-to's. For more information, visit the Adobe Systems Web site (http://www.adobe.com/adobepress/alltitles.html#pmscripting).

MICRO TIP MAC OS / WINDOWS

To avoid long place times in PageMaker 6.0, especially on the Mac, and to minimize publication file size, do not select "Store copy in publication" when placing any graphic file that is roughly 2–5 megabytes or larger. Storing large graphics in publications will also increase the amount of time it takes to convert them from PageMaker 5.0x to 6.0 format. Just make sure you don't delete any graphics you haven't stored in your publication, and transport them with your publication file if you print at a remote site (such as a service bureau).

Using Save for Service Provider Plug-in or CheckList in PageMaker 6.5

Adobe PageMaker 6.5 includes the Save for Service Provider plug-in, rather than the CheckList utility, to enable you to identify problems with a publication before taking it to a service provider. PageMaker 6.0x and earlier for the Macintosh includes the CheckList utility.

The Save for Service Provider plug-in analyzes PageMaker publications for missing fonts, broken graphic links, print settings, and ink settings. You can use its Package command to save the publication with a concise report for your service provider, including details about fonts, linked graphics, print settings, and contact information. Unlike CheckList, the Save for Service Provider plug-in does not scan the system for damaged fonts.

To use the Save for Service Provider plug-in in PageMaker 6.5, choose Utilities > Plug-ins > Save for Service Provider. To analyze and package the open publication, click Preflight Pub. To analyze a PostScript file, click Preflight.PS, then double-click the PostScript file you want to send to the service provider.

You can also use CheckList 2.6 or earlier to analyze a PostScript file printed to disk from PageMaker 6.5:

1. In PageMaker, choose File > Print.
2. Click Options, then select Write PostScript to File, and Normal or For Separations.
3. Name the PostScript file
4. Click Save As, then specify the folder in which you want to save the PostScript file.
5. Click Save.
6. Start CheckList.
7. Select the PostScript file to analyze, then click Open.

PageMaker 6.0's "Use PM5 Custom Settings" Utility

The Use PM5 Custom Settings utility enables you to use PageMaker 5.0x's user dictionaries, non-English dictionaries, custom color libraries, and tracking values in Adobe PageMaker 6.0. The Use PM5 Custom Settings utility copies these files from the Aldus folder (Macintosh) or Aldus directory (Windows), where PageMaker 5.0x stores many of its preferences and user settings, into the appropriate location in the Adobe PageMaker 6.0 folder (Macintosh) or Pm6 directory (Windows). To use the Use PM5 Custom Settings utility, both PageMaker 5.0x and PageMaker 6.0 must be installed.

The Use PM5 Custom Settings utility for the Macintosh is a 68K application that runs in emulation mode on a Power Macintosh.

USING THE USE PM5 CUSTOM SETTINGS UTILITY

To use the Use PM5 Custom Settings utility:

1. Double-click the Use PM5 Custom Settings file (Macintosh) or the Pm5files.exe file (Windows). The Use PM5 Custom Settings utility is installed in the Utilities folder in the Adobe PageMaker 6.0 folder on the Macintosh. The Pm5files.exe file is installed in the Pm6\Rsrc\Usenglsh\Utility directory in Windows.
2. In the Use PM5 Custom Settings dialog box, make sure the folder that contains PageMaker resource files is listed under Aldus Folder. To select an different folder, click Find Aldus Folder.
   NOTE: Aldus Persuasion 2.0x and earlier for the Macintosh create an Aldus Folder in the System Folder, which is different from the folder named Aldus that PageMaker 5.0x and earlier for the Macintosh use.
3. Verify that the folder that contains the PageMaker 6.0 application is listed under PageMaker 6.0 Folder. To select another folder, click Find PM6 Folder.
4. Select the PageMaker 5.0x files (e.g., User Dictionaries, Dictionaries, Custom Color Libraries, Tracking Values) you wish to use in PageMaker 6.0.
5. Click Copy.

MICRO TIP MAC OS / WINDOWS

> If your PageMaker 5.0 publications contain "PS Group it" elements that you might want to ungroup in PageMaker 6.0, run "PS Ungroup it" on the elements before you convert. (PageMaker 6.0 can't ungroup PageMaker 5.0–created "PS Group it" elements.)

PDF Thumbnails Created for First Page of Each Publication in Book List in PageMaker 6.0

ISSUE

When you create a Portable Document Format (PDF) file of booked publications with Thumbnails enabled and the First Page Only option selected from the Thumbnails pop-up menu in the Distiller PDF Job Options dialog box, Adobe PageMaker 6.0 creates a thumbnail for the first page of each booked publication.

SOLUTIONS

Disable Thumbnails when creating a PDF file of a booked publication.

1. Choose File > Create Adobe PDF.
2. In the Create Adobe PDF dialog box, select Override Distiller's Options and click Edit.
3. In the Distiller PDF Job Options dialog box, deselect Thumbnails and click OK.

OR: Leave the First Page Only option selected in the Thumbnails pop-up menu in the Distiller PDF Job Options dialog box to allow the Create Adobe PDF plug-in to create a thumbnail for the first page of each booked publication.

ADDITIONAL INFORMATION

The Create Adobe PDF plug-in treats booked PageMaker publications as individual publications. When you create a PDF file of booked publications in PageMaker 6.0 using the Create Adobe PDF plug-in, and have Thumbnails enabled and the First Page Only option selected from the Thumbnails pop-up menu in the Distiller PDF Job Options dialog box, PageMaker creates a thumbnail for the first page of each publication in the book list.

Kodak Photo CD Image Resolution Choices When Placing in PageMaker 6.0x

Kodak Photo CDs include five different resolutions for each image. Kodak Pro PhotoCDs include an additional resolution, providing a total of six different resolutions for each image.

DEFAULT RESOLUTION SETTING IN PAGEMAKER'S IMPORT FILTER

PageMaker 6.0x's Kodak Photo CD import filter determines the default optimal image resolution based on the default line screen value for the target printer resolution specified in the PageMaker publication. When the target printer resolution does not have an associated default line screen value, the filter uses the closest available printer resolution for which it has a default line screen value. The default optimal image resolution is twice the line screen value for the target printer resolution. For example, in a publication with a target printer resolution of 1200 dpi, which uses a common default line screen value of 110 lines per inch (lpi), PageMaker's Kodak Photo CD import filter, by default, imports the image that has a resolution of twice the default line screen value, or 220 pixels per inch (ppi).

OVERRIDING THE DEFAULT RESOLUTION SETTING

To use a different resolution than the default optimal image resolution in the import filter, select Override PageMaker Resolution, then replace the original number with the desired resolution:

1. Choose File > Place.
2. Double-click on the filename of the Kodak PhotoCD image you want to import.
3. In the Kodak PhotoCD Import Filter dialog box, click Change.
4. Select Override PageMaker Resolution.
5. Select the number in the Resolution dialog box, enter the desired value, then click OK.

PageMaker 6.0x Trapping Options Dialog Box

Adobe PageMaker 6.0x's trapping feature enables you to trap PageMaker-drawn objects and text in your PageMaker publication. The following options in the PageMaker's Trapping Options dialog box give you control over the traps in your publication.

DEFAULT TRAP WIDTH

Specifies the width of the trap for all colors except those that are solid black. The Black Limit setting defines what PageMaker considers solid black. The default trap width is .003 inches.

BLACK WIDTH

Specifies the width of the trap for colors next to or under a solid black. The Black Width is normally 1.5 to 2 times the width of the default trap. The default Black Width is .007 inches.

STEP LIMIT

Specifies the threshold at which PageMaker creates a trap. When the component inks of two colors are at least as different as the step limit, PageMaker traps them. For example, when the step limit is 100%, PageMaker traps no colors. When the step limit is 0%, PageMaker traps all colors. When the step limit is 12%, PageMaker traps colors that vary by at least 12%. The default Step Limit is 10%.

CENTERLINE THRESHOLD

Specifies the threshold at which PageMaker creates a centerline trap (i.e., creates a third color that straddles the border between two colors, instead of spreading the lighter color into the darker one). When the neutral densities of two colors are closer than the Centerline Threshold percentage, PageMaker creates a centerline trap. For example, when the Centerline Threshold is 65%, PageMaker creates a centerline trap if the neutral density of the lighter color divided by the neutral density of the darker color is greater than 65%. When the Centerline Threshold is 0%, PageMaker uses only centerline traps. When the Centerline Threshold is 100%, PageMaker uses only spreads and chokes. The default Centerline Threshold is 70%.

TRAP TEXT ABOVE

Specifies the threshold over which PageMaker traps text. PageMaker traps text larger than the specified point size, and overprints all text at or below this point size, regardless of color. The default Trap Text Above value is 23.9.

BLACK LIMIT

Specifies the percentage of black that a color must contain for PageMaker to consider it a solid black and trap it using the Black Width value. For example, if the Black Limit is 80%, PageMaker considers any color whose black component is 80% or greater to be a solid black. The percentage value refers to the percentage of black (K) in the CMYK components of a color, whether the color was defined as spot or process, RGB, or CMYK. The default Black Limit is 100%.

Saving PageMaker 6.0x Publications in PageMaker 5.0 Format

Because PageMaker 5.0x does not support some features available in PageMaker 6.0x, objects in your publication may not convert or may be modified when saved in PageMaker 5.0 format.

The following PageMaker 6.0x features do not convert to PageMaker 5.0 format or are modified as noted:

- Groups created using the Group command are ungrouped. Transformations (e.g., resizing, rotating) applied to the grouped objects are retained.
- Masked objects are unmasked. The object used to create the mask displays with the masked object.
- Master pages other than the Document Master are deleted, and the Document Master pages are assigned to all pages.
- Locked objects are unlocked.
- Non-printing objects are displayed and printed.
- Color management information and high-fidelity color attributes are removed.
- Polygons, EMF graphics, and objects embedded using OLE 2.0 are removed.
- The following graphic types are removed: Scitex CT; LAB and ICCLAB TIFF images; TIFF images with high-

TIP MAC OS / WINDOWS

Get out your magnifying glass

It's hard to imagine, but we've been told by many customers that sometimes 6-point type just isn't small enough. (We picture this category of users as including lawyers and the publishers of Lilliputian newspapers.)

Here's a way to shrink text further and keep it editable. Create and lay out your type at 6 points. Then choose "Select All" from the Edit menu and "Type Specs..." from the Type menu. Choose "Superscript" from the "Position" drop-down list, then click "Options...." In the "Type Options" dialog box, change the "Super/subscript size" setting to a percentage that fits your needs, and set the "Superscript position" to 0 percent to keep the text on the baseline.

—Submitted by Christopher Drum of Raleigh, N.C.

fidelity colors; indexed TIFF images, except indexed RGB TIFF images; PhotoCD images.

- In Windows, filenames of publications and linked files are truncated when they do not follow DOS naming conventions (i.e., eight characters plus a three character extension). When filenames are truncated, you may need to update publication links and recreate book lists.
- Bookmark and hyperlink information for Portable Document Format (PDF) files are deleted.
- Object-level tints become solid.
- Overprinting and trapping settings specified in the Trapping Options dialog box are removed. When you print color separations, objects assigned PageMaker's default black knock out, and text assigned PageMaker's default black overprints.
- Some custom or pre-defined colors may appear differently.

To avoid changes when you save a PageMaker 6.0x publication in PageMaker 5.0 format, do one or more of the following:

A. Ungroup grouped objects.
B. Create masked objects, polygons, and trapped objects in another application, then import them into the PageMaker 6.0x publication. You can create traps in PageMaker 5.0x for the Macintosh using the TrapMaker addition.
C. Delete any non-printing objects you do not want PageMaker 5.0x to display, or move them to the pasteboard before printing from PageMaker 5.0x.
D. Import graphics for which you have a PageMaker 5.0x graphic import filter installed.
E. Replace object-level tints with color-level tints.
F. Make sure everything functions properly in PageMaker 6.0x (e.g., the publication prints as expected, objects are displayed correctly, text is formatted as expected, publication links are up-to-date).
G. Make a backup copy of the PageMaker 6.0x publication so that if you experience any problems in PageMaker 5.0x, you can return to the PageMaker 6.0x publication.

SAVING A PAGEMAKER 6.0X PUBLICATION IN PAGEMAKER 5.0 FORMAT

To save a PageMaker 6.0x publication in PageMaker 5.0 format:

1. In PageMaker 6.0x, choose File > Save As.
2. Name the new publication. For publications that will be edited in PageMaker 5.0x for Windows, use an eight-character filename with a .PM5 extension.
3. Select 5.0 Publication in the Save As Type dialog box (Windows) or select A Copy in 5.0 Format for the Save As option (Macintosh).
4. Click Save (Windows) or OK (Macintosh).

ISOLATING PROBLEMS AFTER SAVING A PAGEMAKER 6.0X PUBLICATION IN PAGEMAKER 5.0 FORMAT

If an object in the PageMaker 6.0x file does not convert as expected, isolate the problem by doing one or more of the following:

A. Try recreating the problem in the PageMaker 6.0x publication to determine if it is specific to PageMaker 5.0x.
B. Try recreating the problem in another PageMaker 5.0x publication to determine whether it is specific to the converted publication.
C. When problems with linked files occur, make sure all linked files are up to date in the original PageMaker 6.0x publication.
D. When fonts are substituted in the PageMaker 5.0 publication, make sure the same fonts are installed on the computer on which you are opening the PageMaker 5.0 publication. In PageMaker for Windows, select a valid Compose To printer in the Page Setup dialog box.

Using Master Pages in PageMaker 6.0

Adobe PageMaker 6.0x or later enables you to create as many master pages as you need in a publication, increasing layout flexibility and control. When using multiple master pages, planning your publication in advance can prevent unexpected design problems as you create your publication. This document includes general suggestions for using master pages, then explains how inserting publication pages or saving the publication in PageMaker 5.0 format can affect your design.

PLANNING

Planning is the key to using master pages successfully. Before you add any text or graphics, think about how the final publication will look. Identify which elements are common to multiple pages. Will some pages require the same logo, or will some pages use the same column guide format? Then only create master pages for publication pages with these common design elements. Creating a separate master page for every publication page will make your publication unnecessarily complex, so remember your design plans when creating new master pages.

Assigning a master page to a publication page does not affect any objects already placed on the page. To avoid moving objects to conform to new master guides or other master items, assign master pages to publication pages before placing text or graphics in the publication.

INSERTING OR REMOVING PAGES

When inserting or removing an odd number of pages in a double-sided publication, some left-hand pages become right-hand pages, and vice versa. If some of the left-hand pages were assigned the left side of a two-page master spread, PageMaker assigns the right side of the same two-page master spread to them because PageMaker cannot apply the left side of a master spread to a right-hand page, or the right side of a master spread to a left-hand page.

SAVING PAGEMAKER 6.0X PUBLICATIONS IN PAGEMAKER 5.0 FORMAT

When you save your publication in PageMaker 5.0 format, all master pages other than the Document Master are deleted, and all pages are assigned the Document Master pages. Any formatting on additional master pages is lost, but objects specific to the publication pages are retained.

You can preserve the formatting of master pages other than the Document Master by copying the master page objects to their assigned publication pages before saving in PageMaker 5.0 format. You can use the Build Booklet plug-in module, which automatically copies master page objects to their assigned publication pages as it creates a new publication.

Create Adobe PDF Plug-In in PageMaker 6.0x

The Create Adobe PDF plug-in included with Adobe PageMaker 6.0x enables you to convert PageMaker publications to Portable Document Format (PDF) files. These PDF files maintain the layout, graphics, typography, and color of the original document and can include optional links, bookmarks, and articles. You can view or print PDF files using Adobe Acrobat Exchange or Adobe Acrobat Reader for Windows, Macintosh, DOS, or UNIX. The PageMaker 6.0x CD-ROM includes Acrobat Reader 2.1, which may be distributed freely.

MICRO TIP MAC OS / WINDOWS

If you create a PDF from PageMaker using the PDFWriter and your pages end up in reverse order, print your publication to PDF again after selecting the "Reverse order" option in PageMaker's "Print document" dialog box.

The Create Adobe PDF plug-in uses PageMaker's Printer Styles to generate a PostScript file. If you select one or more options (e.g., Link TOC entries, Create Bookmarks) in the PDF Options dialog box, the Create Adobe PDF plug-in inserts PDFMark commands into the PostScript file to create links, bookmarks, or articles. After creating the Post-Script file, the plug-in starts Distiller 2.1 or Distiller 2.1 PE (Private Edition) to convert the PostScript file to a PDF file.

Acrobat Distiller 2.1 PE, which is included with PageMaker 6.0x, can only distill PostScript files created by the Create Adobe PDF plug-in. To distill a PostScript file you created by selecting the Write PostScript to File option in PageMaker's Print Options dialog box, use a full retail version of Acrobat Distiller.

The PDFMark programming language can create bookmarks, links, annotations, and views in a PDF file. You can also create these features manually using Acrobat Exchange. Acrobat Distiller recognizes PDFMark commands, but PostScript output devices (e.g., imagesetters, desktop printers) ignore them. For information about the PDFMark language, see the Pdfmark.pdf file in the Acrobat Help folder in the Distiller folder.

Stacking Order of Objects in PageMaker 6.0

In Adobe PageMaker, a graphic or text block occupies a layer relative to other objects on the page. The order in which objects overlap one another is called the "stacking order." Objects on a forward layer in the stacking order appear in front (i.e., on top) of those that are on a backward layer in the stacking order. When first creating or placing an object into a publication, it appears in front of objects already on the page.

In PageMaker 5.0x and later, menu commands are available for moving an object to the front or to the back of the stack order. PageMaker 6.0 includes menu commands to move an object through one layer of the stacking order at a time.

After you select an object with the pointer tool in PageMaker 6.0, you can use one of four commands on the Arrange menu to change the object's stacking:

- Bring to Front, moves the object to the foremost layer
- Bring Forward, moves the object one layer forward
- Send to Back, moves the object to the backmost layer
- Send Backward, moves the object to one layer backwards

All objects in a PageMaker publication are layered in a stacking order, including text blocks and objects on the pasteboard. After breaking a text block into two threaded text blocks, the original text block remains on the same layer, and the newly created text block moves to the top layer (i.e., moves to the front). To change the stacking order of an object on a layer below overlapping objects, press Command (Macintosh) or Ctrl (Windows) as you click with the pointer tool to select the object on a layer below other objects, where each click on overlapping objects selects the next object down in the stacking order.

TIP MAC OS / WINDOWS

Making "invisible" objects easier to find

When you're working with a PageMaker-drawn object you want to be "invisible" (because you're wrapping text around it or for some other reason), it can be smart to set the fill of the object to "Paper" instead of "None"—this will help you select the object later. To select an object with a fill of "None," you'll need to click exactly on its outside line, which can be difficult when you can't see the object. On the other hand, when an object is filled with the "Paper" color, you can click anywhere within the object to select it. If you use this technique, be aware the "Paper" fill will make your object opaque. —*Mark Rakocy, Bedford, Ohio*

After you group objects in PageMaker 6.0, each object in the group retains their relative stacking order until you use commands from the Arrange menu to change their stacking order.

To change the stacking order of an object in a group:

1. Select the object in the group by pressing Command (Macintosh) or Ctrl (Windows) as you click with the pointer tool to select the object on a layer below other objects, where each click on overlapping objects selects the next object down in the stacking order.
2. Choose Bring to Front, Bring Forward, Send to Back, or Send Backward from the Arrange menu to move the object forward or backwards in the stacking order.

After creating a group, PageMaker assigns the grouped object to the top layer (i.e., the grouped object moves above other objects). After you ungroup objects, the individual objects retain changes made while the objects were grouped. For example, the foremost object remains on the foreground layer, regardless of the object's layer before it was grouped.

WINDOWS

Q *(6.0 only)* **I'm trying to decide whether to upgrade to Windows 95. Am I missing out on any features of PageMaker 6.0 if I stick with Windows 3.11?**

A A few. Adobe PageMaker 6.0 does include features that require a true 32-bit operating system like Windows 95. As a result, PageMaker can't support those features when it's running under a 16-bit operating system like Windows 3.11. By and large, you won't lose much functionality by staying with Windows 3.11, but it may be worthwhile to consider upgrading to Windows 95 if any of the following issues are a concern for you.

- Some "special effects" may not display or print properly to non-PostScript printers. Specifically, clipping paths and masked objects may not print exactly as they do under Windows 95. When you print to a non-PostScript printer, what prints is based on what's displayed—which is why (and how) PageMaker can sometimes print these "special effects" to these printers. But correct display and printing of such objects depends on having sufficient system resources. So while masked objects and clipping paths print fine from PageMaker 6.x in Windows 3.11 to PostScript printers, inadequate memory or resources on your computer or printer may prevent them from printing properly to non-PostScript printers.
- You won't be able to use Adobe Table 2.5. Because Adobe Table 2.5 is not supported by Windows 3.1x, Table Editor 2.11 will be installed instead. Table 2.5 has a number of new features, including improved performance, character-level formatting, and an expanded interface.
- Network installation options are limited. The only PageMaker network installation option you'll have available for Windows 3.11 is to install disk images. You can then install PageMaker onto your workstations from the disk images on the server, instead of from the installation disk set. If you want to be able to install and run PageMaker 6.0x directly from a network drive, you'll need to use Windows 95.
- Enhanced Metafile (EMF) graphics will not import. EMF is a new 32-bit graphic format introduced with Windows 95, and PageMaker will import EMF graphics only while running under Windows 95. Currently, this shouldn't be a significant obstacle, since only Windows 95 itself is supporting this format, but other applications are expected to support it over time.
- Gallery Effects Plug-ins are not compatible. When you install PageMaker 6.0x under Windows 3.1x, the Photoshop Effects function will install 5 filters from Adobe Photoshop LE, instead of the 12 sample Adobe Gallery Effects filters that are installed under Windows 95.
- Open DataBase Connectivity (ODBC) is not operational. ODBC is a Windows-based tool for manipulating and formatting database information from ODBC-compatible sources. PageMaker's ODBC Plug-in is a 32-bit applet; if you want to do any significant amount of database publishing in PageMaker, you should seriously consider the advantages of ODBC, which requires Windows 95.

Preparing to Write PostScript to File for Service Bureau Output in PageMaker 6.0x

Checklist for Preparing PostScript Files for Bureau Output
Talking to Your Commercial Printer & Service Bureau
Ensuring You Have the Right Tools Before Designing Your Publication

Obtaining the Correct WPD, SPD and PPD Files
Determining the Version of Your PostScript Printer Driver
Obtaining the Most Current Version of the PostScript Printer Driver
Installing the PostScript Printer Driver and WPD Files in Windows 3.1x
Installing the PostScript Printer Driver and SPD Files in Windows 95
Installing a PPD File
Connecting Your Printer to a Printer Port
Setting Up Fonts in Windows
Composing Your Publication
Using Color in Your Publication
Writing PostScript to File in PageMaker 6.0x

CHECKLIST FOR PREPARING A POSTSCRIPT FILE FOR SERVICE BUREAU OUTPUT

Use this checklist when preparing for and creating a PostScript file for output at a service bureau:

- Talk to your service bureau and commercial printer.
- Install the correct WPD, or SPD, and PPD for the printer to which the service bureau will print your PostScript file.
- Install the Windows PostScript printer driver version 3.56 or later or Adobe PostScript driver 2.11 later when running under Windows 3.1.x, or install the Windows PostScript printer driver 4.00 or later or Adobe PSPrinter printer driver 4.1 or later when running under Windows 95.
- Ensure your fonts are installed correctly.
- Compose your publication for the printer to which your service bureau will print your PostScript file, and specify the target printer resolution in PageMaker's Document Setup dialog box.
- Use the Save As command to save your PageMaker publication before printing.
- Decide how you will be using color in your publication.
- When printing color separations, make sure you are using graphics that will separate reliably (i.e., Adobe-conforming EPS graphics, DCS files, or CMYK TIFF images).
- Place all graphics from your hard disk, rather than from floppy disks or network drives.
- Check all of your settings in PageMaker's Print dialog box. See the section titled "How to Write PostScript to File in PageMaker 6.0x" for more information.

TALKING TO YOUR COMMERCIAL PRINTER AND SERVICE BUREAU

When preparing files to be printed at an imagesetting service bureau, keep in close contact with your commercial printer and your service bureau throughout the process. From the earliest planning stages to the press check, your commercial printer and service bureau are the experts; do not underestimate their ability to help you avoid costly mistakes.

Before selecting a service bureau, make sure they are willing and able to support you. Here are some questions to ask a prospective service bureau to ensure it meets your needs:

- Is your prospective service bureau comfortable working with Windows PostScript files? If they have IBM-compatible computers and work in Windows, that is certainly a good sign. If they do not, make sure they are familiar with the Windows environment.
- Will your prospective service bureau give you guidelines for providing them with correctly-formatted PostScript files? Can they clearly articulate what they need from you to print your files successfully? Even if you memorize their guidelines, you should work with a service bureau who also understands this process and is willing to help you.
- Will your prospective service bureau arrange for a test print if this is your first time working with them or if you are trying anything new for this project? If possible, try to arrange a test job of two or three pages that will contain the fonts, kinds of graphics, and print settings you intend to use in your final job. If you discover you have made a critical error on the final printout of a long publication, you could waste a lot of money and time.

ENSURING YOU HAVE THE RIGHT TOOLS BEFORE DESIGNING YOUR PUBLICATION

Once you have selected a commercial printer and a service bureau, and have discussed your plans with them, make sure you have the right tools installed before you start designing your publication. You need to have a current Windows printer driver, as well as a PPD and WPD, or SPD, file installed for the printer to which your service bureau will print your PostScript file.

PostScript Printer Driver

When printing from Adobe PageMaker 6.0x, it is essential you use a PostScript printer driver that supports PostScript Printer Description (PPD) files. When printing from Windows 3.1x, the PostScript driver version 3.56 or later (PSCRIPT.DRV) and the Adobe PSPrinter 2.1.1 or later driver (ADOBEPS.DRV) support PPD files. When printing from Windows 95, the Microsoft PostScript printer driver version 4.00 or later or the Adobe PSPrinter printer driver version 4.1 or later support PPD files.

Windows Printer Description File

A Windows Printer Description (WPD) file lists the name of your printer in the Printers Control Panel and makes information about your printer available to Windows applications. In Windows 3.1x, WPD files are located in the Windows\system directory and have a .WPD filename extension. In Windows 95, WPD files are also located in the Windows\system directory, but have either a .SPD or .PPD filename extension.

PostScript Printer Description File

Like a WPD file, a PPD file describes a printer's features (e.g., resolution, fonts, color) to PageMaker 6.0x. PPD files installed with PageMaker 6.0x are located in the pm6\rsrc\usenglsh\ppd4 subdirectory.

Fonts

If you want to include downloadable fonts with your PostScript file, make sure you have all the necessary font files for each style (e.g., bold, italic, roman) installed.

OBTAINING THE CORRECT WPD, SPD AND PPD FILES

Contact your service bureau to determine the type of imagesetter to which they will be printing your publication. If the most current WPD file for their imagesetter is not included with Windows 3.1x or Windows 95, obtain it from your service bureau, or download it from Microsoft's bulletin board or the MSL forum on CompuServe.

If you are using Windows 95, you can obtain SPD files directly from Microsoft or from your printer manufacturer. You can also obtain PPD files from your printer manufacturer or download them from the Adobe BBS.

DETERMINING THE VERSION OF YOUR POSTSCRIPT PRINTER DRIVER

Make sure you have the recommended PostScript printer driver installed. When creating PostScript files from Windows 3.1x, use PostScript driver version 3.56 or later (PSCRIPT.DRV) or the Adobe PSPrinter 2.1.1 or later driver (ADOBEPS.DRV). When creating PostScript files in from Windows 95, use Microsoft PostScript printer driver version 4.00 or later or the Adobe PSPrinter printer driver version 4.1 or later.

To determine the version of the installed PostScript printer driver in Windows 3.1.x:

1. In the Printers Control Panel, select the printer your service bureau will be using (e.g., Linotronic 330).
2. Click Setup, then click About. The About dialog box should say "Windows PostScript Printer Driver" and "Version 3.56" or "PostScript Printer Driver by Adobe" and "Version 2.11."
3. Click OK to exit the About dialog box, click OK to exit the Setup dialog box, then close the Printers Control Panel.

To determine the version of the PostScript printer driver installed in Windows 95:

1. Choose Start > Programs > Windows Explorer.
2. In the Exploring window, locate the file PSCRIPT.DRV or ADOBEPS4.DRV in the Windows\system directory.
3. Right-click the PSCRIPT.DRV file or ADOBEPS4.DRV file, then choose Properties from the pop-up menu.
4. In the PSCRIPT.DRV or ADOBEPS.DRV Properties dialog box, click the Version tab. The PSCRIPT.DRV Properties dialog box should say "File version: 4.00.950," "Product Description: PostScript Printer Driver" and "Copyright...Microsoft Corp." The ADOBEPS4.DRV Properties dialog box should say "File version: 4.10.162" and "Copyright...Adobe Systems Incorporated."

OBTAINING THE MOST CURRENT VERSION OF THE POSTSCRIPT PRINTER DRIVER

You may be able to obtain the most current version of the Windows PostScript printer driver (PSCRIPT.DRV) directly from your service bureau. You can also download the PostScript driver (PSCRIP.EXE) from Microsoft's bulletin board or from the MSL forum on Compuserve. The PostScript driver (PSCRIP.EXE) is a self-extracting file that contains the PostScript driver, text files, and a Help file. The Adobe PSPrinter driver version 4.1 for Windows 95 is available from the Adobe BBS.

If you are unable to obtain the Windows PostScript printer driver from any of these sources, use the PostScript printer driver version 3.58 located on your PageMaker 6.0x diskettes when running under Windows 3.1x. When running under Windows 95, use the PostScript driver version 4.00 located on your Windows 95 diskettes.

NOTE: Microsoft may change the location of files on their online services. If you cannot locate files on Microsoft's online service, contact Microsoft directly.

INSTALLING THE POSTSCRIPT PRINTER DRIVER AND WPD FILES IN WINDOWS 3.1X

To install the WPD file and PostScript printer driver for your printer in Windows 3.1x:

1. Close all your Windows applications.
2. Copy the *.WPD file for your printer and the PostScript driver file to a directory on your hard disk.
3. Move items located in your Startup group to another group. You may move them back to your Startup group after you install the PostScript printer driver.
4. Restart Windows to ensure that a currently-installed PostScript driver is not being used by Windows.
5. Open the Windows Control Panel, then double-click the Printers Control Panel. If the PostScript printer driver and WPD files are located on a floppy disk, insert the floppy disk into your disk drive.
6. In the Printers Control Panel, click Add, then click Install to install an unlisted or updated printer. Windows displays an Install Driver dialog box with an a:\ prompt. If the new driver is on a floppy diskette in drive a:, click OK. If it's in a different location, enter the full drive and path name or click Browse, select the correct location, then click OK.
7. In the Install Driver dialog box, click OK to display a list of printers.
8. Select the printer to which your service bureau will be printing your PostScript file, then click OK. Windows will install the new PostScript printer driver and WPD file.
   NOTE: It is important you do not have more than one file named PSCRIPT.DRV installed. If you installed the PostScript printer driver and WPD file from your hard disk, rename or delete the original PSCRIPT.DRV file located in the directory from which you installed. When installing a printer using the Windows Control Panel, the WPD file and the PSCRIPT.DRV file are added to the Windows\system directory.

INSTALLING THE POSTSCRIPT PRINTER DRIVER AND SPD FOR YOUR PRINTER IN WINDOWS 95

To install the PostScript 4.00 printer driver and an SPD for your printer in Windows 95:

1. Open the Printers window by choosing Start > Settings > Printers, or by double-clicking the My Computer icon on the desktop, then double-clicking Printers in the My Computer window.

2. In the Printers window, double-click the Add Printers icon.
3. In the Add Printer Wizard dialog box, click Next.
4. Select Local Printer, then click Next.
5. Select the manufacturer of the printer to which your service bureau will be printing from the left side of the dialog box, select the printer model from the right side of the dialog box, then click Next.
6. When installing the printer driver from the Windows 95 installation disk set or CD-ROM, click OK. When installing the printer driver from a disk provided by your printer's manufacturer, click Have Disk, insert the disk, locate the driver file on the disk, then click OK.
   NOTE: When installing a printer driver provided by a printer manufacturer, verify it is Windows 95 compatible. If you are unsure whether the printer driver is Windows 95 compatible, install a driver from the Windows 95 installation disk set or CD-ROM.
7. Select the desired printer port from the list of available ports, then click Finish.
8. Accept the default name for the printer or type in the preferred name, select Yes if you want this printer to be the default printer for your Windows applications, then click Next.
9. When installing from the Windows 95 installation disks, ensure the drive indicator for the drive containing the installation disks is correct, then insert the requested disk in the drive. When Windows is unable to locate the disk it requires, it returns the Insert Disk dialog box so that you may locate the file in a different drive or directory. When installing from the Windows 95 CD-ROM, Windows locates the files it requires on the CD-ROM.
10. After installing a printer driver under Windows 95, Windows 95 displays the printer's name in the Printers folder.For instructions on installing the Adobe 4.1 printer driver, see the ReadMe file included with the Adobe 4.1 printer driver.

INSTALLING A PPD FILE

Communicate with your imagesetting service bureau to determine what PPD file you should use for its printer. Adobe PageMaker 6.0x includes many PPD files that may work with your service bureau's printer. To view a list of the PPD files included with PageMaker 6.0x, see the file named PPDLIST.PDF, located in the pm6 directory.

If the PPD file that your service bureau recommends is not included with PageMaker 6.0x, you may also obtain PPD files from these locations:

- The Adobe Technical Support BBS at (206) 623-6984.
- Authorized and registered Adobe Service Bureaus. Contact Adobe Customer Service for a listing of Adobe service bureaus near you.
- The printer manufacturer.

To use a PPD file with PageMaker 6.0x, copy it into the pm6\rsrc\usenglsh\ppd4 directory on your hard disk.

If the PPD you need is included with PageMaker 6.0x, but isn't installed, you can install it from your PageMaker 6.0x disk set or CD-ROM. For instructions, see Further Reading.

CONNECTING YOUR PRINTER TO A PRINTER PORT

When creating a PostScript file from PageMaker 6.0x, your printer may be connected to any port. However, Adobe does not recommend connecting to the port called FILE as it causes the PostScript printer driver rather than PageMaker to generate your PostScript files and may cause PageMaker to create two PostScript files instead of one. Creating two PostScript files does not cause harm, but uses more hard disk space than necessary.

In Windows 3.1.x, the printer port you are connected to is listed in the Printers Control Panel as "[Printer Name] on [Port]." For example, when printing to a Linotronic 330 connected to LPT1, your printer is listed as Linotronic 330 on LPT1.

To change your port designation in Windows 3.1.x:

1. In the Printers Control Panel, select the printer your service bureau will be using.
2. Click Connect.
3. In the Connect dialog box, select the desired port (e.g., LPT1), then click OK.
4. In the Printers Control Panel, click Close.

To determine what printer port you are connected to in Windows 95:

1. Choose Start > Settings > Printers.
2. Right-click the printer your service bureau will be using (e.g., Linotronic 330), then choose Properties from the pop-up menu.
3. In the Properties dialog box, click the Details Tab. The Properties dialog box displays the selected printer port in the from the Print To The Following Port pop-up menu.

To change your port designation in Windows 95:

1. Choose Start > Settings > Printers.
2. Right-click the printer your service bureau will be using (e.g., Linotronic 330), then choose Properties from the pop-up menu.
3. In the Properties dialog box, click the Details tab.
4. Select the desired port from the Print to the Following Port pop-up menu.
   NOTE: When using ATM fonts, connect the printer to which your service bureau will be printing your PostScript file to the same port to which your existing printer is connected. This ensures that the fonts that are available to your existing printer are also available when composing for your service bureau's printer.

SETTING UP FONTS IN WINDOWS

There are many fonts available for use with Windows. Unfortunately, a font that looks nice on your monitor or prints fairly well on your desktop printer may not be ideal for output on an imagesetter. Before you begin designing your publication, ask your service bureau what type of fonts will print best on its equipment. Because PostScript is the standard language for most service bureaus, PostScript fonts

TIP WINDOWS

Different colors for margin, column, and ruler guides

By default, PageMaker's ruler guides are cyan, column guides are light blue, margin guides are pink, and the "floor" (the area that surrounds the pasteboard) is light

yellow. Sometimes these colors aren't very practical—for instance, if you're working with a lot of blue objects, you might not be able to see your column and ruler guides easily. By editing the ALDUS.INI file, you can customize the colors of these elements.

To do so, make a backup copy of your ALDUS.INI file, which is located in the ALDUS\USENGLSH directory, then open it in a text editor such as the Windows Notepad. The colors of these elements are specified as combinations of red, green, and blue components, each of which is defined numerically as a value from 0 to 255. When you open your ALDUS.INI file, you can enter the following lines in the [PageMaker 5] section:

```
ColumnGuideRGB=128 128 255
RulerGuideRGB=0 255 255
MarginGuideRGB=255 128 255
FloorRGB=255 255 128
```

The numbers above are the default settings. The first number in each line is the red setting, the second is the green setting, and the third is for blue. You can experiment with different number combinations to turn your guides and the floor different colors. For example, a setting of 192 0 192 equals purple, a setting of 192 192 192 is light gray, and a setting of 255 128 128 is pinkish orange. Restart PageMaker for your changes to take effect.

Please note that some light colors may not display on a black-and-white screen. Also, changing these settings in your ALDUS.INI file may not affect display color with certain high-resolution video cards, some of which display the guides as black regardless of what the ALDUS.INI settings are.

may be the easiest to print and transport. If you plan to use any other kind of font, be sure to discuss this with your service bureau ahead of time. The rest of this section assumes you're using PostScript fonts with a type management utility (e.g., Adobe Type Manager).

To ensure your fonts print correctly to your service bureau's printer:

- Make sure your final output device is always selected as the Compose To Printer in PageMaker's Document Setup dialog box. This is true even when you are printing proofs to another device. The fonts available in PageMaker (or any other Windows application) depends upon the printer to which you are composing your publication.
- Ensure any PostScript downloadable (or softfonts) you will be using in your publication have been installed for the final output device. Even when softfonts print correctly on your in-house printer, they may not be installed for your final output device. This could happen for two reasons. First, if your in-house printer is a non-Post-Script printer, PostScript softfonts are sent to your printer directly from a type manager such as ATM (Adobe Type Manager) and are not necessarily installed for your PostScript printer. Second, if your in-house printer is a PostScript device, it may not be connected to the same port as your final output device. For example, fonts that download successfully when you print to the port LPT1 may not download when you print to a different port. If you are not sure whether your fonts are installed correctly for the port you are using, use your type manager to reinstall the fonts, then restart Windows.

COMPOSING YOUR PUBLICATION

Once you have finished setting up Windows with all the tools you need, you are ready to start designing your PageMaker publication.

Before placing elements on the page, choose File > Document Setup, select your final output device from the Compose To Printer pop-up menu, then specify your target printer's resolution (i.e., the resolution of your service bureau's printer). PageMaker determines what fonts are available and how to compose your publication (e.g., line endings) based on the printer selected in the Document Setup dialog box. PageMaker also determines what resolution to use when resizing graphics based on the resolution specified in the Document Setup dialog box.

If you want to print to a different printer to proof your publication, do not change the printer that is specified in the Compose To Printer text box. You may, however, choose a different PPD in PageMaker's print dialog box without affecting the composition of your publication.

USING GRAPHICS IN YOUR PUBLICATION

Always place graphics from your local hard disk (i.e., not from a floppy disk or network volume). When you place a graphic file into a PageMaker 6.0x publication, PageMaker creates a link to that file. Placing graphics from your local hard disk ensures PageMaker can find the linked file. Because it takes less time to access files in the local hard drive than to access a files located on a floppy disk or network volume, placing graphics from your local hard disk also improves performance. When PageMaker cannot locate a linked graphic, changes you make to the graphic in the application in which the graphic was created will not be reflected in PageMaker, and the graphic may print poorly or not at all.

If you are planning to print color separations of your publication, import Adobe-conforming EPS graphics (saved with ASCII encoding, as opposed to binary), DCS files, or CMYK TIFF files only. PageMaker cannot print separations of other color graphic formats reliably.

USING COLOR IN YOUR PUBLICATION

Discuss the use of color in your publication with your service bureau and commercial printer ahead of time. Consider the following:

- If you're planning to print color separations, how many plates will you be using? The more plates, the more expensive the job will be.
- Do you want to use spot colors, process colors or both? If you are placing color EPS graphics or CMYK TIFF images into your publication, you will need to print color separations. If you are using single-color graphics and have 3 or fewer colors in your publication, it may be less expensive to use spot colors, as each color corresponds to a separate plate, and fewer plates are less expensive. When you print process colors, you'll pay for 4 plates: Cyan, Magenta, Yellow, and Black.
- What color library should you use when defining your colors? What inks does your service bureau or commercial printer have on hand? What colors would need to be mixed or ordered? Will this work with the deadlines you have?
- Will your service bureau be able to arrange a press-match for you, so you will be able to see exactly what your publication will look like when printed? Remember that your colors will print differently than they display on your computer screen because your computer uses a different color model for on-screen display than your application uses when printing.
- What kind of paper will you be using for your final printed output? The exact same color can look very different when printed to different kinds of media. For example, a specific shade of red might look lighter or brighter when printed on a high-gloss paper; it might look darker on a matte-finished paper. You can demonstrate this yourself by using a magic marker on different kinds of paper. Try using butcher paper or writing paper or the cover of a magazine. Notice how a glossy paper makes the color look different. Also notice how the color of the paper itself affects what the color looks like.

WRITING POSTSCRIPT TO FILE IN PAGEMAKER 6.0X

One you have finished creating your publication, specify the necessary settings in your PageMaker's Print dialog boxes:

1. In PageMaker 6.0x, choose File > Save As, then save your publication to the same name to reduce the file size of your publication.
2. Choose File > Print.
3. In the Print Document dialog box, select the name of the printer to which your service bureau will be printing your publication (e.g., Linotronic 330 on LPT1:) from the Printer pop-up menu, then select the PPD file for that printer from the PPD pop-up menu.
4. Make sure the orientation specified in the Print Document dialog box matches the orientation specified in the Page Setup dialog box; otherwise, the entire page may not print.
5. Ensure the other settings in your Print Document dialog box are correct, then click Paper. In the Print Paper dialog box, choose paper size that is at least as large as the page you specified in the Document Setup dialog box, then click Options.
   NOTE: When printing separations, you must specify a paper size that is at least .875 inches (23 mm) larger in both the horizontal and vertical dimensions of your page to accommodate printer's marks and page information. For example, when printing a publication with Tabloid pages, choose Tabloid Extra for your paper size in the Print Paper dialog box. You can also specify a Custom paper size, as long as its dimensions are at least .875 inches (23 mm) larger than you publication's page size
6. When printing separations, choose Printer's Marks and Page Information in the Print Document dialog box. Otherwise, skip to step 7. When you select these options, PageMaker prints the filename, the separation name, the current date, the page number, crop marks, registration marks, color-control and density-control bars on each page.
7. Click Options. In the Print Options dialog box, select Write PostScript to file, then select Normal. (Choose EPS only if you are taking your PostScript file through Adobe TrapWise, or if you need to create an EPS graphic file for each of your pages. Choose For Prepress only if you need to create an OPI-compatible separation file to use in Adobe PrePrint Pro or another external post-processor.)
8. Select PostScript and TrueType from the Download Fonts pop-up menu. The fonts you have used in your publication will be included in the PostScript file.
9. Click Browse to specify the directory on your hard drive to which you will be saving your PostScript file, then click OK.
   NOTE: Always save to your hard disk and not to a floppy disk or network drive. Saving to your hard disk is faster and more reliable.
10. Click Color. When printing color separations, choose separations in the Print Color dialog box. Otherwise, skip to step 12.
11. Verify only the inks you want to print are selected. If you want to convert all of the colors in your publication to process, click All to Process. Spot colors may shift and specified trapping and overprinting may be lost when converting spot colors to process.
    NOTE: The Angle and Frequency settings in the Print Color dialog box are determined by the selected PPD file. Do not change these settings, unless you know exactly how your changes will affect your printout. There

are also settings in this dialog box for Mirror and Negative. It is important you communicate with your image-setting service bureau about whether or not to choose these settings. Often, these settings are made on the imagesetter itself, and choosing these options in PageMaker could negate settings on the imagesetter.

12. Click Save to save your print job to your hard disk, copy your PostScript file to a floppy disk, then take your diskette to your service bureau to be printed.

    NOTE: The size of your PostScript file will be substantially larger than the size of the PageMaker 6.0x file from which it was created. This is because everything in your PageMaker publication is included in your PostScript file (e.g., fonts and graphic included in your publication). If your PostScript file is too large to fit on a floppy disk, you have three options for transporting your file:

    - Determine what type of large media formats your service bureau can work with. Some examples of large media formats are a Syquest drive, a Bernoulli drive, a Magneto Optical drive, or a modem. Remember that using a modem adds a variable that could cause a problem with your PostScript file after it is transferred.
    - Compress your PostScript file with a file-compression utility such as PKZIP from PKWARE or ARCE.COM by System Enhancement Associates. Again, talk with your service bureau to find out what they can work with. The service bureau needs to have the same utility to decompress your file.
    - Create more than one PostScript file for your publication by specifying several page ranges in the Print Document dialog box. Write PostScript to file for each of the specified ranges, and take all of the *.PS files to your service bureau on separate floppy disks.

Preparing a PageMaker 5.0x Publication for Output at a Service Bureau

TALK TO YOUR COMMERCIAL PRINTER AND SERVICE BUREAU BEFORE YOU START

When preparing files to be printed at a service bureau, keep in close contact with your commercial printer and prepress service provider throughout the process, from the earliest planning stages to the press check. Your commercial printer and prepress service provider are the experts; do not underestimate their ability to help you avoid costly mistakes.

Next, make sure the prepress service provider you select is willing and able to support you. Here are some questions to ask to make sure you have found someone appropriate:

- Is your prospective service bureau comfortable working with Windows PostScript files?

TIP WINDOWS

A mix-and-match Windows/PageMaker guide

Almost everyone reading this has run PageMaker 5.0 under Windows 3.1 or Windows for Workgroups. But in August, Microsoft shipped Windows 95, and lots of folks started asking whether they can use it with PageMaker 5.0 and PageMaker 6.0. Here's a brief explanation of which versions of PageMaker work with which versions of Windows—3.1 and 95, as well as Windows for Workgroups and Windows NT.

Windows 95. PageMaker 6.0 for Windows, a 32-bit application, is specifically engineered for and compatible with Windows 95, and will take full advantage of its user interface, performance enhancements, and memory-management features.

Although PageMaker 5.0 wasn't specifically engineered to work under Windows 95 (Windows 95 wasn't around when PageMaker 5.0 was being developed), it should run well in that environment—Adobe worked closely with Microsoft to ensure that it would. Nevertheless, that doesn't mean you won't encounter some minor problems if you use PageMaker 5.0 (a 16-bit application) with Windows 95 (a 32-bit operating system). If you experience any problems that occur only in Windows 95 with PageMaker 5.0 and other 16-bit applications, you should report those problems to Microsoft.

Windows 3.1 and Windows for Workgroups. You can also run PageMaker 6.0, as well as PageMaker 5.0, in the Windows 3.1 or Windows for Workgroups environment—PageMaker 6.0 ships with the Win32s dynamic linking libraries (DLLs), which were developed by Microsoft to allow 32-bit applications to work under 16-bit versions of Windows (Windows 3.1 and Windows for Workgroups).

Windows NT. Neither PageMaker 5.0 nor 6.0 was specifically developed for Windows NT, and although both products usually work well in that environment you may run into some problems. Adobe Technical Support will help you with any feature-related problems or questions you might have if you're running PageMaker with Windows NT, but it cannot help you with problems or questions related to the system—for instance, system errors, or installation of or problems with printer drivers, video drivers, and so forth. PageMaker technicians will determine if a call is related to PageMaker features or to the NT environment. If you have any problems that only occur when you run within Windows NT, you should report those problems directly to Microsoft.

If they have IBM-compatible computers and know how to work in Windows, that is certainly a good sign. If they do not, that may still be fine as long as they are familiar with the environment in which you are working.

- Will they provide you with any guidelines on how to provide them with correctly formatted PostScript files? Can they clearly articulate what they need from you to print your files successfully?

  Even if you memorize the information in this document, you should work with a service bureau who also understands this process and is willing to help you.
- Will your prospective service bureau arrange for a test print if this is your first time working with them or if you are trying anything new for this project?

  If possible, try to arrange a test job of two or three pages that will contain the fonts, kinds of graphics, and print settings you intend to use in your final job. If you discover you have made a critical error on the final printout of a long publication, you could waste a lot of money and time. Film output from an imagesetter can cost up to $25 or more per page. Paper output from an imagesetter is less expensive; you could do your test print to paper.

MAKE SURE YOU HAVE THE RIGHT TOOLS BEFORE DESIGNING

Once you have selected a commercial printer and a service bureau, and have discussed your plans with them, you will almost be ready to start designing your publication. But before you begin, make sure you have the right tools in Windows.

Windows Printer Description (WPD) File

This file will list the name of the printer that you will be printing to, and make information about that printer available to your Windows applications.

PostScript Printer Driver

PageMaker 5.0x for Windows requires the Microsoft Windows PostScript printer driver 3.56 or later for full printing functionality. The printer driver is included on the PageMaker installation disks. For instructions on installing it, refer to pages 6 to 7 of the PageMaker 5.0 Getting Started manual.

PPD File

PostScript Printer Description files provide applications information about your printer, such as its available fonts, paper sizes, and memory. Make sure you install the PPD file for the imagesetter your PostScript files will be imaged on. PPD files are located in the Aldus\Usenglsh\Ppd4 subdirectory.

Fonts

If you want to include downloadable fonts with the print file, make sure you have all the necessary font files for each style (e.g., bold, italic, roman).

Obtain the Correct WPD File for Your Service Bureau's Printer

Find out from your service bureau what imagesetter or printer they will be printing to. Obtain the WPD file for that printer from your service bureau, or download it from Microsoft's bulletin board (206-637-9009 or 206-936-6735) or from CompuServe in the "MSL" forum.

OBTAIN THE MOST CURRENT VERSION OF THE WINDOWS POSTSCRIPT PRINTER DRIVER

You may be able to get the most current version of the Microsoft PostScript printer driver (Pscript.drv) directly from your service bureau. You can also download the PostScript driver from Microsoft's bulletin board (206-637-9009 or 206-936-6735) or from CompuServe in the "MSL" forum. PageMaker 5.0x includes the Microsoft PostScript driver 3.56 on its installation disks.

INSTALL THE WPD FILE AND POSTSCRIPT DRIVER

To install the WPD file and PostScript printer driver for your printer:

1. Copy the two necessary files (*.wpd and Pscript.drv) to a directory on your hard disk or to a floppy diskette.
2. Exit all Windows applications, then exit and restart Windows. If you have anything that loads in your Startup group of Windows, you may need to temporarily move those items to another group, then exit and restart Windows.
3. Open the Printers Control Panel. 4. If the PostScript driver and WPD files are located on a floppy diskette, put that diskette in your floppy disk drive now.
4. Click Add, then click Install to install an updated or unlisted printer.
5. Windows displays an Install Driver dialog box with an A:\ prompt (it's asking you where the new driver is located). If the new driver is on a floppy diskette in drive A, click OK. If it's somewhere else, type in the full drive and path name, or click Browse and select the correct location from the directory tree listed there.
6. Click OK in the Install Driver dialog box. Windows displays a list of printers.
7. Select the printer your service bureau recommended and click OK. Windows installs the new driver and WPD file.
8. If you've installed these files from a directory on your hard disk, rename or delete the file in that directory called Pscript.drv. Whenever you install a printer using the Windows Control Panel, the WPD file and the Pscript.drv file are added to the Windows\System directory. It is very important that you never have more than one copy of the Pscript.drv file on your computer.

Check the Version of Your PostScript Driver

To check the version of the PostScript printer driver installed on your computer:

1. Open the Printers Control Panel, then select the printer your service bureau will be using.
2. Click Setup, then click About. The About dialog box should read "Windows PostScript Printer Driver" and "Version 3.56" or later.

   NOTE: PageMaker 5.0x for Windows requires the Microsoft Windows PostScript printer driver 3.56 or later.
3. Click OK to close the remaining dialog boxes.

Verify That You are Connected to the Right Port

TIP WINDOWS

Designating a default folder

If you've ever wanted to get PageMaker to look in a certain folder for your publications, there's a great way to do that using a Windows feature.

In Windows 3.1, go to the Program Manager and select your PageMaker icon by clicking on it just once. Select "Properties" from the File menu, and in the "Program Item Properties" dialog box, enter the full path to the directory you want to use for your PageMaker documents in the "Working Directory" field.

In Windows 95, there are a few more steps, but it's essentially the same process.

1. Go to the Start menu and select "Taskbar..." from the Settings submenu.
2. In the "Taskbar Properties" dialog box, choose the "Start Menu Programs" tab and click the "Advanced" button. At this point, an Explorer dialog box should appear.
3. In the left side of the window, double-click on the "Programs" folder, and then double-click on the "Adobe" folder (or navigate to wherever you keep your PageMaker shortcut on the taskbar).
4. Right-mouse click on the "Adobe PageMaker" shortcut icon listed on the right side of the window, and choose "Properties" from the pop-up menu that appears.
5. In the "Adobe PageMaker Properties" dialog box, select the "Shortcut" tab, and in the "Start in" box, enter the full path to the folder you want to use for your documents.
6. Click "OK."

The list of installed printers displays your printer's name and the port that it is connect to by default (e.g., Linotronic 330 on LPT1). You can be connected to any port when writing PostScript files in PageMaker 5.0x, however.

With earlier versions of PageMaker, users would often connect printers that they did not physically have to a port called "FILE." This is no longer necessary with PageMaker 5.0x. In fact, it would be redundant, and it could potentially create two PostScript files instead of one. This would not cause any harm, but it may use up more of your hard disk space.

To change your port designation, click on the name of your service bureau's printer. Then click on "Connect..." and choose an appropriate port. Click "OK," and close out of Printers.

NOTE: If you will be using ATM fonts and you already have a PostScript printer installed, it is a good idea to connect your service bureau's printer to the same port that your existing printer is already connected to. This will ensure that the fonts that are available to your existing printer are also available when composing for your service bureau's printer. For more information about working with fonts see the "Setting up Fonts in Windows" section below.

INSTALLING A PPD FILE

Again, it is important that you contact your service bureau to find out what PPD file you should use for their printer. PageMaker 5.0x includes many PPD files, and one of those might be exactly the one to use. For a list of all of the PPD files that shipped with PageMaker 5.0x, refer to the Ppdlist.wri file, located in the Aldus\Usenglsh\Utility directory.

To install a PPD file for use with PageMaker, simply copy the file to your hard disk in the Aldus\Usenglsh\Ppd4 directory.

To install a PPD file included on the PageMaker installation disks, use the PageMaker 5 Installer to copy and decompress it to the Ppd4 directory:

1. Double-click on PM5Setup (Adobe PageMaker 5.0) or Aldus Setup (Aldus PageMaker 5.0x).
2. Select the PageMaker control file (i.e., Pm5_144.ctl, Pm5_12m.ctl) from the File Name scroll box, then click OK.
3. In the Select Setup Options dialog box, select Printers and click OK.
4. Select the PPD file you want to install in the Select Printer Devices dialog box.
5. Type the drive letter of the drive from which you'll be installing and click OK.
6. Insert the PageMaker disks as prompted, then click OK.
7. Click OK in the Setup Complete dialog box and the Must Install Drivers dialog box.
8. Click Cancel in the Printers Control Panel (the Printers Control Panel launches at the end of the installation process).
9. Click OK in the Setup Complete dialog box, then exit the PageMaker 5 Installer.

SETTING UP FONTS IN WINDOWS

There is a staggering variety of fonts available for use under Windows. But just because something looks nice on your monitor or prints fairly well on your desktop printer does not necessarily mean it's ideal for output on an imagesetter.

Before you begin designing your publication, make sure you ask your service bureau what type of fonts will print best on their equipment. Because PostScript is the standard language for imagesetters, PostScript fonts may be the easiest to print and transport. If you plan to use any other kind of font, be sure to discuss this with your service bureau ahead of time. The rest of this discussion assumes you're using PostScript fonts with a type management utility, such as Adobe Type Manager (ATM).

Here are some basic tips on how to make sure your fonts will print correctly:

- The font list you see in PageMaker (or any other Windows application) is a function of the printer to which you are composing. This is one of the reasons you should make sure your final output device is always selected in the Compose to Printer pop-up menu in PageMaker's Page Setup dialog box.
- If you are using PostScript soft fonts in your publication, make sure you have installed them for your final output device.

  Even if those fonts print correctly on your in-house printer, they may not be installed yet for your final output device. This could happen for two reasons. First, if your in-house printer is a non-PostScript printer, those PostScript soft fonts are probably being sent to your printer directly from a type manager such as ATM (so they are not necessarily installed for your PostScript printer). Second, even if your in-house printer is a PostScript device, it may not be connected to the same port as your final output device (so a successful print job to "LPT1:," for instance, will not necessarily mean all fonts will download correctly to the port you are connected to). If you are not sure whether all your fonts are installed correctly for the port you are using, simply use your type manager to reinstall the fonts, and then restart Windows.

DESIGN YOUR PUBLICATION

Once you have finished setting up Windows with all the tools you need, you're ready to start designing your publication in PageMaker. But before you put anything on the page, choose File > Page Setup and select your final output device from the Compose to Printer pop-up menu. Also, choose the appropriate Target Printer resolution.

The Compose to Printer and Target Printer Resolution options determine how PageMaker composes your publication: they affect what fonts are available, text spacing, graphic resolution, and other aspects of layout. If you need to print to a different printer to proof your publication, do not change the Compose to Printer option; simply select the draft printer and its corresponding PPD file in the Print dialog box.

If you're planning to print color separations, make sure that the only color graphics you use are Adobe-conforming EPS graphics (saved with ASCII encoding, not binary encoding), DCS files, or CMYK TIFF files. Other color graphic formats will not separate reliably.

Always place any graphics from your local hard disk, never from a floppy diskette or network drive. Whenever you import a graphic, PageMaker creates a link to it. PageMaker must be able to access the linked file when you print the publication.

PRINT THE PUBLICATION TO DISK AS A POSTSCRIPT FILE

To print a PageMaker 5.0x publication to disk as a PostScript file:

1. Choose File > Print.
2. Select the output device your service bureau will be using (e.g., Linotronic 330 on LPT1:) from the Print To pop-up menu, then select the corresponding PPD file from the Type pop-up menu.
3. Specify other settings in the Print Document dialog box as desired, then click Paper.
4. Specify a paper size that is at least as large as the page you specified in the Page Setup dialog box. If you will be printing separations, add at least .875 inch (23 mm) to the horizontal and vertical dimensions to accommodate the printer's marks and page information. Many imagesetter PPD files provide "Extra" paper sizes (e.g., Tabloid Extra) that accommodate printer's marks; you can also define a custom paper size. When in doubt, ask your service bureau what to specify.
5. Click Options. If you're printing separations, select Printer's Marks and Page Information.
6. Select Write PostScript to file and Normal.
7. Select Include Downloadable Fonts so the fonts you have used in your publication will be included as part of your PostScript file.
8. Click Browse to specify the directory in which you will be saving your PostScript file. Always save to a directory on your hard disk, not directly to a floppy disk. Once you have selected the directory, click OK.
9. Click Color. If you will be printing separations, select Separations, then select the appropriate inks in the ink list.
10. If your service bureau requires it, select Mirror and Negative.
11. Click Save.

CHECKLIST FOR WRITING POSTSCRIPT TO FILE

- Install the correct WPD and PostScript printer driver version 3.56 or later.
- Install the correct PPD file.
- Ensure your fonts are installed correctly in Windows.
- If you will be printing color separations, make sure that you are using graphics that will separate reliably (Adobe-conforming EPS graphics, DCS files or CMYK tiffs).
- Place all graphics from your hard disk, and never from floppy diskettes.
- Decide how you will be using color in your publication.
- Compose to the correct printer and specify the correct target printer resolution in PageMaker's Page setup dialog.
- Do a save as of your PageMaker publication before printing.
- Check all of your settings in PageMaker's print dialog box. See the section entitled "How to Write PostScript to File in PageMaker 5.0x" for more information.
- Copy your PS file to a floppy diskette to bring to your service bureau for printing.

Removing and Reinstalling Win32s Components for PageMaker 6.0

Adobe PageMaker 6.0 requires Win32s to run in Windows 3.1. Before removing Win32s components from your computer, verify that you have no other 32-bit applications that require these components.

PageMaker 6.0 requires that the Win32s version 1.3a components, which are included with PageMaker, be installed in the Windows\System subdirectory, and that Win32s components installed in any directory be version 1.3a (i.e., 1.30.167.0) or later. If another application requires installed Win32s components in the Windows directory, rename the older files and copy the Win32s components included with PageMaker into the Windows directory.

When removing Win32s files, search for duplicate or older versions of Win32s files in directories other than the Windows\System subdirectory on your hard disk.

To remove Win32s components:

1. Exit PageMaker 6.0.
2. Make a backup copy of your System.ini file, located in the Windows directory.
3. Open the System.ini file in a text editor that can save in text-only format (e.g., Notepad), then delete the following line from the [386Enh] section:
   ```
   device=C:\WINDOWS\SYSTEM\WIN32S\W32S.386
   ```
4. Locate the following line in the [BOOT] section in the System.ini file:
   ```
   drivers=mmsystem.dll winmm16.dll
   ```
5. Remove "winmm16.dll" from the line. For example:
   ```
   drivers=mmsystem.dll
   ```
6. Save the System.ini file in text-only format.
7. From File Manager, delete the WIN32S directory located in the Windows\System subdirectory, then exit Windows.
8. From DOS, delete the following files from the Windows\System subdirectory:
   ```
   Win32s16.dll
   Win32s.ini
   W32sys.dll
   Winmm16.dll
   ```
9. Restart Windows.

To reinstall Win32s components for PageMaker 6.0:

1. Restart Windows, then ensure that Program Manager is the only application running.
2. Turn off virus detection software.
3. Insert the Adobe PageMaker 6.0 Deluxe CD-ROM into your CD-ROM drive, or the last (i.e., highest-numbered) PageMaker 6.0 installation disk into your disk drive.
4. In Program Manager, choose File > Run.
5. When installing from the CD-ROM, type "E:\Pm6\Win32s\Setup.exe" where E: is the CD-ROM drive, then click OK. When installing from the installation disks, type "A:\Setup.exe" where A: is the disk drive, then click OK.
6. Follow the on-screen installation instructions, inserting disks when prompted.
7. When installation is complete, restart Windows to load the Win32s components into memory.

The Win32s installer, included with PageMaker 6.0, adds the following subdirectory and files in the Windows\System subdirectory:

Name	File size in bytes	Created date
Win32s		
Win32s.ini	varies	varies
Ole2prox.dll	51,712	09-06-95
Ole2conv.dll	57,328	08-14-95
Compobj.dll	109,056	09-06-95
Ole2disp.dll	165,008	07-25-95
Storage.dll	157,696	03-02-95
Ole2nls.dll	152,976	07-25-95
Typelib.dll	177,824	07-25-95
Ole2.dll 304,640	09-06-95	
Ole2.reg 28,113	04-16-95	
StdoleE.tlb	5,472	07-25-95
Winhlp32.cnt	930	09-05-95
W32sys.dll	12,112	10-02-95
Winmm16.dll	29,184	10-01-95
Windows.hlp	21,473	09-05-95
Winhlp32.hlp	31,684	09-05-95
Olecli.dll 82,944	09-05-95	
Win32s16.dll	167,424	10-19-95
Winhlp32.exe	329,744	09-11-95

MAC OS

Q I've noticed that you can use either SuperATM, PANOSE, or both to work with missing fonts. Is there a way to determine which is best for me?

A Yes. Anytime you're missing a font, the best thing to do is install the font—that's the only way to ensure that your fonts look the same, retain the same line endings and page breaks, and print the way you intended them to. Sometimes, however, reinstalling a missing font isn't possible or practical. In these cases, use SuperATM to generate a substitute if your font is just missing temporarily. If you need to find a permanent substitution for a missing font, use PANOSE. Here's why.

SuperATM is a special version of Adobe Type Manager that can automatically create a simulated version of a missing font. When it detects a font is missing, it generates a substitute by taking a multiple-master typeface and shaping it according to the missing font's metrics (the exact character-spacing values), which must be available in the "ATM Font Database" file in your System Folder.

Using SuperATM-generated substitute fonts works extremely well when you need to use a different Macintosh temporarily to work on your publication or when you're temporarily missing a font or fonts. That's because SuperATM's substitute fonts reproduce the exact character-spacing values of your missing fonts, allowing you to retain line endings and page breaks. If you frequently move your publication around the office or proof-print from more than one Macintosh, then SuperATM is probably the best font-matching system for you. Just remember that SuperATM-generated fonts are supposed to be temporary substitutes—they won't look exactly like your original fonts, so you shouldn't use them for final output.

If you would like PageMaker to use SuperATM, you must make sure it has been installed successfully and that the "Substitute for missing fonts" option is selected in its Control Panel.

Unlike SuperATM, PANOSE does not generate substitutes for your missing fonts. Instead, it finds or lets you specify the next-best match among your installed fonts. Because PANOSE substitutions are other fonts that may not have the same (or even similar) character-spacing values as your missing fonts, PANOSE substitutions will often cause line endings and page breaks to change.

PANOSE is most useful when you are missing a font that you will not be able to install before you produce final output. It's also valuable when you want to be notified whenever you have a missing font—just make sure the "Show mapping results" option in the "Font matching" dialog box is selected so the "PANOSE font matching results" dialog box appears whenever PageMaker detects a missing font.

For more information on using SuperATM and PANOSE in PageMaker 5.0, see FaxYI document number 215-405, "TechNote: Using font mapping in Aldus PageMaker." FaxYI is at (206) 628-5737.

Optimizing PageMaker 6.0's Performance

Adobe PageMaker 6.0's performance is affected by the installation options you choose, your Macintosh system configuration, and the way you use PageMaker's features. The following guidelines can help you use PageMaker 6.0 efficiently.

PAGEMAKER INSTALLATION OPTIONS

To optimize PageMaker's speed when importing text and graphics, install only those import and export filters you need. PageMaker initializes filters the first time you use the Place Document dialog box; each installed filter increases the time it takes PageMaker to initialize filters.

To optimize PageMaker's printing speed, install only the PostScript Printer Description (PPD) files you need. The first time you choose File > Print, PageMaker creates a printer list. After PageMaker creates the printer list, PageMaker reads the printer list when opening the Print Document dialog box. Each installed PPD file increases the time PageMaker takes to create and read the printer list.

To optimize PageMaker's speed when color managing objects, install only the Kodak Precision Transform (PT) files you need. The first time you use the Kodak Color Management System (CMS) in PageMaker 6.0 (e.g., turn on CMS, place a PhotoCD image), PageMaker reads all installed PTs into memory. The more PTs installed, the longer it takes PageMaker to read the PTs into memory.

MACINTOSH SYSTEM CONFIGURATION

PageMaker 6.0 requires at least 6000K (Macintosh) or 8000K (Power Macintosh) of application RAM. Increasing the amount of memory allocated to PageMaker improves PageMaker's performance. When working with PhotoCD images or using CMS, increase the minimum application memory to 8000K (Macintosh) or 10,000K (Power Macintosh).

PageMaker 6.0 stores temporary files on your startup disk (i.e., volume containing your System Folder) while you work in PageMaker. The amount of free disk space on your startup disk should be at least three times the file size of open publications.

Managing fonts efficiently, by installing only the fonts you need, improves system performance and the performance of application features that require reading each installed font file. Each installed font increases the amount of memory used by the system, which decreases the amount of RAM available to open applications, and increases the amount of time it takes applications to display menus listing font names. Using a font management utility can help you manage many fonts.

When running PageMaker for the Power Macintosh, turn Modern Memory Manager on for increased screen redraw performance. When Modern Memory Manager is turned off, the Memory Manager runs in emulation mode, instead of in native PowerPC mode, resulting in slower performance. Unless you are running an application or extension that is incompatible with Modern Memory Manager, Apple recommends leaving Modern Memory Manager on.

USING PAGEMAKER FEATURES EFFECTIVELY

For faster screen redraw when using graphics, select Gray Out under Graphics Display in the Preferences dialog box.

For faster screen redraw at views smaller than actual size, select a larger pixel size for Greek Text Below in the More Preferences dialog box. Text displays as gray bars when the pixel size of the text at the chosen magnification view is smaller than the number entered for the Greek Text Below preference.

Use the story editor to edit text. The story editor allows you to make text changes without waiting for PageMaker to redraw the screen. To open the story editor, choose Edit > Edit Story. To open an existing story in the story editor, select the text block with the pointer tool, or click an insertion point in the text block, then choose Edit > Edit Story.

Store large graphics externally (i.e., outside your publication) to reduce the publication's file size. The smaller the publication's file size, the faster PageMaker opens, recomposes, and saves the publication.

Use PageMaker's Book feature to manage long publications split into two or more shorter publications. PageMaker opens, recomposes, and saves smaller publications faster.

Text redraw is slower after applying Set Width, small caps, or tracking to text. Apply these features during the final stages of formatting your publication.

COLOR MANAGEMENT'S EFFECT ON PERFORMANCE

The first time you use the Color Management System (CMS) in a PageMaker session, CMS takes several seconds to initialize. CMS initializes the first time you open the CMS Setup dialog box, open a publication that includes a color managed object, or place a PhotoCD image.

To print separations of color images faster, pre-separate bitmap images that are not defined using the CMYK color model (e.g., RGB TIFF). To pre-separate bitmap images, use the Kodak CMS software in PageMaker 6.0, or resave the images in an image editing application (e.g., Adobe Photoshop) in a format that defines color using the CMYK color model (e.g., DCS, CMYK TIFF). PageMaker does not have to perform color conversion calculations when printing images that define colors using CMYK, which decreases the time it takes PageMaker to print color images.

When PageMaker doesn't have enough available memory, printing or displaying color managed images may be slower. Because Precision Transforms (PTs) are cached to memory, insufficient memory forces PageMaker to remove one PT from memory to load another.

Selecting Embed Profiles in Document in the CMS Setup dialog box decreases PageMaker's performance. PageMaker references embedded PTs when copying, pasting, saving, reverting, performing mini-saves, turning pages, and opening publications.

PERFORMANCE DIFFERENCES BETWEEN PAGEMAKER 5.0X AND PAGEMAKER 6.0

PageMaker 6.0 launches slower than PageMaker 5.0x when more than 70 fonts are installed on the system.

Opening two multiple-page publications simultaneously is slower in PageMaker 6.0 than in PageMaker 5.0x.

Running PageMaker 6.0x for the Macintosh with Minimal OLE Files

Adobe PageMaker 6.0x supports the object linking and embedding (OLE) 2.0 protocol, enabling you to link or embed documents from other applications that support OLE. If you do not use OLE functions in PageMaker (e.g., Insert Object, Paste Link) and you want to increase the amount of available random-access memory (RAM) on your Macintosh, you can run PageMaker with a minimal set of OLE files. However, disabling one or more OLE files can cause problems in other applications that require them (e.g., Microsoft Word, Microsoft Excel). Typical problems are the inability to choose Insert Object or Paste Link, or OLE error messages appearing when launching the application.

PAGEMAKER 6.0X FOR THE POWER MACINTOSH

PageMaker 6.0x for the Power Macintosh installs the following Microsoft OLE files in the Extensions folder in the System Folder:

- Microsoft OLE Automation
- Microsoft OLE Extension
- Microsoft OLE Library

PageMaker 6.0 requires the Microsoft OLE Library file to launch, and uses the other two files to activate OLE functions in PageMaker. The Microsoft OLE Library file must be located in the Extensions folder or in the folder that contains the PageMaker application. You can remove Microsoft OLE Automation and Microsoft OLE Extension files if you do not want to use OLE functions in PageMaker 6.0 for the Power Macintosh.

PageMaker 6.01 does not require any OLE files to launch. You can remove all three files if you do not want to use OLE functions in PageMaker 6.01 for the Power Macintosh.

PAGEMAKER 6.0X FOR THE MACINTOSH (68000-SERIES)

PageMaker 6.0x for the Macintosh (68000-series) installs the following OLE file in the Extensions folder in the System Folder:

- Microsoft OLE Extension

It uses the Microsoft OLE Extension file to launch and to activate OLE functions in PageMaker. The Microsoft OLE Extension file must be located in the Extensions folder or in the folder that contains the PageMaker application. It does not use or install the Microsoft OLE Automation or Microsoft OLE Library files.

OPI Support in PageMaker 5.0x and 6.0x

Open Prepress Interface (OPI) is an extension of the PostScript page-description language that lets you design pages with low-resolution images, then replace them with high-resolution images when creating separations. By using low-resolution (i.e., placeholder) images for page layout (e.g., in Adobe PageMaker or QuarkXPress), you can reduce the size of your page layout file and reduce processing time when you work in the file.

The low-resolution version of an image contains OPI comments, which specify the location, placement, and size of the original high-resolution images located on an OPI server. OPI comments also describe the location of bitmap images embedded in an EPS graphic.

PageMaker 5.0x is an OPI Producer. As an OPI producer, PageMaker 5.0x writes OPI comments for placeholder images when printing separations to an OPI server, or when printing a separation (.sep) file. Post-processing applications that reads OPI comments (e.g., PrePrint Pro) open .sep files. PageMaker 5.0x does not include OPI comments when printing a publication to disk as an EPS file or as a composite PostScript (.ps) file.

Like PageMaker 5.0x, Adobe PageMaker 6.0x is an OPI Producer. PageMaker 6.0x writes OPI comments for placeholder images when printing separations to an OPI server, or when printing a .sep or EPS file.

PageMaker 6.0x is also an OPI Consumer. As an OPI consumer, PageMaker 6.0x reads OPI comments for images embedded in EPS graphics when you import the EPS graphics with the OPI Image Links option selected in the EPS Import Filter dialog box (you can access this dialog box by pressing Shift while double-clicking on an EPS graphic in the Place Document dialog box). When you separate the EPS graphics, PageMaker 6.0x uses the OPI comments to locate and print the original high-resolution images, or it writes OPI comments for these images when printing a .sep or EPS file.

PageMaker 5.0x is not an OPI Consumer, which prevents it from reading OPI comments for embedded images in EPS graphics when importing them. As a result, PageMaker 5.0x prints the screen preview of an image embedded in an EPS graphic, rather than the original image. When the embedded image is an RGB image, which PageMaker cannot separate, the image prints as a composite on the black separation.

Calibrating Your Monitor for Use with Adobe PageMaker 6.0x

Accurate monitor calibration ensures consistent display when you use the Kodak Precision Color Management System (CMS) with Adobe PageMaker 6.0x. To calibrate your monitor, you can use commercial calibration software or the Gamma control panel and test images included with PageMaker. If you use commercial calibration software, refer to its documentation for instructions. If you are using the Gamma control panel and test images included with PageMaker, follow the instructions below to adjust your monitor's dials and gamma settings.

PREPARING TO CALIBRATE

Turn your monitor on at least half an hour before you calibrate it. Adjust your environment to neutralize any factors that affect the way you perceive the color of your display, including natural and artificial lighting, the intensity and color of lamps near the monitor, color of the walls, ceiling, desk and floor, desktop patterns, color of windows and title bars displayed, and the color of your clothing, especially if it reflects in the monitor.

ADJUSTING THE MONITOR KNOBS

To adjust the monitor knobs:

1. Increase brightness (e.g., a knob with a symbol of the sun) until the dark area around the edge of the display turns gray.
2. Decrease the brightness slowly until the gray area turns black. Move the knob back and forth until you're certain you've found the point at which it turns from gray to black. If the edge of your display never turns gray, leave the knob at maximum brightness.
3. Adjust the contrast (e.g., a knob with a symbol of a half-moon) until you are comfortable with the white areas on the display (i.e., they are neither too bright nor too dim).

NOTE: Do not adjust the monitor knobs after you have set them. You can tape the knobs in place to avoid accidentally changing them.

ADJUSTING THE MONITOR GAMMA

Adjust the gamma settings whenever you change the position of the monitor knobs (i.e., brightness and contrast), move the monitor to a location with different light sources, use a different monitor, or install a different video card.

You can use the Knoll Gamma control panel, included with PageMaker, to adjust the monitor gamma. Before using the Gamma control panel, make sure the Monitors control panel is set to 256 colors. Most Macintosh monitors use a default gamma value of 1.8, which works well for on-screen display and printed output. If you plan to produce video output with your computer, calibrate to a target gamma of 2.2, which is the gamma value of most television sets.

For instructions on using the Gamma control panel, refer to pages 16-17 of the PageMaker 6.0 for Macintosh Getting Started guide.

NOTE: The "Checking Your Settings" section on page 17 of the Getting Started guide is incorrect. The instructions below are accurate for a gamma setting of 1.8.

If you calibrated with a gamma setting of 1.8, you can use the Gamma 1.8.tif image, which contains squares of gray values represented with horizontal stripes and solid shading, to verify the calibration:

1. In PageMaker 6.0x, choose File > New, then click OK in the Document Setup dialog box.
2. Choose File > Place.
3. Select the Gamma1.8.tif image from the Gamma Control folder in the Utilities folder in the Adobe PageMaker 6.0 folder, then click Open.
4. Place the Gamma 1.8.tif image into the publication.
5. Choose File > Preferences and select High Resolution for Graphics Display, then click OK.
6. Resize the publication window so you can see the image and the Gamma control panel simultaneously.
7. In the Gamma control panel, adjust the Gamma Adjustment slider back and forth until the smaller squares in the test image blend and display the same as the larger squares. You may need to stand a few feet from the monitor to make this adjustment

Unexpected Results

MAC OS / WINDOWS

Q Sometimes when I change the font in a publication, it reverts to a different font when I begin a new text

block. How do you make sure the font is permanently changed for the publication?

A If you want all new text blocks in your publication to use a particular font, what you're after is a new default font: make sure you have no text selected (a good way is to click on a tool in the toolbox) and select the font you want.

In fact, to change any default—text or other settings—make sure you have nothing selected and then change your settings. The new default will affect any new stories you create, new objects you draw, or new graphics you import.

The only exception to this rule is with color. You can have three default color settings—a default color for text, a default color for lines, and a default color for fills (which also functions as the default color for 1-bit and grayscale bitmap graphics). To set a default text color, click on the text tool and select a color from the Colors palette.

To set a default color for both lines and fills, make sure no objects are selected, click on any tool other than the text tool, make sure "Both" is selected in the Colors palette drop-down menu, and select a color from the palette. If you want to have different default colors for fills and lines, the easiest way to set them is to make sure no objects are selected, choose "Fill and line…" from the Element menu, and select your new default colors in the "Fill and line" dialog box.

You can also set application-wide defaults, which will affect all new publications you create thereafter. To do so, close all your publications and then change any settings that aren't grayed out. PageMaker stores these application-wide defaults in a configuration file (PM5.CNF, located in the ALDUS\USENGLSH directory in Windows, or the "PM5.0 Defaults" file located in the Preferences folder within the System Folder on the Macintosh). If you ever want to restore PageMaker's original application-wide defaults, quit PageMaker and delete or rename its configuration file—it will automatically generate a new one the next time you relaunch PageMaker and create or open a publication.

Q Sometimes I check my "Links" dialog box and see unusual characters in front of my linked document or letters for page numbers. What does this stuff mean?

A The symbols that appear to the left of your linked objects convey special information about the status of your links—they appear any time PageMaker detects that one of your linked objects may not be up to date. The characters that appear in the "Page" column to the right of your linked objects describe the objects' page numbers or other positions.

If you're ever unsure what one of the link-status symbols means, just click on the linked object displayed with the symbol and PageMaker will list an explanation of that object's link status in the "Links" dialog box under "Status."

Link-status symbols

NA Indicates the object is not linked to an external document because the object was pasted without links or is an OLE-embedded object.

? Indicates that PageMaker can no longer find the linked object's external file—usually because that file was renamed, deleted, or moved. Unless your external file has been deleted, you can re-establish the link by clicking on the "Info…" button, locating the external file, and clicking "Link."

+ (PC) or (Mac)

Indicates that the object is linked to an external file that has been modified since the link was first established or last updated. Also indicates that you have set that object to update automatically. Therefore, PageMaker will update the object the next time you print or reopen your publication. If you want to update your object sooner, select it and click the "Update" or "Update all" button in the "Links" dialog box. NOTE: In Windows, the "+" also indicates that the object is stored inside the publication.

¥ (PC only)

This is identical to the "+" symbol, except it indicates the object is not stored inside the publication.

- (PC) or (M ac)

Similar to the or "+" symbol—indicates that the object is linked to an external file that has been modified since the object was imported or last updated. However, unlike the or "+" symbols, the " " or "-" symbols indicate that you have not set the object to update automatically. To update the object, select it and click on "Update" or "Update all."

! (PC) or (M ac)

Indicates that the object is linked to an external file and that both the internal and external copies of the object have been modified. If you click on "Update," PageMaker will replace the internal copy of the object with the external copy.

> Indicates the link was established on another platform (Macintosh or Windows), and the object's format isn't completely supported on your current platform (for example, if you chose not to convert metafiles to PICTs, or vice versa, when you opened the publication).

¿ (Unlike the other link-status symbols, this symbol appears in the far right column of the "Links" dialog box.) Indicates the object will not print in high resolution or may not print as expected—for example, because a linked file is missing, a required filter is not available, or the linked file has been modified since it was placed or last updated.

Page/location symbols

UN Object is an inline graphic or text in a story that has not been placed in layout view yet (is part of an unflowed, uncomposed story in the Story Editor).

LM Object is located on the left master page.

RM Object is on the right master page.

PB Object is located on the pasteboard.

OV Object is an inline graphic located in overset text—text that is not displayed in layout view because it has not been completely flowed.

Q I've noticed that my bitmap graphics tend to appear very choppy in PageMaker, even with a high-resolution video card installed. Is there anything I can do to make them appear crisper?

A Yes. In fact, PageMaker has several features that let you control how smooth your bitmap graphics look on screen—you should just be aware that the smoother your bitmap graphics appear, the longer they'll take to redraw.

Before we list all your options, here's a brief overview of how PageMaker handles bitmap graphic display. PageMaker gives you three display choices for your bitmap graphics. These options, which are located in the "Preferences" dialog box, are "Gray out," "Normal" (the default), and "High resolution."

If you choose "Gray out," your screen will redraw at the greatest speed possible, but all your graphics (including vector-based ones) will display as gray boxes. In addition, some grayed-out graphics may not print to non-PostScript devices. If you select "High resolution," PageMaker displays your graphics at the highest resolution possible, using all the data in the graphic files. The trade-off you make is performance—when you use the "High resolution" option, your screen redraw will be slower.

The "Normal" option offers a middle ground between the other two options. When the "Normal" option is selected, PageMaker displays your bitmap graphics using their low-resolution screen images. With the "Normal" setting, your bitmap graphics will redraw pretty quickly but won't look very crisp. Just how chunky they look will depend on the resolution of the screen image PageMaker created when you imported the graphic, and that depends on the "Maximum size of internal graphic" setting in the "Other preferences" dialog box. By default, this option is set at 64K, and you can change it to anything between 8K and 1024K. The smaller you make this setting, the chunkier your screen images will look in "Normal" graphics mode, and the faster they'll redraw. If you alter this setting, the change will only affect graphics you import or update thereafter.

If you have one or a few bitmap graphics that are displaying very poorly in "High resolution" or "Normal" mode (or printing that way), the first thing you should do is check to make sure their links haven't been broken, especially if those graphics aren't stored within your publication. Select "Links..." from the File menu, and in the "Links" dialog box find the name of your graphic. If the link is not up to date or PageMaker cannot locate the graphic's external file, it will display a special symbol next to that item in the list (see the previous question for an explanation of those symbols) and you'll need to reestablish or update that link.

If your links are up to date and your bitmap graphics still look chunky on screen (but print fine), you have several options:

- If you want all your graphics to display at high resolution, use the "High resolution" graphic-display option.
- If the "Normal" setting works for you most of the time, but you want your graphics to display in high resolution occasionally, you can force them to do so using a special keyboard shortcut—just hold down the Control + Shift keys (Windows) or the Control key (Macintosh) while redrawing your page. You can redraw your page by selecting an option from the View submenu of the Layout menu, by double-clicking on your publication window's title bar (Windows), or by clicking on the resize box in the upper-right corner of your publication window (Macintosh).
- If you like using the "Normal" setting but want your graphics to display at slightly higher resolution, you can increase the "Maximum size of internal graphic" setting and reimport your graphics.

Q Occasionally when I place a TIFF in PageMaker, its right side seems to get cut off a little. Why?

A When PageMaker imports a 1-bit (black-and-white) TIFF that contains extra white area around the image, it will automatically crop the graphic for you. Unfortunately, PageMaker occasionally miscalculates where it should crop the graphic, and you end up with a TIFF image slightly clipped—usually along its right side.

Fortunately, it's easy to correct this problem. Just select PageMaker's cropping tool and pull the handles of the TIFF outward to uncrop it. You can also prevent this from occurring by saving your 1-bit image without any extra peripheral white space. If you want to avoid this problem altogether, you can save your 1-bit images in another format (EPS, for instance) that PageMaker will not crop during import.

Q Sometimes I can't get a word to hyphenate, even with a discretionary hyphen—I end up having to use a regular hyphen instead. Why does this happen?

A This generally happens because PageMaker, using a complex system of hyphenation and justification rules, determined that a word break was not necessary at the end of your line. Discretionary hyphens only become active (turn into hyphens and make words break) under special circumstances—in other words, a discretionary hyphen isn't a "forced" hyphen that can make a word break regardless of the word's position. For instance, a discretionary hyphen will never make a word break if that word isn't the last word on the line.

If you're having trouble figuring out why PageMaker thinks it shouldn't break a word that contains a discretionary hyphen, check the following:

Make sure the Hyphenation feature is turned on. If the hyphenation feature is off, discretionary hyphens won't work. Click your text tool somewhere in the paragraph with which you're having the problem, then select "Hyphenation..." from the Type menu. In the "Hyphenation" dialog box, make sure the "On" option is selected.

Check your hyphenation zone—it might be too large. If hyphenation is turned on and you're using left-aligned, unjustified type, the most likely cause of your problem is a hyphenation zone that's too large. Whenever you use left-aligned type, PageMaker uses the hyphenation zone to determine whether it can break a word at the end of a line—

PageMaker will wrap a word to the next line, instead of hyphenating it, if the word begins within the hyphenation zone (the hyphenation zone could have been more aptly named the "no hyphenation zone"). In this manner, the hyphenation zone setting determines how ragged the right side of unjustified type is.

If you think your hyphenation problem may be related to a hyphenation zone that's too large, click inside that paragraph, select "Hyphenation…" from the Type menu, and decrease the "Hyphenation zone" setting until your word hyphenates and you like the amount of raggedness this creates along the right side of your unjustified lines. To achieve a consistent effect throughout your publication, build your hyphenation-zone setting into your styles.

See if your word-spacing settings need fine tuning. If you're using justified type, PageMaker may not be hyphenating your word because it was able to justify your line by expanding or compressing your word spacing within the minimum and maximum word-space values you set in the "Spacing attributes" dialog box. Here's why: There's a special order to the steps PageMaker takes when it tries to justify a line. First, it tries to compress your word spacing to as much as the minimum value you set in the "Spacing attributes" dialog box. Next, it tries to expand your word spacing up to the maximum word-spacing value. Only if these steps don't allow it to justify the line will PageMaker try to hyphenate your word.

If this happens to you, you should try giving PageMaker a little less leeway to compress and expand your word spacing. By default, PageMaker's word-spacing minimum value is 50% and its maximum word-spacing value is 200%. Many professional typographers recommend less extreme minimum and maximum values for more consistent-looking, readable type. Try setting your minimum value to approximately 80% and your maximum value to around 130%.

Check your "Limit consecutive hyphens to" setting. If you're still having problems, check to see if the line immediately preceding the line with which you're having a problem ends in a hyphen. If so, PageMaker may not be hyphenating the next line because of a low "Limit consecutive hyphens to" setting.

Open the "Hyphenation" dialog box and take a look at the "Limit consecutive hyphens to" setting—if it's set at "1," "2," or any other number, PageMaker won't hyphenate any more than that number of consecutive lines. Increase the setting for more hyphenation or, if you want to disable this feature altogether, enter "No limit" for unlimited consecutive hyphens (this is PageMaker's default setting). Doing so might be a good idea for very narrow columns, which tend to have awkward breaks if not adequately hyphenated, but may not be the best choice in other situations—two or more consecutive lines ending in hyphens can be visually disruptive. Be sure to proofread your copy carefully if you use the "No limit" setting.

Make sure that word hasn't been set not to break. If you've tried everything else and your word still won't hyphenate, it could be that you inadvertently did something to prevent it from breaking. Highlight the word and select "Type specs…" from the Type menu. In the "Type specifications" dialog box, make sure the "No break" option isn't turned on—if it's on, select the "Break" option instead to allow your word to break.

If the "No break" option wasn't selected, another possibility is that you entered a discretionary hyphen right before the first character in your word—this will also prevent your word from hyphenating. To make sure there isn't a discretionary hyphen there (it won't be visible) click just to the right of the first character in your word, and press the left arrow once—this should place you between the word and the discretionary hyphen, if there is one there. Then press the backspace key one or more times, until you erase the space before the word, and retype the space.

For more information on PageMaker's hyphenation feature, see Adobe's Straight Talk paper titled, "Hyphenation and Justification in PageMaker 5.0." It's available as document #500307 on the Adobe FaxYI system, (206) 628-5737.

Q When I use the "Display pub info" Addition to see what fonts are in my publication, it often lists fonts I'm sure I didn't use. Where are these fonts coming from?

A The "Display pub info" Addition not only lists the fonts you actually use in your publication, but also those listed in your publication's styles (including ones you didn't use), your publication's defaults, and the font the Story Editor uses to display text. That's because the Addition works by listing all the fonts currently installed on your system and checking which ones are required for your publication.

Here's how you can check your publication to find out where your "mystery" fonts are. First, select "Preferences…" from the File menu, and click "Other…" in the "Preferences" dialog box—that will open the "Other preferences" dialog box, which lists what font the Story Editor uses to display text. If this is a font you're not using elsewhere in your publication, and you don't want "Display pub info" to list it, change your Story Editor font to something you do use elsewhere in your publication.

Next, check your styles. Select "Define styles…" from the Type menu, and in the "Define styles" dialog box scroll through your list of styles, clicking on each one as you go, and make a note of what font it uses—this information will be displayed beneath the style list. It's a good idea to remove styles you don't need—especially if they list fonts you aren't using elsewhere in your publication. Doing so will help reduce the size and complexity of your publication file, as well as prevent the "Display pub info" Addition from listing these fonts.

Finally, you can find out what your default font is by making sure no text is selected (an easy way to do this is by switching to the pointer tool) and selecting "Font…" from the Type menu. Whatever font is selected is your default font. If that's a font you aren't using in your publication, change it to something else.

After you've completed these steps, save your publication by selecting "Save as…" from the File menu, then run the "Display pub info" Addition again. If it still lists fonts you think you didn't use, try opening your publication again and using the Story Editor's Find feature to figure out where the fonts are in your publication—sometimes such fonts are assigned to single characters or are applied to overset text or text on the pasteboard.

If you use the Macintosh version of PageMaker 5.0, you can also use Aldus CheckList to find out what fonts you've used in your publication. Aldus CheckList is a stand-alone application that can analyze a PageMaker or PostScript file and list a variety of information about it. For instance, CheckList can tell you what fonts have been used in a publication, the pages on which each font appears, and whether the font is used in a PageMaker story, a PICT, or an EPS. CheckList also provides information on a publication's styles, links, and print settings. It's available directly from Adobe Customer Services at (800) 628-2320.

Q I have "Autoflow" turned on, but when I'm typing in PageMaker and get to the end of a column, my text doesn't automatically flow into the next column. What's wrong?

A Nothing's wrong. PageMaker's "Autoflow" feature just isn't designed to affect text you enter manually in PageMaker. To use the "Autoflow" feature, you must be flowing text from a loaded text icon. If you have a story in PageMaker that you'd like to autoflow, but it isn't in a loaded text icon, try this:

1. Make sure "Autoflow" is selected (it should have a check next to it at the bottom of the Layout menu).
2. Use the pointer tool to select the last text block in the story you want to autoflow.
3. Click on your story's bottom windowshade handle and roll it up until all your text disappears.
4. Click on the bottom windowshade handle's red arrow. A loaded text icon will appear.
5. Click the loaded text icon where you want the text to begin autoflowing. PageMaker will add pages as necessary until your entire story is flowed. If you want PageMaker to stop, press the spacebar.

For more information on PageMaker's "Autoflow" feature and how to use it, see pages 246–47 in the Aldus PageMaker 5.0 User Manual.

Q Whenever I make a PDF out of a PageMaker file that has a "wide" page setup, the PDF I end up with is turned sideways, cropped, or both. Can I prevent this?

A Yes, you can. You probably need to change your print orientation. How you do that depends on whether you're creating your PDF with the Acrobat Distiller or the PDF-Writer. Here are specific tips for both methods.

If you're using the Acrobat Distiller, there are two things you need to do. First, you need to make sure PageMaker is set to print in the portrait, not landscape orientation. When you're ready to print, select "Print..." from PageMaker's File menu to open the "Print Document" dialog box, and under the "Orientation" options, click on the icon of the person standing upright (not sideways). You'll need to do this for each wide-orientation publication, because by default, PageMaker prints wide publications in landscape orientation. If you're using PageMaker 5.0, you'll need to set your wide publications to print portrait each time you print, since PageMaker 5.0 does not save this particular print setting. If you're using PageMaker 6.0, you'll need to set it only once per publication (PageMaker 6.0 saves this setting). You can even make it part of a printer style for creating PDF files (see the Adobe PageMaker 6.0 User Guide for more information).

The second thing you must do is make sure your paper size is set correctly. In PageMaker's "Paper" print dialog box, select the "Custom..." option from the list of paper sizes, even if you're using a standard paper size such as "letter." (If there's no "Custom..." option listed in your paper sizes, make sure you have the Acrobat Distiller PPD selected under "Type" [PageMaker 5.0] or under "PPD" [PageMaker 6.0] in the "Print Document" dialog box.) PageMaker will display the "Custom paper size" dialog box, where you should make sure your paper's width (the larger value when your page setup is "wide") and height (the smaller value) are in the right place. In PageMaker 5.0, the width measurement should come first, the height second. In PageMaker 6.0 the width and height measurements are clearly labeled.

If you're using the PDFWriter, here's what you need to do to make sure wide-orientation publications print correctly. When you're ready to print, select the PDFWriter driver in the Chooser or by holding your Control key (or other PDFWriter shortcut key) down while you select "Print..." from PageMaker's File menu. In the "Print Document" dialog box, you don't need to change the orientation setting (the PDFWriter ignores it). Instead, click on the "Setup..." button to open the "Acrobat PDFWriter Page Setup" dialog box, where you should click on the landscape-orientation button (the icon of the sideways person). Click "OK" in this dialog box, and in the rest of the PDFWriter dialog boxes, making other changes if you wish, until you're back in PageMaker's "Print document" dialog box. Make other changes to your PageMaker print settings if you want, and click "Print" to create your PDF file.

Q When I open certain publications, the PANTONE colors I've been using in them look wrong, even though they looked fine earlier. What causes this?

A This problem, which occurs only in PageMaker 5.0, is caused by the way PageMaker 5.0 reads the color definitions embedded in your color libraries (including the PANTONE libraries). In PageMaker 6.0, this problem no longer occurs.

Here's exactly what causes the display changes. Most color libraries contain two definitions for each color: one in RGB, which PageMaker uses for screen display, and one in CMYK, which PageMaker uses for printing to PostScript devices. The problem you're experiencing happens because the first time you use a color-library color, PageMaker 5.0 correctly displays the color based on the library's RGB definition for that color. But later, after you've closed and reopened the file, PageMaker 5.0 loses track of that RGB definition from the library and must regenerate an RGB definition for your color based on its CMYK definition, and because of that translation you see the color shift.

Fortunately, if you're using the PANTONE libraries for spot colors in a publication that will be color-separated (and you aren't trying to proof color on screen), this shouldn't be a serious problem for you—no matter how the color displays, or what its exact definition is, it'll still print on its own plate so your printer can use the right PANTONE ink color for your objects. To get the most accurate preview of how that ink will look on print out, refer to the PANTONE swatchbook for coated or uncoated stock. (Using a swatchbook is always a more accurate way to preview colors than viewing them on a monitor.)

If you're using the PANTONE color libraries to print to non-PostScript printers or need more accurate screen display, you may need to take a few steps to ensure that PageMaker 5.0's display problem doesn't interfere with predictable color. One way to do this is to print before you close your publication for the first time. Then, if you need to print after closing and reopening the file, you can redefine your PANTONE colors. (To do so, hold down the Ctrl key [Windows] or Command key [Mac] while clicking on the color in your Colors palette. Then, in the "Edit Color" dialog box, select the appropriate color library from the pop-up list of libraries, select a different color from the library's color swatches, click "OK," and click "OK" again to close the "Edit Color" dialog box. Then Ctrl- or Command-click on that color in your Colors palette, select the same library from the list of libraries in the "Edit Color" dialog box, select the correct color, click "OK," and click "OK" once more.) Since that technique can be too tedious in some situations, we recommend that you upgrade to PageMaker 6.0 if it's extremely important that you get consistent display or non-PostScript output of PANTONE colors. (Or, just use colors you define yourself.) Once you've converted your PageMaker 5.0 documents to 6.0 format, be sure to reimport your PANTONE colors from the libraries that come with PageMaker 6.0.

If you're printing your PANTONE colors as process colors to PostScript devices, you also don't have a serious problem—for PostScript printing, the PANTONE colors will always use the CMYK definitions embedded in each color. To ensure those CMYK definitions are accurate, make sure you're using the updated PANTONE libraries that came with the PageMaker 5.0 Enhancement Packs and with PageMaker 5.0a. Once you have those libraries installed, redefine (reimport) your PANTONE colors from the new libraries. (To do so, hold down the Ctrl key [Windows] or Command key [Mac] while clicking on the color in your Colors palette. In the "Edit Color" dialog box, select the appropriate color library from the pop-up list of libraries, select your color from the library's color swatches, click "OK," and click "OK" again.) If you want to print PANTONE colors with CMYK inks, we recommend that you preview your colors using the PANTONE ProSim library and swatchbook, which include a selection of true process colors.

Q *(6.0 only)* **I saved a PageMaker 6.0 file in 5.0 format, and when I opened it in 5.0 the polygons I'd drawn in 6.0 were gone. Is there a way to get those polygons into PageMaker 5.0? And are other aspects of my publications going to change when I save in 5.0 format?**

A If you draw polygons in PageMaker 6.0 using its new polygon tool, those objects will indeed disappear if you save your publication in PageMaker 5.0 format, because PageMaker 5.0 doesn't have a polygon tool and therefore doesn't support PageMaker 6.0–drawn polygons. (If you have a PageMaker 6.0 publication that contains a PageMaker-drawn polygon as an inline graphic, and you save that publication to 5.0 format, your inline polygon will turn into a rectangle that will take up the same space as your polygon did, so your line endings don't change.)

None of this means it's impossible to get a PageMaker 6.0–drawn polygon into PageMaker 5.0. What you'll need to do is convert that polygon to an EPS, TIFF, or other kind of format that PageMaker 5.0 will accept. Here are a few methods you can use.

- If you're using PageMaker 6.0 for the Macintosh, you can cut your polygon to the clipboard, then paste it back in as a PICT. To do so, select the polygon, and select "Cut" from the Edit menu. Then select "Paste Special…" from the Edit menu, and in the "Paste Special" dialog box, choose "PICT" from the list of formats, and click "OK."
- Using any screen-capture utility, take a screen shot of your polygon (zoom in on it first for the highest-resolution capture possible), and place or paste that capture back into PageMaker in any graphic format PageMaker 5.0 supports.
- Place your polygon on a page by itself, and print that page as an EPS file, which you can then place into PageMaker 5.0. (If you're in Windows, the EPS won't have a screen image. To avoid having to crop an EPS you can't see, you might want to expand your polygon or change your document setup so it fits onto most of your page before you print it to an EPS file.)

Here are a few more things that you might notice in 6.0 publications that have been saved in the 5.0 format.

- OLE 2 objects will appear as boxes and will not print.
- Masked object will appear unmasked.
- Locked objects will no longer be locked.
- Grouped objects will no longer be grouped.
- Photo CD images placed into the publication in PageMaker 6.0 will not appear on the page(s) once the publication has been saved in PageMaker 5.0 format.
- Color Management System tags applied to images won't be included in your publications.
- Tints you've applied to objects using PageMaker 6.0's tint-percentage feature (instead of creating a tint as a separate color and assigning it to objects that way) will appear and print as solid colors.
- HiFi color in general isn't supported in PageMaker 5.0.

PANTONE Hexachrome colors will convert with their names intact, but with process-color definitions and without any references to the Hexachrome library. The colors won't display, print, or separate accurately.

- DCS 2.0 files will display as a gray box with an X in the middle and print as such.
- Nonprinting elements will become printing elements.
- Multiple-master-page elements will not appear on the assigned pages. (All pages will use the Document Master elements.)
- Hypertext-link and bookmark markers (visible in the Story Editor in PageMaker 6.0) will be lost.
- Colors defined in PageMaker 6.0 may display or print somewhat differently in PageMaker 5.0. (See the second question on page 71 for more information.)
- Color names and paragraph styles with the same name but different capitalization will override the default definitions and capitalization in PageMaker 5.0.

Q *(6.0 only)* **When I open my PageMaker 5.0x documents in PageMaker 6.0, my colors look darker on screen. Is this caused by color management?**

A No, color management has nothing to do with this. In PageMaker 6.0, Adobe made some fundamental improvements to the algorithms for converting colors from CMYK to RGB and RGB to CMYK (the algorithms in 6.0 are more accurate). But because of this, you may see some changes in the way colors in converted documents display or print. Here's why this happens, and how you can prevent these changes from causing problems.

Both PageMaker 5.0 and 6.0 need colors to be defined in two ways to display and print them. For printing to non-PostScript printers and for on-screen display, PageMaker needs to use an RGB definition of the color. To print colors to PostScript devices, PageMaker needs a CMYK definition of the color. So, if you have a color defined in one color space (RGB or CMYK) and PageMaker needs it in the other color space to display or print it, PageMaker must convert that color using a conversion algorithm. If you're used to the results you got from the PageMaker 5.0's RGBCMYK algorithm, you may not want a different result from PageMaker 6.0's algorithm, especially if that change occurs on printout.

Here's how to make sure you don't get printed color output that looks different from the printed output you got in PageMaker 5.0. If you're printing to non-PostScript printers, make sure your 5.0 publication's default color model is RGB before you convert your publication to 6.0 format (this will ensure that you get consistent display and non-PostScript output, but your colors may print differently to PostScript devices). If you're printing to PostScript printers, make sure your publication's default color model is CMYK before you convert to 6.0. (This will give you consistent printed output, but your screen colors might look different—possibly a bit darker. But the good news is that your screen display will more accurately represent your printed output.)

To make sure a PageMaker 5.0 publication uses a certain default color model, open it in 5.0, edit any existing color, selecting the desired color model in the "Edit color" dialog box, and save the publication before converting to 6.0.

If you're not satisfied with being able to ensure that your printed output stays the same as it was in PageMaker 5.0—in other words, if you need both non-PostScript/display and PostScript output to stay the same as it was in PageMaker 5.0—there's a way you can get PageMaker 6.0 to use the same RGBCMYK algorithm PageMaker 5.0 uses. The trick is to replace PageMaker 6.0's "dfltcmsg.swb" file (it contains the 6.0 conversion algorithms) with the "dfltcmsg.alt" file, which also came with PageMaker 6.0 and contains the PageMaker 5.0 conversion algorithms. To do so, locate these files on your hard disk (in Windows, look for them under PM6\RSRC\SWITCHB\DFLTCMSG; on the Mac, look for it in Adobe PageMaker 6.0:RSRC:SwitchB:dfltcmsg). Next, while PageMaker 6.0 is closed, rename the "dfltcmsg.swb" file to something like "dfltcmsg.60" to back it up. Then rename the "dfltcmsg.alt" file to "dfltcmsg.swb."

(Later, if you want PageMaker 6.0 to use its own conversion algorithms again, name the "dfltcmsg.swb" file back to "dfltcmsg.alt," and then name the "dfltcmsg.60" file back to "dfltcmsg.swb.")

Although using the PageMaker 5.0 conversion algorithms will ensure that you get the same kind of RGBCMYK conversions you did in PageMaker 5.0, we don't recommend it. You'll sacrifice the more sophisticated PageMaker 6.0 algorithms, which will give you more accurate conversions between RGB and CMYK.

Q *(6.0 only)* **I have a logo that I created in PageMaker a year ago, and I want to edit it now. Unfortunately, I can't seem to ungroup it. What's wrong?**

A Chances are you're trying to use PageMaker 6.0's "Ungroup" command (available on the Arrange menu) to ungroup an object created with PageMaker 5.0x's "PS Group it" Addition—and that simply won't work. PageMaker 6.0 can't ungroup PageMaker 5.0x "PS Group it" objects because they're fundamentally different from PageMaker 6.0 grouped items.

To ungroup the logo, you'll need to reopen the original PageMaker 5.0x publication in PageMaker 5.0x, select the object, then choose "PS Ungroup it" from the Additions submenu of the Utility menu. Save the publication and then reopen it in PageMaker 6.0—you'll then be able to manipulate your logo in any way you want.

A *(6.0 only)* **I installed PageMaker 6.0 and there appears to no longer be a version of the Table Editor. Did Adobe leave it out of PageMaker 6.0?**

A No. PageMaker 6.0 comes with a new table editor, called Adobe Table 2.5 (or, if you're running under Win32s—that is, if you're using Windows 3.1—you can install Table Editor 2.11). If you don't see Adobe Table, chances are you didn't install it, possibly because you used the "Minimal" install option. To install Adobe Table 2.5 on a Macintosh or in Windows 95, do the following:

1. Insert the PageMaker 6.0 CD or floppy disk #1.
2. Locate Setup.exe (Windows) or the PageMaker 6 Installer/Utility (Mac) and double-click on it.
3. Select a language when the Installer prompts you to. Next, choose the "Custom Install" option.
4. Choose to install only Adobe Table 2.5 and click on the "Install" button.
5. (Mac only) Select the folder where you want Adobe Table located, and click "OK."

If you have tables you created in an older table editor, here's what you need to know about converting those tables to Adobe Table 2.5 format.

- Adobe Table 2.5 can open and convert tables from Table Editor 2.x (which shipped with the Windows versions of PageMaker 4.0, 5.0, and 5.0a and the Win32s version of PageMaker 6.0) and Table Editor 1.01 (which shipped with PageMaker 4.x for the Macintosh). To convert tables, select "Open…" from Adobe Table's File menu, and select the table file you want to convert. Adobe Table will open it as an untitled file. Converted tables will retain all their cell grouping and formatting, but any dashed or dotted lines will be converted to solid lines.
- Adobe Table cannot open or convert tables from Adobe Table 1.0, which shipped with Adobe Persuasion 3.0 for Windows and the Macintosh.
- Tables created in Adobe Table 2.5 can be opened in both the Windows and Macintosh versions of Adobe Table 2.5, but not in earlier versions of the Table Editor.

Q *(6.0 only)* **When I use the Create Adobe PDF Plug-in and choose the option to create bookmarks and links for my table of contents and index entries, I notice that Acrobat doesn't take me to the correct pages when I click on these bookmarks or links. What's wrong?**

A There may not be anything serious wrong. If the bookmarks and links take you to the page with the right content, but the page numbers of those pages don't match your PageMaker publication's numbering scheme, you have a relatively benign problem on your hands. However, if your bookmarks and links are taking you to pages that don't contain the elements to which you wanted to link, then you do have a serious problem. Here's an overview of why these problems can occur and how to prevent and fix them.

The first thing you should understand is that PageMaker allows you to create far more complex page-numbering schemes than Acrobat and the PDF format can support. Acrobat and PDF offer one numbering scheme: your first page is always page one, the next page is always page two, and so forth. So, if you're determined to match your Page-Maker publication's page numbers to the numbers Acrobat will assign, you'll need to number your PageMaker publication's pages accordingly—starting on page one, then page two, and so on.

That's not absolutely necessary, though—it's important only if you want your folios, TOC references, and index references to match the Acrobat page number so that navigation seems a little less ambiguous for your readers. But if your readers will be navigating the PDF primarily through links, article threading, and the like—which is especially likely if you're setting up the PDF to run in full-screen mode—then there's little reason to worry about all this. And there are certainly times you wouldn't want to reinvent a PageMaker document's page-numbering scheme (especially in a long document designed for on-paper publication).

But, regardless of the page-numbering scheme you use in PageMaker, the last thing you want is to have someone click on a bookmark or index link and be taken to a page with entirely the wrong content. If you have a booked publication, follow all the steps below to prevent this. If you have a nonbooked publication, just follow steps 3–5.

1. Select "Book…" from the Utilities menu, and in the "Book publication list" dialog box, make sure the right publications, in the correct order, are listed under "Book list." In addition, make sure you've selected the appropriate auto-renumbering option. Click "OK."
2. Hold down your Ctrl (Windows) or Command (Mac) key while selecting "Book…" from the Utilities menu once more. This will copy your book list to the other publications in the book. Doing this whenever you make a change in your book list is a good idea because it ensures that you'll get the right table of contents and index regardless of what publication in the book you're in when you generate them.
3. Just before you create your PDF, generate the table of contents and index. If there are any mistakes in the generated text, don't fix the mistakes by editing the generated text of the table of contents or index—fix them by turning "Include in table of contents" on or off in your styles or local paragraph formatting or by editing index-entry markers. This is critical because the Create Adobe PDF Plug-in doesn't generate bookmarks and index links based on the text of your table of contents and index. Instead, it uses information embedded in special markers that PageMaker creates when it generates the table of contents and index (you can see these markers in the Story Editor if you have the "Display ¶" option on—they look like little triangles).
4. When you run the Create Adobe PDF Plug-in, make sure you use a printer style in which the "Print blank pages" option is turned on (the "Acrobat" printer style that comes with PageMaker 6.0 is one such style). For information on creating and editing printer styles, please see page 343 of the Adobe PageMaker 6.0 User Guide.
5. If generating and laying out your table of contents or index causes the text in the rest of your publication to reflow, it might invalidate some of the page-number references in your table of contents or index. So be sure to set aside space for your table of contents and index before generating their final versions.

Q *(6.0 only)* **I've been creating Web pages using the HTML Author Plug-in in PageMaker 6.0 and something's not right. When I click on certain hyperlinks in my Web browser, the screen jumps to the wrong location. What's the problem?**

A Chances are your hyperlink is taking you to the top of the page that contains your anchor, and it's doing that because that's how the HTML Author Plug-in writes HTML.

In HTML, an anchor is the destination of a hyperlink (it's where you're supposed to end up when you click on the hyperlink in a Web browser). The anchor location is defined with an "anchor tag"—a piece of HTML code that sits next to your anchor but is invisible in a Web browser. PageMaker's HTML Author Plug-in places those anchor tags at the top of the text block that contains the anchor instead of placing them right next to the anchor.

There are two ways you can handle this. First, you can design your document so the anchors go at the top of your text blocks. But if that's not a good workaround, it's pretty easy to edit your HTML code so the anchors go exactly where you want them. Here's how.

1. After exporting the document as HTML from PageMaker, open the HTML document in a text editor.
2. Locate the anchor tag. It'll look something like this:
   ```
   <A NAME="anchor label"> </A>
   ```
   (In the example above, "<A NAME=" is the beginning of the opening tag and "</A>" is the closing tag. The "anchor label" is the label you assigned to the anchor when you created it in the "Create Links" section of the HTML Author Plug-in.)
3. Cut the anchor tag and paste it before the text to which the hyperlink should jump.
4. Save the HTML document in the text-only format.

Keep in mind that if you re-export the HTML document, the HTML Author will completely rewrite the HTML code, erasing any changes you made to it. Therefore, wait until you've exported the final version of your Web page(s) before editing your HTML code.

Q When I type text into a publication, the individual characters overlap one another instead of wrapping to the next line on screen. Sometimes I also get this effect when I print my documents. What is happening, and how do I fix it?

A A few different scenarios can cause this behavior in PageMaker. Generally, text refuses to wrap for one of two reasons. There may be no space characters for PageMaker to use to break the line of text, or the words may be very long (fundamentally the same problem). Or an internal or external factor (for example, type-specifications settings or options chosen in a type manager, respectively) is interfering with the process of breaking the line. Check the following things, listed from most common and easily overlooked to more arcane system-related matters, and see if one of them doesn't solve the problem for you.

- Make sure you've used the space bar on your keyboard to place breaking space characters on each line.
- Make sure the "Line End" option is set to "Break" in the "Type Specifications" dialog box. When the "Line End" option is set to "No Break," the text cannot break or wrap; characters will overlap or stack on top of each other rather than wrap to the next line when the end of the line is reached.
- In a copy of the publication, select the pointer tool and perform a global recompose (Ctrl + "Hyphenation..." on a PC, Option + "Hyphenation..." on a Mac) to ensure that the text is composed with correct font metrics. A global recompose is not to be confused with a diagnostic recompose, which is Ctrl + Shift + "Hyphenation..." on a PC, Option + Shift + "Hyphenation..." on a Mac. A diagnostic recompose, in addition to recomposing text, also checks all links and external connections; that's not necessary in this case.
- Assign a different typeface to the text that won't break. If it then breaks, it may indicate that the original font is damaged, either as applied to a particular piece of text or at a system level. Delete the nonbreaking text, do a "Save As," and then recompose your file, or, for possible system-level font damage, remove and reinstall the typeface.
- Using Adobe Type Manager (ATM) 3.0.1 or earlier with PageMaker 6.0 in Windows 95 may cause text to display or print with incorrect character spacing. If you have this configuration, remove your copy of ATM and install ATM 3.0.2, which is included on the PageMaker 6.0 Deluxe CD-ROM. (For instructions on deinstalling ATM 3.0 or earlier, send an E-mail to techdocs@adobe.com and request document 341402, or obtain FaxYI document 341402.) Versions of ATM prior to 3.0.2 are not compatible with Windows 95.

  To check which version of ATM you have installed, click the Windows 95 "Start" button, then navigate to the ATM Control Panel (from the Main submenu of the Programs menu). You should see the version number in the upper-left corner of the "ATM Control Panel" window.
- If you're printing from PageMaker 5.0x and Windows 3.1x to a Hewlett-Packard LaserJet III printer using the Universal printer driver 3.1.2 and mini-driver 2.0, select the text, then choose "Paragraph..." from the Type menu and click the "Spacing..." button. In the "Paragraph Spacing Attributes" dialog box, deselect the "Pair kerning" check box, or enter a pair-kerning value for "Auto above" that's greater than the point size of the text. This will effectively disable pair kerning for the selected text.

Q When I select "Create Adobe PDF..." in PageMaker, the "Distill now" option is grayed out in the "Create Adobe PDF" dialog box. Why is this happening?

A Most likely because PageMaker can't find Acrobat Distiller. Distiller is the engine that converts PageMaker's PostScript files into PDF form for viewing in Acrobat Reader or Exchange. For PageMaker to automatically convert the document into PDF form, it has to know where the Acrobat Distiller application resides on your hard disk. If PageMaker can't find Distiller for some reason, the "Distill now" option will be unavailable. Resolving the problem is a matter of getting PageMaker to locate the Distiller application. In the short term, don't worry—you can write your PostScript file to disk now, if you like, and distill later.

There are a few reasons why PageMaker may not be able to find Distiller. Before you try anything else, make sure that Adobe Acrobat Distiller version 2.0 or later has been installed. This program is included with PageMaker 6.0x, or you may have installed it separately. If you can't locate the Distiller program on your hard disk, install it from your PageMaker CD or disk set and then make sure it launches. If the "Distill now" option is still dimmed at this point, browse through the following list.

If you use PageMaker 6.x with Windows 3.1 or Windows 95:

- Quit PageMaker, then delete the files "CreatPDF.ini" and "CreatPDF.prf" in the PM6\RSRC\USENGLSH\PLUG-INS directory.
- Hold down the Shift key while choosing "Create Adobe PDF..." from the File menu, then go to the Distiller application when prompted (ACRODIST.EXE or ADISTPE.EXE).

  The path information pointing to the Distiller application is stored in the "CreatPDF.ini" file. The directions listed above are two ways to force PageMaker to relocate the application and re-create the correct path.

If you use PageMaker 6.x on a Macintosh:

- Quit PageMaker, then delete or rename the "Create Adobe PDF.prf" file in the "Plugins" folder in the "RSRC" folder in the "Adobe PageMaker 6.0" folder.
- Rebuild the desktop file by holding down the Command and Option keys while restarting. Keep holding down the keys until you receive the message "Are you sure you want to rebuild the desktop file on the disk [diskname]?" Click "OK." If you are using System 7.5 or later, use the Extensions Manager to turn off all Extensions except Macintosh Easy Open before you rebuild the desktop. A corrupt or out-of-date desktop may not correctly report or locate installed applications, and if your Macintosh can't find it, PageMaker won't be able to find it.
- Before you launch the Create Adobe PDF Plug-in, move the Acrobat Distiller application file to the desktop. After the Create Adobe PDF Plug-in has launched, you can move the Acrobat Distiller application file back to its original location, if desired. Moving Distiller to the desktop may bypass a damaged folder or system that can't properly report its location.

Q *(6.5 only)* **I used to be able to kern text apart by using the Command + Shift + right arrow keyboard shortcut. Now when I use that, it just highlights the rest of the word. What gives?**

A You've run into one of the keyboard-shortcut changes introduced in PageMaker 6.5; there are quite a few others as well. They'll take some time to get used to—especially if you've been using the old ones for a long time, as we have. We sympathize if this causes you any inconvenience, but we hope you'll find them a big improvement in the long run—they were designed with great care to achieve some important goals.

First of all, the new keyboard shortcuts were designed to improve shortcut consistency among Adobe products—which is something Adobe customers have been requesting for a long time (but is also, ironically, something that's hard to implement gracefully since it requires that we all change some very ingrained habits). For instance, the keyboard shortcut you mention above (Command + Shift + right arrow, which is equivalent to Ctrl + Shift + right arrow on the PC) is the new shortcut for selecting right to the end of the word—it's a keyboard shortcut used in other Adobe products, such as Illustrator, and many word-processing applications, including Microsoft Word. The keyboard shortcut for kerning text apart by 1/100th of an em is now Ctrl + Alt + right arrow (Windows) and Command + Option + right arrow (Mac)—the same keyboard shortcut used in Illustrator.

While these shortcuts were being shuffled to improve cross-product consistency, some were also assigned to improve logic and make them easier to remember. For example, all the shortcuts associated with the Frames feature use the F key and various modifiers. Likewise, all the shortcuts for the Group feature are based on the G key.

Another factor that influenced the changes was that PageMaker's old shortcut system (which allowed it to use only Ctrl- and Command-key combinations on main-menu commands) had run out of shortcuts. PageMaker now uses Alt- and Option-key combinations for main-menu commands as well.

PageMaker 6.5 comes with several resources that should help you learn these new shortcuts as quickly as possible. You'll find lists on the Quick Reference card. In PageMaker's online help, there are comprehensive lists that show you which shortcuts are new, which ones have changed, and which ones have equivalents in other Adobe products. To view this information in Windows, select "Shortcuts..." from PageMaker's Help menu. On the Macintosh, select "Shortcuts..." from the help menu () in the upper-right corner of your screen while PageMaker is running. We recommend printing the shortcuts and posting them near your monitor while you're learning them.

Q I've got a tabloid-size document that I want to convert to a smaller layout for publishing online. However, when I use the new "Adjust Layout" feature to make this change, some of the items in my layout end up overlapping or hanging off the edge of the page. Am I doing something wrong?

A Probably not. How complete and predictable an "adjustment" this feature can make depends on the complexity of your document, the magnitude of the changes you're making to its framework, and—most importantly—how thoroughly you've structured it using PageMaker's guides.

You'll often need to make some adjustments manually to complete the transition to the new layout framework. Nevertheless, you can minimize the number of modications you'll have to do manually by using ruler, margin, and column guides effectively. Then, when you adjust your framework (change the columns, margins, or page size) and turn on the "Adjust Layout" feature, PageMaker uses your guides to resize and reposition page elements. When you don't use guides to anchor your elements, PageMaker has little clue how to adjust your layout. (See the illustrations below for an example.)

You'll get the most from automatic layout adjustment if you understand the principles it uses to do its work. Try the tutorial that comes with PageMaker 6.5 for a good overview of this. For more information, see the Adobe PageMaker 6.5 User Guide, pages 88–89. Another helpful resource is the article "Get the lead in" by Tim Cole, Adobe Magazine, May/June 1995, pages 55–59—this article will show you how to set up a full leading grid, which is an excellent way to structure a publication to make layout easier and to ensure a consistent, harmonious look.

Q Sometimes when I save a document and immediately go to close it, PageMaker asks me if I want to save changes (even though I haven't made any). Why can't PageMaker remember that I just saved my document?

A This can occur when you have the text tool and a text-insertion point active just before closing your publication—even if you've just saved it. These "unnecessary" saves aren't about PageMaker trying to save your publication per se, they're about PageMaker trying to save information on where the current text-insertion point is.

In PageMaker 5.0x, when the text tool was active in a paragraph, and the document was saved, the insertion point would disappear—even if you didn't close the publication at that time.

This was remedied in PageMaker 6.0x, which will save the text-insertion point so you can continue working where you left off when you save and don't close the publication (PageMaker does not retain the text-insertion point when you close and reopen your publication). But there's another aspect to this behavior: PageMaker 6.0x will prompt you to save the publication when you close it, regardless of whether you've changed anything in it since the last save. PageMaker 6.5 doesn't do this.

If you don't like the way PageMaker 6.0x behaves in this regard and you don't plan on upgrading to PageMaker 6.5 soon, try this. Switch to the pointer tool just before saving and closing your publication—PageMaker won't prompt you to save it again.

Damaged PageMaker Publication Troubleshooting Guide

ISSUE

When you work in, save, or print an Adobe PageMaker 6.0x or earlier publication, PageMaker returns an error or behaves unexpectedly. You can perform the same tasks in other publications without error.

SOLUTIONS

Open a copy of the publication on the hard disk, then do one or more of the following:

A. Perform a diagnostic recompose:
   1. If you're using PageMaker 6.0 for the Macintosh, temporarily move all imported graphics on master pages to the pasteboard. You do not need to move the graphics if you are using PageMaker 5.0x or 6.01 for the Macintosh, or PageMaker for Windows.
   2. Press Option + Shift (Macintosh) or Control + Shift (Windows) and choose Type > Hyphenation.
   3. After the diagnostic recompose is completed, choose File > Save As, then save the publication to the hard disk.
B. Perform a slide show:
   1. While pressing the Shift key, choose Layout > Go To Page.
   2. After all pages have displayed at least once, press any key to stop the slide show.
   3. Click on the master page icons to display the master pages. In PageMaker 6.0x, click and hold the mouse button on the master page icons (Macintosh) or right-click the master page icons (Windows), then choose each master page from the pop-up menu.
   4. After you have displayed all master pages, choose File > Save As, then save the publication to the hard disk.
C. Unlink files whose links are broken, then save the publication:
   1. Choose File > Links.
   2. Select a file whose name is preceded with a quesion mark (?) or the letters "UN."
   3. Click Unlink.
   4. Repeat steps 2 and 3 for all file names preceded with a question mark or the letters "UN."
   5. Click OK to close the Links dialog box.
   6. Choose File > Save As, then save the publication to the hard disk.
D. For each graphic included in the publication, choose Element > Link Options and deselect Store Copy in Publication. Then choose File > Save As and save the publication to the hard disk.
E. Isolate the object that is causing the error by doing one or more of the following, then replace the object:
   A. Remove empty pages from the publication.
   B. Remove unnecessary or hidden objects, including objects on the pasteboard and nonprinting objects.
   C. Change fonts to a standard font (e.g., Arial, Times New Roman, Helvetica). If the error doesn't occur with this font, reinstall the font you are using in the publication.
   D. In a copy of the publication, remove half the pages and save the publication with a new name. Perform the operations that were causing errors (e.g., printing, copying). If the error or unexpected behavior occurs, there may be a damaged object on one of these pages in the publication; if it doesn't occur, there may be a damaged object on one of the removed pages. Continue to split the publication until you determine the page or pages that cause errors. Remove and replace imported graphics, Page-

Maker-drawn objects, and text blocks on the pages that cause errors.

F. Copy and paste the publication's pages into a new publication using one of the following methods:
Manually copy the pages into a new publication:
1. Choose File > New, then select the desired options in the Document Setup dialog box and click OK.
2. Choose Window > Tile to display both publications.
3. Click on the original publication to activate it.
4. Choose Edit > Select All, then choose Edit > Copy.
5. Click on the new publication to activate it.
6. Press Option + Command + V (Macintosh) or Control + Shift + P (Windows) to paste the objects in the same location on the new page.
7. Repeat steps 3-6 for each page.

OR: In PageMaker 6.0x, create and use a script to copy a publication's objects into a new publication:
1. Choose File > New, then select the desired options in the Document Setup dialog box and click OK.
2. In the new publication, choose File > Save As, then save the file to the hard disk.
3. Choose the original publication from the Window menu.
4. Choose New Script from the Scripts palette menu.
5. Name the script and save it to the Scripts subdirectory.
6. In the Edit Script dialog box, type the following scripting commands, replacing "original publication" with the original publication's filename and path and "new publication" with the destination publication's filename and path:
   selectall —selects all items on current page or page spread
   copy —copies selected items
   window "new publication"—switches to publication named between quotation marks
   multiplepaste 1, 0, 0 —pastes one copy at no offset
   save — saves the publication
   page next —switches to next page or page spread in publication
   window "original publication" —switches to publication named between quotation marks
   page next —switches to next page or page spread in publication
7. Save the script, then double-click on it in the Scripts palette.
8. Double-click the script again for each page or page spread in the publication.

G. In PageMaker 6.0x, save the publication in PageMaker 5.0x format, then open the 5.0x publication in PageMaker 6.0x:
1. Choose File > Save As.
2. Choose 5.0 Publication from the Save As Type pop-up menu.
3. Name the publication with a ".pm5" extension, then click Save.
4. Close the publication.
5. Choose File > Open.
6. In the Open Publication dialog box, choose Older PageMaker Files from the Files of Type pop-up menu.
7. Select the .pm5 publication, then click Open.

NOTE: Features not available in PageMaker 5.0x (e.g., multiple master pages, polygons) are not retained when you save a PageMaker 6.0x publication in PageMaker 5.0x format.

H. Salvage the text by placing the publication's stories into a new publication, then reopen the original publication:
1. Close the publication.
2. Choose File > New, then click OK in the Document Setup (PageMaker 6.0x) or Page Setup (PageMaker 5.0x) dialog box.
3. Choose File > Place.
4. In the Place dialog box, select the PageMaker publication and click Open (PageMaker 6.0x) or OK (PageMaker 5.0x).
5. In the Story Importer dialog box, select the stories to place as one continuous story, then click OK.

ADDITIONAL INFORMATION

When you work in, save, or print a damaged PageMaker publication, PageMaker behaves unexpectedly or returns one of the following errors:

Cannot lock block.
Cannot process publications links. Internal error: Bad Record Index.
Lock not expected but found.
General Protection Fault in Pm5app.exe or Pm6.exe
Win32s Error Unhandled Exception in Storage.dll
Invalid PageFault in Kernel32.dll
Invalid text hole
Internal Error: Bad Class
Invalid PageFault in module unknown
Internal error: Fatal error
Bad Hole Record Index
Cannot place text.
Cannot edit text.
Cannot find hole record.
Type 1
Type 11

A publication may become damaged due to low disk space, low system resources, or system conflicts. When a system error, freeze, or crash occurs while PageMaker is reading from or writing to disk, the open publication may become damaged. Working directly off a network or removable drive (e.g., Syquest) increases the likelihood that communication errors will occur and damage a publication. Damage in a publication may also be caused by a damaged style, font, indexed item, link, or object (e.g., text block, imported graphic, PageMaker-drawn graphic) in the publication.

The diagnostic recompose command is a group of functions that checks the integrity of some structures within a PageMaker publication and repairs specific types of inconsistencies.

PageMaker's slide show feature enables you to display each page of the publication quickly. When PageMaker displays each page, including master pages, it repairs link information.

In PageMaker's Links dialog box, a question mark in front of a linked file indicates that PageMaker cannot locate the linked external file; the letters 'UN" indicate the page number for the text or in-line graphic file is unknown. Unlinking these files prevents PageMaker from attempting to read broken links.

When you deselect Store Copy in Publication in the Link Options dialog box for a graphic, PageMaker stores a screen preview in the publication and maintains a link to the original graphic file. This reduces the file size of the publication and frees up memory.

To avoid damage caused by interrupted communication, work on publications while they are located on local hard disks. To store a publication on a network drive or a removable disk, first save the publication to the local hard disk and close it, then use the Windows 95 Explorer, File Manager, or the Finder to copy the closed publication to the external drive.

Cannot Play QuickTime Movies in PDF Files Exported from PageMaker 6.5

ISSUE

When you click on a QuickTime movie in a PDF file exported from Adobe PageMaker 6.5, the movie does not play.

SOLUTION

Reinstall Acrobat Reader 3.0 from the PageMaker 6.5 CD-ROM:

1. Insert the PageMaker 6.5 CD-ROM.
2. Select Install Acrobat Reader 3.0.
3. Follow the on-screen instructions.

ADDITIONAL INFORMATION

To play QuickTime movies in Acrobat Reader and Acrobat Exchange, you must have the Acrobat Movie plug-in installed. The Movie plug-in for Windows, Movie32.api, which is installed when you install Acrobat Reader from the PageMaker 6.5 CD-ROM, is located in the Acrobat Reader\Plug-ins directory or the Acrobat Exchange\Plug-ins. The Movie Plug-in file for the Macintosh is located in the Plug-ins folder within the Acrobat Reader or Acrobat Exchange folder.

Colors Display Differently in PageMaker 6.5 than in PageMaker 6.0x

Adobe PageMaker 6.5 displays colors defined with CMYK values in third-party color libraries (e.g., PANTONE Coated, Focoltone) differently than does PageMaker 6.0x. To display a color on-screen, PageMaker converts the defined CMYK values to RGB values. Because PageMaker 6.5 uses a different algorithm to convert CMYK values to RGB values than does PageMaker 6.0x, the colors may not appear the same on-screen.

PageMaker 6.5 uses the same algorithm that Adobe Illustrator 6.0x uses, providing more accurate color display than PageMaker 6.0x offers, and enabling consistent color display in graphics created in Illustrator and placed into PageMaker.

Colors applied to objects in a PageMaker 6.0x or earlier publication may be different on-screen when you open the publication in PageMaker 6.5, but the difference in screen display does not affect PostScript printing. However, because non-PostScript devices rasterize what appears on-screen when printing, colors may print to a non-PostScript printer differently from PageMaker 6.5 than they do from PageMaker 6.0x.

Unable to Export PageMaker-Drawn Graphics from PageMaker

ISSUE

You cannot export drawn objects (i.e., lines, boxes, ovals, or polygons) from Adobe PageMaker.

SYMPTOMS

The Export Graphic command in PageMaker 6.5 is dimmed for drawn objects. After you copy a drawn object, you cannot paste it into another application.

SOLUTIONS

Print the page containing the objects to disk as an EPS graphic:

1. Choose File > Print in PageMaker.
2. Verify that a PostScript printer is selected in the Print Document dialog box. If you do not see a PPD pop-up menu, select a PostScript printer in the Print To pop-up menu (Windows) or in the Chooser (Macintosh).
3. Select your printer's PPD file from the PPD pop-up menu.
4. Click Ranges, then type the number of the page that includes the drawn objects.
5. Click Options.
6. Select Write PostScript to File, then select EPS.
7. Click Save.
8. Name the EPS file when prompted. If you will use the EPS graphic in Windows, name it with an ".eps" extension.
9. Click OK.

   NOTE: PageMaker 6.0x and earlier for Windows does not create a screen preview for EPS graphics. When you import the EPS graphic into an application, it will appear on screen as a gray box, but will print as expected to a PostScript printer.

OR: If you're using PageMaker 6.5, capture a screen image of the objects, paste it into PageMaker, then export the screen image:

1. Select the zoom tool, then drag it to draw a marquee around the objects so they are the only objects that appear on screen.
2. Press the Tab key to hide all active palettes.
3. Press Alt + PrintScreen (Windows) or Command + Shift + 3 (Macintosh).
4. Import the screen image by choosing Edit > Paste (Windows), or by choosing File > Place, selecting the Picture 1 file on your hard disk or desktop, and clicking Open (Macintosh).
5. Select the graphic with the pointer tool, then choose File > Export > Graphic.
6. Select a graphic format from the Save As Type pop-up menu.
7. Name the graphic, then click Save.
   NOTE: When you capture an image, it has the same resolution as your monitor (e.g., 72 dpi), which is lower than the resolution of most printing devices.

OR: Capture a screen image of the drawn objects using a screen capture application (e.g., MMedia Lview, Specular Collage, Optomus Snapshot) or the system's screen capture feature. To capture a screen image of the active window in Windows, press Alt + PrintScreen, then choose Edit > Paste in an image-editing application (e.g., Adobe Photoshop, Windows Paintbrush). To capture a screen image on the Macintosh, press Command + Shift + 3. The system creates a PICT graphic on your hard disk named Picture 1.

OR: If you're using PageMaker 6.x, create a PDF file of the publication, then open and save it in an application that can edit PDF files (e.g., Adobe Illustrator):

1. Choose File > Export > Adobe PDF (PageMaker 6.5) or File > Create Adobe PDF (PageMaker 6.0x).
2. Select the desired options in the Export Adobe PDF dialog box (PageMaker 6.5) or the Create Adobe PDF dialog box (PageMaker 6.0x).
3. Click Export (PageMaker 6.5) or Create (PageMaker 6.0x).
4. Name the PDF file, then click Save.
5. Open the PDF file in an application that can edit PDF files (e.g., Adobe Illustrator).
6. Export the file in a standard graphic format (e.g., TIFF).

OR: If you're using PageMaker 5.0x, use the PS Group-It Addition to create a PageMaker group graphic:

1. In PageMaker, select the objects you wish to use as a graphic.
2. Choose Utilities > Additions > PS Group It. PageMaker creates a group (.pmg) file in the directory or folder containing the publication.
3. Open the group file in a drawing application (e.g., Adobe Illustrator).
4. Export or save the graphic in a standard graphic format (e.g., EPS, TIFF)

ADDITIONAL INFORMATION

PageMaker can export or copy and paste imported graphics and text, but not drawn objects.

The Export Graphic command in PageMaker 6.5 enables you to export imported graphics in TIFF, JPEG, GIF89, or DCS format. It also enables you to pre-separate RGB images. The command is dimmed, however, for drawn objects and for imported graphics that are grouped with one or more objects or attached to a PageMaker-drawn object (e.g., frame, keyline).

EPS graphics, PDF files, and PMG files are object-oriented graphics; captured screen images are bitmap images.

The PS Group It Addition for PageMaker 5.0x groups objects by creating an EPS graphic of them, with a bitmap screen preview. You can place this group file into other PageMaker publications, or open it in drawing applications (e.g., Adobe Illustrator). PageMaker 6.x does not include a PS Group It Addition because grouping is fully integrated into the application.

PageMaker 6.0x or Earlier Libraries Don't Convert to PageMaker 6.5

ISSUE

When you open an object library created in Adobe PageMaker 6.0x or earlier, PageMaker 6.5 returns one of the following errors:

PageMaker 6.5 for Windows returns the error "The Library "[filename].pml" was created by an earlier version of PageMaker. You will not be able to place any of its data in PageMaker 6.5 documents. Do you want to open the library anyway?"

PageMaker 6.5 for the Macintosh returns the error "The library "[filename]" cannot be opened because it was created by an earlier version of PageMaker. Please use that version of PageMaker to open the library."

SOLUTION

Recreate the library in PageMaker 6.5:

1. In the version of PageMaker that created the library file (i.e., PageMaker 6.0x or 5.0x), create a new publication.
2. Choose Open Library from the Library palette's pop-up menu.
3. Drag all library objects onto the publication page, then save the publication.
4. In PageMaker 6.5, open the publication and then choose Window > Plug-In Palettes > Show Library.
5. Add the publication's objects to a new object library and then add keywords used in the original library.
6. Repeat steps 1-5 for other libraries you want to use in PageMaker 6.5.

ADDITIONAL INFORMATION

PageMaker transfers objects into libraries using its internal clipboard. Because the internal clipboard format PageMaker 6.5 uses is different from the one PageMaker 6.0x and earlier use, PageMaker 6.5 cannot use libraries created in PageMaker 6.0x or earlier.

When PageMaker 6.5 opens a PageMaker 6.0x or earlier publication, it converts graphics included in the publication, which you can then add to the Library palette in PageMaker 6.5.

Anchors and Sources Disappear from the Hyperlinks Palette after Using Undo in PageMaker 6.5

ISSUE

When you edit or delete text in the Adobe PageMaker 6.5 story editor, then use the Undo command to restore the text, anchors and sources in other stories in the publication no longer appear in the Hyperlinks palette. Anchors and sources in the story you were editing remain unchanged, as do hyperlinks in independent graphics or PageMaker-drawn objects.

SOLUTIONS

Update to PageMaker 6.51.

OR: Recreate the hyperlinks (i.e., anchors and sources) in the affected stories.

ADDITIONAL INFORMATION

PageMaker's Undo command restores a publication to the state it was in just before you performed the last action (e.g., added or deleted text). When you use the Undo command after deleting text in the story editor, the text should reappear and the rest of the publication should be unaffected. However, when you use the Undo command to restore deleted text in the story editor in PageMaker 6.5, sources and anchors in other stories in the publication no longer appear in the Hyperlinks palette, and cannot be recovered by reverting to the last saved version of the publication. Hyperlinks in the story you were editing remain unchanged, as do hyperlinks in independent graphics or PageMaker-drawn objects. When an anchor no longer appears in the Hyperlinks palette, related sources do not appear either.

Using the Undo command to restore deleted text in layout mode in PageMaker 6.5 does not affect hyperlinks. In PageMaker 6.51, you can use the Undo command to restore deleted text in either the story editor or in layout mode without affecting hyperlinks in the publication.

Can't Place Content into Master Page Frame from a Publication Page in PageMaker 6.5

ISSUE

When you place content into a frame in an Adobe PageMaker 6.5 publication, the text or graphic unexpectedly places outside of the frame. The frame is located on a master page.

SOLUTION

Copy the frame from the master page to a publication page, then add content to the frame:

1. In the Master Pages palette, click on a master-page icon to display the master page containing the text frame.
2. Select the text frame, then choose Edit > Copy.
3. Display a page to which you have assigned the master page.
4. Press Option (Macintosh) or Shift (Windows) while choosing Edit > Paste to paste the text frame in its original position (i.e., power paste) on the publication page.
5. Add content to the frame on the publication page.

ADDITIONAL INFORMATION

In PageMaker 6.5, you can use frames as placeholders for unplaced text. To add text to a frame, you can type directly into a frame, use the Attach Content command, or click a loaded text icon on top of a frame. However, you cannot add text to a frame that is located on a master page.

Frames Aren't Automatically Generated When You Flow Text in PageMaker 6.5

Issue When you flow text into a text frame in an Adobe PageMaker 6.5 publication, PageMaker does not generate additional text frames to accommodate text that does not fit into the frame.

SOLUTIONS

Create text frames manually, thread them together, then flow the unplaced text into them:

1. Select one of the Frame tools from the Tool box, then draw text frames in the desired locations on your publication pages. 2. With the pointer tool, select the text frame that contains the placed text.
3. Click the bottom windowshade handle of the selected text frame; the cursor will change to the Thread icon.
4. Click the text frame you want to be threaded to the first frame. The text will flow from the first frame to the next threaded frame.
5. Repeat steps 3-4 for each text frame into which you wish to flow the unplaced text. A plus sign at the bottom of a text frame indicates it's threaded.

ADDITIONAL INFORMATION

In PageMaker 6.5, text frames can be used as placeholders for unflowed text. Unless text frames are threaded, PageMaker won't flow text into more than one frame at a time. Once you have created text frames and threaded them together, you can easily flow text through them.

When you place text directly onto a publication page when Autoflow is selected, PageMaker automatically flows the placed text into threaded text blocks, generating additional publication pages if necessary to accommodate the placed text.

Non-Printing Objects Do Not Have Cyan Handles in PageMaker 6.5x.

ISSUE

When you select a non-printing object in Adobe PageMaker 6.5x, its handles are the same color as the target layer in the Layers palette. In PageMaker 6.0x, non-printing objects have cyan handles.

SOLUTIONS

Create a layer for non-printing objects, rather than using the Non-Printing command:

1. In PageMaker 6.5x, choose Window > Show Layers.
2. Choose New Layer from the Layers palette menu.
3. Enter a name for the layer in the Name text box (e.g., "non-printing objects"), and select a color (e.g., cyan) from the Selection Color pop-up menu, then click OK.
4. Move objects you do not want to print to the new layer. To move an object to the new layer, select the object, then drag the dot that appears on the right side of the Layers palette to the new layer.
5. Before creating or placing new objects that you do not want to print, make the non-printing layer the target layer by selecting it.
   note: The name of the target layer appears in the lower left corner of the Layers palette.
6. Before you print the publication, hide the layer of non-printing objects by clicking on the eye icon to the left of the layer name. When the eye icon is not visible, the layer is hidden and will not print.

OR: Determine whether an object is designated as non-printing by selecting the object, then choosing Element. If a checkmark appears to the left of the Non-Printing command, the object is non-printing.

ADDITIONAL INFORMATION

When you select a non-printing object in PageMaker 6.0x, it has cyan handles. However, because PageMaker 6.5x uses handle colors (e.g., cyan) to denote the layer with which an object is associated, it displays non-printing objects with the same handle color as other objects on its layer.

Layers are publication-wide, so hiding a layer on page 1 hides it throughout the publication, including master pages. When a layer appears on screen, objects associated with that layer also print; when a layer is hidden, its objects do not print. Assigning non-printing objects to a layer enables you to work with the objects on screen, but hide them before printing.

Transparent GIF Images Appear Opaque in HTML Document Exported from PageMaker 6.5

ISSUE

When you view a Hypertext Markup Language (HTML) document exported from Adobe PageMaker 6.5 in a Web browser (e.g., Netscape Navigator), GIF images that are supposed to be transparent appear opaque.

SOLUTION

Make sure the GIF images included in the publication are linked to the original transparent GIF images, then reexport your publication as HTML with the Downsample to 72 dpi option deselected in the Export HTML Options dialog box:

NOTE: PageMaker will overwrite the original transparent GIF images included in the PageMaker publication if the directory you specify for graphics in the Export HTML dialog box is the same directory in which the original transparent GIF images are located. If this has happened, open the GIF images in an image editing application (e.g., Adobe Photoshop 4.0), reapply transparency to them, then relink them in PageMaker before exporting your publication as HTML.

1. Open the PageMaker 6.5 publication and choose File > Links Manager.
2. Make sure the links to any GIF images you wish to appear transparent are up to date, then click OK. 3. Choose File > Export > HTML.
4. In the Export HTML dialog box, click Options.
5. Deselect Downsample to 72 dpi, then click OK.

ADDITIONAL INFORMATION

When you export HTML from PageMaker 6.5 with the Downsample to 72 dpi option selected in the Export HTML Options dialog box, PageMaker's HTML Export plug-in saves copies of the images included in the PageMaker publication into the location specified in the Export HTML dialog box. Because PageMaker's HTML Export plug-in does not support transparency, the copies of the GIF images it creates have a transparency value of "none." GIF images with a transparency value of "none" appear opaque when viewed in a browser. When you deselect the Downsample to 72 dpi option in the Export HTML Options dialog box before exporting HTML from PageMaker 6.5, the HTML Export plug-in will not create opaque copies of transparent GIF images included in the publication.

If the location specified for graphics in the Export HTML dialog box is the directory containing the original transparent GIF images used in the PageMaker publication, PageMaker's HTML Export plug-in will overwrite the transparent GIF images with opaque GIF images.

Unable to Edit Original When Graphic Is Attached to Frame in PageMaker 6.5

ISSUE

When you double-click on an OLE object attached to a frame in Adobe PageMaker 6.5, the OLE server application does not start. Or, when you hold down the Alt key (Windows) or Option key (Macintosh) while double-clicking a placed object attached to a frame in PageMaker 6.5, the application in which it was created does not start.

SYMPTOM

The Edit Original command is dimmed on the Edit menu when you select an object attached to a frame.

SOLUTIONS

Select the object independently of the frame before double-clicking it:

1. Subselect the object by holding down the Control key (Windows) or the Command key (Macintosh) while clicking the object with the pointer tool.

2. Hold down the Alt key (Windows) or the Option key (Macintosh) and double-click the object.

OR: Separate the object from the frame before double-clicking it:

1. Select the frame and its contents with the pointer tool.
2. Choose Element > Frame > Separate Content.
3. Double-click the OLE object, or hold down the Alt key (Windows) or the Option key (Macintosh) and double-click the object.
4. To reattach the object after you have edited it, select the frame and the object, then choose Element > Frame > Attach Content.

ADDITIONAL INFORMATION

In PageMaker 6.5 or earlier, you can edit linked graphics in their original applications by double-clicking them (OLE-linked graphics), or by holding down the Alt key (Windows) or the Option key (Macintosh) while double-clicking them (placed graphics). Because selecting an object attached to a frame also selects the frame, which cannot be a linked object, you must temporarily isolate the object from the frame before you can edit it in its original application. Subselecting the object enables you to edit the object without detaching and reattaching the contents to the frame. If your editing will change the size or shape of the graphic, you may want to separate the object from the frame, then reattach the edited object to a frame .

Wrong Layer Highlighted in Layers Palette When Using Text Tool in PageMaker 6.5

ISSUE

When you select text with the text tool in Adobe PageMaker 6.5, PageMaker does not highlight the text's layer in the Layers palette.

SOLUTION

Select the text object with the pointer tool.

ADDITIONAL INFORMATION

PageMaker's Layers palette assigns objects, but not text, to layers. When you select an object with the pointer tool, the object's handles display in its layer color and PageMaker highlights the layer to which it is assigned in the Layers palette. When you select text with the text tool, PageMaker is unable to display object information (e.g., layer assignment, text block window shade handles).

WINDOWS

Q Whenever I try to draw a rectangle or oval in PageMaker, I get a perfect square or circle—what's the deal?

A Normally, if you want to draw a perfect square or a perfect circle, you use the rectangle or ellipse tool while holding down the Shift key. If you're getting perfect squares and circles even when you don't have the Shift key held down, chances are your problem is being caused by an old driver (dated 1/11/93 or earlier) for a Logitech three-button mouse. To fix it, update the Logitech driver to version 6.24 or later. To do so, download the most current versions of MOUSE.COM and LMOUSE.DRV from the Logitech forum on CompuServe (type GO LOGITECH) or from Logitech's BBS (510-795-0408).

Q Whenever I open certain publications, I get the "PANOSE font matching results" dialog box, which tells me I'm missing a bunch of PostScript fonts in the document. Those fonts are available in other Windows applications, so what's wrong?

A Chances are nothing serious is wrong—your publication might need to be recomposed for the correct printer, you might need to reinstall a font, or you might need to make some other minor adjustment in PageMaker or Windows.

It's entirely possible that PageMaker would think certain PostScript fonts are missing even though they're installed and available in other applications. If you're using the Windows PostScript Driver (PSCRIPT.DRV) or one based on it, and you're using a version of ATM (Adobe Type Manager) prior to 3.0, PageMaker (as well as other Windows applications) won't necessarily recognize all the PostScript fonts installed in Windows—it will recognize only the PostScript fonts installed for PostScript devices on the printer port to which you're targeted.

Sound a bit confusing? Here's some more background information. When you use the Windows PostScript Driver (PSCRIPT.DRV) with a version of ATM prior to 3.0, the driver obtains information about what PostScript fonts are available by looking at the WIN.INI file's [PostScript,Port] section that corresponds to the printer port to which your target printer is attached. Therefore, if your PageMaker publication's "Compose to" printer (which is defined in its "Page setup" dialog box) is some PostScript printer on the LPT2 port, you'll only have access to the fonts listed in your WIN.INI file's [PostScript,LPT2] section. If the list in the LPT2 section is missing fonts installed under another section (for instance, the [PostScript,LPT1] section), and your publication requires those fonts, PageMaker will report them as missing via the "PANOSE font matching results" dialog box.

If you encounter this problem and need to bring back the "missing" fonts for a publication, follow these steps.

1. Open the publication that contains the "missing" fonts. When the "PANOSE font matching results" dialog box appears, allow it to make temporary font substitutions and click "OK."
2. In that publication's "Page setup" dialog box, select the PostScript printer to which your publication should be targeted (select whatever will be your final output device), and click "OK." If PageMaker asks whether you want to recompose your publication, click "OK."

If this doesn't solve your problem, it's possible that the PostScript "Compose to" printer you just selected also doesn't have available to it the fonts that you need. In that case, your best bet is to use ATM to reinstall those fonts.

If you're still missing fonts after reinstalling them and restarting PageMaker, your problem might have a more unusual cause. Try the following:

- See if the font you're "missing" is available on your system, but with a slightly different name. The "missing" font may be a version from another platform (and therefore might be spelled differently) or might be an updated version with a slightly different name.
- Use the Windows File Manager to search your hard drive(s) for WIN.INI files. You should have only one, it should be in your WINDOWS directory, and it shouldn't be larger than 32K. If you have WIN.INI files elsewhere, rename those extra files. Afterward, you may need to reinstall any fonts PageMaker still reports as missing. If your WIN.INI file is too big, try uninstalling fonts you don't use or ask your system administrator to help you reduce the size of your WIN.INI file.
- Exit PageMaker and rename or delete your PageMaker defaults file (if this file is damaged it can cause a variety of odd problems, including font-list anomalies). This file, called PM5.CNF, is located in the ALDUS\USENGLSH directory (or in another language subdirectory, such as the UKENGLSH subdirectory, of the ALDUS directory). Once you restart PageMaker, it will automatically generate a new one.
- Rename or delete the ATMFONTS.QLC file located in the PSFONTS directory and restart Windows. This file is an ATM configuration file that can trigger odd font-list problems if it becomes damaged. ATM will automatically create a new version of the file.

Q When I try to acquire an image in PageMaker 6.0, there's no data source listed in the "Select Source" dialog box. I don't have this problem in Photoshop, so what's going on?

A If you're able to select a data source and acquire images successfully in Photoshop, but can't in PageMaker, you might not be using the most up-to-date set of TWAIN system files (PageMaker requires a more recent set of TWAIN files than Photoshop does). Chances are you need to update one or more of these files.

To start troubleshooting, find the TWAIN.DLL file in your WINDOWS directory. It should be dated 9/11/95 or later. If it's not, you'll need to get a more current version of the file. It's available on the Adobe Bulletin Board System and the Adobe forums on America Online, CompuServe, and the Microsoft Network. (For information on how to use these services, see pages 106–7.) Look in the software-library sections of these forums for a file called "TWAIN.ZIP," then download it and decompress it with the PKUNZIP utility (also available on most online services). It'll expand into a TWAIN.DLL file that you should place in your WINDOWS directory. Restart PageMaker and try to acquire an image.

If you still can't select a data source, your data source (named with a ".DS" extension) might not be in the right place—16-bit data sources must be located in the TWAIN subdirectory under WINDOWS; 32-bit data sources should be located in the TWAIN_32 subdirectory under WINDOWS. If you're not sure whether your data source is 16-bit or 32-bit, check with your scanner manufacturer.

If you're sure your data source files are in the right place but you're still having problems, you'll need to do a bit more homework. Check your hard drive to make sure you have the following files installed and that their dates either match or are more recent than those we list.

In the PM6\RSRC\USENGLSH\PLUGINS directory:

```
ACQUIRE.ADD      10/1/95
```

In the WINDOWS directory:

```
TWAIN_32.DLL     10/11/95
TWUNK_16.EXE     10/19/95
TWUNK_32.EXE     10/19/95
```

(note: The TWAIN_32.DLL and TWAIN32.DLL files aren't the same thing—the latter is an older version that comes with certain programs such as Photoshop—so make sure you look specifically for the TWAIN_32.DLL file.) If you're missing one of these TWAIN-related files or have one that's not current enough, you can reinstall them from the PageMaker 6.0 diskettes or Deluxe CD. Here's how.

1. Make sure PageMaker, Photoshop, and any other programs that might use the TWAIN files aren't running, then find the TWAIN.DLL file in your WINDOWS directory (again, it should be dated 9/11/95 or later).
2. Rename TWAIN.DLL to something else—TWAIN.NEW, for instance. This step is critical because it will ensure that reinstalling other TWAIN files from the PageMaker diskettes or CD won't overwrite your up-to-date version of TWAIN.DLL (PageMaker 6.0 shipped with a version of TWAIN.DLL that isn't adequately up to date).
3. Launch the Setup.exe program (it's located on the "Installer—Disk 1" diskette or in the PM6 folder on the Deluxe CD).
4. When the Setup program prompts you to do so, select the language version you want to install.
5. In the "Type of Install" dialog box, click "Custom."
6. In the "Custom Installation" dialog box, select only the "PageMaker Plug-ins" option and click "Install."
7. From the list of Plug-ins the installer displays, select "Acquire Image" and click "OK." PageMaker will reinstall all the TWAIN-related files you need.
8. Look in your WINDOWS directory to see if PageMaker installed a copy of the TWAIN.DLL file—if it did, delete it (this version isn't current enough).
9. Find the file you renamed in step 2 and change its name back to TWAIN.DLL.

Following this procedure should solve your problem, but if it doesn't, there's one more thing you can try. Sometimes a corrupted defaults file can cause TWAIN-related problems, so try re-creating your PM6.CNF and PM6FLT.CNF files (they're located in your PM6\RSRC\USENGLSH directory). To do so, close PageMaker and rename those files. When you relaunch PageMaker, it'll automatically create new versions of both default files.

Q *(5.x only)* **I recently upgraded my Novell drivers to version 4.x. Now when our licensed users try to launch PageMaker, some get the message "A copy of PageMaker with network ID WPMxxx is already running." Do I need to reinstall or reconfigure my network software?**

A No. If you're using the Adobe version of PageMaker 5.0a, you probably just need to install a two-disk update available from Adobe. This update will eliminate NCD (network copy detection) errors in the following situations:

- When you're using Novell 4.0 with NDS (network directory service) in nonbindery emulation mode;
- If you have a laptop computer that has the Novell VLM drivers loaded, but isn't connected to a network;
- If you want to run PageMaker 5.0 with Personal Netware v. 1.0 or later or noncertified network software that isn't working properly with PageMaker's NCD feature; or
- When you're experiencing NCD errors in Windows 95 after installing Novell's newest 32-bit client software for Windows 95.

To receive this two-disk update, please contact Adobe technical support. Please note that there are other causes and solutions to NCD errors—for more information, see pages 78–81 in the May/June 1995 issue of Adobe Magazine.

Q Sometimes after I've been working in PageMaker, odd things start to happen—I start having strange printing problems, my fonts might look distorted, or sometimes I'll get system errors. I've noticed that this seems to correspond with my free system resources being a little low. Is that causing the problems?

A While there are many things that can cause memory-related problems in PageMaker or other Windows applications, what you're describing does sound like symptoms of low system resources. Here's a bit of information on what those resources are and how you can avoid problems caused by low system resources.

Windows sets aside a fixed portion of memory to handle certain tasks required by PageMaker and other Windows applications, including the display of menus, scroll bars, icons, and so on. This allocated portion of memory is called "system resources." When too much of this portion of memory is in use, Windows can begin to have difficulty managing these tasks, and you might start to see the sort of problems you describe—fonts may appear distorted, menus or other interface items might not display correctly, you might experience non-PostScript printing anomalies (for instance, items might drop off your page or print incorrectly), or system errors like General Protection Faults (Windows 3.1x) or Unhandled Exception Errors (Windows 95) may occur.

These problems can occur in any Windows 3.1x or Windows 95 application, although they tend to occur more frequently in Windows 3.1x because it doesn't set aside as much memory for system resources as Windows 95 does. To prevent problems caused by low system resources when you're using PageMaker (or any other major Windows application), we recommend you keep your free system resources above 50 percent.

To see the amount of free system resources you have, select "About Program Manager" from the Help menu in Windows 3.1x's Program Manager. Or, in Windows 95, you can right-mouse click on the "My Computer" icon, select "Properties," and then select the Performance tab. If you're running a bit low, here are a few things you can try in order to increase free system resources.

1. Close unneeded applications (every program you run uses some system resources). When you close some applications, they may not completely release the system resources they were using. If you run into this, you'll need to use the next step.
2. Restart Windows.
3. Reduce the number of fonts installed on your system.
4. Remove or disable extras like wallpaper, screen savers, and other items that might run in the background while you're working in Windows. Check your startup group for items that load when you start Windows.
5. For your video, try running in 8-bit color mode instead of 16-bit or a higher mode.

If the steps listed above don't do the trick, there are several things you can do within PageMaker to minimize system-resource usage.

1. Close palettes you aren't using.
2. Keep your file sizes small. Use the "Save As" function frequently, make a habit of storing complex graphics outside your publications, and use the "Book" feature to break up your publications whenever possible (see your PageMaker User Guide for more information).
3. When possible, use the "Place" command to bring in graphics and text instead of using the Clipboard.
4. Display your graphics as gray boxes if that won't interfere with your layout process. To do so, open the "Preferences" dialog box (our favorite way is by double-clicking on the pointer tool in the Toolbox) and select "Gray out" as the graphics-display option. This makes PageMaker display gray boxes where your placed graphics are (but of course they'll still print correctly). This setting can be changed on a document-by-document or application-wide basis.
5. Turn off scroll bars when possible. To do so, deselect "Show Scroll Bars" from the Guides and Rulers submenu of the Layout menu.

Can't Automatically Toggle Views by Right-Clicking in PageMaker 6.5

ISSUE
Right-clicking in Adobe PageMaker 6.5 activates a context-sensitive pop-up menu instead of toggling between the Fit in Window and Actual Size views, which right-clicking does in PageMaker 6.0x and earlier.

SOLUTIONS
Hold down the Shift key while right-clicking.
OR: Edit the registry to disable PageMaker's context-sensitive pop-up menu functionality for the right mouse button:

1. Create backup copies of the System.dat and User.dat files (i.e., registry files) in the Windows directory. To view the System.dat and User.dat files in Windows Explorer, choose View > Options, then select Show All Files.
2. Choose Start > Run.
3. Type "regedit" in the Open text box and click OK.
4. In the Registry Editor window, navigate to H_KEY_LOCAL_MACHINE\SOFTWARE\Adobe\PageMaker65-\[language directory]\PageMaker65.
5. Double-click on RightButtonZoom.
6. Enter 1 in the Value Data text box and click OK.

ADDITIONAL INFORMATION
PageMaker 6.5 uses the right mouse button to support Windows 95 and NT 4.0 context-sensitive pop-up menu functionality. For example, when you right-click on a publication page using the pointer tool, PageMaker 6.5 displays a pop-up menu with magnification options. When you right-click on a publication page using the text tool, PageMaker 6.5 displays a pop-up menu with Type menu commands (e.g., Paragraph, Style).

PageMaker 6.0x and earlier use the right mouse button to toggle between the Fit in Window and Actual Size views.

Can't Type Special or Extended Characters in PageMaker 6.5

ISSUE
When you press the Alt key and keys on the numeric keypad to type an extended character in Adobe PageMaker 6.5, no character appears.

SOLUTIONS
Press the Num Lock key on the numeric keypad to enable Num Lock.
OR: Edit your Config.sys file to enable Num Lock when you start your computer:

1. Make a back up copy of the Config.sys file, located at the root of your startup disk.
2. Open the Config.sys file in a text editor that can save in text-only format (e.g., Notepad, Windows Write).
3. Add the following line to the end of the file: numlock=on
4. Save the file in text-only mode, then restart the computer.

ADDITIONAL INFORMATION
The Num Lock key enables you to type numbers using the numeric keypad on your extended keyboard. When Num Lock is disabled, you can use the keys in the numeric keypad to navigate in a document (e.g. Page Down, End). By default, Num Lock is disabled when you start your computer.

Many Windows applications, including PageMaker 6.5, require Num Locks enabled when you press the Alt key and keys on the numeric keypad to type extended characters. In PageMaker 6.0x, you can type these extended characters regardless of whether Num Lock is enabled or disabled.

Cannot Resize Group That Includes Polygonal Text Frame in PageMaker 6.5

ISSUE
After you resize a group that includes a polygonal text frame in Adobe PageMaker 6.5, the text frame snaps back to its original size, the grouped objects disappear, or PageMaker freezes. The group was resized before.

SOLUTIONS
Update to PageMaker 6.51.
OR: Ungroup the objects, resize them, then regroup them:

1. Select the group with the pointer tool, then choose Element > Ungroup.
2. Resize the text frame and other objects.
3. Select the objects you want to group, then choose Element > Group.

ADDITIONAL INFORMATION
The second time you resize a group that contains a polygonal text frame in PageMaker 6.5, the group reverts to its previous size, the grouped objects disappear, or PageMaker freezes. This problem is corrected in PageMaker 6.51.

Keyboard Shortcuts in PageMaker 6.5x Start Other Applications

ISSUE
When you use a keyboard shortcut in Adobe PageMaker 6.5x, another application (e.g., Adobe Photoshop) opens. The keyboard shortcut includes the Ctl + Alt keys.

SOLUTION
Disable or reassign the Windows keyboard shortcut that starts the application:

1. Choose Start > Settings > Taskbar.
2. Click the Start Menu Programs tab, then click Advanced.
3. In the Exploring window, locate the application shortcut whose keyboard shortcut you want to change.

4. Select the application shortcut, then choose File > Properties.
5. Click the Shortcut tab.
6. Click an insertion point in the Shortcut Key field and then press Backspace to change the shortcut to None, or press the key combination you want for the new shortcut. To avoid changing the keyboard shortcut to another one that PageMaker uses, see the list of keyboard shortcuts in PageMaker's online help.
7. Restart Windows.

ADDITIONAL INFORMATION

You can create keyboard shortcuts using the Ctl + Alt keys to start an application in Windows 95 and Windows NT 4.0. In some applications, including PageMaker 6.5x, these shortcuts override the application's shortcuts. In PageMaker 6.5x, if you use a keyboard shortcut that also starts an application in Windows, that application starts.

No keyboard shortcuts in PageMaker 6.0x use the Ctrl + Alt keys.

Multiple Master Page Items Missing in PageMaker 6.0x Publications Converted to PageMaker 6.5

ISSUE

After you open an Adobe PageMaker 6.0x publication in PageMaker 6.5, multiple master pages are listed in the Master Pages palette as expected, but master page items are unexpectedly missing from publication pages, and one or more master pages cannot be selected or applied to publication pages. After you save the publication in PageMaker 6.5x, one or more multiple master pages are missing from the Master Pages palette.

SOLUTIONS

In PageMaker 6.0x, copy items from master pages to new publication pages, open the publication in PageMaker 6.5, then recreate the master pages:

1. In PageMaker 6.0x, open the publication and go to the last page.
2. Choose Layout > Insert Pages add as many new pages as you have master pages.
3. Display a master page, choose Edit > Select All, then Edit > Copy.
4. Turn to a new publication page, then press Option (Macintosh) or Shift (Windows) while choosing Edit > Paste to paste the master page contents in their original position (i.e., power paste) on the new publication page.
5. Repeat steps 3-4 for each master page.
6. Choose Window > Master Pages to display the Master Pages palette.
7. Remove each master page by selecting it and choosing Delete in the Master Pages palette, or by dragging it onto the Trash icon. When the message, "Delete master page "[xxxxx]" and all its contents?" appears, click Delete.
8. Save and close the PageMaker 6.0x publication.
9. Open the publication in PageMaker 6.5.
10. Turn to a new publication page, choose Edit > Select All, then Edit > Copy.
11. Choose Window > Show Master Pages.
12. Create a new master page by choosing New Master from the Master Pages palette Menu, or click the New Master icon.
13. Press Option (Macintosh) or Shift (Windows) while choosing Edit > Paste to paste the new publication page contents in their original position (i.e., power paste) on the new master page.
14. Repeat steps 10-13 until you have recreated all of your master pages.
15. Assign the new master pages to the appropriate publication pages.
16. Delete the new publication pages from the end of the publication. When the message, "Remove pages "[xxx-xx]" and all their contents?" appears, click Delete.

OR: Open the publication in PageMaker 6.0x for Macintosh, open it in PageMaker 6.5 for Macintosh, then open the converted publication in PageMaker 6.5 for Windows.

ADDITIONAL INFORMATION

When opening a PageMaker 6.0x publication, PageMaker 6.5 may flush master pages (e.g., master pages with images) from memory. After you convert a PageMaker 6.0x publication to PageMaker 6.5, master pages list as expected in the Master Pages palette, but items on the master pages are unexpectedly missing from the publication pages and the master pages cannot be selected or applied to publication pages. After you save the converted publication in PageMaker 6.5, master pages are no longer listed in the Master Pages palette.

PageMaker 6.5 converts publication pages as expected, and PageMaker 6.0x for Macintosh coverts both master pages and publication pages correctly.

No Context-Sensitive Pop-Up Menu for Frames in PageMaker 6.5

Adobe PageMaker 6.5 does not include a context-sensitive pop-up menu for frame options. When you right-click on a frame in a publication, PageMaker 6.5 displays a pop-up menu with options for PageMaker-drawn objects (i.e., Fill and Line menu options).

To access frame options in PageMaker 6.5, choose the desired option from the Element > Frame submenu.

Preview Option Unavailable in Export HTML Dialog Box in PageMaker 6.5 for Windows

ISSUE

When you export a publication in HTML from Adobe PageMaker 6.5 for Windows, the Choose a Background dialog box does not include a Show Preview option, as it does in PageMaker 6.5 for the Macintosh.

SOLUTIONS

Preview background images by opening them in an image editing application (e.g., Adobe Photoshop) or by placing them in a PageMaker publication.

OR: Export your publication in HTML from PageMaker 6.5 for the Macintosh.

ADDITIONAL INFORMATION

The Show Preview option in the Choose a Background dialog box in PageMaker 6.5 for the Macintosh displays a thumbnail preview of images, which you can use to preview images before selecting one as the background for your HTML document. PageMaker 6.5 for Windows does not include a Show Preview option in the Choose a Background Image dialog box.

Text Is Fuzzy On Screen in PageMaker 6.5

ISSUE

Text characters in Adobe PageMaker 6.5 appear fuzzy, smeared, or as if they have a gray ring around them on screen. The text prints as expected.

SOLUTION

Disable the Smooth Font Edges on Screen feature in Adobe Type Manager (ATM) 4.0:

1. Click the Settings tab in ATM.
2. Click Advanced.
3. Deselect Smooth Font Edges on Screen in the Type 1 Font Controls section of the Advanced Settings dialog box.
4. Click OK.
5. Exit ATM, then restart Windows

ADDITIONAL INFORMATION

When the Smooth Font Edges on Screen feature in ATM is enabled, ATM smoothes the edges of PostScript fonts on screen by fading the font color into the background color gradually (i.e., anti-aliasing). With some video resolutions, the anti-aliasing is not gradual, so the text may look fuzzy or as if it has a gray ring around it. Disabling the Smooth Font Edges on Screen feature causes ATM 4.0 to display PostScript text with clearly-defined edges.

MAC OS

Q Sometimes when I place a graphic, I get the message: "The document named '[filename]' was not created with the application program 'PageMaker.' To open the document, select an alternate program with or without translation." What's going on?

A You probably have the "Macintosh Easy Open" System Extension installed, and it's interfering with PageMaker's import process. Macintosh Easy Open comes with System 7.5. In addition, some applications such as DataVis MacLink Plus and Aldus Fetch 1.2 automatically put the Extension in your System when they are installed.

Macintosh Easy Open is a software Extension that allows a document to be opened when the application that created it is not available. Macintosh Easy Open also allows documents to be converted into another application's format without actually opening the document.

Unfortunately, Macintosh Easy Open sometimes interferes with PageMaker's import process. If you see this error message while importing, open the Macintosh Easy Open Setup Control Panel (called just Macintosh Easy Open in System 7.5) and either turn off the utility or deselect the "Always show choices" and "Include choices from servers" options (these options are called "Always show dialog box" and "Include applications on servers" in System 7.5).

Q *(6.0 only)* **When I open my PageMaker 5.0x publications in PageMaker 6.0, all I see is a solid black box where my pages used to be. What's wrong?**

A Nothing serious is wrong, even though it probably looks pretty bad. This problem occurs when you convert PageMaker 5.0x publications whose default color space is CMYK to PageMaker 6.0 while you're working on a black-and-white monitor or one that's set to display in black and white. Under these circumstances, PageMaker 6.0 incorrectly converts PageMaker 5.0's white "Paper" color definition to black—and that's why all your pages appear black. (PageMaker's "Paper" color is editable so you can make your pages display in the same color as whatever paper you'll be printing on. The "Paper" color does not affect printing.)

Fortunately, there are several ways to fix this problem. The easiest method is to use your "Monitors" Control Panel to switch from "Black & White" to a different display mode. Another way is to redefine your "Paper" color as white.

To do so, hold down your Command key and click on the "Paper" color in the Colors palette. When the "Edit Color" dialog box appears, select "RGB" from the "Model" pop-up menu. At this point make sure your red, green, and blue components are set to 255—which should equal white. If the color preview swatch in the dialog box still looks black, follow one extra step: set one of the color components to zero instead of 255, and then set it back to 255—that'll force your color-preview swatch to white (as in the illustration above). Click "OK" for the change to take effect.

Q *(6.0 only)* **I can't get the tracking values in PageMaker 6.0 to show any effect on my Power Macintosh. For instance, if I apply "Loose" or "Very Tight" tracking, the spacing of the text doesn't seem to change a bit. What's wrong?**

A This is a problem that occurs in PageMaker 6.0 on Power Macs when the Modern Memory Manager is turned off (when it's off, PageMaker cannot read the information in your "Tracking Values" file). To fix the problem, open your Memory Control Panel, turn on the "Modern Memory Manager" option, and restart your Power Mac—your text should track just fine afterward. Another way to solve the problem is to update to PageMaker 6.01.

The Modern Memory Manager is the Power Mac–native memory manager for System 7.x. Unless you're running an application or extension that is incompatible with it, Apple recommends leaving Modern Memory Manager on for the best possible performance. (When it's off, your Power Mac must run a non-native memory manager in 68K emulation, which will slow things down some.)

Tracking Too Loose, Too Tight, or Doesn't Change in PageMaker 6.0

ISSUE

After applying a track (e.g., Loose, Very Tight) to text in Adobe PageMaker 6.0 for the Power Macintosh, the character spacing of the text does not change or the tracking is tighter or looser than expected.

SOLUTIONS

Update to PageMaker 6.01.

OR: Turn on Modern Memory Manager in the Memory control panel, then restart the Macintosh.

ADDITIONAL INFORMATION

PageMaker accesses tracking information from the Tracking Values file. When Modern Memory Manager is disabled in the Memory control panel, PageMaker 6.0 is unable to read information in the Tracking Values file, and is unable to apply tracks to text. When Modern Memory Manager is enabled in the Memory control panel, PageMaker 6.0 reads information in the Tracking Values file and applies tracks to text as expected.

PageMaker 6.01 is able to read information in the Tracking Values file when Modern Memory Manager is either enabled or disabled.

Modern Memory Manager is the native PowerPC version of System 7.x Memory Manager. When Modern Memory Manager is disabled, the Memory Manager runs in emulation mode, instead of in native PowerPC mode, resulting in slower performance. Unless you are running an application or extension that is incompatible with Modern Memory Manager, Apple recommends leaving Modern Memory Manager on.

Converted PageMaker 5.0x Publication Pages Display Solid Black in PageMaker 6.0

ISSUE

Converted PageMaker 5.0x publication pages display solid black in Adobe PageMaker 6.0 on a monochrome monitor or on a monitor set to Black & White in the Monitors control panel.

SYMPTOMS

The "Paper" color swatch in the Colors palette is solid black instead of white.

SOLUTIONS

Update to PageMaker 6.01.

OR: Change the Monitors control panel setting to an option other than Black & White (e.g., 256, Millions).

OR: Edit the color "Paper" in the PageMaker 6.0 publication:

1. Choose Element > Define Colors.
2. Select "[Paper]," then click Edit.
3. Change the color model to RGB.
4. In the slider control for Red, click the left arrow once to change the "Paper" color to appear white.
5. Click the right arrow to change the value back to 255.
6. Click OK to close the Edit Color dialog box, then click OK to close the Define Colors dialog box.

OR: Before converting the PageMaker 5.0x publication, change the color model:

1. Open the PageMaker 5.0x publication in PageMaker 5.0x.
2. Choose Element > Define Colors.
3. Select the color "Paper" then click Edit.
4. Change the color model from CMYK to RGB, click OK, then save the publication.

OR: Use the PageMaker 5.0x DFLTCMSG.SWB file instead of the PageMaker 6.0 DFLTCMSG.SWB file when displaying PageMaker 6.0 publications:

1. Quit PageMaker 6.0.
2. Open the dfltcmsg folder in the SwitchB folder in the RSRC folder in the Adobe PageMaker 6.0 folder.
3. Rename the "DFLTCMSG.SWB" file to "DFLTCMSG-.PM6."
4. Rename the "DFLTCMSG.ALT" file to "DFLTCMSG-.SWB."

   NOTE: Using the PageMaker 5.0x DFLTCMSG.SWB file affects the algorithm used for color display in all PageMaker 6.0 publications.

ADDITIONAL INFORMATION

When a PageMaker 5.0x publication is saved after the last color model used to define a color is CMYK, PageMaker 6.0 reads the color "Paper" as a CMYK color when opening and converting the PageMaker 5.0x publication. To display color, PageMaker 6.0 uses the DFLTCMSG.SWB file to convert CMYK color values to RGB values. When a PageMaker 5.0x publication is saved after the last color model used to define a color is RGB, PageMaker 6.0 does not perform CMYK to RGB color conversions for display, so the "Paper" color appears as expected.

The "Paper" color is defined in CMYK as C=0, M=0, Y=0, K=0 and in RGB as R=255, G=255, B=255. When PageMaker 6.0 uses the DFLTCMSG.SWB file to convert the CMYK values for the color "Paper" to RGB values for display on a monochrome monitor, PageMaker uses zero for the red, blue, and green color values. R=0, G=0, B=0 is the RGB definition for the color black. Using the DFLTCMS-G.ALT file, PageMaker 6.0 correctly converts the CMYK values to the corresponding RGB color for the color "Paper."

PageMaker 6.0 installs both the DFLTCMSG.SWB and DFLTCMSG.ALT files. The DFLTCMSG.SWB file contains the new color display algorithm developed for PageMaker 6.0. The DFLTCMSG.ALT file contains the color display algorithm for PageMaker 5.0.

Converted PageMaker 5.0x publication pages display as expected in Adobe PageMaker 6.01 on a monochrome monitor or on a monitor set to display Black & White.

Languages Missing in Dictionary Editor Utility Included with PageMaker 6.5

ISSUE

The Dictionary Editor utility included with Adobe PageMaker 6.5 lists only 15 languages in the Language pop-up menu in its New Dictionary dialog box, regardless of how many language dictionaries you have installed.

SYMPTOM

The Catalans and US English dictionaries are not listed in the Language pop-up menu.

SOLUTION

Remove dictionaries you are not using, so that no more than 15 dictionaries are installed:

1. Quit Dictionary Editor.
2. Open the Proximity folder in the Linguistics folder in the RSRC folder in the Adobe PageMaker 6.5 folder.
3. Move dictionary folders that you do not require (e.g., Suomi, Svenska) to a different folder on your hard disk.
4. Restart Dictionary Editor.

ADDITIONAL INFORMATION

Using the Custom option in the PageMaker 6.5 installer, you can install up to 17 language dictionaries. Dictionary Editor for the Macintosh, however, can list only 15 languages in its Language pop-up menu.

Dictionary Editor for Windows lists all languages for which you have dictionaries installed.

Application Errors

MAC OS / WINDOWS

Q I'm getting an error that says I have exceeded the number of concurrent users permitted for this copy of PageMaker, but I know my copy is legal. What's wrong?

A If you receive this error message, either too many people on your network are using a single copy of PageMaker, or you might be running into a symptom of outdated Novell NetWare drivers.

Typically the error you're receiving occurs when more people are trying to run PageMaker than the license for that copy of PageMaker permits. PageMaker 5.0 uses Network Copy Detection (NCD) to record the number of people on the network who are using each copy of PageMaker—if that number exceeds the number permitted by the license, the user who most recently launched PageMaker will receive the error message, and will then have to close PageMaker (PageMaker lets you save your work before it closes).

If your company has purchased enough copies (or licenses) for all its PageMaker users and you're receiving this error message, it could be that the disk set used to install PageMaker on your computer was used to install PageMaker on too many other computers. (Someone in your company may have installed PageMaker from your disk set, mistakenly believing that entering a unique serial number during their installation would prevent NCD errors. However, it won't—NCD doesn't look at serial numbers, but at a unique network ID number embedded in each copy of PageMaker.)

To see your network ID number, select "About PageMaker..." from the Help menu (Windows) or Apple menu (Macintosh)—it'll be the number listed below your serial number. Following it is another number that indicates how many users are licensed to run that copy of PageMaker concurrently. When you receive an NCD error, make a note of that ID number and check with your colleagues to see who else has that ID and is therefore running your copy of PageMaker.

If you receive NCD errors when you and your colleagues are not exceeding the number of concurrent users permitted by your PageMaker license, and you're running the Windows version of PageMaker 5.0, your problem might be a symptom of outdated Novell NetWare VLM drivers.

Check the date of your NETWARE.DRV file in the WINDOWS\SYSTEM directory. If it's 11/24/93 or later, you should be using VLM drivers instead of IPX and NETX drivers. When PageMaker's NCD component queries the network for the name of the server and you're using a version of NetWare prior to 4.02 with the 11/24/93 NETWARE.DRV driver and the version 1.1 VLM drivers, the server returns the wrong information to PageMaker, causing it to report an NCD error.

If you're having this problem, update your NETWARE.DRV file to the version dated 9/22/94 or later and get the VLM drivers version 1.20 or later. These files can be found on Novell's forum on CompuServe. Type GO NOVFILES and download the WINUP9.TXT and DOSUP9.TXT files, which explain what other files you must download and what you should do with them to fix your network problems. If you don't have access to CompuServe, your local Novell reseller may be able to supply you with the files, or you can obtain them directly from Novell by calling (800) NETWARE.

Q *(6.0 only)* **I tried to drag an item from one of my Mac PageMaker 5.0 libraries into a 6.0 document, and I got the message "An error occurred in PageMaker. Cannot read the available Clipboard formats. Cannot paste one or more formats from Clipboard. ID = 6002." Can't I use my old libraries in PageMaker 6.0?**

A Yes and no. PageMaker 5.0x Library-palette libraries aren't compatible with PageMaker 6.0, so you can't use them directly. PageMaker transfers objects into libraries using its internal clipboard. Because the internal clipboard format changed between PageMaker 5.0x and 6.0, PageMaker 6.0 cannot read libraries created in PageMaker 5.0x. Libraries created in Mac PageMaker 5.0x will open in version 6.0, but when you drag a library object into a publication you'll get the error described above. In PageMaker 6.0 for Windows, you won't be able to open 5.0 libraries at all.

Fortunately, it's not too hard to manually reconstruct those libraries for PageMaker 6.0. Here's how.

1. In PageMaker 5.0x, create a new publication.
2. Open a PageMaker 5.0x library in the Library palette.
3. Drag all library objects into the publication, then save and close the publication.
4. Open the PageMaker 5.0x publication in version 6.0.
5. Add the publication objects to a new library, then add any keywords you used in the original library.

Q When I use "Build Booklet" in PageMaker 5.0, I sometimes get the message "Error 7215 Invalid state for requested operation." What's causing this? Will I have this problem in PageMaker 6.0?

A This error usually occurs in PageMaker 5.0x when one of the master pages contains a story with overset text (the tell-tale sign of overset text is a bottom windowshade handle with a red triangle, as in the illustration at left—this indicates that the story contains text that hasn't been flowed yet). To fix the problem, go to the master pages and locate the overset text (zooming out and doing a "Select All" with the pointer tool can help you find the culprit). Click on the red triangle and pull the windowshade handle down until there's no more story left to flow. Finally, save your publication and try using "Build Booklet" again.

Although PageMaker 6.0's "Build Booklet" Plug-in doesn't have a problem with overset text on master pages, you might still get this "Invalid state for requested operation" message. In 6.0 a common cause of this error is locked objects. If you use PageMaker 6.0 for Windows, make sure any master-page text blocks that contain page-number markers aren't locked if you want to use the "Build Booklet" Plug-in. On the Mac, make sure none of your objects are locked.

Q In the March/April issue of your magazine, you had a question about a Build Booklet problem in PageMaker where you receive the error "Invalid state for requested operation." I followed the instructions, but that hasn't solved my problem. What else could it be?

A If the problem isn't solved by checking for overset text or locked items—common reasons for the error you mention—then the publication may be too large, or it may contain at least one problematic graphic or text block on one of the pages. The best method of systematically troubleshooting this type of situation is to break the publication down into progressively smaller and smaller pieces until the problem element has been isolated. Here's a recipe for solving the thorniest of Build Booklet problems.

Step 1: Divide and conquer. First, divide the problem document into two equal halves. The easiest method of doing this is to make two copies (in Explorer, File Manager, or Finder) and remove half the pages from one copy, then the other. Run the Build Booklet Plug-in separately on each of the two new publications. If both halves work independently, it's likely that the size of the document was causing the error message. (This doesn't mean that there is a specific size limit when using Build Booklet; it means that Build Booklet makes interim copies of the file as it creates the new spread, and it needs two to three times the file's size in free disk space to function properly.) If one or both of the newly divided test copies of the publication fail, then proceed to the next step.

Step 2: Find the problem page(s). Divide the test publication(s) that failed into halves again, and run Build Booklet on each. Discard any file that runs Build Booklet without error; repeat the step with the files that fail. Do this until you have narrowed the problem down to the individual pages that don't work with Build Booklet.

Step 3: Isolate the problem element(s). Once you've found the problem page(s), look at the pages for common graphics, styles, or any other elements. Try to "jog" elements you suspect—for instance, change fonts, or relink, reimport, or recreate elements. Or just start dropping objects from the page(s), one by one, and running Build Booklet between each step (after having made a backup copy, of course). When Build Booklet runs on all pages, go to the backup and address problems with the deleted object(s). If the element is a graphic, try re-placing it into the document or, if necessary, re-export the graphic from the application that created it first. If the problem is with a PageMaker-created object, such as text or a shape, try re-creating the object.

Depending upon the size of the document, this can be an arduous process. However, it's relatively foolproof and practically guarantees that once you've reached the end, you'll have an answer to your problem.

Error "Bad record index" or Graphic Links Missing in PageMaker 6.0

ISSUE

The error "Cannot process publication's links. Internal error: Bad record index. 8401:20515" appears when choosing the Links command, or links are unexpectedly deleted in the Links dialog box in a PageMaker 6.0 publication.

SYMPTOMS

A diagnostic recompose (Option + Shift + Hyphenation) was performed on the publication.

One or more imported graphics are located on a master page, and the Link Options command for the graphics is dimmed.

SOLUTIONS

To prevent a "Bad record index" error from occurring or links from being deleted after you perform a diagnostic recompose, update to PageMaker 6.01.

OR: Move imported graphics from all master pages onto the pasteboard or publication pages, perform a diagnostic recompose (Option + Shift + Hyphenation), then relocate the imported graphics on the master pages.

OR: Delete then replace imported graphics located on master pages:

1. Create a backup copy of the publication.
2. Delete all imported graphics located on master pages.
3. Reimport the graphics, relocating the graphics on the publication's master pages.

ADDITIONAL INFORMATION

When you perform a diagnostic recompose in a PageMaker 6.0 publication, PageMaker deletes links to any imported graphics located on the master pages. After the graphic links have been deleted, PageMaker returns the error "Cannot process publication's links. Internal error: Bad record index. 8401:20515" when you choose the Links command, and the publication's file size does not decrease after you choose Save As or Save with the Smaller save preference selected.

Before you perform a diagnostic recompose in PageMaker 6.0, make a backup copy of the publication, then move imported graphics from the master pages onto the pasteboard or publication pages. After you perform the diagnostic recompose, relocate the imported graphic on the master pages.

PageMaker 6.01 does not delete links to imported graphics located on master pages when performing a diagnostic recompose.

Errors Using Build Booklet in PageMaker 6.0 Troubleshooting Guide

ISSUE

When you impose an Adobe PageMaker 6.0 publication using Build Booklet, PageMaker does not complete the imposition or returns an error.

SYMPTOMS

PageMaker 6.0 returns one of the following errors:

- "An error occurred in Build Booklet. 'Invalid state for requested operation.' Error number: 7215"
- Error: 7215 Invalid state for requested operation."
- "This program has performed an illegal operation and will be shut down."
- "Serious internal error"
- "An error occurred in Build Booklet. Object does not exist in pub or on current page(s). Error number: 7229"
- system error (e.g., Type 1, freeze)

SOLUTIONS

Do one or more of the following:

A. Use PageMaker 6.01.

OR: If running PageMaker 6.0 for Windows, unlock page-number markers on master pages.

OR: If running PageMaker 6.0 for the Macintosh, unlock all locked objects.

B. Increase the amount of available disk space by moving files to another volume or deleting them.

C. Move the publication and all linked objects to the local hard disk and then use Build Booklet.

D. For each graphic included in the publication, choose Element > Link Options, deselect Store Copy in Publication, and then choose File > Save As to save the publication to the hard disk.

E. Isolate and then remove or repair any damaged objects:

1. In the publication, choose Utilities > PageMaker Plug-ins > Build Booklet.
2. In the Build Booklet dialog box, select a page of the publication and then click Delete. Pages you delete in the Build Booklet dialog box are not included in the imposition, but remain unchanged in the original publication.
3. Repeat step 2 until you have deleted half of the pages from the imposition.
4. Select the desired imposition options and then click OK. If an error occurs during the imposition, the damaged object is on a page included in the imposition. If no error occurs, the object is on a page that was deleted.
5. Continue to decrease the number of pages imposed until you determine which page or pages contain a damaged object.
6. Remove and replace imported graphics, change fonts, or recreate PageMaker-drawn objects on pages that cause errors.

ADDITIONAL INFORMATION

When you create a booklet, the Build Booklet plug-in copies and pastes objects from the original publication into a new publication. If the plug-in is unable to copy and paste an object, it creates an incomplete imposition or causes PageMaker to return an error.

The Build Booklet plug-in included with PageMaker 6.0 for the Macintosh cannot copy and paste locked objects into a new publication, causing PageMaker to return the error "Invalid state for requested operation. Error 7215" each time the plug-in encounters a locked object in the original publication. The Build Booklet plug-in included with PageMaker 6.0 for Windows can paste all locked objects except for locked page number markers.

In PageMaker 6.01 for the Macintosh and Windows, the Build Booklet plug-in can paste locked objects from the original publication into a new publication.

When creating a booklet using the Build Booklet plug-in, PageMaker creates a temporary file that is three to four times the size of the publication being imposed.

You can unlock an individual object in PageMaker 6.0x by selecting it and choosing Arrange > Unlock. You can also unlock all objects in a publication using an unlock script. To use the script, deselect all items on the publication page and choose Windows > Scripts, then double-click the Unlock Objects On script (Macintosh) or Unlock Layout script (Windows).

Error When Running Add Cont'd Line Plug-in on a Frame With Text Attached in PageMaker 6.5

ISSUE

When you select a frame with text attached and choose Utilities > Plug-ins > Add Cont'd Line in Adobe PageMaker 6.5, PageMaker returns the error, "Plug-in error: Please select a single textblock with the pointer tool first. [8212] 9001:7225" (Macintosh) or "Please select a single textblock with the pointer tool first. [7212] 9001:7225" (Windows).

SOLUTION

Separate attached text from the frame, run the Add Cont'd Line plug-in on the separated text block, then reattach the text to the frame:

1. Select the frame with the pointer tool and choose Element > Frame > Separate Content.
2. Select the separated text block with the pointer tool.
3. Choose Utilities > Plug-ins > Add Cont'd Line.
4. Select the desired Continuation Notice option, then click OK.
5. Hold down the Shift key and select the text block and empty frame with the pointer tool.
6. Choose Element > Frame > Attach Content.

ADDITIONAL INFORMATION

The Add Cont'd Line plug-in can only be used on text blocks selected with the pointer tool. When you run Add Cont'd Line plug-in on a text frame, PageMaker 6.5 returns an error. Separating the attached text from the frame results in an empty frame, and a text block on which you can to run the Add Cont'd Line plug-in.

Error When Running Balance Columns Plug-in on Frame With Text Attached in PageMaker 6.5

ISSUE

When you select frames with attached text and choose Utilities > Plug-ins > Balance Columns in Adobe PageMaker 6.5 for Windows, PageMaker returns the error, "Text frames are not supported by Balance Columns. Cannot run Balance Columns."

After you click OK in the Balance Columns dialog box in PageMaker 6.5 for the Macintosh, PageMaker returns the error, "Plug-in error: Cannot run Balance Columns. Please select only text columns. [8225] 9001:7225."

SOLUTION

Separate the attached text from the frame, run the Balance Columns plug-in on the separated text block, then reattach the text to the frame:

1. Select the frame with the pointer tool and choose Element > Frame > Separate Content.
2. Select the separated text block with the pointer tool.
3. Choose Utilities > Plug-ins > Balance Columns.
4. Select the desired options, then click OK.
5. Hold down the Shift key and select the text block and empty frame from one of the columns with the pointer tool.
6. Choose Element > Frame > Attach Content. 7. Repeat steps 5-6 for each of the remaining columns.

ADDITIONAL INFORMATION

The Balance Columns plug-in can only be used on text blocks selected with the pointer tool. When you run Balance Columns plug-in on text frames, PageMaker 6.5 returns an error. Separating the attached text from the frames results in empty frames, and text blocks on which you can to run the Balance Column plug-in as expected.

Error When Running Headers & Footers Plug-in on Frame With Text Attached in PageMaker 6.5

ISSUE

When you select a frame with attached text and choose Utilities > Plug-ins > Running Headers & Footers in Adobe PageMaker 6.5, PageMaker returns the error, "Text Frames are not supported by Running Headers & Footers. Cannot run Running Headers & Footers." (Macintosh) or "You must select a text block before choosing Running Headers & Footers." (Windows).

SOLUTION

Separate the attached text from the frame, run the Running Headers & Footers plug-in on the separated text block, then reattach the text to the frame:

1. Select the frame with the pointer tool and choose Element > Frame > Separate Content.
2. Select the separated text block with the pointer tool.
3. Choose Utilities > Plug-ins > Running Headers & Footers.
4. In the Running Headers & Footers dialog box, select the desired options, then click OK.
5. Hold down the Shift key and select the text block and empty frame with the pointer tool.
6. Choose Element > Frame > Attach Content.

ADDITIONAL INFORMATION

The Running Headers & Footers plug-in can only be used on text blocks selected with the pointer tool. When you run Running Headers & Footers plug-in on a text frame, PageMaker 6.5 returns an error. Separating the attached text from the frame results in an empty frame, and a text block on which you can to run the Running Headers & Footers plug-in as expected.

Error When Running Script with Commands Separated by Semicolons in PageMaker 6.5

ISSUE

When you run a script that contains commands separated by a semicolon followed by a space character, Adobe PageMaker 6.5 returns the error, "Cannot recognize command. Error in script." (Macintosh) or "'Error in script. Parser can't recognize command.' Script not completed." (Windows). The script runs as expected in PageMaker 6.0x or earlier.

SOLUTION

Make sure each command in the script is on a separate line and that the commands are not separated by a semicolon followed by a space character:

1. In PageMaker 6.5, choose Window > Plug-in Palettes > Show Scripts to display the Scripts palette.
2. Press Command (Macintosh) or Ctrl (Windows) and click the script in the Scripts palette. Or, select the script and choose Edit Script from the Scripts palette menu.
3. In the Edit Script dialog box, select a semicolon and the following space character that separates two commands, then press Return to move the command that follows these character onto its own line. For example:
   If your script contains a line that reads:
   snaptoguides off; snaptorulers off
   Select both the semicolon and space character that separates the two commands, then press Return so the command reads:
   ```
   snaptoguides off
   snaptorulers off
   ```
4. Repeat step 3 for the remaining semicolon and space characters separating commands, then click OK.

ADDITIONAL INFORMATION

PageMaker does not support script commands separated by a semicolon followed by a space character. If you run a script that contains commands separated by a semicolon and space, PageMaker 6.5 returns the error, "Cannot recognize command. Error in script." (Macintosh) or "'Error in script. Parser can't recognize command.' Script not completed." (Windows).

None of the scripts included with PageMaker 6.x and earlier contain commands separated by semicolon and space characters.

Error "Can't Place this File..." or QuickTime Movies Unavailable When Placing QuickTime Movies in PageMaker 6.5

ISSUE

Adobe PageMaker 6.5 does not list any QuickTime movies in its Place dialog box. Or, when you place a QuickTime Movie into a PageMaker 6.5 publication, PageMaker returns the error, "Cant place this file. No filter found for the requested operation 8601:28962."

SOLUTIONS

Do one or more of the following:

A. Install PageMaker 6.5's QuickTime frame import filter from the PageMaker 6.5 software disks or CD-ROM. Then, delete the Pm65filt.cnf file, which is in the Rsrc folder in the Adobe PageMaker 6.5 folder (Macintosh) or in the Pm65\Rsrc\Usenglsh directory (Windows).
B. Install QuickTime 2.1 or later from the PageMaker 6.5 software disks or CD-ROM.
C. Verify the QuickTime movie you wish to place in PageMaker 6.5 is valid by playing it in a QuickTime player (e.g., MoviePlayer).

ADDITIONAL INFORMATION

To import QuickTime movies into PageMaker 6.5, PageMaker's QuickTime frame import filter and QuickTime 2.1 or later must be installed. When PageMaker 6.5 cannot locate QuickTime 2.1 or later or the QuickTime Frame import filter, it does not list QuickTime movies in its Place dialog box and doesn't enable you to place QuickTime files into a PageMaker publication.

When running PageMaker 6.5 on a Macintosh, make sure the QuickTime Frame Import PPC.flt (Power Macintosh only) or QuickTime Frame Import.flt (68k Macintosh only) file is located in the Filters folder in the Rsrc folder in the Adobe PageMaker 6.5 folder.

When running PageMaker 6.5 in Windows 95 or Windows NT 4.0, make sure the Qtimp.flt file is located in the Pm65\Rsrc\Usenglsh\Filters directory.

PageMaker stores information about which filters are installed in the Pm65filt.cnf file. If PageMaker cannot find the Pm65filt.cnf file when accessing filters, it creates a new one with current filter information. Renaming the Pm65filt.cnf file ensures PageMaker recognizes newly installed filters.

Unexpected Behavior or Error When Using Drop Cap Plug-in with Hyperlinked Text in PageMaker 6.5

ISSUE

When you use the Drop Cap plug-in on a paragraph in which the first character is hyperlinked in Adobe PageMaker 6.x, the second character in the selected paragraph unexpectedly becomes a drop cap (Windows), or PageMaker returns the error, "Plug-in error: Cannot complete Drop cap action. Inappropriate first character. [8225] 9001:7225." (Macintosh).

When you use the Drop Cap plug-in to remove a drop cap from hyperlinked text, PageMaker 6.5 for Windows returns the error, "Plug-in error: Cannot compete Drop cap action. Inappropriate first character. [7225] 9001:7225."

SOLUTIONS

In PageMaker 6.5 for Windows, remove the drop cap, remove the hyperlink applied to the text, run the Drop Cap plug-in, then recreate the hyperlink:

1. Click an insertion point anywhere in the paragraph that contains the drop cap you want to remove.
2. Choose Utilities > Plug-ins > Drop Cap.
3. Click Remove to reset the type attributes of the drop cap and remove the inserted tabs and line breaks, then click Close.
4. Select the hyperlinked text, then choose Delete "[name of hyperlink]" from the Hyperlinks palette menu.
5. Click an insertion point anywhere in the paragraph you want to begin with the drop cap.
6. Choose Utilities > Plug-ins > Drop Cap, specify the number of lines to wrap around the drop cap, then click OK.
7. Select the text you wish to specify as a hyperlink, then recreate the anchor or link using the Hyperlinks palette.

OR: In PageMaker 6.5 for Macintosh, remove the hyperlink applied to the text, run the Drop Cap plug-in, then recreate the hyperlink:

1. Select the hyperlinked text, then choose Delete "[name of hyperlink]" from the Hyperlinks palette menu.
2. Click an insertion point anywhere in the paragraph you want to begin with the drop cap.
3. Choose Utilities > Plug-ins > Drop Cap, specify the number of lines to wrap around the drop cap, then click OK.
4. Select the text you wish use as a hyperlink, then recreate the anchor or link using the Hyperlinks palette.

OR: Hyperlink all of the desired text, except the first character in a paragraph, before running the Drop Cap plug-in.

ADDITIONAL INFORMATION

When you hyperlink text, PageMaker 6.5 applies a special character trait to the first character of the hyperlinked text, which the Drop Cap plug-in does not recognize. If you run the Drop Cap plug-in on a paragraph in which the first character is hyperlinked, the Drop Cap plug-in in PageMaker 6.5 for Windows creates a drop cap of the first character in the paragraph it recognizes (i.e., the second character in the paragraph).

If you run the Drop Cap plug-in on a paragraph in which the first character is hyperlinked in PageMaker 6.5 for Macintosh, PageMaker does not create a drop cap and returns the error, "Plug-in error: Cannot complete Drop cap action. Inappropriate first character. [8225] 9001:7225."

Hyperlinking all of the desired text except the first character in a paragraph ensures the Drop Cap plug-in will create drop caps on that paragraph as expected

Error "Do not know how to place this file" Importing JPEG Graphic in PageMaker 6.0

ISSUE

When importing a JPEG graphic into Adobe PageMaker 6.0, the error "Do not know how to place this file." appears.

SYMPTOMS

The JPEG graphic was saved with lossless compression using Picture Press or the Storm Technologies plug-in in Adobe Photoshop.

SOLUTIONS

Resave the graphic in Photoshop using standard JPEG compression:

1. Open the graphic in Photoshop.
2. Choose File > Save As.
3. Select JPEG from the Format pop-up menu, then click Save.
4. In the JPEG Options dialog box, select the desired Image Quality option, then click OK.
5. Replace the graphic in PageMaker.

OR: Save the JPEG graphic in another format and replace it in PageMaker.

ADDITIONAL INFORMATION

Adobe PageMaker 6.0's JPEG filter does not support lossless compression. Standard JPEG compression is "lossy," which means it removes some of the original picture information when compressing an image. Picture Press and the Storm Technologies plug-in for Adobe Photoshop enable you to use "lossless" JPEG compression, which preserves the original image data so the image is the same after compression and decompression.

Alert "You are nearing the maximum number of hyperlinks..." in HTML Author Plug-in in PageMaker 6.0

ISSUE

When creating a hyperlink in an Adobe PageMaker 6.0 publication, the HTML Author plug-in returns the message "You are nearing the maximum number of hyperlinks allowed for a single PageMaker Publication. We suggest that you create multiple publications to reduce the number of hyperlinks per Publication."

SOLUTION

Split the publication into smaller publications, with no more than 50 hyperlinks in each publication, and use hyperlinks to link exported HTML pages to each other.

ADDITIONAL INFORMATION

PageMaker 6.0's HTML Author plug-in supports up to 50 hyperlinks per publication, not 500 hyperlinks per publication as stated in the Adobe PageMaker 6.0 User Guide.

When you create the 46th through 49th hyperlinks in a publication, the HTML Author plug-in returns the message "You are nearing the maximum number of hyperlinks allowed for a single PageMaker Publication. We suggest that you create multiple Publications to reduce the number of hyperlinks per Publication."

When you create the 50th hyperlink, the HTML Author plug-in returns the message "You have reached the maximum number of hyperlinks allowed for a single PageMaker Publication. You will not be able to create further hyperlinks in this publication unless you delete some of the existing ones first." After the 50th hyperlink is created, the Hyperlink option is dimmed in the Create Links pane of the HTML Author dialog box.

Error "Cannot place this file" When Placing CorelDRAW Graphic in PageMaker 6.0x

ISSUE

When you place a CorelDRAW 6.0x CDR file into an Adobe PageMaker 6.0x publication, PageMaker returns the error "Cannot place this file. Format of bitmap not supported. 8101:29731."

SOLUTIONS

Export the file from CorelDRAW in a graphic format other than CDR (e.g., TIFF, GIF, WMF, EMF).

OR: In CorelDRAW, remove the imported bitmap graphic or bitmap texture fill from the file, then resave the file in CDR format.

ADDITIONAL INFORMATION

When you place a CorelDRAW 6.0x CDR file that includes an imported bitmap image or bitmap texture fill into a PageMaker 6.0x publication, PageMaker returns the error "Cannot place this file. Format of bitmap not supported. 8101:29731". PageMaker's CDR import filter converts CorelDRAW 3.0 - 6.0 CDR files into Windows Metafiles (WMF) graphics. The CDR import filter cannot convert CDR files containing bitmap data into WMF graphics.

To determine whether a CorelDRAW file includes an imported bitmap graphic:

1. Open the file in CorelDRAW.
2. Select the selection tool from the tool palette.
3. Select objects in the graphic and read the description field below the horizontal color bars near the bottom of the screen. Objects described as a bitmap file format (e.g., TIFF, BMP, GIF) are imported bitmap graphics.

To determine whether a CorelDRAW file includes a bitmap texture fill:

1. Open the file in CorelDRAW.
2. Select the selection tool from the tool palette.
3. Select objects and look at the palette in the lower right corner of the screen. Objects for which the fill indicator displays a marble effect have been assigned a textured fill.

Error Opening or Running Build Booklet in PageMaker 6.0

ISSUE

When opening or running the Build Booklet plug-in, Adobe PageMaker 6.0 returns an error.

SYMPTOMS

When opening Build Booklet, PageMaker 6.0 for Windows returns the error "There are too many pages in the publication to use Build Booklet."

When opening Build Booklet, PageMaker 6.0 for the Macintosh returns the error "Build Booklet does not work with publications that have more than 499 pages."

When running Build Booklet, PageMaker 6.0 for the Macintosh returns the error "An error occurred in Build Booklet. Invalid command or query argument number 1. Cannot complete requested command. Error number: 7223."

When running Build Booklet, PageMaker 6.0 for Windows returns the error "Error: 7223: Cannot complete requested command. Invalid command or query argument number 1."

SOLUTIONS

Do one or more of the following:

A. Reduce the number of pages in the PageMaker publication to 499 or less.
B. Reduce the number of pages in the booked publications so the number of pages in the imposed publication does not exceed 499.

ADDITIONAL INFORMATION

You can create a single publication with up to 999 pages in PageMaker 6.0, but the Build Booklet plug-in can only impose up to 499 pages. When you open the Build Booklet plug-in in a publication with more than 499 pages, or when you run Build Booklet on a group of booked publications to create an imposed publication with more than 499 pages, PageMaker returns an error.

Alert "Warning: JPEG graphic type ..." When Exporting HTML Document from PageMaker 6.0

ISSUE

When you export an Adobe PageMaker 6.0 publication that contains JPEG graphics to HTML format using the HTML Author plug-in, the plug-in returns the alert "Warning: JPEG graphic type is not part of the HTML 2.0 standard."

SOLUTIONS

Ignore the alert when the HTML document will be viewed in a Web browser that supports the JPEG graphic format (e.g., Netscape Navigator).

OR: Replace JPEG graphics with GIF graphics before exporting your PageMaker publication to HTML format.

ADDITIONAL INFORMATION

The HTML 2.0 standard supports only the GIF graphic format. Because JPEG graphics are not supported by HTML 2.0, JPEG graphics only display as expected when viewed in Web browsers that support the JPEG graphic format (e.g., Netscape Navigator). Because the HTML Author plug-in assigns an image reference tag to graphics saved in unsupported formats when exporting the HTML document from PageMaker, graphics saved in a format that is not supported by the browser do not display, or display as a broken picture icon.

When exporting an HTML document containing a graphic format that is not GIF or JPEG (e.g., EPS, TIFF, PICT, WMF), the HTML Author plug-in returns the message "Graphic type currently not supported by HTML browsers."

Error "The directory was not found" When Applying Photoshop Effects in PageMaker 6.0

ISSUE

When you apply a Photoshop effect to a selected graphic in PageMaker 6.0 by choosing Element > Image > Photoshop Effects, PageMaker returns the error "The directory was not found." and does not apply the effect.

SOLUTION

Rename the folder containing the graphic selected in PageMaker to a name that doesn't include a period (.), replace the graphic in the PageMaker publication, then reapply the Photoshop Effect.

ADDITIONAL INFORMATION

PageMaker 6.0's Photoshop Effects command does not recognize directory (i.e., folder) names that include a period (.) in the name.

Photoshop Effects Plug-in is Slow, Returns Error, or Doesn't Apply Effect in PageMaker 6.0

ISSUE

After you apply an Adobe Photoshop Effect plug-in to a TIFF image in Adobe PageMaker 6.0, the plug-in runs slowly, fails to apply the effect, or returns the error, "Not enough memory to complete this operation."

SOLUTIONS

Reduce the size of the TIFF image to less than 1 MB in an image editing application (e.g., Adobe Photoshop). then replace it into PageMaker.

OR: Apply the effect to the TIFF image in an image editing application before placing it into PageMaker.

ADDITIONAL INFORMATION

Photoshop Effect plug-in filters may run slowly, fail, or return a memory error when you apply them to TIFF images larger than 1 MB in PageMaker 6.0. PageMaker does not have the special memory-handling features included in image editing applications (e.g., Adobe Photoshop) required to apply effects to TIFF images larger than 1 MB. Allocating more random-access memory (RAM) to PageMaker does not affect the performance of the Photoshop Effect plug-in filters.

The file size of TIFF images can be reduced by rescanning the graphic at a lower resolution or resampling the image to a lower resolution or resizing the image in an image editing application.

Reducing the dimensions of the graphic using PageMaker's cropping tool does not affect the size of the TIFF file.

Error "Could not start Rainbow Bridge" When Launching PageMaker 6.0x

ISSUE

When you launch Adobe PageMaker 6.0x, PageMaker returns the error "Could not start Rainbow Bridge: Error 30517.8601:30517." In Windows 3.1x, the error is preceded by the error "Could not load Adobe graphics geng32.dll."

SOLUTIONS

Do one or more of the following:

A. Make sure your computer meets or exceeds the minimum system requirements for running PageMaker 6.0x. For information on PageMaker's minimum system requirements, see Further Reading.

B. If you're using PageMaker 6.0x on a Macintosh, make sure you have enough memory allocated to PageMaker. When virtual memory is disabled, PageMaker 6.0x requires 6000K to 10,000K on a 68000-series Macintosh and 8000K to 12,000K on a Power Macintosh. When virtual memory is enabled, PageMaker 6.0x requires 4000K to 8000K on a 68000-series Macintosh and 6000K to 10,000K on a Power Macintosh. If you are working with large publications, PhotoCD images, or using color management, allocate even more memory to PageMaker if possible.

C. Make sure you have at least 25 MB to 40 MB of free hard disk space available for virtual memory and temporary files.

D. When Virtual Memory is enabled, make sure your Virtual Memory setting is specified at the amount recommended for your operating system. On the Macintosh, open your Memory control panel and make sure Virtual Memory is not set to more than twice your installed

RAM. In Windows 3.1x, open the 386 Enhanced Control Panel, click Virtual Memory, and make sure your virtual memory is set to at least 5 MB. In Windows 95, make sure Windows 95 is managing virtual memory by opening the System Control Panel, selecting the Performance tab, clicking Virtual Memory, then selecting the Let Windows Manage My Virtual Memory Settings option in the Virtual Memory dialog box.

E. Verify the Dfltcmsg.swb and Dfltcmsg.alt files are located in the Pm6\Rsrc\Switchb\Dfltcmsg directory (Windows) or in the Dfltcmsg folder in the SwithchB folder in the RSRC folder in the Adobe PageMaker 6.0 folder. Also make sure the files have the correct file sizes and dates (for the correct file sizes and dates, see Additional Information). If the files are missing or have incorrect file sizes and dates, reinstall them using the Single File Copy command in the PageMaker 6 Installer Utility (Windows), or by double-clicking them on disk 3 of the PageMaker 6.0x installation disk set or folder 3 on the PageMaker 6.0x Deluxe CD-ROM. After you reinstall the files, remove the Pm6.cnf file from the Pm6\Rsrc\Usenglsh directory (Windows), or remove the Adobe PageMaker 6.0P Prefs or Adobe PageMaker 6.0 Prefs from the Preferences folder in the System Folder (Macintosh).

F. Increase the amount of memory available to the system by disabling any programs or extensions (Macintosh) that automatically load during startup.

In Windows 3.1x, create a backup of the Win.ini file, remark out the "Load=" and "Run=" lines in the [Windows] section, then restart Windows:

1. Create a backup of the Win.ini file, located in the Windows directory.
2. Open the original Win.ini in a text editor that can save in text-only format (e.g., Notepad).
3. Insert a semicolon in front of the "Load=" and "Run=" lines in the [Windows] section to remark them out.
4. Save the Win.ini file in text-only format, then restart Windows.

In Windows 95, remove items from the StartUp menu:

1. At the Windows 95 Desktop, choose Start > Settings > Taskbar.
2. In the Taskbar Properties window, click the Start Menu Programs tab.
3. Click Remove.
4. Double-click the StartUp menu Icon, then click Remove.

On the Macintosh, remove any items from the Startup Items folder in the System Folder, then restart with extensions off. To turn all extensions off upon startup, restart the computer while holding the Shift key until the message "Welcome to Macintosh. Extensions Off." appears.

G. If you're using PageMaker for the Macintosh, rebuild the Desktop by holding down the Command and Option keys while restarting the computer. Keep the keys held down until you receive the message "Are you sure you want to rebuild the desktop file on the disk '[diskname]'? Comments in info windows will be lost." then click OK.

H. Verify the hard disk is not damaged or fragmented. In Windows 3.1x or Windows 95, run Scandisk and Defrag at DOS or another disk recovery utility (e.g., Norton Disk Doctor) or optimization utility (e.g., Norton Speed Disk). On the Macintosh, run the Disk First Aid utility included with your system software or another disk recovery utility (e.g., Norton Disk Doctor) and an disk optimization utility (e.g., Norton Speed Disk).

I. Restart with extensions off, then remove and reinstall PageMaker 6.0x:

1. Remove the Pm6.cnf file from the Pm6\Rsrc\Usenglsh directory (Windows), or remove the Adobe PageMaker 6.0 Prefs or Adobe PageMaker 6.0P Prefs file, located in the Preferences folder in the System Folder (Macintosh).
2. Move the publications you created out of the PM6 directory (Windows) or the Adobe PageMaker 6.0 folder (Macintosh), then delete the PageMaker directory or folder.
3. Disconnect any SCSI devices that you do not require for installation.
4. Restart your computer. On the Macintosh, restart with extensions off. If you're installing from a CD-ROM, turn off all extensions but those needed by your Apple CD-ROM drive using an extensions manager, or manually remove extensions and control panels from the System Folder.
5. Reinstall PageMaker 6.0x, then restart the computer.

J. If you're using a Macintosh on which Norton Disk Doubler was installed and then disabled, re-enable Disk Doubler or remove it, then reinstall PageMaker 6.0x.

K. If PageMaker 6.0x was installed to a compressed volume in Windows, remove PageMaker 6.0x, then reinstall it on a volume that is not compressed.

L. If you're launching PageMaker 6.0x from a shortcut (Windows 95) or an alias (Macintosh), delete then recreate the shortcut or alias, or launch PageMaker 6.0x from the application icon.

M. Disable any utilities that increase the amount of RAM available to your system (e.g., Connectix RAM Doubler, Quarterdeck MagnaRam 2).

ADDITIONAL INFORMATION

If you launch PageMaker 6.0x when there is not enough memory available, or when PageMaker, one or more of PageMaker's components, the system, or the hard disk is damaged or missing, or if there is a conflict that prevents one or more of PageMaker's components from loading, PageMaker returns the error "Could not start Rainbow Bridge: Error 30517. 8601:30517." In Windows 3.1x, the error is preceded by the error "Could not load Adobe graphics geng32.dll."

Rainbow Bridge is a component of PageMaker 6.0x that enables PageMaker 6.0x to access Color Management Software, and is one of the first components PageMaker loads when launching. Ensuring there is enough memory available to launch PageMaker and that PageMaker, one or more of PageMaker's components, the system, or the hard disk are not damaged, enables PageMaker to load Rainbow Bridge as expected.

Error "Cannot paste one or more formats..." Pasting from Excel in PageMaker 6.0x

ISSUE

After you choose Edit > Paste Special, select the Paste Link option in the Paste Special dialog box, and then click OK to paste cells selected from an Excel 5.0x or earlier worksheet into Adobe PageMaker 6.0x, PageMaker 6.0x returns one of the following errors:

"Cannot paste one or more formats from Clipboard. PageMaker cannot start the server application. Make sure there is enough memory and that the server is installed properly. 8203:6812."

"Cannot paste one or more formats from Clipboard. Cannot create the linked OLE object because no file exists for it. Save the server document and try again. 8203:6819."

"Cannot paste one or more formats from Clipboard. Internal error: can't retrieve Clipboard data. 8203:-6003."

SOLUTIONS

When you copy cells from a new unsaved Excel worksheet, choose File > Save to save the worksheet before copying selected cells.

OR: In Excel, select the desired cells, then choose Edit > Copy instead of pressing the Shift key and choosing Edit > Copy Picture.

OR: In PageMaker 6.0x, choose Edit > Paste Special, select PICT (Macintosh) or WMF (Windows) in the Paste Special dialog box, then click OK.

OR: When you are copying cells in a worksheet that was originally created in Excel 4.0, rename the worksheet in Excel 5.0 to match standard Excel 5.0 worksheet names (e.g., "worksheet 1"), making sure to remove any existing filename extension (e.g., ".xls").

ADDITIONAL INFORMATION

You can use PageMaker 6.0x's Paste Link option in the Paste Special dialog box to paste link OLE objects only. Before you can paste link an OLE object you must first save the source file (e.g., Excel file) from which you are copying. After you choose Edit > Paste Special, select the Paste Link option in the Paste Special dialog box, and then click OK to paste cells selected from an unsaved Excel 5.0x or earlier worksheet into PageMaker 6.0x, PageMaker 6.0x returns on of the following errors "Cannot paste one or more formats from Clipboard. Cannot create the linked OLE object because no file exists for it. Save the server document and try again. 8203:6819." or "Cannot paste one or more formats from Clipboard. Internal error: can't retrieve Clipboard data. 8203:6003." Saving the Excel worksheet before you copy selected cells to the clipboard enables you to paste link the worksheet as an OLE object in PageMaker 6.0x.

When you copy a worksheet to the clipboard in Excel 5.0x or earlier by choosing Edit > Copy Picture while pressing the Shift key, Excel copies selected cells to the clipboard as a PICT (Macintosh) or a Metafile (Windows) graphic and not as an OLE object. After you choose Edit > Paste Special, select the Paste Link option in the Paste Special dialog box, and then click OK to paste a graphic from clipboard in PageMaker 6.0x, PageMaker 6.0x returns the error "Cannot paste one or more formats from Clipboard. PageMaker cannot start the server application. Make sure there is enough memory and that the server is installed properly. 8203:6812."

Copying selected cells in an Excel worksheet by choosing Edit > Copy enables you to paste link the worksheet as an OLE object in PageMaker 6.0x. Choosing Edit > Paste Special, selecting PICT (Macintosh) or WMF (Windows) in the Paste Special dialog box, and then clicking OK to paste graphics from the clipboard enables you to paste the selected cells as a PICT or Metafile. Once you have pasted a PICT or Metafile, however, the pasted graphic is not linked to the file from which it was copied.

Excel 4.0 only supports one worksheet per file. Excel 5.0x supports multiple worksheets per file. When you open an Excel 4.0 worksheet in Excel 5.0x, Excel uses the filename of the Excel 4.0 file for the name of the converted worksheet. Changing the name of the converted worksheet in Excel 5.0x enables PageMaker 6.0x to recognize the worksheet as a worksheet within an Excel file rather than recognizing it as a separate Excel file.

Error "...Bad colormap..." When Placing Macromedia Xres Graphic into PageMaker 6.0x

ISSUE

When you place a Macromedia Xres 2.0 TIFF image or EPS graphic into an Adobe PageMaker 6.0x publication, PageMaker returns the error " Cannot place this file. Bad colormap - wrong number of entries."

SOLUTIONS

Open the original graphic in an image editing application (e.g., Adobe Photoshop), then save it with a new name.

OR: Place the Macromedia Xres 2.0 graphic into PageMaker 5.0x or earlier.

NOTE: If you convert a PageMaker 5.0x or earlier publication containing Xres graphics to PageMaker 6.0x and print color separations, the Xres graphics will separate as gray or black boxes.

ADDITIONAL INFORMATION

The TIFF (Tagged Image File Format) 6.0 specification defines the tags (i.e., fields) used to write and read TIFF images. Two tags, the colormap tag and the photometric-interpretation tag, specify the image's color lookup tables and color space (i.e., color model). In an Xres TIFF image, the value of the photometricinterpretation tag is incompatible with the value of the colormap tag.

When you place a TIFF image, PageMaker 6.0x reads all tags included in a TIFF image. When PageMaker 6.0x reads the photometricinterpretation tag, then reads the colormap tag, it reports "Cannot place this file. Bad colormap - wrong number of entries." When you import an Xres 2.0 EPS file that was saved with an 8-bit TIFF screen preview, PageMaker 6.0x reads the conflicting tags in the TIFF preview and reports "Cannot place this file. Bad colormap - wrong number of entries."

PageMaker 5.0x imports Xres 2.0 graphics without error because it does not read the colormap tag in the TIFF image.

Many image editing applications (e.g., Adobe Photoshop) save TIFF images with corresponding photometric-interpretation and colormap tags.

WINDOWS

Q When I open some of my publications, I get an error message that says PageMaker can't read from my CD-ROM drive. My publications aren't on a CD, so what's PageMaker doing?

A PageMaker's probably trying to find some TrueType fonts, and Windows is telling PageMaker they're on the CD-ROM drive. Chances are you installed those fonts from a CD, but didn't have the "Copy Fonts to Windows Directory" option (called "Copy fonts to Fonts folder" in Windows 95) selected in the "Add Fonts" dialog box at the time. And because of that, Windows didn't copy the TrueType fonts from the CD onto your hard drive.

To use your PageMaker publication, you'll need to make sure Windows doesn't try to read those fonts from a CD that isn't present. Here are your options:

Leave your fonts CD in the CD-ROM drive. This method might work fine as a temporary solution for the problem (assuming all the fonts you need are located on the same CD), but isn't a permanent one.

Disable your TrueType fonts. If you're using Windows 3.1, need a quick solution, and are willing to use substitute fonts for any TrueType fonts in your publication, try disabling all your TrueType fonts. To do so, double-click on the "Control Panel" icon in the Program Manager's "Main" group of icons, and double-click on "Fonts." In the "Fonts" dialog box, click on the "TrueType..." button. Then, in the "TrueType" dialog box, deselect the "Enable TrueType Fonts" option, and click "OK" in that dialog box and subsequent ones until you've exited the "Fonts" Control Panel. Exit and restart Windows. Unless you've disabled PageMaker's PANOSE font matching feature, the "PANOSE font matching results" dialog box should appear when you open your publication—it will list your missing TrueType fonts and give you the option to assign specific substitute fonts for them.

In Windows 95, there is no quick way to disable TrueType fonts. Instead, you can delete them. Instructions for doing so are listed below under "Remove and then reinstall your TrueType fonts (Windows 95)."

Remove and then reinstall your TrueType fonts (Windows 3.1). If you need a permanent solution to the problem, delete and then reinstall your TrueType fonts so they're located on your hard drive. What method you need to use depends on whether you're running Windows 3.1 or Windows 95—see the next section if you're using Windows 95.

Usually, to delete TrueType fonts from Windows 3.1 all you need to do is select them in the "Fonts" Control Panel and press the "Remove" button. This will work as long as Windows can locate your fonts (if it can't, Windows might give you a system error and freeze)—so, for the easiest fix possible, insert the CD that contains your TrueType fonts and, in the "Fonts" Control Panel, select the fonts you need to reinstall and press the "Remove" button. (If you receive the error message, "System Error. Cannot read from drive [your CD-ROM drive]," that probably indicates that one of the TrueType fonts you selected isn't on your CD-ROM. You'll need to reboot and manually remove your TrueType fonts using the method explained beginning in the next paragraph.) Once the fonts are removed, click on the "Add..." button. In the "Add Fonts" dialog box, make sure the "Copy Fonts to Windows Directory" option is checked, select the fonts you need from your CD, and click "Add."

If you no longer have the CD that contains the TrueType fonts you need and you're using Windows 3.1, you won't be able to reinstall those fonts and you must manually remove them. Here's how.

1. Make a backup copy of your WIN.INI file, then open it in an application, such as the Windows Notepad, that can save in text-only format.
2. Find the section that begins with the line "[fonts]." This section lists all your TrueType and Windows screen fonts.
3. Locate any TrueType lines (they end in .FOT extensions) that refer to fonts you installed from CDs but did not copy to the hard drive. Delete those lines or disable them by inserting a semicolon (;) in front of them.
4. Save the WIN.INI file in text-only format and close it.
5. Restart Windows.

Remove then reinstall your TrueType fonts (Windows 95). To remove TrueType fonts in Windows 95, open the "Fonts" Control Panel by selecting "Control Panel" from the Settings submenu of the Start menu on the Taskbar. In the "Control Panel" window, double-click on the "Fonts" icon to open your Fonts folder window, which lists all your TrueType and Windows screen fonts. It should be easy to pick out any TrueType fonts you installed from a CD without copying them to your hard drive—they should have "shortcut" icons (icons with arrows in their bottom left corners). Select them and press the delete key. When Windows asks whether you want to delete your fonts, click "Yes."

To reinstall your fonts, insert the CD in your CD-ROM drive, then select "Install New Font..." from your "Fonts" folder window's File menu. In the "Add Fonts" dialog box, make sure the "Copy fonts to Fonts folder" option is checked, navigate to whatever folder on your CD-ROM drive contains your fonts, select them, and click "OK."

Q I just installed Windows 95 and reinstalled PageMaker. Now I can't open it without getting the error "Cannot start PageMaker, unable to load icon DLL for this screen. 7527:6622." Am I missing a file?

A No, you're probably not missing anything. This error happens when PageMaker 5.0x or 6.0 is unable to process the system's font information, possibly because you have damaged fonts, a damaged "Fonts" folder, damaged Windows 95 Registry entries, or too many fonts or Registry entries.

Such problems are sometimes caused by installing TrueType fonts with a third-party (non-Microsoft) font-management or -installation utility such as FontMaster 6.0, which ships with CorelDraw! 6.0. According to Corel, there are differences between the way their FontMaster 6.0 utility copies and registers fonts and how the Windows 95 "Fonts" Control Panel performs these tasks. Corel and Microsoft recommend using the Windows 95 "Fonts" Control Panel to install TrueType fonts—especially for users who want to keep a large number of TrueType fonts on their systems. (Corel reports that users who have installed more than 800 fonts using a third-party font-installation utility have experienced erratic system behavior such as difficulty installing additional fonts, the appearance of unusual Desktop and title-bar fonts, incorrect reporting of the number of installed fonts by the "Fonts" Control Panel, and problems launching some programs such as PageMaker.)

Here are a few things you can try in order to get PageMaker to launch.

Restart the computer. Sometimes this will clear up small problems with the "Fonts" folder and Desktop.

Reduce the number of TrueType fonts in your "Fonts" folder. Although Windows 95 doesn't have any fixed limit on the number of fonts you can install, each system has its own practical limit. How many fonts you can install without compromising the stability of your system will depend on how much space you have available on your hard disk, how much RAM you have, the number of applications you run simultaneously, which applications you use, and other factors. To find out how many fonts your system can handle, you may need to experiment. Here's how to remove TrueType fonts.

1. Open the "Fonts" Control Panel by selecting "Control Panel" from the Settings submenu of Windows 95's Start menu and double-clicking on the "Fonts" folder shortcut icon in the Control Panel window.
2. In the "Fonts" Control Panel, remove TrueType fonts by dragging them to another folder. You can also delete them by pressing the Delete key or dragging them to the Recycle Bin, but make sure you have the font files somewhere else before you do so. (If you used a third-party utility to install the fonts, you may be able to remove them with the same utility—consult its documentation for instructions.) You may find it easier to identify the right fonts to remove if you display them in alphabetical order and with file details. To do so, select "Details" from the View menu in the "Fonts" Control Panel.

When you remove TrueType fonts, be careful not to remove the Windows 95 standard fonts, which may be needed by Windows 95 or PageMaker. (A complete list of these fonts is pictured on the previous page.)

Reinstall fonts originally installed with a third-party utility. If you're using a third-party font-installation utility such as FontMaster 6.0, remove any fonts you installed with that utility and reinstall them using the Windows 95 "Fonts" Control Panel. To do so, use the technique described above for removing fonts. Then, in the "Fonts" Control Panel, select "Install New Font..." from the File menu. In the "Add Fonts" dialog box, navigate to the directory that contains the font files, select the fonts you wish to install, and click "OK."

Q *(6.0 only)* **When I run PageMaker 6.0 under Windows 95 I often get "Invalid Page Fault" errors in module KERNEL32.DLL (the error messages cite a variety of memory addresses). What's going on?**

A Those "Page Fault" errors indicate a memory-related or similar problem. They can (and do) occur in a variety of Windows applications. Although Adobe technical support has not been able to isolate the exact cause of these errors, there are several things you can do to get rid of them.

Most of these troubleshooting steps involve memory-management "housecleaning"—cutting back on the number of fonts you have installed, making sure you have a valid temporary-file directory, making more RAM available, checking certain PageMaker settings and files, and so forth. For a complete list of steps you take to eliminate "Invalid Page Fault" errors, send an E-mail with the subject header "316314" to techdocs@adobe.com, or call the FaxYI system and request document 316314.

Error "Kernel32.dll" in PageMaker 6.0 Troubleshooting Guide

ISSUE

When you open or work in an Adobe PageMaker 6.x publication in Windows 95, the system returns the error "PageMaker ... caused an Invalid Page Fault in module Kernel-32.dll." One of the following addresses is included in the error:

0137:BFF9A28C
0137:BFF858FL
014F:BFF9A28C
0137:BFF858CD

014F:BFF858ED
00001:01FEBLLE

SOLUTIONS

If the error occurs when you open a particular publication, repair the publication by placing its stories into a new publication:

1. In PageMaker, choose File > New.
2. Click OK in the Document Setup dialog box.
3. Choose File > Place.
4. In the Place dialog box, select the publication that will not open, then click Open.
5. In the PageMaker 6.0 Story Importer dialog box, click Select All, then click OK.
6. Close the new publication without saving it.
7. Open the original publication.

NOTE: PageMaker 6.5 does not include a story import filter for PageMaker 6.5 publications.

OR: If the error occurs when you work in a particular publication, the publication may be damaged. Recreate the publication or remove damaged objects or pages from it. For instructions, see document 115303 (Damaged Publication Troubleshooting Guide), available from Adobe FaxYI, the Adobe BBS, Adobe Techdocs e-mail, and Adobe's Technical Solutions database on the World Wide Web.

OR: If the error occurs when working in more than one publication, do one or more of the following:

A. Restart Windows and press the F8 key when "Starting Windows 95" displays, then select Safe Mode from the startup menu. If the error does not occur after starting Windows in Safe Mode, one or more device drivers loading into Windows (e.g., mouse driver, video driver) is causing the error. For information on updating a device driver, contact the device manufacturer.
B. If you are using QEMM 8.0, disable it and use Himem.sys as the memory manager. For instructions, see Additional Information.
C. Increase Windows system resources to 55% or greater. To check system resources, right-click on the My Computer icon, then select the Performance tab. For instructions on increasing system resources, see Additional Information.
D. Reduce the number of fonts installed in Windows 95, including Type 1 and TrueType fonts, to 100 or fewer. For instructions, see Additional Information.
E. Use the Windows Standard VGA video driver. If the error does not occur when you use the VGA video driver, contact your video card manufacturer for a Windows 95-compatible video driver. For instructions on specifying the Windows Standard VGA video driver, see Additional Information.
F. Delete or rename the Pm65.cnf file in the Pm65\Rsrc\Usenglsh directory (PageMaker 6.5) or the Pm6.cnf file in the Pm6\Rsrc\Usenglsh directory (PageMaker 6.0x).
G. Make sure there is a valid temporary directory on the system and sufficient hard disk space. By default, Windows 95 creates a temporary directory in the Windows directory. PageMaker requires three to five times the size of the publication in available hard disk space.
H. Exit all applications, then use the Windows Explorer to delete all temporary (*.tmp) files.
I. Make sure there is at least 25 MB of free hard disk space available for Windows 95 to manage virtual memory.
J. Reduce the file size of the Win.ini file to 32K or smaller:
   1. Make a backup copy of the Win.ini file, located in the Windows directory.
   2. Open the original Win.ini file in a text editor that can save in text-only format (e.g., WordPad).
   3. Remove unnecessary lines (e.g., unneeded font entries) and sections. For assistance reducing the size of your Win.ini file, refer to your Windows documentation or contact Microsoft Technical Support.
   4. Save the file in text-only format, then restart Windows.
K. Move font shortcut icons that are not linked to font files out of your Fonts folder to another location (e.g., a temporary folder on the desktop), then restart Windows. To determine whether a font shortcut icon is linked to a font, see Additional Information.
L. Obtain the updated Kernel32.dll file from Microsoft (dated 2/2/96) and install it in your Windows\System directory.
M. Reinstall Windows 95 from your original Windows 95 CD-ROM or installation disks.

ADDITIONAL INFORMATION

Windows 95 returns an Invalid Page Fault in module Kernel-32.dll error when a conflict or illegal operation occurs.

The Kernel, one of the three Windows 95 core components, provides base operating system functionality, including input/output services, virtual memory management, and task scheduling. When you launch an application, the Kernel loads the *.exe and *.dll files for the application, then schedules and runs threads of each process owned by the application. When an application requires software outside of the normal flow of control (i.e., an exception occurs), the Kernel communicates that exception to the application so it can resolve the exception. The Kernel resolves import references and supports demand paging for the application. Using a process called thunking to convert 16-bit code to 32-bit code, the Kernel provides base system functionality to both 16-bit and 32-bit applications. The Kernel32.dll file (411,136 bytes, version 4.00.950) is located in the Windows\System directory.

Starting Windows 95 in Safe Mode bypasses startup files, including the Registry, Config.sys, Autoexec.bat, and [Boot] and [386Enh] sections of the System.ini file. When Windows 95 starts in Safe Mode, only the mouse, keyboard, and standard VGA device drivers are loaded, but you have access to Windows 95 configuration files so you can make any necessary configuration changes and then restart Windows 95 normally. If an error no longer occurs in Safe Mode, you can isolate the conflicting driver by choosing the Step-By-Step Confirmation option in the startup menu (which displays when you restart and press F8) to load particular device drivers. For information on updating a device driver, contact the device manufacturer.

Some font installer utilities create font file shortcuts in the Fonts folder. If a shortcut points to a path that no longer exists, an Invalid Page Fault in module Kernel32.dll occurs.

DISABLING QEMM 8.0 AND ENABLING HIMEM.SYS

To disable QEMM 8.0 and use Himem.sys as the memory manager:

1. Make a backup copy of the Config.sys file, located at the root directory of the C: drive (i.e., C:\Config.sys).
2. In Explorer, note the location of the Himem.sys file with the most recent date.
3. Open the Config.sys file in a text editor that can save in text-only format (e.g., Notepad, WordPad).
4. Locate the line that reads:
   DEVICE=QEMM386
5. Type "REM" in front of the "DEVICE=QEMM386" line to prevent the system from reading the line (i.e., remark out). For example:
   REM DEVICE=QEMM386
6. Type the following text below the "REM DEVICE-=QEMM386" line:
   `DEVICE=C:\WINDOWS\HIMEM.SYS`
   where C:\Windows\Himem.sys is the path to the Himem.sys file with the most recent date on your hard drive.
7. Save the Config.sys file in text-only format, then restart the computer.

INCREASING WINDOWS SYSTEM RESOURCES

To increase Windows system resources to 55% or greater, do one or more of the following:

A. Close all applications.

B. Let Windows 95 manage virtual memory settings:
1. Choose Start > Settings > Control Panel.
2. Double-click the System icon, then select the Performance tab in the System Properties dialog box.
3. Click Virtual Memory.
4. Select the Let Windows Manage My Virtual Memory Settings (Recommended) option, then click OK.
5. Click OK to close the System Properties dialog box, then close the Control Panel.

C. Remove items from the StartUp group:
1. Choose Start > Settings > Taskbar.
2. Select the Start Menu Programs tab in the Taskbar Properties dialog box.
3. Click Remove.
4. In the Remove Shortcuts/Folders dialog box, double-click the StartUp folder.
5. Select each item in the StartUp folder, then click Remove.
6. Click Close, then click OK to exit the Taskbar Properties dialog box.

D. Remark out the Load and Run lines in the Win.ini file:
1. Open the Win.ini file in a text editor that can save in text-only format (e.g., Windows Notepad, WordPad).
2. In the [Windows] section, locate the lines that begin with "Load=" and "Run=."
3. Insert a semicolon (;) at the beginning of the "Load=" line and at the beginning of the "Run=" line to disable the applications listed in those lines.
4. Save the Win.ini file in text-only format, then restart Windows.

E. Disable Adobe Type Manager (ATM) and other utilities.

F. Restart Windows.

REMOVING TRUETYPE FONTS

To remove TrueType fonts in Windows 95:

1. Choose Start > Settings > Control Panel.
2. Double-click the Fonts icon.
3. Select font icons, then delete them or move them to another location (e.g., a temporary folder on the desktop).
4. Restart Windows.

NOTE: Do not remove the TrueType fonts installed by Windows 95, which include:

Arial	*MS Serif 8,10,12,14,18,24*
Arial Bold	*Small Fonts*
Arial Bold Italic	*Symbol*
Arial Italic	*Symbol 8,10,12,14,18,24*
Courier 10,12,15	*Times New Roman*
Courier New	*Times New Roman Bold*
Courier New Bold	*Times New Roman Bold Italic*
Courier New Bold Italic	*Modern.fon*
Courier New Italic	*Times New Roman Italic*
Modern	*WingDings*
MS Sans Serif 8,10,12,14,18,24	

NOTE: Windows 95 also installs several hidden font files (e.g., Marlett.ttf, Dosapp.fon, Vgafix.fon, etc.), which do not display in Windows Explorer or in the Fonts Control Panel, but may display in font management utilities (e.g., Ares FontMinder). Windows requires these hidden font files to run. Do not delete them or remove them from the Fonts directory.

REMOVING POSTSCRIPT FONTS

To disable PostScript fonts in Windows 95, turn off ATM, or remove individual fonts in ATM.

To remove fonts in ATM Deluxe 4.0 or ATM 4.0:

1. If you're using ATM Deluxe 4.0, export your font sets so you can reimport them after re-adding the fonts, rather than recreating the sets. For instructions, see Related Records.
2. Open ATM and click the Sets tab (ATM Deluxe 4.0) or Fonts tab (ATM 4.0).
3. Select the fonts you want to remove from the All Font Sets scrollbox and click Remove.
4. In the Remove Font dialog box, select Remove Fonts from the All Set and Master Font List, and select Remove Font Files from Disk if you are reinstalling fonts from the original installation disks. Then click Yes or Yes to All.

To remove fonts in ATM 3.0x:

1. In the ATM Control Panel, select all the installed fonts from the Installed ATM Fonts list.
2. Click Remove.
3. In the Remove Fonts dialog box, select No Confirmation to Remove Fonts if you don't want a warning dialog box to appear for each font you remove, then click Yes or Yes to All. Do not select Delete Fonts from Disk unless you want to delete the font files from your system.

Identifying Font Shortcut Icons

To determine whether a file is a font file:

1. Choose Start > Settings > Control Panel.
2. Double-click the Fonts icon.
3. Choose View > Large Icons. Icons that display an arrow are font shortcut icons.
4. Double-click on each font shortcut icon. If no font information displays, the font shortcut icon is not linked to a font.

Specifying the Standard VGA Driver

To specify the Windows Standard VGA driver in Windows 95:

1. Right-click on the desktop, then select Properties from the pop-up menu.
2. In the Display Properties dialog box, click on the Settings tab, then click the Change Display Type button.
3. Note the selected Adapter Type, then click Change.
4. In the Select Device dialog box, select the Show All Devices option.
5. Select Standard Display Types from the top of the Manufacturers scroll box.
6. Select Standard Display Adapter (VGA) from the Models scroll box, then click OK.
7. Note the selected Monitor Type, then click Change.
8. In the Select Device dialog box, select Show All Devices.
9. Select Standard Monitor Types from the top of the Manufacturers scroll box.
10. Select Standard VGA 640x480 from the Models scroll box, then click OK.
11. Restart Windows 95.

Win32s Errors in PageMaker 6.0x Troubleshooting Guide

ISSUE

When you run Adobe PageMaker 6.0x in Windows 3.1x, Windows returns the error "Win32s error," "Application error," or "Unexpected DOS -21error."

SOLUTIONS

Do one or more of the following:

A. Make sure you have at least 10 MB of RAM, the minimum requirement for running PageMaker 6.0x in Windows 3.1x.

B. Verify that the Windows\System directory has a Win32s subdirectory. If the Win32s directory is missing, reinstall the Win32s components from your PageMaker 6.0x installation disk set or CD-ROM. For instructions, refer to document 316411, "Removing and Reinstalling Win32s Components for PageMaker 6.0," available from Adobe FaxYI, the Adobe BBS, Adobe Techdocs e-mail, and the Adobe Technical Solutions database on the World Wide Web.

C. Install Win32s 1.3a (i.e., 1.30.167.0) or later:

1. Open the Win32s.ini file, located in the Windows\-System directory, in a text editor that can save in text-only format (e.g., Windows Write, Notepad).
2. Locate the version line in the [Win32s] section. For example:

```
[Win32s]
Version=1.30.167.0
```

3. If the version number is lower than 1.30.167.0, remove the Win32s components and install the version included with PageMaker 6.0x. For instructions, refer to document 316411, "Removing and Reinstalling Win32s Components for PageMaker 6.0."

D. Search the entire startup disk (i.e, the one that contains the Windows\System directory) for older versions or duplicates of Win32s files. The Win32s Installer included with PageMaker 6.0x installs the following files in the Windows\System directory:

Compobj.dll	109,056	09-06-95	12:00a
Ole2.dll	304,640	09-06-95	12:00a
Ole2.reg	28,113	04-16-95	12:00a
Ole2conv.dll	57,328	08-13-95	12:00a
Ole2disp.dll	165,008	07-25-95	12:00a
Ole2nls.dll	152,976	07-25-95	12:00a
Ole2prox.dll	51,712	09-06-95	12:00a
Olecli.dll	82,944	varies	varies
Stdole.tlb	5,472	07-25-95	12:00a
Storage.dll	157,696	03-02-95	12:00a
Typelib.dll	177,824	07-25-95	12:00a
W32sys.dll	12,112	10-02-95	12:00a
Win32s.ini	varies	varies	varies
Win32s16.dll	167,424	10-19-95	12:00a
Windows.hlp	21,473	09-05-95	12:00a
Winhlp32.cnt	930	09-05-95	12:00a
Winhlp32.exe	329,744	09-11-95	12:00a
Winhlp32.hlp	31,684	09-05-95	12:00a
Winmm16.dll	29,184	10-01-95	12:00a

For instructions, refer to document 316315, "Error 'At least one system component...' Installing or Launching PageMaker 6.0."

E. Determine whether there is a conflict with the video driver by using the Windows standard VGA driver. For instructions, refer to document 300604, "Specifying the Windows Standard VGA Driver in Windows 3.1x."

NOTE: Make a backup copy of the System.ini file, located in the Windows directory, before installing a new video driver. If you have difficulty reinstalling your original video driver or want to revert to the original driver, copy the original System.ini file back into the Windows directory.

F. Reset PageMaker's defaults file:
NOTE: PageMaker 6.0x creates the defaults file when launching. On a system where PageMaker 6.0x has never been launched, the defaults file will not exist.
1. Quit PageMaker.
2. In the File Manager, rename the PageMaker preferences file, Pm6.cnf, located in the Pm6\Rsrc\Usenglsh directory.
3. Launch PageMaker.
NOTE: Custom application defaults (e.g., default font, default page size) will be lost.

G. Make sure there is only one copy of each of the Windows system files (i.e., Win.com, System.ini, and Win.ini) installed on your computer. If multiple copies exist, rename the duplicate files (e.g., rename the Win.ini file to Win.old).

H. Make sure you only have one Win.ini file on your system, and that its file size is 32K or smaller.

I. Make sure nothing is loading in Windows by disabling (i.e., remarking out) the "load=" and "run=" lines in the Win.ini file and emptying the StartUp group:
1. Create a backup copy of the Win.ini file, located in the Windows directory.
2. Open the original Win.ini file in a text editor that can save in text-only format (e.g., Windows Write, Notepad).
3. Locate the [Windows] section and insert a semicolon at the beginning of the "load=" and "run=" lines. For example:
```
;load=
;run=
```
4. Save the Win.ini file in text-only format.
5. Remove any program icons from the Start-Up group.
6. Restart Windows.

J. Remove and recreate the Windows swap file:
1. Open the Windows Control Panel, located in the Main group of Program Manager.
2. Double-click the 386 Enhanced icon.
3. Select Virtual Memory in the 386 Enhanced dialog box, then click Change.
4. Select a Drive that is not compressed by a disk compression utility (e.g., Stacker, Disk Doubler).
5. In the New Settings section, select NONE as the Type, then click OK and restart Windows.
6. To reset the Windows swap file, repeat steps 1-3, choose Permanent as the Type in the New Settings section of the Virtual Memory dialog box, change the size of the swap file, if necessary, in the New Size box, then click OK.
NOTE: If you have less than 16 MB of RAM on your system, specify a swap file size of at least 15 MB.
7. Restart Windows.

K. Make sure there is adequate free space on the hard disk to which temporary files are written (i.e., 10 to 20 MB in addition to what is used by Virtual Memory). To determine which directory your temporary files are written to, look at the "Set Temp=" line in your Autoexec.bat file.
To create more free disk space for your temporary files: Exit to DOS and delete all files that have a .tmp extension from the temporary directory.
OR: Delete other files from the hard disk containing the temporary directory.
OR: Edit the "Set Temp=" line in the Autoexec.bat file to set the temporary directory on a non-compressed drive with more free disk space.
NOTE: The temporary directory should be a dedicated directory (e.g., C:\Temp rather than C:\Dos).

L. Set Win32s to load last by editing the System.ini file:
1. Make a backup copy of the System.ini file, located in the Windows directory.
2. Open the original System.ini file in a text editor that can save in text-only format (e.g., Windows Write, Notepad).
3. Locate the [386Enh] section and move the following line to the bottom of the section:
```
device=C:\WINDOWS\SYSTEM\WIN32S\W32S.386
```
4. Save the System.ini file in text-only format, then restart Windows.

M. Use a mouse driver that is compatible with Win32s. To determine if your mouse driver is compatible with Win32s, refer to its documentation or contact the manufacturer.

N. Optimize all partitions on your hard disk using DEFRAG, included with MS-DOS 6.2x, or a third-party disk optimization utility (e.g., Norton Utilities Speed Disk). For instructions, refer to the documentation included with MS-DOS or the third-party disk optimization utility.

O. Use the Windows memory manager, Himem.sys, rather than a third-party memory manager (e.g., QEMM). To temporarily load Himem.sys instead of a third-party memory manager, create a bootable floppy disk with start-up files (i.e., Autoexec.bat, Config.sys) that do not reference the third-party memory manager. For instructions on creating a bootable floppy, see Related Records.

P. Delete and reinstall PageMaker 6.0x.
NOTE: The PageMaker 6.0x Installer, like PageMaker 6.0x, is a 32-bit application. Therefore, video drivers incompatible with Win32s cause conflicts with the Installer as well as PageMaker 6.0x. Use the VGA video driver when running the PageMaker 6.0x Installer. After the installation is complete, launch PageMaker 6.0x. If it launches without error, change to your previous video driver and launch it again. If launching PageMaker 6.0x under your previous video driver returns an error, contact your video manufacturer.

Q. Create a bootable floppy disk with Autoexe.bat and Config.sys files that contain only the information necessary to launch Windows and PageMaker 6.0x.

If no errors occur when you run PageMaker after starting from the bootable floppy disk, software loading at DOS through the Autoexec.bat or Config.sys files is causing the error in PageMaker. To determine which line or lines cause the software conflict, add each removed line back into the Autoexec.bat or Config.sys file on the bootable floppy one at a time, restart the computer, then try to recreate the error in PageMaker. When the error reappears, the line most recently added is the most likely cause of the conflict. Because more than one line in the Autoexec.bat and Config.sys files may be causing the conflict, restart with the addition of each line to determine all lines that are causing the conflict.

If no errors occur when you run PageMaker after starting from the bootable floppy disk, reduce the number of devices loading in Windows or DOS to ensure they are using the memory Windows and PageMaker need to run.

R. In Windows for Workgroups 3.11, remark out the "device=c:\windows\ifshlp.sys" line in the Config.sys file:
   1. Make a backup copy of the Config.sys file, located in the root directory on your hard disk.
   2. Open the original Config.sys file in a text editor that can save in text-only format (e.g., Windows Write, Notepad)
   3. Remark out the "device=c:\windows\ifshlp.sys" line by inserting the word "rem" followed by a space at the beginning of the line. For example:
   rem device=c:\windows\ifshlp.sys
   4. Save the Config.sys file in text-only format, then restart Windows.
S. Install a test version of Windows in a new directory.
T. Deinstall and reinstall Windows, PageMaker 6.0x, and other applications:
   1. Make backup copies of the System.ini and Win.ini files to a bootable floppy disk.
   2. Deinstall and reinstall Windows.
   3. Reinstall Win32s from the PageMaker 6.0x installation disk set or CD-ROM.
   4. Reinstall PageMaker 6.0x and run it to make sure the installation is stable.
   5. If PageMaker 6.0x runs properly, reinstall all other applications, utilities, and fonts. After each installation, run PageMaker 6.0x to make sure the installation is still stable before reinstalling the next application. If PageMaker 6.0x does not run properly, it is conflicting with the last thing you installed.

   NOTE: You must completely deinstall and reinstall Windows. Reinstalling Windows over an old installation is not enough. For instructions on deinstalling and reinstalling Windows, refer to the Windows User Guide or contact Microsoft.

ADDITIONAL INFORMATION

Win32s files are a set of Windows files required to run 32-bit applications on 16-bit operating systems (e.g., Windows 3.1x, Windows for Workgroups). Changes in operating environments can result in incompatibilities with various applications, RAM-resident programs, hardware, or software.

Because Win32s errors occur at the system level, make sure all software (e.g., video driver, mouse driver) running with Win32s is compatible with Win32s applications (e.g., PageMaker 6.0x, Photoshop 3.0x).

The minimum RAM requirement for PageMaker 6.0x in Windows 3.1x is 10 MB.

When your Win.ini file is larger than 32K, Windows may not be able to process it carefully or it may contain damaged information.

Win32s Errors, Application Errors, and DOS Errors received when running PageMaker 6.0x include:

- "Win32s Error. Improper installation. Win32s requires W32s.386 in order to run. Reinstall Win32s."
- "Application Execution Error: One of the library files needed to run this application is damaged. Please reinstall this application."
- "Win32s Error. Pm6.exe unhandled exception detected [oxC0000005]. Application will be terminated."
- "Win32s Error. Pm6.exe. Unhandled Exception detected code 0xc0000005 application will be terminated."
- "Win32s Error. An error has occurred in this application."
- "Win32s Error. One or more system components is out of date..."
- "Application Error. Pm6.exe caused a GPF in Win32s-16.dll at 0001:7ccd"
- "Application Error. Pm6.exe caused a GPF in module Pointer.exe at xxxx:xxxx."
- "Unexpected DOS Error -21"

Build Booklet Returns Error 7214 When Imposing PageMaker 6.5 Publication

ISSUE

When you use the Build Booklet plug-in to impose a PageMaker 6.5 publication, Build Booklet returns the error, "7214" and fails to impose the publication. The publication you are imposing includes a PageMaker-drawn object (i.e., line, box, oval, polygon, or frame) on a master page or on the pasteboard.

SOLUTIONS

Use PageMaker 6.51 to impose the publication. The PageMaker 6.51 updater (Pm65-651.exe) is available on the Adobe Systems Web site (http://www.adobe.com/), Adobe ftp site (ftp://ftp.adobe.com/pub/adobe/), the Adobe BBS, America Online, and CompuServe.

OR: Move PageMaker-drawn objects from the master pages or pasteboard to the publication pages and then impose the publication. OR: Save the publication in PageMaker 6.0 format, then open it and impose it in PageMaker 6.0x.

OR: Create the drawn objects in a drawing application (e.g., Adobe Illustrator), export them in a graphic format (e.g., EPS), and then place them in PageMaker.

OR: Create an EPS file of the master page objects, place the EPS onto the master page, and then impose the publication:

1. Create a new publication with only the master page objects on the page.
2. Choose File > Print.
3. In the Print Document dialog box, enter the number of

the page or pages containing master page objects in the Range text box, then click Options.
4. In the Print Options dialog box, select Write PostScript to File, select EPS, click Browse to specify a name and location for the EPS file, and then click Save.
5. Remove the master page objects from your original publication, then place the EPS on the master page.

ADDITIONAL INFORMATION

When you use the Build Booklet plug-in to impose a PageMaker 6.5 publication, Build Booklet returns the error, "7214" if the publication includes a PageMaker-drawn object (i.e., line, box, oval, polygon, or frame) on a master page or on the pasteboard. The Build Booklet plug-in imposes the same publication as expected in PageMaker 6.51.

Error "Cannot complete requested command..." When Running a Template Script in PageMaker 6.5

ISSUE

When you run a template script in Adobe PageMaker 6.5, PageMaker displays a Missing Font dialog box that contains the error, "'Cannot complete requested command. Invalid argument.' Script not completed."

SOLUTIONS

If you're using Windows 95, install the fonts required for PageMaker's template scripts using ATM 4.0 Deluxe or lite:
1. If ATM 4.0 Deluxe or ATM 4.0 Lite is not installed, install ATM 4.0 Lite from the PageMaker 6.5 CD-ROM. For instructions, see Additional Information.
2. Choose Start > Programs > Adobe > Adobe Type Manager.
3. In the Adobe Type Manager dialog box, click the Add Fonts tab.
4. Navigate to the PM65\Extras\Fonts directory.
5. Select all the fonts, then click Add.
6. In the New Set dialog box, enter a name for the new font set, select Activate New Set, then click OK.
7. Exit ATM.
   OR: If you're using Windows NT, install the fonts required for PageMaker's template scripts using the Fonts control panel:
1. Choose Start > Settings > Control Panel.
2. Double-click the Fonts control panel. 3. Choose File > Install New Font.
4. In the Add Fonts dialog box, navigate to the Pm65\Extras\Fonts directory.
5. Click Select All, then click OK.
6. In the Install Type 1 Font dialog box, click Yes to All.

ADDITIONAL INFORMATION

If you install ATM 4.0 Lite with PageMaker 6.5, the PageMaker 6.5 installer copies the fonts required for PageMaker's template scripts to the hard disk, and then installs them using ATM 4.0 Lite. If you perform a custom installation of PageMaker 6.5 and choose not to install ATM 4.0 Lite, the PageMaker 6.5 installer copies the fonts to the hard disk, but cannot install them. If you run a template script when the fonts required for the script are not available, PageMaker displays an error.

Template scripts and the fonts they require include:

Template Script	Required Font
Biz cards	ITC Officina Serif Book, ITC Officina Sans Book
Brochure 1	ITC Officina Serif Book, ITC Officina Sans Book
Brochure 2	ITC Officina Sans Book, Garamond LightCondensed, Garamond BookCondensed
Brochure 3	ITC Officina Sans Book, Garamond LightCondensed, Garamond BookCondensed
Calendar 2	NupitalScript
Calendar 3	NupitalScript
Invitation	NupitalScript, Woodtype Ornaments 1
Letterhead	ITC Officina Serif Book, ITC Officina Sans Book
Newsletter 1	Garamond BookCondensed, Garamond LightCondensed
Newsletter 2	ITC Officina Sans Book

To install ATM 4.0 Lite from the PageMaker 6.5 CD-ROM in WIndows 95:
1. Insert the PageMaker 6.5 CD-ROM into the CD-ROM drive.
2. In the PM6.5 Autoplay window, select Install PageMaker 6.5.
3. In the PageMaker 6.5 Setup window, click Next.
4. In the Language Setup window, select a language version, then click Next.
5. In the Setup Type window, select Custom, then click Next.
6. In the Select Components window, deselect all options except Adobe Type Manager, then click Next.
7. In the ATM Installer window, click Install.
8. In the Restart Windows window, select Yes, I Want to Restart My Computer Now, then click OK.

Error "...Invalid Page Fault in module Kernel32.dll" When Inserting Table 3.0 OLE Objects into PageMaker 6.5

ISSUE

When you insert multiple OLE objects from Adobe Table 3.0 into an Adobe PageMaker 6.5 publication, the system returns the error, "PageMaker 6.5 caused an Invalid Page Fault in module Kernel32.dll." The error includes one of the following addresses:

```
0137:BFF9A28C
0137:BFF858FL
014F:BFF9A28C
0137:BFF858CD
014F:BFF858ED 00001:01FEBLLE
```

SOLUTION
Update to PageMaker 6.51.

ADDITIONAL INFORMATION
When you insert multiple OLE objects from Table 3.0 into a PageMaker 6.5 publication, the system returns an error. PageMaker 6.51 allows you to insert multiple OLE objects from Table 3.0 as expected.

MAC OS

Q *(6.0 only)* **When I try to launch PageMaker 6.0 I get an error message saying that OLE Extensions from Microsoft aren't installed. What's going on?**
A You're getting this message because the Microsoft OLE Extension files PageMaker requires for OLE 2.0 functionality aren't loading. They might not be loading for a variety of reasons—because one of the Extension files is missing, because there's not enough RAM available, or because of a damaged Desktop file.

Error "Insufficient Memory to generate the preview..." Placing Illustrator Document in PageMaker 6.5

ISSUE
When you place an Adobe Illustrator document in Adobe PageMaker 6.5, PageMaker returns the error "Insufficient memory to generate the preview. Allocate more memory to PageMaker, or create a lower resolution and/or fewer color preview. 5641:5639" or "Insufficient memory to generate the preview. Increase the memory allocation for PageMaker. 5641:5640." After you click Continue in the error dialog box, the Illustrator document imports and appears as a gray box.

SOLUTIONS
Increase the amount of random-access memory (RAM) allocated to PageMaker 6.5:

1. Save and close all PageMaker publications, then quit.
2. Click once on the PageMaker application icon to select it, then choose File > Get Info.
3. In the PageMaker Info dialog box, increase the Minimum Size and Preferred Size settings by 1 MB (1024K) or more.
4. Close the PageMaker Info dialog box and relaunch PageMaker.

OR: Specify a lower resolution or color depth for the screen preview generated by PageMaker:

1. Choose File > Place, then select the Illustrator document in the Place Document dialog box.
2. Press Shift while clicking OK. 3. In the Illustrator 5.0-6.01 Import Filter v1.0 dialog box, enter a lower value in the Resolution text box (e.g., 72 dpi), or set the Color Depth option to 256 Colors, or both, then click OK.

EPS (Encapsulated PostScript) files are PostScript graphics that can include a screen preview. Saving the Illustrator document as an EPS file enables Illustrator to generate the screen preview instead of PageMaker.

System Errors

MAC OS / WINDOWS

Invalid Page Fault or Type 3 Error Running Script in PageMaker 6.0x's Story Editor

ISSUE
When you run a script in Adobe PageMaker 6.0x's story editor, the system returns a Type 3 error (Macintosh) or an Invalid Page Fault in KERNEL32.DLL at 0137:bffb8876 (Windows).

SOLUTIONS
In story editor, choose Story > Display Style Names, then run the script.
OR: Run the script in layout view.

ADDITIONAL INFORMATION
When you run a script in PageMaker 6.0x's story editor while style names are hidden, the system returns a Type 3 error (Macintosh) or an Invalid Page Fault error (Windows). By default, style names display in story editor view.

WINDOWS

Error "A fatal error OD" During Windows 95 Startup After Installing PageMaker 6.5 and ATM 4.0 Lite

ISSUE
When you start Windows 95 after installing Adobe Type Manager (ATM) 4.0 Lite from the Adobe PageMaker 6.5 CD-ROM or installation disk set, Windows returns the error, "A fatal error OD has occurred" or displays a solid blue or gray screen. The error includes the address "2047:00-0011ee" or "204f:2047:000011ee." Windows 95 starts as expected in Safe Mode.

SOLUTIONS
Obtain an updated video driver that is compatible with ATM 4.0 and Windows 95 from your video card manufacturer.
OR: Use the Windows VGA video driver. To specify the Windows Standard VGA driver in Windows 95:

1. Right-click on the desktop, then select Properties from the pop-up menu.
2. In the Display Properties dialog box, click on the Settings tab, then click the Change Display Type button.

3. Note the selected Adapter Type, then click Change.
4. In the Select Device dialog box, select the Show All Devices option.
5. Select the Standard Display Types option from the top of the Manufacturers scroll box.
6. Select the Standard Display Adapter (VGA) option from the Models scroll box, then click OK.

OR: Remove ATM 4.0. If you video driver is compatible with ATM 3.02, install ATM 3.02. For instructions on removing ATM 4.0, see Related Records.

ADDITIONAL INFORMATION

Windows loads the video driver and ATM during startup. If your video driver and ATM are incompatible, Windows will not be able to startup as expected and will return an error. When you start Windows in Safe Mode, Windows disables Startup programs, such as ATM, and loads the Windows standard VGA video driver, which enables Windows to startup as expected. Removing ATM 4.0 or using the Windows VGA video driver enables Windows to startup in Normal mode as expected.

Video drivers that are incompatible with ATM 4.0 lite are also incompatible with ATM 4.0 Deluxe. Video cards whose drivers that are known to be incompatible with ATM 4.0 include the ATI Graphics Pro Turbo PCI Mach64 and Trident 9440 Linera Acceleration.

Error "Invalid Page Fault in Module 'Unknown'" Starting PageMaker 6.0x in Windows 95

ISSUE

When you start Adobe PageMaker 6.0x in Windows 95, the system returns the error, "Invalid Page Fault in module 'unknown'".

SYMPTOM

After you click Close in the error dialog box, an error in Obbc32.dll appears, followed by an error in Krnl386.exe or Kernel32.dll. PageMaker does not start.

SOLUTIONS

Reinstall the ODBC component files:

1. Exit all applications.
2. Insert the PageMaker 6.0x Deluxe CD-ROM.
3. Double-click the Setup.exe file in the Techinfo\Odbc\Disk1 directory (PageMaker 6.0) or in the Techinfo\Odbc\Odbc directory (PageMaker 6.01).
4. In the Microsoft ODBC Setup dialog box, click Continue.
5. In the Install Drivers dialog box, select the ODBC drivers for database file types you want to place in PageMaker, then click OK. Microsoft ODBC Setup copies the ODBC files into your Windows\System directory.
   NOTE: If a DSN Conversion dialog box appears with the error, "No User was selected. DSN conversion will not be performed," ignore the error by clicking OK to close the dialog box.
6. In the Data Sources dialog box, click Close to complete the installation.

OR: Disable PageMaker's ODBC plug-in and filter by renaming the Odbc.add file (e.g., Odbc.old) in the Pm6\Rsrc\Usenglsh\Plugins directory and the Odbcflt2.flt file (e.g., Odbcflt2.old) in the Pm6\Rsrc\Usenglsh\Filters directory.

OR: Disable ODBC by renaming the Odbc32.dll file (e.g., Odbc32.old) and then restarting Windows.

NOTE: Disabling ODBC may affect other applications that support ODBC. To re-enable ODBC, copy the Odbc32.dll file from the Techinfo\Odbc\Disk1 directory on the PageMaker 6.0x Deluxe CD-ROM to the Windows\System directory.

ADDITIONAL INFORMATION

PageMaker 6.0x uses ODBC components to import data from database applications (e.g., FoxPro, dBase, Access, Excel). When PageMaker's ODBC plug-in and filter are installed, PageMaker 6.0x loads the Odbc32.dll file (created 6/6/95, size 64512 bytes) when starting. If the Odbc32.dll file's created date is not 6/6/95 or its file size is not 64512 bytes, PageMaker 6.0x returns the error "Invalid Page Fault in module 'unknown'" after reading the Odbc32.dll file.

Reinstalling the ODBC component files from the PageMaker 6.0x Deluxe CD-ROM replaces damaged or older ODBC component files with the ODBC component files included with PageMaker 6.0x. (The component files are not included on the PageMaker 6.0 installation disk set.) Renaming the Odbc.add and Odbcflt2.flt files disables PageMaker's ODBC plug-in and filter, preventing PageMaker from loading the Odbc32.dll file when starting. If you remove the ODBC plug-in (i.e., Odbc.add file), ODBC no longer appears in the PageMaker Plug-Ins submenu. If you remove the ODBC filter (i.e., Odbcflt2.flt file) and then import a file requiring the filter, PageMaker returns the error, "Do not know how to place file: (filename)."

Renaming the Odbc32.dll file disables ODBC in Windows 95. If PageMaker cannot find the Odbc32.dll file while starting, PageMaker starts without returning an error, but you cannot import data from database applications and ODBC does not appear in the PageMaker Plug-Ins submenu.

Error "Kernel32.dll" When Launching PageMaker 6.0x

ISSUE

When you launch Adobe PageMaker 6.0x in Windows 95, the system returns the error "PageMaker 6.0 caused an Invalid Page Fault in module Kernel32.dll."

SYMPTOMS

One of the following addresses is included in the error:

- 0137:BFF9A28C
- 0137:BFF858FL
- 0137:BFF858CD

SOLUTIONS

Rename the Odbc.add file (e.g., Odbc.old), located in the Pm6\Rsrc\Usenglsh\Plugin folder, then rename the Odbcflt2.flt file (e.g., Odbcflt2.old), located in the Pm6\Rsrc\Usenglsh\Filter folder

OR: If you require the ODBC plug-in and filter, rename the version 2.50 or earlier Odbc32*.dll files, then reinstall the ODBC files included with PageMaker 6.0x. To determine the version of an Odbc32*.dll file, right-click on the Odbc32*.dll file in the Explorer, choose Properties, then click the Version tab. The file's version displays in the Version dialog box.

ADDITIONAL INFORMATION

When you launch PageMaker 6.0x with the ODBC plug-in and filter enabled and version 2.50 or earlier Odbc32*.dll files installed on your computer, the system returns the error "PageMaker 6.0 caused an Invalid Page Fault in module Kernel32.dll."

PageMaker 6.0x uses ODBC components to import data from database applications (e.g., dBase, Microsoft Access, Microsoft Excel). When the ODBC plug-in and filter are installed, PageMaker loads the Odbc32.dll file during launch. If PageMaker loads an Odbc32.DLL file that has a creation date earlier than 6/6/95 or a file size other than 64512 bytes, PageMaker returns the error "Invalid Page Fault" in module "unknown" or module "Kernel32.dll." Renaming the Odbc.add and Odbcflt2.flt files disables PageMaker's ODBC plug-in and filter files, preventing PageMaker from loading the Odbc32.dll file when launching.

Error "?AdobeDirectory<no t found..." Launching PageMaker 6.0x in Windows 3.1x

ISSUE

When launching Adobe PageMaker 6.0x in Windows 3.1x, PageMaker returns the error "?AdobeDirectory<not found. Win.ini setting for AdobeDirectory or PM6LangDir section missing."

SOLUTIONS

Do one or more of the following:

A. Make sure the PageMaker entries in the WIN.INI file include the correct pathnames:
   1. Make a backup copy of the WIN.INI file.
   2. Open the WIN.INI file, located in the WINDOWS directory, in a text editor that can save in text-only format (e.g., Windows Write, Notepad).
   3. In the [Adobe] section, edit the following lines to read:
```
AdobeDirectory=C:\PM6\RSRC
PM6LangDir=USENGLSH
NetAdobeDirectory=NONE
PPD4=C:\PM6\RSRC\USENGLSH\PPD4
```
   where C:\PM6 is the path to the PageMaker directory and USENGLSH is the PageMaker language directory.
   4. Save the file in text-only format.

B. Make sure the PM6RES32.RSL file, located in the PageMaker language directory (e.g., PM6\RSRC\USENGLSH), is 460,800 bytes in size and is dated 10/30/95. If the PM6RES32.RSL file is missing or has the incorrect size and date, use the PageMaker 6.0x Installer to single file copy it into the language directory. The PM6RES32.RSL file is located in the D5\UE_FILES\US\USENGLSH subdirectory on Disk 5 of the PageMaker 6.0x installation disk set or the PageMaker 6.0x Deluxe CD-ROM.

C. Remove and reinstall PageMaker 6.0x.

ADDITIONAL INFORMATION

When launching, PageMaker 6.0x refers to the entries in the [Adobe] section of the WIN.INI file to locate the RSRC, PPD4, and language directories, which contain files PageMaker loads while launching. When the entries in the WIN.INI file are incorrect, PageMaker cannot locate the directories and returns the error "?AdobeDirectory not found. Win.ini setting for AdobeDirectory or PM6LangDir section missing."

PageMaker uses the resources in the PM6RES32.RSL file to launch and run. When PageMaker cannot find the PM6RES32.RSL file or when the file is damaged, PageMaker returns the error "?NetAdobeDirectory<no t found, check win.ini setting."

Error "Cannot create internal clipboard...Make sure Share.exe is running..." When Starting PageMaker 6.0

ISSUE

When you start Adobe PageMaker 6.0 in Windows 3.1x, Windows returns the error "Cannot create internal clipboard. Cannot create temporary file. Make sure Share.exe is running properly. 8201:6022."

SOLUTIONS

If you installed PageMaker 6.0 using the Complete option, or using the Custom option with Photo CD Filter or Kodak Precision CMS selected, restart Windows.

OR: If you installed PageMaker 6.0 using the Minimum option, or using the Custom option without the Photo CD filter or Kodak Precision CMS selected, install Vshare.386 or Share.exe. For instructions, see Additional Information.

ADDITIONAL INFORMATION

Adobe PageMaker 6.0 requires Share.exe or Vshare.386 when running in Windows 3.1x. PageMaker's Photo CD filter and Kodak Color Management System (CMS) require Vshare.386 when running in Windows 3.1x.

When installing the PhotoCD filter or the Kodak CMS (included when the Complete install option is selected), the PageMaker 6 Installer installs Vshare.386 and adds a line to the System.ini file that causes VShare.exe to load with Windows. After installing PageMaker, restart Windows to load Vshare.386. The PageMaker 6 Installer does not install Vshare.386 or Share.exe when the Minimum install option is selected.

Share.exe and Vshare.386 are terminate-and-stay-resident (TSR) programs that enable file sharing and locking in a network or multitasking environment in which programs share files. They keep track of files opened by applications, and prevent two or more applications or processes from modifying the same file at the same time. They are typically loaded as the operating system (i.e., DOS or Windows) initializes.

Share.exe, installed with DOS, is usually referenced in the Autoexec.bat file because it must be loaded before Windows 3.1x. Vshare.386 is a virtual device driver, used instead of Share.exe, that loads in the System.ini when Windows starts.

The Windows for Workgroups 3.11 operating system and some applications require Vshare.386.

To install Vshare.386:

Reinstall PageMaker 6.0 using the Complete option, then restart Windows.

OR: Install the Kodak Color Management System (CMS) or the PhotoCD filter from the PageMaker 6.0 installation disks:

1. Start the PageMaker 6 Installer.
2. Click the desired language option, then click Custom in the Type of Install dialog box.
3. Select PhotoCD Filter or Kodak Precision CMS, then click Install.
4. Follow the on-screen instructions to complete the installation, then restart Windows.

OR: Obtain Vshare.386 from Microsoft and follow the included installation instructions.

To install Share.exe:

1. Locate the Share.exe file on the system and note its path.
2. Make a backup copy of the Autoexec.bat file, which is located in the root directory (e.g., C:\).
3. Open the Autoexec.bat file in a text editor that can save in text-only format (e.g., DOS Editor, Notepad).
4. Insert the following line near the end of the file and before any commands that start Windows (e.g., WIN): c:<path to Share.exe>\Share.exe where <path to Share-.exe> is the complete path of the Share.exe file location.
5. Restart the computer to load Share.exe.

Error "Cannot Run PageMaker 6.0. AdobeDirectory not found" Opening PageMaker 6.0x Publication

ISSUE

After you double-click on an Adobe PageMaker 6.0x publication icon, Windows 95 returns the error "Cannot Run PageMaker 6.0. ?AdobeDirectory<no t found." The publication icon appears a generic Windows 95 icon.

SOLUTIONS

Do one or more of the following:

A. Reinstall PageMaker 6.0x in Windows 95.

B. Make sure the Pm6reg.txt file is in the same folder as the Pm6.exe file. By default, PageMaker installs these files in the Pm6 folder.

C. Edit the Pm6reg.txt file to include the correct values for the Windows 95 Registry:
   1. Make a backup copy of the Pm6reg.txt file, located in the PageMaker folder (e.g., Pm6).
   2. Open the Pm6reg.txt file in a text editor that can save in text-only format (e.g., WordPad, Microsoft Word).
   3. In the [HKEY_LOCAL_MACHINE\SOFTWARE\-Adobe\PageMaker] section, edit the following lines to contain correct path information:
```
"PM6LangDir"="<language>"
"AdobeDirectory"="PageMakerDir\\RSRC"
"NetAdobeDirectory"="None"
"ppd4"="PageMakerDir\\RSRC\<langu-
age>\\PPD4"
```
      where <language> is the PageMaker language dictionary (e.g., Usenglsh).
   4. Save the Pm6reg.txt file in text-only format into the folder containing the Pm6.exe file (e.g., Pm6), then close the Pm6reg.txt file.

D. Make sure the Pm6res32.rsl file in the PageMaker language folder (e.g., Pm6\Rsrc\Us\Usenglsh) has a file size of 460,800 bytes and is dated 10/30/95. If the Pm6res-32.rsl file is missing or has the incorrect size and date, use the PageMaker 6.0 Installer to single file copy the Pm6res32.rsl file into the language directory. The Pm6-res32.rsl file is in the D5\Ue_files\Us\Usenglsh\Pm6-res32.rs_ folder on Disk 5 of the PageMaker 6.0x installation disk set or the PageMaker 6.0x Deluxe CD-ROM.

E. Remove PageMaker 6.0x and then reinstall PageMaker 6.0x in Windows 95.

ADDITIONAL INFORMATION

If PageMaker's values are incorrect in the Windows 95 Registry or if the Pm6res32.rsl file is missing or damaged, double-clicking on a PageMaker 6.0 publication causes Windows 95 to return the error "Cannot Run PageMaker 6.0. ?AdobeDirectory<no t found." When Windows 95 cannot recognize a file's type (e.g., the application that created the file), it displays the file's icon as a generic icon.

After you upgrade to Windows 95, reinstalling applications in Windows 95 enables the application to register in the Windows 95 Registry. When installing PageMaker 6.0x in Windows 95, PageMaker's installer registers PageMaker 6.0x and copies the Pm6reg.txt file into the folder containing the Pm6.exe file. Removing and then reinstalling PageMaker ensures PageMaker's application files are not damaged.

PageMaker 6.0 searches for the Pm6reg.txt file in the folder containing the Pm6.exe file. PageMaker uses the values in the Pm6reg.txt file to update the Windows 95 Registry and to locate the Adobe directory, language directory (e.g., Usenglsh), and Ppd4 directory.

PageMaker requires resources in the Pm6res32.rsl file to start and run.

Error "Adobe Dir. Not found..." When Starting PageMaker 6.0x in Windows NT 3.51

ISSUE

When you start Adobe PageMaker 6.0x in Windows NT 3.51, Windows returns the error, "Adobe Dir. Not found, Registry setting for Adobe dir or PM6langdir key missing or incorrect. Cannot run PM6."

SOLUTION

Log in as an Administrator, start the Registry editor, and specify Full Access to the PageMaker registry key for all users:

1. Log in to the local machine as an Administrator.
2. Start the Registry Editor by double-clciking the Regedt32.exe file, which is located in the Windows\System32 directory.
3. In the Registry Editor window, click the HKEY_LOCAL_MACHINE on Local Machine Key window to bring it to the front.
4. In the left-hand side of the HKEY_LOCAL_MACHINE on Local Machine Key window, select the HKEY_LOCAL_MACHINE\Software\Adobe\Pagemaker registry key.
5. Choose Security > Permissions.
6. In the Registry Key Permissions dialog box, click the Everyone icon.
7. Select Full Control from the Type of Access pop-up menu, then click OK.
8. Exit the Registry Editor, restart the computer, and log in as a user.

disclaimer: PageMaker does not support Windows NT 3.5x or earlier workstations or servers. Adobe did not develop PageMaker for Windows NT 3.5x or earlier, and PageMaker may not meet the expectations of Windows NT 3.5x or earlier users.

ADDITIONAL INFORMATION

The PageMaker installer updates the Windows NT registry with the PageMaker registry key. PageMaker must have access to the information in the PageMaker registry key to run. Be default, Windows NT 3.51 allows only the user who installed PageMaker access to the PageMaker registry key. Because other users cannot access the PageMaker registry key, they receive the error, "Adobe Dir. Not found, Registry setting for Adobe dir or PM6langdir key missing or incorrect. Cannot run PM6." when starting PageMaker.

Error "Call to undefined dynalink" Launching PageMaker 6.0x or PageMaker 6.0x Installer

ISSUE

When you launch Adobe PageMaker 6.0x or the PageMaker 6.0x Installer in Windows 3.1x, Windows returns the error "Call to undefined dynalink." PageMaker then quits or the system freezes.

SOLUTIONS

Do one or more of the following:

A. Increase Windows system resources to 70% or greater. To check system resources, choose Help > About Program Manager. For instructions on increasing system resources, see Additional Information.

B. Verify that the following OLE 2.0 DLL files are located in the Windows\System directory, and that they are the correct size. If one of the files is missing or is not the correct size, remove and then reinstall Win32s. For instructions on reinstalling Win32s components, see Related Records.

```
Ole2.dll 304,640
Ole2conv.dll 57,328
Ole2disp.dll 165,008
Ole2nls.dll 152,976
Ole2prox.dll 51,712
Ole2thk.dll 25,088
```

C. Copy the following OLE files from the Windows\System subdirectory to the Windows directory, then restart Windows.

```
Ole2.dll Ole2conv.dll Ole2disp.dll
Ole2nls.dll Ole2prox.dll Ole2thk.dll
```

ADDITIONAL INFORMATION

When PageMaker 6.0x launches, it asks Windows to load the OLE 2.0 DLL files; when the PageMaker Installer launches, it asks Windows to verify that the OLE 2.0 DLL files are installed. If Windows 3.1x cannot locate or load the OLE 2.0 DLL files while PageMaker or the PageMaker Installer is launching, Windows returns the error "Call to undefined dynalink," causing PageMaker or the Installer to quit or the system to freeze. Windows cannot locate or load the OLE 2.0 DLL files when system resources are low, the DLL files are missing or damaged, or when Windows looks for them in the Windows directory instead of the Windows\System subdirectory.

To increase Windows system resources to 70% or greater, do one or more of the following:

A. Close all applications.

B. Remove icons from the StartUp group in Program Manager, then restart Windows.

C. Disable (i.e., remark out) the Load and Run lines in the Win.ini file:
   1. Open the Win.ini file in a text editor that can save in text-only format (e.g., Windows Notepad, WordPad).
   2. In the [Windows] section, locate the lines that begin "Load=" and "Run=."
   3. Insert a semicolon (;) at the beginning of the "Load=" line and at the beginning of the "Run=" line to disable the applications listed in those lines.
   4. Save the Win.ini file in text-only format, then restart Windows.

D. Disable ATM and other utilities.

E. Restart Windows.

Error "Device AUX" When Using Plug-ins in PageMaker 6.0x

ISSUE

When you use an Adobe PageMaker 6.0x plug-in (e.g., Running Headers and Footers, Build Booklet) in Windows 3.1x, the system returns the error "device AUX" and the mouse no longer responds (i.e., freezes).

SOLUTIONS

Change the mouse driver to "Microsoft, or IBM PS/2" and remove the reference to "pointer.exe" from the Win.ini file:

1. Exit all Windows applications.
2. Make backup copies of the Win.ini and System.ini files located in the Windows directory. 3. Double-click on the Windows Setup icon in the Main group of the Program Manager.
4. Choose Options > Change System Settings.
5. Select "Microsoft, or IBM PS/2" from the Mouse pop-up menu.
6. Click OK and follow the prompts to install the mouse driver. If you receive a prompt asking if you want to use the currently installed driver or install a new one, select to use the currently installed driver. If you need to install a new driver, you will need your Windows installation disk set. Do not restart Windows when prompted.
7. Exit Windows Setup.
8. Open the Win.ini file, located in the Windows directory, in a text editor that can save in text-only format (e.g., Windows Write, Notepad).
9. Locate the "Load=" line in the [Windows] section and then delete the reference to "pointer.exe" including its path (e.g., C:\windows\pointer.exe). After you delete the reference to "pointer.exe", make sure there is one space before all references remaining on the line (e.g., "Load= C<filename>, C<filename>).
10. Save the Win.ini file in text-only format.
11. Restart Windows.

OR: Obtain a device driver that is compatible with Win32s components by contacting the manufacturer of your pointing device (e.g., mouse, tablet).

ADDITIONAL INFORMATION

To start and run in Windows 3.1x, PageMaker 6.0x requires Win32s components. If the device driver for your mouse or other pointer device (e.g., tablet) is incompatible with Win32s, the system returns the error "device AUX" when you run a plug-in (e.g., Build Booklet, Running Headers and Footers) in PageMaker. The "Microsoft, or IBM PS/2" mouse driver is compatible with Win32s.

Win32s components are a set of system files requires to run 32-bit applications (e.g., PageMaker 6.0x, Adobe Photoshop 3.0x) on 16-bit operating systems (e.g., Windows 3.1x, Windows for Workgroups). After installing Win32s components, a system or application error may occur when you run software (e.g., video driver, mouse driver) that is incompatible with Win32s.

Error "Win32s Error. The procedure entry point 'GetSysColorBrush'..." Launching PageMaker 6.0x

ISSUE

When you launch Adobe PageMaker 6.0x in Windows 3.1x, the system returns the error "Win32s - Error. The procedure entry point 'GetSysColorBrush' could not be located in the Dynamic Link Library 'W32scomb.dll'." The error may be followed by: "Application Execution Error. Unexpected DOS error: 21."

SYMPTOM

Adobe Photoshop 3.0x or Adobe Photoshop LE 3.0x was installed after PageMaker 6.0x.

SOLUTION

Remove and then reinstall the Win32s 1.3a or later DLL files, included on the PageMaker 6.0x installation disk set and Deluxe CD-ROM. For instructions on removing and reinstalling Win32s DLL files, see Further Reading and Related Records.

NOTE: When the Win32s 1.0 or 1.1 DLL files are installed after the Win32s 1.3a DLL files, the Win32s.ini file incorrectly states that the currently installed version of Win32s is 1.3a (i.e., 1.30.167.0). Therefore, it is not possible to accurately determine which version of Win32s is installed by looking in the Win32s.ini file.

ADDITIONAL INFORMATION

To run in Windows 3.1.x, PageMaker 6.0x requires Win32s 1.3a or later. If a version of Win32s earlier than 1.3a is installed, the system returns an error when you launch PageMaker.

Photoshop 3.0.x and Photoshop LE 3.0x install a subset of the Win32s 1.0 or 1.1 DLL files, which overwrites the previously installed Win32s 1.3a DLL files.

PageMaker 6.0x Fails to Launch But Doesn't Return an Error

ISSUE

When you launch Adobe PageMaker 6.0x in Windows 95 after launching PageMaker 5.0x, PageMaker 6.0x fails to launch but does not return an error (i.e., nothing happens).

SOLUTIONS

Launch PageMaker 6.0x again. PageMaker 6.0x will launch on the second try.

OR: Launch PageMaker 6.0 before launching PageMaker 5.0x.

ADDITIONAL INFORMATION

When you launch PageMaker 6.0x in Windows 95 after launching PageMaker 5.0x, PageMaker 6.0x fails to launch but does not return an error.

PageMaker 6.0x starts as expected when launched a second time. However, because PageMaker 6.0x failed to launch on the first attempt, PageMaker 6.0x recreates its defaults file, PM6.CNF, on the second launch, which resets your PageMaker 6.0x preferences to the default settings.

Launching PageMaker 6.0x before launching PageMaker 5.0x enables PageMaker 6.0x to start as expected on the first try and prevents PageMaker 6.0x from resetting your PageMaker 6.0x preferences back to the default setting.

System Error (e.g., freeze) When Typing in or Applying Type 1 Fonts in PageMaker 6.0x

ISSUE

When you type in a PostScript font or apply a PostScript (Type 1) font to text in Adobe PageMaker 6.0x, the system returns an error (e.g., freeze).

SYMPTOM

A Matrox Millennium Graphics video card is installed

SOLUTION

Turn off the Use Device Bitmaps Caching option in the Display Control Panel:

1. Choose Start > Settings > Control Panel.
2. Double-click the Display Control Panel.
3. In the Display Properties dialog box, click the MGA Settings tab, then click Advanced.
4. in the Advanced settings dialog box, click the Performance tab, deselect Use Device Bitmaps Caching.

ADDITIONAL INFORMATION

If you type text in a PostScript font or apply a PostScript font to text in PageMaker 6.0x when the Use Device Bitmaps Caching option is enabled for the Millennium Graphics video card, the system will return an error (e.g., freeze).

The Device Bitmaps Caching option improves the video processing performance of the Millennium Graphics video card and improves redraw speed when you reposition bitmap images. Disabling it reduces redraw performance minimally.

MAC OS

Q When I'm working in PageMaker, I sometimes get Type 11 errors and have to restart my computer. They seem to happen randomly, but often at the worst times. What might be causing these and how can I keep them from happening in the future?

A The Type 11 system error is a catchall error that generally indicates a hardware problem, but system software and Extension conflicts are other common causes. Power Macintoshes may experience these errors more frequently than 68K machines, because Power Macs use a software emulator that allows them to run non-native-PPC applications. The emulator may have problems if it encounters incompatible software or hardware while it loads into RAM. If this happens, some of the results show up as Type 11 errors.

Type 11 errors are not unique to PageMaker, and have been reported in other Adobe and non-Adobe products. Although there are no known causes of Type 11 errors specific to PageMaker 6.0, Adobe Technical Support has compiled a Type 11 troubleshooting guide that has proven to be helpful in alleviating the problem for many users. Highlights of that guide appear below; for more detailed information, send an E-mail to techdocs@adobe.com and request document 216316, "Type 1 and Type 11 Errors in PageMaker 6.0 Troubleshooting Guide."

Apple User Assistance recommends that if you are experiencing Type 11 errors, you should troubleshoot first for possible software conflicts before looking at hardware causes. Here are some steps to try, more or less in order of ascending effort on your part.

1. Increase the memory allocated to PageMaker.
2. Increase the amount of available space on the startup disk. Remember that PageMaker requires three times the open publication's file size to create temporary files. So if your publication is 500 K, you'll want to have at least 1500 K available on the drive that your System Folder resides on.
3. Run PageMaker with Extensions disabled to identify and eliminate possible conflicts. Use Extensions Manager to turn off everything that you can (remembering that, on a 68K Macintosh, you need the OLE extensions to run PageMaker). If you're using a Power Mac, you can just restart your Macintosh with the Shift key held down until the message "Extensions Off" appears. If you've copied Extensions (or Control Panels, for that matter) over from an older Macintosh to your Power Macintosh, remember that they may be the cause of some of these conflicts. If you suspect this is the case, you should also consider disabling the Control Panels in question.
4. Disable Virtual Memory, and, on Power Macs, turn off "Modern Memory Manager" in the Memory Control Panel, then restart your computer.
5. Use Disk First Aid, included on your Macintosh System installation disk set, to check the hard disk's directory structure. (Disk First Aid is compatible only with Apple hard disks. If you have a hard drive from another manufacturer, use their recommended diagnostic utility to check the hard disk's directory structure.)
6. Remove and reinstall PageMaker, following the instructions in the Getting Started guide for Adobe PageMaker 6.0.

If you're still experiencing frequent Type 11 errors after trying all of these steps, consider some possible hardware-related conflicts. But before you open up your computer, make sure you understand the hazards and the warranty implications involved in do-it-yourself testing. Contact an authorized Apple reseller or the hardware manufacturer for assistance.

1. Disconnect all external devices (e.g., scanner, hard drive, printer, network) connected to the Macintosh.

2. Update your hard drive's SCSI drivers. Contact the manufacturer of your hard drive or hard-drive utility software to determine whether you have the latest drivers available or for further testing assistance.
3. If you're running PageMaker on a Power Macintosh computer with a cache card installed, remove the cache card.
4. Test RAM modules, including composite SIMMs.

Adobe Technical Support continues to research this issue, and will update their information systems with new information as it becomes available.

Type 1 and Type 11 Error in PageMaker 6.0 Troubleshooting Guide

ISSUE

While working in Adobe PageMaker 6.0, the system error Type 1 or Type 11 occurs.

SOLUTIONS

Ensure software and hardware conflicts are not the cause:

1. Ensure software conflicts are not the cause by doing one or more of the following:
   - A. Increase the memory allocated to PageMaker:
     1. Save and close all publications.
     2. Quit PageMaker.
     3. Select the PageMaker application icon at the Finder.
     4. Choose File > Get Info.
     5. Type a larger value in the Preferred size text box, then close the Get Info window.
   - B. Increase the amount of available hard drive space on the startup disk. PageMaker requires three times the open publication's file size to create temporary files.
   - C. Run PageMaker with Extensions disabled:
     When running PageMaker 6.0 on a Power Macintosh, turn Extensions off upon startup by restarting the computer holding the Shift key down until the message "Welcome to Macintosh. Extensions Off." appears.
     When running PageMaker 6.0 on a Macintosh with System 7.5 or later, use Extensions Manager to enable the System 7.5 Only set, then enable the Microsoft OLE Extension and restart the Macintosh. PageMaker 6.0 on the Macintosh requires the Microsoft OLE Extension to launch.
   - D. Turn off Virtual Memory and the Modern Memory Manager (Power Macintosh only), in the Memory control panel.
   - E. Use Disk First Aid, included on system installation disk sets, to check the hard disk's directory structure. For instructions, see Additional Information.
     NOTE: Disk First Aid is only compatible with Apple hard disks. When using another manufacturer's hard drive, use another hard disk diagnostics utility to check the hard disk's directory structure.
   - F. Ensure PageMaker's preferences file is not damaged by forcing PageMaker to create a new preferences file:
     1. Quit PageMaker.
     2. Rename or delete PageMaker's preferences file, "Adobe PageMaker 6.0P Prefs" (PageMaker for the Power Macintosh) or "Adobe PageMaker 6.0 Prefs" (PageMaker for the Macintosh), located in the Preferences folder in the System Folder.
     3. Restart PageMaker. While launching, PageMaker recreates the preferences file using default settings when an existing preferences file is unavailable.
   - G. Reinstall PageMaker by removing then reinstalling PageMaker and its application files.
2. Ensure hardware conflicts are not the cause by doing one or more of the following:
   NOTE: When troubleshooting possible hardware conflicts, contact an authorized Apple reseller or the hardware manufacturer for assistance. Starting the Power Macintosh without the video card in the Processor Direct Slot (PDS) can damage the computer.
   - A. Disconnect all external devices (e.g., scanner, hard drive, printer, network) connected to the Macintosh.
   - B. Update your hard drive's SCSI drivers. Contact the manufacturer of your hard drive or hard drive utility software to determine whether you have the latest drivers available. For instructions, see Additional Information.
   - C. When running PageMaker on a Power Macintosh computer with a cache card installed, remove the cache card.
   - D. Test RAM modules, including composite SIMMs.

ADDITIONAL INFORMATION

There are no known causes of Type 1 or Type 11 errors in PageMaker 6.0.

The system error "Type 1" or "bus error" occur at the data transfer level in the system, which may be caused by low available RAM or insufficient hard drive space. When the system encounters a conflict or problem and is unable to determine the cause, the system returns the "Type 1" system error.

The "Type 11" system error is a miscellaneous hardware exception error that usually indicates a hardware conflict, but system software and extension conflicts can also cause a "Type 11" system error. When determining the cause of "Type 11" system errors, Apple User Assistance recommends troubleshooting software conflicts before troubleshooting hardware conflicts .

Disabling Modern Memory Manager slows performance and disables automatic tracking in PageMaker, but prevents conflicts between Modern Memory Manager and non-native applications or extensions that are active while PageMaker is running.

Apple Computer reports system errors may be caused by composite RAM SIMMs installed in your Macintosh or Power Macintosh.

To use Disk First Aid to check the hard disk's directory tree:

1. Restart the computer from the "Disk Tools" disk included with the System 7 installation disk set.
2. Launch the Disk First Aid application by double-clicking on its icon.
3. Select or open the hard drive to be verified.
4. Click Verify to check the disk or Repair to check and repair the disk. When Verify is selected, Disk First Aid checks the disk, and returns the option to Repair when problems are found. Choose to Repair the disk when Disk First Aids encounters a problem with the disk.
5. Choose File > Quit.

To update the SCSI drivers:

1. Restart the computer from the "Disk Tools" disk (included with the System 7 installation disk set) or the "System Tools" disk (included with System 6.0.x installation disk set).
2. Launch the HDSC Setup application by double-clicking on its icon.
3. Click Drive until the SCSI drive (hard disk) is selected. NOTE: The error "Drive selection failed. Unable to locate a suitable drive connected to the SCSI port." appears when the hard disk is formatted with a non-Apple utility (e.g., Norton Utilities, MacTools, Symantec Tools for Macintosh, StorWare). Click Continue in the error dialog box to quit HDSC Setup and use the SCSI drive updating utility included with the formatting utility.
4. Click Update button to install updated SCSI drivers to each SCSI disk (e.g., hard disk, cartridge, optical).
5. Choose File > Quit.

System Error (e.g., Type 11) When Choosing Place in PageMaker 6.0 for Power Macintosh

ISSUE

A system error (e.g., Type 11) occurs when you choose File > Place in Adobe PageMaker 6.0 for the Power Macintosh.

SOLUTIONS

Remove the Macintosh Easy Open 1.0.x system extension and the Macintosh Easy Open Setup control panel, then restart the Macintosh.

OR: Upgrade to Macintosh Easy Open 1.1.1 or later, available from Apple Computer.

ADDITIONAL INFORMATION

A system error (e.g., Type 11) occurs if you choose File > Place in PageMaker 6.0 for the Power Macintosh when Macintosh Easy Open 1.0.x is installed. Removing Macintosh Easy Open 1.0.x or upgrading to Macintosh Easy Open 1.1.1 or later prevents the error from occurring when you choose File > Place. Turning off Macintosh Easy Open in the Macintosh Easy Open Setup control panel does not prevent Type 11 errors from occurring when you choose File > Place in PageMaker 6.0.

Macintosh Easy Open enables you to open a document in another application when the application that created the document cannot be found. Macintosh Easy Open 1.0.x includes both the Macintosh Easy Open Setup control panel and the Macintosh Easy Open system extension. Macintosh Easy Open 1.1.1 includes the Macintosh Easy Open control panel. Macintosh Easy Open 1.1.1 is included with System 7.5.x.

Long Import Times or System Freezes When Placing Graphic in PageMaker 6.0x

ISSUE

Adobe PageMaker 6.0x takes longer than expected (e.g., 20 minutes) to place a graphic, or the system appears to freeze. The graphic you're placing is larger than 8 MB.

SOLUTION

Import the graphic without storing a copy of it in the publication by clicking No in the Include Complete Copy in the Publication Anyway? dialog box.

ADDITIONAL INFORMATION

When you import a graphic into a PageMaker publication, PageMaker creates a link to the original graphic file. If the graphic is smaller than the size specified in the More Preferences dialog box, PageMaker also stores the full graphic in the publication.

When you import a graphic larger than the size specified in the More Preferences dialog box, PageMaker enables you to choose whether to store the graphic in the publication. If you click No in the Include Complete Copy in the Publication Anyway? dialog box, PageMaker stores only a low resolution screen version of the graphic in the publication, and uses the linked high resolution graphic when printing. If you will be printing the publication from a different computer or may not have access to the original graphic file later, clicking Yes in the Include Complete Copy in the Publication Anyway dialog box ensures that all the graphic data will be available when you print the PageMaker publication.

Placing a graphic larger than 8 MB in PageMaker 6.0 takes longer than expected (e.g., 20 minutes) when the option to store a copy of the graphic in the publication is selected. Placing the same graphic in PageMaker without including a copy of the graphic in the publication imports as expected.

To prevent PageMaker from storing copies of graphics by default, choose Element > Link Options, then deselect Store Copy in Publication.

Error "... Type 4" When Placing a TIFF or Placed TIFF Displays as Small Gray-and-black Box in PageMaker 6.0x

ISSUE

When you place an Adobe Photoshop TIFF image with a clipping path into a Adobe PageMaker 6.0x publication,

PageMaker returns the error"Application '[Unknown?]' has unexpectedly quit, because an error of Type 4 occurred." and the image does not place. Or, the image places, but displays as small gray-and-black box.

SOLUTION

Open the TIFF image in Photoshop, remove and recreate the clipping path, resave the TIFF image, then place it into the PageMaker publication:

1. Start Photoshop 3.0x and open the TIFF image.
2. In Photoshop, choose Windows > Palettes > Show Paths to display the Paths Palette.
3. In the Paths Palette, select the clipping path (i.e., the path name that is outlined).
4. Choose Delete Path from the Paths Palette menu.
5. Recreate the path by using the pen tool or by making a selection with a selection tool.
6. Choose Make Path from the Paths palette menu.
7. In the Make Path dialog box specify the desired tolerance and click OK.
8. Choose Save Path from the Paths Palette menu.
9. In the Save Path dialog box specify the desired name for the path and click OK.
10. Choose Clipping Path from the Paths Palette menu.
11. In the Clipping Path dialog box, select the saved path from the Path pop-up menu.
12. Enter a flatness value in the Flatness text box, if desired, then click OK.
13. Save the TIFF image and replace it in PageMaker 6.0x.

ADDITIONAL INFORMATION

After you place a Photoshop TIFF image with a clipping path that contains no information (i.e., defined but not drawn), PageMaker 6.0x returns the error

Application '[Unknown?]' has unexpectedly quit, because an error of Type 4 occurred." or the image places, but displays as small gray-and-black box.

PageMaker 6.0x imports and displays a TIFF image with a drawn clipping path as expected.

System Error Using Online Help in PageMaker 6.0C or 6.0K for the Power Macintosh

ISSUE

When you use Online Help in Adobe PageMaker 6.0C Chinese or 6.0K Korean for the Power Macintosh, a system error occurs after you double-click on the Online Help screen or search for text. Localized system software (i.e., Chinese or Korean system software) is installed on the Power Macintosh.

SOLUTIONS

Do one or more of the following:

A. Do not double-click on white space in the Online Help window.
B. Search for titles rather than text in Online Help.

ADDITIONAL INFORMATION

When you run Online Help in PageMaker 6.0C or 6.0K on a Power Macintosh with localized system software, a system error occurs after you double-click on white space in the Online Help window or search for text. The system error does not occur on a 68000-series Macintosh with localized system software, or on a Power Macintosh with US English system software.

Printing Problems

MAC OS / WINDOWS

Q When I apply a color to a grayscale image in PageMaker 5.0a, it prints in plain grayscale to my color PostScript printer. How can I make it print in color?

A This occurs because certain printer manufacturers have recently changed the way their PostScript interpreters process color information (specifically, they render colors based on CMY, not CMYK, data). This makes them unable to render some of the color data PageMaker sends, which is in CMYK form. The problem is known to occur when printing PostScript (not PCL) to the Seiko ColorPoint (PSF), the IBM Lexmark 4079, the HP DeskJet 1200C, and the HP PaintJet XL300; it may also crop up when printing to certain non-Adobe PostScript level 1 color printers.

A similar problem can occur if you're printing from PageMaker 5.0 (that is, if you haven't updated to version 5.0a)—except that colorized grayscale images print without any black in them, rather than without any color.

The solution to either problem is to install a file called ALimage.ps in the ALDUS\USENGLSH directory (Windows) or the Aldus folder within the System Folder (Mac). You can download the file from Adobe's Tech Support BBS (206-623-6984), or from the Adobe forums on America Online (in Adobe\Adobe Support Center\PC Drivers\Filters) or CompuServe (in the Adobe Applications Forum's PC PageMaker library). Once you've installed ALimage.ps, printing colorized grayscale images will be slower to these particular devices, but accurate. Print speeds for other kinds of images won't be affected.

One important caveat: ALimage.ps can interfere with the process of printing color separations—it may make colorized grayscale images print too dark. Before you print separations, be sure to remove ALimage.ps from the ALDUS\USENGLSH directory (Windows) or Aldus folder (Mac). Also, use ALimage.ps only if you're having the specific problem described here—if you're not, the file might cause printing problems.

A I'm creating a contents page list that uses leader dots, but sometimes the dots look different from line to line, or they don't line up correctly along the right-hand edge. What's up?

A PageMaker formats leader-tab dots based on the format of the character immediately preceding the tab. If you have a row of leader dots that aren't lining up with the rest of the column, or that look different from their neighbors, chances are that the character before the tab is formatted differently from those on other lines. For instance, the word before the tab might be in boldface or italic, or set in a different size or typeface than the rest of the text.

The best way to solve the problem is to format all the characters preceding the tabs identically. Assuming you don't want to change the formatting of your text, this means inserting and formatting an invisible character in between the text and the tab. A thin space is the best choice, since it's fairly narrow and remains a consistent width. To type a thin space in PageMaker, press Ctrl + Shift + T (Windows) or Command + Shift + T (Macintosh).

One approach is to do this only on the problem lines, giving each thin space the formatting that the other lines have. Alternatively, you may achieve a more uniform appearance if you insert thin spaces before all the tabs, and then give all those spaces the same formatting. Here's a way to automate the process using the Story Editor's "Change" command. (Be aware, however, that this process affects all tabs in the text you select—if your leader tabs are interspersed with other kinds of tabs, you're probably better off changing the leader tabs manually.)

1. Use the text tool to select the text that contains the leader tabs you want to change. Choose "Edit story" from the Edit menu (Ctrl + E in Windows, Command + E on the Macintosh).
2. Under the Utilities menu, select "Change..." (Ctrl + 9 under Windows, Command + 9 on the Mac). In the "Change" dialog box, make sure "Selected text" is selected in the lower-right corner.
3. In the "Find what" text box, type "^t" (to find all the tabs).
4. In the "Change to" text box, type "^<^t" (to replace each tab with a thin space followed by a tab).
5. Click on the "Attributes..." button. In the "Change attributes" dialog box, leave all the "Find" settings on "Any." Under "Change," choose the attributes you want the thin space and tab to have.
6. Click "OK" to close the "Change attributes" dialog box. Back in the "Change" dialog box, click "Change all."

To check your work, close the Story Editor window.

Even if you aren't having problems with your leader dots looking consistent, this same basic technique can be useful for getting them to look the way you want.

Q *(6.0 only)* **When I print color separations from PageMaker 6.0, some of my text is knocking out instead of overprinting (which it did in PageMaker 5.0). Why?**

A There's a difference between how PageMaker 5.0 and PageMaker 6.0 print text that's been assigned the default process-black color. PageMaker 5.0 always overprinted default-black text; PageMaker 6.0, on the other hand, automatically overprints default-black text only if it's less than 24 points. This approach to overprinting black text is more in sync with what prepress professionals recommend—with large black text, it often looks much better if you trap that text against a colored background instead of overprinting each entire letter.

PageMaker 6.0 gives you the option to perform this kind of trapping, and will also let you change the point-size threshold at which it stops overprinting default-black text. For more information on PageMaker's trapping features, see the Adobe PageMaker User Guide, Version 6.0.

Here's how to change overprinting for default black.

1. Choose "Trapping Options..." from the Utilities menu.
2. In the "Black attributes" section of the "Trapping Options" dialog box, under "Auto-overprint black:," change the number for "Text below XX pts" to whatever you want your new threshold to be. Or, if you want all default-black text to overprint, set that number to 650 points or deselect the "Auto-overprint black:" option. Please note that the settings in the "Black attributes" section of the "Trapping Options" dialog box will affect how your publication prints whether or not you have the "Enable trapping for publication" option selected.

For ultimate control over overprinting black text and other black items, you can set certain black elements to overprint by applying to them a 100% tint of black to which you've assigned the "Overprint" attribute. To prevent certain black elements from overprinting, apply to them a 100% tint of black that you've not assigned the "Overprint" attribute. For more information, refer to your PageMaker 6.0 User Guide.

Q *(6.0 only)* **I was expecting my text to knock out because there's a trap-width setting for text specified in the "Trapping Options" dialog box. But when I print color-separation proofs, some text doesn't knock out. Did I miss a hidden switch?**

A No, you probably didn't miss a special trapping setting for text. There are several reasons why some of your text might not knock out, and we'll outline a few of those reasons for you.

However, before we outline those reasons and before you try to troubleshoot the problem, you should make sure there is a problem. In other words, make sure you know exactly what kind of trapping results you should be getting—it's entirely possible that some of your text will look better if it overprints instead of knocking out. (For instance, black or very dark text often looks fine overprinted. Also, it's usually best to overprint very small type.) If your publication will be printed on a commercial printing press, you shouldn't be making trapping decisions alone—it's critical that you talk to your service providers (whoever will image-set and print your publication). They may advise you not to do any trapping yourself if your job has very complex trapping requirements—for jobs like that, it may be best to use a high-end trapping program like Luminous Corporation's TrapWise.

If you and your service providers decide that PageMaker is the best tool to use to trap your job, work with them to define your settings (trap widths and so forth). With their help, you should get a clear idea exactly what kind of type should and shouldn't knock out. Then, if you do notice text that appears to be overprinting incorrectly when you print color-separation proofs in-house, you should be able to determine what's going on by checking the following list of common reasons why certain text would overprint instead of knocking out.

- Text (and any PageMaker-drawn element, or 1-bit or grayscale imported graphic) will overprint if it's been assigned a color that's set to overprint.
- Text that's a graphic or part of a graphic won't necessarily trap the way other text will—for instance, it won't be affected by the "Trap text above" setting in the "Trapping Options" dialog box. In order for text that's a graphic to knock out, it must be assigned a color that is not set to overprint.
- Text assigned PageMaker's default black will always overprint if it's smaller than the "Text below" setting in the "Black attributes" section of the "Trapping Options" dialog box—even if you do not select "Enable trapping for publication" in that dialog box.
- Bitmap fonts won't trap—trapping works only for TrueType and PostScript Type 1 fonts.
- Text that's ostensibly set to knock out (that is, text that's bigger than the "Trap text above" setting in the "Trapping thresholds" section of the "Trapping Options" dialog box) will appear not to knock out if it's darker than the background behind it and the "Trap width" settings you're using are so large that the knockout area gets completely choked (closed in) by the trap, leaving no knockout area at all.

Hard to visualize that last point? Here's an example that should illustrate the idea. Say you have 30-point, medium-blue, spot-color text sitting on top of a pale-yellow background. Trapping should kick in for the text because it's over the "Trap text above" setting of 23.9 points. And, considering the text is darker than its background, the yellow should "choke" (spread into) the text area (see the illustration at the bottom of the page for an example). But let's say you've set the default trap width rather high—for instance, to 0.05 inches. Unless you're dealing with a typeface that has very thick strokes (thicker than twice the trap width at the point size you're using), the trap will choke out the knockout area.

If you think this scenario describes what you've been experiencing, you should talk with your service providers to find out if you need to adjust any of your trapping settings. But they may very well tell you that the settings are fine, and that your text should overprint in that instance. If that doesn't sit well with you—perhaps because you're concerned about how the text's color will look when it mixes with the background color—you might consider altering your layout.

Q *(6.0 only)* **Every now and then a graphic in one of my PageMaker jobs won't color-separate properly—sometimes an entire color image will print just on the black plate, or the CMYK percentages won't be quite right. What causes this?**

A What usually causes a graphic to color-separate improperly is the format of the graphic. If you're doing high-resolution printing or color separations, there are just three kinds of graphics you should be dealing with: EPS (encapsulated PostScript) and DCS (desktop color separation) graphics and CMYK TIFFs. PageMaker can also color-separate RGB TIFFs if you use its color-management feature (see the PageMaker User Guide for more information). And to ensure that these graphics are color-separating accurately, you'll need to produce your separations on a PostScript device (non-PostScript devices cannot interpret EPS and DCS graphics, and may not accurately separate TIFFs).

If you use any other kind of graphic format—PICT or WMF, for instance—you might not get the color-separation results you're after because those graphic formats simply weren't designed to support accurate color separation. So, before you use the "Place" command to bring in a graphic, check its format. And, whenever possible, do not bring graphics into your publication via the Clipboard. Regardless of the image's original format, bringing it in via the Clipboard will give you a graphic in the Windows bitmap or Windows metafile format or, on the Mac, a bitmap or vector PICT. None of these formats color-separates reliably—Windows bitmaps and bitmap PICTs generally print as composite images on the black separation only; Windows metafiles and vector PICTs may separate, but won't necessarily do so accurately (with correct CMYK percentages).

And here's one more thing you should watch out for. Most of the time you bring objects into an application from the Clipboard using the "Paste" command, but there's another way to bring elements in from the Clipboard: drag and drop. Some applications (Adobe Illustrator 6.0 on the Mac and the Windows 95 Explorer, for example) will let you click on an element and drag it into a document in another application. This technique uses the Clipboard, so in PageMaker what you'll get is some kind of Windows bitmap, Windows metafile, or PICT.

If you have a graphic in your PageMaker publication and you're not certain about its format, click on it and select "Link info..." from the Element menu. If the information listed in the "Kind" field is anything other than TIFF, EPS, or DCS, you might have difficulty separating that image.

Q Why is it that when my PageMaker document is printed on a four-color printing press, my PANTONE colors print differently than what was in the selector guide from PANTONE?

A Chances are you're using a color from one of the PANTONE spot-color libraries, but you're printing that color as a process color made up of some combination of cyan, magenta, yellow, and black process inks, not as a spot color (which would require a special, pre-mixed ink and a separate printing plate). There are two ways you may have changed your spot color to a process color—in the "Edit Color" dialog box you may have changed that color's type from spot to process, or you may have selected the "All to process" option in the "Colors" printing dialog box. The former will convert a spot color to a process color; the latter will temporarily convert all your spot colors to process colors for printing.

The PANTONE spot color libraries and their corresponding swatchbooks won't be very useful tools if you use them for printing four-color process jobs. Briefly, here's why.

PANTONE created a set of library colors based on premixed (also known as solid or spot) inks. PageMaker comes with PANTONE spot-color libraries for coated paper and for uncoated paper. The colors in these libraries are designed to be printed on a printing press using the individual color's ink formula, not a formula based on certain percentages of cyan, yellow, magenta, and black (that is, the traditional process ink colors). The colors in the PANTONE spot-color libraries cover a much larger gamut (range) than what can be reproduced using the traditional CMYK process color inks. Therefore, when you've been using spot colors and basing your expectations of their output on colors from a spot-color swatchbook, but then convert them to process colors for printing (usually in order to have fewer color plates), many of these coated or uncoated colors won't look much like the samples in the swatchbook. The farther a color is out of the CMYK process-color gamut, the greater you can expect the color shift to be.

You can best see the example of the different color gamuts by looking at the PANTONE ProSim selector guide. This color swatchbook displays the spot inks on one side and their closest process-ink equivalents on the opposite side, giving you an approximate idea of what kind of color shift you'll get if you print that spot color as a process color.

How can you prevent this color shift from occurring?

- Use only colors from the PANTONE Process color library when you're going to print process-color separations.
- When you really do want to print a spot color (and can afford to print with an extra plate), use the PANTONE Coated or Uncoated libraries and do not convert the spot inks to process inks at print time.
- Finally, if you're considering a job that'll require two or more spot inks in addition to the four process inks (CMYK), ask your printer whether using PANTONE'S Hexachrome color system might be a good alternative. PANTONE Hexachrome lets you select colors composed of up to six process inks—orange and green plus cyan, magenta, yellow, and black—which gives you a much wider choice of colors than you can get with just CMYK. Depending on what types of colors you were trying to get through spot inks, this might be a great alternative.

Q Sometimes when I try to print to my PostScript printer, the printer light flashes like it's processing, but eventually it stops and nothing comes out. What gives?

A When this occurs with PostScript printers, it usually indicates that there's something in the file that's stopping the job from completing. One of the most common and easy-to-fix causes of this stoppage is a memory-related problem caused by using an incorrect PPD file. To prevent such problems, make sure you're using a PPD file that's right for your printer—see the PageMaker 6.0 User Guide, pages 325–28, for more information on PPDs.

If you've already done that and you're still having a problem, the first thing you should do is go to the "Options" print dialog box (select "Print..." from the File menu and then click the "Options..." button) and select the "Include PostScript error handler" before you try to print again. Doing so downloads a miniature PostScript program, an "error handler," to your PostScript printer. If the PostScript interpreter in your printer is unable to process your print job, most of the time PageMaker's error handler will cause it to print out some information on what caused the problem (the PostScript error and offending command) and some tips on how to resolve the problem. Often it'll print this information along with a partial version of the page that it couldn't process fully.

Depending upon your knowledge of PostScript and experience with these errors, the error information you get from your printer may mean a lot to you, or it may mean nothing. Many of these errors are documented in FaxYI and in our searchable technical-solutions database available on the Adobe Web site (www.adobe.com/supportservice/cust support/tssearchdb.html). Another good source for information on PostScript errors is "Be Your Own Private Eye," by Lynn Powers, Adobe Magazine, November 1995, page 59. This article not only lists several common PostScript errors and offending commands with their general causes, but also outlines a general troubleshooting method for a variety of printing problems.

What does and doesn't print out on the partial page that may accompany the PostScript error information can also provide you with important clues. For example, if you have three graphics on the page, and only two of them printed, this might indicate that the problem is related to the third graphic that didn't print. How do you test your theory? Remove the graphic that didn't print and try printing again. Do you receive an error message? If not, chances are the problem is related to the graphic.

The PostScript error handler isn't the only PageMaker feature that doubles as a troubleshooting tool. The "Proof" and "Download fonts" print options can also really help you narrow down the cause of a problem.

When you select "Proof" in the "Print Document" dialog box, PageMaker won't print any of your imported graphics (instead, it'll print a box with an "X" through it as a placeholder for each graphic). This is a handy way to print your file quickly if you want to proof just the text in your publication. But it's also great for troubleshooting printing problems. If selecting this option enables your file to print, it's likely your problem is related to an imported graphic. If selecting it doesn't allow you to print successfully, you probably have some other text-related problem.

You can also test whether a downloadable font might be the problem. Select the "None" option under "Downloadable fonts" in the "Options" print dialog box. This keeps PageMaker from downloading any fonts when you print. If that enables you to print, you might have a problem with a downloadable font or fonts. If selecting this option does not allow you to print, your problem might be with a font that's permanently downloaded to your printer's hard disk, a problem unrelated to fonts. (Please note that when you select this option, any text in your publication that normally prints as a downloaded font will print as your printer's default font—probably Courier.)

At this point, if you've isolated the problem to a graphic or font, you should test the font or the graphic. This will help you determine whether the problem is directly caused by the graphic or font, or if it's just indirectly related to that element. Try printing the suspect font or graphic by itself from a new publication. If the suspect element is a graphic that won't print from a new publication, try resaving the graphic from the program you used to create it. If the suspect element is a font that won't print from a new publication, remove it from your system and reinstall it.

The methods outlined above are good first steps for troubleshooting a printing problem—by combining them with a little trial and error, you should be capable of solving many printing problems yourself. But if they don't work, and you need to call technical support for assistance, you'll at least be much closer to finding out what's going wrong.

Q When I print my document to a PostScript printer, some of my text doesn't print in the font that I've specified—it prints in Courier instead. The font I was trying to print works just fine from other applications. Is something wrong with PageMaker?

A No, probably not. There are three very common, easy-to-make oversights that can cause this type of behavior in PageMaker. Here's an explanation of these three causes.

Font downloading is not enabled. In the "Print Options" dialog box, make sure the "Download Fonts" option is set to "PostScript and TrueType." If you're using PageMaker 5.0x, make sure "Include Downloadable Fonts" is checked.

When the "Download Fonts" option is set to "None" (PageMaker 6.x) or the "Include Downloadable Fonts" option is unchecked (PageMaker 5.x), PageMaker won't send your downloadable fonts (fonts that reside on your computer) to the printer. And if one of the fonts you're trying to print doesn't already reside at the printer, your printer will have to substitute one of its built-in fonts—often Courier—for that text.

You should set PageMaker not to download fonts using these options only if you're sure the fonts you need to print are built into your printer or have been downloaded to it before print time, or if you want to speed up print times or troubleshoot a problem by letting your printer substitute fonts in this manner.

You're using a PPD file that incorrectly lists your font as resident at the printer. This may sound like a complex, difficult-to-resolve problem, but it usually isn't—the key here is just to make sure you're using the right PPD file for your printer. Here's why.

The PPD (PostScript printer description) file—the thing you select from the "PPD" pop-up menu in PageMaker's "Print Document" dialog box—contains important information about your printer: what paper sizes it supports, how much memory it has, and so forth. It also tells PageMaker what fonts the printer has built into it or downloaded to it. (Using a font-downloading utility, you can download fonts permanently to your printer if it has a hard drive, or download fonts to its RAM before your print job.) At print time, PageMaker doesn't download any font the PPD file says is already at the printer, which can improve print times.

If the font list in the PPD is accurate, this will ensure that your documents print at optimal speed without font substitution. But if your PPD says your printer has a font that isn't built into it or downloaded to it ahead of time, PageMaker won't download that font at print time, and your printer will have to substitute Courier or another font for it.

So how can you tell whether you're using the right PPD file? Check by looking at its name in the "PPD" pop-up menu of PageMaker's "Print Document" dialog box—it should be the same as that of your printer. Or it should be the name of a custom printer file you've created for your PostScript printer—on the Mac, you can use the "Update PPD" utility or Plug-in to create one that contains the correct font list for your printer; in Windows you can use the PPD.EXE version of that utility to select fonts to add to a custom printer file (for more information, see your PageMaker User Guide). If you're in doubt, you can try another PPD, such as the "General" PPD, to see if that helps with your font-substitution problem. If it does, try reinstalling your PPD from your PageMaker disks or CD-ROM, or contact the printer manufacturer for the most up-to-date PPD.

In PageMaker 6.01 for the Mac, there's another way to ensure that PageMaker has accurate information on what fonts are built into and downloaded to your PostScript printer. In the "Print Options" dialog box, select the "Query printer for font and memory information" option (this option won't be available if you have background printing on in the Chooser). This may slow printing somewhat, but can solve font-substitution problems. We still recommend you use the correct PPD for your printer.

Outline or printer font is not available. Font substitution can also occur when you're missing the part of the font PageMaker needs to download to your printer. When this happens, you'll generally have a problem printing that font from all your applications. However, some applications can print a bitmap screen version of the font when the printer font is missing (more on that later).

PostScript fonts come in two primary parts. The first part contains the metric information for your font (this is the information on the font's horizontal spacing characteristics—how much space each character takes up and kerning information). On the PC, this information is stored in a PFM (printer font metric) file. On the Mac, this information is stored in a screen font that also contains a bitmap version of your font (this bitmap version of the font was used for displaying it on screen before the days of Adobe Type Manager—and is still used by some applications for display and printing). This is the part of the PostScript font that applications need in order to list the font as an option on your font menu and to accurately compose each line of text.

The second primary part of a PostScript font is the printer font or outline font—this is the real guts of the font; it's the data that describes the exact shape of each character in the font, and it's the part that applications must download to your PostScript printer so it can print all those characters. On the PC, PostScript printer fonts can be identified by their PFB extension; on the Mac, PostScript printer fonts are easiest to identify in the Finder by viewing their "Kind" description—they'll be listed as "PostScript font." (See the illustration at lower left for more information.)

Sometimes, if you're experiencing font substitution, it may be because you're missing the printer font for that typeface. The easiest way to remedy this problem is to reinstall the font from its original source.

For information on managing fonts, see the PageMaker 5.0 Adobe Commercial Printing Guide, pages 38–39, or "Fonts of Knowledge," by John Cornicello and Glenn Fleishman, Adobe Magazine, March/April 1994, page 43.

Perform on Printer Option Dimmed in PageMaker 6.5's Print Color Dialog Box

ISSUE

The Perform on Printer option is dimmed in Adobe PageMaker 6.5's Print Color dialog box.

SOLUTION

Select a PPD file that supports in-RIP PostScript separations in the Print Document dialog box. To determine whether your printer supports in-RIP separations, contact the printer manufacturer.

ADDITIONAL INFORMATION

Some PostScript Level 2 devices are able to perform color separations in the printer's Raster Image Processor (RIP), enabling you to process separations faster than when PageMaker performs the separations before sending PostScript information to the printer.

The Perform on Printer option in PageMaker's Print Color dialog box is available when you select a PPD file that supports in-RIP PostScript separations. When the Perform On Printer option is selected, PageMaker sends the publication to the printer as a composite so that the printer's RIP, rather than PageMaker, can perform the separations.

When Perform on Printer is not selected, PageMaker performs the color separations itself and sends the separations for each page to the printer's RIP.

To support in-RIP separations, the selected PPD file must be PostScript Level 2 and include the line "*Separation: True." PageMaker considers a PPD file to be PostScript Level 2 if it states it is Level 2, or if it supports a resolution of 1000 dpi or greater and includes custom paper sizes.

Unable to Print Only Desired Printer's Marks from PageMaker 5.0 or Later

ISSUE

When you print from PageMaker 5.0 or later, the option to print only crop marks, registration marks, color-control bars, or density-control bars is not available. The only option available, Printer's Marks in the Paper printing dialog box (PageMaker 6.0x) or Colors printing dialog box (PageMaker 5.0x), prints all printer's marks.

SOLUTIONS

In PageMaker 6.0x, use the Marksmaker plug-in, available from Adobe Plug-in Source.

OR: When printing to a PostScript printer, create a supplemental PostScript file named P6After.ps (PageMaker 6.0x) or AlAfter.ps (PageMaker 5.0x) that instructs PageMaker to print only the desired marks when the Printer's Marks option is selected. For instructions, see Additional Information.

ADDITIONAL INFORMATION

Because most print jobs require both crop marks and density-control bars or all possible printer's marks, PageMaker includes one option for selecting all printer's marks. The Marksmaker plug-in for PageMaker 6.0x enables you to customize printer marks, crop marks, bleed lines, color ramps, and color lists.

The PostScript code that PageMaker 5.0x and later generates can be changed using one or more external PostScript files, which can either replace or append PageMaker's PostScript code. When PageMaker encounters a supplemental PostScript file, it includes the contents of that file in the PostScript code it sends to the printer. PageMaker recognizes files that are named appropriately and located in the RSRC folder (PageMaker 6.0x for the Macintosh), the Pm6\Rscrc\Usenglsh directory (PageMaker 6.0x for Windows), the Aldus folder (PageMaker 5.0x for the Macintosh), or the Aldus\Usenglsh directory (PageMaker 5.0x for Windows). PageMaker 6.0x supplemental PostScript filenames begin with "P6" (e.g., P6Before.ps, P6Error.ps); PageMaker 5.0x supplemental PostScript filenames begin with "AL" (e.g., ALError.ps, ALBefore.ps). Capitalization does not affect PageMaker's ability to recognize the file name.

The P6After.ps and ALAfter.ps files make procedure-specific changes to the way a function behaves in PageMaker by redefining the function. These redefinitions can compensate for printing problems, or can customize routines to fit work needs (e.g., printing only certain printer's marks). These files include code similar to code included in a "*JobPatchFile:" line in a PPD file. The code differs from that of a "*PatchFile:" line in that it is downloaded with every job, regardless of what PPD file is selected. PageMaker can use only one P6After.ps or ALAfter.ps file when printing, but the file can contain multiple PostScript modifications.

To create or modify a P6After.ps file that instructs PageMaker 6.0x to only print crop marks when the Printer's Marks option is selected:

1. Create a new file or open an existing P6After.ps file in a text editor that can save in text-only format (e.g., Windows Write, TeachText).
2. If you're creating a new file, type the following text exactly as shown, including a paragraph return after the last word "end":

```
%%P6After.ps
%%by Olav Martin Kvern
%%To have PageMaker print additional print-
  ers' marks,
%%comment out the line containing the
  appropriate mark,
%%as indicated by the preceding comment.
P6PS begin
%%registration marks
/V‘6 {6{pop} repeat} def
%%density-control bars
/W‘6 {6{pop} repeat} def
%%color-control bars
/X‘6 {5{pop} repeat} def
end
```

OR: If you're modifying an existing P6After.ps file, type the following text exactly as shown before the "end" line:

```
%%registration marks
/V‘6 {6{pop} repeat} def
%%density-control bars
/W‘6 {6{pop} repeat} def
%%color-control bars
/X‘6 {5{pop} repeat} def
```

NOTE: The character " ` " after the characters " /V" is a grave accent, located on the same key as the tilde character (left of the "1" key).

3. Save the file with the name "P6After.ps" in text-only format in the RSRC folder (Macintosh) or the Pm6\Rsrc\Usenglsh directory (Windows).

To instruct PageMaker 6.0x to print other printer mark combinations when the Printer's Marks option is selected, prevent the lines from being read by the PostScript printer (i.e., comment them out) by typing "%%" at the beginning of the line listing the mark you want to print with crop marks. For example, to print crop marks and color-control bars from PageMaker 6.0x, type the following:

```
%%P6After.ps
%%by Olav Martin Kvern
%%To have PageMaker print additional print-
  ers' marks,
%%comment out the line containing the
  appropriate mark,
%%as indicated by the preceding comment.
P6PS begin
%%registration marks
/V‘6 {6{pop} repeat} def
%%density-control bars
/W‘6 {6{pop} repeat} def
%%color-control bars
%%/X‘6 {5{pop} repeat} def
end
```

To create a supplemental PostScript file named AlAfter.ps that instructs PageMaker 5.0x to only print crop marks when the Printer's Marks option is selected:

1. Create a new file or open an existing AlAfter.ps file in a text editor that can save in text-only format (e.g., Windows Write, TeachText).
2. If you're creating a new file, type the following text exactly as shown, including a paragraph return after the last word "end":

```
%%AlAfter.ps
%%by Olav Martin Kvern
%%To have PageMaker print additional print-
  ers' marks,
%%comment out the line containing the
  appropriate mark,
%%as indicated by the preceding comment.
ALPS begin
%%registration marks
/V‘ {6{pop} repeat} def
%%density-control bars
/W‘ {6{pop} repeat} def
%%color-control bars
/X‘ {5{pop} repeat} def
end
```

OR: If you're modifying an existing AlAfter.ps file, type the following text exactly as shown before the "end" line:

```
%%registration marks
/V‘ {6{pop} repeat} def
%%density-control bars
/W‘ {6{pop} repeat} def
%%color-control bars
/X‘ {5{pop} repeat} def
```

NOTE: The character " ` " after the characters " /V" is a grave accent, located on the same key as the tilde character (left of the "1" key).

3. Save the file with the name "AlAfter.ps" in text-only format in the folder named Aldus (PageMaker 5.0x for the Macintosh) or the Aldus\Usenglsh subdirectory (PageMaker 5.0x for Windows).

To instruct PageMaker 5.0x to print other printer mark combinations when the Printer's Marks option is selected, prevent the lines from being read by the PostScript printer (i.e., comment them out) by typing "%%" at the beginning of the line listing the mark you want to print with crop marks. For example, to print crop marks and color-control bars from PageMaker 5.0x, type the following:

```
%%ALAFTER.PS
%%by Olav Martin Kvern
%%To have PageMaker print additional print-
  ers' marks,
%%comment out the line containing the
  appropriate mark,
%%as indicated by the preceding comment.
ALPS begin
%%registration marks
```

```
/V' {6{pop} repeat} def
%%density-control bars
/W' {6{pop} repeat} def
%%color-control bars
%%/X' {5{pop} repeat} def
end
```

Color-Managed Images Print Slowly from PageMaker 6.0

ISSUE

Bitmap images managed with a Color Management System (CMS) in Adobe PageMaker 6.0 print 10 to 20 times slower than bitmap images you haven't color-managed.

SOLUTION

Disable color management for the bitmap images:

1. Select the bitmap image, then choose Element > Images > CMS Source.
2. Select None from the This Item Uses pop-up menu, click OK.
3. Repeat steps 1-2 for other bitmap images.
4. Choose File > Save As to save the publication with a new name or the existing name.

ADDITIONAL INFORMATION

Color management is a resource-intensive process. When you print a PageMaker 6.0 publication that contains color-managed bitmap images, print times are 10 to 20 times longer than when you print the publication without color-managed bitmap images.

Publication file sizes increase when color management is enabled and the Embed Profiles in Document option is selected in the Color Management System Preferences dialog box, but the embedded profiles do not increase print times.

Non-Rotated 1-Bit TIFF Image Prints Low Resolution from PageMaker 6.0

ISSUE

When printing from Adobe PageMaker 6.0, 1-bit (black-and-white) TIFF images print low resolution (e.g., jagged). The TIFF images were not transformed in PageMaker.

SOLUTIONS

Select the Normal option from the Send Image Data pop-up menu in the Print Options dialog box.

OR: Update to PageMaker 6.01.

OR: Resave the image in another format (e.g., EPS, PICT) in an image editing application (e.g., Adobe Photoshop), then replace or relink the image in PageMaker 6.0.

ADDITIONAL INFORMATION

When printing with the Optimized option selected in the Send Image Data pop-up menu in the Print Options dialog box, PageMaker 6.0 incorrectly downsamples 1-bit TIFF images to 72 dots per inch (dpi), instead of downsampling them to the optimum resolution for the output device as expected, causing them to print low resolution. Images printed at a low resolution are more noticeable when printed to a high-resolution device.

When printing with the Normal option selected in the Send Image Data pop-up menu, PageMaker 6.0 does not downsample 1-bit TIFF images, enabling 1-bit TIFF images to print as expected. PageMaker 6.01 does not downsample 1-bit TIFF images to 72 dpi when printing with the Optimized option selected.

PageMaker 6.01 Prints RGB Colors Differently than PageMaker 6.0

ISSUE

Adobe PageMaker 6.01 prints some PageMaker-defined RGB colors differently to a PostScript printer than Page-Maker 6.0. Some RGB colors in Portable Document Format (PDF) files created in PageMaker 6.01 display differently than RGB colors in PDF files created in PageMaker 6.0.

SOLUTION

Remove the PageMaker 6.01 preferences file, rename the PageMaker 6.01 dfltcmsg.swb file, then install the dfltcmsg.swb file from the PageMaker 6.0 installation disk set or Deluxe CD-ROM:

1. Quit PageMaker 6.01.
2. Remove the Adobe PageMaker 6.0 Prefs or Adobe PageMaker 6.0P Prefs file from the Preferences folder in the System Folder (Macintosh), or delete or rename the Pm6.cnf file in the Pm6\Rsrc\Usenglsh directory (Windows).
3. Rename the dfltcmsg.swb file (e.g., "dfltcmsg.601"). The file is located in the SwitchB folder in the RSRC folder in the Adobe PageMaker 6.0 folder (Macintosh) or the PM6\RSRC\SWITCHB directory (Windows).
4. Reinstall the dfltcmsg.swb file from the PageMaker 6.0 disk set or Deluxe CD-ROM. For instructions, see Additional Information.

ADDITIONAL INFORMATION

PageMaker's dfltcmsg.swb file contains color lookup tables that PageMaker uses to convert colors defined using one color model (e.g., RGB) to another color model (e.g., CMYK). PageMaker 6.01 uses an updated dfltcmsg.swb file, which causes it to print some RGB colors differently to a PostScript printer than PageMaker 6.0, and causes some RGB colors to display differently in PageMaker 6.01 PDF files than in PageMaker 6.0 PDF files. Using the PageMaker 6.0 dfltcmsg.swb file with PageMaker 6.01 causes PageMaker 6.01 to convert RGB colors the same way as PageMaker 6.0.

To install the dfltcmsg.swb file from the Macintosh disk set or Deluxe CD-ROM:

1. Insert Disk 3 of your PageMaker 6.0 disk set into your floppy drive, or insert your PageMaker 6.0 Deluxe CD-ROM.

2. Double-click on the dfltcmsg.swb file, located in the SwitchB folder in the RSRC folder on Disk 3 of the installation disk set, or in folder 3 in the Adobe PageMaker 6.0 folder on the Deluxe CD-ROM. The PageMaker 6 Installer launches.
   NOTE: If the error "The document ([filename]) could not be opened, because the application that created it could not be found." occurs, see Additional Information.
3. Navigate to the SwitchB folder in the RSRC folder in the Adobe PageMaker 6.0 folder on the hard disk, then click Save.

To install the dfltcmsg.swb file from the Windows disk set or CD-ROM:

1. Insert Disk 1 of your PageMaker 6.0 disk set into your floppy drive, or insert your PageMaker 6.0 Deluxe CD-ROM.
2. When installing from Disk 1, double-click the Setup.exe file; when installing from the Deluxe CD-ROM, click the PageMaker 6.0 Click to Install option in the PM6-Intro dialog box.
3. In the Language Choice dialog box, select the language version you wish to install.
4. In the Type of Install dialog box, click Custom.
5. In the Custom Installation dialog box, click Single File Copy.
6. In the Copy Single File window, select the file named "dfltcmsg.sw_" located in the D10\Rsrc\Switchb\Dftlcmsg directory.
7. Click Browse, then navigate to the C:\Pm6\Rsrc\Switchb\Dfltmsg directory (where "C" is the drive on which PageMaker 6.01 is installed), then click OK.

In PageMaker 6.0, you can define RGB colors that are outside of the CMYK color gamut (i.e., the RGB color can't be created using Cyan, Magenta, Yellow, and Black inks). When you print the RGB color to a PostScript printer, PageMaker converts it to the closest CMYK equivalent, causing the RGB color to print differently than expected (i.e., shift). To prevent RGB colors from shifting when printed, PageMaker 6.01 includes an updated dfltcmsg.swb file that prevents you from defining RGB colors that are outside of the CMYK color gamut.

When printing to a PostScript printer or using the Create Adobe PDF plug-in, PageMaker 6.0x converts RGB colors to CMYK. PageMaker does not convert RGB colors to CMYK when printing to a non-PostScript printer.

Dfltcmsg.swb File Sizes and Dates

PageMaker 6.0 File	Size	Date
dfltcmsg.swb	42,524	August 11, 1995
PageMaker 6.01 File	Size	Date
dfltcmsg.swb	49,947	February 15, 1996

When you install individual files from the Macintosh installation disk set or Deluxe CD-ROM, double-clicking on a compressed file causes the PageMaker 6 Installer to launch and decompress the file. The PageMaker 6 Installer is automatically installed in the Utilities folder in the Adobe PageMaker 6.0 folder on the hard disk when you select the Easy Install option. If the Installer is not installed or if the Finder cannot locate it, the following error occurs when you double-click on a compressed file: "The document ([filename]) could not be opened, because the application that created it could not be found."

To force the Installer to launch when you double-click on the file, do one or more of the following:

A. Copy the PageMaker 6 Installer, located in the Utilities folder on Disk 1 of the installation disks or folder 1 in the Adobe PageMaker 6.0 folder on the Deluxe CD-ROM, to the Utilities folder in the Adobe PageMaker 6.0 folder on the hard disk.
B. Keep the Utilities folder open in the foreground.
C. Rebuild the desktop file by holding down the Command and Option keys while restarting the computer. Keep the keys held down until you receive the message, "Are you sure you wanted to rebuild the desktop file on the disk '[diskname]'? Comments in info windows will be lost," then click OK.

Non-Printing Objects Are Printing Objects in PageMaker 5.0 Saved from PageMaker 6.0

ISSUE

After saving an Adobe PageMaker 6.0 publication as a PageMaker 5.0 publication, objects that are non-printing objects in the PageMaker 6.0 publication display and print in the PageMaker 5.0x version of the publication.

SOLUTIONS

Delete non-printing objects in the PageMaker 6.0 publication before saving a copy of the publication in PageMaker 5.0 format.

OR: After saving a copy of the PageMaker 6.0 publication in PageMaker 5.0 format, in the PageMaker 5.0 publication, delete the objects or move the objects to the pasteboard before printing.

ADDITIONAL INFORMATION

After saving a copy of a PageMaker 6.0 publication in PageMaker 5.0 format, PageMaker 5.0x is unable to honor new features included in Adobe PageMaker 6.0 that are unavailable in PageMaker 5.0. Because PageMaker 5.0 does not support the non-printing object feature, non-printing objects in PageMaker 6.0 publications saved in PageMaker 5.0 format become PageMaker 5.0 objects, which are printing objects, and lose their non-printing object attribute.

Colors Display and Print Differently in PageMaker 6.0 Than in 5.0x General Information

You can create colors in PageMaker using the RGB (Red, Green, Blue) color model or the CMYK (Cyan, Magenta,

Yellow, and Black) color model. Different output devices use different color models: monitors display colors using the RGB model, PostScript printers print colors use the CMYK model, and non-PostScript printers, which use the screen display to render colors, print colors using the RGB model.

PageMaker uses a mathematical algorithm to convert colors from RGB to CMYK and vice versa for display and printing. PageMaker 6.0 includes a new, more accurate color conversion algorithm, which may cause colors in a PageMaker 5.0x publication to display or print differently after being converted to PageMaker 6.0 format.

CONVERTING PAGEMAKER 5.0X PUBLICATIONS TO 6.0

PageMaker 5.0x defines all colors in a publication using the same color model (i.e., RGB or CMYK). The color model you used when last defining a color becomes the color model for all colors in the publication, regardless of the model you originally specified for a particular color.

When the colors in a PageMaker 5.0x publication are based on the CMYK color model, the colors display differently in PageMaker 6.0 because PageMaker 6.0 uses a different algorithm than PageMaker 5.0x to convert CMYK colors to RGB for screen display. Colors based on the RGB model display identically in PageMaker 6.0 as they display in PageMaker 5.0x because they do not need to be converted for screen display.

A PageMaker 5.0x publication whose colors are based on the CMYK color model print identically to a PostScript printer after conversion to PageMaker 6.0 format because PostScript printers render colors using the color's CMYK color definitions, resulting in the colors requiring no conversion. The colors display and print differently to a non-PostScript printer in PageMaker 6.0 because PageMaker 6.0 uses a different algorithm than PageMaker 5.0x to convert colors to RGB. PageMaker 5.0x colors based on the RGB color model display and print identically to a non-PostScript printer after conversion to PageMaker 6.0 format, but print differently to a PostScript printer.

You can change the defined color model in a PageMaker 5.0x publication before converting it to PageMaker 6.0 format to ensure colors display or print identically in Page-Maker 6.0. For example, if you want the colors to print identically to a PostScript printer from PageMaker 6.0, change the color model in the PageMaker 5.0 publication to CMYK. To ensure the colors display identically in PageMaker 6.0, change the color model in the PageMaker 5.0 publication to RGB.

To change the color model for a publication in PM 5.0x:

1. Choose Element > Define Colors.
2. Select a color other than [Black] or [Registration], then click Edit.
3. Select the color model you want to use, then click OK to close the remaining dialog boxes.
4. Save the publication.

LIBRARY COLORS IN CONVERTED PUBLICATIONS

When you select a color from a color library in PageMaker 6.0, PageMaker 6.0 records both the CMYK and RGB values for that color, ensuring the color displays consistently when you reopen the publication. After you convert the publication to PageMaker 6.0, PageMaker 6.0 uses its color conversion algorithm to convert the CMYK values to RGB for screen display, causing the library color to display differently in PageMaker 6.0 than they displayed in PageMaker 5.0x. To ensure library colors display and print as defined in a color library, redefine all library colors after converting a PageMaker 5.0x publication to PageMaker 6.0.

When you select a color from a color library (e.g., PANTONE, Trumatch) in PageMaker 5.0x, PageMaker records only the color's name and its CMYK values in the publication. While the publication remains open, PageMaker uses RGB values defined in the color library to display the color, but after you close and reopen the publication, PageMaker 5.0x uses its color conversion algorithm to generate RGB values for the color, causing the color to display differently than when first added to the publication.

USING 5.0X S COLOR CONVERSION ALGORITHM IN 6.0

Unlike PageMaker 5.0x's conversion algorithm that is built-in and cannot be modified, PageMaker 6.0's conversion algorithm is contained in an external file named "DFLTCMSG.SWB." You can replace this file with an alternate DFLTCMSG.SWB file that enables PageMaker 6.0 to use an emulation of PageMaker 5.0x's conversion algorithm.

To use PageMaker 5.0x's color conversion algorithm in PageMaker 6.0 for the Macintosh:

1. Quit PageMaker 6.0.
2. Open the Dfltcmsg folder in the SwitchB folder in the RSRC folder in the Adobe PageMaker 6.0 folder.
3. Rename the DFLTCMSG.SWB file to DFLTCMSG.PM6.
4. Rename the DFLTCMSG.ALT file to DFLTCMSG.SWB.
5. Relaunch PageMaker.

To use PageMaker 5.0x's color conversion algorithm in PageMaker 6.0 for Windows:

1. Exit PageMaker 6.0.
2. Open the PM6\SWITCHB\DFLTCMSG subdirectory.
3. Rename the DFLTCMSG.SWB file to DFLTCMSG.PM6.
4. Rename the DFLTCMSG.ALT file to DFLTCMSG.SWB.
5. Restart PageMaker.

SAVING PAGEMAKER 6.0 PUBLICATIONS IN 5.0 FORMAT

When you save a PageMaker 6.0 publication in PageMaker 5.0 format, all colors in the PageMaker 5.0 publication are defined using the CMYK model, regardless of the color model you used when defining the color in PageMaker 6.0.

Because PageMaker 5.0x uses a different algorithm than PageMaker 6.0 to convert CMYK colors to RGB for screen display, colors created in the PageMaker 6.0 publication display differently in PageMaker 5.0x. The colors print identically to a PostScript printer from PageMaker 5.0x unless you color-managed the colors in PageMaker 6.0 using a color management system (CMS). The colors print differently to a non-PostScript printer from PageMaker 5.0x because non-PostScript printers render colors using the RGB screen display.

DCS 2.0 Images Don't Print On Hexachrome Separations From PageMaker 6.0x

ISSUE

When you print PANTONE Hexachrome (CMYKOG) color separations from Adobe PageMaker 6.0x, DCS 2.0 images do not print on the PANTONE Hexachrome separation plates as expected.

SOLUTION

Reexport the image from Adobe Photoshop 3.0.x in DCS 2.0 format using the PlateMaker plug-in, change the names of the color separation plates (i.e., channels) to match the names of PageMaker's PANTONE Hexachrome process colors, then replace the DCS 2.0 image in PageMaker 6.0x:

1. In Photoshop 3.0.x, open the image from which you created the DCS 2.0 image.
2. Choose File > Export > PlateMaker.
3. In the DCS 2.0 dialog box, change the names of the color channels to match the names of PageMaker's PANTONE Hexachrome process colors:
   - Hexachrome Cyan
   - Hexachrome Yellow
   - Hexachrome Magenta
   - Hexachrome Black
   - Hexachrome Green
   - Hexachrome Orange
4. Click OK.
5. In the Save As dialog box, click Save.
6. In PageMaker 6.0x, replace the existing DCS 2.0 image with the updated DCS 2.0 image.

ADDITIONAL INFORMATION

To ensure a DCS 2.0 image prints on the desired separation plates from PageMaker 6.0x, the color names included in the image must be identical to color names defined in PageMaker.

WINDOWS

Q Whenever I print from PageMaker, I get the error "PROGMAN.EXE caused a GPF in WINMM16.DLL." What is the WINMM16.DLL file, and how do I prevent this from happening?

A WINMM16.DLL is part of Win32s, which is a Windows subsystem developed by Microsoft. It's installed with, and allows you to run, 32-bit applications (such as PageMaker 6.0 or Photoshop 3.0) in Windows 3.11, which is a 16-bit environment. (A 32-bit application is one that takes advantage of the 32-bit architecture of a program like Windows 95.) The purpose of the WINMM16.DLL file is to allow 32-bit applications to perform multimedia functions in a 16-bit environment. The Win32s installer is its own discrete program, and installs its components automatically, regardless of whether they are specifically needed or not.

The simplest way to prevent this error from happening again is to disable the WINMM16.DLL file. Of course, that might not be prudent if you have 32-bit applications on your system that need to use it—check with the manufacturer of your non-Adobe applications to see if they require WINMM16.DLL. PageMaker, Illustrator, Photoshop, and Persuasion don't require this file.

To disable the WINMM16.DLL file, you must remove the reference to it in the [boot] section of your SYSTEM.INI file. Here's how to do that.

1. Make a backup copy of the SYSTEM.INI file located in your WINDOWS directory.
2. Open the original SYSTEM.INI file in a text editor that can save in text-only format (e.g., WordPad, Notepad).
3. Locate the line in the [boot] section that reads
   `drivers=mmsystem.dll winmm16.dll`
4. Edit the line to read
   `drivers=mmsystem.dll`
   (that is, remove the reference to WINMM16.DLL). Don't remove any other line or section of this line.
5. Save in text-only format and restart Windows.

If you can't disable the WINMM16.DLL file because you need it for a certain 32-bit application, one way you can work around this problem temporarily is to replace your current video driver with the standard Windows VGA driver. (WINMM16.DLL needs at least 256 colors to run; using the VGA driver, which runs at 16 colors, will effectively disable the WINMM16.DLL.) For instructions on installing the Windows VGA driver, send an E-mail to techdocs@adobe.com and request document 300604, "Specifying the Windows Standard VGA Driver." (Or you can find it on the PageMaker 6.0 Enhancement Pack CD-ROM—see the tip on page 79.)

Q I've got some text that has a color applied to it, and when I print it to a black-and-white printer, the text comes out solid black instead of the shade of gray that I'm expecting. What can I do?

A First, you should click on the "Color" button in the "Print Document" dialog box to check whether you've got "Print colors in black" selected. If you do, deselect that option, and you're probably home free.

If not, chances are that your problem has to do with printing TrueType fonts to a PCL printer. When PageMaker prints colored TrueType fonts to a black-and-white PCL printer, the characters are rasterized (converted to a series of dots your printer understands) by the Windows Graphical Device Interface (GDI), a Windows subsystem that controls many printing and display functions. The GDI rast-erizes colored text as either black or white instead of approximating the color saturation using a shade of gray. Fortunately, it's pretty easy to get around this, using one of the following methods.

- Rotate or skew the text block to force the text to print correctly—even .01 degree will do it, and it won't be noticeable. Black-and-white PCL printers use a different set of GDI commands to process transformed text than they do for regularly set text.

- Reformat the text using a PostScript Type 1 font (installed via Adobe Type Manager). Type 1 fonts are generally bypassed by the GDI, so they won't experience the symptoms commonly seen with TrueType fonts.
- Print to a PostScript or color PCL printer, if one's available.

Troubleshooting Printing Problems in PageMaker 5.0x

Use this fax to resolve printing problems in PageMaker 5.0x without a technician's assistance; it contains the techniques used by Adobe Technical Support staff. Using these techniques, you should be able to resolve many of your printing problems on your own. Also, this fax will better prepare you to provide a technician with the information needed to resolve especially difficult printing problems.

DETERMINE THE LEVEL OF THE PROBLEM

The first step in resolving a technical issue is to determine at what level the problem occurs. When the problem is repeatable in other applications, it is occurring at the system level. When the problem only occurs in PageMaker, it is occurring at the application level. However, even when the problem only occurs in PageMaker, there may be other factors contributing to the problem. Determine whether the problem occurs in all, some, or just a single publication. If you can isolate the printing problem to a few similar publications or a single publication, try to isolate the printing problem to a single page or group of pages.

DETERMINE IF THE PRINTING PROBLEM IS OCCURRING AT THE SYSTEM LEVEL

To determine whether the printing problem is occurring at the system level, print from another application, such as Windows Write. If nothing prints from any application, contact Microsoft Technical Support or the printer manufacturer. Always check the physical connection between the printer and the computer before calling, as the solution may be as simple as reconnecting a loose cable.

Also, consider what has changed on your system recently that may be impacting printing. For example, have you:

- Updated your hardware?
- Added new software?
- Updated existing software?
- Deleted software?
- Installed new fonts?
- Added hardware components?
- Recently connected to a network?
- Cleaned up the hard drive?
- Encountered random system errors?

Often, a change on your system directly corresponds to the appearance of a printing problem. Keeping a record of changes made to your system can be an excellent resource for troubleshooting printing and other problems.

When determining if the printing problem occurs in other Windows applications, make sure you're making valid print comparisons. If the problem only occurs when attempting to print certain fonts or a particular graphic, try printing the same elements from the other application. If the elements you're trying to print from PageMaker are damaged or corrupt, the same printing problem should surface when printing those elements from any other application. Damaged fonts or graphics should be reinstalled or resaved.

DETERMINE WHETHER THE PRINTING PROBLEM IS RELATED TO THE PAGEMAKER APPLICATION

To determine if the PageMaker application is the cause of your printing problem, try printing a different PageMaker publication. Create a new publication containing only a PageMaker-drawn box, then print the publication. If the page prints, add text and graphics one element at a time, printing after each addition. If the file won't print after adding a certain element, create another file that just contains that element and print.

Also try printing a publication that has printed successfully before. The absence of printing problems in each of these tests indicates that your printing problem is publication-specific and does not indicate a problem with the PageMaker application.

ISOLATE THE PRINTING PROBLEM WITHIN THE PAGEMAKER PUBLICATION

To determine whether the entire publication or just certain pages won't print, try printing single pages of the publication. If some pages print as expected, while one or more other pages do not print, isolate which elements (i.e.., text or graphics) are preventing the publication from printing.

TROUBLESHOOTING PRINTING PROBLEMS

When the printing problem occurs in only one or a few similar PageMaker publications, do one or more of the following to isolate problematic elements:

A. Make sure a valid printer is selected in the "Compose to:" box of the "Page setup" dialog box. When a printer name preceded by a question mark or "Display on none" is selected in the "Page setup" dialog box, your publication may not print as expected.

B. Print the publication as a proof print:
   1. Choose "Print..." from the File menu.
   2. Select "Proof" in the "Print document" dialog box, then print the file.

   Selecting "Proof" in the "Print document" dialog box tells PageMaker not to send any graphic information to the printer. If the publication prints when "Proof" is selected in the "Print document" dialog box, one or more of the graphic elements on the page may be damaged. Isolate the element or elements causing the print problem, then delete and replace them. You may need to re-export the graphic from the application in which it was created.

   Successful printing with "Proof" selected in the "Print document" dialog box may also indicate you don't have enough printer memory. Common symptoms of insufficient printer memory include font substitution and missing data. Simplify the publication to see if it will print with fewer elements.

C. Deselect "Include downloadable fonts" in the "Options" printing dialog box:
   1. Choose "Print..." from the File menu.
   2. Click on "Options...," then deselect "Include downloadable fonts."

   Deselecting "Include downloadable fonts" in the "Options" printing dialog box will result in font substitution of any non-printer resident fonts. However, if your file prints as expected when this option is deselected, the printing problem may be related to one or more of the installed fonts used in the publication. You may have a damaged text block or one or more damaged fonts.

   For more information on font-related printing issues, refer to FaxYI documents 315605 and 315604.

D. Send the PostScript error handler to the printer:
   1. Choose "Print..." from the File menu.
   2. Click on "Options..." then choose "Include PostScript Error Handler" in the "Options" printing dialog box.

   The PostScript error handler will print a page with any PostScript errors that are occurring when you print. For help interpreting PostScript errors, refer to FaxYI document 200103, "PostScript Error Troubleshooting Guide."

E. Verify that all links in the publication are valid:
   1. Choose "Links..." from the File menu.
   2. Unlink or relink any graphic or text file whose name is preceded by a question mark or other symbol in the "Links" dialog box. For explanation of the various symbols that may appear in PageMaker"s "Links" dialog box, refer to page 332 of the PageMaker 5.0 User Manual.

   When graphic and text elements are placed into PageMaker, a link is formed to the original graphic or text file. PageMaker relies on the original graphic or text file for information used to display and print the file correctly. If an element is not stored in the PageMaker publication (an option in the "Links option" dialog box) and the link is broken (e.g., the original file is moved or deleted), PageMaker is unable to locate the original file at print time and the element may not print correctly. For more information on links in PageMaker, refer to the PageMaker 5.0 User Manual.

F. Recompose the publication:
   1. Hold down the Control and Shift keys while choosing "Hyphenation..." from the Type menu.
   2. Hold down the Shift key while choosing "Go to page..." from the Layout menu. PageMaker will cycle through the pages of your publication. Once it has cycled through once completely, hit any key to make the slide show stop.
   3. Choose "Save as..." from the File menu to save the file to a new name.

   The Control + Shift + "Hyphenation..." and Shift + "Go to page" keyboard commands initiate internal checks that look for and repair a small number of inconsistencies. Using the "Save as" command rather than the "Save" command reduces file size and may eliminate corrupted information from your publication.

G. When printing to a non-PostScript printer, deselect "Allow PCL Halftoning" in the "Colors" printing dialog box:
   1. Choose "Print..." from the File menu.
   2. Click on "Colors" then deselect "Allow PCL Halftoning."

   "Allow PCL Halftoning," which is selected by default in the "Colors" printing dialog box, gives the printer control of the halftoning process. When "Allow PCL Halftoning" is deselected, the halftoning is done before the data is sent to the printer. When "Allow PCL Halftoning" is selected, special effects created using PageMaker"s "Image Control" feature are ignored.

H. Make sure you have adequate free memory in Windows to print your publication. To check the amount of available memory:
   1. Leave PageMaker open and use the Alt + Tab or Ctrl + Esc keyboard combinations to switch to Program Manager.
   2. Choose "About Program Manager" from the Help menu.

   If you're printing a complex PageMaker publication, your system may freeze when system resources fall below 50%. To increase system resources, close all applications not needed for printing. You may need to close all applications and restart Windows to refresh the free system resources.

   PageMaker 5.0 requires a minimum of 4MB of memory. Approximately 1MB of memory is used when Windows is launched. Loading other items (e.g., fonts, Startup group items, applications) reduces the free system resources, causing PageMaker to perform poorly, if at all.

OR: When the printing problem occurs in all PageMaker publications, do one or more of the following:

NOTE: Publication-specific printing problems may also be resolved using the following techniques.

A. Rename or delete the PageMaker defaults file, PM5.CNF, located in the ALDUS<LangDir> subdirectory. The PM5.CNF file stores information about application-wide defaults, which are used each time a new file is created. Printing problems may occur when the PM5.-CNF file is damaged; PageMaker creates a new PM5.CNF file when the original is renamed or deleted.

B. Make sure you have the correct printer driver installed for the printer to which you're printing. To check the version of the printer driver:
   1. Open the Windows Control Panel and double-click on the "Printers" icon.
   2. Select the printer to which you're printing, then click on "Setup...."

3. Click on "About" to see the printer driver version.
   NOTE: Some printer drivers do not have an "About" dialog box; printer driver versions may also be listed in the "Setup" and "Options" dialog boxes.
   When printing to a PostScript printer, the installed printer driver should be the Microsoft PostScript printer driver version 3.56 or later or the Adobe PostScript printer driver version 2.1.1 or later. Contact the printer manufacturer for information on printer driver updates.

C. When printing to a PostScript printer driver, make sure you have the correct PostScript Printer Description (PPD) file installed:
   1. Choose "Print..." from the File menu.
   2. The PPD file selected in the "Type:" drop-down box of the "Print document" dialog box should match the actual output device (i.e., don't choose a Linotronic PPD file when printing to a Hewlett-Packard LaserJet IIIsi).
      Print using the General or Color General PPD file if print problems occur when using the PPD file designed specifically for your printer. Some PPD files were updated after PageMaker 5.0 was released; contact the printer manufacturer for information on updated PPD files.
      For more information on PPD files, refer to the PageMaker 5.0 User Manual or PageMaker 5.0 Commercial Printing Guide.

D. Use the Windows File Manager to search all drives and directories for duplicate printer driver files. If your PageMaker files are stored on a network drive, check that drive for printer drivers as well. Printer drivers should only be located in the WINDOWS\SYSTEM directory; if located in other directories, they may cause printing problems.

E. Use the Windows File Manager to search all drives and directories for multiple WIN.INI files. If your PageMaker files are stored on a network drive, check that drive for WIN.INI files as well. The WIN.INI file should be located in the WINDOWS directory; multiple WIN.INI files can cause various problems, ranging from error messages to no output from the printer.

F. When using ATM, make sure the installed version is 2.5 or later. To check the installed version of ATM, double-click on the "ATM Control Panel" icon, typically located in the Main group of Windows Program Manager. The version number is located in the upper left corner of the "ATM Control Panel" dialog box.
   Versions of ATM earlier than 2.5 were not tested and are not supported with PageMaker 5.0.

G. Verify the "Set Temp=" line is present in the AUTOEXEC.BAT file and that it points to a valid drive and directory. There should be at least 10MB of free disk space on the drive listed in the "Set Temp=" line. To verify the "Set Temp=" line points to a valid drive and directory:
   1. Exit Windows and type the word "set" at a DOS prompt.
   2. Change to the directory listed after the equal sign. For example, if the directory listed in the "Set Temp=" line is C:\WINDOWS\TEMP, type:

```
CD C:\WINDOWS\TEMP
```

   If a message appears stating that the directory is invalid, either create the directory using the DOS MD or "Make Directory" command or edit the "Set Temp=" line in the AUTOEXEC.BAT file to point to a valid directory. Make a backup copy of the AUTOEXEC.BAT file before editing it. For more help editing the AUTOEXEC.BAT file, contact Microsoft Technical Support.

H. Deselect "Fast printing direct to port" in the Windows Printer Control Panel:
   1. Open the Windows Control Panel and double-click on the "Printers" icon.
   2. Select the printer to which you're printing from the "Installed printers" list, then click on "Connect."
   3. Deselect "Fast printing direct to port," then click "OK" to close the Printers Control Panel.
      When "Fast printing direct to port" is selected in the Printers Control Panel, Windows uses the network device driver to send data directly to the printer's port. Some printing enhancements, such as those that allow a network user to output documents on a printer attached to a server, rely on communications with MS-DOS. Deselecting "Fast printing direct to port" passes the data through DOS, allowing these print enhancements to function properly.
      Deselecting "Fast printing direct to port" should not noticeably affect printing performance. However, if deselecting this option does not resolve your printing problem, reselect it.

I. Turn off Print Manager:
   1. Open the Windows Control Panel and double-click on the "Printers" icon.
   2. Deselect "Use Print Manager," then click "OK" to close the Printers Control Panel.
      When Print Manager is active, all print jobs are spooled to its print queue. Print Manager works in the background, allowing you to continue work in Windows while it sends data to the printer. You should have at least 12MB free hard disk space when Print Manager is active.

J. When printing to a non-PostScript printer, use the Windows VGA video driver rather than a high resolution third-party driver:
   1. Make a backup copy of the SYSTEM.INI file, located in the WINDOWS directory.
   2. Open Windows Setup, typically located in the Main group of Program Manager.
   3. Choose "Change System Settings..." from the Options menu.
   4. Choose "VGA" from the "Display:" drop-down list, then follow the prompts to load the VGA video driver.
   5. Restart Windows.

If you can print your publication without error when using the Windows VGA video driver, there may be a conflict between your original video driver and PageMaker. Contact the video card manufacturer to make sure you have the most current video driver. If the driver you have is the most current available, try using a different video resolution (e.g., 800 x 600 rather than 1024 x 768).

K. When printing to an early-model printer, make sure the firmware version of your printer or PostScript cartridge version is current. Contact the printer manufacturer for assistance in identifying the firmware version.

L. Print to a different printer. If your publications print as expected to other printers, you may have damaged hardware or cables.

M. Print your publication from a different computer. If the publication prints to the same printer when sent from a different computer, the printing conflict may be specific to one system. Compare the hardware and software on each machine to identify which component(s) are involved in the printing conflict.

N. When printing over a network, hook your computer directly to the printer and try printing again. If you can't hook up direct to the printer, print your publication to disk and send the file to the printer from DOS on a machine that can be hooked up direct to a printer.

O. Print to disk and copy the file to the printer from a DOS prompt. For instructions on creating a PostScript file, refer to the PageMaker 5.0 User Manual.

To copy a PostScript file to the printer from DOS:

1. Exit to DOS and change to the directory in which your PostScript file is located.
2. Type the following command to send the PostScript file to the printer:

```
copy filename.ps LPT1
```

(assuming your printer is connected to the port LPT1)

If the publication prints when sent to the printer from a DOS prompt, one or more Windows-specific elements are contributing to the printing conflict. Common Windows-specific causes of print conflicts include low system resources, a damaged Print Manager, or a WIN.INI file that is larger than 32K or is damaged.

P. Make sure the printer to which you're printing supports the current printing operations. For example, you should not print color separations of EPS graphics to a non-PostScript printer. For more information about your printer's capabilities, contact the printer manufacturer.

PostScript Type 1 Fonts Print as Courier from PageMaker 6.5

ISSUE

When you print from Adobe PageMaker 6.5 to a PostScript printer, text formatted with printer-resident PostScript Type 1 fonts prints in Courier.

SOLUTIONS

Print from PageMaker 6.51. You can download the PageMaker 6.51 updater (Pm65-651.exe) from Adobe's FTP site (ftp://ftp.adobe.com/pub/adobe/pagemaker/win/6.x/updaters), Adobe's Web site (http://www.adobe.com/), the Adobe BBS (206-623-6984), America Online (Keyword: Adobe), or CompuServe (GO ADOBEAPP). You can also obtain the updater on disk from Adobe Customer Services.

OR: Install the screen fonts or *.pfm files for the printer-resident fonts. If the screen fonts were not included with your printer, obtain them from the printer manufacturer:

1. Open Adobe Type Manager (ATM).
2. Click the Add Fonts tab (ATM Deluxe 4.0) or the Fonts tab (ATM 4.0).
3. Choose Browse for Fonts from the Source pop-up menu.
4. Locate the folder that contains the font files you want.
5. Select the fonts you want to install, then click Add.
6. Close ATM.

OR: Turn off ATM 4.0:

1. In ATM, click the Settings tab.
2. Click Off in the ATM System section of the dialog box.
3. Close ATM, then restart Windows.

NOTE: If you turn off ATM, PostScript fonts will be substituted on screen with other fonts (e.g., Times, Arial), although they will print correctly.

ADDITIONAL INFORMATION

PageMaker 6.5 queries ATM for the font metrics for those fonts used in the publication. When the screen font for a printer-resident font is installed, ATM provides the font metrics to PageMaker and the font prints as expected. If ATM does not have font metric information (e.g., the screen font is not installed), PageMaker substitutes Courier, whether the font is listed in the PostScript Printer Description (PPD) file or is resident on the printer.

When you turn ATM 4.0 off, PageMaker relies on the PPD file to determine which fonts are available at the printer, and does not substitute printer-resident fonts. When ATM is off, PostScript fonts are substituted on screen with other fonts (e.g., TrueType fonts), but they print correctly.

PageMaker 6.51 queries the PPD file when font metrics aren't available from ATM; PageMaker 6.51 only substitutes Courier if ATM does not provide font metrics and the font is not listed in the PPD file as a printer-resident font.

Error "The filter required to print this graphic is not installed" for PIC or HPGL Graphic in PageMaker 6.0

ISSUE

When printing or viewing the link status of a Lotus PIC or HPGL graphic, Adobe PageMaker 6.0 returns the error "The filter required to print this graphic is not installed. This graphic cannot be printed in high resolution." The publication was converted from PageMaker 5.0x.

SOLUTION

Force-update the link to the graphic in PageMaker 6.0:

1. Select the graphic's filename in the Links dialog box, then click Info.
2. In the Link Info dialog box, locate the linked source file.
3. Press the Shift key and double-click on the source file.

ADDITIONAL INFORMATION

When converting PageMaker 5.0x publications, PageMaker 6.0 reimports placed graphics using the updated PageMaker 6.0 filter. When reimporting Lotus PIC or HPGL (Hewlett-Packard Graphics Language) graphics, PageMaker 6.0 does not use the installed PageMaker 6.0 filter, resulting in PageMaker converting the publication without reimporting Lotus PIC or HPGL graphics. Because the Lotus PIC or HPGL graphics were not reimported by PageMaker 6.0 during conversion, PageMaker assumes the import filter is unavailable for the Lotus PIC or HPGL graphics, causing the error "The filter required to print this graphic is not installed. This graphic cannot be printed in high resolution." when choosing the Links or Print command.

After force-updating the link to the graphic, PageMaker 6.0 reimports the graphic using the installed PageMaker 6.0 filter.

For PageMaker 6.0, the Lotus PIC filter is IMPRC9.FLT, and the HPGL filter is IMPHGL9.FLT.

Creating a Custom Printer File to Address Slow Print Times to PostScript Printers from PageMaker 6.0x

ISSUE

Print files are larger or print more slowly than expected when printing to PostScript devices from Adobe PageMaker 6.0x.

SOLUTIONS

Use the Update PPD utility to create a custom printer file that supplements the PostScript Printer Description (PPD) file you're using and correctly reflects the available memory on your printer. The Update PPD utility (Ppd.exe), located in the Pm6\Rsrc\Usenglsh\Utility subdirectory, can be used in Windows 3.1 or Windows 95.

OR: If you are using Windows 3.1, manually create a custom printer file to supplement the PostScript Printer Description (PPD) file and accurately reflect the memory available on your printer:

1. Copy the file Testps.txt, located in the Windows\System directory, to your printer from a DOS prompt using the following command (where LPTx is your printer port):

   ```
   Copy TESTPS.TXT LPTx
   ```

   On the resulting printout, find the line that reads "Max Printer VM (KB):XXXX." XXXX represents the amount of virtual memory available on the printer (i.e., the amount of memory available to print your publications). PageMaker prints most efficiently when the FreeVM setting in the custom printer file is 90-95% of the printed number. The Testps.txt file reports memory in terms of kilobytes; the custom printer file you'll create reports memory in bytes.

   To determine the FreeVM setting for the custom printer file, multiply the Max Printer VM setting by 0.9 and add three zeros. For example, if the Max Printer VM setting is 500KB, multiply by 0.9 to get 450, then add three zeros to arrive at 450000.
2. Open the PPD for your printer in a text editor (e.g., Windows Write, Notepad) and write down the lines beginning *PPD-Adobe, *Product, *ModelName, and *NickName. Then close the PPD without saving it.
3. In the DOS Editor, type in the skeleton custom printer file shown below. Type the lines beginning *PPD-Adobe, *Product, *ModelName and *NickName to match the lines you copied from the PPD. This example creates a custom printer file for the Hewlett-Packard LaserJet 4Si. In the *NickName line, the "+" character differentiates the custom printer file from the PPD itself. PostScript is very particular about typographical errors so go slowly and proofread your file carefully. The *Include line refers to the actual filename of your PPD, not the nickname. Type it in uppercase because PPD files are case sensitive.

   NOTE: Use DOS editor because other text editors (e.g., Windows Write, Notepad) sometimes add extraneous characters to text files, which make the custom printer file invalid. To use the DOS editor, exit Windows, then, at a DOS prompt, type "Edit." If the DOS directory is not in your path statement, you may need to change to the DOS directory before typing "Edit."

   ```
   *PPD-Adobe: "4.0"
   *Product: "(HP LaserJet 4Si)"
   *ModelName: "HP LaserJet 4Si"
   *NickName: "+HP LaserJet 4Si v2011.110"
   *FreeVM: " "
   *Include: "HP4SI6_1.PPD"
   ```
4. Between the quotes in the line beginning *FreeVM: , type the number you arrived at in step 1. In this example, the line looks like this:

   ```
   *FreeVM: "450000"
   ```
5. Save the file, naming it with a .ppd extension.
6. Use the Windows File Manager or DOS COPY command to copy the custom printer file into the Pm6\Rsrc-\Usenglsh\Ppd4 directory.
7. When you print from PageMaker, choose the custom printer file from the PPD pop-up menu in the Print Document dialog box. The custom printer file appears as it is listed in the *NickName: line. In this example, the custom printer file is listed as +HP LaserJet 4Si v2011.110.

ADDITIONAL INFORMATION

If PageMaker 6.0x prints slower than expected or its print files are larger than expected, the virtual memory (FreeVM) setting in your PPD file may not accurately reflect the memory available on the printer. Creating a custom printer

PageMaker to substitute the correct memory ...on when using the PPD for your printer.

... FreeVM setting dictates the amount of data sent to ...printer, including how often fonts are downloaded. If the setting is too low, PageMaker flushes and redownloads fonts often to avoid overloading the printer's memory. When the memory available on the printer is larger than the PPD reports, PageMaker downloads fonts more often than necessary, resulting in large print files and slow print times.

PageMaker 6.0x and earlier use PPD files when printing to a PostScript printer to determine a printer's features, including the amount of memory available on the printer, predefined paper sizes, optimized screen settings to use in printing color separations, and fonts resident on the printer. Because PageMaker uses this information to determine what information to send to the printer, it is important the PPD reflect the printer's features accurately. Adobe recommends using a PPD specifically written for your PostScript printer.

Error or Objects Don't Print as Expected to HP LaserJet 4 from PageMaker 6.0

ISSUE

When printing from Adobe PageMaker 6.0 to a Hewlett-Packard LaserJet 4 using the HP LaserJet 4 PCL printer driver, objects do not print as expected, an error occurs, or partial pages print.

SYMPTOMS

Reversed (i.e., white) PageMaker-drawn lines print transparent and don't knock out objects beneath them.

PageMaker-drawn objects with pattern fills and a color other than Black applied print solid black.

PageMaker-drawn objects with pattern fills and the color Paper applied print gray.

The error "Error 21 (data complexity)" appears on the printer's display.

SOLUTIONS

Do one or more of the following:

A. Print with Use Raster Graphics selected, instead of Use Vector Graphics, for the Graphics Mode option when printing with the HP LaserJet 4 PCL printer driver. For instructions, see Additional Information.

B. When running PageMaker on a computer with a high-resolution video card installed:
   Use the Windows VGA video driver.
   OR: Use an updated video driver, available from your high-resolution video card manufacturer.

C. Create the fill in another application, export the fill as a graphic, then place the graphic in PageMaker.

ADDITIONAL INFORMATION

When printing with the Use Vector Graphics option selected in the Graphics Mode section of the Print Setup dialog box, the error "21 - Print Overrun" appears on the printer's display, or documents do not print as expected. The ReadMe file, included with LaserJet 4 printers, recommends selecting the Use Raster Graphic options instead of the Use Vector Graphics option when the printer returns the "21 - Print Overrun" error or when documents do not print as expected. The Use Vector Graphics and Use Raster Graphics options for the LaserJet 4 printers optimize printing to reduce print times.

PCL printers (e.g., HP LaserJet 4) print graphics and text by using the rasterized screen representation. When using a high-resolution video driver, rasterizing screen information for printing is memory intensive. When insufficient memory is available, objects may print differently to a PCL printer than they display. Because some high-resolution video cards are not written to Windows specifications, they may have interface problems with complex Windows application.

To enable the Raster option in the Windows 95 Printers HP LaserJet 4's Properties dialog box:

1. Choose Start > Settings > Printers from the taskbar.
2. Right-click on the HP LaserJet 4 printer icon, then choose Properties.
3. Click the Graphics tab.
4. Select Use Raster Graphics.
5. Click Apply, then click OK.

To enable the Raster option in the Windows 3.1 Printers Control Panel:

1. Open the Control Panel icon in the Main group in Program Manager.
2. Open the Printers Control Panel.
3. From the list of Installed Printers, select the LaserJet 4 printer, then click Setup.
4. In the Setup dialog box, click Options.
5. Select Raster from the Graphics Mode options.
6. Click OK in the Options dialog box, click OK in the Setup dialog box, then close the Printers Control Panel.

Rotated Images Print Distorted to PCL Printers from PageMaker 6.0 in Windows 95

ISSUE

When you print from Adobe PageMaker 6.0 to a PCL printer using the Universal Printer driver included with Windows 95, rotated images print distorted.

SOLUTIONS

Select a dithering method other than Error Diffusion in the Graphics section in PageMaker's Print Setup dialog box.
OR: Deselect Allow Printer Halftones in PageMaker's Print Color dialog box.

ADDITIONAL INFORMATION

To perform Error Diffusion dithering on an image while printing, the Universal 4.00.950 printer driver, which is included with Windows 95, dithers pixels in each horizontal row of the image. Because pixels in a rotated image may not be positioned horizontally as assumed by the Universal printer driver, rotated images print distorted from PageMaker 6.0 with Error Diffusion is selected.

The Allow PCL Halftoning option in PageMaker's Print Color dialog box enables the printer driver to control dithering (i.e., halftoning), overriding changes made in PageMaker's Image control dialog box. Deselecting the Allow PCL Halftoning option disables dithering by the printer driver.

Error "You have printer and display fonts... mismatched..." Printing from PageMaker 6.0x

ISSUE

When you print to a PostScript printer from Adobe PageMaker 6.0x running in Windows 95, the error "You have printer and display fonts that are mismatched. Text may not print as expected. To correct this, refer to the Readme.wri." occurs after the first page prints. Clicking Continue in the error dialog box prevents the error from reoccurring, but text does not print as expected (e.g., text appears smudged, kern pairs vary with printer resolution, fonts are substituted, line endings change). Clicking Cancel in the error dialog box cancels the print job, resulting in only one printed page.

SOLUTIONS

Do one or more of the following:

A. Print using the Adobe PostScript 4.1 printer driver (AdobePS), which is included on the PageMaker 6.01 Enhancement Pack.

B. Remove all your installed fonts from Adobe Type Manager (ATM) 4.0, remove font references from the Win.ini file and the Atm.ini file, re-add fonts in ATM, then check the size of the Win.ini file:

1. Make backup copies of the Win.ini and Atm.ini files.
2. In ATM, export your sets (ATM Deluxe only) and remove all installed fonts. For instructions, see Additional Information.
3. Open the Win.ini file, located in the Windows directory, in a text editor that can save in text-only format (e.g., Notepad, WordPad).
4. Delete any lines that begin with "softfont" (e.g., softfonts=20).
5. Delete all lines that refer to an MFD file (e.g., ADMFDFile=C:\Windows\Ad434af1\ Mfd).
6. Save the Win.ini file in text-only format.
7. Open the Atm.ini file, located in the Windows directory, in a text editor that can save in text-only format (e.g., NotePad, WordPad).
8. Delete any lines in the [Fonts] section (e.g., "Helvetica=C:\Psfonts\Pfm\Hv_______.pfm; C:\Psfonts\Hv_______.pfb").
9. Save the Atm.ini file in text-only format.
10. Delete all Atmfonts.qlc files, then restart Windows.
11. In ATM, re-add your fonts. For instructions, see Additional Information.
12. Choose Start > Find > Files or Folders, then locate the Win.ini file in the Windows directory. Check the size of the Win.ini file in the search results window and make sure it is smaller than 32K. If the Win.ini file is larger than 32K, make a backup of the file, then open the original Win.ini in a text editor that can save in text-only format and remove lines or sections no longer needed.

OR: Remove all your installed fonts from ATM 3.0x, remove font references from the Win.ini file and the Atm.ini file, re-add font in ATM, then check the size of the Win.ini file:

1. Make backup copies of the Win.ini and Atm.ini files.
2. In the ATM Control Panel, select all fonts in the Installed ATM Fonts list, then click Remove.
3. In the Remove Fonts dialog box, select No Confirmation to Remove Fonts if you don't want the dialog box to appear for each font you remove, then click Yes or Yes to All. Avoid selecting Delete Fonts from Disk unless you want to delete the font files from your system.
4. Open the Win.ini file, located in the Windows directory, in a text editor that can save in text-only format (e.g., Notepad Windows Write).
5. Delete all lines that begin with the word "softfont" (e.g., softfonts=20).
6. Delete all lines that refer to an *.mfd file (e.g., Admfdfile=C:\Windows\Ad434af1.mfd).
7. Save the Win.ini file in text-only format.
8. Open the Atm.ini file, located in the Windows directory, in a text editor that can save in text-only format (e.g., Notepad, WordPad).
9. Delete all lines in the [Fonts] section (e.g., "Helvetica=c:\psfonts\pfm\Hv_______.pfm; c:\psfonts\Hv_______.pfb").
10. Save the Atm.ini file in text-only format.
11. Delete all Atmfonts.qlc files, then restart Windows.
12. Open the ATM Control Panel, then click Add.
13. In the Add Fonts dialog box, locate the drive and directory containing your fonts are located (e.g., C:\Psfonts\Pfm, A:\Psfonts).
14. Select the font you want to install from the list of available fonts, then click Add.
15. Restart Windows.
16. Choose Start > Find > Files or Folders, then locate the Win.ini file in the Windows directory. Check the size of the Win.ini file in the search results window to make sure it is smaller than 32K. If the Win.ini file is greater than 32K, make a backup of the file, open the original Win.ini in a text editor that can save in text-only format and remove lines or sections no longer needed.

C. Remove all installed fonts from ATM 4.0, remove multiple [PostScript, <port>] sections from your Win.ini file, then reinstall your PostScript fonts:

1. Make sure you have your Windows 95 CD-ROM or installation disks available.

2. In ATM, remove all installed fonts.
3. Choose Start > Settings > Printers to open the Printers folder.
4. In the Printers Control Panel, select a PostScript printer, then choose File > Delete. Repeat for each PostScript printer.
   NOTE: To determine whether a printer is a PostScript printer, select the printer and choose File > Properties. When there is a PostScript tab in the printer's properties dialog box, the printer is a PostScript printer.
5. Make a backup copy of the Win.ini file located in the Windows directory.
6. Open the Win.ini file in a text editor that can save in text-only format (e.g., WordPad).
7. In the Win.ini file, delete all [PostScript,<port>] sections. Remove the printers listed between the brackets, the ATM=placeholder line, and all lines that begin with "softfont" underneath the ATM=placeholder line. For example:

```
[PostScript,lptl]
ATM=placeholder
softfonts=45
softfontl=c:\psfonts\pfm\zgrg____.pfm,c:\ps-
  fonts\zgrg____.pfb
softfont2=c:\psfonts\pfm\zgrg____.pfm,c:\ps-
  fonts\zgrg____.pfb
[PostScript,\\Lilith\bob]
ATM=placeholder
softfonts=45
softfontl=c:\psfonts\pfm\zgrg____.pfm,c:\ps-
  fonts\zgrg____.pfb
softfont2=c:\psfonts\pfm\zgrg____.pfm,c:\ps-
  fonts\zgrg____.pfb
```

8. Delete all lines that refer to an *.mfd file (e.g., Admfdfile=C:\Windows\Ad434af1.mfd).
9. Save the Win.ini file in text-only format.
10. Install your PostScript printer. For AdobePS, see the installation instructions on the PageMaker 6.01 Enhancement Pack. For the Windows PostScript printer driver installation instructions, see your Windows 95 documentation.
11. Add your fonts in ATM.
12. Restart Windows 95.

D. Make sure there is only one Win.ini file, and that it is located in the Windows directory. Rename duplicate Win.ini files.

E. To ensure the font is not damaged, reinstall it in ATM from the original disks.

ADDITIONAL INFORMATION

When the Microsoft PostScript printer driver is installed, ATM adds *.pfm and *.pfb font references to each [Postscript,<port>] section in the Win.ini file that references a separate port. The Microsoft printer driver searches for available fonts in the targeted printer's [Postscript,<port>] section in the Win.ini file. PageMaker 6.0x returns the error "You have printer and display fonts that are mismatched. Text may not print as expected. To correct this, refer to the Readme.wri." after printing the first page when the Microsoft printer driver cannot find a font used in the publication in the targeted printer's [Postscript,<port>] section in the Win.ini file. Multiple [PostScript, <port>] sections, incorrect font references, or outdated font references in the Win.ini file may also prevent the Microsoft printer driver from locating a font in the Win.ini file.

The Adobe PostScript printer driver 4.1 (AdobePS) searches for available fonts in the Atm.ini file.

Removing and then reinstalling your fonts, removing multiple [PostScript, <port>] sections from the Win.ini file, removing duplicate Win.ini files, or reinstalling a font from the original installation disks enables the printer driver to locate font references in the Win.ini file or Atm.ini file for printing.

To export your sets in ATM Deluxe 4.0:

1. In ATM, click the Sets tab.
2. Select one or more sets to export.
3. Choose File > Export.
4. In the Export dialog box, specify a filename and location for the AFS file, then click Save.

To remove your fonts in ATM 4.0:

1. In the All Font Sets pane of the Sets tab (ATM Deluxe 4.0) or the Fonts tab (ATM 4.0), select the fonts you want to remove, then click Remove.
2. In the Remove Font dialog box, select the Remove Fonts from All Set and Master Font List option, select the Remove Font Files from Disk option if you are reinstalling your fonts from the original installation disks, then click Yes or Yes to All.

To re-add your fonts in ATM 4.0:

1. Click the Add Fonts tab (ATM Deluxe 4.0) or the Fonts tab (ATM 4.0), then select Browse for Fonts from the Source pop-up menu.
2. Navigate to the drive and directory where your fonts files are located (e.g., C:\Psfonts\Pfm, A:\Fontdisk).
3. Select the fonts you want to add from the Source pane scrollbox, then click Add.

To import your sets in ATM Deluxe 4.0:

1. With Browse for Fonts still selected in the Source pop-up menu, navigate to the drive and directory where your AFS file is located. ATM lists the sets you exported in the AFS file.
2. Select the sets you want to import, then click Add.
3. Remove any duplicate fonts outside your sets by selecting them and clicking Remove.

PostScript Error "undefined..." When Printing Publication Containing Metafiles from PageMaker 6.0x

ISSUE

When you print an Adobe PageMaker 6.0x publication containing multiple metafile graphics (e.g., WMF, OLE object, CGM, WPG, DXF, Plot-10, ADI) on the same page, the

PostScript error "undefined: OffendingCommand; [various]" occurs.

SOLUTIONS

If you are running PageMaker 6.0x in Windows 3.1x, print using the Microsoft Windows PostScript printer driver 3.58. OR: If you are running PageMaker 6.0x in Windows 95, print using the Microsoft Windows PostScript printer driver 4.0 or the Adobe PSPrinter printer driver 4.0 or later (AdobePS).

ADDITIONAL INFORMATION

To print a metafile from PageMaker 6.0x, the PostScript printer driver first downloads PostScript resources for printing metafiles into the printer's memory. If the printer's memory begins to run low, PageMaker 6.0x manages the printer's memory by flushing the printer driver's PostScript resources from the printer's memory. When PageMaker 6.0x flushes the printer driver's PostScript resources for printing metafiles from the printer's memory before it prints all metafiles on a page, the PostScript error "undefined: OffendingCommand; [various]" occurs.

The Microsoft Windows PostScript printer driver 3.57 and earlier, and the Adobe PostScript printer driver 3.01 and earlier (AdobePS) can only download the PostScript resources for printing metafiles once. The Microsoft 3.58 and 4.0 printer drivers and AdobePS 4.0 and later can redownload the PostScript resources for print metafiles after the resources are flushed by PageMaker 6.0x.

Windows 3.1x and earlier are 16-bit operating system environments, which do not support 32-bit software. Because the Microsoft 4.0 printer driver included with Windows 95 is a 32-bit printer driver, it is incompatible with Windows 3.1x and earlier.

MAC OS

Q I've been having printing problems ever since I installed QuickDraw GX and the LaserWriter GX driver. Aren't they compatible with PageMaker?

A No, QuickDraw GX and the LaserWriter GX driver aren't entirely compatible with PageMaker. Unfortunately, in the last issue of Adobe Magazine (March/April 1995), the "So What Is GX, Anyway?" article incorrectly stated that the LaserWriter GX driver works "just fine" with PageMaker 5.0.

If you print from PageMaker using the LaserWriter GX driver, extra blank pages may print and some PICT graphics may not print at all from some publications. Also, the LaserWriter GX driver is incompatible with the current version (1.7) of the "Update PPD" Addition and utility. If you try to use Update PPD with this driver, you'll receive the error message, "Update PPD v1.7 will not run with QuickDraw GX enabled. Please disable it to run Update PPD." In addition, when Desktop Printing is disabled, Background Printing is enabled and the option to disable Background Printing is unavailable in the Chooser. If you remove the PrintMonitor from the System Folder, you'll receive the error, "Nothing can be printed now, because PrintMonitor could not be found. To print, put Print-Monitor into the Extensions folder in the System Folder."

If you encounter these problems you have a few options:

- You can restore standard printing for all your applications by removing QuickDraw GX files, restoring Type 1 fonts, and setting up a PostScript printer.
- You can disable the "QuickDraw GX" and "PrinterShare GX" Extensions, restore Type 1 fonts, and set up a PostScript printer.
- You can restore standard PostScript printing for PageMaker 5.0 while retaining QuickDraw GX's Desktop Printing for other applications.

For more information on the LaserWriter GX driver and PageMaker, or for instructions on how to restore standard Macintosh printing for some or all of your applications, see FaxYI document 215135, "Unable to Print from PageMaker 5.0 After Installing QuickDraw GX . . ."

By the way—the PageMaker printing problems related to the LaserWriter GX driver need not prevent you from installing System 7.5. As of early March, there is only one known, confirmed problem between PageMaker 5.0 and one of System 7.5's components. The "Macintosh Easy Open" Control Panel, which is installed with System 7.5 by default, can interfere with some PageMaker 5.0 filters (this problem is not difficult to resolve). For more information on this problem, see FaxYI document 215604, "Error, 'The document named [filename] was not . . .'"

Q Sometimes when I apply bold or italic to certain fonts, they don't print as bold or italic to my PostScript printer. I seem to have to go back and assign the bold or italic attribute through the Font menu. Why does this happen? Is it better to assign these attributes through the Font menu anyway?

A It isn't necessarily better to assign bold or italic through the Font menu than it is to assign these attributes as character formatting (by selecting bold and/or italic from the Type Style menu; by using the keyboard shortcuts Command + Shift + B for bold or Command + Shift + I for italic; or by clicking on the "B" or "I" button in the Control palette). When everything's working right, both methods will get you the same printed output.

Nevertheless, there are some distinct workflow advantages to assigning bold and italic as character formatting instead of through the Font menu. But before we explain what those advantages are and why assigning bold and italic sometimes doesn't work unless you do it through the Font menu, we need to take a step back and explain how bold and italic work in the PostScript world.

Many PostScript typeface families come with several fonts—a regular (sometimes called "Book" or "Roman") font, a bold font, a bold-italic font, and an italic font. Some typeface families also come with Semibold, Light, and other special fonts. Each font has a separate screen font and printer font file. You must have both these files for ATM to display your font accurately (or for that font to print to a non-PostScript printer), and you must have the printer font file for the font to print on a PostScript printer.

When you select a font (regular, bold, italic, or other version) from the Font menu, you're selecting that font's screen- and printer-font files directly. When you apply bold or italic character formatting to a font, you're selecting your screen and printer fonts indirectly. Say you have some text set in the regular version of Stone Sans, and then apply bold to it. The regular version of that font is designed to know which one of its sibling fonts should be used when bold is applied to it—in this case, that font would be Stone Sans Semibold. If you apply bold formatting to text set in Stone Sans Semibold, that font knows that it should substitute the font Stone Sans Bold.

Sometimes a typeface family isn't encoded to know how to perform these automatic substitutions when bold or italic formatting is applied to some or all fonts within the family. When this occurs, ATM will simulate a bold or italic effect on screen by fattening or slanting your Roman font (which won't look nearly as good as a specially designed bold or italic version of that typeface). If you then print to a non-PostScript printer, you'll get the same simulation of bold or italic that you see on screen. But if you print to a PostScript printer, you'll probably get some kind of font substitution (for instance, your text might print in the regular version of the font instead). In such cases, you'll need to select the version of the font you need from the Font menu.

One advantage to using the Font menu to gain access to bold and italic versions of your fonts is that doing so allows you to keep track of all the fonts within that family (and can help keep you from accidentally trying to use a nonexistent bold, italic, or bold-italic version of a typeface). But these are fairly minor advantages. There are quite a few more advantages to applying bold and italic as character formatting:

- Assigning bold and italic as character formatting can help facilitate easier, smoother transfer to and from the Windows platform, without unnecessary font substitution. (In Windows, you can usually only assign bold and italic as character attributes, so Windows applications like PageMaker often don't know that they're supposed to map the Macintosh font "B Sabon Bold," for instance, to the Roman version of Sabon with a bold attribute.)
- In PageMaker, assigning bold and italic as character attributes for local formatting (that is, for just part of a paragraph) ensures that assigning a style to that paragraph won't cause this kind of local formatting to change. Say you have a paragraph mostly formatted as Times Roman, with just a book title with the italic attribute applied as character formatting. If you then apply a new paragraph style that contains Helvetica with bold formatting, the book title will remain italicized—it'll become Helvetica with bold and italic attributes. On the other hand, if the book title was originally set as Times Italic via the Font menu, applying the new style would make the whole paragraph, including the book title, display and print as Helvetica Bold.

Q *(6.0 only)* **In Macromedia FreeHand 5.0x I created an EPS that contains a scanned image. When I place it in PageMaker, the scanned image won't print. Why not?**

A The scanned image probably isn't printing because it isn't actually embedded in your EPS file and PageMaker can't correctly link to the version of it on your hard disk.

A combination of things probably happened for this to occur. First, when you saved the EPS in FreeHand, you probably left the "Omit Image Data" option selected, so the scanned image wasn't actually embedded in the EPS file. Second, you probably imported the EPS while PageMaker's EPS import filter had its "Read embedded OPI image links" option selected (which it is by default)—this option is located in PageMaker's "EPS import filter v2.0" dialog box, which you can open by selecting an EPS graphic and holding the Shift key down while clicking "Open" (Windows) or "OK" (Mac) in PageMaker's "Place" dialog box.

OPI comments in an EPS file allow a scanned image to be linked to the EPS instead of being embedded in it. However, FreeHand structures those comments differently than PageMaker expects them to be structured, and because of that, PageMaker treats the OPI comments as invalid and omits the scanned image.

Fortunately, this problem shouldn't be hard to fix. Here's what you should do.

1. Open the original file in FreeHand.
2. Select "Output Options" from the File menu.
3. In the "Output Options" dialog box, select "Binary" under "Image Data" to include TIFF image data in the EPS graphic, and click "OK."
4. Select "Export" from the File menu and export your artwork in EPS format.
5. In PageMaker, select "Place" from the File menu.
6. Find the EPS graphic, click on it once, and then hold down the Shift key while you click "Open" (Windows) or "OK" (Mac).
7. In the "EPS import filter v2.0" dialog box, deselect "Read embedded OPI image links" and click "OK." Your EPS file should import and print correctly.

   Please note that when you change options in the "EPS import filter v2.0" dialog box, PageMaker will observe the changed options for any EPS you import until you reset those options or quit and relaunch PageMaker.

Q *(6.01 only)* **When I print a TIFF graphic from PageMaker 6.01, the right side of the image prints with a vertical line of solid-colored pixels. This didn't happen in PageMaker 6.0. Is there a way to prevent this?**

A Yes. As you may have discovered, this problem occurs only in 6.01 and affects only QuickDraw printers. The problem has been fixed in PageMaker 6.5. But if you won't be upgrading right away, here are some workarounds.

- Rotate or skew the image by a negligible amount, such as .01%.
- Open the TIFF in an image-editing application such as Photoshop and save it in PICT format, then replace it in PageMaker 6.01.

- Print to a PostScript printer.
- Print your publication from PageMaker 6.0.
- Save the publication in PageMaker 5.0 format, then print it from PageMaker 5.0x.

Q Each time I print something to my PostScript printer from PageMaker, I get a blank page after the job. What's causing this?

This problem is caused by a conflict between the LaserWriter 8.4.1 printer driver and PageMaker. To correct the problem, use LaserWriter 8.4 or earlier, or print using the Adobe PSPrinter driver that's included with PageMaker, or update to the LaserWriter 8.4.2 driver available from Apple. If you're not sure which version of the LaserWriter driver you're using, select the "LaserWriter 8" icon in the "Extensions" folder of your System Folder, and choose "Get Info" from the Finder's File menu.

Bitmap Images in Macromedia FreeHand 5.0x EPS Don't Print from PageMaker 6.0

ISSUE

When printing an Adobe PageMaker 6.0 publication that contains a Macromedia FreeHand 5.0x EPS graphic, bitmap images included in the EPS graphic do not print. Other elements in the Macromedia FreeHand 5.0x EPS graphic print as expected.

SYMPTOMS

The Macromedia FreeHand 5.0x EPS graphic was imported with Read Embedded OPI Image Links selected in PageMaker's EPS Import Filter v2.0 dialog box.

SOLUTION

Update to PageMaker 6.01.

OR: Resave the Macromedia FreeHand 5.0x EPS graphic to include the image data, then deselect Read Embedded OPI Image Links in PageMaker's EPS Import Filter v2.0 dialog box when reimporting:

1. Open the original file in Macromedia FreeHand.
2. Choose File > Output Options.
3. For Image Data, select Binary data to include TIFF image data in the EPS graphic.
4. Choose File > Export and export the graphic in EPS format.
5. In PageMaker, choose File > Place.
6. Select the EPS graphic, then hold the Shift key and click OK.
7. In the EPS Import Filter v2.0 dialog box, deselect Read Embedded OPI Image Links, then click OK.

ADDITIONAL INFORMATION

When printing a Macromedia FreeHand EPS graphic placed into PageMaker 6.0 with Read Embedded OPI Image Links selected, PageMaker 6.0 compares OPI image bounding box comments with the EPS graphic's bounding box comments. When the bounding box comments begin from unexpected coordinates (i.e., when the OPI image comments in the EPS graphic do not use the lower left corner of the page for the zero point), PageMaker 6.0 interprets the OPI image comments as invalid and omits the bitmap image included in an EPS graphic.

When printing a Macromedia FreeHand EPS graphic containing bitmap image data and placed into PageMaker 6.0 with Read Embedded OPI Image Links deselected, the bitmap image contained in the EPS graphic prints as expected.

When printing a Macromedia FreeHand EPS graphic containing bitmap image data and placed into PageMaker 6.01 with Read Embedded OPI Image Links selected, PageMaker 6.01 compares OPI image bounding box comments with the EPS graphic's bounding box comments, then prints the bitmap image contained in the EPS graphic prints as expected.

Blank Pages Print When Tiling to Non-PostScript Printer from PageMaker 6.0

ISSUE

When tiling an Adobe PageMaker 6.0 publication to a non-PostScript printer, tiles print blank.

SOLUTIONS

Update to PageMaker 6.01.

OR: Print the page by grouping the objects on the page, then positioning each section of the group that makes the tiled pages on a smaller page:

1. Select all objects on the page.
2. Choose Arrange > Group.
3. Choose File > Document Setup.
4. In the Document Setup dialog box, change the page size to match the desired size of the tiles (e.g., the paper size in the printer).
5. Position the first section, or tile, of the grouped object within the printable area of the page (e.g., 1/2" from the upper left corner).
6. Choose File > Print, then click Paper.
7. In the Print Paper dialog box, select None from the Tiling pop-up menu.
8. Click Print.
9. Move the grouped object on the page as desired to print each additional tile.

OR: Use PageMaker's Tiling feature to tile the publication to a PostScript printer.

OR: Print the publication using scaling instead of tiling by selecting the Reduce to Fit option in PageMaker's Print Paper dialog box.

ADDITIONAL INFORMATION

When you print tiles to a non-PostScript (e.g., QuickDraw, fax) printer from PageMaker 6.0, the tiles print blank. When you print tiles to a non-PostScript printer from PageMaker 6.01, the tiles print as expected.

Tiles print as expected to a PostScript printer from PageMaker 6.0x.

PageMaker 6.5 or Earlier Prints Incorrectly When QuickDraw GX is Installed

ISSUE

After you install QuickDraw GX, Adobe PageMaker 6.5 or earlier prints incorrectly (e.g., omits PICT graphics, prints extra blank pages) to a PostScript printer.

SYMPTOMS

Only QuickDraw GX printer drivers appear in the Chooser, instead of the Adobe PSPrinter 8.x or the Apple LaserWriter 8.x printer driver, even when Desktop printing is disabled.

After you disable Desktop printing, the system enables Background printing and dims the option to disable Background printing in the Chooser.

When you remove PrintMonitor, the system returns the error, "Nothing can be printed now, because PrintMonitor could not be found. To print, put PrintMonitor into the Extensions folder in the System folder."

SOLUTIONS

Restore standard Macintosh printing for all applications by removing QuickDraw GX files, restore Type 1 fonts, and setup a PostScript printer. For instructions, see Additional Information.

OR: Disable the QuickDraw GX and PrinterShare GX system extensions, restore Type 1 fonts, and setup a PostScript printer. For instructions, see Additional Information.

OR: Restore PostScript printing to PageMaker while retaining QuickDraw GX Desktop printing for other applications:

1. On the QuickDraw GX Install disk, double-click the Install QuickDraw GX installer control file to start the Apple Installer.
2. In the Installer dialog box, select Custom Install from the pop-up menu.
3. Click the arrow to the left of the QuickDraw GX Utilities selection to view additional options, then select the QuickDraw GX Helper option.
4. Specify the volume containing the system software as the Destination Disk, then click Install to install the QuickDraw GX Helper system extension.
5. When installation is complete, restart the Macintosh.
6. Remove the LaserWriter 7.x printer driver (named "LaserWriter" in the Finder) by using an extensions manager or by manually removing it from the Extension folder.
7. Move PostScript outline font files from the Archived Type 1 Fonts folder or other specified Type 1 font archive folder to the Fonts folder in the System Folder.
8. Start PageMaker, then select Turn Desktop Printing Off from the Apple menu.
9. When the system returns the alert, "Click OK to use the 'LaserWriter 8' driver for printing from this application. To continue using desktop printing from this application, click Cancel." click OK. PageMaker 5.0x and later will print by spooling using Background printing. If the alert refers to the LaserWriter driver instead of LaserWriter 8.x printer driver, repeat step 6.

Additional Information Apple's QuickDraw GX, included with Apple Macintosh System 7.5, is an updated version of QuickDraw, the language that controls Macintosh display and printing. To support QuickDraw GX printing, applications must recognize GX printer drivers and include QuickDraw GX options in the Print and Page Setup dialog boxes. To support QuickDraw GX TrueType fonts, applications must recognize their extended character set and their line layout capabilities for text composition.

QuickDraw GX supports only QuickDraw GX printer drivers. PostScript printer drivers (e.g., Apple LaserWriter, Adobe PSPrinter) and QuickDraw printer drivers are unavailable in the Chooser. You can access PostScript printer drivers using the QuickDraw GX Helper extension, which is included with QuickDraw GX. QuickDraw GX printer drivers included with System 7.5 include the ImageWriter GX, ImageWriter LQ GX, LaserWriter 300 GX, LaserWriter GX, LaserWriter IISC GX, PDD Maker GX, and StyleWriter GX printer drivers.

Printing when QuickDraw GX is installed is called "Desktop printing" because print jobs are controlled through Desktop Printer icons that appear on the desktop. Desktop Printers (Desktop Printer icons) are print queues that spool print jobs targeted to specific printers using a QuickDraw GX printer driver. Desktop Printers replace PrintMonitor with added functionality. To print after you install QuickDraw GX, you create a Desktop Printer icon in the Chooser. If you print before you create at least one Desktop Printer icon, the system returns the message, "Your request could not be completed because there are no desktop printers. Select Chooser from the Apple menu to create a desktop printer."

PageMaker 6.x and earlier do not support Desktop printing when you print to a PostScript printer. To print to a PostScript printer from PageMaker, you must remove or disable QuickDraw GX and restore PostScript Type 1 fonts. Restarting with extensions off, or disabling the QuickDraw GX and QuickDraw GX Helper extensions, disables QuickDraw GX and restores standard Macintosh printing. Restoring PostScript Type 1 fonts prevents fonts used in your PageMaker publications from printing as the printer's default font (e.g., Courier).

The QuickDraw GX Helper system extension enables you to bypass Desktop printing for the active application by choosing Turn Desktop Printing Off from the Apple menu. If you installed QuickDraw GX by selecting the Easy Install installation option, the Apple Installer does not install the QuickDraw GX Helper system extension. To use QuickDraw GX Helper to bypass Desktop printing and to enable PageMaker to find outline fonts when printing, move PostScript outline (printer) font files from the Archived Type 1 Fonts folder, or from another folder you specified as the Type 1 font archive folder, to the Fonts folder in the System Folder. If PageMaker cannot find outline fonts when printing, it returns the error, "One or more fonts in your publication could not be found. Be sure all of the printer fonts you need are installed on your computer. 7812:5824."

When you choose Turn Desktop Printing Off from the Apple menu, the system disables Desktop printing for the active application and returns the alert, "Click OK to use the '[driver name]' driver for printing from this application. To continue using Desktop printing from this application, click Cancel." The printer driver name included in the alert is the name of the printer driver that is compatible with the default GX printer created in the Chooser (e.g., LaserWriter, StyleWriter). For PostScript printers, QuickDraw GX Helper selects the LaserWriter 7.2 PostScript printer driver by default, when it is installed. If this compatible printer driver is unavailable, QuickDraw GX Helper selects the LaserWriter 8.x PostScript printer driver.

The Apple Installer installs the LaserWriter 7.x and LaserWriter 8.x printer drivers. PageMaker requires the LaserWriter 8.x, PSPrinter 8.x, or LaserWriter 8.x-compatible printer driver for PostScript printing. To ensure QuickDraw GX Helper selects a compatible QuickDraw GX printer driver, remove the LaserWriter 7.x printer driver from the Extensions folder and then, in PageMaker, choose Turn Desktop Printing Off from the Apple menu. If QuickDraw GX Helper cannot find a compatible QuickDraw GX printer driver, it returns an alert requesting that you to install a compatible QuickDraw GX printer driver.

To restore standard Macintosh printing for all applications:

1. Start the Apple Installer by double-clicking the Install QuickDraw GX installer on the QuickDraw GX Install disk.
2. In the Installer dialog box, select Custom Remove from the pop-up menu.
3. For the Custom Remove options, select Base QuickDraw GX Software for This Macintosh, Base QuickDraw GX Software for Any Macintosh, QuickDraw GX Utilities, ATM for QuickDraw GX, and All QuickDraw GX Drivers for Apple Printers.
4. Specify the disk containing the system software as the Destination Disk (click Switch Disk to change the selected disk), then click Remove.
5. When the installer is finished, restart the Macintosh.

To restore PostScript Type 1 fonts:

1. Move all enabled font suitcases, which are in the Fonts folder in the System Folder by default, to a different location. Enabled suitcases contain converted TrueType versions of the PostScript Type 1 font in addition to the bitmap (screen) fonts.
2. Move fonts contained in the Archived Type 1 Fonts folder in the System Folder to the Fonts folder, then delete the empty Archived Type 1 Fonts folder.
3. Move other fonts enabled using the Type 1 Enabler application to another folder not accessed by any font management utility (e.g., Suitcase). Move the original archived copy of the Type 1 font back to the desired folder to make it available to the font management utility.
4. Reinstall any version of Adobe Type Manager except for ATM/GX 3.7.

To set up a PostScript printer in the Chooser:

1. Select the Chooser from the Apple menu, then click the PSPrinter or LaserWriter 8.x printer driver icon.
2. Select a PostScript printer from the Select a PostScript printer list, then click Setup.
3. Click Auto Setup in the Current Printer Description File (PPD) Selected dialog box, and then click OK to set up the PostScript printer. An icon appears to the left of the printer's name in the Chooser indicating it is set up using the PSPrinter or LaserWriter 8 printer driver.

NOTE: When Auto Setup is selected, the PSPrinter or LaserWriter 8.x printer driver locates the PostScript Printer Description (PPD) file for the printer. If the LaserWriter 8.x printer driver cannot find a corresponding PPD file, click Select PPD and select another appropriate PPD file, or click Use Generic in the Select a PostScript Printer Description File dialog box.

To disable the QuickDraw GX and PrinterShare GX system extensions:

In Apple's Extensions Manager control panel (included with System 7.5 and later), deselect the QuickDraw GX and PrinterShare GX system extensions, then restart the Macintosh.
OR: Manually remove the QuickDraw GX and PrinterShare GX system extension.

PostScript Error Printing CMYK TIFF Image to Agfa Imagesetter from PageMaker 6.0

ISSUE

When printing separations of an Adobe PageMaker 6.0 publication containing a CMYK TIFF image to an Agfa imagesetter, the PostScript error "invalidaccess; OffendingCommand: put" occurs. The Agfa imagesetter is calibrated with Southwest Software's Color Encore 3.4 or earlier.

SOLUTIONS

Calibrate the Agfa Imagesetter using Color Encore 3.5 or later.
OR: Open the CMYK TIFF image in an image editing application (e.g., Adobe Photoshop), export the image as an EPS graphic, then replace the graphic in PageMaker.

ADDITIONAL INFORMATION

When printing separations of a PageMaker publication containing a CMYK TIFF image to an Agfa imagesetter that was calibrated with Color Encore 3.4 or earlier, the PostScript error "invalidaccess; OffendingCommand: put" occurs. When printing separations of the same PageMaker publication to an Agfa imagesetter that was calibrated with Color Encore 3.5 or later, the publication prints as expected.

When printing separations of a PageMaker publication containing an EPS graphic to an Agfa imagesetter that was calibrated with Color Encore, the publication prints as expected.

Tints from PageMaker 6.0 Print Solid from TrapWise and PrePrint Pro

ISSUE

When you print an Adobe PageMaker 6.0 separation (.sep) or EPS file from Adobe TrapWise 2.5 or Adobe PrePrint Pro, grayscale images with a process or high-fidelity tint applied in PageMaker print solid. The graphics separate as expected from PageMaker 6.0.

SOLUTIONS

Print separations from PageMaker 6.0.

OR: Apply a spot color or a different color library (e.g., PANTONE) tint to grayscale images before printing the publication as a separation or EPS file.

OR: Apply the tint to grayscale images in another application (e.g., Adobe Photoshop, Adobe Illustrator) before importing them into PageMaker and printing the publication as a separation or EPS file.

ADDITIONAL INFORMATION

When printing, PageMaker 6.0 includes Open Prepress Interface (OPI) 2.0 comments to identify color tints applied to images. PageMaker 6.0 writes incorrect OPI comments for images with process or high-fidelity tints applied, causing these tints to print solid from applications that read OPI 2.0 comments (e.g., TrapWise 2.5, PrePrint Pro).

PageMaker 6.0 Unexpectedly Downloads Fonts Installed on Printer's Hard Disk

ISSUE

Adobe PageMaker 6.0 downloads fonts installed on the printer's hard disk when printing with the Query Printer For Font and Memory Information option selected in the Print Options dialog box.

SOLUTIONS

Upgrade to Adobe PageMaker 6.01.

OR: Install a P6After.ps file containing PostScript code that enables PageMaker 6.0 to detect fonts installed on the printer's hard disk in the RSRC folder in the Adobe PageMaker 6.0 folder. A P6After.ps file containing this PostScript code is available on the Adobe BBS.

OR: Select a PPD file that includes the fonts installed on the printer's hard disk from the PPD pop-up menu in the Print Document dialog box.

OR: Create a custom printer file that includes the fonts installed on the printer's hard disk:

1. In PageMaker 6.0, choose Utilities > PageMaker Plug-ins > Update PPD.
2. In the Update/Customize PPD dialog box, click Options.
3. Select Include Fonts on the Printer's Hard Disk in the Update PPD Options dialog box, then click OK.
4. Click Update in the Update/Customize PPD dialog box.
5. When prompted, save the custom printer file in the Printer Descriptions folder in the Extensions folder in the System Folder.
6. Select the custom printer file in the PPD pop-up menu in the Print Document dialog box.

ADDITIONAL INFORMATION

PageMaker 6.0 does not detect fonts installed on the printer's hark disk when printing with the Query Printer For Font and Memory Information option selected, causing it to download PostScript fonts installed on the printer's hard disk. When you install a P6After.ps file containing PostScript code that enables PageMaker 6.0 to detect fonts installed on the printer's hard disk, PageMaker 6.0 does not download fonts installed on the printer's hard disk when printing with the Query Printer For Font and Memory Information option selected.

When printing, PageMaker 6.0 references the External Font Information section in the selected PPD or custom printer file, which lists the fonts installed in the printer's hard disk. Printer manufacturers only include fonts built in the printer (i.e., included in the printer's ROM) in PPD files.

When you select the Query Printer For Font and Memory Information option in the PageMaker 6.0 Print Options dialog box, PageMaker detects the amount of virtual memory available at the printer, then creates a list of the fonts in the printer's RAM, ROM, and hard disk. From this font list, PageMaker 6.0x determines what PostScript fonts to download when printing with the PostScript and TrueType option selected in the Download Fonts pop-up menu. PageMaker does not download PostScript fonts when the TrueType or None option is selected. PageMaker 6.01 does detect fonts installed on the printer's hark disk when printing with the Query Printer For Font and Memory Information option selected, which prevents it from downloading PostScript fonts installed on the printer's hard disk.

The PostScript code PageMaker 6.0 generates when printing can be changed using one or more external PostScript files, which contain a complete replacement of or an addendum to PageMaker's PostScript code (e.g., P6After-.ps). When PageMaker 6.0 encounters a supplemental PostScript file in the RSRC folder, it includes the contents of that file in the PostScript stream in the appropriate place. P6After.ps was created to allow modifications to PageMaker's PostScript code without having to make changes to the application code.

The following PostScript code prevents PageMaker 6.0 from downloading fonts installed on the printer's hard disk when printing with the Query Printer For Font and Memory Information option selected:

```
%Copyright: (C) Copyright 1995 Adobe Sys-
  tems, Inc.  All Rights Reserved.
%PM6 P6After.ps, Version 1.0
%Disk Font Patch—Mac Only
%This file, when placed within the RSRC
  folder, will append the PageMaker 6.x
%PostScript header (P6PS.ps) with an updated
  query for fonts on a printer.
```

TIP MAC OS

Avoid last-minute printing worries

When you're planning a long-awaited vacation, you may tend to ignore, until the last minute, the mundane process of packing. It's not that different when you're knee-deep in an important design job—consumed with the creative process, the last thing you're thinking about is what you need to bring with you to get it printed, and how you're going to get it there. It's wise to have a checklist when you're preoccupied and packing, and it's wise to have the CheckList utility when you're packing up a big job for the service bureau.

CheckList 2.6 reports on font usage, printer settings, style sheets, and linked graphic files in PageMaker 6.0x publications. It also analyzes font and print-setting information for EPS files and PostScript print-to-disk files. The analysis can then be printed in a report form, or pasted to another application. In short, CheckList provides you with an easy way of gathering information about the contents of your publications before taking them to be printed at a remote location, such as a service bureau.

CheckList has an integrated "Packager," which can compress publications and then split the compressed file across several disks. The Packager can also include necessary graphics, screen and printer fonts, tracking values, and prep files in the compressed package. The resulting compressed file is self-expanding, so CheckList needn't be present to unpack the information.

Even if you don't ever print your documents remotely, CheckList can still be useful to you. CheckList can download EPS and PostScript files, with the option to download all necessary fonts first. The downloader can query the printer for installed fonts before the download, so only the missing fonts are downloaded. In addition, you can use CheckList to help you manage your fonts. CheckList will automatically generate a report indicating damaged, duplicate, or conflicting fonts, or the presence of competing font technologies (for example, TrueType and PostScript versions of the same typeface). And it's free.

CheckList 2.6 comes with PageMaker 6.01 for the Macintosh. You can find it in the "Utilities" folder, which is inside the "Adobe PageMaker 6.01" folder.


```
%Use this file if PageMaker's two-way printer
  communications is not finding
%fonts resident on a printer's hard disk,
  and downloading them during printing.
P6PS begin
/AskFont{save/sv exch def/str(fonts/)def/st2
  128 string def
st2 cvs dup FontDirectory exch known{pop(Y
  R)}{/filenameforall where{pop str
exch st2 cvs dup length/len exch def 6 exch
  putinterval str 0 len 6 add
getinterval mark exch{}st2 filenameforall
  counttomark 0 gt{cleartomark(Y H)}{
cleartomark(NnN)}ifelse}{pop(NnN)}ifelse}
  ifelse = flush sv restore}bind def
end
```

PostScript Error or Font Substitution in PDF Created in PageMaker 6.0

ISSUE

When you use Adobe PageMaker 6.0's Create Adobe PDF plug-in to create and distill a PostScript file that includes TrueType fonts, Adobe Acrobat Distiller substitutes Courier for TrueType fonts, or returns the PostScript error "invalidfont; OffendingCommand: findfont."

SOLUTIONS

Before creating the PDF in PageMaker, select Include Downloadable Fonts in the Create Adobe PDF dialog box. OR: Select Prepare PostScript File for Distilling Separately in the Create Adobe PDF dialog box, then distill the file. OR: Use PageMaker to create the PostScript file with TrueType Only selected in the Download Fonts pop-up menu in PageMaker's Options printing dialog.

ADDITIONAL INFORMATION

Because Acrobat Distiller cannot interpret TrueType fonts, it relies on the PostScript printer driver to convert TrueType fonts to PostScript Type 1 fonts. When TrueType fonts are not included in the PostScript file generated by PageMaker, the printer driver cannot convert TrueType fonts to PostScript Type 1 fonts. Without font information, Distiller cannot embed fonts, and either substitutes Courier for the TrueType fonts or returns the PostScript error "invalidfont; OffendingCommand: findfont."

Type 1 Fonts Print Substituted from PageMaker 6.0 After Installing QuickDraw GX

ISSUE

PostScript Type 1 fonts print as the printer's default font (usually Courier) from Adobe PageMaker 6.0 after QuickDraw GX has been installed.

SYMPTOMS

The message "PageMaker 6.0 does not support, and is not compatible with QuickDraw GX. Remove QuickDraw GX and restore Type 1 fonts to ensure proper printing with PageMaker." appears when printing, followed by the message "One or more fonts in your publication could not be found. Be sure all of the printer fonts you need are installed on your computer. 7812:5824."

SOLUTION

De-install QuickDraw GX, restore Type 1 fonts in the system, and set up a PostScript printer in the Chooser. For instructions, see Additional Information.

ADDITIONAL INFORMATION

Adobe PageMaker 6.0 and earlier are not compatible with QuickDraw GX fonts and printer drivers.

PostScript Type 1 fonts located in the Fonts folder in the System Folder during QuickDraw GX installation are "enabled" by the Apple QuickDraw GX installer. Enabled suitcases contain converted TrueType versions of PostScript Type 1 outline fonts and bitmap (screen) fonts. The original PostScript bitmap and outline fonts are copied into the Archived Type 1 Fonts folder, located in the System Folder. PostScript Type 1 fonts not present in the Fonts folder during QuickDraw GX installation may be enabled by using the Type 1 Enabler utility included with System 7.5x.

After removing QuickDraw GX, PostScript Type 1 fonts must be "restored" manually by moving them from the Archived Type 1 Fonts folder into the Fonts folder in the System Folder or into a folder accessed by a font management utility (e.g., Suitcase 2.x). When printing, PageMaker searches for outline fonts in the Fonts folder or in the folder specified by a font management utility. When PageMaker cannot locate outline fonts during printing, the error "One or more fonts in your publication could not be found. Be sure all of the printer fonts you need are installed on your computer. 7812:5824." occurs and PostScript fonts print as the printer's default font (usually Courier) .

To remove or de-install QuickDraw GX, Apple recommends using the Apple installer's "Custom Remove" option.

To restore PostScript Type 1 fonts after de-installing QuickDraw GX:

1. Remove all "enabled" font suitcases. By default, enabled fonts suitcases are located in the Fonts folder in the System Folder. Enabled fonts may also be located in a folder accessed by a font management utility (e.g., Suitcase).
2. Move the original Type 1 fonts into the Fonts folder in the System folder or into a folder accessed by a font management utility. Original Type 1 fonts are located in the Archived Type 1 Fonts folder or in a folder specified when using the Type 1 Enabler utility.
3. Delete the empty Archived Type 1 Fonts folder or folder specified when using the Type 1 Enabler utility.

CorelDRAW WMF Converted to PICT Prints with Extra Lines from PageMaker 6.0

ISSUE

When printing to a PostScript printer from Adobe PageMaker 6.0, a CorelDRAW Windows Metafile (WMF) graphic prints with extra lines. The graphic displays in the publication as expected.

SOLUTIONS

Export the graphic from CorelDRAW in TIFF or EPS format, then replace the graphic into PageMaker.

OR: Before exporting the graphic in WMF format from CorelDRAW, avoid converting text to curves.

ADDITIONAL INFORMATION

When printing to a PostScript printer from PageMaker 6.0, a CorelDRAW WMF graphic that includes text converted to curves prints with extra lines, but displays in the publication as expected.

CorelDRAW TIFF images and EPS graphics print from PageMaker 6.0 as expected.

Adobe PageMill®

Adobe PageMill was the world's first visual HTML-page creator. Adobe acquired it as well as Adobe SiteMill when it acquired Ceneca in 1995. PageMill version 2.0 for MacOS and Windows was released in 1997. PageMill makes building Web pages as easy as "drag and drop." While you don't have to know a thing about HTML, tags, anchors, frames, URLs or any of the other Internet protocols, PageMill's powerful technology enables even veteran HTML programmers to use PageMill as the prototyping tool of choice. Adobe SiteMill 2.0 was released in 1997.

Contents

Adobe PageMill®

Feature Techniques

MAC OS

Q I get tired of typing long URLs into PageMill 1.0's Link Locator bar, and a friend tells me PageMill 2.0 has some way to make this easier. Is that so?

A Yes, it is. Although there's no way around the fact that some URLs are long and unwieldy, PageMill 2.0 introduces a feature called "assisted URL entry" that makes the process a little easier.

When you're typing an address in the Link Locator bar at the bottom of PageMill's application window, try entering only the first one or two characters of the URL's protocol (the protocol is the first part of a URL, such as "ftp://," "http://," or "telnet://") and then pressing the Tab key. You'll see that PageMill completes the protocol. For example, if you were to type "fi" and press Tab, PageMill would finish the protocol by entering "file://" into the Link Locator bar.

When the URL's protocol is done, pressing the Tab key again automatically enters "www." for the domain section of the URL (most Web URLs begin with "www.").

Next, you must enter a server name followed by a period (e.g., "adobe."). Finally, PageMill can complete the domain when you enter the first character of the closing section of the domain name and press Tab. For example, if you type "o" and press the Tab key, PageMill enters "org" into the Link Locator bar. Alternatively, you can press Tab several times and the entry will rotate among "com" (the default), "org," "edu," "net," "gov," and "mil."

Here's a complete example of using this feature. Let's say you want to enter the URL http://www.adobe.com into the Link Locator bar. You'd press "h" and the Tab key to enter the "http://" protocol. Next, another Tab enters "www." You'd type in "adobe." and then press Tab again to complete the URL with "com."

Q When I double-click on an image in my PageMill 2.0 document, I don't see any way for me to make areas of the image transparent. What happened to the image window that I used in PageMill 1.0?

A The image window is still part of the PageMill application, but, because support for client-side image maps has been added in PageMill 2.0, you access the image window differently in the new version of the program. The two options you have for accessing the image-editing tools in PageMill 2.0 are illustrated below and to the right.

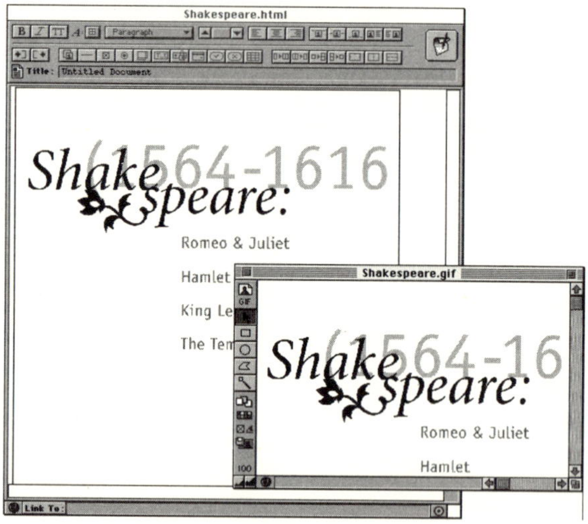

Hold down the Command key as you double-click, and the image window will open, with all its familiar tools and options.

When you double-click on an image in PageMill 2.0 (without holding down Command), you are actually opening PageMill's in-place image editor—the way you can tell it's open is that a wide grey border appears around your image and a set of drawing tools appears on the second line of the toolbar. The drawing tools are for defining "hot spots" as part of creating client-side image maps.

Q *(2.0 only)* **Can I import my Excel worksheet into PageMill?**

A Yes, PageMill 2.0 allows you to import data from an Excel worksheet, and automatically places the data into a table in the document. To import Excel data into a PageMill 2.0 document:

1. Copy the Excel worksheet you want to import. Select all the cells in that worksheet and choose "Copy" from the Edit menu.
2. Paste the worksheet into PageMill. Switch to PageMill, and click the globe icon to switch to Edit mode. Click the cursor where you want the table to be inserted, and choose "Paste" from the Edit menu.

Using Dartmouth University's Fetch to Upload Files to a Web Server

CONFIGURING FETCH PREFERENCES

Fetch is a File Transfer Protocol (FTP) utility for the Macintosh, written by Jim Matthews at Dartmouth University. Adobe Systems recommends using Fetch 3.0 to transfer Adobe PageMill or Adobe SiteMill files.

A File Transfer Protocol is a way of moving files between computers according to a common set of rules, or protocol. The protocol guides all aspects of the process, from connecting the two sites and identifying which and what kind of files are to be moved, to determining how the files are transmitted over the connection and stored. FTP protocol involves a client and server: the computer initiating the connection and making a request is the client and the computer receiving the connection is the server. Fetch is an FTP client and can interact with computers (servers) that recognize and use the FTP protocol.

NOTE: Do not confuse Fetch with Adobe Fetch. Adobe Fetch is a commercial utility from Adobe Systems that catalogs files. Fetch and Adobe Fetch have completely different feature sets.

To upload your Web files using Fetch, use the following procedures.

Configuring Fetch Preferences

Fetch has preference settings that must be configured before you upload files to the Web server. Proper preference settings ensure that you preserve links in uploaded files, and that images in HTML documents display as expected in a Web browser.

1. Launch Fetch and click Cancel in the New Connection dialog box.
2. Choose Customize > Preferences.
3. Click the Upload tab.
4. For the default text format, select Text from the pop-up menu.
5. For the default non-text format, select Raw Data from the pop-up menu.
6. Deselect the Add .txt Suffix to Text Files option.
7. Click OK.

Connecting to the Web Server

Your Internet Service Provider (ISP) should provide you with instructions and login information so that you can connect to the Web server. If you have not received this information, contact your ISP before proceeding.

1. Choose File > New Connection.
2. Enter the Web server's hostname.
3. Enter your User ID.
4. Enter your password.
5. Enter the name of the directory where you will upload your Web site. Many ISPs name this directory "public_-html."
6. Click OK.

Uploading the Site

If you using System 7.5 or later, simply select Automatic in the Fetch window, then drag your site folder into the Fetch window.

If you are using System 7.1.2 or earlier, use these steps to upload your Web site:

1. Choose Remote > Put Files and Folders.
2. Locate the file or folder you wish to upload, and click Add.
3. When you are finished adding files, click Done.
4. Click OK to confirm your selection. Make sure the Text File format is Text and the Other Files format is Raw Data.

Retrieving Files and Folders

When you make changes to your Web site, you may need to download a file from the server. Fetch can download files and folders from any directory on the Web server that you have permission to alter. If you are using System 7.5 or later, simply select Automatic in the Fetch window, then drag your site folder from the Fetch window onto your desktop.

If you are using System 7.1.2 or earlier, use these steps to download files from your Web site:

1. Launch Fetch and connect to the Web server.
2. Click Automatic in the Fetch window.
3. Select the file or folder you wish to download and click Get File.
4. Set the Text File format to Text and the Other Files format to Raw Data.
5. Navigate to the location you wish to save the file or folder.
6. Click OK.

To stop uploading or downloading during a file transfer, click the Stop button. If the server you are connected to does not recognize the Stop command, the transfer will continue. To stop the transfer at this stage, close the transfer window or quit Fetch.

Using Anchors in Adobe PageMill 1.0.x and Adobe SiteMill 1.0.x

An anchor is a link that enables you to go to or jump to a specific location within the same Hypertext Markup Language (HTML) document or to a location in another HTML document. For example, when the HTML document you are creating for use on the World Wide Web is long, you can incorporate anchor links from a list of topics at the beginning of the HTML document to the related information in the body of the document. This type of anchor is an internal anchor. You can also use anchors to establish links between HTML documents. Creating a link to an anchor within another HTML document enables the reader to go directly to a specific location within the document, instead of to the top of the document. This type of anchor is an external anchor.

To create internal and external anchors in PageMill and SiteMill:

1. In PageMill or SiteMill, save your HTML document while in Edit mode.
2. Choose Edit > Show Anchors.
3. Drag the Page Proxy icon to a location near the text or image for which you want to create a link.
4. Select the text or image to which you want to link, then drag the anchor icon onto the selected element.
5. Select the anchor, and cut and paste it in the desired destination (i.e., the location the link jumps to within the same HTML document, or within a different HTML document).

After establishing anchors within PageMill and SiteMill HTML documents, the anchor name can be changed. The standard HTML naming convention for an anchor is: "#anchorname." PageMill and SiteMill generate a name for each anchor using the convention: "anchorxxxxxxx," where xxxxxxx is a randomly generated 7-digit number (e.g., anchor1234567).

NOTE: Change anchor names before creating links to the anchors. If you change an anchor's name after linking it to an object within an HTML document, that link will be broken, and the anchor will no longer preview as expected. Do not use HTML-reserved characters (e.g., pound symbol "#," or ampersand "&") within anchor names.

To change the name of an anchor in PageMill and SiteMill:

1. Open the HTML document in PageMill or SiteMill.
2. Click the Globe icon to switch to Edit mode.
3. Choose Edit > Show Anchors.
4. Select the anchor that you wish to change.
5. Choose Window > Show Attributes Inspector
6. Click on the Image button.
7. Enter the new name of the anchor in the Name field, and press Return.

After establishing anchors within PageMill and SiteMill HTML documents, the anchor link color can be changed. PageMill and SiteMill indicate established links by changing the appearance and color of linked objects. Linked text displays in a different color, and is underlined. Linked images display with a colored border. The default link color for PageMill and SiteMill is blue. You can change the color of linked objects in PageMill and SiteMill HTML documents in the Attributes Inspector.

To select the default link color for text, and the default border color for linked images:

1. Open the HTML document in PageMill or SiteMill.
2. Click the Globe icon to switch to Edit mode.
3. Choose Window > Show Attributes Inspector.
4. Click the Page button.
5. Under Link Color, select Custom from the Normal pop-up menu.
6. Make a color selection, and click OK.

Creating Links to Acrobat PDF Files in PageMill 1.0.x and SiteMill 1.0x General Information

Because Adobe PageMill 1.0.x and Adobe SiteMill 1.0.x do not support importing Portable Document Format (PDF) files, you can't insert them using the Insert command or drag-and-drop. You can, however, create links to PDF files, which enables Internet users to view the files using their Web browser and a helper application (e.g., Acrobat Reader, Acrobat Exchange).

Creating a Mirror Folder

HTML (Hypertext Markup Language) documents include links to external files, rather than the contents of external files. To make sure the links are maintained after you upload your files to the Web server, create a mirror folder of your Web site on a local volume that contains all your HTML documents and linked PDF files.

Formatting Links to PDF Files

The format (i.e., syntax) of the link that you enter in the Link Location field varies depending on where the PDF file is located.

When the PDF file is located within the same folder as the HTML document, enter only the name of the PDF file. For example:

```
my_PDF.pdf
```

When the PDF file is located in a folder called "pdf_files" that is within the same folder as the HTML document, enter the path to the file followed by the filename. For example:

```
pdf_files/my_PDF.pdf
```

When the PDF file is located in a folder called "pdf_files" that is in the same folder as the folder containing the HTML document, enter "../" followed by the path to the file and the filename. For example:

```
../pdf_files/my_PDF.pdf
```

When the PDF file is located on a remote Web server, enter the PDF file's Uniform Resource Locator (URL). For example:

```
http://www.adobe.com/PDFs/my_PDF.pdf
```

Linking to a PDF File in a PageMill HTML Document

1. Move the PDF file to the location in the mirror folder where it will reside when uploaded to the Web server.
2. Make sure the PDF filename includes a ".pdf" extension.
3. Open the HTML document in which you want to create a link to the PDF file.
4. Click the globe icon to switch to PageMill's Edit mode.
5. Select the object (i.e., text or image) that you want to link to the PDF file.
6. Activate the Link Location Bar at the bottom of the Page View Window by pressing Enter.
7. Type the PDF file's pathname, including the PDF file's name, then press Return or Enter.

Linking to a PDF File in a SiteMill HTML Document

1. Move the PDF file to the location in the mirror folder where it will reside when uploaded to the Web server.
2. Choose Site > Load, and select the local mirror folder of your Web site.
3. Open the HTML document in which you want to create a link to the PDF file.

4. Click the globe icon to switch to SiteMill's Edit mode.
5. Select the object (i.e., text or image) that you want to link to the PDF file.
6. Drag the PDF file from SiteMill's Site view, and drop it on the selected object.

Previewing Links to PDF Files

PageMill and SiteMill cannot preview links to PDF files. To preview the links, use a Web browser.

Linking to Movie and Sound Files in PageMill 1.0.x and SiteMill 1.0.x General Information

Adobe PageMill 1.0.x and Adobe SiteMill 1.0.x do not support importing sound or movie files. While you cannot insert sound or movie files using the Insert command or drag-and-drop, you can create links to sound and movie files, enabling Internet users to view the files using their Web browser and a helper application (e.g., Sparkle, RealAudio Player).

PageMill 2.0 supports importing and previewing sound and movie files when the plug-in corresponding to the file type of the sound or movie file is installed in the Browser Plug-ins folder in the PageMill Plug-ins folder.

Creating a Mirror Folder

HTML (HyperText Markup Language) documents include links to external files, rather than to the contents of external files. To make sure links are maintained after you upload your files to the Web server, create a mirror folder of your Web site on a local volume that contains all your HTML documents and linked sound and movie files.

Formatting Links to Sound and Movie Files

The format (i.e., syntax) of the link that you enter in the Link Location field varies depending on where the sound or movie file is located.

When the file is located within the same folder as the HTML document, enter only the name of the file. For example:

```
my_sound.au
```

When the file is located in a folder called "media_files" that is within the same folder as the HTML document, enter the path to the file followed by the filename. For example:

```
media_files/my_sound.au
```

When the file is located in a folder called "media_files" that is in the same folder as the folder containing the HTML document, enter "../" followed by the path to the file and the filename. For example:

```
../media_files/my_sound.au
```

When the PDF file is located on a remote Web server, enter the PDF file's Uniform Resource Locator (URL). For example:

```
http://www.adobe.com/media_files/my_sound.au
```

Sound File Formats and Filename Extensions

Sound File Format	Extension	Platform
AU/U-law	.au, .snd	Sun/UNIX
AIFF/AOFC	.aiff, .aif	Macintosh
WAV	.wav	Windows
MIDI	.midi, .mid	Any
MPEG audio	.mp2	Any
RealAudio	.ram	Any

Movie File Formats and Filename Extensions

Movie File Format	Extension	Platform
AVI	.avi	Windows
MPEG	.mpg, .mpeg	Any
QuickTime	.qt, .mov	Macintosh
QuickTime VR movie	.mov	Macintosh

Linking to a Sound or Movie File in a PageMill HTML Document

1. Move the file to the location in the mirror folder where it will reside when uploaded to the Web server.
2. Make sure the filename includes an extension.
3. Open the HTML document in which you want to create a link to the file.
4. Click the globe icon to switch to PageMill's Edit mode.
5. Select the object (i.e., text or image) that you want to link to the file.
6. Activate the Link Location Bar at the bottom of the Page View Window by pressing Enter.
7. Type the file's pathname, including the file's name, then press Return or Enter.

Linking to a Sound or Movie in a SiteMill HTML Document

1. Move the file to the location in the mirror folder where it will reside when uploaded to the Web server.
2. Choose Site > Load, then select the local mirror folder of your Web site.
3. Open the HTML document in which you want to create a link to the file.
4. Click the globe icon to switch to SiteMill's Edit mode.
5. Select the object (i.e., text or image) that you want to link to the file.
6. Drag the file from SiteMill's Site view and then drop it on the selected object.

Previewing Links to PDF Files

PageMill and SiteMill cannot preview links to sound or movie files. To preview the links, use a Web browser.

Creating Image Maps in PageMill 1.0.x and SiteMill 1.0.x General Information

CONTACT YOUR INTERNET SERVICE PROVIDER

An image map is an inline graphic in a Hypertext Markup Language (HTML) document that has multiple links associated with it. Different areas of an image map, called hot spots, have separate hyperlinks assigned to them—when you click on a hot spot, the Web browser accesses the hyperlink associated with it.

Image maps can be either server-side or client-side image maps. Server-side image maps are processed on a Web server, and client-side image maps are processed by the Web browser viewing the document. PageMill and SiteMill create server-side image maps, and don't directly support the creation of client-side image maps.

To create a server-side image map in an HTML document, you create a separate image map (.map) file, which contains information about the hot spot areas of the image map and their hyperlinks. When you click on an image map graphic, the .map file is read by the Web server software or passed to a CGI-script. The server or CGI-script matches the coordinates of the area clicked on the graphic to the correct hyperlink, then sends the requested HTML document or external link to the Web browser.

To preview a server-side image map on your local computer, use PageMill's or SiteMill's Preview mode, which simulates a map application or script on a Web server and enables you to check the image map links to pages within your own site.

When creating an image map, use the following guidelines to ensure your image map works as expected when you publish your HTML documents on a Web server. Because of the number of servers and configurations available, you need to obtain specific instructions for your Web server from your Internet Service Provider (ISP).

CONTACT YOUR INTERNET SERVICE PROVIDER

Before creating an image map, ask your ISP these questions:

- Does the Web server support image maps?
- What is the final URL of your Web site?
- What image map file type does the Web server require (i.e., NCSA or CERN)?
- What path is used to invoke image map support on the Web server?
- Is there any documentation available for configuring an image map to run on the Web server?

Your ISP must provide you with the path for invoking your image map on the Web server. The path is similar to a URL, and often begins with the URL of the mapserver application followed by additional information (e.g., the path to the map file). When your ISP does not know the path for invoking support for your image map on the Web server, ask for a URL of a page on their Web server that contains a working image map. Adobe Systems cannot provide this information.

CREATE A SITE FOLDER

Create a main site folder on a local volume, and place all of your HTML documents and images into the folder before creating links. Once you complete the Web site, upload the contents of this folder (either all at once, or file-by-file) to the Web server.

Creating and maintaining a pair of mirrored site folders (i.e., one copy on the local volume, and the other copy on the Web server) ensures your links are maintained throughout the site creation and editing process. It also ensures that image maps you create in PageMill or SiteMill work successfully.

SET UP PREFERENCES IN PAGEMILL AND SITEMILL

PageMill and SiteMill include several preference settings which affect how links behave, and what path information appears in .map files. Before you create image maps in PageMill or SiteMill, choose Edit > Preferences to configure preference settings as follows:

A. Page Preferences

Line Breaks

Select the platform on which you will publish your HTML documents. Web servers require supported line break characters at the end of each line in .map files.

B. Image Preferences

Default Folder for Images

Select a folder within the local mirror of your Web site as the Default Folder for Images. The folder you specify will contain the PICT graphics converted by PageMill or SiteMill. Select a folder within the local mirror of your Web site, which will ensure your links are maintained after you upload your site onto a Web server.

Map format

Select the map format specified by your Internet Service Provider (ISP). Web servers require map files to be in either NCSA or CERN format.

Remote Server Preference

Select the Remote Server option when using image maps in your HTML document. Enabling the remote server option makes the Local Root Folder and Remote Root Directory settings active. If you mount the external volume that serves as your Remote Root Directory, leave this preference unchecked.

Local Root Folder

Select the root level of your local site folder. PageMill and SiteMill write path information in .map files using this setting as a point of origin.

Remote Root Directory

Enter your Web site's remote root directory path, whose pathname begins and ends with a forward slash (/). The pathname you enter for your Web site's remote root directory path is often your Web server's Universal Resource Locator (URL) address without the protocol (http:/) and domain (/www.name.com/). If you have domained your Web site (i.e., purchased or licensed your own domain name) type a single forward slash (/) character as the Remote Root Directory.

PageMill and SiteMill append Remote Root Directory information to the beginning of each path statement in .map files. These path statements must be accurate for your image map links to work as expected on the Web server.

If you make changes to PageMill's or SiteMill's preference settings after you create an image map, resave the .map file to reflect the changes. To resave a .map file, double-click the image map image to open the Image View window. Make a minor change (e.g., move one of the hot spots slightly, then move it back) and choose File > Save.

CREATE HOT SPOTS

To create image map hot spots in PageMill and SiteMill, double-click the image to open it in the Image View window. Select a hot spot tool, then click and drag on the image to create the hot spots. After you draw hot spots in the

Image View window, you can select, move, or reshape them using the pointer tool.

You can change the color of each hot spot to increase its visibility. To change the color of a hot spot, select it with the pointer tool, click the color icon, and select the desired color.

LAYER OVERLAPPING HOT SPOTS

PageMill and SiteMill number each hot spot you create, to represent the layering order. Smaller-numbered hot spots are in front of higher-numbered ones. When hot spots overlap, those in front take precedence over those in back. To ensure the correct hot spot link is used when someone clicks the image map, you can change the layering order of the hot spots. Select the desired hot spot, click the layer icon, then select Bring to Front, Send to Back, Shuffle Forward, or Shuffle Back.

SPECIFY A DEFAULT IMAGE MAP LINK

Specify a default link to another page so that if readers miss the hot spots, they link to a default location. Most Web servers require map files to contain a default link. To add a default link to an image map, drag a page icon, an image icon, or an anchor, and drop it anywhere on the image not covered by a hot spot.

ADD LINKS TO REMAINING HOT SPOTS

To add links to the remaining hot spots, drag a page icon, an image icon, or an anchor, and drop it onto each hot spot. Alternatively, you can select each hot spot and type the link's URL into the Link Location Bar in the Image View window and press Enter.

When you finish creating links, save the image map by choosing File > Save. PageMill and SiteMill create a .map file using the image's name plus the .map extension, and save the .map file into the folder as the image.

CHANGE THE IMAGE TO AN IMAGE MAP

Change your image to an image map by selecting your graphic in Page view, opening the Attributes Inspector, and clicking Map in the Image Attributes panel.

SPECIFY THE MAP LOCATION FOR THE WEB SERVER

For image maps to work when uploaded to a Web server, you must link the mapped graphic to the .map file using the path provided by your ISP. Select the graphic in Page view, open the Attributes Inspector, type the path in the Location text box in the Text Attributes panel, then press Enter.

Designing Web Pages General Information

Before designing your Web page, contact your Internet Service Provider (ISP) to obtain requirements and limitations (e.g., available disk space on the Web server, URL address) for your Web site. Then decide whether you want to distribute information using Hypertext Markup Language (HTML), the command language used to create Web pages, or using a combination of HTML and Portable Document Format (PDF) files.

HTML, the command language used to create Web pages, is a semantic markup language that controls the content of a Web page, with few controls over the layout of the Web page. You can use HTML styles to control the appearance (e.g., font, point size, bold, italic) of text in a Web page, but the Web browser (e.g., Netscape Navigator) has final control over how text in a Web page displays. Create HTML documents to distribute information electronically when you do not require control over layout. You can create HTML documents by saving HTML commands in a text-only format file or by using an HTML authoring tool.

PDF files enable you to control layout and typography attributes in documents distributed electronically. You can create PDF files using Adobe Acrobat, which can convert a PostScript file into a PDF file. Acrobat 2.1 and later can include embedded hyperlinks to a Web location in a PDF file.

When designing a Web page, consider your audience's hardware and software limitations. Larger image files take longer to download than smaller image files. Web pages that use advanced HTML features (e.g., image maps, forms) require the Internet services provider to help implement your HTML documents on the Web server.

After deciding to use HTML or a combination of HTML and PDF files to distribute your information, determine the structure of your pages to minimize the need to relink pages. For example, decide on using linked pages or longer pages with anchors for your Web page, the number of Web pages in your Web site, and the theme of each Web page.

HTML documents include references, or links, to images in an external location. To ensure your links remain intact after being copied to the Web server, create a mirror folder, which is a folder that duplicates the folders and their contents for your Web site, on your hard drive.

PageMill 1.0.x and SiteMill 1.0 automatically convert inserted PICT and Scrapbook files, which are incompatible with browsers, to GIF files then saves converted GIF files into the folder specified as the Default Folder for Images. When using PageMill 1.0.x or SiteMill 1.0 to create HTML documents, prevent broken links to images by specify your mirror folder as the Default Folder for Images in the PageMill Preferences dialog box.

Using PageMill's and SiteMill's Pasteboard

You can use the Pasteboard in Adobe PageMill 1.0.x and Adobe SiteMill 1.0.x to store text, images, and links that you use frequently in your HTML documents.

To add an object to the Pasteboard, select the object in your document and then drag it to the Pasteboard. PageMill and SiteMill create a copy of the object in the Pasteboard. When you select and drag multiple objects to the Pasteboard, PageMill and SiteMill group them in the Pasteboard. Then, when you copy them to your HTML document, they ungroup the objects.

To add a copy of an object stored in the Pasteboard to your document, select the object and then hold down the Option key while you drag the object to your document. To remove an object from the Pasteboard, drag it to your document and press the Delete key.

The Pasteboard contains five pages. To flip to a different page in the Pasteboard, click the turned-up page flap in the lower-left corner of the Pasteboard to display the next page, or click the lower-left corner, below the turned-up page flap, to display the previous page.

PageMill's and SiteMill's <NATURALSIZEFLAG> HTML Tag

When you insert an image into an Adobe PageMill or Adobe SiteMill document, PageMill and SiteMill create a reference for the image in the HTML document that includes the name, dimensions, and alignment of the image, and writes the <NATURALSIZEFLAG="x"> HTML tag, where "x" is a value of 0, 1, 2, or 3. For example:

```
<IMG SRC="IMAGE.GIF" WIDTH="287" HEIGHT=
"122" ALIGN=bottom NATURALSIZEFLAG="3">
```

PageMill and SiteMill use the <NATURALSIZEFLAG="x"> tag to specify an image's actual or resized dimensions. PageMill and SiteMill determine the display size of an updated image using either the original image's actual dimensions, or by scaling the original image's dimension based on the <NATURALSIZEFLAG="x"> tag's value.

Browsers ignore the <NATURALSIZEFLAG="x"> tag. If you remove the <NATURALSIZEFLAG="x"> tag from a PageMill or SiteMill HTML document, PageMill or SiteMill restores the <NATURALSIZEFLAG="x"> tag after opening and saving the HTML document.

`<NATURALSIZEFLAG="x"> Tag Values`

`<NATURALSIZEFLAG="0">`

The value "0" indicates a horizontally and vertically resized referenced image. When updating or replacing the referenced image, PageMill or SiteMill scales the updated image to maintain the dimensions of the original image.

`<NATURALSIZEFLAG="1">`

The value "1" indicates a vertically resized image. When updating or replacing the referenced image, PageMill or SiteMill scales the updated image to maintain the only the height dimension of the original image.

`<NATURALSIZEFLAG="2">`

The value "2" indicates a horizontally resized image. When updating or replacing the referenced image, PageMill or SiteMill scales the updated image to maintain only the width dimension of the original image.

`<NATURALSIZEFLAG="3">`

The value "3" indicates an actual size image. When updating or replacing the referenced image, PageMill or SiteMill displays the updated image using the image's PageMill dimensions, and not the original image dimensions.

Linking Images in PageMill and SiteMill General Information

You can link to images into an Adobe PageMill or an Adobe SiteMill document using drag-and-drop, copy and paste, or the Insert command. Because HTML is a semantic markup language and cannot contain binary image data, PageMill and SiteMill create HTML code that contains references, or paths, to the externally-stored image file. When the browser application reads a HTML document, it locates the external image file then loads it into the appropriate location on the Web page. When the path to the image is incorrect, a broken graphic icon or question mark appears on the Web page in place of the image.

PageMill and SiteMill automatically convert inserted PICT and Scrapbook files to 72 dpi GIF files. PageMill 1.0.x and SiteMill 1.0.x save the converted files into the folder specified in the Preferences dialog box as the Default Folder for Images. PageMill 2.0 saves converted files into the folder specified in the Preferences dialog box as the PageMill Resources folder. To specify the location of converted files, choose Edit > Preferences.

PageMill and SiteMill define the path to a linked image contained in an HTML document when saving the HTML document. After the HTML document is uploaded to the service provider, the path to a linked image file is not automatically updated. PageMill and SiteMill write the link to the inserted image file relative to the location of the HTML file when the HTML file was saved in PageMill or SiteMill. When the HTML file and the image are located in the same folder, PageMill and SiteMill indicate the link to the image file with the <img src="[image file name]"> tag. For example:

```
<img src="graphicname">
```

When the HTML file is located in a folder that contains the linked image file in an additional folder (e.g., linked GIF files in the Images folder), PageMill indicates the link image with the <img src="[folder name]/[image file name]"> tag. For example:

```
<img src="images/graphicname">
```

The forward-slash "/" is the UNIX character that separates the directories or folders in a path statement. The "/" command instructs the browser to link to the image file in a folder located with the HTML document. When the image file is located in a folder containing the HTML document, PageMill indicates the linked graphic with the <img src="../"[image file name]"> tag. For example:

```
<img src="../graphicname">
```

The "../" characters instructs the browser to locate the linked image in the folder hierarchically above the HTML document. Each instance of "../" instructs the browser to look for the linked graphic one level higher in the folder hierarchy. For example, the tag <img src="../../graphicname"> instructs the browser to search for the linked graphic two folders above the folder containing the HTML file.

When the folder structure of the volume containing the HTML documents is changed, the browser viewing the HTML document displays a broken link icon in place of the image. Because PageMill's and SiteMill's drag-and-drop architecture enables you to easily insert graphics from many different locations (e.g., servers, disks, hard disks), your HTML document may preview correctly on your computer, but the images may not appear when you view the document on a server. To preserve the links to images referenced in your HTML document, create a folder structure on your local volume that mirrors the structure of folders on the sever where your HTML document and linked images will be uploaded.

Changing PageMill's and SiteMill's Default Font

Adobe PageMill and Adobe SiteMill use the font Times to display text in Hypertext Markup Language documents. You can change the font PageMill and SiteMill use to display text by editing the PageMill or SiteMill application in a resource editor (e.g., ResEdit).

To change PageMill or SiteMill's default font:

DISCLAIMER: This procedure is not supported by Adobe Systems Incorporated and is only provided as a guideline. Experience using ResEdit is highly recommended, since it can change or remove any resource from any file. Always modify a copy of the file to be edited. Never modify an open file. If the wrong resource is modified or alterations are incorrectly performed, the application can be damaged. In the event of problems, revert to the original copy.

PageMill and SiteMill calculate the position of the cursor and text selection areas using integer (i.e., whole number) font widths. Most proportional fonts contain real (i.e., fractional number) font widths, which Adobe Type Manager (ATM) uses to compose text to the screen. Because of this, the font you specify as PageMill's or SiteMill's default font may cause the cursor and selection areas to be incorrect in PageMill or SiteMill while ATM is active.

1. At the Finder, make a copy of the PageMill or SiteMill application by selecting it and choosing File > Duplicate.
2. Open the copy of the PageMill or SiteMill application in Resedit 2.11 or later.
3. In Resedit's Adobe PageMill or Adobe SiteMill copy window, double-click the FOND resource.
4. Choose File > Open, then navigate to the Fonts folder in the System Folder.
5. Select the desired font suitcase, then click Open.
6. In the [Fontname] window, double-click the FOND resource.
7. In the FONDs from [Fontname] window, select the desired font FOND resource, then choose Edit > Copy.
   NOTE: Because Bold or Italic font styles may cause poor on-screen text display, it is best to choose a basic (e.g., plain, roman) font style.
8. Close the FONDs from [Fontname] window.
9. Click the FONDs from the Adobe PageMill or Adobe SiteMill copy window, then choose Edit > Paste.
10. In FONDs from the Adobe PageMill or Adobe SiteMill copy window, delete the "Times" FOND resource.
11. Select the pasted font FOND resource, then choose Resource > Get Resource Info.
12. Enter "20" in the ID field, then choose File > Save.
13. Quit ResEdit.
14. Use the copy of the PageMill or SiteMill application to create HTML documents.

Creating Web-Based Forms that Return Data by E-mail

Web-based forms enable Internet users to send data to a Web server, which stores, analyzes, or acts on the data entered into your form. For a Web server to process data entered in your form, your Internet Service Provider (ISP) must associate a Common Gateway Interface (CGI) script with the form. However, if your ISP does not provide support for CGI scripts, you can configure your form to send data to an Internet e-mail address when an Internet user clicks the Submit button.

To link a Submit button to an Internet e-mail address in Adobe PageMill or Adobe SiteMill:

NOTE: The following information is provided to assist you in retrieving form data when your ISP or Webmaster does not provide access to form-processing CGI scripts. Adobe Systems recommends linking your form to a form-processing CGI script, rather than retrieving form data through e-mail.

1. In PageMill or SiteMill, open the HTML document.
2. Click the globe icon to switch to Edit mode.
3. Select the Submit button.
4. Choose Window > Show (Attributes) Inspector.
5. In PageMill 2.0, click the Inspector's Form tab. In PageMill 1.0.x or SiteMill 1.0.x, click the Inspector's Page button.
6. Click inside the Action text box.
7. Enter the e-mail address using the "mailto:" protocol (i.e., mailto:user@address), then press Return or Enter. For example:
   ```
   mailto:jdoe@company.com
   ```
   NOTE: Do not enter space characters before or after the colon. The word "mailto" must be in lowercase characters.
   Internet users send the data they enter into your form to the specified e-mail address by clicking the Submit button.

The Web server encodes data when sending it to an e-mail address, making the data difficult to read in e-mail form. For example, when you view data entered into a form in an e-mail application (e.g., Lotus cc:Mail), space characters display as a "+" (plus sign) or "&" (ampersand), and paragraph returns display as "&0D."

To make form data easier to read in an e-mail application, create a description for each form element:

1. Open the HTML document.
2. Click the globe icon to switch to Edit mode.
3. Select a form element (e.g., text entry box).
4. Choose Window > Show (Attributes) Inspector.

5. In PageMill 1.0.x, or SiteMill 1.0.x, click the Inspector's Page button. (PageMill 2.0 displays the appropriate tab in the Inspector.)
6. In the Name text box, enter a description of the form element, then press Enter or Return.

After you create a description for each form element, the form data that is sent to an e-mail address includes the description of the contents of each form element, as well information entered into the form fields.

Using Clipping Files with PageMill or SiteMill

Adobe PageMill and Adobe SiteMill support creating and importing clipping files, which are either in PICT format (i.e., picture clippings) or text format (i.e., text clippings). You create clipping files by dragging selected items from an application that supports Macintosh drag and drop (e.g., PageMill, SiteMill, Photoshop 3.0.4, Scrapbook, SimpleText) onto the desktop or into an open window in the Finder.

Dragging and dropping from an application that supports Macintosh drag and drop into another application that supports Macintosh drag and drop requires both applications to be running and visible. Because clipping files are created by dragging selected items to the Finder, you can use clipping files to exchange data from an application that supports Macintosh drag and drop into another without having both applications running and visible.

To create clipping files from an application that supports Macintosh drag and drop, install the Clipping Extension system extension when running System 7.5 or later. When running System 7 Pro (Finder 7.1.3), install both the Clipping Extension and the Macintosh Drag and Drop system extension.

To create a clipping file from a PageMill or SiteMill Hypertext Markup Language (HTML) document:

1. In PageMill or SiteMill, open the HTML document from which you want to create a clipping file.
2. Click the globe icon to switch to Edit mode.
3. Select the item or items you want to include in the clipping file.
4. Drag the selected item or items from PageMill or SiteMill and drop them onto the desktop or into an open window in the Finder.

When dragging a single GIF image or JPEG image from a PageMill or SiteMill HTML document to the Finder, PageMill and SiteMill convert the image to PICT format to create a picture clipping file. When dragging text or a combination of text, form, and image objects from a PageMill or SiteMill HTML document to the Finder, PageMill and SiteMill create a text-only format clipping in which all text formatting is lost, and replace images and form elements with pound (#) characters.

Because PageMill and SiteMill do not maintain text and image formatting in clipping files, drag and drop objects directly from one PageMill or SiteMill HTML document to another, instead of using clipping files, to maintain text and image formats. Use PageMill or SiteMill clipping files when transferring data from a PageMill or SiteMill HTML document into another application that supports Macintosh drag and drop.

Using Progressive JPEG Images in PageMill and SiteMill

Baseline JPEG images contain graphic information stored in a single, top-to-bottom scan. Because the image loads in one pass, it can be time-consuming to download over a slow modem connection. Interlaced GIF images load more quickly by dividing graphic information into a series of scans, but they support only 8-bit color.

Progressive JPEG images were introduced to provide fast loading while maintaining color depth. They support up to 32-bit color, and load quickly by dividing graphic information into a series of scans. The first scan, a low-resolution copy of the image, serves as a placeholder in the document and provides a preview of the image. Successive scans improve the quality of the image, until the image appears at the intended resolution and quality. Each scan adds to the data already present, so that the total storage requirement is roughly the same as for a baseline JPEG image.

Adobe PageMill and Adobe SiteMill cannot preview progressive JPEG images. When you insert a progressive JPEG image into a PageMill or SiteMill document, the image displays as a missing graphic icon (i.e., a small square containing a question mark), although it previews correctly in a Web browser. Do not resize the bounding box of the missing graphic icon, which could cause the image to resize unexpectedly in a Web browser.

To successfully use a progressive JPEG image with PageMill or SiteMill, create a baseline copy of the image. Add this copy to the document and use it as you would any other image file. Then, before you upload the document to a Web server, remove the baseline copy from the site folder and add the progressive JPEG image, renaming it with the name used by the baseline copy.

The latest versions of Netscape Navigator and Microsoft Internet Explorer support progressive JPEG images.

Animated GIF Images General Information

A short tour on the Internet today reveals an array of special effects on Web pages, from animated icons to virtual reality scenes. Among the simplest effects are animated GIFs.

Animated GIFs contain multiple images assembled into one file. An application or script (e.g., GifBuilder, Imaging Machine) collects individual images and compiles them into frames within a single file. When previewed, each frame displays in sequence to simulate animation.

Animated GIF images are possible because of features added to the two latest versions of the Compuserve GIF file format (i.e., GIF87a and GIF89a). Both formats enable you to store multiple images within the core data stream of a single file. In addition, the GIF89a format adds several features that enhance the creation of animated GIFs, including transparency, interlacing, timing delay between frames, and the ability to animate a portion of an image.

When you view an animated GIF in a compliant browser (e.g., Netscape Navigator 2.0), each frame displays sequentially, and the sequence repeats itself to achieve the appearance of true animation. When you view an animated GIF in a non-compliant browser (e.g., America Online Browser 1.0), the first or the last frame of the file displays, or the frame sequence displays once instead of looping. When you place an animated GIF into a PageMill or SiteMill document, only the first frame displays.

You add animated GIFs to Hypertext Markup Language (HTML) documents as you would any other image. Use animated GIFs at display-intended size, as resizing an animated GIF affects the resolution of the images. Animated GIFs are typically too large to use as background images, and will not animate as expected (e.g., a single frame displays rather than an animation).

Creating Thumbnail Links in PageMill and SiteMill General Information

You can design HTML documents in Adobe PageMill and Adobe SiteMill with thumbnail links to larger graphic images. The thumbnail link displays in a Web page as a small, low-resolution version of the original image, which downloads to the Web browser quickly. Clicking on the low-resolution image causes the Web browser to download a larger, higher resolution copy of the image.

PageMill and SiteMill cannot downsample images, so you must first create the thumbnail in an image editing application (e.g., Adobe Photoshop). Thumbnails should be smaller than 256 x 256 pixels in size, have a resolution no higher than 72 pixels per inch, and be saved in a supported format (i.e., GIF, JPEG, or PICT). After creating the thumbnail image, you can link it to the original image in PageMill or SiteMill.

To link the thumbnail image to the original image in PageMill or SiteMill:

1. Insert the thumbnail image into a PageMill or SiteMill HTML document.
2. Select the thumbnail image on the page.
3. Choose File > Open and open the original image to which the thumbnail will be linked.
4. Drag and drop the image icon from the image window to the selected thumbnail on the page.

Unexpected Results

MAC OS

Q Centered elements in my PageMill document sometimes do not appear centered when I open the document in Netscape. What's happening?

A Netscape Navigator doesn't reliably display elements that are centered using tags, and may display some of them as left-aligned. The only way to work around this is to use different alignment tags—of which there are several.

PageMill 2.0 lets you choose which tags get automatically used to align text and objects within your documents. You can use the tag (the paragraph tag), the <DIV> tag (a tag proprietary to Netscape that creates divisions within text), or the <CENTER> tag, which is supported by a number of browsers, including Netscape. (Using a combination of the tags is not an option unless you tag your HTML code manually in a text editor, after you've finished all your PageMill work on the document—if you open it again in PageMill, all those tags will be converted back to the tag you specified as your preference.) When elements have been centered using either <DIV> tags or <CENTER> tags, Netscape Navigator displays those elements correctly.

Here's how to set it up in PageMill 2.0.

1. Select the <DIV> or <CENTER> tag as your default. Choose "Preferences..." from the Edit menu, and click the "HTML" icon in the left panel of the "Preferences" dialog box to access HTML code preferences. Then, in the "HTML Syntax" section on the right side of the "Preferences" dialog box, choose either the <DIV> tag or the <CENTER> tag from the Alignment pop-up menu. (The default preference is the tag.) Click "OK" to close the "Preferences" dialog box.
2. Save your document.
3. Test the results. Open the document in Netscape Navigator to verify that your elements align as expected.

For more information on the alignment tags, see the "Behind the Scenes" tip at the top right of this next page.

Q Sometimes when I indent something to the right in PageMill, the element moves beyond the right margin of the window, and I can't select it. How can I get it back?

A When you indent something beyond the right margin of the PageMill document window, the only way to get it back is to indent it back to the left. To indent the element back into editable range, click an insertion point in the line where the element is located. (If nothing seems to happen when you click there, it's because the cursor isn't visible either—it's over by the object that's outside the window. To be sure you're putting the cursor in the correct place, try clicking an insertion point at the end of the previous line, then pressing the right arrow key once to advance the insertion point a single character.) Press the left-indent button until the element is visible.

Images in PageMill 1.0x or SiteMill 1.0.x HTML Documents Display as "?" in Browser

ISSUE

When viewing a HTML document in a Web browser, a GIF or JPEG image linked to a HyperText Markup Language (HTML) document displays with a question mark icon, but displays as expected when previewed in Adobe PageMill 1.0.x or Adobe SiteMill 1.0.x.

SOLUTIONS

Do one or more of the following:

A. Change the browser's preferences to display GIF and JPEG images automatically.

B. Add the ".GIF" filename extension to GIF image files and the ".JPG" or ".JPEG" filename extension to JPEG image files, then reinsert or relink the image in PageMill or SiteMill.

C. Change the name of your Web site's images and folders to names that conform to UNIX file naming conventions, then reinsert or relink the image in PageMill or SiteMill.

D. Upload the image to the Web server as Raw Data. For more information on uploading images to a Web server using your FTP application (e.g., Dartmouth Fetch), refer to your FTP application's documentation.

ADDITIONAL INFORMATION

When opening an HTML document, browsers display images, and images located in folders, whose names do not conform to UNIX naming conventions as a question mark icon. When opening a HTML document, PageMill and SiteMill replace characters in the path statement for the referenced image that do not conform to the UNIX file naming conventions with HTML code equivalents in the HTML document, which enables the images in the HTML document to preview as expected in PageMill and SiteMill. For example, when opening an HTML document that contains space characters in a path statement for a referenced image, PageMill and SiteMill replace the space characters with their HTML code equivalent, "%20."

UNIX filenames are case sensitive, can only include alphanumeric characters and the period (.), underscore (_), and hyphen (-) punctuation characters, and cannot include the forward slash or two consecutive periods.

Unable to Apply Text Wrap to Images in PageMill 1.0.x or SiteMill 1.0.x

ISSUE

Adobe PageMill 1.0.x or Adobe SiteMill 1.0.x do not display text wrap around images specified with ALIGN tags in Preview mode. When opening an HTML document, PageMill 1.0.x or SiteMill 1.0.x do not display text wrap around images as expected in Preview mode.

SOLUTIONS

Use PageMill 2.0.

OR: When your Web browser supports Netscape extensions to the HTML 3.2 language (e.g., Netscape Navigator 1.1n or later), open the PageMill or SiteMill document in a text editor (e.g., SimpleText, TeachText), then manually add the ALIGN tags.

DISCLAIMER: Adobe Systems does not support modifying an HTML document with a text editor. Familiarity with opening HTML files in a text editor and saving in text-only (e.g., ASCII) format is required. Experience with HTML language is highly recommended. Always modify a copy of the original HTML file. If alterations are incorrectly performed or the file is saved in the wrong format, the HTML file or sections of the HTML file can be unreadable. In the event of problems, revert to the original copy.

ADDITIONAL INFORMATION

PageMill 1.0.x and SiteMill 1.0.x support HTML 2.0 tags and some Netscape extensions to the HTML 2.0 language. Because ALIGN tags are Netscape extensions to the HTML 3.0 language, which PageMill and SiteMill do not support, PageMill and SiteMill do not display text wrap around images specified with ALIGN tags in Preview mode.

Because PageMill 2.0 supports HTML 3.2 tags, and some Netscape extensions to the HTML 3.2 language, PageMill supports using text wrap in HTML documents.

PageMill 1.0 incorrectly rewrites the ALIGN HTML tags and displays them in the Raw HTML style (i.e., red text). For example:

```
<IMG SRC=(image name) WIDTH=228 HEIGHT=105
  ALIGN=left>
```

is rewritten by PageMill 1.0 to read:

```
<IMG SRC=(image name) WIDTH=228 HEIGHT=105
  ALIGN=bottom NATURALSIZEFLAG=0>
```

Because PageMill 1.0.x and SiteMill 1.0.x do not rewrite ALIGN tags, avoid opening and saving HTML documents that contain ALIGN tags in PageMill 1.0.

Question Mark Icon Displays Instead of Image in SiteMill 1.0.x or PageMill 1.0.x and Later

ISSUE

A question mark icon and path statement appear instead of the expected image in an Adobe SiteMill 1.0.x or Adobe PageMill 1.0.x or later document.

SYMPTOMS

A GIF or JPEG image in the HTML document, or one of the folders containing the image, was moved, deleted, or renamed.

The HTML document was copied from another hard disk, but the linked images included in the HTML document were not.

The HTML document was created in another HTML editing application or in a text editor.

TIP MAC OS

Behind the scenes

When you center an element using the tag, PageMill writes the alignment attributes within the paragraph tag (i.e., <P ALIGN=CENTER>). When you center elements using the <DIV> tag, PageMill writes alignment attributes using Netscape's <DIV> tag (i.e., <DIV ALIGN=CENTER>). When you center elements using <CENTER> tags, PageMill writes alignment attributes separate from the paragraph tag (i.e., <CENTER>centered text </CENTER>).

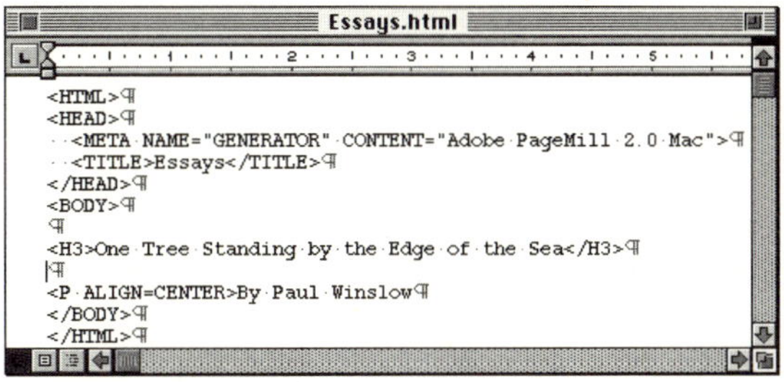

SOLUTIONS

In PageMill, relink to the image files in Edit mode:

1. Click the Globe icon to switch to Edit mode.
2. Double-click the question mark icon.
3. Select the image's filename, then click OK.
4. Repeat steps 2-3 for each additional image included in the HTML document.

OR: In SiteMill, relink to the image files using the drag-and-drop error correction feature:

1. Choose Site > Load.
2. Select the site folder, then click Open.
3. In SiteMill's Errors window, note the filename of the missing image.
4. In SiteMill's Site window, select the missing image's file icon and then drop it on the corresponding icon in the Errors window.
5. Click OK at the Modify Files prompt.
6. Repeat steps 3-5 for all image files that appear in the Errors window.

OR: Increase the amount of memory (RAM) allocated to PageMill or SiteMill:

1. Quit all open applications.
2. Choose About This Macintosh from the Apple menu.
3. Note the Largest Unused Block value (i.e., available memory), then close the About This Macintosh window.
4. Select the PageMill or SiteMill application icon, then choose File > Get Info.
5. Enter a larger value in the Preferred Size text box (System 7.1 or later), not exceeding the Largest Unused Block value you noted in step 3.
6. Close the Get Info window.

ADDITIONAL INFORMATION

When opening an HTML (Hypertext Markup Language) document that contains an image, PageMill and SiteMill create a link to the image by including its path statement (i.e., the description of its location on the hard disk) in the document. If PageMill or SiteMill cannot locate the image because its path is different than the path statement in the HTML document, they cannot display the image. In its place they display a question mark icon and path statement. After you relink the image, PageMill and SiteMill update its path statement in the HTML document, which enables them to locate and display the image as expected.

When you create an HTML document with a text editor or other HTML editor and define the link to an image file as an absolute link or Uniform Resource Locator (URL) link instead of a relative link, PageMill and SiteMill cannot locate the image. After you relink the image in PageMill or SiteMill, PageMill and SiteMill update the path statement for the image with a relative path, which enables them to locate and display the image as expected.

When PageMill and SiteMill do not have enough memory to display an image, they display a question mark icon and path statement in its place.

Center Aligned Objects in PageMill or SiteMill HTML Documents Display Left Aligned in Mosaic

ISSUE

Center aligned objects in an Adobe PageMill or an Adobe SiteMill document display left aligned in NSCA Mosaic 2.x and earlier.

SOLUTIONS

When using PageMill 2.0, align objects using <ALIGN> tags:

1. Click the Globe icon to switch to Edit Mode.
2. Choose Edit > Preferences, then click the HTML icon.
3. In the HTML Syntax section, choose tag from the Alignment pop-up menu, then click OK.
4. Choose Edit > HTML Source to switch to HTML Source view.
5. Choose Edit > HTML Source to switch to Page Edit mode.

OR: After saving the HTML document in PageMill or SiteMill, replace <CENTER> tags with <x ALIGN=CEN-TER> tags, where "x" is the text style attribute (e.g., P, H1), in a text editor:

DISCLAIMER: Adobe Systems does not support modifying a HTML document with a text editor. Familiarity with opening HTML files in a text editor and saving in text-only (e.g., ASCII) format is required. Experience with HTML language is highly recommended. Always modify a copy of the original HTML file. If alterations are incorrectly performed or the file is saved in the wrong format, the HTML file or sections of the HTML file can be unreadable. In the event of problems, revert to the original copy.

1. Save the HTML document in PageMill or SiteMill.
2. Open a copy of the HTML document in a text editor that can save in text-only format (e.g., SimpleText, Microsoft Word).
3. Replace <CENTER> tags with <x ALIGN=CENTER> tags, where "x" is the text style attribute (e.g., P, H1).
4. Save the HTML document in text-only format.

ADDITIONAL INFORMATION

Mosaic 2.x does not recognize the Netscape <CENTER> tag. Because PageMill 1.0.x and SiteMill 1.0.x use the Netscape <CENTER> tag to center align objects, objects aligned using the <CENTER> tag display left aligned in Mosaic. Mosaic only displays objects aligned using the <ALIGN=CENTER> HTML tag as center-aligned objects.

PageMill 2.0 enables you to select which HTML tag to use when aligning elements; <ALIGN>, <CENTER>, or <DIV>. When you select the <ALIGN> tag in PageMill's Preferences dialog box, and toggle between HTML Source view and Page Edit mode, PageMill rewrites the file using <ALIGN> tags to align document elements. Elements aligned using <ALIGN> tags display as expected in Mosaic 2.x.

PageMill or SiteMill Always Requests Registration Information When it Starts

ISSUE

Every time PageMill or SiteMill starts it displays the Registration dialog box requesting your registration information, even after you've entered your registration information in the Registration dialog box and clicked OK.

SOLUTIONS

Restart with extensions off, personalize PageMill or SiteMill, then restart with extensions on:

1. Restart without all extensions by holding the Shift key while restarting until the message "Welcome to Macintosh. Extensions Off." appears.
2. Start PageMill or SiteMill, enter the requested information in the registration dialog box, then click OK.
3. Quit PageMill or SiteMill, then restart the Macintosh.

OR: Restart with extensions off, remove then reinstall PageMill or SiteMill, then personalize PageMill or SiteMill:

1. Delete the Adobe PageMill Prefs (Preferences) and Adobe PageMill Pasteboard files from the Preferences folder in the System Folder.
2. Delete the Macintosh Drag and Drop and ObjectSupportLib system extensions from the Extensions folder in the System Folder.
3. Move the HTML documents you created from the PageMill or SiteMill folder, then delete the PageMill or SiteMill folder.
4. Restart without all extensions by holding the Shift key while restarting until the message "Welcome to Macintosh. Extensions Off." appears.
5. Install then launch PageMill or SiteMill, enter the requested information in the registration dialog box, then click OK.
6. Quit PageMill or SiteMill, then restart the Macintosh.

ADDITIONAL INFORMATION

If PageMill or SiteMill is unable to write registration information into the PageMill or SiteMill application file because of an extension conflict or because the PageMill or SiteMill application is damaged, they will request product registration information every time they start.

The first time PageMill or SiteMill starts, it displays the product Registration dialog box. When you click OK in the product Registration dialog box, PageMill or SiteMill writes your registration information into its application file.

PageMill or SiteMill Forms Don't Work on Web Server Troubleshooting Guide

ISSUE

After you upload an Adobe PageMill or an Adobe SiteMill document that contains a form, nothing happens after submitting information entered into the form.

SOLUTIONS

Do one or more of the following:

DISCLAIMER: Adobe does not provide technical support for Common Gateway Interface (CGI) scripts or Web Servers, which HTML forms require.

A. Set up the form by doing one or more of the following:
   A. Include a submit button in the form.
   B. Verify the Uniform Resource Locator (URL) listed for the Submit button in the Action field of the Page Attributes Inspector and the GET or POST option in the pop-up menu to the right of the Action field for the customer's CGI script requirements are correct.
   C. For each individual form elements (e.g., radio buttons, text fields), associate a name that can be understood by a CGI script in the Object panel of the Attributes Inspector.
   D. Name all radio buttons in a group using the same name.
B. Test the form to ensure it submits information as expected by using a test CGI script from the National Center for Supercomputing Applications (NCSA):
   1. Open the page containing the form in PageMill or SiteMill.
   2. Choose Window > Show Attributes Inspector.
   3. Click the Page icon in the Attributes Inspector palette to display the Page Attributes Inspector.

4. In the Page Attributes Inspector, type the following into the Action field, then press Return: http://hoohoo.ncsa.uiuc.edu/cgi-bin/test-cgi
5. Select GET from the pop-up menu to the right of the Action field.
6. Choose File > Save As and save the page to the local hard disk.
7. Open the page in a browser that reads forms (e.g., Navigator Netscape, NCSA Mosaic, MacWeb).
8. Fill out the form and click the submit button. When the form is set up to submit information correctly, you receive a page back from the NCSA hoohoo Web server containing information indicating the name of your browser, connection, and the form's information received.

ADDITIONAL INFORMATION

After creating an interactive HTML form for the Web in PageMill or SiteMill, your Internet Service Provider must create the interactions using the CGI scripts associated with form. You can associate an e-mail address with your form so the data entered into the form can be sent to a specified e-mail address. Because data entered into a form is encoded when it is sent to an e-mail address, data entered into an HTML form is not easy to read when viewed in an e-mail application. For example, when viewing data entered into an HTML form in an e-mail application, space characters entered into a form display as a "+" or "&" character, line breaks display as the "&0D" characters. To ensure data received from the HTML forms is easy to read, associate your form with a CGI script.

PageMill and SiteMill embed HTML commands within a document. Browsers that support HTML forms (e.g., Netscape Navigator, NCSA Mosaic) use these embedded HTML commands to display text fields, radio buttons, submit buttons, and other form related elements. Browsers that support forms also support sending the information entered into the form to the Web address specified in the form. To send information entered into a HTML form, browsers require an associated CGI script to submit the information. When the reader presses a submit button in an HTML form in a browser, the server invokes the associated CGI script.

CGI scripts are written using a scripting language (e.g., AppleScript, Perl).

Horizontal Rules in HTML Documents Preview Incorrectly in Web Browser

ISSUE

After you edit an HTML document in Adobe PageMill 1.0.x or Adobe SiteMill 1.0.x, horizontal rules do not display at the expected width in a Web browser. The horizontal rule previewed as expected in a Web browser before you saved the document in PageMill or SiteMill.

SOLUTIONS

Use PageMill 2.0.

OR: Remove the percentage sign from the <HR WIDTH> tag: disclaimer: Adobe Systems does not support modifying an HTML document with a text editor (e.g., SimpleText, TeachText). Familiarity with opening HTML documents in a text editor and saving in text-only (e.g., ASCII) format is required. Experience with HTML language is highly recommended. Always modify a copy of the original HTML document. If alterations are incorrectly performed or the file is saved in the wrong format, the HTML document can be further damaged. In the event of problems, revert to the original copy.

1. Open a copy of the HTML document in a text editor that can save in text-only format (e.g., SimpleText, TeachText).
2. Locate the <HR WIDTH> tag that contains a percent sign. For example:
```
<HR WIDTH="120%">
```
3. Remove the percent sign from the tag. For example:
```
<HR WIDTH="120">
```

ADDITIONAL INFORMATION

PageMill 1.0.x and SiteMill 1.0.x express the width of horizontal rules as a percentage of the current screen width. Other HTML editors (e.g., World Wide Web Weaver) enable you to express the width of horizontal rules as either a percentage of the current screen width, or as a fixed number of pixels. When opening HTML documents created in other HTML editors, PageMill 1.0.x and SiteMill 1.0.x add a percent sign to values for the width of horizontal rules, causing the horizontal rule to preview incorrectly in Web browsers.

PageMill 2.0 supports horizontal rules expressed as a percentage of the current screen width, and a fixed number of pixels.

Text Entered into PageMill or SiteMill HTML Documents is Unexpectedly Hyperlinked

ISSUE

When you type text in an Adobe PageMill or an Adobe SiteMill document, the text appears to be hyperlinked (i.e., blue and underlined).

SOLUTION

Remove the link from the text by selecting the text and choosing Edit > Remove Link.

ADDITIONAL INFORMATION

When you enter new text into a PageMill or SiteMill HTML document, it takes on the attributes of any text at the insertion point. If text at the insertion point contains a hyperlink, so will the new text. Choosing Edit > Remove Link removes any hyperlink attributes from the selected text.

Images Dragged into PageMill or SiteMill Documents Display with Fewer Colors

ISSUE
When you drag and drop an indexed color image from an image editing application into Adobe PageMill or Adobe SiteMill, the image appears posterized (i.e., it contains fewer colors).

SOLUTIONS
Convert the image to RGB mode before you drag and drop it into the PageMill or SiteMill document.
OR: Save the image in GIF or JPEG format from an image editing application, then use the Insert Image command to add it into the PageMill or SiteMill document.

ADDITIONAL INFORMATION
When you add a PICT image to an HTML document, PageMill and SiteMill convert a copy of the PICT image to GIF format. PICT images support 24-bit color (16.7 million colors) and GIF images support 8-bit color (256 colors). When converting the image, PageMill and SiteMill must discard color information from the copy of the PICT image to conform to GIF specification. PageMill and SiteMill discard color information from all placed PICT images.

When you drag and drop an indexed color image into a PageMill or SiteMill document, the system software converts the image to a 24-bit PICT, even though indexed color images contain a maximum of 256 colors (8-bit color). This conversion adds no additional colors to the image. PageMill and SiteMill must discard color information from the PICT image to convert it to GIF format. The loss of additional colors from the image causes it to appear posterized in the HTML document.

RGB images support 24-bit color. When you drag and drop an RGB image into a PageMill or SiteMill document, the system software converts the image to a 24-bit PICT image. PageMill and SiteMill still discard color information from the PICT image to convert it to GIF format but no additional color loss occurs.

PageMill and SiteMill do not discard color information from GIF or JPEG images you add using the Insert Image command.

Can't Drop Text, Graphic, Link, or Anchor onto Page in PageMill or SiteMill

ISSUE
You cannot drop text, links, anchors, or images onto a page in Adobe PageMill or Adobe SiteMill.

SOLUTION
Click the globe icon in the upper-right corner of the page to switch from Preview mode to Edit mode (Pen and Paper icon).

ADDITIONAL INFORMATION
You cannot edit documents while in Preview mode in PageMill and SiteMill. Preview mode simulates the way a document and its links will appear in a Web browser. To edit a document in PageMill or SiteMill, click the globe icon to switch to Edit mode.

You use the Mode button to switch between Preview mode and Edit mode in PageMill and SiteMill. When a document is in Preview mode, a globe icon appears on the Mode button. When a document is in edit mode, a pen and paper icon appears on the Mode button.

Paragraph Changes After Applying Style in PageMill or SiteMill

ISSUE
When you apply a heading style to a line of text in Adobe PageMill or Adobe SiteMill, the entire paragraph changes to the new heading style, instead of only the selected text.

SOLUTION
Apply a type style (e.g., bold, strong) from the Style menu, instead of a different heading style.

ADDITIONAL INFORMATION
Because HTML does not support multiple styles within a paragraph, when you apply a heading style to a line of text, PageMill and SiteMill apply the heading style to the entire paragraph.

HTML supports multiple type styles (e.g., bold, strong) in a paragraph. To emphasize selected text in a paragraph without changing the attributes of the entire paragraph, apply a type style (e.g., bold, strong) from the Style menu.

Pop-up Menus in PageMill or SiteMill HTML Documents Don't Work in Netscape 1.1N

ISSUE
When you preview an Adobe PageMill or Adobe SiteMill document in Netscape Navigator 1.1N or earlier, form pop-up menus display as text entry boxes.

SOLUTIONS
Specify a default menu choice for the pop-up menu:
1. Open the HTML document containing the pop-up menu in PageMill or SiteMill.
2. Click the globe icon to switch to Edit mode.
3. Double-click the pop-up menu.
4. Drag the triangle that appears on the right side of the pop-up menu to the menu choice that you wish to be selected by default.
5. Click outside of the pop-up menu.

OR: Preview the document in Netscape Navigator 2.0 or later.

ADDITIONAL INFORMATION

Netscape Navigator 1.1N or earlier does not support form pop-up menus without a specified default menu. When you preview a PageMill or SiteMill HTML document in Netscape Navigator 1.1N or earlier, form pop-up menus that do not have a default menu choice specified behave as text entry boxes, which enable you to type text into a Web-based form.

Browser Displays Gibberish Characters in Web Pages Uploaded to America Online

ISSUE

A Web browser displays gibberish characters (i.e., binary data) when you view an Adobe PageMill or Adobe SiteMill document uploaded to America Online.

SOLUTION

Follow the instructions provided by America Online for uploading the HTML document. For instructions, contact the America Online FTP administration department by Internet e-mail (ftpadmin@aol.com) or America Online e-mail (ftpadmin).

ADDITIONAL INFORMATION

After uploading your Web site to America Online's My Home Page section, America Online compresses the Web site files into a StuffIt archive. When you view the compressed files in a browser, the browser displays the compressed file's binary data instead of the HTML document.

Anchor Links Don't Function in IBM's Web Explorer 1.0.x

ISSUE

After you edit an HTML document in Adobe PageMill or Adobe SiteMill, anchor links in the document do not function in IBM's Web Explorer 1.0.x (i.e., nothing happens when you click on a linked image or text).

SOLUTION

Open the HTML document in a text editor that can save in text-only format and replace the reference to the linked object:

DISCLAIMER: Adobe Systems Incorporated does not support modifying an HTML document with a text editor. Familiarity with opening HTML documents in a text editor and saving in text-only (e.g., ASCII) format is required. Always modify a copy of the original HTML document. If you perform alterations incorrectly, or the file is saved in the wrong format, the HTML document can be further damaged. In the event of problems, revert to the original copy.

1. Open the HTML document that contains the non-functioning anchor in PageMill or SiteMill.
2. Choose Edit > Show Anchors.
3. Select the icon for the anchor that does not function.
4. Choose Window > Show (Attributes) Inspector.
5. If you're using PageMill 1.0.x or SiteMill 1.0.x, click the Object Attributes button.
6. Note the name of the anchor in the Name field.
7. Close the document.
8. Open the HTML document in a text editor that can save in text-only format (e.g., SimpleText, Microsoft Word).
9. Locate the line containing the anchor name you noted in step 6. For example:

```
<A NAME="anchor402671"></A> this is the
destination
```

   In the original HTML document (i.e., before it was saved in PageMill or SiteMill) the text "this is the destination" was the object of anchor 402671. In this example, PageMill or SiteMill has moved the text outside of the anchor tag.

10. Move the reference for the text or graphic back inside the anchor tag. For example:

```
<A NAME="anchor402671">this is the destina-
tion</A>
```

11. Save the HTML document in text-only format.

ADDITIONAL INFORMATION

PageMill and SiteMill use an anchor icon to denote the destination of anchor links in HTML documents, and do not include a text or graphic reference in anchor tags. When you open and save an HTML document containing an anchor link with a text or graphic destination, PageMill and SiteMill rewrite the anchor reference, moving the destination text or graphic outside of the anchor tag.

IBM's Web Explorer 1.0.x cannot follow an anchor link without a text or graphic destination, like those created by PageMill or SiteMill.

PICT Image Placed into PageMill or SiteMill Document Loses Colors

ISSUE

When you insert a PICT image in an Adobe PageMill or Adobe SiteMill document, the image is displayed with fewer colors than expected.

SOLUTION

Use an image editing application (e.g., Adobe Photoshop) to convert the PICT image to JPEG format, then insert the JPEG image into the PageMill or SiteMill document.

ADDITIONAL INFORMATION

PageMill and SiteMill automatically convert PICT images to GIF format during import. GIF images support up to 8-bit color (a maximum of 256 colors). If the PICT image contains more than 256 colors, color data is discarded when PageMill or SiteMill converts it to GIF format.

PageMill and SiteMill import JPEG images, which support 24-bit color (up to 16,777,216 colors).

Unable to Drag and Drop from Finder into PageMill or SiteMill

ISSUE

After you drag one or more items from the Finder into an Adobe PageMill or an Adobe SiteMill document, PageMill's or SiteMill's Pasteboard, or the (Attributes) Inspector's Image Well, the items do not appear.

SOLUTIONS

To drag and drop an item into PageMill or SiteMill, do one or more of the following:

A. Drag and drop one item at a time into the document or Pasteboard.
B. Use System 7 Pro (Finder 7.1.3) or later.
C. Save the file to be dragged and dropped in GIF, PICT, or JPEG format.
D. Select Show Desktop When in Background in the General Controls control panel.

OR: When using PageMill 1.0.x or SiteMill 1.0.x, use the Insert Image button to import an image.

OR: When using PageMill 2.0, use the Insert button, or choose File > Place to import an image.

OR: To import an image you wish to use as a background in a PageMill or SiteMill HTML document, insert the image into the document, then drag the image from the document window and drop it into the Image Well in the Inspector.

OR: Copy and paste the image into the PageMill or SiteMill HTML document.

ADDITIONAL INFORMATION

PageMill and SiteMill do not enable you to add multiple items into an HTML document or the Pasteboard by dragging and dropping them from the Finder.

System 7.1 or earlier does not support drag and drop functionality between applications (e.g., between the Finder and PageMill). When running System 7.1 or earlier, PageMill and SiteMill installs the Macintosh Drag and Drop extension in the Extension folder in the System Folder, which enables drag and drop within PageMill and SiteMill only.

System 7 Pro includes system extension documents and an updated Finder that supports drag and drop functionality. System 7.5.x and later includes drag and drop functionality integrated in the system software, instead of in system extension documents.

To drag and drop from the Finder into an application, the Desktop must be visible.

Application Errors

MAC OS

Error "At least one of the files in this site is locked..." Occurs in SiteMill 1.0.x

ISSUE

Adobe SiteMill 1.0.x displays the error "At least one of the files in this site is locked. Changes may result in broken links since SiteMill cannot repair links inside locked files" after you load a Web site or attempt to preview an anchor link.

SOLUTIONS

Ensure none of the files in the site is in use by SiteMill or another application.

OR: Find and unlock any locked files in the site folder:

1. In SiteMill, choose Site > Load.
2. Load each folder in the site separately, progressing through the site hierarchy.
3. When the error message "At least one of the files...is locked..." occurs, verify that all files in the loaded folder are not locked by selecting each file in the Finder, and choosing File > Get Info.
4. Repeat steps 1-3 until the site loads successfully.

OR: Remove extra pound (#) characters from anchor names in all documents in the site:

1. Open a file from the loaded folder in SiteMill.
2. Click the globe icon to switch to SiteMill's Edit mode.
3. Choose Edit > Show Anchors.
4. Select an anchor icon on the page.
5. Choose Window > Show Attributes Inspector and click on the Object Attributes button to display the anchor attributes.
6. Remove pound characters from the anchor name in the Name field, and press Return.
7. Repeat steps 4-6 for each anchor in the document.
8. Choose File > Save and close the document.
9. Choose Site > Load.
10. Repeat steps 1-9 until the folder loads successfully.

OR: When "@è#anchorxxxxxx" displays in the Errors window, correct the damaged anchor link:

1. Click the Incoming Links pop-up menu to the right of the anchor.
2. Select the page shown in the pop-up menu.
3. Click the globe icon to switch to Edit mode.
4. Choose Edit > Show Anchors.
5. Select an anchor icon on the page.
6. Choose Window > Show Attributes Inspector and click the Object Attributes button.
7. Compare the name of each anchor and determine which anchor name most closely matches the anchor listed in the Errors window.
8. In the SiteMill document, delete and recreate the anchor.
9. Repeat steps 1-8 until the site loads successfully.

ADDITIONAL INFORMATION

SiteMill displays the error "At least one of the files in this site is locked. Changes may result in broken links since SiteMill cannot repair links inside locked files" after you load a Web site or attempt to preview an anchor link.

When a file within the site folder is open in another application (e.g., SimpleText, BBEdit) or when you have locked a file within the site folder, SiteMill cannot access the file to verify and change links. Closing the file when open in another application, or unlocking the file enables SiteMill to load the site as expected.

When an anchor link within a site file contains additional pound characters, SiteMill returns the error "At least one of the files in this site is locked. Changes may result in broken links since SiteMill cannot repair links inside locked files." Removing the additional pound characters enables SiteMill to load the site as expected.

After you create anchor links in PageMill and SiteMill HTML (Hypertext Markup Language) documents, you can change the anchor name. The standard HTML naming convention for an anchor is "#anchorname." PageMill and SiteMill generate a name for each anchor using the convention "anchorxxxxxx," where xxxxxx is a randomly generated 6-digit number (e.g., anchor123456).

If you use a character other than a letter, number, underscore "_" or hyphen "-" in an anchor name, PageMill and SiteMill cannot interpret the HTML code. Do not use HTML-reserved characters (e.g., pound symbol "#" or ampersand "&") within anchor names.

Error "...unable to find file: default.cgi..." When Clicking Linked Image in Netscape Navigator

ISSUE

After you click on a linked image in an Adobe PageMill or an Adobe SiteMill HTML document in Netscape Navigator, Netscape returns the error "Netscape is unable to find the file: /pathname/default.cgi. Check the file name and try again."

SOLUTION

Apply the Picture attribute to the image in PageMill or SiteMill:

1. Open the HTML document in PageMill or SiteMill.
2. Click on the globe icon to switch to Edit mode.
3. Select the graphic then choose Window > Show (Attributes) Inspector.
4. In PageMill 1.0.x, and SiteMill, click on the Object button to display the Object Attributes.
5. Select Picture from the Behavior options.
6. Save and close the HTML document, then reopen the HTML document in Netscape.

ADDITIONAL INFORMATION

When you click on a linked graphic with a Button attribute applied in a PageMill or SiteMill HTML document in Netscape 2.0 or earlier, Netscape returns the error "Netscape is unable to find the file: /pathname/default.cgi. Check the file name and try again." Linked images with the Picture Behavior attribute applied, instead of the Button attribute, behave as links in PageMill or SiteMill HTML documents when viewed in Netscape.

Error "File is busy" When Saving Document in PageMill or SiteMill

ISSUE

Adobe PageMill or Adobe SiteMill returns the error "File is busy" when saving a file.

SOLUTION

Close the HTML document in any other applications in which it is open (e.g., TeachText).

ADDITIONAL INFORMATION

PageMill and SiteMill cannot save an HTML document when it is in use by another application.

Message "Save changes...before closing?" When No Changes Made in PageMill 2.0

ISSUE

After you preview a link in an Adobe PageMill 2.0 document, PageMill displays the message "Save changes to the PageMill document [filename] before closing?" You made no changes to the document.

SOLUTION

Click Don't Save in the message dialog box.

ADDITIONAL INFORMATION

If your PageMill document contains an image that you also used for the document's background image, the message "Save changes to the PageMill document [filename] before closing?" appears the first time you preview a link. Clicking Don't Save prevents PageMill from continuing to prompt you to save the document during the current PageMill session.

Each time you quit and relaunch PageMill and then preview a link in the same document, PageMill displays the same message.

Error "An internal error has occurred" When Viewing or Inserting PDF in PageMill 2.0

ISSUE

When you open a document containing a PDF file or place a PDF file into an Adobe PageMill 2.0 document, PageMill returns the error "An internal error has occurred."

SOLUTIONS

If you have more than 24 MB of built-in memory:

1. Quit all applications, then restart the Macintosh.

2. Start PageMill.
3. Start Adobe Acrobat Exchange 3.0 or later or Adobe Acrobat Reader 3.0 or later.
4. Insert the PDF into the PageMill document.

If you have less than 24 MB of built-in memory on your system, do one or more of the following:

A. Remove the PDFViewer plug-in, then reinsert the PDF:
   1. Quit PageMill.
   2. Drag the PDFViewer plug-in from the Browser Plug-ins folder in the PageMill Plug-ins folder, to the desktop.
   3. Start PageMill, then insert the PDF file into the document.

NOTE: The PDF file displays as a broken plug-in icon when the PDFViewer plug-in is not located in the Browser Plug-ins folder. The PDF previews as expected in a Web browser.

B. Install additional RAM.

ADDITIONAL INFORMATION

To preview PDF files in documents, PageMill requires Acrobat Reader or Exchange, the PDFViewer plug-in, and 24 MB of physical (built-in) RAM. The error "An internal error occurred," displays when you place a PDF file or open a document containing a PDF file on a system with less than 24 MB of physical RAM.

If you have more than 24 MB of physical RAM installed, quitting all applications and restarting the system clears the memory buffer to free the maximum amount of system memory. Starting PageMill and Acrobat Exchange or Reader ensures that enough memory is available for both applications to run, and that you can insert the PDF file as expected.

If you have less than 24 MB of physical RAM installed, removing the PDFViewer plug-in enables PageMill to embed the PDF without previewing it.

Error "PageMill 2.0 requires Apple's Drag and Drop Extension..." When Starting PageMill 2.0

ISSUE

When you start Adobe PageMill 2.0, it returns the error, "PageMill 2.0 requires Apple's Drag and Drop Extension in order to run." PageMill is running in System 7.1.

SOLUTION

Install the Macintosh Drag and Drop extension using PageMill's Custom Install option:

1. Insert the PageMill 2.0 CD-ROM, or the first PageMill 2.0 software disk.
2. Double-click the Install Adobe PageMill 2.0 icon on the CD-ROM or software disk.
2. Select Custom Install from the pop-up menu in the Install Adobe PageMill dialog box.
3. Select the Macintosh Drag and Drop option, then click Install.
4. Restart the Macintosh.

ADDITIONAL INFORMATION

When running in System 7.1, PageMill requires the Macintosh Drag and Drop extension. PageMill 2.0 does not install the Macintosh Drag and Drop extension when you select the Easy Install option in the Install Adobe PageMill window.

When running in System 7.5 or later, PageMill does not require the Macintosh Drag and Drop extension.

Error "...'ObjectSupportLib' could not be found" When Starting PageMill 2.0

ISSUE

When you start Adobe PageMill 2.0, PageMill returns the error "The application 'Adobe PageMill 2.0' could not be opened because 'ObjectSupportLib' could not be found." PageMill is running in System 7.1 on a Power Macintosh.

SOLUTIONS

Run PageMill in System 7.5 or later.

OR: Install the ObjectSupportLib system extension file into the Extensions folder in the System Folder. The ObjectSupportLib system extension file is available from the Claris FTP site (ftp://ftp.claris.com/pub/USA-Macintosh/Updaters/ObjectSupportLib1.1.bin).

OR: Install PageMill for the Macintosh (68K version):

1. Delete the currently installed PageMill folder.
2. Double-click the Install Adobe PageMill 2.0 application.
3. In the Installer window, select Custom Install from the pop-up menu.
4. Select the Adobe PageMill 2.0 68K custom install option.
5. Click Install and then complete the installation by following the on-screen instructions.
6. When installation is complete, click Restart.

ADDITIONAL INFORMATION

PageMill 2.0 requires the ObjectSupportLib system extension file to run on a Power Macintosh. If the ObjectSupportLib system extension is not installed when you start PageMill, PageMill returns the error, "The application 'Adobe PageMill 2.0' could not be opened because 'ObjectSupportLib' could not be found."

PageMill 2.0 for the Macintosh (68K version) does not require the ObjectSupportLib system extension to run. The PageMill 2.0 installer does not install the ObjectSupportLib system extension, which is included with System 7.5 or later.

Error Occurs When Previewing Movie File in Web Browser

ISSUE

When you preview a link to a QuickTime movie on the local hard disk, the Web browser returns the error "Couldn't open the file 'filename' because the file is not a movie file."

SOLUTIONS

Flatten the movie (i.e., remove its resource fork) using a video editing application (e.g., Adobe Premiere, FlattenMooV).

OR: Upload the movie to a Web server as Raw Data.

ADDITIONAL INFORMATION

Web browsers do not support previewing movie files that contain resource forks. When you try to preview a link to a QuickTime movie on the local hard disk, the Web browser returns the error "Couldn't open the file 'filename' because the file is not a movie file." Flattening the movie (i.e., removing its resource fork) with a movie editing application (e.g., Adobe Premiere, FlattenMooV) enables you to preview it locally.

When you upload a movie file to a Web server as Raw Data, the resource fork is removed, enabling the Web browser to preview the movie file as expected.

Error When Selecting Local Alias Folder Preference in PageMill 2.0

ISSUE

When you select a Local Alias folder in the Adobe PageMill 2.0 Preferences dialog box, PageMill returns the error, "A local alias can not be a subfolder of an existing local alias." or "A local alias can not be a parent folder of an existing alias."

SOLUTIONS

Do one or more of the following:

A. Remove Local Alias preference settings you no longer need and then select a Local Alias folder. For instructions, see Additional Information.

B. Move the folder you want to make a Local Alias folder out of a previously specified Local Alias folder.

C. Move previously specified Local Alias folders out of the folder you want to make a Local Alias folder.

D. If the folder you want to make a Local Alias folder shares the root name (e.g., "site," "sites") of a previously specified Local Alias folder and is at the same nested level, move or rename it or its parent folder. For example, to rename a Local Alias folder with the path:

`MYDRIVE:Websites:Client:Site`

when you want to select a Local Alias folder with the path:

`MYDRIVE:Websites:Clients:PizzaHaus:Pepperoni:Site`

rename the Clients folder so it does not share the same root name as the Client folder at the same level in your original Local Alias folder's pathname. For example, rename the Clients folder:

`MYDRIVE:Websites:Accounts:PizzaHaus:Pepperoni:Site`

E. Delete the PageMill 1.0 and 2.0 Preferences files:

1. Quit PageMill.
2. Delete the Adobe PageMill 2.0 Prefs file and Adobe PageMill Preferences file from the Preferences folder in the System Folder.
3. Start PageMill.

ADDITIONAL INFORMATION

Selecting a Local Alias folder in PageMill 2.0 enables you to create URL links, rather than relative links, to items (e.g., documents, images) in your documents. Because Local Alias settings apply to contents of a folder, including the contents of its subfolders, Local Alias folders cannot contain or be within another Local Alias folder.

If you select a Local Alias folder that is in another Local Alias folder, PageMill returns the error, "A local alias can not be a subfolder of an existing local alias." If you select a Local Alias folder that contains a previously specified Local Alias folder, PageMill returns the error, "A local alias can not be a parent folder of an existing alias."

PageMill cannot create links correctly when the currently selected Local Alias folder, or its parent, shares the same root name as a previously selected Local Alias folder. Changing the name or case of it or its parent folder, or moving either folder, enables you to use either the folder as a Local Alias folder.

If the Adobe PageMill Preferences file created by PageMill 1.0.x or SiteMill 1.0.x is in the Preferences Folder in the System Folder, PageMill 2.0 uses the Local Alias preference settings specified in this file.

To remove Local Alias preference settings you no longer need and select a Local Alias folder:

1. In PageMill, close all files.
2. Choose Edit > Preferences and then click the Server icon.
3. In the Local Aliases section, locate references for the folder that is a parent or subfolder of the folder you want to make a Local Alias.
4. Click in the text field to the right of the globe icon above the Local Alias you located in step 3.
5. Choose Edit > Select All and then press the Delete key.
6. Press Return.
7. Select the folder you want as your Local Alias folder.

Error "File or folder missing" Saving Image or Document in PageMill 2.0

ISSUE

When you save a file, Adobe PageMill 2.0 returns the error "File or folder missing."

SOLUTIONS

Do one or more of the following:

A. Mount the volume or disk that contains the last saved version of your file and then choose File > Save.

B. If you changed the name of your file, or a folder, volume, or disk containing your file, while working in PageMill, rename the file, folder, volume, or disk back to its original name.

C. Save the file to a local volume (e.g., internal hard disk) or disk and then copy the file to a remote volume.

D. Choose File > Save As to save a copy of the file.

E. If you made a change to PageMill's remote root directory preference while working in the file, remove and then reinsert all images in the document, recreate the document's server side image maps, and then save the file.

F. Rebuild the desktop file on the volume containing the file and on all volumes containing documents or images linked to the file. To rebuild the desktop file in System 7.1 and later, hold down the Command and Option keys while restarting the computer. Keep the keys held down until you receive the message "Are you sure you want to rebuild the desktop file on the disk '[diskname]'?" then click OK.

G. Check for hard disk problems (e.g., damaged media) using a hard disk utility (e.g., Norton Utilities for Macintosh, Disk First Aid).

ADDITIONAL INFORMATION

When you open a file, PageMill stores its name and location in memory. When you save the file, PageMill searches for your file using the information it stored in memory. If PageMill cannot find your file, it returns the error, "File or folder missing." Changing the name of the file, folder, volume, or disk back to the original name, or remounting the remote volume enables PageMill to locate the file and save it without returning the error message.

PageMill cannot find your file and save changes if you rename the file, rename the folders, volume, or disk containing the file, or rename or unmount the remote volume containing the last saved version of your file while the file is open in PageMill. Hard disk problems (e.g., damaged media) may prevent PageMill finding your file, and network problems (e.g., loose connections, heavy traffic) may prevent PageMill from finding a file on a remote volume.

When you insert an image located in a folder that has a Local Alias, PageMill uses the Local Alias setting to locate the image on the volume or disk. If you change PageMill's remote root directory path in the Local Alias preference while the image is open in the Image View window, PageMill can no longer locate the image on the disk and returns the error, "File or folder missing" when you save the image. Closing the image without saving your changes, removing and reinserting all images in the document, and then recreating the document's server-side image maps enables you to remove all references to the former remote root directory from the file. After you remove references to the previous remote root directory in the file, PageMill saves the file without returning the error.

If your file, or a document or image liked to your file, is on a volume that has an out-of-date or damaged desktop file, PageMill returns the error "File or folder missing" when you save the file. Rebuilding the volume's desktop file, which your system uses to keep track of files on the volume, ensures it is up-to-date and not damaged.

Error "Internal error - An assertion failed" Previewing Link in PageMill 2.0

ISSUE

When you preview a link to a file with a ".gif," ".jpeg," or ".jpg" filename extension in Adobe PageMill 2.0, the error "Internal error- An assertion failed" occurs.

After you place a file with a ".gif," ".jpeg," or ".jpg" filename extension into PageMill 2.0, the file appears as a broken plug-in icon or text link.

SOLUTION

Rename the file with an ".htm" or ".html" filename extension, then relink it in PageMill.

ADDITIONAL INFORMATION

Because the HTML specification requires HTML documents to have an ".htm" or ".html" filename extension, PageMill does not support previewing links to HTML documents with other filename extensions (e.g., ".gif"). When you preview a link to an HTML document with a ".gif" or ".jpg" or ".jpeg" filename extension in PageMill, the error "Internal error- An assertion failed" occurs. Renaming the linked HTML document with an ".htm" or ".html" filename extension and relinking it enables PageMill to preview the link as expected.

PageMill cannot create links to HTML documents with filename extensions other than ".htm" or ".html." When you choose File > Place and select an HTML document with a different filename extension, PageMill either displays a broken plug-in icon or creates a text link to the file. Renaming the HTML document with an ".htm" or ".html" filename extension and replacing it enables PageMill to create a link to the document as expected.

Error "Internal error - An assertion failed." When Starting or Switching to PageMill 2.0

ISSUE

After you copy data from Microsoft Excel, the error, "Internal error- An assertion failed" occurs when you start Adobe PageMill 2.0 or make it the active application.

SOLUTIONS

Copy multiple rows of Excel data, start or switch to PageMill, paste the data into the PageMill document, and then delete extra data from the document.

OR: Clear the Excel data from the clipboard by copying another object (e.g., single character), then start or switch to PageMill.

ADDITIONAL INFORMATION

If the system clipboard contains Excel data from multiple cells in the same row, the error, "Internal error- An assertion failed" occurs when you start or make PageMill the active application (e.g., choose PageMill from the application menu). If the clipboard contains other information (e.g., more than one row of Excel data, a space character, a rectangle), PageMill starts or becomes the active application, as expected.

Error "Specified file cannot be found," or "Viewing remote files is currently disabled..." When Opening an Image in PageMill 2.0

ISSUE

When you open an image in the Image window, Adobe PageMill 2.0 returns the error "Specified file cannot be found" or "Viewing remote files is currently disabled. To enable this feature use the Preferences command."

SYMPTOMS

You changed PageMill's Local Alias settings.

If you save the document containing the image, the error "File or folder is missing" occurs.

A question mark appears in place of the image if you toggle to HTML Source view and back to Page Edit mode, or close and reopen the document.

A broken plug-in icon appears in place of the plug-in object if you toggle to HTML Source view and back to Page Edit mode, or close and reopen the document.

SOLUTIONS

Remove document links to elements stored in the Local Alias folder, then recreate the document links and server-side image maps.

OR: If you did not intend to change the remote root directory for your Local Alias, respecify the former remote root directory:

1. Close all files without saving changes.
2. Choose Edit > Preferences and click the Server icon.
3. Respecify the former remote root directory and press Return.
4. Click OK.
5. Reopen the document.

ADDITIONAL INFORMATION

To keep link information straight in server-side image maps, you can use local a

liases for remote folders when you create HTML documents in PageMill 2.0. When you create a link to elements within a local alias folder, PageMill adds the l

ocal alias' corresponding remote root directory path to the beginning of the link reference. For example, if a local alias folder has a remote root directory path of "http://www.adobe.com/," and you insert a file named "image.gif" from the local alias folder into a document that is also located in the local alias folder, PageMill writes the link to "image.gif" as <A HREF="http://www.adobe.com/image.gif">.

If you change the remote root directory path for a local alias folder while a document containing elements or links to elements in that folder in that folder is open in PageMill, PageMill cannot resolve links to the elements, and returns an error message if you open an image into the Image window, try to save the image, save the document, or close and reopen the document.

If you remove the links to the elements in the local alias folder and then recreate the links, PageMill rewrites the link references using the new remote root directory path. If you close all the documents without saving any changes and then reset the remote root directory path for the local alias folder, PageMill can resolve the link references in the document.

Adobe Systems recommends you make changes to your local alias settings in PageMill with no documents open.

System Errors

MAC OS

PageMill 2.0 Beta Documents Cause System Crash When Opened in Final Release of PageMill 2.0

ISSUE

When you open a document created in a beta version of Adobe PageMill 2.0 in the final release of PageMill 2.0, a system error (e.g., Type 1, Type 11, Type 28) occurs.

SOLUTION

Recreate the document in the shipping (i.e., non-beta) version of PageMill 2.0.

ADDITIONAL INFORMATION

Beta, or pre-release, software may contain errors, and other problems that could cause system failures. Consequently, Adobe disclaims any warranty of beta software, and cannot support beta software, or guarantee the integrity or performance of files created using beta software.

Recreating the document using the shipping version of PageMill 2.0 ensures the file does not contain HTML errors which may lead to system errors when opening documents.

System Error in PageMill 2.0 When Opening a Document that Contains an Unclosed Tags

ISSUE

A system error occurs (e.g., freeze, Type 11) when you open a document in Adobe PageMill 2.0. The document contains a tag following an unclosed tag (i.e., an opening tag without the closing </FONT SIZE> tag), within an <A HREF> tag.

SOLUTION

Open the document in a text editing application, remove the SIZE attribute from all tags, and then add relative font size formatting in PageMill:

DISCLAIMER: Adobe Systems does not support modifying an HTML document with a text editor. Familiarity with opening HTML documents in a text editor and saving in text-only (e.g., ASCII) format is required. Experience with HTML language is highly recommended. Always modify a copy of the original HTML document. If alterations are performed incorrectly or the file is saved in the wrong format, the HTML document can be further damaged. In the event of problems, revert to the original copy.

1. Open a copy of the HTML document in a text editing application that can save files in text-only format (e.g., SimpleText, BBEdit). 2. Locate the tag with a SIZE attribute. For example:

```
<A HREF="http://www.adobe.com/">
la
<FONT SIZE=+2 COLOR=#000000>
</A>
```

3. Delete the SIZE attribute from the tag. The remaining code appears as:

```
<A HREF="http://www.adobe.com/">
la
<FONT COLOR=#000000>
</A>
```

4. Repeat steps 2 and 3 until you remove all instances of the SIZE attribute from all tags in the document.
5. Save and close the file.
6. Open the document in PageMill and apply the desired relative font size to the text.

ADDITIONAL INFORMATION

PageMill cannot open documents that contain a tag followed by an unclosed tag within an <A HREF> tag. Opening a document that contains this series of tags will cause a system error (e.g., freeze, Type 11). Removing the SIZE attribute from all tags in a text editor enables you to open the file in PageMill without error. Applying the desired relative font size to the text within PageMill ensures that tags are properly formatted, and text is the desired size in the document.

System Error Inserting Image on Page containing Embedded PDF in PageMill 2.0

ISSUE

A system error (e.g., illegal instruction, Type 8, Type 10) occurs when you insert an image into an Adobe PageMill 2.0 document that contains one or more embedded PDFs.

SOLUTIONS

Do one or more of the following:

A. Remove all PDFs from the document, insert the image, then reinsert the PDFs.
B. Quit PageMill, remove the PDFViewer plug-in from the Browser Plug-ins folder in the PageMill Plug-ins folder, then start PageMill, reopen the document, and insert the image.
C. Increase the amount of memory allocated to PageMill:
    1. Quit all applications.
    2. Start Adobe Acrobat Reader 3.0 or Exchange 3.0.
    3. Choose Apple > About this Macintosh.
    4. Note the Largest Unused Block value (i.e., available memory) and close the window.
    5. Click once on the PageMill application icon and choose File > Get Info.
    6. Enter a value in the Preferred Size text field (System 7.1 or later) that is larger than the original value but does not exceed the value you noted in step 4.
    7. Close the Get Info window, then restart PageMill.

ADDITIONAL INFORMATION

When Acrobat Reader 3.0 or Acrobat Exchange 3.0, and the PDFViewer plug-in are installed, PageMill displays thumbnails of any PDFs embedded in a PageMill document. When you add a PDF to a PageMill document, the amount of memory PageMill requires to display the document increases substantially. Depending on the free system resources, a system error can occur when you insert an image into a document containing one or more PDFs. However, a system error will not occur if you insert a PDF after inserting an image.

When installed in the Browsers Plug-ins folder in the PageMill Plugins folder, the PDFViewer plug-in enables you to view PDFs inside a PageMill document. Disabling the PDFViewer plug-in enables you to insert both images and PDFs without causing a system error. When you disable the PDFViewer plug-in, PageMill displays Netscape plug-in icons rather than the actual PDFs, but the PDFs will display as expected in a Web browser. Allocating more memory to PageMill enables simultaneous display of both images and PDFs.

System Error or Freeze When Pasting Cells from Excel Spreadsheet in PageMill 2.0

ISSUE

A system error (e.g., freeze, Type 1, Type 11) occurs after you paste cells from a Microsoft Excel spreadsheet into an Adobe PageMill 2.0 document.

SOLUTION

Restart the Macintosh and then do one or more of the following:

A. Increase the amount of memory allocated to PageMill.
    1. Quit all applications.
    2. Choose About This Macintosh from the Apple menu.
    3. Note the Largest Unused Block value (i.e., available memory) and then close the About This Macintosh window.
    4. Select the PageMill application icon and then choose File > Get Info.
    5. Enter a larger value in the Preferred Size text box (System 7.1 or later) that does not exceed the Largest Unused Block value you noted in step 3.

NOTE: The amount of memory required to copy and paste data between Excel and PageMill depends on the size of the data you copy and paste. For example, when you paste a large Excel file into a PageMill document, PageMill can require up to 20 MB of RAM and may pause before displaying the pasted data.

6. Close the Get Info window and then restart PageMill.

B. Disable added extensions by doing one or more of the following:

   A. When you use System 7.5 or later, restart your Macintosh with the Shift key held down until the message "Welcome to Macintosh. Extensions off." appears. Because this method does not enable you to select which extensions you want to disable, use it for troubleshooting extension conflicts when you don't require a specific extension (e.g., CD-ROM driver, QuickTime).

   B. Use an extensions manager (e.g., Apple Extensions Manager, Casady & Greene Conflict Catcher, Now Startup Manager) to selectively disable extensions. Any extension you use to disable other extensions is suspect itself. When you use System 7.1, PageMill requires the Macintosh Drag and Drop extension be active.

   C. Manually move extensions out of the System Folder. Although this method takes time and requires you to be familiar with the contents of your System Folder, you have more control over which extensions you disable. To manually disable extensions:

      1. Move the Control Panels and Extensions folders from the System Folder to a new location (e.g., desktop).
      2. Restart your Macintosh. The system searches for system preferences files and the Control Panels and Extensions folders in the System Folder. When your system cannot find the folders it needs in the System Folder, it creates new ones.
      3. When you use System 7.1, move the Macintosh Drag and Drop extension from your previous Extensions folders into your new, empty Extensions folder in the System Folder.
      4. Restart your Macintosh.

C. Open the Excel file in PageMill, rather than using copy and paste:

   1. If you do not want to import the entire Excel spreadsheet, create a new spreadsheet consisting of only the cells you want to import into the PageMill document.
   2. In PageMill, choose File > Open.
   3. In the Open dialog box, select All Readable from the File Type pop-up menu.
   4. Select the desired file, then click Open.

ADDITIONAL INFORMATION

When you copy and paste data from Excel into a PageMill document, PageMill converts the Excel data into PageMill objects in application memory (RAM). If PageMill runs out of available memory while converting data, a system error occurs. Increasing PageMill's memory partition (i.e., that amount of memory allocated to PageMill) enables PageMill to convert and paste objects as expected.

If an extension is conflicting with PageMill or the system software when you copy and paste, a system error occurs. Restarting the Macintosh without added extensions enables you to copy and paste data into PageMill as expected.

When you open an Excel file in PageMill by choosing File > Open, PageMill converts the Excel file using an Adobe File Utilities import filter, which requires less memory.

System Error When PageMill 2.0 Opens Table with Baseline-Aligned Cell and Horizontal Rule

ISSUE

When you open an Adobe PageMill 2.0 document with a table containing a baseline-aligned cell and a horizontal rule, a system error (e.g., Type 11, Type 1) occurs.

SOLUTIONS

Remove the BASELINE attribute from the table cell before you open the document:

1. Open the document in a text editing application that can save files in text-only format (e.g., BBEdit, SimpleText).
2. Locate the code for the table cell with the BASELINE alignment attribute. For example:

```
<TR >
<TD  VALIGN="BASELINE">
</TD>
</TR>
```

3. Remove the BASELINE attribute from the code so it appears as follows:

```
<TR >
<TD >
<HR></TD>
</TR>
```

4. Save the document in text-only format.

OR: Remove the horizontal rule from the table cell before you open the document:

1. Open the document in a text editing application that can save files in text-only format (e.g., BBEdit, SimpleText).
2. Locate the code for the horizontal rule in the table cell. For example:

```
<TR >
<TD >
<HR></TD>
</TR>
```

3. Remove the horizontal rule from the code so it appears as follows:

```
<TR >
<TD >
</TD>
</TR>
```

4. Save the document in text-only format.

ADDITIONAL INFORMATION

A system error (e.g., Type 11, Type 1) occurs in PageMill if you open a document including a table containing a baseline-aligned cell and a horizontal rule. Removing the BASELINE alignment attribute or the horizontal rule from the table cell prior to opening the file prevents the error from occurring.

PageMill does not prevent you from creating a table that contains both a baseline-aligned cell and a horizontal rule.

Printing Problems

MAC OS

Cannot Print White Text from PageMill or SiteMill

ISSUE

White text does not print from Adobe PageMill or Adobe SiteMill.

SOLUTIONS

Apply a color to the white text before printing the document, then change the text back to white after printing.
OR: Select Print Page Background in the Print dialog box.
OR: Print the document from a Web browser (e.g., Netscape Navigator, NCSA Mosaic).

ADDITIONAL INFORMATION

PageMill and SiteMill support printing white text. However, white text is not visible when printed on a white background. Printing the document background or changing the color of the text makes the text visible when printed.

Web browsers print white text in black, making the text visible when printed on white paper.

Print Command Dimmed in PageMill or SiteMill

ISSUE

The Print command is dimmed in Adobe PageMill or Adobe SiteMill.

SOLUTIONS

Close the Image View window.
OR: Click on the document window to make active.

ADDITIONAL INFORMATION

When the Image View window is active (i.e., the foremost window), PageMill and SiteMill disable the Print command. Clicking on the document window activates it (i.e., brings it to the foreground).

Background Image or Color Does Not Print from PageMill or SiteMill

ISSUE

When you print an Adobe PageMill or Adobe SiteMill document, its background color or tiled background image does not print.

SOLUTION

Select Print Page Background in the Print dialog box.

ADDITIONAL INFORMATION

PageMill and SiteMill only print the background color or tiled background image of an HTML document when Print Page Background is selected in the Print dialog box.

Installation Issues

WINDOWS

Unable to Download or Install PageMill 2.0 for Windows Beta

ISSUE

You cannot download the Adobe PageMill 2.0 beta from the Adobe Web page or start the downloaded installer because an error occurs (e.g., "Extract failed: return from extract=-9"), the Web browser halts when downloading, or the downloaded file cannot be found.

SOLUTIONS

Do one or more of the following:

A. Use a Web browser that can download the Install Adobe PageMill file (e.g., Netscape Navigator 1.2 and later, Microsoft Internet Explorer 2.x and later, America Online).
B. If the downloaded installer (Pmlw2r18.exe) will not start, make sure its file size is 4,259,508 bytes. If its file size is not 4,259,508 bytes, redownload the file from the Web.
C. If your Web browser stops before finishing the download, do one or more of the following:
   A. Download the Install Adobe PageMill file when there is less activity on the Internet (e.g., late in the evening, early in the morning).
   B. If you are connected to the Internet using a standard phone line, disable call waiting and make sure voice communication is free of noise and static by checking the line for clarity.
   C. Make sure your Internet connection is not the cause of the problem by downloading a different file (e.g., Acrobat Reader).
D. If you cannot locate the Install Adobe PageMill file after downloading it, choose Start > Find > Files or Folders and search for "a6instal." After locating the file, move it to a convenient location for installation (e.g., the desktop).

ADDITIONAL INFORMATION
You may not be able to download the PageMill 2.0 beta from the Adobe Web page if your Web browser does not support downloading files, if there is much activity on the Internet, or if you establish a poor Internet connection. The PageMill 2.0 beta installer will not start if it was downloaded incompletely.

MAC OS

Error When Installing PageMill or SiteMill on UNIX Workstation

ISSUE
When installing Adobe PageMill 1.0.x or Adobe SiteMill 1.0.x onto a UNIX workstation with Apple's Macintosh Application Environment (MAE) software, the installer returns the error "The selected disk named "diskname" is a network server volume. The installer cannot install in a network server volume."

SOLUTION
Install PageMill or SiteMill on a Macintosh, then move the installed components to the UNIX workstation.

ADDITIONAL INFORMATION
The Adobe PageMill or Adobe SiteMill installer does not support Apple's Macintosh Application Environment (MAE) software, which emulates the Macintosh operating system on Sun Microsystems SPARCstations and HP Series 700 workstations.

PageMill and SiteMill support System 7.1 and later. MAE for UNIX emulates System 7.1, but Adobe does not support running PageMill and SiteMill in this configuration.

Unable to Install PageMill from a Copy of the PageMill CD-ROM

ISSUE
When you double-click the "Install Adobe PageMill 2.0" icon on a copy of the PageMill CD-ROM, the system beeps and the PageMill Installer does not start.

SOLUTION
Install PageMill by double-clicking the "Install Adobe PageMill" icon in the Disk 1 folder in the Adobe PageMill 2.0 folder.

ADDITIONAL INFORMATION
The "Install Adobe PageMill 2.0" icon located on the Adobe PageMill 2.0 CD-ROM is a launcher application that starts the PageMill Installer. The launcher application locates the PageMill Installer using a specific pathname, which includes the name of the PageMill CD-ROM. If you create a copy of the CD-ROM, the launcher application may not be able to find the installer.

You can bypass the launcher application and install PageMill by double-clicking the PageMill Installer in the Disk 1 folder in the Adobe PageMill 2.0 folder

Unable to Install WebSTAR Application from PageMill 2.0 CD-ROM

ISSUE
When you run the WebSTAR installer on the Adobe PageMill 2.0 CD-ROM, it returns the message, "Please insert the disk: WebSTAR." A WebSTAR disk is not included with PageMill.

SOLUTION
Download and install the WebSTAR software from the Quarterdeck/StarNine Corporation Web site (http://www.-starnine.com/).

ADDITIONAL INFORMATION
When you run the WebSTAR installer on the PageMill 2.0 CD-ROM, it returns the message, "Please insert the disk: WebSTAR." Because the disk is not included with PageMill, you cannot complete the installation.

General Information

MAC OS

Q What is an animated GIF, and how do I add one to my PageMill or SiteMill document?

A Animated GIFs contain multiple images assembled into one file. An application or script (e.g., GifBuilder, Imaging Machine) collects individual images and compiles them into frames within a single file. When the file is previewed in a compliant Web browser or application, each frame displays in sequence, creating the appearance of movement.

You add an animated GIF to a PageMill or SiteMill document just as you would add any other graphic file—either by dragging the file into your document, by clicking on the appropriate button ("Place Object" in PageMill 2.0, "Insert Image" in PageMill/SiteMill 1.0x), or by using PageMill 2.0's "Place..." command. Once you've placed the file, if you're using PageMill 2.0 you can switch to Preview mode and you'll see the animated GIF as it will appear in most browsers. In PageMill 1.0.x and SiteMill 1.0.x, only the first frame will be displayed, but the file can be opened in Netscape or other compatible browser to view the animation.

While you can resize your animated GIF in PageMill or SiteMill without stripping out the built-in resource code for the animation, it's best to place your graphics at the size at which you'll want them to display. Resizing GIF images affects their resolution, and PageMill and SiteMill do not perfectly preserve image resolution when you resize graphics.

Q What is the "Preformatted" option in PageMill and SiteMill?

A "Preformatted" is one of the paragraph-level HTML attributes that you apply to text within a PageMill or SiteMill document. Paragraph-level attributes affect all the text within any given paragraph. You can find all the paragraph-level HTML attributes listed under the Format menu in both PageMill and SiteMill.

The preformatted text format is handy when you want to preserve spacing within HTML documents. When you enter multiple spaces or returns into a PageMill or SiteMill document that hasn't been preformatted, multiple spaces are condensed into a single space character, and some Web browsers display multiple returns as a single return. To preserve those multiple spaces or returns, you simply select them as a block, then choose "Preformatted" from the Format menu. Because of the way the format is defined in HTML, Web browsers must honor all space characters and returns within a block of text that is preformatted—that is, bounded by the preformatted tag.

Both PageMill and SiteMill display preformatted text using the Courier font. Many Web browsers also use Courier to display preformatted text, but each Web browser has its own definition of how to display preformatted text. In all cases, preformatted text is displayed in a monospaced (fixed-width) font.

Within blocks of preformatted text, you can include anchors, hyperlinks, and horizontal rules. You can apply any character style to preformatted text, including bold, italic, teletype, strong, emphasis, citation, sample, keyboard, code, and variable. All these character styles are found under the Style menu in PageMill and SiteMill. You cannot apply any additional format found under the Format menu to a block of preformatted text.

Top Issues: Adobe PageMill 2.0

This document summarizes the latest and most common issues we're hearing in Adobe Technical Support about Adobe PageMill 2.0. Numbers are included for documents that describe related issues in more detail. These documents are available from the following sources:

- The Adobe Technical Solutions database on the World Wide Web (http://www.adobe.com/supportservice/custsupport/tssearchdb.html)
- Adobe's automated faxing system, Adobe FaxYI, at 206-628-5737
- Adobe's auto-response e-mail system, techdocs@adobe.com
- The Adobe BBS at 206-623-6984

For an index of all FaxYI documents available for PageMill, see document 260099.

The latest version of Adobe PageMill for the Macintosh is PageMill 2.0. For pricing and availability information, visit the Adobe PageMill home page: (http://www.adobe.com/prodindex/pagemill/main.html) or call Adobe at 1-800-42-ADOBE (23623).

This document was last revised February 5, 1997. New and updated issues are indicated with an asterisk (*).

1. Centered Elements in a PageMill 2.0 Document Display Left-Aligned in Netscape Navigator

   PageMill 2.0 enables you to use tags, <DIV> tags, or <CENTER> tags to center objects in documents. Netscape Navigator does not reliably display elements centered using tags, and may display some elements you center using the tag as left-aligned. Netscape Navigator displays elements centered using either <DIV> tags or <CENTER> tags more reliably.

   For more information, see document 202124.

2. Error "PageMill 2.0 requires Apple's Drag and Drop Extension..." When Starting PageMill 2.0

   When you run PageMill in System 7.1, PageMill requires the Macintosh Drag and Drop extension. PageMill 2.0 does not install the Macintosh Drag and Drop extension when you select the Easy Install option in the Install Adobe PageMill window. If you start PageMill when the Macintosh Drag and Drop extension is not installed, PageMill returns the error, "PageMill 2.0 requires Apple's Drag and Drop Extension in order to run."

   For more information, see document 202131.

3. Error "...'ObjectSupportLib' could not be found." When Starting PageMill 2.0

   PageMill 2.0 requires the ObjectSupportLib system extension file to run on a Power Macintosh. If the ObjectSupportLib system extension is not installed when you start PageMill, PageMill returns the error, "The application 'Adobe PageMill 2.0' could not be opened because 'ObjectSupportLib' could not be found." The PageMill 2.0 installer does not install the ObjectSupportLib system extension, which is included with System 7.5 or later.

   For more information, see document 202135.

4. Target Hyperlinks in PageMill 2.0 Documents

   When you create a hyperlink in an Adobe PageMill 2.0 frame document, you can target the link, which forces the linked document to open in a specific location. PageMill enables you to specify whether the linked document opens within the current frameset or outside of the current frameset, and the window or frame in which a linked document will load.

   To specify targets for links in a document, select each link and apply a target value, or specify a base target for the entire document when you want all links in the document to open in the same manner (e.g., all links open in a new browser window). Manually specifying a target for an individual link overrides the base target you've specified for the document. If you do not specify a target for a linked document, the document opens in the frame that contains the link to the document. PageMill includes five targeting options: Default, New Window, Parent Frameset, Same Frame, and Same Window. For more information, see document 202147.

5. Unable to Insert or Preview Plug-in Object in PageMill 2.0 Troubleshooting Guide

PageMill 2.0 uses Netscape Navigator 2.0.x compatible plug-ins to insert and preview plug-in objects (e.g., PDF files, QuickTime movies) in a document. When you insert a plug-in object, PageMill searches for the plug-in that corresponds to the object's filename extension in the Browser Plug-ins folder in the PageMill Plug-ins folder. If the corresponding plug-in is not in the Browser Plug-ins folder, or if the plug-in object has no filename extension or one for which there is no corresponding plug-in, PageMill cannot find the plug-in it needs to display the object, and so it displays the broken plug-in icon instead.

If you do not have enough memory allocated to PageMill, PageMill returns an out of memory error. Increasing the amount of memory allocated to PageMill enables it to display or preview complex documents.

If you have several plug-ins installed that perform the same or similar function (e.g. QuickTime, MoviePlayer), they may interfere with PageMill's ability to display and preview plug-in objects. Other installed extensions may interfere with PageMill's ability to display and preview plug-in objects.

If a plug-in object does not preview as expected in Navigator when the corresponding plug-in is installed, the plug-in object will not preview as expected in PageMill. Several plug-ins require Macintosh System 7.5.3 or later.

For more information, see document 202151.

6. Creating Tables in PageMill 2.0

Adobe PageMill 2.0 enables you to control a table's appearance and structure in an HTML document. Table, cell, and column width constraints influence the appearance and behavior of a table, so achieving the table design you want can be confusing. In PageMill, you can create dynamic table which resize to the size of the Web browser window, you can create fixed tables, which remain the same size regardless of the size of the Web browser window, and you can also create hybrid tables, which have the attributes of both dynamic and fixed tables.

A hybrid table combines attributes of both dynamic and fixed tables by using pixel constraints for some columns and no constraints for others. When the sum of a table's constraints does not equal 100% of the Web browser window, many browsers expand the table so that it fills the entire window so columns with no constraint behave dynamically. PageMill ignores the specified pixel constraint of the first column once you add content to the second column. After you create a hybrid table in a PageMill document, preview the document in a Web browser to make sure the table appears correctly. To preserve the constraint of a cell when you add text, add line breaks by holding down the shift key while pressing Return.

For more information, see document 202152.

7. Using Alignment Options in PageMill 2.0

PageMill 2.0 enables you to select which tags it uses to align text and objects within HTML documents. Each yields different results when used in combination with other tags and previewed in a Web browser. You can align elements in PageMill documents using the tag, the <CENTER> tag, or the <DIV> tag. To change the alignment tag that PageMill uses, choose Edit > Preferences, click the HTML icon, and then select one of the options from the Alignment pop-up menu in the HTML Syntax section.

When you select a different alignment tag option in PageMill's Preferences dialog box, PageMill rewrites all alignment tags in the active document the next time PageMill parses the file. PageMill parses the file when you switch between HTML Source view and Page Edit mode, and when you save the file. PageMill does not support using more than one type of alignment tag in a document.

For more information, see document 202127.

8. Compatibility Between PageMill 2.0 and SiteMill 1.0.x General Information

One of the new features of Adobe PageMill 2.0 is support for many HTML (HyperText Markup Language) 3.2 tags. Because Adobe SiteMill 1.0.x supports only HTML 2.0 tags and some Netscape Navigator extensions for the HTML 2.0 language, some PageMill 2.0 features are not supported by SiteMill 1.0.x.

For more information on the compatibility issues that arise when you use Adobe SiteMill 1.0x and Adobe PageMill 2.0 to author and maintain a Web site containing client side image maps, embedded objects, tables, font size and color, placeholders, invisible elements, text wrap, pixel-based horizontal rules, basefont settings, and frames, see document 201902.

9. PageMill_Resource Folder Keeps Appearing on Hard Disk

When you insert a PICT image, copy and paste an image, or import a file with an embedded PICT or WMF image, PageMill 2.0 converts the image to GIF and stores it in the Resource folder. By default, this folder is named "PageMill_Resource" and is located at the root level of the hard drive where you installed PageMill.

If you delete the default PageMill_Resource folder and specify a different Resource folder, PageMill does not use the specified Resource folder and instead recreates the default PageMill_Resource folder. PageMill uses the specified Resource folder only for documents that are open when you specify the folder, and only during that session.

Open all PageMill documents in which you want to insert PICT images, choose Edit > Preferences and specify the desired Resource Folder location, then insert the PICT images into the open documents. This workflow forces PageMill to use the selected Resource Folder for the active session.

About this Macintosh Shows Little or No Memory Available for PageMill or SiteMill

Because Adobe PageMill and Adobe SiteMill do not report their memory usage to the Finder, the About This Macintosh dialog box indicates there is little or no free memory available for PageMill or SiteMill after you run PageMill or SiteMill for awhile.

The About This Macintosh dialog box displays horizontal bars which report the amount of memory allocated to each currently running application. The shaded part of the bar indicates how much memory an application is using, and the unshaded part indicates the amount of reserved system memory available to an application.

When launched, PageMill and SiteMill load the amount of memory allocated to the PageMill or SiteMill application, which includes the memory they require to run and additional system memory (i.e., the system heap). Right after you launch PageMill or SiteMill, you can view the division between the amount of memory PageMill and SiteMill require to run and the amount of available system memory reserved for PageMill or SiteMill in the About this Macintosh dialog box.

Like other Macintosh applications, when PageMill and SiteMill perform tasks that require additional memory (e.g., generating a .map file), they acquire memory from the system heap. But unlike other applications, PageMill and SiteMill do not notify the Finder when they are no longer using system memory. Instead, they monitor their memory usage and the amount of available system memory, reusing available system memory as needed. Because they do not report their memory usage to the Finder, the Finder indicates there is little or no free memory available for PageMill or SiteMill in the About This Macintosh dialog box.

Browser's Default Window Widths General Information

Because the default window width at which each browser displays Web pages may be unique, it can be difficult to determine how wide to create your Hypertext Markup Language (HTML) documents in Adobe PageMill 1.0.x or Adobe SiteMill 1.0.x.

PageMill's and SiteMill's default window width for displaying HTML documents is 480 pixels. You can resize PageMill's and SiteMill's document window to display images that are wider than the default window width. The dimensions of a resized document window are not saved in the HTML document. When opening a new or existing HTML document, PageMill and SiteMill display the HTML document at the default width window.

Netscape Navigator 2.0 and earlier for the Macintosh is the browser most commonly used to preview PageMill and SiteMill HTML documents. The default window width for Netscape is 468 pixels, which equals 6.5 inches on a 72 dpi monitor. In Netscape, an actual size (100%) 72 dpi image that is approximately 480 pixels or wider displays cropped in Netscape's default window. Because you can resize Netscape's window, Netscape's default width should not be considered a limitation when creating HTML documents in PageMill or SiteMill. Like PageMill and SiteMill, Netscape opens and displays HTML documents at the default window width.

Each browser available for the Macintosh has its own default window width for displaying HTML pages. Before creating HTML documents, determine the default window width of the browser in which you wish to view your PageMill or SiteMill HTML documents.

To determine your browser's default window width:

1. Move the browser's preferences file, located in the Preferences folder in the System Folder, to another location (e.g., desktop).
2. Launch your browser.
3. When the browser's main window is open, perform a screen capture (Command + Shift + 3), then quit your browser. The screen capture is a PICT file named "Picture [x]" where "x" is a number (e.g., Picture 2), and is located in the root folder on your hard disk.
4. Open the screen capture in Adobe Photoshop 3.0.x.
5. Crop the screen capture so all that remains is the browser window.
6. Choose Image > Image Size, then change the measurement system for the Width to pixels. The dimension listed in the Width field is the width of the default window in the browser.
7. Quit Photoshop 3.x, then move the browser's preferences file back into the Preferences in the System Folder.

Using .HTML or .HTM Filename Extensions General Information

HTML (Hypertext Markup Language) is the command language used to display information on the World Wide Web. The filenames of HTML documents must conform to HTML file naming conventions (i.e., they must include an ".HTM" or ".HTML" extension), and meet the requirements of the operating system running the Web server on which they reside.

You can select the default filename extension, or suffix, for HTML documents you create Adobe PageMill and Adobe SiteMill from the File Suffix pop-up menu in the Preferences dialog box. When saving HTML documents, PageMill and SiteMill display the default filename extension in the Save dialog box. The file naming conventions for UNIX, DOS, Windows 95, Windows NT, and Macintosh operating system are described below.

UNIX Web Servers

UNIX filenames are case-sensitive, and can contain up to 255 characters. If you'll be uploading your PageMill or SiteMill HTML documents to a UNIX Web server, or if you'll be copying your HTML documents to a UNIX computer for editing or previewing, set the File Suffix option to .HTML.

DOS Web Servers
DOS filenames (i.e., DOS and Windows 3.1.x) contain up to eight alphanumeric characters followed by a period and a three-character extension (e.g., document.htm). If you'll be uploading your PageMill or SiteMill HTML documents to a DOS Web server, or if you'll be copying your HTML documents to a DOS computer for editing or previewing, set the File Suffix option to .HTM before inserting images or creating links.
Windows 95 Web Servers
Windows 95 filenames can contain up to 255 characters. If you'll be uploading your PageMill or SiteMill HTML documents to a Windows 95 Web server, or if you'll be copying your HTML documents to a Windows 95 based computer for editing or previewing, set the File Suffix option to either .HTM or .HTML.
NOTE: If you'll be copying files to a DOS-formatted floppy disk in order to transfer them to Windows 95, long filenames are truncated to the DOS naming conventions described above. If you will be transferring your files using DOS-formatting floppy disks, set the File Suffix option to .HTM.
Windows NT Web Servers
Windows NT filenames can contain up to 255 characters, including the extension. If you'll be uploading your PageMill or SiteMill HTML documents to a Windows NT Web server, or if you'll be copying your HTML documents to a Windows NT computer for editing or previewing, set the File Suffix option to either .HTM or .HTML.
Macintosh Web Servers
Macintosh filenames can contain up to 31 characters. If you'll be uploading your PageMill HTML documents to a Macintosh Web server, set the File suffix option to either .HTM or .HTML.

PageMill 2.0 Preferences General Information

PageMill stores preference data in the Adobe PageMill 2.0 Prefs file, and the Adobe PageMill Pasteboard file, which are located in the Preferences folder in the System folder. The Adobe PageMill 2.0 Prefs file contains most of the user-customizable settings. The Adobe PageMill Pasteboard file contains information about items stored on the Pasteboard, as well as custom color values you specify in PageMill's Color Panel. Deleting these files restores PageMill's preferences to their default settings.

When you start PageMill 2.0, it reads the Adobe PageMill Preferences file (PageMill 1.0.x stores preference data in the Adobe PageMill Preferences file) and moves any comparable settings (e.g., line breaks, file suffix, and Default Folder for Images location) to the Adobe PageMill 2.0 Prefs file.

To customize your settings in PageMill 2.0, choose Edit > Preferences.

GENERAL PREFERENCES
Tiling
When you choose Window > Tile, PageMill tiles all active windows into the application screen. Select vertical or horizontal to determine which direction PageMill divides the application window.
Pasteboard
When you select Sound Effect, PageMill makes a flipping sound when you change pages in the Pasteboard.
Browsing
Open Pages In: Choose Edit or Preview from the Open Pages In pop-up menu to determine the mode in which PageMill opens documents.
Local Links: When you choose Same Window from the Local Links pop-up menu, PageMill previews document links by opening new documents into the same application window. When you choose New Window, PageMill previews document links by opening new documents into a separate application window (like PageMill 1.0.x).
Remote Links: Choose Select Browser from the Remote Links pop-up menu to specify a Web browser to enable you to preview external links.

PAGE PREFERENCES
Appearance
PageMill enables you to choose custom colors for your HTML documents. You can specify default colors for document text, document background, links, active links, and visited links from each respective pop-up menu in the Appearance section. You can also choose a default background image for your HTML documents. Use the Insert button, or drag and drop the desired image into the Background Image Well in the Appearance section. To remove the default image, press the Trash button.
NOTE: You cannot drag color chits from PageMill's Color Panel into the Preferences dialog box.
Line Breaks: Select the platform on which you will publish your HTML document to ensure line breaks display as expected.
Suffix: Select the filename extension to accommodate the platform on which you will publish your HTML document (i.e.,".htm" for IBM-compatible, ".html" for Macintosh or UNIX).

RESOURCES
Resource Folder
Select a folder within the local mirror of your Web site as the Resource Folder. The folder you specify as the Resource Folder contains the PICT graphics converted by PageMill. Selecting a folder within the local mirror of your Web site ensures links are maintained after you upload your site onto a Web server.
Map Format
Select the map format specified by your Internet Service Provider (ISP). Web servers require server-side image map files to be in either NCSA or CERN format.

SERVER
When you wish to create server-side image maps, or cause PageMill to write full URL pathnames when creating links,

you must set up your Server Preferences. PageMill's Server Preferences enable you to specify remote URLs that correspond to folders on your hard disk. Set up a Local Alias (Remote Root Directory and Local Root Folder) for each Web site you will author.

Remote Root Directory (Globe icon): Enter your Web site's remote root directory path, whose pathname begins and ends with a forward slash (/). Accurate path statements within image map files enable your image map links to work as expected on the Web server. The pathname you enter for your Web site's remote root directory path is often your Web server's Uniform Resource Locator (URL) address without the protocol (http:/) and domain (/www.name.com/).

Local Root Folder (Folder icon): Select the root level of the local mirror of your Web site to preview and maintain links in your HTML document locally and on the Web server.

HTML

HTML Source View

Comment color: Choose Custom from the Comment color pop-up menu when you wish to specify which color PageMill uses to display HTML Comments in HTML Source View. By default PageMill displays HTML Comments in red.

Tag color: Choose Custom from the Tag color pop-up menu when you wish to specify which color PageMill uses to display HTML tags in HTML Source View.

HTML Syntax

Font Size: When you wish PageMill to specify the relative size of text in a document using tags, choose SIZE Attribute from the Font Size pop-up menu. When you wish PageMill to specify the relative size of text in a document using <BIG> and <SMALL> tags, choose <BIG> & <SMALL> tags from the Font Size pop-up menu.

Alignment: PageMill enables you to select which tags it uses to align text and objects within HTML documents. Each yields different results when used in combination with other tags. For more information, see the record "PageMill 2.0 Alignment Options General Information."

When you choose Tag from the Alignment pop-up menu, PageMill writes alignment attributes as part of the paragraph tag (i.e., <P ALIGN="CENTER">). When you choose <DIV> Tag from the Alignment pop-up menu, PageMill writes alignment attributes using Netscape's <DIV> tag (i.e., <DIV ALIGN="CENTER">). When you choose <CENTER> Tag from the Alignment pop-up menu, PageMill writes alignment attributes outside of the paragraph tag (i.e., <CENTER>centered text</CENTER>).

SWITCH TO

The Switch To preference enables you to add and remove applications from PageMill's Switch To submenu. When you wish to add an application, click the Diamond icon, and select an application from the dialog box. When you wish to remove an application, press the Trash icon beside the application's name.

PageMill 2.0 Download Statistics General Information

Adobe PageMill 2.0's Download Statistics feature enables you to approximate the length of time it takes to download a PageMill document and its associated files (e.g., images, plug-in objects) based on the speed of an Internet connection. Download times in the Download Statistics dialog box do not include background images.

The Download Statistics feature measures data transfer in kilobits per second (kbps) and supports a range of calculation from 9.6 kbps to 128 kbps (i.e., the speed of an ISDN connection). The speed at which information travels across the Internet is affected by many variables, including your connection to the Web server, the speed of your computer, the amount of Internet traffic, the route the information takes (e.g., intermediate servers, routers, "detours"), and the quality of the phone line. Because so many variables exist, the Download Statistics feature can only approximate download times in a best-case scenario.

The Download Statistics dialog box contains three sections: the Object section, the Page section, and the Frameset section. The Object section shows the approximate download time for a selected object in hours:minutes:seconds format, and the selected object's file size in bits. The Page section shows the approximate download time for the composite document (i.e., the active document plus its linked files) in hours:minutes:seconds format, and the composite document's file size in bits. If the active document is a frameset, the Frameset section shows the approximate download time for the frameset, including all source documents and linked files. The section shows the download time in hours:minutes:seconds format, and the composite document's file size in bits.

PageMill represents download times graphically in each section using a pie chart. The green pie chart represents the first minute of download time. If the download time is longer than one minute, PageMill represents download time using a blue pie chart within the green pie chart.

PageMill 2.0 Import Filters General Information

Adobe PageMill 2.0 includes import filters that enable you to add information from a wide variety of sources to your PageMill documents. PageMill's import filters enable you to import files in RTF, ASCII (text-only), and HTML format, as well as files from the following applications:

- AmiPro/Word Pro 1.x, 2.x, and 3.x for Windows
- ClarisWorks 3.0 for Windows and for the Macintosh
- Lotus 123 1A, 2.x, 3.x, 4.x, and 5.0 for Windows
- MacWrite Pro 1.0 for the Macintosh
- Microsoft Excel 3.0, 4.x, and 5.a for the Macintosh

- Microsoft Excel 2.1, 3.x, 4.x, 5.0, and 7.0 for Windows
- Microsoft Word 3.x, 4.x, 5.x, and 6.0 for the Macintosh
- Microsoft Word 1.x, 2.x, 6.x, and 7.0 for Windows
- WordPerfect 1.0, 2.x, 3.x, and 3.5 for the Macintosh
- WordPerfect 5.x, and 6.1 for Windows

To import a file in PageMill 2.0, choose File > Open, select All Readable from the File Type pop-up menu, select a file, and then click Open. PageMill reads the file's header information to determine which import filter to use. PageMill then creates a temporary HTML file while importing and converting the file. After converting the file, PageMill names the temporary HTML file "untitledx.html," where "x" is the next unused sequential document in the PageMill session (e.g., untitled1.html, untitled2.html). You can edit, drag and drop, or copy and paste the contents of the untitledx.html document, just like you can in any other document you create in PageMill.

When importing text files, PageMill's import filters preserve HTML-supported text formatting (e.g., bold, italic, font size. The import filters discard formatting not supported by HTML (e.g., tabs). PageMill's import filters convert spreadsheet files from Microsoft Excel and Lotus 123 into fully-editable tables.

If your text or spreadsheet file contains images in TIFF, PICT, JPEG, or WMF format, PageMill converts them to JPG format and then saves them in the PageMill Resources folder. PageMill names the converted image file "

GRxxxxxx.JPG," where "xxxxxx" is the next unused sequential number for files in the Resources folder. PageMill does not convert images saved in other formats, so these images do not appear in converted files.

PageMill does not use import filters when you copy information in another application and then paste the information in PageMill.

Adobe SiteMill®

Feature Techniques

MAC OS

Tips for Creating Web Pages in PageMill and SiteMill

TALK TO YOUR INTERNET SERVICE PROVIDER (ISP)

The Adobe PageMill and Adobe SiteMill documentation explains how to use the software, but when creating a Web page you will also need additional information that can not be provided by Adobe. This document supplements the manuals with additional information to help you avoid common problems encountered when constructing Web pages.

TALK TO YOUR INTERNET SERVICE PROVIDER (ISP)

Before creating your Web site, ask your ISP the following:

1. Is the Web server running on a Macintosh, UNIX workstation, or IBM-compatible?
2. What is the path to the root directory of your Web site on the server?
3. Does your ISP make any CGI (Common Gateway Interface) scripts available to subscribers? CGI scripts are necessary to implement image maps and forms on most Web servers. Obtain instructions from your ISP to use CGI scripts successfully.
4. Which image map file format does the Web server use?
5. What is the correct procedure to use when you are ready to upload your Web site to the server? Many ISP's (e.g., America Online) have specific rules that govern how files are uploaded to the server.

SET UP PAGEMILL OR SITEMILL PREFERENCES

With the answers your ISP provides, you can correctly set up PageMill's or SiteMill's preferences. Customizing preference options before creating your Web site ensures your site's links will work as expected when the site is uploaded on a World Wide Web server.

To customize preferences in PageMill and SiteMill, choose Edit > Preferences. In the Preferences dialog box, you can customize the following options.

General Preferences

Page Flip Sound: When this option is selected, PageMill and SiteMill make a flipping sound when you change pages in the Pasteboard.

Page Preferences

Line Breaks: Select the platform on which you will publish your HTML documents to ensure line breaks display as expected.

File Suffix: Select the filename extension to accommodate

the platform on which you will publish your HTML documents (i.e.,".HTM" for IBM-compatible, ".HTML" for the Macintosh or UNIX). Without a filename extension, some Web browsers display the code of the HTML file, rather than the formatted page.

Image Preferences

Default Folder for Images: Select a folder within the local mirror of your Web site as the Default Folder for Images. The folder you specify as the Default Folder for Images contains the PICT graphics converted by PageMill or SiteMill. Selecting a folder within the local mirror of your Web site ensures links are maintained after you upload your site onto a Web server.

Map format: Select the map format specified by your Internet Service Provider (ISP). Web servers require map files to be in either NCSA or CERN format.

Remote Server Preference: Select the Remote Server option when using image maps in your HTML document. Enabling the remote server option makes the Local Root Folder and Remote Root Directory settings active.

Local Root Folder: Select the root level of the local mirror of your Web site to preview and maintain links in your HTML document locally and on the Web server.

Remote Root Directory: Enter your Web site's remote root directory path, whose pathname begins and ends with a forward slash (/). Accurate path statements within image map files enable your image map links to work as expected on the Web server. The pathname you enter for your Web site's remote root directory path is often your Web server's Universal Resource Locator (URL) address without the protocol (http:/) and domain (/ www.name.com/).

CREATE A MIRROR FOLDER

HTML documents include links to external files, rather than the contents of external files. To ensure links in your Web site remain valid, you must preserve your file's relative positions after you create links. You can preserve relative file positions by creating and using a pair of mirrored site folders, one on the local hard disk, and one on the Web server. When you initially upload your local site folder to the Web server, both folders should be identical. Any changes made to the local folder need to be made to the site folder to preserve the mirror relationship.

If you are unable to upload your entire site folder at the same time, create a folder structure on the Web server that matches the folder structure of your local site folder, then upload the site files into the appropriate folders.

NAME YOUR HTML DOCUMENTS

HTML documents need a filename extension appropriate to the platform from which you publish them. If your Web server is a Macintosh or UNIX workstation, use ".HTML." If the Web server is an IBM-compatible, use ".HTM." Files without filename extensions display the code of the HTML file in a Web browser, rather than the formatted document.

Use alphanumeric characters when you name HTML documents, and for the greatest compatibility use eight-character, single-word filenames (e.g., document.html). If you must use more than one word when you name HTML documents, use an underscore ("_") or hyphen ("-") rather than a space character. When you name a file using space characters, the space characters become ASCII-encoded, and links to the file are broken.

Many Web server packages are case-sensitive. When you create links manually, make sure you match the case of the file to which you are linking.

LOCATE AND NAME YOUR GRAPHIC FILES

PageMill and SiteMill can import images in GIF, JPEG, and PICT format. When importing PICT images, PageMill and SiteMill convert the PICT image into a GIF image, and store the GIF image file in the Default Folder for Images folder. To specify a Default Folder for Images, choose Edit > Preferences and select a folder within your local site folder. Then place graphics you wish to use into this folder before inserting them into your HTML documents.

PageMill and SiteMill name autoconverted PICT files using this format: "image1.gif," "image2.gif," "image3.gif," in numeric order. If you want more control over the names of graphic files within your Web site, convert PICT files to either GIF or JPEG format before you import them.

Graphic files need a filename extension appropriate to the platform from which you publish them. If the Web server is a Macintosh or UNIX workstation, use ".GIF" or ".JPEG." If your Web server is an IBM-compatible, use ".GIF" or ".JPG." Files without filename extensions display the code of the graphic file in a Web browser, rather than the graphic.

Use alphanumeric characters when you name graphic files, and for the greatest compatibility use eight-character, single-word filenames (e.g., photo.gif). If you must use more than one word when you name graphic files, use an underscore ("_") or hyphen ("-") rather than a space character. When you name a file using space characters, the space characters become ASCII-encoded, and links to the file are broken.

UPLOAD YOUR WEB SITE

When you upload your Web site to the server, send HTML files as text, and all other files as raw data. If you upload files using a different format, links will not work as expected, and graphics will not display. When you upload your Web site using a standard FTP utility (e.g.,Dartmouth Fetch) refer to support documentation for answers to questions. Adobe Systems does not support FTP utilities or uploading Web site files.

HAVE REALISTIC EXPECTATIONS

PageMill and SiteMill are versatile and easy to use, but have their limitations. PageMill and SiteMill support the last standardized HTML specification, HTML 2.0, and some Netscape extensions (e.g., visited link color). The majority of Web pages published on the Internet contain some elements included in the proposed HTML 3.2 specification (e.g., tables, frames, text wrap, different typefaces). Later releases of PageMill and SiteMill will support newer HTML elements, but it's difficult to write an application to support a still-evolving standard.

Different Web browsers interpret HTML differently. For example, some formatting or objects in your HTML documents may look different in Netscape Navigator than they do in the America Online Web browser.

Linking to Director Movies for Use With Shockwave in PageMill 1.0.x and SiteMill 1.0.x

The Macromedia Shockwave plug-in for Netscape Navigator 2.0x enables Netscape to play movies made in Macromedia Director 4.0.4 or later on a World Wide Web page.

To play Director movies using the Shockwave plug-in, open and save your Director movies in Macromedia Afterburner. Afterburner compresses Director 4.0.4 or later movies so they can be transmitted efficiently over the Internet, and adds the extension ".dcr" to the saved movie to enable the Shockwave plug-in to recognize them.

After saving Director movies in Afterburner, you can create links to them in Adobe PageMill 1.0.x or Adobe SiteMill 1.0.x using the <EMBED> Hypertext Markup Language (HTML) 3.0 tag.

To link to a Director 4.0.4 or later movie in PageMill or SiteMill:

1. Open your PageMill or SiteMill HTML document, then click the globe icon to switch to Edit mode.
2. Position the mouse where you would like the Director movie to appear, then click to create an insertion point.
3. Choose Style > Raw HTML.
4. Type the <EMBED> tag, including within it the pixel height, pixel width, and location of the Director movie. For example, to embed a Director movie named "Movie.DCR" that has a height and width of 100 pixels and is located in the same folder as the HTML document in which it is embedded, type:
   <embed height=100 width=100 SRC="movie.dcr">
5. Save the PageMill or SiteMill HTML document. You can preview the Director movie by opening the PageMill or SiteMill HTML document in Netscape 2.0x with the Shockwave plug-in installed. PageMill 1.0.x and SiteMill 1.0.x cannot preview Director 4.0.4 or later movies.

To play your Director movies in Netscape after they are uploaded to a Web server, the Web server must be configured to interpret and attach the correct MIME header to .dcr files. To determine whether your Web server supports .dcr files, contact your Internet Service Provider.

Unexpected Results

MAC OS

Links Defined as Absolute Paths List as Errors in SiteMill 1.0.x

ISSUE

After loading a Web site, Adobe SiteMill 1.0.x lists links defined as absolute paths in the Errors window.

SOLUTIONS

Choose Edit > Replace Links, and change the link definition from an absolute path to a relative path.

OR: If the linked file is within the Site folder, use drag-and-drop error correction to change the link definition to a relative path:

1. Load the site, then choose Window > Tile to display both the Site window and the Errors window.
2. Locate the missing file or anchor in the Site window.
3. Drag the file from the Site window, and drop it over the corresponding file in the Errors window.
4. Click OK to update the links.
5. Repeat steps 2-4 until all links defined as absolute paths no longer display in the Errors window.

OR: Change the link definition for links listed in the Errors window from an absolute path to a URL:

1. In SiteMill's Errors window, click the file's Inbound Link button.
2. Open the file that contains the link definition in SiteMill by selecting its name from the inbound links pop-up menu.
3. In SiteMill's Edit mode, select the element using an absolute path link definition.
4. Enter the linked file's URL address in the Link Location bar, then press Return.
5. Repeat steps 1-4 for additional links listed in the Errors window.

ADDITIONAL INFORMATION

When loading a Web site, SiteMill defines the loaded site folder as the root level of the directory structure. Because absolute path definitions begin at the root level of the directory structure on the hard disk, and not at the loaded site folder, SiteMill displays links defined as absolute paths in the Errors window.

When you choose Edit > Change Links and change link definitions from absolute paths to relative paths, SiteMill does not verify the link starting with the root level of the hard disk. SiteMill verifies the link based on the relative path within the loaded site folder, and can verify the link as expected.

If the linked file is within the site folder, SiteMill can resolve the error using drag-and-drop error correction.

SiteMill does not verify links defined using a URL address on the local hard disk.

Errors Window Displays Image Map Links in SiteMill 1.0.x

ISSUE

After loading a Web site in Adobe SiteMill 1.0.x, links in image map files list in the Errors window.

SOLUTIONS

Choose Edit > Preferences and revert to the Remote Server preference settings made when you created the image map files and reload the site.

OR: Replace links to files listed in the Errors window:

1. Position the Site window and the Errors window so that both are visible on-screen.
2. In the Site window, locate the file icon or anchor icon listed as missing in the Errors window.
3. Drag the icon from the Site window and drop it on the missing icon in the Errors window. Click OK.
4. Repeat steps 2-3 for each missing link listed in the Errors window.

OR: Remove forward slash characters (/) from the name of the hard disk and any site folders and replace links to image map hotspots:

1. Rename the hard disk and any site folders without using forward slash characters.
2. Choose Edit > Preferences.
3. Click the Local Root Folder icon, select the site folder, and click In Here.
4. Choose Site > Reload.
5. Position the Site window and the Errors window so that both are visible on-screen.
6. In the Site window, locate the file icon or anchor icon listed as missing in the Errors window.
7. Drag the icon from the Site window and drop it on the missing icon in the Errors window.
8. Click OK.
9. Repeat steps 6-8 for each missing link listed in the Errors window.

ADDITIONAL INFORMATION

When loading a Web site, SiteMill uses the Remote Server preference settings to verify links in image map files. If the Remote Server preferences are different from the settings specified when you create the image map files, SiteMill cannot locate the linked items in the image map. When you revert to the Remote Server preferences specified when creating the image map files SiteMill can locate the linked items in the image map files.

When Remote Server information changes, recreate image map files by making new preference selections, reloading the Web site, and relinking files listed in the Errors window.

A forward slash character indicates a change of directory for UNIX machines, Web browsers, and SiteMill. When the name of your hard disk, or the name of any site folder contains a forward slash character, SiteMill cannot resolve image map the links inside map file properly. Removing the forward slashes, resetting the Local Root Folder, reloading the site, relinking and fixing any errors enables SiteMill to resolve image map links as expected.

Line Break Missing From Top of Page After Reopening HTML Document in SiteMill 1.0.x

ISSUE

After opening a Hypertext Markup Language (HTML) document that was previously saved in Adobe SiteMill 1.0.x, one less line break (i.e., paragraph return) appears at the beginning of the page than expected.

SOLUTIONS

Insert one more line break than desired at the beginning of the page.

OR: Left-align the first object on the page, then reinsert the missing line break.

ADDITIONAL INFORMATION

When SiteMill 1.0.x reopens an HTML document that begins with two or more line breaks (i.e., <BR> tags) followed by a center-aligned object, SiteMill removes one line break from the beginning of the page. Because SiteMill removes the line break only once, inserting an extra line break causes the desired number of line breaks to appear the next time you open the HTML document. Left-aligning the first object on the page prevents SiteMill from removing a line break when you reopen the HTML document.

Can't Select Multiple Files in Site Window in SiteMill 1.0.x

ISSUE

After loading a Web site in Adobe SiteMill 1.0.x, multiple files cannot be selected simultaneously in the Site window.

SOLUTION

Select only one file at a time in SiteMill's Site window.

ADDITIONAL INFORMATION

SiteMill does not support selecting multiple files simultaneously in the Site window.

Map Files Don't Display in Site Window in SiteMill 1.0.x

ISSUE

Image map (.map) files do not appear in the Site window in Adobe SiteMill 1.0.x.

SOLUTION

Verify the location of .map files at the Finder.

ADDITIONAL INFORMATION

SiteMill 1.0.x does not display .map files in the Site window. When you move an image file using SiteMill, however, SiteMill also moves any corresponding .map files.

After you create an image map in a PageMill or SiteMill HTML document, PageMill or SiteMill creates a separate .map file, which contains information about the hotspots on the image map and their hyperlinks. By default, PageMill and SiteMill store .map files in the same folder as the corresponding image file.

Image Inserted Using Replace Links Command is Wrong Size in SiteMill 1.0.x

ISSUE

After you use the Replace Links command in Adobe SiteMill 1.0.x to replace an image in a Hypertext Markup Language (HTML) document, the new image does not display as expected (e.g., stretched or shortened).

SOLUTION

Scale the original image to its actual size before replacing it:

1. Open the HTML document containing the resized image in SiteMill.
2. Click on the Globe icon to switch to Edit mode.
3. Select the resized image.
4. Choose Window > Show Attributes Inspector.
5. Click the Object button to show the image attributes.
6. Select Scale to Height.
7. Select Scale to Width.
8. Save and close the document.
9. Replace the image using the Replace Links command.

ADDITIONAL INFORMATION

When you resize an image in a SiteMill document, and then replace it using the Replace Links command, the new image will display at the resized dimensions of the original image. If an image is not resized, and you replace the image using the Replace Links command, the new image will display as expected.

When you use the Replace Links command in SiteMill, SiteMill alters only the target file of the image link, and does not alter any of the information added to the HTML code of the file for the original graphic (i.e., height, width, border).

Bullet Style Changes in HTML Document Opened in PageMill or SiteMill

ISSUE

When you open an Adobe PageMill or Adobe SiteMill document, bullets in unordered lists, menu lists, or directory lists display as solid circles (discs) instead of open circles or open squares as expected.

SOLUTION

After saving the HTML document in PageMill or SiteMill, open a copy of the document in a text editor that can save in text-only format (e.g., Microsoft Word, SimpleText), then replace the <UL> tags with <UL TYPE=disc>, <UL TYPE-=circle>, and <UL TYPE=square> tags, or replace the <LI> tags with <LI TYPE=disc>, <LI TYPE=circle>, and <LI TYPE=square> tags.

DISCLAIMER: Adobe Systems does not support modifying an HTML document with a text editor. Familiarity with opening HTML files in a text editor and saving in text-only (e.g., ASCII) format is required. Experience with HTML language is highly recommended. Always modify a copy of the original HTML file. If alterations are incorrectly performed or the file is saved in the wrong format, the HTML file or sections of the HTML file can be unreadable. In the event of problems, revert to the original copy.

ADDITIONAL INFORMATION

PageMill and SiteMill do not support the Netscape TYPE attribute for defining bullets in unordered, menu, or directory lists, or for individual list items. When opening a document that contains bullets defined using TYPE attribute tags, PageMill and SiteMill convert <UL TYPE=disc>, <UL TYPE=circle>, and <UL TYPE=square> tags to the <UL> tag, and convert <LI TYPE=disc>, <LI TYPE=circle>, and <LI TYPE=square> tags to the <LI> tag.

PageMill and SiteMill use the <UL> and <LI> tags to display solid circle (disc) bullets for all list items in unordered, menu and directory lists.

The Netscape TYPE attribute can be used to define bullets for list items in browsers that support Netscape's TYPE attribute. The <UL TYPE=> tags define bullets for all list items, while the <LI TYPE=> tags define bullets for individual list Items.

Can't Move File or Folder to Site Root Folder in SiteMill 1.0.x

ISSUE

When moving a file or folder to the root level of a loaded Web site folder in the Site window in Adobe SiteMill 1.0.x, the file or folder does not move (i.e., nothing happens).

SOLUTIONS

Create a new Hypertext Markup Language (HTML) document in SiteMill, save it in the root folder of the Web site, then reload the Web site:

1. In SiteMill, choose Site > Load, then select your Web site folder.
2. Choose File > New.
3. Choose File > Save, save the HTML document into the root folder of your Web site, then close the document.
4. In the Site view window, drag and drop the desired file or empty folder onto the new HTML document in the Web site's root folder.

OR: Choose Site > Load, then load the folder in which your Web site folder resides.

ADDITIONAL INFORMATION

SiteMill 1.0.x supports moving files or folders to the root folder of a loaded Web site folder in the Site view when there are no files located in the root of a loaded Web site.

When loading the folder that contains your Web Site folder, SiteMill considers the Web site folder as a separate folder within the loaded site, instead of as the root level of your Web site.

Multiple Instances of the Same File Display in the Site Window in SiteMill 1.0.x

ISSUE

Multiple instances of the same folder or file with case variances (e.g., myfile.html, Myfile.html, MyFile.html) display unexpectedly in the Site window in Adobe SiteMill 1.0.x.

SOLUTIONS

Change all duplicate instances of a folder or filename to match the corresponding name in the Finder:

1. Switch to the Finder and note the exact case of the duplicated folder or filename in the Site window.
2. In SiteMill's Site window, change the spelling of the duplicate object.
3. Rename the object with the desired name and case.
4. Repeat steps 1-3 for each duplicate folder or filename.
5. Choose Site > Reload.

OR: Use SiteMill's Replace Links feature to rename duplicated folders or filenames:

1. Switch to the Finder and note the exact case of the duplicated folder or filename in the Site window.
2. In SiteMill, choose Site > Replace Links.
3. Drag the icon for a duplicate file or folder from the Site window, and drop it in the Find text box.
4. Drag the icon for the file with the desired name and case from the Site window to the Replace text box.
5. Click Replace All, and click OK.
6. Repeat steps 1-5 for each duplicate folder or filename.
7. Choose Site > Reload.

ADDITIONAL INFORMATION

When you manually link to a local file using its Uniform Resource Locator (URL) without matching the case of each folder and filename in the path to the linked object, multiple instances of the same folder or file display unexpectedly in SiteMill's Site window. When you change all duplicate instances of a folder or filename in the Site window to match the corresponding name in the Finder, or update the links using SiteMill's Replace Links feature, SiteMill displays the folders or files as expected (i.e., a single instance of the folder or file with correct case).

When the file is present on the local hard drive, use drag and drop to link to the file. SiteMill uses the case of the folders and filenames in the Finder to create links.

Case Changes to Folder or Filenames in SiteMill 1.0.x Don't Occur in Finder

ISSUE

When you change the case of a file or folder name in SiteMill 1.0.x's Site view, the change does not occur in the Finder.

SOLUTION

Change the spelling of the file or folder name in Site view, then change it back to the desired name and case.

ADDITIONAL INFORMATION

When you change the case of a file or folder name in SiteMill's Site view, SiteMill updates all linked site files to reflect the change, but the Finder does not update the case change. When you change the spelling of a filename or folder name in Site view, the Finder does update the case change.

When a file or folder name in Site view is different from the corresponding name in the Finder, erroneous broken links appear and disappear in SiteMill's Errors window, and SiteMill may not display the "This change requires modifying xx files" message when you change the name.

Globe Cursor Keeps Spinning when Loading Site in SiteMill 1.0x

ISSUE

When you load a Web site in Adobe SiteMill 1.0.x, the globe cursor continues to spin, the progress bar freezes, and the site does not load.

SOLUTION

Remove colon (:) characters from anchor names in all HTML documents in the site:

1. Note the filename that displays in SiteMill's progress bar when the system freezes.
2. Restart the Macintosh.
3. Launch SiteMill and open the file you noted in step 1.
4. Click the globe icon to switch to Edit mode.
5. Choose Edit > Show Anchors.
6. Select an anchor icon on the page.
7. Choose Window > Show Attributes Inspector, then Object Attributes.
8. Remove colon characters from the anchor name in the Name field, and press Return.
9. Repeat steps 6-8 for each anchor in the document.
10. Choose File > Save and close the document.
11. Choose Site > Load.
12. Repeat steps 1-11 until the Web site loads successfully.
13. Fix broken anchor links by dragging the anchor icons in SiteMill's Site view to the corresponding anchor icons in SiteMill's Errors window.

ADDITIONAL INFORMATION

SiteMill does not support anchor names that include colon characters. When you load a site with documents in which one or more anchor names includes a colon, the globe cursor continues to spin, the progress bar freezes, and the site does not load.

SiteMill supports anchor names that use only alphanumeric, hyphen (-), or underscore (_) characters. The HTML specification reserves the colon character for defining protocols (e.g., http://, ftp://, gopher://, mailto:, news:) and port numbers in URL addresses (e.g., http://www.company-.com:8080/).

Application Errors

MAC OS

Error "Unknown Error..." or "..file can not be found" Clicking Image in PageMill or SiteMill

ISSUE
When you double-click on an image in an Adobe PageMill or an Adobe SiteMill document, PageMill or SiteMill returns the error "Unknown exception error" or "The specified file can not be found."

SOLUTIONS
Delete, then reinsert the image into the PageMill or SiteMill document.
OR: When using SiteMill, change the name of the image or the folder containing it back to its original name:

1. Choose Site > Load.
2. Select the Web site containing the image.
3. In the Site window, change the name of the image or the folder containing it back to its original name.

OR: When using SiteMill, rename files and folders in your Web site in the Site window instead of in the Finder.

ADDITIONAL INFORMATION
After you insert an image into a PageMill or SiteMill HTML document, renaming the image or the folder containing it breaks PageMill's or SiteMill's link to the image. When you double-click on an image with a broken link in an HTML document, PageMill or SiteMill returns the error "Unknown exception error" or "The specified file can not be found." PageMill and SiteMill recreate the link to an image when you reinsert it.

Error "Loading this site failed..." in SiteMill 1.0.x

ISSUE
When you load a Web site in Adobe SiteMill 1.0.x, SiteMill returns the error "Loading this site failed, since the folder hierarchy is too deep."

SOLUTION
Restructure your web site so that no folder in the site is nested more than 24 levels deep.

ADDITIONAL INFORMATION
Adobe SiteMill 1.0.x cannot load sites with folders nested deeper than 24 levels.

Error "default.cgi" Appears in SiteMill's Errors Window

ISSUE
After loading a Web site in Adobe SiteMill 1.0.x, the error "default.cgi" displays in SiteMill's Errors window.

SOLUTIONS
Do one or more of the following:

A. When the Hypertext Markup Language (HTML) document causing the error contains form objects, create a link to the CGI script that will be associated with the document on the Web server:
    1. In the SiteMill Errors window, click and hold down the Incoming Links button, which is to the right of the error message. A pop-up menu containing the names of the HTML documents causing the error displays.
    2. Select one of the listed documents to open it.
    3. In the HTML document, click the globe icon to switch to Edit mode.
    4. Choose Window > Show Attributes Inspector.
    5. In the Attributes Inspector, click Page.
    6. In the Action text box, enter the Uniform Resource Locator (URL) of the CGI script that will be linked to your HTML document on the Web server , then press Enter.
    7. Repeat steps 2 to 6 for each HTML document that appears in the Incoming Links pop-up menu.

    NOTE: Avoid linking your HTML document to the default.cgi file included with SiteMill. The default.cgi file is a placeholder text file associated with the EWOrder.html file, which is part of the SiteMill tutorial, and not a CGI script.

B. When the HTML document that causes the error contains an image that is not intended to be a submit button for a form, apply the Picture attribute to the image:
    1. In the SiteMill Errors window, click and hold down the Incoming Links button, which is to the right of the error message. A pop-up menu containing the names of the HTML documents causing the error displays.
    2. Select one of the listed documents to open it.
    3. In the HTML document, click the globe icon to switch to Edit mode.
    4. Select the image, then choose Window > Show Attributes Inspector.
    5. In the Attributes Inspector, click Object.

6. For the Behavior option, select Picture.
7. Repeat steps 4-6 for each image in the HTML document.
8. Repeat steps 2-7 for each HTML document that appears in the Incoming Links pop-up menu.

ADDITIONAL INFORMATION

Establishing a link to the CGI script that will be associated with your HTML document, or applying the Picture attribute to images not intended to act as submit buttons for HTML forms, prevents the error "default.cgi" from displaying in SiteMill's Errors window after loading a Web site in SiteMill.

Interactive HTML forms require a Common Gateway Interface (CGI) script to communicate information between the Web browser and the Web server. When you load a Web site containing an HTML document that is not linked to a CGI script, but does includes a form object (e.g., submit button, check box) or an image with the Button attribute applied, SiteMill displays the error "default.cgi" in the Errors window.

Error "...only empty directories may be moved..." When Moving Folder in SiteMill 1.0.x

ISSUE

When moving a folder into another folder in the Site view window, SiteMill 1.0.x returns the error "Sorry - only empty directories may be moved in this version." SiteMill 1.0x does not move the folder.

SYMPTOM

A triangle appears to the left of the folder, indicating that the folder contains files.

SOLUTION

In SiteMill create an empty folder in the desired location, then move the files into that folder:

1. In SiteMill's Site view window, choose Site > Create Folder to create an untitled folder.
2. Move the untitled folder to the desired destination.
3. Rename the untitled folder with the desired folder name.
4. Move files individually into the new folder.
5. At the Finder, delete the original folder.
6. In SiteMill, choose Site > Reload.

ADDITIONAL INFORMATION

Adobe SiteMill 1.0.x supports moving empty folders and single files in the Site window, but does not support moving folders containing files or folders, or moving multiple files in the Site window.

Error "An Error Occurred While Reading the Site Directory" in SiteMill 1.0.x

ISSUE

The error "An Error Occurred While Reading the Site Directory" occurs when you load a site in Adobe SiteMill 1.0.x.

SOLUTIONS

Do one or more of the following:

A. Mount the volume that contains the site folder.
B. Remove or rename all files that end with the .dir filename extension.
C. Remove any unnamed files (e.g., Count WWWebula 1.2.1 includes a file in the Counters folder that has no name).
D. If the site folder is on a DOS-formatted disk network drive, copy it to a Macintosh volume or hard disk.
E. Rename or disconnect any mounted volume that shares the same name as the volume containing the site folder.
F. Make sure the hard disk or mounted volume name does not contains HTML-reserved characters (e.g., the characters "." and "..").
G. Change hyperlinks to folders (e.g., "folder1/folder2") into hyperlinks to documents (e.g., "folder1/folder2/document.html").
H. Move a folder from within the site folder to the desktop, then load the site. Continue to move folders one at a time from within the site folder to the desktop, until the site loads without displaying an error message. When the site loads correctly, load the last folder moved to the desktop by itself in SiteMill. If an error occurs, remove half the files from that folder and load it again. Continue to isolate files from the folder to determine which files are causing the error.
I. Increase SiteMill's memory partition:
   1. Quit all applications.
   2. Choose Apple > About this Macintosh.
   3. Note the Largest Unused Block value (i.e., available memory), then close the window.
   4. Select the SiteMill application icon and choose File > Get Info.
   5. Enter a larger value in the Preferred Size text box (System 7.1 or later), but not exceeding the Largest Unused Block value you noted in step 3.
   6. Close the Get Info window, then restart SiteMill and load the site.
J. Run SiteMill with all extensions off to verify that added extensions are not the cause. To turn off all extensions upon startup in System 7, restart the computer while holding the Shift key down until the message "Welcome to Macintosh. Extensions off." appears. (Non-Apple keyboards may have a different method for restarting the Macintosh with extensions off.)
K. Recreate the SiteMill preferences file:
   1. Quit SiteMill.
   2. Delete the Adobe PageMill Preferences file, located in the Preferences folder in the System Folder.
   3. Restart SiteMill.

L. Restart with extensions off, then remove and reinstall SiteMill:
   1. Delete the Adobe PageMill Preferences and Adobe PageMill Pasteboard files, located in the Preferences folder in the System Folder.
   2. Delete the Macintosh Drag and Drop and ObjectSupportLib system extensions, located in the Extensions folder in the System Folder.
   3. Move the HTML documents you created out of the SiteMill folder, then delete the SiteMill folder.
   4. Restart with all extensions turned off by holding down the Shift key while restarting the Macintosh until the message "Welcome to Macintosh. Extensions off." appears.
   5. Reinstall SiteMill, then restart the Macintosh.

M. Rebuild the desktop file for all volumes (hard disks). To rebuild the desktop file, hold down the Command and Option keys while restarting the computer. Keep the keys held down until you receive the message "Are you sure you want to rebuild the desktop file on the disk '[disk-name]'? Comments in info windows will be lost." Then click OK.

N. Check for hard disk problems. For instructions, see Additional Information.

ADDITIONAL INFORMATION

When you wish load a Web site in SiteMill that you stored on an external volume, mount the external volume before loading the site.

An error occurs when you load a site that contains files ending with the .dir filename extension, or files that have no name. Removing or renaming these files enables SiteMill to load the site as expected.

SiteMill does not support loading a site from DOS-formatted floppy disks. Copy your site to your Macintosh's hard disk before you load the site.

If an error occurs when you load a site stored on a network volume, copy the site to the local hard disk before loading it.

When more than one hard disk on the desktop shares the same name, or when a hard disk is named using HTML-reserved characters (e.g., "." or ".."), SiteMill cannot resolve link references in the site, and returns an error. When you resolve hard disk naming issues by disconnecting from or renaming the hard disk, SiteMill loads the site as expected.

Because the HTML specification requires you to specify file names in links, SiteMill produces an error when you load a site containing links to folders, rather than files. Open all HTML documents containing links to folders, and replace them with links containing filenames.

A damaged or conflicting file may be cause SiteMill to return the error "An Error Occurred While Reading the Site Directory" when you load a site. When you remove one folder at a time from the site folder, and try to recreate the error, you can determine which folder or file is causing the error. Systematically isolating the problem file or folder until your site loads as expected, and recreating the problem item enables you to prevent the error from occurring.

When your site contains many links and images, SiteMill may use all available memory and generate an error. Increasing the preferred memory allocated to SiteMill enables the site to load as expected.

SiteMill may return an error while loading a site if there is an extension conflict, damaged preferences file, the desktop file is corrupt, or the hard disk is damaged or heavily fragmented. Run SiteMill with all extensions disabled, recreate the preferences file, rebuild the desktop file, or check the hard disk for damage.

To check a hard disk's directory structure with Disk First Aid:

1. Start the Macintosh from the Disk Tools disk included with your System 7 installation disks.
2. Double-click on the Disk First Aid application.
3. Select or open the drive to be verified or repaired.
4. Click Verify to check the disk or Repair to check and repair the disk. If you click Verify, Disk First Aid tells you if there is a problem with the disk and asks you if you want to repair it. Always repair the disk when prompted.
5. Choose File > Quit.

To check for hard disk problems, do one or more of the following:

A. Use Disk First Aid, included on the system software installation disk sets, to check the hard disk's directory structure. For instructions on using Disk First Aid, see Additional Information.

B. Update all SCSI drivers to ensure they are not damaged and are compatible with the current system. For instructions on updating SCSI drivers, see Additional Information.

C. Use a third-party disk utility (e.g. Norton Utilities, MacTools, Symantec Tools for the Macintosh) to ensure damaged sectors are tagged as unusable. For instructions, refer to the utility's documentation.

D. Defragment and optimize your hard disk using a disk utility (e.g., Norton Utilities, MacTools).

System Errors

MAC OS

System Error (e.g., Freeze) Saving HTML Document into Loaded Web Site in SiteMill 1.0.x

ISSUE

When saving a Hypertext Markup Language (HTML) document into a loaded Web site in Adobe SiteMill 1.0.x, a system error (e.g., freeze) occurs and the HTML document is not saved.

SOLUTION

Remove the colon (:) character after anchor names in the HTML document:

1. Open the HTML document SiteMill's Edit mode.

2. Choose Edit > Show anchors.
3. Choose Window > Show Attributes Inspector, and then click Object Attributes.
4. Select an anchor icon on the page.
5. In the Name text box, delete the colon (:) character in the anchor's name, and then press Return.
6. Repeat steps 4-5 for each anchor on the page.

ADDITIONAL INFORMATION

When SiteMill is unable to save an HTML document because an anchor's name contain unsupported characters, a system error (e.g., freeze) occurs.

SiteMill supports anchors and form element names using alphanumeric, hyphen (-), and underscore (_) characters. The HTML specification reserves the colon character for defining protocols (e.g., http://, ftp://, gopher://, mailto:, news:) and port numbers in Uniform Resource Locators (URL) addresses (e.g., http://www.company.com:8080/).

System Error (e.g., Freeze) After Web Site is 100% Loaded in SiteMill 1.0.x

ISSUE

When you load a World Wide Web site in Adobe SiteMill 1.0.x, a system error (e.g., freeze) occurs after its progress bar is 100% full.

SOLUTION

Remove references to embedded URL-encoded Apple Scripts from the HTML documents, load and modify your Web site in SiteMill 1.0.x, and then re-add the URL-encoded AppleScripts into the HTML documents:

DISCLAIMER: Adobe Systems does not support modifying an HTML document with a text editor (e.g., SimpleText, Teach Text). Familiarity with opening HTML documents in a text editor and saving in text-only (e.g., ASCII) format is required. Experience with HTML language is highly recommended. Always modify a copy of the original HTML document. If alterations are incorrectly performed or the file is saved in the wrong format, the HTML document can be further damaged. In the event of problems, revert to the original copy.

1. Open a copy of the HTML document containing embedded URL-encoded AppleScript in a text editor that can save in text-only format (e.g., SimpleText, TeachText).
2. Locate the embedded URL-encoded AppleScripts, which are located within anchor tags and use the "ascpt:" protocol. For example:
```
<A HREF="ascpt:tell%20application%20Netscape
 2.0%20to%20say%20%27Hello,%20%27%22"></A>
```
3. Select the embedded URL-encoded AppleScript and then choose File > Cut. After cutting the embedded URL-encoded AppleScript, the anchor tags should read:
```
<A HREF=></A>
```
4. Open a new document and then choose File > Paste. For HTML documents that contain multiple embedded URL-encoded AppleScript, cut and paste each embedded URL-encoded AppleScript into the new document.
5. Save the new document containing the URL-encoded AppleScript with the name "script.txt."
6. In the HTML document, enter placeholder text (e.g., "deleted_AppleScript") to replace the embedded URL-encoded AppleScript in the anchor tag. For example:
```
<A HREF="deleted_AppleScript"></A>
```
7. Save the HTML document in text-only format, and then close the document.
8. Repeat steps 1 to 7 for each HTML document that contains embedded URL-encoded AppleScripts.
9. In SiteMill, choose Site > Load, then select your Web site folder. The modified HTML document appears in SiteMill's Errors window.
10. Modify your Web site as desired, then quit SiteMill.
11. Re-open the script.txt file and the HTML document from which you removed the embedded URL-encoded AppleScript in a text editor.
12. In the script.txt file, select the URL-encoded AppleScript, and then choose Edit > Cut.
13. In the HTML document, select the placeholder text, and then choose Edit > Paste to replace the placeholder text with the embedded URL-encoded AppleScript. For HTML documents that contain multiple embedded URL-encoded AppleScript, cut and paste each embedded URL-encoded AppleScript back into the HTML document, replacing the placeholder text.
14. Save the HTML document in text-only format.

ADDITIONAL INFORMATION

SiteMill does not support the "ascpt:" protocol, which embeds an URL-encoded AppleScript in HTML documents. When loading a Web site in SiteMill 1.0.x that includes HTML documents containing the "ascpt:" protocol, a system error (e.g., freeze) occurs after SiteMill's progress bar is 100% full.

Printing Problems

MAC OS

Transparent Areas of GIF Prints Gray to PostScript Printer from PageMill or SiteMill

ISSUE

When you print to a PostScript printer from Adobe PageMill or Adobe SiteMill, transparent pixels in GIF images print gray. The GIF images display as expected on screen.

SYMPTOM

The GIF image was exported from Adobe Photoshop 3.0.5 in GIF89a format with transparency applied.

SOLUTIONS

Print the PageMill or SiteMill document from a Web browser that can print transparent pixels in GIF images (e.g., Netscape Navigator 1.1 or later).

OR: Resave the image from Photoshop 3.0.x in GIF format, insert the image in PageMill or SiteMill, then apply transparency to it:

1. Open the image in Photoshop 3.0.x.
2. Choose File > Save As.
3. In the Save As dialog box, select CompuServe GIF from the Format pop-up menu, then click Save.
4. Open the HTML document that contains the original image.
5. Click the globe icon to switch to Edit mode.
6. Select the original image, then press the Delete key.
7. Insert the resaved GIF image.
8. Press Command and double-click on the image.
9. In the Image View window, select the Transparency tool, then click the area on then image that contains the color you wish to make transparent.
10. Choose File > Save, then close the Image View window.

ADDITIONAL INFORMATION

Photoshop 3.0.5 does not specify transparent pixels correctly in GIF89a images. When you print a Photoshop GIF89a image to a PostScript printer from PageMill or SiteMill, transparent pixels in the GIF image print gray, although they print transparent from Web browsers that support transparent GIF images (e.g., Netscape Navigator 1.1 or later).

GIF89a is the only version of the GIF format that supports transparency. When you save a Photoshop image in CompuServe GIF format, Photoshop creates a GIF87a image, which does not support transparency. If you then insert the image in PageMill or SiteMill, apply transparency to it, and save it in the Image View window, PageMill or SiteMill converts the image to GIF89a format and specifies the transparent pixels correctly, causing the image to print transparent to a PostScript printer as expected.

Reapplying transparency to pixels in a Photoshop GIF-89a image in PageMill or SiteMill does not cause the image to print transparent, because PageMill or SiteMill does not convert the image to GIF89a format and specify the transparent pixels in the image.

The GIF89a Export plug-in included with Photoshop 3.0.5 enables you to export GIF images in GIF89a format from Photoshop.

General Information

MAC OS

HTML Tags and Netscape Extensions Supported in SiteMill 1.0

Adobe SiteMill 1.0 supports writing and previewing Hypertext Markup Language (HTML) 2.0 tags as specified in the HTML Level 2 Definition Type Document (DTD), and a select set of commonly used Netscape extensions to the HTML 2.0 language. SiteMill 1.0 supports the following Navigator Netscape extensions and HTML tags. Information about what HTML language level the tag uses, whether the tag is a Netscape extension, and how the tag is supported by SiteMill 1.0 follows each listed Netscape extension and HTML tag.

SiteMill 1.0 rewrites HTML tags when opening an HTML document created in a different application. To easily revert back to the original HTML document, create a backup of your HTML documents created in another application before opening and saving these in SiteMill 1.0. Adobe Systems Incorporated does not support the HTML 3.0 programming language.

SITEMILL 1.0 SUPPORTED NETSCAPE EXTENSIONS

- Netscape centering
- Borders
- Thickness
- Width percent scaling on horizontal rules
- Solid horizontal rules
- Background colors
- Tiled backgrounds
- Text colors
- Link colors
- Visited (traversed) link colors
- Active link colors
- Image dimensions

Legend for SiteMill 1.0 Mupported HTML Tags

Y	Supported
N	Not supported; SiteMill 1.0 displays in Raw HTML style (i.e., red text)
R	Rewritten by SiteMill 1.0
P	Passthrough; SiteMill does not display formatting, but passes it through unaltered unless otherwise indicated
2.0	HTML version 2.0
3.0	HTML version 3.0
N1.0	Netscape 1.0 style
N1.1	Netscape 1.1 style
N2.0	Netscape 2.0 style
?, xxx	Represents a number, series of numbers, or text

SiteMill 1.0 Supported HTML Tags

SiteMill 1.0, HTML, Description, Tag Supported, Version

General

Y 2.0 Prologue <!DOCTYPE HTML PUBLIC "-//IETF// DTD HTML 2.0//EN">
N 3.0 Prologue <!DOCTYPE HTML PUBLIC "-//W3O/ /DTD W3 HTML 3.0//EN">
Y 2.0 Document Type <HTML></HTML>
Y 2.0 Title <TI TLE></TITLE>
Y 2.0 Header <HEAD></HEAD>
Y 2.0 Body <BODY></BODY>
Y 2.0 Next ID <NE XTID N=xxx>

Hard Formatting or Physical Styles

Y 2.0 Bold </B>
Y 2.0 Italic </I>
N 3.0 Underline </U>
N N1.0 Strikeout <S></S>
Y 2.0 Typewriter <TT ></TT>
N N1.0 Blinking <BLINK></BLINK>

Soft Formatting or Logical Styles

Y 2.0 Headings <H?></H?>
Y 2.0 Emphasis <EM></EM>
Y 2.0 Strong Emphasis <STRONG></STRONG>
Y 2.0 Preformatted <PRE></PRE>
Y 2.0 Width <PRE WIDTH=?></PRE>
N 2.0 Pre/No Tags <XMP></XMP>
Y 2.0 Citation <CITE></CITE>
Y 2.0 Code <CODE></CODE>
N 2.0 Plaintext <PLAINTEXT>
Y 2.0 Sample Output <SAMP></SAMP>
Y 2.0 Keyboard Input </KBD>
Y 2.0 Variable <VAR></VAR>
Y 2.0 Definition <DFN></DFN>
Y 2.0 Listing <LISTING></LISTING>
N N1.0 Font Size <FONT SIZE=?></FONT>
N N1.0 Change Font Size <FONT SIZE=+|-?></FONT>
N N1.0 Base Font Size <BASEFONT SIZE=?>

Alignment

Y 2.0 Block Quote <BLOCKQUOTE></BLOCKQUOTE>
N/R/P 3.0 Align Text <P ALIGN=LEFT|CENTER|RIGHT></ P>

NOTE: *SiteMill 1.0 does not support aligning text using these Netscape extensions. SiteMill 1.0 rewrites <P ALIGN=LEFT></ P> to and displays this alignment as aligned left. SiteMill 1.0 rewrites <P ALIGN=CENTER></P> to <CENTER></CENTER> and displays this alignment as centered. SiteMill 1.0 enables <P ALIGN =RIGHT></P> to passthrough without alteration, and displays this alignment attribute in Raw HTML style.*

N/R 3.0 Align Heading <H? ALIGN=LEFT|CENTER|RIGHT> </H?>

NOTE: *SiteMill 1.0 does not support aligning headings using these Netscape extensions. SiteMill 1.0 rewrites <H? ALIGN=LEFT></ H?> to <H?></H?>, <H? ALIGN=CENTER> to <H?><CENTER></H?>, and displays <H? ALIGN=RIGHT></H?> in Raw HTML style.*

Y N1.0 Center <CENTER></CENTER>

Links and Graphics

Y 2.0 Link <A HREF="URL"></A>
Y 2.0 Link to Target <A HREF="URLxxx"></A> <A HREF="xxx"></A>
Y 2.0 Define Target (Anchor) <A NAME="xxx"></A>
Y 2.0 Display Image <IMG SRC="URL">
Y 2.0 Alignment <IMG SRC="URL" ALIGN=TOP|BOT-TOM|MIDDLE>
N/P N1.0 Alignment <IMG SRC="URL"ALIGN=LEFT|RIG-HT|TEXTTOP|ABSMIDDLE|BASE-LINE|ABSBOTTOM>

NOTE: *SiteMill 1.0 does not support aligning images using these Netscape extensions. SiteMill 1.0 enables these image alignment attributes to passthrough without alteration, but does not display these alignment attributes in Raw HTML style. SiteMill 1.0 displays the images with <ALIGN=LEFT> and <ALIGN=RIGHT> and <ALIGN=TEXT TOP> as if they were aligned using <ALIGNTOP>. SiteMill 1.0 displays images with <ALIGN=ABSMIDDLE> as if they were aligned using <ALIGN=MIDDLE>. SiteMill 1.0 displays images with <ALI GN=ABSBOTTOM> and <ALIGN=BASELINE> as if they were aligned using <ALIGN=BOTTOM>.*

Y 2.0 Alternate <IMG SRC="URL" ALT="xxx">
Y 2.0 Image Map <IMG SRC="URL" ISMAP>
N N2.0 Client-side Image Maps <IMG SRC="URL" USEMAP="#xxx"> <MA P NAME="xxx"> <AREA SHAPE="RECT" COORDS ="xxx" HREF="URL"> </MAP>
Y N1.0 Dimensions <IMG SRC="URL"WIDTH="?" HEIGHT="?">
Y N1.0 Border <IMG SRC="URL" BORDER=?>
N/P N1.0 Runaround Space <IMG SRC="URL" HSPACE=? VSPACE=?>

NOTE: *SiteMill 1.0 does not support running space around images using these Netscape extensions. SiteMill 1.0 enables these attributes to passthrough without alteration, but does not display the image with the surrounding space and the HSPACE or VSPACE attributes in Raw HTML style.*

N/R N1.0 Low-Res Proxy <IMG SRC="URL" LOW-SRC="URL">

NOTE: *SiteMill 1.0 does not support referencing low-res proxy images using this Netscape extension. SiteMill 1.0 enables this attribute to passthrough but does not display these alignment attributes in Raw HTML style. SiteMill 1.0 removes the quototation marks around the URL reference to the image.*

Dividers

Y/R 2.0 Paragraph

NOTE: *SiteMill 1.0 converts the paragraph tag to <BR>.*

N 3.0 Paragraph </P>
Y 2.0 Line Break
N N1.0 Clear Textwrap <BR CLEAR=LEFT|RIGHT|ALL>
Y 2.0 Horizontal Rule (shaded) <HR>
N/P N1.0 Alignment <HR ALIGN=LEFT|RIGHT|CENTER>

NOTE: *SiteMill 1.0 does not interpret or rewrite the alignment, nor display it in Raw HTML style.*

Y N1.0 Thickness <HR SIZE=?>

N/R N1.0 Width <HR WIDTH=?>

NOTE: SiteMill 1.0 interprets and rewrites the width tag as <HR WIDTH=?%>

Y N1.0 Width Percent <HR WIDTH=?%>
Y N1.0 Solid Horizontal Rule (unshaded) <HR NOSHADE>
N N1.0 No Break <NO BR>
N N1.0 Word Break <WB R>

Lists

Y 2.0 Unordered List <UL><LI></UL>
N/R N1.0 Bullet Type <UL TYPE=DISC|CIRCLE|SQUARE> <LI TYPE=DISC|CIRCLE|SQUARE>

NOTE: SiteMill 1.0 interprets and rewrites the bullet type attributes as: <UL> and <LI> and displays them with the default attribute DISC.

Y 2.0 Ordered List <OL><LI></OL>
N N1.0 Outline Type <OL TYPE=A|a|I|i|1> <LI TYPE=A|a|I|i|1>
N N1.0 Starting Number <OL VALUE=?> <LI VALUE=?>
Y 2.0 Definition List <DL><DT><DD></DL>
Y 2.0 Menu List <ME NU><LI></MENU>
Y 2.0 Directory List <DIR><LI></DIR>

Backgrounds and Colors

Y N1.1 Background Color <BODY BGCOLOR="#$$$">
Y N1.1 Tiled Background <BODY BACKGROUND="URL">
Y N1.1 Text Color <BODY TEXT="xxx">
Y N1.1 Link Color <BODY LINK="xxx">
Y N1.1 Visited Link <BODY VLINK="xxx">

NOTE: SiteMill 1.0 does not display visited link colors in Preview mode. To Preview visited link colors, open the HTML document in a browser that supports visited link colors.

Y N1.1 Active Link <BODY ALINK="xxx">

Special Characters

Y 2.0 Special Character &#?;

NOTE: SiteMill 1.0 does not read the special character " ." SiteMill 1.0 displays the " " characters in the Raw HTML style and reserves it as a non-defined character, while some browser applications do read and understand this character.

Y 2.0 < <
Y 2.0 > >
Y 2.0 & &
Y 2.0 " "
Y/R 2.0 Registered TradeMark ®

NOTE: SiteMill 1.0 reinterprets and rewrites the registered trademark (tm) tag as: ®

Y N1.0 Registered TradeMark ®
Y/R 2.0 Copyright ©

NOTE: SiteMill 1.0 reinterprets and rewrites the copywrite tag as the © tag.

Y N1.0 Copyright ©

Forms

Y 2.0 Define Form <FORM ACTION="URL" METHOD= GET|POST></FORM>
Y 2.0 Input Field <INPUT TYPE="TEXT|PASSWORD|-CHECKBOX|RADIO|IMAGE|SUB-MIT|RESET">

NOTE: SiteMill 1.0 does not support hidden fields (i.e., <INPUT TYPE=HIDDEN>). SiteMill 1.0 enabless the hidden field tag to passthrough without alteration, but does not display the hidden field tag in Raw HTML style.

Y 2.0 Field Name <INPUT NAME="xxx">
Y 2.0 Field Value <INPUT VALUE="xxx">
Y 2.0 Checked <INPUT CHECKED>
Y 2.0 Field Size <INPUT SIZE=?>
Y 2.0 Max Length <INPUT MAXLENGTH=?>
Y 2.0 Selection List <SELECT></SELECT>
Y 2.0 Name of List <SELECT NAME="xxx"></SELECT>
Y 2.0 Number of Options <SELECT SIZE=?></SELECT>
Y 2.0 Multiple Choice <SELECT MULTIPLE>
Y 2.0 Option <OPTION>
Y 2.0 Default Option <OPTION SELECTED>
Y 2.0 Input Box Size <TE XTAREA ROWS=? COLS=?></ TEXTAREA>
Y 2.0 Name of Box <TE XTAREA NAME="xxx"></ TEXTAREA>

Tables

N 3.0 Define Table <TABLE></TABLE>
N 3.0 Table Border <TABLE BORDER></TABLE>
N N1.1 Table Border <TA BLE BORDER=?></TABLE>
N N1.1 Cell Spacing <TA BLE CELLSPACING=?>
N N1.1 Cell Padding <TA BLE CELLPADDING=?>
N N1.1 Desired Width <TA BLE WIDTH=?>
N N1.1 Width Percent <TA BLE WIDTH=%>
N 3.0 Table Row <TR ></TR>
N 3.0 Alignment <TR ALIGN=LEFT|RIGHT|CEN TER VALIGN=TOP|MIDDLE |BOTTOM>
N 3.0 Table Cell <TD ></TD>
N 3.0 Alignment <TD ALIGN=LEFT|RIGHT|CEN TER VALIGN=TOP|MIDDLE |BOTTOM>
N 3.0 No linebreaks <TD NOWRAP>
N 3.0 Columns to Span <TD COLSPAN=?>
N 3.0 Rows to Span <TD ROWSPAN=?>
N N1.1 Desired Width <TD WIDTH=?>
N N1.1 Width Percent <TD WIDTH=%>
N 3.0 Table Header <TH ></TH>
N 3.0 Alignment <TH ALIGN=LEFT|RIGHT|CEN TER VALIGN=TOP|MIDDLE |BOTTOM>
N 3.0 No Linebreaks <TH NOWRAP>
N 3.0 Columns to Span <TH COLSPAN=?>
N 3.0 Rows to Span <TH ROWSPAN=?>
N N1.1 Desired Width <TH WIDTH=?>
N N1.1 Width Percent <TH WIDTH=%>
N 3.0 Table Caption <CAPTION></CAPTION>
N 3.0 Alignment <CAPTION ALIGN=TOP |BOTTOM>

Frames

N N2.0 Define Frames </FRAMESET>
N N2.0 Frame Columns <FRAMESET COLS="50%,50%">

N	N2.0	Frame Rows	<FRAMESET ROWS="50%,50%">
N	N2.0	Frame	
N	N2.0	Frame Source	<FRAME SRC="URLxxx"> <FRAME SRC="xxx.html">
N	N2.0	Frame Name	<FRAME NAME="window_name">
N	N2.0	Frame Width	<FRAME MARGINWIDTH="value">
N	N2.0	Frame Height	
N	N2.0	Frame Scrollbar	<FRAME SCROLLING="yes|no|auto"
N	N2.0	Frame Sizing	
N	N2.0	Alternative Content	<NO FRAMES>

Miscellaneous Tags

N/P	2.0	Comment	<!— xxx —>

NOTE: *SiteMill 1.0 supports entering comments in Raw HTML style. SiteMill 1.0 enables the comment tag to passthrough without alteration, but like most browsers, SiteMill does not display the common tag in Raw HTML style.*

Y	2.0	Author's Address	<ADDRESS></ADDRESS>
N	2.0	Searchable	<ISINDEX>
N	N1.0	Prompt	<ISINDEX PROMPT="xxx">
Y	2.0	Send Search	<A HREF="URL?xxx"></A>
N	2.0	URL of This File	<BASE HREF="URL">
N	2.0	Relationship	<LINK REV="xxx" REL="xxx" HREF="URL">
N/P	3.0	Meta Information	<META>

NOTE: *SiteMill 1.0 does not support entering meta information. SiteMill 1.0 enables the <ME TA> tag to passthrough without alteration, but like most browsers, SiteMill does not display the meta tag in Raw HTML style.*

System Requirements for SiteMill 1.0.x

MINIMUM SYSTEM REQUIREMENTS

- Macintosh II series (68020 or later processor)
- Macintosh System 7 Pro or System 7.1 or later
- 3 MB of application RAM
- Hard drive with 5 MB or more of available space for installation
- 4-bit (16 shades) grayscale monitor
- StuffIt Expander for installation from the World Wide Web (WWW)
- 3.6 MB of hard disk space to install the online manual, included with SiteMill from the WWW
- Adobe Acrobat Reader for viewing the online manual, when included
- High-density disk drive for installation from disk set

RECOMMENDED SYSTEM REQUIREMENTS

- 68040 Macintosh or Power Macintosh
- Macintosh System 7 Pro or System 7.5 or later for full drag and drop functionality
- 4 MB of application RAM (NOTE: more RAM may be required for loading large sites or opening large graphics).
- Color monitor

SiteMill 1.0 Documentation Errors

ADOBE SITEMILL 1.0 USER GUIDE

Page 3 (Online User Guide is correct)

Adobe SiteMill requires a Macintosh or Power Macintosh running System 7 or later, 3.5 megabytes (MB) of unused RAM, 5 MB of unused hard disk space, and a 4-bit display or higher.

Should be

Adobe SiteMill requires a Macintosh or Power Macintosh running System 7.1 or later, a minimum of 3 megabytes (MB) of unused RAM (4 MB preferred), 5 MB of unused hard disk space, and a 4-bit display or higher. To install the online manual included with the online version of SiteMill, you need an additional 3.6 MB of hard disk space.

Page 67 (Page 70 of Online User Guide)

To resize while keeping the most recent proportions of the rule, press Shift as you drag the botton right corner handle.

Should Be

To resize while keeping the most recent proportions of the rule, press Shift before you drag the botton right corner handle.

Page 74 (Page 77 Online User Guide)

file:// opens a file on a mounted volume

Should Be

file:/ opens a file on a mounted volume

Page 82 (Page 85 of Online User Guide)

The text in the Remote Root Directory in the screenshot of the Preferences dialog reads: /www.company.com/departments/marketing/

Should be

Either http://www.company.com/departments/marketing/ or /departments/marketing/

Adobe Persuasion®

Adobe Persuasion joined the Adobe team when Aldus Corporation merged with Adobe in 1994. The newest version, Adobe Persuasion 4 was released in early 1997. Persuasion is the presentation tool for veteran road warriors who've seen it all. It produces sophisticated presentations in any medium, including the Web. Add hypertext links, movies, and sounds to your presentations; drag and drop URL links directly from Netscape Navigator and insert links to other slides, presentations, and even Web pages. Then export the file to Adobe Portable Document Format (PDF) with links intact, ready for publishing on the Web.

Contents

Adobe Persuasion®

Feature Techniques

MAC OS / WINDOWS

Q *(Player)* **How can I include QuickTime movies in a Player file so that they will play on either platform?**

A There are two prerequisites for successful cross-platform transfer of QuickTime movies with a Player file. One is that you have QuickTime installed on both platforms; the other is that you have the Persuasion Player version 3.01.

To tell which version of the Player you have, launch the Player and look at the startup screen. You should see "3.01" in small type in the screen's lower-right corner (PC) or lower- left corner (Mac). If the Player is already running, you can choose "About Persuasion Player..." from the Help menu (PC) or the Apple menu (Mac) to view the startup screen. Or, on the PC, you can check the date of PLAYERW.EXE in File Manager—it will be 9/12/94 for version 3.01. On the Mac, you can see what's listed next to "Version" in the Player's "Get Info" dialog box (click once on the Player application in the Finder, and choose "Get Info" from the File menu).

If you don't have version 3.01, see the box on page 86 for information on how to get it.

Once you've got QuickTime installed and have version 3.01 of the Player, here are the steps on each platform for creating a transferrable file.

PC

1. In Windows Persuasion 3.0, export the presentation as a Player file (see chapter 10 of the User Manual for detailed instructions). For convenience, you may want to select "Copy Links: Movies," which will copy all linked movies into the same directory as the exported Player file, but it's not necessary to do so.
2. Transfer the resulting Player file and all the QuickTime movies that were used in the file into a single folder on the Macintosh.
3. On the Mac, launch Player version 3.01 and play the file normally.

Mac

1. In Mac Persuasion 3.0, export the presentation as a Player file (see chapter 10 of the User Manual for detailed instructions), but do not select "Package movies."
2. Still on the Mac, open the resulting Player file using Persuasion Player version 3.01.
3. Press Command + M to display the menu bar. Choose "Save as..." from the File menu. Give the file a name with up to eight characters and a .ppf extension (for example, "show.ppf"). Select "Package movies" and "All Persuasion Players." Click "OK."
4. If you're saving to the same folder and with the same filename as the existing file, you'll be asked whether you wish to replace the existing file. Click "Replace."

   This "Save as" procedure creates a separate file for each occurrence of a movie or sound in the Player file. Each movie or sound will be assigned the name of the Player file followed by a number and a .mov extension. (So, for the Player file named show.ppf, the movies and sounds will be named show_pp1.mov, show_pp2.mov, and so on.) If the Player filename already has eight characters, it will be truncated to allow room for the numbers.
5. Transfer the Player file you just created and all its associated .mov files into a single directory on the Windows-based computer. Launch Player version 3.01 under Windows to play the file.

Q *(3.0 only)* **How do I control the position of the labels on a pie chart? I want them to be on the pie slices.**

A Label positions are controlled through the "Slice feeler size" dialog box—whether or not slice feelers (the lines that connect labels with pie slices) are turned on. You can position labels individually or as a group. Here's how.

1. Display slice labels by opening the "Display status" dialog box (choose "Display status..." from the Chart menu) and selecting "Slice names" and/or "Slice values." Click "OK."
2. If you want to move only certain labels, click to select them (hold down the Shift key to select more than one). If you don't select any labels, they'll all be changed.
3. Choose "Slice feeler size..." from the Chart menu. Enter 0 in the "Horizontal" and "Feeler length" text boxes. Then enter a value between 0 and 100 for "Center distance"—the number expresses the distance from the center as a percentage of the pie's radius. (The dot on the sample diagram moves as you enter values, so you can see the effect of what you're doing.)
4. When you're satisfied, click "OK." The labels should be on top of the pie slices.

TIP MAC OS / WINDOWS

Stop-and-go Player files *(3.0 only)*

Sometimes—like for self-running demos—it would be nice to have a presentation that was advanced manually by the viewer for a while, then would display a sequence of slides automatically, and then waited again to be advanced by the viewer. Impossible, you say? Here's a technique that accomplishes it, by stringing together a series of Player files that autojump to one another. Let's say you have a 12-slide presentation and you want the first 3 slides to advance manually, the next 5 to advance automatically, and the final 4 to advance manually. Here's how to set it up.

1. Once you've created the presentation, choose "Slide sorter" from the View menu. Shift-select slides 1, 2, and 3. Choose "Export…" from the File menu, make sure "Selected slides" is chosen in the "Export" dialog box, and export the group as a Player file. Name it something that will remind you what slides are in it, like 1_3.PPF. (For more information on creating Player files, see page 169 of the Windows Persuasion 3.0 User Manual or page 187 of the Macintosh Persuasion 3.0 User Manual.)
2. Repeat the process for slides 4 through 8, naming the exported file 4_8.PPF, and for slides 9 through 12 (name it 9_12.PPF). Don't worry about autojumps or transition effects yet—you're going to overwrite these files later in the procedure.
3. Still within Persuasion itself (not the Player), return to Slide view and go to slide 3. Create an autojump hotspot. You can do this either by selecting an object or text block and choosing "Autojump" from the Draw menu, or—if you want the hotspot to be invisible to the audience—by dragging an area with the Autojump tool from the Tools palette. In the "Autojump" dialog box, choose "Presenta-tion" (Windows) or "Jump to player presentation" (Macintosh) and select the Player file called 4_8.PPF.
4. If you created a visible hotspot but only want it to show up after the other layers have displayed, use the Layer pop-up menu at the bottom of the Persuasion window to assign the hotspot to the last layer on the slide.
5. Go to slide 8, the last slide in the second group, and repeat this process, creating an autojump hotspot that will jump to the third Player file, 9_12.PPF.
6. Choose "Slide show" from the View menu and select "Transitions" from the submenu. In the "Slide" list box, select slide 8 and assign the maximum delay to that slide (600 seconds in Windows, 100 seconds on the Mac). Select the last layer for that slide and assign the max-imum delay for that layer. (You'd repeat this process if you had another group of automatically advancing slides that were jumping to a manual-advance group.) When you're finished, click "OK."
7. Return to "Slide sorter" view and again export the three groups of slides as Player files, giving them the same names as the first time—thus replacing the existing Player files.
8. Exit Persuasion and launch the first exported Player file. Press Ctrl + T (Windows) or Command + T (Macintosh) to bring up the "Settings" dialog box. Select manual advance, and click "Continue." Then press the Esc key (Windows) or Command + period (Macintosh) to close the Player file. Save the changes when prompted. Open the next file and choose automatic advance; finally, open the last file and choose manual advance.
9. To show the presentation, launch the first Player file and advance it manually. When it stops on slide 3, click the hotspot. The file containing slides 4 through 8 will launch seamlessly and advance automatically. When the show pauses on slide 8, click the hotspot before your time is up—on Windows you have 1,200 seconds, or 20 minutes; on the Mac, you have 200 seconds, or 3 minutes and 20 sec-onds. The final file will launch, and you can click your way through slides 9 through 12.

Q *(3.0 only)* **When people view the presentations I create, they sometimes accidentally click somewhere on the slide, and advance to the next slide without meaning to. Is there a way I can set up a button to take them to the following slide—and make clicking elsewhere do nothing?**

A There is, although it's a little devious: essentially, you make the entire slide area into an autojump "hot area" leading back to the same slide. As long as this autojump area is behind the other autojump buttons, the buttons will work, but any mouse click outside the buttons will appear to do nothing. Here's how to do it.

1. First, set up the autojump button leading to the next slide, as well as any other visible autojumps you want. For information on creating an autojump button, see the online help, or pages 148–49 (Windows) or 162–63 (Mac) of the Aldus Persuasion 3.0 User Manual.
2. With nothing selected, click the autojump tool and drag to select an area the size of the entire slide.
3. In the "Autojump" dialog box, click "Jump to slide." In

the "Slide" pop-up menu, scroll to the slide you're presently on. Click "OK."

4. Select the autojump area by clicking on its edge, and choose "Send to back" from the Draw menu.
5. To check your work, choose "Show all slides…" from the "Slide show" submenu under the View menu. Make sure manual advance is specified, and then click "Play." You'll notice that the mouse cursor looks like a pointing finger no matter where it is positioned on the slide. Clicking on the visible autojump buttons will jump to the appropriate destination as usual, but clicking anywhere else on the slide will result in no change.

NOTE: This will work only as long as the user clicks within the slide area. If a Player file's display resolution is greater than 640 x 480, each slide will display with a black area around it—and clicking in this area will still cause the presentation to go to the next slide.

Q *(3.0 only)* **I usually want my tables to fit into a particular amount of space, so I create them by dragging the table tool. But then if I want to add another row or column, the table gets bigger—and if I resize it on the slide, it gets distorted. How do I get the size I want with the right number of rows and columns?**

A The best solution is to preset the table defaults to the desired number of rows and columns before dragging the tool to create your table. Here's how.

1. Once you know how many rows and columns you want, launch Table by dragging the table tool. (It doesn't matter what size you drag—you're not going to save this table.)
2. Select "Table format…" from the Edit menu.
3. Enter the number of rows and columns you want and click the "Set default" button. Then close the dialog box by clicking "Cancel" (not "OK").
4. Choose "Close" from the File menu and, when prompted, choose not to update.
5. Now you're ready to create your table. With the table tool, drag an area that's the size you want the table to be. When Table launches, it will have the correct number of rows and columns for your table. (Be sure that your table is contained within the white area in the Table application. If it spills over onto the gray boundary region, close the table without updating and drag a smaller area on the slide.) Then, as long as you don't do anything that will force a cell's size to increase (such as adding more text than the cell can hold), your final table will match the size you specified when dragging the tool.

Q *(3.0 only)* **I wish I could mix automatic and manual advance in a single slide show. For instance, I sometimes want the layers to advance automatically, but slide advance to be manual; other times, I'd like some slides to advance automatically and others manually. Can you help?**

A The simplest way to create the impression of mixed automatic and manual advance is to make all the advances automatic, but put the longest possible delay on the ones that will be advanced manually—since clicking will always advance a slide or layer. The maximum delay possible in Persuasion for Windows is 600 seconds, or 10 minutes, while on the Mac it's 100 seconds, or over a minute and a half; however, you can double these numbers by assigning that delay both to a slide and to its last layer. For many presentations, that will be plenty of time to essentially create "true" manual advance.

Here's how to set up a slide show in which layers advance automatically but slides advance manually (unless you wait too long before clicking).

1. Once you've created your presentation and assigned layers, choose "Set default transitions…" from the "Slide show" submenu under the View menu.
2. In Windows, enter the value "600" in the "Set default transitions" dialog box next to "Delay between slides," then click "OK." On the Mac, click on the pop-up menu next to "Slide delay" and select "Other"; enter "100" in the "Slide delay" dialog box; and click "OK" to close both dialog boxes.
3. From the View menu, select "Slide show" and then "Transitions…." Ensure that each slide in the "Slide" list box shows the delay assigned in step 2. If there are any slides that don't, select that slide in the list box and click "Defaults" (Windows) or "Use defaults" (Mac).
4. Still in the "Transitions" dialog box, select the first slide in the "Slide" list box and then that slide's last layer in the "Layer" list box. In Windows, enter 600 seconds in the box at the bottom of the dialog box under "Delay." On the Macintosh, click on the pop-up menu at the bottom of the dialog box under "Delay" and choose "Other…." Enter 100 seconds in the "Layer delay" dialog box. Repeat this step for each slide. When you're done, click "OK."
5. Finally, choose "Show all slides…" from the "Slide show" submenu under the View menu. Set the slide advance for the presentation to "Automatic." Make sure that all the other options are set the way you want.

When this presentation is shown, either as a slide show or as a Player file, the layers will display automatically, but there will be a long pause at the end of each slide (20 minutes in Windows, 3 minutes and 20 seconds on the Mac), giving you plenty of time to click and advance manually.

If you want to mix the way slides advance—some manual, some automatic—you can use the same basic technique. Set the default transition to the maximum time, and then assign a short time (like 2 seconds) to the individual slides that you want to have advance automatically.

Alternatively, if the presentation you're creating is destined to be a Player file, there's a way to actually mix groups of slides that advance manually and automatically—see the tip below.

Q Is there an easy way to delete the text on my slides that says "Click here for title," "Click here for subtitle," and so on?

TIP MAC OS / WINDOWS

Motion control *(3.0 only)*

You probably know that Persuasion's "Autoanimate" feature can cause objects (graphics or text blocks) to move around the screen in simple ways—entering or exiting from the edges, for instance. What you may not realize is that a couple of the options in the "Autoanimate" dialog box can give you more control over when and how objects appear or disappear—especially if you pull a few tricks with invisible objects, grouping, and layers.

For instance, let's say you want to create the effect of a man rushing across the slide and through a doorway. Follow these steps.

1. Draw a rectangle near the right-hand edge of the slide to represent your doorway. Give it a solid-color fill.
2. Draw another, smaller rectangle with a solid-color fill to represent the person, or import a drawing of a rushing man (there's one supplied with Persuasion's clip art called "Dashing.wmf" on the PC and "Dashing" on the Mac). If necessary, resize it relative to your doorway.
3. Position this figure near the left edge of the slide, with its bottom edge aligned with the bottom of the "doorway" (you may want to Shift-select both objects and use the "Align/Distribute" command).
4. With the line tool, draw a line that extends from the figure to the right edge of the doorway opening. Assign it a line weight of "none" (PC) or no fill (Mac). This makes it invisible.
5. With the invisible line still selected, hold down the Shift key and select the figure on the left. Choose "Group" from the Draw menu.
6. Select the new grouped figure and assign it to layer 2 using the layer pop-up menu at the bottom of the slide.
7. With the grouped figure still selected, choose "Autoanimate..." from the Draw menu. In the "Autoanimate" dialog box, choose "Exit to right" for the animation direction and "Cropped" for the play area.
8. Preview your slide, first making sure that both "Animations" and "Layers" are selected in your slide- show settings.

The key to this process is that when an animation is set to "Cropped," it will move only as far as its selection handles. By grouping the rushing figure with an invisible object whose handles were positioned at the desired exit point, we extended the figure's play area.

Granted, it's not Toy Story, but playing around with variations of this technique can create quite a few interesting animated effects.

A These "Click here for . . ." text blocks in Persuasion 3.0 are optional prompts. If you don't find them helpful, simply uncheck "Prompt text" from the Placeholder submenu under the Show menu. This submenu also offers you the chance to show or hide the placeholder's dotted-line boundaries.

Of course, even when displayed, the prompts and boundaries will not show up in the slide show, in printed output, or on 35-mm. slides.

Q I'd like to get my Persuasion presentation into Premiere, so I can incorporate it into a QuickTime movie I'm working on. Do I need some kind of fancy equipment to do this?

A No, no special equipment is needed. You simply export the slides in your presentation as Windows Metafiles (on the PC) or PICT files (on the Mac), and then batch-import them into Premiere. Be aware, though, that this means you'll lose any time-based effects you created in Persuasion (such as transitions, animations, or imported movies or sounds). Chances are, of course, that you can create similar effects within Premiere. Also, for best results be sure that the aspect ratio (width to height) of your Persuasion slides matches that of your Premiere project (usually 4:3).

Here are the steps to follow in order to get your presentation into Premiere:

1. Create an empty folder (directory) for storing the slides. Then open your Persuasion file and choose "Export..." from the File menu.
2. In the "Export" dialog box, select a file type to export. On the PC, choose "Windows metafile (*.wmf)" under "Export as file type"; on the Macintosh, select "PICT" under "File format."
3. Navigate to the folder you created in step 1, then give the file a name—for example, "myshow.wmf" on the PC, or "my show" on the Mac. (It's helpful to keep the name short, especially on the PC, since additional characters will be added later.)
4. Make sure the other options in the "Export" dialog box are set the way you want them—including "All slides" if you want the whole show to be exported—and click "OK" (PC) or "Export" (Mac).
5. When the export is complete, exit Persuasion and open the folder you created in step 1. In it you'll see a series of numbered files, one for each slide—on the PC, they'd be "myshow1.wmf," "myshow2.wmf," and so on, while on the Mac they'd be called "my show.001," "my show-.002," and so on.

6. Launch Premiere, and open or start the project into which you wish to insert your presentation.
7. On the PC: Choose "Directory..." from the Import submenu of the File menu, then select the folder/directory you created in step 1; the entire folder will appear in the Project window. Drag the folder to the desired track in the Construction window. The slides will fall into the track at a default rate of one frame per second.

   On the Mac: Choose "File..." from the Import submenu of the File menu. Navigate to the folder you created in step 1 and select the first of the numbered PICTs (in our example, the one called "my show.001") and click "Import." The entire numbered series will be imported as a single filmstrip. By default, the images are assigned a frame rate of one frame per second.

Q My Player file is a bit too big to fit on one disk. How can I make the file smaller without removing slides?

A Use one or more of several techniques for reducing the complexity of the Player file. Choose from the following:

A. Minimize the number of graduated fills in the presentation, using solid fills instead of graduated ones. (Graduated fills occupy more space than solid ones.)

B. When you use graduated fills, select ones that graduate from top to bottom (for example, a vertical graduated fill or vertical A-B-A graduated fill). Due to the way Player files are compressed, horizontal or diagonal graduated fills don't compress as much as vertical fills. Here's a list of graduated fills, from largest Player size to smallest:
   - A-B-A horizontal (left to right)
   - A-B horizontal
   - Diagonal and square radial
   - Rounded radial
   - Square radial with center in upper-left, lower-left, upper-right, and lower-right corners
   - A-B-A vertical (top to bottom)
   - A-B vertical

C. Minimize the number of bitmap images (e.g., scanned graphics) in the presentation. If you want to use a particular image on multiple slides, put a single copy on a slide master or background.

D. Minimize the number of objects that have Auto-animation applied. Persuasion stores animated objects as compressed images in the Player file. When an animated object passes under or over other objects as it moves, the portions that overlap are stored as additional images within the Player file.

E. Reduce the resolution (dpi) and color depth (e.g., 8-bit, 16-bit) of imported bitmap images in an image editing program before you import them into Persuasion. (In Photoshop, you reduce an image's resolution by choosing "Image Size..." from the Image menu, and the color depth by choosing "Indexed Color..." from the Mode menu.) Player files are designed to display 256 colors at 72 dpi, so this reduction shouldn't make a noticeable difference in the quality of your images; however, it's a good idea to review the Player file after you've made these modifications to make sure the graphics still look good.

F. Reduce the number of layers in the file.

Q *(4.0 only)* **I've noticed that when I bring a graphic into Persuasion, sometimes it gets listed in the "Links" dialog box and sometimes it doesn't. Do I have any control over what links and what doesn't?**

A Basically, no—linking and embedding options are determined based on the graphic format. You have no control over this; however, if a graphic comes in linked, you can usually unlink it through the "Links" dialog box (which you open by choosing "File Info" from the File menu, then choosing "Links..."). Linked graphics are not fully contained in the Persuasion file—a low-resolution screen image serves as a graphic placeholder, and Persuasion tracks the location of the original file. When Persuasion needs access to the graphic information for display or printing, it follows the link to the external file. When a graphic is embedded, all the graphic information that Persuasion needs is included within the Persuasion file. The table shows which graphic formats link and which embed.

Graphic Formats, which Link and which Embed

Format	Mac	Windows
Native Illustrator	Linked	Linked
"Illustrator" format files generated by third-party products are not supported.		
Native Photoshop	Embedded	Embedded
Transparency is preserved for display (when imported without flattening layers) but is lost on PostScript output or PDF.		
EPS	Linked	Linked
All level-1 EPS files are rasterized. Screen previews are used for level-2 EPS.		
TIFF	Linked	Linked
JPEG and IT8 compression are not supported. LZW and RLE compression are supported.		
JPEG	Linked	Embedded
RGB and grayscale JPEG files are supported, baseline DCT compression only.		
GIF	Embedded	Linked
GIF89a and older GIF formats are supported.		
Photo CD	Embedded	Linked
Movies/Sounds	Linked	Linked
Movies and sounds cannot be unlinked.		
WMF	Linked	Linked
Popular Windows format. Supported but not recommended on Macintosh.		
PICT	Linked	Linked
Popular Macintosh format. Supported but not recommended for Windows.		

PCX, CGM, PLT	not supported	Linked
Can be included in an interchange file but not supported for direct import on the Macintosh.		
BMP	Linked	Linked
RLE compression is not supported.		

Q *(4.0 only)* **I see that I can now export to PDF and use Acrobat Reader to display my slide show. In the past I've always used Player. Now that I have a choice, I'm not sure which one to use. What advice can you give me?**

A Persuasion Player and Acrobat Reader each have their advantages; which one you choose will depend on which features you think will be most important for a particular presentation. You may even want to consider making both a Persuasion Player and an Acrobat Reader version of some presentations to use under different circumstances or with different audiences.

HERE ARE SOME OF THE DIFFERENCES TO KEEP IN MIND

Color and resolution: Player is limited to a resolution of 640 by 480 pixels and to a color depth of 256 colors per slide. With Acrobat, the resolution and color depth at which your presentation displays will be limited only by the capabilities of the display system you're using.

Animations: Player can display animated objects. Reader does not support animation.

Movies and sounds: Both Player and Reader can play movies and sounds. Playback can be either manual or automatic in Player; in Reader it is manual only.

Printing: You can't print Player presentations, but you can print PDFs from Reader.

Consecutive play: In Player you can create a Show List to play a series of Player files in order without further input from the presenter. Reader does not have a similar feature.

Operating systems: Player runs either in Windows or on a Macintosh; Acrobat Reader is available for Windows, Macintosh, OS/2, and UNIX. Furthermore, PDF files can be viewed on the World-Wide Web.

If you have Adobe Acrobat Exchange, you can also merge full or partial PDFs and add or rearrange PDF pages. Remember, however, that Acrobat Exchange is not included with Persuasion.

Q (4.0 only) There now appear to be two ways to create an Adobe Acrobat PDF from Persuasion 4.0. I can choose to export to an Acrobat PDF, or I can choose to print to a PostScript file and then distill it, which is what I did with Persuasion 3.0 files. Are there any differences between the results of these two methods?

A Yes, there are. Both methods create the same basic PDF file, viewable in Acrobat Reader or Exchange, but there is a difference in feature support. The process of creating a PostScript file and then distilling it is the "generic" way to create a PDF from almost any application on your computer; it's not customized to support special features of Persuasion (or any other "source" application). The "Export to Acrobat PDF" option, on the other hand, supports particular active and interactive features of both Persuasion and Acrobat. Therefore, when you export slides to PDF you have the following extra benefits:

- The PDF page size matches the Persuasion page (slide) size.
- Transition effects and hyperlinks are retained in the PDF.
- Links to movies and sounds placed on the slides are retained. Both can be played manually in the PDF.
- Persuasion outline entries are included as bookmarks.
- The file size is optimized. Both the initial PostScript file and the final PDF are significantly smaller than their print-to-disk counterparts when you export to PDF.

TIP MAC OS / WINDOWS

Preview transition effects on the go

(3.0 only) Here's how you can view your transition effects as you assign them.

From the View menu, choose "Show all slides..." from the Slide show submenu. In the "Slide show" dialog box, select the range of slides to which you want to assign transitions, then set the "Slide advance" option to "Manual." Under "Show," select "Menu bar," "Layers," "Transition effects," and any other options that might apply to your presentation, then click "Play." When the first layer of your first slide appears, choose "Show transitions..." from the Slide show submenu of the View menu. Drag the floating transitions palette to a convenient place and start assigning the desired transitions for each slide and layer. To view the assigned transition, click "Preview." To advance to the next layer or slide, press the right arrow on your keyboard or click anywhere on the slide. To move backward one layer or slide, press Shift + the left arrow. (Note that in Persuasion for Windows, if the transitions dialog box is the active window, you will have to click twice on the slide in order to advance or go back.)

If you don't want to change your slide-show settings, or you want to work with transitions on only your current slide, you can bypass the setup information described above by choosing "Preview current slide" from the "Slide show" submenu of the View menu (or press Ctrl + Shift + P in Windows, or Command + Shift + P on a Mac). When the slide is showing, use Ctrl + M (Windows) or Command + M (Mac) to bring up the menu bar.

Bringing Freelance 2.x Slides into Persuasion 3.x

EMBEDDING A FREELANCE SLIDE IN PERSUASION

Lotus Freelance Graphics 2.x slides can be imported into Persuasion 3.x by embedding the Freelance slide in a Persuasion slide, pasting the Freelance slide onto a Persuasion background using the Paste Special and Picture commands, or exporting individual Freelance slides as a graphic (e.g., TIF, WMF) and importing the Freelance graphic onto a Persuasion slide using the Import command.

EMBEDDING A FREELANCE SLIDE IN PERSUASION

After choosing to import a Freelance slide using the Insert Object command in Persuasion, the Insert Object command resaves the Freelance slide as an OLE object then embeds the OLE Freelance slide into Persuasion slide. The Insert Object command embeds the entire Freelance Graphic slide including the background. Double-clicking the embedded Freelance slide launches the Freelance application, when installed, allowing you to edit the embedded Freelance slide in Freelance.

To OLE-embed a Freelance slide in Persuasion:

1. Start Persuasion 3.0.x and view the slide on which you wish to place the Freelance slide.
2. Choose Edit > Insert Object.
3. In the Insert Object dialog box, select the Freelance Presentation Object Type and click OK.
3. When Freelance starts, create one slide to be imported into Persuasion.
4. When the slide is complete, choose Freelance Graphics File > Update Adobe Persuasion, then choose File > Exit to return to Persuasion 3.0.x.
5. Click Yes when prompted to update your Persuasion presentation.

To OLE-embed a Freelance slide in Persuasion:

1. Start Freelance and open the Freelance presentation containing the desired slide.
2. Choose View > Page Sorter.
3. Select the desired slide from the Page Sorter dialog box then choose Edit > Copy.
4. Start Persuasion and open the desired Persuasion file.
5. Go to the side where you want to import the Freelance slide.
6. Choose Edit > Paste link or Edit > Paste Embed.
7. Resize and position the Freelance slide as needed.

PASTING FREELANCE SLIDES INTO PERSUASION

To import a Freelance slide without a link import the Freelance slide into Persuasion with the Paste or Paste Special commands. The Paste Special command import as an existing Freelance slide without the slide background. To edit a Freelance slide in a Persuasion presentation, select the Freelance object and choose Draw > Ungroup.

To paste a Freelance slide into Persuasion:

1. Start Freelance and open the desired slide.
2. Choose Edit > Select > All.
3. Choose Edit > Copy.
4. Start Persuasion 3.0.x and view the slide on which you wish to place the Freelance slide.
5. Apply a background to the Persuasion slide that contrasts with the pasted Freelance objects.
6. Choose Edit > Paste Special.
7. In the Paste Special dialog box, select the Picture option, then click Paste.

IMPORTING A FREELANCE SLIDE INTO PERSUASION

Persuasion 3.0.x for Windows imports Freelance slides exported in PICT, TIF, TGA, WPG, WMF, PCX, GIF, CGM, BMP, and EPS file format. For smooth display and printing from Persuasion 3.0.x, export your Freelance slides in Windows Metafile (i.e., WMF) or TIF format. Freelance TIF files display and print smoothly from Persuasion, but cannot be edited or ungrouped. WMF files display and print smoothly from Persuasion, and can be ungrouped for editing within Persuasion. To ungroup a WMF file in Persuasion, select the WMF graphic and choose Draw > Ungroup.

A Freelance slide can be exported in EPS format and imported into Persuasion 3.0.x for Macintosh or Persuasion 3.0.x for Windows. EPS file cannot be ungrouped or edited within Persuasion. Freelance EPS screen preview does not display in Persuasion for Macintosh. PostScript outline font information is not included within a Freelance EPS file. When the outline font is unavailable in the computer or at the printer, the text in the EPS file prints as the printer's default font (usually Courier).

To export and import a Freelance slide into Persuasion:

1. Start Freelance and open the desired Freelance slide.
2. Choose File > Export.
3. In the Export dialog box, select the Windows Metafile (WMF) or .TIF File Type, name the file, then click OK.
4. Start Persuasion 3.0.x and view the slide on which you wish to place the Freelance Graphic slide.
5. Choose File > Import.
6. Select the desired Freelance graphic in the Import dialog box, then click Import.
7. Resize and position the imported graphic as needed.

Rotating Text with Type Twister in Persuasion 3.0.2

Adobe Type Twister 1.0 is included on the Adobe Persuasion 3.0.2 CD-ROM. Type Twister is an OLE server application that enables you to create special text effects such as rotated text.

INSTALLING TYPE TWISTER INCLUDED IN PERSUASION 3.0.2

To install Type Twister from the Persuasion 3.0.2 for the Macintosh CD-ROM, double-click Type Twister Installer in the Adobe Type Twister folder in the Bonus CD folder.

To install Type Twister from the Persuasion 3.0.2 for Windows CD-ROM, double-click Setup.exe in the Bonuscd\Typtwstr\Disk1 subdirectory.

Creating Plain, Rotated Text in Persuasion with Type Twister

1. In Persuasion, display the slide on which you want to insert rotated text.
2. Choose Edit > Insert Object > Type Twister Text (Persuasion for the Macintosh) or choose Edit > Insert Object, select Type Twister Text in the Insert Object dialog box, then click OK (Persuasion for Windows).
3. Enter text into the Type Twister text box.
4. Select Plain from the Effect pop-up menu, select Rectangle from the Shape pop-up menu, and select a font from the Font pop-up menu.
5. Select Custom from the Colorset pop-up menu, then choose Options > Custom Color.
6. In the Custom Color dialog box, specify a color for the Background, Background Outline, Face, and Face Outline. For colored text with no outline or background fill, click the "X" in the upper-left corner of the color palette while Background, Background Outline, and Face are selected.
7. Resize the text by dragging any of the selection points that surround the text in the preview window or select 100% from the Zoom pop-up menu to view the text at the same size it appears in your presentation.
8. Rotate the text by dragging the lever that extends from the center of the text block in the preview window. (You may need to select a smaller magnification from the Zoom pop-up menu to display the rotation lever.) Press Shift while dragging the lever to constrain the rotation to 15 degree increments.
9. Click Done, then click Yes to update the slide.

ACCESSING TYPE TWISTER ONLINE HELP

To access Online Help in Type Twister for the Macintosh, choose ? (Help) > Show Balloons.

To access Online Help in Type Twister for Windows, choose Help > Help Contents.

Setting Up Playback Time for a Player File General Information

Many variables can affect the playback speed of an Adobe Persuasion presentation slide show or a Persuasion Player file slide show. Because of these variables, you may find it difficult to set up a presentation or Player file to play within a specific length of time. Estimating the required time when creating a presentation, exporting the presentation as a Player file, then specifying a specific time frame in the Player, enables you to better control playback time. The Player generally displays slide shows faster than the Persuasion internal slide show, so allow some leeway for slide shows taking less time to display in the Player.

Presentation playback time can be affected by many factors, including:

- Delay time between slides (i.e., how long each slide displays during automatic playback after all slide activity such as transitions or movies has stopped)
- Delay time between layers

MICRO TIP MAC OS / WINDOWS

To apply autolayering to an individual text block, select the text block with the pointer tool and choose "Autolayer…" from the Draw menu. To autolayer all the text blocks in a presentation at once, navigate to the slide master and apply autolayering to the text placeholder.

- Slide complexity (i.e., number and details of slide elements such as graphics and movies)
- Transition frequency and complexity
- Hardware limitations (e.g., amount of RAM, hard drive space and fragmentation, processing speed)

The combination of all these factors can prevent you from precisely calculating the amount of time a presentation will require to display as a slide show. However, estimating the delay times while creating a presentation, then using the Player's timing settings, enables you to calculate the required playback time more closely.

Because most systems can reduce the playing speed of a slide show more efficiently than they can increase the speed, you may want to create your presentation to be slightly shorter than the desired playback time (e.g., nine minutes and 30 seconds instead of ten minutes). Then you can reduce the timing speed within the Player, causing the slide show to display in the desired time (e.g., ten minutes).

To enable a slide show to play within a certain time frame in the Player:

1. When creating a presentation in Persuasion, choose View > Slide Show > Transitions, estimate and set your preferred slide and layer delay times (e.g., 2 seconds) in the Transitions dialog box, then click OK.
2. After you've completed the presentation, choose File > Export, select Slide Show (Player File) as the File Format, then click Export.
3. In the Player, choose File > Open.
4. In the Open dialog box, select the Show Settings option, locate and select your Player file, then click Open. The Settings dialog box appears.
5. In the Settings dialog box, select Automatic as the Slide Advance option to enable the Timing button, then click Timing.
6. Move the Estimated Presentation Timing slider to increase or decrease the file's playback time, then click Play.

Transferring Presentations Between Persuasion 3.0 for the Macintosh and Persuasion 2.1 for Windows

You can transfer a presentation you created in Persuasion 3.0 for the Macintosh to Persuasion 2.1 for Windows and vice versa by saving the presentation as an interchange file with an eight-character filename and a .PRF filename extension. Persuasion 3.0 for the Macintosh presentations cannot be transferred to Persuasion 2.0 or earlier for windows.

Both Persuasion 3.0 and 2.1 for the Macintosh presentations transfer the same features to Persuasion 2.1 for Windows presentations (e.g., masters, backgrounds, subtitles, graduated fills, and AutoTemplates do not transfer). Because Persuasion 3.0 has features not supported by Persuasion 2.1, some objects do not transfer.

CHARTS AND TABLES

Charts and tables do not transfer from Persuasion 3.0 for the Macintosh to Persuasion 2.1 for Windows because they are OLE objects. The interchange format does not support OLE objects when you transfer Persuasion 3.0 for the Macintosh presentations to Persuasion 2.1 for Windows, although it does when you transfer Persuasion 3.0 for the Macintosh presentations to Persuasion 3.0 for Windows.

To transfer a chart or table, convert it to a PICT graphic and then ungroup it:

1. Select the chart or table.
2. Choose Convert to Picture on the object's badge pop-up menu.
3. Choose Draw > Ungroup.

Charts and tables do transfer from Persuasion 2.1 to Persuasion 3.0. After you open an interchange file containing a chart or table in Persuasion 3.0 for the Macintosh, Persuasion displays and prints the charts and tables as Chart 1.0 or Table 1.0 icons until they are redrawn. When you edit a chart or table, Persuasion returns the message "This chart/table was created in a prior version of Persuasion. Replotting will significantly alter its appearance. Replot anyway?" Persuasion returns this same message when you convert a Persuasion 2.1 for the Macintosh chart or table to Persuasion 3.0 for the Macintosh. When you replot the chart or table, Persuasion retains the data, but the chart or table changes appearance because Persuasion 3.0 uses different charting and table routines than Persuasion 2.1 does.

AUTOTEMPLATES

The AutoTemplates included with Persuasion 3.0 for the Macintosh were not included with Persuasion 2.1 for Windows. When you open a Persuasion presentation that uses an unavailable AutoTemplates, Persuasion uses the substitute AutoTemplate you selected or uses a default blank slide master and blank background (Macintosh) or a default AutoTemplate (Windows).

NEW FEATURES

New Persuasion 3.0 features do not transfer to Persuasion 2.1 (e.g., AutoLayering, AutoJump, Autoanimation, edited arrowheads, color systems), and when you transfer the presentation back to Persuasion 3.0. Opening the presentation in Persuasion 2.1 permanently removes new features included in Persuasion 3.0, but not supported in Persuasion 2.1.

WINDOWS

Q *(3.0 only)* **Whenever I start a new presentation, every object I draw with any tool has a shadow. I'm constantly turning off shadows! Is there any way to have them off by default?**

A Most of the AutoTemplates that shipped with Persuasion 3.0 have "Show object shadow" turned on as the default setting. You can either turn it off in each original AutoTemplate you use, so that files made using those AutoTemplates will start out with shadows off, or you can turn off the default in each new presentation after you open it.

To open and modify an AutoTemplate:

1. Select "Open presentation..." from the startup screen.
2. In the dialog box that appears, select "Persuasion 3.0 autotemplate (*.at3)" from the "List files of type..." drop-down list.
3. Navigate to the directory where your AutoTemplates are and click once on the AutoTemplate you want to modify.
4. Under "Open," click on "Original" (instead of "Copy"), and then click "OK" to open the file.
5. In slide view, check the bar at the top of the window to make sure you opened the AutoTemplate you intended to. Make sure nothing is selected and choose "Shadow offset..." from the Draw menu.
6. In the "Shadow offset" dialog box, uncheck "Show object shadow" (click on it once to make the "x" disappear). Click "OK."
7. Close the file, saving your changes. Repeat this process for each AutoTemplate you want to alter.

If you prefer to modify individual presentation files rather than AutoTemplates, follow the same basic procedure. As long as nothing is selected when you uncheck "Show object shadow," new objects you create in that presentation won't have shadows.

Q I have some decorative fonts that I would like to use for bullet characters. How can I find the character I want and make it into a bullet?

A Get acquainted with Character Map. This is a Windows tool for viewing all the characters within a font (or typeface). Character Map is located in Windows Accessories. (If you did not install this accessory, add it from your Windows disks or CD-ROM. Refer to your Windows documentation or call Microsoft Windows Technical Support if you need help adding the Character Map accessory.)

Open Character Map and select your decorative font from the font list. All the characters in the font appear in a grid. Click on the character that you want as your bullet. In the lower-right corner of the Character Map window, note the keystroke for the selected character. For example, "Keystroke: t" means that typing the lowercase "t" on your keyboard will produce the selected character when you're using this font. Sometimes the keystroke will be a combination of the Alt key and a 4-digit number (for example, "Keystroke: Alt+0213"). In this case, hold down Alt and enter

0213 using the numeric keypad at the right side of your keyboard (making sure NumLock is on).

Once you know the correct keystroke, select a text placeholder, then choose "Define bullets…" from the Master menu in Persuasion to open the "Define bullets" dialog box (see pages 48 and 49 in the Adobe Persuasion User Manual for further instructions on formatting bullets).

Click in the box that shows the bullet level you want to change, and enter the keystroke you found in Character Map. Select the font, color, and other formatting for the bullet and click "OK." If there are certain characters in your decorative font that you would like to use often, you may want to print a list of those characters and their keystrokes to refer to.

You can also copy the desired character from Character Map and paste it into the "Define bullets" dialog box. Refer to the tip on page 48 of the manual for details.

MAC OS

Q *(3.0 only)* **I'd like to have some music from a music CD play in the background during an entire slide show. Is there a way I can do this?**

A There certainly is. You'll need QuickTime version 1.6 or higher and an Apple series 300 CD-ROM drive (or compatible model). Also, be sure that you won't be violating any licensing or copyright restrictions by duplicating the music. Then follow these steps.

1. Open your presentation and, from the View menu, choose "Slide show" and then "Transitions…."
2. In the "Transitions" dialog box, select slide 1 from the "Slide" list box and layer 1 from the "Layer" list box.
3. Choose "Import..." from the pop-up list underneath "Sound effect."
4. Select "Audio CD" from the Desktop and click "Open…."
5. Select the desired track and click "Convert...."
6. In the next dialog box that appears, before saving, click "Options…"
7. Select the desired settings, including the start and stop points. To keep the size of the file at a minimum, import only the portion of the track that you want. Click "OK."
8. Give the audio clip a name and specify the desired folder for storage. Click "Save."
9. You'll now be back in the "Transitions" dialog box. The name you gave your sound will be in the sound-effects box for layer 1. Select "Continue" from the pop-up menu to the right of the sound effects menu (under "During sound playback")—this allows the slide show to continue while the sound is playing.
10. Click "OK" to close the "Transitions" dialog box.

Q How can I get more than one slide on each notes page? We don't have a lot of notes for each slide, and using a whole page for each one seems wasteful.

A Although Persuasion itself doesn't offer the ability to print more than one slide on a notes page, there is a way to do it—by using the two-up and four-up printing options offered by the LaserWriter 8.x driver.

When designing your Notes master, keep in mind that everything will be scaled down to fit 2 or 4 notes pages on one page—beware of type becoming unreadably tiny. When you are ready to print the notes, select "Page setup…" from the File menu. From the Layout drop-down box, select "2 Up" or "4 Up". (NOTE: This option is not available in the LaserWriter 7.x driver). Click "OK," and then click "OK" again in the "Presentation setup" dialog box when it appears. Select "Print…" from the File menu and, in the "Print" dialog box, be sure you select only "Notes" for "Print choices."

Once you've printed your notes pages, be sure to reset the layout to "1 Up" for the rest of your printing.

Q Is there an easy way to get a total or an average of a row or column of data in the data sheet?

A Definitely. The Chart data sheet supports various simple math functions. In addition to basic math calculations—multiplication, division, addition, and subtraction—you can use the data sheet to derive the sum, minimum, maximum, or average of columns, rows, or cells that you specify.

To use these functions, first select the cell in which you want the result of the calculation or function to appear. Then simply begin typing the appropriate formula; it will appear in the long field just above the data display. Once you've finished typing your formula, hit Return and the appropriate value will appear in the cell you selected.

The formula must always begin with an equals sign (=). Individual cells are designated by column letter followed by row number (B7), and a range of cells is designated by the first (upper left) and last (lower right) cells in the range separated by a colon (B4:D6). Here are some examples:

=**SUM(B7,C2,A5)** will give you the sum of the values in cells B7, C2 and A5;

=**AVG(A3:B6)** will give you the average (arithmetic mean) of the values in cells A3, A4, A5, A6, B3, B4, B5, and B6;

=**100-MIN(B3:D10)** will determine the smallest number in the range of cells from B3 to D10, and subtract that value from 100; and

=**SUM(AVG(A1:A5),B10)** will add the value in cell B10 to the average value of cells A1 through A5.

You can find more detailed information on the math functions in Chart's online Help under "Math features of the data sheet." To open Help, choose "Help" from the Apple menu while Chart is running.

Persuasion for the Macintosh Damaged Presentation Troubleshooting Guide

ISSUE

When you open or work in an Adobe Persuasion presentation, Persuasion returns an error or behaves unexpectedly.

SYMPTOMS

One of the following errors occurs:

- "The application '[application name or unknown]' has unexpectedly quit because an error of Type 1 occurred."
- "An internal inconsistency has been found."
- "Internal error: Bad table index."
- "An error has occurred. ffff:ffd9"

SOLUTIONS

To recover an unopenable presentation, do one or more of the following:

A. In Persuasion, open a copy of the presentation by selecting Copy in the Open dialog box, selecting the presentation, and then clicking Open.

B. While Persuasion opens the presentation, hold down the Command key and press the arrow keys to change views.

C. Make a copy of the presentation in the Finder by using the Duplicate command, then open the copy in Persuasion.

D. Allocate more memory to Persuasion:
1. Quit Persuasion.
2. In the Finder, select the Persuasion application icon, then choose File > Get Info.
3. In the Persuasion Info window, increase the Preferred Size (System 7.1 or later) or Current Size (System 7.0x) value, then close the Info window.

E. Increase the amount of available hard disk space by moving or deleting files from the hard disk.

F. Move the Fonts and Preferences folders from the System Folder to another location (e.g., desktop), restart the Macintosh with extensions disabled, and then open the presentation. To quickly disable added or non-essential extensions, restart with the Shift key held down until the message "Welcome to Macintosh. Extensions off." appears, or use an extensions manager.

G. Select a different printer driver in the Chooser, then open the presentation.

H. Open the presentation on a different Macintosh.

I. Open a backup copy of the presentation.

J. Import the text and slide masters into a new presentation:
1. Open the presentation in a text editor that can save in text-only format (e.g., TeachText, Microsoft Word).
2. Delete all code characters in the file, then save it in text-only format.
3. Create a new Persuasion presentation, then import the text file into the outline.
4. Save the presentation, close it, and then open a copy of the presentation.
5. Choose File > Change Design > Replace Masters.
6. In the Replace Masters dialog box, select the original presentation as the source for your masters, then click Import.

To repair damage in an openable presentation, do one or more of the following:

A. Choose File > Save As to save the presentation with a different name. If possible, save the presentation on your startup disk (e.g., hard disk containing the active system).

B. Allocate more memory to Persuasion.
1. Save the presentation with a different name.
2. Quit Persuasion.
3. In the Finder, select the Persuasion application icon, then choose File > Get Info.
4. In the Persuasion Info window, increase the Preferred Size (System 7.1 or later) or Current Size (System 7.0.x) value, then close the Info window.

C. Save the presentation with a different name, then quit Persuasion. Restart the Macintosh with extensions disabled, then open the presentation. To quickly disable added or non-essential extensions, restart with the Shift key held down until the message "Welcome to Macintosh. Extensions off." appears, or use an extensions manager.

D. Save the presentation with a different name, then quit Persuasion. Remove the Persuasion preferences file (i.e., Adobe Persuasion 4.0 Prefs, Persuasion 3.0ppc Preferences, Persuasion 3.0 Preferences) from the Preferences folder in the System Folder, then reopen the presentation.

E. Copy slides into a new presentation:

In Persuasion 4.0, create a new presentation with the same page setup as your original presentation, then copy slides by dragging them from the original presentation's slide sorter window to the new presentation's slide sorter window.

OR: In Persuasion 3.0.2 or earlier:
1. In the slide sorter view, choose Edit > Select All, then choose Edit > Copy.
2. Create a new presentation with the same page setup as your original presentation.
3. In the slide sorter view, choose Edit > Paste.

F. Replace the masters:
1. Save a copy of the presentation with a different name.
2. In the copy of the presentation, choose File > Change Design > Replace Masters.
3. In the Replace Masters dialog box, select an Auto-Template with masters that use the same page setup as your presentation, then click Import.

G. Save a copy of the presentation with a different name. In the copy of the presentation, delete unused masters or custom masters, then assign standard imported masters to all slides.

H. Determine if the error is caused by damaged graphics by choosing File > Preferences, then selecting Hide Big PICTs, then try to recreate the error. If the error does not reoccur, delete and then replace the graphics in the presentation.

I. Save the presentation as an interchange file.

NOTE: Persuasion does not include graphics in interchange files.

J. Save a copy of the presentation with a different name, then quit Persuasion. Drag the Fonts folder from the System Folder to another location (e.g., desktop), restart the Macintosh, then open the presentation. If the error does not reoccur, isolate the damaged font, then reinstall that font.
K. Save the presentation in an earlier Persuasion version format, then open it in that earlier version of Persuasion. For example, in Persuasion 3.0.2, save the presentation in Persuasion 2.x format, then open the Persuasion 2.x presentation in Persuasion 2.x.
L. Open a backup copy of the presentation.
M. Copy the text and masters into a new presentation:
   1. In outline view, choose Edit > Select All, then choose Edit > Copy.
   2. Create a new Persuasion presentation with the same page setup as your original presentation.
   3. In outline view, click on the first slide icon, then choose Edit > Paste.
   4. Save the presentation, close it, and then open a copy of the presentation.
   5. Choose File > Change Design > Replace Masters.
   6. In the Replace Masters dialog box, select the original presentation as the source for your masters, then click Import.
   7. Assign the masters to the slides in your new presentation.
N. Isolate the damaged item or items in the presentation:
   1. Open a copy of the presentation.
   2. In slide sorter view, delete half of the slides.
   3. Choose File > Save As to save the file with a different name.
   4. If the error does not reoccur when you work in this half of the file, open the copy of the full presentation and delete the other half of the slides. Then save that file with a different name and work in it to see if the error reoccurs.
   5. Continue to remove one or more slides until you isolate the damaged slide or group of slides.
   6. After you have isolated the damaged slide or slides, identify a common element that may be causing the problem (e.g., font, graphic, master, background).
   7. Delete the suspect element or the entire slide, then reimport or recreate it.

ADDITIONAL INFORMATION

Persuasion returns an error or behaves unexpectedly when damage in a presentation prevents Persuasion from opening the presentation or from performing other actions. Common causes of damaged presentations include low or badly fragmented disk space, low system resources, system errors, and saving files to damaged media (e.g., damaged sector on a disk). A damaged graphic, font, master, or AutoTemplate in a presentation can also cause an error or unexpected behavior when you work in Persuasion.

Matching Colors from Other Applications in Persuasion 2.1.2 and Earlier

Aldus Persuasion 2.12 and earlier define colors using red, green, and blue (RGB) values from the Apple Color Picker model. The Apple Color Picker describes red, green, and blue as values between zero (0) and 65535. To match colors in Persuasion to colors defined in other applications that do not use the same model, convert the colors to the model by describing the colors red, green, and blue using values between 0 and 65535.

When you convert colors between applications, rounding errors and differences in how each application generates colors may result in differences colors defined with the same values in each application.

MATCHING COLORS FROM PAGEMAKER AND ALDUS FREEHAND

When you define colors in PageMaker and Aldus FreeHand, specify colors using the RGB color model, which defines colors using a percentage value. To calculate the whole numbers to enter in Persuasion, change the color value percentage to a decimal number and multiply by 65535.

For example, a color is defined in PageMaker or Aldus FreeHand as:

Red: 40%
Green: 13%
Blue: 100%

To compute the RGB color value for the new color in Persuasion, multiply the percentage by 65535:

Red: .40 X 65535 = 26214
Green: .13 X 65535 = 8520
Blue: 1.00 X 65535 = 65535

The results are the colors value you use to define a custom color in Persuasion:

Red: 26214
Green: 8520
Blue: 65535

MATCHING COLORS FROM ADOBE PHOTOSHOP

When you define colors in Adobe Photoshop, specify colors using the RGB color model, which defines colors using values between 0 and 255. To calculate the whole numbers to enter in Persuasion, change the color value to a percentage of 256, multiply by 65535, then round to the nearest whole number.

For example, a color is defined in Adobe Photoshop as:

Red: 100
Green: 42
Blue: 151

To compute the RGB color value for the new color in Persuasion, calculate the color value's percentage and then multiply by 65535:

Red: (100/256) x 65535 = 25599.6 = 25600
Green: (42/256) x 65535 = 10751.8 = 10752
Blue: (151/256) x 65535 = 38655.4 = 38655

The results are the colors value you use to define a custom color in Persuasion:

Red: 25600
Green: 10752
Blue: 38655

MATCHING COLORS FROM ADOBE ILLUSTRATOR

This application defines colors in a CMYK format only. To match colors in Persuasion, save the Illustrator file as an Illustrator 1.1 EPS file or Illustrator 3.0 with EPS Exchange, then open it in Adobe Photoshop or Aldus FreeHand to determine RGB values for Persuasion as described above.

Unexpected Results

MAC OS / WINDOWS

Q I want to use one of the arrows from Persuasion's clip art, but it's pointing in the wrong direction and the options under "Rotate/Flip" are grayed out. Why can't I rotate the arrow?

A Imported graphics (such as clip art) have to be ungrouped before "Rotate/Flip" can be applied. To ungroup an object, select it and, from the Draw menu, choose "Ungroup" (Ctrl + F7 in Windows, Option + Command + U on the Mac). Now the various "Rotate/Flip" options can be applied—the "Rotate" options turn the object 90 degrees, while "Flip" turns it 180 degrees.

By the way, once the graphic has been ungrouped, you can immediately regroup it without losing the "Rotate/Flip" options. Regrouping is often a good idea, since it will keep you from accidentally disassembling your graphic when you try to move it.

Q *(3.0 only)* **I've created a line chart, but the points are falling between the vertical grid lines, not on them. Is there a way I can get them onto the grid lines?**

A It depends what kind of data you're trying to graph. If you want a data axis consisting of numbers and a category axis consisting of words—say, you're plotting sales figures by the month—then you want a line chart. In that case, there is unfortunately no way to get Chart to plot the data points on the grid lines. That's because it treats the categories as areas of the chart, and plots the data points in the middle of those areas. You may be able to add the grid lines you want by drawing them onto the chart in Persuasion (although you'll have to move them manually if the chart is resized or updated).

However, if you want an X and Y axis that are both numerical—for scientific data, for instance—you can use a scatter chart, in which the data points can be plotted on the grid lines. As long as you treat the data for each line as its own series, you can then choose to have the points connected by lines. Here's how.

1. Begin a new chart and select "Scatter" from the Standard Gallery list. Select the sample "Scatter" (Windows) or "Scatter.3df" (Mac) and click "OK."
2. With the sample chart on the screen, go to the Gallery menu and make sure "Xy scatter" is selected on the Scatter submenu. (This procedure assumes you don't want each point labeled individually; if you do, choose "Xy with labels," and adjust steps 4 and 5.)
3. Click on the upper-right icon in the toolbox (technically called the Control palette) to enter the data sheet. It's generally most convenient to enter your x and y values for each line vertically, so—since all the points for a given line must be in the same series—choose "Data orientation..." from the Data menu, and then in the "Data orientation" dialog box, click on "Columns are data series" and "Cells for a data point are side-by-side." Click "OK."
4. Drag-select cells A6 through D12 and choose "Cut" from the Edit menu. Then select cell D5 and cut the word "label" (unless you're creating a chart with data-point labels—see step 2).
5. Enter the x and y values for each point in the first line under the "x" and "y" headings. (Enter them in the order in which you want the line to connect them.) If you're going to show more than one line, use the next two columns (D and E) to enter the x and y values for the second line. Follow the same pattern for each additional line.
6. If you want your chart to have a legend, enter the legend labels in the cells above each series (B4, D4, etc.).
7. Drag-select all the cells containing the x and y values. In the cell assignment drop-down list, choose "Data range," and then click the "Set data range" button.
8. If you entered legend labels in step 6, drag-select that row. In the cell assignment drop-down list, choose "Column headers," and then click the "Set column headers" button.
9. Now view the chart by clicking on the upper-right icon in the toolbox. Click to select one of the points in your first series. Choose "Curve fit & stat lines..." from the Chart menu and choose "Connected line." Click "OK." You'll see a line connecting all the points in that series. Repeat this step for each additional series.

If you want more vertical grid lines than you're seeing, choose "Grid lines..." from the X-axis submenu of the Chart menu. Checking "Show minor grid lines" under "Minor divisions" lets you specify the interval at which the grid lines will be drawn.

Q *(3.x only)* **When I transfer a file from my Macintosh version of Persuasion 3.0 to the PC version, the "Inter-**

change master selection" dialog box comes up, and I select to use the masters in the transferred file. But then some of the slides come up with no background at all—just plain white! Other slides in the same file have the appropriate background. How can I fix this?

A To understand the reason this is occurring, you need to have a grasp of the three "levels" Persuasion operates on: slides, slide masters, and background masters. A slide master is a master design that governs one or more slides; a background master is a master design that governs slide masters.

Your problem is happening because the Mac version of Persuasion allows you to have multiple background masters, while PC Persuasion does not—all slide masters use a single background master. So when PC Persuasion opens an Interchange file, it looks for the most-used background master, and makes that the background master for the file. But it doesn't discard the other background masters you created on the Mac: it turns them into regular slide masters.

In PC Persuasion, take a look at the "Slide master" submenu under the View menu. There, you'll see not only the names of the slide masters you already had (such as "Text" and "Org Chart"), but also the new ones made from your Mac background masters (which might be called, say, "Background 2" and "Background 3"). To make the situation right, you need to put those backgrounds back together manually with the elements on the slide masters.

There are two ways to do it. If only one master lost its background, you can use the copy-and-paste approach outlined in "Method A" below to get all the master elements consolidated onto a single slide master. If several masters lost the same background, it'll be easier to use method B, which restores the lost background to each master by using the "Set background..." command.

METHOD A

Let's assume you had created a specially colored background master on the Mac called "Background 2," and had assigned it only to the "Text" master. When you opened the presentation on the PC, all the slides using the "Text" master had white backgrounds.

1. Choose "Slide master" from the View menu, and pick "Text" from the list of masters.
2. You're now looking at the "Text" master (with its white background). From the Edit menu, choose "Select all" and then "Copy."
3. From the View menu, choose "Slide master" again and click "Background 2" (which is now a regular slide master, not a true background master). It will contain the background fill you want, but no placeholders.
4. Choose "Paste" from the View menu. Now your "Background 2" slide master has all the elements you wanted on the "Text" master—including the correct background.
5. Select "Slide sorter" from the View menu. Hold down the Shift key and select all the slides using the "Text" master. From the pop-up menu at the bottom of the screen, choose "Background 2."

Now all the slides that used to be assigned the "Text" master will use "Background 2" instead, and will look the way they did on the Mac.

METHOD B

Let's assume that, on the Mac, you had created a specially colored background master called "Background 2," and had applied it to the "Text" and "Title" masters. When you opened the presentation on the PC, all slides using the those masters appeared with white backgrounds.

1. In Slide view, choose "Slide master" from the View menu, and from the "Slide master" submenu select "Background 2" (which is now a regular slide master, not a background master). It should have no placeholders on it.
2. From the Master menu, select "Set background...." Make a note of the background fill pattern and the color assignments for color 1 and color 2. Click "Cancel" to close the dialog box.
3. If there are any other elements (text or graphics) on the master, choose "Select all" and then "Copy" from the Edit menu. (If there aren't other elements on the master, skip this step.)
4. Select "Slide master" from the View menu and select the "Text" master from the list. From the Master menu, choose "Set background..." and select the fill and colors that you noted in step 2. Click "OK."
5. If you copied elements in step 3, choose "Paste" from the Edit menu. (Otherwise, skip this step.)

Your "Text" master now has the same fill it had in the Mac version of the presentation. Repeat these steps for the other masters that lost their backgrounds.

Q I often try to ungroup charts or imported graphics so I can edit them on a slide, but I've run into two problems. Sometimes the "Ungroup" option is grayed out, and sometimes ungrouping an object changes it significantly. What can I do to avoid these problems?

A First, think about whether you really need to ungroup the graphic. If you still have the original graphic file and the application in which it was made (or a similar one), you might get better results by reopening the graphic in that application, doing any editing there, and then reimporting it into Persuasion. If you have the application but not the original version of the file that's native to it, copying the version you do have within Persuasion and pasting it into the application might work as well. If the object in Persuasion is an OLE-embedded graphic, just double-clicking it will activate the link to its originating application and reopen it for editing there.

It's also important to understand that, when Persuasion ungroups a graphic, it's actually converting the elements in the graphic to Persuasion elements—things that can be made with Persuasion's tools, like lines or polygons.

When a graphic can be ungrouped, because its elements are being reinterpreted into elements that can be made with Persuasion's tools, you may see shifts in size, position, and color, or even substituted characters or flipped text. Different programs work with different color and measurement systems, and Persuasion tries to approximate elements created with other programs' systems. But the process can lead to the sorts of shifts you're referring to, and if they bother you, you might be better off editing the graphic in its originating application, as discussed above. Common file formats that can be ungrouped are Windows metafiles (.WMF) and computer graphic metafiles (.CGM) on the PC, and object-oriented PICTs on the Macintosh.

Sometimes the differences between the system used by the originating application and Persuasion are too great. If the graphic contains objects that can't be reinterpreted with Persuasion's tools, such as some fill patterns, it can't be ungrouped and either the "Ungroup" option will be grayed out or you'll get a message that the image contains objects that can't be ungrouped. Persuasion also can't ungroup EPS graphics or bitmap graphics such as TIFFs.

Q When I use highlighted layers for the bullet points in my body text, all the layers highlight after the last bullet point and before the next slide. How can I keep this from happening?

A Highlighted layers—which are available as part of the "Autolayer" feature, found under the Draw menu—do indeed cause all the layers to highlight at the end. However, it's not too hard to avoid this. The solution varies depending on whether you're creating an on-screen presentation or imaging to slides.

For a Persuasion slide show or Player file, create an invisible autojump button and set it up to jump to the next slide. During the presentation, click on the autojump button after reaching the desired final layer. Once the button is clicked, Persuasion skips the last layer (where all the bullet points are highlighted) and goes to the next slide.

To create an invisible autojump button:

1. On the first layer of the slide, use the autojump tool to draw a rectangle where you want an invisible button. (To make sure the button really is invisible when the slide show is running, choose "Show all slides..." from the "Slide show" submenu under the View menu and make sure "Badges" is unchecked.)
2. When the "Autojump" dialog box appears, specify that you want to jump to a slide. Then, from the "Slide" pop-up menu, select "Next slide"; from the "Layer" pop-up menu, select "First layer." Click "OK."

For 35-mm. slides, image to a film recorder that allows you to delete slides from the imaging queue (for example, Presentation Technologies' ImageQ), and go into the queue to remove the slides that show the final build layer.

Q I used ruler guides on my text master to position the top and left edges of the body text placeholder. The text in the placeholder on the master is positioned just the way I want. But when I look at the slide, the text is starting above the ruler guide and is not as far to the left as I want it to be. Reapplying the master doesn't help. I know it should work; what am I missing?

A You're missing only the use of the Anchor feature. A text placeholder is designed to expand to accommodate the amount of text you enter. You can control the directions in which that growth occurs by using anchoring. In your case, you want to "fix" or "anchor" the top and left edges of the placeholder at your ruler guides, allowing the right and bottom edges to move outward to fit your text. Here's how:

1. Go to the appropriate slide master.
2. Select the placeholder with the pointer tool.
3. Choose "Anchor placeholder..." from the Master menu.
4. Select "Top" for the vertical anchor and "Left" for the horizontal anchor.
5. Click "OK" and return to the slide view.

If you've manually moved the text on your slide, you may need to reapply the placeholder position:

1. Select the text block on your slide with the pointer tool.
2. Select "Reapply placeholder..." from the Master pop-up box along the bottom of the slide window.
3. Select "Position" and click "OK."

By selectively reapplying specific attributes of a single placeholder in this way, you can preserve other slide-specific changes you may have made to your text.

For more information regarding anchoring, refer to the Persuasion User Manual (pages 52–53 in the Windows manual, pages 58–59 in the Macintosh manual).

Q Recently someone told me I should delete my Persuasion preferences file, and now that I've done so, Persuasion won't launch. What exactly is a preferences file, and what happened?

A Let's answer your questions in the order in which they were received. The "Persuasion 3.0ppc Preferences" (on a Power Mac) or "Persuasion 3.0 Preferences" (on a 68K machine) file includes information on:

- The status of the palettes (whether they're opened or closed, and their locations on the screen);
- The available OLE servers (i.e., the Chart and Table applications) that show up as tools in the Tools palette;
- The save reminder time (if any); and
- The location of Persuasion's support files (default AutoTemplate, Help files, spelling files, etc.).

Persuasion reads the preferences file when it launches, and—based on data in that file—sets up the look of the screen when the program opens and determines the availability of necessary files. In general, if you're having trouble launching Persuasion, it could be because the preferences file has somehow become damaged.

Many things could cause a file to become damaged: a large number of setup changes, not enough disk space, fragmentation on the drive, a "blip" in your power supply, to name a few. If you witness surprising behavior in the program, it could indicate this kind of damage.

Deleting the preferences file is a common troubleshooting procedure. What does Persuasion do when there is no preferences file? Every time Persuasion opens, it searches the "Preferences" folder in your System Folder, and any folders within the "Preferences" folder, for this file. If it can't locate a Persuasion preferences file, it creates a new one. This, of course, takes care of problems caused by damage.

However, if you've just deleted the preferences file and suddenly you are unable to run Persuasion, it's probably not due to a corrupted preferences file. Something else may be preventing Persuasion from starting up, or at least making it seem like it won't. The more files there are in the "Preferences" folder, the longer it can take for Persuasion to determine whether a preferences file exists. When the "Preferences" folder contains an extremely large number of files, it may appear that Persuasion is not going to launch at all.

A large number of files are present in the "Preferences" folder when you've got the World-Wide Web browser Netscape Navigator installed. Netscape stores recently visited Web pages in the "Cache" folder in the "Netscape" folder in the "Preferences" folder. (When you request a page that is stored in Netscape's cache, Netscape retrieves the page from the cache more quickly than retrieving the page again from its location on the Web.) This cache may contain hundreds of files. If, for whatever reason, you have no Persuasion preferences file, it's a good idea to clear the Netscape cache before attempting to launch Persuasion.

Q I recently upgraded to Illustrator 6.0, and now when I import EPS files, they are much smaller than they should be and their backgrounds are opaque instead of transparent like they used to be. What is happening?

A You're seeing a new and different version of the image; it's the document thumbnail (new to Illustrator 6.0), not the screen preview you're accustomed to. (The thumbnail is used to show a preview of the file while in the "Open" or "Import" dialog box of most applications.) By default, Illustrator 6.0 includes a document thumbnail in its EPS files. If the thumbnail is present, Persuasion uses it to display the EPS on the slide instead of using the screen preview that Illustrator also includes in the file. If you want your old screen preview back, follow these steps to resave your Illustrator EPS and eliminate the document thumbnail.

1. Open the EPS in Illustrator.
2. Choose "Save As..." from the File menu to open the "Save As" dialog box.
3. Select "Illustrator EPS" from the Format menu, specify a location, name the file, and click "Save."
4. Deselect the "Include Document Thumbnails" option in the "Options" section of the "EPS Format" dialog box, and then click "OK."
5. Reimport the file into Persuasion.

If you are printing your slides to a PostScript device and the screen appearance is of no concern, you don't need to eliminate the document thumbnail. Just resize the graphic on the slide to the correct dimensions of the original graphic's bounding box, if you have them. (Since the thumbnail is square, if your original graphic isn't square, trying to maintain the proportions that you see on the screen by resizing with the Shift key will actually distort the graphic when it's printed.) The graphic will look distorted and very bitmapped on the screen, but will print correctly.

Q I often use scanned images in my presentations and they look fine as long as I am printing or using the Persuasion internal slide show, but if I export my file as a Persuasion Player file, my images tend to look bitmapped and spotty. Is there any solution for this?

A When you display the presentation in Persuasion's internal slide show, the color depth and resolution of your slides are limited only by your monitor settings (for example, thousands of colors and 1,024 by 768 pixels per inch) and by the makeup of the graphics themselves.

Player files, on the other hand, are internally limited to 256 colors per slide and 640 by 480 pixels per inch. Persuasion creates a new 256-color (8-bit) palette for each slide in a Player file. If your scanned images have a higher resolution or greater color depth than Player supports, then Persuasion will downsample and index (that is, reduce the resolution and color depth of) the images whenever you export the presentation as a Player file.

The quality of Persuasion downsampling may vary depending on your images, so we recommend that you save your images to the correct size, resolution, and color depth before you import them into Persuasion. To do this, open the graphic in an image-editing application, such as Photoshop, and change the height and width of the image to the final size you'll want in Persuasion, so you don't have to resize it when you get there. You may want to experiment with your image resolution to determine what setting gives you the best results; 150 dpi should be enough resolution to give you excellent results in any medium, and for some images 72 dpi will be sufficient for optimal on-screen display. If you're using Photoshop, go to the Mode menu and change your image to "Indexed Color." In the "Indexed Color" dialog box, select the following options: "8-bit" for "Resolution," "Adaptive" for "Palette," and "None" for "Dithering." Save the images as TIFF (Windows) or PICT (Macintosh) files and import them in Persuasion.

If you've got multiple images on a single slide, use the same color palette for all the images, so they all share the same 256 colors. To do this, copy and paste into one new Photoshop file all the images that you want to use on the slide. Change the mode of this new composite image to Indexed Color, using the options listed above. When that's done, open all your original images and change them to Indexed Color mode as well, setting the "Palette" option to "Previous." This applies the color palette that was just created from the composite image. (You could also create a custom color palette from the composite image and later choose that custom palette in the "Indexed Color" dialog box when you convert each image to Indexed Color mode.)

The 256-color palette that Persuasion uses for a slide will be set according to all the colors on the slide, so keep the colors used outside the scanned images to a minimum. In particular, avoid using graduated fills either in the background or in drawn objects.

Q *(Win 95/Mac, 4.0 only)* **The version of ATM that came with Persuasion gives me an on-screen font-**

smoothing feature that has really improved the appearance of my slide show. But sometimes it seems that my "jaggies" come back. I haven't changed anything in ATM, so why would this happen?

A ATM 4.0's font-smoothing option anti-aliases only PostScript fonts for better on-screen display. It doesn't apply anti-aliasing to TrueType fonts, so if you're using a combination of TrueType and PostScript fonts in your presentation, you're probably seeing some smooth and some jagged fonts for this reason.

Another possibility is that you have changed your display settings from thousands or millions of colors to 256 colors (8-bit). ATM doesn't attempt to anti-alias colored text in 256-color mode because there are not enough colors to do a good job. It will attempt to anti-alias black text; however, it is recommended that you not use font smoothing unless your black text is against a white background. Also, if you plan to use the Persuasion slide show on a 256-color display, we recommend that you turn off the font-smoothing option in the ATM Control Panel.

Q *(4.0 only)* **Sometimes when I open a file and select some text, the font name doesn't appear in either the text palette or the text dialog box. The place where the font name would normally appear is blank. Why does this happen, and what can I do about it?**

A This is Persuasion's way of telling you a particular font isn't available on the current system. When Persuasion can't locate a particular font it's supposed to use, in Windows you'll see the font name in brackets ({}), or, on a Macintosh, the area where Persuasion would normally display the font name is blank. The solution is to use the "Font Summary" dialog box (new in Persuasion 4.0) to identify and globally replace any missing fonts.

1. Open the file in Persuasion 4.0.
2. From the File menu, select "File Info," then "Fonts...."
3. The "Font Summary" dialog box appears, listing all the fonts used in the presentation. Font names followed by asterisks are missing fonts.
4. If you have the font but it is not active (for instance, if you're using a font-management utility and have disabled the font), close Persuasion and activate the font. If you do not have the font, click on the font name in the "Font Summary" dialog box and then click on the "Replace" button.
5. Select a replacement font from the drop-down list, and then click "OK."

Q *(4.0 only)* **The Player files that I've created in Persuasion 4.0 display in different sizes on my screen than they did when I created them in Persuasion 3.0. Sometimes a Player file is too big for the screen, and gets cropped. What has changed?**

A The ability to control the size of your Player files is what has changed. A Player file exported from Persuasion 3.0 was always 640 by 480 pixels in size, regardless of the slide size of the Persuasion presentation or the resolution of the monitor. Because of this, the only way you could get a full-screen Player file was to set the monitor resolution to 640 by 480.

In Persuasion 4.0, you can determine the dimensions of your screen presentations by altering the slide size in your Persuasion file. The Player file dimensions are the pixel equivalent of the original presentation's page size at 100%. When it's exporting to a Player file, Persuasion uses the current dpi of your monitor (for example, 72 dpi) to convert the inch measurement of the page size to a corresponding number of pixels. This makes it possible to create a full-screen Player file, even for a monitor that is set to a resolution greater than 640 by 480. For more detailed information on this topic, request document 124103 from FaxYI (206-628-5737) or from techdocs@adobe.com, or look up the same document in the Adobe Web site technical database.

To see or change your slide-size settings, go to the File menu and choose "Page Setup" and then "Slide Setup..." (Windows) or simply "Page Setup..." (Macintosh). You can choose a predetermined setting from a list in the "Slide Setup" (Windows) or "Page Setup" (Macintosh) dialog box. However, to further tailor your presentations and make the best use of this new feature, you can set a custom slide size to match a particular screen size and resolution, using the following guidelines.

Calculating screen size for various monitor resolutions. As we mentioned earlier, Persuasion converts inch measurements to pixels to calculate the correctly sized Player file. Therefore, to create an accurate custom setting, you'd have to do the same. To calculate the appropriate slide size, you need to know the dpi of your monitor (for example, 96 dpi) and the resolution being displayed (for example, 800 by 600). (Please note that although the number of pixels displayed on your monitor is commonly referred to as dpi, it's actually ppi—pixels per inch.)

The basic formula is pixels/dpi = inches. In other words, divide the resolution of your screen (in pixels) by the number of pixels per inch of your screen to get the inch measurement for your presentation. Calculate this for both the horizontal and vertical axes of your screen.

For example, if your monitor is 72 dpi and the monitor's resolution has been set to 832 by 624, you would calculate the size for your Persuasion presentation like this (rounding up):

```
832 / 72 = 11.56 inches wide by 624 / 72 =
  8.67 inches tall
```

Below are the dimensions (in inches) needed to create a slide for a number of common screen resolutions.

For 72- dpi resolution (typical for Macintosh monitors)

Screen size (in pixels)	Page/slide size
320 x 240	4.44" x 3.33"
512 x 384	7.11" x 5.33"
640 x 400	8.89" x 5.56"
640 x 480	8.89" x 6.67"
800 x 600	11.11" x 8.33"

832 x 624	11.56" x 8.67"
1024 x 768	14.22" x 10.67"
1280 x 1024	17.77" x 14.22"
648 x 486	9.0" x 6.75"

For 96-dpi resolution (typical for Windows monitors)

Screen size (in pixels)	Page/slide size
320 x 240	3.33" x 2.5"
512 x 384	5.33" x 4.0"
640 x 400	6.67" x 4.17"
640 x 480	6.67" x 5.0"
800 x 600	8.33" x 6.25"
832 x 624	8.66" x 6.5"
1024 x 768	10.67" x 8.0"
1280 x 1024	13.33" x 10.67"

(This is a portion of the table shown in Persuasion's Online Help under the topic "Using the Pasteboard.")

PICT Images in Persuasion 3.x File Drop Out after Transferring Across Platforms

ISSUE

When you transfer an Adobe Persuasion 3.x file from the Macintosh to Windows, PICT images contained in the file drop out.

SOLUTIONS

When the original PICT files are available, do either or both of the following:

A. Rename the PICT files with a DOS- and Windows-compatible eight-character name (e.g., Slide1-1.PCT), transfer them from the Macintosh to Windows, then import them into the converted Windows presentation.

B. Open each PICT file in an image editing application (e.g., Photoshop), edit it if desired, then save it as an EPS file or a TIFF file. Import the EPS or TIFF files into the Persuasion presentation, save the presentation in interchange format, then transfer the interchange file to Windows.

OR: When the original PICT files are not available, do one or more of the following:

A. Select each PICT image in the presentation, then choose Draw > Ungroup to ungroup it. Save the file in interchange format, then transfer it to Windows.

B. Select and then copy each PICT image in the presentation, then paste it into a graphic editor (e.g., Photoshop). Edit the image if desired, save it as an EPS or TIFF file with a DOS- and Windows-compatible eight-character name (e.g., Image1.EPS, Image1.TIF), then transfer it to Windows. In Windows, import each EPS or TIFF file into the presentation.

C. Export each slide containing a PICT image as a PICT file, then open it in a graphic editor (e.g., Photoshop). Edit the image if desired, then save it as an EPS or TIFF file. Import the EPS or TIFF files into the Persuasion presentation, save the presentation in interchange format, then transfer the interchange file to Windows.

D. Export each presentation slide in PICT format with a DOS- and Windows-compatible eight-character name (e.g., Slide1-1.PCT). Transfer the files to Windows. In Windows, import the PICT files into a new Persuasion presentation.

E. Export the presentation as a Player file, then transfer the Player file to Windows. Open the Player file in Windows, then copy and paste each slide into a new Persuasion presentation.

ADDITIONAL INFORMATION

Because Persuasion's interchange format cannot contain PICT format information, PICT images drop out when you transfer a Macintosh file containing them to the Windows platform. Transferring the PICT files to the Windows platform and then importing them into your presentation, using another graphic file format, ungrouping each PICT, or copying and then pasting the image from a Player file enables you to transfer your images from the Macintosh to Windows as expected.

When you transfer a PICT file from the Macintosh to Windows, then import it into a Persuasion presentation, Persuasion converts the PICT information to WMF information, which is compatible with Windows.

Ungrouping a PICT image in a Persuasion presentation converts its data to native Persuasion format, which the interchange format can transfer to Windows.

Adobe recommends using file formats other than PICT (e.g., EPS, TIFF) for images you will be transferring from the Macintosh platform to the Windows platform.

Transition Sounds Don't Play or Continue in Persuasion 3.x

ISSUE

Sound files imported in Persuasion 3.x do not play or do not continue playing when advancing the slide.

SYMPTOMS

The sound files are imported as transitions and set to Continue.

The file is being played by Persuasion for Windows, or Persuasion Player for Macintosh or Windows, with the Layers option disabled.

SOLUTIONS

Select the Layers option before playing the slide show by doing one or more of the following:

A. When playing the slide show in Persuasion for Windows, choose View > Slide show > Show all slides, select Layers, then click Save.

B. When playing the slide show in Persuasion Player, select Layers in the Settings dialog box:

1. To make the menu bar visible, press Command + M (Macintosh) or Control + M (Windows).
2. Choose File > Settings, then select Layers.
3. Click Restart or Continue to resume playing the slide show.

OR: When using Persuasion Player, set the slide advance to Automatic:

1. To make the menu bar visible, press Command + M (Macintosh) or Control + M (Windows).
2. Choose File > Settings, then select Automatic.
3. Click Restart or Continue to resume playing the slide show.

OR: When using Persuasion Player for Macintosh, advance slides using the right arrow key instead of the mouse.

ADDITIONAL INFORMATION

Setting transition sounds to Continue enables the sound to play throughout a presentation while other slides and slide layers are shown. Setting transition sounds to Wait causes Persuasion to play the entire sound before advancing to the next slide or layer in automatic mode.

Transition sounds set to Continue stop playing when Persuasion advances in manual mode to a slide or layer that contains additional transition sounds.

Slide Show Runs Slowly or Performs Poorly in Persuasion 4.0 or Earlier

ISSUE

When you play a slide show in Adobe Persuasion 4.0 or earlier, the slide show starts, advances from slide to slide or from layer to layer, or completes an AutoJump to another slide slowly, or the slide show performs transitions, sounds, or movies included in the slide show poorly (e.g., transitions do not appear as expected, sounds or movies are cut or play roughly).

SOLUTIONS

In Persuasion 4.0, export the presentation as a PDF file, then view it in Acrobat Reader 3.0.

OR: Use the Persuasion Player instead of Persuasion's internal slide show.

NOTE: The Player supports all internal slide show features and can render slides and layers faster than the internal slide show. The Player is limited to 640 x 480 pixels and 256 or fewer colors.

OR: Increase the efficiency of the internal Persuasion slide show by doing one or more of the following:

A. Change the monitor's color mode to 16-bit (i.e., thousands of colors) or 24-bit (i.e., millions of colors) to reduce the time Persuasion requires to allocate colors for each slide:

   On the Macintosh, open the Monitors control panel and set the Colors option to Thousands or Millions, then click OK.

   In Windows 95, right-click on the desktop, then select Properties from the pop-up menu. In the Display Properties dialog box, click the Settings tab, select the desired color option from the Color Palette pop-up menu, and then click OK and restart Windows.

   In Windows 3.1x, open Windows Setup and choose Options > Change System Settings. In the Change System Settings dialog box, select the desired color option from the Display pop-up menu, click OK, and then restart Windows.

B. Use an image editing application (e.g., Adobe Photoshop) to resave color images so that they are the same bit depth as the monitor on which you are presenting the slide show, and then reimport them into Persuasion. For example, if the monitor display is 8-bit (256 colors), use 8-bit images in the slide show.

C. For images scaled in Persuasion, use an image editing application (e.g., Adobe Photoshop) to scale images to the desired size, and then reimport them into Persuasion.

D. Use an image editing application (e.g. Adobe Photoshop) to reduce the resolution of graphics in the presentation (e.g., from 150 ppi to 72 ppi), and then reimport them into Persuasion.

E. Move graphics you use throughout the presentation onto the background master.

F. Reduce the number of complex graphics (e.g., gradient fills, gradient backgrounds, line art, bitmap images) in the presentation.

G. Replace complex elements (e.g., glitter transition, animation) with simpler elements (e.g., wipe transition, fewer animations).

H. Designate the slide shape as Screen for the monitor on which you are presenting the slide show so that Persuasion does not scale each slide to fit the monitor during the slide show. For instructions, see Additional Information.

I. Allocate additional memory to Persuasion by doing one or more of the following:
   A. Quit other applications.
   B. Turn on virtual memory.
   C. On the Macintosh, increase the amount of memory allocated to Persuasion:
      1. Quit Persuasion.
      2. Select the Persuasion application icon in the Persuasion folder, then choose File > Get Info.
      3. In the Persuasion Info window, increase the value for Preferred Size (System 7.1 or later), Current Size (System 7.0x), or Application Size (System 6.0.x).

J. Alternate slide complexity for consecutive slides (i.e., place a simple slide containing few elements after a complex slide containing a graphic, gradient fill, sound or movie).

K. On the Macintosh, disable added or nonessential extensions:

   If your presentation contains no movies or sounds, press the Shift key while restarting the Macintosh.

   NOTE: Disabling extensions with the Shift key disables

the QuickTime extension, which Persuasion requires for movies or sounds.

OR: Use Extensions Manager to select the System 7.5.x set, which enables only those extensions included with System 7.5.x. The System 7.5.x extensions include QuickTime, which Persuasion requires for movies and sounds.

OR: Move all extensions except a printer driver (e.g., Apple LaserWriter 8.x, Adobe PSPrinter 8.x, HP LaserJet) from the Extensions folder in the System Folder to a different folder (e.g., new folder on the desktop). If the presentation contains movies or sounds, leave the QuickTime extension in the Extensions folder.

L. For more efficient playback for movies and sounds in a presentation, do one or more of the following:
   A. Use the Screen slide size or one that is smaller than the original movies. Do not enlarge movies.
   B. Use a 24-bit (millions of colors) monitor instead of an 8-bit (i.e., 256 color) monitor.
   C. Defragment the hard disk.

ADDITIONAL INFORMATION

When Persuasion doesn't have enough random access memory (RAM) to display a slide show, it displays or advances it slowly. Increasing the amount of memory available to Persuasion enables it to display the presentation quickly. Persuasion speeds its displaying by storing both the current slide and the following slide in memory (RAM). When Persuasion doesn't have enough memory to store two complex slides (e.g., slides containing gradient fills, bitmap images, transitions, sounds, or movies), Persuasion displays slides slowly. Alternating slide complexity for consecutive slides reduces the amount of memory Persuasion needs, and enables Persuasion to display slides quickly.

In 8-bit (256 color) mode, Persuasion reallocates the color palette for each slide, which improves color display, but increases the time Persuasion takes to display each slide. Setting the display to 16-bit or 24-bit color mode enables Persuasion to reallocate colors more quickly. When the monitor's resolution (e.g., 70 to 85 dpi) is less than the resolution of a scanned or bitmap image, monitors cannot display all the image's information. Persuasion determines how to display images that contain more color information than your monitor can display (e.g., a 16-bit image displaying on an 8-bit monitor) each time it appears in your slide show. Reducing the resolution or bit depth of images contained in the presentation, or increasing the bit depth setting for your monitor, enables Persuasion to display images quickly. Setting the slide shape as Screen enables Persuasion to quickly compose its display specifically for your monitor.

Because background master elements redraw faster than slide graphics, putting graphics on the background master enables Persuasion to display them quickly. The more complex graphics (e.g., gradient fills, gradient backgrounds, line art, bitmap images) a presentation contains, the longer Persuasion takes to display them. Reducing the number of complex graphics in each slide enables Persuasion to display them quickly. Because complex elements require more time to display, replacing complex elements with simpler elements enables Persuasion to display them quickly.

Macintosh extensions may interfere with Persuasion's slide show display. You can verify that added extensions are not slowing the display by running Persuasion with all extensions off except a printer driver. Persuasion requires a printer driver installed in the Extensions folder in the System Folder to launch.

QuickTime displays the movies in Persuasion presentations. For movies in a presentation, maintaining or reducing the size of the original movie enables QuickTime to display it quickly. Because QuickTime must reduce the bit depth of a 24-bit movie to display it on an 8-bit monitor, using a 24-bit monitor instead of an 8-bit monitor for a 24-bit movie enables QuickTime to display the movie quickly. Adobe recommends using On-Screen/Video AutoTemplates instead of 35mm Slide or Overhead AutoTemplates for a presentation containing a movie.

When Persuasion runs a slide show of the presentation, it allocates colors during the slide show, increasing the time it takes to render the display. The Persuasion Player does not allocate colors while running a presentation because Player allocates color when you export a presentation as a player file.

The Player does not scale the slides during the presentation because it is limited to 640 x 480 pixels. When showing a presentation on a larger monitor, Persuasion scales every slide during the slide show. Because presentations exported as player files are a series of bitmap images containing no font information, Player can display presentations more quickly than Persuasion.

Unlike the Player's color and size limitations, Acrobat Reader 3.0 can display the maximum number of colors and sizes your monitor is capable of.

To designate the slide shape as Screen for the monitor in Persuasion for the Macintosh:

1. Open a copy of the original presentation.
2. Choose File > Page Setup.
3. Click OK in the Page Setup dialog box to close it, leaving the Presentation Setup dialog box on-screen.
4. Select the Screen option for Slide Shape, then click OK.
5. If the Adjust Graphics dialog box with the message "Page size of slides, notes, and handouts has changed" appears, change the dialog box options as desired, then click OK.

To designate the slide shape as Screen for the monitor in Persuasion for Windows:

1. Open a copy of the original presentation.
2. Choose File > Slide Setup, then select Display from the Printer pop-up menu.
3. Select the Screen option for the Slide Type, then click OK.
4. If the Adobe Persuasion dialog box with the message "Warning: Slide size and/or orientation has been changed. Slide appearance may be adversely affected." appears, click OK.

WINDOWS

Q *(3.0 only)* **I've always used my right mouse button to toggle between 100% and Fit in Window views, but it doesn't work anymore. What gives?**

A In Persuasion 3.0 there are four ways to change the view magnification when you're in slide view.

- Press Ctrl + Alt + left mouse button to toggle between Fit in Window and 100% views (what you used to do with the right mouse button).
- Select specific views from the Magnification submenu of the Show menu.
- Use keyboard shortcuts to go to those same views: Ctrl + W (Fit in Window), Shift + Ctrl + W (Fit Pasteboard in Window), Ctrl + 7 (75% view), Ctrl + 1 (100% view), Ctrl + 2 (200% view), and Ctrl + 4 (400% view).
- Use one of the new magnifying-glass tools in the toolbox. Select either the zoom-in tool (with a plus sign in it) or the zoom-out tool (with a minus sign) and click on the area where you want to zoom.

The right mouse button has a new function in Persuasion 3.0. When you're in slide view, clicking the right mouse button on any object with a badge (whether the badge is being displayed or not) will display its badge menu. Objects that have badges include OLE objects, movies and sounds, and objects with Autoanimation or Autojump applied. Also, in Aldus Chart, clicking the right mouse button while pointing to any chart object will display a pop-up list of menu items that you can use to modify the object.

Vertical Lines with Arrowheads Don't Display Straight in Persuasion 3.x

ISSUE

Vertical lines with one arrowhead display jagged rather than straight when you view the slides, run a slide show in Persuasion, or run a Persuasion Player file. The lines were drawn while pressing the Shift key.

SOLUTIONS

Disregard the appearance of the lines on screen. The lines will print straight.

OR: Remove the arrowheads from the lines, then draw arrowheads using the polygon drawing tool.

OR: Use lines that have arrowheads at both ends.

OR: Use imported arrows from Persuasion's PR3\CLIPART directory.

ADDITIONAL INFORMATION

Straight vertical lines with arrowheads at one end only may display jagged in Persuasion 3.x. The lines print straight as expected.

Pressing Shift while drawing with the Line tool constrains the line to either a horizontal or vertical segment. You must use the Line tool when adding line ends (e.g., arrowheads).

PostScript Text Dithers or Changes Color in Slide Show

ISSUE

Colored text formatted with a PostScript font dithers (i.e., displays ragged or spotty) or changes color in an Adobe Persuasion or Player slide show. The text may also display poorly in the Persuasion presentation after you run the slide show. Text formatted with a TrueType font displays as expected.

SYMPTOM

The video card is an ATI Mach 32 2.6 or later, with display set at 256 or fewer colors.

SOLUTIONS

Set the video card to display more than 256 colors:

1. Quit all applications.
2. Back up the System.ini file, located in the Windows directory.
3. Open the Mach FlexDesk Control Panel.
4. In the Control Panel, select a color option that displays more than 256 colors (e.g., 65 thousand, 16.7 million). If other color options are not available, select a different screen size (e.g., 1024 x 768) or consult your video card documentation.
5. Close the Control Panel, then restart Windows.

OR: Format the text with a TrueType font instead of a PostScript font.

OR: Change the color of the text.

ADDITIONAL INFORMATION

The ATI Mach 32 2.6 or later video card may not display colors as expected in a Persuasion or Player slide show when it is set to display 256 or fewer colors, causing colored PostScript text to appear dithered or change color. Setting the video card to display more than 256 colors, using a TrueType font, or changing the color of the text may enable Persuasion and Player to display the text as expected.

MAC OS

Q *(3.0 only)* **In "Slide sorter" view, how can I tell the slide number of a slide that's selected? It used to show up in the lower-left corner, but it doesn't in 3.0.**

A Although the slide number doesn't display automatically in Persuasion 3.0's slide sorter, there are two easy ways to find it. One is to select a slide and press Command + Shift + G. This brings up the "Go to slide" dialog box with the number of the selected slide displayed. Press the Escape key or click "Cancel" to close the dialog box.

Alternatively, you can select the slide and then click and hold on the slide button in the upper-right corner of the window. This displays a drop-down list of all the slides, with a check mark next to the one that's currently selected.

There is a way to make a number temporarily appear on the slides themselves in "Slide sorter" view—which can be particularly handy if you're rearranging a large number of slides. Here's how.

1. From the View menu, choose "Background," and then select the current background from the submenu.
2. In Background view, choose "Add page number" from the Master menu. This inserts a page-number placeholder (reading "XXXXX") on the background.
3. With the page-number placeholder still selected, assign it a large point size (try 72-point) and a color that's easily visible against the background. If necessary, use the pointer tool to resize or move the text block.
4. Repeat steps 1 through 3 for each of the backgrounds used in the presentation.

Now, when you return to "Slide sorter" view, you'll see a slide number on each slide. Each number will remain with its slide as you rearrange them (unless you redraw the screen or leave "Slide sorter" view). When you don't need the slide numbers anymore, return to the background, select the placeholder with the pointer tool, and delete it.

Q I want to use a PowerBook in combination with an LCD panel to display my Player presentations; however, I've found that some of my slides suddenly display in black and white even though I still see them in color on my PowerBook screen. How can I prevent this?

A First, you should know the technical reason that this is happening (which basically amounts to a memory problem). After that, we will give you some suggestions to help you work around the problem.

Most PowerBook computers have 512 K of video memory or VRAM, which can't be expanded. When the computer doesn't have enough VRAM to display full-screen, full-color, complex slides on two monitors at once, images on the secondary monitor (which is usually the LCD panel) tend to display in black and white—black-and-white images require less VRAM.

Simply designating the LCD panel as the startup monitor may be enough to take care of the problem. To do this, first turn off video mirroring in the Control Strip or PowerBook Control Panel. Then open the Monitors Control Panel and move the Monitor 1 title bar to Monitor 2. Close the Monitors Control Panel and turn video mirroring back on. Now restart and test your slide show. In most cases, this will transfer the color display from your PowerBook to the LCD panel. If this doesn't work, try turning off video mirroring altogether. With all VRAM now dedicated to the LCD panel, you should see the color display properly.

If neither of these solutions works, you may have to simplify your screen presentation. Turning off transition effects may be enough. To turn off transitions for a Persuasion slide show, choose "Show all slides..." from the Slide show submenu of the View menu. In the "Slide show" dialog box, deselect "Transition effects." To turn off transition effects in a Player file, press Command + T to show the "Settings" dialog box. From there, deselect "Transition effects" and click "Restart."

Here are a few other suggestions for how you might simplify your presentation:

- Insert blank slides with black backgrounds before and after the slides that display in black and white. Persuasion creates a new 256-color palette for each slide and preloads the next slide into RAM. "Sandwiching" the color-intensive slides between black slides that require less VRAM for display will allow Persuasion Player to dedicate more VRAM to the slide that contains the image.
- Rescan or downsample images to a smaller number of dots per inch.
- Change the background fill to a solid color rather than a gradient fill. Gradient fills, as you know, contain many colors.

Unable to Start Persuasion 4.0 Troubleshooting Guide

ISSUE

When you try to start Adobe Persuasion 4.0, a system error (e.g., Type 1, Type 11) occurs or Persuasion freezes.

SOLUTIONS

Do one or more of the following:

A. Disable all extensions except Apple Event Manager and Shared Code Manager, then restart Persuasion.
B. Rebuild the desktop file by holding down the Command and Option keys while restarting the computer. Keep the keys held down until you receive the message "Are you sure you want to rebuild the desktop file on the disk '[diskname]'?", then click OK.
C. In the Chooser, select a printer driver or select a different printer driver.
D. Move the Persuasion application to the startup volume, and ensure at least 5 MB of free disk space is available on the startup volume.
E. Delete the Persuasion 4.0 Preferences file, which is located in the Preferences folder in the System Folder, then restart Persuasion.
F. Move the Support folder from the Persuasion folder to another location (e.g., desktop), then restart Persuasion.
G. Reinstall Persuasion with all extensions disabled. Before installing Persuasion, delete the Apple Event Manager file, Shared Code Manager file, and Shared Code folder from the Extensions folder in the System Folder. Delete the Embedding Preferences, Shared Code Preferences, Adobe Chart Preferences, Adobe Table Prefs, Adobe Persuasion 4.0 Preferences files from the Preferences folder in the System Folder.
H. Ensure the installation media are not damaged:

   If you are installing from a Persuasion CD-ROM, examine the CD-ROM for dirt, dust, fingerprints or scratches. Wipe the unprinted side of the CD-ROM gently, from the center outward, with a soft, lint-free cloth.

Examine the CD-ROM caddy or loading tray for your CD-ROM drive. If it is dirty, wipe it with a clean, lint-free cloth. If the CD-ROM is scratched, contact Adobe Customer Services for a replacement disc.

OR: If you are installing from disks, verify that your Macintosh can read the disks. In the Finder, copy the contents from each disk to the hard drive. If the Macintosh is unable to read a disk made from a disk image on the CD-ROM, recreate that disk using a new disk and the disk image from the CD-ROM. If the Macintosh is unable to read a disk from Adobe, recreate that disk using a new disk and the disk image from the CD-ROM, or contact Adobe Customer Services for a replacement disk set.

I. When installing from backup disks, make sure they are named with the same names as the original disks or the disk images on the CD-ROM, and that they contain the same items in the same folder hierarchy.

J. When using System 7.1 or later, move the Control Panels, Extensions, Fonts, and Preferences folders from the System Folder to another location (e.g., desktop), then restart the Macintosh. For instructions, see Additional Information.

K. When using System 7.x, reset the Macintosh's Parameter RAM (PRAM) by choosing Special > Restart and immediately pressing Command + Option + P + R. Keep the keys held down until the Macintosh restarts a second time.

NOTE: Resetting, or zapping, the PRAM resets the Macintosh back to its default settings. You may need to reset custom settings (e.g., Monitors and Network control panel options) after you reset the PRAM.

L. Reinstall the system software to ensure it is not damaged.

M. Disconnect added hardware (e.g., SCSI devices, accelerator boards, video cards).

n. Reformat the hard disk with a utility compatible with the version of the system software you are running.

ADDITIONAL INFORMATION

Extension conflicts or a damaged preferences file, application file, system, system files, or desktop file can prevent Persuasion from starting.

Because Persuasion requires that a printer driver be selected in the Chooser, a damaged or incompatible printer driver can prevent Persuasion from starting. If Persuasion starts without error after you choose a different printer driver in the Chooser, continue using the currently selected printer driver, or reinstall the original printer driver. Before you reinstall the original printer driver, remove its preference files from the Preferences folder in the System Folder.

The Support folder in Persuasion 4.0 contains Persuasion's dictionaries, Adobe Chart Help and Adobe Table Help. If Persuasion starts successfully after you move the Support folder, recreate the folder using the Finder's New Folder command, then move each of the files contained in the folder back to the new folder in its original location, one at a time. Restart Persuasion after you move each file into the new folder. If Persuasion is unable to start after you move a file into the new folder, the file is damaged. Delete and reinstall the damaged file.

If you delete Persuasion's preferences file, Persuasion will create a new preferences file when you close the application.

When you move the Control Panels, Extensions, Fonts, and Preferences folders from the System Folder and restart the Macintosh, the Finder creates new, empty folders with the same names in the System Folder. If Persuasion starts successfully, move the contents of the original folders into the appropriate newly-created folders, one by one, until you determine which file is damaged, then delete and reinstall the damaged file.

Persuasion 4.0 and Earlier Damaged Presentation Troubleshooting Guide

ISSUE

When you open or work in an Adobe Persuasion 4.0 or earlier presentation, Persuasion returns an error or behaves unexpectedly.

SYMPTOMS

One of the following errors occurs:

- "The application '[application name or unknown]' has unexpectedly quit because an error of Type 1 occurred."
- "An internal inconsistency has been found."
- "Internal error: Bad table index."
- "An error has occurred. ffff:ffd9" "Insufficient memory to refresh screen."
- "Insufficient memory to proceed. ffff:ff94"

SOLUTIONS

To recover an unopenable presentation, do one or more of the following:

A. In Persuasion, open a copy of the presentation by selecting Copy in the Open dialog box, selecting the presentation, and then clicking Open.

B. While Persuasion opens the presentation, hold down the Command key and press the arrow keys to change views.

C. Make a copy of the presentation in the Finder by using the Duplicate command, then open the copy in Persuasion.

D. Allocate more memory to Persuasion:
   1. Quit Persuasion.
   2. In the Finder, select the Persuasion application icon, then choose File > Get Info.
   3. In the Persuasion Info window, increase the Preferred Size (System 7.1 or later) or Current Size (System 7.0x) value, then close the Info window.

E. Increase the amount of available hard disk space by moving or deleting files from the hard disk.

F. Move the Fonts and Preferences folders from the System Folder to another location (e.g., desktop), restart the Macintosh with extensions disabled, and then open the presentation. To quickly disable added or non-essential extensions, restart with the Shift key held down until the message, "Welcome to Macintosh. Extensions off." appears, or use an extensions manager.

G. Select a different printer driver in the Chooser, then open the presentation.

H. Open the presentation on a different Macintosh.

I. Open a backup copy of the presentation.

J. Import the text and slide masters into a new presentation:
   1. Open the presentation in a text editor that can save in text-only format (e.g., TeachText, Microsoft Word).
   2. Delete all code characters in the file, then save it in text-only format.
   3. Create a new Persuasion presentation, then import the text file into the outline.
   4. Save the presentation, close it, and then open a copy of the presentation.
   5. Choose File > Change Design > Replace Masters.
   6. In the Replace Masters dialog box, select the original presentation as the source for your masters, then click Import.

To repair damage in an openable presentation, do one or more of the following:

A. Choose File > Save As to save the presentation with a different name. If possible, save the presentation on your startup disk (e.g., hard disk containing the active system).

B. Allocate more memory to Persuasion.
   1. Save the presentation with a different name.
   2. Quit Persuasion.
   3. In the Finder, select the Persuasion application icon, then choose File > Get Info.
   4. In the Persuasion Info window, increase the Preferred Size (System 7.1 or later) or Current Size (System 7.0.x) value, then close the Info window.

C. Save the presentation with a different name, then quit Persuasion. Restart the Macintosh with extensions disabled, then open the presentation. To quickly disable added or non-essential extensions, restart with the Shift key held down until the message, "Welcome to Macintosh. Extensions off." appears, or use an extensions manager.

D. Save the presentation with a different name, then quit Persuasion. Remove the Persuasion preferences file (i.e., Adobe Persuasion 4.0 Prefs, Persuasion 3.0ppc Preferences, Persuasion 3.0 Preferences) from the Preferences folder in the System Folder, then reopen the presentation.

E. Copy slides into a new presentation:
   In Persuasion 4.0, create a new presentation with the same page setup as your original presentation, then copy slides by dragging them from the original presentation's slide sorter window to the new presentation's slide sorter window.

OR: In Persuasion 3.0.2 or earlier:
   1. In the slide sorter view, choose Edit > Select All, then choose Edit > Copy.
   2. Create a new presentation with the same page setup as your original presentation.
   3. In the slide sorter view, choose Edit > Paste.

F. Replace the masters:
   1. Save a copy of the presentation with a different name.
   2. In the copy of the presentation, choose File > Change Design > Replace Masters.
   3. In the Replace Masters dialog box, select an AutoTemplate with masters that use the same page setup as your presentation, then click Import.

G. Save a copy of the presentation with a different name. In the copy of the presentation, delete unused masters or custom masters, then assign standard imported masters to all slides.

H. Determine if the error is caused by damaged graphics by choosing File > Preferences, then selecting Hide Big PICTs, then try to recreate the error. If the error does not reoccur, delete and then replace the graphics in the presentation.

I. Save the presentation as an interchange file.
   NOTE: Persuasion does not include graphics in interchange files.

J. Save a copy of the presentation with a different name, then quit Persuasion. Drag the Fonts folder from the System Folder to another location (e.g., desktop), restart the Macintosh, then open the presentation. If the error does not reoccur, isolate the damaged font, then reinstall that font.

K. Save the presentation in an earlier Persuasion version format, then open it in that earlier version of Persuasion. For example, in Persuasion 3.0.2, save the presentation in Persuasion 2.x format, then open the Persuasion 2.x presentation in Persuasion 2.x.

L. Open a backup copy of the presentation.

M. Copy the text and masters into a new presentation:
   1. In outline view, choose Edit > Select All, then choose Edit > Copy.
   2. Create a new Persuasion presentation with the same page setup as your original presentation.
   3. In outline view, click on the first slide icon, then choose Edit > Paste. 4. Save the presentation, close it, and then open a copy of the presentation.
   5. Choose File > Change Design > Replace Masters.
   6. In the Replace Masters dialog box, select the original presentation as the source for your masters, then click Import.
   7. Assign the masters to the slides in your new presentation.

N. Isolate the damaged item or items in the presentation:
   1. Open a copy of the presentation.
   2. In slide sorter view, delete half of the slides.
   3. Choose File > Save As to save the file with a different name.
   4. If the error does not reoccur when you work in this half of the file, open the copy of the full presentation and delete the other half of the slides. Then save that file with a different name and work in it to see if the error reoccurs.
   5. Continue to remove one or more slides until you isolate the damaged slide or group of slides.
   6. After you have isolated the damaged slide or slides,

identify a common element that may be causing the problem (e.g., font, graphic, master, background).

7. Delete the suspect element or the entire slide, then reimport or recreate it.

Additional Information Persuasion returns an error or behaves unexpectedly when damage in a presentation prevents Persuasion from opening the presentation or from performing other actions. Common causes of damaged presentations include low or badly fragmented disk space, low system resources, system errors, and saving files to damaged media (e.g., damaged sector on a disk). A damaged graphic, font, master, or AutoTemplate in a presentation can also cause an error or unexpected behavior when you work in Persuasion.

Application Errors

MAC OS / WINDOWS

Error When Saving Persuasion 3.0x Presentation as Interchange File

ISSUE

When saving a Persuasion 3.0x presentation as an interchange file, the error "Cannot complete this operation, Internal Program Error" appears in Persuasion for Windows, or the error "Unable to save the document xxx.prf. An error has occurred." appears in Persuasion for Macintosh. The file saves as a presentation without error.

SOLUTIONS

When the presentation contains an organization chart, remove invisible items from the organization chart master:

1. Make a backup copy of the presentation.
2. Choose "Org Chart" from the "Slide master" submenu of the View menu.
3. Choose "Select all" from the Edit menu, then choose "Clear" from the Edit menu.
4. Re-add the desired placeholders from the Master menu, positioning and formatting them as desired.
5. View a slide that was assigned to the organization chart master, then select "Reapply master" from the middle popup menu at the bottom of the window. Repeat for other slides assigned to the organization chart master.

OR: When an organization chart is not used in the presentation, delete the organization chart master:

1. Select "Text" from the "Slide master" submenu of the View menu.
2. Select "Define masters..." from the Master menu.
3. In the "Define masters" dialog box, select "Org Chart" in the scroll box and click "Remove" (Macintosh) or "Delete" (Windows).
4. Click "OK" to close the dialog box.

ADDITIONAL INFORMATION

An invisible object in some organization chart masters (e.g., PINUPOH.AT3 included with Persuasion 3.0x for Windows) causes an error to occur when saving a Persuasion 3.0x presentation as an interchange file. The object can only be selected for deletion by using the "Select all" command.

Error "Cannot open file" or Type 11 When Opening a Persuasion 4.0 Interchange File

ISSUE

When you open an Adobe Persuasion 4.0 interchange file in Persuasion 4.0 for Windows, Persuasion returns the error, "Cannot open file. Internal Program Error. [Error number]."

When you open a Persuasion 4.0 interchange file in Persuasion 4.0 for the Macintosh, the system returns a Type 11 error.

Symptom

The interchange file was saved from Persuasion 4.0 for the Macintosh directly to a Windows-compatible disk.

SOLUTION

Save the interchange file from Persuasion 4.0 for the Macintosh to the Macintosh hard disk, then copy the interchange file to a disk.

ADDITIONAL INFORMATION

When you save an interchange file from Persuasion 4.0 for the Macintosh directly to a Windows-compatible disk, the file becomes damaged, causing an application or system error to occur when you open it.

Error "No Player files specified..." When Trying to Run Persuasion Slide Show

ISSUE

When you try to run a slide show using the Aldus Persuasion Player 1.0, Player returns the error "No Player files specified. Check filename and try again. Note that Player cannot display standard GIF 87a/89a files."

SOLUTION

Re-export the original presentation as a Player file from Aldus Persuasion 2.1 or later.

ADDITIONAL INFORMATION

The Persuasion Player 1.0 can play files exported from Persuasion 2.1 or later for the Macintosh or Windows. If you try to play a file that was created an application other than Persuasion, Player 1.0 returns the error "No Player files specified. Check file name and try again. Note that Player cannot display standard GIF 87a/89a files." If the file was created in Persuasion, the error indicates the presentation is damaged.

Re-exporting and retransferring the presentation ensures the Player file is not damaged.

The GIF 87a/89a file structure was developed for CompuServe. The Persuasion Player uses a modified version of this file type and cannot display the unmodified version, used by other applications.

System Errors

MAC OS / WINDOWS

Freeze or Error Importing CMYK JPEG Image into Persuasion 4.0

ISSUE

When you import a CMYK JPEG file into Adobe Persuasion 4.0 for the Macintosh, Persuasion returns the error, "Image Import Error. This image file is not supported."

When you import a CMYK JPEG file into Adobe Persuasion 4.0 for Windows, Persuasion freezes with the progress bar approximately 50% full, or returns the error, "Cannot complete this operation. Cannot place this file."

SOLUTIONS

Open the file in an image editing application (e.g., Adobe Photoshop), change its color mode from CMYK to RGB or grayscale, then save the image and import it into Persuasion.

OR: If you need to retain the CMYK color information, open the file in an image editing application (e.g., Adobe Photoshop), save it in TIFF or Photoshop format, then import it into Persuasion.

ADDITIONAL INFORMATION

Because Persuasion can import only RGB or Grayscale JPEG files, it returns an error when you import a CMYK JPEG file. Saving the file in another color mode enables Persuasion to import it without returning an error. Persuasion can import CMYK TIFF or Photoshop files.

The Persuasion 4.0 CD-ROM Disc 2 includes several CMYK JPEG images, in the Digital Vision folder in the Photos folder in the Image Club folder in the 3rd Party folder (Macintosh) or in the 3rd_part\Imagclub\Photos\Dig_vis subdirectory (Windows).

The CMYK JPEG images on the Persuasion 4.0 CD-ROM Disc 2 are:

Couple.jpg
Crowds.jpg
Earth.jpg
Mother.jpg
Mountain.jpg
Phone.jpg

WINDOWS

Error or Freeze When Checking Spelling In Persuasion 3.0 on a Network

ISSUE

An error occurs or the computer freezes when checking spelling in Aldus Persuasion 3.0 when Persuasion is installed on a network volume.

SYMPTOMS

The error "Problem initializing spell. Proximity DLL was not found" occurs after selecting "Spelling" from the Edit menu.

The error "Cannot run spell. Linguist support file failed to open, file:2" occurs after clicking on the "Start" button in the "Spelling" dialog box.

SOLUTIONS

Do one or more of the following:

A. Copy the Persuasion dictionary files from the original installation disks to the network server, replacing any currently installed files:
  1. Insert Disk 1 of the Persuasion 3.0 installation disk set, then choose "Run..." from the File menu in Program Manager or File Manager.
  2. In the "Run" dialog box, type X:\ALDSETUP in the "Command Line:" text box, where "X" is the drive in which Disk 1 is inserted.
  3. In Aldus Setup, select "Single file copy..." from the File menu.
  4. In the "Copy single file" dialog box, navigate to the ALDUS\USENGLSH directory in the "Files in:" list box.
  5. Select the file named ALDUSN.BP_ then type the full path to the USENGLSH directory on the network server in the "Enter target directory:" text box and click "OK."
  6. Repeat step 5 for the files ALDUSN.NF_, ALDUSN00.VP_, and PRXLNGST.RS_.
  7. Leaving the "Copy single file" dialog box open, eject Disk 1 and insert Disk 3.
  8. In the "Files in:" list box, select the file PRXLNGST.DL_, located in the ALDUS directory on Disk 3.
  9. Type the full path to the directory containing the USENGLSH subdirectory on the network server (e.g., ALDUS) in the "Enter target directory:" text box, then click "OK."
  10. Choose "Exit" from the File menu to exit Aldus Setup.

  NOTE: For a directory structure of the copied files, see Additional Information.

B. Ensure the [aldus] section of the WIN.INI indicates the correct path to the Persuasion network directories:
  1. Make a backup copy of the WIN.INI file.
  2. Open the original WIN.INI file, located in the WINDOWS directory, in a text editor that can save in text-only format (e.g., Windows Write, Notepad).
  3. Ensure the following lines appear exactly as follows:

```
PR3SharedDirectory=x:\xxxx
PR3LangDir=USENGLSH
```

Where x:\xxxx is the drive letter and full path to the network directory containing the USENGLSH subdirectory (e.g., ALDUS).
4. Save the WIN.INI file in text-only format and restart Windows.

C. Ensure you have write access to the network directory containing the USENGLSH subdirectory (e.g., ALDUS).

D. Remark out all other entries in the [aldus] section of the WIN.INI file:
1. Make a backup copy of the WIN.INI file.
2. Open the original WIN.INI file, located in the WINDOWS directory, in a text editor that can save in text-only format (e.g., Windows Write, Notepad).
3. Type a semicolon before each line in the [aldus] section except for the "PR3SharedDirectory" and "PR3LangDir" lines. For example:

```
PR3SharedDirectory=x:\xxxx
PR3LangDir=USENGLSH
;ChartSharedDir=C:\ALDUS
;ChartLangDir=USENGLSH
```

4. Save the WIN.INI file in text-only format and restart Windows.
NOTE: If spelling checks successfully in Persuasion, remove each semicolon one by one, until the entry that is misdirecting Persuasion is found. Other applications (e.g., Aldus PageMaker, Aldus FreeHand) write lines to the [aldus] section of the WIN.INI file. When those lines are remarked out, the applications may not launch.

ADDITIONAL INFORMATION

Persuasion 3.0 uses the five dictionary files noted below when checking spelling. If the files are not installed, are installed in the wrong location, or are damaged, Persuasion cannot check spelling. If Persuasion cannot locate the files due to incorrect entries in the WIN.INI file, or if Persuasion cannot access the files because it does not have write access to the network directory containing them, Persuasion cannot check spelling.

The five dictionary files should be installed in the following locations (the disks from which they are copied are noted in parentheses):

```
NET DIRECTORY (e.g., ALDUS)
prxlngst.dll  (Disk 3)
USENGLSH
 aldusn.bpx (Disk 1)
 aldusn.nfo (Disk 1)
 aldusn00.vpx (Disk 1)
 prxlngst.rsl (Disk 1)
```

Error "Cannot complete this operation. OLE server failed to open document" in Persuasion

ISSUE

After you select Copy Linked Files in the Save As dialog box, Persuasion returns a Sharing Violation message or the error "Cannot complete this operation. OLE server failed to open document; possible invalid link."

SOLUTION

Close OLE applications (e.g., Microsoft Excel) before choosing File > Save As in Persuasion.

ADDITIONAL INFORMATION

When saving a Persuasion presentation containing OLE graphics, Persuasion automatically copies linked files when the Copy Linked Files option is selected. When saving and copying linked graphics, Persuasion sends an update to OLE servers (e.g., Excel) that includes the new file's location.

Printing Problems

MAC OS / WINDOWS

Q Is there any way that I can print the data sheets for my Persuasion charts?

A Yes, there is. While the Chart application can't print charts (they need to be pasted or embedded into some other application in order to be printed), it can print data sheets. In Chart, make sure that the data sheet window is the active window. If you want to print only a portion of the data sheet, select the cells you want to print.

Your exact printing options vary between platforms; here are the specifics:

On the PC: On the File menu are two printing choices: "Print all data" and "Print selection." Choosing either opens the standard Windows "Print Setup" dialog box, where you can specify your printer and choose the page orientation. If you have a lot of data and are printing to a PostScript printer, you may want to select "Options…" in this dialog box and enter a scaling percentage to make your data sheet fit on the page. With either print selection, your printout will include the name of the chart for that data sheet, the data sheet's column and row labels, and a page number. "Print all data" prints all the cells that contain information, while "Print selection" prints only the selected cells. Be aware that the cells will print as they appear on the screen. This means that if you only see a portion of the text because the cell is too narrow to display it all, that's the way it will print. You can drag the edge of the column to make it wider so that it can display and print all of the text.

On the Macintosh: First, choose "Page setup…" from the File menu to select the orientation of your page and to reduce or enlarge the output. Then, either select "Print…"

from the File menu to print all the cells that contain information, or choose "Print selection..." to print only the selected cells. The data sheet's row and column labels don't print. Neither do page numbers or file-names, so if you want this information on the printout you'll want to enter it in the cells of the data sheet. One wrinkle: Text that is too long for a narrow cell may print completely by overlapping the next cell, or may "abbreviate" part of the cell text with ellipses. To avoid this, drag the edge of the column to make it wide enough to display all of its text.

Q Can I print the Slide Sorter view from Persuasion?

A The Slide Sorter view can't be printed, but if you just want to print thumbnails of all your slides, you can do so by using Persuasion's handouts feature. What this does is allow you to create an arrangement of slide thumbnails on a handout master page. Persuasion then uses that master to arrange thumbnails of all of your slides the same way on each page, regardless of how many pages are needed to accommodate them all.

(Note for Windows users: Persuasion 3.x doesn't support the Adobe PostScript driver version 4.0 and earlier, including the version shipping with Windows 95. When you use this driver, certain printing problems occur—for instance, the first page of Persuasion handouts doesn't print at all. For more information on this issue call FaxYI, Adobe's free fax-information service, at 206-628-5737 and request document 300120.)

1. Go to your handout master by selecting "Handout master" from the View menu.
2. Select all (Ctrl + A in Windows, Command + A on the Mac), then press the backspace or delete key on your keyboard. This leaves you with a blank page.
3. From the Master menu, select "Add slide copy." The first thumbnail, or copy placeholder, appears on the page. (This doesn't show your own copy, but it does represent one of your real slides: when you print, your copy will appear on the miniature version created by this master.) Drag the placeholder to the place you want it to go on your printout—usually, in the upper-left-hand corner.
4. Repeat step 3, placing each thumbnail where you want it to go. Keep going until you have run out of slides or until "Add slide copy" is grayed out (this indicates that you've reached the maximum number of placeholders on a page—12 on the PC, 8 on the Mac). You may want to make use of Persuasion's rulers and guides in positioning your slide placeholders. To do that, look under "Rulers" and "Guides" in the Show menu, and make sure "Show rulers" and "Show guides" are both checked; then click inside the rulers and drag the guides to where you need them.
5. To print the handouts, select "Print..." from the File menu. In the "Print" dialog box, select only the "Handouts" check box (under "Print choices" on the Mac, under "Notes printer" on the PC).

Macintosh users who are printing with the LaserWriter 8.x driver have a further option for getting additional slides on the page. In Persuasion, select "Page setup..." from the File menu. Then, in the "Layout" drop-down menu, select "2 Up" or "4 Up" to get 16 or 32 thumbnails, respectively, per printed handout page. If you do this, don't forget to reset the layout to "1 Up" before printing the slides themselves.

WINDOWS

Q *(3.0 only)* **In Persuasion 2.x, I used to use the "Proof print" option when I wanted a quick black-and-white printout of my presentation. I tried using 3.0's new "Draft" option in the "Print" dialog box, but my graphics don't print. How do I get a proof print?**

A Persuasion 3.0 doesn't include any exact equivalent of 2.x's "Proof print" option, which printed all lines and text as black, and all colors, fills, and backgrounds as white. However, you can use Persuasion's "Grayscale" mode to preview how your presentation will look on a black-and-white laser printer, and adjust it as needed for legibility.

To convert your presentation to grayscale, select "Grayscale mode" (Crtl + Shift + G) from the Show menu. In grayscale mode, Persuasion-created objects are displayed in inverse grayscale (dark colors become light shades of gray, while light colors become dark shades of gray) and imported graphics are displayed in standard grayscale (dark colors become dark shades of gray, while light colors become light shades of gray).

Before you print, it's a good idea to look through all your slides to make sure that all the slide elements can be distinguished from one another—two contrasting colors can sometimes convert to very similar shades of gray. You can use the Colors/Fills palette to change the shade of gray or the fill pattern assigned to any object. These changes won't affect the color version of your presentation.

If your background color converts to a shade of gray and you'd prefer white, you can deselect "Background" in the "Print" dialog box. This will drop out the background fill, while leaving the background graphic elements.

If you want to change a whole series of objects that are assigned the same gray shade, you can edit the grayscale table, or you can import an entire grayscale table from another presentation or AutoTemplate. For more detailed information on Grayscale Mode, see pages 110–15 of the Persuasion 3.0 User Manual.

Objects or Pages Don't Print from Persuasion 3.0.x Using Windows 95 PostScript Driver

ISSUE

When you print from Persuasion 3.0.x using the Microsoft Windows PostScript printer driver 4.0, Persuasion doesn't print pattern fills, bitmap images, the first handout page, or the first notes page, or prints one or more pages blank.

SOLUTIONS

Use Persuasion 4.0 or later.

OR: Print using the Adobe PostScript printer driver 4.1 (AdobePS).

ADDITIONAL INFORMATION

Persuasion 3.0.x is incompatible with the Microsoft Windows 4.0 printer driver. If you print from Persuasion 3.0.x using the Microsoft Windows 4.0 printer driver, Persuasion does not print pattern fills, bitmap images, the first handout page, or the first notes page, or prints one or more pages blank. Persuasion 4.0 or later is compatible with the Microsoft Windows 4.0 printer driver.

Persuasion 3.0 and later print as expected when you print using AdobePS 4.1. AdobePS 4.1 is designed for use in Windows 95 and does not work with previous versions of Windows.

Persuasion 3.0.x is compatible with Windows 95, but is not Windows 95 logo-compliant. Applications that are Windows 95 logo-compliant have the "Designed for Microsoft Windows 95" logo and support all Microsoft Windows 95 design criteria (e.g., 32-bit design, long filename capability, OLE 2.0).

Installation Issues

MAC OS / WINDOWS

Q I want to keep Persuasion 3.0 on my system for a while after I install Persuasion 4.0. Can I do that?

A Yes, you certainly can. The two versions are completely separate (each will be installed in its own folder) and won't affect each other in the least. You'll be able to open your 3.0 presentations directly in Persuasion 4.0; as always, the first time you open an older-version file in a new version it'll open as an untitled presentation.

Persuasion 4.0 is backward-compatible (like Persuasion 3.0 before it); you can save a presentation in either 4.0 or 3.0 format, or, to transfer a presentation across platforms, you can save it as an Interchange file.

WINDOWS

Adobe Persuasion 3.0.2 Network Installation Guide

This document describes how to install Adobe Persuasion 3.0.2 on a network server for access by multiple users. These instructions supplement the steps described in the "How to install Persuasion 3.0 on a network" card and in the Adobe Persuasion 3.0 User Manual. The steps listed here for the first installation method are simpler and more automated than those described on the network install card.

There are two ways you can install Adobe Persuasion 3.0.2 on a network server using the Persuasion 3 Setup program:

- Install on network server

  Install Persuasion and its supporting files on a network server. Users run Persuasion from the network server, with just a few personalized files installed on their hard drives, which makes it easy to update Persuasion's files for all users at once.
- Install disks on server

  Copy the Persuasion disk images to the network server so that users can install Persuasion on their hard drives themselves. Because the disk images are on the network server, you don't have to distribute the original disks to each user.

To install Persuasion on a network server, you need supervisor-level access to the network. At this level, you should have read/write access to any directory on the network server and be able to create new directories. If your access privileges are restricted, contact your network supervisor for help.

INSTALL ON NETWORK SERVER

There are two parts to installing Adobe Persuasion 3.0.2 on a network server: the network administrator portion and the user portion.

NETWORK ADMINISTRATOR PORTION

To installing Adobe Persuasion 3.0.2 on a network server:

1. Log onto the network server on which you want to install Persuasion.
2. Start Windows 3.1 and insert Persuasion Disk 1.
3. In Program Manager, choose "Run..." from the File menu and type A:\PR3SETUP A:\NET\NET.CTL, then click "OK." If the disk was not inserted in drive A, substitute the correct drive letter for "A."
4. In the "Installation Logfile Creation" dialog box, specify where you want the logfile (i.e., a text file with a detailed record of the installation) to be created and click "OK."
5. Read the Network Licensing Agreement that appears on your screen. Click "OK" to confirm that you have full access privileges to the network server.
6. In the "Persuasion 3 Setup Main Window," select "Install on network server" in the "Select setup options:" list box and click "Setup...."
7. In the "Select directory" dialog box, specify the drive letter and directory where you want to install Persuasion. For example, if you want to install Persuasion in the APPS directory on the Q: drive, type Q:\APPS\-NETALDUS.
8. In the "Select dictionaries" dialog box, select at least one dictionary from the "Available for installation" list box, then click "OK." If you click "OK" without selecting any dictionaries, the alert "At least 1 items must be installed" appears and returns you to this dialog box.

NOTE: The amount of free disk space listed at the bottom of this dialog box refers to the amount of free disk space on the local drive, not on the network server.

9. In the "Personalize your program" dialog box, enter your name, serial number, and company name, then click "OK."
10. Follow the instructions on your screen, inserting disks as prompted, until Persuasion is installed. Click "OK" at the message confirming successful installation, then select "Exit" from the File menu in the "Persuasion 3 Setup Main Window."

USER PORTION

To install Adobe Persuasion 3.0.2 on a network server:

1. When another Adobe or Aldus product (e.g., PageMaker, Aldus FreeHand) is installed on the workstation from which you want to run Persuasion, remark out the "AldusDirectory=" line in the WIN.INI file before completing the user portion of the installation:
   1. Make a backup copy of the WIN.INI file.
   2. Open the original WIN.INI file, located in the WINDOWS directory, in a text editor that can save in text-only format (e.g., Windows Write, Notepad).
   3. In the [aldus] section, insert a semicolon before the "AldusDirectory=" line so that it reads:
      `;AldusDirectory=x:\xxxx`
      where x:\xxxx is the full path to the ALDUS directory on the local drive.
   4. Save the WIN.INI file in text-only format and restart Windows.
   5. After completing the installation steps below, remove the semicolon from the "AldusDirectory=" line, save the WIN.INI file, and restart Windows.
2. At the workstation from which you want to run Persuasion, log on to the network server where Persuasion is installed.
3. In File Manager, double-click on the NETINST.EXE file in the NETALDUS\USENGLISH\PR3USER subdirectory on the network server to launch the installation program.
4. In the "Installation Logfile Creation" dialog box, specify where you want to create the logfile, then click "OK."
5. In the "Persuasion 3 Setup Main Window," select "Install Persuasion 3.0" and click "Setup...."
6. In the "Select directory" dialog box, type the path to the PR3USER directory on the network server (e.g., Q:\APPS\NETALDUS\USENGLSH\PR3USER), then click "OK."
7. Personalized files are copied to the local drive, the WIN.INI file is customized, an Adobe group is created in the Program Manager if one didn't previously exist, and icons for Persuasion, Chart, and Player are created. Click "OK" at the message confirming successful installation, then select "Exit" from the File menu in the "Persuasion 3 Setup Main Window."

INSTALL DISKS ON SERVER

There are two parts to installing disk images on a network server: the network administrator portion and the user portion.

NETWORK ADMINISTRATOR PORTION

To installing disk images on a network server:

1. Log on to the network server on which you want to install Persuasion.
2. Start Windows 3.1 and insert Persuasion Disk 1.
3. In Program Manager, choose "Run..." from the File menu and type A:\PR3SETUP A:\NET\NET.CTL, then click "OK." If the disk was not inserted in drive A, substitute the correct drive letter for "A."
4. Read the Network Licensing Agreement that appears on your screen. Click "OK" to confirm that you have full access privileges to the network server.
5. In the "Persuasion 3 Setup Main Window," select "Install disks on server" in the "Select setup options:" list box and click "Setup...."
6. In the "Select directory" dialog box, specify the drive letter and directory where you want to install Persuasion. For example, if you want to install Persuasion in the PR3IMAGE directory on the Q: drive, type Q:\PR3-IMAGE.
7. Follow the instructions on your screen, inserting disks as prompted, until Persuasion is installed. Click "OK" at the message confirming successful installation, then select "Exit" from the File menu in the "Persuasion 3 Setup Main Window."

USER PORTION

To installing disk images on a network server:

1. At the workstation from which you want to run Persuasion, log on to the network server where Persuasion is installed.
2. In Program Manager, choose "Run..." from the File menu and type X:\PR3SETUP in the "Command Line:" edit box, where X is the drive letter and path to the network directory where the disk images are located (e.g., Q:\PR3IMAGE\PR3SETUP), then click "OK."
3. If a dialog box prompting you to select a ".ctl" file appears, select the PR3_144.CTL file from the directory where the disk images are located, then click "OK."
4. Follow the normal installation instructions described in the Adobe Persuasion 3.0 User Manual, beginning with Step 3 on page 7.

General Information

WINDOWS

Q Can I use Persuasion with Windows 95?

A Yes. Although Persuasion 3.0x was not designed to be Windows 95–compliant, you should still be able to install and run it under the new operating system. But there are two issues you'll want to be aware of.

The first is that launching Chart from Persuasion will give you an "Assertion Failed!" error message. The error dialog box asks you whether to "Abort," "Retry," or "Ignore." Choose "Ignore." Chart will then launch as usual and you will see the standard "Select a Chart Template" dialog box. (One side effect of ignoring the error message, though, is that the "Select a Chart Template" dialog doesn't display completely. To correct this, simply do something to force a screen redraw, such as dragging the dialog-box window slightly.) To get more info about this, call Adobe's FaxYI number (206-628-5737) and request FaxYI document 300320 (to learn more about FaxYI, see "Adobe Products and Services," page 106–107 of this issue).

The other issue is with the 4.0 version of the PostScript driver, which shipped with Windows 95. You'll experience three things because of this driver or third-party drivers based on it: the first page of handouts will not print at all, slides containing bitmaps will not print at all, and objects with pattern fills will not print correctly. There's a FaxYI document with more information on this problem and how to work around it; call for document 300120.

Finally, if you need to remove Persuasion from Windows 95, FaxYI document 300420 will tell you how.

MAC OS

NTSC Video "Safe" Zones for Persuasion

When creating a file for video in Aldus Persuasion or other application, the "action safe" and "title safe" areas of the screen standard in National Television Standards Committee (NTSC) should be considered. By keeping important movement and text within the action and title safe zones, they won't get cut off when played back on video monitors (i.e., television screen). When creating a screen size presentation in Persuasion for Macintosh, the presentation will use the Macintosh's standard screen size of 640 x 480 screen pixels or 8.89 x 6.67 inches.

ACTION SAFE AREA

The action safe area is approximately 10% smaller than the standard screen size, 576 x 432 screen pixels or 8.0 x 6.0 inches.

TITLE SAFE AREA

The title safe area is approximately 20% smaller than the standard screen size for text, 512 x 384 screen pixels or 7.10 x 5.32 inches.

Persuasion 3.0.x and 4.x Color Systems General Information

Adobe Persuasion for the Macintosh includes the Standard color system and six other color systems, each containing a predefined sets of colors designed to be easily produced by a particular output device. Each of the six other color systems are a subset of the Standard color system, so when you edit colors in the Standard color system, the other color systems reflect the changes you made. If you edit a color in the Standard color system and then edit the same color in another color system, Persuasion does not change the color. If you edit a color in a color system before editing the same color in the Standard color system, however, Persuasion applies the changes you made in that color system.

STANDARD COLOR SYSTEM

The Standard color system uses the RGB (Red, Green, Blue) color model and contains a default set of colors optimized for color monitors, film recorders, and color printers.

GRAYSCALE COLOR SYSTEM

The Grayscale color system includes only shades of gray optimized for grayscale monitors and laser printers. Persuasion uses the formula [(Red value x 30) + (Green value x 59) + (Blue value x 11)] / 100 to convert RBG colors to the Grayscale color system.

INVERSE GRAYSCALE SYSTEM

The Inverse Grayscale color system, which includes only shades of gray, is optimized for proofing slides on a laser printer. Persuasion uses the formula [100 - ((Red value x 30) + (Green value x 59) + (Blue value x 11))] / 100 to convert RGB colors to the Inverse Grayscale color system.

NTSC VIDEO SYSTEM

The National Television Standard Committee (NTSC) color system dims vibrant colors to match the color standards for American television. In the NTSC color system, the highest possible percentage for the red, blue, or green value is 81.25%. If the red, blue, or green color value percentage is higher than 81.25%, Persuasion reduces it to 81.25% or lower, rounding to the nearest 1%.

PAL SYSTEM

The Phase Alternation Line (PAL) color system matches the color standards for European television. In the PAL system, the highest possible percentage for the red, blue, or green value is 81.25%. If the red, blue, or green color value percentage is higher than 81.25%, Persuasion reduces it to 81.25% or lower, rounding to the nearest 1%.

BLACK AND WHITE SYSTEM

The Black and White color system changes white text to black, eliminates shadows, drops fills for objects created in Persuasion, and converts color charts to grayscale. It also converts imported graphics to grayscale or outline depending on the application that created it and whether it contains embedded PostScript comments. Persuasion uses the formula [(Red value x 30) + (Green value x 59) + (Blue value x 11)] / 100 to convert RGB colors to the Black and White color system.

CUSTOM SYSTEMS

The Custom color systems include default colors from the Standard color system, which you can modify to produce the colors you want from your output device (e.g., film recorder, laser printer).

Adobe Photoshop®

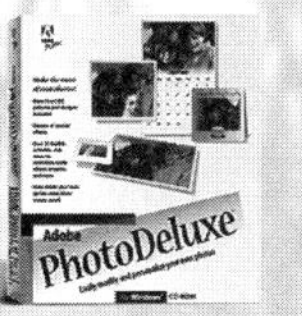

Adobe Photoshop, initially developed by the Knoll brothers, was acquired from BarneyScan by Adobe in 1988. After vast engineering improvements, it was first released in 1989. It has since become a world-wide standard, especially with Photoshop 4.0, released in November 1996. Adobe Photoshop is used to create, retouch, and enhance images for virtually every medium—from print to the Web and everything in between. Whether you're a graphic designer, photographer, multimedia specialist, videographer, or webmaster, Photoshop is it. Adobe PhotoDeluxe, a consumer product that shares the same application engine, has sold millions of copies.

Contents

Adobe Photoshop®

Feature Techniques

MAC OS / WINDOWS

Q How can I configure memory to get the best performance from Photoshop? Will virtual memory help?

A Your overall strategy should be to ensure that Photoshop can do as much of its work as possible in actual RAM, not virtual memory. Here's why.

Virtual memory is hard-disk space that your system and applications use as though it's RAM. But, compared to RAM, virtual memory is relatively slow. Information in RAM is held in a live, electrical current that your computer can read from and write to at extremely high speeds. On the other hand, when your computer reads and writes to your hard disk, it must use a much slower mechanical process.

You'll get the fastest performance if Photoshop has access to an amount of RAM equal to 3–5 times the size of the graphic file you're editing—that will be enough RAM to hold both your graphic file and the data Photoshop needs to perform calculations on it.

Here's some more specific information on how to configure memory for Photoshop.

PHOTOSHOP FOR WINDOWS

To find out the amount of RAM to which Photoshop currently has access, select "Memory" from the Preferences submenu of the File menu. In the "Memory Preferences" dialog box, check the "Available RAM" number—that's the amount of RAM Photoshop has access to (it isn't the total amount your computer has—it doesn't include the RAM Windows is already using or a certain amount of RAM Photoshop leaves available for Windows, scanner drivers, and other applications). Make sure the "Used by Photoshop" amount is set to 100% of the available RAM.

If your "Available RAM" amount doesn't equal 3–5 times the size of the image you're editing, turn off any TSR (terminate-and-stay-resident) utilities, such as drivers, screen savers, and so forth, and then relaunch Photoshop. If that doesn't give you enough RAM, consider purchasing more. *Here are some additional tips that will help you get the best performance from Photoshop for Windows:*

- Set up a Windows permanent swapfile (a type of Windows-based virtual memory) that is at least as large as your total amount of RAM. This will ensure that if Windows needs to use virtual memory, it will run as fast as possible. If you're not sure what a permanent swapfile is or how to create one, consult your Microsoft Windows Users' Guide.
- Make sure Photoshop's scratch disk is set to a hard disk that contains a large amount of unused, unfragmented space. Photoshop's scratch disk is the disk it uses to create its own virtual memory, in which it temporarily stores image data when it doesn't have enough actual RAM. To set a scratch disk, select "Memory" from the Preferences submenu of the File menu. Then, in the "Memory Preferences" dialog box, select a disk from the Scratch Disk drop-down menu.
- If you use the same disk for your scratch disk and your Windows permanent swapfile, don't make your Windows swapfile a great deal larger than it needs to be, especially if you don't have a lot of free space on the disk or if you also use that disk for your temp directory (your temp directory is defined in the AUTOEXEC.BAT file's "SET TEMP=" line). This will ensure Photoshop has access to more space to use its own type of virtual memory, the "scratch disk," and that you'll minimize the chance of encountering "Scratch Disk Full" errors.

Photoshop for the Mac and Power Mac

If possible, do not use the System's virtual memory with Photoshop. There are only a few cases in which you might benefit from using System virtual memory with Photoshop:

- If you're using a Macintosh that doesn't have enough RAM to allow you to launch Photoshop without virtual memory, and you're willing to run Photoshop at what might be an extremely slow speed, or
- If you want to be able to run several applications at once and you can tolerate a performance downgrade.

Unless one of these scenarios describes your situation, turn off System virtual memory by opening the Memory Control Panel, selecting the "Off" option under "Virtual memory," and restarting your Macintosh.

Then, if possible, allocate to Photoshop an amount of RAM equal to 3–5 times the size of the graphic file you're editing. To do so, start by finding out how much RAM you can allocate to Photoshop. At the Finder, with no applications running, select "About This Macintosh..." from the Apple menu. Make a note of the "Largest unused block" size and multiply that number by 0.9. (If the result is a lot less than 3–5 times the size of the sort of graphic files you usually edit, you should consider purchasing more RAM.) Then, select the Photoshop application icon (by clicking on it once), and enter the new value in the "Preferred size" field.

Here are some additional memory-management tips.

- Make sure Photoshop's scratch disk is set to the fastest available hard disk that contains a large amount of free, unfragmented space. Photoshop's scratch disk is the disk it uses to create its own virtual memory, in which it temporarily stores image data when it doesn't have enough actual RAM. To set a scratch disk, select "Memory..." from the Preferences submenu of the File menu. Then, in the "Memory Preferences" dialog box, select a disk from the Scratch Disk pop-up menu.
- Set your Disk Cache to the lowest possible setting—in System 7.x, that's 32K. To change your Disk Cache, open the Memory Control Panel and select a new setting from the Disk Cache pop-up menu.

Q What's the difference between layers and channels?

A If you used a version of Photoshop prior to 3.0, you're probably already familiar with channels—they're essentially 8-bit, single-color components that combine to form your image. For instance, an RGB image has three channels: a red, a green, and a blue channel. CMYK images have cyan, magenta, yellow, and black channels. In this sense, channels correspond to separation plates. In addition to these basic channels, you can also create and use "alpha channels" in Photoshop images. Alpha channels consist of 8-bit, grayscale data that you can save with your images and use in a variety of ways: to save selection areas, to mask portions of your image, and so forth.

Layers, which are new to Photoshop 3.0, offer much more flexibility than channels. Layers act a lot like acetate sheets on which you can store full-color image data, selection areas, masks, and so forth. Furthermore, you can create different composite effects with layers by altering their opacity, blending modes, and other features.

Q Is there a way I can export a non-rectangular shape from Photoshop, or a way to make parts of my image invisible if I use it in another program?

A Yes. One way to get a transparent image is to use a bitmap (one-bit or black-and-white) image. In one-bit images, the "white" areas are always transparent, or "invisible." If you want part of another type of image to be "invisible" when you export it to another program, you can use a clipping path.

Photoshop lets you export clipping paths drawn with the pen tool and saved with your image in EPS format. For an overview of how to use clipping paths, see the Adobe Photoshop 3.0 User Guide, pages 88–91.

Q I can't seem to save my Photoshop files in any format other than Photoshop's native file format, but I can open all kinds of files. Can't Photoshop save to other formats?

A Photoshop can save to many file formats, but virtually all file formats have some limitations on the kind of data they support. Before attempting to save a Photoshop document to any specific format, check to be sure it contains appropriate data. Here are some guidelines on the kinds of data that can limit your "Save As" format options.

If your document contains layers or transparent pixels, the only format you'll be able to save to is the Photoshop 3.0 format, since that's the only format that supports layers and transparency. (By the way, documents saved in Photoshop 3.0 format can be opened in Photoshop 2.5 if saved with the "Photoshop 2.5 Format Compatibility" option checked in the "More Preferences" dialog box.) If you flatten the image (select "Flatten Image" from the Layers palette menu), many other file-format options should become available.

Just be sure to save a copy of your document with the layers intact first if you want to be able to manipulate the layers later. Alternatively, you can choose "Save a Copy..."

TIP MAC OS / WINDOWS

Creating drop shadows for text *(3.0 only)*

Here's an easy, flexible way to create a drop shadow for text using layers.

1. Create a new layer and call it "shadow." To do so, click on the new-layer icon in the Layers palette.
2. Type your text, without anti-aliasing, in black on the new layer. Leave it selected.
3. Duplicate this layer by clicking on it in the Layers palette and dragging it onto the new-layer icon. Name it "text."
4. Set the foreground color to be the color you want to use for your text.
5. Select "Fill" from the Edit menu. In the "Fill" dialog box, select "Foreground Color" from the "Use" list and make sure the "Preserve Transparency" option is selected. Click "OK."
6. Move the colored text slightly to offset it from the underlying black text, which will become its shadow.
7. Select the "shadow" layer by clicking on it in the Layers palette.
8. Deselect the text, then select "Gaussian Blur" from the Blur submenu of the Filter menu. In the "Gaussian Blur" dialog box, set a radius of approximately 2 to 3 pixels and click "OK."
9. If it's too dark, try reducing the shadow layer's opacity in the Layers palette.

TIP MAC OS / WINDOWS

Easy dodging and burning *(3.0 only)*

With Photoshop 3.0's Layers feature, you can use different painting tools to apply dodging and burning without having the changes affect your image until you're satisfied with the results. Here's how.

1. Click the new-layer icon in the Layers palette to open the "New Layer" dialog box. Enter a name, like "dodge and burn," select "Soft Light" from the Mode pop-up menu, and select the "Fill with Soft-Light-neutral color (50% gray)" option. This fills the new layer with a 50% gray color, which indicates no changes in the "dodge and burn" layer.
2. Make sure both the Background and "dodge and burn" layers are visible. (You'll know a layer is visible when it appears with an eye icon in the Layers palette.)
3. Using any of the painting tools, such as the paintbrush or airbrush tools, paint on your dodging and burning effects. Paint with white where you want to lighten the image; paint with black where you want to darken. To paint on subtle effects, reduce the painting tools' opacity or pressure settings in the Options portion of the Brushes palette. To get a quick look at how much dodging and burning you've done, make your Background layer invisible (click on its eye icon in the Layers palette) and look at your "dodge and burn" layer—the black parts are where you've darkened the image and the white parts are where you've lightened it. Any neutral gray areas represent parts of the image you haven't changed.

If you want to undo all your work, you can delete the entire "dodge and burn" layer. Or, if you want to return only certain parts of your image to their original state, try this: Make your background layer temporarily invisible (click on its eye icon in the Layers palette) so you'll just see the "dodge and burn" layer. Using the eyedropper tool, click in a 50% gray area to make your foreground color 50% gray. Then make the Background layer visible again (but keep your "dodge and burn" layer the target layer) and use the painting tools set at 50% gray to paint the areas you want to return to their original lightness value.

from the File menu, which automatically saves a flattened copy of the image without affecting the original.

Extra channels ("alpha" channels, which are generally used for storing masks and selection areas) will also prevent you from saving your image in most formats. The only file formats that support alpha channels are Photoshop 2, Photoshop 3, TIFF, PICT, TARGA, and the RAW file format. So if your document contains alpha channels you'll need to discard them by dragging them to the trash icon in the Channels palette before saving to other formats.

Some of the file formats that Photoshop can save to also require that a Plug-in be installed, so if you can't seem to save to a particular file format, check to be sure you have the necessary Plug-in installed in Photoshop's Plug-ins folder. File formats that require Plug-ins include Amiga IFF, Amiga HAM, BMP, CompuServe GIF, Filmstrip, MacPaint, PCX, Pixar, PixelPaint, and Targa.

Some file formats also require that a specific color mode be used. For example, only files in Indexed Color, Bitmap, or Grayscale mode can be saved in CompuServe GIF format; before an image can be saved in the Scitex CT format, it must be in RGB, CMYK, or Grayscale mode; and the MacPaint format requires Bitmap mode.

There are also a few file formats that have special restrictions or requirements. For example, Photoshop can open Kodak Photo CD files but can't save to the Kodak Photo CD format, and Photoshop can save to the Filmstrip format only if the file being saved originated as a Filmstrip-format file and you haven't done anything to change the image's file size in Photoshop.

One more note: remember that not all file-format saving options are located in the "Save As" dialog box. The Export submenu of the File menu is the place to go for the "Amiga HAM..." and "Paths to Illustrator..." options.

Q I have Photoshop images containing transparent areas, but they don't stay transparent when I import them into other programs. Is there a way to do this?

A Yes. Transparency—or the appearance of transparency—can be achieved in several ways. Each method has certain advantages and disadvantages. Here's an overview of the various options.

Use a clipping path. If your image will be printed to a PostScript device, the best way to achieve transparency in a color or grayscale image is probably to use a clipping path.

Essentially, a clipping path does to your image what a cookie-cutter does to cookie dough: the shape of the clipping path "clips" the image, so only the area within the shape gets used. When you print an image with a clipping path, it tells your PostScript printer which portions of the image to print, and which portions to ignore.

If you're not sure how to define a clipping path, see your Photoshop manual.

After defining your clipping path, you'll need to save it with your image in one of two ways. Most applications that can recognize clipping paths saved with images can only do so if that image is saved in the EPS format. To save an image as an EPS with a clipping path, select "Save As..." from Photoshop's File menu, and in the save dialog box, select "EPS" from the "Format" pop-up menu (if it's grayed out, you probably have extra channels or layers that you'll need to flatten by selecting "Flatten Image" from the Layers palette's pop-up menu), and click "Save." When Photoshop displays the "EPS Format" dialog box, select your clipping path from the "Path" pop-up menu, and click "OK."

Some applications, like PageMaker 6.0, support TIFFs with clipping paths. If you'd like to save your image as a TIFF with a clipping path (which offers certain advantages over the EPS format—for instance, you'll be able to use compression on the image, print it to non-PostScript devices, and edit it more easily), you'll need to follow one extra step before saving. Select "Clipping Path..." from the Paths palette's pop-up menu. In the "Clipping Path" dialog box, select your clipping path from the "Path" pop-up menu, and click "OK." Then, save your image as a TIFF—Photoshop will embed the clipping path in it automatically.

Save black-and-white images in the "Bitmap" (one-bit) mode. Most applications treat the "white" pixels in one-bit images as transparent, so if you're working with a black-and-white image you'll be importing into another program, all you need to do to achieve transparency is to make sure you're working in the "Bitmap" mode and save your image in an appropriate format.

If you'll be importing that image into PageMaker or another application that treats one-bit TIFFs as transparent, save your image as a TIFF. Then, if you want to assign a color to that image, you can do so in the other program. In most applications, one-bit TIFFs behave as transparent images whether you print to a PostScript or non-PostScript device.

If you want to use your image in an application that doesn't support TIFFs or that doesn't treat one-bit TIFFs as transparent (for instance, Illustrator), save your image as an EPS. Select "Save As..." from Photoshop's File menu, and in the save dialog box, select "EPS" from the "Format" pop-up menu. Click "Save." When Photoshop displays the "EPS Format" dialog box, select the "Transparent Whites" option and click "OK." All the white pixels in your EPS will be treated as transparent pixels when you print to any PostScript device.

For World-Wide Web pages, use transparent GIFs. If you're creating an image for an HTML page on the World-Wide Web, save it as a GIF with a transparent background. A new Plug-in for the Macintosh version of Photoshop makes it possible to export files to the GIF89a format, with transparent backgrounds and interlacing. This Plug-in, called "GIF89 Export" is now available on Adobe's BBS, Adobe's World-Wide Web home page, and Adobe forums on America Online and CompuServe. For information on how to use these services, see pages 118–19.

To use the new GIF89 Export Plug-in, simply copy the Plug-in to your Photoshop Plug-ins folder and restart Photoshop. Once the new Plug-in is loaded, you can choose "GIF89 Export" from the Export submenu of Photoshop's File menu. In the "GIF89 Export" dialog box, you have the option to designate a color to behave as though it's transparent, and you also have the option to save the file as an interlaced GIF (a GIF that draws on screen in several stages of increasingly higher resolution), for quicker display in Netscape and other World-Wide Web browsers. For additional information on the GIF89 Export Plug-in, refer to the "ReadMe" file included with the Plug-in.

There are also shareware programs that can take a GIF file and designate one of its colors as transparent. For the Macintosh, "Transparency" by Aaron Giles is available from http://guru.med.cornell.edu/~giles/projects.html. For the PC, there's "LView Pro" by Leonardo Haddad Loureiro, which can be downloaded from ftp://oak.oakland.edu/SimTel/win3/graphics/lviewp1b.zip.

Q Whenever I print a document from Photoshop, it prints centered on the page. How can I get it not to be centered?

A Photoshop always places your image in the center of the page when printing. If you want your image placed elsewhere on the page, there are two options available.

The easiest way is usually to save your Photoshop document in a file format that can be placed into another application (such as TIFF or EPS), then place the image in a page-layout or illustration program and simply move it to where you want it to appear on the printed page.

You can also change where Photoshop places your image on a printout by increasing the size of the canvas. Select "Canvas Size..." from the Image menu. In the "Canvas Size" dialog box, you can enter numerical values for height and width; if you increase either dimension, you can control which side of the image the space gets added to by clicking parts of the "Placement" diagram. (The extra space it adds will be filled with your current background color, so be sure you've set your background color to white.) Photoshop will still center the canvas on the page when it prints, but your image will be off-center within the canvas. Note that achieving the exact page placement you want will probably take some trial and error. Also, be aware that increasing the canvas size increases the size of the file.

Q *(3.0 only)* **I'd like to use nonprinting guides in a Photoshop document, like the ones I use in PageMaker. Is there any way to do this?**

A Not directly, but you can create lines on a separate layer and use them as guides to help you arrange objects in your document. First create a new layer, select it, and delete all the pixels in it (press Ctrl + A in Windows or Command + A on the Mac, and then press the Backspace or Delete key),

MICRO TIP MAC OS / WINDOWS

When you use the drag-and-drop method to transfer a selection area or an entire layer to a new layer in another image, you can constrain the placement of that selection area or layer by holding down your Shift key while you place it—that will ensure the selection area or layer is positioned in the center of the target image.

making the layer transparent. Then use Photoshop's line tool to draw whatever guide lines you want.

On the Macintosh, there's also a shrewdly designed Plug-in called "Grid" by Chris Cox that will draw you a grid of regularly spaced lines in the currently selected layer of your Photoshop document; you can specify the spacing and thickness of horizontal and vertical lines, and whether you want them drawn using your current background or foreground color. "Grid" is shareware; to find it on America Online, go to the Macintosh Graphics Forum (keyword MGR) and search for "ChrisCox."

However you generate these lines, remember that they are not nonprinting—before you print, make their layer invisible or delete it. If you're flattening your document, you'll have to delete the layer first or the grid lines will become a permanent (and visible) part of your image.

Q *(3.x only)* **I've been creating images in Photoshop for my World-Wide Web page, and I need to make the backgrounds transparent. I've tried using a shareware application and a Photoshop Plug-in to achieve transparency, but it doesn't make my background completely transparent. Is there any way to get it right?**

A There are several programs and Plug-ins to help you achieve the appearance of transparency in GIF images for Web pages, but they all depend on your having a single, pure color in the image that you can designate as your background color; then, when viewed in some Web browsers (such as Netscape Navigator), the designated color is treated as if it were transparent. You can get into trouble, though, if your image's background contains more than one color. You could edit the image in Photoshop and change all the background pixels to a single color, or you could use Adobe's new GIF89a Export Plug-in. The Plug-in is available for both Windows and the Macintosh, and can be downloaded at no charge from Adobe's online sites (see the end of the first answer in this section for details). The Windows version is downloadable as a separate file; the Mac version is available only as part of the 3.0.5 update to Photoshop (see the first question).

One of the handy features of the new GIF89a Export Plug-in is that it allows you to select multiple colors for transparency. You can also designate a channel to be used to generate the transparency mask. (See the illustrations on this page for more detail.)

Q *(3.x only)* **I'm interested in writing my own Plug-ins for Photoshop. Is there an easy way to do this?**

A That depends on your definition of "easy." If you're an experienced programmer, you might want to get a copy of the Photoshop Plug-ins Software Developers Kit (SDK). There are separate Windows and Macintosh Photoshop SDKs available on Adobe's Web site, which you can download and use at no charge (the URL is http://www.adobe.com/Support/ADA.html). You'll need experience writing in C or C++ in order to write Plug-ins using the SDK. If you're interested in developing commercial Plug-ins, you may also want to consider joining the Adobe Developers Association (ADA); information and membership applications are available at the URL listed above. If you don't have access to the Web, you can call the ADA at (415) 961-4111.

If you're not a programmer, you can still try your hand at creating Photoshop Plug-ins by using Photoshop's Filter Factory Plug-in. The Filter Factory Plug-in, which ships on all Photoshop 3.0x CDs, allows you to create custom effects and then save them as your own Plug-ins, which can then be used like other Photoshop Plug-ins. The Filter Factory Plug-in is not installed automatically, so you may never have run across it: you need to locate it on the Photoshop 3 Deluxe CD-ROM and copy it to your Plug-ins folder. You can find the Filter Factory Plug-in (as well as some examples and documentation on its use) in the GOODIES\FFACTORY directory (Windows) or the "Filter Factor" folder in the "Other Goodies" folder (Macintosh). Once you've copied the Filter Factory Plug-in to your Plug-ins folder and restarted Photoshop, you should see a new category in your Filters menu called "Synthetic." For information on how the Filter Factory's controls work, refer to the documentation that accompanies it.

Achieving a specific effect with the Filter Factory Plug-in can require a strong knowledge of Photoshop and mathematics, but even if you're a mathophobe you can easily come up with some interesting effects by experimenting.

Q **I want to upgrade my computer so it can run Photoshop faster. Am I better off investing my money in more RAM or in getting a faster CPU?**

A It's impossible to answer definitively without knowing what kind of system you have and what kind of work you do, but generally you'll get more of a performance boost

TIP MAC OS / WINDOWS

Cross-cloning

Photoshop's rubber-stamp tool is very handy for cloning one part of an image into another. But did you know you can clone from one open Photoshop document into another, as long as they share the same color mode (such as RGB, CMYK, etc.)? Simply open both documents side by side; you'll need to arrange the windows so you can see both the place in your source document from where you'll be cloning and the portion of the target document where you want the material to end up. Then, with your source document active, choose the rubber-stamp tool and Alt/Option-click to define your source point; then move the cursor over the target document, click once to make it active, and simply paint with the stamp tool, cloning pixels right out of the source document.

TIP MAC OS / WINDOWS

Using Color Range to make a mask

Certain images lend themselves to using separate colors or combinations of colors to make a mask. In this example, the apple is made up mostly of red. By isolating the red, you can easily make a mask for the apple. You can also add other colors to build more complex masks using the Color Range feature.

1. Open the image containing the object you want to make a mask of. Using the lasso tool, make a rough selection just outside the object.
2. Choose "Color Range..." from the Select menu. When the "Color Range" dialog box appears, move it to the side of the screen so you can view your image. Make sure the "Select" pop-up menu is set to "Sampled Colors" and that the "Selection" option (not the "Image" option) is selected.
3. Click on the predominant color in your selection with the plain eyedropper in the "Color Range" dialog box. This will select any like-colored pixels located within the boundary you "lassoed" in step 1.
4. To add more pixels to the selection, place the eyedropper either on the image selection or on the mask in the "Color Range" dialog box, and click while holding down the Shift key. To delete pixels, hold down the Ctrl key (Windows) or Command key (Macintosh) while clicking the eyedropper tool.
5. Once your selection mask looks nearly correct, move the "Fuzziness" slider in the "Color Range" dialog box to fine-tune the mask. When the mask looks cor-rect, click "OK." Or, to create the inverse of the selection area, hold down your Alt key (Windows) or Option key (Mac-intosh) as you click "OK."
6. If you want to reuse the selection, choose "Save Selection" from the Select menu and save it as a new channel.

from additional RAM. Photoshop is very RAM-dependent, and the more RAM you make available to Photoshop, the faster it will execute most of its operations.

Certainly a much speedier processor than you have now (a Pentium instead of a 386, or a PowerPC instead of a 68040) will perform many tasks faster, but upgrading just your processor can give you disappointing results if other parts of your setup—including RAM, bus type, and amount of free hard-disk space—are acting as bottlenecks. (For more on upgrade options, see "A Separate Piece," by James Larkin, Adobe Magazine, November 1995, page 27.)

Q I'm shopping for a new display for my computer. What benefit would I derive from getting extra VRAM? Would it make Photoshop run faster?

A More VRAM (Video RAM) wouldn't make Photoshop run any faster, but it may allow you to display more colors and/or a higher resolution on a larger screen. If you're already able to display millions of colors at high resolution on your monitor, and you're not switching to a bigger monitor, you wouldn't realize any performance benefit from adding more VRAM.

Q When I copy an object from one Photoshop document into another, I often have to resize the object being copied. I usually just make an estimate, resize the original document using the "Image Size" command, then copy it. But if I guess wrong, I have to go back and start over. Isn't there an easier way?

A Yes. Go ahead and copy the object at its present size, and paste it into the target document. Then, while it's still a floating selection in the target document, select "Scale" from the Effects submenu of the Image menu. You'll get draggable handles at the corners of the selection that allow you to resize it visually. You can hold the Shift key down to keep things proportional as you resize.

Q Is there any way that I can paint pixels with type?

A Sure—just define a custom brush, using your type character as the brush definition. When you define your own brushes, you can use anything you want: type, dingbats, squiggles, a scan of your cat—although the brush can contain only grayscale or bitmap information. Here's how.

1. If you want to use a pre-existing image as a brush, open it in Photoshop; if you want to use type or create artwork from scratch, create a new, blank document, and then enter your type or doodle away.
2. Select the artwork you want to use as a brush.
3. Double-click the brush tool in the toolbox. In the Brushes palette, click the Brushes tab and select "Define Brush" from the pull-down menu in the corner. You'll get a new, custom brush shape appended to your current brushes (look at the end of the palette—you may have to scroll down a bit to see it).
4. You can now simply choose the brush and use it like any other brush. For more control over its action, double-click it in the Brushes palette; this brings up the "Brush Options" dialog box, where you can control the spacing of the brush's effect.

Your custom brush can be up to 1,000 by 1,000 pixels—although if you make it that large, you'll see only a small portion of it in the Brushes palette. If you want to use the same brush in the future, be sure to save your current Brushes palette as a brushes file. (Choose "Save Brushes..." from the drop-down menu in the Brushes palette. To load the file later, choose "Load Brushes..." from the same menu.)

TIP MAC OS / WINDOWS

Exporting transparent drop shadows

All bitmap images, except one-bit images, are opaque. That doesn't mean it wouldn't occasionally be nice to have a color image with some parts that are transparent—say, for instance, you have a color image in Photoshop that you'll be exporting to use in a page-layout program like PageMaker, and you want that image to include a see-through shadow with soft edges. Impossible? It would be if you tried to make the shadow a part of your color image. But if you create a separate, one-bit image for your shadow, and layer that image behind a color image with a clipping path, you can do it. Here's how.

1. Save your image as an EPS with a clipping path around the area you want to be opaque. If you're not familiar with clipping paths, see the Adobe Photoshop 3.0 User Guide, pp. 88–91.
2. Select the area that will have the drop-shadow applied to it (this should be that same area around which you created the clipping path). You can do this using any of the selection tools or you can convert the clipping path to a selection area.
3. Open the Channels palette by selecting "Show Channels" from the "Palettes" submenu of the Window menu. Select the channel that gives the best grayscale representation of your selected image. Select "Copy" from the Edit menu to copy your selection to the Clipboard.
4. Select "New…" from the File menu and create a grayscale file with the same dimensions as your original image. Paste the grayscale data from your original image into your new one.
5. If your image looks too dark or light to be a shadow, adjust it using the "Levels" or "Curves" dialog box. If you do so, save your selection first by clicking the "Save" icon in the Channels palette. If your grayscale data has a lot of highlights and shadows that will give you an uneven shadow, you can flatten the gray values using the "Curves" dialog box or by using a combination of the "Add Noise" and "Blur" filters.
6. With your image still selected (or after reloading your selection area from the Channels palette), select "Border…" from the Modify submenu of the Select menu and type a value of 2–4 pixels in the "Border" dialog box. This will give you a selection area that consists of just the border of your image.
7. Select "Gaussian Blur…" from the "Blur" submenu of the Filters menu, and in the "Gaussian Blur" dialog box set a low value. (Try starting with a value of 1.5 pixels and experiment until you find a blur value that will give your shadow the right look. It'll help if you zoom in on one of your image's edges and turn the "Preview" option on in the "Gaussian Blur" dialog box.)
8. Once you're happy with the shadow edge of your image, select "Bitmap…" from the Mode menu. When Photoshop displays the "Bitmap" dialog box, select the "Diffusion" pattern option and enter an output resolution value appropriate for your final output device. If your final output will be to a printer that uses laser toner, try 200 dpi. If you'll be imagesetting to film for printing on a commercial press, try 600 dpi. If you want to fine-tune the effect, work with your service providers to print some test images.
9. Save your image as a TIFF.
10. When you bring the images into your page-layout or illustration program, place the opaque, full-color EPS on top of and slightly offset from the TIFF shadow image. If the shadow image overlays any background elements, make sure it's set to overprint. (In PageMaker, create a 100% tint of Black and turn on the overprinting attribute for that color. Then assign the new color to your shadow.)

Here are a few more tips if you use PageMaker. Be sure not to use the "Image control" feature on your shadow image (this would convert it to a grayscale, opaque image). If you import the shadow image as a TIFF, PageMaker will automatically crop extra border areas, so if you want the TIFF to be its original size (to help you place it accurately), use the cropping tool to uncrop it.

This technique is based on a tip from Michael Tompert of tompert design, Palo Alto, Calif.

You probably already have some interesting, alternative brush shapes you can try out—they're part of Photoshop's default installation. On Windows, they're in a file called ASSORTED.ABR located in the PHOTOSHP/BRUSHES folder; on the Mac, the file is called "Assorted Brushes," and it's in the "Brushes & Patterns" folder within the "Goodies" folder, which is in the same folder as the Photoshop application. To try them out, use the "Load Brushes…" command on the Brushes palette.

Q I have a grayscale image I want to print in a 60% tint of a Pantone ink. How can I accomplish this?

A There are several ways. The simplest might be to import the grayscale image into a page layout program, then tint it there with the PMS color. Another way to accomplish the same thing would be to use Photoshop's Duotone feature to convert the file to a "monotone," tinted with the PMS color, and then save it as an EPS file. Here's how.

1. With your grayscale image open, choose "Duotone..." from the Mode menu. In the "Duotone Options" dialog box, choose "Monotone" from the Type pop-up menu.
2. Click on the color square (which will probably be black) to open the "Custom Colors" dialog box. If this brings up the "Color Picker" dialog box instead, click the "Custom" button to open the "Custom Colors" dialog box. In the "Custom Colors" dialog box, select the Pantone color upon which you want to base your tint, then click "OK" to close the "Custom Colors" dialog box.
3. Back in the "Duotone Options" dialog box, click on the curve box (between the color square and the words "Ink 1"). Then, in the "Duotone Curve" dialog box, enter your desired tint value (in this case, 60%) in the field labeled 100% (the 0 field should have a 0 in it, and all other fields should be blank). The resulting curve should be a straight line beginning in the lower-left corner (0) and ending along the right edge at 60%.
4. Click "OK" to close the "Duotone Curve" dialog box, then once more to exit the "Duotone Options" dialog box. Save the file in EPS format.

Q When I'm making a complex selection using the lasso tool, my hand sometimes gets fatigued—but if I release the mouse button, the selection area completes itself in a straight line. Is there any way to give my hand a rest as I work on a selection?

A There are a couple of keys that can help. The Shift key allows you to add to a selection area, so you may be able to make part of your selection, give your hand a rest, and then hold down the Shift key and add some more to the selection. However, this can get tricky—it's easy to wind up with unselected zones sticking into your desired selection area.

If you want the luxury of stopping and starting while using the lasso tool, you can use the Alt (PC) or Option (Mac) key to give your hand a break. When you hold down Alt/Option while using the lasso tool, it draws a straight line to the next place you click the mouse. If you want to rest your mouse hand while lassoing, hold down Alt/Option and then release the mouse button (and the entire mouse, if you want). As long as you don't let go of the Alt/Option key, Photoshop will wait patiently for your next mouse click. When you're ready to mouse around some more, carefully reach for the mouse again and—without moving it—click down the mouse button and then let go of the Alt/Option key. You should be right back to where you were when you gave your hand a break.

Q In Illustrator and FreeHand, you can cut a path using the scissors or knife tool. Is there any way to do this with a path in Photoshop?

A There's no tool specifically designed to cut paths, but you can accomplish the same thing easily. First, it's a good idea to zoom in to a highly magnified view of the part of the path you want to cut. Then use the Path palette's pen+ tool () to add three points close to each other along the path. Switch to the arrow tool and select the middle point of the three, then press the Delete key on your keyboard, deleting that point. Your path should now be cut in two.

Q *(3.0 only)* **When I'm compositing images, irregularly shaped elements often seem to bring a "halo" of their background with them, no matter how carefully I've selected them. Is there any way to get rid of this without a lot of painstaking, pixel-by-pixel handwork?**

A Fortunately, there usually is: Photoshop's "Matting" feature. While the element in question is still a floating selection, choose "Matting..." from the Select menu and you'll see three choices: "Defringe...," "Remove Black Matte," and "Remove White Matte." If the halo around your element is black or white, try one of the latter two options. If it's a different color (or a mixture of colors), or if you want more control over the effect, choose "Defringe...."

In the "Defringe" dialog box, you can enter the width, in pixels, of the "halo" or fringe you want to eliminate. When you click the "OK" button, Photoshop recolors those pixels with the colors of nearby ones. In many cases this will eliminate a halo entirely, even one containing multiple colors.

These functions can work wonders and give you a realistic composite, but it's important to be careful when using them. If used too often or carelessly, "Remove Black Matte" and "Remove White Matte" can make your edges too well defined to look realistic. And "Defringe" can affect areas other than the edge, so watch for surprises elsewhere in your selection area.

Q Space on my hard drive is pretty tight. Until I get a new, bigger drive, will it work for me to run Photoshop off a server?

A In a word, no. We recommend running Photoshop only off a local hard drive. If you try to run it over a network (which may or may not work at all), you probably won't like the speed at which Photoshop runs. The Photoshop application itself, your operating-system software, and Photoshop's designated scratch disk(s) should all be on local, nonremovable media drives.

We also suggest working on your documents locally, rather than over a network. That is, if you want to work on a file that resides on a network drive, copy that file to your local drive, then open it in Photoshop and work on it there; when you're done, save it (on the local drive), then copy it back to the server.

TIP MAC OS / WINDOWS

Lose weight without dieting! *(3.x only)*
Unless you regularly need to open your Photoshop 3.0x documents in version 2.5, you can make your files that use layers a lot smaller by turning off the "2.5 Format Compatibility" option (which is on by default). To turn it off, choose "General..." from the Preferences submenu on the File menu; in the "General Preferences" dialog box, click the "More..." button. In the "More Preferences" dialog box, uncheck "2.5 Format Compatibility." For those individual instances when you really do want 2.5 format compatibility, you can simply open the file in Photoshop 3.0, turn that option back on, and resave the file.

Q Which is a better format for saving Web graphics, GIF or JPEG?

A That depends on what kind of image you have, and what you want to do with it. Each file format has its advantages and disadvantages (as well as its proponents and detractors), and most browsers in common use support both.

GIF89a (the latest version of the GIF format) allows you to create files with interlacing, meaning that they appear in most Web browsers as a low-res image that increases in "stripes" toward sharp resolution; GIF89a also supports transparency, so that designated areas of the image allow the background to show through. But since GIF files must by definition be in Indexed Color mode, your image can contain no more than 256 colors. For many graphics, 256 colors is plenty. But if you have a photographic-type image, or an image with many subtle gradations in color, your image may not look quite right if saved as a GIF.

JPEG files, in contrast, can be saved in full 24-bit color (millions of colors), so they lend themselves well to images that require high-quality color. However, they don't support transparency or interlacing. (There is a new file format, Progressive JPEG, which displays in a series of increasingly high-resolution images, but it's not widely supported yet.)

Compression is intrinsic to the JPEG format, and GIF supports compression. JPEG compression is "lossy"—that is, some image data is discarded—so it's a good idea to avoid saving an image in JPEG format repeatedly, since the image quality will degrade slightly each time the image is compressed (saved) and decompressed (opened). GIF compression is nonlossy—but, of course, only 256 or fewer colors can be present in the image.

Q I work with AutoCAD files all the time. Is there any way to save a Photoshop file to DXF format?

A Not directly, but there's a Plug-in from Knoll Software called CyberMesh that will let you export a grayscale Photoshop file as a 3-D model in DXF (Data eXchange Format) or ElectricImage FACT format. Gray levels are interpreted as heights, with black treated as lowest, white as highest; models can be rectangular, spherical, or cylindrical. For information on CyberMesh, which sells for $49, contact Knoll Software at (415) 453-2471.

Q I have some Photoshop artwork I want to wrap around a globe. Is there any way to do this in Photoshop, or do I need to get a 3-D rendering application?

A You can't do this manually in Photoshop, but there's a Plug-in that will let you wrap Photoshop images around simple shapes. Andromeda Software's Series 2 filters allow you to apply any Photoshop image to spheres, planes, and rectangular solids while controlling lighting, shading, viewpoint, and other settings. It's not a substitute for a full-blown rendering application, but if your needs are modest, it may be all the 3-D rendering you need. It retails for $79.95; contact Andromeda Software at (805) 379-4109.

Q An artist has supplied me with some EPS files that I want to open in Photoshop; I have Illustrator, but they weren't created in Illustrator. Is there any way to get them into Photoshop?

A You have a couple of options. If you're on the Mac and you have Illustrator 6.0, chances are you're in luck. Although previous versions of Illustrator could generally open only EPS files that it had created (and PDF files), Illustrator 6.0 will open EPS files from most applications. Once a file is opened in Illustrator, save it as a standard Illustrator file, which Photoshop will be able to open and rasterize.

If you're using a PC, or you're on the Mac but don't have Illustrator 6.0, there are also several third-party applications and utilities that can convert and/or rasterize EPS files so that Photoshop can open them. These include epsConverter (Mac, shareware), from Artemis Software, which comes on the Photoshop 3.0 Deluxe CD (in the "Third Party Products" folder in the "Other Goodies" folder); TransverterPro (PC/Mac), from TechPool Inc., (216) 382-1234; and Epilogue (Mac), from Total Integration Software, (708) 776-2377.

Q I have lots of Plug-ins, and would rather not load all of them every time I launch Photoshop. Is there any way to load various "sets" of Plug-ins for different purposes?

A Certainly there is, as long as you don't mind restarting Photoshop every time you change Plug-in sets. There are two basic approaches you can take.

One is simply to create a series of folders (or directories), each with a different name, and each containing a group of Plug-ins you want to load for a given purpose. Then, from within Photoshop, choose "Plug-ins..." from the Preferences submenu of the File menu. Navigate to the folder you want to load and click the appropriate button ("OK" in Windows or "Select [folder name]" on the Mac). Then quit and restart Photoshop.

Alternatively, you can manipulate folder names and locations when Photoshop isn't running, taking advantage of the fact that, by default, Photoshop will load whatever Plug-ins folder it last loaded (unless you've deleted Photoshop's preferences file, that is). So, for instance, if Photoshop last loaded a folder called "Plugins1," you can simply give that folder a different name, and name the one you now want to load "Plugins1." As long as it's in the same location as the identically named folder was before, Photoshop will load those Plug-ins when it next launches.

On the Mac, you have an additional option. If Photoshop isn't already running, you can hold down the Command + Option keys when launching it; a dialog box will appear asking you to choose a Plug-ins folder.

Q I've begun authoring Web pages and have a graphic I want to use as an image map. Can I save an image map from Photoshop?

A No, Photoshop can't save image maps (areas of a graphic that act as clickable links on the Web). But you can save your Photoshop document as a PICT, JPEG, or GIF file and import that into a Web page you're creating in PageMill. Once it's in PageMill, you can create your image map there.

Q Is there any way to kern type in Photoshop?

A Not in the sense that you do in PageMaker or Illustrator, with precise, numerical control over spacing. If you want that kind of control over your kerning in Photoshop, you should probably set and kern the text in Illustrator, then import and rasterize it into Photoshop. However, it's possible to do some manual "kerning" of letters as graphic objects, by selecting and moving them.

The best way to accomplish this is probably to create a new, transparent layer and type your text onto it. Then you can select individual letters with the lasso tool and use the left and right arrow keys on your keyboard to nudge the selection in either direction.

If you don't want to create a new layer (or can't, since you're using a version of Photoshop prior to 3.0), you have an alternative, though it's trickier. Click Photoshop's type tool in your image, type your text in the "Type Tool" dialog box, and click "OK." While the type is still a floating selection, hold down the Ctrl key (PC) or the Command key (Mac); the type tool will temporarily change to the lasso tool. Drag the tool around the letter or letters you don't want to move, deselecting them. You can then use the arrow keys to nudge those that are still selected. Of course, this technique's usefulness is limited by the fact that, once a given letter is deselected, you can't move it anymore. (Even if you can manage to select it, moving it will leave blank pixels underneath.)

TIP MAC OS / WINDOWS

Creating rainbow blends

It's easy to make a two-color blend in Photoshop, but how can you make a multicolored rainbow blend, like the one shown here? It's easy—just follow these steps.

1. Create a new layer by clicking on the New Layer icon in the Layers palette. When the "New Layer" dialog box appears, select "Screen" from the Mode pop-up menu and click "OK."
2. With the new layer selected, use the marquee tool to make a selection roughly the width that you want the rainbow to be. Next, select the brightest red in the spectrum for the foreground color, and a bright magenta for the background color.
3. Double-click the gradient tool to open the Gradient Tool Options palette. Select "Counterclockwise Spectrum" from the "Style" pop-up menu, set "Midpoint" to 60%, and select "Linear" from the "Type" pop-up menu. With the gradient tool selected, place the cursor at the top of the selection area. Drag to the bottom of the selection, holding down the Shift key to ensure the gradient angle is perfectly vertical.
4. Press Ctrl + D (Windows) or Command + D (Mac) to deselect the rainbow, and then rotate the entire image 90° clockwise by selecting "90° CW" from the Rotate submenu of the Image menu.
5. Run the Shear filter on the rainbow layer by choosing "Shear" from the Distort submenu of the Filter menu. Move one or more points slightly along the curve to shape the rainbow like an arc and select the "Repeat edge pixels" option. Click "OK." Next rotate the entire image back to its original position by selecting "90° CCW" from the Rotate submenu of the Image menu.
6. Fine-tune the posi-tion of the arc by selecting "Free" from the Rotate submenu of the Image menu and dragging one of the handles to adjust the rainbow's angle. Click inside the selection when you're done. Finally, use the move tool if you want to move your rainbow.
7. With the layer still selected, choose "Gaussian Blur..." from the Blur submenu of the Filter menu. Adjust the radius value until the rainbow has a soft blur in the preview window.
8. Use the eraser tool to erase any extra rainbow area.

This technique came to us from Russell Brown, senior art director at Adobe Systems.

Q *(3.0.x only)* **Is there any way to perform operations on more than one layer at once—like applying effects, or moving them around?**

A You can't edit more than one layer at once, but you can move multiple layers simultaneously. To do so, click in the Layers palette on one of the layers you want to move, to make sure it's the active layer. Then, in the second column in the Layers palette, click on any additional layers you want to move together. The link icon (which looks just like the move tool) will appear, indicating which layers are linked. Then select the move tool from the toolbox and, in the main document window, drag the linked layers to the desired position.

Q I have a friend who has a copy of Adobe Photo-Deluxe. Can we exchange files?

A Sure, although there are some limitations you should be aware of due to the fact that PhotoDeluxe's feature set is more limited than Photoshop's.

Photoshop can open any file saved from PhotoDeluxe. But if you're saving a Photoshop file that's bound for PhotoDeluxe, your best bet is to save it in native Photoshop format or TIFF. Also, because PhotoDeluxe works in RGB only, you'll get the most predictable results if you convert the image to RGB in Photoshop before saving it.

PhotoDeluxe supports a maximum of six layers, so if you try to open a Photoshop file containing more layers than that, PhotoDeluxe gives you a warning message and then, if you elect to proceed, flattens the image. Similarly, PhotoDeluxe supports only five blending modes, so if you've used a Photoshop blending mode that's not one of those five, you'll get a message warning you that PhotoDeluxe will convert that mode to "Normal." Paths are not supported at all in PhotoDeluxe, so all path information in a Photoshop file gets discarded.

Note that PhotoDeluxe always opens an untitled copy of a Photoshop file, so there's no danger of losing data in your original file.

Q I'm new to Photoshop and am a little overwhelmed. I'd like to do some color correction on scanned photos, but the "Levels," "Curves," and "Color Balance" dialog boxes are a bit over my head right now. Are there any easier ways to adjust color?

A The easiest way to make color adjustments on screen is to use the "Variations" dialog box (choose "Variations…" from the Adjust submenu of the Image menu). It's easy to use and gives you simple, direct feedback on basic color corrections. In the main part of the dialog box, your image sits inside a circle of slightly altered samples (see below). You can nudge your image's color in any direction by clicking the sample on a given side; to nudge it in the opposite direction, click the sample on the opposite side. Similarly, the images in the right-hand section let you control overall darkness and lightness. Meanwhile, at the top of the dialog box is your unaltered original next to a sample of what you've done to it.

As you become more sophisticated in your understanding of color correction, or if your needs are more exacting, you'll want to turn to the "Levels" and "Curves" dialog boxes, since they give you much more precise control over color adjustments. For a guide to using them, see "Picture Fixes," by Bruce Fraser (Adobe Magazine, July/August 1996, page 61).

TIP MAC OS / WINDOWS

Selecting transparent or opaque pixels

Ever want to select all the transparent or all the opaque pixels in a layer? There are a few methods you can use.

The long way is to use the magic-wand tool to select some of the transparent pixels, then choose "Similar" from the Select menu. If you want all the opaque pixels selected, choose "Inverse" from the Select menu.

Another way to do this is to select all the pixels in your layer by pressing Ctrl + A (Windows) or Command + A (Mac), then press one of the cursor (arrow) keys to move everything one pixel—this also changes the selection to just the nontransparent pixels. To move your image back to its original position, hit the opposite arrow key. If you want all your transparent pixels selected, you'll need to choose "Inverse" from the Select menu.

Another technique involves using Photoshop's transparency mask. On any layer in Photoshop 3.0 containing transparent pixels, there is an implied or "hidden" transparency mask that Photoshop 3.0 uses to distinguish the opaque pixels from the transparent ones on the layer. This mask can be loaded as a selection quickly and easily. Here's how.

1. Click on the layer in the Layers palette to target it.
2. Choose "Load Selection…" from the Select menu.
3. In the "Source" field, under "Channel," choose "Layer X Transparency" (where "Layer X" equals the name of the target layer)—this will select the opaque pixels. If you'd rather select the transparent pixels, check the "Invert" box. Click "OK."

To make this technique even faster, use the keyboard shortcut for loading the transparency mask. Click on the appropriate layer in the Layers palette and press Ctrl + Alt + T (Windows) or Command + Option + T (Mac)—all your opaque pixels in your layer will be selected.

Q *(4.0 only)* **When I perform scaling or some other transformations in Photoshop 4.0 and then decide to cancel them, I can't seem to find the right way to do so. What am I doing wrong?**

A The way you cancel transformations has changed. In Photoshop 3.0, when your cursor is over your transformed selection it changes to a gavel (or hammer). To make the transformation changes take effect, you click inside the selection with the hammer. If you instead want to cancel the changes, you can move the cursor outside the selection, where the hammer changes to a "cancel" cursor (a circle with a slash through it); click the "cancel" cursor and your changes are canceled.

In Photoshop 4.0, the hammer and cancel cursors are gone. There are three ways to accept a transformation: press the Enter (or Return) key; double-click inside the selection; or choose another tool and, in the resulting dialog box, click the "Apply" button. If you want to cancel your transformation, just press the Esc key (or, on the Mac only, press Command + period).

Q I want to trace the outlines of a bitmap image, and then use that outline in Illustrator. Is there any way to do that in Photoshop?

A Your best bet is a dedicated autotracing program like Adobe Streamline. However, in a pinch, you may be able to accomplish it in Photoshop. Here's how.

First, use any of Photoshop's selection tools and techniques to select the area you want to trace. Then convert that selection to a path: from the Paths palette, choose "Make Path..." (or, in version 4.0, "Make Work Path..."), then enter a value for "Tolerance" in the resulting dialog box. A low tolerance will generate a path that closely follows your selection—but be careful, since you might create a very complex path composed of so many points that it will be difficult or impossible to print. A higher tolerance will simplify the selection somewhat.

Once you've got the path defined, you can export it—from the Export submenu of the File menu, choose "Paths to Illustrator...," enter a filename, and check the "Write" window to ensure you're exporting the correct path (if there's more than one in your document). You should then be able to open the file in Illustrator (or Macromedia FreeHand), where your path will be fully editable.

Q I'm trying to make an image look like an engraving. Is there any way to do this in Photoshop?

A Try converting to a high-resolution bitmap file using a custom pattern that you've defined in Photoshop (for information on how to do this, see Adobe Magazine, September/October 1996, page 85). For your custom pattern, try using some sort of line-art scan such as wood grain.

Alternatively, you may want to check out Andromeda Software's Series 3 "Screens" Plug-in (call Andromeda at 800-547-0055 or 805-379-4109 for information).

MICRO TIP MAC OS / WINDOWS

Need to convert a floating selection to a layer? Try any of these quick methods: double-click on the floating selection in the Layers palette, or drag the floating selection on top of the new-layer icon in the Layers palette, or select "Make Layer..." from the Layer palette's pop-up menu. All these methods will open the "Make Layer" dialog box. If you usually just click "OK" to accept the default settings in that dialog box, you can bypass it by holding down the Alt key (Windows) or Option key (Mac) while double-clicking on the floating selection in the Layers palette.

Creating Transparent Images in Photoshop

An image's file format determines whether it is transparent or opaque. File formats that support transparency include 1-bit (black-and-white) TIFF images, 1-bit EPS images, and indexed color GIF images. File formats that do not support transparency include color or grayscale images saved in PICT, TIFF, or EPS format. You can create transparent images or the appearance of transparency in Adobe Photoshop 3.0.x using several file formats.

BITMAP IMAGES

Bitmap images (i.e., black-and-white, 1-bit, and line art images) designate black pixels as "on" and white pixels as "off." Because TIFF images do not specify whether the white pixels appear transparent or opaque, the application you import a 1-bit TIFF image into determines whether the white pixels are opaque or transparent. Most page layout applications (e.g., Adobe PageMaker, QuarkXPress) designate the white pixels in 1-bit TIFF images as transparent.

The white pixels in a 1-bit EPS file saved in Photoshop can be either transparent or opaque. To save a 1-bit (Bitmap mode) EPS file with transparent white pixels:

1. Choose File > Save As.
2. In the Save As dialog box, select EPS from the Format pop-up menu.
2. Name the file and click OK (Windows) or Save (Mac).
3. In the EPS Format dialog box, select the Transparent Whites option, then click OK.

GRAYSCALE AND COLOR IMAGES

Grayscale images describe each pixel as a shade of four to 256 grays, rather than using black pixels to form patterns that simulate gray shades. The white pixels in grayscale images are always opaque, because they are defined as a shade of gray.

Color images describe each pixel as a color. RGB images describe colors using red, blue, and green values, and CMYK images describe colors using cyan, magenta, yellow, and black values. Index (Palette) images are similar to grayscale images, except that they use an index to map colors into an existing RGB color lookup table. The white pixels in color TIFF, PICT and EPS files are always opaque, because they are defined as a shade of color.

CLIPPING PATH TRANSPARENCY

You can create the appearance of a transparency in opaque images using a clipping path. A clipping path is an vector path that masks areas in an image. The pixels outside the clipping path are treated as if they are transparent, and the areas inside the clipping path treated as if they are opaque. (note: If you use a clipping path to mask an object with a feathered edge, the clipping path defines the edge of the image and the image prints with a hard edge instead of a feathered edge.) Photoshop 3.0.x can include clipping paths in images saved in Photoshop, EPS or TIFF file formats; Photoshop 2.5.x and earlier can include clipping paths in Photoshop or EPS images.

EPS files containing a clipping path appear transparent when saved with a Macintosh screen preview (i.e., PICT preview), but display opaque when saved with a Windows screen preview (i.e., TIFF preview). The EPS files print transparent to a PostScript printer, however, when saved with either type of preview.

To save an EPS file with a clipping path:

1. Create a selection around the portion of the image you want to be opaque.
2. Choose Windows > Palettes > Show Paths.
3. Select Make Path from the Path palette pop-up menu.
4. In the Make Path dialog box, set the tolerance value, then click OK.
5. Select Save Path from the Path palette pop-up menu.
6. Name the path, then click OK.
7. Choose File > Save As.
8. Select EPS from the Format pop-up menu.
9. Name the EPS file, then click OK (Windows) or Save (Macintosh).
10. In the EPS Format dialog box, select the path from the Clipping Path pop-up menu, set the other format options (e.g., Encoding, Preview), then click OK.

For more information about clipping paths in Photoshop, refer to the Adobe Photoshop User Guide, the Clipping Paths.PDF file in the Photoshop Tech Notes folder in the Technical Library folder on the Photoshop 3.0 for the Macintosh Deluxe CD-ROM, or the 4254.PDF file in the techlib\tecnotes subdirectory on the Photoshop 3.0 for Windows Deluxe CD-ROM.

TRANSPARENT GIF FILES

When you save an indexed color image as a GIF file using the GIF89a plug-in, you can designate certain colors as transparent. (GIF files created by selecting the CompuServe GIF file format in the Save As dialog box are opaque.) Photoshop 3.0.5 includes the GIF89a plug-in.

To export a transparent GIF file in Photoshop using the GIF89a plug-in:

1. Install the GIF89a Export plug-in into Photoshop's Plug-ins folder (Windows) or the Acquire/Export folder in Photoshop's Plug-ins folder (Macintosh).
2. Restart Photoshop, then open the your file and convert it to Indexed Color mode by choosing Mode > Indexed Color. You must convert to Indexed Color mode to access transparency options in the GIF89a Export dialog box.
3. Choose File > Export > GIF89a Export.
4. In the GIF89a Export dialog box, select the colors you want to designate as transparent, then click OK.
5. Name the GIF file, then click Save.

Several applications and utilities can designate an opaque color in a GIF file as transparent, including Adobe PageMill, the Transparency shareware utility for the Macintosh, and the LView Pro shareware utility for Windows.

Creating Clipping Paths in Photoshop

To mask or crop an image, Adobe Photoshop includes a clipping path option. Clipping paths create the illusion of a transparent background for an opaque image (e.g., grayscale TIFF image, color TIFF image) by cropping or masking out areas of the image. PostScript's clipping path command "clippath" describes a path that masks out areas of an image outside of the clipping path, so only the area of the image within the clipping path displays and prints. The EPS (Encapsulated PostScript) graphic format supports clipping paths.

A clipping path is a PostScript object, and although the path is invisible when printed, the printer interprets the path as it does other PostScript objects. Clipping paths are often too complex for PostScript devices to print. When a clipping path's complexity exceeds the printer's available memory, the printer returns the limitcheck PostScript error or fails to print the object or file containing the clipping path. By simplifying clipping paths, you can avoid PostScript printer errors caused by insufficient memory.

TIP MAC OS / WINDOWS

Getting back to basics

Sometimes, when you've been altering settings in one of Photoshop's dialog boxes, things get out of hand to the point where you'd rather just start that task over. Fortunately, you don't have to cancel out and re-enter that dialog box. In most of Photoshop's dialog boxes you can reset all the values to what they were when you entered that dialog box. Hold down the Alt key (Windows) or the Option key (Mac) and the "Cancel" button should change to "Reset"; click on it, and all the dialog box's settings will be reset to their previous values.

TIP MAC OS / WINDOWS

Penless clipping paths

Have you ever tried to create a clipping path, only to end up frustrated with the pen tool or disappointed by a path that doesn't look quite right? Working with clipping paths doesn't have to be difficult—there are lots of ways to create them, and some methods are more efficient than others.

It's natural to assume that you need to define a clipping path using the pen tool—after all, the pen tool lives in the Paths palette—but that isn't so. The pen tool can be a great way to draw simple, geometric paths, yet it can be rather awkward if you need to draw along an irregularly shaped object, or you're not used to pen-tool drawing. In many cases, you might be better off creating a selection area for your object and converting that selection area to a path. Here's how.

To get the selection you want, you can use any of the selection tools and/or techniques that you're comfortable with: loading a saved selection, using the lasso or magic-wand tools, selecting by color with the "Color Range" feature, painting a mask, and so forth. See "Chapter 4: Working with Selections" in your Adobe Photoshop User Guide for more information.

Once you're satisfied with your selection, go to the Paths palette (if you don't see the Paths palette, select "Show Paths" from the Palettes submenu of the Windows menu). Then select "Make Path..." from the Paths palette's pop-up menu. In most cases you can just click "OK" in the "Make Paths" dialog box to accept the default "Tolerance" value of 2 pixels. (This setting tells Photoshop how exactly to follow your selection outline when making a path. If your selection is very complex, a low tolerance value may result in a path that's too complex for your printer to process, in which case you may need to enter a higher value.) After clicking "OK" in the "Make Path" dialog box, you should see "Work Path" listed in the Paths palette. Finally, save your path. You can do so either by double-clicking on "Work Path" or by selecting "Save Path..." from the Paths palette's pop-up menu. When the "Save Path" dialog box appears, enter a name for your path and click "OK.".

To create a clipping path in Photoshop 3.0.x and 2.5.x:

1. In Photoshop, choose Windows > Palettes > Show Paths (Photoshop 3.0.x) or Window > Show Paths (Photoshop 2.5x).
2. Draw a path by using the pen tool or by making a selection with a selection tool, then choose Make Path from the Paths palette menu.
3. Save and name the path by choosing Save Path from the Paths palette menu.
4. Specify the path as a clipping path by choosing Clipping Path from the Paths palette.
5. In the Clipping Path dialog box, select the saved path from the Path pop-up menu in the Clipping Path dialog box.
6. Enter a flatness value in the Flatness text box, if desired, then click OK.
7. Choose File > Save As.
8. In the Save dialog box, select EPS from the Format pop-up menu.
9. Specify the desired options in the EPS Format dialog box, then click OK.

SIMPLIFYING COMPLEX CLIPPING PATHS

PostScript devices cannot print complex paths when the number of straight lines that describe the path exceeds the printer's internally defined limit. The higher the printer's resolution, the more straight lines are required to describe a curve, which requires more printer memory. Because curve or complex paths require less printer memory when printed to a low-resolution device (e.g., 300dpi) compared to a high-resolution device (e.g., 2400dpi), ensure the file containing a complex path prints to a low-resolution device before printing the file to a high-resolution device.

To simplify paths in Photoshop, do one or more of the following:

A. Decrease the number of points used to describe the path by deleting points or by using the pen tool to redraw a path created by the Make Path command.
B. Increase the flatness by entering a higher value in the Flatness text box in the Clipping Path dialog box. Specifying a flatness value enables the PostScript printer to flatten curves, where the higher the flatness values the fewer the number of straight lines are required to describe the curve. Setting a flatness value that is too high causes the curve to become angular, which decreases the quality of the curve. The flatness value required to print a complex path at acceptable quality varies depends on the resolution of the printer. As a guideline, specify a Flatness value of 8 to 10 for high-resolution printing and a Flatness value of 0 to 3 for low-resolution printing.
C. Increase the Tolerance value in the Make Path dialog box. The Tolerance value can range from 0.5 to 10 pixels. The higher the tolerance, the fewer anchor points are used to draw a path.
D. Specify that Photoshop write the PostScript code for clipping paths using the non-zero winding number rule,

instead of the even-odd rule. When using Photoshop 3.0.x, install the Even-Odd to Winding Rule plug-in, included with Photoshop 3.0.x, by moving the Even-Odd to Winding Rule plug-in and the About Even-Odd to Winding Rule ReadMe file from the Optional Extensions folder on the Install-Disk 1 installation disk to the Photoshop Plug-ins folder. When using Photoshop 2.5x, select the Even-Odd to Winding Rule option in the Clipping Path dialog box.

Creating Mezzotints in Adobe Photoshop

This technical note applies to both the Macintosh and the Windows versions of Adobe Photoshop. Please note that the Control and Alt keys in the Windows version function as the Command and Option keys in the Macintosh version, respectively. In the following text, the Windows key is given after the Macintosh key.

A mezzotint is a random, nondirectional pattern produced in traditional printing, by exposing an image to a specially designed halftone screen. The mezzotint image, when magnified, appears composed of randomly shaped dots. This technical note describes how to create a mezzotint pattern in Adobe Photoshop and how to apply the pattern to your image as a halftone screen.

In Adobe Photoshop, you can create a true mezzotint only in Bitmap mode by using a mezzotint custom pattern when you convert a Grayscale mode image to Bitmap. In all other modes, you can simulate the appearance of a

TIP MAC OS / WINDOWS

Creating seamless tiles in Photoshop *(3.0 only)*

Seamlessly tiled images used as backgrounds for World-Wide Web pages are becoming increasingly popular with the growing use of Netscape 1.1 (which, unlike some Web browsers, supports background images). Seamless tiles—images that when laid out in a grid appear to be one continuous image—are easy to create in Photoshop.

There are two basic approaches: using an existing image and modifying it so it tiles well, and creating a new tileable image from scratch. (In either case, make sure the image is small—128 pixels by 128 pixels works best in most cases.)

If you're using an existing image, chances are you'll have to do some editing along its edges to make it tile well. The easiest way to do so is to choose "Offset…" from the "Other" submenu of the Filter menu. Choose values for the horizontal and vertical offset that are roughly half the image's dimensions along those axes, and set the "Undefined Areas" option to "Wrap Around." This will let you see how the edges will work when you tile. Then, using the rubber-stamp tool, sample portions of the image and clone them over the vertical and horizontal seams. Resample from many different sources within the image so you don't get a noticeable repetition. If you're careful, you should be able to eliminate any remnants of the seams. (When you're finished fixing the seam, you can leave the image offset—that won't affect how it tiles—or, if you prefer, you can use the Offset filter again with identical but negative values, to put the image back together.) To check your work, see the instructions in the last paragraph of this tip.

Making your own tileable image offers a lot more flexibility. Several filters that ship with Photoshop will create seamless images that don't require any additional modification. Version 3.0's Clouds and Difference Clouds filters (found on the Render submenu of the Filters menu) are underappreciated filters that generate beautiful, organic-looking cloud textures based on your foreground and background colors.

Images created using these filters are likely to tile well as long as your tile size is 128 pixels by 128 pixels (or some multiple of 128 pixels). Photoshop's Add Noise and Extrude filters can also create quick and easy seamless tiles.

Once you've generated a texture using one of these filters, you can use other filters (or other techniques) to make them more interesting. For example, applying the Adobe Gallery Effects Emboss Plug-in to a clouds texture creates an interesting, stucco-like effect. (Note that some filters can cause changes to the edges of your tile that will need to be cleaned up using the "Offset" filter, as described above.)

Other third-party Plug-ins open up limitless possibilities for seamless tiles, including KPT Texture Explorer and KPT Seamless Welder, from HSC Software; Alien Skin's Textureshop; MicroFrontier's Pattern Workshop; Andromeda's Series-1 Designs; and Xaos Tools' Terrazzo (which stands out for its ability to create nonrectangular images reminiscent of kaleidoscopes or mystical symbols).

When you're done creating or modifying your image, check to make sure it really tiles seamlessly. Select the entire image (press Ctrl + A in Windows or Command + A on the Mac) and choose "Define Pattern" from the Edit menu. Next, open up a new document that's large enough to fit the tile in many times over. In the new document, select "Fill…" from the Edit menu; in the "Contents" field of the "Fill" dialog box, select "Pattern." Click "OK." Your document will be filled with your tiles. If it checks out OK, you can then save your tile document into whatever format you're using for your Web-page graphics.

mezzotint by creating a pattern and applying it to an image, but Adobe Photoshop will print the image with a regular halftone dot. You must use traditional printing methods to print a true mezzotint that uses a randomly shaped halftone dot.

Adobe Photoshop supplies patterns, created in Adobe Illustrator (and Adobe Illustrator for Windows), which can be used to apply mezzotint effects. The patterns are located in the PostScript Patterns folder (in the Brushes & Patterns folder in the Adobe Photoshop folder or on the Adobe Type Manager disk in Photoshop 2.0) and in the Adobe Collectors Edition: Patterns and Textures, which is a collection of artwork that can be used with Adobe Illustrator and Adobe Photoshop to paint objects with patterns. You can also create your own pattern by using one of the following procedures.

To create a mezzotint pattern in Adobe Photoshop:

1. Open a new grayscale document.
2. Choose Noise>Add Noise from the Filter menu. In the Add Noise dialog box, set the noise amount, and select Gaussian distribution to distribute the pixels randomly.
3. Apply a softening filter, such as the Blur or Blur More filter, to the pattern.
4. Choose All from the Select menu (Command/Ctrl+A); choose Define Pattern from the Edit menu. The defined pattern remains in memory until you quit Adobe Photoshop or define another pattern. You can use this pattern to create a mezzotint effect.

To define an existing Adobe Illustrator pattern as an Adobe Photoshop pattern:

1. Make sure that you are running both Adobe Photoshop and Adobe Illustrator.
2. In Adobe Illustrator, open a pattern, and select the pattern tile. Deselect Mask in the Paint Style dialog box in the Paint menu to remove any masks. Hold down the Option/Alt key while choosing Copy from the Edit menu; this command sequence places a PICT (TIFF) version of the pattern on the Clipboard.
3. In Adobe Photoshop, open a new grayscale document, and paste the pattern into the document. Choose Paste As Pixels and Antialiased. Click OK. To eliminate white space around the pattern, crop the image so that it contains only the pattern.
4. Blur the pattern using the Blur or Blur More filter.
5. Choose All from the Select menu (Command/Ctrl+A); choose Define Pattern from the Edit menu. The defined pattern remains in memory until you quit Adobe Photoshop or define another pattern. You can use this pattern to create a mezzotint effect.

To apply a mezzotint to a black-and-white image:

1. Create a Photoshop pattern or define an Adobe Illustrator pattern as a Photoshop pattern, as described in the preceding procedures.
2. Open the image to which you will apply the mezzotint pattern. If necessary, choose Grayscale from the Mode menu to convert the image to Grayscale mode.
3. Choose Bitmap from the Mode menu to convert the Grayscale image to Bitmap. In the Bitmap dialog box, select the following options:

   Resolution: For the best results, increase the output resolution to a value higher than the input resolution. This produces a larger file, but of higher-quality output.

   OR: Method: Custom Pattern.
4. Click OK. The mezzotint pattern is applied to the Bitmap image. Print the Bitmap image for a true mezzotint.

You can also display and print the image with a mezzotint effect in modes other than Bitmap. To do so, choose Grayscale from the Mode menu to convert the image back to Grayscale mode. In the Grayscale dialog box, make sure that the Size Ratio is set to the default of 1. Click OK.

To apply a mezzotint to an RGB image:

1. Create a Photoshop pattern or define an Adobe Illustrator pattern as a Photoshop pattern, as described in the preceding procedures.
2. Open the RGB image to which you will apply the mezzotint pattern.
3. Choose Split Channels from the Channels palette menu. Splitting the RGB channels results in three separate files of the image: Red, Green, and Blue.
4. For each Red, Green, and Blue file, choose Grayscale from the Mode menu to convert the file to Grayscale mode.
5. For each Red, Green, and Blue file, choose Bitmap from the Mode menu to convert the file to a bitmap. In the Bitmap dialog box, select the following options:

   Resolution: For best results, increase the output resolution to a value higher than the input resolution. This produces a larger file but yields better-looking results.

   OR: Method: Custom Pattern.
6. Click OK. The mezzotint pattern is applied to the Bitmap image.
7. For each Red, Green, and Blue file, choose Grayscale from the Mode menu to convert the image back to Grayscale mode. In the Grayscale dialog box, make sure that the Size Ratio is set to the default of 1. Click OK. (Important: You must convert all three channels back to Grayscale to be able to merge them in the next step.)
8. Choose Merge Channels from the Channels palette menu. In the Merge Channels dialogue box choose the Mode and number of channels. Click OK. Specify the three separate RGB channels that you created in step 2, and click OK. Click OK again. This step converts all three channels to RGB mode. Any additional channels contained in the file will be lost when the channels are merged.

Using Separation Tables from Other Applications

Adobe Photoshop allows you to use separation tables created in other applications to convert images to CMYK mode. This feature enables you to replicate a separation from other applications that perform color separations, such as ColorStudio, Cachet, and Color Access.

Once you create a table for RGB-to-CMYK conversions, you can also create a table for the CMYK-to-RGB conversions that Adobe Photoshop uses to display the CMYK image on the monitor (monitors are RGB devices) and ensure the most accurate on-screen display of separated colors.

CREATING SEPARATION TABLES IN OTHER APPLICATIONS

The following procedures outline the steps involved in creating a separation table in another application. For detailed information about a specific application, please refer to that applications documentation. The second section in this document provides step-by-step information on creating a table from EFI Cachet.

1. In Adobe Photoshop 2.5, open the Lab.Tif file located in the Calibrate folder.
2. Convert the file to RGB mode.
3. Save the file as a TIFF file, giving it a descriptive name such as PhotoRGB.Tif.
4. In the other application, open the Photoshop RGB file, and convert it to the CMYK mode using the desired separation options.
5. Save the file as a TIFF file, giving it a descriptive name such as CachtSWP.Tif.
6. In Adobe Photoshop, open the TIFF file and save the file in the Raw format using the following dialog box settings: Header: 0; Interleaved Order. This creates a table that gives Adobe Photoshop access to the mode-conversion algorithm used in the other application.
7. To use the table, close the file in Photoshop, then rename it to replace the .TIF extension with an .AST extension.
8. Choose "Separation Tables" from the "Preferences" submenu of the File menu, then use the "Load" button in the "Separation Tables" dialog box to load the .AST file renamed in step 7. When you convert an RGB image to the CMYK mode, Photoshop will use the separation algorithm in this table.

To create a table for CMYK-to-RGB conversions in most applications:

1. In the other application, open the CMYK Colors file in the Adobe Photoshop Calibrate folder.
2. Convert the file to RGB mode.
3. Save the file as a TIFF file, giving it a descriptive name such as CachetRGB.Tif.
4. In Adobe Photoshop, open the RGB TIFF file, and convert it to Lab mode.
5. Save the file in the Raw format, using the same dialog box settings shown in the previous illustration. This creates a table you can load through the "Separation Setup" dialog box, as described in the previous section.

Creating Separation Tables in EFI Cachet

The following procedures describe how to create and use separation tables from EFI Cachet both to separate RGB documents and to display CMYK documents on your RGB monitor. After creating both tables, use them to create a single, two-directional table, following the instructions in the final section of this document.

To create an RGB-to-CMYK table in Cachet:

1. Open the Lab Colors file located in the Calibration folder in Adobe Photoshop.
2. Convert the file to RGB mode.
3. Save the file as a TIFF file, giving it a descriptive name such as PhotoRGB.Tif.
4. In Cachet, open the Adobe Photoshop RGB file as a file intended for corrections.
5. Choose "Save Separations" from the File Menu.
6. Select the desired separations options, and save the file with a descriptive name such as CachetSWP.Tif.
7. In Adobe Photoshop, open the file you just saved.
8. Save the file in the Raw format with the options shown in the Raw Options dialog box in the preceding section of this tech note.

Load the separation table in the Adobe Photoshop "Separation Tables" dialog box using the procedure described in the first section of this tech note.

To create a CMYK-to-RGB table in Cachet:

To ensure that Adobe Photoshop accurately displays your custom CMYK separations on an RGB monitor, create a custom CMYK-to-RGB table for using Adobe Photoshop. This gives you the closest possible match between the screen and printed output.

NOTE: You must have Cachet v1.0.1 to open a CMYK file.

1. In Cachet, choose "Import" from the File menu. Select the Cachet Importer and import the file for corrections.
2. Import the file CMYK Colors from the Adobe Photoshop Calibration folder using the TIFF format.
3. In the "Cachet Importer Setup" window, select a color space profile such as "Swop Coated."
4. Click "Translate" to convert the file to RGB mode.
5. Save the file as a TIFF file with a descriptive name such as CachtRGB.Tif.
6. In Adobe Photoshop, open the TIFF file you just saved.
7. Convert the file to Lab Color mode.
8. Save the file in the Raw format with the options shown in the Raw Options dialog box in the preceding section of this tech note.

Load the separation table in the Adobe Photoshop "Separation Tables" dialog box using the procedure described in the first section of this tech note.

TIP MAC OS / WINDOWS

A finer grid for curves

Ever wished you could increase the number of grid squares displayed in Photoshop's "Curves" dialog box? You can. Simply Alt-click (Windows) or option-click (Macintosh) anywhere within the grid area to toggle between four and ten grid divisions.

TIP MAC OS / WINDOWS

Putting the pieces back together

If you've received the preseparated C, M, Y, and K plates from a Photoshop DCS (desktop color separation) file, but you need to go back into the file to make revisions, you can easily reassemble the composite image from the DCS separations—even if you don't have the original composite file that was used to create them.

To do so, open all four plates—they should each have a common file name followed by a .C, .Y, .M, and .K extension. (If you're using Photoshop on a PC, you'll need to select "Open As…" from the File menu, and make sure "*.*" is entered in the "File Name" text box and that "EPS" is selected in the "Open File as Format Type" drop-down menu.)

Then, from Photoshop's Channels palette, select "Merge Channels…." In the "Merge Channels" dialog box, choose "CMYK Color" from the "Mode" pop-up menu, and in the "Merge CMYK Channels" dialog box, you map the four DCS separations to the CMYK channels (and if the file names follow standard naming conventions, they should be mapped correctly by default). Click "OK" and you should wind up with a single, untitled CMYK composite file. You can then make your changes and save the image back into DCS format.

CREATING A TWO-DIRECTIONAL SEPARATION TABLE

Once both tables are loaded in the "Separation Tables" dialog box, create a single, two-directional separation table that Adobe Photoshop can use for both RGB-to-CMYK conversion and CMYK-to-RGB conversion. To do this, click the "Save" button in the "Separation Tables" dialog box. Give the table a name you will easily recognize, such as Cachet.Ast or Colortab.Ast. Use the "Load" button to load the table.

The new table will be used for all future mode conversions. To quit using the table, select the "Use Separation Setup" and "Use Printing Inks Setup" options in the "Separation Tables" dialog box.

Working with Type in Adobe Photoshop

To work effectively with type in Adobe Photoshop, it helps to understand a few fundamental concepts.

Pixels are small squares that make up a digital image; an object defined by pixels is called a bitmap. Type in Adobe Photoshop does not look as sharp as type printed from a vector-based application such as Adobe Illustrator because Adobe Photoshop is a pixel-based application that generates bitmapped type at the resolution of the image. In contrast, vector-based applications generate type as mathematically described outlines that can be scaled and manipulated independently of the image resolution.

To improve the way fonts are displayed on-screen, make sure that you have installed the Adobe Type Manager (ATM) software included with Adobe Photoshop. ATM rasterizes or creates bitmap versions of PostScript language outline fonts. Therefore, you must install outline fonts on your Macintosh for the best display and printed results. For Windows, the fonts must be stored in the PSFONTS directory as both .PFM and .PFB files. If type in Photoshop appears extremely blocky on-screen, ATM is probably not installed or is installed incorrectly. See the "Adobe Photoshop Getting Started" guide for information on installing and using ATM.

The image resolution is defined by the pixels per inch (ppi). In Photoshop, image resolution determines the highest resolution at which an image can be displayed or printed. If your image resolution is 72 ppi, the image will print at a resolution of 72 dots per inch (dpi) on a printer, even if the printer can print at 2540 dpi.

Continuous-tone images, such as photographs, don't need a high image resolution to look good when printed. This is because the images are typically halftoned when printed. Halftoning simulates the gray values with screens of small dots. Continuous-tone images need an image resolution about twice as large as the line screen used to print the images (for example, 300 ppi for an image printed with a halftone screen of 150 lines per inch).

To produce type with sharp edges, however, the image resolution must be significantly higher. Type is usually not halftoned. In a pixel-based application like Photoshop, the sharp edges of type must be reproduced pixel by pixel. To produce type in Photoshop with the sharpness of a 2540-dpi printer, the image containing the type would need a resolution of 2540 ppi. However, a 2540-ppi image would create an enormous file that would be difficult, if not impossible, to edit and print.

One way to achieve type with sharp edges in Adobe Photoshop is to use the Anti-aliased option in the type tool options dialog box. Turning on this option blurs the edges of type and minimizes the pixelization of the type, making it appear sharper and less jagged.

To achieve the best-looking type, you should create type in a vector-based application such as Adobe Illustrator. If you have a continuous-tone image to which you want to add type, you can import the image into Adobe Illustrator and then add the type using Adobe Illustrator tools. You can also place type created in Adobe Illustrator into your Adobe Photoshop image. Creating type in Adobe Illustrator gives you much more flexibility and control.

TIP MAC OS / WINDOWS

Recipe cards for Photoshop

Many users overlook Photoshop's "File Info" features. Selecting "File Info..." from Photoshop's File menu opens a dialog box containing several fields that can store text, which gets saved along with your file. These fields are designed to be used for photo captions, credits, and the like, as well as category and keyword information that can be searched using Adobe Fetch or other image-cataloging applications. But you can enter any kind of text information you want.

Have you ever achieved cool Photoshop effects one day, only to be unable to remember weeks or months later how it was you got that effect? You can use the "File Info" feature to store production notes on your techniques. The "Caption" field can hold up to 2,000 characters in an editable, scrollable field.

Try keeping a small text editor (such as SimpleText or Notepad) open as you work, and record the steps you use along with dialog-box settings. This can serve as a text "recipe" of how you achieved your final effects. When you're finished with your document, copy the text from the text editor, switch over to Photoshop, select "File Info...," and paste your recipe into the "Caption" window. Months later, if you want to recreate the same effect, you can retrieve your recipe from the file's caption and follow the same steps.

Using the Emboss Filter with Layers

This technical note applies to both the Macintosh and the Windows versions of Adobe Photoshop. Please note that the Control and Alt keys in the Windows version function as the Command and Option keys in the Macintosh version, respectively. In the following text, the Windows key is given after the Macintosh key.

Adobe Photoshop provides a wide range of possibilities for special effects. The following technique illustrates an effect you can create with color images using the Emboss filter and layers. Although the following procedure applies to an RGB image, the same procedure works with other types of color images.

To use the Emboss Filter with Layers in Adobe Photoshop:

1. Copy the image by choosing All from the Select menu (Command/Ctrl+A) and Copy from the File menu (Command/Ctrl+C).
2. Convert the image to grayscale by choosing Grayscale from the Mode menu. When prompted whether you want to discard the color information, click OK.
3. Choose Stylize from the Filter menu and Emboss from the submenu. Accept the default values by clicking OK. Experiment with inverting the image by choosing Map from the Image menu and Invert from the submenu (Command/Ctrl+I); choose Undo from the Edit menu (Command/Ctrl+Z) to toggle between the image and the inverted image. You may prefer the embossed, raised look, or you may prefer the concave look.
4. To increase the contrast of the image, choose Adjust from the Image menu and Brightness/ Contrast from the submenu (Command/Ctrl+B). Increase the contrast and brightness as appropriate. This adjustment adds more definition to the image.
5. Choose RGB from the Mode menu to return to RGB mode.
6. Choose Paste Layer from the Edit menu to paste the image from the Clipboard; this pastes the contents of the clipboard onto a new layer.
7. Choose Color from the Mode menu in the Layers palette to replace only the color values (not the lightness values) of the underlying pixels with the pixels in the pasted image.
8. Experiment with these Mode options to create unusual effects: Darken, Lighten, Color, Multiply, and Screen. You can also use the opacity slider setting to affect the opacity of the layers. For more information about layers, see Chapter 8 of the "Adobe Photoshop User Guide."

Exporting CMYK Files to Other Applications

When your project involves process color printing, your RGB image must eventually be separated into four pieces of film or paper. Each piece of film or paper will be printed with a different color ink usually cyan, magenta, yellow, and black (CMYK). Adobe Photoshop does an excellent job of separating images by converting your RGB images to CMYK. See the "Adobe Photoshop User Guide" for more information about creating separations.

EXPORTING CMYK FILES TO OTHER APPLICATIONS

Most illustration and page-layout programs support the Encapsulated PostScript file (EPS) format. EPS is also the preferred format for exporting CMYK files to these applications or to save CMYK files in TIFF format. When exporting CMYK files in the EPS file format to other applications, specify various options to enhance printing and processing in the EPS Format dialog box. The options are described in detail in the following sections.

Before you export a CMYK file to another application:

1. Make sure that your file is in CMYK mode.
2. Choose Save As from the File menu.
3. Choose EPS from the File Format pop-up menu. The EPS Format dialog box appears.
4. Select the desired options, as described in the following sections; then click OK.

To export files to Adobe Illustrator:

1. Choose Save As from the File menu and EPS from the File Format pop-up menu. The EPS Format dialog box appears.
2. Select a Preview option, as described in the following section, "EPS preview options."
3. Select the ASCII or Binary encoding option (Binary is recommended). For more information, see "EPS encoding options" later in this note.
4. Click Off under the Desktop Color Separation options; then click OK.

To export files to QuarkXPress:

1. Choose Save As from the File menu and EPS from the File Format pop-up menu. The EPS Format dialog box appears.
2. Select a Preview option, as described in the following section, "EPS Preview Options."
3. Select the ASCII or Binary encoding option (Binary is recommended.) For more information, see "EPS Encoding Options" later in this note.
4. Select a Master File option from the Desktop Color Separation options. The Master File options affect a composite proof only; they do not affect the high-resolution information in the file. For more information, see "Desktop Color Separation Options" later in this note.
5. Click OK.

To export files to Aldus PageMaker:

1. Choose Save As from the File menu and EPS from the File Format pop-up menu. The EPS Format dialog box appears.
2. Select a Preview option, as described in the following section, "EPS Preview Options."
3. Select ASCII encoding. For more information, see "EPS Encoding Options" later in this note.
4. Click Off under the Desktop Color Separation options; then click OK.

EPS FORMAT DIALOG BOX OPTIONS

Several EPS format dialog box options exist to enhance the printing and processing of your color separations. A detailed description of these options follows.

EPS preview options

Some graphics applications, like Adobe Illustrator, display or preview a PICT (TIFF in Windows) representation of a PostScript

language image saved in EPS format. The PICT (TIFF) preview image approximates the image when it is printed and accurately places the image on the page. Your choice of preview affects only the display, not the printout. Although your image is in color, a 1-bit black-and-white preview may be adequate and generates a much smaller file than an 8-bit preview. Select either an IBM PC or Macintosh preview.

EPS encoding options

The encoding options control the type of information that is saved in the document—either ASCII or binary. The binary option results in a file that is about half the size of an image saved with the ASCII encoding option and takes half as long to transfer to the printer. However, some applications (such as Aldus PageMaker and Aldus FreeHand) might not support binary EPS documents. For these applications, select the ASCII encoding option. In addition, some commercial print-spooling software does not support binary encoding. If you experience printing errors, your print spooler may require ASCII encoding.

Check the manufacturers suggestions, or experiment to determine whether to use ASCII or Binary encoding.

Include Halftone Screens Option

Adobe Photoshop allows you to set your screens in the Page Setup dialog box and then include those screen settings

TIP MAC OS / WINDOWS

Customizing the Commands palette

Are you a keyboard-shortcuts person? If not, is it because you have trouble remembering which shortcuts are assigned to which keys? In either case, you can probably get a lot out of Photoshop's Commands palette.

Using the palette, you can assign keystrokes to most of Photoshop's menu items, which means you can perform those operations from the keyboard without having to grab the mouse. And if you have the Commands palette showing, you'll also have an on-screen reminder of what keyboard shortcuts you've assigned (not to mention clickable buttons for those commands, if you prefer).

Select "Show Commands" from the Palettes submenu of the Window menu, then select "Edit Commands..." from the palette's drop-down submenu. You can then assign new keyboard shortcuts, delete or edit existing commands from the palette, and reconfigure the layout of the commands. Other options on the drop-down menu let you save a set of commands (say, for different types of projects), load a saved set of commands, reset to the default set, or even combine two different sets (by choosing "Append Commands...").

By default, the commands are listed in a single column (right), but many users find it's handy to configure the Commands palette as a thin bar extending across the bottom of the monitor (below). The maximum number of buttons that can be displayed side by side depends on the width of your monitor. In the "Edit Commands" dialog box, try entering 9 or 10—if it's too many, Photoshop displays an alert box and enters the maximum that there's room for.

TIP MAC OS / WINDOWS

Photoshop as a calculator

If you're working with an image and find yourself wondering how big the file would be at a particular size and resolution, you don't have to switch to your Windows or Mac calculator—let Photoshop do the math. Simply choose "Image Size…" from the Image menu and, in the bottom half of the "Image Size" dialog box, enter your values for width, height, and resolution. The size of the resulting file will appear where it says "New Size." (NOTE: This works only if "File Size" isn't checked in the "Constrain" line at the bottom of the dialog box.) You can do the same thing in the "New" dialog box (choose "New…" from the File menu), and there you can also specify what color mode you want. In either case, just press the "Cancel" button if you don't want to resize or create the resulting file.

when you save the files in EPS format. If you want another application, such as Adobe Separator, to set the screens — perhaps because you have additional art from other applications—deselect the Include Halftone Screens option. Check with your print shop if you don't know what screen settings to use. If you print to an imagesetter with Accurate Screens, Balanced Screens, or HQS Screens, get the manufacturers recommendations for screen settings.

Include Transfer Functions option

Transfer functions compensate for miscalibrated imagesetters. You can adjust the Transfer functions in the Transfer Functions dialog box by clicking Transfer in the Page Setup dialog box under the File menu. If you have adjusted the Transfer functions, select the Include Transfer Functions check box in the EPS Format dialog box when you save the EPS file.

For more information about Transfer functions, see the Adobe Photoshop User Guide.

Desktop Color Separation (DCS) option

The DCS option is an extension of the standard EPS format developed by Quark, Inc. for use with QuarkXPress and other applications that support the extension. If you are unsure about whether your application accepts DCS files, contact the manufacturer.

The DCS option creates five files on your hard disk: a master file and a file for cyan, magenta, yellow, and black. The master file contains a PICT (TIFF) preview of the image and a link to the other four files. All five files must be kept together in the same folder or directory. Place the master file in the host applications document. In addition, the master file may contain a low-resolution EPS image in CMYK color or grayscale for printing proofs. The low-resolution EPS image does not affect the final print separations.

Choose one of the following options to generate print separations:

- Select the Master File: No composite PostScript option to print separations only. This option does not allow you to print a composite of the placed Photoshop image.
- Select the Master File: 72 pixels/inch grayscale option to print a 72-dpi grayscale composite of the Adobe Photoshop image.
- Select the Master File: 72 pixels/inch CMYK option if you want to send a 72-dpi color composite of the Adobe Photoshop image to a color printer.

EXPORTING CMYK FILES WITH CLIPPING PATHS

The Clipping Path feature in Adobe Photoshop lets you use a path drawn with the pen tool in the Paths palette as a mask for placed files in Adobe Illustrator and other page layout applications including Aldus PageMaker and QuarkXPress. For information on using this feature, see Chapter 5 of the "Adobe Photoshop User Guide" and the technical note, "Working with Clipping Paths."

Creating a Hard-edged Border in Photoshop

Using the "Border..." command (by selecting "Modify" under the Select menu) on a rectangular selection creates an anti-aliased, rounded-corner border in Adobe Photoshop 2.01 and later. To create a border that is a non anti-aliased line with square corners, follow the instructions below.

To create a hard-edged border in Photoshop:

1. Create a selection using the rectangle selection tool.
2. Under the Edit menu, select "Stroke...".
3. Enter the desired stroke width in the "Width" box (measured in pixels).
4. Select the "Inside" option under "Location." Selecting any option other than "Inside" when stroking will not create a completely squared edge.
5. Click "OK."

ADDITIONAL INFORMATION

Anti-aliasing partially fills the pixels surrounding a selection area so they are semitransparent, making the transition between the edges of the selection and surrounding pixels more subtle. The Border command is anti-aliased by default.

MAC OS

Q I have a document I created in PageMaker that I would like to bring into Photoshop. Is there any way to do this?

A There are several ways to bring a PageMaker document into Photoshop. One way is to convert your PageMaker file to a PDF (Portable Document Format) file, open the PDF in Illustrator and save it there, then rasterize the Illustrator file in Photoshop. For more information, see Olav Martin Kvern's Desktop Science column "On the High Wire," in the March/April 1995 issue of Adobe Magazine (page 57).

Another way to get a PageMaker page into Photoshop is to print that page as an EPS, then use a conversion utility to convert that EPS to Illustrator format (one conversion utility that'll do the trick is epsConverter by Artemis Software). Once the EPS is in Illustrator format, you can open and rasterize it in Photoshop. For more information on epsConverter and other utilities that can convert EPS files to Illustrator format, see page 83 of the May/June 1995 issue of Adobe Magazine.

Q I have a Photoshop document in indexed color mode, and I want to be able to use that palette of colors in another application. Is there a way to do that?

A Yes there is, but you'll need some kind of utility that can convert a Photoshop document's color palette to formats other applications can read.

One such program is Debabelizer, a graphics-processing application that can (among other things) extract, manipulate, and convert an image's color palette and save it to many different formats. For more information on Debabelizer, contact Equilibrium Technologies at (415) 332-4343.

Another utility that will do the trick is Praxisoft's Color Compass, which creates and converts color palettes. Although it's primarily designed for creating custom color libraries, Color Compass will also open, convert, and save color palettes to formats compatible with most popular applications including Photoshop, Illustrator, and PageMaker. It can even extract color tables from CLUT resources (color-lookup tables) and PICT files. For more information on Color Compass, contact Praxisoft at (800) 557-7294.

Q *(3.x only)* **I have lots and lots of images on my hard drive and I sometimes have a hard time tracking down the document I want. Got any suggestions?**

A One often-overlooked feature in Photoshop is its "Find" function. When you choose "Open…" from within Photoshop, the resulting dialog box contains a "Find…" button. Navigate to the disk or volume on which you want to search, and then click the button. It brings up a dialog box where you can enter the name—or a part of the name—of the file you're trying to find.

If you're looking for a more sophisticated way to catalog and search for image files, you may want to consider a dedicated cataloging application.

TIP MAC OS / WINDOWS

Selectively applying—and unapplying—effects

Have you ever wished you could paint with a special-effects filter? For example, let's say you want to play around with a Gallery Effects filter, applying it to various parts of an image with varying degrees of opacity—and you even want to "erase" the effect in certain places. By creating a new layer and then painting on a layer mask, you can. Try this:

1. In the Layers palette, select your original layer and choose "Duplicate Layer…" from the drop-down menu. We'll call the new layer "Affected layer," and it should be above the original layer.
2. Run your special-effects filter on this layer, or make any other radical changes you want. Don't worry—you're going to have unlimited "undo" options.
3. Add a layer mask to the affected layer by choosing "Add Layer Mask" from the drop-down menu on the Layers palette (be sure you've targeted the "Affected layer").
4. Fill the layer mask with solid black. The quickest way is to press the D key and then press Alt + delete (Windows) or option + delete (Mac). (Pressing D sets colors to their defaults, with black as the foreground color and white as the background; Alt/option + delete fills the layer with the foreground color.) On your screen, the layer mask will mask out (that is, hide) the affected layer completely, and you should see only the original, unaffected pixels.
5. Now swap the background and foreground colors by pressing the X key; this sets your foreground color to white and background color to black.
6. Now, with the layer mask targeted, you can paint with most of the painting tools (the paintbrush, pencil, airbrush, and so on—even the type tool for interesting type effects). Wherever you paint, the affected pixels from the layer below will be revealed. If you make a mistake and want to undo portions, just hit the X key to swap the foreground and background colors, and paint back over that area—the original pixels will be painted back.

With this technique, the only pixels you're really changing are those in the layer mask, hiding or revealing the original or affected layers as you choose. You can use the various painting modes available on the drop-down menu in the painting tool's "Paintbrush Options" palette (Normal, Dissolve, Screen, Difference, etc.) to control how your painting affects the layer mask; you can also control how the affected layer interacts with the original layer by using the drop-down menu on the Layers palette (Normal, Difference, Hue, Color, etc.). When you're satisfied and ready to make your work irrevocable, simply merge your layers or flatten the document.

TIP MAC OS / WINDOWS

Stealing splash screens

(2.x and later) If you publish any information about computers, chances are you sometimes need to reproduce a program's "splash screen"—the identifying screen that appears as the program boots up. Sure, you can catch it as you launch the program by using the Mac's built-in screen-capture capability (press Command + Shift + 3) or a dedicated screen-capture utility, and then paste or open it in Photoshop. But there's a simpler way: taking advantage of Photoshop's ability to directly acquire PICT resources.

In Photoshop, choose "PICT Resource..." from the Acquire submenu on the File menu. In the resulting dialog box, navigate to the program whose splash screen you want, and click "Open." Unless there are no PICT resources present, you'll next see the "Pict Resource" dialog box, which tells you how many PICT resources Photoshop found. Click the "Preview" button to see what they look like; the arrow buttons on each side of it scroll to previews of the other PICTs present. When you've found the one you want, click "OK."

The PICT resources that you'll find within programs (or documents) will vary, but you can usually get a program's splash screen and some other elements; a document will often yield only a preview or thumbnail. (Also, you can't acquire PICT resources from within Photoshop itself—it has a strong instinct for self-preservation.) Of course, these images will always be low-resolution, so they won't be of much use for print unless you're reducing their size considerably, but they're fine at full size for a Web page or other on-screen use. Also, remember that some of the images you extract may be copyrighted, so be sure to get permission if you have any doubt about the legality of how you're using them.

Q I have a small monitor, and it's a pain to move around a large image to zoom in and make minute changes. Can you suggest an easier way to do this?

A Yes, in a word: PhotoNavigator. This is a free Plug-in from Extensis Corporation that directly addresses your problem. PhotoNavigator is a resizable floating palette that displays a small version of whatever image you have open at the time. In this thumbnail view, you can click, drag, or use keyboard combinations to specify what area of your image you want to concentrate on. When you select an area in the PhotoNavigator window, that area displays in the large image window without redrawing.

PhotoNavigator works with Photoshop 3.0.4 or later. You can download it from the Extensis Web site at www.extensis.com.

Importing Illustrator Artwork into Photoshop

When opening Adobe Illustrator 5.x and earlier documents and EPS files, Adobe Photoshop 2.5.x or later converts Illustrator artwork into a bitmap image. When copying Illustrator 5.x elements to the system clipboard, Illustrator copies the elements in Adobe Illustrator Clipboard (AICB) format, which Photoshop is able to paste and convert into a bitmap image. Photoshop 3.0.x can paste Illustrator-drawn paths as object-oriented or bitmap formats.

Photoshop 3.0.x uses the Adobe Illustrator Parser plug-in filter to convert Illustrator artwork. When Photoshop 3.0.x cannot access the Adobe Illustrator Parser plug-in, it is unable to place, paste, and open Illustrator documents. When Photoshop 3.0.x opens an Illustrator EPS file when the Adobe Illustrator Parser plug-in is unavailable, Photoshop converts the Illustrator EPS file's 72 dpi screen preview instead of the Illustrator EPS file's PostScript code. Photoshop cannot access plug-ins when they are not installed in the folder selected in the Plug-ins Preferences dialog box or when the "Adobe Photoshop 3.0 Prefs" or "Photoshop Prefs" file is damaged. Deleting the "Adobe Photoshop 3.0 Prefs" or "Photoshop Prefs" file and relaunching Photoshop forces Photoshop to create new preferences file.

Photoshop 2.x and earlier includes built-in support for converting Illustrator files.

When opening, placing, or pasting an Illustrator document containing an unsupported fill (i.e., pattern, gradient), Photoshop converts the object's fill to a solid gray or black fill. Photoshop converts stroked text into unstroked text, but converts stroked objects, which includes text converted to outlines, with the stroke attribute. When Photoshop opens or places an Illustrator document containing an EPS file, Photoshop is unable to convert the EPS file, resulting in the placed EPS file being omitted in the converted Photoshop document. Photoshop converts Illustrator 5.x elements masked by text as unmasked and without the type; Photoshop converts elements masked by type converted to outlines as masked and with the type.

Photoshop 3.x is unable to convert the following elements in Illustrator documents:

- Imported EPS files
- Pattern fills and strokes
- Stroked text

Photoshop 2.5.x is unable to convert the following elements in Illustrator documents:

- Gradient fills
- Imported EPS files
- Pattern fills and strokes
- Stroked text
- Illustrator 5.x type that masks other elements

To open an Illustrator document in Photoshop:

1. Save the artwork in Illustrator 5.x or earlier format, in EPS file format, or for Illustrator 5.x documents containing gradient fills save in Illustrator 3 format to convert the gradient fill into a blend element.
2. Close the Illustrator document.
3. In Photoshop, choose File > Open, select the desired Illustrator file, then click Open.
4. In the Rasterize Adobe Illustrator Format dialog box (Photoshop 3.0.x) or the EPS Rasterizer dialog box (Photoshop 2.5.x), select the desired image dimensions, resolution, and color mode, then click OK.

To place an Illustrator document in Photoshop:

1. Save the artwork in Illustrator 5.x or earlier format, in EPS file format, or for Illustrator 5.x documents containing gradient fills save in Illustrator 3 format to convert the gradient fill into a blend element.
2. Close the Illustrator document.
3. In Photoshop, create a new or open an existing image.
4. Choose File > Place, select the desired Illustrator file, then click Open.
5. The Illustrator artwork imports as a floating selection inside a box centered in the image. Click on the box border or "X" to reposition; click and drag the box handles to resize.
6. Once the imported artwork's box is sized and positioned, move the pointer outside the selection box, then click when the Arrow tool changes to a Gavel to place the Illustrator document.

To paste an Illustrator path into Photoshop 3.0.x:

1. Select the path in Illustrator, then choose Edit > Copy.
2. In Photoshop, create a new or open an existing image.
3. Choose Edit > Paste.
4. In the Paste dialog box, select Paste As Path then click OK.

Acquiring or Opening a Low-Resolution Image from a DCS File in Photoshop

When a Photoshop DCS file includes a Macintosh preview, the screen preview in the main DCS file can be opened as an EPS PICT Preview or acquired as a PICT Resource. When you open the DCS main file as an EPS PICT Preview or PICT Resource, Photoshop opens the DCS file's screen preview as a 72 dpi indexed color image. When you acquire the DCS file's screen preview using the Acquire > PICT Resource command, Photoshop opens the screen preview as a 72 dpi RGB PICT graphic with the same dimensions as the original screen preview.

After Photoshop saves a DCS file with a preview icon and a screen preview, it includes in the DCS main file a 72 dpi PICT graphic the same size as original screen preview and a 72 dpi PICT graphic that is 1.5-by-1.5" or smaller. When you select the Thumbnail Preview option in the Photoshop 3.x General Preferences dialog box, Photoshop includes a preview icon. When you select the Save Preview option in Photoshop 2.x, it includes a preview icon in files.

To acquire a low-resolution (72 dpi) RGB version of an image from the main file of a DCS file:

1. Start Photoshop 2.x or later.
2. Choose File > Acquire > PICT Resource.
3. In the Acquire PICT Resource dialog box, select the DCS main file, then click OK.
4. In the PICT dialog box, click the arrow buttons to select the PICT you want to open, then click OK.

To open a low-resolution (72 dpi) Indexed Color version of an image from the main file of a DCS file in Photoshop 3.x:

1. Choose File > Open.
2. In the Open dialog box, select Show All Files, then select the DCS main file.
3. Select EPS PICT Preview from the Format pop-up menu, then click Open.

To open a low-resolution (72 dpi) Indexed Color version of an image from the main file of a DCS file in Photoshop 2.x:

1. Choose File > Open As.
2. In the Open As dialog box, select the DCS main file.
3. Select PICT Resource from the Format pop-up menu, then click Open.

Unexpected Results

MAC OS / WINDOWS

Q In my illustration program, I tried to create a CMYK background color that would match a CMYK color in a Photoshop image. I used the same color definition, but they printed differently. What happened?

A If you create two CMYK colors—one in Photoshop and another in a page-layout or illustration program—and print

TIP MAC OS / WINDOWS

On-off switch for layers

(3.0 and later) To turn off a layer mask without discarding it, you can simply Ctrl-click (PC) or Command-click (Mac) on the layer mask in the Layers palette. A red X appears in the layer mask's thumbnail in the Layers palette indicating that the layer is turned off. Simply click on the layer-mask thumbnail to turn the mask back on.

This keyboard shortcut is the equivalent of checking and unchecking the "Do not Apply to Layer" option in the "Layer Mask Options" dialog box. You can open that dialog box—which also offers controls for the mask's color, position, and opacity—by double-clicking the layer-mask thumbnail in the Layers palette.

TIP MAC OS / WINDOWS

Dots and dashes

If you need dotted or dashed lines in your Photoshop document, and don't want to (or can't) create them in an illustration program such as Illustrator, try this trick.

Say you want to create a dotted line—that is, a line made up of circular dots. Double-click the pencil tool (you can use the paintbrush tool, but your dots will have soft edges) to open the Pencil Options palette. Click the Brushes tab, pick out a circular brush of about the size you want your dots to be, and double-click it to open the "Brush Options" dialog box. Set the "Spacing" value to about 200 percent—this will cause the dots in your line to be separated by about one diameter. (If your brush shape is not symmetrical, you may need to set the spacing much higher.) Click "OK," and you're ready to draw your line. Remember that you can hold down the Shift key while dragging to make a straight horizontal or vertical line.

If you prefer drawing lines by using the pen tool, first select the pencil tool and customize the brush as described above. Then define your path with the pen tool and choose "Stroke Subpath..." from the Paths palette's pop-up menu; in the "Stroke Subpath" dialog box, select the pencil tool and click "OK." Then you can delete the path, leaving the dots.

Want a dashed line instead—that is, one with squares or rectangles instead of circles? You'll need to create or load a square brush, but be aware that it's going to work best for vertical or horizontal lines, since the squares don't rotate with the line direction. Here's how to create and use your own square brush. (Alternatively, skip steps 1 and 2 below and instead choose "Load Brushes..." from the Brushes palette menu; then navigate within your Photoshop folder to Goodies:Brushes & Patterns:Square Brushes, which will load your Brushes palette with a series of square and rectangular brushes.)

1. Create a new, small Photoshop document.
2. Click on the rectangular-marquee tool and hold down Shift while dragging to select a square of the size you want your dashes to be. Choose "Fill..." from the Edit menu and fill it with black.
3. While the square is still selected, double-click the pencil tool, click on the Brushes tab in the palette, and choose "Define Brush" from the pop-up menu on the right side. Your black square will appear as one of the brushes in the palette (you may need to scroll down in the Brushes palette to see it).
4. Double-click your new square brush. In the "Brush Options" dialog box, give it a spacing of 200 percent or more. Click "OK."

Now you can draw lines using the pencil tool as described above.

Finally, you can use a similar procedure to create rectangular dashes, but because the rectangles won't rotate with the direction of the line, you'll have to create a horizontally oriented rectangle for horizontal lines, and a vertically oriented one for vertical lines. However, if you need a lot of such lines, it may well be worth the trouble.

those colors to film on a CMYK device for color separations, your colors should match exactly if you used identical CMYK percentages. However, if you print the colors to a composite color device (or any non-CMYK device), chances are the printout of the two colors won't match exactly because Photoshop and several page-layout and illustration programs use different calibration methods for these devices.

There are several ways to address this problem. First, you can make sure both Photoshop and your page-layout or illustration program use the same calibration values for output—see their documentation for information on how to alter their calibration values. Unfortunately, that may take more time that you want to spend.

Another approach is to make the Photoshop image large enough to cover the desired area, fill its background with the color you want, and import the expanded image into your page-layout or illustration program. That, however, can result in a very large file. Instead, make a low-resolution background that results in a much smaller file.

1. In Photoshop, open the image that needs a background.
2. Select the eyedropper tool, and while holding down the Alt key (Windows) or Option key (Macintosh), sample the color that you would like to be the background color. (By holding the Alt or Option key, you'll assign your background fill color to be the color you're sampling.)
3. Select "New..." from the File menu, and in the "New" dialog box, enter the width and height needed for your background, select a resolution of one pixel per inch, choose "CMYK" from the Mode pop-up menu, and select "Background" from the "Contents" options. Click "OK." Photoshop will open your low-resolution background image, which will look very small on screen (don't worry, it's not displayed at actual size).
4. Save the file as an EPS and place it in your page-layout or illustration program.

Q I can't seem to open some of my EPS files in Photoshop. What should I do?

A Photoshop can only open EPS files saved in the Adobe Illustrator EPS format. If you want to use another kind of EPS file in Photoshop, you'll need to convert it first. Fortunately, there are several ways to do that.

TransverterPro: This application, which is available for both the Macintosh and Windows, offers a variety of features. It lets you open any PostScript or EPS file and convert it to an Illustrator 3.0– or 1.1–compatible file, which you can then rasterize into bitmap PICT or TIFF formats. In addition, it allows you to batch-process your EPS or PostScript files for conversion.

If you use TransverterPro to convert EPS or PostScript files so you can use them in Photoshop, we recommend that you not rasterize them in TransverterPro (instead, just convert them to Illustrator format). You can rasterize the file when you open or place it in Photoshop 3.0, which will offer you more rasterization options, such as anti-aliasing.

For more information on TransverterPro, contact its developer, TechPool Inc., 1463 Warrensville Center Road, Cleveland, OH 44121-2676; phone (216) 382-1234.

epsConverter: This Macintosh utility can convert almost any EPS file into an Adobe Illustrator–compatible EPS, which Photoshop can open and rasterize. If you've upgraded to Photoshop 3.0, you have epsConverter—it comes on the Photoshop 3.0 Deluxe CD. Look for it in the "Third Party Products" folder inside the "Other Goodies" folder.

epsConverter is a shareware product from Artemis Software. For more information on epsConverter, see the "About epsConverter" text file in the "epsConverter" folder on the Photoshop 3.0 Deluxe CD. You can contact Artemis Software via mail at P.O. Box 11488, Bainbridge Island, WA 98110-5488; via fax at (206) 780-0271; via E-mail at artemisSW@aol.com; or through the Artemis Software forum on America Online.

Epilogue: A collection of applications from Total Integration, Inc., Epilogue uses a configurable PostScript Level 2 interpreter to rasterize EPS and PostScript files so they can be opened in Photoshop 3.0. The Epilogue PS Plug-in module lets you preview, crop, and select an area of EPS or PostScript file to interpret, and supports anti-aliasing up to four levels (none, low, medium, and high).

Q Some of my Plug-ins aren't showing up in the Filters menu. What's wrong?

A There are several reasons why some Plug-ins might not show up on your Filters menu. If you run into this problem, try the following:

First, double-check your Plug-ins directory or folder to make sure that the Plug-in(s) you're not seeing are there or in one of its subdirectories or subfolders. In Windows, your Plug-in directory is PHOTOSHP\PLUGINS by default; on the Macintosh, it's probably in your "Plug-ins" folder within your "Adobe Photoshop 3.0" folder. If your "missing" Plug-in isn't there, find it, move it to your Plug-ins folder, and restart Photoshop.

If that doesn't work, retarget your Plug-ins folder. To do so, select "Plug-ins..." from the Preferences submenu of the File menu. In the dialog box that appears, click on your Plug-ins folder or directory to select it (do not double-click it—that will open it instead of selecting it) and click "OK" (in Windows) or "Select [name of your Plug-ins folder]" on the Macintosh. (If you're using Photoshop 2.5x on the Macintosh, click the button labeled "[name of your Plug-ins folder].") Close and restart Photoshop for your change to take effect.

If you're still having problems, you may have a damaged preferences file—try creating a new one. To do so, quit Photoshop. Then, if you're in Windows, use the File Manager to rename your Photoshop preferences file (it's called PHOTOS30.PSP if you're using Photoshop 3.0, or PHOTOSHP.PSP if you're using Photoshop 2.5x) to something like PSHOPPSP.BAK. If you're on the Macintosh, go to the "Preferences" folder within your System Folder, and rename the file "Adobe Photoshop Prefs" (if you're using Photoshop 3.0) or "Photoshop Prefs" (if you're using Photoshop 2.5x) to something like "PShop Prefs Backup." The next time you launch Adobe Photoshop it will create a new preferences file. If you had previously customized your preferences, you'll need to do that again.

If you're using Photoshop 3.0 in Windows NT and some of your third-party Plug-ins (Plug-ins not supplied by Adobe) aren't showing up in your Filters menu, chances are they aren't 32-bit and therefore aren't being recognized by Windows NT, which is a 32-bit operating system. Contact the developers of your Plug-ins to find out if they've released 32-bit versions of them.

TIP MAC OS / WINDOWS

Round 'em up!

Looking for a way to set type on an ellipse or circle? Certainly the best way is to set it up in a drawing program such as Adobe Illustrator and then import it into Photoshop. However, you can get some interesting effects in Photoshop. Try this: Set a line of type, select it using the rectangular-marquee tool, then run the Polar Coordinates filter (choose "Polar Coordinates..." from the Distort submenu on the Filters menu; in the "Polar Coordinates" dialog box, choose the "Rectangular to Polar" option and click "OK"). Your type will be distorted around a circular or elliptical shape, with the exact effect depending on the shape of the selection you chose. You may need to experiment a bit to achieve predictable results, the range of effects is limited, and the type itself becomes distorted (a result you can avoid when putting type on a path in Illustrator). But with a little creative play, you can get some pretty interesting results.

TIP MAC OS / WINDOWS

Merging individual layers

(3.0.x only) In a multilayer document, you can automatically create a new layer that consists of the data in all visible layers, without actually merging the individual layers. From Photoshop's Layers palette, hold down the Alt (Windows) or xOption (Mac) key and select "Merge Layers" from the drop-down menu. This will create a new layer that includes the merged data from all visible layers; your original layers remain unaffected. (note: To hide a layer, click its eye icon.)

Q I have a Kodak Pro Photo CD but can't open the highest-resolution images. What's up?

A If you can't open the highest-resolution Pro Photo CD images (the 75-MB or "Base 64" images), you probably need to get an updated Photo CD Plug-in.

On the PC, the version of Kodak's Photo CD Plug-in that shipped with Photoshop 3.0 won't allow users to open Pro Photo CD images at the "Base 64" resolution in Windows 3.1 or Windows for Workgroups 3.11 (but should work under Windows NT). An updated Kodak Photo CD Plug-in that does allow these images to be opened is available on Adobe's BBS (206-623-6984) and Adobe's forums on CompuServe and America Online. Download the file PCD32.ZIP, decompress it, and copy the resulting file PCDLIB32.DLL to your Windows directory, overwriting the version that shipped with Photoshop.

On the Mac, you should be able to open the "Base 64" files using the Kodak CMS Photo CD Plug-in, either version 3.0 (which shipped with Photoshop), or version 3.1.1, which is written in "fat binary" code so it contains both a 68K and a native Power Mac version of the Plug-in. Both versions are on Adobe's BBS and Adobe's forums on CompuServe and America Online.

If you have one of the correct Photo CD Plug-in versions for the Mac, but you still can't select the "Base 64" import option, some or all of the System extensions required to access those files may be missing. Be sure that the following files are present in your "Extensions" folder: "Apple Photo Access," "ISO 9600 File Access," "Foreign File Access," and "High Sierra File Access." If they're not, you can reinstall them from the System 7.5 disks (choose "Custom Install" and pick just the "CD-ROM" option under the "Multimedia" install option). If you're using an earlier version of the System software, you can get these files off the disks that came with your CD-ROM drive. If these files are present, but you're still having a problem, one or more of those files might be damaged—try reinstalling them.

Q I have a Photoshop image with a strange checkerboard pattern covering certain areas. I know I didn't put the checkerboard there. Where did it come from?

A The checkerboard pattern is just there to show you what parts of your image contain transparent pixels; the pattern displays on screen but won't print. If you want Photoshop to display the transparent pixels differently, select "Transparency..." from the Preferences submenu of the File menu. In the "Transparency Options" dialog box, you can set the transparency checkerboard to display in another color, or not at all. Although transparency is supported in Photoshop's native file format, it isn't currently supported in other formats. (Note that having "transparent" areas within Photoshop isn't the same thing as having invisible or transparent parts of an image that's been exported from Photoshop and viewed in another application. For details, see Adobe Magazine, May/June 1995, pages 84 and 86.)

Q I've recently upgraded to Photoshop 3 from version 2.5.1. I think the upgrade is great, but what happened to "Composite Controls"?

A Composite Controls are still in Photoshop, they're just in a different place now.

In Photoshop 2.5, you can control how a floating selection blends with the underlying image by selecting "Composite Controls..." from the Edit menu. In Photoshop 3.0.1, you can get the same control over how one layer blends with the layer below it by double-clicking on the layer in the Layers palette (or by selecting "Layer Options..." from the Layers palette's pop-up menu). In the "Layer Options" dialog box you'll find the same controls as those in Photoshop 2.5's "Composite Controls" dialog box.

In Photoshop 2.5 you can apply composite controls to a floating selection. However, in Photoshop 3.0 (Windows) or 3.0.1 (Mac) you can use these controls only if you're working with a layer. To manipulate blending for a floating selection in Photoshop 3.0.1, you first need to convert the floating selection into a layer.

The option to use composite-control features on a floating selection has been restored in Photoshop 3.0.4, which should be available by the time you read this (3.0.4 will be sent, on CD, to all registered owners of Photoshop 3.0). When you have a floating selection in Photoshop 3.0.4, you can choose "Float Controls..." from the Select menu to gain access to the composite-control features offered in version 2.5 (and available only for layers in Photoshop 3.0.1).

Q I have a Filmstrip file that I opened in Photoshop for some editing and retouching. Now I want to save it so I can take it back to Premiere, but Photoshop won't let me select the Filmstrip format. What's up?

A Filmstrip files—used with Adobe Premiere—can be opened in Photoshop and worked with in much the same manner that one works with any file, but if you change certain image parameters (resolution, dimensions, or color mode), Photoshop won't let you save it back into Filmstrip format. In addition, the file must have been in Filmstrip format when you brought it into Photoshop (in other words, you can't create an image from scratch or from something that started out in another format, and save it as a Filmstrip file). For more information on Filmstrip files, see the Adobe Premiere User Guide.

Q *(3.x only)* **I downloaded the Photoshop GIF89a Export Plug-in from an online service, but it doesn't seem to work with my copy of Photoshop. Should it? I'm using version 3.0.1.**

A No, the Plug-in was only designed and tested to work with version 3.0.4 and later. (Some users report that it works fine with earlier versions of Photoshop, but Adobe doesn't guarantee that it will.) Photoshop version 3.0.4 was sent free on CD to all registered users of Photoshop 3.0 late last year; since then Adobe has issued an update to version 3.0.5, which is available on disk (for Windows users) or as an online "patcher" (for Mac users). For details, see page 73 of our January/February 1996 issue, or call (800) 628-2320.

Q I think there's something wrong with the cropping tool in my copy of Photoshop. I'm trying to crop down to a 2-inch-by-2-inch section of a document. So, in the Cropping Tool Options palette, I've checked the "Fixed Target Size" box and entered my desired crop dimensions (2" x 2" at 150 pixels per inch). But when I use the cropping tool, it lets me select any size square—and then it takes that area and resizes it! What's going on?

A Your cropping tool is working fine, but it's not the right tool for the job you're trying to do. By entering a fixed target size of 2 by 2, you're telling Photoshop to take whatever area you select, crop out everything else, and scale the resulting area up or down to fit your target size. If all you want to do is crop down to a certain area, don't use the cropping tool—use the rectangular marquee tool instead. Here's how.

1. Double-click the rectangular marquee tool in the toolbox to open the Marquee Options palette.
2. Select "Fixed Size" from the Style drop-down menu, and enter your desired width and height in the text boxes. You have to enter them in pixels, but the math's not hard: just multiply your desired dimensions (in inches or centimeters, for instance) by the resolution (in pixels per inch or centimeter). In your case—2 inches square at 150 ppi—you want 300 pixels for each dimension.
3. Click the tool in your document to make your selection area appear. If it's not positioned exactly where you want it, hold down Control + Alt (Windows) or Command + option (Macintosh) and drag the selection area to its desired location.
4. Once it's where you want it, select "Crop" from the Edit menu, and Photoshop will crop away everything except the selected portion—without resizing it.

Q *(3.0.4 and 3.0.5 only)* **I'm having trouble with Photoshop's GIF89a Export Plug-in. Some of my GIFs are showing up on my Web pages with transparency in places I wasn't expecting. What's going on?**

A Because of a problem in the GIF89a Export Plug-in, sometimes the GIF files you export from Photoshop with a

TIP MAC OS / WINDOWS

Avoiding lost actions

(4.0 only) As you may know, one of Photoshop 4.0's niftiest new features is the Actions palette. You can record commands or sequences of commands, and have them handy the next time you need them, right there in the palette—unless, that is, you haven't saved them and you delete your preferences file.

Photoshop always stores certain settings in its preferences file. On the PC, this file (actually it's two files, one named CCOLORSD and the other named either PHOTO30.PSP for version 3.0.x or PHOTOS40.PSP for version 4.0) is located either in the WINDOWS directory (versions 3.0.1 and 3.0.4) or in the PREFS directory within your Photoshop directory (version 3.0.5 or newer). On the Mac, this file (named "Adobe Photoshop 3.0 Prefs" or "Adobe Photoshop 4.0 Prefs") is located in the "Preferences" folder inside your System folder.

Every time you launch Photoshop, the program looks for a preferences file. If it finds one, it will load it; if it doesn't, it will create a fresh one. One of the most common (and easiest) troubleshooting steps you can take if you're having problems with Photoshop is to delete or rename the preferences file and then relaunch Photoshop. In many cases it's the only thing you have to do to get Photoshop working again if it starts misbehaving.

But when you delete or rename the preferences file, all your settings that are stored there (the locations of your palettes, your color settings, etc.) will be reset to the defaults. In most cases this is no big deal, but in Photoshop 4.0 you will also lose any unsaved actions—actions that you've named and created, so they appear in the Actions palette, but that you haven't saved to a file using the "Save Actions..." command in the palette's drop-down menu.

Since deleting Photoshop's preferences file is a common troubleshooting step that you may need to take someday (and since Photoshop's preferences file, like any other file, can become unusable), it's prudent to use the "Save Actions..." command on any actions you don't want to risk losing.

palette of 256 colors can wind up with incorrect colors appearing transparent once they're displayed in a Web browser. Try this: When you convert to Indexed Color mode—or when converting from within the GIF89a Export Plug-in's dialog box—use 255 (or fewer) colors. That should result in more predictable transparency.

Q I've found that after I rotate an image in Photoshop, it often isn't as sharp as it was before rotating. What's going on?

A Interpolation. Remember, an image in Photoshop (like any bitmap image) is defined as the colors applied to a grid of square pixels. When you rotate an image, you're not rotating the pixel grid—just the colors that are applied to it.

If you rotate your image in a multiple of 90 degrees, Photoshop can simply move the color information around—it still lines up with the grid, pixel for pixel. But if you rotate it any other amount, the color information won't fit perfectly into the pixel grid anymore, so Photoshop has to do some calculations to determine what color values to assign to the resulting pixels. When that interpolation occurs, the results will never be quite the same as the original pixel data.

If you've got a document with a high enough resolution, the interpolated image should still be of high quality. But every time interpolation takes place, there is the potential for image degradation (just as if you were to start with a low-resolution scan and resample it up to a higher resolution—a bad idea!), so be careful whenever you perform any operation that results in interpolation.

Incidentally, Photoshop's "General Preferences" dialog box offers the choice among several interpolation schemes; the default, "Bicubic," provides the highest-quality results.

Q I saved an EPS file with JPEG encoding, and it printed fine to my laser printer, but my service bureau can't get it to print properly on their imagesetter. Is it because the file's corrupt?

A Probably not—the JPEG encoding option works correctly only when printed to PostScript Level 2 devices. While there are many laser printers with Level 2 interpreters, the majority of imagesetters use Level 1 RIPs. If you're sure that the device you're printing to is a Level 2 device, you can safely use this option, which does reduce file size. But if there's any chance your document will end up printed to a Level 1 RIP, you should use a different option. If you need to save your file as an EPS, use the "ASCII" (if you're on a PC) or "Binary" (on a Mac) encoding option. Alternatively, you might consider using another file format entirely—such as TIFF, which offers LZW compression options.

Q I scanned in some wood grain that I want to use as a custom screening texture for bitmap images. But when I try to convert my grayscale images to bitmap, the "Custom Pattern" option is never available—it's always grayed out. How come?

A It's because you need to tell Photoshop what your custom pattern is before you convert the image. First, open the image you want to use as a pattern (in your case, the wood-grain scan) and make a rectangular selection. Then choose "Define Pattern" from the Edit menu. Now close that image, open the one you want to convert to bitmap mode, and choose "Bitmap…" from the Mode menu. In the "Bitmap" dialog box, the "Custom Pattern" option should now be available.

TIP MAC OS / WINDOWS

Give your image a quick makeover

(3.0.x only) Don't despair if you find a washed-out image staring up from your page. You can quickly, and often dramatically, improve a bland picture without a lot of time-consuming color work. All you have to do is duplicate the layer the image is on, then set the duplicate layer's blending mode to "Overlay" using the drop-down menu in Photoshop's Layers palette. The "Overlay" mode increases contrasts while preserving the tonal values of both the highlights and the shadows of the image. (note: To duplicate a layer, drag it onto the new layer icon.)

Q *(3.0.4/3.0.5 only)* **I'm using the GIF89a Export Plug-in to create graphics for Web pages, but I can't seem to get any of the transparency options to work anymore. I've found and used them in the past, but now, no matter what I do, I don't see any of the options for a transparency. What's gone wrong?!**

A You probably stopped working in Indexed Color mode. Remember that you will have access to the transparency options only if your image is already in Indexed Color mode when you use the GIF89a Export Plug-in. The GIF89a Plug-in will allow you to export images that are in either Indexed Color mode or RGB mode. Depending on which mode your document is in when you select the GIF89a Export module, you will see different options for saving the document. When you export an RGB document, it will be converted to Indexed Color by the GIF89a filter, but you won't be able to specify any of the transparency options. When you first convert the document to Indexed Color mode in Photoshop, and then export it, you'll have access to all the transparency options from within the "GIF89a Export" dialog box. You can select colors within the document or select an alpha channel for transparency, and also choose to interlace the image.

Q *(4.0 only)* **I just received the Photoshop 4.0 upgrade and can't find the Commands palette that I liked in Photoshop 3.0. Am I overlooking it, or has the Commands palette gone away?**

A The Commands palette has indeed disappeared, but if you've become accustomed to using it to assign function keys to certain commands, don't worry—you can do that and a lot more with the new Actions palette, which replaces the Commands palette.

The Actions palette is like a complete macro-automation program within Photoshop; it allows you to automate just about anything you can do in

Photoshop, including complex sequences of commands. You can save, edit, and modify your actions, and can also use them to batch-process entire folders of images. Photoshop 4.0 ships with a handful of sample actions; you can create any others you find useful.

To assign a function-key shortcut to an action in the Actions palette, first make sure "Button Mode" is unchecked in the palette's drop-down menu. Then double-click the action (or click once on the action to select it and choose "Action Options..." from the drop-down menu). In the "Action Options" dialog box, you can choose a function key that will activate the action. You can also rename the action and assign it a color.

Q I've been working with some JPEG images and they seem to be getting uglier and uglier as time goes by. Any idea what could be wrong?

A Avoid repeatedly resaving files in JPEG format. One of JPEG's advantages is that it uses compression to reduce file size, but its compression method is "lossy": that is, whenever a file is saved in JPEG format, some color information is discarded, and that data is gone forever. When the file is opened back up, the image is decompressed, but the data is permanently altered. Doing this only once or twice may not result in any visible degradation, but saving in JPEG format repeatedly will eventually result in poor-quality images.

This means that it's a good idea to save files in JPEG format only when they are "finished." If you want to save a file in a compressed format that retains all the data, use TIFF and select the LZW compression option. LZW compression is "lossless"—that is, when you open and decompress a file, it retains every bit of data that was in the file when it was saved.

Q Occasionally, when I try to resize a Photoshop file using the "Image Size" dialog box, all sorts of weird things happen. Sometimes I get an error message telling me that an integer between 1 and 30,000 is required, or that it requires a number between 0.001 and 416.667; other times the number in the "Resolution" field goes crazy. What's going on?

A You're running up against the upper limit of the number of pixels Photoshop can handle: a maximum of 30,000 pixels in either dimension.

MICRO TIP MAC OS / WINDOWS

> If you add a font to your system while Photoshop is running, it normally won't become available to you until you quit and relaunch Photoshop. But you can force Photoshop to rebuild its internal list of available fonts by pressing the Alt (Windows) or Option (Mac) key and clicking with the type tool (anywhere in an open document window) at the exact same time. The timing is critical, so you may have to try it a few times. You'll know you got it right when you see a message saying "Building the font menu. This may take a minute or so...."

If you have "Pixels" chosen as your "Width" and "Height" units and you try to create a file that exceeds that limit (or to enlarge a file so that it would), Photoshop will refuse to accept the value you try to enter, and will force you to use a value between 1 and 30,000.

The changes in the "Resolution" field happen when you're using a unit of measurement (such as inches) for "Width" and "Height" and you enter a value that would make either dimension top 30,000 pixels—Photoshop will reset the value in the "Resolution" field to 1.

There is also a limit to the total amount of information that can be contained in a Photoshop file; the current limit is 2 gigabytes (2,048 MB). If you try to create a file larger than that, Photoshop will display a message reading, "This image would be too large to store in a file. Decrease the dimensions or the resolution."

Q *(4.0 only)* **I recently upgraded to Photoshop 4.0, and now it's taking forever to open my files. The same files opened faster in Photoshop 3. Why?**

A There are several common causes for this kind of performance slowdown. Here are a few things to check.

Try turning down the image-cache setting. To do so, select "Memory & Image Cache..." (in Windows) or "Image Cache..." (on the Mac) from the Preferences submenu on the File menu. The default "Memory & Image Cache" (Windows) or "Image Cache" (Mac) setting level is 4; valid settings can range from 1 to 8.

When Photoshop 4.0 opens a file, it builds and stores (or "caches") multiple views of your document. These additional views speed up zooming, panning, and compositing within the document, but creating them in the first place takes time when you open the file. Higher "Memory & Image Cache" or "Image Cache" settings result in more views cached; this results in faster performance when panning and zooming, but causes opening files to take longer. If you prefer to forgo the cached views altogether, simply set the cache level down to 1, which should make images load at the same speed as they did in Photoshop 3.0.x. (Of course, you'll then lose the performance benefits of image caching, but you can't have it both ways.)

Note that a high image-cache setting has a particularly pronounced effect on the time it takes to open TIFF files saved with LZW compression. If you're using files saved this way, you may want either to turn down the image-cache setting or to resave the TIFF files without LZW compression (or in some other graphics file format).

Disable the Detect Watermark plug-in if you don't use it frequently. Another thing to watch for is the Detect Watermark plug-in. When installed, this plug-in will check every image you open for an embedded digital watermark, which slows down the opening process. If you have this plug-in installed but don't actually use it often, you may want to disable it until you really need it. To disable the plug-in, just move it to someplace outside of the Photoshop folder and its subfolders, and then restart Photoshop. By the way, the Detect Watermark plug-in is not installed by default; if you do want to use it you'll need to copy it to your Photoshop plug-ins folder from the Photoshop 4.0 application CD-ROM. You'll find it in the GOODIES\-PLUG_INS\DIGIMARC\DIGIOPEN.8BE folder (Windows) or in the Optional Plugins:Digimarc:Detect Watermark folder (Mac).

If you're on a Power Mac or AV Quadra, try the Enable Async I/O plug-in. Here's one last item for Mac users to check. On Mac O/S computers using Power PC processors, Photoshop's Enable Async I/O plug-in can speed up all disk operations, including opening files. This plug-in allows asynchronous read/write operations to the hard disk under system 7.5.1 or later.

Under Photoshop 3.0.x, the Enable Async I/O plug-in is installed and enabled automatically, but under Photoshop 4.0 the plug-in is installed but disabled—its folder name has an Option + L character ("¬") in it, making it invisible to Photoshop. To enable the plug-in, open the "Extensions" folder within your Photoshop plug-ins folder. Look for the folder called "¬ Enable Async I/O" and simply remove the special "¬" character, changing the folder's name to "Enable Async I/O." Then restart Photoshop.

By the way, you can tell whether asynchronous read/write operations are enabled by looking in the efficiency indicator in the lower-left corner of your image window—make sure "Efficiency" is chosen from the drop-down menu there. If, next to the efficiency value, you see a "dagger" character (†) in Mac Photoshop 3.0.5 or an asterisk (*) in Mac Photoshop 4.0, you're getting the benefit of asynchronous disk operations. Note that for asynchronous disk operations to work on the Mac, a number of conditions must be met: you must be using an AV Quadra or a MacO/S computer with a Power PC processor; you must be running Photoshop 3.0 or later; Photoshop's Enable Async I/O plug-in must be loaded; and your hard disk must be formatted with a utility that's compatible with Apple's SCSI Manager 4.3.1 or newer.

Q *(4.0 only)* **What has happened to the Amiga IFF plug-in? I used it all the time in Photoshop 3.0.x, and now it's gone. How can I get it back?**

A Don't worry, it hasn't vanished. Several of the less widely used Photoshop plug-ins are no longer installed by default, but are nonetheless included on the Photoshop application CD. These include both the Amiga IFF and Amiga HAM plug-ins. To use these plug-ins, just copy them from the Photoshop 4.0 application CD-ROM to Photoshop's designated plug-ins folder, and then restart Photoshop. On Windows, the Amiga IFF plug-in is called "Aiff8b.8bi," and is located inside the GOODIES\-PLUG-INS folder; on the Mac, it's called "Amiga IFF" and can be found in Other Goodies:Optional Plugins:File Format.

Q *(4.0 only)* **I work in a service bureau where we routinely save high-resolution DCS EPS files from drum-scanner software. When I try to open these files in Photoshop 4.0, I get a dialog box asking for information about how to rasterize this "generic" EPS file; once the file is opened, it looks awful—like a low-resolution image. Also, my Scitex CT files with clipping paths open up in Photoshop 4.0 minus the clipping paths and all the image data that was outside the paths! These files used to open in Photoshop 3 just fine. What's going on here?**

A These problems are probably caused by the new generic EPS Parser in Photoshop 4.0. We'll explain in a minute, but first, the solution: simply remove the EPS Parser plug-in from Photoshop's plug-ins folder. Under Windows, the file's called EPSParsr.8by, and it's located in PLUGINS\-FORMATS; on the Mac, it's called "EPS Parser," and is in the "Parser" folder inside Photoshop's "Plug-ins" folder. Now restart Photoshop. Your EPS DCS and Scitex CT files should open properly.

Here's what's going on. Photoshop 3.0.x had no generic EPS parser—that is, no way to open EPS files created by most applications other than Photoshop or Illustrator. This meant that when Photoshop 3 opened your EPS DCS or Scitex CT files, they appeared to be files written by Photoshop, so it simply opened them up without any rasterization (conversion).

Photoshop 4.0 includes a generic EPS Parser that can rasterize most EPS files created by other applications (as long as they're

TIP MAC OS / WINDOWS

Diagonal marquees

Wouldn't it be nice if you could rotate the rectangular-marquee tool, to select a diagonal rectangle? Well, you can't, but you can achieve the same result by using Photoshop 4.0's new polygonal-marquee tool, or—in version 3.0—using the lasso tool while holding down Alt (Windows) or Option (Mac). By clicking from point to point, you can select any polygonal shape, at any orientation you wish.

TIP MAC OS / WINDOWS

How to scale paths

After you've drawn a path with the pen tool, sometimes you may wish it were a little larger or smaller overall. Sure, you can switch to the direct-selection (pointer) tool and start pulling points around, but here's an easier way. Using the direct-selection tool, select the path you want to scale, either by drawing a selection marquee around it or by Alt-clicking (Windows) or Option-clicking (Mac) on it. Then create a new, empty document, copy the path(s) into it, and use the "Image Size..." command to scale the entire document up (or down). Then return to your original document, make sure the original path isn't highlighted in the Paths palette, and copy the resized path(s) back in. Your path will be scaled as desired.

written correctly by the creating application). With the EPS Parser plug-in installed, when Photo-shop 4.0 encounters an EPS file it checks to see whether it was written by Photoshop. If it finds that it was written by Photoshop, Photoshop opens the file directly (i.e., with no conversion). If it finds that the file was written by Illustrator, it uses the generic EPS Parser to open it. And if it sees a file that appears to have been written by another application, Photoshop also invokes the generic EPS rasterizer—even if the image data doesn't need to be rasterized (as in the case of your EPS DCS or Scitex CT files).

As long as you don't need to open and rasterize vector EPS files (e.g., EPS files from Illustrator), you can leave the parser outside the Photoshop folder.

Q I'm working with a Photoshop image and when I try to rotate it, my only choices are to rotate it in 90-degree increments (180°, 90° CW and 90° CCW). I've rotated other documents to all different angles. Also, the Effects submenu of the Image menu is grayed out. What am I doing wrong?

A You're not doing anything wrong, you're probably just working in Bitmap mode. Many features available in the color modes and Grayscale mode are not supported in Bitmap mode, including the "Free" and "Arbitrary" rotation options and all the options under the Effects, Map, and Adjust submenus of the Image menu. To enable these features, change from Bitmap mode to Grayscale mode; if you want, you can change the image back to Bitmap mode before saving.

Image Changes Size After Being Pasted into Photoshop Document

ISSUE

After pasting an image into a new or existing document in Adobe Photoshop 2.5 and later, the image displays and prints larger or smaller than expected.

SOLUTION

Ensure the resolution of the image to be copied and the destination document are the same:

1. With both images at the same magnification view (e.g., 1:1, 1:2), note the Current Size resolution value of both images by choosing Image > Image Size.
2. For either image, increase or decrease the Resolution value in the Image Size dialog box so the resolution of both images are the same value.

NOTE: Increase or decrease the image's dimensions (i.e., height and width) to change the image's resolution without changing the image's dimensions. Because increasing or decreasing an image's dimensions may change the image's quality (e.g., more pixelation, darker, lighter), rescanning instead of resizing the image ensures control of the image's quality.

ADDITIONAL INFORMATION

When displaying an image, Photoshop determines the size of the image by its resolution, and not by the image's dimensions (i.e., width and height). After pasting an image into another document, Photoshop forces the pixels (resolution) of the pasted image to occupy the same number of pixels (resolution) in the destination document.

Unable to Change Background Layer to Normal Layer in Photoshop 3.0x

ISSUE

After you double-click on the Background layer in Adobe Photoshop 3.0x's Layers palette, the Make Layer dialog box does not appear as expected, preventing the Background layer from being converted to a Normal (i.e., non-Background) layer.

SOLUTION

Choose the Mode command to change the image's color mode to Grayscale, Duotone, RGB Color, CMYK Color, or LAB color.

ADDITIONAL INFORMATION

Because Photoshop 3.0x layers do not support Indexed Color, Multichannel, or Bitmap color modes, images using these color modes are limited to using the Background layer, preventing the Make Layer dialog box from appearing after you double-click on the Background layer in the Layers palette. After you change the image's color mode to one supported by the layers feature (i.e., Grayscale, Duotone, RGB Color, CMYK Color, or LAB color), the Make Layer

TIP MAC OS / WINDOWS

What was that color?

Ever have trouble remembering what custom color you've been using in your document? Just add the color to Photoshop's Swatches palette. Here's how.

First, select your custom color in the Color Picker. Then move the cursor over an unused section of the Swatches palette, and it should change to the paint bucket. Click the paint bucket to create a new swatch of your custom color. If your custom color is a Pantone color, note that when you move the cursor over that swatch, the tab at the top of the Swatches palette displays the name of the color.

dialog box appears as expected after you double-click on the Background layer.

Photoshop's Background layer:

- appears with the name "Background" in italic type
- appears at the bottom of the list of layers in the Layers palette since it is the back-most layer
- cannot contain a hidden transparency mask
- cannot contain transparent pixels

Black Areas Display on CMYK Channels in Photoshop

ISSUE

After you convert an RGB image to a grayscale or CMYK image in Adobe Photoshop 2.5x or later, the black and gray pixels display in the cyan, magenta, yellow, and black channels in the Channels palette. The black areas of the image print muddy (i.e., rich black) instead of as a pure or simple black (i.e., 100% black, 0% cyan, 0% magenta, and 0% yellow).

SOLUTION

Change the Black Generations setting to Maximum in the Separation Setup dialog box:

1. With the grayscale or RGB image open in Photoshop, choose File > Preferences > Separation Setup.
2. Select Maximum from the Black Generation pop-up menu and click OK.
3. Choose Mode > CMYK Color to convert the image to a CMYK image.

NOTE: The Black Generation setting affects all subsequent CMYK conversions.

ADDITIONAL INFORMATION

The Black Generation preference controls how Photoshop generates black when converting an image to CMYK mode. When the default setting, Medium, is selected as the Black Generation preference, Photoshop adds cyan, magenta, and yellow values to black areas for a richer black. When Maximum is selected for Black Generation, Photoshop converts all black pixels onto the Black channel, creating a simple or pure black. When None is selected for Black Generation, Photoshop defines black using cyan, magenta, and yellow; no pixels assigned to the black channel.

Scanned Images Display with Moire, Screen, or Plaid Pattern in Photoshop

ISSUE

A scanned image displays and prints with a moire, screen, or plaid pattern, or with colored or gray blotches, in Adobe Photoshop.

SOLUTIONS

Rescan the image from original artwork or photographs.

OR: To minimize the moire pattern, do one or more of the following:

NOTE: Minimizing the moire pattern may decrease the image's detail.

A. Rescan the image at twice the resolution, use Photoshop's Gausssian Blur filter to reduce the moire pattern, resample the image, then use the Unsharp Mask filter:
   1. Scan the image at twice the recommended resolution.
   2. With the image open in Photoshop, select Filter > Blur > Gaussian Blur.
   3. Select Preview in the Gaussian Blur dialog box, then move the slider under Radius until the moire pattern disappears or is acceptably decreased.
   4. Select Image > Image Size and resample the image to the recommended resolution.
   5. Select Filter > Sharpen > Unsharp Mask.
   6. Select Preview in the Unsharp Mask dialog box and move the Amount, Radius, and Threshold sliders to regain sharpness in the image.

B. Rescan the image at twice the resolution, resample the image, use Photoshop's Gausssian Blur filter to reduce the moire pattern, then use the Unsharp Mask filter:
   1. Scan the image at twice the recommended resolution.
   2. Select Image > Image Size and resample the image to the recommended resolution.
   3. With the image open in Photoshop, select Filter > Blur > Gaussian Blur.
   4. Select Preview in the Gaussian Blur dialog box then move the slider under Radius until the moire pattern disappears or is acceptably decreased.
   5. Select Filter > Sharpen > Unsharp Mask.
   6. Select Preview in the Unsharp Mask dialog box and move the Amount, Radius, and Threshold sliders to regain sharpness in the image.

c. Rescan using a scanning application (e.g., ScanPrep, ScanPrepPro, Ofoto) that includes an option (e.g., Descreening) that can compensate for scanning halftoned artwork.

NOTE: Adobe Photoshop 3.0 Deluxe CD-ROM for Macintosh includes a demo version of ScanPrep, located in the Third Party Products folder in the Other Goodies folder.

ADDITIONAL INFORMATION

Previously-printed material (i.e., a picture from a magazine, book, brochure, newsletter, poster) has already been broken up into a halftone pattern for reproduction. Because scanners convert light and dark areas into a dot pattern, or halftone, creating a dot pattern of areas that are already dot patterns produces a moire pattern.

Image Size does not Increase Correctly when Constrained in Photoshop 3.0x

ISSUE

When increasing the size of an image with both "Proportions" and "File Size" selected as "Constrain:" options in the "Image Size" dialog box in Adobe Photoshop 3.0x, the new image size dimensions are not retained.

SYMPTOMS

After clicking "OK" then reopening the "Image Size" dialog box, the new dimensions aren't listed in the "Width:" and "Height:" boxes.

SOLUTIONS

Reset the new "Width:" and "Height:" values in the "Image Size" dialog box:

1. Choose "Image Size..." from the Image menu.
2. Enter the desired values in the "Width:" and "Height:" edit boxes, then click "OK."
3. To check the new image dimensions, reopen the "Image Size" dialog box and make sure the values in the "Width:" and "Height:" edit boxes match those entered in step 2, then click "OK" or "Cancel."

OR: Use Photoshop 2.5x.

ADDITIONAL INFORMATION

Photoshop 3.0x does not increase an image's size to the dimensions (i.e., "Width:" and "Height:") first entered in the "Image Size" dialog box. To increase an image's size, you must enter the desired values in the "Width:" and "Height:" edit boxes in the "Image Size" dialog box and click "OK," then reopen the "Image Size" dialog box and reenter the values.

When increasing the "Width:" and "Height:" dimensions in the "Image Size" dialog box, the "Resolution:" value does not decrease below a certain number. For example, when a 7" by 5" image with a resolution of 300 dpi is increased to 112" by 80", the constrained resolution value becomes 21 dpi, which is mathematically incorrect (the resolution should be 18.75 dpi). Clicking "OK" then reopening the "Image Size" dialog box reveals the new dimensions are 100" by 71.429", which does match the 21 dpi resolution value, but are not the desired dimensions.

Photoshop 2.5x does increase an image's size to the dimensions first entered in the "Image Size" dialog box.

Photoshop 3.0 Only Format Available When Saving in Photoshop 3.x

ISSUE

When you use the Save or Save As commands in Adobe Photoshop 3.0.x, Photoshop 3.0 is the only file format available. Other formats are dimmed.

SOLUTIONS

Use the Save a Copy command to create a copy of the file without alpha channel or layer information:

1. Choose File > Save a Copy.
2. In the Save a Copy dialog box, select the desired file format, then click OK.

OR: Flatten all layers before using the Save or Save As command:

1. Choose Flatten Image from the Layers palette menu.
2. Choose Save or Save As from the File menu.
3. In the Save or Save As dialog box, select the desired format, then click OK.

NOTE: All layers are discarded and cannot be recovered after you flatten and save an image.

TIP MAC OS / WINDOWS

Gray be gone

Are you tired of seeing that dull gray background when you're working in Photoshop's full-screen mode with the menu bar? (That's the mode you get by clicking the middle icon at the bottom of the toolbar; also, you can cycle through the three modes by pressing the F key on your keyboard.) You can change it to any color you like. Simply define a foreground color (click once on the foreground-color icon in the toolbar), then Shift-click with the paint-bucket tool anywhere on the gray background. Your foreground color fills the entire area.

Altering this background is probably not a good idea if you're doing serious color work, since the background color can skew your color perception (a neutral gray minimizes this effect).

To get back to the neutral gray, define a foreground color of neutral gray (for instance, 0% C, 0% M, 0% Y, and 50% K, or 128 R, 128 G, and 128 B) and use the paint-bucket trick again.

MICRO TIP MAC OS / WINDOWS

Any selection can be "nudged" one pixel up, down, left, or right by using the arrow keys. To nudge a selection ten pixels, hold down the Shift key while using the arrow keys.

ADDITIONAL INFORMATION

When you add one or more layers to an image in Photoshop 3.0.x, Photoshop 3.0 is the only available file format in the Save and Save As dialog boxes. Layers are a proprietary feature of Photoshop 3.0.x and are only supported by the Photoshop 3.0 (.psd) file format. Flattening an image merges all layers into the background layer, which enables the image to be saved in other formats.

Most file formats do not support alpha channels. The Save a Copy command creates a copy of the image, removing any alpha channels and flattening the layers. When saving an image with the Save a Copy command, all the file formats supported by the image's color mode appear in the Save a Copy dialog box.

The Photoshop 3.0 file format is the only image format that supports layers.

The following file formats support alpha channels:

File Format	Color Mode
Photoshop 3.0	CMYK, RGB, and Grayscale
Photoshop 2.0	CMYK, RGB, and Grayscale
PICT File	RGB
PICT Resource	RGB
Pixar	RGB, Grayscale
Raw	CMYK, RGB, and Grayscale
Targa	RGB
TIFF	CMYK, RGB, and Grayscale

File formats supported by each color mode:

File Format	Color Mode
Photoshop 3.0	Multichannel, Lab Color, CMYK, RGB, Indexed, Duotone, Grayscale, Bitmap
Photoshop 2.0	Multichannel, CMYK, RGB, Indexed, Duotone, Bitmap
Amiga IFF	RGB, Indexed, Grayscale, Bitmap
BMP	RGB, Indexed, Grayscale, Bitmap
CompuServe GIF	Indexed, Grayscale, Bitmap
EPS	Lab Color, CMYK, RGB, Indexed, Duotone, Grayscale, Bitmap
FilmStrip	RGB
JPEG	CMYK, RGB, Grayscale
MacPaint	Bitmap
PCX	RGB, Indexed, Grayscale, Bitmap
PICT File	RGB, Indexed, Grayscale, Bitmap
PICT Resource	RGB, Indexed, Grayscale, Bitmap
Pixar	RGB, Grayscale
PixelPaint	Indexed, Grayscale, Bitmap
Raw	Multichannel, Lab Color, CMYK, RGB, Indexed, Duotone, Grayscale
Scitex CT	CMYK, RGB, Grayscale
Targa	RGB, Indexed, Grayscale
TIFF	Lab Color, CMYK, RGB, Indexed, Grayscale, Bitmap

Transparency Options Unavailable When Exporting to GIF89a File Format in Photoshop

ISSUE

When you export a file using Photoshop's GIF89a Export plug-in, the transparency options are unavailable in the GIF89a Export dialog box.

SOLUTION

Convert the file to Indexed Color mode before choosing File > Export > GIF89a.

ADDITIONAL INFORMATION

Photoshop's GIF89a Export plug-in enables you to export and save RGB or Indexed Color files in GIF89a format. When you export an Indexed Color file, you can select one or more colors as transparent, designate an additional channel to use as a transparency mask, and select a transparency index color in the GIF89a Export dialog box. When you export an RGB file, these transparency options are unavailable.

Unable to Print Tiles from Photoshop 2.0 and Later

ISSUE

Unable to print tiles from Adobe Photoshop 2.0 and later.

SOLUTIONS

Import the image into an application that supports printing tiles (e.g., Adobe PageMaker, QuarkXPress).

OR: Print one portion of the image at a time from Photoshop:

1. Double-click the Marquee tool to open the Marquee Options palette.
2. In the Marquee Options palette, select Rectangular for Shape and Fixed Size for Style.
3. For Width and Height, enter the printable area of your paper size dimensions in pixels. For instructions on determining the printable area of your printer in pixels, see Additional Information.
4. Click the cursor over the image and hold the mouse button down to draw a marquee the size of the desired portion of the image to print.
5. Choose File > Page Setup, then select the desired paper size and orientation for the first portion of the image to be printed.

6. Choose File > Print, then select Selection for Print Range.
7. Repeat steps 2-6 until all desired portions of the image are printed.

NOTE: Overlap between tiles may be desired to ensure there are no gaps in the image after printing.

ADDITIONAL INFORMATION

Photoshop does not support printing tiles.

To determine the printable area of your printer:

1. Choose File > New.
2. In the New dialog box, specify Image Size dimensions that are larger than the paper size you are printing to, select Pixels/Inch and type "30" for Resolution, then click OK.
2. Color the entire image 50% gray.
3. Select the paper size and orientation in the Page Setup dialog box.
4. Choose File > Print.
5. When the message "The image is larger than the paper's printable area. Some clipping will occur" appears, click Proceed.
6. Measure the width and height of the area that prints 50% gray. This is the printable area of your printer.

   To determine your page size in pixels:

   1. Choose Image > Image Size and note the current resolution of your image.
   2. Multiply the size of the paper size that you are printing to by the resolution of your image. For example:

```
Page size = 8.5 x 11 (portrait) and image's
  resolution = 100
Width = (8.5 x 100) pixels or 850 pixels
Height = (11 x 100) pixels or 1100 pixels
```

Rubber Stamp Tool Has No Effect in Photoshop 3.0.x

ISSUE

When you use the rubber stamp tool in Adobe Photoshop 3.0.x, no pixels in the image are affected or changed. No alert dialog appears.

SOLUTIONS

Do one or more of the following:

A. Click the Standard mode tool (i.e., the icon with a circle on a white background) in Photoshop's toolbox to use the rubber stamp tool in Standard mode, rather than Quick Mask mode.

B. Reset Photoshop's preferences file:

   When running Photoshop for the Macintosh:

   1. Quit Photoshop.
   2. At the Finder, open the Preferences folder in the System Folder.
   3. Delete the Adobe Photoshop Prefs file.

   When running Photoshop for Windows:

   1. Quit Photoshop.
   2. Use the Windows File Manager to rename or delete the Photos30.psp file, which is located in the Windows directory.

   NOTE: Custom preference settings will be lost.

ADDITIONAL INFORMATION

Photoshop's rubber stamp tool is not designed to work in the Quick Mask mode.

Filters Dimmed in Filter Menu in Photoshop 3.0x

ISSUE

Filters are dimmed in Adobe Photoshop 3.0x's Filter menu.

SOLUTION

Change the image's mode to RGB color by choosing Mode > RGB Color.

ADDITIONAL INFORMATION

When listing filters in the Filter menu, Photoshop lists filters that support the image's mode (e.g., Bitmap, RGB Color). Photoshop dims filters in the Filter menu when the filter does not support the image's color mode. All filters included with Photoshop 3.0 support the RGB Color mode.

The Lighting Effects, Lens Flare, and NTSC Colors filters support the RGB Color mode only.

The De-interlace filter supports the RGB Color, Grayscale, Duotone, Lab Color, and Multichannel modes.

The Texture Fill and Difference Clouds filters support the RGB Color, CMYK Color, Grayscale, Duotone, and Multichannel modes.

All other filters support all modes except for the Indexed Color and Bitmap modes.

Pencil Tool Doesn't Use Hardness Settings for Brush Options

The Pencil tool is a hard-edged tool and will only allow hard strokes in Adobe Photoshop 2.5x and later. While the option to change the hardness settings is available in the "Brush Options..." drop-down list from the Brushes palette when the pencil tool is selected, changing the settings will still only allow hard strokes with the pencil tool.

The Paintbrush, Airbrush and Dodge and burn tools are soft-edged tools and allow the hardness settings to be changed using the "Brush Options..." choice from the drop down list from the Brushes palette.

WINDOWS

Q I've just switched from Windows 3.1 to Windows NT, and now most of my Photoshop Plug-ins won't work anymore. What's wrong?

A You're probably running into an incompatibility between your Plug-ins and Windows NT. Most Plug-ins are written for a 16-bit environment, such as Windows 3.1. Windows NT, however, is a 32-bit operating system. In order for Photoshop Plug-ins to function properly in a 32-bit environment like Windows NT or Windows 95, they need to be specifically rewritten for a 32-bit environment.

Most Plug-in manufacturers are currently updating their Plug-ins for 32-bit environments. Contact the developers of your Plug-ins for information on the status and availability of 32-bit updates.

If you're sure a Plug-in has been updated for a 32-bit environment, but you're still having problems, don't forget to try basic Plug-in troubleshooting techniques. Delete or rename your Photoshop preferences file, which is named "PHOTOS30.PSP" (for Photoshop 3.x) or PHOTOSHP.PSP (for Photoshop 2.x) and is located in the Windows NT directory. (Note that deleting or renaming this file will cause you to lose any preferences you've set.) Next, make sure Photoshop is looking in the right place for your Plug-ins—select "Plug-ins..." from the Preferences submenu of Photoshop's File menu, and in the "Select Plug-ins Directory" dialog box, make sure your Plug-ins directory is selected (usually, this directory is called PLUGINS). Finally, make sure the Plug-in you're trying to use is located in your Plug-ins directory and is installed correctly (for instance, it should not be compressed or located in a subdirectory of the Plug-ins directory).

Q I can't seem to get text to align vertically (as illustrated on page 113 of the manual). When I try to use the vertical-alignment options, my text isn't aligned vertically—it's merely rotated 90 degrees. What's going on?

A You're right, the feature doesn't work as it's supposed to. Fortunately, there's an easy fix: adding a line of text to your PHOTOS30.INI file.

The PHOTOS30.INI file is a text-only file that contains options for customizing certain Photoshop functions. To enable true vertical text alignment in Windows Photoshop, open the PHOTOS30.INI file in a text editor such as Notepad. Where you'll find the file may vary depending on your version of Photoshop: if you're using version 3.0.1 or 3.0.4, the file will be in the WINDOWS directory (or folder); the installation for Photoshop 3.0.5 places the file in the PREFS folder within the PHOTOSHP folder (which is, by default, in the WIN32APP folder). Note to Windows 95 users: if you're looking for the file in the Explorer, it may appear only as PHOTOS30, with no .INI extension, depending on the viewing options you've set up.

Once you've opened it, add the following line at the end:

```
RealVerticalText=1
```

Make sure you type it exactly as shown, without any spaces between the characters. Then save the file (still in text-only format) and restart Photoshop. You should now be able to get text to align vertically using all three of the vertical-alignment options.

Q *(3.0.x only)* **I've been using Photoshop to work with images on Photo CDs for months, but suddenly I can't seem to open any of them. Other kinds of images—TIFFs, EPSs, etc.—will open fine, but my Photo CD images don't appear in the "Open" dialog box. Got any ideas about what's wrong?**

A Yes, if you've recently installed a copy of Kai's Power Goo. Kai's Power Goo, from MetaTools Software, installs two files that interfere with Photoshop's ability to open Photo CD files. The two files are KPSYS32.DLL and PCDLIB32.DLL. Photoshop has already installed those two files in your WINDOWS directory. Kai's Power Goo installs a second copy of these two files in the WINDOWS\SYSTEM directory. Having these files installed in both directories prevents Photoshop from opening Photo CD files.

The solution is to eliminate the duplicate files. Search for the files KPSYS32.DLL and PCDLIB32.DLL and rename or delete any iterations of them that are not located in the WINDOWS directory. Relaunch Photoshop, and you should be able to open Photo CD files. Power Goo will still work fine.

Q I've saved some Targa files from Photoshop. When I saved them, they were at 300 dpi. When I went back to work on them again, they opened at 72 dpi. It seems as if every Targa file I open comes in at 72 dpi—it doesn't seem to matter what resolution they were saved at. Am I losing my mind?

A No—Targa files always open at 72 dpi on a PC, no matter what resolution you save them at. On the Macintosh, the resolution information for a Targa file is written to the file's resource fork (Macintosh files generally consist of two parts: a resource fork and a data fork). Since PC files don't contain resource forks (or forks of any kind, for that matter), when a Targa file is opened on a PC, the resolution always defaults to 72 dpi.

You probably noticed that when a Targa file opens at 72 dpi, its dimensions are also larger than they had been. The total number of pixels hasn't changed; only the resolution has changed. To bring your image back to the desired resolution, choose "Image Size..." from the Image menu and enter a new resolution, making sure to check "File Size" in the "Restrain" section.

Q I've been having all kinds of problems with Photoshop lately. The marquee tool isn't working properly, I'm having trouble resizing images, and whenever I use any of the paint tools there's a strange line that begins at the end of the brushstroke and continues up at a 45-degree angle. Any ideas what's wrong?

A We've seen this occur on several laptops (including Toshibas and IBM ThinkPads) and some desktop PCs. Check to see if you have Logitech Mouseware for Windows installed; if you do, try removing it. We have found that in some installations it conflicts with Photoshop and can cause erratic selection and painting behavior. For information on removing it, contact Logitech.

Q *(4.0 only)* **Photoshop was running fine before I switched video cards. Now that I have a Matrox MGA card, the redraw in Photoshop is excruciatingly slow. What should I do?**

A Start by making sure that you're using the latest driver for your video card. There's also an adjustment you can make that will considerably increase performance with your card.

First, quit out of Photoshop if it's running. Locate the file called "Photos40.ini" (it's in the "Prefs" folder inside your Photoshop folder), make a backup copy of it, and open it in a text editor—if you double-click on this file, it should open up in Notepad. Anyplace following the [Photoshop] line, add a new line and type the following text:

```
INVERTDIB=0
```

(Note that the character at the end of that line is a zero, not a capital letter O as in "Orange.") Then save the file in text format. Relaunch Photoshop and things should be much speedier.

Plug-in Filters Unavailable in Photoshop Running Under Windows 95

Issue

Plug-in filters do not list, or are missing, in the Filter menu in Adobe Photoshop 3.0 or later running under Windows 95.

SOLUTIONS

Do one or more of the following:

A. Ensure that the plug-in filters are located in Photoshop's Plug-ins (PLUGINS) directory, but are not located in a subdirectory in the PLUGINS directory.

B. Deinstall previous versions of Photoshop then install Photoshop 3.0.5 or later.

OR: When Photoshop 3.0.4 is installed, deinstall previous versions of Photoshop, reinstall Photoshop 3.0.4, then install the 16-bit Plug-in Update (i.e., PSUT9532.DLL and PSUT9516.DLL files dated 9/14/95). For information on installing the 16-bit Plug-in Update, see Additional Information.

NOTE: To ensure you are using Photoshop 3.0.4 or later, choose Help > About Adobe Photoshop in Photoshop. Photoshop 3.0.4 and later display the version number in small black type on the right side of the window.

C. Reset the location of the Photoshop Plug-ins directory:
   1. Launch Photoshop, then choose File > Preferences > Plug-ins.
   2. Select the plug-ins directory that installed with Photoshop 3.0.4 or later, then click OK.
   3. Restart Photoshop.

D. Recreate the Photoshop Preferences file:
   1. Quit Photoshop.
   2. Delete the PHOTOS30.PSP file from the WINDOWS directory (Photoshop 3.0.4) or the WIN32APP\PHOTOSHP\PREFS directory (Photoshop 3.0.5).

E. Disable the "PHOTOSHP=0x00208000" line in the [Compatibility32] section of the WIN.INI file:
   1. Make a backup copy of the WIN.INI file, located in the WINDOWS directory.
   2. Open the WIN.INI file in a text editor that can save in text-only format (e.g., Notepad).
   3. In the [Compatibility32] section, locate the line that reads "PHOTOSHP=0x00208000."
   4. Disable the "PHOTOSHP=0x00208000" line by inserting a semicolon before the word "PHOTOSHP" in the "PHOTOSHP=0x00208000" line. For example:
      `;PHOTOSHP=0x00208000`
   5. Save the WIN.INI file in text-only format then restart Windows.

F. Use a 32-bit version of the plug-in, available from the plug-in's manufacturer.

ADDITIONAL INFORMATION

Photoshop 3.0.5 is Windows 95 logo-compliant and includes the built-in 16-bit Plug-in Update, which enables Photoshop 3.0.5 to recognize most 16-bit plug-ins when running under Windows 95. Photoshop 3.0.4 is Windows 95 compatible, but is not Windows 95 logo-compliant. When running under Windows 95, Photoshop 3.0.4 recognizes some 16-bit plug-in filters, and recognizes additional 16-bit plug-ins after the 16-bit Plug-in Update is installed. Photoshop 3.0 was released before Windows 95 and is not Windows 95 compatible.

16-bit plug-in filters are designed for use in 16-bit operating systems (e.g., Windows 3.1x), but are not designed for use in 32-bit operating systems (e.g., Windows 95). Both Photoshop 3.0.5 and Photoshop 3.0.4 with the 16-bit Plug-in Update installed are optimized to recognize many 16-bit plug-in filters installed under Windows 95, but 16-bit plug-ins that are unavailable after updating to Photoshop 3.0.5 are incompatible with 32-bit applications running in Windows 95 (i.e., 32-bit operating system).

The 16-bit Plug-in Update, 16BUPDAT.ZIP, which contains the compressed files PSUT9516.DLL, PSUT9532.DLL, and README.TXT, is available on the Adobe BBS, Adobe's World Wide Web Page, CompuServe, and America Online.

When installing under Windows 95, Photoshop's installer installs Photoshop 3.0.4 and later, by default, in the C:\WIN32APP\PHOTOSHP directory, and Photoshop 3.0, by default in the C:\PHOTOSHP directory. Installing Photoshop 3.04 or later using the default install location does not overwrite Photoshop 3.0. Deinstalling Photoshop 3.0 before installing Photoshop 3.0.4 or later ensures you have only one version of Photoshop installed and you are using the latest version.

To recognize plug-ins and list them in the Filters menu, Photoshop requires plug-in files to be installed in Photoshop's plug-ins directory. When a plug-in is not installed in Photoshop's plug-ins directory, Photoshop's link to its plug-ins directory is broken, or Photoshop's preferences file is damaged, Photoshop is unable to list the filter in its Filter menu.

Windows 95 adds the "PHOTOSHP=0x00208000" line to the WIN.INI file to enable Photoshop 3.0 to run under

Windows 95. When running Photoshop 3.0.4 or later, disable or remove the "PHOTOSHP=0x00208000" line.

To install the 16-bit Plug-in Update for Photoshop 3.0.4:

1. Rename the existing PSUT9532.DLL and PSUT9516.DLL files (dated 5/18/95) in the PHOTOSHP dir.
2. Copy the new PSUT9532.DLL and PSUT9516.DLL files (dated 9/14/95) into the PHOTOSHP directory.

Desired File Format Unavailable When Saving in Photoshop 3.0.x for Windows

ISSUE

When you save a file, Adobe Photoshop 3.x does not list the desired file format in the Save or Save As dialog box.

SOLUTIONS

Do one or more of the following:

A. Use the Save a Copy command to create a copy of the file without layer information.

B. Ensure the selected color mode is supported by the file format in which you want to save the file. For example, CompuServe GIF supports images in Indexed, Grayscale, and Bitmap color mode. See Additional information for a list of file formats and supported color modes.

C. Ensure the image's dimensions do not exceed the maximum dimensions supported by the file format in which you want to save the file. For example, MacPaint format supports images with dimensions up to 576 x 720 pixels.

D. Install the desired File Format plug-in file for the desired file format into the Photoshop Plug-ins directory. By default, Photoshop installs the Targa8b.8bi, Pixar8b.8bi, Pixpnt8b.8bi, Pcx8b.8bi, Macpnt8b.8bi, Gif8b.8bi, Filmst8b.8bi, Bmp8b.8bi, and Aiff8b.8bi File Format plug-in files in the Photoshp/Plugins directory.

E. Recreate Photoshop's preferences file:
   1. Quit Photoshop.
   2. Delete the Photos30.psp file located in the Win32app\Photoshp\Prefs directory (Photoshop 3.0.5) or the Windows directory (Photoshop 3.0 and 3.0.4).

   NOTE: Custom preference settings will be lost.

F. Reset the location of the Photoshop Plug-ins directory:
   1. Start Photoshop, then choose File > Preferences > Plug-ins.
   2. In the Select Plug-in Directory dialog box, click once on the Plugins directory to select it, then click OK.
   3. Restart Photoshop.

G. If external SCSI devices (e.g., external hard drives, removable media drives, optical drives, external CD-ROM drives, scanner) are connected to the computer, ensure SCSI connection devices, cables, or termination are not the cause by turning the computer and SCSI devices off, disconnecting all SCSI devices, and restarting the computer.

ADDITIONAL INFORMATION

Photoshop 3.0.x uses File Format plug-in files to save documents in Amiga (IFF), Windows Bitmap (BMP, RLE), CompuServe Graphic (GIF), FilmStrip (FLM), MacPaint (MPT, MAC), PCX (PCX), Pixar (PXR), Pixel Paint 1.0/2.0 (PX1), and TARGA (TGA) file format. When the File Format plug-in file required to save one of these formats is not installed in Photoshop's plug-ins (Plugins) directory, Photoshop's link to its plug-ins directory is broken, or Photoshop's preferences file is damaged, Photoshop is unable to list the file format in the Save, Save As, or Save a Copy dialog box.

Because the ability to save documents in Photoshop 3.0, EPS, JPEG, PICT, RAW, Scitex CT, and TIFF file formats are built into Photoshop 3.0.x, Photoshop does not require an installed File Format plug-in file to list these file formats in the Save, Save As, or Save a Copy dialog box.

Photoshop does not list file formats in the Save, Save As, and Save a Copy dialog box that do not support the Photoshop features used in the image (e.g., Color mode, layers, alpha channels).

Most file formats do not support alpha channels or layers. The only image format that supports layers is the Photoshop 3.0 file format. The Save a Copy command creates a copy of the image and flattens the layers. When saving an image using the Save a Copy command, all file formats supported by the image's color mode appear in the Save a Copy dialog box.

Photoshop is unable to create FilmStrip files. The full retail builds of Photoshop 2.0 and later can open and save FilmStrip files created in other applications (e.g., Adobe Premiere 4.0). Once a FilmStrip file is opened in Photoshop and saved in another format (e.g., EPS, Photoshop), Photoshop dims the FilmStrip format and is unable to resave the file in FilmStrip format.

Problems with connected SCSI devices (e.g., unterminated SCSI devices, damaged connection cables or cards) can cause problems in Windows, which in turn may affect the applications you run in Windows.

The following file formats support alpha channels:

File format	Supported color mode
Photoshop 3.0	CMYK, RGB, and Grayscale
PICT	RGB
Pixar	RGB, Grayscale,
Raw	CMYK, RGB, and Grayscale
Targa	RGB
TIFF	CMYK, RGB, and Grayscale

Color modes supported by Photoshop file formats:

File format	Supported color mode
Photoshop 3.0	Multichannel, Lab Color, CMYK, RGB, Indexed, Duotone, Grayscale, Bitmap
Amiga IFF (IFF)	RGB, Indexed, Grayscale, Bitmap
Windows Bitmap (BMP, RLE)	RGB, Indexed, Grayscale, Bitmap
CompuServe GIF (GIF)	Indexed, Grayscale, Bitmap
EPS (EPS)	Lab Color, CMYK, RGB, Indexed, Duotone, Grayscale, Bitmap

FilmStrip (FLM)	RGB
JPEG	CMYK, RGB, Grayscale
MacPaint (MPT, MAC)	Bitmap
PCX (PCX)	RGB, Indexed, Grayscale, Bitmap
PICT File (PCT, PIC)	RGB, Indexed, Grayscale, Bitmap
Pixar (PXR)	RGB, Grayscale
PixelPaint 1.0/2.0 (PX1)	Indexed, Grayscale, Bitmap
Raw (RAW)	Multichannel, Lab Color, CMYK, RGB, Indexed, Duotone, Grayscale
Scitex CT (SCT)	CMYK, RGB, Grayscale
Targa (TGA)	RGB, Indexed, Grayscale
TIFF (TIF)	Lab Color, CMYK, RGB, Indexed, Grayscale, Bitmap

Photoshop installs the following File Format plug-in files into the Photoshp\Plugins folder:

Plug-in File	Format
TARGA8B.8BI	Targa (TGA)
PIXAR8B.8BI	Pixar (PXR)
PIXPNT8B.8BI	PixelPaint 1.0/2.0 (PX1)
PCX8B.8BI	PCX (PCX)
MACPNT8B.8BI	MacPaint (MPT, MAC)
GIF8B.8BI	CompuServe Graphics Interchange Format (GIF)
FILMST8B.8BI	FilmStrip (FLM)
BMP8B.8BI	Windows Bitmap (BMP, RLE)
AIFF8B.8BI	Amiga Interchange File Format (IFF)

Gallery Effects Volume One Filters Not Available in Windows Photoshop 2.5.1 or Later

ISSUE
After you install Gallery Effects Volume One, the filters do not display under the Filter menu in Adobe Photoshop 2.5.1.

SOLUTION
Update to Gallery Effects Volume One version 1.5.2 or later.
OR: When you using Windows 95 or Windows NT, use version 1.5.2 of Gallery Effects Volume One and Photoshop 3.0.5 or later.

ADDITIONAL INFORMATION
Version 1.5 and earlier of Gallery Effects Volume One are not compatible with Photoshop 2.5.1 or later. Version 1.5.2 and later of Gallery Effects Volume One are compatible with Photoshop 2.5.1 and later when you use Photoshop in a 16-bit version of Windows (i.e., Windows 3.1x). Version 1.5.2 of Gallery Effects Volume One is compatible with Photoshop 3.0.5 when you use Photoshop in a 32-bit version of Windows (i.e., Windows 95 and Windows NT).

Photoshop 3.0.1 Deluxe Tutorial Displays Bottom Half of Screen Only

ISSUE
Only the bottom half of the video picture is visible in the Adobe Photoshop 3.0.1 Deluxe CD-ROM Tutorial. The top half of the video picture is black.

SOLUTION
Make sure your video driver is compatible with Photoshop 3.0.1 and QuickTime 1.1.1 or later. For information on whether your video driver is compatible with Photoshop 3.0.1 and QuickTime 1.1.1 or later, or to obtain an updated video driver, contact the video card manufacturer.

ADDITIONAL INFORMATION
Incompatible video drivers for installed video cards (e.g., Western Digital video card) cause the Photoshop 3.0.1 Deluxe CD-ROM Tutorial to display incorrectly (i.e., only the bottom half of the screen).

Plug-ins Don't Appear in Photoshop 3.0x Running on Windows NT

ISSUE
When you run Adobe Photoshop 3.0x in Windows NT 3.5, third-party plug-ins do not appear under the Filter or Acquire menus. When you select a third-party plug-in, a system error (e.g., freeze) occurs.

SOLUTIONS
Use the standard (i.e., non-optional) 32-bit Photoshop plug-ins included with Photoshop 3.0x.
OR: Instead of using a third-party plug-in to scan an image, use the scanner software outside of the Photoshop application, when available.
OR: Run Photoshop in Windows 3.1x or Windows for Workgroups 3.11.
OR: Use the updated, 32-bit version of the plug-in.

ADDITIONAL INFORMATION
Plug-ins written for a 16-bit operating environment are not 32-bit compatible. Because Windows NT 3.5 is a 32-bit operating environment, Photoshop 3.0x only supports 32-bit plug-ins when you run in Windows NT. The standard (non-optional) plug-ins included with Photoshop are 32-bit plug-ins. The optional, third-party plug-ins included on the Photoshop 3.0.x Deluxe CD-ROM are 16-bit plug-ins.

Unable to Use Distort Filter on 16 MB or Larger Image in Photoshop 3.0.x

ISSUE
The error "Could not complete your request because there is not enough memory (RAM)" appears when applying a

Distort filter (e.g., Pinch, Ripple, Twirl) to an image larger than 16 MB in Adobe Photoshop 3.0.x.

SOLUTIONS

Apply the Distort filter to an image that is smaller than 16 MB.
OR: Apply the Distort filter to each of the image's channels (e.g., Red, Green, Blue).
OR: Use the Distort filter in Photoshop running under Windows 95 or Windows NT.

ADDITIONAL INFORMATION

When running Photoshop 3.0.x on a computer with WIN-32s installed, applying a Distort filter to an image larger than 16 MB causes the error "Could not complete your request because there is not enough memory (RAM)" because Win32s cannot allocate memory in blocks larger than 16 MB.

Windows 95 and Windows NT can allocate memory in blocks larger than 16 MB.

MAC OS

Q My pen tool seems awfully slow compared to the rest of Photoshop's features. How can I speed it up?

A Chances are your pen tool is being slowed down by the "DirectBits" Plug-in, which is supposed to improve the performance of the Bezier (pen) tool. However, the "DirectBits" Plug-in that shipped with Photoshop 3.0 wasn't written in native PowerMac code, so it actually degrades Bezier-tool performance instead of improving it.

To maximize your pen tool's performance, upgrade to the "fat" version of DirectBits, which includes a native PowerMac version of DirectBits. It's on the free Adobe Technical Support BBS—call (206) 623-6984 and download the "DirectBits (Fat).SEA" self-extracting archive from the File Library: Photoshop: Photoshop-Mac section. The same file is also available in the Macintosh Files library of the Aldus forum on America Online (use the Keyword "ALDUS" or "ADOBE" to enter this forum). On CompuServe, you can find the upgraded version of DirectBits in the Adobe forum (type GO ADOBEAP and download the DIRBIT.SEA file from the Photoshop Mac library).

Q My cursor sometimes disappears when I'm working in a Photoshop document. I thought my copy of Photoshop might be damaged so I reinstalled, but it still happens. What's wrong?

A This problem is usually caused by a conflict between an extension and the DirectCursors Plug-in that shipped with Photoshop 3.x. It can also be caused by an old version of DirectCursors from Photoshop 2.5.

To find out what the cause is, reboot with extensions off (hold down the Shift key at startup until you see the message "Extensions Off" on the "Welcome" screen). Try using your cursor in Photoshop again; if it doesn't disappear anymore, your problem was being caused by an extension conflict, and you'll have to do some troubleshooting to track down which extension is the culprit.

If rebooting with extensions off doesn't fix the problem, check to be sure you don't have more than one DirectCursors Plug-in installed. If you do find more than one, you'll want to delete all except one copy of version 3.0 of the Plug-in. You can check the version numbers by selecting the Plug-in file (click on it once in the Finder) and pressing Command + I to display the "DirectCursors Info" window. The version number appears just above the "Comments" box.

If all else fails, you can eliminate your problem by disabling the DirectCursors Plug-in—just move it from your "Plug-ins" folder (it should be located inside the "Extensions" folder inside the "Plug-ins" folder) to someplace outside Photoshop's designated "Plug-ins" folder, and then restart Photoshop.

If you disable DirectCursors your cursor should stop disappearing, but you will lose some functionality. The DirectCursors Plug-in allows Photoshop to display large brush cursors (up to 300 pixels!) if the "Brush Size" option is checked in Photoshop's "General Preferences" dialog box. Without DirectCursors, your brush cursor can only display up to 16 pixels. DirectCursors also allows the crosshair cursor (displayed when the Caps Lock key is pressed) to show up against a 50% neutral gray background—if the Plug-in is disabled, the crosshair cursor may be difficult to see against a 50% gray or similar background.

Q Sometimes when I'm using Photoshop and entering text I get strange characters, some of which look like they're from a foreign language. What's going on?

A You're probably running into one of System 7.5's little-known features. When you press the Command and space-bar keys together (which happens to be the keyboard shortcut for Photoshop's zoom tool), you switch your system from one keyboard layout to another if you have more than one keyboard layout installed. If you did the default installation of System 7.5, you almost certainly have a bunch of extra foreign-language keyboard layouts available.

Unfortunately, when you change your keyboard layout using this shortcut, System 7.5 doesn't tell you that you've just switched to Portuguese or Danish (or whatever happens to be next in line). And there's no way to stop the System software from doing this every time you use that keystroke in any application, unless you remove the extra keyboard layouts.

To put a stop to this unwanted language-switching, you can either upgrade to System 7.5.1 (which no longer supports this language-switching convenience), or remove from the "Keyboard" Control Panel all your keyboard layouts except the one you want to keep (probably U.S. English). To do so, close all your applications and drag extra keyboard layouts out of your System suitcase (which is located in your System Folder).

Q I've used the Gamma Control Panel to set the gamma for my monitor as part of the calibration process, but every time I boot my Power Mac, the gamma settings seem to be ignored. What's up?

A This problem is unique to PCI-based Power Macs running System 7.5.2. What happens is that adjustments made to the Gamma Control Panel (which is made by Knoll Software and comes free with Photoshop) are ignored at startup—in fact, if you watch carefully, you may notice that the gamma adjustments get made when the Control Panel loads, but then are lost just before the Desktop appears. Updating to System 7.5.3 sometimes eliminates the problem. But if it doesn't, or you don't want to update, there are a couple of ways around it.

Probably the easiest is to make an alias of the Gamma Control Panel and place it in your System Folder's "Startup Items" folder. This will cause the gamma settings to load again after all other Extensions have loaded. (You could also simply open and then close the Gamma Control Panel, but you'd probably get tired of doing this every time you boot your Mac.) Another option is to delete the "Display Preferences" file from the "Preferences" folder in the System Folder and restart—but again, this can get tedious.

Incidentally, if you don't find the Gamma Control Panel in your "Control Panels" folder, it's probably still in the "Calibration" folder in the "Goodies" folder inside your Photoshop folder, which is where a default installation puts it. If it's not there (because you performed a custom installation), you can grab it from the equivalent location on the Photoshop Deluxe CD-ROM.

Q Sometimes when I enter type that has long ascenders or descenders in Photoshop, the tops and bottoms of longer characters get clipped off. Changing the leading doesn't seem to fix it. Are my fonts corrupted? Is Photoshop?

A Neither. It's probably the result of a setting in Adobe Type Manager (ATM), which Photoshop uses to rasterize type—that is, to turn it into bitmaps. The problem occurs with only a few fonts (such as certain script faces) that have exceptionally long ascenders and/or descenders. To fix it, open the ATM Control Panel and, under "Preserve," select the "Character shapes" option (by default, "Line spacing" is selected). Close the ATM Control Panel and restart your Mac. Back in Photoshop, type your text again, and it will appear with its ascenders and descenders intact.

ATM's default setting to preserve line spacing is appropriate for typographically oriented programs—such as PageMaker, Illustrator, and many others. In fact, be sure to set ATM back to the "Line spacing" setting and restart your Mac again before using type in any such program. (Don't worry, the type you already entered in Photoshop will still look fine—all that matters is ATM's setting at the moment you click "OK" in Photoshop's "Type Tool" dialog box, which is when the rasterization takes place.)

If you need to switch back and forth between Photoshop and other programs frequently, all this restarting of your Mac isn't too practical. In that case, it's probably a better idea to set your type in Illustrator, convert it to outlines, and import it into Photoshop.

Q I have an object-oriented PICT file that was created in Canvas. I know Photoshop can read PICTs, but this one looks awful when I open it—very jagged. Can you tell me what is going on with this PICT?

A There are PICTs and then there are PICTs—they're not quite as unique as snowflakes (thank goodness), but they're not all the same. Most PICT files you come across, including those Photoshop writes, are pixel-based or bitmap PICTs. You open them just like any other pixel-based file. Some applications, however, such as Canvas or ClarisDraw, write out object-oriented PICT files in which the image data is described as a series of shapes rather than as a grid of pixels.

As you've seen, Photoshop will let you open object-oriented PICTs "conventionally," but you'll probably wind up with a file in Bitmap mode—pure black and white. If your image contained colors or gradual tone transitions, all of them will be lost. The better choice is to open such a file as an anti-aliased PICT. To do so, choose "Acquire" from the File menu, and select "Anti-aliased PICT." (Note that to enable this option, you must have Photoshop's Anti-Aliased PICT Plug-in installed. You can find it on the Adobe Photo-shop 3.0 Deluxe CD-ROM in the Adobe Photoshop 3.0.5:-Adobe Photoshop 3.0.5 Universal:Plug-ins:Acquire/Export folder, or you can use the "Easy Install" option to install from diskettes, which will install all Plug-ins.) Since an object-oriented PICT file is resolution-independent, you can enter dimensions (in pixels) in the "Anti-Aliased PICT" dialog box to scale the image up or down as it's being rasterized—the same way you can specify dimensions when you're rasterizing an EPS file. Once you've opened it in Photoshop, the image will be composed of pixels like any other Photoshop document, with no loss of color or quality.

Q *(3.0.x only)* **I'm trying to get Photoshop running on my Performa 6300 but it refuses to launch, saying there isn't enough RAM. I recently upgraded to 32 MB of RAM, and it still says there isn't enough memory to launch. How much RAM do I have to throw at Photoshop to make it go?**

A Actually, you probably had enough RAM to begin with —but don't worry, you'll be glad you bought more (RAM prices have been so low, and anyway you can't have too much memory). The problem you describe stems from the PowerPC 603 chip in your Performa. On any PowerPC-based Macintosh running this chip, you need to have the Macintosh Easy Open Control Panel loaded; otherwise you will get that memory alert no matter how much RAM is installed. (This condition occurs not only in Photoshop, but in many other applications as well.) The Macintosh Easy Open Control Panel has an "Automatic document translation" feature that may interfere with normal operations (such as placing a TIFF file into PageMaker). You can turn off "Automatic document translation," but Macintosh Easy Open has to load at startup in order to prevent the erroneous memory alert—so remember, if you disable the Macintosh Easy Open Control Panel by using an Extensions manager or by rebooting with the Shift key held down to bypass all Extensions, the problem will return.

Q *(3.0 and later)* **Sometimes when I run the Displace filter on an image, things just seem to go haywire. The displacement doesn't work correctly, and I get some strange, hard-to-read text over my image that sometimes looks like it's in a bunch of different languages. What's going on here?**

A Don't worry—it isn't speaking in tongues. The problem stems from trying to use a file containing layers as your displacement map. Photoshop can't use files that contain layer information for a displacement map; when you try to use one, it displays text across your file warning you that something has gone wrong. Although it can be hard to read (it depends on your document), the text should say, "Photoshop 3.0 is required to open this file" in English and six other languages. Just save a flattened copy of the image you're using for your displacement map, and it should work correctly.

Another way to prevent this is to save your files with the "2.5 Format Compatibility" option selected in the "More Preferences" dialog box (Photoshop 3.0) or the "Saving Files" portion of the "Preferences" dialog box (Photoshop 4.0). When you save a document with this on, Photoshop saves a flattened version of your image within your Photoshop file so Photoshop 2.5 (which doesn't support layers) can open it. By default this option is selected, but you may have deselected it in order to reduce the size of the Photoshop-format files you save.

Gamma Control Panel Turns Off After Extensions Have Loaded on PCI Power Macintosh

ISSUE

When you start a PCI-based Power Macintosh or MacOS clone running System 7.5.2, Knoll Software's Gamma 2.0 control panel loads and applies a gamma adjustment to the monitor display. Then, after all other extensions load, the monitor display reverts to its pre-gamma display.

SOLUTIONS

Place an alias of the Gamma control panel in the Startup Items folder in the System Folder.

OR: Open and close the Gamma control panel after startup.

OR: Delete or remove the Display Preferences file from the Preferences folder in the System Folder.

OR: Upgrade to System 7.5.3, then delete the Display Preferences file and the Sound & Displays or Monitors control panel, if installing the system software does not delete them.

ADDITIONAL INFORMATION

When you restart the Macintosh after changing the settings in System 7.5.2's Sound & Displays (Power Macintosh 7500, 8500) or Monitors (Power Macintosh 7200, 7500) control panel, the Gamma 2.0 control panel loads and then appears to turn off because the new settings override the adjustment made by the Gamma control panel. The settings are saved in the Display Preferences file, so deleting the Display Preferences file restores the default settings for the control panels, which do not override the Gamma control panel's gamma adjustment. Deleting the Display Preferences file does not affect custom color depth or screen resolution settings.

Because items in the Startup Items folder load after all other extensions, placing an alias of the Gamma control panel forces the system to reload the Gamma control panel after reading the Display Preferences file, which restores the Gamma control panel's gamma adjustment.

Opening and closing the Gamma control panel at any time forces the system to read the Gamma control panel's settings, which restores the Gamma control panel's adjustment.

System 7.5.3 controls video and sound using the Monitors & Sound control panel, instead of the Sound & Displays or Monitors control panel. Changing settings in the Monitors & Sound control panel does not override the Gamma control panel's gamma adjustment.

Unable to Save in MacPaint Format in Photoshop 3.0.x

ISSUE

When saving a document, Adobe Photoshop 3.0.x dims the MacPaint file format in the Save, Save As, or Save a Copy dialog box.

SOLUTIONS

Do one or more of the following:

A. Change the color mode to Bitmap to convert the image to a 1-bit format.

B. Ensure the image is smaller than 576 x 720 pixels.

ADDITIONAL INFORMATION

The MacPaint file format only accepts bitmap (i.e., black-and-white, 1-bit) images smaller than 576 x 720 pixels. Photoshop 3.0.x dims the MacPaint file format in the Save, Save As, and Save a Copy dialog box when you're saving an image in a color mode other than Bitmap (e.g., RGB, Grayscale), or when saving an image larger than 576 x 720 pixels.

Photoshop does not list the MacPaint file format in the Save, Save As, or Save a Copy dialog box when the MacPaint plug-in is missing, Photoshop's link to the plug-ins folder is broken, or the Adobe Photoshop 3.x Prefs file is damaged.

DCS Files Named Differently Than Expected in Photoshop 3.0x

ISSUE

After saving an image, whose filename includes the .EPS extension, in DCS format from Adobe Photoshop 3.0x,

Photoshop names the main file as expected (e.g., Filename.EPS), but does name the separation files as expected (e.g., Filename.C, Filename.M, Filename.Y, and Filename.K instead of Filename.EPS.C, Filename.EPS.M, Filename-.EPS.Y, and Filename.EPS.K).

SOLUTION

Before saving the image in DCS format in Photoshop, remove or change the .EPS extension in the image's filename.

ADDITIONAL INFORMATION

When saving a DCS image than includes the .EPS extension in its filename, Photoshop replaces the .EPS extension for the separation files with the separation file extensions (e.g., .C, .M, .Y, ".K) to ensure cross-platform compatibility. Photoshop replaces only the .EPS extension, and does not replace other filename extensions, when saving an image in DCS format.

The main, or master, DCS file uses filename extensions (e.g., .C, .M, .Y, .K) to locate the separation files. DCS files with multiple extensions other than .EPS (e.g., Filename-.FOO.M) separate as expected on the Macintosh, as the Macintosh or DCS file format does not require a single filename extension. DOS-compatible files use filename extensions (e.g., .EPS) to indicate a file's type or creator. DOS-compatible computers support only filenames containing eight or less characters followed by an extension containing three or less characters.

Photoshop 3.0.1 Displays Incorrect Version Number for TWAIN Plug-in

ISSUE

When you select About Plug-in > TWAIN Acquire from the Apple menu in Adobe Photoshop 3.0.1, Photoshop displays the incorrect version number (i.e., 1.0) for the TWAIN plug-in file. The TWAIN Info dialog box displays the correct version number (i.e., 3.0).

SOLUTIONS

Verify the correct version number of the TWAIN plug-in file in the TWAIN Info dialog box:

1. At the Finder, double-click the Acquire/Export folder in the Photoshop's plug-ins folder.
2. Single-click to select the TWAIN plug-in file, then choose File > Get Info.
3. In the TWAIN Info dialog box, the correct version (i.e., 3.0) is displayed after "Version:" toward the bottom of the window.

OR: Update to Photoshop 3.0.4.

ADDITIONAL INFORMATION

Photoshop 3.0.1 displays the incorrect version number (i.e., 1.0) for the TWAIN plug-in file when you choose About Plug-in > TWAIN Acquire from the Apple menu. The correct version number is displayed in the TWAIN Info dialog box.

Photoshop 3.0.4 and later display the correct version number of the TWAIN plug-in file when you choose About Plug-in > TWAIN Acquire from the Apple menu.

JPEG Compressed PICT Graphic Appears with Only Top Half

ISSUE

After you save a PICT graphic with JPEG compression in Adobe Photoshop 2.5x or later, Photoshop 2.5x displays on the top half of the the JPEG image and Photoshop 3.0 displays the entire JPEG image in the top half with distortion. The bottom half of the JPEG image displays as white.

SYMPTOMS

The JPEG image was saved on a Macintosh with QuickTime 2.0 and the RasterOps 24STV, 24MxTV, 24XLTV, or MediaTime video capture card installed.

SOLUTIONS

Disable the RasterOps video capture card.

OR: Temporarily disable the RasterOps Video 3.0 control panel by moving it out of the Control Panels folder in the System Folder and then restart the Macintosh.

NOTE: Disabling the RasterOps Video control panel disables RasterOps video digitizing and codec (compression/decompression) components for QuickTime.

ADDITIONAL INFORMATION

Because of a conflict between QuickTime 2.0 and the RasterOps Video 3.0 control panel, PICT graphics saved with JPEG compression in Adobe Photoshop 2.5x and later display incorrectly. The RasterOps Video control panel supports various video capture cards and includes the video digitizing and codec components for QuickTime. Installing the Apple MultiMedia Tuner 2.0.1 does not prevent PICT graphics saved with JPEG compression from displaying incorrectly. Versions of QuickTime earlier than QuickTime 2.0 may be incompatible with other applications.

Desired Color Mode Unavailable in Photoshop 2.5 or Later

ISSUE

The desired color mode is dimmed in Adobe Photoshop 3.0.x and earlier's Mode menu.

SOLUTIONS

Do one or more of the following:

A. Choose an intermediate color mode, then select the desired mode. For a list of mode conversion options available from each mode, see Additional Information.
NOTE: Mode conversions change the data in a document, which can result in data loss.

B. Delete one or more channels in the file so that the total number of channels in the file after mode conversion will not exceed 24 (Photoshop 3.0x) or 16 (Photoshop 2.5x).

C. Save a copy of the file without alpha channels or layers.

ADDITIONAL INFORMATION

Adobe Photoshop 3.0.x includes eight modes under the Mode menu. Available mode conversion options change depending on the current mode, with unavailable modes dimmed.

Photoshop dims modes in the Mode menu when the mode conversion would add channels to the file in excess of Photoshop's channel limit, which is 24 channels (Photoshop 3.0x) or 16 channels (Photoshop 2.5.x). Photo-shop files have one, three, or four channels, and you can create additional channels (i.e., alpha channels) in any file. Photoshop adds channels to a file when you convert to a color mode that uses more channels than the current mode. For example, the RGB mode uses three channels and the CMYK mode uses four, so converting from RGB to CMYK adds one channel to the file.

Because the Multichannel mode does not add channels but converts a file's channels to generic channels, Multichannel may be available when other modes are dimmed.

Mode	*Mode conversion options available*
Bitmap	Grayscale
Grayscale	Bitmap, Duotone, Indexed Color, RGB Color, CMYK Color, Lab Color, Multichannel
Duotone	Bitmap, Grayscale, Indexed Color, RGB Color, CMYK Color, Lab Color, Multichannel
Indexed Color	Grayscale, RGB Color, CMYK Color, Lab Color
RGB Color	Grayscale, Indexed Color, CMYK Color, Lab Color, Multichannel
CMYK Color	Grayscale, RGB Color, Lab Color, Multichannel
Lab Color	Grayscale, RGB Color, CMYK Color, Multichannel
Multichannel	Bitmap, Grayscale, RGB Color (for files containing 3 channels), CMYK Color (for files containing 4 channels), Lab Color

Cursor Disappears in Photoshop 3.0.x for Macintosh

ISSUE

When you position the cursor over an image in Adobe Photoshop 3.0.x, the cursor (e.g., paintbrush, pencil, magic wand, marquee, lasso) disappears or is faint.

SOLUTIONS

Do one or more of the following:

A. Restart the Macintosh with extensions off, then launch Photoshop to verify that added extensions or control panels are not causing the problem. To turn all extensions off upon startup in System 7, restart the computer while holding down the Shift key until the system returns the message "Welcome to Macintosh. Extensions Off." When the problem does not reoccur after disabling added extenstions, troubleshoot extension conflicts.

B. Ensure that you are using the version of the DirectCursors plug-in that corresponds to your version of Photoshop. To determine your plug-in version, single-click the DirectCursors plug-in, located in the DirectCursors folder in the Extensions folder in Photoshop's Plug-ins folder, then choose File > Get Info. For corresponding Photoshop and DirectCursors version numbers, see Additional Information.

C. Disable the DirectCursors plug-in to prevent it from loading when you launch Photoshop:
   1. Quit Photoshop.
   2. Rename the DirectCursors folder by typing Option + l (lowercase "L") at the beginning of the DirectCursors folder name, or move the DirectCursors plug-in to another location (e.g., desktop).
   3. Restart Photoshop.

D. Ensure only one DirectCursors plug-in is installed in Photoshop's Plug-ins folder or subfolder of the Plug-ins folder.

E. Recreate Photoshop's preferences file:
   1. Quit Photoshop.
   2. Delete or remove the Adobe Photoshop 3.0 Prefs file, located in the Preferences folder in the System Folder.
   3. Launch Photoshop.

ADDITIONAL INFORMATION

The cursor disappears or is faint after you position it over an image in Photoshop 3.0.x when one or more extensions conflicts with the DirectCursors plug-in, more than one DirectCursors plug-in is installed in the Plug-ins folder, a version earlier than DirectCursors 3.0 plug-in is installed in the Plug-ins folder, or when the Photoshop preferences file is damaged.

Multiple DirectCursors plug-ins or an earlier version of the DirectCursors plug-in are commonly installed when the contents of the Plug-ins folder from a previous version of Photoshop are copied into Photoshop 3.0.x's Plug-ins folder.

The DirectCursors plug-in enables several display-related cursor features. Selecting the Brush Size option in the General Preferences dialog box enables the DirectCursors plug-in to display brush cursors larger than 16 pixels. Disabling the DirectCursors plug-in limits the display size of the cursor to Photoshop's maximum size of 16 pixels. The DirectCursors plug-in also enables the crosshair cursor to contrast against a 50% neutral gray background. Disabling the DirectCursors plug-in may cause the crosshair cursor to be invisible against a neutral 50% gray, or similar shade background.

Photoshop Version	Corresponding DirectCursors Version
3.0.5	3.0.5
3.0.4	3.0.4
3.0.3	3.0
3.0.1	3.0

Thumbnail Preview Doesn't Appear in Photoshop 3.0.x's Open Dialog Box

ISSUE

When you open a file in Adobe Photoshop 3.0.x, the file's thumbnail preview and the Show Thumbnail option do not appear in the Open dialog box.

SOLUTIONS

Do one or more of the following:

A. Delete then reinstall QuickTime 2.x or later:
   1. Quit all applications.
   2. Disable extensions by restarting the computer while holding the Shift key until the message "Welcome to Macintosh. Extensions Off." appears.
   3. Delete the QuickTime and QuickTime PowerPlug (Power Macintosh only) extensions from the Extensions folder in the System Folder.
   4. Restart the Macintosh
   5. Insert the Photoshop 3.0.x Deluxe CD-ROM, then double-click the Adobe Photoshop Installer.
   6. Select Custom Install, select QuickTime from the available options, then click Install.
   7. Restart the Macintosh, and restart Photoshop.

B. Disable all extensions, except the QuickTime and QuickTime PowerPlug (Power Macintosh only) extensions, by removing them from the System Folder then restarting the Macintosh or by using Extensions Manager to verify that other extensions or control panels are not the cause.

C. Reinstall Photoshop 3.0.x.

D. Reinstall the Macintosh system software.

ADDITIONAL INFORMATION

Photoshop 3.0.x uses QuickTime 2.x to display thumbnail previews in the Open dialog box. When QuickTime 2.x is not installed or is damaged, Photoshop is unable to display thumbnail previews or the Show Thumbnail option in the Open dialog box.

Extension conflicts, damaged application software, or damaged system software may also prevent Photoshop from displaying thumbnail previews in the Open dialog box.

When the Show Thumbnail option is available and checked but a file's thumbnail preview does not display, then the file may not have been saved with a preview file.

Thumbnail preview files are PICT files compressed using QuickTime compression.

Performance Doesn't Improve Using PowerPC Accelerator or AV DSP Plug-in with Photoshop 2.5.1 LE

Adobe's AV DSP (Audio Visual Digital Signal Processor) plug-in and PowerPC Accelerator plug-in improve the performance and speed of Adobe Photoshop 2.5x, but not in Photoshop 2.5x LE, on AV Macintosh computers (e.g., 840AV) and Power Macintosh computers. The AV DSP and PowerPC Accelerator plug-ins were written for and designed to speed up the full version of Photoshop 2.5x only.

Installed Plug-ins do not Appear in Photoshop 2.0

ISSUE

Photoshop 2.0 does not list installed plug-ins or acquire modules in its Filter menu the Acquire submenu of its File menu.

SOLUTION

Make sure there is only one Photoshop preference file, "PS Prefs," on the system and that it is located in the same directory as the plug-in modules.

1. Quit Photoshop.
2. Use the Finder to locate the Photoshop preferences file, "PS Prefs."
3. If there is more than one "PS Prefs" file, delete all but one and move that one to the "Plug-ins" folder in the Photoshop folder.
4. Start Photoshop.

NOTE: A dialog box may appear and ask "Where is the preferences file?" If so, navigate to and select the "PS Prefs" file in the Plug-ins folder.

ADDITIONAL INFORMATION

The Photoshop preferences file, "PS Prefs," must be located in the same folder as the plug-in filters and acquire modules for those filters and modules to appear in Photoshop 2.0x Filter or Acquire menus.

Photoshop 3.0.x Displays Apple Color Picker

ISSUE

When you modify the foreground or background color in Adobe Photoshop 3.0.x, the Apple Color Picker (i.e., color wheel) displays instead of the Adobe Photoshop color picker. The Custom button and CMYK color model do not appear in the Apple Color Picker dialog box.

SOLUTION

Select the Adobe Photoshop color picker in the General Preferences dialog box.

1. Choose File > Preferences > General.
2. In the General Preferences dialog box, select Photoshop from the Color Picker pop-up menu, then click OK.

ADDITIONAL INFORMATION

The color picker selected in the General Preferences dialog box determines the color model options available in the Color Picker dialog box. When the Apple Color Picker is selected in the General Preferences dialog box, the Apple color wheel appears in place of the square Photoshop color field, and the Custom button and CMYK color model do not appear in the Color Picker dialog box.

The Apple Color Picker defines colors using the HSB or RGB color model. The Adobe Photoshop color picker enables you to define a color using the CMYK, HSB, RGB color models, or choose a color from a custom color library (e.g., PANTONE, APNA, TRUMATCH).

Photoshop 3.0's default color picker is the Adobe Photoshop color picker.

Application Errors

MAC OS / WINDOWS

Q Often when I've been working in Photoshop and I switch to another open application, I see a message on the screen that says "Exporting Clipboard," with a progress bar that sometimes takes quite a while to fill up. Is there any way to stop this from happening, and if so, is it a bad idea to do so?

A Photoshop uses its own proprietary clipboard format for copying and pasting within Photoshop. The message you refer to is telling you that Photoshop is transferring whatever's in its own clipboard to the Windows or Macintosh clipboard, in case you want to paste it into another application.

This function works a little differently on Windows and the Mac. In Windows, when you quit Photoshop you receive a message reading, "There is image data on the Clipboard. Do you want this data to be available to other applications?" If you click "Yes," the progress bar and "Exporting Clipboard" message appear at the bottom of the screen. On the Mac, when you quit or switch to another application, you aren't presented with a choice—you simply get the "Exporting Clipboard" message and the progress bar.

In either case, you can prevent this message from appearing at all by choosing "General" from the Preferences submenu of the File menu and then, in the "General Preferences" dialog box, clicking the "More…" button. In the "More Preferences" dialog box, uncheck "Export Clipboard." The only thing this will disable is your ability to copy data from Photoshop into other applications via the Windows or Macintosh clipboard—which may or may not be a good idea anyway, since those clipboards don't support many of the file formats and data types commonly used in Photoshop.

Q I keep getting "Scratch Disk is Full" errors even though I think I have enough free disk space. I understand that you need to allow 3 to 5 times the size of the document for Photoshop's scratch file. I'm working on a 40-MB bitmap, and I have about 200 MB of disk space free. Shouldn't that be enough?

A Yes—and no. The "3 to 5 times the file size" rule of thumb holds true much of the time; you understand correctly that Photoshop will usually create a temporary (scratch-disk) file that's 3 to 5 times the size of your document while it's working on it. However, there's an exception to this rule; it doesn't hold true for files in Bitmap mode (that is, pure black-and-white images). For files in Bitmap mode, Photoshop may require up to ten times the size of the document for its scratch-disk file. Obviously, for large, high-resolution Bitmap mode files, the scratch-disk space requirement can be substantial. For example, if your Bitmap mode file is 40 MB, you could need up to 400 MB of free space for your scratch-disk file.

Q *(4.0 only)* **I see that Photoshop 4.0 can save files in PDF format, but it doesn't always seem to be able to open PDF files. What's up with that?**

A Photoshop can open only those PDFs that were written by Photoshop. Other PDF files (such as those created by Adobe Acrobat or Illustrator) show up in Photoshop's "Open" dialog box, but when you try to open one, Photoshop displays an error message reading, "Could not open [filename] because this is not an Adobe Photoshop PDF image file."

There is a way to get such a PDF file into Photoshop if you have Illustrator 5.5 or later: Use the "Open…" command within Illustrator to open the file, resave it as an Adobe Illustrator file, and then open and rasterize it in Photoshop.

Error Parsing EPS File in Photoshop 2.5.1 and Earlier

ISSUE

When opening an EPS file, Adobe Photoshop 2.5.1 or earlier returns the error "Could not open [Filename] because of a problem parsing the EPS file." The EPS file was saved with JPEG encoding.

SOLUTION

Open the EPS file in an application that can open a JPEG-encoded EPS file (e.g., Photoshop 3.0.x), and resave it with ASCII or Binary encoding.

ADDITIONAL INFORMATION

Photoshop 2.5.1 and earlier does not support JPEG encoding. JPEG-encoded EPS files must be opened in an application that supports them (e.g., Photoshop 3.0.x), then resaved with either Binary or ASCII encoding for before you can open them in Photoshop 2.5.1 or earlier.

JPEG-encoded files are smaller than both ASCII- and Binary-encoded files, but the compression is "lossy," which means the JPEG encoding can reduce the quality of your output. JPEG encoding is supported only when printed to a PostScript Level 2 output device.

ASCII-encoded files are larger than Binary-encoded files. The characters used in Binary and JPEG encoding may interfere with network protocols.

Error "Out of memory" or "Disk or Scratch Disk is full" Opening Image in Photoshop 3.0.x

ISSUE

When opening an image, Adobe Photoshop 3.0.x returns the error, "Out of memory" or "Disk or Scratch Disk is full"

SOLUTION

Make sure you have free disk space equal to 3-5 times the size of the file you're trying to open.

ADDITIONAL INFORMATION

Because Photoshop's native Photoshop format uses Run Length Encoded (RLE) compression, files saved in Photoshop's native format, PSD, are often larger in size when opened in Photoshop than when saved on the hard drive. The more alpha channels and layers in a PSD file, the more disk space Photoshop requires to open the file. When a file has many channels and many layers, Photoshop's status bar may indicate a file size more than 10 times the file size as indicated by the system software. For example, a saved 25 MB file with many layers and channels on the hard drive opens as a 500 MB file in Photoshop.

Flattening an image and simplifying or deleting unneeded channels before saving in Photoshop format reduces the amount of disk space Photoshop requires to open the file. RLE is better at compressing channels that do not contain complex information (e.g., a blend). The amount of free disk space Photoshop requires to open a file equals 3-5 times the size of the file you're opening.

WINDOWS

Q *(3.0 only)* **After I launch Photoshop I get the error "GROWSTUB caused a General Protection Fault in module POINTER.DLL." What's wrong?**

A This error message occurs due to a conflict between the Microsoft Mouse driver version 9.01 and the Win32s system—it can happen in any 32-bit application, such as Adobe Photoshop 3.0, that uses Win32s under Microsoft Windows 3.1 or Windows for Workgroups 3.11. Sometimes the same problem can cause different symptoms, such as the mouse "freezing" when the 32-bit application launches. To fix the problem, update your mouse driver or switch to a different driver.

To update your mouse driver, you'll need to obtain version 9.01b of the POINTER.DLL file. This file is available as a self-extracting archive called HD1061.EXE, and can be obtained on the Microsoft BBS at (206) 936-6735 (use any standard telecommunications software to connect), via the Internet at ftp.microsoft.com:Softlib/MSLFILES, or directly from Microsoft.

If you can't get the new POINTER.DLL file as fast as you need it, or want another fix, you can also eliminate the error by changing the mouse driver to "Microsoft, or IBM PS/2" and removing the reference to "pointer.exe" from the WIN.INI file. Follow these steps:

1. Exit all applications.
2. Double-click on the Windows Setup icon in the Main group of the Program Manager.
3. Choose "Change System Settings" from the Options menu.
4. Select "Microsoft, or IBM PS/2" from the "Mouse" drop-down menu.
5. Click "OK," follow the prompts to install the mouse driver, then exit Windows Setup.
6. Make a backup copy of your WIN.INI file, then open it in a text editor, such as Windows Write or Notepad, that saves in text-only format.
7. Locate the "load=" line in the [Windows] section and delete the reference to "pointer.exe," including the path to that file. Do not delete the equals sign following the word "load." Here's an example of how the line should look before and after this step:
   Before:
   ```
   load=c:\windows\pointer.exe nwpopup.exe
   ```
   After:
   ```
   load=nwpopup.exe
   ```
8. Save the WIN.INI file as text-only and restart Windows.

Changing your mouse driver to the "Microsoft, or IBM PS/2" driver will fix the "GROWSTUB" errors, but you'll lose some of the special functionality of the Microsoft Mouse driver—for instance, larger pointer icons, reverse-video pointers, and different mouse tracking and mouse trails.

Q *(3.0.5 for Windows 3.x)* **When I launch Photoshop I get a message saying "At least one system component is out of date" and telling me that I need to reinstall PHOTOSHP.EXE. I've reinstalled many times, but I can't get past that error message. Help, please!**

A Help is on the way. Photoshop, not surprisingly, installs its system files in the directories where it needs them (see the following list). But other Windows applications may install their own, possibly older versions of the same system files into the same or other directories. When Photoshop launches, it sees an unexpected version or location of a necessary component installed by another program, and returns the "component is out of date" message.

To address this conflict, you'll have to search for the system files that Photoshop requires, and remove duplicate files from any directories where they don't belong (at least from Photoshop's perspective). You may want to create a separate directory into which to move the duplicates, or you can rename them and leave them where they were.

The system files listed below are installed by and required by Photoshop.

In the WINDOWS directory:

```
Ctl3d.dll     Kpsys32.dll
Ctl3d32s.dll  Pcdlib32.dll
Kpapi32.dll   Twain.dll
Kpcms.ini     Twunk_16.exe
Kpcp32.dll    Twunk_32.exe
```

In the WINDOWS\SYSTEM directory:

```
Compobj.dll   Penwin.dll
Ctl3d32.dll   Stdole.tlb
Msvcrt10.dll  Storage.dll
Msvcrt20.dll  Typelib.dll
Ole2.dll      W32sys.dll
Ole2.reg      Win32s16.dll
Ole2conv.dll  Windows.hlp
Ole2disp.dll  Winhlp32.cnt
Ole2nls.dll   Winhlp32.exe
Ole2prox.dll  Winhlp32.hlp
Ole2thk.dll   Winmm16.dll
```

Search for duplicates of all of these files, and note their locations. You'll want to delete, move, or rename these duplicates; make sure to exit Windows and do this at a DOS prompt. (You don't want to—and usually can't—alter Windows system files while Windows is running.) If you move the files, put them in a directory other than WINDOWS. Relaunch Windows once you've dealt with any duplicates; you should then be able to launch Photoshop.

Q Sometimes when I try to open a Photoshop TIFF, the file doesn't open and I get an error message saying the file is not a TIFF file, or that Photoshop could not parse the file. This also sometimes happens with other file formats. Are my files really becoming corrupt?

A This could happen because of a damaged file, but don't jump to that conclusion until you've investigated a more likely (and much easier to fix!) problem: the document may simply have been given the wrong file extension.

Photoshop will try to open a file in whatever format the extension indicates. (See the table below for a few of the commonest three-letter extensions for image files.) For example, if you have a file named PICTURE.JPG, Photoshop will try to open it as a JPEG file. But if that file is actually in some other format (for example, TIFF), Photoshop won't be able to open it correctly and will give you an error message. If you know a file has a format that's different from its three-character extension, either rename the file, or use the "Open As..." command from Photoshop's File menu and choose the correct file type in the "Open As" dialog box.

By the way, when you're saving a file in Photoshop 3.0.4 or later, the program will automatically append the correct filename extension based on the file type you specify in the "Save File as Format Type" field.

Common file-format extensions

.PSD	Photoshop native format
.GIF	Graphics interchange format
.TIF	TIFF (tagged image file format)
.JPG	JPEG (Joint Photographic Experts Group)
.EPS	Encapsulated PostScript
.PCD	Photo CD

Q I've been running Photoshop under Windows for some time without any trouble, but now I'm getting program errors. I can't open any new or existing files, I can't save files—it won't even let me scan! What could the problem be?

A If you've recently installed fax software, your problem is probably caused by having a fax-modem driver designated as your Windows default printer. Photoshop checks the default printer driver whenever it opens, creates, or saves a file, and when you're scanning from within Photoshop. If the driver returns information that Photoshop can't understand, it will generate one of these errors. Nonstandard drivers—especially fax-modem drivers—often will return nonstandard information.

The solution is to change your default printer to something more conventional, such as a PostScript printer (for instance, the HP LaserJet 4/4M PostScript driver works fine). It isn't necessary that you pick a printer you actually have.

To change your default printer in Windows 95, choose "Printers" from the Settings submenu of Windows 95's Start menu; in the "Printers" window, click on the printer driver you want and choose "Set As Default" from the File menu. (For instructions on changing your default printer in Windows 3.1 or NT, check your documentation.)

If that doesn't help, or if you haven't recently installed fax-modem software, your printer driver may be damaged or outdated. If it's damaged, reinstalling it off your Windows disks or CD should take care of the problem. If you think the printer driver may not have been updated for your version of Windows (either Windows 95, Windows 3.1, or Windows NT), contact the printer manufacturer for an updated driver.

Scanning Errors in Photoshop 3.0x under Windows NT

Adobe Photoshop 3.0x has built-in support for TWAIN32, an image-acquiring (scanning) technology designed for use with a 32-bit operating system (e.g., Windows NT). The TWAIN-32.DLL file, necessary to use TWAIN32, does not exist.

Because there is no TWAIN32.DLL file, the error "Could not complete your request because there is no scanner installed" appears when selecting "Select TWAIN32 Source..." from the "Acquire" submenu of the File menu and the error "Could not initialize TWAIN. Make sure that the TWAIN32.DLL is installed in the Windows directory" appears when selecting "TWAIN32" from the "Acquire" submenu of the File menu in Photoshop 3.0x when running under Windows NT.

It is the responsibility of scanner manufacturers to develop the TWAIN32.DLL file or a TWAIN32-compatible file.

Error "Scratch Disk Full" When Starting Photoshop 3.0

ISSUE

When starting, Adobe Photoshop 3.0 returns the error "Could not initialize Photoshop because the primary scrat-ch disk is full. We suggest you free some space on your scratch drive before continuing." The Photoshop primary scratch disk is on a volume containing more than 2 gigabytes (GB) of available disk space. The scratch disk volume and the startup volume contains adequate available disk space for the Windows Swap file, the Temp directory, and Photo-shop's scratch disk.

SOLUTIONS

Use Photoshop 3.0.4 or later.

OR: Reduce the amount of available disk space to 2 GB or less by moving files onto the hard disk or by partitioning the hard disk.

ADDITIONAL INFORMATION

Photoshop 3.0 cannot start when its scratch disk is on a volume containing 2 GB or more of available disk space, or when the startup volume and scratch disk volume have insufficient disk space for Photoshop's scratch disk, the Windows Swap file, and the Temp directory.

When Photoshop starts, it queries the startup volume or targeted scratch volume to determine the amount of free disk space available for the scratch disk. By default, Photoshop creates the primary scratch disk on the startup volume. Photoshop 3.0 cannot use a scratch disk that is larger than 2 GB. When Photoshop starts and queries a scratch disk on a volume containing 2 GB or more of available disk space, Photoshop reads the available disk space as a negative value and returns the error "Could not initialize Photoshop because the primary scratch disk is full. We suggest you free some space on your scratch drive before continuing."

Photoshop 3.0.4 can use a scratch disk on a volume containing 2 GB or more of available disk space. Scratch disks for Photoshop 3.0.x use a maximum of 2 GB for each scratch disk.

Error "...unable to parse the PostScript" When Opening an EPS File in Photosho 2.5.x

ISSUE

When you open an EPS file in Adobe Photoshop 2.5.x running under Windows NT Workstation 3.5 or Windows NT Server 3.5, Photoshop returns the error "Could not open [filename] because Photoshop was unable to parse the PostScript."

SOLUTION

Upgrade to Photoshop 3.0 or later.

ADDITIONAL INFORMATION

Unlike Photoshop 3.0 and later, Photoshop 2.5.x does not support Windows NT Workstation 3.5 and NT Server 3.5.

Error "...Sharing Violation On Drive [x]" Opening PhotoCD Image in Photoshop 3.0.x and Later

ISSUE

When you open a PhotoCD (*.pcd) file in Adobe Photoshop 3.0.x and later, the system returns the error "System Error: Sharing Violation on drive [x]." After you click Cancel, the Kodak Precision CMS PhotoCD dialog box appears. After you click OK in the dialog box, the error "Error- Call Failed" appears. After you click OK again, the error "Error- Memory Error Occurred" appears. After you click OK a third time, Photoshop returns but does not open the PhotoCD file.

SOLUTIONS

Remove Share.exe and install Vshare.386. When Share.exe is installed, the Autoexec.bat file includes a reference to it. To remove Share.exe and then install or reinstall Vshare.386, obtain and run the Ww1000.exe file, available from the Microsoft BBS, CompuServe, and GEnie, which expands to the Vshare.386 file and a ReadMe file, which provides instructions for removing Share.exe and installing Vshare.386.

OR: If Vshare.386 is already installed, rename and reinstall the Vshare.386 file. The Ww1000.exe file, available from the Microsoft BBS, CompuServe, and GEnie, expands to the Vshare.386 file and a ReadMe file, which provides instructions for installing Vshare.386.

ADDITIONAL INFORMATION

Photoshop 3.0.x requires the Vshare.386 file to open PhotoCD images. If the Vshare.386 file is missing or damaged, the error "System Error: Sharing Violation on drive [x]" appears when you open a PhotoCD image in Photoshop.

The Ww1000.exe file contains Vshare.386 version 3.11.-0.402, which is compatible with Windows 3.1x and Windows for Workgroups 3.1x.

Error "...not enough memory (RAM)..." When Starting Photoshop 3.0.x in Windows 3.1x

ISSUE

When you start Adobe Photoshop 3.0.x in Windows 3.1x, Photoshop 3.0.x returns the error "There is not enough memory (RAM) to launch Photoshop."

SOLUTIONS

Do one or more of the following:

A. Run Photoshop 3.0.x on a computer with at least 10 MB of RAM, which is Photoshop's minimum requirement.

B. Verify the Windows swap file is equal to or greater than the amount of installed RAM in size. When Photoshop's minimum requirement of installed RAM (10 MB) is installed, specify your swap file size to be at least 15 MB.

C. Recreate Photoshop's preferences files, named Photos30.psp and Ccolorsd, by quitting Photoshop, renaming or deleting the existing Photos30.psp and Ccolorsd files located in the Photoshp\Prefs directory (Photoshop 3.0.5) or Windows directory (Photoshop 3.0 and 3.0.4), then restarting Photoshop.

NOTE: Custom preference settings will be lost.

D. Recreate the Windows swap file:
1. Open the Windows Control Panel, located in the Main group of Program Manager.
2. Double-click the 386Enhanced icon.
3. Select Virtual Memory in the 386 Enhanced dialog box, then click Change.
4. In the Virtual Memory dialog box, select NONE as the Type in the New Settings section, then click OK and restart Windows.
5. To reset the Windows swap file, repeat steps 1-3, choose Permanent as the Type in the New Settings section of the Virtual Memory dialog box, change the size of the swap file to an amount equal to or greater than the amount of RAM in the New Size box, then click OK.
6. Restart Windows.
7. Recreate Photoshop's preferences file, named Photos30.psp, by quitting Photoshop, renaming or deleting the existing Photos30.psp file located in the Windows directory, then restarting Photoshop.

E. Ensure there is at least 20 MB of free contiguous hard disk space. When Photoshop and Windows are installed on different hard disks, ensure there is approximately 20 MB of free contiguous hard disk space on both hard disks.

F. Ensure there is at least 10-20 MB of free disk space for the directory containing temporary files, which is specified by the "Set Temp=" line in your Autoexec.bat file. To create more free disk space for your temporary files:

Exit to DOS then delete all existing temporary files (i.e., files with a *.TMP extension) located on the disk and directory listed in the "Set Temp=" line in the Autoexec.bat file.

OR: Delete other files to which the "Set Temp=" line points from the hard disk.

OR: Edit the "Set Temp=" line in the Autoexec.bat file to point to a disk with more free disk space.

NOTE: The "Set Temp=" line should point to a non-compressed disk and a directory containing only temporary files (e.g., C:\Temp).

ADDITIONAL INFORMATION

When starting Photoshop 3.0.x on a computer with less than 10 MB of memory (RAM) installed, with a small Windows swap file, or when the Photoshop preferences file or Windows swap file is damaged, Photoshop 3.0.x returns the error "There is not enough memory (RAM) to launch Photoshop." Photoshop requires a minimum of 20 MB of free contiguous hard disk space, 10 MB of RAM, and a Windows swap file specified to be at least equal to the amount of installed RAM, but no smaller than 15 MB, in size.

Error "GPF in Module Photoso2.dll" When Opening an EPS File in Photoshop 2.5.x

ISSUE

When you open an EPS file in Adobe Photoshop 2.5.x running under Windows NT Workstation 3.5 or Windows NT Server 3.5, the system returns the error "General Protection Fault in module Photoso2.dll at 0007:42FD."

SOLUTION

Upgrade to Photoshop 3.0 or later.

ADDITIONAL INFORMATION

Unlike Photoshop 3.0 and later, Photoshop 2.5.x does not support Windows NT Workstation 3.5 or NT Server 3.5.

Error After Selecting Gallery Effects Plug-in in Photoshop 3.x

ISSUE

When you select an Adobe Gallery Effects 1.5.1 plug-in in Adobe Photoshop, Photoshop returns the error, "Settings file (.set) extension is an old version. Please delete file and run extensions again."

SOLUTION

Reset the Gallery Effects preferences file:
1. Exit Photoshop.
2. Delete the Classic.set file, which is located in the Photoshp\Plugins directory.
3. Restart Photoshop, then select the Gallery Effects plug-in to enable Gallery Effects to create a new Classic.set file.

NOTE: You will need to reset custom Gallery Effects preferences.

ADDITIONAL INFORMATION

The Classic.set file created by Gallery Effects 1.5 and earlier is not compatible with Gallery Effects 1.5.1. If a Classic.set file created by Gallery Effects 1.5 or earlier is located in the Plugins directory, Gallery Effects 1.5.1 will return the error, "Settings file (.set) extension is an old version. Please delete file and run extensions again." when you select a Gallery Effects plug-in in Photoshop.

Gallery Effects creates the Classic.set file to store its custom settings.

Error "Could not initialize... file is locked" When Starting Photoshop 3.0.x

ISSUE

When starting, Adobe Photoshop 3.0.x returns the error "Could not initialize Photoshop because the file is locked. Use the 'Properties' command in the File Manager to unlock the file."

SOLUTION

Recreate Photoshop's preferences file:

1. Quit Photoshop.
2. Delete the Photos30.psp file located in the Win32-app\Photoshp\Prefs directory *(Photoshop 3.0.5)* or the Windows directory *(Photoshop 3.0 and 3.0.4).*

NOTE: Custom preference settings will be lost.

ADDITIONAL INFORMATION

When Photoshop 3.0.x cannot write to its scratch disk, it returns the error "Could not initialize Photoshop because the file is locked. Use the 'Properties' command in the File Manager to unlock the file." Photoshop cannot write to its scratch disk when you do not have write privileges on the volume specified as the primary scratch disk.

If Photoshop cannot find its preferences file when starting, it creates a new preferences file, which includes default settings. Photoshop's default setting for the primary scratch disk is the startup disk.

Error "Invalid Page Fault" Opening EPS or Illustrator File in Photoshop 3.0.4 in Windows 95

ISSUE

When you open or import an EPS file or Illustrator (*.ai) file in Adobe Photoshop 3.0.4 running in Windows 95, the system returns the error "This program has performed an illegal operation and will be shut down. If the problem persists, contact the program vendor." After you click Details in the error dialog box, the system returns the error "PHOTOSHP caused an invalid page fault in module [filename]," where the module's filename is Kernel32.dll, Agm.dll, or Aiparser.8by.

When you choose File > Open As, Photoshop 3.0.4 returns the error "Unable to parse the Postscript information, open preview instead?"

SOLUTIONS

Use Photoshop 3.0.5 or later.

OR: Reduce the number of fonts installed in Windows 95, including PostScript Type 1 and TrueType fonts, to 100 or less. For instructions, see Additional Information.

ADDITIONAL INFORMATION

If you run Photoshop 3.0.4 in Windows 95 with more than 100 TrueType or PostScript Type 1 fonts installed, the system returns the error "PHOTOSHP caused an invalid page fault in module Kernel32.dll." when you open or import an EPS file or Illustrator (*.ai) file. Reducing the total number of installed fonts to less than 100, although you may need to have no more than 50, or Using Photoshop 3.0.5 or later prevents the system error when you open or place files in Photoshop.

To reduce the number of installed fonts in Windows 95:

Remove TrueType fonts from the Windows Fonts folder except those that Windows installs:

1. Choose Start > Settings > Control Panel.
2. Double-click the Fonts icon.
3. Select font icons, then delete them or move them to another location (e.g., temporary folder on the Windows 95 desktop).
4. Restart Windows.

To disable PostScript Type 1 fonts:

Turn off ATM Deluxe 4.0 or ATM 4.0:

1. Choose Start > Programs > Adobe > Adobe Type Manager Deluxe or Adobe Type Manager.
2. Click the Settings tab.
3. Select Off in the ATM System section.
4. Exit ATM and restart Windows.

Turn off ATM 3.0x:

1. Choose Start > Programs > Main > ATM Control Panel.
2. Select the Off option.
3. Exit ATM and restart Windows.

Exporting your sets in ATM Deluxe 4.0 and then removing your fonts enables you to reimport your sets, instead of recreating them, after you re-add your fonts.

To export your sets in ATM Deluxe 4.0:

1. In ATM, click the Sets tab.
2. Select one or more sets to export.
3. Choose File > Export.
4. In the Export dialog box, specify a filename and location for the AFS file, then click Save.

To remove your fonts in ATM Deluxe 4.0 or ATM 4.0:

1. In the All Font Sets pane of the Sets tab (ATM Deluxe 4.0) or the Fonts tab (ATM 4.0), select the fonts you want to remove, then click Remove.
2. In the Remove Font dialog box, select Remove Fonts from All Set and Master Font List, select Remove Font Files from Disk if you are reinstalling your fonts from the original installation disks, then click Yes or Yes to All.

To re-add your fonts in ATM Deluxe 4.0 or ATM 4.0:

1. Click the Add Fonts tab (ATM Deluxe 4.0) or the Fonts tab (ATM 4.0), then select Browse for Fonts from the Source pop-up menu.
2. Navigate to the drive and directory containing your fonts files (e.g., C:\Psfonts\Pfm, A:\Fontdisk).
3. Select the fonts you want to add from the Source pane scroll box, then click Add.

To import your sets in ATM Deluxe 4.0:

1. With Browse for Fonts still selected in the Source pop-up menu, navigate to the drive and directory containing your AFS file. ATM lists the sets you exported in the AFS file.
2. Select the sets you want to import, then click Add.
3. Remove any duplicate fonts outside your sets by selecting them and then clicking Remove.

To remove your fonts in ATM 3.0x:

1. In the ATM Control Panel, select installed fonts from the Installed ATM Fonts list.
2. Click Remove.
3. In the Remove Fonts dialog box, select No Confirmation to Remove Fonts if you don't want the dialog box to appear for each font you remove, then click Yes or

Yes to All. If you want to delete the font files from your hard disk, select the Delete Fonts from Disk option.

MAC OS

Q *(3.0 only)* **I tried to select a color from the Color Picker and got the error, "Insert the disk [name of hard drive]." Is something wrong with my hard drive?**

A No, there probably isn't anything wrong with your hard drive. You should be able to use the Apple Color Picker in Photoshop. The problem you're seeing is the result of a conflict between System 7.5 and certain third-party, hard-disk formatting utilities.

Usually, this problem is caused by APS (Allied Peripheral Systems) drivers prior to version 3.0, SCSI Director drivers older than version 3.09, some CMS Enhancements drivers, and certain drivers from Transoft, a company that used to develop APS and SCSI Director drivers. These drivers incorrectly set the hard drive as "ejectable." This, in turn, causes the system to look for an ejectable hard disk (which you don't actually have) when you try to use the Apple Color Picker. And that's when the system gives you the message, "Insert the disk [name of your hard drive]."

There are several ways you can fix this problem. One way is to disable the System 7.5 Color Picker extension by pulling it out of the "Extensions" folder within your System Folder. Or you can change your hard-disk formatter driver. Check with the manufacturer of your hard drive to find out which drivers are compatible. You can also upgrade your driver to a more current version that doesn't have this problem. To do so, contact the developer of your driver. If you don't want to change your driver, you may be able to use a disk formatting utility to set your hard disk as a non-ejectable drive. Contact your hard-drive manufacturer for more information.

Q *(3.0.4 or later)* **I'm having trouble with some of Photoshop's distortion Plug-ins, like Ripple and Twirl. When I try to use them, I get some strange error message about there being a problem with the "Macintosh Code Fragment Manager." What am I doing wrong?**

A You're probably trying to use Photoshop 3.0.5 with the distortion Plug-ins that shipped with Photoshop 3.0.1. When Photoshop 3.0.4 shipped, the distortion Plug-ins—Displace, Pinch, Polar Coordinates, Ripple, Shear, Spherize, Twirl, Wave, and ZigZag—were updated (along with lots of other changes), and the older Plug-ins won't work with the newer versions of the Photoshop application. To make sure that you're using the updated Plug-ins, trash your existing Plug-ins folder and insert the Photoshop 3.0.4 or 3.0.5 CD (or floppies), choose "Custom install," and select only the Plug-ins in the "Custom install options" dialog box. If you use any third-party Plug-ins with Photoshop (i.e., Plug-ins that didn't come with Photoshop), back up your Plug-ins folder (or at least those third-party Plug-ins) before you trash and reinstall.

Q Sometimes, when I import an Adobe Illustrator document into Photoshop, I get an error message saying that one of the fonts used in the publication is not currently available. This happens even if I have just created the file on my Mac and I know the font is there. If I continue and open the file in Photoshop, the type looks fine. What's going on?

A When you have both PostScript and TrueType versions of a font installed, Photoshop's EPS Rasterizer generates this erroneous alert. Open the font suitcase and remove the TrueType version, and the message about missing fonts should no longer crop up.

Q *(2.5 and later)* **When I try to save files in the PICT format, I sometimes get an error message that says the image is too wide to be saved as a PICT. Is there some kind of width limit I'm exceeding?**

A Unfortunately, there is: Photoshop cannot save RGB PICT files that are wider than 4,096 pixels. To determine how wide your image is, choose "Image Size..." from the Image menu and, in the "Image Size" dialog box, set the "Width" field's unit to pixels. If the number there is greater than 4,096 (and your document is in RGB mode), you'll need to save the file in some format other than PICT, reduce the image's resolution or width, or change to some color mode other than RGB—the PICT format also supports the "Bitmap," "Grayscale," and "Indexed Color" modes.

Q *(4.0 only)* **I can't seem to get Photoshop 4.0 to run on my Mac. When I try to launch it I get a message that says something about DragLib. What on earth is DragLib?**

A DragLib is actually a shared library component that's part of the MacO/S software in System 7.1.3 and earlier. If you run System 7.1.2 and try to launch Photoshop, you'll get a message saying that DragLib is missing and Photoshop can't be launched. Fortunately, the fix is right there on your Photoshop 4.0 application CD.

Simply install the tryout version of Adobe PageMaker that you'll find inside the "Product Tryouts" folder on the CD (the "Minimum Install" option will work just fine)—doing so will install the files you need to fix the DragLib problem. Reboot your Mac, and Photoshop should launch successfully.

Error "Could Not Initialize Photoshop Because of a Disk Error" Troubleshooting Guide

ISSUE

The error "Could not initialize Photoshop because of a disk error" occurs when launching Adobe Photoshop 2.0x or later, preventing Photoshop from launching.

SOLUTIONS

Do one or more of the following:

A. Recreate the Photoshop preferences file:
   1. Quit Photoshop.
   2. Delete the Photoshop preferences file. For preference filenames and locations, see Additional Information.
   NOTE: Custom preferences will be reset.
B. Use a utility (e.g., MacTools, Norton Utilities for Macintosh) to locate and repair damaged media (i.e., bad sectors) on the hard drive containing Photoshop and the system software and other volumes designated as a Photoshop scratch disk.

NOTE: Other installed extensions may interfere with Photoshop 3.0x. Restart with all extensions off to verify that added extensions are not the cause. To turn all extensions off upon startup in System 7, restart the computer while holding the Shift key until the message "Welcome to Macintosh. Extensions Off." appears.

ADDITIONAL INFORMATION

The Photoshop preferences file stores location and content information about a variety of Photoshop settings. When the information contained in the preferences file becomes damaged, Photoshop is unable to initialize while launching, and returns the error "Could not initialize Photoshop because of a disk error." Photoshop creates a preferences file after launching successfully. A preferences file may be available when Photoshop creates an incomplete preferences file while attempting to launch, or when another copy of Photoshop was previously installed.

Photoshop's preferences filenames and locations:

Photoshop Version	Filename
Photoshop 3.0	Adobe Photoshop 3.0 Prefs
Preferences folder in the System Folder	
Photoshop 2.5.x	Photoshop Prefs
Preferences folder in the System Folder	
Photoshop 2.5.x LE	Photoshop LE Prefs
Preferences folder in the System Folder	
Photoshop 2.0x	PS Prefs
Photoshop plug-ins (default location)	

Error "...not enough memory (RAM)" in Photoshop 3.0x Troubleshooting Guide

ISSUE

The error "Could not complete your request because there is not enough memory (RAM)" occurs while running Adobe Photoshop 3.0x.

SOLUTIONS

Increase the amount of memory available to Photoshop by doing one or more of the following:

A. Allocate more memory to Photoshop:
   1. Quit Photoshop and all other applications.
   2. At the Finder, choose About This Macintosh or About This Mac OS Computer from the Apple menu.
   3. Note the Largest Unused Block value, then close the dialog box.
   4. Select the Photoshop application icon, then choose File > Get Info.
   5. In the Photoshop Info dialog box, increase the Preferred size value, not exceeding 90% of the Largest Unused Block value noted in step 3.
   6. Close the Photoshop Info dialog box.
B. Reduce the image's resolution to reduce the memory requirements of the image:
   1. With the image open in Photoshop, choose Image > Image Size.
   2. In the Image Size dialog box, deselect the File Size option, decrease the Height, Width, or Resolution values, then click OK.
   NOTE: Reducing the image resolution may result in lower image quality.
C. Temporarily reduce the number of installed Photoshop plug-ins:
   1. Quit Photoshop.
   2. At the Finder, move plug-ins that are currently not in use from your designated Photoshop Plug-ins folder to another location (e.g., desktop, new temporary folder).
D. When editing a Photoshop 3.0, Scitex CT, or uncomp-ressed TIFF image, open a portion of the file using Quick Edit:
   1. Install the Quick Edit plug-in file in the Plug-ins folder.
   2. In Photoshop, choose File > Acquire > Quick Edit.
   3. Select the file you want to edit, then click Open.
   4. In the Acquire Quick Edit dialog box, drag-select a portion of the image, or select a portion using the Grid option, then click OK.
   5. After completing your edits, save the portion of the file back into the original file by choosing File > Export > Quick Edit Save.
E. Edit one channel at a time in a multi-channel document by selecting a single channel in the Channels palette.
F. Restart the Macintosh to defragment the memory.
G. Enable virtual memory in the Memory control panel. Because virtual memory can severely degrade Photoshop's performance, disable virtual memory when memory requirements of Photoshop or the currently open document decrease.

NOTE: Other installed extensions may cause Photoshop to return low-memory errors. Run Photoshop with all extensions off to verify that added extensions are not the cause. To turn extensions off upon startup in System 7, restart the computer while holding the Shift key until the message "Welcome to Macintosh. Extensions Off." appears.

ADDITIONAL INFORMATION

When Photoshop has insufficient memory (RAM) while performing most operations, Photoshop writes to its scratch disk. Because some memory-intensive operations (e.g., using the Distort filter) can only be executed in RAM, Photoshop returns the error "Could not complete your request because there is not enough memory (RAM)" and does not complete the operation while attempting to perform one of these operations.

Because installed plug-ins load with Photoshop and use Photoshop's allocated memory, reducing the number of installed plug-ins increases the amount of memory available to Photoshop for other operations.

Launching and exiting applications repeatedly can fragment the Macintosh's memory. When memory is fragmented (i.e., not available in a single, contiguous block), applications may be unable to access all their allocated memory. Restarting the Macintosh defragments its memory.

Error "...not enough RAM" When Using Quick Edit Module in Photoshop 3.0.x

ISSUE

After you select the Quick Edit Save command in Adobe Photoshop 3.0.x, Photoshop returns the error "Could not complete your request because there is not enough RAM."

SOLUTIONS

Do one or more of the following:

A. Allocate an amount of memory that is no more than 10% less than the largest unused block to Photoshop. The largest unused block is noted in the About this Macintosh dialog box.
B. Set the Cache Size to 32K and Virtual Memory to Off in the Memory control panel.
C. Delete Quick Edit's Adobe Photoshop Quick Edit preference file, which is located in the Preferences folder in the System Folder.
D. Quit all applications, then restart Photoshop.
E. Decrease the amount of memory allocated to Photoshop.
F. Edit and save a smaller Quick Edit file.
G. Restart the Macintosh.

NOTE: Other installed extensions or control panels may interfere when using the Quick Edit Save module in Photoshop 3.0.x. Run Photoshop with all extensions off to verify that added extensions or control panels are not the cause. To turn all extensions off upon startup in System 7, restart the computer while holding the Shift key until the message "Welcome to Macintosh. Extensions Off." appears.

ADDITIONAL INFORMATION

Quick Edit requires a contiguous block of memory (RAM). When working on a large image file, Quick Edit may request a memory allocation that exceeds the largest contiguous block.

Quick Edit is a Photoshop 3.0 plug-in that enables you to open and edit a portion of a large file, which reduces the image's memory requirements and processing time. The Quick Edit Save command exports the file back to its original file.

While working on the Macintosh, memory can become fragmented; usually as a result of launching and quitting applications repeatedly. Although a large amount of memory may be available to Photoshop, if the memory is fragmented (i.e., not contiguous), memory-intensive operations may not be able to be completed. Restarting the Macintosh defragments memory. Memory allocated to Photoshop is available for both the Photoshop application and opened image files.

To increase or decrease the amount of memory allocated to Photoshop:

1. Save and close all Photoshop images, then quit Photoshop.
2. At the Finder, select the Photoshop application icon, then choose File > Get Info.
3. In the Photoshop Get Info window, set the Preferred size (System 7.1 or later) or Current size (System 7.0.x) to a higher or lower value for Memory Requirements, then close the Get Info window.

Error "Application Has Expired" When Launching Photoshop 3.0

ISSUE

The error "Application Has Expired. This is an expired beta version." appears when you launch Adobe Photoshop 3.0.

SOLUTIONS

Update to Photoshop 3.0.1 or later.

OR: When the system clock date is set prior to January 1, 1994 or after December 31, 1994, temporarily reset the system clock to a date in 1994.

ADDITIONAL INFORMATION

Adobe Photoshop 3.0 includes a security code time constraint that causes Photoshop 3.0 to return the error "Application Has Expired. This is an expired beta version." when the system clock date is set prior to January 1, 1994 or after December 31, 1994. Photoshop 3.01 and later do not include the security code time constraint.

System Errors

MAC OS / WINDOWS

Photoshop 3.0.x Doesn't Support SoftWindows

Adobe Photoshop 3.0.x for Windows does not support Insignia Solutions SoftWindows 1.0x, SoftWindows 2.0x, SoftWindows 3.0x, and SoftWindows 95 for the Power Macintosh.

SoftWindows 2.0x, SoftWindows 3.0x, and SoftWindows 95 for the Power Macintosh emulate an Intel 80386 processor on a Power Macintosh.

SoftWindows 1.0x for the Power Macintosh emulates Windows 3.1 Standard mode running on an Intel 80286 processor. Photoshop 3.0.x requires an Intel 80386 or later processor (e.g., i386, i486, Pentium), and does not support Windows 3.1's Standard mode.

WINDOWS

Q *(3.0 only)* **The other day, I got a "Win32s - Error" message that said I had to reinstall Photoshop. What is Win32s and how can I keep these errors from happening again?**

A Win32s is a Windows subsystem, developed by Microsoft Corporation, that allows 16-bit versions of Windows (including Windows 3.1 and Windows for Workgroups 3.11) to run 32-bit applications like Photoshop. When you install Photoshop 3.0 under Windows 3.1 or Windows for Workgroups 3.11, it adds several Win32s files to your WINDOWS\SYSTEM and WINDOWS\SYSTEM\WIN32S directories. Photoshop does not install the Win32s files if you're running under Windows NT, which has built-in support for 32-bit applications and therefore doesn't require Win32s.

If you try to launch Photoshop and your screen blanks out and returns to the Program Manager without starting Photoshop, or if you receive a "Win32s - Error" message, chances are one or more of your Win32s DLL files is missing or damaged. If this happens, reinstall Photoshop. When you launch Photoshop's Setup program, just select "Photoshop" from the list of installation options (you don't need to select any other options) and click "Install." Whenever you install the Photoshop program files, the Setup program also adds the Win32s files to your system.

If you receive the error "Win32s - Error. Improper installation. Win32s requires Windows to run with virtual memory enabled. Re-install Win32s," you may not need to reinstall Photoshop. This error can occur if you turn off Windows'

virtual memory feature, which Win32s requires. To fix the problem, define your Windows swapfile as a permanent swapfile that's at least as large as the amount of RAM you have installed, and no smaller than 8MB. If you're not sure how to set up a permanent swapfile in Windows, check the Microsoft Windows Users' Guide. If you have a lot of free hard disk space but can't create a large enough swapfile, try optimizing (defragmenting) your hard drive with an application such as Norton Utilities.

Q I'd like to run Photoshop under Windows NT 4.0, but whenever I try to launch it I get error messages, usually about memory. Is Photoshop compatible with NT?

A Photoshop 3.0.5 is compatible with Windows NT 3.5.1, but was not tested with NT 4.0. Photoshop 4.0, which was recently released (see page 14), is supported under Windows NT 4.0.

Win32s Errors in Photoshop 3.0.x Troubleshooting Guide

ISSUE

When you run Photoshop 3.0.x, Windows returns one of the following Win32s errors:

"Improper installation. Win32s requires W32s.386 in order to run. Reinstall Win32s Application Execution Error: One of the library files needed to run this application is damaged. Please reinstall this application."

"Photoshp.exe Unhandled Exception detected code [0xC0000005]. Application will be terminated."

"Win32sxxxx An error has occurred in this application."

"Application Error Photoshp.exe caused a GPF in Win-32s16.DLL at 0001:7ccd"

"Unexpected DOS Error -21"

"Unexpected DOS Error 21"

SOLUTIONS

Do one or more of the following:

A. Verify that your hard disk contains a Win32s directory. When installing, Photoshop 3.0 creates a Win32s directory in the Windows\System directory. If the Win32s directory does not exist, remove and reinstall Photoshop.

B. Recreate Photoshop's preferences files:
   1. Quit Photoshop.
   2. Delete the Photos30.psp and Ccolorsd files, which are located in the Win32app\Photoshp\Prefs directory (Photoshop 3.0.5) or the Windows directory (Photoshop 3.0 and 3.0.4).

   NOTE: Custom preference settings will be lost.

C. Make sure you have at least 10 MB of memory (RAM), the minimum amount Photoshop requires to run.

D. Make sure there is sufficient free disk space on the hard disk targeted as Photoshop's scratch disk. To process an image, Photoshop requires at least 3-5 times the size of the image on the Photoshop scratch disk and in memory (RAM).

E. Make sure there is at least 20 MB of free disk space on the hard disk where Windows is installed.

F. Ensure there's adequate free space on the hard disk for temporary files (at least 10-20 MB free on the disk to which the temporary files are written) by doing one or more of the following:
   1. Exit to DOS, then, from each connected drive's root directory, delete all files with a *.tmp extension.
   2. Delete other files on the volume specified in the "Set Temp=" line in the Autoexec.bat file.
   3. Edit the "Set Temp=" line in the Autoexec.bat file to specify a directory on a non-compressed disk that has sufficient free disk space.

G. Remove and reinstall Photoshop and its Win32s components:
   1. Move your documents out of the Photoshp directory and its subdirectories.
   2. Delete the Photoshp directory and its subdirectories.

3. If Photoshop 3.0 or 3.0.4 is installed, delete the following files from the Windows directory:
   `Photos30.ini`
   `Photos30.psp`
   `Ccolosd`

NOTE: Photoshop 3.0.5 installs these files in the Win32-app\Photoshp\Prefs directory, which was deleted in step 2.

4. Delete the Windows\System\Win32s directory and its files.
5. In DOS, delete, move, or rename the following files in the Windows\System directory:
   `Winmm16.dll`
   `Win32s16.dll`
   `Win32s.ini`
   `W32sys.dll`
6. Reinstall Photoshop.

H. Use a video driver that is compatible with Win32s, Win32s-based applications, and 256 or more colors. To determine whether your video driver is compatible with Win32s, specify another video driver that is compatible (e.g., Windows Super VGA video driver), refer to the video driver's documentation, or contact the video driver's manufacturer.

NOTE: Make a backup copy of the System.ini file, located in the Windows directory, before changing your video driver. If you are unable to reinstall your original video driver or want to revert to the original driver, you can copy the original System.ini file back into the Windows directory.

I. Use a mouse driver that is compatible with Win32s. To determine if your mouse driver is compatible with Win32s, refer to its documentation or contact the manufacturer.

J. Use the Windows memory manager Himem.sys, rather than a third-party memory manager (e.g., QEMM). To temporarily load Himem.sys instead of a third-party memory manager, create a bootable floppy disk containing startup files (i.e., Autoexec.bat, Config.sys) that reference Himem.sys, instead of the third-party memory manager.

K. Make sure nothing is loading in Windows by disabling (i.e., remarking out) the "load=" and "run=" lines in the Win.ini file:
1. Make a backup copy of the Win.ini file in the Windows directory.
2. Open the original Win.ini file in a text editor that can save in text-only format (e.g., Windows Write, Notepad).
3. In the [windows] section, insert a semicolon at the beginning of the "load=" and "run=" lines. For example:
```
;load=
;run=
```
4. Save the Win.ini file in text-only format, then restart Windows.

L. Specify an uncompressed disk (i.e., a disk that is not compressed by a disk compression utility) for Photoshop's scratch disk and the Windows swap file (i.e., virtual memory).

M. Recreate and resize the Windows swap file (i.e., virtual memory):
1. Open the Windows Control Panel, located in the Main group of Program Manager.
2. Double-click the 386 Enhanced icon.
3. In the 386 Enhanced dialog box, select Virtual Memory, then click Change.
4. In the Virtual Memory dialog box, select NONE from the Type pop-up menu in the New Settings section, click OK, then restart Windows.
5. Repeat steps 1-3 to reset the Windows swap file.
6. In the Virtual Memory dialog box, choose Permanent from the Type pop-up menu in the New Settings section, and change the size of the swap file in the New Size text box to a value that equals or approximates the amount of your computer's installed RAM. When you have the minimum amount of RAM required to run Photoshop (10 MB), specify a swap file size of at least 15 MB.
7. Click OK, then restart Windows.

N. Make sure there is only one copy of each of the Windows system files (i.e., Win.com, System.ini, and Win.-ini) installed on your computer. If multiple copies exist, rename the duplicate files (e.g., rename the Win.ini file "Win.old").

O. Reduce the size of your system's Win.ini file to 32K or less by removing unneeded entries, sections, or font lines (e.g., TrueType fonts listed in the [fonts] section, PostScript fonts listed in the [PostScript,LPTx] section).

P. Set Win32s to load last by editing the System.ini file:
1. Make a backup copy of the System.ini file in the Windows directory.
2. Open the original System.ini file in a text editor that can save in text-only format (e.g., Windows Write, Notepad).
3. In the [386Enh] section, add or move the following line to the end of the [386Enh] section:
```
device=C:\WINDOWS\SYSTEM\WIN32S\W32S.386
```
4. Save the System.ini file in text-only format, then restart Windows.

Q. Reduce the amount of memory (RAM) reserved for Photoshop:
1. Choose File > Preferences > Memory.
2. In the Physical Memory Usage section of the Memory Preferences dialog box, change the Used By Photoshop value to 80%, then click OK.
3. Restart Photoshop.

R. Optimize all partitions on your hard disk using the SCANDISK and DEFRAG commands, included with MS-DOS 6.2x and later, or a disk optimization utility (e.g., Norton Utilities).

S. Create a bootable floppy disk with Autoexec.bat and Config.sys files that contain only the information necessary to launch Windows and Photoshop. If the Win32s error does not reoccur after you start from the bootable floppy disk, do one or more of the following:

A. Determine which line or lines in the Autoexe.bat or

Config.sys file is loading software at DOS that is conflicting and causing the Win32s error in Photo-shop. To isolate the conflicting line or lines, add each removed line back into the Autoexec.bat or Config.-sys file on the bootable floppy disk one at a time, restart the computer, then try to recreate the error in Photoshop. If the Win32s error reappears, the line most recently added is most likely the cause of the conflict. Because more than one line in the Auto-exec.bat and Config.sys files may cause a conflict, reboot after adding each additional line to determine all conflicting lines.

B. Reduce the number of devices listed in the Autoexec.bat and Config.sys files that are loading in Windows or DOS to increase the amount of memory available to Windows and Photoshop.

T. Install an updated version of Win32s (e.g., 1.2 or later), available from Microsoft and included with many Win-32s applications. Photoshop 3.0.5 includes Win32s version 1.30.167.

U. When running Photoshop in Windows for Workgroups 3.11, disable (i.e., remark out) the "device=c:\windows\ifshlp.sys" line in the Config.sys file:

1. Make a backup copy of the Config.sys file, located in the root directory on your hard disk.
2. Open the original Config.sys file in a text editor that can save in text-only format (e.g., Windows Write, Notepad).
3. Disable the "device=c:\windows\ifshlp.sys" line by adding the word "rem" followed by a space at the beginning of the line. For example:

```
rem device=c:\windows\ifshlp.sys
```

4. Save the Config.sys file in text-only format, then restart Windows.

V. Save backup copies of your System.ini and Win.ini files onto a volume other than your startup volume, then reinstall Windows.

OR: Install a second copy of Windows in a new directory to determine if the original copy of Windows is causing the error. For instructions, see Additional Information.

NOTE: After reinstalling Windows, you may need to reinstall your Windows applications. For instructions on deleting and reinstalling Windows, refer to the Windows User Guide or contact Microsoft.

ADDITIONAL INFORMATION

Win32s components enable 32-bit applications (e.g., Photoshop 3.0x, Adobe PageMaker 6.0) to run in 16-bit operating systems (e.g., Windows 3.1x, Windows for Workgroups). If the system encounters a conflict or error when running Win32s, the system returns a Win32s error.

When you run a Win32s-based application in Win32s, incompatible software (e.g., video driver, mouse driver), conflicting software (e.g., duplicate system files), insufficient memory, or damaged software can cause a system error to occur.

The maximum valid size for Windows initialization files (e.g., the Win.ini file) is 64K. Applications running in Windows may be unable to read *.ini files when they exceed 32K. If the size of the Win.ini file exceeds 32K or 64K, Windows or applications running in Windows behave unpredictably (e.g., system configuration changes are not implemented, fonts are missing, printer information is missing, application's default information is not saved).

The "Set Temp=" line in your Autoexec.bat file specifies the directory containing your temporary files.

Video drivers using the S3 chip may not be compatible with Win32s-based applications.

To install a second copy of Windows in a new directory to determine if the original copy of Windows is causing the error:

1. Create a new directory (e.g., named "Testwin"), then install Windows into the new directory. For instructions on installing Windows, refer to the Microsoft Windows User's Guide.
2. Start Windows from the Testwin directory by exiting to DOS, navigating to the Testwin directory by typing "cd testwin" at the DOS prompt, then typing "win" to launch the new installation of Windows.
3. Install Photoshop.
4. Reboot the computer, then start Windows from the Testwin directory. Windows uses the system files located in the newly created directory (e.g., "Testwin") instead of the Windows directory.
5. Before launching Photoshop, rename the Win.com, System.ini, and Win.ini files located in the Windows directory and its subdirectories (e.g., rename these files "Wincom.old," "System.old," and "Winini.old") to ensure Windows does not use system files located in the original Windows directory and its subdirectories.
6. Attempt to recreate the Win32s error while running Photoshop by performing the same actions that previously caused the error. When the Win32s errors do not reoccur when running Photoshop in the installed copy of Windows, delete your previously installed Windows system files.

Error "At least one system component is out of date" When Starting Photoshop 3.0.5 in Windows 3.1x

ISSUE

When you start Adobe Photoshop 3.0.5 in Windows 3.1x, the error "WIN32s Error: At least one system component is out of date. Please reinstall C:\Photoshp\Photoshp.exe." appears and is followed by one of the following errors:

"WIN32s Error. Initialization of a dynamic link library failed. The process is terminating abnormally."
"Application execution error. Application requires Microsoft Win32s extensions."
"Undefined Call to Dynalink"
"Invalid Call to Dynalink"
"Invalid Call to a Dynamic Link Library"
"Invalid Dynamic Link call to a DLL file"
"DOS Error 21"

SOLUTION

Remove duplicate system files required by Photoshop from the hard disk:

1. In File Manager choose File > Search.
2. In the Search For text box, enter the name of a system files required by Photoshop. For a list of system files required by Photoshop, see Additional Information.
3. In the Start From text box, enter the location of the Windows 3.1x directory (e.g., C:\Windows).
4. Select the Search All Subdirectories option, and click OK.
5. When you find duplicate files on the hard disk, note the location and name of each file.
6. Repeat steps 2-5 for each file listed below.
7. In File Manager, double-click the root level of the hard disk containing Windows, then choose File > Create Directory.
8. Enter the name of the temporary directory where you want to move all duplicate files, then click OK.
9. Exit Windows.
10. At the DOS prompt, move duplicate instances of the files noted in step 5 into the directory created in steps 7-8.
11. Restart Windows, then launch Photoshop 3.0.5.

ADDITIONAL INFORMATION

Photoshop 3.0.5 installs the system files it requires into the Windows and Windows\System directories. When other applications install duplicates of these files in the Windows directory structure, Photoshop returns the error "WIN32s Error: At least one system component is out of date. Please reinstall C:\Photoshp\Photoshp.exe" when launching under Windows 3.1x.

System files located in the Windows\System directory required by Photoshop 3.0.5:

Name	Date	Size in Bytes
Compobj.dll	09-06-95	109,056
Ctl3d32.dll	09-16-94	26,112
Msvcrt10.dll	07-23-93	210,944
Msvcrt20.dll	01-20-95	244,736
Ole2.dll	09-06-95	304,640
Ole2.reg	04-16-95	28,113
Ole2conv.dll	08-14-95	57,328
Ole2disp.dll	07-25-95	165,008
Ole2nls.dll	07-25-95	152,976
Ole2prox.dll	09-06-95	51,712
Ole2thk.dll	09-06-95	25,088
Penwin.dll	05-30-92	130,816
Stdole.tlb	07-25-95	5,472
Storage.dll	03-02-95	157,696
Typelib.dll	07-25-95	177,824
W32sys.dll	10-02-95	12,112
Win32s16.dll	10-19-95	167,424
Windows.hlp	09-05-95	21,473
Winhlp32.cnt	09-05-95	903
Winhlp32.exe	09-11-95	329,774
Winhlp32.hlp	09-05-95	31,684
Winmm16.dll	10-01-95	29,184

System files located in the Windows directory required by Photoshop 3.0.5:

Name	Date	Size in Bytes
Ctl3d.dll	09-16-94	20,976
Ctl3d32s.dll	09-16-94	26,112
Kpapi32.dll	varies	varies
Kpcms.ini	varies	varies
Kpcp32.dll	varies	varies
Kpsys32.dll	varies	varies
Pcdlib32.dll	varies	varies
Twain.dll	varies	varies
Twain_32.dll	varies	varies
Twunk_16.exe	varies	varies
Twunk_32.exe	varies	varies

Error "Stack overflow" When Launching Photoshop 3.0.x in Windows 3.1x

ISSUE

When you launch Adobe Photoshop 3.0.x in Windows 3.1x, the error "Stack overflow" occurs.

SOLUTIONS

Do one or more of the following:

A. Make sure the "Stacks=" line in the Config.sys file is set to 9,256 and that it is written correctly:
   1. Make a backup copy of the Config.sys file.
   2. Open the original Config.sys file, located in the root directory, in a text editor that can save in text-only format (e.g., Windows Write, Notepad).
   3. Locate the "Stacks=" line and make sure the line appears exactly as shown below:

   `STACKS=9,256`

   NOTE: Make sure there are no space characters and that "Stacks" is plural.
   4. Save the Config.sys file in text-only format.
   5. Restart the computer.

B. Recreate and resize the Windows swap file (i.e., virtual memory):
   1. Open the Windows Control Panel, located in the Main group of Program Manager.
   2. Double-click the 386 Enhanced icon.
   3. In the 386 Enhanced dialog box, select Virtual Memory, then click Change.
   4. In the Virtual Memory dialog box, select None from the Type pop-up menu in the New Settings section, click OK, then restart Windows.
   5. Repeat steps 1-3 to reset the Windows swap file.
   6. In the Virtual Memory dialog box, choose Permanent from the Type pop-up menu in the New Settings section, and change the size of the swap file in the New Size text box to a value that equals or approximates the amount of your computer's installed RAM. If you have the minimum amount of RAM required to run Photoshop (10 MB), specify a swap file size of at least 15 MB.

7. Click OK, then restart Windows.

C. Increase the number in the "Stacks=" line in the Config.sys file to 9,512, following the instructions in step A.

D. Run Windows in a "minimized" configuration:

1. Ensure nothing is loading in Windows by disabling (i.e., remarking out) the "load=" and "run=" lines in the Win.ini file:
   a. Make a backup copy of the Win.ini file located in the Windows directory.
   b. Open the Win.ini file in a text editor that can save in text-only format (e.g., Windows Write, Notepad).
   c. In the [windows] section, insert a semicolon at the beginning of the lines that begin "load=" and "run=". For example:

```
;LOAD=
;RUN=
```

   d. Save the Win.ini file in text-only format, then restart Windows.
2. Prevent programs from loading when you start Windows by removing their icons from the Startup group:
   a. In Program Manager, double-click the Main group, then double-click the Startup group.
   b. Drag all icons from the Startup group to another group.
   c. Restart Windows.
3. Restart the computer from a bootable floppy disk with Autoexec.bat and Config.sys files that contain only the information necessary to launch Windows and Photoshop. For instructions on creating a bootable floppy disk for Windows and Photoshop, see Additional Information. If the "Stack overflow" error does not reoccur when you launch Photoshop after booting from the bootable floppy disk, do one or more of the following:
   A. Determine which line or lines in the Autoexec.bat or Config.sys file are loading software in DOS that is causing the "Stack overflow" error in Photoshop. To isolate the conflicting line or lines, add each removed line back into the Autoexec.bat or Config.sys file on the bootable floppy disk one at a time, restart the computer, then attempt to recreate the error in Photoshop. If the "Stack overflow" error reappears, the line most recently added is most likely the cause of the error.
   B. Reduce the number of devices that are loading in Windows or DOS to reduce the amount of hardware interrupts sent to the CPU, which ensures Windows and Photoshop can run successfully.

ADDITIONAL INFORMATION

Stacks handle hardware interrupts, which are commands sent to the coprocessor (CPU) from the computer's hardware components (e.g., keyboard, mouse, disk drives). For example, each time you press a key on the keyboard, one or more hardware interrupts are sent to the CPU and added to a stack. Terminate-and-stay-resident (TSR) programs, MS-DOS device drivers, and system BIOS software may examine the hardware interrupts using a technique known as "hooking" the interrupt. Each hardware interrupt hook may require more stack space. When too much stack space is used, a stack overflow error occurs.

The stacks setting in the Config.sys file is always two numbers separated by a comma (e.g., 9,256). The first number is the number of stacks, and the second number is the number of bytes in each stack. For example, a stacks setting of 9,256 means that Windows creates nine stacks of 256 bytes each.

To create a bootable floppy disk for Windows and Photoshop:

1. At the DOS prompt, insert a floppy disk and then type the following command:

```
FORMAT A: /s
```

   where A: is the floppy disk drive letter. The "/s" switch, which is required, tells DOS to create a "boot sector" on the floppy disk and copy three additional files necessary for DOS to function.

   OR: In Windows, open File Manager and choose Disk > Make System Disk. Insert a floppy disk and then click Yes when prompted, "Are you sure you want to copy system files onto the disk in drive A:?"
2. Use the COPY command at the DOS prompt or the Copy command in File Manager to copy the Autoexec.bat and Config.sys files from the root directory of the hard disk to the floppy disk.
3. Minimize the Autoexec.bat file on the floppy disk:
   A. Open the Autoexec.bat file on the floppy disk in a text editor that can save in text-only format (e.g., Windows Write, Notepad).
   B. Delete all but the following lines:

```
PROMPT $p$g
PATH=
SET TEMP=
```

   NOTE: The entries after "Path=" (or "Set Path=") and "Set Temp=" (or "Temp=") vary from one computer to another.

   C. Save the Autoexec.bat file on the floppy disk in text-only format.
4. Minimize the Config.sys file on the floppy disk:
   A. Open the Config.sys file on the floppy disk in a text editor that can save in text-only format (e.g., Windows Write, Notepad).
   B. Delete all but the following lines:

```
DEVICE=C:\WINDOWS\HIMEM.SYS
FILES=
BUFFERS=
STACKS=
```

   NOTE: The Files, Buffers, and Stacks lines are followed by numbers which vary from one computer to another. The Himem.sys file may be located in either the Dos or Windows directory.

   C. Save the Config.sys file on the floppy disk in text-only format.

5. Restart the computer with the bootable floppy disk in the floppy disk drive.

Error "...because of a program error" When Opening or Saving a Document in Photoshop 3.0.x

ISSUE

When opening a document, Adobe Photoshop 3.0.x returns the error "Could not open file [filename] because of a program error." When saving a document, Photoshop 3.0.x returns the error "Could not save file [filename] because of a program error."

SOLUTIONS

Do one or more of the following:

A. Reset the Windows swap file or Photoshop's scratch disk to a disk that is not compressed. For instructions on resetting the Windows swap file or Photoshop's scratch disk, see Additional Information.

B. When running Windows for Workgroups 3.1.1, use Photoshop 3.0.4 or later.
OR: Disable virtual memory's 32-bit File Access option:
1. Open the Windows Control Panel, located in the Main group of Program Manager.
2. Double-click the 386 Enhanced icon.
3. Click Virtual Memory.
4. Click Change.
5. Deselect the Use 32-Bit File Access option.
6. Click OK, then click OK again to restart Windows.

NOTE: Disabling 32-bit File Access may cause other Windows applications to run slower.

ADDITIONAL INFORMATION

When 32-bit File Access is enabled in Windows for Workgroups 3.1.1, Photoshop 3.0, 3.0.1, and 3.0.3 create thousands of lost clusters, resulting in diminished free disk space and random errors (e.g., "Could not open file [filename] because of a program error."). Photoshop 3.0.4 or later does not create thousands of lost clusters when 32-bit File Access is enabled.

Errors may occur when opening and saving files if either the Windows swap file or Photoshop's scratch disk is set to a compressed disk.

To reset Windows Virtual Memory swap file to an uncompressed disk:

1. Open the Windows Control Panel, located in the Main group of Program Manager.
2. Double-click the 386 Enhanced icon.
3. Click Virtual Memory.
4. Click Change.
5. Change Drive to an uncompressed drive.
6. Click OK, then click OK again to restart Windows.

To reset Photoshop's scratch disk to an uncompressed disk:

1. In Photoshop, choose File > Preferences > Memory.
2. Change Primary to an uncompressed drive.
3. Click OK to close the Memory Preferences dialog box, then restart Photoshop.

Error "Invalid Page Fault" When Running Photoshop 3.0.4 Under Windows 95

ISSUE

When running Adobe Photoshop 3.0.4 under Windows 95, the system returns the error "This program has performed and illegal operation and will be shut down. If the problem persists, contact the program vendor." After clicking Details in the error dialog box, the system returns the error "PHOTOSHP caused an invalid page fault in module KERNEL32.DLL."

SOLUTIONS

Use Photoshop 3.0.5 or later.

OR: Use Photoshop 3.0.4 or earlier under Windows 3.1x, instead of under Windows 95.

ADDITIONAL INFORMATION

The system error "PHOTOSHP caused an invalid page fault in module KERNEL32.DLL." may occur in Photoshop 3.0.4 when cutting, pasting, magnifying, or moving a floating selection at a magnification view greater than 1:1. Because Photoshop 3.0.5 is Windows 95 logo-compliant, the system error "PHOTOSHP caused an invalid page fault in module KERNEL32.DLL." does not occur in Photoshop 3.0.5 when cutting, pasting, magnifying, or moving a floating selection.

System Error Launching or Running Photoshop 3.0 Deluxe CD Tutorial Troubleshooting Guide

ISSUE

A system error (e.g., General Protection Fault error, crash, freeze) occurs when starting or running the Adobe Photoshop 3.0.x Deluxe CD Tutorial.

SOLUTIONS

Do one or more of the following:

A. Make sure your video driver is compatible with QuickTime 1.1.1 (Photoshop 3.0 and 3.0.4) or QuickTime 2.0.1 or later (Photoshop 3.0.5). For information on whether your video driver is compatible with QuickTime, contact the video card manufacturer or Apple Computer, Inc. To obtain an updated video driver, contact the video card manufacturer.

B. Update the drivers for the sound card or Windows Sound System.

C. When you receive a General Protection Fault error in Gdi.exe at 0001:0F6A on a computer with an ATI video card installed, turn Devicebitmap to OFF in the Mach32

TIP WINDOWS

Photoshop 3.0.x Doesn't Support OS/2 and OS/2 Warp

Adobe Photoshop 3.0.x does not support any version of OS/2, including OS/2 3.0 (also known as OS/2 Warp). As stated on the Photoshop 3.0.x product box and in the Getting Started manual, Photoshop 3.0.x only supports Windows 3.1x, Windows NT 3.5x, and Windows 95 (Photoshop 3.0.4 and later).

Photoshop 3.0.x, as a 32-bit application, requires Win32s to run in a 16-bit operating system (e.g., Windows 3.1x, OS/2 Warp). Photoshop 3.0.x supports Win32s 1.15a and later, but OS/2 and OS/2 Warp support Win32s 1.1 and earlier.

or Mach64 video driver Flexdesk Control Panel. You can also turn Devicebitmap to off by editing the Win.ini (Mach32) or System.ini (Mach64) file.

D. Determine whether a conflict with something loading in the Config.sys or Autoexec.bat files is preventing you from starting the Deluxe Tutorial by booting from a floppy disk containing startup files (i.e., Autoexec.bat, Config.sys) that load only the CD-ROM drive. CD-ROM drives normally load in the Config.sys file. Consult the CD manufacturer manual for the exact "Load" statement for the CD-ROM drive.

E. Make a backup copy of your System.ini file, then change the resolution and numbers of colors (e.g., 256 colors) in your video driver settings.

F. Delete, then reinstall QuickTime.

G. Contact Apple Computer, Inc. for the latest version of QuickTime for the version of Windows you are using.

H. Run the Photoshop 3.0 Deluxe CD Tutorial under Windows 3.1x, instead of Windows NT.

ADDITIONAL INFORMATION

Adobe Photoshop Deluxe CD-ROM Tutorial requires that QuickTime, Photoshop, the Deluxe Tutorial, and Windows are installed, that the directory containing QuickTime is included in the path statement in the Autoexec.bat file, and that you use a 256-color (or more) video driver.

When you install Photoshop from the CD-ROM, Photoshop installs QuickTime for Windows. When you install Photoshop from the disk set, Photoshop does not install QuickTime.

Removing, then reinstalling QuickTime files ensures QuickTime is not damaged. Apple Computer, Inc., the manufacturer of QuickTime, recommends setting your video driver to display 256 colors.

Adobe Photoshop Deluxe CD-ROM Tutorial requires Windows NT 3.51 or later to run in Windows NT.

Error "GROWSTUB... in module POINTER.DLL" or Mouse Freezes in Photoshop 2.5 or Later

ISSUE

When launching Adobe Photoshop 2.5 and later, the mouse freezes or the system returns the error "GROWSTUB caused a General Protection Fault in module POINTER.DLL."

SOLUTIONS

Do one or more of the following:

A. Remove the reference to Pointer.exe in the WIN.INI file and change the mouse driver to Microsoft, or IBM PS/2:

1. Exit all Windows applications.
2. Make backup copies of the WIN.INI and SYSTEM.-INI files located in the WINDOWS directory. For instructions on making backup copies of the WIN.-INI and SYSTEM.INI files, see Additional Information.
3. Open the WIN.INI file located in the WINDOWS directory in a text editor that can save in text-only format (e.g., Windows Write, Notepad).
4. In the "Load=" line in the [Windows] section, delete the reference to Pointer.exe including its path (e.g., C:\Windows\Pointer.exe). After deleting the reference to Pointer.exe, there should be one space between any references remaining in the "Load=" line (e.g., Load=[reference] [reference] [reference]).
5. Save the WIN.INI file in text-only format, then exit the text editor (e.g., Windows Write, Notepad).
6. Double-click the Windows Setup icon in the Main group of the Program Manager.
7. Choose Options > Change System Settings.
8. In the Mouse pop-up menu, select Microsoft, or IBM PS/2, then click OK. If Windows asks you whether you want to use the currently installed driver or install a new one, select Current. If you choose New, you will need your Windows installation disk set.
9. Restart Windows.

B. Ensure there's only one MOUSE.DRV file installed and that it is located in the directory listed in the "mouse.-drv=" line in the [boot] section in the SYSTEM.INI file. When the "mouse.drv=" line reads "mouse.drv=mouse.drv," the system is accessing the MOUSE.DRV file located in the WINDOWS\SYSTEM directory, which is the where Windows installs the mouse driver by default. When the "mouse.drv=" line does not point to the correct location of the MOUSE.DRV file, open the SYSTEM.INI file in a text editor that can save in text-only format (e.g., Notepad, Windows Write), then edit the line so that it points to the correct location of the MOUSE.DRV file. Delete or rename MOUSE.DRV files that are not located in the directory listed in the "mouse.drv=" line in the SYSTEM.INI file.

C. Ensure the file size of the MOUSE.DRV file is correct. The correct file size of the MOUSE.DRV file for the

Microsoft, or IBM PS/2 mouse driver is either 10672 bytes or 10144 bytes. When the MOUSE.DRV file size is not 10672 or 10144 bytes, reinstall the MOUSE.DRV file by first installing a different mouse driver, then reinstalling the desired mouse driver to force Windows to overwrite the current mouse driver. For instructions, see Additional Information.

D. Reinstall the MOUSE.DRV file by first installing a different mouse driver, then reinstalling the desired mouse driver to force Windows to overwrite the current mouse driver. For instructions, see Additional Information.

E. Use Windows File Manager to search all volumes for multiple WIN.INI and SYSTEM.INI files. The WIN.INI and SYSTEM.INI files should be located in the WINDOWS directory. Rename duplicate WIN.INI and SYSTEM.INI files that are located in directories other than the WINDOWS directory.

F. Obtain an updated mouse driver from your mouse manufacturer.

ADDITIONAL INFORMATION

When launching Photoshop 2.5 and later, the mouse freezes or the system returns the error "GROWSTUB caused a GPF in module POINTER.DLL" when the mouse driver and its Pointer.exe file are incompatible with Win32s, the mouse driver is incorrectly referenced in the SYSTEM.INI file, the mouse driver file is damaged, or when you have multiple WIN.INI and SYSTEM.INI files.

When the size of the MOUSE.DRV file for the Microsoft, or IBM PS/2 mouse driver is not 10672 bytes or 10144 bytes, the file may be damaged. When there are multiple copies of the WIN.INI and SYSTEM.INI files, which store information about your mouse, the mouse information in each file may differ, resulting in conflicting mouse information that causes a system error (e.g.," GROWSTUB caused a GPF in module POINTER.DLL," freeze).

To make backup copies of your SYSTEM.INI or WIN.INI file:

1. In the Windows File Manager, locate either the SYSTEM.INI or WIN.INI file in the WINDOWS directory, then click once to select it.
2. Choose File > Copy.
3. Insert a blank formatted disk into the disk drive.
4. In the To text box of the Copy dialog box, enter the appropriate drive indicator (e.g., "A:\,""B:\"), then click OK.

NOTE: You can copy the backup WIN.INI and SYSTEM.INI files back into the WINDOWS directory to restore original settings.

To reinstall the MOUSE.DRV file by first installing a different mouse driver, then reinstalling the desired mouse driver to force Windows to overwrite the current mouse driver:

1. Ensure you have your Windows installation disks or CD-ROM, then exit Windows.
2. From a DOS prompt, type "cd windows" to change to the WINDOWS directory.
3. Type "setup" then press Enter to open Windows Setup.
4. Arrow up to the Mouse line, then press Enter to open the list of mouse choices.
5. Select No Mouse or Other Pointing Device, then press Enter.
6. Press Enter to accept the configuration.
7. If Setup prompts you for an installation disk, insert your installation disk then enter the path to the designated drive and directory to locate the required files. For example, on the Dell Windows 3.1 CD-ROM, the necessary Windows files are in the WINDOWS.310 directory. Setup automatically returns to DOS after locating and copying the necessary files.
8. At the WINDOWS DOS prompt, type "setup."
9. Arrow up to the Mouse line.
10. Press Enter to open the list of mouse choices.
11. Select Microsoft, or IBM PS/2, then press Enter.
12. Press Enter to accept the configuration.
13. When Setup displays the message "This driver for Mouse is already installed on your system..." press the Esc key to replace the currently installed driver.
14. When Setup prompts you for an installation disk, insert your installation disk and enter the path to the designated drive and directory to locate the required files. For example, on the Dell Windows 3.1 CD-ROM disk, the required Windows files are located in the WINDOWS.310 directory. Windows Setup installs the MOUSE.DRV file in the WINDOWS\SYSTEM directory by default, and automatically returns to DOS after locating and copying the required files.
15. At the DOS prompt, type "win" to restart Windows.
16. Verify the file size of the MOUSE.DRV file is either 10672 bytes or 10144 bytes.

Photoshop 3.0x Fails to Launch, Freezes, or Displays Dialog Boxes Incorrectly

ISSUE

Adobe Photoshop 3.0x fails to launch, generates Win32s errors, freezes, or doesn't display dialog boxes correctly (e.g., splash screen does not display, palettes don't are incomplete).

SOLUTIONS

When using a video card based on the S3 chip set, edit the System.ini file:

1. Make a backup copy of the System.ini file located in the Windows directory.
2. Open the original System.ini file in a text editor that can save in text-only format (e.g., Windows Write, Notepad).
3. Change the "aperture-base=100" line in the [Display] section to read:
   `aperture-base=0`
4. Save the System.ini file in text-only format.
5. Exit, then restart Windows.

OR: Use an updated video driver, which is available from the video driver's manufacturer and online services:

NOTE: When using a video card based on the S3 chip, make sure the updated driver is Win32 or Win32s-compatible.

To determine whether your video card has an S3 chip, refer to the documentation included with the video card or contact the manufacturer of the card.
OR: When using an Orchid Farenheit 1280 with BIOS earlier than version 3.0, update the video driver to version 5.11 or later.
OR: When using an Orchid Farenheit 1280 card with the 3.0 BIOS and 7.0 software, update the video driver to version 7.10.82 or later.
OR: When using a Diamond Stealth, update the video driver to version 3.0 or later.
OR: When using an Actix Graphics, Elsa Winner, Metheus Premier, Micronics, Number 9, STB Powergraph and Wind/x or other video card using the S3 chip, contact the appropriate manufacturer for driver updates.
OR: Use a different video driver or mode of the same driver. When running Windows for Workgroups 3.11, install a Windows SVGA driver (e.g., 640 x 480 x 256 colors). When running Windows 3.1, use a different mode specifically for your video card (e.g., 800 x 600 x 256 colors, instead of 1024 x 768 x 256 colors).
NOTE: Photoshop 3.0x does not support running with less than 256 colors.

ADDITIONAL INFORMATION

Photoshop is a 32-bit application. Because Windows 3.1x is a 16-bit operating system, running Photoshop in Windows 3.11 requires installing Win32 components to enable Windows 3.1x to support 32-bit applications. Some video drivers for video cards based on the S3 chip are not compatible with 32-bit applications.

Video cards based on the S3 chip include:

```
ACTIX GRAPHICS ENGINE
ACTIX GRAPHICS ENGINE 32 PLUS
DIAMOND STEALTH 24
DIAMOND STEALTH 24 VLB
DIAMOND STEALTH Pro&Pro VLB
DIAMOND STEALTH VRAM
DIAMOND STEALTH 64
ELSA WINNER 1000
METHEUS PREMIER 928
METHEUS PREMIER VL-BUS 928
MICRONICS VL-BUS
NUMBER 9 GXE
ORCHID FAHRENHEIT 1280
ORCHID FAHRENHEIT VA
ORCHID FAHRENHEIT VA/VLB
STB POWERGRAPH X-24
STB POWERGRAPH VL-24
STB WIND/X HC
```

MAC OS

Q *(3.0 only)* **Ever since I started using Photoshop 3.0 I've been getting some strange errors, like "The application 'unknown' has unexpectedly quit due to a type -11 error," a "type -2" error, and some disk errors. What's wrong?**

A You may be experiencing a problem related to your SCSI devices, and it's showing up in Photoshop because Photoshop installs with a special Plug-In, "Enable Async I/O," that speeds disk access but also makes Photoshop more sensitive to problems in your SCSI setup.

To find out if this is the cause and to provide a temporary fix, disable the "Enable Async I/O" Plug-In. You can do so either by dragging the "Enable Async I/O" Plug-In out of its folder (also called "Enable Async I/O") located within the "Plug-Ins" folder—drag the Plug-In anywhere but the "Plug-Ins" folder or one of its subfolders. You can also disable "Enable Async I/O" by changing the name of the "Enable Async

I/O" folder to "¬Enable Async I/O" (add the special character "¬" at the beginning of its name by holding down the Option key while typing a lowercase L).

If disabling the "Enable Async I/O" Plug-In eliminates the problems you've been having, you may want to try to find the root cause of the problem. (Disabling "Enable Async I/O" isn't an ideal solution, since it will decrease Photoshop's performance.) Try the following:

- Check your SCSI setup. Bad or loose SCSI cables or terminators can cause your machine to hang if you're using "Enable AsyncI/O." If you have a problem in your SCSI setup, you should fix the SCSI problems—if you don't fix them, you could lose data.
- Install Apple's System Update 3.0 (you need to be running System 7.1 to do so). This update fixes several Async I/O–related problems. If you're using a Quadra, we recommend installing System 7.5, which makes Async I/O available for most 68040 machines (Quadras and some Performa models). And, if you're using an AV Macintosh or a Power Macintosh, make sure you're using the SCSI Manager (version 4.3) that comes with System Update 3.0 and System 7.5 and is available on the major bulletin-board systems—it fixes some minor SCSI-related problems on those machines.
- Find out if you're working with prototype hardware. Some of the beta Power Macintosh computers Apple shipped to developers and beta test sites have reported SCSI problems.

Q Sometimes while I'm working in Photoshop, my Mac crashes and I get an error message that says something about a "floating point coprocessor" not being installed. I'm pretty sure that my Mac came with a math coprocessor, so what's the deal?

A Error messages about a missing math coprocessor can be caused by many conditions, most of which have absolutely nothing to do with the presence or absence of a math coprocessor. Your may be experiencing an extension conflict or other problem.

A math coprocessor, also referred to as a floating-point unit or FPU, is circuitry (either on a separate chip or built into the computer's main processor) designed to speed certain math calculations. If a program is written to take advantage of a coprocessor, and if one is present, it will run much faster. Photoshop uses a Mac's math coprocessor (if one is present) to speed up many of its operations. Most high-performance Macs have math coprocessors—all the Power Macs, almost all Centris and Quadra models, and many other Mac models have them, but some Performa and LC models do not.

In most cases a "coprocessor not installed" error is caused by extension conflicts, a problem with the Mac's SCSI chain, damaged software, or some other problem unrelated to math coprocessors.

If you receive this message when you quit Photoshop, you might be experiencing a conflict between Photoshop and version 3.0 of the Norton FileSaver Control Panel. To fix this conflict, try the updated version (3.1.3) of FileSaver, which is available from Symantec at (800) 441-7234.

If you have a Power Mac and receive this message, it might be caused by an old Photoshop Plug-in that really does require a coprocessor. If that Plug-in hasn't been rewritten in Power Mac native code, it won't be able to take advantage of your Power Mac's built-in math coprocessor (non-native applications run through the Power Mac's 68K emulation program, which doesn't have an FPU). Such Plug-ins include Kai's Power Tools version 2.0 or earlier (the KPT Plug-ins version 2.1, which contains native code for Power Macs, should work properly).

If you need to upgrade your KPT Plug-in, contact HSC Software at (805) 566-6200. If you have another 68K Plug-in that requires a math coprocessor, contact that Plug-in's developer to see if an upgrade is available.

Q *(3.0 only)* **I have a new Performa 6200 and I can't get Photoshop to run. Every time I try to launch the program it tells me there's not enough memory. I have 64 megabytes of RAM—isn't that enough?**

A That should be plenty of RAM. You've encountered a problem with the new Power Mac 5200 and Performa 6200 series models, which are based on the PowerPC 603 chip. If you don't load the "Macintosh Easy Open" Control Panel when you start up one of these Macs, Photoshop won't launch. The solution: either use Extensions Manager (or a similar utility) to activate Macintosh Easy Open, or manually move it into the "Control Panels" folder in the System Folder. Then restart your Mac. Photoshop should now launch just fine. If you don't want Easy Open to be active, you can go to the "Macintosh Easy Open" Control Panel and turn it off (and you may not want it active, since it can cause importing problems in PageMaker)—but the control panel itself does need to load at startup.

Q Suddenly, all my Photoshop documents show up as "GE Sumi-e" files when I look at them in the Finder. What on earth has happened? Have my files been corrupted?

A Don't worry—your files are OK. But there is something wrong with the way your Macintosh is seeing them.

This problem usually occurs immediately after you've installed the Adobe Gallery Effects Plug-ins that were included on the Illustrator 6.0 CD-ROM. In most cases the file type indicates that it's a "GE Sumi-e" file, but it could say it's any kind of Gallery Effects filter file (e.g., GE Stamp, GE Watercolor, etc.). Fortunately, in almost all cases, the solution is relatively simple.

The first thing to try is rebuilding your Macintosh's desktop file (which is a good thing to do periodically anyway). Here's how. First, if you're running SuperATM, go to the ATM Control Panel and turn it off temporarily (if you don't, all your documents may show up as generic documents after rebuilding the desktop). Then restart your Mac with Extensions off (hold down the Shift key at startup) and, before the hard drive(s) appear on the Macintosh desktop, hold down the Command + Option keys. You should see a message asking if you really want to rebuild the desktop; click "OK." If you have more than one hard disk connected to your Macintosh, you'll need to rebuild the desktop on each volume (click "OK" when prompted for each one).

If that doesn't solve the problem, reinstalling Photoshop and then rebuilding the desktop almost certainly will. First, remove Photoshop from your Mac (if you have more than one copy installed, be sure to get rid of them all), and then reinstall it. Be sure you do this after the Gallery Effects Plug-ins have been installed. After reinstalling Photoshop, rebuild the desktop on all volumes that are connected to the Macintosh, as described in the preceding paragraph.

In the unlikely event that removing Photoshop, reinstalling it, and rebuilding the desktop doesn't fix the problem, you'll need to run a utility that can change a file's "bundle bits" flag (a part of every file that helps the Mac system software identify it). Norton Disk Doctor can do this, as can certain shareware utilities. After running the utility and telling it to fix the bundle bits of the Gallery Effects filters, rebuild the desktop as described earlier in this answer. That should solve the problem.

A revised Illustrator 6.0 CD-ROM containing updated Gallery Effects Plug-ins that don't cause this problem is available at no charge from Adobe Customer Services. To obtain the CD, call (800) 833-6687.

Q *(3.0.x only)* **I'm having a lot of problems with Photos-hop ever since I updated to System 7.5.3. It's become very unstable, and there are times when I can't get it to launch at all. Is Photoshop compatible with System 7.5.3?**

A Absolutely. Photoshop will run great on a Mac under System 7.5.3, as long as the system software is in good shape. The same is true of any version of system software: if the system software is damaged—even slightly—Photoshop may stop working correctly (even while other applications are running fine).

No matter what version of the system you're running, if you have reason to believe that your system software may not be in the pink, it may be worth reinstalling it in what's known as a "clean install." And one key indicator of system-software problems, of course, is if your problems began immediately after updating to a new version, such as System 7.5.3.

The updater to System 7.5.3 that most people are using (called System Update 2.0) requires that an existing system already be installed—that is, your Mac must already have a System 7.5.x folder, which can be updated to version 7.5.3. Unfortunately, Adobe Tech Support has found that many users experience problems after updating to 7.5.3 if they run the updater on a "dirty" System Folder—that is, one that's been in use for a while, and is therefore loaded with a lot of extra enablers, Extensions, preferences, fonts, and all the other files that tend to accumulate in a System Folder that's been around the block a few times. Although some users report no problems after running the updater on a "dirty" System Folder, many do have trouble.

Fortunately, you can avoid most of these problems (or fix them) if you do a clean install of a new System Folder, then run the updater on that system. The first step is to perform a clean install of whatever version of System 7.5 you have prior to 7.5.3 (that is, System 7.5, 7.5.1, or 7.5.2). Here's how. (A reminder: It's always a good idea to back up your data before installing system software.)

1. Launch the installer, then click "Continue…" in the first screen that comes up (the one that says "Welcome to System 7.5.x").
2. In the main installer screen (the one that lets you choose "Easy Install" or "Custom Install"), type Command + Shift + K. A small dialog box will appear that asks you to choose the type of installation you want: "Update Existing System Folder" or "Install New System Folder." Choose "Install New System Folder," and click "OK" to return to the main installer window.
3. The button that used to be labeled "Install" should now say "Clean Install." This step is critical: if you don't see the "Clean Install" button, quit out of the Installer and repeat steps 1 and 2. Provided you do see it, click "Clean Install" and wait while the installation completes.

After it's finished, you should have a brand-new, squeaky clean System Folder; your old System Folder—with all the stuff you've accumulated—is still there, but it has been renamed "Previous System Folder." For now, leave your "Previous System Folder" alone.

Run the System 7.5.3 updater on your new, clean System Folder. After your system has been updated, reinstall Photoshop from the CD (or floppies). Photoshop should launch and run without a hitch.

Assuming it does, the final step in this process is to reconcile the files from your old System Folder with those in your new one. Simply drag the files from your previous System Folder to your new one, following one unbreakable rule of thumb: don't overwrite any files in your new, clean System Folder with identically named files from your old one. Copying files one at a time is the safest course, since anytime there's a duplication in filenames you'll get an alert box that lets you cancel the operation for that one file; however, going one by one may just take too long. There's no reason you can't move the files several at a time, or even a whole bunch at a time, but pay close attention, and when you receive an alert that says, "Some items in this location have the same names as items you're moving. Do you want to replace them with the ones you're moving?" be sure to click "Cancel" and figure out which files in the batch are the duplicates.

System Error (e.g., Type 11, Type 1, Type 3) Running Photoshop 3.0.x Troubleshooting Guide

ISSUE

The system error "Type 11," "Type 1," or "Type 3" occurs when you run Adobe Photoshop 3.0.x.

SOLUTIONS

Do one or more of the following:

A. Allocate additional memory (RAM) to Photoshop. Photoshop for the Macintosh requires a minimum of 6 MB of memory, and Photoshop for the Power Macintosh requires at least 11 MB of memory.

B. Recreate the Photoshop preferences file:
   1. Quit Photoshop.
   2. Delete the Adobe Photoshop 3.0 Prefs file in the Preferences folder in the System Folder.

   NOTE: Custom preferences must be reset.

C. Reinstall Photoshop:
   1. Move any documents in the Photoshop 3.0 folder to another location.
   2. Delete the Photoshop 3.0 folder and the Adobe Photoshop 3.0 Prefs file, which is located in the Preferences folder in the System Folder.
   3. Reinstall Photoshop from the software disks, following the on-screen instructions.

D. Turn Virtual Memory off in the Memory control panel.

E. Set the Cache Size option for Disk Cache in the Memory control panel to a value equal to or less than 96K.

F. Run Photoshop with all extensions off to verify that added extensions are not the cause:
   1. To turn all extensions off upon startup in System 7, restart the computer with the Shift key held down until the message "Welcome to Macintosh. Extensions Off." appears.

      NOTE: Non-Apple keyboards may have a different method for restarting the Macintosh with Extensions off.
   2. If "Type 11" errors recur after you restart with the Shift key held down, move the Fonts folder, Extensions folder, Control Panels folder, Startup Items folder, Adobe Photoshop 3.0 Prefs file, control panels, and system extensions from the System Folder to another location (e.g., the desktop), then restart the Macintosh.

G. Run Photoshop without the Enable Async I/O folder:
   1. Quit Photoshop.
   2. Move the Enable Async I/O folder, located in the Ex-

tensions folder in the Photoshop 3.0's Plug-ins folder, to another location (e.g., the desktop).

H. Disable automatic drive or file compression utilities (e.g., AutoDoubler, TimesTwo).

I. If you're using more than one hard disk, set Photoshop's scratch disk to the internal hard disk, making sure the amount of available hard disk space is 3 to 5 times the size of the image, or 10 times the size of bitmap mode images being opened. To set Photoshop's scratch disk location, choose File > Preferences > Scratch Disks. Then set the Primary location to the internal hard disk.

J. Check the hard disk for errors, damage, or fragmentation by doing one or more of the following:

   A. Use Disk First Aid, which is included on the system software Disk Tools disk, to check the hard disk's directory structure. For instructions on using Disk First Aid, see Additional Information.
   NOTE: Disk First Aid is only compatible with Apple hard disks. If you're using another manufacturer's hard disk, use a different diagnostics utility to check the hard disk's directory structure.

   B. Update all SCSI drivers to ensure they are not damaged and are compatible with the current system. For instructions on updating SCSI drivers, see Additional Information.

   C. Use a third-party disk utility (e.g. Norton Utilities, MacTools, Symantec Tools for the Macintosh) to ensure damaged sectors are tagged as unusable. For instructions, refer to the utility's documentation.

   D. Defragment and optimize your hard disk using a disk utility (e.g., Norton Utilities, MacTools).

K. If external SCSI devices (e.g., external hard drives, removable media drives, optical drives, external CD-ROM drives, scanner) are connected to the Macintosh, ensure SCSI connection devices, cables, or termination are not the cause by turning the computer and SCSI devices off, disconnecting all SCSI devices, and restarting the computer.

L. Make sure hard disk drivers and all media formatting are compatible with SCSI Manager 4.3. For information about formatting software's compatibility with SCSI Manager 4.3, contact the manufacturer of the drive mechanism.
NOTE: Reformatting your hard disk after updating the hard disk driver is not required, but reformatting may prevent "Type 11" errors.

M. Reinstall the system software by performing a Clean Install (i.e., install new system software into a new System Folder, instead of installing over the existing system software).

n. Upgrade to System 7.5.1 or later.

n. Troubleshoot hardware conflicts by doing one or more of the following:
DISCLAIMER: When troubleshooting hardware conflicts, contact an Apple reseller or the hardware manufacturer for assistance. Making changes to your Macintosh hardware may void the warranty on your computer. Starting the Power Macintosh without the video card in the Processor Direct Slot (PDS) can damage the computer. Contact Apple User Assistance or an authorized Apple reseller for hardware support.

   A. Turn off your computer, then remove accelerator, cache, and other cards installed in the Macintosh.

   B. If you're using a 68K Macintosh with a PowerPC upgrade card, turn off the computer, remove the upgrade card from the computer, restart the computer, then reinstall the 68K or Universal version Photoshop.

   C. Use the built-in video rather than a third-party video card. To check the video card in use:
      1. Open the Monitors control panel.
      2. Click Options in the Monitors dialog box. The video card is listed in the upper-left corner of the Options dialog box.
      3. If you're using a 68K Macintosh with a third-party video card, turn off your computer, then plug the monitor into the built-in video rather than the third-party video card.
      NOTE: Starting the Power Macintosh without the video card in the Processor Direct Slot (PDS) can damage the computer.

   D. Ensure that the RAM SIMMs are installed properly and are not the cause by doing one or more of the following:
      A. Remove and then reinstall the same SIMMs to ensure the SIMMs are seated properly.
      B. In Photoshop's Get Info dialog box, set the Minimum Size and Preferred Size values to the same value as the Suggested Size.
      C. If a large number of SIMMs are installed, remove one or more of them.
      D. Change the order of the SIMMs installed.
      E. Install new SIMMs.
      f. Remove composite RAM SIMMs. Composite RAM SIMMs are not recommended by Apple; check with your dealer to determine if composite RAM SIMMs are installed.
      G. Ensure that your SIMMs are the same speed and same size, and are from the same manufacturer. Check with your dealer to determine the speed, size, and manufacturer of the SIMMs installed.

   E. Run from a different hard drive installed in the Macintosh or the same hard drive installed in a different Macintosh.

   F. Reset the Parameter RAM (PRAM) by holding down the Command + Option + P + R keys when restarting the computer. Hold these keys down until you hear the startup beep twice, then release the keys.
   NOTE: Resetting the Parameter RAM resets the system's preferences to the default settings (e.g., Black and White in the Monitors control panel, LocalTalk Built In in the Network control panel).

   G. Replace the computer's motherboard.

ADDITIONAL INFORMATION

The "Type 11" system error is a miscellaneous hardware exception error, which is caused by a hardware conflict, or by system software or extension conflicts. Apple User Assistance recommends ruling out software conflicts before troubleshooting hardware conflicts.

If removing the Enable Async I/O folder prevents the Type 11 error, there may be an incompatibility between the hardware, system, or drivers on the system and asynchronous input/output.

Common hard disk formatting software that is compatible with SCSI Manager 4.3 include:

- Apple's HDSC 7.3 or later (for Apple hard disks)
- FWB's Hard Disk Toolkit 1.62 or later
- La Cie's SilverLining 5.54, 5.6 or later.

To check a hard disk using Disk First Aid:

1. Start up from the System Software or Disk Tools disk included with your System 7 software disks.
2. Double-click on the Disk First Aid application.
3. Select or open the drive to be verified or repaired.
4. Click Verify to check the disk or Repair to check and repair the disk. If you click Verify, Disk First Aid tells you if there is a problem with the disk and asks you if you want to repair it. Always repair the disk when prompted.
5. Choose File > Quit.

To update SCSI drivers:

1. Start up from the System Software or Disk Tools disk included with your System 7 software disks.
2. Double-click the HDSC Setup application.
3. Click the Drive button until your SCSI drive (i.e., hard disk) is selected.

   NOTE: If your disk drive has been formatted with a third-party disk utility (e.g. Norton Utilities, MacTools, Symantec Tools for Macintosh), HDSC Setup returns the message, "Drive selection failed. Unable to locate a suitable drive connected to the SCSI port." Clicking Continue quits HDSC Setup. You must use the Disk Tools disk from that utility's disk set for these steps. For instructions, refer to the utility's documentation.
4. Click Update to install updated SCSI drivers to each SCSI disk (i.e., hard disk, cartridge, optical).
5. Choose File > Quit.

Printing Problems

MAC OS / WINDOWS

Exported Duotones Print an Extra Plate from Photoshop 2.5 and Later

ISSUE

When you print duotones created in Adobe Photoshop 2.5 and later from a page layout application (i.e., Adobe Illustrator, Quark XPress, Adobe PageMaker), a PANTONE process color duotone prints on a separate plate, rather than on the appropriate process color plate. For example, if the duotone contains "PANTONE Process Black CV," a separate plate, called "PANTONE Process Black CV" prints in addition to the black plate.

SOLUTION

Rename the process color used in the duotone:

1. Choose Mode > Duotone to open the Duotone Options dialog box.
2. In the Duotone Options dialog box, rename the process color "Black" (or "Cyan," "Magenta," or "Yellow"). Make sure that the first letter or the color name is capitalized.
3. Resave the duotone as an EPS and reimport the file into the page layout application.

ADDITIONAL INFORMATION

Process colors in page layout applications are always named "Cyan," "Magenta," "Yellow" and "Black." Process colors from the PANTONE Coated list in Photoshop are named "PANTONE Process <Colorname> CV." Renaming the duotone color in Photoshop to match its counterpart in the page layout application ensures separations print correctly.

Grays in RGB Images Print with Color Cast in Photoshop 2.0 and Later

ISSUE

The gray, shadow, or black areas of an RGB image print with a color cast (i.e., colored tint) from Adobe Photoshop 2.0 and later.

SOLUTION

Enable Photoshop to create the image's gray and black tones:

1. Choose File > Preferences > Separation Setup.
2. In the Separation Setup dialog box, select Maximum from the Black Generation pop-up menu, then click OK.
3. Choose Mode > CMYK to convert the RGB image to CMYK mode.

ADDITIONAL INFORMATION

When you print an RGB image from Photoshop 2.0 or later to a color printer, Photoshop 2.0 accesses the printer's built-in color conversion tables. The printer adds cyan, magenta, and yellow to make a rich black, which results in a color cast.

Photoshop creates a black defined as 100% black, 0% cyan, 0% yellow, and 0% magenta when Maximum is selected for Black Generation in the Separation Setup dialog box. Converting the image to CMYK mode ensures Photoshop defines the color conversion, instead of the printer.

By default, Photoshop adds cyan, magenta, and yellow to make a rich black when defining black in an RGB image.

Enabling PostScript Level 2 Printer to Convert RGB to CMYK for Photoshop

RGB graphics created in Adobe Photoshop 2.5 and later include RGB tags. When RGB tags are enabled, they instruct Photoshop to use its RGB to CMYK algorithm to convert all RGB data to CMYK data when printing separations.

You can disable Photoshop's RGB tags in Photoshop 2.5 and later, with the exception of Photoshop 3.0.1. Disabling RGB tags enables a PostScript Level 2 printer to convert RGB data to CMYK data for separations using its conversion algorithm.

To disable RGB Tags in Photoshop 2.5x, Photoshop 3.0, or Photoshop 3.0.4 or later for Macintosh:

Move the Don't Tag RGB PostScript plug-in from the Optional Extensions folder, located on the Install-Disk 1 Photoshop installation disk or in the Install-Disk 1 folder on the Photoshop Deluxe CD-ROM, into the Photoshop 3.0 Plug-in folder (Photoshop 3.0 or later) or Photoshop Plug-in folder (Photoshop 2.5x).

To disable RGB tags in Photoshop 2.5 or later for Windows, add the "DISABLERGBTAGS=1" line in the [Adobe Photoshop] section of the PHOTOS30.INI (Photoshop 3.0x) or PHOTOSHP.INI (Photoshop 2.5x) file:

1. Exit Photoshop.
2. Make a backup copy of the PHOTOS30.INI file (Photoshop 3.0.x) or the PHOTOSHP.INI file (Photoshop 2.5.x) located in the WIN32APP\PHOTOSHP\PREFS directory (Photoshop 3.0.5) or the WINDOWS directory.
3. Open the original PHOTOS30.INI or PHOTOSHP.INI file in a text editor that can save in text-only format (e.g., Windows Write, Notepad).
4. Add the "DISABLERGBTAGS=1" line in the [Adobe Photoshop] section, exactly as shown:
   `DISABLERGBTAGS=1`
5. Save the file in text-only format.

Painting on Black CMYK Image Creates Halo Around Stroke in Photoshop 2.x or Later

ISSUE

In Adobe Photoshop 2.x or later, a halo (e.g., ring of lighter color) appears around the brush stroke after painting on a black (e.g., 100% K) background in a CMYK image using the Airbrush or Paint brush tool.

SYMPTOMS

The foreground color of the brush stroke does not transition smoothly into the black background color.

When painting in RGB color mode, foreground color of the brush stroke fades smoothly into the background color.

SOLUTIONS

Paint in LAB or RGB color mode with the Airbrush or Paint brush tool:

1. Choose LAB or RGB Color from the Mode menu.
2. Paint with the Airbrush or Paint brush tool.
3. Choose Mode > CMYK Color to return to CMYK color mode.

OR: Darken the display of the image by increasing the dot gain (e.g., 30% or 40%):

1. Choose File > Preferences > Printing Inks Setup.
2. Increase the Dot Gain percentage, then click OK.

NOTE: Photoshop uses a 20% dot gain by default.

ADDITIONAL INFORMATION

In Photoshop 2.x and later, painting with the Paint brush and Airbrush tools creates an anti-aliased brush stroke.

When you paint in Photoshop's CMYK mode using the Airbrush or Paint brush tool on a color composed of Black and less than 100% of Cyan, Magenta, or Yellow, Photoshop creates an anti-aliased transition of a lighter color (e.g., a halo) between the brush stroke and background. When a brush stroke is anti-aliased in CMYK color mode, the transition between the background and foreground color is composed of tints of the CMY colors in the background color and decreasing percentages of Black (K) in the foreground color. For example, when anti-aliasing a 100% Black brush stroke painted over a background color of 100% Cyan and 100% Magenta, the transition color created by anti-aliasing contains 33% Cyan, 33% Magenta, and 67% Black. The light color transition between the edge pixels of the brush stroke and the background color creates the appearance of a halo around the anti-aliased brush stroke.

The larger the percentages of CMY in the black background color, the less distinct the halo around the brush stroke appears. The fewer the percentages of CMY in the black background color, the lighter and more distinct the halo around the brush stroke appears.

Dark colors in RGB color mode are composed of decreasing amounts or Red, Green, and Blue. Black is composed of 0 Red, 0 Green, and 0 Blue. When you paint with the Airbrush and Paint brush tools in RGB color mode, the anti-aliased edge pixels of the brush stroke are composed of RGB, seamlessly blending the brush stroke into the background.

Increasing the dot gain percentage in the Printing Inks Setup dialog box lessens the halo around the brush stroke by darkening the overall appearance of the image.

Creating Predictable Separations

To generate reliable color separations in Adobe Photoshop, it's important to understand the role of calibration. This document outlines the issues involved in calibration. For more detailed information about calibration in Adobe Photoshop, refer to the "Adobe Photoshop User Guide."

MONITOR CALIBRATION

Colors displayed on the monitor can look different from those that are printed. However, you can control certain factors to ensure predictable printed results.

Lighting and viewing conditions
It is important to work in a controlled environment where the ambient light in the room does not change during the course of the day. Any change can affect your perception of colors on the monitor. Ideally, you should work in an artificially lit room with the same brightness level at all times. You can control the environment by closing your room off to external light sources and taping down the monitor and room lighting controls once they are set.
Colors
Screen colors can be affected by a monitors age and temperature. Such factors can create a color cast on the monitor. If your monitor does display a color cast, follow the manufacturers instructions to be sure that it is adjusted properly. Let the monitor warm up for an hour after it is turned on before making color corrections to an image. Also, do not leave the monitor running overnight. However, you can leave your computer and disks running but you should turn the monitor off.
Monitor color cast
Most uncalibrated monitors tend to display a bluish cast. Use the monitor calibration feature supplied with the Adobe Photoshop Gamma Control Panel (or another more sophisticated calibration program) to eliminate the cast. For example, if the color cast remains, add yellow and red to an image to compensate for the blue cast; the result is a printed image with a yellow and red color cast.
Gamma
All monitors tend to display images with a shift in the midtone values, causing an image to look darker or lighter. This midtone shift varies among manufacturers, and even between monitors from the same manufacturer. A built-in value is used to compensate for this effect. Give the adjustment value terminology to Adobe Photoshop so that the affected midtone areas can be printed accurately. The default monitor gamma value is 1.8 for both monitor setup and Gamma Control Panel. To print or display the image with another application or on another platform, use a gamma of 1.8; this value is the closest match for uncorrected gamma. Images intended for video and film recorders should have a target gamma of 2.2, which is the typical gamma of most television sets. The higher value is due to the luminosity value of video. See Chapter 2, Calibrating Your System, in the "Adobe Photoshop User Guide" for more information.

The Monitor Setup dialog box (accessible through the Preferences submenu of the File menu) includes options that give Adobe Photoshop information about lighting, viewing, and monitor configurations. This data is then used to create separations.

Other factors also influence the integrity of the printed image. Make the following adjustments to your imagesetter to produce high-quality output:

- Adjust it for varying dot densities.
- Adjust it for dot gain that occurs when plates are burned and on-press gain.

Other factors can also affect color image quality. For example, the quality of the final output can vary dramatically with the imagesetter, the strength and mixture of the chemicals, the batch of film, the paper stock, and the type of press.

IMAGESETTER MISCALIBRATION

Unless the imagesetter and processor are well maintained, the dot percentage requested may not be the actual percentage measured with a densitometer on film. For example, if you specify a 65-percent halftone tint, the actual reading from a densitometer can vary by as much as 15 to 20-percent. Images that were meant to look identical can print differently unless the dot density produced by the imagesetter is well calibrated. A well-calibrated densitometer is required to measure dot densities for accurate halftones. Calibration of an imagesetter should be performed at least once a day and color separation output should be checked with each new roll of film and batch of chemicals in the process.

If you select the Calibration Bars option in the Page Setup dialog box, an 11-step gray wedge is printed on your separations. By using this gray wedge, you can record densities at different levels from a given imagesetter. Adobe Photoshop can compensate for these density changes with a function called Transfer. If you enter information about the density that is recorded at different levels, Adobe Photoshop makes the necessary adjustments to ensure linearization (to ensure that the requested tints closely match the output). See the "Adobe Photoshop User Guide" for more details. For best results, however, use the calibration utility provided by the manufacturer of your imagesetter rather than the Adobe Photoshop Transfer function.

DOT GAIN ON-PRESS

Even if the dot percentages recorded on film are accurate, they may change during printing due to dot gain on the printing press. Dot gain occurs when halftone dots reproduce larger on paper (in varying degrees depending on the paper stock) than they do on film. They can cause oversaturated colors and in accurate reproduction. A certain amount of dot gain always occurs on-press, but you can compensate for it if you know what to expect.

For each project, ask the printer how much dot gain to anticipate. Adobe Photoshop compensates for gain on-press with easily selectable lookup tables in the Printing Inks Setup dialog box. The lookup tables take into consideration the nature of the paper stock, how colors reproduce on the stock, and the level of dot gain expected on the stock at the 50-percent mark. Adobe Photoshop uses this 50-percent value to generate a curve that applies dot gain compensation throughout the image.

OTHER CONSIDERATIONS

Other considerations, such as the way the color separations are set up, and using the Lab Color mode, can affect the quality of your separations.
Separation setup
When preparing color separations, it is important to select the correct separation options in the Separation Setup dialog box.

The two types of separations you can choose are Gray Component Replacement (GCR), the default, and Undercolor Removal (UCR). Contact your printer to find out which method for generating the black plate they have the most experience with. Many printers are more comfortable with the UCR method of printing.

Other options in the dialog box—such as Black Ink Limit, Total Ink Limit, and UCA Amount—involve conditions specific to the press on which your separations will be printed. Contact your printer for advice on entering these values.

Lab color mode

Adobe Photoshop uses the Lab color mode as an intermediary in most mode conversions. Lab color is a device-independent color mode that appears the same no matter what type of monitor or printer youre using, as long as the devices are calibrated. If printing to a PostScript Level 2 printer, convert the document to Lab Color mode, and let the Level 2 interpreter perform the conversion to CMYK mode. For more information about Lab color, see the technical note "The Lab Color Mode."

Questions to Ask Your Printer

To get the best results from four-color separations in Adobe Photoshop, it is important to maintain a dialogue with the different agencies involved in getting the job printed. This may involve talking with the professionals at a color house for scans, at a service bureau for producing film, and finally, at a print shop for printing the job on-press.

Of all these relationships, the dialogue with your printer is the most crucial. To begin the search for a good print shop, you should consult with several printers and tour their facilities. When you take a tour, ask to see printed samples of their work and spec sheets for their equipment. Many good printers provide information geared to working with desktop files. Be sure to find out about their printing press capabilities.

When you pick a printer and are ready to start working on a project, do not hesitate to ask any questions. Asking the right questions helps you to establish a good rapport with the printer, can avoid surprises, and build confidence about producing good separations.

The following sections detail the most important information you need from your printer to produce good color separations in Adobe Photoshop:

- The press's ability to handle screen frequencies
- Press conditions and potential dot gain
- Method for generating black separation plates
- Ink limitations of the press and the ink density of the black plate
- The printers role in producing film

Your printer may also be able to guide you in selecting and modifying images that print well, and perhaps can recommend a color house for high-end scans.

SCREEN FREQUENCY AND IMAGE RESOLUTION

When you first talk with your printer, determine the screen frequency potential of the press. The screen frequency may vary depending on the plates. Also, a higher screen frequency may be more expensive. The screen frequency directly affects the resolution of the scanned image in Adobe Photoshop. In general, the image resolution needs to be 1.5 to 2 times the screen frequency at which the file is printed. For example, if the press can support a 150-line screen, you won't need an image resolution greater than 300 pixels per inch (ppi). A higher image resolution won't yield significantly better results, but will generate a much larger file size. On the other hand, a lower resolution for your image may create a file that looks blockish, or pixelated, when printed.

For more information about issues related to scanning, see Chapter 3 of the Adobe Photoshop User Guide.

DOT GAIN ON PRESS

Be sure to ask how much dot gain the printer experiences on-press for a given paper stock. Ask how much dot gain is expected on-press from the film stage to press sheet in the midtones. Many printers will tell you the amount of dot gain expected from the proof stage to the press sheet, but this is an incorrect value to use in Adobe Photoshop.

In general, coated stock registers a dot gain of 18% to 25% in the midtones. Dot gain for uncoated stock and newsprint varies from 30%t to 40%. Because midtones register the greatest amount of gain on-press, Adobe Photoshop uses the gain in the midtones as a good indication of the gain that occurs over the rest of the image. If your printer is unsure of the dot gain value, use the default values provided for each type of paper stock in the

Printing Inks Setup dialog box:

- Ink Colors: SWOP (Coated)
- Dot Gain: 20%
- Gray Balance: C: 1.00; M: 1.00; Y: 1.00; K: 1.00
- Use Dot Gain for Grayscale Images should be selected

GENERATING THE BLACK SEPARATION PLATE

Adobe Photoshop offers two ways to generate the black separation plate: Undercolor Removal (UCR) and Gray Component Replacement (GCR). The options appear in the Separation Setup dialog box.

The difference between the two methods affects mainly the black plate. GCR generates black throughout the image, beginning in the highlights. UCR generates black mainly in the 3/4-tones and in the black part of the image, thus holding shadow detail better. See how the two methods distribute black ink by observing the black in the Gray Ramp when you choose either GCR or UCR. (Notice also that the supporting C, M, and Y are adjusted.)

For best results, choose GCR or UCR, depending on which method the print shop has more experience and is more comfortable. Many printers are more comfortable with UCR. For more information about UCR and GCR, refer to the "Adobe Photoshop User Guide."

Ink Limits
Also ask your printer about the total ink limit the press can support and the total ink density used for the black plate. Enter this information in the Separation Setup dialog box. Many small to medium-sized print shops may not be able to provide this information. If you are unsure, use the default values.

THE PRINTER S ROLE IN PRODUCING FILM
A close working relationship with your printer in producing film can save many headaches as well as wasted time and money. Ask your printer what role the print shop will play in producing film. Pick a printer who assumes this function in-house or who is willing to work closely with your imaging house or service bureau.

Working with Slide Film Recorders

The term film recorder may refer to one of two types of devices: a slide film recorder or a high-end film recorder.

A slide film recorder outputs instant film (sometimes called Polaroids), slides, and transparencies. The film recorder is a black-and-white CRT (cathode-ray tube) attached to a 35mm camera. The larger the CRT, the smaller the spot size, or size of each pixel on the face of the CRT, and the better the quality of the resulting image. Leading vendors of slide film recorders include Agfa Matrix and ChromaScript, Lasergraphics, Mirus, GCC Technologies, and Presentation Technologies.

A high-end film recorder, sometimes called a laser plotter, is used to generate output from color prepress systems. These high-resolution devices differ from most PostScript imagesetters in the way they generate output and in their output speed two to twenty times faster than most PostScript imagesetters. Unlike the flatbed design of earlier PostScript imagesetters, all high-quality film recorders use a rotary-drum design. The halftone screening often is generated through built-in proprietary hardware; in many cases the screening algorithms are licensed from Hell Graphics systems (now merged with Linotype-Hell).

This tech note discusses slide film recorders and some of the issues to be aware of when working with these devices.

QUICKDRAW SUPPORT
Most slide film recorders available today support only the Apple QuickDraw format, not PostScript output, and they support only 35 commonly used fonts. If you download an Encapsulated PostScript (EPS) file to a film recorder that supports only QuickDraw, the film recorder produces only a low-resolution PICT preview associated with the EPS file. The result is a coarse image.

To compensate for the QuickDraw limitation, many vendors incorporate into their recorders the software-based PostScript clone Freedom of Press or the driver Professional Output Manager by Visual Business Systems (VBS), which acts as a PostScript compatible interpreter.

RGB MODE AND GAMMA
Slide film recorders operate only in RGB mode, similar to the RGB mode in Adobe Photoshop. You cannot send CMYK images to these devices.

In addition, the gamma of the film used in slide film recorders is much higher than that of a monitor. The gamma of most commercial slide film recorders is 2.2. If you work with images that will be output to a film recorder, for best results, set the gamma in your application to 2.2 to match that of the film recorder. If you do not calibrate your system for the film recorder, out- put will probably be darker than expected.

A quick and simple way to calibrate your system for the film recorder is to print a slide and use the Gamma CDEV or a similar monitor calibration utility to make the screen look like the slide. (See Chapter 2, Calibrating Your System, in the "Adobe Photoshop User Guide" for instructions.) The gamma adjustment should improve the image quality by adjusting for overall light- ness and darkness.

FILM RECORDER AND OUTPUT RESOLUTION AND SIZE
Another issue that affects working with film recorders is resolution. Film recorders measure resolution as the size of the image the recorder can output; the image is output as individually colored pixels. The resolution measures the actual number of pixels (height by width) that the film recorder can output. Most film recorders output film with a resolution of at least 4K (4096 by 2732 pixels); more sophisticated film recorders output images with a resolution of 8K (8192 by 5460 pixels) or 16K (16,384 by 10,928 pixels).

Think of the film recorder as having a number of grids, one for each resolution the film recorder can output (2K, 4K, etc.). To be output by the film recorder, the height and width of an image (in pixels) must be smaller than or equal to the height and width of the grid. If the image size is

Resolution	Pixel count (height x width)	Appropriate file size	Suggested use
2K	2048 x 1366	10 MB	35 mm slides; separations for printing at low and medium resolution
4K	4096 x 2732	35 MB	Up to 4x5-inch slides; near-photographic quality; most workable file size
8K	8192 x 5464	150 MB	Up to 8x10-inch slides; excellent resolution; very large file size
16K	16,384 x 10, 928	600 MB	Up to 8x10-inch slides; exceptional resolution, but prohibitive file size

greater than a given resolution, the film recorder will output the image using a finer (higher-resolution) grid, and the resulting image will have to be resized.

For example, an image measuring 2000 pixels by 1350 pixels fits within the 2K grid; however, an image measuring 2000 pixels by 1400 pixels fits the horizontal but not the vertical limits of the grid. As a result, the film recorder will output the image at the next-highest resolution that can accommodate the image, 4K; the resulting image would be scaled to 50 percent to fit on the higher-resolution grid.

As with other types of output, the resolution of the film recorder output directly affects the file size and the quality of the output. The higher the resolution of the output, the better is its quality but the larger the file size and the greater the processing time. A slide with a resolution of 8K can take up to an hour to process. In addition, the advantage of outputting film at a higher res- olution is lost if the resolution exceeds that of the film. For example, using a resolution higher than 4K exceeds the resolution of commonly used slide films such as Ektachrome.

Photoshop Image Doesn't Print with Expected Custom Halftone Screen from Other Applications

ISSUE

Imported Photoshop 2.5.1 or later images do not print with the expected custom halftone screen, as specified in Photoshop's Halftone Screens dialog box.

SOLUTIONS

In Photoshop, resave the image as an EPS (*.eps) file by choosing EPS from the Format pop-up menu then selecting Include Halftone Screen in the EPS Format dialog box. OR: Specify a custom halftone screen for the image within the printing application (e.g., QuarkXPress, PageMaker).

ADDITIONAL INFORMATION

Only the EPS file format includes custom halftone screen information. When printing an imported Photoshop EPS file from another application, custom halftone screens included in the EPS file override the printing application's default halftone screens.

Photoshop images saved in other file formats (e.g., TIFF, PICT) do not contain custom halftone screen information, as these formats are unable to include custom halftone screen information. Imported Photoshop images saved in formats other then EPS print from other applications using the application's default halftone screen or with the halftone screen assigned to it in the application.

To set custom halftone screens for a CMYK image:

1. Open a CMYK image.
2. Choose File > Page Setup, then click Screen.
3. In the Halftone Screens dialog box, deselect Use Printer's Default Screens.
4. Select Cyan from the Ink pop-up menu, then enter the desired screen frequency and angle.
5. Select each remaining ink (i.e., Magenta, Yellow, Black) from the Ink pop-up menu, and enter the desired screen frequency and angle.
6. Click OK.

To set a custom halftone screen for a grayscale image in Photoshop:

1. Open a grayscale image.
2. Choose File > Page Setup, then click Screen.
3. In the Halftone Screen dialog box, deselect Use Printer's Default Screen.
4. Enter the desired screen frequency.
5. Click OK.

How to Print Photoshop Images in Different Places on a Page General Information

When you print an image from Adobe Photoshop, it centers the image on the page. To print an image off-center, you must use Photoshop's Canvas Size feature to add white space (pixels) to the sides, top, or bottom of your image. Then, when you print the image on white paper, Photoshop centers the entire image area, including the canvas, so that the original image area prints off-center in the desired location on the page.

Because adding canvas to an image increases file size and slows printing, you may want to export your Photoshop images to a page layout application (e.g., Adobe PageMaker, QuarkXPress), position it on the page, then print. Both printing methods are detailed below.

To print a Photoshop image from a page layout application:

1. In Photoshop, choose File > Save to save your Photoshop image in a file format (e.g., TIFF, EPS) that can be imported into a page layout program.
2. Import your Photoshop image into the page layout application, then move it to the desired location on the page.
3. Print the image.

To add canvas to an image and print from Photoshop:

1. Open your image in Photoshop.
2. Click the Default Colors icon (small black and white squares) in Photoshop's toolbox to set the background color to white, so that the canvas you add to your image is white.
3. Choose Image > Canvas Size.
4. In the New Size section, enter a Width and Height for the canvas, so that the canvas, when centered on your page, will include the area of the page where you want your image to print. For example if you are printing on 8.5" x 11" paper, and you want to print your image in the top left corner of the page, enter a Height of approximately 10" and a Width of approximately 7", depending on the imageable area of your printer.
5. For Placement (Photoshop 3.0.x) or Anchor (Photoshop 4.0), click the square on the grid that represents where you want your image to be located on the canvas. For

example, if you want your image to be placed in the lower left corner of your canvas, click the lower left square on the grid.

NOTE: Adding canvas to an image increases file size, which can slow image processing (e.g., screen redraw, printing). Add only enough canvas to shift the image to desired location on the page. For example, to print an image at the top center of the page, change only the Height to the maximum imageable area of your printer, then click the top center square for Placement/Anchor.

6. Click OK.
7. To preview the new image size (including canvas) on the page, click the box in the lower-left corner of the document window, where the file size is displayed.
   NOTE: The dimensions of the page shown in the page preview box correspond to the page size selected in the Page Setup dialog box.
8. Print the image from Photoshop.

WINDOWS

Q *(3.0.x only)* **I have a color printer, but when I print a color document from Photoshop under Windows 95, all I seem to get is black-and-white output. Any ideas what's wrong?**

A There are several reasons this could be happening. Here are a few suggested steps to take, one of which will probably correct the problem.

- Double-check in Photoshop's "Print" dialog box to make sure you're really sending color data—if you have the "Gray" option checked under "Print as," you certainly won't get color output.
- Check with your printer's manufacturer to make sure the printer driver you're using is updated for Windows 95; if it's not, you may have trouble printing in color (or at all).
- If you're printing to a PostScript printer, look in the "Encoding" section of the "Print" dialog box to see if "Binary" in selected; if it is, try checking the "ASCII" option.
- Another tactic if you're printing to a PostScript printer is to add a "switch," or setting, to your PHOTOS30.INI file that will bypass the printer driver, so that the PostScript code Photoshop generates will be sent directly to the printer. In some cases this solves the problem. Use a text editor such as Notepad or WordPad to open your PHOTOS30.INI file (located in the WINDOWS directory for Photoshop 3.0.4, or in the PHOTOSHP\PREFS directory for Photoshop 3.0.5). Once the file's open, add the following, on its own line, anywhere in the text after the [Photoshop] line:

```
PRINTMODE=1
```

Save the file as text only, restart Photoshop, and try printing again. If your problem doesn't disappear, undo what you just did—delete the new line from PHOTOS30.INI, save it again, and restart Photoshop.

Q I can't seem to print anything from Photoshop to my HP DeskJet 550c. The printer just sits there and does nothing. Isn't Photoshop compatible with this printer?

A Yes, Photoshop is compatible with your printer, but version 5.0 of the HP 500 series driver (used with the Hewlett-Packard DeskJet 500, 500c, 510, 520, 540, 550c, and 560c) doesn't work correctly with Photoshop and other 32-bit applications. If you can't print to one of these printers, you probably need to change your driver.

You can check to see which version of the driver you're using by opening the Control Panel in the "Main" program group in Program Manager, then double-clicking on the Printers icon. In the "Installed Printers" list, select your HP5xx printer (for example, HP 550c) and click "Setup...." In the printer driver's main dialog box, click once on the Control menu (see the illustration above) and select "About..." to display the version of the driver.

If you are using version 5.0, get the newer version. Version 6.10, which solves this problem, is now available from Hewlett-Packard. Contact HP at (303)339-7009 to obtain the updated driver, or download it from HP's BBS at (208) 344-1691—the file is named DJ100EN.EXE. If you have Internet access, the new driver can also be downloaded from HP's FTP site at:

```
ftp://ftp-boi.external.hp.com/pub/printers/
djet_pjet_dwriter/win_dos
```

Changing to an older version of the driver, such as 4.x, will also fix the problem. This driver is available on the HP BBS as D5WN31.EXE (it may also be on the disks that came with your printer). Once you've installed and switched to the newer (or older) driver, your documents should print properly from Photoshop.

If you can't get a different driver and you need another fix, you can save your Photoshop image in a format that'll import into another program (TIFF or EPS, for example), and print your image from the other application.

Installation Issues

MAC OS / WINDOWS

Q *(3.0 only)* **I recently received a CD in the mail with an update to Photoshop 3.0.4. What does it do?**

A The 3.0.4 update was sent out in August on CD free of charge to all registered users of Photoshop 3.0. The 3.0.4 update is a "maintenance release" that includes a few new features, and adds enhancements for 604-based Power Mac systems and improved support for Windows 95.

New features in both the Macintosh and Windows versions of Photoshop 3.0.4 include the addition of a "Scratch Disk Efficiency" indicator that lets you know the amount of time Photoshop is accessing the scratch disk; a Float Controls feature that allows users to control how a floating selection interacts with the layer(s) below it; improved import of

Adobe Illustrator files; added support for TWAIN 36- and 48-bit scanners; and support for online registration.

The Windows version includes improved performance with Win32s and improved support for many 16-bit Plug-ins and the HP 16-bit TWAIN scanning module. There is also extensive optimization for Windows 95, including right mouse-button configuration for Photoshop's Commands palette; support for filenames up to 256 characters; registry of application and file icons; and support for Universal Naming Convention (UNC) path names.

The Macintosh version includes improved support for the new Power Macintosh computers that use the Motorola PowerPC 604 processor (including the Power Macintosh 8500 and 9500 series)—several functions (including Skew, Rotate, Gaussian Blur, and many path operations) will execute significantly faster than in version 3.0. Also included are an HSB/HSL Plug-in, a fat-binary Kodak Photo CD Plug-in, an improved DirectBits Plug-in, and a fat-binary version of Adobe Type Manager.

All registered users of Photoshop 3.0 should have received a copy of the 3.0.4 update by now, free of charge, on CD. If you haven't received it, contact Adobe Customer Services at (800) 628-2320.

Q *(3.x only)* **I have some version of Photoshop 3 on my computer, but I'm not sure if I have the latest update installed or not. Is there any easy way to tell what version I'm running so I don't have to reinstall?**

A Sure. On the PC, with Photoshop running, select "About Adobe Photoshop..." from Photoshop's Help menu. In the "Adobe Photoshop 3.0" dialog box, look below the artwork over on the right side underneath the eye. If you don't see any number there, you're running version 3.0. If you see a number, that's the version number you're running—3.0.4 is the latest version.

On the Mac, select the Photoshop 3.0 program icon while in the Finder, and choose "Get Info" from the File menu (or type Command + I) to open Photoshop's "Info" dialog box. The version number is listed on the line just above the "Comments" box. If you've got the latest update, the version number should be 3.0.4.

Q *(3.x only)* **I recently heard about Photoshop 3.0.5, but it wasn't too long ago that I received a Photoshop 3.0.4 update CD in the mail from Adobe. Why is there a 3.0.5 update? Do I need to install it?**

A Yes, you'd probably benefit significantly from installing 3.0.5. Like most other major software programs, Photoshop is updated frequently to improve performance and compatibility with the latest hardware and operating systems. When this issue went to press, the most recent revision to Photoshop was version 3.0.5, on both Mac and Windows.

Users of Macintosh Photoshop 3.0.4 (or Photoshop LE 3.0.4) can update to version 3.0.5 by downloading the 3.0.5 Update from Adobe's Web site and other online sources (see the last paragraph of this answer for more detailed instructions). Note that the 3.0.5 updater can update only Photoshop 3.0.4—that is, it will not work on previous versions. Version 3.0.5 fixes a file-preview problem and an error that results in a crash upon quitting on some Power Macs. It also includes several new Plug-ins, including a GIF89a Export Plug-in that supports transparent and interlaced GIF files for use in World-Wide Web pages; a PowerPC Accelerator Plug-in, which accelerates certain functions on Power Macs; and improved DirectCursors, Adobe Illustrator Parser, and PCX Plug-ins.

The Windows 3.0.5 upgrade is designed to meet the Windows 95 certification requirements, and it should be available by the time you read this. (For pricing and availability information, contact Adobe Customer Services at 800-628-2320.) The Windows upgrade also includes an improved "Universal Thunker" to fix problems some users have encountered when attempting to use some 16-bit Plug-ins and 16-bit scanning modules under Windows 95. The "Universal Thunker" files (compressed into a file called THUNK.ZIP) can be downloaded at no charge from Ado-be's online sites.

To download these files from Adobe's World-Wide Web home page at http://www.adobe.com, click "Adobe Products," then "Applications," then "Adobe Photoshop"; scroll down the Photoshop page until you see the appropriate file listed. On CompuServe, go to the Adobe Applications Forum (GO ADOBEAPP), click "Browse Libraries," and open the "Photoshop Mac" or "Photoshop PC" library. If you're using America Online, use the keyword "Adobe," then double-click "Adobe Software Libraries" and navigate to the appropriate area from there. Finally, you can call Adobe's free Tech Support BBS (206-623-6984), open the "File Library," and then open either the "Photoshop-Mac" or "Photoshop-Windows" folder.

Q *(3.x only)* **I read in a recent issue of Adobe Magazine that I could save a Photoshop TIFF file with a clipping path, but I can't get it to work. I've been able to get clipping paths to work in EPS files in the past, but it doesn't seem to be working with TIFF files that I place in QuarkXPress. Am I doing something wrong?**

A You can indeed save a clipping path as part of a TIFF file from Photoshop 3.0. (To do so, follow the instructions on pages 77–91 of the Adobe Photoshop User Guide, but choose the TIFF rather than EPS format when saving.) However, the only page-layout program that currently supports clipping paths in TIFF files is PageMaker 6.0. So if you're using some other page-layout program, you'll have to save your Photoshop file with a clipping path in the EPS format, which most page-layout programs (including all versions of PageMaker and QuarkXPress) accept.

Q I recently got Photoshop 3.0.5, and I'm having trouble installing the program from the Photoshop Deluxe CD. Got any suggestions?

A There are several things that can interfere with Photoshop's installer program. To get around these conflicts, try the following steps.

If you're running Windows 95, copy the install files (the entire directory labeled PHOTOSHP) from the Deluxe CD to the hard drive, then restart your PC in Windows 95's Safe mode and run the installer directly from the hard drive. To boot in Safe mode, restart your PC and, as you see the message "Starting Windows 95," press and hold down the F5 key until the Windows 95 logo appears. Booting in Safe mode allows Windows to launch without loading certain drivers and other memory-resident utilities that sometimes conflict with Photoshop's installer. Once you've completed the installation, you'll need to restart Windows in normal mode (just restart and don't hold down any keys) in order for Photoshop to launch.

On a Macintosh, use an Extensions manager to temporarily disable all Extensions except the ones you need to be able to use your CD-ROM drive (such as the Apple CD-ROM Extension), then try running the installer. If you still have problems with the installer, you can simply drag a preinstalled copy of Photoshop from the CD to your hard drive. Open the folder labeled "Adobe Photoshop 3.0.5" on the Photoshop Deluxe CD and drag the folder named "Adobe Photoshop 3.0.5 Universal" to your Mac's hard drive. This folder contains all the files you'll need to get Photoshop up and running, and will work on both Power Macs and 68K (non-PowerPC) Macs. The only things this method doesn't give you are the files that the installer places in your System Folder, including Adobe Type Manager (ATM), Adobe Type Reunion, QuickTime, and the Kodak Photo CD color management files.

WINDOWS

Q *(3.0 only)* **I just installed Windows 95 and Photoshop on my PC. Photoshop seems to run fine, but the box didn't have one of those Windows 95 stickers on it. Should I expect problems?**

A Photoshop should run just fine under Windows 95. Photoshop is a 32-bit application, and the 3.0.4 update (see the question at the bottom right of this page) is specifically written to take advantage of Windows 95. Adobe is also currently working on an additional update to Photoshop that will meet all the Windows 95 logo-certification requirements; this update is expected to be available within 90 days after the final release of Windows 95, for a price that hadn't been determined at press time. Packages shipped after that will come with the Windows 95 sticker on the box.

Removing and Reinstalling Win32s Components from Photoshop 3.0.x

To remove and reinstall Win32s components installed by Photoshop 3.0.x from your system:

NOTE: Other applications may also use Win32s files. Instead of deleting these files, moving or renaming them enables you to restore these files should another application require them.

1. Exit Photoshop.
2. Delete the WINDOWS\SYSTEM\WIN32S directory and the files it contains from your hard disk.
3. Open the SYSTEM.INI file, located in the WINDOWS directory, in a text editor that can save in text-only format (e.g., Notepad), then delete the following line from [386Enh] section:
   `device=C:\WINDOWS\SYSTEM\WIN32S\W32S.386`
4. Save the SYSTEM.INI file in text-only format, then exit Windows.
5. From DOS, delete the following four files from the WINDOWS\SYSTEM directory:
   `WIN32S16.DLL`
   `WIN32S.INI`
   `W32SYS.DLL`
   `WINMM16.DLL`
6. If Photoshop has been launched at least once, delete the PHOTOS30.PSP, PHOTOS30.INI, and CCOLORSD files in the WIN32APP\PHOTOSHP\PREFS directory (Photoshop 3.0.5) or the WINDOWS directory (Photoshop 3.0 and 3.0.4).
7. Restart Windows, then reinstall Photoshop.

GPF Error or Screen Turns Black When Installing Photoshop 3.0.5 in Windows 3.1x

ISSUE

When you install Adobe Photoshop 3.0.5 in Windows 3.1x, the Photoshop 3.0.5 Installer returns the error "IS INST30 caused a GPF error in module unknown," or the Installer screen turns black after loading the InstallShield Wizard.

SOLUTIONS

Do one or more of the following:

A. Install the Windows Standard VGA video driver, install Photoshop, then revert to your regular video driver. For instructions on installing the Windows Standard VGA video driver, see Additional Information.
   NOTE: Photoshop requires a video driver that displays at least 256 colors to run. After you install Photoshop using the Standard VGA video driver, change to a video driver that displays 256 or more colors.
B. Change the resolution of your video driver (e.g., 1024 x 768, 256 colors, instead of 800 x 600, 256 colors). To change the resolution of your video driver, follow steps for installing the Windows Standard VGA video driver in Additional Information, but choose a display driver other than VGA (e.g., 1024 x 768, 256).
C. Install an updated driver for your video card, available from your video card manufacturer, then reinstall Photoshop.

ADDITIONAL INFORMATION

The Photoshop 3.0.5 Installer is incompatible with some older video drivers, causing an error to occur or the Installer screen to turn black. Changing to the Windows Standard VGA video driver, changing the resolution of your video driver, or updating your video driver enables Photoshop to install successfully.

To install the Windows Standard VGA video driver in Windows 3.1x:

1. Make a backup copy of the System.ini file:
   1. At the DOS prompt, change to the Windows directory by typing:

   CD WINDOWS

   2. At the C:\WINDOWS prompt type:

   `COPY SYSTEM.INI SYSTEM.BAK`

   3. Press Enter. This creates a backup copy of the System.ini file named "System.bak" in the Windows directory.

   NOTE: You can use the backup file to restore your original video settings at any time by copying the backup file over the newer System.ini file at a DOS prompt by typing:

   `CD WINDOWS`

   And then at the C:\WINDOWS prompt type:

   `COPY SYSTEM.BAK SYSTEM.INI`

   Press Enter. This copies your original System.ini file (e.g., System.bak) over the newer System.ini file.
2. Start Windows.
3. Double-click the Windows Setup icon in the Main group of Program Manager, or choose File > Run and type "setup" in the Command line text box, then click OK.
4. In Windows Setup, choose Options > Change System Settings.
5. Select VGA from the Display pop-up menu, then click OK.
6. Follow the on-screen instructions to install the VGA video driver, inserting Windows installation disks if prompted.
7. Restart Windows.

Error "MS Setup Toolkit API Error..." When Installing Photoshop 3.0x

ISSUE

When you start the Adobe Photoshop 3.0x Installer (Setup.exe), the system returns the error "MS Setup Toolkit API Error, Bad Arg 3:AddSectionFiles to CopyList, [PhotoCD PT, D:\Photoshop\Disk1\, C:C:\Windows\PhotoCD]." The drive, directory, path, and disk information in the error message varies depending on whether you are starting the Installer from the CD-ROM or software disk.

SOLUTIONS

Do one or more of the following:

A. Rename the file Kpcms.ini file in the Windows directory, then restart Windows.

B. Make sure at least 10 MB of random-access memory (RAM) is available.

C. Make sure at least 20 MB of nonfragmented disk space is available on the volume (e.g., internal hard disk) where you are installing Photoshop.

D. Recreate the Windows swap file. For instructions, refer to the Microsoft Windows User's Guide.

ADDITIONAL INFORMATION

The Kpcms.ini file contains information about the location of KPCMS components and modules. If a Kpcms.ini file is installed (e.g., with Aldus PhotoStyler) when you install Photoshop, it can prevent the Photoshop Installer from starting. The Installer requires sufficient memory and disk space to start.

Installation Options Require Zero KB When Installing Photoshop 3.0x

ISSUE

After you select the Tutorial Files, Patterns, Duotone Files, or Plug-In Filters installation options in Photoshop, the Adobe Photoshop 3.0x installer returns the message that 0K (zero KB) of hard disk space is required.

SOLUTIONS

Ignore the message that 0K of hard disk space is required and continue the installation.

OR: Delete the currently installed items before reinstalling.

ADDITIONAL INFORMATION

The Photoshop 3.0x installer returns the message that Photoshop requires 0K of hard disk space if you select the Tutorial Files, Patterns, Duotone Files, or Plug-In Filters installation options when these items are already installed.

To ensure all files are replaced when reinstalling an application (e.g., Photoshop), first delete the currently installed files.

Removing Photoshop 3.0.x in Windows 3.1x

When you install Adobe Photoshop 3.0.x under Windows 3.1x, the installer creates a Photoshp directory, adds several lines to the System.ini file, and adds files to the Windows and Windows\system directories.

Some files Photoshop installs may be used by other applications. Instead of deleting these files, moving or renaming these files enables you to restore these files should another application require them.

To remove Photoshop 3.0.x installed files:

1. Move all personal files out of the Photoshp directory and its subdirectories.
2. Delete the Photoshp directory and its subdirectories.
3. Delete the following files located in the Windows directory (Photoshop 3.0.4 and earlier):

   `Photos30.ini`
   `Photos30.psp`
   `Ccolorsd`
4. Delete the following files located in the Windows directory:

   `Psdeluxe.ico`

```
Kpsys32.dll
Kpapi32.dll
Pcdlib32.dll
Kpcp32.dll
Winfile.ini
```

NOTE: Photoshop only installs the Psdeluxe.ico file when installing from the Photoshop CD-ROM.

5. Delete, move, or rename the Kpcms.ini file and Twain.dll file, located in the Windows directory.
6. Delete, move, or rename the following QuickTime files located in the Windows\System directory:

```
Mciqtenu.dll
Mciqtw.drv
Msvcrt10.dll
Mavg.qtc
Playenu.dll
Playenu.hlp
Player.exe
Viewenu.dll
Viewenu.hlp
Viewer.exe
```

7. Delete, move, or rename the Qtw.ini file located in the Windows directory.
8. When Photoshop's Deluxe CD Tutorial was installed, delete, move, or rename the following files located in the Windows\System directory:

```
Qcmc.qtc
Qtcvid.qtc
Qthndlr.dll
Qtim.dll
Qtimcmgr.dll
Qtipeg.qtc
Qtmovie.vbx
Qtmsvc.qtc
Qtnotify.exe
Qtole.dll
Qtipic.vbx
Qtraw.qtc
Qtrle.qtc
Qtrpza.qtc
Qtrt21.qtc
Qtsmc.qtc
Qtvhdw.dll
Qtyvu9.qtc
```

9. Delete the Windows\System\Win32s directory and the files it contains.
10. Exit Windows, then in DOS delete, move, or rename the Olecli.dll file located in the Windows\System directory, then rename the Olecli.w31 file, located in the Windows\System directory, to Olecli.dll:

    NOTE: When installing, Photoshop renames the existing Windows installed Olecli.w31 file then installs a new Olecli.dll file.

    To delete the Olecli.dll file, type the following DOS command at the DOS prompt:

    ```
    del C:\WINDOWS\SYSTEM\Olecli.dll
    ```

    OR: To move the Olecli.dll file, type the following DOS command at the DOS prompt:

    ```
    move C:\WINDOWS\SYSTEM\Olecli.dll
      newpathname\filename
    ```

    OR: To rename the Olecli.dll file, type the following DOS command at the DOS prompt:

    ```
    ren C:\WINDOWS\SYSTEM\Olecli.dll
      C:\WINDOWS\SYSTEM\newfilename
    ```

    To rename the Olecli.w31 file to Olecli.dll, type the following DOS command at the DOS prompt:

    ```
    ren C:\WINDOWS\SYSTEM\Olecli.w31
      C:\WINDOWS\SYSTEM\Olecli.dll
    ```

11. In DOS, delete, move, or rename the following files located in the Windows\system directory:

    ```
    Winmm16.dll
    Win32s16.dll
    Win32s.ini
    W32sys.dll
    Adobekey.drv
    Adobemse.drv
    ```

    To delete these files, type the following DOS command at the DOS prompt for each file to be deleted:

    ```
    del C:\WINDOWS\SYSTEM\filename
    ```

    OR: To move these files, type the following DOS command at the DOS prompt for each file to be moved:

    ```
    move C:\WINDOWS\SYSTEM\filename
      newpathname\filename
    ```

    OR: To rename these files, type the following DOS command at the DOS prompt for each file to be renamed:

    ```
    ren C:\WINDOWS\SYSTEM\filename
      C:\WINDOWS\SYSTEM\newfilename
    ```

To remove the lines Photoshop adds to the System.ini file:

1. Make a backup copy of the System.ini file located in the Windows directory.
2. Open the System.ini file in a text editor that can save in text-only format (e.g., Windows Write, Notepad).
3. In the [boot] section, locate the "drivers=" line (e.g., "drivers=mmsystem.dll winmm16.dll"), which may include multiple references in the "drivers=" line, then delete only the text " winmm16.dll" (i.e., space followed by "winmm16.dll").
4. Delete the following "device=c" line located in the [386Enh] section:

    ```
    device=c:\windows\system\win32s\w32s.386
    ```

5. Delete the "adobekey" and "adobemse" lines located in the [drivers] section. For example:

    ```
    adobekey=adobekey.drv
    adobemse=adobemse.drv
    ```

6. Save the System.ini file in text-only format, then restart Windows.

Error "Insufficient Disk Space" When Installing Photoshop 3.0x Under Windows 3.1x

ISSUE

The error "Insufficient Disk Space" occurs when installing Adobe Photoshop 3.0x under Windows 3.1x.

SOLUTIONS

Do one or more of the following:

A. Ensure that the volume (e.g., hard disk) or partition where Windows operating system software is installed has at least 3-4 MB of free disk space.

B. Ensure that the volume (e.g., hard disk) or partition where Photoshop is being installed has at least 20 MB of free disk space.

ADDITIONAL INFORMATION

Photoshop 3.0x installs Win32s into the WINDOWS\SYSTEM subdirectory on the startup volume (i.e., volume containing Windows operating system). Photoshop requires at least 3-4 MB of free disk space to install.

Manually Deinstalling Photoshop 3.0.5 in Windows 95

The Add/Remove Programs feature in Windows 95 automatically uninstalls Windows 95 logo-compliant applications, but does not guarantee a complete uninstall. To remove Photoshop completely from your system, deinstall it manually.

When you install Adobe Photoshop 3.0.5 in Windows 95, Photoshop creates a Win32app\Photoshp directory and a Windows\Photocd directory, and adds files to the Windows and Windows\System directories. Other applications may also use the files installed by Photoshop in the Windows or Windows\System directory. Instead of deleting these files when you remove Photoshop, move or rename them so you restore the files should another application require them.

To manually deinstall Photoshop 3.0.5 in Windows 95, delete or rename the Photoshop files, then remove the lines that Photoshop adds to the Win.ini and System.ini files.

To delete the Photoshop 3.0.5 files:

1. Move your documents out of the Photoshop directory and its subdirectories.
2. Delete the Photoshop directory and its subdirectories.
3. Delete the following Start menu shortcut files from the Windows\Start Menu\Programs\Adobe directory:
   ```
   Photoshop 3.0.5 (Adobep~1.lnk )
   Photoshop 3.0.5 Deluxe CD (Photos~1.lnk )
   Photoshop 3.0.5 ReadMe (Photos~2.lnk )
   Register Adobe Photoshop 3.0 (Regist~1.lnk)
   ```
4. Delete the following files from the Windows\Photocd directory:
   ```
   Adobergb.pt
   cp01
   Phcdcn01.pt
   Phcdek01.pt
   Phcdko01.pt
   Pslabexp.pt
   ```
5. Delete the following files from the Windows directory:
   ```
   Kpapi32.dll
   Kpcp32.dll
   Kpcsys32.dll
   Pcdlib32.dll
   Psdeluxe.ico (only installed from the
     Photoshop Deluxe CD-ROM)
   Uninst.exe
   ```
6. Delete, move, or rename the following files in the Windows directory:
   ```
   Kpcms.ini (Required by PhotoStyler)
   Playenu.dll
   Player.exe
   Playenu.hlp
   Qtw.ini
   Twain.dll
   Twain32.dll
   Twunk_16.exe
   Twunk_32.exe
   Viewenu.dll
   Viewenu.hlp
   Viewer.exe
   ```
7. If the Photoshop Deluxe CD-ROM Tutorial is installed, delete, move, or rename the following files in the Windows\System directory:
   ```
   Dhio_dh.qtc
   Mciqtenu.dll
   Mciqtw.drv
   Msvcrt10.dll
   Navg.qtc
   Qcmc.qtc
   Qtcvid.qtc
   Qthndlr.dll
   Qtimcmgr.dll
   Qtim.dll
   Qtiv32.qtc
   Qtivu9.qtc
   Qtjpeg.qtc
   Qtmovie.vbx
   Qtnotify.exe
   Qtold.qtc
   Qtole.dll
   Qtpic.vbx
   Qtraw.qtc
   Qtrle.qtc
   Qtrpza.qtc
   Qtrt21.qtc
   Qtsmc.qtc
   Reelmgic.qtc
   ```
8. If Photoshop 3.0 was previously installed, delete, move, or rename the following files in the Windows\System directory:
   ```
   Qtmsvc.qtc
   Qtvhdw.dll
   Qtyvu9.qtc
   ```

To remove the Photoshop lines from the Win.ini file:

1. Make a backup copy of the Win.ini file, located in the Windows directory.
2. Open the original Win.ini file in a text editor that can save in text-only format (e.g., Windows Write, Notepad).

3. In the [mci extensions] section, remove the following line:
   `mov=QTWVideo`
4. In the [Extensions] section, remove the following lines:
   `psd=C:\WIN32APP\PHOTOSHP\photoshp.exe ^.psd`
   `mov=C:\WINDOWS\player.exe ^.mov`
5. In the [Mach] section, remove the following line:
   `devicebitmap=off`
6. In the [Embedding] section, remove the following line:
   `Photoshop.Image.3=Adobe Photoshop Image,Adobe Photoshop Image,C:\Win32App\Photoshp\photoshp.exe,picture`
7. In the [Compatibility32] section, remove the following line:
   `PHOTOSHP=0x00208000`
   NOTE: Windows 95 adds the "PHOTOSHP=0x00208000" line to improve Photoshop 3.0's compatibility with Windows 95. Photoshop 3.0.4 and later do not use the "PHOTOSHP=0x00208000" line.
8. Save the Win.ini file in text-only format, then restart Windows.

To remove the Photoshop lines from the System.ini file:

1. Make a backup copy of the System.ini file, located in the Windows directory.
2. Open the original System.ini file in a text editor that can save in text-only format (e.g., Windows Write, Notepad).
3. In the [MCI] section, delete the following line:
   `QTWVideo=C:\WINDOWS\SYSTEM\mciqtw.drv`
4. In the [Macx] section, delete the following line:
   `DeviceBitmap=OFF`
5. Save the System.ini file in text-only format, then restart Windows.

General Information

MAC OS / WINDOWS

Q *(4.0 only)* **I have oodles of "third party" plug-ins—those from companies other than Adobe—that worked fine in Photoshop 3.0.x. Will they work in 4.0?**

A It depends on the plug-in. Some will undoubtedly work without a hitch in Photoshop 4.0, but others may need to be updated for compatibility. If you're having trouble with an older plug-in, contact the plug-in developer to see if an update is available.

The Lab Color Mode

The Lab color mode in Adobe Photoshop is a new feature that allows you to work in a truly device-independent color space. This document provides a brief overview of device independence and the Lab Color model, and offers tips and suggestions on using the Lab Color mode in Adobe Photoshop.

THE NEED FOR DEVICE-INDEPENDENT COLOR

Because different devices reproduce colors differently, maintaining consistent color from device to device has been a technical obstacle. Color reproduction in an image may not only vary with the type of device monitor, printer, or slide imager—but may also vary with similar devices from different manufacturers, or even with different units from the same manufacturer. Because of this variability, producing consistent color on different devices is often a logistical nightmare. The purpose of device-independent color, therefore, is to give users a way to create consistent color documents regardless of the device used to image the file.

Different methods of reproducing color use different color models. Certain color models, such as the RGB and CMYK models, comprise a subset of the visible spectrum. The key to device-independent color is a standardized color model that comprises all colors; such a model can then provide a system for translating color from device to device.

THE LAB COLOR MODEL

In 1931, the Commission Internationale d'Eclairage (CIE), an international organization formed to standardize color measurement, developed a color model based on the way the human eye perceives color. This model is the basis for all colorimetric measurement. In 1976, the CIE proposed two additional color systems based on their original model; one of these systems is CIE L* a* b*.

The Lab Color model defines color using the values L, a, and b, where L defines the lightness of the color, and "a" and "b" define the color along a red/green and blue/yellow axis, respectively.

USING THE LAB COLOR MODE IN ADOBE PHOTOSHOP

Like other CIE color models, the Lab model comprises all colors in the visual spectrum and is device-independent. It is therefore extremely useful for converting colors between other color models—for example, from an RGB model to a CMYK model. It also provides a way to preserve original color values when colors are transferred from one color reproduction system to another. The following are just some of the benefits that Lab Color mode brings to Adobe Photoshop.

MODE CONVERSION

Internally, Adobe Photoshop uses the Lab Color mode when converting color values from one mode to another. Because Lab Color mode provides a system for defining color values in all modes, using Lab as an intermediate mode for color conversions ensures that colors are not altered in the conversion process, other than the necessary clipping of out-of-gamut colors. L = 100

For example, when converting an RGB image to CMYK mode, Adobe Photoshop first converts the RGB color values to Lab mode using the information in Monitor Setup. Adobe Photoshop then uses information in Printing Inks Setup and Separation Setup to build a color table and convert the image to CMYK mode. Once the image is in CMYK mode, Adobe Photoshop must reconvert the color values to RGB to be displayed on an RGB monitor. To do this, Adobe Photoshop converts the CMYK values back to Lab (using the same color table if no values in Printing Inks Setup or Separation Setup have been changed) and then back to RGB (again using the Monitor Setup information).

WORKING WITH PHOTO CD IMAGES

When opening Photo CD images in Adobe Photoshop, open the image in Lab Color mode instead of RGB mode. Opening a Photo CD image in Lab Color mode preserves all colors in the image. This is because the native color space of Photo CD images, Photo YCC, is another implementation of a CIE Color model and is therefore device-independent. After you open the image in the Lab Color mode, convert the image to RGB mode for editing, or convert the image to CMYK mode for separations.

PRINTING TO POSTSCRIPT LEVEL 2 PRINTERS

Because Level 2 printers support device-independent color, convert Adobe Photoshop images to Lab Color mode when printing to such a printer directly from Adobe Photoshop. The printer then performs the conversion from Lab to CMYK. Before sending the image to the printer, select the appropriate Monitor Setup options; this will ensure the best possible match between the printed image and the monitor screen.

SELECTIVE COLOR CORRECTION

Because the Lab Color mode separates the lightness component (channel L) from the other color components (color channels "a" and "b"), use this mode to edit just the lightness values in an image. Similarly, use Lab Color mode to edit just the red/green component or the yellow/ blue component in the image. The following tips are just two examples of how to use this feature:

- To create a grainy quality in a color image, the appearance of speckled color, apply the Add Noise filter to adjust the "L" channel of an image in Lab Color mode.
- Noise in the "L" channel does not expand the pixels for a speckled appearance.
- To create painterly effects in a grayscale image, convert the image to Lab Color mode. Create a horizontal gradient fill from black to white in the a channel and a vertical gradient fill from black to white in the b channel. This creates a blend in the color channels of the image without affecting the image detail in the lightness channel.

Scanning Basics

This technical note gives an overview of scanning technology, issues that affect scanning results, and techniques that will help you achieve the best results when using desktop scanners. The note also discusses the types of scanners and other image-capture devices available.

Scanners play a pivotal role in today's digital imaging applications. These devices convert continuous-tone photographic prints and transparencies into digital images that can be manipulated on a computer. Although technology that allows cameras to capture images directly into digital form is under development, an understanding of scanning technology is important for users of current digital imaging software.

SCANNER TECHNOLOGY

Scanners work by reflecting light from or transmitting light through the photograph or transparency being scanned. The reflected or transmitted light is directed to the scanning head, which typically consists of an array of charge-coupled devices (CCDs) or light-sensitive diodes. A diode or device measures the amount of light striking it and uses this measurement to generate an intensity value between 0 and 255 for each of the three additive primary colors: red, green, and blue (RGB). The scanner then combines these RGB samples to produce a 24-bit, full-color image (8 bits for each primary color).

A wide range of scanners exist: there are slide scanners that are designed to scan transparencies; low-end desktop scanners, which typically have a flatbed design; and high-end drum scanners, or laser plotters, which are used by expensive color systems (such as Scitex and Crosfield) that color separate images as part of the scanning process. Images can also be captured directly from image-capture devices (such as still-video cameras or digital cameras) and converted into digital data.

SCANNER TYPES

A more detailed discussion of scanner types follows:

- Slide scanners, like those marketed by Nikon, Barneyscan/PixelCraft, and Kodak, are designed to scan small-format transparencies such as 35mm slides and 2.25-inch transparencies at resolutions up to 4000 lines per inch. These scanners use linear arrays of CCDs to capture a single line of data at a time. Three passes, each using a different color filter, are made over the image to capture RGB information. This three-pass process increases both scanning time and the likelihood of motion-based scan lines and defocusing.
- Flatbed scanners, such as those from Microtek, Sharp, and Howtek, can accommodate reflective art in a variety of sizes and can also handle transparencies (using an optional transparency holder). The effective resolution of flatbed scanners is usually 300 to 400 dpi, although some can reproduce resolutions up to 600 dpi. Like slide scanners, most flatbed scanners make three passes over the image for a full-color scan.
- Drum scanners made by Isomet, Optronics, Crosfield, Diamechi, and other manufacturers, are generally considered high-end, professional devices. The operator fixes the original artwork to a cylinder that spins in front of the scanning head, which also focuses a point of light onto the image. These devices generally use photo-mul-

tiplier tubes (PMTs) to record the light intensity. The consistency of the light beam and the accuracy of the focusing optics result in high-quality scans.

OTHER IMAGE-CAPTURE DEVICES

Still-video cameras capture images directly into NTSC video format, which video capture boards can convert into RGB data for computer manipulation. (Some so-called video-graphics boards can also digitize individual frames from videotape or from a live video feed.) The resolution of images captured from video is fixed at about 640 pixels by 480 pixels, and color accuracy is greatly limited by the constraints of broadcast video standards. These two drawbacks limit the usefulness of video image capture in print applications.

A new digital camera developed by Kodak uses a standard Nikon F3 camera body that accepts all Nikon lenses. The camera converts the images directly into 24-bit digital data, at a resolution of 1024 by 1280 pixels. This is the approximate resolution needed for a 4-by-5-inch magazine-quality print. The camera is attached to a processing unit and hard disk drive that can store up to 160 megabytes of data (about 40 images). These digital photographs can then be loaded directly into a Macintosh computer.

ISSUES AFFECTING THE QUALITY AND ACCURACY OF A SCANNED IMAGE

A number of issues affect the quality and accuracy of the digital file captured during a scan, including the scanner resolution, dynamic range and illumination, focusing accuracy, and recognition of black and white points.

Scanner resolution

Most desktop scanners use CCDs. The density of the CCDs determines the scanners resolution; the more CCDs in a given area, the greater is the scanner resolution as measured in dots per inch (dpi). Each CCD records color information and outputs one 24-bit color value. This value makes up an individual pixel in the digital image. The higher the resolution of the scan, the greater is the number of data points recorded, and the larger the file size.

A full-width scan along one axis is called "a line of resolution." High-end scanners scan information as lines; they can achieve resolutions of up to 10,000 lines per inch. Desktop scanners, which scan information as dots (pixels), cannot achieve such high resolution; this is one of the obvious differences between high-end and low-end scanners. Typically, desktop scanners have a resolution of 300 dots per inch (dpi), which generally is high enough for reproductions of usable quality

Dynamic range and illumination

Dynamic range is the range of discrete colors that a scanner can distinguish. Variations in dynamic range impact the quality of the scan more than simple resolution does. High-end scanners are more sensitive to the range of colors in the spectrum and can record minor differences between two almost-identical colors. A scanner with a lower dynamic range records the two similar colors as the same value.

Several variables determine a scanners dynamic range—pixel depth (number of bits per pixel per color), sensitivity of the CCD, accuracy of the focusing optics, and precision of the measurement of the black and white points.

Illumination can also affect the quality of the scan. For instance, CCD arrays require a consistent light source to illuminate the image evenly. Variations in illumination across the original can produce unwanted artifacts in the digital image.

Focusing accuracy

The accuracy with which light is focused onto the scanning head is one of the primary distinguishing qualities between desktop scanners and the high-end devices used in prepress houses. To receive the most accurate reading from any point on the image, CCDs in the scanning head require a finely controlled optical aperture.

The color information for one pixel in the original image is focused precisely onto one, and only one, CCD in a scanner with excellent optics. This yields a very crisp scan with distinct colors. In a scanner with less refined optics, the pixels original color information is diffused slightly across several adjacent CCDs. The diffusion tends to soften or muddy the colors and edges in the resulting digital image. Therefore, if one of the devices has better optics, two scanners with identical resolution and illumination characteristics can produce scans of radically different quality.

Because accurate focus is so important in scanning, any vibration or movement of the CCD degrades the quality of a resulting image. Such unwanted movement has the same effect as poor focusing optics. Motion during a scan can also create image slips, which occur if the movement of the drum or bed holding the original artwork is not smooth and continuous. In such a case, the scanned image has a seam or line through it. Image slips occur most often on desktop scanners.

Black-and-white points

The accuracy with which a scanner senses the original images black-and-white points also greatly affects the dynamic tonal range of the final digital image. If a scanner does not accurately recognize the darkest point in an image and set that point as black (or does not let the user define it as black), the tonal range of the resulting digital file is lessened. A similar reduction in tonal range occurs if the scanner incorrectly determines the white point (the lightest point in the image.)

Because most desktop scanners do not automatically seek an images black-and-white points, these scanners generally clip the original images dynamic range. Most high-end scanners automatically and accurately determine white and black points and spread out the range of tones to be scanned.

BEFORE SCANNING

The choices you make before scanning an image will affect the quality and usefulness of the resulting digital file. Before scanning, consider the resolution at which the image will be scanned, determine the optimal dynamic range, and determine whether the image contains unwanted color casts that could be eliminated during scanning.

DETERMINING THE CORRECT SCAN RESOLUTION

The most important consideration in assuring the quality and usefulness of the scanned image is determining the correct resolution for your scan. The optimal resolution depends on how the image will be printed or displayed. For example, if the image will be used as a screen display, then its resolution need not be greater than the resolution of the target screen area—about 640 pixels by 480 pixels. On the other hand, if the final image will be a full-bleed magazine cover, you'll need considerably more data with which to work.

If the image resolution is too low, the PostScript language may use the color value of a single pixel to create several halftone dots. This results in pixelization, or very coarse-looking output. If the resolution is too high, the file contains more information than the printer needs. The file size directly affects how long it takes Adobe Photoshop to process the image, and the printer to output the image. The size of a file is proportional to its image resolution. For example, the file size for an image with a resolution of 200 ppi is four times greater than an image of identical dimensions and a resolution of 100 ppi. Try to balance ideal resolution with a manageable file size.

The scanning resolution of printed output depends on the target line screen as well as on the resolution of the printer and the size of the original document compared to the scanned image. Because different color-separation software utilities suggest different pixel-to-line-screen ratios, check with your service bureau and print shop before scanning.

A good rule of thumb for images that will be color separated is to capture pixels at twice the line frequency of the screen to be used for printing. For example, if you are producing a magazine cover that measures 10 inches tall by 7 inches wide and will be printed using a 133-line-per-inch screen, a good scanning resolution would be 2660 pixels for the height (133 lpi by 10 inches by 2 inches), or 266 ppi. Note that if your image resolution is more than 2.5 times the screen ruling, you will get an alert message. This means that the image resolution is higher than the printer can accommodate and is unnecessarily increasing the file size and print time.

The size of the final image compared to the original image is also a consideration in setting scan resolution. When making the image larger, additional data is necessary to produce a final image with the correct image resolution. If the final image will be smaller than the original, less data is needed. Determine what the file size must be to contain the pixel information by creating a dummy file in Adobe Photoshop. For more information, see Chapter 3, Scanning, Importing, and Exporting Images, in the "Adobe Photoshop User Guide.

DETERMINING THE OPTIMAL DYNAMIC RANGE

Because the human eye can detect a wider tonal range than what can be printed, consider adjusting the scanning parameters to pick up the details that are of the most interest in the final image. However, because each primary color has to be assigned a discrete value between 0 and 255, limiting values to a certain range may cause valuable detail to be lost. Some scanners can capture 12 bits per pixel per color, which allows them to capture a larger range of detail. Emphasize specific tonal areas in the image by carefully setting the white-and-black points in an image before scanning it.

COMPENSATING FOR AN UNWANTED COLOR CAST

Before scanning, determine whether the original image has an unwanted color cast that you might be able to eliminate during the scan. Use the following procedure to make sure that the scanner itself is not introducing a color cast. While color cast is sometimes used for aesthetic effect, its typically undesirable when it is created as part of the scanning process.

Calibrate your monitor using the Gamma CDEV included in Adobe Photoshop or a monitor calibration utility. For more information about this process, see Chapter 2, Calibrating Your System, in the "Adobe Photoshop User Guide." Calibration compensates for any color casts and shifts in gamma caused by the monitor display. It is critical to calibrate your monitor before attempting the following test.

To ensure that the scanner does not create an unwanted color cast:

1. Create a file in Adobe Photoshop containing an 11-step gray wedge. (Or use an 8-inch by 10-inch, 18 percent neutral gray card and an 11-step gray wedge purchased from a photographic supply store for this test.)
2. Print the file, and then scan the printed output back into Adobe Photoshop in the RGB or CMYK mode.
3. Sample the grays in the image to see whether they contain any hue or color tint by using the Info palette and the eyedropper tool. If the grays contain a hue or color tint, then the scanner is adding a color cast.
4. Eliminate the color cast with the Adobe Photoshop Levels controls and record the resulting gamma and the white-and-black point settings.
5. Use the values recorded in step 4 to compensate for the color cast by using the controls (or plug- in module) provided with your scanner. Rescan the gray wedge to verify that the cast has been removed.

Understanding Digital Halftones

In traditional photographic reproduction, a continuous-tone image (such as a photograph) is prepared for printing by reducing the tonal image to two values: black and white. This process is known as making a halftone. This document outlines some of the issues involved in choosing screen sets for digital halftones. For more detailed information, see "PostScript Screening: Adobe Accurate Screens" by Peter Fink, published by Adobe Press.

In conventional graphics printing, a halftone is produced by projecting light onto a photograph through a screen that converts the image into dots. The screen divides the image into a grid of halftone cells, with each cell containing one halftone dot. The dots provide room for the ink to spread and indicate the relative darkness of the photograph at any specific point. The relative sizes of the halftone dots produce the shades of black, white, and gray the human eye perceives. When the halftone cell dots are large, we see black. When the dots are very small (or there is none at all), we see white. Gray shades are made by dots whose sizes increase as the degree of darkness increases.

Digital halftones are produced in much the same way—by breaking the image down into halftone cells, with each cell containing a single halftone dot. With digital halftones, however, the halftone cell is made up of digital picture elements, called pixels, which are either turned on (making them black) or turned off (leaving them white) when the laser beam in the imagesetter scans across them. The size and shape of a halftone dot are determined by the pixels turned on in that cell.

An imagesetter's resolution, measured in dots per inch (dpi), is the number of pixels per inch the imagesetter can produce. The screen frequency, also called line screen or screen ruling, is the number of halftone cells produced per unit of measurement. A standard laser printer has a resolution of 300 dpi and uses a 53 lines per inch (lpi) screen frequency.

The Challege of Digital Separations

In traditional color separations, a photograph or image is photographed four times using a different color filter for each exposure. The halftone screen grid is rotated to a different angle for each color (cyan, magenta, yellow, and black). If you look at a high-quality printed image under a magnifying glass, you see that the four different-colored dots form a rosette pattern. Dots that interfere with one another can produce repeating patterns, called moirÇ patterns. The rosette pattern produces the least amount of moirÇ patterns in images and is generated by a careful balancing of screen angle, screen frequency, and halftone dot shape. In actuality, nearly every four-color prepress process results in some degree of moirÇ.

In theory, a 30-degree distance between screen angles is ideal for forming a rosette pattern. Keep in mind, however, that the angles 90 and 0 produce exactly the same screen; this means that adjustments must be made to accommodate a fourth screen. Typically, black is assigned an angle of 45 degrees, because 45 degrees is the least visible screen orientation. Magenta and cyan are each rotated 30 degrees from the black screen; the 75-degree and 15-degree angles are considered equally visible and therefore interchangeable. The lightest color, yellow, is assigned the fourth angle (90 degrees) to produce the least noticeable deviation possible in the rosette pattern.

Digital color separations pose yet another complication for halftone screening because each halftone screen must line up with the pixels of the device. Specifically, the corners of the halftone cells must align with corners of the device pixels. Similarly, the screen frequency that can be achieved in a digital halftone is constrained by the device pixels, because the number of halftone cells per inch (lpi) is related to both the size of the halftone cell (pixels per cell) and the device resolution (pixels per inch). Most traditional screen frequencies are ideal values and cannot be exactly reproduced on electronic output devices.

To illustrate the effect that device constraints can have on actual screen angles and frequency in digital separations, suppose that you specify a resolution of 2540 and a screen of 150 in the Adobe Photoshop Auto Screens dialog box (click the Screens button in Page Setup dialog box to open Auto Screens). The screen sets that are actually generated using a typical digital screen method are the following: black at 45 degrees and 149.7 lpi; cyan at 18.4 degrees and 133.9 lpi; magenta at 71.6 degrees and 133.9 lpi; and yellow at 90 degrees and 141.1 lpi.

Remember that adding or subtracting 90 degrees from an angle results in exactly the same screen rotation; therefore, the screen angles 90 and 0 are identical, as are the pairs 105 and 15, 108 and 18, 161 and 71, and so on. The screen angle and frequency combinations produced by Adobe Photoshop have been tested and shown to produce the least moirÇ patterns for the output device resolution and frequency specified. Newer technologies, such as Adobe Accurate Screens, are able to calculate screen sets that more closely approach ideal values. These technologies are available on many different output devices. See the technical note, "Digital Screening Technologies," for more information on advanced screening technologies.

Terminology

The following terms for creating traditional halftones are also used in digital halftones:

Grid Pattern: The shape of the halftone screen dots. Some common shapes are linear, elliptical, and round. Different shapes cause different effects in the final output. Adobe Photoshop allows you to specify a diamond dot, which is supported on some of the newer imagesetters. Contact your vendor to find out whether your imagesetter supports the diamond dot function.

Screen Angle: The angle at which a screen is rotated for printing. The angle affects the way the halftone dots are laid down on each separation film. If the dots do not align correctly, moirÇ patterns appear when the films are placed on top of one another.

Screen Frequency: The number of halftone cells per unit of measurement in a screen; the higher the frequency, the finer the screen. A screen of 30 lines per inch is made up of dots that are one-third the size of the dots in a screen of 10 lines per inch.

Output Resolution: The dots per inch (dpi) of the output device (high-end imagesetters can support various resolutions). The higher the screen frequency, the higher is the output resolution required to maintain 256 shades of gray.

MoirÇ: An undesirable effect that results when halftone screen patterns become visible. This pattern is often caused by misaligned screens.

Rosette: The pattern created when all four CMYK color halftone screens are printed at traditional angles, shown to produce the best results in printed color output. The rosette pattern is noticeable only under magnification.

Plug-in File Type and Extensions for Photoshop 3.0x General Information

Adobe Photoshop 3.0x plug-ins are separate files containing code that extends Photoshop functions. Plug-ins enable Adobe Systems and third-party developers to enhance Photoshop without modifying the base application. Photoshop supports five kinds of plug-ins, including Acquisition, Export, Filter, File Format, Parser, and Hardware Accelerator plug-ins.

Acquisition

Acquisition plug-ins open an image in a new window. Acquisition plug-ins are used to interface to scanners or frame grabbers, read images in unsupported or compressed file formats, and to generate synthetic images. You can access these plug-ins in Photoshop by selecting File > Acquire.

Export

You can use Export plug-ins to output images. Export plug-ins are used to print to devices that do not have Chooser-level driver support (Macintosh), and to save images in unsupported or compressed file formats. You can access these plug-ins in Photoshop by selecting File > Export.

Filter

Filter plug-ins modify a selected area of an existing image. You can access these plug-ins in Photoshop by selecting the Filter menu.

File Format

File format plug-ins provide support for additional image import and export formats. These additional formats appear in Photoshop's Open, Save As, and Save a Copy dialog boxes, accessed from the File menu.

Parser

Parser plug-ins enable Photoshop to open third-party file formats. These additional file formats list in Photoshop's List Files of Format Type pop-up menu in the Open dialog box.

Hardware Accelerator

Hardware accelerator plug-ins, or extension plug-ins, enable Photoshop to access hardware accelerators (e.g., Adaptive Solutions Powershop). The hardware uses the plug-in to route data to be accelerated through the hardware accelerator and back through the main processor.

Plug-in Type	Macintosh file type	Windows extension
General (any type of plug-in)	8BPI	.8bp
Acquisition	8BAM	.8ba
Export	8BEM	.8be
Filter	8BFM	.8bf
File Format	8BIF	.8bi
Parser	8BYM	.8by
Hardware Accelerator (extension)	8BXM	.8bx

Out of Gamut Colors in Photoshop 3.0.x General Information

Each color model (e.g., RGB, CMYK) has a unique range of colors, or gamut. Because each color model has a different gamut, certain colors that are reproducible (i.e., within the gamut of) one color model may not be reproducible (i.e., out of gamut) in another color model.

Monitors display color using the RGB color model, which uses beams of red, green, and blue light that combine in different intensities to display colors. The four-color printing process produces color using the CMYK color model, which uses cyan, magenta, yellow, and black inks that absorb light and reflect different wavelengths, depending on the pigment, to create the CMYK spectrum of colors. Monitors can display colors that cannot be reproduced in the printing process, as the RGB color model has a larger gamut (i.e., more reproducible colors) than does the CMYK color model.

Because monitors and printers use different color models, which have different color gamuts, matching colors using monitor display and printer output may not be possible. RGB colors that are out of the CMYK gamut are "out of gamut colors." Out of gamut colors cannot use the four color printing process to reproduce the RGB color, resulting in color differences between monitor display and printed output.

Adobe Photoshop 3.0.x provides a number of methods to identify and correct out of gamut colors:

Gamut Warning

Photoshop builds a color conversion table, based on the Monitor Setup and Printing Inks Setup options, and identifies out of gamut colors by displaying their names in gray. To access Gamut Warning, choose Mode > Gamut Warning.

CMYK Preview

Choose Mode > CMYK Preview to have Photoshop represent the color on screen using the CMYK color model. Photoshop temporarily displays the CMYK equivalent of the colors in the image using the current Separation Setup, Monitor Setup, and Printing Inks Setup options, but no actual conversion takes place. To return to the image in RGB preview, deselect CMYK Preview.

Color Range

The Color Range command creates a specified color selection, which can then be color corrected. To display out of gamut colors in black, choose Select > Color Range then choose Out of Gamut from the Select pop-up menu.

Exclamation Point Warning in Color Picker

A warning, or exclamation point with a small color patch, appears to the right of the two color swatches in the Color palette to indicate the selected color cannot be reproduced using CMYK colors (i.e., out of gamut). The color patch in the warning indicates the closest reproducible color.

Exclamation Point in Info Palette

An exclamation point appears in the Info palette to the right of the CMYK percentages when the color is out of gamut.

Entering Color Coordinate Values in Photoshop 3.0.x General Information

A spectrophotometer is an instrument used to read colors values and translate them into coordinate values for several different color measurements (e.g., RGB, YCC, CIELAB, and Y, x, y). Adobe Photoshop 3.0.x uses the Y, x, y values to determine its Printing Inks Setup.

To enter color coordinate information from a spectrophotometer in Photoshop 3.0.x:

1. Print a calibration file (e.g., Ole No Moire [Macintosh], Testpict.jpg [Windows], which are included with Photoshop) to your output device.
2. Read the values of the individual color swatches with the spectrophotometer.
3. Choose File > Preferences > Printing Inks Setup.
4. In the Ink Colors section of the Printing Inks Setup dialog box, click Custom.
5. In the Ink Colors dialog box, with color swatches on one side and a table with Y, x, y values for the individual colors on the other side, enter the spectrophotometer readings.
6. Click OK to save these settings. They will remain the active settings until they are replaced with new ones. The settings can also be saved and reloaded using the Load and Save options in the Ink Colors dialog box.

To enter color coordinate information using color calibration information obtained visually:

1. Print a calibration file (e.g., Ole No Moire [Macintosh], Testpict.jpg [Windows], which are included with Photoshop) to your output device.
2. Choose File > Preferences > Printing Inks Setup.
3. In the Ink Colors section of the Printing Inks Setup dialog box, click Custom.
4. Select the individual color swatches in the Ink Colors dialog box to access the color picker, then select the colors on the screen that best match your printed output.
5. Click OK to save these settings. They will remain the active settings until they are replaced with new ones. The settings can also be saved and reloaded using the Load and Save options in the Ink Colors dialog box.

Adobe PhotoDeluxe®

Feature Techniques

MAC OS / WINDOWS

Recommended Scanning Resolutions for PhotoDeluxe

Scanning resolution affects both the quality and file size of an image. When the scanning resolution is too low, the image's quality is decreased, and the image appears blocky or coarse. When the scanning resolution is too high, the quality of the image does not increase and the image's file size is unnecessarily large, requiring more random access memory (RAM) to display. Images that require more RAM than you have available display slowly in Adobe PhotoDeluxe 1.0, and special effects commands (e.g., smudge, twirl) take longer to perform.

To determine the optimum scanning resolution for your photographs, determine how you plan to display or print your final artwork, then refer to the chart below for recommended scanning resolutions.

For optimum output on:	Scan at this resolution:
Macintosh monitor	72 pixels per inch (ppi)
IBM-compatible monitor	96 pixels per inch (ppi)
300 dpi laser printer	100 pixels per inch (ppi)
600 dpi laser printer	150 pixels per inch (ppi)
725 dpi inkjet printer	150 pixels per inch (ppi)
1200+ dpi image setter	1.5 times the screen frequency

Unexpected Results

MAC OS / WINDOWS

Image Changes Size When Added to Another Image in PhotoDeluxe

ISSUE

When you add one image to another (e.g., by cutting and pasting, or by using PhotoDeluxe's Hold Photo command) in PhotoDeluxe, the added image displays larger or smaller in the target image than in the source image.

SOLUTIONS

When the added image is too large, resize it:

1. After adding the image to the target image, choose File > Long Menus.
2. Choose Size > Resize, then drag the corners to decrease the image's dimensions.

OR: When the added image is too small, do one or more of the following:

A. Resize the added image:
   1. After adding the image to the target image, choose File > Long Menus.
   2. Choose Size > Resize, then drag the corners to increase the image's dimensions.

   NOTE: Increasing an image's dimensions decreases the image's resolution, which may noticeably decrease its quality (e.g., more pixelation, blurrier). View or print your lower-resolution image before you save it to ensure you are satisfied with the results.

B. Ensure the resolutions of the source image and the target image are the same by decreasing the higher resolution image to match the lower resolution image:
   1. Start PhotoDeluxe.
   2. Choose File > Open File, select your source image (i.e., the image you want to add to the target image), then click Open.
   3. Choose File > Long Menus.
   4. Choose Size > Photo Size.
   5. In the Current Size section, note the Resolution value, then click OK.
   6. Choose File > Close to close the source image.
   7. Choose File > Open File, select your target image (i.e., the image you want to add the source image to), then click Open.
   8. Choose Size > Photo Size.
   9. In the Current Size section, note the Resolution value, then click OK.
   10. When the two noted resolutions are different, open the image, either target or source, that has the higher resolution.
   11. Choose Size > Photo Size.
   12. At the bottom of the Photo Size dialog box, deselect File Size.
   13. In the New Size section of the Photo Size dialog box, change the Resolution value to match the lower resolution file (target or source).
   14. Click OK.
   15. Choose File > Save As, then, if you want to retain the higher resolution version of the file, rename the file and click Save.
   16. Recombine the images.

   NOTE: Decreasing an image's resolution may noticeably decrease the image's quality (e.g., more pixelation, blurrier). View or print your lower-resolution image before you save it to ensure you are satisfied with the results.

ADDITIONAL INFORMATION

When you combine images with different resolutions, PhotoDeluxe resamples (i.e., changes the resolution) of the added image to match the resolution of the target image. Resampling an image changes its dimensions. When you resample down (i.e., decrease resolution), PhotoDeluxe distributes the image's pixel information over a larger area, which increases the dimensions of the image. When you resample up (i.e., increase the resolution), PhotoDeluxe compresses the image's pixel information into a smaller area, which decreases the dimensions of the image. For example, if you add a 50 pixels per inch (ppi) image to a 100 ppi image, PhotoDeluxe resamples the 50 ppi image up to 100 ppi, which causes the dimensions of the image to be halved, because the resolution of the target file (100 ppi) is two times the resolution of the source file (50 ppi).

WINDOWS

Guidelines In Guided Activity Templates Disappear In PhotoDeluxe 1.0

ISSUE

Guidelines in an Adobe PhotoDeluxe Guided Activity (e.g., Greeting Cards, Report Covers) disappear at lower magnifications (i.e., while "zoomed out").

SOLUTION

Zoom in on the document by clicking the magnifying glass tool with the plus sign (+) inside it until the guidelines reappear.

ADDITIONAL INFORMATION

Guidelines are thin (one pixel) lines that may disappear at lower magnifications as PhotoDeluxe resizes the document to display it on-screen.

Application Window Doesn't Open Full Screen in PhotoDeluxe 1.x

ISSUE

After you launch Adobe PhotoDeluxe 1.x in Windows 3.1 or later, PhotoDeluxe's application window is smaller than expected (i.e., minimized or not full-screen).

SOLUTIONS

Manually resize the application window by dragging its corners with your mouse, then exit and restart PhotoDeluxe.

OR: Modify the "Maximized=" line in PhotoDeluxe's pd.ini file:

1. Make a backup copy of the pd.ini file.

TIP MAC OS

PhotoDeluxe Uses RGB Color for All Supported Images

PhotoDeluxe's default image color model is RGB (red, green, blue). When opening an Indexed color, Grayscale, or Bitmap image, PhotoDeluxe 1.0 automatically converts the image to an RGB color image, and opens the image in an Untitled window to prevent PhotoDeluxe's RGB version of the file from replacing the original image file. Because PhotoDeluxe supports the 24-bit RGB color mode only, PhotoDeluxe does not support opening color images whose colors are not defined using RGB colors [e.g., CMYK (cyan, magenta, yellow, black), Lab color].

After using PhotoDeluxe's Color to Black and White command to remove color from an image, the image is still an RGB color image, defining shades of gray using RGB color values.

2. Open the original pd.ini file, located in the Windows directory, in a text editor that can save in text-only format (e.g., Windows Write, Notepad).
3. Locate the line that begins "Maximized=" in the [PhotoDeluxe 1.0] section.
4. Edit the line to read:
   ```
   Maximized=1
   ```
5. Save the pd.ini file in text-only format and restart Windows.

OR: When running PhotoDeluxe in Windows 95, locate the shortcut for PhotoDeluxe, then set the shortcut's properties to open PhotoDeluxe with a maximized application window:

1. Choose Start > Settings > Taskbar.
2. In the Taskbar Properties dialog box, click the Start Menu Programs tab.
3. Click the Advanced button. The Windows Explorer window appears, and lists your Start Menu folder.
4. Open the Adobe folder, located in the Programs folder in the Start Menu folder.
5. Right-click the Adobe PhotoDeluxe 1.0 shortcut icon, then select Properties from the pop-up menu.
6. In the PhotoDeluxe Properties window, click the Shortcut tab, select Maximized Window from the Run pop-up menu, then click OK.

OR: When running PhotoDeluxe in Windows 3.1 or later, modify PhotoDeluxe's pd.ini file to reflect the video card's maximum resolution size in pixels:

1. Make a backup copy of the pd.ini file.
2. Open the original pd.ini file, located in the Windows directory, in a text editor that can save in text-only format (e.g., Windows Write, Notepad).
3. Locate the line that begins with "Window_Pos=." For example:
   ```
   Window_Pos=[3,7,700,453]
   ```
4. Change the first two values to "0" and "0" and the second two values to the number of your screen's maximum resolution size in pixels. For example:
   ```
   Window_Pos=[0,0,800,600]
   ```
   NOTE: The first two values are the (x,y) coordinates of the top left corner of PhotoDeluxe's application window, and the second two values are the (x,y) coordinates of the bottom right corner. When you're unsure of your screen's maximum resolution size in pixels, use a common resolution size (i.e., [0,0,640,480], [0,0,800,-600], or [0,0,1024,768]) or contact your video card manufacturer to help you determine your video card's current resolution setting. If the Windows 95 or Windows NT taskbar obscures a portion of PhotoDeluxe's application window, modify your values to accommodate the taskbar. The Windows 95 taskbar is approximately 32 pixels high when at the top or bottom edge of the screen, or 32 pixels wide when at the left or right edge of the screen.
5. Save the pd.ini file in text-only format and restart Windows.

ADDITIONAL INFORMATION

When you launch PhotoDeluxe for the first time after installing it, PhotoDeluxe does not start up with a maximized application window. After the first launch, PhotoDeluxe starts up with a maximized application window if you manually resize the window, if you modify the "Window_Pos=" line in the pd.ini file, if you modify the "Maximized=" line in the pd.ini file, or if you select the Maximized Window option from the Run pop-up menu in the shortcut's Properties tab in Windows 95.

MAC OS

Scanned Images Display with Moire, Screen, or Plaid Pattern in PhotoDeluxe

ISSUE

Adobe PhotoDeluxe displays and prints a scanned image with a moire, screen, or plaid pattern, or with colored or gray blotches.

SOLUTIONS

Rescan the image from the original artwork or photograph, instead of from an already halftoned or previously printed copy.

OR: Minimize the pattern or blotches by doing one or more of the following:

NOTE: Minimizing the pattern may also decrease the image's detail.

A. Rescan the image at twice the recommended resolution, use PhotoDeluxe's Blur filter to reduce the moire pattern, resample the image, then use the Sharpen filter:
   1. Scan the image at twice the recommended resolution (e.g., 300 ppi, instead of 150 ppi, for a photograph that you are printing to a 600 dpi laser printer).
   2. In PhotoDeluxe, open the image and then click in sequence: On Your Own, Modify, the Effects tab, Special Effects, the Blur tab, Soften.
   3. In the Soften dialog box, select Preview, move the slider under Radius until the moire pattern disappears or is acceptably decreased (.5 pixels is a good place to start), then click OK.
   4. Select the Done tab.
   5. Select the Size tab, then select Photo Size.
   6. Deselect the File Size option, enter the recommended resolution in the Resolution text box, and then click OK.
   7. Select the Quality tab, and then click Sharpen.

B. Rescan using a scanning application (e.g., ScanPrep, ScanPrepPro, Ofoto) that includes an option (e.g., Descreening) to compensate for scanning halftoned artwork.

ADDITIONAL INFORMATION

Previously printed material (e.g., a picture from a magazine, book, brochure, newsletter, poster) has already been broken up into a halftone pattern for reproduction. Because scanners convert light and dark areas into a dot pattern, or halftone, creating a dot pattern of areas that are already dot patterns produces a moire, screen, or plaid pattern, or colored or gray blotches.

Nothing Happens After Clicking Step Tab in PhotoDeluxe's Guided Activities

ISSUE

After clicking a step tab other than the next or previous step tab in an Adobe PhotoDeluxe Guided Activity, PhotoDeluxe does not change the step tab.

SOLUTION

Click each step tab sequentially without completing the instructions for the step or steps you want to skip. For example, if you are on step 3 and you want to skip step 4 and 5 and proceed to step 6, click step tab 4, then click step tab 5, then click step tab 6.

ADDITIONAL INFORMATION

Because many of PhotoDeluxe's Guided Activities cannot be completed without following the instructions in each step sequentially, you cannot click a step tab other than the next or previous step tab. You can click step tabs sequentially without completing the instructions in the step, but doing so may prevent you from completing the next step or the Guided Activity.

To leave a Guided Activity at any time, click the Done tab.

Acquire Command Dimmed or Plug-ins Don't Appear in PhotoDeluxe 1.0

ISSUE

The Acquire command or submenu is dimmed, or plug-in modules (e.g., Apple QuickTake, Kodak DC-40) do not appear in the Acquire submenu in Adobe PhotoDeluxe 1.0.

SOLUTIONS

Do one or more of the following:

A. Ensure the plug-ins are located in PhotoDeluxe's Plug-ins folder.

B. Update the link to the Plug-ins folder:
   1. Quit PhotoDeluxe.
   2. At the Finder, press the Command key and double-click the PhotoDeluxe application icon.

C. Retarget the Plug-ins folder:
   1. In PhotoDeluxe, choose File > Preferences > Plug-ins.
   2. In the Select the Plug-ins Folder dialog box, click once on the Plug-ins folder to select it.
   3. Click the Select 'Plug-ins' button, located in the lower-right corner of the Select the Plug-ins Folder dialog box.
   4. Restart PhotoDeluxe.

D. Recreate PhotoDeluxe's preferences file:
   1. Quit PhotoDeluxe.
   2. At the Finder, open the Preferences folder in the System Folder.
   3. Delete the Adobe PhotoDeluxe Prefs file.

   NOTE: Deleting PhotoDeluxe's preferences file restores PhotoDeluxe's default preferences settings, and custom preferences settings are lost.

ADDITIONAL INFORMATION

PhotoDeluxe's Acquire command loads import plug-in modules (e.g., scanner plug-ins) from the Plug-ins folder. If PhotoDeluxe cannot access the plug-ins, it dims the Acquire command or does not list plug-ins in the Acquire submenu.

PhotoDeluxe's preferences file stores location and content information about the Plug-ins folder. If the Plug-ins folder name or location changes and the preferences file is not updated with these changes, or if the preferences file is damaged, PhotoDeluxe cannot access plug-ins. Deleting the preferences file and relaunching PhotoDeluxe forces PhotoDeluxe to create a new preferences file that contains updated plug-in folder and file information, and default preferences settings.

Application Errors

MAC OS

Error "...not enough memory (RAM)" in PhotoDeluxe Troubleshooting Guide

ISSUE

The error "Could not complete your request because there is not enough memory (RAM)" occurs when running Adobe PhotoDeluxe 1.0.

SOLUTIONS

Increase the amount of memory available to PhotoDeluxe by doing one or more of the following:

A. Allocate more memory to PhotoDeluxe:
 1. Quit PhotoDeluxe and all other applications.
 2. At the Finder, choose About This Macintosh from the Apple menu.
 3. Note the Largest Unused Block value, then close the dialog box.
 4. Select the PhotoDeluxe application icon, then choose File > Get Info.
 5. In the PhotoDeluxe Info dialog box, increase the Preferred size value, not exceeding 90% of the Largest Unused Block value noted in step 3.
 6. Close the PhotoDeluxe Info dialog box.

B. Reduce the image's resolution to reduce the memory requirements of the image:
 1. With the image open in PhotoDeluxe, choose Size > Photo Size.
 2. In the Photo Size dialog box, deselect the File Size option, decrease the Height, Width, or Resolution values, then click OK.
 NOTE: Reducing the image resolution may result in lower image quality.

C. Temporarily reduce the number of installed Photo-Deluxe plug-ins:
 1. Quit PhotoDeluxe.
 2. At the Finder, move plug-ins that you don't intend to use from your designated PhotoDeluxe Plug-ins folder to another location (e.g., desktop, new temporary folder).

D. Restart the Macintosh to defragment its memory.

E. Recreate PhotoDeluxe's preferences file:
 1. Quit PhotoDeluxe.
 2. Delete or move the Adobe PhotoDeluxe Prefs file, which is located in the Preferences folder in the System Folder.
 NOTE: Deleting the Adobe PhotoDeluxe Prefs file restores PhotoDeluxe's default preferences settings. To save custom preferences settings, move the Adobe PhotoDeluxe Prefs file to another location (e.g., in the trash but do not empty the trash). If the original Adobe PhotoDeluxe Prefs file is not the cause of the system error, replace the new Adobe PhotoDeluxe Prefs file with the original Adobe PhotoDeluxe Prefs file to restore custom preference settings.

F. Enable Virtual Memory in the Memory control panel. Because virtual memory enables applications to use hard disk space as memory, PhotoDeluxe's performance decreases when memory relies on hard disk access speeds, which is slower than installed RAM access speeds. Disable virtual memory when memory requirements of PhotoDeluxe or the currently open document decrease. For instructions on enable Virtual Memory, see Additional Information.
NOTE: Other installed extensions may cause Photo-Deluxe to return low-memory errors. Run PhotoDeluxe with all extensions off to verify that added extensions are not the cause. To turn extensions off upon startup in System 7, restart the computer while holding the Shift key until the message "Welcome to Macintosh. Extensions Off." appears.

ADDITIONAL INFORMATION

PhotoDeluxe uses both installed memory (RAM) and scratch disk memory to perform most operations, but some operations (e.g., using the Distort filters) run exclusively in RAM. When PhotoDeluxe has insufficient RAM to perform these operations, PhotoDeluxe returns the error "Could not complete your request because there is not enough memory (RAM)."

Because installed plug-ins load with PhotoDeluxe and use the memory allocated to PhotoDeluxe, reducing the number of installed plug-ins increases the amount of memory available to PhotoDeluxe for other operations.

Launching and exiting applications repeatedly can fragment the Macintosh's memory. When memory is fragmented (i.e., not available in a single, contiguous block), applications may be unable to access all their allocated memory. Restarting the Macintosh defragments its memory.

When PhotoDeluxe's preferences file is damaged, Photo-Deluxe may return the error "Could not complete your request because there is not enough memory (RAM)." Deleting PhotoDeluxe's preferences file and relaunching Photo-Deluxe forces PhotoDeluxe to create a new preferences file that contains default preferences settings.

To enable Virtual Memory:

1. Choose Control Panels from the Apple Menu.
2. Open the Memory control panel.
3. In the Virtual Memory section of the Memory control panel, select On.
4. Select the hard disk you want to use for virtual memory from the Select Hard Disk pop-up menu.
5. Use the arrow buttons to specify the amount of total memory you want. For best performance, enter a value equal to or less than twice the amount of installed memory (i.e., built-in memory).
6. Choose Special > Restart. After you restart the computer, its total memory includes virtual memory.

Error "Could not connect to camera. It may not be turned on." Acquiring Images from a Digital Camera

ISSUE

Adobe PhotoDeluxe 1.x returns the error "Could not connect to the camera. It may not be turned on." when acquiring images from a digital camera.

SOLUTIONS

Do one or more of the following:

A. Ensure the camera is turned on, and is in ready mode (i.e., not in sleep mode).

B. Ensure the connecting cables are securely fastened to the camera and computer.

ADDITIONAL INFORMATION

PhotoDeluxe returns the error "Could not connect to the camera. It may not be turned on." when your digital camera is turned off, is in sleep mode, or is not connected securely to the computer.

Adobe PostScript®

Adobe PostScript

Adobe® PrintGear™

Adobe PostScript was first developed in the early 1980s at Xerox PARC by John Warnock and Chuck Geschke, CEO and president of Adobe. Not only did PostScript give birth to Adobe Systems, but it started a revolution that continues to this day. PostScript is the software for describing to a printer the appearance of a page, including text, graphics, and scanned images. Adobe works with more than 70 industry-leading manufacturers to produce more than 300 output devices that bear the Adobe PostScript mark of excellence. PostScript Level 3 was announced in April of 1997.

Contents

Adobe PostScript®

Feature Techniques

MAC OS / WINDOWS / UNIX

Understanding PostScript Error Messages

If a PostScript file fails to print because of an error, the experience can be frustrating, time-consuming, and, ultimately, expensive. Because the printing systems that support the PostScript language are complex, their error messages can be varied and difficult to diagnose. With some knowledge of the PostScript language and the environment in which it operates, though, these experiences can be reduced or even eliminated. This appendix provides a basis for understanding PostScript errors and ways to interpret and correct them.

WHAT IS A POSTSCRIPT ERROR?

When you print a page on a desktop printer or a RIP (see "What Is a RIP?" page 101) that supports the PostScript language, the printer or RIP executes an electronic file that is a representation of the page in PostScript code. More accurately, the printer or RIP contains software called the PostScript interpreter, which is responsible for executing the PostScript file and creating a second representation of the page (often called the raster image) that can be understood by a printer engine. The engine then prints the raster image on paper or film.

When the interpreter executes a PostScript file, the usual result is that the corresponding page or pages are printed by the printer engine. If there is something wrong with the PostScript code in this file, however, the interpreter will detect an error—a PostScript error. When such an error occurs, the interpreter executes special code, called an error handler, designed to address that particular error. The error handler records information in the RIP's memory about the error and then executes a command to stop processing the file.

At this point, the PostScript code in the file may ignore the command to stop processing so that the interpreter may continue executing the file. For example, a file's request for duplex (two-sided) printing on paper will likely cause an error if it's sent to a printer that prints on only one side of the paper. If so, the internal error handler for that error executes the command to stop the job. But the PostScript file may ignore the command to stop as well as the request for duplex printing (the source of the error). Although the job will not fail in this case, it will print only single-sided pages. If the PostScript code does not ignore the command to stop, the interpreter processes the information recorded earlier by the internal error handler, which usually produces a message that looks like this:

```
%%[ Error: <error name>; OffendingCommand:
  <command name> ]%%
%%[ Flushing: rest of job (to end-of-file)
  will be ignored ]%%
```

The first line shows the name of the error as well as the name of the PostScript command that caused the error. The second line states that the rest of the job will not be processed. (This particular error message is very useful, although you may not always be able to see it. See "Displaying Error Messages," page 102, for information on how to find error messages.) The interpreter will then stop executing the file.

The RIP may create other error messages that look like the one shown above. If the messages have a similar format but do not contain the words Error and OffendingCommand, however, they are very likely not PostScript errors. For example, you may see a message containing the label PrinterError, such as:

```
%%[ PrinterError: Media jam ]%%
```

This type of message does not represent an error in the PostScript file detected by the interpreter. It represents a different type of problem that was detected by some other part of the system, in this case by the printer engine.

UNDERSTANDING ERROR MESSAGES

Although you need to take some action to correct a PostScript error, you may not understand what the error is when you see the message corresponding to that error.

```
%%[ Error: limitcheck; OffendingCommand:
  sethalftone ]%%
```

If you see this message, for instance, you know that an error called limitcheck occurred when a command called sethalftone was executed in the file, but this message doesn't tell you much about the source of the problem. In some cases, you may get a clue from the name of the error or command involved. In this example, you might guess that the error was produced by some limit that was reached while attempting to set up a halftone screen.

You can make more educated guesses by learning about the types of commands and errors contained in the PostScript language. The PostScript Language Reference Manual (second edition) is the official specification for the PostScript language. It contains descriptions of all of the standard commands and errors contained in Level 2 of the PostScript language. The standard commands are commonly referred to as operators. Section 8.1, "Operator Summary," groups all of the operators in the PostScript language into twenty-four categories. It also contains a brief summary of the thirty possible PostScript errors.

When analyzing an error message, look first at the offending command to determine what type of operation failed. Then look at the name of the error to determine what kind of failure occurred. In both steps, use Section 8.1 as a guide. The error name alone is meaningless without also knowing the offending command. For example, a limitcheck error message means that some limit in the RIP's design was exceeded; by itself, however, a limitcheck error message tells you nothing about which limit or even what kind of limit was exceeded.

The offending command.

The OffendingCommand statement identifies which PostScript operator failed. Operators may be divided into two groups: those that influence the appearance of a page and those that do not. In particular, operators in the first group influence the appearance of the three types of objects supported in the PostScript language: text, graphics, and images (images include rasterized artwork that has been generated digitally or scanned to capture pixel data). The distinction between the two groups is important: You may be able to correct errors resulting from operators in the first group by modifying the document from within the application that you used to create it. Operators in the second group, however, are used for the programming aspects of a PostScript file and require a great deal of experience with the PostScript language to understand and troubleshoot.

The first group of operators can be broken down further using the categories in Section 8.1 of the PostScript Language Reference Manual, which are described in Table 1: Graphics State, Device-Independent; Graphics State, Device-Dependent; Path Construction; Painting; Form and Pattern; Device Setup; and Character and Font. The large number of operators represented by these seven categories may be overwhelming, but bear in mind that within each category, some operators are seldom used. For example, the Painting operator `fill` occurs often because it is used to paint graphics; however, the Painting operator ueo`fill` is rarely used because it is more specialized.

When you see an operator name in an error message's OffendingCommand statement, find its category in Section 8.1. This will help you identify the type of operation that produced the error. For example, the show operator is in the Character and Font category; therefore, if you see an error whose offending command is the show operator, you should suspect that there is a problem with the text in the PostScript file. Table 1 (page 102) lists the seven operator categories, along with their descriptions and common examples.

You may see some commands in error messages that you will not find in the PostScript Language Reference Manual because they are not standard PostScript com-

TABLE 1: POSTSCRIPT OPERATORS

OPERATOR CATEGORY	CATEGORY DESCRIPTION	SAMPLE OPERATORS	OPERATOR DESCRIPTIONS
Graphics State, Device-Independent	Used to control how objects are painted; results should not vary from one type of output-device engine to another	`setcolor` `setlinewidth`	Establishes the color for an object to be painted Establishes the thickness of painted lines
Graphics State, Device-Dependent	Used to control how objects are painted; results usually vary from one type of output-device engine to another	`sethalftone` `setflat`	Establishes a requested halftone screen Establishes the flatness of curves

Path Construction	Used to create graphics such as polygons and curves	`lineto`
		`curveto`
		`arc`
			Draws a line
			Draws a curve
			Draws part or all of a circle

Painting	Used to paint graphics and images	`stroke`
		`fill`
		`image`
			Paints the outline of graphics
			Paints the interior of graphics
			Paints images

Form and Pattern	Used to generate repeatable forms and patterns	`setpattern` `execform`	Establishes a pattern Paints a form
Device Setup	Used to set up printing attributes	`setpagedevice`	Installs requested device features
Character and Font	Used to manipulate fonts and parts of fonts, such as characters	`findfont` `show`	Looks for and loads a requested font Paints a character or group of characters

TABLE 2: POSTSCRIPT ERROR MESSAGES			
ERROR NAME	USUAL MEANING	OFFENDING COMMANDS	COMMON PROBLEMS AND SOLUTIONS
<fontname> `not found, using Courier.`	The requested font was not supplied by the RIP or was not within the PostScript file. (This error message is formatted differently; it has no offending command.)	Not applicable	Download the missing font to the RIP, include it in the document, or choose a different font.
`configurationerror`	A requested feature setting cannot be satisfied; often accompanied by an extra `ErrorInfo` field in the error message indicating the requested feature.	`setpagedevice`	Do not request the feature from the printer driver, use a different printer support file, or configure the RIP to support the feature.
`dictfull`	There is no more room in PostScript data structures called dictionaries; this problem is more common with PostScript Level 1 than with Level 2.	`store, put, def`	These operators store objects in dictionaries; error requires advanced debugging.
`invalidaccess`	An attempt was made to put an object into a read-only data structure.	`store, put, def`	These operators store objects in various PostScript data structures; error requires advanced debugging.
`invalidfont`	There was an attempt to install a malformed or an improperly licensed font in the RIP's memory.	`findfont, definefont, selectfont`	Replace or reinstall the font on the RIP and/or computer.
`invalidrestore`	There is a programming problem with memory management.	`restore`	There is likely a problem with the printer driver; requires advanced debugging.
`ioerror`	An input/output error occurred while the RIP was processing a file; the file in question could be the actual job or another file referenced by the job file.	`image, colorimage`	The amount of data supplied is incorrect; scan, edit, or import the image again.
		Random characters	These characters may indicate a problem with the communications link; move or replace the communications line, check communications settings, disable spoolers, or run the job again.
`limitcheck`	An implementation limit was exceeded.	`show, fill, stroke, clip,` other painting operators	A graphic is too complex (this occurs very rarely when using PostScript Level 2); increase flatness, split paths, simplify the graphic, or lower the printer engine's resolution.
		`sethalftone`	The internal representation of the requested halftone screen is too large or too small; consult your RIP vendor.
		`image`	The image is too large, its resolution is too high, or it cannot be rotated. Reduce the size or resolution, rotate the image at a different angle, or rotate it in an image editing application such as Adobe Photoshop.

mands. This situation is much more common in products that support only Level 1 of the PostScript language than in those that support Level 2 as well (see "PostScript Level 2," page 104).

The error name.

After identifying the offending command in the error message, note the error name that was also reported in the message. The more common errors and their meanings are listed in Table 2 (pages 104-105), along with examples of offending commands and common problems and solutions for those combinations of errors and offending commands. Some of the examples are more complicated programming errors that require advanced debugging techniques and knowledge of the PostScript language to evaluate and correct. In such a case, you should call a local expert, the application vendor, or your RIP vendor for assistance.

You will find that the solutions offered in Table 2 do not always apply to the errors that you experience. There are too many possible errors— offending command combinations, circumstances that produce errors —and possible solutions to list in a single table. Instead, this information is intended to give you an idea of the usual meanings of common errors and how they vary.

To learn more about operators and errors, see Section 8.2, "Operator Details," of the PostScript Language Reference Manual; the rest of the manual describes the principles of operation regarding PostScript operators and errors. There are also a number of books and classes that discuss the PostScript language in more practical terms (see "Suggested Reading" and "Training Courses and Seminars," page 108).

DISPLAYING ERROR MESSAGES

After the interpreter creates an error message, several things can happen to it, depending on the printer or RIP you are using. The message, perhaps in a different format than described earlier, may be recorded somewhere in the RIP, or it could be sent back to the computer that sent it to the RIP.

TABLE 2: POSTSCRIPT ERROR MESSAGES (CONTINUED)			
ERROR NAME	USUAL MEANING	OFFENDING COMMANDS	COMMON PROBLEMS AND SOLUTIONS
`rangecheck`	A value provided to the operator was outside the acceptable range.	`setpapertray` (Level 1)	The requested paper tray does not exist; request a different tray from the printer driver.
		Several operators	Requires advanced debugging
`stackoverflow`	This is a programming problem concerning the filling up of an internal data structure called the operand stack.	Several operators	May indicate a printer driver problem or interference from a separate utility; requires advanced debugging.
`stackunderflow`	The operator expected one or more values to be available on the operand stack, but there were none.	Several operators	May indicate a printer driver problem or interference from a separate utility; requires advanced debugging.
`timeout`	A time limit for an operation has been exceeded.	Several operators	A time-out threshold is set too low or there is a communications problem. Use administration software or the printer driver to reset the time-out value on the RIP, or try a different driver.
`typecheck`	The operator expected a certain type of value on the operand stack, but the wrong type was provided instead.	Several operators	May be a printer driver problem or interference from a separate utility; requires advanced debugging.
		Random or no characters	This could indicate a problem with the communications link or with the leftover data in the job; try a different communications line or printer driver. This problem may also occur if a PostScript file is saved, transferred to a different computer platform, and downloaded from that computer; try saving the file in ASCII or Text Only rather than binary format.
`undefined`	The name specified in the OffendingCommand is not known to the RIP.	`md`	This is not a PostScript operator; it indicates that the required PostScript code has not been included in a PostScript file saved on the Macintosh. Resave the file.
		Several operators	The job contains a nonstandard operator that is not recognized by the RIP; check the driver settings or select a different printer support file.
		Random characters	Too much data for an image may have been supplied; scan, edit, or import the image again.
`VMerror`	The RIP has run out of PostScript virtual memory (VM) during the job.	Several operators	Reboot the RIP to clear its memory; this error should be very rare when using PostScript Level 2.

If your RIP does not record messages or is unable to send them to an attached computer, the messages will be lost. In this case, it is best to use an error handler utility. Error handler utilities are PostScript files that change the way error messages are processed and displayed by the interpreter. For example, they may print the error information at the RIP or write it to the RIP's disk so that it may be read later. Some error handler utilities also provide more information than just the error message, but this additional information typically requires in-depth knowledge of the PostScript language. Contact your RIP vendor for information on available error handler utilities. Adobe Systems also provides a simple error handler utility via modem or the Internet (see "Accessing Adobe Files," page 103).

Even if the RIP can send error messages back to your computer, you may not see the error message at all or it may flash by too quickly on your computer's display to be read or understood. In this case, the printer driver on your computer is ignoring or intercepting messages sent back from a RIP. (Examples of printer drivers include Apple Computer's LaserWriter driver, Microsoft's PSCRIPT™ driver, and Adobe Systems' PSPrinter™ and ADOBEPS™ drivers for the Macintosh and Windows platforms, respectively.)

Further, if the printer driver detects that the message represents an error, it may post an uninformative message such as -8133, which indicates that a PostScript error has occurred. Be aware that not all generic error messages indicate a PostScript error. For example, the messages -4100 or The job is OK but can't be printed. on the Macintosh may indicate a problem in the communications link between the Macintosh and the RIP.

You can use an error handler utility in this case, but this is not always the best choice. An error handler utility that instructs the RIP to print the error information on paper or film, for instance, could be an expensive waste of media. A better method is to look for an option to display error messages when you print. The PSPrinter and LaserWriter

8.0 printer drivers (from Adobe Systems and Apple Computer, respectively) both provide this option.

If this feature is not available to you, the next best method is to save the PostScript file on your computer's hard disk drive and download it separately to the RIP. Look for an option to save the PostScript file when you print. After saving the file, send it to the RIP using a downloader utility. (Examples of downloader utilities are font downloader software, LaserTalk™, and SendPS™, all of which are available from Adobe Systems; your RIP vendor may also offer downloader utilities.)

Typically, downloader utilities either show you the error message on-screen after sending the file or write any information returned by the RIP to a "log file" on your computer's hard disk drive. Alternatively, if your error handler utility provides additional information from the RIP with the error message and does not print on media, install it and then download the saved PostScript file. This allows you to see the more complete information returned by the error handler utility.

Follow these steps to help you determine which method to use to display complete error messages:

1. If the RIP can record or display error messages, consult the RIP documentation on how to read them. If not, go to step 2.
2. If the RIP is unable to send messages back to your computer, use an error handler utility. If it can send messages back, go to step 3.
3. If you are able to see complete error messages when you print, begin using them. If not, go to step 4.
4. If your printer driver has an option to display complete error messages, enable this option when you print. If not, go to step 5.
5. If your printer driver has an option to save PostScript files, save the file, then use a downloader utility to send the file to the RIP.
6. Finally, try running the PostScript file through the Adobe Acrobat Distiller. If the Distiller detects the same error, you should be able to see what that error is.

If none of these methods works, you will need to use more advanced techniques. Consult with a local expert or contact your RIP vendor for assistance.

CAUSES OF POSTSCRIPT ERRORS

In order to correct a PostScript error, you first need to know at which point in the printing process it was introduced. Although printing a document is a complex operation that varies slightly from one printing environment to another, generally there is a common sequence of steps. If you become familiar with these steps, you will be better able to isolate the cause of the errors you encounter. The following list describes each step in the printing process, along with common problems associated with it and suggested solutions.

1. You compose a document on your computer using an application. The application uses its own graphics language to represent the document on your monitor. The document may also include files imported from other applications. If there is a problematic object in this document or an error in one of the imported files, remove or modify the offending object or imported file.
2. When you print the document, you select the destination RIP as well as various settings for printing the document on that RIP, such as paper size, hardware resolution, or flatness. If you selected settings that are inappropriate for the RIP, try selecting different ones.
3. The printer driver then converts the document into a PostScript file. The driver translates the representation of the document from the application's graphics language into the PostScript language. If the PostScript code created by the printer driver is faulty, the translation will produce an error. Try a different printer driver or try modifying the document from within the application.
4. Some printer drivers add information to the PostScript code, such as details about fonts, images, and other resources required by a document. Such information can be formatted according to the Document Structuring Conventions (DSC) described in the PostScript Language Reference Manual or the Open Prepress Interface (OPI) specification. If there is a mistake in the added information, a problem in the PostScript code may be introduced later if a spooler is attached to the RIP. Try using a different driver, changing the fonts, or changing the structure of the document (by moving or deleting pages, for example).
5. The printer driver may insert extra PostScript code into the file (see "Sending the Right File," this page) that requests specific features of the destination RIP. Some printer drivers obtain this code from printer support files, such as PostScript Printer Description (PPD) files from Adobe Systems (see "Customizing a PPD File," page 108). These support files contain product-specific code so that the printer drivers don't have to include it. If you or the printer driver chooses the wrong printer support file for the destination RIP, go back and select the appropriate printer support file for the RIP. If the information in the printer support file is incorrect, contact your RIP vendor or try using a printer support file for a very similar RIP.
6. The PostScript file is sent or transferred to the RIP, usually by the printer driver. If there is a problem with the way that the file is sent to the RIP, either in the physical connection or in the software that is sending the file, try a different way of sending the file. For example, try a different cable, using a different type of communications link, or using the same link but a different printer driver, downloader, or file transfer software.
7. If a spooler or OPI server is on the network or part of the RIP, the spooler or server intercepts the file. (A spooler is software that coordinates the delivery of files to a RIP.) Some spoolers and servers modify the file according to the DSC or OPI information in the file before passing it on to the PostScript interpreter within

the RIP. If the DSC or OPI information is incorrect or if the spooler handles the information incorrectly, an error will result. Disable the spooler if possible, or check that the resources required by the file are available at the RIP.

8. Finally, the interpreter executes the file—this is when errors are actually detected. Problems within the interpreter itself are less common than errors introduced in the previous steps. Some utilities, such as those for color calibration, make subtle changes to the interpreter's operation that can interfere with the proper operation of the interpreter. If there is a problem in the interpreter or if a utility is interfering, try either using a different RIP or restarting the RIP without using specialized utilities. If this does not help, contact your RIP vendor to report the problem.

If all else fails, one final solution that you can try is to save the PostScript file, modify it directly, and download it to the RIP. This requires explicit knowledge of the PostScript language and of DSC, however. Alternatively, you can contact your RIP vendor for assistance.

ISOLATING THE CAUSE OF THE ERROR

Note that one common action in the suggested solutions is to replace, remove, or otherwise change a particular part in the process, such as the printer driver, printer support file, or spooler. The best way to find the cause of an error is to isolate it by systematically changing one part of the process at a time and then observing whether the error still occurs. If you make a change and the problem disappears, you have located the cause of the problem and solved it as well; otherwise, try changing another part of the process.

Replacing the printer driver is a common change, since the driver is involved in several of the steps in the printing process. If you try a different driver, you are sending different PostScript code for the same document. (Some applications, such as Adobe Photoshop, Adobe Illustrator, and QuarkXPress, generate their own PostScript code, so changing the driver may not have an effect in these cases.) If the error persists, then you need to look at the other parts of the process, such as modifying the file from within the application or changing the way the file is transferred to the RIP.

If you modify the file in the application, you can use a similarly systematic approach by replacing, removing, or modifying pages or objects on the page. Again, the error information may guide you in determining which objects to change.

There are several ways to change the method for transferring a file to the RIP. You can try different physical connections, such as LocalTalk® or EtherTalk® (both from Apple Computer) or serial or parallel cables. Or you can save a PostScript file using the printer driver and then send it to the RIP separately with a downloader utility. In this case, you are using the downloader utility software to transfer the file to the RIP; if the error disappears, you know it had to do with the way the printer driver transferred the file.

When you save a PostScript file using a printer driver, however, you may introduce some new problems. Because the driver adds device-dependent code to the file, it may not be appropriate to send the file to another type of RIP; either the file will fail or you will not get the printing features you requested. Also, if you transfer a saved PostScript file from a Windows or DOS machine to a Macintosh, there may be nonprinting characters (also called binary characters) within the file that will cause an undefined error when the file is downloaded to the RIP. In general, files with binary characters are much more difficult to transfer from one computer platform to another. It's safest to save files in ASCII text format rather than binary format.

Another method for transferring the PostScript file is to store the file on the RIP's internal disk, if it has one, and run it from there. This is similar to downloading and storing a font to the RIP's internal disk. When you run the file from the RIP's disk, you no longer need to send the file to print it, which effectively removes the communications step from the printing process. (Note, however, that if the file had binary characters in it when you stored it on the RIP's disk, those characters may have been lost if you used a serial or parallel connection.)

Some downloader utilities allow you to store a PostScript file to the RIP's internal disk. If one is not available, use a text editor (in ASCII format) to add the following PostScript code to the beginning of a PostScript file:

```
%!
/rf currentfile def
/wf (myfile.ps) (w) file def
/str 65535 string def
 //rf //str readstring
 //wf 3 -1 roll writestring
 not {exit} if
} bind loop
```

You can change the name of the file by replacing myfile.ps in the code with your file name (retain the parentheses). It's best to keep the name simple and to avoid using spaces or nonalphanumeric characters. You can then send this new file to the RIP using a downloader utility. If there are no problems, the PostScript file will now be stored on the RIP's internal disk. Next, from within the text editor, create another PostScript file that contains only this simple code:

```
%!
(myfile.ps) run
```

Again, substitute the placeholder myfile.ps with the name of the file you stored previously on the RIP's internal disk. Save (also in ASCII format) and download this simple file to the RIP. The file myfile.ps will be executed. You can send this file as many times as you want to run myfile.ps. If the error persists, then the source of the problem is not in the communications line or the way that the printer driver sent the file to the RIP. Once you have finished testing for the error's source, you must delete the myfile.ps file; to do so, create and download another PostScript file to the RIP that contains this code:

```
%!
(myfile.ps) deletefile
```

Your RIP vendor may have utilities or methods available for performing these kinds of operations with PostScript files. For example, on some software-based RIPs that run on workstations, it may be possible to store a PostScript file on the workstation's file system so that it can be executed by the RIP.

This systematic approach can be time-consuming, since the printing process has so many parts and steps. Bear in mind, however, that the PostScript error message will often provide clues about the type of operation that failed and how it failed. For example, if you see an ioerror message with random characters rather than an operator name as the offending command, you should suspect a problem with the communications link to the RIP. But if you see an ioerror message associated with the image operator (related to a scanned image), you should either suspect the communications link or the application that you used to create and save the scanned image.

With time and experience, you will discover that intuitive hunches play a part in determining the causes of PostScript errors. Yet even when you are able to make such intuitive leaps, it will always be a good idea to return to basic principles: Know the steps in the printing process, know how to display the complete error message, know how to interpret the elements of the error message, and know that successful troubleshooting requires systematically isolating possible sources of the problem.

SUGGESTED READING

Braswell, Frank. Inside PostScript. Berkeley, Calif.: Peachpit Press, 1989.

Fink, Peter. PostScript Screening: Adobe Accurate Screens. Mountain View, Calif.: Adobe Press/MacMillan Computer Publishing, 1992.

Glover, Gary. Running PostScript from MS-DOS. Blue Ridge, Pa.: Windcrest Books, 1989.

McGilton, Henry, and Mary Campione. PostScript by Example. Reading, Mass.: Addison-Wesley, 1992.

Adobe Systems Incorporated. PostScript Language Reference Manual. 2d ed. Reading, Mass.: Addison-Wesley, 1990.

Reid, Glenn. Thinking in PostScript. Reading, Mass.: Addison-Wesley, 1990.

Roth, Stephen. Real World PostScript. Reading, Mass.: Addison-Wesley, 1988.

Smith, Ross. Learning PostScript: A Visual Approach. Berkeley, Calif.: Peachpit Press, 1990.

TRAINING COURSES AND SEMINARS

PostScript Language Training, Levels 1 and 2 Acquired Knowledge 619-587-4668

PostScript Concepts Seminar Systems of Merritt 205-660-1240

Customizing a PPD File

A PostScript Printer Description (PPD) file—a printer support file in ASCII text format created by Adobe Systems or one of its original equipment manufacturers (OEMs)—describes the specifications and features of a specific Post-Script printing device in its original manufactured state. Applications such as Adobe Separator and PageMaker, as well as printer drivers from Adobe Systems and Apple Computer, use PPD files, which may be distributed by the application vendor or OEM. PPD files allow the user to select settings for different features, such as paper sizes, tray options, halftone screens, and output resolutions. Sometimes you may need to add to or modify a PPD file for a particular printing environment. This section—which is addressed primarily to prepress operators—discusses common ways of customizing PPD files.

In general, modifying a PPD file requires knowledge of the PPD format and often of the PostScript language itself. Although neither Adobe Systems nor its OEMs support PPD file customization, with careful attention to detail, it can be done successfully.

CUSTOMIZATION METHODS

Changes can be made to a PPD file in two ways: by editing the PPD file directly with a text editor, or by creating and editing a separate PPD file, called an editable customization file, that refers to the original PPD file. If you edit the PPD file, save a copy of the original and edit the copy, not the original. Use any text editor to modify or create the PPD file and always save the file in Text Only or ASCII format.

To create an editable customization file, create a new file in a text editor and type the following line:

```
*Include: "filename"
```

Replace filename (keep the quotes) with the name of the original PPD file that is to be customized. Add the custom PPD entries you want before this line so it will override the information in the original PPD file. The custom PPD entries must conform to the PPD specifications. Save the customization file with a unique name that represents the changes you made or the particular device for which you made those changes (for example, MyPrntr.PPD). The .PPD extension (it is not case-sensitive) should be preserved because many applications and print managers search for files with that extension. Store both the original PPD file and the customization file in the same location.

Whenever possible, use the editable customization file method rather than editing a PPD file directly. There are several advantages to using an editable customization file over modifying the PPD file. First, the editable customization file method allows you to isolate errors more easily. Second, the original PPD files are still supported by Adobe Systems and its OEMs because they remain unchanged. Third, you can create a naming convention for the editable customization files that will make it easy to track future modifications. The disadvantage of using an editable customization file is that you must know the PPD file specifications in order to make the correct entries.

The only time you should edit the original PPD file is when you wish to make a small number of simple changes. In general, if you are making several customizations, you should use the editable customization file method instead.

APPLICATIONS

This section provides some examples of PPD file customizations.

Editing halftone screen information.

The ColorSepScreenAngle and ColorSepScreenFreq entries in either an original PPD or a customization file correspond to a particular halftone screen angle and frequency for each process and custom color, usually at a certain output resolution. Although you may select a 132-lpi screen frequency and a 2540-dpi output resolution in the dialog boxes of an application such as Adobe Separator, the actual settings may not represent an exact 132-lpi screen. To set your own custom screen frequency and angle, follow these steps.

1. Search for the ColorSepScreenAngle and ColorSepScreenFreq entries in the PPD file (they are usually near the end).
2. Locate the group of lines representing the screen frequency and output resolution combination (in lpi and dpi, respectively) you wish to modify (132/2540 in this example). You will find lines of code similar to these:

```
*% For 132 lpi / 2540 dpi
*ColorSepScreenAngle
  ProcessBlack.132lpi.2540dpi/132 lpi / 2540
  dpi: "45.0"
*ColorSepScreenAngle
  CustomColor.132lpi.2540dpi/132 lpi / 2540
  dpi: "45.0"
*ColorSepScreenAngle
  ProcessCyan.132lpi.2540dpi/132 lpi / 2540
  dpi: "18.4349"
*ColorSepScreenAngle
  ProcessMagenta.132lpi.2540dpi/132 lpi /
  2540 dpi: "71.565"
*ColorSepScreenAngle
  ProcessYellow.132lpi.2540dpi/132 lpi / 2540
  dpi: "0.0"
*ColorSepScreenFreq
  ProcessBlack.132lpi.2540dpi/132 lpi / 2540
  dpi: "119.737"
*ColorSepScreenFreq
  CustomColor.132lpi.2540dpi/132 lpi / 2540
  dpi: "119.737"
*ColorSepScreenFreq
  ProcessCyan.132lpi.2540dpi/132 lpi / 2540
  dpi: "133.871"
*ColorSepScreenFreq
  ProcessMagenta.132lpi.2540dpi/132 lpi /
  2540 dpi: "133.871"
*ColorSepScreenFreq
  ProcessYellow.132lpi.2540dpi/132 lpi / 2540
  dpi: "127.0"
```

3. At the end of each ColorSepScreenAngle line, edit the value within the quotation marks. This will change the angle of the screen used to create the halftone. These numbers must contain a decimal point, so follow each whole number with a decimal point and a zero. For example, enter 45 degrees as "45.0" (include quotation marks). If you are using the customization file method, copy these entries and place them in the customization file before the line containing *Include. Then edit the values in the customization file.
4. At the end of each ColorSepScreenFreq line, edit the value within the quotation marks. This will change the screen frequency used to create the halftone. These numbers must also have a decimal point, so follow each whole number with a decimal point and a zero. For example, enter 127 degrees as "127.0" (include quotation marks).

CHANGING MENU ITEM NAMES

Applications and drivers use translation strings to describe some menu items. Translation strings translate potentially cryptic PPD file entries into easily identifiable names or phrases, even in natural programming languages. To identify a translation string in a PPD file, look for a phrase preceded by a solidus (/) and followed by a colon (:). By editing these strings, you can use names that are more useful to you than the printer vendor's names.

For example, many imagesetter PPDs have a paper-size selection called Letter.Transverse, for letter-sized paper that is fed into the printer by its long edge. It may be more intuitive to be able to select the Long-edge-feed Letter paper size than it is to select the Letter.Transverse size in the appropriate dialog box. You can customize the PPD file to change the name of this paper size.

The latest drivers from Adobe Systems and Apple Computer use the *PageSize entries in the PPD file to display the names of the available paper sizes in the appropriate dialog box. When the entry shown below exists, it causes the printer driver to display Letter.Transverse, since there is no translation string. (In a PPD file, these entries are placed with other *PageSize entries; in a customization file, they are placed above the line that contains *Include.)

```
*PageSize Letter.Transverse: "<PostScript
  language code>"
```

Change the menu item by adding the following translation string :

```
*PageSize Letter.Transverse/Long-edge-feed
  Letter: "<PostScript language code>"
```

In this case, as a result of this new entry, the name of this paper size will now be displayed as Long-edge-feed Letter the next time you elect the same PPD file. Do not change the PostScript language code between the quotes.

Changing the nickname of your printer.

There may be times when you'll need to identify a PPD file by the function of the printer it represents, rather than the name of the product. The PSPrinter driver from Adobe Systems, for example, is able to display an alternate name for a PPD file when you select the printer in the Chooser on a Macintosh. Changing the *NickName entry in the PPD file changes this alternate name.

First, find the *NickName entry, which is usually near the beginning of the PPD file. It will look something like this:

```
*NickName: "ACME Color Printer 1000
 v2013.114"
```

You may change the nickname to something more useful to you by changing the *NickName statement to read:

```
*NickName: "ACME Color Proofer"
```

The new nickname should be no longer than thirty-one characters. f it is longer, add this entry: ShortNickName: "<desired name>"

Adding Fonts to a Custom Printer File Using a Text Editor

Custom printer files supplement PPD (PostScript Printer Description) files, allowing printer information to be customized for a particular printer (e.g., resident fonts, paper sizes, virtual memory).

The External Font Information section in the selected PPD or custom printer file indicates what fonts are installed in the printer's hard drive. From this list of fonts, applications that read PPD files determine what fonts to download. Most PPD files list fonts in the printer's ROM only. The advantages of listing all fonts at the printer will depend on your work flow and how many fonts are always installed on the printer's hard drive. Listing fonts in the printer's RAM is not recommended, as those fonts are deleted from memory when the printer is reset.

To add fonts available at the printer to a custom printer file using a text editor:

1. Retrieve a list of PostScript font names available at the printer. For instructions, see "Retrieving List of PostScript Font Names."
2. Open the custom printer file in a text editor that can save in text-only format (e.g., Microsoft Word, TeachText, MS-DOS Editor).
   NOTE: Some text editors (e.g., Microsoft Write, Notepad) add invisible characters (e.g., end-of-file, line feed) to the file that prevent the PPD file from being parsed.
3. Before the "*Include" line, add the printer fonts using the syntax:

```
*Font fontname: encoding "(version)" charset
 status
For example, ROM resident fonts:
*Font Courier: Standard "(001.004)" Standard
 ROM
*Font Symbol: Special "(001.003)" Special
 ROM
For example, fonts residing on the printer's
 hard disk:
*Font Palatino-Bold: Standard "(001.002)"
 Standard Disk
*Font Palatino-BoldItalic: Standard
 "(001.002)" Standard Disk
*Font Palatino-Italic: Standard "(001.002)"
 Standard Disk
*Font Palatino-Roman: Standard "(001.001)"
 Standard Disk
*Font MinionMM-Ep: Expert "(001.000)" Expert
 Disk
*Font MinionMM-It: Standard "(001.000)"
 Standard Disk
*Font AGaramondAlt-Italic: Special
 "(001.001)" Special Disk
*Font AGaramondAlt-Regular: Special
 "(001.001)" Special Disk
```

   NOTE: The encoding, version, charset, and status are not used by most applications (e.g., Adobe PageMaker). Aldus TrapWise requires the correct font encoding, version, charset, and status. If the custom printer file is used only in PageMaker or Aldus PrePrint, the only information required after the PostScript font name is "Standard" for encoding, "001.000" for version, "Standard" for charset, and "Disk" or "ROM" for status. For example:

```
*Font Palatino-Bold: Standard "(001.000)"
 Standard Disk
```

4. Save the custom printer file in text-only format in the Printer Descriptions folder (Macintosh) or in the ALDUS\USENGLSH\PPD4 subdirectory (Windows).

RETRIEVING LIST OF POSTSCRIPT FONT NAMES ON THE MACINTOSH

Create a Font catalog using Apple LaserWriter 8.0 Utility v 7.4.1:

1. Use Apple LaserWriter 8.0 Utility v 7.4.1 or later to print a Font catalog to disk.
2. Open the file in a text editor, and search for the PostScript font names in parentheses (e.g., Helvetica-ExtraCompressed) listed in the section "Fonts on printer."
   OR: Use a PostScript file downloading utility (e.g., Adobe Font Downloader 5.04) to print or display a list of PostScript font names.
   NOTE: PostScript font names displayed by Adobe Font Downloader 5.04 cannot be copied from the displayed list.

OR: Download a PostScript routine to query for fonts at the printer, and return a list of these fonts in a text file:

1. Open a new file in a text editor that can save in text-only format.
2. Type the following PostScript code (Color Central User Manual, p. 71):

```
statusdict begin save
/SC 100 string def
FontDirectory{pop = flush}forall
(fonts/*){dup length 6 sub 6 exch
  getinterval = flush} SC filenameforall
restore
```

3. Save in text-only format.
4. Download the PostScript routine file using a utility able

to return a text or log file (e.g., Apple LaserWriter 8.0 Utility v 7.4.1). The log file returned will contain the every font name resident in the printer's RIP (i.e., ROM, RAM, hard drive).

OR: Copy the FontName line in the PostScript font's AFM file, included with PostScript fonts.

OR: Use ResEdit to open the printer font and retrieve the font name from the POST resource number 501.

OR: Use the Update PPD Addition or PPDShell.ps PostScript routine file included with Adobe PageMaker 5.0x to query and list available fonts at the printer in the generated custom printer file.

NOTE: The fonts listed in the custom printer file generated by the Update PPD Addition or "PPDShell.ps" PostScript routine file can be copied into other custom printer files.

RETRIEVING LIST OF POSTSCRIPT FONT NAMES IN WINDOWS

Use a PostScript file downloading utility to print a list of PostScript font names.

OR: Copy the FontName line in the PostScript font's AFM file, included with PostScript fonts.

Creating Smooth and Efficient Gradations or Blends for PostScript

PostScript creates a graduated effect digitally by generating a series of halftone bands. Each band is a different shade or tint; the series of tint bands create the illusion of a gradation. The thinner the tint bands, the smoother the gradation will appear. Thick bands create a gradation that appears "banded."

It is possible to calculate the size of tint bands in a gradation (i.e., gradient fill, radial fill, or blend) to predetermine banding and ensure efficient blends for PostScript output. These calculations aid in creating gradations with the optimum number of steps to prevent noticeable banding while decreasing imaging times. As a general guideline, gradations with tint bands less than 3 points wide appear smooth; tint bands 3 points or wider appear banded.

When creating blends, do not add extra blend steps to create a smoother effect. The number of tints produced is related to the variables listed below. Specifying more blend steps than the number of available tints adds extra information that the printer cannot use but still has to process, making the print time longer with no increase in quality.

The following information is needed to calculate tint band widths:

- The printer resolution in dots per inch (dpi).
- The screen frequency in lines per inch (lpi).
- The change in color between the beginning and ending tints in the gradation described as a percentage.
- The physical distance between the beginning and ending tints of the gradation described in points.

CALCULATING TINT BANDS FOR GRADATIONS

To calculate available tints and band widths, use the following three formulas in the order listed:

```
([Resolution (dpi)] / [Screen frequency
  (lpi)]) [squared] + 1 = [a]
[a] x [amount of tint change in gradation] =
  [b]
[length of area to be filled] / [b] = [c]
```

Where:

[a] is the initial number of tints available.

[b] is the actual number of tints available for the gradation.

[c] is the size of each band or how visible it will be.

To calculate tints available and band size using the above formulas:

1. Divide the printer resolution by the chosen screen frequency. Square the integer value (discard any remainder or decimal), then add 1 to the result. This is the approximate number of tints the printer is capable of producing using this resolution and screen frequency.
```
([Resolution (dpi)] / [Screen frequency
  (lpi)]) [squared] + 1 = [initial number of
  tints available]
```
2. When the number calculated for initial number of tints available is higher than 256, reduce to 256. PostScript cannot create more than 256 different tints per ink.
   For example, when printing to a device with resolution set at 1270 dots per inch (dpi) and line frequency specified at 150 lines per inch (lpi), the formula calculates roughly 72 available tints. Changing the resolution to 2540 dpi, while keeping the screen frequency at 150 lpi, results in 287 available tints. Because PostScript is only capable of 256 tints, you must use the number 256.
3. Multiply the initial number of tints available by the amount of tint change in the gradation, expressed as a decimal.
```
[Initial number of tints available] x
  [amount of tint change in gradation] =
  [actual number of tints available for the
  gradation]
```
   For example, for a 20% black to 80% black gradation, the tint change is 60% or .60 when expressed as a decimal. Because a tint change of less than 100% uses less that 100% of the total available range of tints (e.g., 60% of 256 tints is 153 tints), you must calculate the actual number of tints available.
4. Measure the object in the direction of the gradation and convert that length to points (72 points per inch).
5. Divide the length of the gradation by the actual number of tints available to determine the width of each tint band or the minimum width of objects used to create a blend.
```
[length of area to be filled] / [actual
  number of tints available] = [size of each
  tint band]
```
   For example, when the gradation is 4 inches (288 points) in length with 153 tints available, each tint band will be about 1.9 points wide.

CALCULATING TINT BANDS FOR PROCESS COLOR GRADATIONS

When predetermining band widths for process color gradations, calculate band widths for each of the four process inks involved. You can calculate banding for the ink that has the most change in color, and the ink with the least change to determine the complete spectrum of expected band widths. Banding in a lighter color (i.e., yellow) is less evident when the final product is printed than banding in a darker color (i.e., black).

REDUCING BANDING

Variables that affect banding are: resolution, screen frequency, tint change in the gradation, and the length of the gradation.

Adjust variables to reduce the width of tint bands by doing one or more of the following:

A. Increase the resolution until the gray bands are thin enough or until the number of initially available grays passes PostScript's limit of 256 gray levels. Raising resolution after passing 256 tints is pointless because PostScript can only produce 256 tints per ink.

B. Lower the screen frequency value until the formula shows the bands are thin enough or until the number of initially available tints passes PostScript's limit of 256 gray levels. Lowering screen frequency after passing 256 tints is pointless because PostScript can only produce 256 tints per ink.

C. Increase the difference in color between the starting and ending tints in the gradation.

D. Decrease the length of the gradation.

OR: Diffuse the hard edges of the tint bands by applying noise to the gradation in an application that can open and rasterize the gradation (e.g., Adobe Photoshop), or by choosing an ink or absorbent paper stock that will aid in diffusing the tint bands.

OR: Replace the gradation by having your printer strip in a pre-made gradation or by printing to a PostScript processing system (e.g., Scitex system) that replaces gradations with a proprietary smooth rasterized gradation.

PostScript Level 2 General Information

PostScript, developed by Adobe in 1985, is a page description language for printing and displaying documents that integrate text, graphics, images, and color. PostScript implementations are organized into levels (i.e., Level 1, Level 2). Several extensions have been made to the PostScript language to adapt to new technology and to incorporate new functionality and flexibility. PostScript extensions are collections of language features that are not a standard part of the language level.

PostScript Level 1 interpreters implement all Level 1 features documented in the first edition of the PostScript Language Reference Manual.

PostScript Level 2 introduces new language features as well as optimized text and graphic operators. Level 2 features include CMYK color extensions, composite font extensions, and many of the Display PostScript extensions that apply to raster devices. Because Level 2 supports Level 1 features and operators, applications that support printing to Level 1 interpreters also support printing to Level 2 interpreters. PostScript Level 1 does not support all Level 2 features and operators. PostScript language applications that support Level 2 operators and features do not automatically support printing to Level 1 interpreters.

POSTSCRIPT LEVEL 2 NEW LANGUAGE FEATURES

PostScript Level 2 provides improved and enhanced support for the following features:

Composite font

PostScript Level 2 incorporates the composite font extension. Composite fonts are a hierarchical collection of base fonts (i.e., individual character descriptions) that support character sets larger than 256 characters and complex character positioning. In PostScript Level 1, fonts are limited to 256 characters. Languages such as Japanese and Chinese require character sets larger than 256 characters.

Data Compression and Decompression Filters

Data Compression and Decompression filters transform data as it is being read from or written to a file. The PostScript Level 2 language supports filters for ASCII HEX coding, ASCII85 coding, LZW compression, Run-length compression, CCITT fax compression (i.e., Group 3 and Group 4), and JPEG compression.

Device-independent Color

PostScript Level 2 supports several device-independent color spaces based on the international standard CIE 1931 (Commission International de l'Eclairage) as well as the CMYK and RGB color models. CIE is a system for specifying color values in a way that is related to human visual perception. The CIE color models are based on visual color perception rather than color production. The CIE color system allows for device-independent color, which enables you to create, view, and print color information with more predictable results on a variety of displays and printers.

Forms

A form is a self-contained description of graphics, text, or images painted multiple times on any number of pages by using Form caches. To optimize the repeat uses of the same from, the form cache uses a location in memory to store recently used forms. When the form is requested, it is retrieved from the form cache. If the form is not requested within a predetermined amount of time, the form is deleted from memory.

Improved Halftoning Algorithms

PostScript Level 2 devices provide improved accuracy of angles and frequencies for imagesetter halftone screens. Halftone screen calculations are based on parameters such as the exact screen angle and frequency requested, resolution of the device, and memory available for use by the algorithm. PostScript Level 2 uses device-specific halftone dictionaries to ensure hardware specific adjustments. A halftone dictionary (e.g., type 1, type 3) is a self-contained description of a halftoning process.

Improved Memory Management

Memory in a PostScript Level 2 device is available to all resources, resulting in dynamically-shared memory for increased efficiency. In PostScript Level 2, the VM, stacks, paths, font cache, form cache, and the page buffer expand when necessary, sharing memory as needed. PostScript Level 2 supports the removal of individual entries from dictionaries and the removal of font definitions in an order unrelated to the order in which they were created. Virtual memory (VM) is reclaimed automatically for composite objects.

Patterns

PostScript Level 2 allows printers to paint with patterns in addition to solid colors. Painting operators are used to tile a pattern cell at fixed intervals to cover the area being painted. The pattern cache is a location in memory where recently used patterns are stored, optimizing the repeated use of the same pattern. When the pattern is requested, it is retrieved from the pattern cache. If the pattern is not requested in a predetermined amount of time, it is deleted from memory.

Resource Management

PostScript Level 2 enables quick storage and retrieval of resources (e.g., fonts, forms, patterns, font encoding vectors, and CIE-based color-rendering dictionaries). A resource is a collection of named objects that either reside in VM or can be located and brought into VM on demand. There are separate categories of resources with independent name spaces.

Printer-specific features

The "setpagedevice" operator provides a device-independent framework for specifying the requirements of a page and for controlling both standard features (e.g., number of copies) and optional device features (e.g., duplex printing, multiple paper trays).

PostScript Level 2 Operators

The following Level 2 operators, along with the Level 1 operators documented in the first edition of the PostScript Language Reference Manual, are present the Level 2 implementation of the PostScript language.

```
<<
>>
arct
colorimage
cshow
currentblackgeneration
currentcacheparams
currentcmykcolor
currentcolor
currentcolorrendering
currentcolorscreen
currentcolorspace
currentcolortransfer
currentdevparams
currentglobal
currentgstate
currenthalftone
currentobjectformat
currentoverprint
currentpacking
currentpagedevice
currentshared
currentstrokeadjust
currentsystemparams
currentundercolorremoval
currentuserparams
defineresource
defineuserobject
deletefile
execform
execuserobject
filenameforall
fileposition
filter
findencoding
findresource
gcheck
globaldict
GlobalFontDirectory
glyphshow
gstate
ineofill
infill
instroke
inueofill
inufill
inustroke
ISOLatin1Encoding
languagelevel
makepattern
packedarray
printobject
product
realtime
rectclip
rectfill
rectstroke
renamefile
resourceforall
resourcestatus
revision
rootfont
scheck
selectfont
serialnumber
setbbox
setblackgeneration
setcachedevice2
setcacheparams
setcmykcolor
setcolor
setcolorrendering
setcolorscreen
setcolorspace
```

```
setcolortransfer
setdevparams
setfileposition
setglobal
setgstate
sethalftone
setobjectformat
setoverprint
setpacking
setpagedevice
setpattern
setshared
setstrokeadjust
setsystemparams
setucacheparams
setundercolorremoval
setuserparams
setvmthreshold
shareddict
SharedFontDirectory
startjob
uappend
ucache
ucachestatus
ueofill
ufill
undef
undefinefont
undefineresource
undefineuserobject
upath
UserObjects
ustroke
ustrokepath
vmreclaim
writeobject
xshow
xyshow
yshow
```

Converting PostScript Files to EPS Graphics

To convert a PostScript file to an EPS graphic, you must open it in a text editor and add lines that identify it as an EPS graphic and specify the dimensions, or bounding box, of the image contained in the file. Adding these lines does not guarantee the file will conform to the EPSF specification, but it may enable you to import a PostScript file into an application when no other options are available.

To convert a PostScript file to an EPS graphic using a text editor:

1. Using any PostScript downloading utility, download the original PostScript file to a PostScript printer to ensure it prints as expected.
2. Draw a box around the printed image that includes the entire image, with a minimum of white space. This box represents your bounding box.
3. Measure distance "a" from the lower-left corner of the bounding box to the left edge of the paper. Note measurement "a" in points. (To calculate points: 1 inch=72 points, and 1 pica=12 points.)
4. Measure distance "b" from the lower-left corner of the bounding box to the bottom edge of the paper. Note measurement "b" in points.
5. Measure distance "c" from the upper-right corner of the bounding box to the left edge of the paper. Note measurement "c" in points.
6. Measure distance "d" from the upper-right corner of the bounding box to the bottom edge of the paper. Note measurement "d" in points.
7. Open the PostScript file in a word processing application. The lines at the top of the file are the header. The subsequent lines are the PostScript description of the image.
8. Edit your PostScript file so that it begins with the following lines:
   ```
   %!PS-Adobe-2.0 EPSF-1.2
   %%Creator: name
   %%CreationDate: date
   %%Title: filename
   %%BoundingBox: a b c d
   %%EndComments
   ```
   where "name" is your name or initials, "date" is today's date in any format (e.g., 9/18/57 or September 18, 1957), "filename" is the name of the PostScript file, and "a," "b," "c," and "d" are the measurements you noted in steps 3 - 6.

   NOTE: Do not insert blank lines between the lines of the header.
9. Save the file in text-only format.

   NOTE: EPS files do not automatically include a screen preview. If you import an EPS file that doesn't contain a screen preview into an application, the application displays a gray box. Inside the gray box are the title, creator, and creation date of the graphic, if those comments are found inside the EPS file. Saving an EPS file that contains a screen image in text-only (ASCII) format will eliminate the screen preview.

Adding Custom Paper Sizes to a Custom Printer File Using a Text Editor

Creating a custom printer file to supplement a PPD file enables you to customize the printer information (e.g., resident fonts, paper sizes, virtual memory) your printer's PPD file contains. Most sheet-fed, desktop laser printers (e.g., Apple LaserWriter II NTX) do not support custom paper sizes. As a result, the PPDShell.ps PostScript routine and the Update PPD Addition or utility are unable to add custom paper size information to a custom printer file when they query these printing devices. Printing devices that support variable paper sizes (e.g., imagesetters) support custom paper size information and include the "*VariablePaperSize: True" line in their PPD file.

The following example creates a custom paper size named "MyCustomPage" with dimensions of 3" x 4.5". Not all PPD files include the "*PageRegion" keyword as the "*PageSize" keyword can function as both the "*PageSize" and "*PageRegion" keywords. The "*PageRegion" keyword specifies input options, which are contained in the "*PageSize" keyword.

To add a new custom paper size to a custom printer file using a text editor:

1. Open the custom printer file in a text editor that can save in text-only format (e.g., Microsoft Word, TeachText, MS-DOS Editor).
   NOTE: Some text editors (e.g., Microsoft Write, Notepad) add invisible characters (e.g., end-of-file, line feed) to the file that prevent applications or printer drivers from parsing, or reading, the PPD file.
2. In the section containing the "*PageSize" keywords, add a custom paper size after the last "*PageSize" line using the following syntax:
   For Normal orientation (1):
   ```
   *PageSize MyCustomPage: "216 324 1
     statusdict begin setpage end"
   ```
   where:
   "MyCustomPage" represents the name of your page, with no spaces.
   "216" is the small page dimension in points (72 points = 1 inch).
   "324" is the large page dimension in points.
   For Transverse orientation (0):
   ```
   *PageSize MyCustomPage.Transverse: "324 216
     0 statusdict begin setpage end"
   ```
   where:
   "MyCustomPage.Transverse" represents the name of your page, with no spaces.
   "324" is the large page dimension in points.
   "216" is the small page dimension in points.
   NOTE: When adding large paper sizes, low memory at the printer causes a failed print job, cropped print job, or a PostScript error. The total width plus margin of the paper size must be less than or equal to the imageable width of the imagesetter.
3. In the section containing the "*PageRegion" keywords, add a line for the custom paper size after the last "*PageRegion" line using the following syntax:
   For Normal orientation (1):
   ```
   *PageRegion MyCustomPage: "216 324 1
     statusdict begin setpage end"
   ```
   For Transverse orientation (0):
   ```
   *PageRegion MyCustomPage.Transverse: "324
     216 0 statusdict begin setpage end"
   ```
4. In the section containing the "*ImageableArea" keywords, add a line for the custom paper size after the last "*ImageableArea" line using the following syntax:
   ```
   *ImageableArea MyCustomPage: "0 0 216 324"
   ```
   where "0 0 324 216" sets the bounding box of the imageable area for the page size.
5. Locate the "*PaperDimension" keywords, add a line for the custom paper size after the last "*PaperDimension" line using the following syntax:
   For Normal orientation (1):
   ```
   *PaperDimension MyCustomPage: "216 324"
   ```
   For Transverse orientation (0):
   ```
   *PaperDimension MyCustomPage: "324 216"
   ```
6. Save the custom printer file in text-only format in the Printer Descriptions folder (Macintosh) or in the PPD4 subdirectory (Windows).

Creating a Minimum Custom Printer File Using a Text Editor

PostScript Printer Description (PPD) files, provided by the printer manufacturer, describe a printer's standard configuration. To provide more detailed information to your applications about your printer (e.g., custom page sizes, linescreen and resolution combinations), supplement the PPD file by creating a custom printer file.

Information in the custom printer file preceding the "*Include" line overrides the same information in the PPD file. The actual file name of the custom printer file is optional. The line *Include: "PPD NAME HERE" specifies which PPD file the custom printer file will supplement.

To generate a basic custom printer file using a word processor or text editor:

1. Open a new file in a text editor that can save in text-only format (e.g., Microsoft Word, TeachText, MS-DOS Editor).
   NOTE: Some text editors (e.g., Microsoft Write, Notepad) add invisible characters (e.g., end-of-file, line feed) to the file that prevent the PPD file from being parsed.
2. Type the following lines:
   ```
   *PPD-Adobe: "4.0"
   *Include: "PPD NAME HERE"
   *% End of Aldus PPD local customization file.
   ```
3. In the custom printer file, replace "PPD NAME HERE" after the "*Include:" line with the corresponding PPD file's name, ensuring the straight quotes are not deleted around the PPD file's name. For example:
   ```
   *Include: "LaserWriter II NTX v51.8"
   ```
4. Add custom page sizes, printer resident fonts, and custom line screen information between the *PPD-Adobe: "4.0" and *Include: lines.
5. Save the file as text-only (ASCII) in the Printer Descriptions folder in the Extensions folder (Macintosh) or in the Aldus\Usenglsh\Ppd4 subdirectory (Windows).

Updating PPD Files to Reflect Available Virtual Memory Using a Text Editor

Custom printer files supplement PPD files, enabling you to customize printer information for a particular printer (e.g., resident fonts, paper sizes, virtual memory). The "*FreeVM" line in the selected PPD or custom printer file indicates the amount of virtual memory (VM) in bytes available at the printer. From available VM specified in the PPD file, applications that read PPD files determine how much VM is needed to rasterize the page, and allocate the remaining VM for downloadable fonts. When a document contains complex graphics or several fonts that must download, and the amount of available VM in the target printer is low, low printer memory symptoms (e.g., long print times, "VMerror" and "limitcheck" PostScript errors, font substitution) or excessive print spooling times occurs.

To modify a custom printer file to reflect available VM of a printer using a text editor:

1. Determine the amount of available VM the printer has. For instructions, see below.
2. Open the custom printer file in a text editor that can save in text-only format (e.g., Microsoft Word, TeachText, MS-DOS Editor).
   NOTE: Some text editors (e.g., Microsoft Write, Notepad) add invisible characters (e.g., end-of-file, line feed) to the file that prevent applications and printer drivers from parsing the PPD file.
3. Find or add the "*FreeVM" line before the "*Include line." For example:
   ```
   *FreeVM: "x" (where "x" is the value of
     virtual memory in bytes)
   ```
4. Select the VM value between the quotes and then change the value to reflect the actual value of FreeVM in bytes.
5. Save the custom printer file in text-only format in the Printer Descriptions folder (Macintosh) or in the Aldus\Usenglsh\Ppd4 subdirectory (Windows).

Options for Determining the Available Virtual Memory (VM) at the Printer:

A. Use the Apple LaserWriter 8.x printer driver's or the Adobe PSPrinter 8.x printer driver's Printer Info feature.
B. Download a PostScript routine that prints the value of virtual memory in bytes.
C. Create a custom printer file using the Update PPD Addition or PPDShell.ps PostScript routine file.

A. To determine the available VM using the LaserWriter 8.x printer driver's or the PSPrinter 8.x driver's Printer Info feature:
   1. Open the Chooser and select the LaserWriter 8.x or PSPrinter 8.x printer driver.
   2. In the Chooser, select the printer, then click Setup.
   3. Click Printer Info. If Printer Info is dimmed, click More Choices and then Printer Info.
   4. Click Update Info, then scroll through the Printer Information list to locate the Total Memory Available and note the value.
   5. Multiply the Total Memory Available number by 1,048,576 to convert from megabytes to bytes. The value in bytes is the available virtual memory value used in the *FreeVM line in the custom printer file.

B. To download a PostScript routine that prints the value of virtual memory in bytes:

   Print the VM value by downloading a PostScript routine to query the printer:
   1. Open a new file in a text editor that can save as text-only (e.g., Microsoft Word, TeachText, MS-DOS Editor).
   2. Type the following text exactly as shown to print the amount of available VM:
      ```
      %!PS
      % Prints the FreeVM value
      /Courier-Bold findfont 24 scalefont
        setfont
      vmstatus
      100 500 moveto
      (*FreeVM: ) show
      16 string cvs show
      pop pop
      showpage
      ```
   3. Save this file in text-only format with the name "vmstatus.ps."
   4. Using a PostScript downloading utility (e.g., Adobe Font Downloader version 5.04, Apple LaserWriter 8.0 Utility), download the vmstatus.ps file to the printer.
   5. The printer prints the value of the printer's available virtual memory in bytes. This is the available virtual memory value used in the *FreeVM line in the custom printer file.

OR: Create a log file (i.e., text file) with the available VM by downloading a PostScript utility to query the printer:
   1. Open a new file in a text editor that can save as text-only (e.g., Microsoft Word, TeachText, MS-DOS Editor).
   2. Type the following text exactly as shown to save the amount of available VM in a log file:
      ```
      %!PS
      % Returns FreeVM value in a log file
      vmstatus
      (*FreeVM: ) = =
      pop popf
      ```
   3. Save this file in text-only format with the name "vmstatus.ps."
   4. Using a PostScript downloading utility (e.g., Apple LaserWriter 8.0 Utility version 7.4.1 or later), download the vmstatus.ps file to the printer.
   5. The printer prints the value of the printer's available virtual memory in bytes. This is the available virtual memory value used in the *FreeVM line in the custom printer file.
      NOTE: The FreeVM value in the log file may yield some special characters in the number (e.g., *FreeVM: L234454). Delete these special characters before copying the FreeVM value (e.g., *FreeVM: 234454).

C. Both the Update PPD Addition and the PPDShell.ps PostScript routine file included with PageMaker 5.0x create a custom printer file that includes the available virtual memory for the targeted printer. You can copy and paste the available virtual memory value in the generated custom printer file into other custom printer files.

Unexpected Results

MAC OS / WINDOWS / UNIX

PostScript Error Troubleshooting Guide

PostScript errors are caused by miscommunication between a printer and computer: either the PostScript code is not understood by the interpreter at the printer, or it exceeds one or more of the limits built into the PostScript language. Printing to a printer that is low on memory, for example, can give unpredictable results or generate a PostScript error.

There are two parts to a PostScript error: the error and the offending command.

```
%%[Error: limitcheck; OffendingCommand:
  image ]%%
```

The error (e.g., limitcheck) provides information as to what type of PostScript error occurred. The offending command (e.g., image) notes what was being processed at the time the error occurred, and may at times appear to be merely a string of nonsense characters. While it can be helpful to know the meaning of the error or offending command, many PostScript error issues can be resolved without this information.

PostScript errors don't display or print automatically—you need to set up your computer to do so. If the display or printing of PostScript errors is disabled on your computer when a PostScript error occurs, your printer may appear to process data but then stop without printing anything. To view PostScript errors on the Macintosh, disable the Background Printing option in the Chooser. To print PostScript errors in Windows, set up your printer driver to do so.

To print PostScript errors in Windows 95:

1. Choose Start > Settings > Printers.
2. Right-click on your target printer, then select Properties from the pop-up menu.
3. In your printer's Properties dialog box, click the PostScript tab.
4. Select the Print PostScript Error Information option, then click OK.

To print PostScript errors in Windows 3.1x:

1. In Program Manager, open the Control Panel in the Main group.
2. Double-click on the Printers icon.
3. Select your target printer from the list of installed printers.
5. Click Setup, then click Options, then click Advanced.
6. In the Advanced Options dialog box, select the Print PostScript Error Information option.
7. Click OK to close the remaining dialog boxes.

Some applications, such as Adobe PageMaker, have the ability to download their own error handlers. Refer to your product user manual to verify whether your application has this functionality. (In Adobe PageMaker, select the Include PostScript Error Handler option in the Print Options dialog box to download PageMaker's error handler.) Error handler utilities can also be used with all applications.

The information that follows is divided into four sections: common causes of PostScript errors, techniques for isolating the cause of an error, common PostScript errors with their likely causes, and common Offending Commands with their likely causes. While you may be able to interpret an error message and quickly pinpoint the source of a problem, you will most likely need to use troubleshooting techniques as well.

COMMON CAUSES OF POSTSCRIPT ERRORS

- Element on the page (text, or imported graphics such as EPS, PICT, or WMF)
- Data corruption
- Damaged font
- Complexity (exceeds printers available memory)
- Communication error (devices on other ports, loose wires, system level issues, problems with printer hardware)
- Damaged printer driver
- Printing to a PostScript emulator (printer using a non-Adobe licensed version of PostScript)

ISOLATING POSTSCRIPT ERRORS

To isolate a PostScript error, first determine when it occurs. Do you receive the error:

- When printing from just this application on this computer, or from all applications on this computer?

  If all applications generate the same error or exhibit problematic behavior, you need to isolate which piece of your system is not working properly. These PostScript errors are typically communication errors, so potential causes include damaged fonts, damaged system files, a damaged printer driver, network spooling issues, or problems with your printer hardware. Make sure that your printer is turned on and check all cable connections. Contact your printer manufacturer or system software support for assistance in isolating the problem.
- When printing a particular file created in this application, or when printing any file created in the same application?

  Since PostScript errors can be related to file complexity, individual elements on a page, or even a SCSI port connection (e.g., for a scanner or external hard drive), you will want to know just how widespread the problem is. If every file created in this application generates a PostScript error when printed, you may need to reinstall the application. It's possible that your printer is using a PostScript emulator (e.g., Pacific Page cartridge, Phoenix PostScript Interpreter) that handles

PostScript generated by older or simpler applications, or by older printer drivers that cannot process data from updated or more demanding software and drivers. If you know that your printer is a PostScript emulator, or it's simply an older printer, try printing to a device that uses a current version of Adobe licensed PostScript (e.g., Apple LaserWriter II NTX, HP LaserJet 4 PostScript printer). If you're not certain whether you have a PostScript emulator or your printer is capable of supporting newer versions of PostScript, contact your printer manufacturer.

It is also possible that you are using a particular font or graphic in all of the files receiving a PostScript error. As a test, try creating a new file, drawing a simple box or line on the page and printing it. If your test file prints, you'll want to determine which element (text or graphic) common to your files is causing the error. You may need to update or reinstall one or more of your fonts. If a specific graphic or all graphics from a particular application seem to generate the error, you may need to ensure the graphic isn't damaged or too complex, use a different graphic format, or inquire about updates to either application. Contact technical support for your product if you need this kind of information.

- When printing all pages or just one?

If you can isolate the problem to one or several files, you may also find that the problem occurs only when printing specific pages. To troubleshoot problems occurring when printing multiple pages, look for common elements. Perhaps you are using the same element (graphic or text) on more than one page. Items like a company logo or corporate font are suspect if they appear on problematic pages.

Whether the error is specific to one page in a single file, or whether it occurs on several pages of different files, use the following techniques to isolate the problem. Open a copy of your file and try printing half of the elements on the page. If you still receive an error, try printing the other half of the page. Try deleting elements from the page until you are able to print. No output, even when all elements have been removed, indicates the file itself is probably damaged. To ensure the file is not damaged, copy and paste all of the elements from this file into a new one, save it with a different name, and print. If you are able to print by reducing the information on your page, you most likely have an element on the page that contains some bad information, or your file is simply too complex for your printer's capabilities.

In the process of deleting elements from the page, you may already have identified which item is causing the error. If not, try printing text and drawn elements but no imported graphics. Some applications, such as Adobe PageMaker, give you the option to proof print a file (i.e., print all elements on a page except imported graphics). Check your application's user manual to see if this option is available. An imported graphic can cause a PostScript error if it contains damaged or poorly written information, or if it is extremely complex (e.g., contains custom fills, complex type effects, nested objects, or many points on a path). It's possible to create a graphic or file of such complexity that even a high-end printing device cannot process the data required to output it. Also, graphic formats are updated periodically, so an EPS file created from an application purchased four years ago isn't based on the same standard as an EPS file created in a newer application.

Once you've identified which graphic seems to generate the error, try re-importing it into your file. If this does not work, try re-exporting it from the source application in the same or a different format, and then re-importing it. Check whether the graphic prints from your application if it is the only element in a new file. It may be complex enough that combining it with other elements on a page is too much for your printer. A graphic that won't print as the only element in a new file is damaged. A graphic that prints, but not in combination with other elements, is generating errors related to printer memory.

You may also find that the error can be isolated to a particular piece of text on the page, or to any text assigned a specific font. Try retyping the text you've identified as the source of problems. If you suspect a font rather than specific text, assign a different font for all occurrences of the suspicious font. Your original font may be damaged, or may not meet industry standards for font specifications.

- When printing complex files, or files containing complex elements?

If this is the case, you need to consider simplifying your file. Some applications, such as Adobe PageMaker, are not designed to create complex elements, but do allow you to import such elements from other sources. Applications like Adobe Illustrator or Adobe Photoshop enable you to create complex files without importing any data. To simplify a file in an application like PageMaker, you may need to use fewer imported items or fewer fonts that must be downloaded to your printer. If your application can generate complex elements, you may need to user fewer points on a path, reduce the number of items that have been copied or cloned multiple times, or simplify customized fills or gradients. Errors related to complex text effects (e.g., text that has been skewed, rotated, or kerned) may be eliminated by converting the text information to outlines or paths. EPS files can often be identified as the source of a PostScript error because they may contain complex information.

The information included in this publication is by no means an exhaustive reference for understanding and troubleshooting PostScript issues. You will be able to handle many of your own PostScript printing problems by using these techniques, and in the case of exceptionally difficult issues, you will be much better prepared to provide a technician with information needed to resolve your issue quickly.

Complexity Errors

error	description	likely cause	solution
dictfull	Related to a PostScript dictionary being mismanaged, too full, or damaged.	-Imported graphic -Damaged font -Data corruption	Isolate problem element.
fatal system error at [number string]	Indicates the printer is completely out of memory, while the number following the error is a memory location in the printer.	-The printer memory requirements of the file are too high for the current memory state of the printer.	Simplify your publication, restart your printer.
limitcheck	A PostScript implementation limit has been exceeded.	-Printer memory requirements of file, or a limit as defined in PostScript has been reached.	Check offending command
VMerror	Out of printer memory. The offending command is where processing stopped stopped when memory ran out. An attempt was made to create a new composite object (string, array, or dictionary) that would exhaust Virtual Memory resources.	Printer memory requirements of file.	Simplify page, or modify PPD file if applicable.

Communication Errors

error	description	likely cause	solution
ioerror	Bad data transmission, cannot read or write data.	-Communication error -Binary image data (TIFF, EPS, or DCS graphics) -Disk errors -Damaged Printer Driver	Try printing from a different application, reinstall printer driver, omit graphic data.
timeout	A time limit has been exceeded (e.g., communication limit between the computer and printer).	-Large imported graphics -Complex fill patterns -Complex type effects -Network problems -Nested grouped elements	Isolate element, increase timeout settings.

postscript code errors

error	description	likely cause	solution
invalidrestore	Improper attempt to restore.	-Imported graphic -Data corruption	Isolate element.
stackoverflow, stackunderflow	There are either too many objects (values or commands) on one of the PostScript stacks (overflow) or an object is missing (underflow).	-An offending element -Imported graphic -Memory problem -Data corruption -Communication error	Isolate element, simplify page.
typecheck	An object or value does not match PostScript expectations Typecheck does not necessarily imply problems with text.	-An offending element -Imported graphic -Data corruption	Isolate element, copy and paste data to new file.
undefined	A keyword, value, or object is encountered that cannot be defined.	-A printer prep file or PostScript dictionary is missing -Imported graphic -Damaged font -Data corruption -Communication error -Missing PostScript header information	Isolate element, try printing from a different application, copy and paste data to a new file, if converted from a previous version, try printing again from that version.

Offending Commands Related to Complexity

Command	Likely Cause
charpath	Complex text or text effects.
clip, eoclip	Graduated or radial fills, complex or compound paths, text effects, masks.
curveto	Complex curve paths.
fill, eofill	Complex or compound paths.
lineto, moveto	Paths composed of many points (may include converted PICT graphics).
makefont	Text effects (includes scaled, skewed, rotated, or reflected text).
stroke	Complex paths, paths with complex fills and outline strokes, or converted PICT graphic.
	note: A complex path can be described as one that contains many points; a path may be too complex for the current flatness settings of an element in your illustration application. Refer to your user manual for more information about flatness settings.

Offending Commands Related to Printer Memory

Command	Likely Cause
def	Printer memory, printer fonts, or imported graphics.
dict	Printer memory, printer fonts (see errors related to system components).
framedevice	Printer memory, printing from an older application, using an outdated printer driver (PostScript level 1 only).
index	Printer memory, imported graphics.

Offending Commands Related to One or More Elements on a Page

Command	Likely Cause
ashow, widthshow	Offset text (e.g., kerned text, super or subscripted text, custom letter or word spacing)
awidthshow	or damaged font.
colorimage	Color bitmap images.
currentpoint	Imported graphic, elements created in application.
def	Imported graphic (may also be related to printer fonts or printer memory).
exch	Imported graphic (may also be related to a damaged font).
get	Imported graphic.
image	Bitmap or paint-type images.
imagemask	1-bit or paint-type bitmap image, bitmap fonts.
index	Imported graphic (may also be related to low printer memory).
itransform	Very small element.
kshow	Kerned text, including pair kerning.
nostringval	An offending element, perhaps an imported graphic (may also be related to a damaged font).
packedarray	Imported graphics (may also be related to data corruption, or printing to a PostScript emulator).
put	Custom fills (may also be related to a damaged font).
setdash	Custom PostScript line, imported graphic with custom lines.
setgray	Tints, imported EPS files, fonts created with old versions of Fontographer.
setlinecap	Custom PostScript line, imported graphic with custom line.
setlinejoin	Custom PostScript line, imported graphic with custom line.
show	Text (includes text in an imported EPS graphic).
stringwidth	Text (includes text in an imported EPS graphic).
character string	Imported image file (damaged, very high resolution, poorly written), data corruption.

Offending Commands Related to Damaged System Components

def	Printer fonts (also imported graphics, printer memory).
dict	Printer fonts (also printer memory).
exch	Damaged font (also imported graphics).
flxproc	Damaged font.
nostringval	Damaged font (also specific element on the page).
put	Damaged font (also related to custom fills in graphic elements).
setpageparams	Page or paper size selected in application exceeds the imageable area defined in the PPD for this printer. PPD may have been incorrectly edited.

Printer Inaccuracy General Information

When PostScript code contains accurate numbers, inaccurate output from a PostScript printing device is due to the printing device itself. It is up to the printer to control paper feed and paper stretch for accurate output. When paper or film stretches, or other printer adjustments are needed, output will vary from specified.

A test file containing PostScript code describing one easily measured element (e.g., 4-by-4" square), can be downloaded to check printer accuracy and eliminate software as a cause of inaccuracy.

The following PostScript file creates a 4-by-4" box, which you can downloaded directly a printer several times. If the result is slightly, but consistently off, the printer, not the software, is the source of the inaccuracy. Because of paper stretch, this inaccuracy is usually in length, rather than width.

If you print the same PostScript box to another printer, the result will be consistent on that printer, but may be different from the output on another printer.

To create a PostScript file describing a 4-by-4" square:

1. In a word processing program that can save in text-only (e.g., Microsoft Word, TeachText) type the following code:

```
%% 4 inch black box with no stroke
144 288 moveto
0 288 rlineto
288 0 rlineto
0 -288 rlineto
closepath
fill
showpage
```

2. Save as text-only with the name "4 inch box.ps."
3. Download the 4 inch box.ps file to the printer using a downloading utility (e.g., Adobe's Font Downloader, Apple's LaserWriter Font Utility).

Error Opening or Separating a DCS File with a Name Beginning in a Space

ISSUE

An error occurs when you open or print a DCS file whose name begins with a space character.

SYMPTOMS

When opening a DCS file, Adobe Photoshop 2.5.1 returns the error, "Could not open a DCS color plate because File not found."

When separating a linked DCS file, PageMaker 5.0x returns the error, "Some DCS files could not be found. Check main DCS link and re-link if necessary. Make sure DCS files are kept in same folder as the main file. 7816:5827."

When separating a linked DCS file, QuarkXPress 3.3 returns the error, "Couldn't find the DCS plate '[file name.C]' for '[file name]' OK to print missing plates in low resolution?"

SOLUTIONS

Remove the space character from the beginning of each of the DCS separation files. For example, change " filename.C" to "filename.C."

OR: Open and print the DCS file from Photoshop 3.0.

ADDITIONAL INFORMATION

Desktop Color Separation (DCS) files consist of five files: a main composite file and four process separation files (e.g., "filename.C," "filename.M," "filename.Y," and "filename.K"). When a DCS file is opened or separated, information in the main file is used to link to each of the separation files. Some applications (e.g., Photoshop 2.5.1, Page-Maker 5.0x, QuarkXPress) cannot link to DCS separation files when any of their filenames begin with the space character. For example, when you open a DCS main file that links to separation files whose names begin with a space (e.g.," filename.C") in Photoshop 2.5.1, Photoshop returns the message, "Could not open a DCS color plate file because File not found."

PostScript Error "Undefined; OffendingCommand: featurecleanup" When Printing

ISSUE

When you print a document using the LaserWriter 8.1.1 printer driver, the PostScript error, "Undefined; Offending-Command: featurecleanup" appears.

SYMPTOMS

In the LaserWriter 8.1.1 printer driver, the printer is set up with a PPD (PostScript Printer Description) file that contains the "*JobPatchFile:" or "*PatchFile:" keyword.

The PPD file selected in the application's print dialog box (except PageMaker 5.0x's) contains the "*JobPatchFile:" or "*PatchFile:" keyword.

You are printing from PageMaker 5.0x with Background Printing enabled.

You are printing a PageMaker 5.0x publication containing a PICT, CGM, WMF, DXF, or OLE PICT graphic.

SOLUTIONS

If you're printing from PageMaker 5.0x, turn off Background Printing in the Chooser.

OR: Make sure an imported graphic is not causing the error by printing the file or page without any imported graphics (e.g., select the Proof option). After isolating an offending graphic, resave the graphic and replace.

OR: If you're printing from an application other than PageMaker 5.0x, do one or more of the following:

A. In the Chooser, select the LaserWriter 8.1.1 printer driver, select your printer and click Setup, click the Select PPD option, then change the printer's associated PPD file to one that doesn't contain the *JobPatchFile or *PatchFile keyword.

B. In the printing application, select a PPD file that doesn't contain the *JobPatchFile or *PatchFile keyword.
OR: Print using the LaserWriter 8.0 or earlier printer driver.

ADDITIONAL INFORMATION
When you print using a PPD file that contains a *JobPatchFile or *PatchFile keyword, the "featurecleanup" command is needed to handle the *JobPatchFile or *PatchFile keyword. The LaserWriter 8.1.1 driver uses the "featurecleanup" command before it is defined in PostScript, resulting in the PostScript error "undefined; OffendingCommand: featurecleanup."

PPD files modified to prevent TIFF images from printing too dark or light from PageMaker 5.0, the Apple LaserWriter PPD file included with PageMaker 5.0, and other PPD files (e.g., AccelaWriter 8000 [PM50] and AccelaWriter 4000 [PM50]) contain the a *JobPatchFile or *PatchFile keyword.

If you choose File > Print in PageMaker without pressing the Option key, PageMaker generates the PostScript code for the publication itself, with the exception of PostScript fonts and PICT graphics. PageMaker 5.0x uses the LaserWriter 8.x printer driver to convert PICT files (including converted CGM, WMF, DXF or OLE PICT graphics) to EPS graphics. PageMaker uses the LaserWriter printer driver to generate the PostScript code for the entire publication you hold down the Option key while choosing File > Print.

If you print from PageMaker 5.0x with Background Printing enabled, the PPD file associated with the printer specified in the LaserWriter 8.1.1 printer driver is read, causing the "undefined; OffendingCommand: featurecleanup" PostScript error when the associated PPD file contains either the *JobPatchFile or *PatchFile keyword.

Low Line Screens Not Printing as Specified

ISSUE
When you print a document to a PostScript device, it prints at a higher line screen frequency than the low value you specified.

SOLUTIONS
Disable screening or calibration software at the imagesetter's RIP (raster image processor).
OR: Print to another device capable of printing the desired line screen value.

ADDITIONAL INFORMATION
The lowest line screen (lpi) value that a printer can image varies from printer to printer. Screening or calibration software (e.g., Agfa Balanced Screens, HQS screens) may prevent some custom screen frequencies from printing, because it optimizes screen and angle rulings for the imagesetter.

You can determine the lowest line screen value possible for your printer by downloading a PostScript file to it that draws a tinted box set to 1 line per inch (lpi). To create the file:

1. Create a new file in a text editor that can save in text-only format (e.g., TeachText, Notepad) 2. Type the following text exactly as shown:

```
gsave
1  %% This number is the screen frequency
45  %% This number is the screen angle
{180 mul cos exch 180 mul cos add 2 div}  %%
  This is the spot function
setscreen
%% 4 inch box, 20% fill, 1 pt. black stoke
144 288 moveto
0 288 rlineto
288 0 rlineto
0 -288 rlineto
closepath
gsave
.8 setgray
fill
grestore
stroke
grestore
showpage
```

2. Name the file "20box.ps" and save it in text-only format.
3. Disable all calibration and screening software at the imagesetter.
4. Download the PostScript file to the printer.
5. Measure the line screen value in the 4-inch box. This is the lowest lpi value your printer can produce.

General Information

MAC OS / WINDOWS / UNIX

PostScript Printer Memory General Information

PostScript printer memory (RAM) is divided into sections, which are used in the following order:

1. Frame buffer (builds the page with pixels).
2. Prep files (dictionaries used by the printer to define PostScript).
3. Fonts manually downloaded using a downloader utility.
4. PostScript information describing each print job.
5. Fonts downloaded to RAM during printing.

The majority of PostScript printer memory is dedicated to the frame buffer to build the page. The higher the resolution and the larger the page, the more memory the frame buffer requires. For example, when you print a letter-size page to a standard Apple LaserWriter NTX printer at 300 dpi, there is 150K to 300K of available memory for prep files, fonts downloaded to memory, and the PostScript file you're trying to print. Although imagesetters come with more memory than laser printers, they require more to create more pixels to print high resolution.

Troubleshooting PostScript Errors

PostScript errors are caused by PostScript code that is not understood by the printer's PostScript interpreter, or PostScript code that exceeds one or more of the limits built into the PostScript page description language. PostScript error messages include a PostScript error type, which is one of a relatively limited number of different types, and an offending command, which can be any combination of ASCII characters. PostScript errors usually look like:

```
%%[Error: <type>; OffendingCommand: <offending command> ]%%
```

For example, the PostScript error %%[Error: dictfull; OffendingCommand: def]%% contains the PostScript error type "dictfull" and the offending command "def." The error type indicates what kind of problem the PostScript interpreter had; the offending command is the last command it tried to process, and is sometimes, but not always, the command that caused the problem.

Some PostScript errors will point you right to the cause of the problem, and some will get you looking in the right direction. If your printer appears to process data but then stops without printing anything, it may have encountered a PostScript error. If you don't get the PostScript error readout, you can coax one from your printer in any of these ways:

In Windows 95:

1. Choose Start > Settings > Printers.
2. Right-click on your target printer, then select Properties from the pop-up menu.
3. In your printer's Properties dialog box, click the PostScript tab.
4. Select the Print PostScript Error Information option, then click OK.

In Windows 3.1x:

1. In Program Manager, open the Control Panel in the Main group.
2. Double-click on the Printers icon.
3. Select your target printer from the list of installed printers.
5. Click Setup, then click Options, then click Advanced.
6. In the Advanced Options dialog box, select the Print PostScript Error Information option.
7. Click OK to close the remaining dialog boxes.

On the Macintosh:

- Select either Summarize on Screen or Print Detailed Report in the PostScript Error pop-up menu in the Apple LaserWriter 8.x or Adobe PSPrinter 8.x Print Options dialog box.
- Disable print spoolers, including Background Printing. To disable Background Printing, in the Chooser, select your printer driver and then select Off for the Background Printing option.

In Windows or on the Macintosh:

Use an error handler utility designed to work with multiple applications or use an error handler supplied by your application, if available. For example, Adobe PageMaker offers the Include PostScript Error Handler option in the Print Options dialog box.

UNDERSTANDING POSTSCRIPT ERRORS

To begin troubleshooting your printing problem, use the PostScript Error Types and the PostScript Offending Command sections below. The PostScript Error Types section lists common error types under a general cause, and the PostScript Offending Command section lists common offending commands under what most likely caused the error.

For example, to use these sections after you receive the PostScript error, %%[Error: limitcheck; OffendingCommand: image]%%, locate the "limitcheck" type and "image" offending command in the sections. The PostScript Error Types section lists "limitcheck" under "Exceeds printer's memory or PostScript language limit." The PostScript Offending Command section lists the "image" offending command under "bitmap data." By putting these two together, you have a probable cause—a bitmap image exceeds the printer's available memory (or other PostScript language limit). In such a case you'd probably need to simplify the bitmap graphic by resampling or rescanning it at a lower resolution, or by printing to a printer that has more available memory.

Some PostScript errors won't help you pinpoint a likely cause. For example, if you receive the PostScript error, %%[Error: undefined; OffendingCommand: (random characters)]%%, the PostScript Error Types section lists "undefined" under "Errors that indicate unintelligible PostScript code" and the PostScript Offending Command section lists "[random characters]" under "any element or file." In this case, you'll need to continue troubleshooting to isolate the cause of the problem.

POSTSCRIPT ERROR TYPES

Errors that indicate something exceeds the printer's memory or a PostScript-language limit:

```
dictfull
fatal system error at [various]
limitcheck
VMerror
Errors that indicate communication problems:
interrupt
ioerror (May also be caused by a disk
  problem, such as a bad sector, on the
  printer's hard disk.)
timeout
Errors that indicate unintelligible
  PostScript code:
dictstackoverflow
dictstackunderflow
execstackoverflow
handleerror
invalidaccess
```

```
invalidexit
invalidfileaccess
invalidfont
invalidrestore
nocurrentpoint
rangecheck
stackoverflow
stackunderflow
syntaxerror
typecheck
undefined
undefinedfilename
undefinedresult
unmatchedmark
unregistered
```

POSTSCRIPT OFFENDING COMMANDS

Offending commands associated with specific text or font element:

```
ashow
awidthshow
charpath
definefont
findfont
imagemask
kshow
makefont
selectfont
show
stringwidth
widthshow
```

Offending commands associated with specific masks (clipping paths):

```
clip
eoclip
```

Offending commands associated with fills and lines, often in imported object-oriented, or vector, graphics (EPS files or PICT graphics, for instance):

```
arc
arcto
currentpoint
curveto
eofill
fill
lineto
moveto
rcurveto
rlineto
setdash
setlinecap
setlinejoin
stroke
```

Offending commands associated with bitmap data:

colorimage

```
image
imagemask (Associated with 1-bit image
  bitmap graphics and bitmap fonts.)
```

Offending commands associated with any element or file:

```
array
def
dict
exch
get
index
itransform
nostringval
packedarray
put
restore
save
setgray
setpageparams
setscreen
[random characters]
```

TROUBLESHOOTING PRINTING PROBLEMS

While many PostScript error quickly pinpoint the source of a problem, you'll need to troubleshoot your printing problem if you don't receive an PostScript error message, or if the PostScript error doesn't limit the number of likely causes. To troubleshoot your printing problem, isolate when the problem occurs to determine if it is a system-level, application-specific, file-specific, or element-specific problem. After narrowing down when the problem occurs, eliminate likely causes until you solve the problem.

ISOLATING SYSTEM-LEVEL PRINTING PROBLEMS

Do you receive the error when you print from multiple applications? If the same problem occurs when you print from multiple applications, the cause is most likely a problem at the system level. System-level problems are commonly caused by damaged fonts, damaged system files, damaged printer drivers, insufficient hard disk space, network problems, or hardware problems.

Check for loose cables or faulty connections by securing loose cables by unplugging and replugging them. If there are any other devices that your print job needs to travel through (like a switch box), check their connections, too. Problems caused by severed connections have unambiguous symptoms: your printer won't receive data, so it won't do anything—none of its readouts will blink, and it certainly won't print anything. But when you have a loose connection, the symptoms of your problems might be more ambiguous: small jobs might print, but larger jobs won't, and on a Macintosh, the printer in your Chooser might appear and disappear intermittently.

Make sure you are using an up-to-date PostScript printer driver, or use the version of the PostScript printer driver required by your application. You also need plenty of free hard-disk space to print, especially when you print large documents. And for fast and efficient printing, make sure your free hard-disk space is unfragmented, especially on the disk your system uses to create temporary files, which is usually the disk that contains your operating system.

If your printer is an older PostScript printer or one that uses a PostScript emulator (e.g., Pacific Page cartridge, Phoenix PostScript Interpreter), it may not understand the newer PostScript code generated by your application or printer driver. To rule out this cause, try printing your file to a device that uses a more current or up-to-date version of Adobe licensed PostScript.

ISOLATING APPLICATION-SPECIFIC PROBLEMS

Do you receive the error when you print any file from a single application? You can easily determine if you only receive the error in a single application by creating a new test file that contains only a simple element, such as a rectangle or line. If this test file prints, continue troubleshooting for file-specific causes. If you receive a PostScript error when you print any file from the same application, rule out damaged application software as the cause by reinstalling the application, including its support files and preferences file.

ISOLATING FILE-SPECIFIC PROBLEMS

Do you receive the error when you print a specific file, or specific files, from a single application? If the error occurs when you print a specific file, the file may be damage, or it may contain a damaged element or an element that doesn't print because of another reason. Begin troubleshooting by checking your file's print settings against those of a file that does print.

To rule out file damage as the cause, copy the file's elements into a new file, save your file using the Save As command, delete elements you don't need to print, or run any built-in diagnostic routines your application offers. In PageMaker, for instance, you can repair certain file problems by using its Diagnostic Recompose feature: deselect all elements in the file, then choose Type > Elements while you hold down the Ctrl and Shift keys (Windows) or the Option and Shift keys (Macintosh). If, after you rule out file-specific causes, you still receive the error when you print the file, troubleshoot file-specific problems.

ISOLATING ELEMENT-SPECIFIC PROBLEMS

Do you receive the error when you print only a specific page or elements on a page? After you've ruled out a damaged file as the cause, the cause of your printing problem is most likely a damaged or incorrectly written element or font, or by an element or combination of elements on a page that requires more printer memory than is available. If you receive the error when you print a range of pages, look for common elements. If you can print all elements individually or in small groups, but not all at the same time, the combination of elements you are printing requires more printer memory than your printer has available.

To isolate the element, or elements, causing your problem, make a copy of your file and print groups of pages, and then one page at a time, until you've narrowed down the problem to a specific page or range of pages. After narrowing down which page or page range is causing the problem, isolate the element causing the problem by removing an element from the page and then printing. Continue until you can print the file without receiving the error. (You can also remove elements in groups to narrow down the problem faster. For example, remove half of the elements in your file and then print your file. If the error doesn't reoccur, print the other half of the elements.) Some applications, such as PageMaker, offer an option that enables you to print some elements but not others. For example, when you print from PageMaker by selecting the Proof Print option, PageMaker prints the text but not the graphics. Using this option, you can quickly determine if your problem is caused by an imported graphic or other element in your PageMaker publication.

If the element causing your problem is text or an element you've created in the application, recreate the element. For text elements, also try using a different font (e.g., reformat the text using a different kind of font or a printer-resident font). If your file prints when you use a different font, reinstall the original font to eliminate damaged font files as the cause.

If the element causing the problem is an imported graphic, first try reimporting the graphic. If the printing problem still occurs, open the graphic in the application in which it was created, resave it, ensure it prints from this application, then reimport the graphic. If you still can't print the imported graphic, try resaving it in a different format, exporting it from a different application, or simplifying it so that it requires less printer memory.

An imported graphic can cause a PostScript error if it contains damaged or incorrectly written information, or if it too complex for your printer (i.e., it requires more memory than your printer has available). To begin simplifying a file, use fewer imported graphics, use fewer fonts that must be downloaded to your printer, use fewer text effects (e.g., skewed or rotated text, type effects), delete elements you don't need, create paths using fewer points, or resample or rescan bitmap images at a lower resolution. Graphic formats such as EPS are updated periodically, so older applications may use an older standard that newer software or hardware may not understand.

Adobe PSPrinter®

Feature Techniques

WINDOWS

Adding Printers Using AdobePS 4.1 Setup Utility

The AdobePS 4.1 PostScript Printer Driver supports Windows 95, but does not support Windows 3.1x, Windows for Workgroups, or Windows NT.

To install printers with AdobePS 4.1:

1. Launch the AdobePS 4 Setup Utility by choosing Start > Programs > AdobePS4.
2. In the AdobePS 4 PostScript Printer Driver Setup dialog box, click Next.
3. When your printer is connected directly to your computer, select Local Printer, then click Next in the Printer Type dialog box.
   OR: When your printer is connected through a network, select Network Printer, then click Next in the Printer Type dialog box. In the Network Path dialog box, type the network path or queue name, or click Browse to locate the printer, then click Next.
4. In the Install PostScript Printer from PPD dialog box, install PPD files by doing one or more of the following:
   A. Locate the folder on your hard disk that contains PPD files (e.g., C:\PM6\RSRC\USENGLSH\PPD4), then select one or more PPD files by double-clicking the printer's name, or clicking the printer's name then clicking Next.
   B. To install PPD files included on the AdobePS 4.1 CD-ROM:
      1. In the Drives list, select the drive indicator for your CD-ROM drive.
      2. In the Directories list, open the PPDs folder located in the Drvrdisk folder in the Adobeps folder on the CD-ROM.
      3. Open the folder with the name of your printer's manufacturer (e.g., Agfa, Hewlett-Packard, IBM).
      4. Select the printer you want to install by double-clicking the printer's name, or clicking the printer's name then clicking Next.
      5. When installing a local printer, select a port from the list of available ports in the Local Port Selection dialog box, then click Next.
6. In the Add Printer dialog box, accept the default name for the printer, or type in the preferred name, select Yes if you want this printer to be the default printer for your Windows applications, select Yes if you want to print a test page, then click Next.
7. In the Properties dialog box, adjust the Properties for your printer as desired, then click OK to return to the AdobePS 4 PostScript Printer Driver Setup.
8. In the Setup dialog box, either click Exit to quit AdobePS 4 PostScript Printer Driver Setup or click Add Another then repeat steps 3-8 to add another printer.

MAC OS

Setting up Spooling Location for PSPrinter 8.x

When you spool print jobs using the Adobe PostScript printer driver 8.x (PSPrinter), you can use PSPrinter's default spooling location, or you can change the default spooling location so that PSPrinter spools files to another local hard disk or Macintosh on the network.

USING THE DEFAULT SPOOLING LOCATION

By default, PSPrinter 8.x spools print jobs to the startup hard disk, using its available hard disk space to store information. When Background Printing is Off, PSPrinter spools files to the temporary folder it creates, which it names Printing Temp Folder (PSPrinter 8.1 and later) or PSPrinter Temp Folder (PSPrinter 8.0) and locates in the Extensions folder in the System Folder. When you print with Background Printing enabled, Apple's PrintMonitor spools files to the PrintMonitor Documents folder in the System Folder. After Print-Monitor spools the file to the Printing Temp Folder, PSPrinter Temp Folder, or PrintMonitor documents folder, PSPrinter converts it to PostScript code, compresses it for faster transmission to the printer, then sends it to the printer.

If there is not enough disk space for the spooled file on the hard disk, PSPrinter returns a Disk Full error. To prevent a Disk Full error, remove files on the startup disk (i.e., volume containing the active system software) to ensure there is sufficient available disk space, or spool to another volume (local or remote hard disk) that has more available space.

SPOOLING TO ANOTHER LOCAL HARD DISK

You can set up PSPrinter to spool to another local hard disk (e.g., external hard disk) when you print in Foreground printing mode (i.e., Background Printing is turned Off in the Chooser).

To set up PSPrinter to spool to another local hard disk:

1. On the disk you want to spool to, create a new folder and name it "Printing Temp Folder" (PSPrinter 8.1 and later) or "PSPrinter Temp Folder" (PSPrinter 8.0).
2. Create an alias of the newly created folder by selecting it and then choosing File > Make Alias.
3. Move the alias into the Extensions folder in the System Folder.
4. Select the alias and rename it "Printing Temp Folder" (PSPrinter 8.1 and later) or "PSPrinter Temp Folder" (PSPrinter 8.0).
5. In the Chooser, select PSPrinter, select Off for Background Printing, and then close the Chooser.

SPOOLING TO ANOTHER MACINTOSH ON THE NETWORK

Before setting up PSPrinter to spool documents to another Macintosh on the network:

- Install System 7.x on both Macintosh computers.
- Install the same version of PSPrinter 8.x (e.g., PSPrinter 8.3) on both Macintosh computers.
- Enable Background Printing in the Chooser on both Macintosh computers. When Background printing is enabled, any error generated by PrintMonitor appears only on the local Macintosh.
- Install the same fonts on both Macintosh computers.
- Disable virus protection utilities (e.g., Symantec AntiVirus, Norton Utilities) on both Macintosh computers.

To set up PSPrinter to spool to a Macintosh on the network:

1. On the remote Macintosh (i.e., the Macintosh that you are spooling to), open the Chooser.
2. In the Chooser, select PSPrinter, select a destination printer, select On for Background Printing, then close the Chooser.
3. Open the Sharing Setup control panel, click Start in the File Sharing section, then close the control panel.
4. In the Finder, select the System Folder, then choose File > Sharing.
5. In the Sharing dialog box, select the option labeled "Share this item and its contents." For the Everyone options, select See Folders, See Files, and Make Changes. Select the option labeled "Can't be moved, renamed or deleted" and then close the Sharing dialog box.
6. In the System Folder, select the PrintMonitor Documents folder and then choose File > Make Alias. The Finder creates a file named "PrintMonitor Documents alias" in the System Folder.
7. On the local Macintosh (i.e., the Macintosh that you are printing from), open the Chooser and then select PSPrinter and a destination printer. Print jobs will not print to the printer you selected in this step, but PSPrinter requires that you select one.
8. Select On for Background Printing and then select AppleShare.
9. In the Select a File Server window, select the remote Macintosh and then click OK.
10. Log into the remote Macintosh as Guest, select the remote volume's System Folder, click OK, then close the Chooser. The System Folder icon will appear on the local Macintosh desktop.
11. Copy the file named "PrintMonitor Documents alias" from the remote hard disk's System Folder to the local hard disk's System Folder.
12. In the System Folder on the local Macintosh, delete the PrintMonitor Documents folder, then rename the PrintMonitor Documents alias file to "PrintMonitor Documents".
13. On the remote Macintosh, delete the PrintMonitor Documents alias file.

Unexpected Results

WINDOWS

Fonts Tab Dimmed in AdobePS 3.0.1 Setup

ISSUE

After selecting Setup in the AdobePS PostScript Printer Driver 3.0.1 printer driver running in Windows 3.1x, the Fonts tab is dimmed, preventing you from downloading fonts and PostScript files to the printer by clicking the Font Downloader button in the Fonts tab. Other tabs (e.g., Features, PostScript) are available.

SOLUTIONS

Enable TrueType fonts in the Fonts Control Panel:

1. Double-click the Control Panel icon in the Main Group in Program Manager.
2. Double-click the Fonts icon.
3. Click TrueType.
4. Select Enable TrueType Fonts, click OK, then close the Fonts Control Panel.

OR: Launch the Font Downloader (WINDOWN.EXE) by choosing the Run command in Program Manager:

1. In Program Manager, choose File > Run.
2. In the Run dialog box, type "C:\WINDOWS\SYSTEM\WINDOWN.EXE" in the Command Line text box, then click OK.

ADDITIONAL INFORMATION

Because the AdobePS PostScript Printer Driver 3.0.1's Fonts tab contains the TrueType font substitution options, the Fonts tab is dimmed when TrueType fonts are not enabled in the Fonts Control Panel. When TrueType fonts in the

Fonts Control Panel are enabled, the AdobePS PostScript Printer Driver 3.0.1's Fonts tab is available.

Clicking Font Downloader in the Fonts tab or typing "C:\WINDOWS\SYSTEM\WINDOWN.EXE in the Program Manager's Run dialog box launches WINDOWN.EXE, which enables you to download fonts and PostScript files to a printer.

Virtual Memory Information Omitted on Installed Printer's Test Page

ISSUE

After choosing to print a test page for an installed printer using the AdobePS 4.1 printer driver, the test page lists no virtual memory information. Other test page information (e.g., printer name, driver name) prints as expected.

SOLUTION

Reinstall the printer, then print a test page from the AdobePS 4 Setup Utility, instead of from the printer's Properties sheet:

1. Launch the AdobePS 4 Setup Utility by choosing Start > Programs > AdobePS4 or by double-clicking Setup.exe in the Drvrdisk folder in the Adobeps folder on the PageMaker 6.01 Updater CD-ROM.
2. Follow the on-screen instructions to install the printer, accepting the default name for the printer or type in the preferred name, selecting Yes if you want this printer to be the default printer for your Windows applications, and selecting Yes to print a test page in the Add Printer dialog box.

ADDITIONAL INFORMATION

When you print a test page in Windows 95 by selecting Print Test Page in the General pane of your installed printer's Properties window, the Windows 95 Printer Test Page, which does not include the printer's virtual memory information, prints. When you print a test page by selecting Yes to print a test page in the Add Printer dialog box in the AdobePS 4 Setup Utility, the AdobePS 4 PostScript Printer Driver Printer Test Page, which includes the printer's virtual memory information, prints.

The AdobePS 4.1 Readme.doc incorrectly states that "You can get printer memory information by printing a test page from the General properties dialog box."

When you reinstall a printer, the installer creates a copy of the installed printer's icon, named "[Printer Name] (Copy 1)," in the Printers Control Panel. After printing a test page to your printer, you can delete the copy of the installed printer by selecting the copy of the installed printer's icon, then pressing the Delete key.

Font Menus in Windows 95 List Fonts Removed from ATM

ISSUE

After you remove fonts in Adobe Type Manager (ATM) 3.0x in Windows 95, application font menus continue to list the removed fonts. The AdobePS 4.1 printer driver is installed and set as the default printer.

SOLUTIONS

Upgrade to ATM 4.0.

OR: With no other applications running, add or remove fonts in Ares FontMinder 3.0.5.

OR: Temporarily remove any font in ATM, rename the Psfonts folder, then launch Wordpad:

1. Remove a font (e.g., Anna) from the ATM Control Panel, then exit ATM.
2. Rename the Psfonts folder (e.g., Psfontss).
3. Choose Start > Programs > Accessories > WordPad.
4. Quit WordPad.
5. Rename the Psfonts directory to its original name (i.e., Psfonts).
6. Readd the font you removed in step 1.
7. Restart Windows 95.

OR: Update the font list using the AdobePS 4.1 Update Soft Fonts option:

1. Make sure the fonts have been removed in the ATM Control Panel.
2. Rename the Psfonts folder (e.g., Psfontss).
3. Choose Start > Settings > Printers to open the Printers Control Panel.
4. Right-click on any printer that uses the AdobePS 4.1 printer driver, then choose Properties from the pop-up menu.
5. In the Fonts pane of the Properties dialog box, click the Update Soft Fonts button.
6. Click OK to close the Printers Control Panel.
7. Choose Start > Programs > Accessories > WordPad.
8. Quit WordPad.
9. Rename the Psfonts directory to its original name (i.e., Psfonts).
10. Restart Windows 95.

OR: Edit the Windows 95 Registry to remove PostScript font references:

1. Choose Start > Run, then type "regedit" in the Open textbox and click OK.
2. Make a backup copy of the Registry by choosing Registry > Export Registry File.
3. In the Export Registry File dialog box, choose a location and name for the backup file, then click Save.
4. Open the Hkey_Local_Machine \Software\Microsoft\-Windows\CurrentVersion\PostscriptFonts key (i.e., directory).
5. Select all the Postscript font values (i.e., files) and press the Delete key to remove them. Do not remove the Default value or SerialNumber value.
6. Exit the Registry Editor, which saves your changes to the Registry, then restart Windows 95.

ADDITIONAL INFORMATION

When the AdobePS 4.1 printer driver is set as the default printer and you add fonts in ATM 3.0x, references to the fonts are added to the Atm.ini file, the Windows 95 Registry, and Windows 95 MFD files. When you remove fonts in ATM 3.0x, the font references are updated only in the Atm.ini file, causing the removed fonts to continue to display in font menus.

ATM 4.0 removes font references from the Registry, causing fonts to display in font menus as expected.

FontMinder 3.0.5 removes the PostScriptFonts key from the Registry when you add or remove a font. When the incorrect font references are removed with the PostScriptFonts key, font menus display fonts as expected. FontMinder must be the only application running when you add or remove a font.

When you remove a font or use the AdobePS 4.1 Update Soft Fonts option, then change the name of the Psfonts folder and launch WordPad, the font references should be updated so only the installed ATM fonts display in font menus. If the font references do not update, you must remove the font values from the Registry manually.

Removing or editing MFD files does not cause font menus to display correctly.

LaserJet 4MPlus Uses Upper Paper Cassette Instead of Lower with AdobePS 2.1.1

ISSUE

When you print to an HP LaserJet 4MPlus using the AdobePS 2.1.1 printer driver with the Upper Cassette option selected in the printer's Paper options, the printer uses paper from the Lower Cassette.

SOLUTIONS

Print using AdobePS 2.1.2 or later.

OR: Print using another printer driver (e.g., Microsoft PostScript 3.58 printer driver).

OR: Print to another printer (e.g., HP LaserJet 4M).

ADDITIONAL INFORMATION

The AdobePS 2.1.1 printer driver causes the HP LaserJet 4MPlus to use paper from the Lower Cassette when the Upper Cassette option is selected in the Paper pane of the printer's properties dialog box. Using AdobePS 2.1.2 or later, another printer driver, or another printer enables you to print from the Upper Cassette as expected.

PostScript Print Options Missing in FreeHand When Using AdobePS 4.1

ISSUE

When you print using the Adobe PostScript printer driver 4.1 (AdobePS), some options (e.g., Separations, Composite) are missing in the Macromedia FreeHand 5.0 Print dialog box.

SOLUTIONS

Print using the Microsoft Windows PostScript printer driver.

OR: Use Macromedia FreeHand 5.0b or later.

ADDITIONAL INFORMATION

Macromedia FreeHand 5.0 displays all options in the Print dialog box when you print using the Microsoft PostScript printer driver. Macromedia FreeHand 5.0b displays all options in the Print dialog box when you print using either the AdobePS 4.1 or the Microsoft printer driver.

MAC OS

Characters Appear Clipped in PDFs from PageMaker and QuarkXPress

ISSUE

Text characters formatted with a TrueType font appear clipped or do not display in a Portable Document Format (PDF) file. The PDF file was distilled from a PostScript file created by an application that generates its own PostScript code (e.g. Adobe PageMaker, QuarkXpress) using the Adobe PSPrinter 8.2.1 or earlier printer driver.

SOLUTIONS

Print the PostScript file to disk using the PSPrinter 8.3 or later printer driver.

OR: Print the PostScript file to disk using the Apple LaserWriter 8.0 or later printer driver.

OR: Use PostScript fonts instead of TrueType fonts.

OR: Print the PostScript file to disk using an application that does not generate its own PostScript code (e.g., Microsoft Word, WordPerfect, ClarisWorks).

ADDITIONAL INFORMATION

The Adobe PSPrinter 8.2.1 or earlier printer driver returns a random value for TrueType font bounding boxes when converting TrueType fonts to PostScript. When you print a PostScript file to disk from an application that generates its own PostScript code, the driver provides the application with incorrect font bounding box values. Because Acrobat Distillerrequires font bounding box information when distilling PostScript files, it cannot generate PDF characters correctly, causing them to appear clipped or not to display.

Other printer drivers (e.g., PSPrinter 8.3 or later, LaserWriter 8.0 or later) return accurate values for TrueType font bounding boxes, enabling the converted characters to be distilled correctly by Distiller. Printing from an application that does not generate its own PostScript code enables PSPrinter 8.2.1 or earlier to generate the PostScript code itself, preventing it from returning random values for TrueType font bounding boxes.

Application Errors

WINDOWS

Error "PS_ENUM.DLL version is incompatible with AdobePS" When Printing or Opening Application

ISSUE

After launching an application (e.g., Adobe PageMaker, WordPad), choosing File > Print, or selecting a printer, the error "PS_ENUM.DLL version is incompatible with AdobePS version. Exit Windows and re-install the printer." appears. Both Adobe Illustrator 4.x and the AdobePS PostScript Printer Driver 3.0.1 are installed.

SOLUTION

Remove then reinstall the AdobePS PostScript Printer Driver 3.0.1.

ADDITIONAL INFORMATION

Because the AdobePS PostScript Printer Driver 3.0.1 requires both the PS_ENUM.DLL file (modified 5/5/95) and RUN_ENUM.EXE file (modified 5/5/95) to print, the AdobePS PostScript Printer Driver 3.0.1 returns the error "PS_ENUM.DLL version is incompatible with AdobePS version. Exit Windows and re-install the printer." after you launch an application, choose the Print command, or select a printer when a different version of the PS_ENUM.DLL file or RUN_ENUM.EXE file is installed.

The AdobePS PostScript Printer Driver 3.0.1installs both the PS_ENUM.DLL file (modified 5/5/95) and RUN_ENUM.EXE file (modified 5/5/95), overwriting existing PS_ENUM.DLL and RUN_ENUM.EXE files.

When installing Illustrator 4.x after installing the AdobePS PostScript Printer Driver 3.0.1, clicking Yes in Illustrator's message that asks whether you want to overwrite the existing C:\WINDOWS\SYSTEM\PS_ENUM.DLL or C:\WINDOWS\SYSTEM\RUN_ENUM.EXE file instructs Illustrator to replace the existing PS_ENUM.DLL or RUN_ENUM.EXE file with the PS_ENUM.DLL or RUN_ENUM.EXE file included with Illustrator 4.x.

Alert "...may not be compatible with watermark or page layout" Printing with AdobePS 3.0.1

ISSUE

When printing a document using the AdobePS 3.0.1 printer driver's watermark or page layout (n-up) feature, the following alert appears: "This application may or may not be compatible with the watermark [or page layout (N-up)] feature you selected in Printer Setup. You may cancel the job or try to print it."

SOLUTION

Print the document from an application that supports AdobePS 3.0.1's watermark or page layout feature (e.g., Microsoft Word).

ADDITIONAL INFORMATION

When you print a document from an application that does not support the watermark or page layout feature, the AdobePS 3.0.1 printer driver displays the alert "This application may or may not be compatible with the watermark [or page layout (N-up)] feature you selected in Printer Setup. You may cancel the job or try to print it."

Error "Not enough memory available for this task" Changing Settings in AdobePS

ISSUE

When you change settings (e.g., paper orientation) in the AdobePS PostScript printer driver 3.0.1 and earlier Setup dialog box, the driver returns the error "Not enough memory available for this task. Quit one or more applications to increase available memory, and then try again." The driver is connected to a printer port whose reference in the [Ports] section of the Win.ini file does not have a colon following it (e.g., LPT1.DOS)

SOLUTION

Add a colon to the printer port reference in the [Ports] section of the Win.ini file (e.g., LPT1.DOS:):

1. Open the Win.ini file in a text-editor that can save in text-only format (e.g., Windows Write, Notepad).
2. In the [Ports] section, add a colon to the appropriate printer port reference.
3. Save the Win.ini file in text-only format.

ADDITIONAL INFORMATION

When AdobePS is unable to locate a colon following a printer port reference in the [Ports] section of the Win.ini file, it returns the error "Not enough memory available for this task. Quit one or more applications to increase available memory, and then try again." Adding a colon enables you to set up the driver without error.

MAC OS

Error "Printer could not be opened" When Using Downloader 5.0.1 or Earlier

ISSUE

The error "Printer could not be opened." appears when downloading a font using Adobe Downloader 5.0.1 or earlier in System 7.x.

SOLUTIONS

Use Downloader 5.0.4 or later.

OR: When using Downloader 5.0.1, move the printer driver (e.g., Apple LaserWriter, Adobe PSPrinter) from the Extensions folder in the System Folder into the System Folder, then download the fonts. After downloading the fonts, move the printer driver back into the Extensions folder.

ADDITIONAL INFORMATION

Downloader 5.0.1 and earlier return the error "Printer could not be opened." while downloading a font when the printer driver is installed in the Extensions folder.

Downloader 5.0.1 and earlier searches for printer drivers in the System Folder when downloading fonts, and cannot locate printer drivers installed in the Extensions folder. Downloader 5.0.1 and earlier are designed to run in System 6.x. In System 6.x, printer drivers are installed in the System Folder. In System 7.0 and later, printer drivers are installed in the Extensions folder in the System Folder.

Downloader 5.0.4 is designed to run in System 7.0 and later, and can locate printer drivers installed in the Extensions folder.

PostScript Error Downloading PostScript Level 1 File to PostScript Level 1 Printer

ISSUE

When you download a PostScript file saved as Level 1 Compatible to a PostScript Level 1 printer, a PostScript error occurs (e.g., "syntaxerror; OffendingCommand: nostringval"). The printer driver you used to print the PostScript file to disk is set up with a PostScript Printer Description (PPD) file for a PostScript Level 2 printer (e.g., Apple LaserWriter Pro 810, Apple LaserWriter Pro 810f).

SOLUTIONS

Download the file to a PostScript Level 2 printer.

OR: Set up the printer driver with a different PostScript Level 2 PPD file (e.g., HP LaserJet 4M) in the Chooser.

OR: Set up the printer driver with a Level 1 PPD file or generic PPD file (i.e., click Use Generic) in the Chooser.

ADDITIONAL INFORMATION

When you print a PostScript file to disk using a printer driver set up with a PostScript Level 2 PPD file, you can select the Level 1 Compatible option or the Level 2 Only option in the Format dialog box, which appears after you click Save in the Print dialog box. When you select the Level 1 Compatible option, some PostScript Level 2 PPD files (e.g., Apple LaserWriter Pro 810, Apple LaserWriter Pro 810f) cause the printer driver to generate PostScript Level 2 code, instead of PostScript Level 1 code as expected. Because a PostScript Level 1 printer cannot interpret the Level 2 code, a PostScript error occurs when you download the file to a PostScript Level 1 printer.

Using a different PostScript Level 2 PPD file (e.g., HP LaserJet 4M), a Level 1 PPD file, or a generic PPD file enables the printer driver to write the PostScript file with Level 1 code only, but may limit your printing options (e.g., paper size, feed options).

To determine the PostScript Level of a PPD file:

1. Open the PPD file in a text editor (e.g., SimpleText, Microsoft Word).
2. Locate the "*Language Level:" line, which indicates the PostScript level of the PPD file. For example:

```
*LanguageLevel: "1"
```

System Errors

MAC OS

System Error (e.g., Freeze) After Clicking Setup for Birmy PowerRip in PSPrinter

ISSUE

After you click Setup in the Chooser to set up a Birmy PowerRIP 3.1f35 or earlier raster image processor using the Adobe PostScript printer driver 8.3 (PSPrinter), a system error (e.g., freeze) occurs.

SOLUTIONS

Use the Birmy PowerRIP 3.1f36 or later raster image processor.

OR: Use another printer driver (e.g., PSPrinter 8.2.x or earlier, Apple LaserWriter 8.x).

ADDITIONAL INFORMATION

Because PSPrinter 8.3 is incompatible with the Birmy PowerRIP 3.1f35 and earlier

raster image processor, the system returns an error (e.g., freezes) after you click Setup in the Chooser to set up the PowerRIP raster image processor using PSPrinter 8.3. Using the Birmy PowerRIP 3.1f36 or later raster image processor or another printer driver enables you to set up the PowerRIP printer in the printer driver without causing the system to return an error.

The PowerRIP for the Macintosh and Windows is a software raster image processor that uses Adobe PostScript Level 2. When the PowerRIP application is running, the Chooser lists the PowerRIP as an available printer after you select a PostScript printer driver.

Printing Problems

WINDOWS

TrueType Font Character Strokes Print with White Spaces with AdobePS 4.1

ISSUE

When you print text formatted with a TrueType font using the Adobe PostScript Printer Driver (AdobePS) 4.1 PostScript printer driver, characters print with gaps (i.e., white spaces) at the intersection of one or more character strokes. For example, the number 8 prints with a white spot or line at the point where the upper and lower circles of the character should meet. Text formatted with a PostScript font prints as expected.

SOLUTION

Format the text with a PostScript font.

ADDITIONAL INFORMATION

When PostScript character strokes overlap, they create a knock-out effect, causing a white space to appear where they overlap. Because of this knockout effect, PostScript fonts do not contain overlapping character strokes and print as expected. However, TrueType fonts contain overlapping character strokes. The AdobePS 4.1 PostScript printer driver converts TrueType font information to PostScript information, causing the TrueType font's overlapping character strokes to knockout when printed.

MAC OS

Bold Text Prints as Random Characters Using PSPrinter 8.0 or LaserWriter 8.0

ISSUE

Text formatted with a PostScript font and a bold type style prints as random characters using the Adobe PSPrinter 8.0 or Apple LaserWriter 8.0 printer driver. Text formatted in the same font but without the bold style prints as expected.

SOLUTIONS

Install the PostScript outline (printer) font for the bold type style (e.g., TrajaBol).
OR: Do not apply the bold type style to the text.
OR: Print the text using the PSPrinter 8.1.1 or later or LaserWriter 8.1.1 or later printer driver.

ADDITIONAL INFORMATION

When you apply a bold type style to text formatted with a PostScript font, but the outline font for the bold type style (e.g., TrajaBol) is not installed, the font should print in the roman typeface (e.g., Trajan Regular). The PSPrinter 8.0 and LaserWriter 8.0 printer drivers, however, print random characters instead of the roman typeface.

The PSPrinter 8.1.1 or later and LaserWriter 8.1.1 or later printer drivers print the font in the roman style when the outline font for the bold style is not installed.

Cannot Print to LaserWriter Select 310 Using PSPrinter or LaserWriter Printer Driver

ISSUE

When you select the PSPrinter, LaserWriter 8.x, or LaserWriter printer driver in the Chooser, the LaserWriter Select 310 does not display in the Select a PostScript Printer list.

SOLUTION

Select the LW Select 310 printer driver in the Chooser.

ADDITIONAL INFORMATION

The LaserWriter Select 310 uses a serial port and requires a modified LaserWriter 7.x printer driver for serial communication. All other PostScript printers use an AppleTalk port, and can be targeted in the Chooser using the PSPrinter, LaserWriter 8.x, or LaserWriter printer driver, which are AppleTalk printer drivers.

Because the Apple LaserWriter Select 310 uses a modified version of the LaserWriter 7.x printer driver, applications that require the PSPrinter 8.x or LaserWriter 8.x printer driver (e.g., PageMaker 5.0x or later) may not print as expected to the LW Select 310.

Text Formatted in Font with Long Name Doesn't Print

ISSUE

When printing using the Adobe PSPrinter 8.0x and Apple LaserWriter 8.0 printer driver, text prints as a blank area or no output is received. The text is formatted with a font whose name contains 32 or more characters (e.g., Helvetica Condensed Black Oblique, Futura Condensed Extra Bold Oblique, ITC Garamond Condensed Ultra Italic).

SOLUTIONS

Print using the Adobe PSPrinter 8.1 or later printer driver.
OR: Print using the Apple LaserWriter 8.1 or later printer driver.

ADDITIONAL INFORMATION

The PSPrinter 8.1 or later printer driver, and the LaserWriter 8.1 or later printer driver, support printing fonts whose names contain 32 or more characters. The PSPrinter 8.0x and the LaserWriter 8.0 printer drivers limit the length of font names they can print, which causes missing text or no output when printing fonts whose names contain 32 or more characters (e.g., Helvetica Condensed Black Oblique,

Futura Condensed Extra Bold Oblique, ITC Garamond Condensed Ultra Italic).

Installation Issues

WINDOWS

No Printer Icon Appears in Printers Folder After Installing PSPrinter 3.0.1 in Windows 95

ISSUE

After you install the AdobePS 3.0.1 PostScript printer driver in Windows 95, an icon for the selected printer does not appear in the Printers folder.

SOLUTIONS

Restart Windows 95.

OR: Install AdobePS 4.1 or later, or the Microsoft PostScript printer driver 4.0 or later.

ADDITIONAL INFORMATION

Because the AdobePS 3.0.1 printer driver is not Windows 95 logo-compliant, it does not update the Windows 95 Registry during installation so that an icon for the selected printer appears in the Printers folder. Instead, it adds entries to the WIN.INI file. Windows 95 reads the WIN.INI file when it restarts and incorporates the entries into the Registry, creating an icon for the installed printer in the Printers folder.

When you install a Windows 95 logo-compliant printer driver (e.g., AdobePS 4.1 or later), it updates the Windows 95 Registry, causing an icon for the selected printer to appear in the Printers folder.

The AdobePS PostScript 3.01 printer driver is a 16-bit application specifically designed for 16-bit versions of Microsoft Windows (e.g., Windows 3.1, Windows for Workgroups). AdobePS 3.0.1 is compatible with Microsoft Windows 95, a 32-bit operating system, but is not Windows 95 logo-compliant. Windows 95 logo-compliant programs meet the required Windows 95 Logo criteria, which include support of system level features (e.g., long filenames, 32-bit addressing, new user interface shell) and additional functionality (e.g., OLE 2.0).

Error "Attempt to install an older version" When Installing AdobePS 4.1

ISSUE

When you install a printer using the Adobe PostScript printer driver (AdobePS) 4.1 setup utility from a CD-ROM, the setup utility returns the error, "Error: Attempt to install an older version. Setup has detected that you are trying to install one or more files that are older than what you already have installed on your system. This operation is not permitted."

SYMPTOM

AdobePS 4.1.1 is installed.

SOLUTION

Rename the Adobeps4.drv file in the Windows\System directory, then reinstall AdobePS.

OR: Install a printer using the AdobePS 4.1.1 setup utility.

ADDITIONAL INFORMATION

After you install AdobePS 4.x, you can run the AdobePS setup utility from your hard drive (if you installed it there) or from a CD-ROM. When you run the setup utility from the hard drive, it automatically uses the installed version of AdobePS (i.e., the installed version of the Adobeps.drv file) to install a printer. When you install AdobePS 4.1.1 and then install a printer using the AdobePS 4.1 setup utility from a CD-ROM, the setup utility returns the error, "Error: Attempt to install an older version," because it cannot replace AdobePS 4.1.1's newer Adobeps.drv file with AdobePS 4.1's older Adobeps.drv file. Renaming the previously installed Adobeps4.drv file (i.e., the one installed for AdobePS 4.1.1) enables the setup utility to install AdobePS 4.1.

AdobePS 4.1 is included on the Adobe Type Manager (ATM) Deluxe 4.0 CD-ROM, while AdobePS 4.1.1 is included on the PageMaker 6.5 CD-ROM. The Adobeps4.drv file used by AdobePS 4.1.1 has a date of 05/24/96, while the Adobeps4.drv file used by AdobePS 4.1 has a date of 03/01/96. You can check the printer driver version in Windows 95 in an installed printer's Properties dialog box by clicking the Paper tab and then clicking About in the Properties dialog box.

Error "Invalid printer name" When Installing Printer for AdobePS 4.x

ISSUE

When you install a printer with Adobe PostScript printer driver (AdobePS) 4.x, the AdobePS Setup Utility returns the error, "Invalid printer name [name]." The printer is connected via a Novell Netware 4.x network using Netware Directory Services (NDS).

SOLUTIONS

Install the printer driver as a local printer using the AdobePS Setup Utility, then set up the printer as a network printer:

1. Using the AdobePS 4 Setup Utility, install the printer as a local printer. For instructions, see document 370411.
2. Choose Start > Settings > Printers.
3. In the Printers Control Panel, right-click the newly installed printer, then select Properties from the pop-up menu.
4. In the Properties dialog box, click the Details tab, then click Add Port.

5. In the Add Port dialog box, click Browse. Navigate to the network printer, select it, then click OK. Click OK again to return to the Properties dialog box.
6. Click OK to close the Properties dialog box.

OR: Configure the path to a network printer so its pathname does not contain a period. Consult your network administrator or the Netware documentation for assistance.

OR: Disable NDS. Contact your network administrator or the Netware documentation for assistance.

ADDITIONAL INFORMATION

By default, NDS creates pathnames with periods (e.g., \\Press-\.LP3-Vari2.courier) for networked printers. Because AdobePS does not support pathnames with periods, the AdobePS Setup Utility will return an error when you add a network printer whose pathname contains a period. Disabling NDS, creating pathnames without periods, or setting up the printer as a local printer before setting it up as a network printer enables you to add a printer without error.

Installing the AdobePS 2.1.2 Driver from the Type On Call 4.0 CD-ROM

To install the Adobe PostScript printer driver 2.1.2 (AdobePS) included on the Adobe Type On Call 4.0 CD-ROM in Windows 3.1x:

1. Open the Printers Control Panel, then click Add.
2. Select the Install Unlisted or Updated Printer option from the List of Printers, then click Install.
3. In the Install dialog box, type "X:\Free\PC\Adobedrv\Install," where X is your CD-ROM drive, then click OK. The Add Unlisted or Updated Printer dialog box appears.
   OR: Click Browse, select your CD-ROM drive from the Drives pop-up menu, select the Free\PC\Adobedrv\Install directory from the Directories list, then click OK. Click OK again in the Install dialog box. The Add Unlisted or Updated Printer dialog box appears.
4. In the Add Unlisted or Updated Printer dialog box, select the printer you want to install, click OK, then click OK again.
5. Close the Printers Control Panel.

Password Requested When Installing AdobePS 4.1 with Copstalk Installed

ISSUE

When you use the AdobePS 4 Setup Utility to install the Adobe PostScript printer driver 4.1 (AdobePS) for a network printer connected via a Copstalk 1.2 network, a dialog box appears requesting a user name and password, and the installation fails.

SOLUTIONS

Upgrade to Copstalk 2.0 or later.

OR: Install the printer driver as a local printer using the AdobePS 4 Setup Utility, then set up the printer as a network printer:

1. Using the AdobePS 4 Setup Utility, install the printer as a local printer. Select No when prompted to print a test page.
2. Choose Start > Settings > Printers.
3. In the Printers Control Panel, right-click the newly installed printer, then select Properties from the pop-up menu.
4. In the Properties dialog box, click the Details tab, then click Add Port.
5. In the Add Port dialog box, click Browse. Navigate to the network printer, select it, then click OK. Click OK again to return to the Properties dialog box.
6. Click OK to close the Properties dialog box.

ADDITIONAL INFORMATION

Because Copstalk 1.2 is not Windows 95 logo-compliant, it does not support all Windows 95 network features. The AdobePS 4 Setup Utility, which uses Windows 95 network features to add a network printer, is unable to install a printer on a Copstalk 1.2 network. You can use AdobePS with a network printer on a Copstalk 1.2 network by first installing the printer as a local printer, then setting up the printer driver for the Copstalk 1.2 network.

Copstalk 2.0 or later is Windows 95 logo-compliant and is compatible with the AdobePS 4 Setup Utility.

MAC OS

Adobe Printer Driver 8.x for Macintosh: Installation and Troubleshooting

This technical note covers how to install the Adobe Printer Driver for Macintosh (represented by the PSPrinter 8.x icon) and how to perform its troubleshooting procedures. The contents of this technical note are:

PSPRINTER 8.X VERSUS APPLE LASERWRITER 8.X

PSPrinter 8.x and LaserWriter 8.x are the same program. Apple Computer, Inc. and Adobe Systems, Incorporated wrote the program jointly, but use different distribution channels for it. Therefore, the only differences are in the representative icon and in the PPDs (PostScript Printer Description files) that are distributed with the product. Apple ships only Apple PPDs with LaserWriter 8.x and Adobe ships PPDs from all manufacturers that have granted Adobe permission to do so.

Aldus Corporation, Frame Technologies, and other software manufacturers have also decided to distribute the driver with their products. All companies distributing the product have agreed to support their own distribution. For example, if your copy of LaserWriter 8.x comes with PageMaker 5.0, then Aldus Corporation provides support. If you purchased PSPrinter directly from Adobe, then Adobe provides support. Support for specific features enabled by PPDs are provided by the printer manufacturers.

INSTALLATION INSTRUCTIONS

How to install Adobe Printer Driver:

1. Quit all running applications, then insert Disk 1 into the floppy disk drive. The Disk 1 window opens.
2. Double-click the Adobe PSPrinter Installer program icon. The installer dialog box appears.
3. Click Install and the installation process begins. *The installer program copies the Adobe Printer Driver and the Printer Descriptions folder (for PPD files) into the System Folder as follows:*
   - For a Macintosh running System 7.x software, the installer places these files in the Extensions folder inside the System Folder.
   - For a Macintosh running System 6.x software, the installer places these files in the System Folder, along with new versions of the Backgrounder, PrintMonitor, LaserWriter, and Laser-Prep utilities.

TROUBLESHOOTING

This section describes some problems you may face during and after installation, and how to solve them.

SPOOLING FILES TO A HARD DRIVE

One of the features of PSPrinter 8.x is speed. In order to print faster, PSPrinter 8.x spools the print job to the startup hard drive. This spooling process then allows the driver to convert the file to PostScript code, compress it for speed of transmission, and then send it to the printer. If there is not enough disk space to spool the file to the hard drive, then the job may fail, resulting in a Disk Full error. If a print job has failed because you do not have enough storage on your startup hard drive, clear space on the drive by removing files, then try your print job again. You may also wish to return to version 7.x of the LaserWriter driver.

FOREGROUND SPOOLING

To Another Local Hard Drive This section provides workarounds for inadequate space on your startup drive to allow PSPrinter to create spool files. If you cannot remove files to create additional space on your startup drive, try one of these workarounds or use LaserWriter version 7.1.2.

If you have an additional hard drive attached to your Macintosh, and are using System 7 or greater, you can force PSPrinter to spool the printer file to that drive. However, this works only in Foreground Printing mode.

You select Foreground or Background printing mode in the Chooser when you select the printer. Apple's PrintMonitor program controls Background Printing, which requires that spooled files be placed in the PrintMonitor Documents folder of the active System Folder. Therefore, with Background Printing on, you must spool to your startup disk's System Folder or to a System Folder on a remote Macintosh (see the next section). The PostScript printer driver controls spooling during Foreground Printing.

To control how your computer spools its print jobs:

1. Select the disk that you wish to use for spooling and create a new folder. PSPrinter 8.0 users must name this folder "PSPrinter Temp Folder," and LaserWriter 8.0 users must name it "LaserWriter Temp Folder." If you have version 8.1 or later of the driver, then name the folder "Printing Temp Folder."
2. Select the folder you just created and choose Make Alias from the File menu.
3. Copy the alias into your Extensions folder (located in your System Folder), and delete the string "alias" from the file name.
4. Start the Chooser, select the Adobe PostScript printer driver and click Background Printing Off.
5. Print as usual. The document prints in the foreground after spooling to the disk on which you created the new spooling folder.

BACKGROUND SPOOLING

To Another Macintosh on the Network If you have another Macintosh computer on the same network as your computer, you can use it for spooling documents. For this to work, both computers must have the same version of PSPrinter 8.x (or LaserWriter 8.x, or HPLaserJet 8.x), and you must be running System 7.0 or higher in order to share files between the two computer. In the following instructions, the Macintosh from which you are printing is the "local" computer and the Macintosh that you are using for spooling purposes is the "remote" computer.

1. On the remote computer, choose the Chooser from the Apple menu. Select the Adobe PostScript printer driver, then choose a destination printer. Background Printing should be on.
2. On the remote computer, double-click the startup disk and select the System Folder. Choose Sharing from the File menu. Turn on Sharing for the System Folder and all enclosed folders, and select "Everyone" for the "See all folders," "See files," and "Make changes" options.
3. On the remote computer, open the System Folder. Select the PrintMonitor Documents folder, then choose Make Alias from the File menu.
4. On the local computer, choose Chooser from the Apple menu. Select the Adobe PostScript printer driver, choose a destination printer, then turn on Background Printing. Close the Chooser.
5. On the local computer, open the Chooser again and select the AppleShare icon. Log onto the remote computer's System Folder as "guest." Copy the file, "PrintMonitor Documents alias" from the remote computer's System Folder into the local computer's System Folder.
6. Delete the local computer's folder called "Print Monitor Documents" and change the name of the file "PrintMonitor Documents alias" to "PrintMonitor Documents." (If you select the PrintMonitor Documents folder, then choose Get Info from the File menu, you will see that the original file of this alias resides in the remote computer's System Folder.)

7. On the remote computer, delete the file "PrintMonitor Documents alias." You no longer need this file.
8. Now you may print your files as usual from the local computer. Observe the spool dialog on the local computer. Immediately after you print from the local computer, a temporary spool file is created on the remote computer in the "PrintMonitor Documents" folder. The system on the remote computer will find the spooled documents and print them.

Important notes on this procedure:

- Any error messages you receive from PrintMonitor show up only on the remote computer.
- Some virus protection software flags this process as suspicious activity. You may get a message that you are attempting to bypass the Resource Manager. This is expected behavior for this workaround.
- The remote computer must have all fonts that the print jobs require because the local computer does not send fonts to it. If the required fonts are not available on the remote computer, font substitution may occur, and Courier will be substituted.

LARGER PRINT AREA DIMMED

Most PPDs, but not all, have two printable area dimensions included within the file. Those PPDs which do not have two dimensions included dim the Larger Print Area option, in which case the largest print area is the default. Choosing the Generic PPD will make the larger print area option available, although it is not necessary to have this option because the PPD automatically selects the largest print area.

ERRORS WHILE PRINTING CERTAIN FONTS

PSPrinter 8.0 does print the following fonts:

- Helvetica Condensed Black Oblique
- Futura Condensed Extra Bold Oblique
- ITC Garamond Condensed Ultra Italic

The problems associated with printing these fonts have been fixed in PSPrinter 8.1.1. You should upgrade to the 8.1.1 driver if you wish to print using these fonts.

PSPrinter 8.0 does not print any font that has been stylized through the Style menu if the specific outline font is not available. For example, if you choose Bold from the Style menu for text in the Futura type face, and the Futura Bold outline font is not installed, then the job will not print. PSPrinter 8.1.1. produces a bold version of the regular typeface even if you have not installed the bold version of that typeface on the system.

TYPE ALIGN PRINTING PROBLEMS

Type Align files print as Courier when printed with PSPrinter 8.x from within TypeAlign or when exported as PICT files or as Cut-and-Paste via the Clipboard. Files exported as EPS print but will not have a preview.

If you are experiencing problems printing from the Adobe Type Align program with printer driver 8.0, 8.1, or 8.1.1, try using Apple printer driver version 7.x. The 8.x series of the printer driver is incompatible with Adobe Type Align.

PROBLEMS WITH PPDS & OBTAINING PPDS

Problems concerning specific features in PPDs are handled by the original manufacturer. One example of a PPD issue would be the Larger Print Area being dimmed, as discussed earlier in this technical note.

Updated PPDs and PPDs not distributed with PSPrinter 8.x should be obtained from the printer manufacturer.

Error "Please insert the disk PSPrinter" When Installing PSPrinter 8.3.1

ISSUE

When you install the Adobe PostScript printer driver (PSPrinter) 8.3.1, the Installer returns the error "Please insert the disk PSPrinter" followed by the error "An error occurred while installing on the active startup disk [disk name]. Installation was not able to be completed, but your original software has been restored." Renaming the disk does not enable the Installer to recognize it.

SYMPTOM

You downloaded PSPrinter from the Adobe World Wide Web site or the Adobe BBS and then copied it to a disk.

SOLUTION

Name the disk "PSPrinter" and make sure it contains only the following files and folder:

Name	Size	Kind
Chooser	54K	desk accessory
Installer	152K	application program
Printer Descriptions folder:		
PSPrinter	708K	Chooser extension
PSPrinter Instal	168K	Installer document
PSPrinter ReadMe	13K	Simple text document

Additional Information When you download the Psp831-.sit file and decompress it, it creates the following files and folder:

- 8.3.1 User Guide.pdf
- PSPrinter folder
- ReadMe First

If you copy PSPrinter onto a disk to install it, you must copy the contents of the PSPrinter folder only, then name the disk "PSPrinter." If the disk is not named "PSPrinter" or contains unexpected contents (e.g., the PSPrinter folder instead of only the contents of that folder), the PSPrinter Installer returns the error "Please insert the disk PSPrinter."

The ReadMe First file includes the following installation instructions:

"PSPrinter is systems software and, as such, cannot be installed to the same disk on which it resides. Copy the contents of the PSPrinter folder onto a diskette. When creating the diskette, please ensure to name on the disk appears exactly as it does on the decompressed folder, paying special attention to capitalization."

Adobe Premiere®

Adobe Premiere was the world's first desktop digital video, nonlinear editing system. It's current version is 4.2 and is available for both Mac OS and Windows computing platforms. Create digital movies or videos, by combining video, still images, animation, and graphcis. Export them in a variety of formats. The economical solution for professional video needs, you can edit on-line or off-line, add graphics and special effects with the same high quality as proprietary editing systems. True to the leading technology of the day, costly special effects hardware or production services are not required.

Contents

Adobe Premiere®

Feature Techniques

MAC OS / WINDOWS

Using Miniatures in Premiere

The Miniatures feature in Adobe Premiere creates miniature clips out of original clips, which can be used to edit projects containing hardware-compressed clips on a computer without a hardware compression board. It also speeds editing of large frame size movies (i.e., quarter-screen or larger) or movies compressed with a slow playback compression/decompression scheme (codec). Miniatures should not be used if the Image Pan filter will be applied to a clip in the project.

MAKING MINIATURE CLIPS

After capturing the original source clips, use the Miniatures command to create the miniature clips used in editing. Be sure to create miniatures of clips captured with hardware compression on the computer where the hardware compressor is installed.

To create miniature clips in Premiere:

1. Move all source clips on which the miniatures will be based to a single folder or directory.
   NOTE: If any of the source clips or still images contain alpha channels, move them into a different folder or directory and make a separate miniature pass with a compressor that supports a color depth of Millions of Colors+ (i.e. Animation or None), which will retain the alpha channel information.
2. In Premiere, choose File > Tools > Miniatures.
3. Select the the folder or directory in which the source clips are located, then click Select [foldername] (Macintosh) or OK (Windows). The Create Miniatures Folder/Directory dialog box appears, with the default output and compression options displayed.
4. To change the output options, click Output Options. The goal is to work with small, low-quality images and basic sound. For best results, select an image size of either 120-by-90, 160-by-120 or 320-by-240, and a sound setting of 11 kHz, 8 Bit, Mono. For information on other Output Options settings, see Further Reading.
   NOTE: If the computer where you are editing the project has a hardware compression card and you are working with full-frame images, 320-by-240 is recommended.
5. To change the compression options, click Compression. Unless hardware compression will be available on all computers used to edit the project, select a fast software compressor (e.g., for QuickTime movies, select Apple Video (Macintosh) or Video (Windows), and for Video for Windows (AVI) movies select Microsoft Video 1). Move the Quality slider to the left to maximize compression but retain an acceptable quality level. For more information on compression options, see Further Reading.
6. Name the Miniatures folder or directory and click OK. Premiere creates a new folder or directory of the miniature clips, whose file names are the same as their source clips.
7. To import all the miniature clips into the project at once, choose File > Import > Folder (Macintosh) or File > Import > Directory (Windows). Select the folder in which the miniature clips are located, then click Select [foldername].

REPLACING MINIATURE CLIPS WITH SOURCE CLIPS

After you finish editing the Project, use the Re-Find Files command to replace the miniature clips with their source clips. If a project containing the source files already exists, you can use the Re-Find Files command to replace the originals with the miniatures, then use the command again to restore the original clips.

To replace miniature clips with their source clips:

1. Save the project.
2. Choose Project > Re-Find files, then click OK to the warning message indicating that the operation cannot be un-done.
3. Select the source clip indicated at the top of the dialog box, then click OK or Find (Macintosh only) to locate the source clip.
4. After locating the first source clip, Premiere automatically exchanges the miniature clips in the Project window and Construction Window with the source clips located in the same folder or directory. If miniature clips from other folders or directories were used, you must locate each folder or directory individually.
   NOTE: To skip one clip and locate the next, click Skip in the Re-Find dialog box.

Adding a Graphic to the Back of the Page Peel Transition in Premiere 4.x

The Page Peel transition in Adobe Premiere 4.x peels a clip on Track A away from a clip on Track B, displaying a reflection of the Track A clip on the back of the page as it peels. You can replace the reflected Track A clip with a logo or graphic by nesting transitions.

To add a logo or graphic to the back of the Page Peel transition:

1. Drag the first clip (i.e., the one that peels away) onto Track A of the Construction Window.
2. Drag the Page Peel transition from the Transitions window to Track T.
   NOTE: In Premiere 4.0x for Windows, click on the upper left corner of the Transition Settings dialog box that appears so the transition peels from upper left to lower right.
3. Choose Project > Add Color Matte, then select a bright blue color from the color picker and click OK.
4. In the Color Matte dialog box, enter a name in the Name text box and an effect duration in the Duration text box, then click OK.
   NOTE: You cannot specify an effect duration in the Color Matte dialog box in Premiere 4.0x for Windows. Manually stretch the matte after adding it to the Construction Window so it aligns with the other clips.
5. Drag the matte from the Project window to Track B.
6. Select the first clip, the transition, and the color matte with the block select tool.
7. Move the cursor over the selected block so it turns into a virtual clip tool, then click and drag the virtual clip onto Track S1.
   NOTE: You can also compile the selected items into a movie, import the movie into a new project, then drag it onto Track S1.
8. Drag the logo or graphic from the Project window to Track A.
   NOTE: The image will be rotated and mirrored in the transition, so you may want to rotate or mirror the image in an image editing application before importing it into Premiere.
9. Drag the Page Turn transition onto Track T.
10. Drag the second clip (i.e., the one revealed by the effect) onto Track B.
11. Align the clips and transition vertically.
12. Select the virtual clip or movie on Track S1, then choose Clip > Transparency.
13. In the Transparency Settings dialog box, select Blue Screen from the Key Type pop-up menu, then change other settings as desired and click OK.
    NOTE: You can click on the page peel icon in the Transparency Settings dialog box to preview the effect while adjusting settings.

Edit Decision List (EDL) and Off-line Editing with Premiere

Traditionally, there have been two ways to edit videotape: on-line and off-line. With on-line editing, you work with the original tapes to produce a master tape that can be broadcast or otherwise distributed. Traditional on-line editing requires high-end video tools such as switchers, mixing boards, and video tape recorders. For most video producers, these tools are too expensive to purchase or rent.

With off-line editing, you use copies of the original tapes and relatively low-cost equipment to make editing decisions. Your editing decisions are recorded in an Edit Decision List (EDL). The EDL contains a list of all of the clips, transitions, and special effects in the movie. It is used later on a postproduction system that builds the distribution master from the original tapes. Adobe Premiere lets you create EDLs in a variety of popular formats.

Off-line editing requires considerably less equipment than on-line editing does. For a list of the hardware components needed for off-line editing with Premiere, see Related Records.

MAXIMIZING HARD DISK SPACE FOR CAPTURE FILES

The first step in off-line editing is making copies of your original video tapes in Apple QuickTime format. This digitizing process is called "video capture."

Captured QuickTime files can be extremely large. You can save hard disk space by applying compression to the clips as you capture them. Because you're working with copies of the original tapes, you should use as much compression as possible rather than be concerned about image quality—the final master will be produced from the original tapes.

Other ways to conserve hard disk space include capturing video in black and white (if your video capture card allows it) and capturing at fewer than 30 frames per second (fps). Black-and-white clips can be more than 50 percent smaller than color clips, and the time code in the EDL will be valid even if you capture at 15 fps. You should capture at 30 fps if there are specific frames you want to include in your movie. For detailed instructions on capturing video, see your Adobe Premiere User Guide.

WORKING WITH EDIT DECISION LISTS

After you edit your clips and assemble your movie in Premiere, you can generate the EDL. Premiere can export EDLs in many different formats, including CMX 3400, CMX 3600, Grass Valley, Sony BVE, and formats provided through third-party plug-in modules. A Plug-in Developers Kit to help you create your own plug-in modules is available from Adobe. Registered users of Premiere can obtain a Plug-in Developers Kit free of charge by calling Adobe Technical Support. For specific instructions on generating an EDL, see your Adobe Premiere User Guide.

EDITING WIPE PATTERNS

With the exception of the Cross Dissolve and Direct transitions in Premiere, all transitions are interpreted as wipes by the EDL module. Video switchers interpret wipe patterns as codes. You can map the wipe patterns in the EDL to the wipe pattern codes used by your postproduction facility. If you are using Premiere 2.0, the EDL must be edited in a word processing program. When editing an EDL with a Macintosh word processor, save your work in text format with line breaks—EDLs require a line break at the end of each line in a file.

In Premiere 3.0, you can use the Wipe Code Editor to edit the codes. For specific instructions on using the Wipe Code Editor, see your Adobe Premiere User Guide.

USING A CORRECTLY FORMATTED TRANSFER DISK

Most postproduction systems use a disk formatting system known as MFM (Modified Frequency Modulation). The Macintosh uses a different format known as GCR (Group Code Recording). You will need a utility program that lets you mount an MFM-formatted disk onto your Macintosh so that you can move the EDL to a transfer disk. Because the IBM PC uses MFM format, any program that lets you mount PC-formatted disks will give you access to MFM-formatted disks.

Some older CMX postproduction systems used a proprietary format created by Digital Equipment Corporation (DEC). Digital FX has a program called FX Press, which allows you to access a Digital Computer-formatted disk on your Macintosh.

Using Device Controllers with Premiere

This record describes how to use device control in Adobe Premiere 4.x, and lists several device controllers for the Macintosh and Windows.

USING DEVICE CONTROL IN PREMIERE

Device controllers let you control your tape deck or video camera from within Adobe Premiere using a timecode address (i.e., by identifying individual frames), which allows frame-accurate capture of video clips.

If you have Premiere and a video tape recorder (VTR) or video camera that supports device control, you can:

- control the tape deck from the computer screen instead of by pressing buttons on the tape deck
- set In and Out points for clips in the Movie Capture or Clip Logging dialog box, then record those video segments automatically using the Batch Capture feature, or export an Edit Decision List (EDL) for offline editing
- stamp timecode onto the digitized movie when your deck is capable of variable playing speeds
- when your deck is capable of variable playing speeds, capture movies at low frame rates, then increase the frame rate when rendering your final movie
- automatically advance your tape deck to the frame displayed in the In or Out field of the Movie Capture window by pressing Option and clicking the In or Out button in the Movie Capture window

NOTE: Device control is not supported in Premiere LE.

To capture video using device control, you must use source footage that has been recorded with timecode, called burned-in timecode, visual timecode, or window dubs. The timecode's format should follow one of the standards set by the Society of Motion Picture and Television Engineers (SMPTE), the European Broadcasting Union (EBU), or Sony's RC timecode.

When you capture burned-in timecode in Premiere using a video capture card other than the Radius Telecast, Premiere only reads the timecode address of the first frame that is captured; the remaining frames in the captured clip are automatically numbered by Premiere. For this reason, the timecode address of some frames in a captured clip may not match the timecode address of the burned-in timecode.

TIMECODE

Timecode identifies the duration of a video clip, or its starting and ending points. Timecode enables video editors to locate frames accurately, and to synchronize picture and audio elements, or frame-accurate synchronization. SMPTE timecode identifies each frame with a unique address in the "hours:minutes:seconds:frames" form. SMPTE timecode can be Longitudinal Timecode (LTC), which is recorded in the second audio track of a video tape, or can be Vertical Interval Timecode (VITC), which is recorded in the vertical space between frames.

There are several SMPTE timecode standards that are used with different frame rates. Since the SMPTE timecode for National Television Standards Committee (NTSC) video assumes a frame rate of 30 frames per second (fps), even though the actual NTSC standard is 29.97 fps, there is a 0.1 percent discrepancy between real playing time and the timecode's duration measurement. The drop-frame format, developed to address this discrepancy, drops two frame counts (i.e., actual frames are not dropped) from the count every minute, for 9 out of 10 minutes. The nondrop-frame timecode ignores this discrepancy and is not duration accurate.

While SMPTE is the standard timecode used in North America, EBU is the standard timecode used in Europe. EBU is based on PAL or SECAM video signals which have a playback rate of 25 fps, and is a nondrop-frame standard only.

CONNECTIVITY AND PROTOCOL

To determine whether your VTR or video camera supports device control, look for an outlet labeled "Remote" or "VISCA" on the back of the VTR or video camera. For more information on using device control with your recording device, refer to the manufacturer's documentation.

Device controllers are connected from the RS-232, RS-422 or VISCA ports on the video tape recorder (VTR) to the printer/modem serial port (Macintosh) or COM port 1-4 (IBM-compatible). Most VTRs use a 9-pin RS-422 interface (e.g., Sony PVW or BVW). The RS-232 ports on some decks (e.g., Sony UVW series) require a DB-9 to DB-25 adapter to accommodate their 25-pin outlets.

Sony VISCA is a common device control interface that is built into many VTRs. It connects to the computer's serial port using an 8-pin DIN connector (Macintosh) or 9-pin connector (IBM-compatible). VISCA requires a control panel device (included with Premiere in the Third Party Stuff folder) when used with Premiere for Macintosh.

Sony Control-L and Control-C interfaces are similar to VISCA, and can be used with Sony's V-Box to make a consumer-grade VCR capable of device control.

EZ by Telcom Research can be used to make an ordinary VCR capable of device control. The EZ provides a RS-422 interface that can be used by any device controller that supports RS-422. The EZ can read burned-in timecode, enabling Premiere to create an Edit Decision List (EDL), but does not enable batch capture.

DEVICE CONTROLLERS

Device controllers are either video controllers or animation controllers. Video controllers capture video in real time, while animation controllers capture video frame by frame (nonreal-time).

The following device controllers are video controllers (real time):

- DQ-TimeCoder (Macintosh)
  The Diaquest DQ-TimeCoder includes a Premiere plug-in and cable, and uses RS-422 protocol. The DQ-TimeCoder supports both SMPTE and EBU timecode, and is similar to VISCA protocol, though it does not use Sony's proprietary RC timecode. Diaquest can be reached at 510-526-7167.
- MacAnimator Control Plug-In (Macintosh)
  The MacAnimator Control plug-in supports any broadcast or professional quality VTR with an RS-422 remote control port and built-in SMPTE timecode reader. The MacAnimator Control plug-in requires Premiere 4.0 or later. The MacAnimator Control plug-in can only be used with VTRs that support SMPTE timecode, which includes consumer-grade VTRs, Camcorders using Control-L or Control-S protocols, but not Sony VISCA recorders. The MacAnimator Control plug-in requires System 7.x and QuickTime 2.x. The MacAnimator Control plug-in is available from McQ Productions/Software Systems at 800-659-4755.
- MediaMotion (Macintosh and Windows)
  MediaMotion (formerly Video Toolkit [VTK] Plug-In Pack) includes a control cable and software (Macintosh or Windows compatible) for use with Premiere. MediaMotion supports consumer-level and professional VTR using Control-L, Control-M (Macintosh only), RS-422, RS-232, and VISCA protocols. MediaMotion control devices use LTC, VITC, and RC timecode, and support batch capture. Videonics (formerly Abbate Video, Inc.) can be reached at 800-338-3348.
- ProVTR (Macintosh and Windows)
  The Pipeline Digital ProVTR includes the ProVTR plug-in for use with Premiere, a Mac-to-VTR cable, and has an internal timecode reader. The ProVTR uses 9-pin protocol for RS-422 compatible VTRs. You can use RS-232 VTRs with an adapter. The ProVTR is bundled with the Radius VideoVision Studio capture card, or is available separately for $99. Pipeline Digital can be reached at 800-798-8793.
- Pipeline Recorder (Macintosh)
  The Pipeline Recorder includes all the features of the Pipeline ProVTR, plus support for insert edits on RS-422 9-pin VTRs, and assemble-edit capability for RS-232 25-pin and VISCA VTRs. You can use the Pipeline Recorder with the Radius VideoVision Studio or Telecast capture card (using Radius Studio Player 2.6 or later), or the Truevision Targa 1000 or Targa 2000 capture card. Pipeline Digital can be reached at 800-798-8793.
- V-LAN (Macintosh and Windows)
  VideoMedia's V-LAN controller box, called the Alix, controls a wide range of videotape, digital disk recorder, and video switchers for animation, desktop video, and broadcast television production. VideoMedia's AutoPICTs application writes compiled movies to tape as sequentially numbered PICT frames. V-LAN does not require a system extension or control panel device. To use V-LAN with Premiere, install the compatible version of V-LAN's EPROM software. VideoMedia can be reached at 408-227-9977.

The following device controllers are animation controllers (nonreal-time):

- ARTI (Macintosh and Windows)
  The ARTI controller requires no system extensions or control panel devices. The higher-end model can write timecode to a VTR. Advanced Remote Technologies can be reached at 408-374-9044.
- Diaquest DQ-Animaq (Macintosh)
  Diaquest's DQ-Animaq is a NuBus card that controls most professional and broadcast video recorders in NTSC and PAL formats. Diaquest's Animaq 1.5 software utility, included with the DQ-Animaq card, works in conjunction with the user's video capture card to digitize video frame by frame, saving numbered PICT, PIC, TARGA, or QuickTime files. DQ-Animaq requires a control panel device, and requires DQ Timecoder software when the video capture card does not record timecode from digitized clips. Diaquest can be reached at 510-526-7167.
- MacAnimator Export Plug-In (Macintosh)
  The MacAnimator Export plug-in enables you to record uncompressed movies frame by frame from Premiere's Clip window or Preview window. The MacAnimator Export plug-in requires a video capture card that produces NTSC or PAL video signals (e.g., Truevision Targa 1000, Truevision Targa 2000, Radius VideoVision Studio), or a Power Macintosh AV computer with

enough Video RAM (VRAM) to support two monitors (e.g., 4 MB). The MacAnimator Export plug-in requires a VTR with an RS-422 port and AutoEdit functionality, and requires System 7.x and QuickTime 2.x. The MacAnimator Export Plug-in is available from McQ Productions/Software Systems at 800-659-4755.

Calculating File Sizes for Premiere

CALCULATING IMAGE SIZE IN PREMIERE

To calculate the size in kilobytes (K) of one frame of uncompressed video, use the following formula:

- Frame size K = ((Pixel Width*Pixel Height*Bit Depth)/8)/1024

Where 8 represents an 8-bit byte, and 1024 equals the number of bytes per kilobytes. For example, the size in kilobytes of an uncompressed frame of full-size (i.e., 640 pixels by 480 pixels), 24-bit video is:

Frame size K = ((640*480*24)/8)/1024 = 900K

To determine the file size of one second of uncompressed video, multiply the image size by the number of frames per second (fps). For example, one second of uncompressed, full-size, full-speed (30 fps), 24-bit video is:

```
900K*30 = 27MB
```

To determine how compression affects file size, divide the file size by the compression ratio. For example, a 10:1 compression ratio will make a 27 megabyte (MB) file 2.7 megabytes per second.

When processing an image pan, Premiere requires three image buffers, plus up to 3MB of memory for application overhead. To determine how much memory is need to process an image pan:

```
Memory MB = ((image size)*3)+3
```

For example, an 8MB image requires 27MB of memory to process an image pan.

CALCULATING AUDIO SIZE IN PREMIERE

To determine the size of an audio file, use the following formulas:

- For 8-bit mono: (Seconds)*(kHz)=(Size)
- For 16-bit mono: ((Seconds)*(kHz))*2=(Size)
- For 8-bit stereo: ((Seconds)*(kHz))*2=(Size)
- For 16-bit stereo: (((Seconds)*(kHz))*2)*2=(Size)

For example, the file size of 30 seconds of 16-bit, 11kHz mono audio is:

```
30*11*2=660k
```

The resulting value is an approximation only because 1 kilobyte equals 1,024 bytes, not 1000 bytes, but the results are accurate enough to estimate data rates.

Field Rendering

Field rendering is the process of creating a movie from a sequence of interlaced fields rather than frames. Many video playback and broadcast systems, including National Television Standards Committee (NTSC) and Phase Alternating Line (PAL) formats, display one field at a time, rather than one frame at a time. Movies created as a sequence of frames will look stuttered when played back on a system that displays sequences of fields. This record describes the process of field rendering and the field rendering options available in Adobe Premiere.

FRAMES AND FIELDS

Each video frame consists of consecutively numbered horizontal lines, which are divided between two different fields. One field consists of all odd-numbered lines, and the other consists of all even-numbered lines.

Standard video equipment records and displays fields one after the other, alternating between odd-numbered and even-numbered fields, a process referred to as "interlaced video." A field whose first line is the topmost line is called an upper field, an odd field, or field 1; a field whose first line is second from the top is called a lower field, an even field, or field 2.

FIELD DOMINANCE

Field dominance (i.e., field rendering order) is the order in which video tape equipment renders fields (i.e., upper field first or lower field first). When a movie is rendered, the movie's field rendering order should match the playback equipment's field rendering order. For example, if the playback equipment is "field 1-dominant," then field 1 should be rendered first when making the movie. A movie whose field dominance is opposite that of the playback system will play with stuttered movement. Most 640 x 480 pixel movies are field 1-dominant, while most movies that are 648 x 480 pixels or larger are field 2-dominant.

FIELD RENDERING OPTIONS

To set the field rendering order in Adobe Premiere 4.x, choose Make > Output Options. In the Project Output Options dialog box, select one of the following options from the Type pop-up menu:

FULL SIZE FRAME

Select the Full Size Frame option when rendering a movie with video capture boards that do not process separate fields in a NTSC video frame. If clips within the project contain separate field, only the upper field will be used to render the frame.

- Field 1

  Select the Field 1 option for field 1-dominant boards that process full-frame, 60-field video.
- Field 2

  Select the Field 2 option for field 2-dominant boards that process full-frame, 60-field video.
- 1/2 Horizontal

  Select the 1/2 Horizontal option for boards that capture full-frame video by capturing half of each alternating field in a 320-pixel by 480-pixel configuration.

- 1/2 Vertical
  Select the 1/2 Vertical option for boards that capture full-frame video by capturing half of each alternating field in a 640-pixel by 240-pixel configuration.
- Field 1 - 1/2 H
  Select the Field 1 - 1/2 H option for field 1-dominant boards that process half of each alternating field in a 320-pixel by 480-pixel configuration.
- Field 2 - 1/2 H
  Select the Field 2 - 1/2 H option for field 2-dominant boards that process half of each alternating field in a 320-pixel by 480-pixel configuration.
  NOTE: The 1/2 Horizontal, 1/2 Vertical, Field 1 - 1/2 H, and Field 2 - 1/2 H option do not appear in the Type pop-up menu when the Simple Fields plug-in is installed in the Adobe Premiere Plug-Ins folder.

Premiere's "Replace with Source" Feature Summary

FEATURE

The "Replace with Source" feature in Adobe Premiere 3.0x and later replaces a virtual clip with its source clips.

Implementation

To use the command, select a virtual clip and choose "Replace with Source" from the Clip menu. In the dialog box that appears, specify output and compression options, which correspond to the project's output and compression options by default, then name the file and click "OK."

DETAIL

The "Replace with Source" feature compiles a movie from the source clips of a virtual clip, then imports the source clip and replaces the virtual clip with it. The compiled source movie displays more quickly in previews, and you can delete the original source clips from the Construction window after creating one.

Creating an Inset Without Cropping

After you add a video clip to a project, Adobe Premiere automatically resizes it to the project's dimensions. To create a scaled inset (i.e., play a smaller clip inside a larger clip), you can use transitions or motion settings.

To create an inset using the Zoom transition in Premiere 4.x or Premiere 4.x LE:

1. Drag the background clip (i.e., the larger clip) from the Project window to Track A in the Construction Window.
2. Drag the inset clip (i.e., the smaller clip) to Track B in the Construction Window.
3. Drag the Zoom transition from the Transition window to Track T in the Construction Window, then adjust its duration to equal the duration of the inset clip.
4. Double-click the Zoom transition to open the Zoom Settings dialog box, then select Show Actual Sources.
5. Reduce the inset clip by dragging the sliders beneath the right and left images until the zoom percentage is the same for both the start and finish (e.g., Start=50%, End=50%).
6. If you want the inset clip to be off-center, position the cursor in the center of the left-hand clip (i.e., until the cursor changes to a pointing hand), then press the mouse button and drag the clip to the desired location.
7. Click OK to close the Zoom Settings dialog box.

To create an inset using Motion Settings in Premiere 4.x:

1. Drag the background clip (i.e., the larger clip) from the Project window to Track A in the Construction Window.
2. Drag the inset clip (i.e., the smaller clip) to Track S1 in the Construction Window.
3. Select the inset clip, then choose Clip > Motion.
4. In the Motion Settings dialog box, select the Start point and drag it to a position within the Visible Area.
5. Enter a scaling value in the Zoom text box to adjust the size of the inset clip.
6. Drag the Finish point directly on top of the Start point, then enter the same scaling value in the Zoom text box.
7. Click OK to close the Motion Settings dialog box.
   NOTE: If the scaled clip loses quality (e.g., artifacts appear), you can apply the Resize filter to the clip to resize the image to its final output size using interpolated scaling.

Deleting Preview Files from Premiere's Construction Window

The preview files in an Adobe Premiere project are not deleted automatically, so you can use them again if you want to make changes to the project. Once you have made a move, however, the preview files are unnecessary and take up disk space. Deleting them increases available disk space.

To delete all preview files (i.e., temporary clips) in a Premiere project from the Construction Window:

1. Press Command + Option + Shift (Macintosh) or Ctrl + Alt + Shift (Windows).
2. Position the cursor over the preview files bar (i.e., between the yellow work area bar and the time ruler).
3. Click when the cursor displays as a trash can.

Creating Movies with Transparent Backgrounds in Premiere

Alpha channels are invisible 8-bit channels reserved for masking or other transparency information in an image. You can use alpha channels to create movies with transparent backgrounds in Adobe Premiere. The compiled movie can be used in any application that supports alpha channels.

To create a movie with a transparent background:

1. Import a video clip containing source footage shot against a blue screen or green screen.

2. Drag the clip from the Project window to the S1 track in the Construction window. Make sure there are no other clips above or below it.
3. Choose "Transparency" from the Clip window, then select "Blue Screen," "Non-Red" for footage shot against a blue screen, or "Green Screen" for footage shot against a green screen from the "Key Type:" popup menu.
4. Select "Mask Only," then select "None" from the "Smoothing:" popup menu.
5. Click the Collapse Preview icon to display the sample image in the "Preview" window, then click the checkerboard or page peel icon.
6. Adjust the "Threshold=" and "Cutoff=" sliders until the sample image displays black and white or as close as possible to black and white, then click "OK."
7. In the Construction window, select the clip by dragging with the block select tool.
8. Move the pointer over the selected clip so it turns into a virtual clip tool, then click and drag the virtual clip to the B track in another area of the Construction window.
9. Drag a copy of the original video clip from the Project window to the A track, aligning it above the virtual clip.
10. Drag the "Channel Map" transition from the "Transitions" palette to Track T, aligning it with the two clips.
11. In the "Channel Map Settings" dialog box that appears, set the four popup menus as follows, then click "OK."
    Source A Red to Red
    Source A Green to Green
    Source A Blue to Blue
    Source B Gray to Alpha
12. Position the Work Area bar over the two clips.
13. Choose "Movie..." from the Make menu, then click "Compression...."
14. In the "Compression" dialog box, select "Animation" or "None" from the video compressor popup menu, select "Millions of Colors+" from the color popup menu, then click "OK."
15. In the "Make Movie" dialog box, click on "Output Options...."
16. Select "Work Area" from the "Output:" popup menu, then click "OK."
17. Name the movie and click "OK."

Applying Data Rate Limits in Premiere and After Effects

Applying a data rate limit when you capture or render digital video prevents your computer from dropping frames, which causes video to appear stuttered or jerky. The data rate you choose for video capture depends on the capabilities of your system and hardware configuration, while the data rate you choose for playing or previewing video depends on the target playback system.

If your movie will be played or previewed on your local hard drive, you should limit the data rate to the maximum video data rate of your local system and hardware configuration (e.g., the optimal capture rate you found when choosing an appropriate data rate for video capture).

If your movie will be played on other systems (e.g., on a CD-ROM or Web servers), you should limit the data rate to the maximum video data rate of those playback systems. For example, a realistic data rate for CD-ROM movies is 90-100 K/sec for single-speed (1x) CD-ROM drives, 150-200 K/sec for double-speed (2x) drives, and 350-500 K/sec for quad-speed (4x) drives.

CHOOSING A DATA RATE LIMIT FOR CAPTURING VIDEO IN PREMIERE 4.X

When capturing (i.e., digitizing) video, the amount of data you capture should not exceed the capacity of your capture drive and video capture card, otherwise your computer will drop frames. Because the amount of data you can capture is affected by your system and hardware configuration, the only way to determine an appropriate data rate is to test the system yourself.

To determine your system's maximum data rate for video capture using Adobe Premiere 4.x:

1. Make sure you have followed your device manufacturer's instructions for optimizing your system and hardware configuration. Adobe also provides optimization instructions for some capture cards.
2. In Premiere 4.x, choose File > Preferences > Scratch Disks.
3. Choose the hard drive you will use to capture video from the Temp/Captured Movies pop-up menu (Macintosh) or from the pop-up menu that appears (Windows), then click OK.
4. Choose File > Capture > Movie Capture to activate the Movie Capture menu.
5. Follow the instructions provided with your video capture card for entering a data rate limit. The procedure for most capture cards is as follows:

   In Premiere 4.x for the Macintosh, choose Movie Capture > Video Input. Select your hardware compressor from the pop-up menu in the upper-left corner, enter a data rate limit, then click OK.

   In Premiere 4.x for Windows, choose Movie Capture > Recording Options, then click Compression. Enter a data rate limit, click OK to close the Video Compression dialog box, then click OK to close the Recording Options dialog box.

   NOTE: The data rate limit you enter should be an initial estimate of your system's capabilities. To assist you in making this estimate, review the specifications of your capture drive and capture card, or use a hard disk utility to perform a test of the drive.
6. Disable audio input by making sure Sound Off is checked on the Movie Capture menu (Macintosh), or Record Audio is unchecked on the Movie Capture menu (Windows).
7. Click Record in the Movie Capture window, wait for a few seconds, then click the mouse to stop recording.

8. When the Clip window appears, choose File > Save. Name the file, specify a target location, then click Save.
9. Choose File > Tools > Movie Analysis. In the dialog box that appears, locate and select the movie you just saved, then click Analyze (Macintosh) or Open (Windows).
NOTE: The Movie Analysis tool is not available in Premiere 4.0 LE for Windows. To analyze your movie's data rate in Windows 95, select your movie in the Windows Explorer, then choose File > Properties and click the Details tab. The data rate is reported in the Video Format section in KB/sec. To analyze your movie's data rate in Windows 3.x, open your movie in Media Player, then choose Devices > Configure. Your movie's data rate is reported in the Information section of the Video Playback Options dialog box. For additional support using Windows to analyze your movie's data rate, contact Microsoft Technical Support.
10. In the Analysis window, scroll to the Video section. If the first line reads "This movie appears to have dropped frames," your capture data rate was too high, and you should repeat steps 4-9 using a lower data rate limit (try using the average data rate reported in the Movie Analysis window). If the Video section does not report dropped frames, repeat steps 4-9 using a higher data rate limit. Once you have found the highest data rate limit possible without dropping frames, use this data rate as the limit when capturing video. You may need to adjust this limit as your configuration or source video changes.
NOTE: This process determines the maximum capture rate achievable at the time you execute this procedure. If you find you are unable to capture at this rate without dropping frames in the future, you should repeat steps for optimizing your system and hardware configuration.

CHOOSING A DATA RATE LIMIT FOR PREMIERE 4.X PROJECTS

To find an appropriate data rate limit for movies that are previewed and played on your local system in Premiere 4.x:

1. Open your Premiere project, then choose Make > Movie (Macintosh) or Make > Make Movie (Windows).
2. Click Compression. In the Compression Settings dialog box, choose the compressor you will use for your final output from the Compressor pop-up menu (Macintosh) or Method pop-up menu (Windows).
3. Select Limit Data Rate To, then enter an initial estimate of your system's maximum video data rate in the adjacent text box. For example, you could enter the maximum capture rate you found when choosing an appropriate data rate for video capture, or you could enter the average data rate reported by the Movie Analysis tool for the clips in your project.
NOTE: Some compressors require a slightly different procedure for entering a data rate limit, while other compressors don't support data rate limits. If you are using a Motion-JPEG (MJPG) hardware compressor, refer to your compressor's documentation for information on applying a data rate limit. If you are using one of the software compressors included with QuickTime, QuickTime for Windows, or Video for Windows, the Limit Data Rate To option will be dimmed if that compressor does not support data rate limits.
4. Click OK to close the Compression Settings dialog box.
5. Choose Project > Preview.
6. Watch the preview and evaluate how smoothly it plays. If your movie stutters or jerks when played, repeat steps 1-5 using a lower data rate limit. If your entire movie plays smoothly, repeat steps 1-5 using a higher data rate limit. Once you have found the highest data rate limit possible without stuttered playback, set this data rate as your limit in the Compression Settings dialog box. You may need to adjust this limit as your configuration or source video changes.

CHOOSING A DATA RATE LIMIT FOR AFTER EFFECTS 3.X PROJECTS

To find an appropriate data rate limit for movies that are played on your local system in Adobe After Effects 3.x:

1. Open your After Effects project, then choose Composition > Make Movie.
2. Name your movie, specify a target location, and click Save.
3. In the Render Queue dialog box, select Custom from the current composition's Output Module pop-up menu.
4. In the Output Module Settings dialog box, click Format Options in the Video Output section.
5. In the Compression Settings dialog box, choose the compressor you will use for your final output from the Compressor pop-up menu.
6. Select Limit Data Rate To, then enter an initial estimate of your system's maximum video data rate in the adjacent text box. For example, you could enter the maximum capture rate you found when choosing an appropriate data rate for video capture, or, if you have Adobe Premiere, you could enter the average data rate reported by Premiere's Movie Analysis tool for the clips in your project.
NOTE: Some compressors require a slightly different procedure for entering a data rate limit, while other compressors don't support data rate limits. If you are using a Motion-JPEG (MJPG) hardware compressor, refer to your compressor's documentation for information on applying a data rate limit. If you are using one of the software compressors included with QuickTime, the Limit Data Rate To option will be dimmed if that compressor does not support data rate limits.
7. Click OK to close the Compression Settings dialog box, then click OK to close the Output Module Settings dialog box.
8. In the Render Queue dialog box, click Render.
9. Play your movie and evaluate how smoothly it plays. If your movie stutters or jerks when played, repeat steps 1-8 using a lower data rate limit. If your entire movie

plays smoothly, repeat steps 1-8 using a higher data rate limit. Once you have found the highest data rate limit possible without stuttered playback, set this data rate as your limit in the Compression Settings dialog box. You may need to adjust this limit as your configuration or source video changes.

Converting Movies Between QuickTime and Video for Windows Formats

This document describes the process of converting digital movies between QuickTime and Video for Windows formats.

BEFORE CONVERTING MOVIES

Compression

When you capture (digitize) video and audio data, use the least lossy compression scheme available. Lossy compression schemes remove information during capture that cannot be recovered. Because additional information is lost when the final movie is rendered and the frames are recompressed, capture movies with more video and audio data than you need for final output.

When you render movies that will be converted, use a compression/decompression algorithm (codec) that is compatible with both QuickTime and Video for Windows. Cinepak, supported by Apple QuickTime, QuickTime for Windows, and Video for Windows, provides complete compression and playback functionality, is optimized for compressing 16-bit and 24-bit video, and attains a high compression ratio.

Intel Indeo R3.2 is supported by both Video for Windows and QuickTime for Windows. An Apple QuickTime codec is available from Intel for compressing, editing, and playing back video on the Macintosh.

The Apple Video, Graphics, RLE, and JPEG codecs are supported by QuickTime for Windows, but not by Video for Windows. The Apple Animation codec is read-only (uneditable) in Windows.

The Video for Windows Utilities include the Windows Compressor extension that enables Microsoft RLE, Microsoft Video 1, and Microsoft Full Frame compression. Apply these codecs to movies created on the Macintosh that will be played on the Windows platform, but not when they will be played on the Macintosh, as they have not been optimized for use with QuickTime.

Audio Interleaving

In Premiere's Project Output Options dialog box, the number you choose from the Blocks pop-up menu (Macintosh) or Interleave pop-up menu (Windows) determines the amount of audio stored in the movie between blocks of video. You can specify the amount of audio information stored between blocks of video (i.e., the audio interleaving), by a number of frames or by a length of time in seconds or minutes.

Video for Windows interleaves audio and video based on a specified number of frames, while QuickTime interleaves according to a specified amount of time. Video for Windows files should be interleaved at a 1:1 ratio (i.e., one frame of video for each sample of audio) by choosing 1 Frame from the Interleave pop-up menu (Windows) in the Project Output Options dialog box. QuickTime files should be interleaved at one half second of sound for every half second of video by choosing 1/2 Sec from the Blocks pop-up menu (Macintosh) or the Interleave pop-up menu (Windows) in the Project Output Options dialog box.

Audio Frequency

For movies that will be played back on the Windows platform, specify an audio frequency of 11.025 kHz, 22.050 kHz, or 44.100 kHz.

To set the audio frequency, do the following:

1. Set the appropriate audio frequency by choosing Make > Output Options.
2. In the Project Output Options dialog box, choose Other from the Rate pop-up menu.
3. In the Audio Rate dialog box, choose 11025 Hz, 22050 Hz, or 44100 Hz from the pop-up menu, or enter 11025, 22050, or 44100 in the Rate text box, then click OK.
4. Click OK in the Project Output Options dialog box.

Depending on the method used to convert movies to a Windows compatible format, you may be able to change the audio frequency during conversion.

Color Palettes

QuickTime enables you to attach custom color palettes to QuickTime movie files to optimize display on 8-bit monitors. Video for Windows only supports custom color palettes for some codecs.

Gamma Correction

Because of color display differences between the Macintosh and Windows platforms, movies created on a Macintosh may appear darker when played on a Windows computer. When you create movies in Premiere for the Macintosh that will be played back on a Windows computer, apply the Gamma Correction filter to accommodate color display differences. In the Gamma Correction Settings dialog box, specify a 0.7 or 0.8 gamma level. The Gamma Correction filter lightens the image by adjusting the brightness levels of the midtones.

When you use Premiere for Windows to convert Video for Windows (AVI) files to QuickTime movies, apply the Gamma Correction filter and specify a 1.2 or 1.3 gamma level.

FLATTENING MACINTOSH QUICKTIME MOVIES BEFORE CONVERSION

QuickTime for Macintosh files must be flattened before they can be played in Windows applications. Flattening a movie removes its resource fork and puts all video and audio information into a single data fork, making the file self-contained.

QuickTime for Macintosh movies, like other Macintosh files, have data organized into resource forks and data forks. Windows and DOS applications do not use resource forks, storing all information in a single data fork. Flattening a movie appends its resource fork information (e.g., type and creator information, references to data in other files) to the end of the data fork.

You can flatten movies using Adobe Premiere 3.0x and later, FusionRecorder 1.1, MoviePlayer 2.0, Movie Converter 1.0, and FlattenMooV.

To flatten existing QuickTime movies in Premiere 3.0x and later:

1. Open the movie to be flattened.
2. Choose File > Export > Flattened Movie.
3. Name the file according to MS-DOS naming conventions (e.g., Filename.mov), then click Save.

To flatten movies as they are compiled from the Construction Window in Premiere 4.x:

1. If you're using Premiere 4.0x, install the Make Flattened plug-in in the Adobe Premiere Plug-Ins folder. The Make Flattened plug-in is installed by the Premiere installer into the Additional Plug-Ins folder in the Goodies folder in the Adobe Premiere 4.0 folder.
2. Launch Premiere 4.x and open a completed project in the Construction Window.
3. Choose Make > Movie, then click Output Options.
3. In the Project Output Options dialog box, select Flatten, make other appropriate selections, then click OK.
4. Click Compression, then make the appropriate selections and click OK.
5. Name the movie, then click OK.

To flatten a QuickTime movie in Video Fusion 1.5, FusionRecorder 1.1, MoviePlayer 2.0, or Movie Converter 1.0:

1. Open the movie then choose File > Save As.
2. Select Make Movie Self-contained and select Cross-Platform (Video Fusion only) or Playable on Non-Apple computers.
3. Name the file using the MS-DOS naming convention (e.g., Filename.mov), then click Save.

To flatten a QuickTime movie using the FlattenMooV application:

1. In FlattenMooV, open the movie to be flattened in the list box that appears.
2. Click the close box in the upper-left corner of the movie window.
3. When prompted, specify a location for the saved movie, then click OK.

CONVERTING QUICKTIME MOVIES TO VIDEO FOR WINDOWS MOVIES

You can convert QuickTime movies to Video for Windows movies using the Microsoft Video for Windows Converter (Macintosh), TRMOOV (Windows), or SmartCap (Windows).

The Video for Windows Converter does not interleave QuickTime movies in Video for Windows (AVI) format. You can interleave QuickTime movies in Video for Windows format after conversion using a utility (e.g., VidEdit). The Video for Windows Converter cannot convert movies with Indeo compression unless you modify the Video for Windows Converter utility using a resource editing utility (e.g., Apple ResEdit). For instructions on modifying the Video for Windows Converter, see Further Reading.

TRMOOV should only be used when the original file and the converted file use the same codec (i.e., Cinepak or Indeo). TRMOOV does not support resampling audio or retaining color palettes attached to the movie file. Audio tracks in long movies converted with TRMOOV may play out of sync with their video tracks.

Intel's SmartCap can only convert movies saved with Indeo compression. SmartCap does not support resampling audio, and removes custom color palettes attached to the movie file. For instructions on using SmartCap, see Further Reading.

To convert QuickTime movies to AVI files using the Video for Windows Converter:

1. Launch the Video for Windows Converter utility.
2. In the Video for Windows Converter dialog box, click Open Source.
3. Locate and open the folder containing the movie or movies to be converted, select one of the movie names in the list box, then click Open. All movies in the folder appear in the Source Folder list within the Video for Windows Converter dialog box.
4. Select the movie or movies to be converted in the Source Folder list.
5. Designate a folder for the converted movies by clicking Open Destination in the Video for Windows Converter dialog box. Then, in the dialog box that appears, select the desired folder and click Select Folder.
6. In the Video for Windows Converter dialog box, click Convert. In the dialog box that appears, select the desired compression and audio resampling options.
   NOTE: If the movie was created with a compatible compressor, choose Direct Transfer from the pop-up menu next to Video. If the movie was created with an incompatible audio frequency, choose Resample Audio from the pop-up menu next to Audio.
7. Click OK. The Video for Windows Converter automatically names the files using a MS-DOS compatible filename (e.g., Filename.avi).

To convert QuickTime movies to AVI files using TRMOOV:

1. After generating a flattened QuickTime movie on a Macintosh computer, transfer the movie to a computer running Windows.
2. Launch Trmoov.exe on the Windows computer.
3. Select the Source Movie and Target Movie, then click Start.

CONVERTING VIDEO FOR WINDOWS MOVIES TO QUICKTIME MOVIES

Microsoft's AVI to QT Utility (Macintosh), Premiere for Windows, TRMOOV (Windows), SmartCap (Windows), or SmartVid (DOS) can covert Video for Windows movies to QuickTime movies.

The AVI to QT Utility cannot resample audio, and may reduce the quality of converted movies when applying a new codec to the movie file. Video for Windows (AVI) files compressed with Cinepak for Windows 1.5.0.29 and earlier may display streaks or artifacts when played back on a

Macintosh computer. Use the AVI to QT Utility when your AVI files are compressed with Cinepak for Windows 1.5.0.-198 or later. To determine which version of Cinepak for Windows is installed, use the Windows Drivers applet.

Use TRMOOV only when the original file and the converted file use the same codec. TRMOOV cannot resample audio or consistently retain color palettes attached to movie files. Audio tracks in long movies converted with TRMOOV may play out of sync with their video tracks.

SmartCap can only convert files compressed with the Indeo codec, and removes custom color palettes attached to movie files. For instructions on using SmartCap, see Further Reading.

SmartVid converts movie files compressed with any codec. Because SmartVid does not modify the compression scheme, movies that are not compressed with a Quick-Time-compatible codec may not play as expected after conversion.

To convert AVI files to QuickTime movies:

1. Launch the AVI to QT Utility.
2. In the dialog box that appears, select the movie or movies to be converted, then click Add.
3. After adding movies to the conversion list, click Convert.
4. In the dialog box that appears, select Save Self-Contained Movie, designate a folder for the converted movie, then click Choose [Folder Name].

To convert AVI files to QuickTime movies using Premiere for Windows:

1. Add the AVI file to the Construction Window.
2. Apply the Gamma Correction filter with a gamma level of 1.2 or 1.3.
3. Choose Make > Movie, then click Output Options. Choose 1/2 Second from the Interleave pop-up menu, make other appropriate selections, then click OK.
   NOTE: When using the Cinepak codec and a frame size that is not a QuickTime standard, specify a frame height and width in pixels that are multiples of four. Standard QuickTime frame sizes are 120 x 90, 160 x 120, 240 x 180, and 320 x 240.
4. In the Make Movie dialog box, click Compression, make the appropriate selections, then click OK.
5. Name the file using a MS-DOS compatible filename (e.g., Filename.mov), then click OK.

AVAILABLE CONVERSION UTILITIES

FusionRecorder is included with the system software for all Power Macintosh and Macintosh AV computers, and is available on the World Wide Web.

MoviePlayer and Movie Converter are available from Apple Programmer & Developer Association (APDA), and on the World Wide Web. Movie Converter is included with the Apple QuickTime Starter Kit, and is also available from Apple Programmer & Developer Association (APDA).

FlattenMooV, a freeware application written by Robert Hennessy, is available on the World Wide Web.

The Video for Windows Converter and the AVI to QT Utility are included with the Video for Windows Utilities, available from Microsoft.

SmartCap and SmartVid are available from Intel.

TRMOOV is available from San Francisco Canyon Company and on the World Wide Web.

Creating Photoshop Alpha Channels for use in Premiere and After Effects

An alpha channel is an invisible 8-bit channel assigned to an image, often used for creating masks that isolate part of the image. You can use Adobe Photoshop to create alpha channels for images that you import into Adobe Premiere and Adobe After Effects.

NOTE: You must use the full retail version of Photoshop 2.x or later to create alpha channels. Photoshop LE, which is included with Premiere LE, cannot create alpha channels.

To create an alpha channel in Photoshop 2.x or later:

1. Choose Mode > RGB Color.
2. Select the area that you wish to remain opaque in Premiere or After Effects.
3. Choose Select > Save Selection. In Photoshop 3.x's Save Selection dialog box, select New Channel, then click OK.
   NOTE: Photoshop uses the information in the fourth channel to create the alpha channel. If your new channel is not listed in the fourth position in the Channels palette, drag the channel within the palette to the fourth position.
4. Choose File > Save As.
5. When saving files for use on a Macintosh computer, select Photoshop, Pict File, or Targa from the Format pop-up menu. When saving files for use in Windows, select Photoshop, Pict File, Targa, or TIFF from the Format pop-up menu.
   NOTE: The Photoshop file format retains layer information for use in After Effects.
6. Click Save. In the dialog box that appears when saving Targa or Pict files, select 32 bits/pixel for the resolution and None for the compression method, then click OK.

Importing Timecode Logs for Batch Capture in Premiere 4.x

You can import a timecode log for batch capturing in Adobe Premiere 4.x. The timecode log is a tab-delimited text file that contains a list of clips with their associated capture parameters.

To import a timecode log in Premiere 4.x:

1. Choose File > Capture > Batch Capture.
2. Choose Batch Capture > Import From Text File.
3. In the dialog box that appears, double-click the text file containing your timecode log.

For Premiere to correctly interpret the information in your timecode log, include one set of capture parameters for each clip, separating each capture parameter by a tab character and each clip by an end-of-paragraph character. For example, the text file could contain:

```
001 00:00:00:00 00:00:23:23 Cat Blue-Screen
001 00:00:33:33 00:00:45:45 Dog Green-Screen
```

Premiere imports each parameter based on the order the parameters appear in the Batch List window: Reel Name, In, Out, File Name, and Comment. You can change the order Premiere uses to import each parameter by choosing Batch Capture > Import/Export Settings.

Maintaining Aspect Ratio and Transparency in Premiere 4.x

When you add a video clip to a project, Adobe Premiere 4.x resizes the clip to the project dimensions by default. The height-to-width ratio (i.e., aspect ratio) of the resized clip may change considerably, causing the clip to display distorted. You can prevent this distortion by constraining the aspect ratio, which adds a black field between the video clip's borders and the project dimensions rather than resizing the clip. In Premiere 4.2 and later, you can edit the black field to display a different color. You can also make this field transparent so the clip can be superimposed on another background.

To prevent clips from distorting when you import them into Premiere 4.x:

Select the clip in the Project window or Construction Window, then choose Clip > Maintain Aspect Ratio.

OR: Before importing clips, choose File > Preferences > Still Image, select Lock Aspect (Windows) or Lock Aspect Ratio (Macintosh), then click OK.

To edit the field color around your clip's borders in Premiere 4.2 and later:

1. Make sure Maintain Aspect Ratio is checked on the Clip menu.
2. Select the clip, then choose Clip > Aspect Color (Windows) or Clip > Aspect Fill Color (Macintosh).
3. In the dialog box that appears, select a color, then click OK.

To make the field around a video clip transparent:

Crop the clip's borders in the Transparency Settings dialog box:

1. Drag the video clip from the Project window to the S-track in the Construction Window.
2. Select the clip in the Construction Window, then choose Clip > Transparency.
3. Reposition the clip handles in the Sample box to crop out the added black areas, then click OK.

   NOTE: To constrain cropping, press Shift, then position the crosshair over the outside edge of the clip and drag to crop.

OR: Select RGB Difference from the Key Type pop-up menu, select the fill color with the dropper, and set the Similarity slider to 0, then click OK. Blocks with matching RGB values are keyed out.

Unexpected Results

MAC OS / WINDOWS

Ceiling, Floor, or Walls Stretch to Infinite Points in Premiere 360-Degree Presentation

ISSUE

When creating a 360-degree Adobe Premiere presentation as described in the Adobe Premiere User Guide, the rear edge of the ceiling, floor, or walls stretch to a point, rather than a straight edge, in previews and movies. There is no rectangular frame defined for the back wall.

SOLUTIONS

Turn off field rendering when making the movie:

1. Choose "Output Options" from the "Make" menu.
2. Choose "Full Size Frame" from the menu next to "Type."

   OR: Disregard the appearance of the ceiling, floor, and walls and continue to add a back wall. The final preview and movie appear as expected.

ADDITIONAL INFORMATION

When "Field 1" or "Field 2" is selected in the "Project Output Options" dialog box, the movie or preview may appear differently than shown in the Premiere 4.0 User Guide.

The "Type" setting in the "Project Output Options" dialog box should match the video display board's method of processing NTSC or PAL video. The "Full Size Frame" option is selected when the board does not process the separate fields in a NTSC video frame.

Boards that can process the separate fields in a NTSC video frame are designated either field 1 dominant or field 2 dominant. "Field 1" or "Field 2" is selected for the "Type" setting depending on the field dominance of that board. Most boards are field 1 dominant, including Radius VideoVision, SuperMac DigitalFilm, and RasterOps MoviePak.

A 360-degree presentation, as described in the Adobe Premiere 4.0 User Guide, uses virtual clips to create a three-dimensional space effect with movies playing on five separate "walls."

Audio Plays with Clicking Noise When Previewed or Compiled in Premiere

ISSUE

Audio tracks play with a clicking noise when previewed or compiled in Adobe Premiere. The source files play correctly.

SOLUTION

Conform the captured clips to the project's time base:

1. **In Premiere, choose File > Tools > Conform Movie (Macintosh) or File > Tools > Conform AVI Movie (Windows).**

2. Select the captured clip then click Conform (Macintosh) or OK (Windows), or select a folder containing captured clips and click Conform [foldername] (Macintosh only).
3. Enter "30.00" in the Conform Movie To text box in the Conform Movie dialog box.

ADDITIONAL INFORMATION

When you capture video clips at 29.97 frames per second (fps) and import them into an Adobe Premiere project whose time base is set to 30 fps, the video clips preview and compile as expected. Audio tracks captured with the video clips do not scale to the 30 fps time base, causing them to play with a clicking noise in Premiere. Conforming the captured clips to the project's time base enables the audio tracks to play without a clicking noise.

Transitions Don't Shift to Second Track in Premiere 4.x

ISSUE

Transitions rendered in Adobe Premiere 4.x modify track A or track B, but do not shift from one track to the next.

SOLUTION

Use a time-variant transition, instead of a non-time-variant (i.e., Channel Map, Direct, Displace, Luminance Map, PICT Mask, Take, Texturize, Three-D, or Transition Factory) transition.

ADDITIONAL INFORMATION

Non-time-variant transitions in Premiere 4.x do not shift from one track to the next; rather, one track modifies the appearance of the other. In non-time-variant transitions, the mix of the two tracks remains constant from start to finish, but the content of one track processes or modifies the signal of the other track throughout the duration of the transition. Non-time-variant transitions can be identified in the Transition window by their icons, which are not animated like the icons of the time-variant transitions.

When using time-variant transitions in Adobe Premiere 4.x, the transition frames display a varying mix of tracks A and B. For example, the first frame of the transition may display 100% of track A and 0% of track B; as the transition progresses, the percentage of track A decreases while the percentage of track B increases, until the last frame displays 0% of track A and 100% of track B. This type of transition is called time-variant because the mix of the two tracks varies over time.

Non-Time-Variant Transitions

Non-Time-Variant Transitions	Description
Channel Map	Selected channels from images A and B map to the output.
Direct	Image B plays instead of image A.
Displace	The red and green channels of image A displace the pixels of image B.
Luminance Map	The luminance of image A maps onto image B.
PICT Mask	A user-selected PICT masks image B onto image A.
Take	Image B plays instead of image A.
Texturize	Image A maps onto image B.
Three-D	Source image maps into the red and blue output channels.
Transition Factory	A user-defined set of expressions defines the transition.

Movies with Still Images Compile with Dropped Frames or Repeated Transitions

ISSUE

Movies containing still images (e.g., Adobe Illustrator files, titles, mattes) preceded or followed by a video clip compile with dropped frames or repeated transitions in Adobe Premiere 3.0 or later for the Macintosh or in Premiere 4.x for Windows. You're using a Motion-JPEG (MJPG) video capture card.

SOLUTIONS

Do one or more of the following:

A. If you're using Premiere 4.0.1 or later for the Macintosh, deselect Optimize Stills in the Output Options dialog box.
   NOTE: If the Optimize Stills option is unavailable in Premiere 4.0.1, move the Make Flattened plug-in file from the Additional Plug-Ins folder to the Adobe Premiere Plug-Ins folder, then relaunch Premiere.
B. If you're using Premiere 4.x for Windows, deselect Optimize Stills in the Compression Settings dialog box. If you're using Premiere 3.0 or 4.0 for the Macintosh, apply a filter to the image:
   1. Select the still image in the Construction Window, then choose Clip > Filters.
   2. In the Filters dialog box, select any filter, then click Add.
      NOTE: You can apply the Image Pan filter to the clip without affecting how the clip displays.
   3. If the filter displays a settings dialog box, click OK to close the dialog box.
   4. Click OK to close the Filters dialog box.

ADDITIONAL INFORMATION

When you render movies that include still images, Premiere 3.0 or later for the Macintosh and Premiere 4.x for Windows reduce rendering time by not rendering each frame of the still image (i.e., they optimize stills). Many MJPG capture cards have difficulty switching between compiling every frame of a video clip and processing less information for the still image, resulting in dropped frames. Rendering every frame of the still image prevents these capture cards from dropping frames when compiling movies.

Deselecting Optimize Stills in Premiere 4.0.1 or later for the Macintosh and Premiere 4.x for Windows causes Premiere to render each frame of a still image. Applying a filter to the still image forces Premiere 3.0 and 4.0 for the Macintosh to render each frame.

The Optimize Stills option is only available in Premiere 4.0.1 when the Make Flattened plug-in is installed. Premiere installs the Make Flattened plug-in in the Additional Plug-ins folder in the Goodies folder in the Adobe Premiere 4.0.1 folder.

Movies are Pixelated or Distorted After Compiling in Premiere

ISSUE

After you compile a movie in Adobe Premiere, the entire movie, or clips with transitions, filters, motion, or overlays (i.e., titles) applied, display pixelated, blurred, or distorted.

SYMPTOMS

Video clips were captured using a hardware compression/decompression scheme (CODEC).

The Quality slider in the "Compression Settings" dialog box was used to set compression when compiling the movie.

SOLUTIONS

When using Premiere 3.0 or later for Macintosh or Premiere 4.0 or later for Windows, determine an average data rate using the Movie Analysis command and compile the movie with the data rate limiting function:

1. Use the Movie Analysis command to determine the average data rate of each clip or a sampling of clips in the project. For information on the Movie Analysis command, refer to the Adobe Premiere User Guide.
2. Average the Average Data Rate values of all the clips.
3. In the Compression Settings dialog box, select Limit Data Rate To and enter the average value in the corresponding text box, then recompile the movie.

OR: When using Premiere 1.x for Windows, determine an average data rate using Media Player, included with QuickTime for Windows, and compile the movie using Premiere's data rate limiting function:

1. Start Media Player, then open the clips used in the project.
2. Select Device > Configure. The data rate of each clip displays in the Information section of the Video Playback Options dialog box.
3. Average the data rate values of all the clips.
4. In Premiere's Compression Settings dialog box, select Limit Data Rate To and enter the average value in the corresponding text box, then recompile the movie.

ADDITIONAL INFORMATION

When compiling a movie in Adobe Premiere using compression, you can either set a consistent compression level with the Quality slider or control the amount of data being transferred to the hard disk using the Limit Data Rate To option. When using the Quality slider, Premiere applies the same level of compression to every portion of the movie, so complex areas of the movie (e.g., clips with motion, transitions, or filters applied to them) that contain more data to be processed are compressed the same amount as less complex areas of the movie (e.g., still images). The amount of data transferred in more complex areas may exceed the capabilities of the computer, causing data to be lost during compilation. The movie displays pixelated or distorted in those areas.

When the Limit Data Rate To option is selected, Premiere automatically adjusts compression levels to maintain the specified data rate: it increases compression in more complex areas of the movie and decreases compression in simpler areas, so that the computer's capabilities are not exceeded. You can determine the achievable playback rate of the computer where the video clips were captured or created by determining the clips' average data rate.

The entire movie may display distorted when Force Recompression is selected in the Project Output Options dialog box (Premiere 1.x for Windows), Recompress Always is selected in the Compression Settings dialog box (Premiere 4.0.x for Windows), or QuickTime Movie is selected as the output file type in the Project Output Options dialog box (Premiere for Macintosh).

Red "X" Appears in Preview Window in Premiere

ISSUE

A red letter "X" appears in the Preview window during transitions, filters, and special effects when previewing in Adobe Premiere. The previews are uncompiled.

SOLUTIONS

Generate a compiled preview by doing one or more of the following:

A. Choose Project > Preview, or press Enter.
B. Choose Make > Snapshot. When the Controller appears, use it to play the preview.

OR: Position the cursor in the time ruler so that the cursor changes to a down arrow, press and hold the mouse button, then drag the cursor through the time ruler.

ADDITIONAL INFORMATION

When playing uncompiled previews in Premiere, a red letter "X" appears in locations that require compiling to be previewed accurately (e.g., transitions, filters).

Uncompiled previews don't require processing time, but they lack the detail or accuracy of compiled previews. Uncompiled previews are displayed by dragging the cursor through the Construction window's edit line when the cursor displays as a triangle, or by clicking the Play button in the Construction window or Controller.

Audio in Captured Movie Clip Plays Too Fast or Too Slow in Premiere

ISSUE

Audio tracks play at an incorrect speed, instead of unsynchronized, or video tracks play with dropped frames in movies captured in Adobe Premiere 4.0x.

SOLUTIONS

Deselect the Conform Movie To option in the Recording Settings dialog box, then recapture the movie.

OR: Do one or more of the following:

A. Update to Premiere 4.2 or later.

B. Determine the data rate of the computer, then select that value from the Conform movie to pop-up menu in the Recording Settings dialog box:

1. Choose File > Movie Capture, then in the Movie Capture window, choose Movie Capture > Recording Settings.
2. In the Recording Settings dialog box, enter the desired frame dimensions in the Record At text boxes, deselect Conform Movie To, then click OK.
3. Choose Movie Capture > Video Input, then select Compression from the pop-up menu at the top left of the Video dialog box.
4. Adjust the Quality slider, or select Limit Data Rate To then enter the desired data rate in the text box.
5. Enter the desired value in the Frames Per Second text box, then click OK.
5. Choose Movie Capture > Sound Input, specify desired options, then click OK.
6. Capture a few seconds of video then save the captured file.
7. Choose File > Tools > Movie Analysis, select the captured file, then click Analyze.
8. Note the Average Frame Rate value, then close the Analysis window.
   NOTE: When the average frame rate reported is lower than desired, reduce the frame size dimensions in the Recording Settings dialog box, or adjust the Quality slider or data rate limit in the Video dialog box, then recapture the movie. Continue adjusting these settings until an acceptable average frame rate is reported in the Analysis window.
9. In the Frames Per Second text box in the Video dialog box, enter the average frame rate value noted in step 8, then click OK.
10. From the Conform Movie To pop-up menu in the Recording Settings dialog box, select a value close to the average frame rate noted in step 8, click OK, then recapture the movie.

ADDITIONAL INFORMATION

The Conform Movie To option in Premiere 4.x's Recording Settings dialog box is a time-base corrector that ensures all captured frames have exactly the same duration (e.g., video tape decks can produce frame rate errors). When the Conform Movie To option is selected, Premiere conforms movies by adding or reducing the number of frames in the captured clip to match the frame rate selected from the pop-up menu, then scaling the entire movie to match the duration of the captured clip.

Premiere 4.0x incorrectly conforms movies when the requested capture rate exceeds the actual capture rate, causing the playback speed of conformed video clips to increase. Premiere 4.2 does not alter the playback speed of conformed video clips, except in extreme cases of dropped frames.

When using Premiere 4.0 for the Macintosh, QuickTime 2.0 without Apple Multimedia Tuner 2.0.1 incorrectly interprets the Conform Movie To option with time base and frame rate options, causing the movie to play too fast or too slow and with an incorrect duration. Updating QuickTime 2.0 with the Apple Multimedia Tuner 2.0.1, included with Premiere 4.0.1, causes QuickTime to correctly interpret the Conform Movie To option.

When using Premiere 4.0x for Macintosh or Windows, frames drop when recording a movie when the frame rate selected from the Conform Movie To pop-up menu exceeds the computer's maximum data rate. When scaling the captured movie to the specified duration, Premiere also scales the audio, causing the movie too play too fast or too slow. For example, when conforming a movie to 30 frames per second (fps) on a computer that can only record at 10 fps, Premiere adds frames to the captured movie to make it 30 fps, extends the audio, then scales the entire movie to its original duration, causing the audio to play back three times faster than it was recorded.

You can also conform movies after they have been captured with the Conform Movie command. After selecting the Conform Movie command, select a frame rate close to the average data rate in the Conform Movie dialog box to prevent distortion.

Cannot Add Video Clip with Audio to Premiere's Construction Window

ISSUE

When you add a video clip containing audio to a video track in Adobe Premiere's Construction window, Premiere does not highlight the video track, and the clip outline disappears after you release the mouse button.

SOLUTIONS

Ensure an equal number of audio and video tracks are listed in the Add/Delete Tracks dialog box.

OR: Remove audio clips from the corresponding audio track.

ADDITIONAL INFORMATION
When you add video clips containing audio to Adobe Premiere's Construction window, Premiere places video and audio on corresponding tracks. When there is no corresponding audio track or a separate audio clip has been added to the corresponding audio track, Premiere is unable to add the video clip.

Rendered Stills Flicker, Shake, or "Strobe" in Premiere

ISSUE
When you play an Adobe Premiere movie on an NTSC monitor or print to video, still images in the movie flicker or shake ("strobe").

SYMPTOMS
The still images contain high-contrast, one-pixel lines, hard-edged objects, or many diagonal lines.

SOLUTIONS

When using Premiere 4.01 and later, activate Flicker Removal:

1. Select the still image in the Construction window, then choose Clip > Field Options.
2. In the Field Options dialog box, select Flicker Removal, then click OK.

When using Premiere 4.0 or earlier, do one or more of the following:

A. Deinterlace the video fields:
   1. Select the clip in the Construction window, then choose Clip > Field Options.
   2. In the Field Options dialog box, select Always Deinterlace, then click OK.

B. Deinterlace individual frames:
   1. Select the image in the Construction window, then choose Clip > Frame Hold.
   2. In the Frame Hold dialog box, select Deinterlace, then click OK.

C. Apply the Camera Blur filter to the image:
   1. Select the image in the Construction window, then choose Clip > Filters.
   2. In the Filters dialog box, select Camera Blur from the Available list box, then click Add.
   3. In the Camera Blur Settings dialog box, adjust the Start and End sliders to a value between 2 and 5%, then click OK to close the remaining dialog boxes.

D. Apply a slight (e.g., 0.5 to 1.0 pixel) Gaussian Blur to the image using Adobe Photoshop. For more information, refer to the Adobe Photoshop User Guide.
   NOTE: The Gaussian Blur filter in Premiere is not suitable for this solution, because it does not contain settings adjustments and automatically blurs images by a large amount.

ADDITIONAL INFORMATION
NTSC monitors display still images in two alternating fields ("interlaced video"). One-pixel lines, diagonal lines, or hard horizontal edges in an RGB image appear to flicker when displayed in the alternating frames. Zoomed images may contain lines resized to one pixel, causing the same behavior.

The Flicker Removal feature in Adobe Premiere 4.0.1 and later softens still images so they do not appear to flicker when converted to interlaced video.

The Always Deinterlace feature in Premiere 4.0 and earlier averages the two alternating fields into a single frame of video with no discernible fields. The Deinterlace feature in the "Frame Hold" dialog box removes any jittering that could be caused by freezing a frame.

Applying a slight (2-5%) Camera Blur to the image in Premiere, or applying a Gaussian Blur to it in Photoshop, unfocuses the image enough to prevent the appearance of flickering.

Alpha Channel Not Transparent in Animated Movie Imported into Premiere

ISSUE
The alpha channel in a movie created by an animation application (e.g., LogoMotion) displays opaque when the movie is placed on the S-track of the Construction Window and keyed out with the Alpha Channel key type in Adobe Premiere 3.0x and later.

SOLUTION
Recreate the movie in the animation application with compression set to Animation or None with Millions of Colors+ (i.e., 32-bit color) selected.

ADDITIONAL INFORMATION
Alpha channels are invisible, 8-bit grayscale channels reserved for masking or other color information. When the Alpha Channel key type is selected in Premiere's Transparency Settings dialog box, the black areas in a movie's alpha channel become transparent.

Alpha channels can only be created in movies saved in 32-bit color (i.e., Millions of Colors+). A compression/decompression algorithm (codec) offering only one color option (e.g., Color) in the Compression Settings dialog box is 24-bit color. Files compressed without 32-bit color do not support alpha channels.

Captured Video is Fuzzy or Distorted and Picture Rolls in Premiere

ISSUE
Captured video displays fuzzy, distorted, or with a rolling picture in Adobe Premiere.

SOLUTIONS

Do one or more of the following:

A. Secure any loose cable connections.
B. Connect the video source (e.g., VCR, camera, source tape) to the computer with a different set of cables.
C. Capture video from a different video source.

ADDITIONAL INFORMATION

When capturing video, loose or damaged cables or damaged equipment can weaken the video signal and, in turn, weaken the vertical synchronization (i.e., "sync") and analog data. Weak vertical sync cannot hold the picture in place, causing rolling. Weak analog (i.e., videotape) data causes analog noise to be as strong as the picture, resulting in fuzziness or distortion.

When the source videotape is degraded, the captured video is also of low quality.

Sequence Files Import at the Wrong Duration in Premiere 4.x

ISSUE

Adobe Premiere 4.x imports numbered sequence files with a duration of 1 second, regardless of the duration specified in the Still Image preferences dialog box.

SOLUTIONS

Change the movie's playback rate in the Clip Speed dialog box:

1. Select the imported clip in the Project or Construction Window.
2. Choose Clip > Speed, then select New Rate.
3. Enter a percentage rate adjustment in the New Rate text box, then click OK. To calculate your new rate adjustment, multiply your project's timebase by the desired duration of each image (in frames), then multiply by 100 to get the percentage rate adjustment. For example, if your project's timebase is 30 frames per second (fps) and you would like each still image to last 1 frame, enter 3000 in the New Rate text box (30 x 1 x 100 = 3000).

OR: Change the movie's duration in the Clip Speed dialog box:

1. Select the imported clip in the Project or Construction Window.
2. Choose Clip > Speed, then select New Duration.
3. Enter a new duration in the New Duration text box, then click OK.

ADDITIONAL INFORMATION

When Premiere opens or imports a series of numbered still images, it assigns the images a frame rate of 1 fps. The default frame duration you set in your Still Image dialog box does not apply to numbered sequence files.

Movies are Pixelated or Banded with 8-bit Cinepak Compression in Premiere 4.2.x

ISSUE

Movies rendered in Adobe Premiere 4.2.x with Cinepak compression and 8-bit color (i.e., 256 colors) are pixelated, banded, or dithered.

SYMPTOM

A custom color palette is not attached to the movie.

SOLUTION

Render the movie with 24-bit color (i.e., Millions of Colors) and attach an 8-bit palette to it:

1. Choose Make > CD-ROM Movie.
2. In the CD-ROM Movie Options dialog box, select Cinepak from the Compression pop-up menu, then select 24 Bit from the Colors pop-up menu.
3. Select Playback Palette. (If the CD-ROM Movie Options dialog box doesn't have a Playback Palette option, click More Options in the lower-left corner of the dialog box.)
4. In the Playback Palette section, select Calculate New if you want QuickTime to generate a custom palette for your movie, or select Load From File to attach an existing color palette.
5. Make other appropriate selections, then click OK.
6. Name the file, specify a target location, then click Save.
   NOTE: To use the attached custom color palette on a 16-bit (256 color) monitor, play the movie using Apple Movie Player 2.x. Premiere does not use custom color palettes when playing movies on 16-bit monitors in order to avoid the color flashes that appear when your Macintosh changes display palettes.

ADDITIONAL INFORMATION

When you create an 8-bit, Cinepak-compressed movie in Premiere 4.2.x without attaching a custom color palette to the movie, Premiere uses the system palette to render the movie, which causes it to appear pixelated, banded, or dithered. You can use Premiere's CD-ROM Movie Maker to attach an 8-bit custom color palette to the movie, which causes it to render without pixelation, banding, or dithering. (QuickTime and Cinepak are optimized to compress 24-bit movies, so a 24-bit Cinepak movie with an attached 8-bit palette requires less disk space than an 8-bit Cinepak movie.)

Audio Clip Plays with Static in Premiere

ISSUE

An audio clip plays with static (i.e., tinny, scratchy) in an Adobe Premiere preview or movie, but plays correctly in other applications (e.g., the Finder).

SOLUTIONS

Do one or more of the following:

A. Make sure the preview's audio playback rate and format match those of the captured audio clip: 1. Select the clip in the Construction Window, then note the audio rate and format displayed in the Info window.
   2. Choose Make > Preview Options.
   3. Select the values noted above from the Rate and Format pop-up menus, then click OK.
   4. Choose Project > Preview to recreate the preview.

B. Make sure the movie's audio playback rate and format match those of the captured audio clip:
   1. Select the clip in the Construction Window, then note the audio rate and format displayed in the Info window.
   2. Choose Make > Movie, then click Output Options button.
   3. Select the values noted above from the Rate and Format pop-up menus, then click OK.
   4. Name the movie and click OK to recompile it.

C. Before recording audio on a Macintosh AV computer, disable voice recognition and GeoPort software:
   1. Removing or disable the Speech Setup file in the Control Panel folder and the following PlainTalk files in the Extensions folder:
      PlainTalk Text-To-Speech
      PlainTalk Speech Recognition
      Speech Manager
      Speech Recognition,
      SR Monitor
      SR North American English
   2. Remove or disable the Express Modem file in the Control Panels folder, and the following GeoPort Telcom Adapter (or GeoPort Pod) files in the Extensions folder:
      GeoPort TM Telecom
      Shared Library Manager
      Fax Sender
      GeoPort TM Extension
      GeoPort TM Telecom Adapter
      Fax Extension
      Serial Extension

ADDITIONAL INFORMATION

If Adobe Premiere creates a preview file whose audio playback rate is slower than the audio capture rate, the preview's audio quality is poor but the preview is created quickly.

When you compile a movie, output rates should be identical to audio capture rates to ensure that sound quality in the final movie matches the quality of captured audio. Interference occurs when you record audio on a Macintosh AV computer with voice recognition and GeoPort software installed.

AV Macintosh computers are optimized to record sound at 44 kHz, 16-bit, stereo.

Audio Clips Appear as Gray Bars in Construction Window in Premiere 4.x

ISSUE

Adobe Premiere 4.x displays audio clips as gray bars instead of as waveforms in the Construction window.

SOLUTIONS

Do one or more of the following:

A. Disable the preference setting that approximates audio waveforms:
   1. Choose File > Preferences > Audio.
   2. In the Audio Preferences dialog box, select No Views from the Approximate Audio For pop-up menu, then click OK.

B. Select a Construction window Track Format option that includes video frames:
   1. Click the Construction window to make it active, then choose Windows > Construction Window Options.
   2. In the Construction Window Options dialog box, select either the first or second Track Format option (i.e., one of the two options that include video frames), then click OK.

ADDITIONAL INFORMATION

Premiere 4.x displays audio clips as gray bars or as waveforms, depending on your display preferences. If you set your audio preferences to approximate audio waveforms, or if you set your track format to display only the filename of each clip in the Construction window, then Premiere displays audio clips as gray bars.

If your time unit in the Construction window is small, Premiere displays audio clips faster with gray bars than with waveforms.

The Premiere 4.0 User Guide for Macintosh describes the Audio Preferences dialog box as it appears in Premiere 3.0.

MAC OS

Q Some transitions seem to work differently than others—for example, the Luminance Map transition. Instead of gradually changing from displaying a clip on the A track to displaying the clip on the B track, the clip changes appearance immediately. Why is this happening?

A Adobe Premiere has two types of transitions: time-variant and nontime-variant. Examples of nontime-variant transitions include Luminance Map, Channel Map, Direct, Displace, PICT Mask, Take, Texturize, Three-D, and Transition Factory.

Nontime-variant transitions in Premiere do not shift from one track to the next; rather, one track modifies the appearance of the next. In other words, the mix of the two tracks remains constant from start to finish, and the content of one track processes or modifies the signal of the other track throughout the duration of the transition. You can tell which transitions are nontime-variant by looking at their icons in the Transitions window; time-variant transitions are animated (nontime-variant transitions are not).

In time-variant transitions, the transition frames display a varying mix of tracks A and B. For example, the first frame of the transition may display 100 percent of track A and 0 percent of track B. As the transition progresses, the percentage of track A that appears decreases, while the percentage of track B that appears increases, until the last frame displays 0 percent of track A and 100 percent of track B. This type of transition is called time-variant because the mix of the two tracks varies over time.

Q I often capture video clips from an NTSC source, edit them, and then output them back to videotape. However, the final videotape sometimes has "jittery" playback. Why?

A When you capture video from an NTSC source, edit it in Premiere, and then output it to videotape, you're making a round trip from analog to digital form and back again. At each step, certain characteristics of analog and digital video can cause artifacts, such as jittery playback, to creep into your work. However, if you have a good idea of what happens at each step, you can take steps to achieve the high-quality results you want.

Each frame of NTSC video comprises 526 scan lines—horizontal lines of information that make up the image in the frame. When a television displays NTSC video, it draws each frame one scan line at a time, starting at the top of the screen. However, television display systems can't display all 526 lines in one rapid sequence—if they did, the lines at the top of the screen would start to flicker and fade before the lines at the bottom had been drawn.

To compensate for this problem, the television industry long ago divided each frame into two fields. One field contains all of the even lines in the frame, while the other field contains all of the odd lines. A television displays one field of information, and then the other, very quickly (at approximately 30 frames or 60 fields per second) in a process called video interlacing. The human eye resolves these sequences of fields as moving pictures.

When you capture NTSC video, the video card combines each pair of fields into a single frame (or bitmap). The video capture card determines the order in which the fields will be incorporated into the frame based on the frame size you specify. In general, when you capture frames at 640 by 480 pixels, the video capture card starts with field 1. When you capture frames at 648 by 480 pixels, field 2 dominates. The video plays back smoothly as long as you maintain the set field order. However, if the field order becomes reversed, the movie looks jittery when you play it back.

A number of tasks in Premiere may cause the field order to reverse. For example, applying the "Backwards (Video)" filter to a clip plays it in reverse—but it also reverses the final field order as it renders the movie. Applying speed changes, motion, or freeze-frame effects to clips can result in similar field disruption.

You can easily correct a clip to prevent the jittery playback. Simply select it in the Construction Window in Premiere. Choose "Field Options..." from the Clip menu. In the "Field Options" dialog box, select "Always deinterlace." Click "OK" to close the dialog box, then render the movie again. Premiere will recognize the original order of the fields in the clip. If you're planning to apply motion or effects to your clips, or alter their speed, setting the deinterlacing option before you work with captured NTSC video prevents the jitter problem from occurring at all.

Top Issues: Adobe Premiere 4.2.x for the Macintosh

This document summarizes the latest and most common issues we're hearing in Adobe Technical Support about Adobe Premiere 4.2.x for the Macintosh. This document was last revised October 24, 1996. Issues that are new or updated from the previous revision are indicated with an asterisk (*).

Numbers are included for documents that describe related issues in more detail. These documents are available on our automated faxing system, Adobe FaxYI at 206-628-5737, on the Adobe BBS at 206-623-6984, and on the Adobe home page on the World Wide Web (http://www.adobe.-com/). For an index of all FaxYI documents available for Premiere, see document 310099.

The latest version of Adobe Premiere for the Macintosh is Premiere 4.2.1. For pricing and availability information, visit the Adobe Premiere home page (http://www.adobe.-com/prodindex/premiere/) or call Adobe at 1-800-42-ADOBE (23623).

*1. New QuickTime 2.5 Setting Causes Render Problems

QuickTime 2.5 includes a new frame rate setting, 29.97 fps. If you select this frame rate in the Compression Settings dialog box when rendering a movie in Premiere, the frame rate is converted to 29 fps, causing stuttered playback and frames with unusual durations. To prevent this problem, set the compression frame rate to 30 fps for projects with a time base of 29.97 or 30 fps. Premiere treats a 30 fps frame rate as 29.97 fps if the project's time base is set to 29.97 fps, or as 30 fps if the time base is set to 30 fps.

2. Unable to Capture or Play Video

Many of the problems encountered in Premiere 4.x are related to video or audio capture and playback. To determine if the problem is caused by Premiere or by the system and hardware configuration, capture or play your audio or video files in another application (e.g., FusionRecorder, MoviePlayer). If the capture or playback problem occurs in another application, then the problem lies with your system or hardware configuration rather than your capture or playback application. Contact Apple or the capture card manufacturer

for configuration and compatibility information.
For more information, see document 243310.

3. Red "X" Appears in Preview Window

A red letter "X" appears in the Preview window during transitions, filters, and special effects in uncompiled previews.

To compile a preview, choose Project > Preview, press Enter, or choose Make > Snapshot and use the Controller to play the preview.

4. Audio Synchronization Problems

Audio and video tracks play out of sync in movies created from Premiere 4.2 and earlier at 29.97 frames per second (fps), or audio and video play out of sync in movies captured in Premiere 4.2.1 and earlier.

To prevent sync problems in 29.97 fps movies, render the movies in Premiere 4.2.1 or later. The Premiere 4.2 to 4.2.1 Updater is available on Adobe's World Wide Web site, the Adobe BBS, America Online, and CompuServe.

To prevent sync problems when you capture movies, install the Movie Capture 4.2.2 plug-in file before capturing. To install the Movie Capture 4.2.2 plug-in file, download the Movcap.sit.hqx file from Adobe's World Wide Web site, the Adobe BBS, America Online, or CompuServe. Double-click the Movcap.sit.hqx file to decompress the Movie Capture plug-in file and its installation instructions.

5. Error -2209 Capturing Video with Targa Video Capture Card

The Targa 2000 and Targa 1000 video capture cards require the Movie Capture window to display on a 24-bit monitor connected to the Targa video capture card. If the Movie Capture window does not display on the monitor connected to the Targa video capture card, the error -2209 occurs when you capture video.

To prevent this error, make sure the Movie Capture window displays on the monitor connected to the Targa video capture card, and set the monitor to display millions of colors (i.e., 24-bit color).

6. Problems Making Movies with the CD-ROM Movie Maker

When rendering movies with the CD-ROM Movie Maker in Premiere 4.2.x, Premiere returns an error, reports exceptionally long rendering times, or appears inactive (e.g., hangs, freezes).

This problem may result from a damaged Premiere preferences file, or because De-Interlace is inappropriately selected in the Special Processing dialog box for video source clips smaller than 640-by-480 pixels. To prevent this problem, deselect De-Interlace in the Special Processing dialog box and reset Premiere's preferences file.

To reset Premiere's preferences file, quit Premiere, delete the Adobe Premiere 4.2 Prefs file in the Preferences folder, then relaunch Premiere. Note that a damaged preferences file may result from hardware and software configuration problems.

7. Decreased Quality After Compiling a Preview or Movie

After you compile a movie in Premiere, the entire movie, or clips with transitions, filters, motion, or overlays (i.e., titles) applied, display pixelated, blurred, or distorted. The movie was compressed with a Motion-JPEG (MJPG) compressor, and either an incorrect data rate or no data rate was set for Compression.

To prevent this problem, apply a data rate limit when rendering the movie instead of using the Quality slider.

8. Type 1 or Type 11 Errors in Premiere 4.x

Type 1 and type 11 errors often occur in Premiere when there are software and hardware compatibility conflicts on your system (e.g., a damaged or incompatible system extension is installed). The error can occur when you launch Premiere or while you work in Premiere.

To prevent this problem, troubleshoot your system for software and hardware conflicts.

9. Poor Capture Performance with Motion-JPEG Video Capture Card

When you capture video with an MJPG video capture card, the captured video clip has dropped frames or its data rate is lower than expected.

To prevent dropped frames or low data rates, your hardware and system configuration should be optimized to capture video at its highest capabilities. Use only the latest recommended software, and minimize the number of system extensions you have installed. Follow the guidelines set by your video capture card and hard drive manufacturers to optimize your hardware config-ration.

10. Errors Occur When Printing to VideoVision Studio

An error may occur when you export previews, movies, or sequences from Premiere 4.x using the Print to VideoVision Studio command.

To prevent this problem, make sure all clips are the same size, set an appropriate data rate limit, and apply Radius Studio compression to all clips in the project.

11. Problems Recording to Video Tape from an AV Macintosh

When recording movies to a VCR from an AV Macintosh, Premiere 4.x must display the movie on an NTSC (i.e., television) monitor.

Your monitor configuration and the method you use to display Premiere movies on your NTSC monitor vary with the type of AV Macintosh you have.

For more information, see document 243126.
Revision 4.0

Application Errors

WINDOWS

Error "This feature is not supported in this try-out version..." in Premiere 4.0a

ISSUE

After clicking OK in the Build Custom Transition dialog box, Adobe Premiere 4.0a returns the error "This feature is not supported in this try-out version. Please call Adobe Systems at 1-800-833-6687 (U.S. and Canada), or contact your authorized Adobe distributor."

SOLUTIONS

Upgrade to Premiere 4.2.

OR: Before launching Premiere 4.0a, make a copy of the Transition Factory plug-in file, named fx-fact.prm and located in the Premiere 4.0 PLUGINS directory, then move the copy into the Premiere 4.0a PLUGINS directory.

OR: Build and save your custom transition in Premiere 4.0, then copy the custom transition from the Premiere 4.0 PLUGINS directory to the Premiere 4.0a PLUGINS directory. The custom transition appears in the Transitions window the next time you launch Premiere 4.0a.

ADDITIONAL INFORMATION

Premiere 4.0a's Transition Factory plug-in (62,464 bytes, created 6/20/95) causes an error to appear when building custom transitions. Premiere 4.2's Transition Factory plug-in (51,200 bytes, created 4/23/96) and Premiere 4.0a's Transition Factory plug-in (64,512 bytes, created 12/8/94) does not cause errors to appear when building custom transitions.

Premiere 4.0a can use the Transition Factory plug-in included with Premiere 4.0, and can use custom transitions created in Premiere 4.0 using Premiere 4.0's Transition Factory plug-in.

Error "Invalid Serial Number" When Starting Premiere LE Bundled with FAST FPS-60

ISSUE

After you enter the serial number as prompted as Adobe Premiere 4.x LE starts, Premiere returns the error "Invalid serial number." The serial number entered is from the registration card included with the FAST Electronics FPS-60 video capture board bundled with Premiere LE.

SOLUTION

When the serial number does not begin with the characters "MSW400B," contact Adobe Customer Services to receive a valid serial number.

ADDITIONAL INFORMATION

Some FAST Electronics FPS-60 video capture boards bundled with Premiere LE include a European serial number. The U.S. version of Premiere LE requires a U.S. serial number.

Error Saving Project Containing Clips with Long Filenames in Premiere 4.2

ISSUE

When you save a project in Adobe Premiere 4.2, Premiere returns the error, "An error occurred while saving your project." The project contains clips with long filenames (i.e., greater than 30 characters).

SOLUTION

Rename and replace any clips whose filenames exceed 30 characters before saving your project:

1. In Premiere's Project window, locate the clips whose filenames exceed 30 characters.
2. Select each clip, then press Delete. In the dialog box that appears, click OK.
3. Locate the clips using Windows Explorer, then rename the clips so their filenames do not exceed 30 characters.
4. Reimport the clips into your Premiere project.

ADDITIONAL INFORMATION

Premiere 4.2 cannot save projects that contain clips whose filenames exceed 30 characters.

QuickTime for Windows and Video for Windows limit filenames to 35 characters, although Windows 95 supports filenames as long as 255 characters. Premiere 4.2 cannot import, open, or save movies whose filenames exceed 35 characters.

Premiere 4.0x and earlier adheres to the MS-DOS naming convention (e.g., Filename.mov).

Memory-Related or "MCI Error" Error on Playback in Premiere

ISSUE

When you play a clip or compile a movie, Adobe Premiere returns the error "MCI Error" or the system returns a memory-related error.

SOLUTIONS

Do one or more of the following:

A. When the error occurs on a computer with a 64-bit graphic display card installed, disable (i.e., remark out) the Direct Control Interface (DCI) lines in the System.ini file:
   1. Make a backup copy of the System.ini file.
   2. Open the System.ini file, located in the Windows directory, in a text editor that can save in text-only format (e.g., Windows Write, Notepad).
   3. Locate the line or lines in the [Drivers] section that read:
      ```
      DCI=[varies]
      ```
   4. Disable or remark out the DCI line or lines in the [Drivers] section by typing a semicolon at the beginning of the line. For example:
      ```
      ;DCI=[varies]
      ```
   5. Locate the line or lines in the [Drivers] section that begin with "VIDS" or "VIDC.S." For example:
      ```
      VIDS.DRAW=udh.dll
      ```
   6. Disable or remark out the VIDS or VIDC.S line or lines by typing a semicolon at the beginning of the line. For example:
      ```
      ;VIDS.DRAW=udh.dll
      ```

7. Save in text-only format, then restart Windows.

B. When MS-DOS 6.x is installed, use MemMaker to optimize conventional memory. For instructions, refer to the MS-DOS 6 User's Guide.

C. Change the order in which device drivers and programs load to free additional conventional memory by editing the Config.sys and Autoexec.bat files. For instructions, refer to the Microsoft MS-DOS 6 User's Guide.

D. Remove unnecessary device drivers and TSRs (memory-resident programs) by editing the Config.sys and Autoexec.bat files. For instructions, refer to the Microsoft MS-DOS 6 User's Guide.

E. Disable applications that start automatically when you start Windows by disabling (i.e., remarking out) the "Load=" and "Run=" lines in the Win.ini file or by moving their icons out of the StartUp group in Program Manager.

F. When using MJPEG compressed clips that have a data rate of 1 MB/sec or higher, recapture or recompile the clips to have a data rate less than 1 MB/sec.

G. When network connections are not required, do not load any network drivers.

H. In Windows Setup, select a video driver compatible with the computer's monitor with a resolution of 640x480 and 256 colors.

I. Use the Program Manager (Progman.exe) as the Windows shell.

ADDITIONAL INFORMATION

When you play a Video for Windows (AVI) file, Premiere requires specific Video for Windows DLL files loaded into conventional memory. When there isn't enough memory to load these files, Premiere returns the error "MCI Error."

Direct Control Interface (DCI) provides faster screen redraw for video cards by enabling direct communication between the system and the video card. Video for Windows 1.1 and earlier and QuickTime for Windows 2.02 and earlier do not support DCI, causing system errors (e.g., freeze, General Protection Fault) to occur when you quit Windows after running Adobe Premiere 4.0x, or when you play movies in Premiere. Disabling DCI slows screen redraw, but does not affect overall system performance.

DOS uses conventional memory to load DOS startup files, the Config.sys file, and the Autoexec.bat file into conventional memory, then these startup files load drivers, utilities, and applications that in turn use conventional memory. Windows requires at least 256K of free conventional memory, but having 535K or more of free conventional memory before you start Windows is recommended.

You can increase the amount of free conventional memory by minimizing the amount of memory used by DOS, device drivers, and other memory-resident programs (TSRs). MemMaker, included with MS-DOS 6.x, modifies the Config.sys and Autoexec.bat files so that device drivers and other TSRs load into upper memory, instead of into conventional memory.

Clips compressed with MJPEG compression may cause Premiere to return the "MCI Error" when their data rate exceeds 1 MB/sec.

To determine the amount of available conventional memory you have when using MS-DOS 5.x or later:

1. In Program Manager, double-click MS-DOS Prompt in the Main group.
2. At the C:\ prompt, type "mem" to display the amount of available conventional memory.
3. Type "exit" to return to Windows.

Error "Call to Undefined Dynalink" in Premiere Troubleshooting Guide

ISSUE

The error "Call to Undefined Dynalink" occurs while using Adobe Premiere in Windows 3.x. The error occurs when launching Premiere, opening or importing movies, capturing video, or during video playback.

SOLUTIONS

Do one or more of the following:

A. When the error occurs while capturing or playing Video for Windows (.AVI) movies, reinstall Video for Windows using the Premiere installation disks:

1. In File Manager, delete the following files from the Windows\system directory:
```
avicap.dll
avifile.dll
mciavi.drv
msvidc.drv
msvideo.dll
```
2. Insert Disk 1 of the Premiere installation disk set, or insert the Premiere 4.x Deluxe CD-ROM.
3. Choose File > Run in Program Manager.
4. When using the installation disk set, type "a:\setup-.exe" in the Run dialog box (where "a:\" indicates the drive containing the Premiere installation disk), then click OK.

   When using the Premiere 4.0x Deluxe CD-ROM, type "d:\Premiere\disk1\setup.exe" in the Run dialog box (where "d:\" indicates the CD-ROM drive), then click OK.

   When using the Premiere 4.2 Deluxe CD-ROM, type "d:\Premiere\win3x\disk1\setup.exe" in the Run dialog box (where "d:\" indicates the CD-ROM drive), then click OK.
5. In the Adobe Premiere Installer window, deselect Adobe Premiere program, deselect QuickTime and Tutorial Files, then click Install.
6. Continue the installation by following the on-screen instructions, then click OK when installation is completed.
7. Reinstall the software drivers for your video capture card.
8. Restart Windows.

B. When the error occurs while opening or importing QuickTime movies in Windows 3.x, remove and reinstall all QuickTime for Windows files:

1. In File Manager, search for and remove all qt*.* and *.qtc files. For a listing of QuickTime files, see Additional Information.
   NOTE: Do not remove the qtiface.dll file, located in the Premiere directory, or non-QuickTime application files (e.g., Quicken files, personal files beginning with the letters "qt" or ending with the extension ".qtc").
2. Insert Disk 1 of the Premiere installation disk set, or insert the Premiere 4.x Deluxe CD-ROM.
3. In Program Manager, choose File > Run.
4. When using the installation disk set, type "a:\setup.-exe" in the Run dialog box (where "a:\" indicates the drive containing the Premiere installation disk), then click OK.
   When using the Premiere 4.0x Deluxe CD-ROM, type "d:\Premiere\disk1\setup.exe" in the Run dialog box (where "d:\" indicates the CD-ROM drive), then click OK.
   When using the Premiere 4.2 Deluxe CD-ROM, type "d:\Premiere\win3x\disk1\setup.exe" in the Run dialog box (where "d:\" indicates the CD-ROM drive), then click OK.
5. In the Adobe Premiere Installer window, deselect all installation options, select QuickTime, then click Install.
6. Continue the installation by following the on-screen instructions, click OK when installation is completed, then restart Windows.

C. When the error occurs on a computer with a 64-bit graphic display card installed, disable (i.e., remark out) the Direct Control Interface (DCI) lines in the system.ini file:

1. Make a backup copy of the system.ini file.
2. Open the system.ini file, located in the Windows directory, in a text editor that can save in text-only format (e.g., Windows Write, Notepad).
3. Locate the line or lines in the [Drivers] section that read:
   ```
   DCI=[varies]
   ```
4. Disable or remark out the DCI line or lines in the [Drivers] section by typing a semicolon at the beginning of the line. For example:
   ```
   ;DCI=[varies]
   ```
5. Locate the line or lines in the [Drivers] section that begin with "VIDS" or "VIDC.S." For example:
   ```
   VIDS.DRAW=udh.dll
   ```
6. Disable or remark out the VIDS or VIDC.S line or lines by typing a semicolon at the beginning of the line. For example:
   ```
   ;VIDS.DRAW=udh.dll
   ```
7. Save in text-only format, then restart Windows.

D. If the error occurs while you open or import QuickTime movies in Premiere 1.x with QuickTime 2.x is installed, update Premiere 1.x with the qtpatch.exe file, so that it is compatible with QuickTime for Windows 2.0 or later. The qtpatch.exe file is available from Adobe Systems, the Adobe BBS, CompuServe, and America Online.

OR: Remove all QuickTime for Windows files, then install QuickTime 1.0 using the Premiere installation disks:
NOTE: Other applications may be incompatible with QuickTime 1.0.

1. In File Manager, search for and remove all qt*.* and *.qtc files. For a listing of QuickTime files, see Additional Information.
   NOTE: Do not remove the qtiface.dll file, located in the Premiere directory, or non-QuickTime application files (e.g., Quicken files, personal files beginning with the letters "qt" or ending with the filename extension ".qtc").
2. Insert Disk 1 of the Premiere installation disks, then choose File > Run in Program Manager.
3. Type "a:\setup.exe" in the Run dialog box (where "a:\" indicates the drive containing the Premiere installation disk), then click OK.
4. In the Adobe Premiere Installer dialog box, deselect all installation options, select QuickTime, then click Install.
5. Continue the installation by following the on-screen instructions, click OK when installation is completed, then restart Windows.

ADDITIONAL INFORMATION

When damaged or incompatible versions of Video for Windows Dynamic Linked Library (DLL) files are installed, the error "Call to Undefined Dynalink" occurs when you capture video or play an AVI file in Premiere 4.x. Removing damaged or incompatible Video for Windows DLL files before reinstalling Video for Windows and video capture drivers ensures a successful reinstallation.

If damaged, incompatible, or multiple versions of QuickTime DLL files are installed, the error "Call to Undefined Dynalink" occurs when you open or import a QuickTime movie in Adobe Premiere. Removing all QuickTime files and reinstalling them using the Premiere installation disks ensures the latest versions of the .DLL files are installed. The Premiere installer only replaces QuickTime files located in the Windows\system subdirectory. Deleting QuickTime files not located in the Windows\system directory ensures you do not install duplicate QuickTime files.

Direct Control Interface (DCI) provides faster screen redraw for video cards by enabling direct communication between the system and the video card. Video for Windows 1.1 and earlier and QuickTime for Windows 2.02 and earlier do not support DCI, causing system errors (e.g., freeze, General Protection Fault) to occur when you quit Windows after running Adobe Premiere 4.0x, or when you play movies in Premiere. Disabling DCI slows screen redraw, but does not affect overall system performance.

Adobe Premiere 1.x is designed for use with QuickTime 1.0 for Windows. When you use Premiere 1.x with QuickTime 2.0, update the application using the qtpatch.exe file so that it is compatible with QuickTime 2.0. Instructions for using the patch are included in the qtpatch.txt file.

QuickTime 2.x files located in the Windows directory:

```
qcmc.qtc
qtcvid.qtc
qthndlr.dll
```

qtim.dll
qtim32.dll
qtimcmgr.dll
qtiv32.qtc
qtiyvu9.qtc
qtipeg.qtc
qtmovie.vbx
qtnotify.exe
qtold.qtc
qtole.dll
qtole32.dll
qtpic.vbx
qtraw.atc
qtrle.qtc
qtrpza.qtc
qtrt21.qtc
qtsmc.qtc
qtvhdw.qtc
qtviewer.exe
qtw32.cpl
qtwcp.hlp
qtwmci32.dll

QuickTime 2.x files located in the Windows\system directory:

qtw.ini
qtw.qtw

QuickTime 1.x files located in the Windows directory:

qcmc.qtc
qtcvid.qtc
qthndlr.dll
qtim.dll
qtimcmgr.dll
qtiv32.qtc
qtiyvu9.qtc
qtipeg.qtc
qtnotify.exe
qtole.dll
qtraw.atc
qtrle.qtc
qtrpza.qtz
qtrt21.qtc
qtsmc.qtc
qtvhdw.qtc

QuickTime 1.x files located in the Windows\system directory:

qtw.ini

MAC OS

Error Selecting "Capture" or Using Device Controller in Premiere 4.0x

ISSUE

An error or unexpected behavior occurs when using a device controller (e.g., VISCA, ARTI, V-LAN) with Adobe Premiere 4.x on a Power Macintosh 8100/100 or greater, or on a Macintosh with System 7.1 or earlier installed.

SYMPTOMS

A system error (e.g., Type 1, freeze) or inappropriate error (e.g., "No VCR is available" when a VCR is available) occurs when choosing File > Capture.

The device controller behaves unexpectedly (e.g., the indicator light is on, but the source deck is inactive).

When attempting to set up a V-LAN device in the Device Control dialog box, Premiere returns an error indicating that a V-LAN device controller cannot be found.

SOLUTIONS

Do one or more of the following:

A. Use Premiere 4.0.1 or later. When using a V-LAN device controller, use Premiere 4.2.

B. Use System 7.5 or later.
NOTE: Do not use System 7.5.3 with Digital Pipeline's ProVTR unless you have a PCI-based Macintosh computer (e.g., Power Macintosh 7500, 8500, or 9500). If you have a NuBus-based Macintosh computer (e.g., Power Macintosh 8100, Quadra 840av), use System 7.5.1 with Digital Pipeline's ProVTR. Use Serial DMA 2.02 only on PCI-based Macintosh computers with System 7.5.2 installed.

C. When using a Macintosh Quadra 840AV with System 7.1 or earlier installed, install System Enabler 088 1.1.

D. When using a Power Macintosh 6100, 7100, or 8100 with System 7.1 or earlier installed, install System Enabler 1.0.

E. When using Sony VISCA on a Power Macintosh 8100/100 or later, with the exception of the Power Macintosh 8500, install a device controller other than VISCA (e.g., Videonics's MediaMotion, Pipeline Digital's ProVtr).

F. Delete the System Update 3.0 file from the System Folder, and then restart the Macintosh.

G. Disable the GeoPort Telecom Adapter or GeoPort Pod:
   1. Remove the following files from the Extensions folder in the System Folder:
      GeoPort TM Telecom
      Shared Library Manager
      Fax Sender
      GeoPort TM Extension
      GeoPort TM Telecom Adapter
      Fax Extension
      Serial Extension
   2. Remove the Express Modem control panel from the Control Panels folder in the System Folder.
   3. Restart the Macintosh.

H. Remove the Serial Port Arbitrator system extension from the Extensions folder in the System Folder, and then restart the Macintosh.

ADDITIONAL INFORMATION

Premiere 4.0.1 corrects specific device control and batch capture problems in Premiere 4.0. Premiere 4.2 corrects V-LAN compatibility problems between Premiere 4.0.1 and Power Macintosh models.

The Sony VISCA 1.2 control panel and Chooser extension documents are incompatible with the System 7.0x and

7.1 Enabler files, and with the Enabler files included with the Power Macintosh 8100/100 and the Power Macintosh 8100/110. System 7.5 does not require system enablers except for the Power Macintosh 8100/100 and later models.

The ARTI device control plug-in is not compatible with the serial ports on Power Macintosh 8100/100 and Power Macintosh 8100/110 computers.

System Update 3.0, available for System 7.0x and 7.1, is incompatible with serial port device controllers, such as Sony VISCA.

Batch capture and device control in Adobe Premiere 4.0 may conflict with the GeoPort Telecom Adapter or GeoPort Pod.

The VISCA Control Panel version 1.2 may conflict with AppleTalk Remote. Removing the Serial Port Arbitrator extension disables AppleTalk Remote.

Error -5000 Saving Premiere Project to Network Server

ISSUE

The error "An error occurred while saving this file. -5000." appears when saving a Premiere project to a network server or when saving a Premiere project that includes video or audio clips stored on a network server.

SOLUTION

Resave the project to the same location.

NOTE: If the error "An error occurred. File is in use. Premiere or another application is currently using this file. Delete any clips which refer to this file or close this file from any other applications." occurs, click "OK." Because the file is not in use, the error is false.

ADDITIONAL INFORMATION

The error "An error occurred while saving this file. -5000." may appear when saving a Premiere project to a network server or when saving a Premiere project that includes video or audio clips stored on a network server. The project resaves as expected.

Creating a project using video or audio clips stored on a server may cause jerky motion or dropped frames, due to slow data transfer rates to the server.

Error "File is busy or damaged" Capturing Movies in Premiere

ISSUE

The error "File is busy or damaged" appears when capturing movies in Adobe Premiere.

SOLUTIONS

Do one or more of the following:

A. When using more than one monitor, drag the Movie Capture window onto the monitor that is connected to the video capture card.
B. Reduce the bit depth of the screen display to 16-bit color (i.e., Thousands of colors) or less.
C. Capture video with a separate capture utility (e.g., Apple FusionRecorder, Radius Video Studio) to determine whether the system and hardware configuration is capable of capturing video.
D. Reinstall the software used to operate the video capture card.
E. Disable all extensions except QuickTime, and those used to operate the video capture card and external disk drives.

ADDITIONAL INFORMATION

Video RAM (VRAM) memory is used for screen display and related functions (e.g., playing movies). When the amount of free VRAM is limited by running two monitors or by displaying colors at a high bit-depth, Premiere returns the error "File is busy or damaged" when capturing movies.

The Power Macintosh 8500 has 2 MB of VRAM, which is not enough to run two monitors simultaneously. The Power Macintosh 8500 computer can be upgraded to 4 MB of VRAM, as described in the Power Macintosh 8500 user manual.

Error "Not enough memory to play movie" in Premiere 3.0x or Later

ISSUE

The error "Not enough memory to play movie" appears when you play a compiled movie in Adobe Premiere 3.0x or later. When you print to video from a sequence, Premiere 3.0x returns the error "Movie must be flattened" or "Movie area 'snapshot x' is not self-contained."

SOLUTIONS

Upgrade to the Video Vision Studio 2.0 or later drivers, available from Radius, Inc.

OR: With 8 MB or more of RAM allocated to Premiere, flatten the movie clip:

1. At the Finder, select the Premiere application and choose File > Get Info.
2. In the Premiere Info window, enter a value of 8192 or more in the Preferred Size text box, then close the window.
3. Open the Premiere project, then choose File > Export > Flatten Movie.
4. Name the movie and click Save.

OR: If there is not enough disk space to create a flattened movie clip, recompile the movie as a QuickTime movie:

1. In Premiere, choose Project > Make > Movie, then click Output Options.
2. Select QuickTime Movie from the output file type pop-up menu in the Project Output Options dialog box.
3. Click OK, then name the movie and click OK.

ADDITIONAL INFORMATION

The Video Vision Studio 1.7 or 1.6 drivers do not correctly compress Premiere 3.0x or later movies when compiling them as QuickTime Composite files. Little or no compression is applied to the movies, causing the error "Not enough memory to play movie" to appear when you play them. Video Vision Studio 2.0 or later drivers compile the movies correctly.

Compiling a Premiere movie as a QuickTime Movie creates a smaller file that requires less memory to play, because compression is applied to the entire movie file rather than only to modified clips. Flattening a movie clip also creates a smaller file by compressing all movie data into a single data fork. Ample hard disk space must be available to flatten the clip, as the process creates an additional file that may be as large as the original movie.

QuickTime Error Occurs When Starting Premiere 3.x or Later

ISSUE

When you start Adobe Premiere 3.0 or later, an error appears indicating that QuickTime is not installed or that an incorrect version of QuickTime is installed.

SYMPTOMS

Premiere 4.0.1 or later returns the error "Adobe Premiere Requires QuickTime. (Version 1.6 or greater for 68000 Macintoshes, version 1.6.2 or greater with the QuickTime PowerPlug for Power Macintoshes)."

Premiere 4.0 returns the error "Adobe Premiere Requires a newer version of QuickTime than what is currently installed. (Version 1.6 or greater for 68000 Macintoshes, version 1.6.2 or greater with the QuickTime PowerPlug for Power Macintoshes)."

Premiere 3.0x returns the error "Adobe Premiere Requires QuickTime version 1.6 or greater."

SOLUTIONS

Do one or more of the following:

A. Install QuickTime 1.6 or later.

B. If you are running Premiere on a Power Macintosh, install compatible versions of QuickTime and QuickTime Power Plug. QuickTime 2.5 requires the QuickTime PowerPlug 2.5, QuickTime 2.1 requires the QuickTime PowerPlug 2.1, QuickTime 2.0 requires the QuickTime PowerPlug 2.0, and QuickTime 1.6.2 requires the QuickTime Power Plug 1.0.

C. Ensure sufficient memory is available to the Finder for QuickTime resources to load:
   1. In the Finder, select the Premiere application icon, then choose File > Get Info.
   2. Note the Preferred Size value, then close the window.
   3. Choose About This Macintosh from the Apple menu.
   4. Subtract the Preferred Size value you noted in step 2 from the value listed for Total Memory. The Largest Unused Block value should be at least 1 MB or 10% of this sum, whichever is greater. If the Largest Unused Block value is less than 1 MB or 10% of this sum, quit other applications or decrease the amount of memory allocated to Premiere.

ADDITIONAL INFORMATION

When you start the Macintosh, QuickTime 1.6 and later loads a minimal set of components into memory (RAM). QuickTime loads additional resources when you start Premiere and when you import, play, preview, and create QuickTime files. QuickTime requires approximately 10% of the memory available to the Macintosh when Premiere is running, or a minimum of 1 MB, to load these additional resources.

Error "-8961" When Playing or Previewing VideoVision Studio Clips in Premiere 3.0 and Later

ISSUE

The error "Error -8961. 0-10% completed, file is busy, in use by another application, close this file from other open applications" appears when playing or previewing Radius VideoVision Studio clips in Adobe Premiere 3.0 and later.

SYMPTOM

An error appears when playing or previewing the Radius VideoVision Studio clips with the Radius Studio Player utility.

SOLUTIONS

Do one or more of the following:

A. Reinstall the VideoVision Studio software 2.5.1 or later.

B. Make sure the VideoVision Studio capture card is securely installed in its slot.

ADDITIONAL INFORMATION

The error "Error -8961. 0-10% completed, file is busy, in use by another application, close this file from other open applications" occurs when applications and system software cannot communicate with the VideoVision Studio capture card. Applications and system software cannot communicate with the VideoVision Studio card when the VideoVision Studio software is damaged or when the board is not securely installed in its slot.

Error Importing QuickTime for Windows Movie in Premiere 4.0 for Macintosh

ISSUE

When importing a QuickTime for Windows movie, Adobe Premiere 4.0 for the Macintosh returns the error "The file [filename.mov] could not be imported. The file is either corrupted, an unsupported type or in use by another program."

SOLUTIONS

Update to Premiere 4.0.1 or later.

OR: Open the file in Premiere 4.0 instead of importing it:

1. Choose File > Open, select the QuickTime for Windows, then click Open.
2. When the message "The file xxx.mov appears to be a QuickTime movie. Do you wish to change the filetype and open it as a QuickTime movie?" appears, click Change & Open.
3. When the movie's Clip window opens, choose Project > Add This Clip to add the movie to the Project window. The file can now be imported directly into other Premiere 4.0 projects.

ADDITIONAL INFORMATION

QuickTime for Windows movies are assigned the file type "TEXT" when transferred to a Macintosh computer. When Premiere 4.0 attempts to import a QuickTime file with the file type "TEXT," it treats the file as a text file and returns the error "The file [filename.mov] could not be imported. The file is either corrupted, an unsupported type or in use by another program."

When opening, not importing, a QuickTime movie with the file type "TEXT," Premiere 4.0 recognizes the file as a QuickTime movie and changes the file's type to "MooV." After the file type is changed to "MooV," it can be imported into other Premiere 4.0 projects.

Premiere 4.0.1 recognizes QuickTime files that have the file type "TEXT" as valid QuickTime files when importing or opening.

Error -2209 Capturing Video with Targa Video Capture Cards in Premiere 4.x

ISSUE

When capturing video using a Truevision Targa 2000 or Targa 1000 video capture card, Adobe Premiere 4.x returns the error, "Error -2209. File is either damaged, an unsupported type, locked or in use by another application."

SOLUTIONS

Do one or more of the following:

A. Make sure the Movie Capture window displays on the monitor connected to the Targa video capture card.
B. Set the monitor connected to the Targa video capture card to display millions of colors (i.e., 24-bit color).
C. Make sure the dimensions of the Movie Capture window do not exceed the resolution of the monitor connected to the Targa video capture card. You can change the dimensions of the Movie Capture window in Premiere's Recording Settings dialog box.

ADDITIONAL INFORMATION

The Targa 2000 and Targa 1000 video capture cards require the Movie Capture window to display on a 24-bit monitor connected to the Targa video capture card.

Premiere 4.x cannot capture video when the resolution of the Movie Capture window (i.e., its dimensions) exceeds the resolution of the capture monitor.

System Errors

WINDOWS

GPF in Module Tliw32p3.drv When Launching Premiere 4.0

ISSUE

A General Protection Fault (GPF) error in module Tliw32p3.drv occurs when you start Adobe Premiere 4.0 on a computer with a miroVIDEO DC1 video capture card.

SOLUTION

Change the color mode to 256 colors.

To change the color mode in Windows 95:

1. Right-click on the desktop, then select Properties from the pop-up menu.
2. In the Display Properties dialog box, click the Settings tab.
3. Select 256 Color from the Color Palette pop-up menu, then click Apply.
4. Restart Windows 95.

To change the color mode in Windows 3.x:

1. Make a backup copy of the System.ini file.
2. Double-click the Windows Setup icon, located in the Main group of Program Manager.
3. Choose Options > Change System Settings.
4. From the Display scrollbox, select a video driver that displays 256 colors and is compatible with the installed display card.
5. Click OK, then restart Windows.

ADDITIONAL INFORMATION

Adobe Premiere is incompatible with some video display cards when they display 32-bit color (e.g., MiroVIDEO DC1), causing a GPF error to occur when launching. Changing to 256 colors enables Premiere to launch without error.

MiroVIDEO supplies the Tliw32p3.drv file, which loads on startup with the video driver, to support Miro's video overlay feature. Video overlay (i.e., video-in-a-window) displays live video input on-screen without burdening the coprocessor, which is useful when making real-time capture decisions. Because the Tliw32p3.drv file requires 32-bit color, when you change the color mode to 256 colors in Windows the file does not load and the video overlay feature is disabled.

To use video overlay, switch the color mode to 32-bit color and capture the footage using Testcap.exe (Windows

3.x), Captest16.exe (Windows 3.x), or Captest32.exe (Windows 95). Then, switch back to 256 colors, launch Premiere, and import the footage for editing. Testcap.exe is located on Disk 4 of the Premiere 4.0x installation disks and in the Premiere\Disk4 subdirectory on the Premiere 4.0x Deluxe CD-ROM. Captest16.exe and Captest32.exe are located in the Support directory on the Premiere 4.2 Deluxe CD-ROM.

GPF Error in Msvfw32.dll When Starting Premiere 4.2

ISSUE

When you start Adobe Premiere 4.2, a General Protection Fault (GPF) error in module Msvfw32.dll or a Divide Error at Msvfw.dll occurs. Premiere is installed on a computer that has a Matrox Millennium video display card installed.

SOLUTIONS

Update to Millennium software drivers 2.23 or later.

OR: Use Premiere 4.0a. To install Premiere 4.0a from the Premiere 4.2 CD-ROM:

1. Double-click on the Setup.exe file located in the Premiere\Win3x\Disk1 directory on the Premiere 4.2 Deluxe CD-ROM.
2. Specify a target directory for Premiere 4.0a, then click Install.

NOTE: To leave Premiere 4.2 unchanged after you install Premiere 4.0a, install Premiere 4.0a into a different directory than Premiere 4.2. The default directory for Premiere 4.0a is C:\Premiere, while the default directory for Premiere 4.2 is C:\Win32app\Premiere 4.2 (where C:\ indicates the root level of the boot volume).

ADDITIONAL INFORMATION

The Millennium video display card requires software drivers 2.23 or later to be compatible with the 32-bit version of Microsoft Video for Windows. Premiere 4.2 initializes Video for Windows' Dynamic Link Library (Msvfw32.dll) when starting, causing a GPF error in module Msvfw32.dll or a Divide Error at Msvfw.dll to occur when the Millennium video display drivers are incompatible with the 32-bit version of Video for Windows.

Premiere 4.0a is a 16-bit application and does not use the 32-bit version of Video for Windows.

System Error or Freeze During Playback in Premiere 1.x

ISSUE

If you play clips or movies in Adobe Premiere 1.x when a 64-bit or PCI video card (e.g., Matrox, ATI, Stealth, Viper, Number Nine) is installed, the system returns an error or freezes.

SOLUTION

Disable (i.e., remark out) the Direct Control Interface (DCI) lines in the System.ini file:

1. Make a backup copy of the System.ini file, which is located in the Windows directory.
2. Open the original System.ini file in a text editor that can save in text-only format (e.g., Windows Write, Notepad).
3. Locate the line(s) in the [Drivers] section that read:
   `DCI=[varies]`
4. Disable the DCI line(s) in the [Drivers] section by typing a semicolon at the beginning of the line. For example:
   `;DCI=[varies]`
5. When one of the DCI lines reads "DCI=Display," locate the line in the [Drivers] section that begins with "VIDS" or "VIDC.S." For example:
   `VIDS.DRAW=udh.dll`
6. Disable the VIDS or VIDC.S line by typing a semicolon at the beginning of the line. For example:
   `;VIDS.DRAW=udh.dll`
7. Savethe System.ini file in text-only format, then restart Windows.

ADDITIONAL INFORMATION

Direct Control Interface (DCI) provides faster screen redraw for high-end video cards by enabling direct communication between the system and the video card. Video for Windows 1.1 and earlier, and QuickTime for Windows 2.02 and earlier are not compatible with DCI.

MAC OS

Error Using VISCA, ARTI, or V-LAN Device Control in Premiere 4.x on Power Macintosh

ISSUE

When using a VISCA, ARTI, or V-LAN device controller with Adobe Premiere 4.x on a Power Macintosh, an error (e.g., "Type 1," "No VCR is available," cannot find the V-LAN device controller) occurs or the device controller behaves unexpectedly (e.g., the indicator light is on, but the source deck is inactive).

SOLUTIONS

When using the VISCA controller, do one or more of the following:

A. When running Premiere on a Power Macintosh 8500, capture video using Avid VideoShop, included with the Power Macintosh 8500.
B. Capture video using a different device controller (e.g., Videonics MediaMotion).

OR: When using the V-LAN controller, do one or more of the following:

A. Use Premiere 4.2 or later.
B. Capture using Premiere 4.0 installed on a Power Macintosh.
C. Capture using Premiere 4.0.1 installed on a 68000-series Macintosh.

ADDITIONAL INFORMATION
When using a device controller with Adobe Premiere 4.x on a Power Macintosh, an error (e.g., "Type 1," "No VCR is available," cannot find the V-LAN device controller) occurs or the device controller behaves unexpectedly (e.g., the indicator light is on, but the source deck is inactive) when the device controller is incompatible with installed software or your hardware configuration.

The VISCA device control is not compatible with the System Update file included with System 7.5.1, 7.1, and 7.1.1 and the system enabler, included with System 7.5.x, required by the Power Macintosh 8100/100 and later.

The V-LAN device control is not compatible with Premiere 4.0.1 running on a Power Macintosh, but is compatible with Premiere 4.0 and 4.2 running on a Power Macintosh.

The ARTI device control's ARTI plug-in is not compatible with the Power Macintosh 8100/100 and Power Macintosh 8100/110 serial ports.

System Error (e.g., Freeze) Capturing or Rendering 240 x 180 Pixel Movie in Premiere 4.x

ISSUE
A system error (e.g., freeze) occurs when capturing or rendering 240 x 180 pixel movies using a VideoVision Studio capture card and Radius Studio compression.

SOLUTIONS
Capture or render movies at a size other than 240 x 180 pixels (e.g., 160 x 120 pixels, 320 x 240 pixels, 640 x 480 pixels).
OR: Select a compressor/decompressor (CODEC) other than Radius Studio when capturing or rendering movies.

ADDITIONAL INFORMATION
The VideoVision Studio capture board can capture video without error when the movie's size is 160 x 120, 320 x 240, or 640 x 480 pixels. The Radius Studio CODEC cannot compress frames that are 240 x 180 pixels.

System Error Launching Premiere 4.0.1 When Running System 7.5.1

ISSUE
When launching Adobe Premiere 4.0.1 on a Macintosh computer running System 7.5.1, a system error (e.g., freeze) occurs.

SOLUTIONS
Do one or more of the following:
A. Delete the Adobe Premiere 4.0 Prefs file located in the Preferences folder in the System Folder, then relaunch Premiere.
B. Remove or disable all system extension and control panel files except QuickTime, then restart the Macintosh.
C. When a beta version of the System 7.5 Update file is installed in the System Folder, install the System 7.5 Update release version 1.0.2 (created March 7, 1995) or later. To check which version of the System 7.5 Update is installed, select the System 7.5 Update file, located in the System Folder, then choose File > Get Info. The version displays in the System 7.5 Update Info dialog box.
D. Remove the System 7.5 Update file from the System Folder, then restart the Macintosh.

ADDITIONAL INFORMATION
The System 7.5 Update file is part of a set of software files that update System 7.5 to System 7.5.1. When launching Adobe Premiere 4.0.1, a system error (e.g., freeze) occurs when a beta version of the System 7.5 Update is installed, when the Premiere preferences file is damaged, or when there is an extension conflict.

Premiere is compatible with the System 7.5 Update. The ReadMe file included with the TrueVision Targa 2000 video capture board states that Adobe Premiere 4.0.1 is incompatible with System 7.5.1, and that Adobe is working to address the problem. TrueVision tested the Targa 2000 board with Premiere 4.0.1 on a Macintosh computer running a beta version of the System 7.5 Update. TrueVision recommends running the Targa 2000 with the System 7.5 Update for improved performance, but the update is not required.

System Error (e.g., Freeze) or Stuttered Playback When Previewing VVS Clips in Premiere 4.x

ISSUE
When previewing high data-rate (e.g., 3 MB/sec or greater) VideoVision Studio clips in Adobe Premiere 4.x by pressing Return or choosing Project > Preview, a system error (e.g. freeze) occurs, or the preview plays with stuttered, jerky motion.

SOLUTIONS
Do one or more of the following:
A. View the Preview Window on the monitor connected to the VideoVision Studio card.
B. Choose Make > Preview Options and enter a smaller Preview Window size in the Preview Options dialog box.
C. Preview projects using Print to VideoVision Studio:
NOTE: For best performance when previewing using Print to VideoVision Studio, use VideoVision Studio software 2.5.1 or later and Studio Player Component

2.5.2, which improves playback when previewing with Print to VideoVision Studio.

1. When previewing only a portion of the Construction Window, position the yellow Work Area bar over the section to be previewed.
2. Choose Make > Output Options.
3. In the Output Options dialog box, choose either Entire Project or Work Area from the Output pop-up menu, then click OK.
4. Choose File > Export > Print to VideoVision Studio. NOTE: If Print to VideoVision Studio is not available on the Export submenu, move the Print to VideoVision Studio plug-in to the Adobe Premiere Plug-Ins folder and re-launch Premiere. The Print to VideoVision Studio plug-in is located in the For Adobe Premiere folder in the Plug-In Modules folder in the Goodies folder in the Utilities folder of the VideoVision System disk.
5. In the VideoVision Studio Player dialog box, select Current from the Video Output pop-up menu to display the movie on the current video screen, then click Play.
   NOTE: If the error "Can't open Movie Work Area. Snapshot [filename]" appears, choose Make > Output Options, choose QuickTime Movie from the Output As pop-up menu, then repeat steps 1-4.

D. Preview projects by dragging the cursor through the time ruler in the Construction window.

ADDITIONAL INFORMATION

When previewing projects in Premiere 4.x by pressing Return or choosing Project > Preview, Premiere 4.x uses QuickTime 2.x to preview the project. Because QuickTime 2.x does not process high data-rate clips (e.g., 3 MB/sec or greater) correctly, Premiere 4.x returns a system error (e.g., freeze) or generates stuttered playback when previewing clips with high data rates.

When previewing projects using Print to VideoVision Studio, Premiere 4.x uses the VideoVision Studio software to generate the preview rather than QuickTime 2.x. VideoVision Studio software produces smooth previews at high data rates.

VideoVision Studio software 2.5.1 and Studio Player Component 2.5.2 correct playback problems for movies containing more than 12 clips or edits. When Premiere 4.x returns an error when using Print to VideoVision Studio, outputting as QuickTime Movie instead of QuickTime Composite facilitates the preview process.

VideoVision Studio software 2.5.x is available from Radius's World Wide Web site, the Radius BBS, America Online, and CompuServe.

Printing Problems

MAC OS / WINDOWS

Print to Video Command Dimmed When Exporting Sound File from Premiere

ISSUE

When you export a sound file from Adobe Premiere, the Print to Video command is dimmed.

SOLUTION

Activate the Construction window.

ADDITIONAL INFORMATION

When you export a sound from Premiere, the Print to Video command is available only if the Construction window is active.

No Output or Elements Missing When Printing to Non-PostScript Device from Premiere

ISSUE

When you print from Adobe Premiere to a non-PostScript (e.g., QuickDraw, PCL) device, no output is generated or the output does not print as expected (e.g., characters, lines, or other elements are missing).

SOLUTION

Print to a PostScript device.

ADDITIONAL INFORMATION

Adobe Premiere does not correctly cache pages when printing to a non-PostScript device, causing elements on the page to disappear or resulting in pages not printing.

MAC OS

Printing to VideoVision Studio in Premiere 4.x Troubleshooting Guide

ISSUE

When you choose Print to VideoVision Studio to export a preview, movie, or sequence in Adobe Premiere 4.x, playback stops, stutters, drifts out of sync, or an error message appears.

SYMPTOMS

One of the following error messages appears:

"Error looking for video data."

"Can't open Movie Work Area. Snapshot [filename]."

"Too many tracks."

"Sorry, but the playback of video tracks with different characteristics (width, height, colors) is not supported in this version. Unable to play movie [filename]."

SOLUTIONS

Do one or more of the following:

A. Make sure your system and hardware are configured correctly by doing one or more of the following:

A. Use the latest recommended software for compressing video:

- Use Premiere 4.2.1 and the Movie Capture 4.2.2 plug-in.
- Install the Radius VideoVision 2.5.1 software and the Radius StudioPlayer 2.6.2 software, which includes the Studio Player Component 2.6.2 system extension, Studio Player 2.6.2 application, and Print to VideoVision Studio 2.6.2 plug-in.
- Install System 7.5.1 (System 7.5 and the System 7.5 Updater 1.0).
NOTE: Radius does not recommend using System 7.5.3 or later with the NuBus VideoVision Studio capture card.
- Install QuickTime 2.5 and, if you are using a Power Macintosh, install QuickTime PowerPlug 2.5.

B. Limit the data rate of your output to match the maximum video data rate of your system:

1. Choose Make > Compression.
2. In the Compression Settings dialog box, select Radius Studio from the Compressor pop-up menu, then click Options.
3. In the VideoVision Studio Compression Options dialog box, select Adaptive Compression and Maintain Data Rate Of, then enter the maximum video data rate of your system.
NOTE: If you do not know the maximum video data rate of your system, use Premiere's Movie Analysis tool to determine the average data rate of the clips in your project, then enter the highest data rate in the Maintain Data Rate Of text box.
4. Click OK to close the VideoVision Studio Compression Options dialog box, then click OK to close the Compression Settings dialog box.

C. Make sure your Preview and Output Options are set correctly for the VideoVision Studio capture card:

1. Choose Make > Preview Options.
2. In the Preview Options dialog box, enter 640 in the height (h) text box and 480 in the width (w) text box for Preview Window Size.
3. Click More Options, if available.
4. Select Process At, then enter 640 in the height (h) text box and 480 in the width (w) text box.
5. Select Field 1 from the Type pop-up menu, make other desired selections, and then click OK.
6. Choose Make > Output Options.
7. In the Output Options dialog box, enter 640 in the height (h) text box and 480 in the width (w) text box for Size.
8. Select Field 1 from the Type pop-up menu, deselect Optimize Stills, and then select Flatten.
9. Make other selections as desired, then click OK.

B. Make sure all portions of your project are compressed with Radius Studio compression by doing one or more of the following:

A. When the majority of your project contains clips that are not compressed with Radius Studio compression, recompile your entire project using Radius Studio compression:

1. Choose Make > Output Options, select Entire Project from the Output pop-up menu and QuickTime Movie from the As pop-up menu, and then click OK.
2. Choose File > Export > Print to VideoVision Studio.

B. When scattered portions of your project contain clips that are not compressed with Radius Studio compression, recompile those portions using Radius Studio compression:

1. Position the yellow Work Area Bar over any portion of your project containing clips that are not compressed with Radius Studio compression (e.g., stills, animations, mattes, titles, or areas where there are no transitions, filters, or applied motion).
2. Choose Make > Output Options, select Work Area from the Output pop-up menu and QuickTime Movie from the As pop-up menu, and then click OK.
3. Choose File > Export > Print to VideoVision Studio.
4. Repeat steps 1-3 as needed to compress all portions of your project with Radius Studio compression.

C. If audio and video drift are out of sync when you print to video from the Construction Window, render your project from the Construction Window with QuickTime 2.5 installed, then play the resulting movie with Radius StudioPlayer 2.6.2.

D. When playback stops, stutters, or an error message occurs while exporting (i.e. printing to VideoVision Studio) from a movie's Clip window, make sure the clip has only one video track and one type of video data (i.e., Radius Studio) by doing one or more of the following:

A. Make sure the movie has only one video track:

1. Choose File > Tools > Movie Analysis, then double-click the movie you want to export.
2. In the Video section of the Analysis window, make sure only one video track appears. If more than one video track appears, open the movie in a Clip window, choose File > Export > Flattened Movie, name the file and specify a target location, and then click Save. 3. Print to VideoVision Studio from the newly-saved movie.

B. Make sure the movie's video track has only one type of video data:

1. Choose File > Tools > Movie Analysis, then

double-click the movie you want to export.

2. In the Video section of the Analysis window, make sure that the video track has only one type of video data and that the video data's Compressor is Radius Studio. If there is more than one type of video data, or if the video data is not compressed with Radius Studio compression, recompile the movie in Premiere using Radius Studio compression.
3. Print to VideoVision Studio from the newly-saved movie.

E. When playback stops, stutters, or an error message occurs while exporting (i.e., printing to VideoVision Studio) from the Sequence window, export your clips from the Construction Window:

1. Choose File > New > New Project, then double-click the Radius Studio - Full Screen NTSC Preset.
2. Make sure your Output Options are set correctly for the VideoVision Studio capture card:
   1. Choose Make > Preview Options.
   2. In the Preview Options dialog box, enter 640 in the height (h) text box and 480 in the width (w) text box for Preview Window Size.
   3. Click More Options, if available.
   4. Select Process At, then enter 640 in the height (h) text box and 480 in the width (w) text box.
   5. Select Field 1 from the Type pop-up menu, make other desired selections, and then click OK.
   6. Choose Make > Output Options.
   7. In the Output Options dialog box, enter 640 in the height (h) text box and 480 in the width (w) text box for Size.
   8. Select Field 1 from the Type pop-up menu, deselect Optimize Stills, and then select Flatten.
   9. Make other selections as desired, then click OK.
3. Import each of the movies that were in your Sequence window, then place them in sequential order on Track A of the Construction Window.
   NOTE: Your clips should have the identical dimensions and frame rate, and similar data rates. If a clip cannot be exported successfully as a stand-alone clip, it will prevent you from exporting your entire project.
4. Choose File > Export > Print to VideoVision Studio.

F. Output to video using Radius StudioPlayer 2.6.2:

1. Render your project as a QuickTime movie using Radius Studio compression.
2. Open the movie in Radius StudioPlayer and then output to video.

G. When playback stops, stutters, or an error message occurs while rendering movies that have a file size larger than 2 GB, export to video from a Referencing Movie in Premiere 4.2.x:

1. Choose File > New > New Project, then double-click the Radius Studio - Full Screen NTSC Preset.
2. Import each of the movies you want to export as one movie, then place them in sequential order on Track A of the Construction Window.
3. Choose Make > Referencing Movie.
   NOTE: If the Referencing Movie command does not appear on your Make menu, move the Referencing Movie plug-in from the Additional Plug-Ins folder inside the Goodies Folder to the Adobe Premiere Plug-Ins folder, then restart Premiere.
4. Click Output Options or Compression to modify your output settings.
5. Name the file, specify a target location, and then click OK.
6. Open the newly-saved movie in Studio Player, then output to video.

ADDITIONAL INFORMATION

Premiere 4.2.1, VideoVision Studio software 2.5.1, and QuickTime 2.5 improve playback of high data rate files (e.g., full-frame, full-motion video). System 7.5.3 is incompatible with VideoVision Studio software and interferes with SCSI data throughput on NuBus Macintosh computers.

Movies play stuttered or jerky when their data rate exceeds the maximum video data rate of your system. Setting an appropriate data rate for your output ensures your movies play back smoothly. The average data rate of your captured clips is nearly identical to the maximum video data rate of your system at the time of capture.

Incorrect preview and output options may cause Premiere to return an error when exporting to video. Setting all processing dimensions to the same size (i.e. 640 x 480) prevents errors when exporting to video. Deselecting the Optimized Stills option enables Premiere to maintain a smooth data rate. When you render or print to video, Radius recommends flattening movies that generate errors.

When you export movies by choosing Print to VideoVision Studio in Premiere, the StudioPlayer Component system extension controls the movie's playback. Because Studio Player Component only plays movies that are compressed with Radius Studio compression, ensure that all your clips are compressed with Radius Studio compression.

Printing to VideoVision Studio from the Construction Window instead of the Sequence window may prevent errors from occurring when you export video. Premiere exports Motion-JPEG (MJPG) movies (e.g., Radius Studio compressed movies) incorrectly from the Sequence window, causing poor playback or error messages to appear when exporting.

The Macintosh system limits individual files to 2 GB in size. When you encounter errors rendering movies that have a file size larger than 2 GB, render your project in segments where each segment's file size is less than 2 GB. You can record each shorter segment to video to make one long movie by creating a Referencing Movie in Premiere 4.2.x. Referencing Movies have small file sizes as they only contain references to the location of other movies.

When rendering projects as QuickTime Composites, Premiere only compiles areas that have been modified (e.g., transitions, filters, motion, transparency), leaving other areas in their original condition (i.e., Premiere doesn't change their compressor or compression settings). To display video on an NTSC monitor, the Radius Studio Player Component system extension file requires all portions of the movie to be compressed with Radius Studio compression. Rendering projects as QuickTime movies ensures Premiere applies Radius Studio compression to the entire project.

Premiere cannot export some movies that play as expected in Studio Player 2.6.

Error "Can't open Movie Work Area. Snapshot [filename]" Printing to VideoVision from Premiere

ISSUE

When printing to VideoVision from Adobe Premiere's Construction or Sequence window, Premiere returns the error "More tracks than supported in the movie work area. Snapshot [filename]" or "Can't open Movie Work Area.Snapshot [filename]." Premiere returns the error at different times while printing and includes different filenames in the error.

SOLUTIONS

Use Studio Player 2.0.1, available from Radius and included with the VideoVision Studio 2.0.2 upgrade.
OR: Print to VideoVision from the Preview Window.
OR: Compile and print the movie from Premiere's Clip window, then print the movie from the Radius Print to VideoVision Studio application. For instructions on printing from Premiere's Clip window, see Additional Information.
OR: Use the Print to VideoVision Studio 2.0 or later plug-in.

ADDITIONAL INFORMATION

Print to VideoVision 2.0 can only print 12 or less edits or separate files. When printing from Premiere's Construction or Sequence window using the Print to VideoVision Studio 1.7 plug-in, Premiere returns the error "Can't open Movie Work Area.Snapshot [filename]."

When using the Print to VideoVision plug-in in Premiere, the Radius Studio Player application compiles the movie in real time. Studio Player 2.0 and earlier cannot locate or process files that include different dimensions, compression schemes, filters, or multiple audio or video tracks, causing the error "Can't open Movie Work Area.Snapshot [filename]." Creating a QuickTime movie combines the contents of the Construction window into a single, linear file that the Radius Studio Player can compile.

To output a movie from Premiere's Clip window:

1. Choose Make > Movie, then click Output Options.
2. Select Entire Project and QuickTime Movie from the Output pop-up menu, then click OK.
3. Click Compression.
4. Select Radius Studio from the Video pop-up menu, specify a value for Quality, then click OK. For instructions on specifying a compression quality value, refer to the Radius VideoVision Studio User's Manual and ReadMe files.
5. Name the file, then click OK.
6. When the compiled movie appears in the Clip window, choose File > Export > Print to VideoVision to record to videotape.

Frames Drop When Printing to VideoVision Studio in Premiere

ISSUE

Frames drop when you print to VideoVision Studio in Adobe Premiere.

SOLUTIONS

Do one or more of the following:

A. Print using Adobe Premiere 4.0.1, QuickTime 2.0, Apple Multimedia Tuner 2.0.1, and the VideoVision Studio 2.0.2 update, available on the Radius ftp site (ftp.radius.com), the Radius BBS, and America Online.
B. When using the Adaptive Compression option in the VideoVision Studio Compression Options dialog box, determine an average data rate using the Movie Analysis command and compile the movie with the data rate limiting function:
   1. Use the Movie Analysis command to determine the average data rate of each clip or a sampling of clips in the project.
   2. Average the Average Data Rate values of all the clips.
   3. In the VideoVision Studio Compression Options dialog box, select Maintain Data Rate Of and enter the average value in the corresponding text box, then recompile the movie.
C. When the Project contains still images (e.g., stills, titles, mattes), do one or more of the following:
   A. Use Premiere 4.0.1 and deselect Optimize Stills in the Output Options dialog box, if available.
   B. Apply a filter to the image (e.g., apply the Image Pan filter, which does not affect the image):
      1. Select the still image clip in the construction window.
      2. Select Clip > Filters.
      3. In the Filters dialog box, select Image Pan, then click Add.
      4. Click OK in the Image Pan Settings dialog box and in the Filters dialog box.

ADDITIONAL INFORMATION

Premiere 4.0.1, QuickTime 2.0, and the VideoVision Studio 2.0.2 drivers include performance improvements that prevent dropped frames.

When recording a movie using adaptive compression, you can regulate movie quality using either the Quality or the Maintain Data Rate Of option. The data rate of a movie is a more precise indicator of movie quality because it takes into account the varying complexity of images. By determining the performance capability of a computer system and constraining the rate to that limit, movies can be recorded and played back for Printing to VideoVision at the best quality supported by the system.

When recording movies that include still images, Premiere 3.0 and 4.0 optimize still images by not compiling each frame. The VideoVision Studio capture card has difficulty switching between compiling every frame and processing less information for the still image, resulting in reported or actual dropped frames. Applying a filter to the still image forces Premiere to compile every frame of the image, preventing dropped frames.

Premiere 4.0.1 processes a still image by rendering a single frame and duplicating it. The Optimized Stills option, available when the Make Flattened plug-in is installed, causes Premiere 4.0.1 to process still images using the Premiere 4.0 method. The Make Flattened plug-in is included in the Additional Plug-ins folder in the Goodies folder.

General Information

MAC OS / WINDOWS

Standard Video and Film Format Aspect Ratios

Listed below are video aspect ratios for standard video and film formats.

NTSC IMAGE SIZES

Conventional Size: 640 x 480 pixels
Aspect Ratio (w:h): 1.33:1
Pixel Aspect Ratio (w:h): 1:1
Adjusted Aspect Ratio (w:h): 1.333:1 (4:3)

D1 Image
Size: 720 x 486 pixels
Aspect Ratio (w:h): 1.48:1
Pixel Aspect Ratio (w:h): 0.9:1
Adjusted Aspect Ratio (w:h): 1.333:1 (4:3)

D2 Image
Size: 752 x 480 pixels
Aspect Ratio (w:h): 1.567:1
Pixel Aspect Ratio (w:h): 0.859:1
Adjusted Aspect Ratio (w:h): 1.346:1

PAL IMAGE SIZES

Conventional Size: 668 x 576 pixels
Aspect Ratio (w:h): 1.33:1
Pixel Aspect Ratio (w:h): 1:1
Adjusted Aspect Ratio (w:h): 1.333:1 (4:3)

D1 Image
Size: 720 x 576 pixels
Aspect Ratio (w:h): 1.25:1
Pixel Aspect Ratio (w:h): 1.067:1
Adjusted Aspect Ratio (w:h): 1.333:1 (4:3)

D2 Image
Size: 752 x 576 pixels
Aspect Ratio (w:h): 1.31:1
Pixel Aspect Ratio (w:h): 1.019:1
Adjusted Aspect Ratio (w:h): 1.330:1

HDTV IMAGE SIZES

#1
Size: 1280 x 720 pixels
Aspect Ratio (w:h): 1.78:1
Pixel Aspect Ratio (w:h): 1:1
Adjusted Aspect Ratio (w:h): 1.78:1 (16:9)

#2
Size: 1920 x 1080 pixels
Aspect Ratio (w:h): 1.78:1
Pixel Aspect Ratio (w:h): 1:1
Adjusted Aspect Ratio (w:h): 1.78:1 (16:9)

FILM IMAGE SIZES

Full Aperture
Size: 2048 x 1536 pixels
Aspect Ratio (w:h): 1.33:1
Pixel Aspect Ratio (w:h): 1:1
Adjusted Aspect Ratio (w:h): 1.333:1 (4:3)

Academy Aperture
Size: 1828 x 1332 pixels
Aspect Ratio (w:h): 1.37:1
Pixel Aspect Ratio (w:h): 1:1
Adjusted Aspect Ratio (w:h): 1.37:1

Recommended Key Frames for Cinepak and Indeo Compression

When compiling a movie in Adobe Premiere, the manufacturers of Cinepak (SuperMac) and Indeo (Intel) recommend specific key frame rates for optimal playback.

Recommended compression schemes and their corresponding key frame rate are:
Cinepak: 7
Indeo: 4

To compile a movie and specify a compression setting:

1. Choose Project > Make > Movie.
2. Click Compression.
3. In the Compression Settings dialog box, select a compression method from the Video pop-up menu.
4. Enter the appropriate key frame rate value for the selected compression method in the Key Frame Rate Every _ Frames text box, then click OK.
5. Name the file, then click OK.
6. Verify the key frame rate each time you recompress the movie.

Videotape Formats General Information

VIDEOTAPE CATEGORIES

Video cameras differ in the way they encode color information into a video signal. Some cameras process separate signals for each color component while others encode color information into a single signal. These different methods can be broken down into three categories: composite, S-Video, and component.

COMPOSITE FORMATS

This format is most commonly used in consumer-level equipment, but offers the lowest-fidelity audio and video. Composite video modulates the brightness and color information comprising the video signal into a single channel. Audio is carried on separate left and right channels. Composite videotapes range in size from 8mm to 1". Formats include Standard VHS, 8mm, 3/4" Umatic, 3/4" Umatic SP, 1", Unihi, Laservision (ODC), and Laserdisc (ASACA). Composite video is transmitted over a cable with an industry-standard RCA connector or via RF/coaxial connectors like those on "cable ready" television.

S-VIDEO FORMATS

S-Video formats separate analog video into color (chrominance) and brightness (luminance) components, carrying them on separate left and right channels. This category offers the next-best video fidelity. Formats are currently limited to S-VHS and Hi8. S-VHS uses an S-video cable for video, and phono cables for audio. The S-video cable has connectors similar to those on a Mac serial cable. Hi8 video equipment has S-Video ports and professional Hi8 equipment also has BNC outputs to make it compatible with other equipment using BNC connectors, such as 3/4" and 1" decks.

COMPONENT FORMATS

Component video provides the highest quality representation of video, separating the video signal into three channels. These channels are encoded either as RGB information, with discrete channels for red, green and blue color information, or as YUV (Yellow Under Violet), with one channel carrying information describing the image's intensity and the other two used for color data. Equipment that supports component formats also outputs a fourth channel that carries a video synchronizing signal. Sound is carried on two independent channels. Component tape formats are usually in 1/2", 3/4", or 1" tape sizes, and include Betacam, BetaSP, Digital Betacam, MII, D-1, DCT and Laserdisc. Component video is transmitted via cables with BNC connectors, a common video connector with a locking mechanism that ensures a good connection. The audio is sent over XLR cables. An XLR connector has three pins and a locking mechanism.

CONSUMER QUALITY FORMATS

All of these formats suffer from dropout, a defect in the tape medium that causes metal particles on the tape to fall off, producing white streaks in the image or, at worst, synchronization problems. The greater width of VHS tapes makes them less susceptible to this problem than 8mm.

VHS

VHS uses 1/2" media with 240 line horizontal resolution (H-res). It can record up to two hours at regular speed (also known as standard play [SP] mode). Because of the large number of machines available, VHS is the standard for video distribution. It is not acceptable for production or post-production tasks.

8mm

This consumer composite format is made by Sony and is used mainly for palm-sized camcorders. It has 260 line Hi-res and can record up to two hours in standard mode. This format requires an 8mm-compatible deck for playback.

VHS-C

This format is designed to fit smaller camcorders. VHS-C has the same format specs as VHS but only records up to 30 minutes per tape. When loaded in an adapter, it can be played back from any VHS tape player.

INDUSTRIAL QUALITY FORMATS

These formats are more robust than consumer formats and there are also more editing facilities available that handle them.

S-VHS

S-VHS uses S-Video format and has 400 lines H-res. Like VHS, S-VHS uses standard metal 1/2" tape but adds two high-fidelity and two linear audio channels. Hi-fi audio has a much greater frequency response than the standard linear audio. Hi-fi is recorded in the same area as the video signal so you can't add hi-fi audio to a prerecorded tape during editing without recording over the preexisting video. S-VHS machines can both play and record VHS tapes. S-VHS C is a smaller format to reduce camera weight; it uses cassettes that hold from 20 to 30 minutes of footage. These tapes need a special adapter to be played back on standard S-VHS video decks.

Hi8

Hi-8mm also uses S-Video format with 400 lines H-res. Hi8 dominates the high-end "prosumer" camcorder market. Besides support of the S-video format, the basic difference between Hi8 and 8mm tape is that on Hi8 the Y signal's overall frequency range is greater, allowing a larger overall bandwidth to record video information. The sound capabilities are quite good since it uses both hi-fi and PCM (pulse code modulation, a form of digital audio) recording technology to provide high-fidelity sound.

3/4" and 3/4" SP Umatic

Now being replaced by S-VHS as an industrial video production standard, 3/4" is a composite format with 280 lines H-res and two linear audio channels. Sony introduced 3/4" SP as an upgrade to the format, enhancing the image resolution with 330 line H-res and two hi-fi channels. Because of the media size, 3/4" tapes can only record one hour per tape.

PROFESSIONAL BROADCAST FORMATS

At the professional level, the cost-per-tape and the cost of production and postproduction equipment increases rapidly. These formats are designed to withstand many generations of use, and also to be able to record the most detailed image possible. The media is more resilient with the backing on the tape twice as thick and the outside case much stronger. The hardware needed to record and play back is both more sophisticated and much more expensive than the industrial formats.

Betacam and Betacam SP

These are the most common professional tape formats available. Both are 1/2" component formats by Sony. Betacam SP adds better image quality (360 line H-res) and audio capabilities to the regular Betacam format (330 H-res). While portable Betacam decks and camcorders can only record up to 30 minutes of material, larger video decks can record up to 90 minutes of material.

MII

MII is a 1/2" component format from Panasonic, with 440 lines H-res and four audio channels. This tape is very robust even after going down several generations from the master tape. Because the tape moves faster than normal, it can only hold maximum of 20 minutes of video per tape.

1" C

1" C is an open-reel composite formation with 330 lines H-res and three linear audio channels, which pales in comparison to the hi-fi audio on Betacam, MII, or S-VHS decks. This format is being replaced by Betacam SP and some of the new digital formats.

DIGITAL FORMATS

At the very high end of the format spectum, digital formats are used at ultra high-end production and postproduction companies. Instead of recording analog signal to tape, these formats convert the source video signal into digital video data, resulting in no generational degradation as long as the data stays digital. The digital formats are separate formats, not enhancements on each other.

D-1

D-1 is a digital component format and currently the highest-quality video format commercially available (460 lines H-res). This is the first format with four channels of CD-quality digital audio.

D-2

D-2 is a 3/4" composite format with 440 lines H-res and four channels of CD-quality audio. Video quality tends to be much brighter than other composite formats. Many editing studios edit their final masters to D-2.

D-3

D-3 is Panasonic's version of D-2. It has 440 lines H-res but is based on 1/2" tape. D-3 is lightweight and often used in the field as a production format.

FUTURE FORMATS

- Sony's Digital Betacam format
- Panasonic's D-5, a component 1/2" digital format
- Ampex's DCT, a digital component format
- HDTV (high definition television), which is a new analog video standard with a wide-screen 16:9 aspect ratio

Video Capture Cards Bundled with Premiere General Information

VIDEO CAPTURE CARDS BUNDLED WITH PREMIERE FOR WINDOWS

MediaSpace
Company: VideoLogic
Phone: (415)-875-0606
Maximum Capture Rate: 30 fps @ 320 x 240
Compression: MJPG

MegaMotion
Company: Alpha Systems Labs
Phone: (714) 252-0117
Maximum Capture Rate: 30 fps @ 320 x 240
Compression: MJPG, CL-550 Single field 320 x 240

MiroVideo DC1
Company: Miro Computer
Phone: (415) 855-0940
Maximum Capture Rate: 30 fps @ 640 x 480
Compression: MJPG

MovieMachine Pro
Company: Fast Electronics
Phone: (415) 802-0772
Maximum Capture Rate: 30 fps @ 640 x 480
Compression: MJPG (optional)

MovieMan
Company: Logitech
Phone: (510) 795-8500
Maximum Capture Rate: 15 fps @ 320 x 240, 30 fps @ 160 x 120
Compression: none

RealMagic Producer
Company: Sigma Design
Phone: (510) 770-0100
Maximum Capture Rate: 30 fps @ 352 x 240
Compression: Editable MJPG (i-frame only)

Targa 2000
Company: Truevision
Phone: (317) 841-0332
Maximum Capture Rate: 30 fps, 60 fields @ 1024 x 768
Compression: MJPG

Videola
Company: Orchid Technology
Phone: (510) 683-0300
Maximum Capture Rate: 30 fps @ 240 x 180, 15 fps @ 320 x 240
Compression: JPEG CL-550 single field 4:2:2

Videola Premium
Company: Orchid Technology
Phone: (510) 683-0300
Maximum Capture Rate: 30 fps @ 320 x 240
Compression: JPEG CL-550 single field 4:2:2

VideoStar
Company: Diamond Computer
Phone: (408) 736-2000
Maximum Capture Rate: 30 fps @ 160 x 120
Compression: VideoStar Proprietary (YUV-6)

VideoStar Pro
Company: Diamond Computer
Phone: (408) 736-2000
Maximum Capture Rate: 30 fps @ 320 x 240
Compression: MJPG, Zoran (4:1:1, 320 x 240, single field)

VIDEO CAPTURE CARDS BUNDLED WITH PREMIERE FOR MACINTOSH

*Targa 2000**
Company: Truevision
Phone: (317) 841-0332
Maximum Capture Rate: 30 fps, 60 fields, @ 648 x 486, 16-bit/48.8kHz audio (DAT)
Compression: MJPG

*Targa 2000 Pro**
Company: Truevision
Phone: (317) 841-0332
Maximum Capture Rate: 30 fps, 60 fields, @ 648 x 486, 16-bit/48.8kHz audio (DAT)
Compression: MJPG

*Telecast***
Company: Radius
Phone: (408) 541-6100
Maximum Capture Rate: 60 fps, 120 fields @ 640 x 480, 16-bit/48.8kHz audio (DAT)
Compression: MJPG (Radius)

VideoVision Studio
Company: Radius
Phone: (408) 541-6100
Maximum Capture Rate: 30 fps, 60 fields @ 640 x 480, 16-bit/44kHz audio
Compression: MJPG (Radius)

* Targa 2000 is a single-slot NuBus card; Targa 2000 Pro is a dual-slot NuBus card. PCI versions are available.

** Radius Telecast is bundled with Premiere 4.0.1t (distributed through Radius), which supports Telecast timecode.

VIDEO CAPTURE CARDS THAT SUPPORT AUDIO CAPTURE

Alpha Systems Labs MegaMotion
Truevision Targa 2000
VideoLogic MediaSpace
Video Capture Cards That Support Video Out
Alpha Systems Labs MegaMotion
Fast Electronics Movie Machine Pro (with MJPG option)
Miro Computer MiroVideo DC1
Orchid Technology Videola Pro (with optional MJPG compressor)
Orchid Technology Videola Premium
Sigma Design RealMagic Producer
Truevision Targa 2000

VIDEO CAPTURE CARDS THAT ARE NOT INDUSTRY STANDARD ARCHITECTURE (ISA)

Sigma Design RealMagic Producer - PCI (Peripheral Component Interconnect)
Truevision Targa 2000 - EISA (Extended Industry Standard Architecture)

File Size Limitations in Premiere General Information

PREMIERE FOR THE MACINTOSH

The maximum size of still images supported by Macintosh system software is 4000 x 4000 pixels. To increase Premiere's default size limit of 2048 x 2048 pixels, choose File > Preferences > General, then select 4000 x 4000 from the Maximum Image Size pop-up menu. The maximum size of Premiere's Title window is 2048 x 2048 pixels.

The maximum frame size for QuickTime movies is 2048 x 1536 pixels. The minimum frame size for QuickTime movies is 60 x 45 pixels.

Because of a file size limit in Macintosh system software, files can be no larger than 2 GB. Because of a Finder limitation, the maximum number of sequential PICT files that can be imported into Premiere from one folder is 1000, though 300 or less is recommended.

PREMIERE 4.X FOR WINDOWS

The maximum size of still images in Premiere 4.2 is 4096 x 4096 pixels. To increase Premiere's default size limit of 2048 x 2048 pixels, choose File > Preferences > General, then select 4096 x 4096 from the Maximum Image Size pop-up menu.

Because of a size limitation in Windows 3.x, the maximum size of still images in Premiere 4.0x is 2000 x 2000 pixels. To increase Premiere's default size limit of 2048 x 2048 pixels, choose File > Preferences > General, then select 4000 x 4000 from the Maximum Image Size pop-up menu.

The maximum frame size for .AVI and QuickTime movies is 2048 x 1536 pixels. The minimum frame size for .AVI and QuickTime movies is 60 x 45 pixels.

Because of a file size limit in Video for Windows running on Windows 3.11, Video for Windows (.AVI) movies larger than 1 gigabyte (GB) do not play as expected, and may not open in Premiere 4.x. The 32-bit version of Video for Windows running on Windows 95 enables Premiere to play .AVI movies larger than 1 GB.

Clips longer than 60 minutes cannot be placed in the Construction window in Adobe Premiere 4.x.

PREMIERE 1.X FOR WINDOWS

The maximum size of still images is 4000 x 4000 pixels. To increase Premiere's default size limit of 2048 x 2048 pixels, choose File > Preferences > General, then select 4000 x 4000 from the Maximum Image Size pop-up menu.

The maximum frame size for .AVI and QuickTime movies is 2048 x 1536 pixels. The minimum frame size for .AVI and QuickTime movies is 60 x 45 pixels.

Because a file size limit in Video for Windows running on Windows 3.11, Video for Windows (.AVI) movies larger than 1 GB do not play as expected, and may not open in Premiere 1.x.

Compression and Data Rates General Information

This record describes the relationship between compression and data rates, and how changes in compression method affect the data rates of the movies you render.

COMPRESSION AND DATA RATES

Compression is the process of removing or restructuring data to decrease the size of a file, and is accomplished by a compressor/decompressor (codec). Codecs achieve greater compression when the source video is simple and has fewer changes between frames (e.g. very little motion, a lot of color similarity, high quality source footage, etc.).

The data rate (sometimes called the data transfer rate) of digital video is defined as the amount of data per second for any given point in a movie. For example, a movie may begin with a data rate of 1500K/second, but increase to 1800K/sec in areas that are more complex (e.g., transitions, filters, motion, audio). As movies increase in size, complexity, and image quality, the data rate increases as well.

Disk drives (e.g., hard disk drives, CD-ROM drives, disk arrays) are also rated in terms of their data transfer rate. A drive with a high data rate (e.g., a SCSI hard drive) can read and write more information per second than a drive with a low data rate (e.g., CD-ROM drive). While drive speed is often analyzed or reported in terms of the SCSI transfer rate or maximum sustained transfer rate, these figures do not directly correspond to the drives video data rate (i.e., the highest rate at which the drive can play video without dropping frames).

Your digital movies should have the highest data rate possible without exceeding the video data rate of the capture or playback drive. If the data rate of your digital video exceeds the video data rate of your drive, either during video capture or video playback, your computer will drop frames (i.e., some frames will not be recorded to disk during video capture, or they will not be displayed during playback). Movies with dropped frames appear stuttered or jerky when played. On the other hand, if your movie's data rate is too low you will compromise image quality. For this reason, you should adjust the data rate of your movies so they match the video data rate of the capture and playback drives.

USING DATA RATES TO CONTROL COMPRESSION QUALITY

You can alter the data rate of your movies by adjusting the level and type of compression (e.g., hardware compression vs. software compression). All codecs allow you to adjust the ratio of compression (e.g., 10:1, 15:1) by means of a Quality slider. When the Quality slider is set to its highest point, the least amount of compression is applied, resulting in higher data rates and better image quality. As the Quality slider is lowered, compression increases while the data rate and image quality decrease.

When you use the Quality slider to adjust your movies data rate, a constant level of compression is applied to the entire movie, regardless of the movies content. For example, if the Quality slider is set to its highest point, each frame in the movie is compressed by the ratio corresponding to the position of the Quality slider (e.g., 16:1), whether the frame contains 100 k of raw data or 1000 k of raw data.

The drawback of applying a constant level of compression is that some frames are compressed unnecessarily, while the data in other frames exceeds the limits of the playback system. For example, if your playback system supports a data rate of 1500 k/sec, you need to compress the portions of your movie that are higher than 1500 k/sec, but you don't need to compress areas that are already less than 1500 k/sec. A constant level of compression would compress both the complex and simple portions of your movie by the same ratio, which often results in data spikes (i.e., sudden data increases) in some areas and compression artifacts (i.e., streaks or specks) in others. To compress only those portions of your movie that exceed a certain data rate, you should apply a data rate limit instead of adjusting the Quality slider.

A data rate limit defines the maximum amount of data per second for your movie. For example, if you apply a data rate limit of 1500 k/sec, your codec will only compress the portions of your movie that exceed 1500 k/sec; all other portions will remain unchanged.

However, your codec is limited by its maximum compression ratio, and may not achieve the data rate you specify. When a codec cannot remove enough information to meet the data rate limit, the data rate of the final movie is higher than the data rate limit. For example, when your codec can only compress frames as low as 150 k/sec, and the requested data rate limit is 90 k/sec, the data rate of your final movie is still 150 k/sec for those frames. If it is essential that your movies do not exceed a certain data rate (e.g., when making movies for CD-ROM distribution), but your codec cannot meet the requested data rate limit using its maximum compression ratio, you must either choose another codec or reduce the content and complexity of your movie (e.g., reduce the frame size, lower the frame rate, minimize special effects and transitions).

Frame Rate vs. Time Base in Premiere

Frame rate may be the most misunderstood and misused option in Adobe Premiere. The frame rate you specify when setting up a compression method should not be confused with the time base you set up when you create a new project.

FRAME RATE

The frame rate determines the playback rate of the movie. In general, higher rates yield better results, with smoother, more natural-looking motion. You should select a rate that matches the maximum playback rate of the computer system on which the finished movie will be played. Selecting a rate that cannot be achieved by the playback system results in dropped frames and possible flutter when the movie is played.

The maximum rate of the playback system depends on the speed of its components, the CPU speed, the hard drive or CD-ROM performance, data-transfer limits, compression abilities, the video card, and the color depth settings of the monitor. Playback is also affected by movie settings such as frame size, color depth and the selected compression/decompression scheme (codec).

You can specify the frame rate for compiling Adobe Premiere movies in the Compression Settings dialog box, which appears when you choose Make > Compression, or when you click the Compression button in the Make Movie dialog box. You can set the frame rate for previews in the Preview Options dialog box, which appears when you choose Make > Preview Options.

TIME BASE

Although the time base is expressed as frames per second (fps), it determines how Adobe Premiere interprets imported clips and lets the application know how many frames make 1 second of a movie for editing. It can be the rounded National Television Standards Committee (NTSC) standard of 30 fps, 25 fps (the norm for Europe's Phase Alternation Line [PAL] and Systeme Electronique Couleur Avec Memoire [SECAM]) or 24 fps (film). In Premiere 4.x, the time base can be 29.97 fps, the true NTSC standard. The time base affects both the timecode frame numbers and the Construction Window's time ruler.

Although the time base is not the same as the frame rate, consider the frame rate of your final movie when setting the time base for a project. Doing so ensures data will not be lost through interpolation when Adobe Premiere translates data from the project frame rate into the compiled movie's frame rate. Select a time base that's an even multiple of the final movie. For example, if you want to output a final movie at 15 fps, you should set the time base to 30 fps, because 30 is evenly divisible by 15 (every two frames will be duplicates).

The time base also limits the maximum frame rate of the compiled movie. For example, if the project's time base is set to 25 and the new movie is set to 30 frames per second, the compiled movie will only have 25 fps despite compression settings that appear to be creating 30 fps.

You can set the time base in Premiere 4.x by selecting a preset in the New Project Presets dialog box, which appears when you choose File > New > New Project. Because Premiere 4.x can import projects into other projects, if the imported project has a different time base, the receiving project's time base is used.

Premiere Preview Files General Information

Adobe Premiere creates preview files when compiling a preview if the video mode in the Preview Options dialog box is set to Effects to Disk. Premiere for the Macintosh saves the preview files in an Adobe Premiere Preview Files folder inside the folder where the project is located, or on the disk specified for Video Preview Temps in the Scratch Disks dialog box. Premiere for Windows always saves preview (.tmp) files in a Projname.tmp directory in the directory where the project is located.

The preview files help Premiere preview and compile movies more quickly. Once a section of the project has been compiled, it does not have to be recompiled unless you change the preview or output options, or modify that section of the project (e.g., apply a transition to a video clip). To ensure smooth previews in the Effects to Disk mode, make sure the dimensions of the original clips match the Process At dimensions in the Preview Options dialog box. If the dimensions do not match, Adobe Premiere must resize the clips while it plays the preview, which may result in stuttered (e.g., jerky) playback.

Premiere automatically relocates the preview files when opening a project. If you have done any of the following, Premiere prompts you to locate the preview files when opening a project:

- moved or deleted the preview files.
- changed the name of the preview files folder.
- made changes in a project without saving them.
- changed preview options.
- pressed Command + Option + Shift and click on the work area bar to delete preview files.

If the preview files are not available, press Control (Macintosh) or Ctrl (Windows) and click Skip to skip all preview files. If the preview files are available but Macintosh Premiere cannot locate them, try rebuilding the desktop by pressing Command + Option while restarting the Macintosh.

WINDOWS

Top Issues: Adobe Premiere 4.x for Windows

This document summarizes the latest and most common issues we're hearing in Adobe Technical Support about Adobe Premiere 4.x for Windows. This document was last revised November 11, 1996. Issues that are new or updated from the previous revision are indicated with an asterisk (*).

Numbers are included for documents that describe related issues in more detail. These documents are available on our automated faxing system, Adobe FaxYI at 206-628-5737, on the Adobe BBS at 206-623-6984, and on the Adobe home page on the World Wide Web (http://www.adobe.-com/). For an index of all FaxYI documents available for Premiere, see document 310099.

The latest version of Adobe Premiere for Windows is Premiere 4.2. For pricing and availability information, visit the

Adobe Premiere home page (http://www.adobe.com/prodindex/premiere/) or call Adobe at 1-800-42-ADOBE (23623).

1. *Unable to Select Premiere 4.2 (32-bit version) in Adobe Premiere Installer Dialog Box

    The Premiere Installer is incompatible with the Microsoft Windows 95 OEM Service Release 2, which causes the Premiere 4.2 (32-bit version) option to be dimmed in the Adobe Premiere Installer dialog box. Service Release 2 is pre-installed with Windows 95 and Windows NT on most PCs purchased after October 1996. To install Premiere 4.2 on a computer running Service Release 2, you need to bypass the Premiere Installer.

    If Service Release 2 is installed, the words "Microsoft Internet Explorer" appear below the Windows flag in the Windows startup screen. You can also check for Service Release 2 by right-clicking on My Computer and selecting Properties from the pop-up menu. If Service Release 2 is installed, the system version listed is 4.00.950 B.

    To manually install Premiere 4.2 in Windows 95 or Windows NT, double-click the Setup.exe file in the Premiere\Win95&nt\Disk1 directory on the Premiere 4.2 Deluxe CD-ROM.

    To manually install the English version of Premiere 4.2 LE in Windows 95 or Windows NT, double-click on the Setup.exe file in the English\Premle\Win95&nt\Disk1 directory on the Premiere 4.2 LE CD-ROM. To install the German or French version of Premiere LE, double-click on the Setup.exe file in Deutsch\Premle\Win95&nt\Disk1 or Francais\Premle\Win95&nt\Disk1, respectively.

    For more information, see document 343427.

2. Unable to Output to Videotape from TrueVision Bravado 1000 with ActiveMovie Installed

    When you videotape a movie compiled with TrueVision Bravado compression, the video signal must be played back on an external NTSC monitor connected to the outputs on the Bravado 1000 card. If ActiveMovie is installed, however, the video signal is redirected to your computer monitor. To direct the video signal to the NTSC monitor, you must disable ActiveMovie.

    To disable ActiveMovie in Windows 95:

    1. Choose Start > Settings > Control Panel, then double-click Multimedia.
    2. In the Multimedia Properties dialog box, click the Advanced tab, double-click Media Control Devices, then double-click ActiveMovie MCI Driver.
    3. Select "Do not use this Media Control device" to disable ActiveMovie.
    4. Repeat steps 2-3 for any listings for ActiveX, DirectX, or Direct Draw.

    ActiveMovie is a cross-platform digital video technology created by Microsoft for the desktop and the Internet. ActiveMovie is installed with Netscape Navigator 3.x or later, Microsoft Internet Explorer, ActiveMovie technology, ActiveX technology, Diamond Stealth display cards, and Matrox display cards.

3. Online Documentation for Premiere 4.2 LE

    The Adobe Premiere 4.2 LE and Adobe Photoshop 3.0.5 LE User Guides are included on the Adobe Premiere LE CD-ROM in Portable Document Format (PDF). You can view, search, and print the documentation using the Adobe Acrobat Reader, which is also included on the CD-ROM. In addition, you can click on references in the Index to automatically display the appropriate page.

    The Premiere LE User Guide and Photoshop LE User Guide PDF files are located in the Documentation folder in the English folder on the CD-ROM.

    To order a printed copy of the Premiere 4.2 LE User Guide for US$20, enter your order information on the reverse side of your Premiere LE registration card, or contact Adobe Customer Services at 800-833-6687.

4. Red "X" Appears in Preview Window

    A red letter "X" appears in the Preview window during transitions, filters, and special effects in uncompiled previews.

    To compile a preview, choose Project > Preview, press Enter, or choose Make > Snapshot and use the Controller to play the preview.

5. Project Trimmer Converts Audio Data in AVI Files to 8-bit Mono, 22 kHz

    When trimming projects using the Project Trimmer in Premiere 4.2, Premiere converts the audio data in Video for Windows (AVI) files to 8-bit mono, 22 kHz sound.

    To prevent this problem install the revised H-proj.prm plug-in file, available in compressed form (H-proj.zip) on Adobe's World Wide Web site, the Adobe BBS, America Online, and CompuServe. Installation instructions are included with the H-proj.zip file.

    For more information, see document 343338.

6. Unable to Save Projects Containing Clips with Long Filenames in Premiere 4.2

    A system error (e.g., freeze) occurs, or Premiere 4.2 returns an error when saving projects that contain clips with long filenames (i.e., greater than thirty characters).

    To prevent Premiere from returning an error when saving, remove all clips with long filenames from the project. Rename the clips with filenames that do not exceed thirty characters before importing them into Premiere.

7. Invalid Page Fault Error When Saving Projects with Custom Presets in Premiere 4.2

    Premiere returns an invalid page fault error when saving projects created using a custom preset (e.g., DPS Perception Video Recorder (PVR), DPS Personal Animation Recorder (PAR).

    To prevent this problem, install the revised H-proj.prm plug-in file, available in compressed form (H-proj.zip) on Adobe's World Wide Web site, the Adobe BBS, America Online, and CompuServe. Installation instructions are included with the H-proj.zip file.

8. Capture and Display Drivers are Outdated for Windows 95 and Windows NT

One of the most common causes of system errors (e.g., General Protection Fault, freeze) in Windows 95 or Windows NT is outdated video display drivers or video capture drivers. For instructions on determining the version of your drivers, see below.

- TrueVision Bravado 1000

  If you're using the TrueVision Bravado 1000 video capture card in Windows 3.1 or Windows 95 with version 1.1 or earlier of the TrueVision Bravado driver, contact TrueVision (800-522-8783) to obtain an updated driver.

- Quadrant Q-Motion PCI

  If you're using the Quadrant Q-Motion PCI video capture card in Windows 3.x or Windows 95, install version 1.41 or later of Quadrant's Q-Motion PCI software drivers. Q-Motion PCI software drivers are available from Quadrant International's World Wide Web site.

- Miro DC-20

  If you're using the Miro DC-20 video capture card in Windows 95 or Windows NT, install version 1.05 or later of Miro's software drivers. Miro software drivers are available from Miro's BBS (415-855-9944).

- DPS Perception (PVR)

  If you're using the DPS Perception (PVR) video capture card, install version 2.52 or later of DPS's software drivers. DPS software drivers are available from DPS's FTP site (ftp://ftp.dps.com/pvr/NTSC) or BBS (416-754-8368). DPS recommends using Premiere 4.2 in Windows NT, and Premiere 4.0a in Windows 95. Other configurations are not supported by Adobe Technical Support.

- Matrox Millennium

  If you're using the Matrox Millennium video display card, install version 2.30 or later of Matrox's software drivers. Matrox software drivers are available from Matrox's World Wide Web site (http://www.matrox.com/mgaweb/ftp_mw95.htm) or BBS (514-685-6008).

To determine the version of your capture card driver in Windows 95:

1. Choose Start > Settings > Control Panel, then double-click Multimedia.
2. In the Multimedia Properties dialog box, click the Advanced tab, double-click Video Compression Codecs, then double-click the name of your hardware compressor/decompressor (codec).
3. Verify that the message "Device is enabled and functioning properly" displays in the Codec section, then click Settings to view the version of your capture card driver.

To determine the version of your capture card driver in Windows NT 3.51:

Double-click the Drivers Control Panel in the Main group in Program Manager, then double-click the name of your hardware codec to view its version number.

To determine the version of your video display driver in Windows 95:

1. Choose Start > Settings > Control Panel, then double-click Display.
2. In the Display Properties dialog box, click the Settings tab, then click Change Display Type. The version number displays in the Adapter Type section.

To determine the version of your video display driver in Windows NT 3.51:

Double-click the Display Control Panel in Program Manager's Main Group, then click Change Display Type to view the version of your video display driver.

9. Errors Launching or Importing in Premiere 4.0 LE with
   - Miro DC-20 Video Capture Card

   Errors occur when launching or importing files in Premiere 4.0 LE when a Miro DC-20 video capture card is installed.

   The Miro DC-20 video capture card requires its compressor/decompressor (codec) to remain open when you work in Premiere. To ensure that the codec remains open, launch the Miro DC-20 Control application before launching Premiere, or add instructions to the Premiere.ini file to keep the codec open.

10. Video Does Not Display on NTSC (TV) or Computer Monitor

    If video displays on the computer monitor instead of the NTSC monitor after you choose Print to Video, make sure your control or display application is set to send the video display signal to your NTSC monitor.

    If video switches between the NTSC and computer monitors during playback, make sure the MJPG codec is selected in the Compression Settings dialog box, and all portions of your project have been compressed with that codec.

    If video displays gray or black on the computer monitor and no NTSC monitor is attached, make sure your control or display application is set to send the video display signal to the computer monitor, not to an NTSC monitor.

11. Audio and Video are Out of Sync During Playback

    When audio and video drift out of sync during playback, it's usually because the audio and video clips were captured using separate audio and video capture cards. To make sure the movie was rendered correctly, pause it when it is playing out of sync, then continue playback. If the movie now plays in sync, you know that it was rendered correctly but is drifting out of sync because of timing differences between the audio and video capture cards.

    To minimize audio and video sync problems, use the Sync option in Premiere 4.2's Project Output Options dialog box.

12. Unable to Capture or Play Video

    Many video or audio capture and playback problems encountered in Premiere are caused by system or hardware configuration problems. To determine if you have a configuration problem, capture or play your audio or video files in another application (e.g., TestCap, Sound Recorder, Media Player). If the capture or playback problem occurs in another application, then the problem lies with your system or hardware configuration rather than your capture or playback application. Contact the video or sound card manufacturer for configuration and compatibility information.

13. Poor Video Quality During Transitions, Filters, and Motion

If movies play with poor quality (e.g., pixelated, blurred, distorted) during transitions, filters, and motion, the data rate may have been set incorrectly when the movie was rendered.

The data rate limit in the Compression Settings dialog box should match the data rate of the video clips in the project.

MAC OS

Uncompressed Audio Data Rates

Sample Rate (Hertz)	Channels	Bit Depth	Kbytes/ Second
11000	Mono	8	11
11000	Mono	16	22
11000	Stereo	8	22
11000	Stereo	16	44
11025	Mono	8	11.025
11025	Mono	16	22.05
11025	Stereo	8	22.05
11025	Stereo	16	44.1
22000	Mono	8	22
22000	Mono	16	44
22000	Stereo	8	44
22000	Stereo	16	88
22050	Mono	8	22.05
22050	Mono	16	44.1
22050	Stereo	8	44.1
22050	Stereo	16	88.2
24000	Mono	8	24
24000	Mono	16	48
24000	Stereo	8	48
24000	Stereo	16	96
44000	Mono	8	44
44000	Mono	16	88
44000	Stereo	8	88
44000	Stereo	16	176
44100	Mono	8	44.1
44100	Mono	16	88.2
44100	Stereo	8	88.2
44100	Stereo	16	176.4
48000	Mono	8	48
48000	Mono	16	96
48000	Stereo	8	96
48000	Stereo	16	192

Adobe Premiere's Hardware Requirements

REQUIREMENTS FOR ONLINE VIDEO EDITING

With online editing, you work with the original video tapes to produce a movie for broadcast or other type of distribution. Using the Adobe Premiere program as a real-time video editing device requires the following high-end video hardware.

Required hardware:

- A fast computer. To produce full-screen, full-motion (30 frames per second) video, you need a computer with a 68040 or better processor.
- A large hard disk with a sustained data transfer rate of 4 MB per second or higher.
- A high-end audio-video capture board that supports hardware compression and video output for capturing and playing back full-screen, full-motion video, such as those offered by SuperMac, Radius, RasterOps, and TrueVision.
- At least 20 MB of available RAM. To play QuickTime movies directly from RAM, you may need more than 20 MB of RAM.

Optional hardware:

- A device controller (such as ARTI, V-LAN, DQ Animaq, or VISCA) and a controllable tape deck that supports SMPTE (Society of Motion Picture and Television Engineers) time code. These devices let you control your tape deck from the computer during video capture.
- An array system (i.e., a high-speed hard drive configuration in which two or more drives act as one).

REQUIREMENTS FOR OFF-LINE VIDEO EDITING

With off-line editing, you review video tapes copied from the original tapes, then edit and sequence the material and record editing decisions in an Edit Decision List (EDL). The EDL is used later to build the distribution tape. Off-line editing enables you to use lower-end, lower-cost equipment for the bulk of the editing work and keeps expensive online editing time to a minimum. Off-line editing requires considerably less equipment than does online editing.

Off-line video editing requires the following equipment:

- A midrange computer, such as a Macintosh IIci or better with at least 8 MB of RAM. Although you can run Adobe Premiere on a slower computer, you need at least a IIci to work with images that are 240 pixels by 160 pixels or more at 10 frames per second or faster.
- A hard disk with at least 200 MB of free space. Even small QuickTime movies require a lot of free disk space.
- An audio-video capture card. While full-screen, full-motion capability and video output are not necessary with off-line editing, you may want to output your movie to videotape so you can compare it to the final product generated from the EDL. A capture card such as the SuperMac Video Spigot & Sound, the RasterOps Media Time, or the Radius VideoVision should be sufficient.
- A tape deck, preferably one with device control. If your tape deck supports SMPTE time code, Premiere notes

the time code information on your tape. If your tape deck does not understand time code, your tapes must have visible time code readings (i.e., window dubs) so that you can enter the time code information manually in Premiere.

REQUIREMENTS FOR MULTIMEDIA EDITING

When you edit video for inclusion in multimedia applications, you create QuickTime movies and then import them into an application such as Macromedia Director or Adobe Persuasion. For video that you want to include in multimedia applications, you can use the following basic hardware configuration.

Basic hardware configuration:

- A computer with color capability. Because you do not know the on which computer model your multimedia application will be viewed, consider developing on a slower computer to ensures your application runs on slower computers. When putting the application together on a slower computer is too tedious, use a Macintosh IIci or better for your development work and check the application on a slower computer such as an Macintosh LC.
- A hard disk with 200 MB or more free disk space.
- An audio-video capture card. As in off-line editing, your clips probably will be smaller than 240 pixels by 160 pixels so a high-end capture card and a high-speed hard drive are unnecessary. A card such as the SuperMac Video Spigot & Sound, the RasterOps Media Time, or the Radius VideoVision should be sufficient. If you want to export your final product to tape, you will need a board or converter box with video output capability.
- A good multimedia package, such as Macromedia Director, that lets you combine your video clips with full-screen text and graphics.

Uncompressed Video File Size and Data Rates

The following table lists the size in bytes of a single frame of uncompressed video and the data rate required to capture or play back the video at 24 or 30 fps (frames per second).

Frame	Size	Pixels/	Depth	Bytes/	24fps	30fps		
Horiz	Vert	Frame	(bits)	Frame	KB/Sec	MB/Min	KB/Sec	MB/Min
80	60	4800	8	4800	115	7	144	9
80	60	4800	16	9600	230	14	288	17
80	60	4800	24	14400	346	21	432	26
80	60	4800	32*	19200	461	28	576	35
160	120	19200	8	19200	461	28	576	35
160	120	19200	16	38400	922	55	1,152	69
160	120	19200	24	57600	1,382	83	1,728	104
160	120	19200	32*	76800	1,843	111	2,304	138
240	180	43200	8	43200	1,037	62	1,296	78
240	180	43200	16	86400	2,074	124	2,592	156
240	180	43200	24	129600	3,110	187	3,888	233
240	180	43200	32*	172800	4,147	249	5,184	311
320	240	76800	8	76800	1,843	111	2,304	138
320	240	76800	16	153600	3,686	221	4,608	276
320	240	76800	24	230400	5,530	332	6,912	415
320	240	76800	32*	307200	7,373	442	9,216	553
400	300	120000	8	120000	2,880	173	3,600	216
400	300	120000	16	240000	5,760	346	7,200	432
400	300	120000	24	360000	8,640	518	10,800	648
400	300	120000	32*	480000	11,520	691	14,400	864
480	360	172800	8	172800	4,147	249	5,184	311
480	360	172800	16	345600	8,294	498	10,368	622
480	360	172800	24	518400	12,442	746	15,552	933
480	360	172800	32*	691200	16,589	995	20,736	1,244
560	420	235200	8	235200	5,645	339	7,056	423
560	420	235200	16	470400	11,290	677	14,112	847
560	420	235200	24	705600	16,934	1,016	21,168	1,270
560	420	235200	32*	940800	22,579	1,355	28,224	1,693
640	480	307200	8	307200	7,373	442	9,216	553
640	480	307200	16	614400	14,746	885	18,432	1,106
640	480	307200	24	921600	22,118	1,327	27,648	1,659
640	480	307200	32*	1228800	29,491	1,769	36,864	2,212

** Requires 32 bits for images containing alpha-channel information.*

Adobe Type Library®

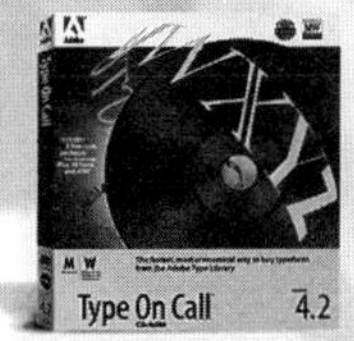

The Adobe Type Library is the world's largest collection of Type 1 digital typefaces comprising over 2,100 typefaces and growing. It encompasses type families from the world's best known type foundries, as well as Adobe Originals, developed by Adobe's award-winning type designers. Groupings and pairings from the library are common, and you can even purchase type from Adobe's Web site, www.adobe.com. Digital type technology is a serious concern of Adobe's. New Adobe typefaces, type products, and innovative software engineering are a blending of Adobe's commitment to the art and technology of digital communications.

Contents

Adobe Type Library®

Feature Techniques

MAC OS / WINDOWS

Phonetic Fonts

Adobe's Phonetic typefaces (i.e., ITC Stone Phonetic Sans, ITC Stone Phonetic Serif, and Times Phonetic) each include an International Phonetic Association (IPA) font and an Alternate font and represent spoken sound.

The IPA font conforms to the alphabet approved by the International Phonetic Association at its 1989 conference in Kiel, West Germany, but does not include the Association's contour tones. The Alternate font supplements the IPA font, containing glyphs that are in current use or of historical significance but not included with the IPA font.

Phonetic typefaces enable you to compose glyphs to represent a language phonetically. Glyphs are graphic shapes that include diacritical marks, or accents; tone marks, or symbols, that represent five different pitches; and regular characters such as "r" or "t." You compose glyphs by using a single keystroke for the most common glyphs, or by using a combination of keystrokes to attach a diacritic to a symbol.

The phonetic typefaces contain some diacritics that are higher or lower than normal for tall or deep glyphs such as "l" or "g," but do not use special diacritics for wide or narrow glyphs. Because the dots over the "i" and "j" characters can interfere with diacritics, the IPA font includes versions of "i" and "j" without the dots.

Most diacritics map to the numeral keys. To place a diacritic below a glyph, press [glyph] + [numeral key]. To place a diacritic above a glyph, press [glyph] + (Shift + [numeral key]). For example, to produce a long "a" in a phonetic IPA typeface, type "a" followed by (Shift + 4).

KERNING PAIRS

Because using "fixed width" or "zero-width" diacritics (i.e., different versions of diacritics are designed for each variation) results in an unacceptably large number of characters, Adobe's phonetic font designers used kerning pairs to create a wide selection of glyphs and diacritics without using multiple fonts. Applications that support font kerning information (e.g., Adobe PageMaker, QuarkXPress) can use phonetic font kerning pairs. You can use phonetic typefaces with applications that do not support kerning information, but you may have to kern the diacritic and glyph manually.

Kerning pairs eliminate the white space between a pair of adjacent glyphs and enable shapes to overlap when placing diacritics above or below a preceding glyph. To compose glyphs using kerning pairs, type the diacritic after the base glyph. Applications that support kerning information kern the diacritic automatically and attach it to the base glyph.

TIE LIGATURES, LINKS, AND THINSPACES

Phonetic typefaces contain top and bottom tie ligatures and a link suprasegmental (used to indicate stress, pitch or juncture) to create ligatures and links between a pair of glyphs.

Use the IPA font to access the top tie ligature: Press Shift + Option + x (Macintosh) or Alt + 0220 on the number keypad (Windows). For example, to produce b-d with a top tie ligature on the Macintosh, in the IPA font type b + (Shift + Option + x) + d. To produce b-d with a top tie ligature in Windows, in the IPA font type b + (Alt + 0220) + d.

Use the Alternate font to access the bottom tie ligature: Press Shift + Option + X (Macintosh) or Alt + 0220 on the number keypad (Windows). For example, to produce d-s with a bottom tie ligature on the Macintosh, in the Alternate font type d + (Shift + Option + X) + s. To produce d-s with a bottom tie ligature in Windows, in the Alternate font type d + (Alt + 0220) + s

Use the IPA font to access the linking character, which occupies a full character width: Press Shift + Option + 7 (Macintosh) or Alt + 0217 on the number keypad (Windows). For example, to produce k-h with a bottom link on the Macintosh, in the IPA font type k + (Shift + Option + 7) + h. To produce k-h with a bottom link in Windows, in the IPA font type k + (Alt + 0217) + h.

Press 5 in the IPA or the Alternate font to add a thinspace character, which adds extra space when automatic kerning places a diacritic too close to a glyph or when your application limits the amount of kerning between characters.

KEYBOARD LAYOUT INFORMATION

The IPA and Alternate fonts map diacritics identically. The keyboard layouts maintain a visual mnemonic connection between a Roman letter key and a similar phonetic glyph shape, with basic Roman characters in their standard positions. Use Character Map (Windows) or the KeyCap utility (Macintosh) to display keyboard layout and keystroke information.

Optical Size Axis in Multiple Master Typefaces General Information

In traditional metal typefounding, each style and size of a typeface was cut by hand. Subtle adjustments to letter proportion, weight, contrast, and spacing were made to optimize readability in every point size. Digital type technologies generally scale type using mathematical formulas that do not allow for variations at different sizes for enhanced readability. Most digital type is optimized for use at 12 point text size. For optimal readability, smaller type sizes require additional space between characters, and larger sizes require less space.

Multiple master typefaces that include the optical size axis enable you to generate fonts that are optically adjusted for use at specific point sizes, where smaller text is clear and easy to read, and larger sizes are refined and elegant. As the optical size increases in a multiple master typeface, the space between the characters decreases, the space within the characters (counters) becomes smaller, the serifs become finer, the overall weight becomes lighter, and the x-height gradually decreases in size.

When specifying the optical size axis for a multiple master typeface, begin by specifying the same value as the text's point size. For example, for 10-point text, specify 10 points for the optical size; for 96-point text, specify the closest optical size value, which is usually 72. Unlike other multiple master axes, the optical size axis is non-linear, which causes noticeable changes to the shape of characters depending on the text's point size. For example, a change to the optical size by 2 points for 10-point text is more noticeable than for 72-point text, and the difference in character shape is noticeable for 9-point text with an optical size axis value greater than 9 points.

Creating Fractions Using Fraction Fonts

Adobe's fraction typefaces (i.e., Helvetica-Fraction, Helvetica-FractionBold, NewCenturySchlbk-Fraction, NewCenturySchlbk-FractionBold) for the Macintosh and for Windows include standard numbers and numerical characters that comprise numerators and denominators with a diagonal slash or horizontal line. Applications that support fractional character widths (e.g., Adobe PageMaker, WordPerfect, Microsoft Word for Windows, AmiPro) support fraction typefaces.

To create fractions using a fraction typeface, type the numerator then the denominator that you want. The fractional typefaces use all keys for their numerical characters, which enables you to create fractions using any key, not only the number keys. Each key types a number, beginning with 1 on the left, in numerical order to the right.

When following the instructions below to create fractions using fractional typefaces:

- first-row refers to the top row of keys, 1 through 0.
- second-row refers to the Q through P keys.
- third-row refers to the A through Semicolon keys.
- fourth-row refers to the Z through Slash keys.

To create standard numbers:

Use lowercase first-row keys (i.e., 1, 2, 3, 4, 5, 6, 7, 8, 9, 0).

To create diagonal-slash fractions:

1. Use Shift + fourth-row keys (e.g., Shift + Z, Shift + C, Shift + B, Shift + M, Shift + /) for numerator digits.
2. Use "\" (backslash character) to create the dividing slash (/).
3. Use fourth-row keys (e.g., z, c, b, m, /) for denominator digits.

For example:

To create	*Type the following sequence*
Two-thirds (2/3)	(Shift + X) + \ + c
One and one-half (1 1/2)	1 + (Shift + Z) + \ + x
Seven-sixteenths (7 1/16)	(Shift + M) + \ + z + n

To create horizontal-line fractions with single-digit numerators and denominators:

1. Use Shift + first-row keys (e.g., Shift + 1, Shift + 3, Shift + 5, Shift + 7) for the numerator digit.
2. Use third-row keys (e.g., a, d, g, j, l) for the denominator digit.
3. Press Space to complete the fraction (Windows only).

For example:

To create	*Type the following sequence*
One-half (1/2)	(Shift + 1) + s + Space
Seven-eighths (7/8)	(Shift + 7) + k + Space
One and two-thirds (1 2/3)	1 + (Shift + 2) + d + Space

To create horizontal-line fractions with vertically-offset numerators and denominators:

1. Use Shift + third-row keys (e.g., Shift + A, Shift + D, Shift + G, Shift + J, Shift + L) for numerator digits.
2. Use second-row keys (e.g., q, e, t, u, o) for denominator digits.
3. Press Space for denominators that are larger than their numerators (e.g., two-thirteenths, 24 over 135).

For example:

To create	*Type the following sequence*
Two-thirteenths (2/13)	q + (Shift + S) + e + Space
13 over 2 (13/2)	(Shift + A) + w + (Shift + D)
24 over 135 (25/135)	q + (Shift + S) + e + (Shift + F) + t + Space
135 over 24 (135/24)	(Shift + A) + w + (Shift + D) + r + (Shift + G)

To create horizontal-line fractions with vertically-aligned numerators and denominators:

NOTE: You cannot create horizontal-line fractions with vertically-aligned numerators and denominators for fractions that have a larger numerator than denominator (e.g., 135 over 2).

1. Use Shift + second-row keys (e.g., Shift + Q, Shift + E, Shift + T, Shift + U, Shift + O) for numerator digits.
2. Use second-row keys (e.g., q, e, t, u, o) for denominator digits.
3. Press Space after each denominator digit.
For example:

To create	*Type the following sequence*
2 over 134 (2/135)	q + Space + (Shift + W) + e + Space + r + Space
13 over 24 (13/24)	(Shift + Q) + w + Space + (Shift + E) + r + Space
135 over 246 (135/246)	(Shift + Q) + w + Space + (Shift + E) + r + Space + (Shift + T) + y + Space

Copying Windows Font Files to a Network Server or Disk

You can transfer font files from one Windows workstation to another by first copying them to a network server or a disk. After you have copied the files, you can install the font on another workstation using Adobe Type Manager (ATM). Make sure you adhere to your font manufacturer's licensing agreement when copying font files to other locations.

To copy Windows font files, you first need to know the name of the PostScript font files. Font filename prefixes often do not resemble the font's actual name (e.g., Akzidenz Grotesk font files begin with GF, Centaur font files begin with NR). PostScript font filenames have eight-character prefixes. Font filenames consist of one to five characters, followed by underscore characters to make a total of eight characters. For example, the complete filename prefix for the Helvetica font file is "Hv______."

PostScript font filename information for all Adobe fonts is listed in the document Fntnames.pdf, available on the Type On Call CD-ROM. You can download the same document from Adobe's World Wide Web site at http://www.adobe.com (document number 5090). Additionally, if a font is installed in ATM on the workstation from which you are copying, you can open ATM's Atm.ini file, located in the Windows directory, to view its filename.

Make sure to copy all a font's components. A single master PostScript font is composed of a PFM file and a PFB file (e.g., Com_____.pfm and Com_____.pfb). A multiple master base font is composed of a PFM file, a PFB file, and an MMM file (e.g., Zjrg____.pfm, Zjrg____.pfb, and Zjrg____.mmm). A multiple master instance is composed of a PFM file and a PSS file (e.g., Zjrg_iyc.pfm and Zjrg_iyc.pss).

To copy font files from a Windows 95 workstation to a network server or floppy disk:

1. Identify the names of your font files.
2. Choose Start > Programs > Windows Explorer.
3. In Windows Explorer, navigate to your fonts directory (e.g., C:\Psfonts). The fonts directory usually contains a sub-directory that holds other font files (e.g., C:\Psfonts\Pfm).
4. To copy font files to a network server, select the desired font files from the fonts directory and from any subdirectory inside the fonts subdirectory, then copy them to the desired location on the network server. For example, copy the file Com_____.pfb from the Psfonts directory and the file Com_____.pfm from the Psfonts\Pfm subdirectory.
   OR: Select the desired font files from the fonts directory and from any subdirectory inside the fonts subdirectory, then copy them onto a disk.
5. Choose File > Close to exit Explorer.

To copy font files from a Windows 3.1x workstation to a network server or floppy disk:

1. Identify the names of your font files.
2. Open File Manager.
3. In File Manager, navigate to your fonts directory (e.g., C:\Psfonts). The fonts directory usually contains a subdirectory that holds other font files (e.g., C:\Psfonts\Pfm).
4. To copy font files to a network server, select the desired font files from the fonts directory and from any subdirectory inside the fonts subdirectory, then copy them to the desired location on the network server. For example, copy the file Com_____.pfb from the Psfonts directory and the file Com_____.pfm from the Psfonts\Pfm subdirectory.
   OR: Select the desired font files from the fonts directory and from any subdirectory inside the fonts subdirectory, then copy them onto a disk.
5. Choose File > Exit to exit File Manager.

Font Style Linking General Information

PostScript fonts display different names when accessed on the Macintosh and in Windows. While each PostScript font has a unique PostScript name that is identical on the Macintosh and in Windows, the same PostScript font displays a different name in font menus on the Macintosh, in font menus in Windows, and in Adobe Type Manager (ATM) for Windows. These name differences can lead to a perception that fonts are missing in Windows, and can cause fonts to substitute to other fonts when you transfer files across platforms.

Although fonts may display different names on different platforms, once you understand font name style links, you can use them to access your fonts on both platforms and avoid font matching problems.

FONT NAMES AND STYLE LINKS

Windows can display a maximum of four styles (e.g., normal, bold, italic, bolditalic) per family in application font menus. Because of this limitation, many font families have bold, semibold, or italic members that do not appear in font menus. To access them, you must apply a style link—that is, apply the bold or italic type style to text formatted with a regular (roman) font.

The Macintosh doesn't limit the number of font family styles that can display in font menus, so you can apply any font style in two ways: you can select the font in any available style directly from the font menu, or select the regular font and then apply a type style to it.

Because of the different ways you can access a font, the same PostScript font may display a different name in a font menu on the Macintosh than it does in a font menu in Windows. Additionally, fonts installed in ATM for Windows may display different names in ATM than in font menus. In ATM, each member of a style-linked family is listed by its Windows menu name, plus the style link after a comma in ATM 4.0 (e.g., "Fontname, Style link") or in capital letters in ATM 3.0x and earlier (e.g., "Fontname, STYLE LINK").

For example, the font Futura-Bold displays these variations:

PostScript name	Futura-Heavy
Macintosh font menu name	Futura Heavy
Windows font menu name	Futura Medium
ATM 4.0 font name, Style link	Futura Medium, Bold

In other words, Futura Heavy does not appear in font menus in Windows, so you must access it using a style link: format text with Futura Medium and then apply the bold type style. Futura Heavy does appear in Macintosh font menus, so you can format text with the font directly. You can also select Futura Medium from the font menu, then apply the bold type style to your text, which will print the exact same font as if you directly selected Futura Heavy from the font menu.

However, selecting a font style directly from the font menu on the Macintosh (i.e., not selecting the regular font and then applying a type style) may cause problems when you transfer files from the Macintosh to Windows. If the Windows version of the font style does not have the same font menu name, you may receive a font matching error or your text may display in an unexpected font. To prevent these problems, format text on the Macintosh using style links.

WHERE TO GET STYLE LINK INFORMATION FOR YOUR FONTS

PostScript font name and style link information for all Adobe fonts is listed in the document Fntnames.pdf, available on the Type On Call CD-ROM. You can also download the same document from the Adobe World Wide Web site at http://www.adobe.com/ (document number 5090). Additionally, the ReadMe documents that are included with some font packages, as well as the Type On Call CD-ROM, contain information about the style linking options for each package.

If you are using the font Futura on the Macintosh and you will be transferring your file to the Windows platform, use the style link options (i.e., the options listed in the "Windows Menu, STYLE NAME" column) for Futura-Heavy, Futura-Oblique, Futura-HeavyOblique, and Futura-ExtraBoldOblique, instead of selecting these fonts directly from the font menu.

WINDOWS

Calculating Characters per Pica in Windows

You can calculate characters per pica (cpp) for PostScript Type 1 fonts to help calculate the page count for books and periodicals. For example, a document that has 8.7532 cpp, 20 picas per line, and 100,000 characters requires approximately 571 lines. You can multiply the required number of lines by the line height to calculate column-inches and page count. You can calculate only an approximate cpp value, however, since variables such as the application or printer driver you are using affect the cpp value.

To calculate approximate cpp:

1. Open the font's AFM file in a text editor that can save in text-only format (e.g., WordPad, Notepad).
2. Locate the character values that follow the StartCharMetrics line. For example, the letter "A" appears as:
   ```
   C 65 ; WX 481; N A ; B -22 0 491 704 ;
   ```
3. Add the 3- or 4-digit WX (i.e., width of the x-axis) values for all the uppercase and lowercase letters (i.e., A to Z and a to z), then divide the total by 52 to determine the average letter width value. The resulting value is T.
4. Close the font's AFM file.
5. Determine the point size (e.g., 10, 12) for which you want to calculate cpp. The point size value is p.
6. Multiply T by p. The resulting value is Tp.
7. Enter Tp in the following equation:
   ```
   340,722 ^ Tp = cpp
   ```
   The number 340,722 represents the results of the equation:
   ```
   12 ^ [((T ^ 26.5) x p) ^ 1000]
   ```
   This equation represents the algebraic equivalents for:

- In the PostScript page description language, one point is equivalent to 99.62% of a traditional typographer's point, where the digital point is 1/72" and the traditional printer's point is 1/72.29".
- The sum of the widths of all lowercase characters from a to z are divided by 26.5 to account for punctuation variances for cpp output.
- Since a pica is 12 points, the cpp value is expressed in units of 12. Therefore, the total width of all lowercase characters, divided by 26.5 and multiplied by the point size, is normalized to units of 12.

MAC OS

Calculating Characters per Pica on the Macintosh

You can calculate characters per pica (cpp) for PostScript Type 1 fonts to help calculate the page count for books and periodicals. For example, a document that has 8.7532 cpp, 20 picas per line, and 100,000 characters requires approximately 571 lines. You can multiply the required number of lines by the line height to calculate column-inches and page count. You can calculate only an approximate cpp value, however, since variables such as the application or printer driver you are using affect the cpp value.

To calculate approximate cpp:

1. Open the font's AFM file in a text editor that can save in text-only format (e.g., SimpleText, TeachText).
2. Locate the character values that follow the StartCharMetrics line. For example, the letter "A" appears as:
   `C 65 ; WX 481; N A ; B -22 0 491 704 ;`
3. Add the 3- or 4-digit WX (i.e., width of the x-axis) values for all the uppercase and lowercase letters (i.e., A to Z and a to z), then divide the total by 52 to determine the average letter width value. The resulting value is T.
4. Close the font's AFM file.
5. Determine the point size (e.g., 10, 12) for which you want to calculate cpp. The point size value is p.
6. Multiply T by p. The resulting value is Tp.
7. Enter Tp in the following equation:
   `340,722 ^ Tp = cpp`
   The number 340,722 represents the results of the equation:
   `12 ^ [((T ^ 26.5) x p) ^ 1000]`
   This equation represents the algebraic equivalents for:
   - In the PostScript page description language, one point is equivalent to 99.62% of a traditional typographer's point, where the digital point is 1/72" and the traditional printer's point is 1/72.29".
   - The sum of the widths of all lowercase characters from a to z are divided by 26.5 to account for punctuation variances for cpp output.
   - Since a pica is 12 points, the cpp value is expressed in units of 12. Therefore, the total width of all lowercase characters, divided by 26.5 and multiplied by the point size, is normalized to units of 12.

Differentiating TrueType Fonts and QuickDraw GX-Enabled Fonts

When you enable a PostScript Type 1 font for use in QuickDraw GX, the enabler adds an SFNT resource to the font file, causing it to display the same icon in the Finder as a TrueType font (i.e., three "A"s). Because these font formats use the same icon, distinguishing TrueType font files from QuickDraw GX-enabled font files requires either viewing their screen font names or using a resource editing application (e.g., ResEdit).

TO DETERMINE IF A FONT FILE IS A TRUETYPE FONT FILE OR A QUICKDRAW GX-ENABLED POSTSCRIPT TYPE 1 FONT FILE:

Open the font's suitcase to view the names of its screen font files. Fonts with names that include a number indicating a point size (e.g., 10, 12, 24) are enabled PostScript fonts. Fonts with names that do not include a number are TrueType fonts.

OR: Use a resource editor (e.g., ResEdit) to view the font file's SFNT resource:

DISCLAIMER: This procedure is not supported by Adobe Systems Incorporated and is only provided as a guideline. Experience using a resource editor is highly recommended, since it can change or remove any resource from any file. Always modify a copy of the file to be edited. Never modify an open file. If the wrong resource is modified or alterations are incorrectly performed, the file can be damaged. In the event of problems, revert to the original copy.

1. In the resource editor, open the font's SFNT resource.
2. Note the first four letters of the text that appears. If the first four letters are "typ1," the font is a PostScript Type 1 font, or a PostScript Type 1 font enabled for use in QuickDraw GX. If the first four letters are "true," the font is a TrueType font.

Unexpected Results

MAC OS / WINDOWS

Incorrect PostScript Font Substitution After Cross Platform Transfer

ISSUE

When opening a document created in the same application on a different platform, font substitutions occur (e.g., text formatted as Helvetica in a Macintosh document displays as Gill Sans in a Windows document).

SOLUTIONS

When font substitution occurs with stylized fonts (e.g., Helvetica Bold, Helvetica Italic), apply the style (e.g., bold, italic) to plain text, instead of selecting stylized fonts from the Font menu, before transferring.

OR: When using Adobe fonts, use the renamed or revised version of the font.

OR: Update the destination application's font matching table or other font matching feature used when opening documents created on another platform, when available.

ADDITIONAL INFORMATION

On the Macintosh, stylized fonts (e.g., Helvetica Bold, Helvetica Italic) can be specified by selecting the stylized font from the Font menu or by applying a style (e.g., bold, italic) to the plain font (e.g., Helvetica). In Windows, stylized fonts must be specified by applying a style to the plain font, as stylized fonts are not available in font menus.

When transferring files between Macintosh and Windows computers, apply styles to plain fonts, instead of selecting stylized fonts from the Font menu, before transferring. Many Adobe fonts have been renamed to make Macintosh and Windows plain font's menu names identical.

When opening documents transferred from a different platform, applications attempt to match the name of the font requested by the document to a name of a font currently installed in the system. When no match is found, the application performs its method of font substitution.

Application font matching features include:

- Microsoft Word 6.x matches fonts using the font's menu names.
- PageMaker 5.x and later matches fonts using the PANOSE font matching system to look at alternate font names when no match is found.
- QuarkXPress 3.x matches fonts using the encrypted PostScript font name.

Expert Fonts Display Boxes or Other Unexpected Characters

ISSUE

Text formatted in an Expert font (e.g., Minion Expert) displays as boxes or unusual characters (e.g., ligatures, fractions).

SOLUTION

Apply a standard font instead of an Expert font to the text (e.g., apply Minion instead of Minion Expert).

ADDITIONAL INFORMATION

When text containing an unsupported character is formatted with an expert font, the text displays formatted with the Expert font, which includes non-standard characters. Adobe Expert (e.g., Minion Expert) fonts do not contain standard characters (e.g., alphanumeric, punctuation, common symbols) included in standard fonts (e.g., Minion). Expert fonts contain selected characters designed to enhance a standard font package (e.g., ligatures, fractions).

Characters Formatted in Cyrillic Font Change After Transferring Across Platform

ISSUE

Text formatted in an Adobe Cyrillic font changes (i.e., words contain unexpected characters) after transferring then viewing the file on a different platform (e.g., Macintosh to Windows).

SOLUTION

Convert the file to a Portable Document Format (PDF) document using Adobe Acrobat Distiller or PDF Writer, then transfer the PDF file to the other platform.

ADDITIONAL INFORMATION

Because characters in Cyrillic fonts map differently on each platform, characters formatted in an Adobe Cyrillic font change after transferring the file to a different platform. Creating a PDF document enables Cyrillic characters to display and print as expected.

Adobe Cyrillic fonts include Baskerville Cyrillic, Excelsior Cyrillic, Helvetica Cyrillic, Minion Cyrillic, and Times Ten Cyrillic.

Incorrect Spacing or Size of Em Dashes

ISSUE

There is too much or too little space on either side of em dashes. Em dashes are longer in one typeface and shorter in another at the same point size.

SOLUTIONS

Use a font other than Berthold when em dashes that don't have a thin space on each side and are the same length as the point size are desired.

OR: Use Berthold fonts when em dashes that have a thin space on each side and are shorter than the point size are desired.

OR: Use kerning to achieve the desired character spacing.

ADDITIONAL INFORMATION

Unlike most Adobe proportional fonts that follow the Anglo-American approach to typesetting, fonts that follow the German approach to typesetting (e.g., Adobe Berthold) design the em dash symbol shorter with a thin space, instead of no space, on either side.

Fonts use either the Anglo-American or German approach to typesetting to design the em dash. The Anglo-American approach to typesetting designs the em dash character's width (i.e., the amount of horizontal space required by a letter, number, or symbol including enough space to set it apart from the next character) to include an em dash symbol the same length as the point size, with no additional space on either side. The German approach to typesetting designs the em dash character's width to include an em dash symbol that is shorter than the Anglo-American version, with a thin space on either side.

An em is a unit of measurement the exact width and height of the point size set. For example, in 10 point type, an em is 10 points wide and 10 points high. This unit of measurement was traditionally the width of the capital M in a given typeface, because an M was usually cast on a square body.

Em Dashes Are Different Lengths or Have Different Spacing

ISSUE

There is too much or too little space on either side of an em dash. Em dashes are longer in one typeface and shorter in another at the same point size.

SOLUTIONS

Use a font other than a Berthold font when you want to use em dashes that do not have a thin space on both sides and

are the same length as the point size.
OR: Use a Berthold font when you want to use em dashes that have a thin space on both sides and are shorter than the point size.
OR: Use kerning to achieve the character spacing you want.

ADDITIONAL INFORMATION

Fonts use either the Anglo-American or German approach to typesetting to design the em dash. The Anglo-American approach designs the em dash character's width (i.e., the amount of horizontal space required by a letter, number, or symbol, including enough space to set it apart from the next character) to include an em dash symbol the same length as the point size, with no additional space on either side. The German approach designs the em dash character's width to include an em dash symbol that is shorter than the Anglo-American version, with a thin space on either side. The Adobe font Berthold follows the German approach to typesetting design.

An em is a unit of measurement the exact width and height of the point size. For example, for 10-point type, an em is 10 points wide and 10 points high. The em unit of measurement was traditionally the width of the capital letter "M" in a given typeface because it was usually cast on a square body.

Adobe distributes the following Berthold fonts:

Berthold Font
Berthold Akzidenz Grotesk
Berthold Baskerville
Berthold Bodoni
Berthold Caslon Book
Berthold City
Berthold Garamond
Berthold Imago
Berthold Script
Berthold Walbaum
Block Berthold

Glyphs in Phonetic Fonts Do Not Appear Above Characters

ISSUE

Glyphs in phonetic fonts (e.g., Stone Phonetic, Times Phonetic) do not appear above main characters.

SOLUTION

Use an application that supports automatic pair kerning (e.g., Adobe PageMaker, QuarkXPress, MacWrite II).
NOTE: Because character widths vary, the space between a phonetic character and the character that follows it might be too tight. If characters overlap, manually kern the characters for the desired spacing.

ADDITIONAL INFORMATION

Phonetic characters are composed of two characters kerned together with negative pair kerning, which requires applications that support automatic pair kerning. Other space formatting (e.g., tracking) may affect the placement of the diacritic relative to the character.

Microsoft Word 5.0 and WordPerfect do not support pair kerning.

WINDOWS

Slow Screen Redraw When Using Multiple Master Font in QuarkXPress 3.31 or Earlier

ISSUE

When you format text in a QuarkXPress 3.31 or earlier document using Adobe Type 1 fonts (e.g., Ex Ponto), the text redraws slower than expected.

SOLUTION

Avoid formatting the text with fonts that contain 2,000 or more built-in kern pairs.

ADDITIONAL INFORMATION

Applications that read kern pair information (e.g., Adobe PageMaker, QuarkXPress) redraw text slowly when the text is formatted with a font that contains a large number of built-in kern pairs. QuarkXPress for Windows redraws text even more slowly than expected when the text is formatted in a font that contains a large number of built-in kern pairs.

Because each instance of a multiple master font is considered a separate font, each additional multiple master font on a page slows redraw performance in QuarkXPress. Disabling automatic pair kerning in QuarkXPress's Typographic Preferences dialog box or increasing the size of the ATM font cache does not affect QuarkXPress's screen redraw performance. Formatting text using a font with over 2,000 kern pairs in QuarkXPress 3.x for the Macintosh does not cause slower than expected screen redraw.

Fonts containing a large number of built-in kern pairs include Ex Ponto, which contains more than 3900 kern pairs, and Nueva, which contains more than 2,000 kern pairs.

Multiple Master Font Doesn't Display or Print in Windows

ISSUE

Text formatted with multiple master fonts does not appear on screen or when printed.

SOLUTIONS

Do one or more of the following:

A. Install Adobe Type Manager (ATM) 3.0 or later.
B. Increase the amount of memory available to ATM and the system by doing one or more of the following:
  A. When viewing or printing more than one typeface

on a page or document, increase the size of the font cache in ATM.

B. Reduce the number of installed PostScript fonts by removing them from ATM.

C. Exit applications you are not using.

C. Make sure the Atm.ini file has the correct font references:

Make sure the path and font file references listed in the [Fonts] and [MMFonts] sections of the Atm.ini file are accurate.

OR: Remove the fonts using ATM, then reinstall them from the original installation disks.

ADDITIONAL INFORMATION

ATM 2.x and earlier do not support multiple master font technology. Multiple master fonts do not display or print as expected when the application or system has insufficient memory. Increasing the font cache (i.e., the amount of memory ATM uses to store font data) in ATM increases the number of bitmap typefaces ATM can store for screen display. This decreases screen redraw times when more than one typeface is used in a document, but reduces the amount of memory available to the system or other applications.

When many fonts are installed, reducing the number of installed fonts increases the amount of memory available to the system and applications, and reduces the number of font references in system files Windows must read. When applications are running in the background, exiting applications not in use frees up system resources that ATM needs to display and print multiple master fonts as expected.

When the path and font file references listed in the [Fonts] and [MMFonts] sections of the Atm.ini file are incorrect or missing, the fonts are unavailable in font menus or to ATM. The [Fonts] section of the Atm.ini file lists the *.pfm and *.pfb files for each installed PostScript Type 1 font and the *.pfm and *.pss file for each multiple master font. The [MMFonts] section lists the *.mmm and *.pfb files for each installed multiple master font. *.pfm and *.mmm files contain font metrics information, and *.pfb and *.pss files contain the outline or printer information of the typeface.

Removing and reinstalling fonts rewrites the font's references in the Atm.ini file, which corrects errors in filenames and path names.

Univers Typefaces Missing from Font Menu

ISSUE

After you install Adobe Univers typeface package 37 (Univers) or 38 (Univers-Condensed), typeface styles expected in a Windows application's Font menu are missing.

SYMPTOMS

After you install Univers package number 37, Univers 65 Bold, Univers 65 BoldOblique, Univers 75 Black and Univers 75 BlackOblique do not appear in Font menus.

After you install Univers package number 38, Univers 67 CondensedBold and Univers 67 CondensedBoldOblique do not appear in Font menus.

SOLUTION

Apply the appropriate type style to a related font (e.g., apply the Bold style to the Univers 45 font to use Univers 65 Bold).

NOTE: When moving files from the Macintosh to Windows computers, use style linking to ensure consistent and accurate cross-platform font mapping.

ADDITIONAL INFORMATION

Windows can display a maximum of four styles per font. The Univers typeface packages include more than four font styles, so some of the styles do not appear in Font menus. These styles must be accessed by applying the appropriate type style to a related font.

Fonts Don't Display On Screen When Using ATM 2.6 or Later

ISSUE

After installing Adobe Type Manager (ATM) 2.6 or later, text formatted with a PostScript font does not display (i.e., blank spaces display instead of the text characters), but prints as expected to PostScript printers.

SOLUTIONS

Use an updated version of the Type 1 PostScript font.

OR: Use a different Type 1 PostScript font that conforms to Adobe Type 1 font specifications.

ADDITIONAL INFORMATION

ATM 2.6 and later supports only fonts that conform to Adobe Type 1 font specifications (e.g., Adobe Type 1 PostScript fonts). ATM 2.6 and later cannot render fonts on screen that do not conform to Adobe Type 1 font specifications, causing blank spaces to display instead of the font's characters. ATM 2.5 and earlier can render fonts on screen that do not conform to Adobe Type 1 font specifications, resulting in non-conforming Type 1 PostScript fonts to display on screen as expected.

Manufacturers of Type 1 PostScript Fonts that may not conform to Adobe Type 1 font specifications include:

LaserMaster
DTC
Cassedy & Green
Corel

Duplicate Font Names Display in WordPad Font Menus in Windows 95

Because of its method for listing font names, WordPad in Windows 95 displays duplicate font names in font menus.

When you start WordPad, it queries Windows 95 for a list of available fonts. It then queries the printer driver for a list of available fonts. When both Windows and the printer driver return the same font name, WordPad lists the font twice in its font menu. When the same font is installed in Adobe Type Manager (ATM), ATM provides the font name to WordPad, which adds yet another listing of the font name to its font menu. You cannot prevent WordPad from listing duplicate font names.

MAC OS

Unexpected Character After Typing Extended or Expert Character

ISSUE

When typing an option, extended, or special character (i.e., characters typed using the Option or Option + Shift keys) or when using Adobe Expert Collection fonts, an unexpected character displays.

SOLUTIONS

Use a keyboard character map utility (e.g., Key Caps) or refer to the ATM & Adobe Type Library User Guide to obtain the keyboard commands for the desired characters available from the installed system software.

OR: When running System 7.1 or later, select the keyboard layout for the desired system version (e.g., U.S. - System 6) in the Keyboard control panel.

OR: Select the U.S. - English keyboard layout in the Keyboard control panel or Keyboard Layout menu.

NOTE: The Keyboard Layout menu is activated with the KMT (Keyboard Menu Toggle) application included with Type On Call 4.0 Macintosh Cyrillic Utilities. When clicking on the Keyboard Layout Menu's flag icon, which is located between the Balloon Help and Application menus, a list of available keyboard layout options appear.

ADDITIONAL INFORMATION

System 7 maps 14 extended characters to a different location on the keyboard than does System 6, and accesses four characters that System 6 does not. All characters available in System 6 are available in System 7.

System 7 remaps 11 keys used by Adobe Expert Collection fonts. All expert collection characters available in System 6 are available in System 7. To determine the keyboard commands to access the remapped characters in System 7, use a keyboard character map utility (e.g., Key Caps), or refer to the ATM & Adobe Type Library User Guide.

System 7.1 or later includes a System 6 keyboard resource, enabling choosing between the System 6 and System 7 keyboard layouts. To access extended characters using the System 6 keyboard commands, choose the U.S. - System 6 option in the Keyboard control panel.

The U.S. English keyboard layout may have a different character map than non-U.S. English keyboard layouts. To access extended characters or use the Adobe Expert font collection as specified in the ATM & Adobe Type Library User Guide, select the U.S. keyboard layout in the Keyboard control panel or in the Keyboard Layout menu.

Unexpected Font Displays When Creating Text in QuarkXPress

ISSUE

When creating text in QuarkXPress 3.3x, the font that displays is different than the font selected in the font menu.

SOLUTION

In Suitcase 2.1.4x, deselect the Update Existing Font Menus When a Font Suitcase is Opened or Closed option, located in Fonts Preferences dialog box when the Sets & Suitcases or Resources window is open, then quit and relaunch QuarkXPress.

ADDITIONAL INFORMATION

QuarkXPress is not compatible with Suitcase 2.1.4x's ability to update existing font menus after opening or closing a font suitcase. When typing in QuarkXPress 3.3x with Suitcase's Update Existing Font Menus When a Font Suitcase is Opened or Closed option selected, the font that displays on screen is different than the font selected in the font menu.

The alert "May not work with, or may cause problems with, some applications!" appears after selecting the Update Existing Font Menus When a Font Suitcase is Opened or Closed option in Suitcase.

Box or Unexpected Characters for Font Names Appear in Font Menu

ISSUE

Boxes or unusual characters appear in an application's font menu instead of font names.

SOLUTION

Disable extensions (e.g., WYSIWYG Menus) that enable font names in an application's font menu to appear in their own typeface.

NOTE: Other installed system extensions or control panel documents may interfere with the display of font names in an application's font menu. Run with the extensions off to verify that added extensions are not the cause. To turn extensions off upon startup in System 7.x, restart the computer while holding the Shift key down until the system returns the message "Welcome to Macintosh. Extensions Off."

ADDITIONAL INFORMATION

Box or unusual characters may appear in an application's font menu instead of font names when an extension (e.g.,

WYSIWYG menus) that modifies the way font names appear in an application's font menu is installed. Extensions that modify an application's font menu change how the system displays font names by constructing the name from the letters using the actual typeface (e.g., the Palatino font name in an application's font menu appears in the Palatino typeface) instead of in the system's menu font (e.g., Chicago). When a typeface includes unusual characters (e.g., Expert fonts), unavailable characters indicated by the box character or the typeface's unusual characters appear in the font menu.

Myriad Roman, Nueva Roman, or Sanvito Roman Displays Jagged and Prints as Courier

ISSUE

Text formatted with the Adobe PostScript font Myriad Roman, Nueva Roman, or Sanvito Roman is jagged on screen and prints in the printer's default font (e.g., Courier). The font was copied from the Adobe Originals Sampler 1 (Package 906) or the Adobe Originals Sampler 2 (Package 907) on the Adobe Type On Call 4.1 CD-ROM.

SOLUTIONS

Rename the Myriad Roman font's outline file from "MyriaReg" to "MyriaRom".

OR: Rename the Nueva Roman font's outline file from "NuevaReg" to "NuevaRom".

OR: Rename the Sanvito Roman font's outline file from "SanviReg" to "SanviRom".

ADDITIONAL INFORMATION

PostScript fonts have two components: a bitmap (screen) font, which is used to display text on screen, and an outline (printer) font, which is used to print text. Adobe Type Manager (ATM) uses the outline font file to rasterize fonts (i.e., smooth font edges) on screen. To determine which outline font file to rasterize, ATM reads the bitmap font file, which provides ATM with the appropriate outline font file's name. When the bitmap font file refers to a specific outline font file but ATM is unable to locate that outline font file, ATM cannot rasterize the outline font file.

The outline font files for Myriad Roman, Nueva Roman, and Sanvito Roman included on the Type On Call 4.1 CD-ROM were incorrectly named "[fontname]Reg" instead of "[fontname]Rom." ATM cannot rasterize the misnamed font files because it cannot locate the font files named "MyriaRom," "NuevaRom," and "SanviRom," causing text to which the fonts are applied to appear jagged. Printer drivers cannot download the misnamed font files, causing text formatted with the fonts to print in the printer's default font.

Type On Call 4.1.1 and later include correctly-named outline font files for Myriad Roman, Nueva Roman, and Sanvito Roman.

PostScript Font Option Characters Display Jagged When Using ATM 3.9 or Earlier

ISSUE

After you press Option + [character] to type a special character, the character appears jagged on-screen, but appears as expected (i.e., smooth) on the printout from a PostScript printer. The text is formatted with a PostScript Type 1 font and Adobe Type Manager (ATM) 3.9 or earlier is installed.

SOLUTIONS

Install the Symbo file, which is the PostScript outline font file for the Symbol font, into the Fonts folder in the System Folder.

OR: Install the Symbol TrueType font included on the System 7.5.x software disks.

OR: Use ATM Deluxe 4.0 or ATM Lite 4.0.

ADDITIONAL INFORMATION

Because the Symbol font included with Macintosh system software contains the special characters listed below, most Macintosh PostScript fonts do not contain these characters. ATM uses the PostScript outline or TrueType font file to display the character's outline on-screen. If the PostScript outline or TrueType font file for the Symbol font is not installed, these characters appear jagged on-screen. These characters appear smooth on the printout when you print to a PostScript printer because the printer uses the Symbol PostScript font file resident in the printers memory. The Symbol font is a printer-resident font in most PostScript printers.

Installing the PostScript outline file for the Symbol font enables ATM 3.9 or earlier to display the characters on-screen as expected (i.e., smooth). Installing the TrueType Symbol font enables the system to display the characters on-screen as expected (i.e., smooth). ATM 4.0 displays these characters as expected.

Symbol Characters

Keystroke Character	Character Name
Option + b	Integral; integration
Option + d	Differential; derivative
Option + j	Delta
Option + p	Pi
Option + v	Square root
Option + w	Sigma; sum
Option + x	Approximately
Option + z	Omega; ohm
Option + 5	Infinity
Option + =	Not equal to
Option + ,	Less than or equal to
Option + .	Greater than or equal to
Shift + Option + k	Apple Closed Apple
Shift + Option + v	Open diamond

PostScript Fonts Display Incorrectly at Large Point Sizes in Word 6.0.1

ISSUE

Text formatted with a PostScript font in a very large point size (i.e., 150 points or larger) in Microsoft Word 6.0.1 displays incorrectly (e.g., characters squeeze together, overwrite the right margin, or display in Geneva instead of the specified font).

SOLUTION

Apply a smaller point size to the text (i.e., 149 points or smaller).

ADDITIONAL INFORMATION

Microsoft Word may incorrectly display text formatted with PostScript fonts at a very large point size (i.e., 150 points or larger). Using PostScript fonts at smaller sizes (i.e., 149 points or smaller) enables Word to display the text characters as expected.

Text Descenders and Ascenders Don't Display or Are Truncated

ISSUE

Character ascenders or descenders (e.g., the upper stem of the letter "b" or the lower stem of the letter "p") appear truncated on-screen and when printed to a QuickDraw printer.

SYMPTOMS

Adobe Type Manager (ATM) is installed.

The ascenders or descenders appear truncated regardless of the applied leading value.

SOLUTIONS

To display character ascenders and descenders on-screen, select Character Shapes, instead of Line Spacing, for the Preserve option in the ATM Control Panel.

OR: Disable ATM to use only the bitmap (screen) font file for display.

OR: Print to a PostScript printer.

ADDITIONAL INFORMATION

Ascenders or descenders that fill or extend past a character's bounding (i.e., the distance between the character's ascender and descender is equal to or larger than its point size) do not display.

Adobe Type Manager's Preserve Character Shapes option enables PostScript Type 1 fonts to display as accurately as possible on-screen. Adobe Type Manager's Preserve Line Spacing option enables the line lengths of text formatted with a PostScript Type 1 font to display as accurately as possible on-screen. When printing to a QuickDraw printer, QuickDraw printer drivers use the screen display for printing.

Text Doesn't Appear After You Apply a Different Font

ISSUE

Text disappears after you apply a PostScript font to it. The text may print as expected to a PostScript printer.

SOLUTIONS

Do one or more of the following:

A. Increase the size of the Adobe Type Manager (ATM) Font Cache in the ATM control panel, then restart the Macintosh.

B. Reinstall the font from the original disk. For instructions, see Additional Information.

C. Disable other extensions, reinstall ATM, then run ATM with all other extensions disabled:

1. Move the Extensions and Control Panels folders from the System Folder to another location (e.g., desktop).
2. Restart the Macintosh. After the Macintosh restarts, the Finder creates new, empty Extensions and Control Panels folders in the System Folder. 3. Install ATM from the original disks into the new Control Panels folder in the System Folder.
4. Restart the Macintosh.

D. Install an updated version of the font.

ADDITIONAL INFORMATION

Text may disappear on screen after you apply a PostScript font to it if ATM's Font Cache is too small, a font file or the Fonts folder is damaged, an extension conflict exists, or you're using an old version of a font. Increasing the size of the Font Cache, reinstalling font files, recreating the Fonts folder, eliminating extension conflicts, or updating the font files may enable the PostScript Type 1 font to appear on-screen and print as expected.

ATM's Font Cache is an allotment of memory that ATM uses to store font data. When ATM has insufficient memory in the Font Cache to create or display a font, the font appears bitmapped or does not appear on-screen at all. The default size of the Font Cache is 256K. You should increase this size to 512K or more when working with a document that uses five or more typefaces or uses a Multiple Master typeface (e.g., Jenson, Ex Ponto, Tekton). You can adjust the size of the font cache in the ATM control panel, clicking the up or down arrows to increase or decrease its size. The changes do not take effect until you restart the Macintosh.

To reinstall a PostScript font in System 7.1 or later:

1. Quit all applications.
2. Move the Fonts folder from the System Folder to the desktop, then restart the Macintosh. After the Macintosh restarts, the Finder creates a new, empty Fonts folder in the System Folder.
3. Copy the outline and bitmap font files from the original disks into the Fonts folder in the System Folder.

To reinstall a PostScript font in System 7.0x:

1. Quit all applications.
2. Remove the PostScript outline fonts from the Extensions folder in the System Folder.
3. Remove bitmap font suitcases from the System suitcase in the System Folder.
4. Copy the PostScript outline fonts from the original disks into the Extensions folder in the System Folder.
5. Copy the bitmap font files from the original disks into the System suitcase in the System Folder.

Typeface Has No Apostrophe or Quotation Marks Character

ISSUE

Apostrophe or quotation mark characters in a display typeface (e.g., Lithos, Parisian, or Blackoak) display as a blank space or unexpected character.

SOLUTIONS

To create an apostrophe in a display typeface, type Option + Shift +].

To create a quotation mark in a display typeface, type Option + Shift + [.

ADDITIONAL INFORMATION

Display typefaces (i.e., typefaces designed to be displayed at larger point sizes) do not map apostrophe or quotation mark characters to the standard keyboard locations.

Wrong Font Appears When Typing in QuarkXPress 3.3x

ISSUE

When you type text in QuarkXPress 3.3x, the font that appears on-screen is different than the font you selected in the font menu.

SOLUTION

In Symantec Suitcase 2.1.4x, deselect the "Update Existing Font Menus When a Font Suitcase Is Opened or Closed" option, which is located in the Fonts Preferences dialog box when the Sets & Suitcases or Resources window is open, then quit and restart QuarkXPress.

ADDITIONAL INFORMATION

QuarkXPress does not support the Suitcase 2.1.4x "Update Existing Font Menus When a Font Suitcase is Opened or Closed" option that updates font menus after you open or close a font suitcase. If you type text in QuarkXPress 3.3x with this option selected, the font that appears on-screen is different than the font you selected in the font menu.

Application Errors

MAC OS / WINDOWS

Error "Insert the same Type On Call CD-ROM used for installation" When Unlocking Fonts

ISSUE

When you unlock new fonts or copy previously unlocked fonts from a Type On Call 4.1x CD-ROM, the Adobe Type On Call Purchaser returns the error, "To copy items, you must insert the same Type On Call CD-ROM used for installation."

SOLUTIONS

Unlock or copy the fonts from the original Type On Call 4.1x CD-ROM:

1. Quit the Purchaser.
2. Remove the Type On Call CD-ROM from the CD-ROM drive.
3. Insert the Type On Call CD-ROM from which you originally installed Type On Call. 4. Start the Purchaser, then unlock or copy the fonts you want.

OR: Reinstall Type On Call from the inserted CD-ROM, then obtain new unlocking codes from the Type On Call unlocking center.

ADDITIONAL INFORMATION

Once you install Type On Call, it requires that you use the same CD-ROM to unlock new fonts or copy previously unlocked fonts. Type On Call records information about the Type On Call CD-ROM you used to install in its preferences files. If you insert a different Type On Call 4.1.x CD-ROM disc, you can start the Purchaser because it can use the installed preferences files to start, but when you unlock or copy fonts, it returns the error, "To copy items, you must insert the same Type On Call CD-ROM used for installation."

Type On Call 4.1.1 or later is on Type On Call CD-ROM discs labeled version 4.1 with a pressing number of 16 or later. To determine your Type On Call CD-ROM pressing, locate the number (i.e., xxxxxx-x) on the inside rim on the bottom of the CD-ROM (i.e., the side without a printed label). The two numbers preceding the dash indicate the pressing number. For example, the number "999901-2" indicates CD-ROM pressing 1. The number "999914-2" indicates CD-ROM pressing 14.

Type On Call CD-ROM discs are included with most Adobe products, so you may have multiple Type On Call CD-ROM discs.

WINDOWS

Error "Internal error GL 1" in FontMonger

ISSUE

When you switch between two or more open fonts, Adobe FontMonger 1.0.8 returns the error, "Internal error GL1." At least one font is in Character Chart view at the same time at least one font is in Keyboard Layout view.

Solutions Do one or more of the following:

A. View all fonts in the same layout view (i.e., only in Character Chart view or only in Keyboard Layout view).

B. Open only one font at a time.

ADDITIONAL INFORMATION

FontMonger's Keyboard Layout view displays character locations on a keyboard, while the Character Chart view displays characters in their positions within the ANSI character set. If you switch between two or more open fonts when one or more of the fonts is open in a different view, FontMonger may return the error "Internal error GL1."

MAC OS

Alert "Error: ATM -22." Appears When Creating Multiple Master Instance

ISSUE

After you click Create in Font Creator to generate an instance from a multiple master base font, the alert "Error: ATM -22. Volume, file, or suitcase is read-only." appears.

SOLUTION

Remove the multiple master font from Suitcase 3.0 before creating an instance of that font:

1. In the Suitcase control panel, open the set containing the font from which you want to create an instance.
2. Select the font, choose Edit > Remove Selected Items, then click Remove.
3. Install the font in the Fonts folder in the System Folder.
4. Create the multiple master instance.
   OR: If the font is not installed in Suitcase 3.0 but its suitcase is locked, unlock it:
   1. Select the font suitcase.
   2. Choose File > Get Info.
   3. Deselect the Locked option, then close the Get Info window.

ADDITIONAL INFORMATION

When you create a multiple master instance, Font Creator writes the new font information in the font's suitcase. When a font's suitcase is designated read-only or is locked, Font Creator is unable to write to the suitcase, so it returns the error "ATM -22. Volume, file, or suitcase is read-only." Suitcase 3.0 designates font suitcases as read-only. Removing the font from Suitcase 3.0 so it is writable or unlocking the font's suitcase enables Font Creator to create a multiple master instance without error.

Suitcase 2.1.4 includes a Shared Suitcase option that enables you to designate a font suitcase as writable and prevent the error "ATM -22" from occurring. Suitcase 3.0 does not include this option.

System Errors

MAC OS

System Error "Type 11" When Moving Font File or Opening Suitcase

ISSUE

When you open a font suitcase or move a font file in the Finder (i.e., desktop), a system error (e.g., "Type 11," "Suitcase Error Type 11", "Finder Error Type 11") occurs.

SOLUTIONS

In the Adobe Type Manager (ATM) control panel, select Substitute for Missing Fonts, then restart the Macintosh.
OR: Install ATM 3.5.x, ATM 3.6.x, or ATM 3.9, then restart the Macintosh.
OR: Remove the ATM Font Database file from the System Folder, then restart the Macintosh.

ADDITIONAL INFORMATION

When ATM 3.8.x is installed and the Substitute for Missing Fonts option is deselected in the ATM 3.8.x Control Panel, a system error (e.g., "Type 11") occurs when you open a font suitcase or move a font file in the Finder. When ATM 3.8.x is installed and the Substitute for Missing Fonts option is selected, or when ATM 3.5.x, ATM 3.6.x, or ATM 3.9 is installed, a system error (e.g., "Type 11") does not occur when you open a font suitcase or move a font file in the Finder.

With Suitcase II and ATM 3.8.x are installed and Substitute for Missing Fonts is deselected in the ATM Control Panel, the error "Suitcase Error Type 11" occurs when you open a font suitcase or move a font file in the Finder.

ATM 3.5 and later simulate substitute fonts for unavailable fonts when SuperATM's ATM Font Database file is installed in the System Folder. After ATM finds the SuperATM ATM Font Database file (file size 1 MB or larger) in the System Folder, it includes the Substitute for Missing Fonts option in the ATM Control Panel. If ATM cannot find the SuperATM ATM Font Database file in the System Folder, ATM does not include the Substitute for Missing Fonts option in the ATM Control Panel.

Error "-39" or "Font in use" When Removing Font in System 7.x

ISSUE

When you remove a font from the Fonts folder in the System Folder, System 7.1 or later returns the error "Error -39" or "You cannot remove this font because it is in use by the system."

SOLUTION

Move the Fonts folder from the System Folder, restart, then move the font:

1. Move the Fonts folder in the System Folder to another the location (e.g., desktop), then restart the Macintosh. After restarting, the system creates a new, empty Fonts folder in the System Folder.
2. Move the PostScript bitmap (screen) and outline (printer) font files of the font you want to remove from the Fonts folder to another location (e.g., desktop).
3. Move the fonts you want installed from the copy of the Fonts folder to the newly created Fonts folder in the System Folder.

ADDITIONAL INFORMATION

When a font file or the Fonts folder is damaged, the system returns the error "Error -39" or "You cannot remove this font because it is in use by the system" when you remove the font from the Fonts folder in the System Folder. When you move the Fonts folder to another location and then restart the Macintosh, the system creates a new, empty Fonts folder in the System Folder. During restart, the system searches for the Fonts folder in the System Folder. When the system is unable to find a Fonts folder in the System Folder, it creates a new, empty Fonts folder in the System Folder. Because the system is unable to use a Fonts folder that is not located in the System Folder during startup, you can remove font files from it.

Printing Problems

MAC OS

PostScript or Communication Error Printing Jenson Multiple Master Font

ISSUE

When printing the Adobe Jenson or Adobe Jenson Expert multiple master font, a PostScript error (e.g., "rangecheck; OffendingCommand: makeblendedfont") or a communication error (e.g., "Because of a communication error, [document name] from [application] could not be printed on [printer name]") occurs.

SOLUTION

Print Adobe Jenson using the Adobe PSPrinter 8.3 or later printer driver.

ADDITIONAL INFORMATION

Because the Adobe Jenson and Adobe Jenson Expert multiple master fonts incorporate new multiple master font technology, they require the Adobe PSPrinter 8.3 or later printer driver to print. When you print the Adobe Jenson or Adobe Jenson Expert multiple master font using the LaserWriter printer driver, or the Adobe PSPrinter 8.2.1 or earlier printer driver, a PostScript error or a communication error occurs.

Type 1 Font Prints Without Bold, Italic or BoldItalic Style

ISSUE

Text formatted with a plain (e.g., Goudy) typestyle and an applied style (e.g., Bold, Italic) displays stylized, but prints in the plain typeface to a PostScript printer. For example, text formatted in Microsoft Word 6.0 with Goudy and the style Bold applied displays as Goudy Bold, but prints as Goudy.

SOLUTIONS

Do one or more of the following:

A. Install the printer font file (e.g., GoudyBol) for the stylized typeface (e.g., Goudy Bold).

B. Delete then reinstall the font's screen (bitmap) and printer (outline) font files.

C. Apply the stylized typeface (e.g., Goudy Bold) to the text, instead of applying a style (e.g., Bold) to the plain typeface (e.g., Goudy).
   NOTE: Other installed extensions or control panels may interfere with fonts being downloaded to the printer. Run the application with all extensions off to verify that added extensions or control panels are not the cause. To turn all extensions off upon startup in System 7, restart the computer while holding the Shift key until the message "Welcome to Macintosh. Extensions Off." appears.

ADDITIONAL INFORMATION

Text formatted with a plain, or Roman, typeface and an applied style (e.g., Bold, Italic) prints in a plain typeface when the stylized printer font file is not installed (e.g., GoudyBol), the font does not include a designed stylized typeface (e.g., Oxford, Zapf Chancery), the font's printer font file is damaged, or an extension conflicts with the printing application.

Document Containing Multiple Master Font Doesn't Print to PostScript Level 1 Printer

ISSUE

When you print a document containing multiple master fonts to a PostScript Level 1 printer (e.g., Apple Personal LaserWriter NT, Hewlett-Packard Series II or III printer using a PostScript Level 1 cartridge, NewGen Turbo PS 480), nothing prints. The printer display indicates it has begun processing, then returns to idle.

SOLUTIONS

Print to a PostScript Level 2 printer (e.g., Apple LaserWriter Pro 630).
OR: Print to a different PostScript Level 1 printer (e.g., Apple LaserWriter II NTX).
OR: Specify type using PostScript Type 1 or TrueType fonts instead of multiple master fonts.

ADDITIONAL INFORMATION

The PostScript code used in multiple master fonts is not compatible with all versions of PostScript Level 1. When you print a document containing multiple master fonts to an incompatible PostScript Level 1 printer, the printer display indicates it has begun processing, then returns to idle, and nothing prints.

Some PostScript Level 1 printers can be upgraded to PostScript Level 2. For more information, contact your printer manufacturer.

Multiple master fonts include:

- ITC Avant Garde Gothic MM
- Caflisch Script
- Ex Ponto MM
- ITC Garamond MM
- Graphite
- Jenson
- Mezz
- Minion MM
- Minion MM Expert Collection
- ITC Motter Corpus
- Myriad
- Nueva
- Penumbra
- Sanvito
- Tekton MM
- Viva
- AdobeSanXMM (multiple master substitution font included with SuperATM and Adobe Acrobat)
- AdobeSerifMM (multiple master substitution font included with SuperATM and Adobe Acrobat)

Multiple Master Fonts Don't Print to Imagesetter

ISSUE

When you print to an imagesetter using Kodak Precision Color 1.26 and earlier, multiple master fonts do not print (e.g., characters drop out, a PostScript error occurs). The multiple master fonts print as expected to a laser printer.

SOLUTIONS

Use Kodak Precision Color 1.27 or later.
OR: Print the document without Precision Color installed:

1. Uninstall Precision Color. For instructions, see the Precision Color documentation.
2. Restart the imagesetter to flush Precision Color from memory (RAM).
3. Print the document containing multiple master fonts.
4. Reinstall Precision Color.

OR: Download the following patch to the imagesetter before printing:

DISCLAIMER: This procedure is not supported by Adobe Systems Incorporated and is only provided as a guideline. For support, contact Eastman Kodak.

1. Type the following text in a text editor that can save in text-only format (e.g., Microsoft Word, MS-DOS Editor):

```
%!PS-Adobe-2.0 Exitserver
%%Title: Patch to fix multiple master/
  Precision ILS compatibility issue
%%Creator: Southwest Software
%%CreationDate: Thursday, September 17, 1992
%%make sure that findfont is defined in
  userdict
serverdict begin 0 exitserver
/findfont
dup load def
```

2. Save the file in text-only format.
3. Download the file to the imagesetter using a file downloader (e.g., WINDOWN, Adobe Font Downloader).

ADDITIONAL INFORMATION

Because Kodak Precision Color 1.26 and earlier is incompatible with multiple master fonts, a PostScript error occurs when you print multiple master fonts to an imagesetter calibrated with it, or the fonts do not print. Upgrading, removing, or patching Precision Color 1.26 and earlier enables the fonts to print as expected.

Precision Color is a color calibration utility. Precision Color 1.26 and earlier create a copy of the PostScript interpreter's system dictionary (systemdict), giving the copy the same name as the original. The original systemdict is read-only, but the copy of systemdict can be written to.

When you print a document containing multiple master fonts, the multiple master software tries to add multiple master functionality to the PostScript findfont command in systemdict. The multiple master software cannot write to the read-only systemdict, and is incompatible with Precision Color 1.26 or earlier's copy. When the multiple master software is unable to locate a systemdict it can write to, it tries to redefine findfont in the read-only systemdict, which causes a PostScript error to occur.

Installation Issues

MAC OS

Fonts Copy Slowly or System Error When Installing Font Files

ISSUE

When you copy outline (printer) font files from a CD-ROM (e.g., Type On Call, Font Folio) or a different volume to a Macintosh running System 7.1 or later, font files copy slower than expected or hard drive activity appears to stop (e.g., freeze, hang).

SOLUTIONS

Wait for the fonts to finish copying. Because the process of copying fonts can take several minutes per font, the system appears to freeze while copying fonts.
OR: Use a utility (e.g., CopyDoubler included with SuperDoubler by Symantec/Fifth Generation Systems) to copy outline font files.
OR: Rebuild the desktop file on the destination volume by holding down the Command and Option keys while restarting the computer. Keep the keys held down until you receive the message "Are you sure you want to rebuild the desktop file on the disk '[diskname]'? Comments in info windows will be lost," then click "OK."

ADDITIONAL INFORMATION

When copying outline font files at the Finder from a CD-ROM or a different volume to a Macintosh running System 7.1 or later, font files copy slower than expected or hard drive activity appears to stop.

Adobe and other font providers include a bundle (bndl) and icon (icn#) resource in each outline font to associate the font's icon with the font. The bundle and icon resource cause the Finder to assume the outline font file is an application. When the Macintosh Finder 7.1 or later copies an application from one volume to another, it references each application's file Type and Creator resource located in the desktop file. Referencing the desktop file for each file slows the copying process. When copying many font files, copying times can become extremely slow.

File copying utilities (e.g., CopyDoubler or SuperDoubler by Symantec/Fifth Generation Systems) copy outline font files faster than the Finder by bypassing the Finder's requirement to look up the file's Type and Creator resource in the desktop file.

The retail version of Adobe Font Folio 7.0 includes SuperDoubler. The upgrade version of Font Folio 7.0 does not include SuperDoubler.

Installing Fonts in System 7.0 and Later

To install font files, you move them into the appropriate folder. A font file is either a TrueType font file, a bitmap (screen) font suitcase, or a PostScript outline (printer) font file. For more information on font files, see document number 241313.

INSTALLING FONTS IN SYSTEM 7.1 AND LATER

Move your font files into the Fonts folder in the System Folder.
OR: Move font files onto the System Folder icon so the system automatically places them in the proper location.

INSTALLING FONTS IN SYSTEM 7.0 AND 7.0.1

Move bitmap font suitcases into the System suitcase in the System Folder and move outline font files into the Extensions folder in the System Folder.
OR: Move all font files onto the System Folder icon so the system automatically places them in the proper location.

Font/DA Mover Does Not List Font to Install

ISSUE

The Apple Font/DA Mover 3.7 and earlier does not list a bitmap font as available to install.

SOLUTIONS

Install the font using Font/DA Mover 3.8 or later.
OR: Upgrade to System 7.0 or later and install the fonts by dragging them into in the System Folder.

ADDITIONAL INFORMATION

PostScript fonts created before 1988 include the font resource FONT. PostScript fonts created later than 1988 include the font resource NFNT (newfont). Because Font/DA Mover 3.7 and earlier was created before the NFNT resource was introduced, it does not recognize fonts with the resource NFNT. Font/DA Mover 3.8 or later and System 7.0 or later recognize both the FONT and NFNT resources.

System 6.x requires the Font/DA Mover to install bitmap fonts. System 7.0 or later does not require the Font/DA Mover to install bitmap fonts.

The NFNT resource was introduced with the Macintosh 128K ROM. It enables the Macintosh to load more than 256 fonts at one time.

General Information

MAC OS / WINDOWS

Type Terminology

AFM
Adobe Font Metrics. A text file that defines metric and pair kerning information. See also INF and PFM.
Ascender
The portion of a lower case character that rises above its x-height. For example, the letters b, d, h, k, and l have ascenders.
Adobe Type Manager (ATM)
A system software utility that rasterizes type at any size using a Type 1 outline font file. See also AFM, INF, PFB, PFM, and Rasterizing.
Base Font
See Multiple Master Base Font.
Baseline
The imaginary line that runs under each character.
Bitmap font
A pattern of dots (bits) that forms a character shape in a given typeface, point size, rotation, and resolution, usually used for on-screen display. See also PFM.
Bold
Designates a heavier-weight typeface. See also Roman and Italic.
Cap Height
The height of a capital letter from the baseline to the top of the letter.
Condensed
A typeface that has been designed to be thinner and more compact than the original typeface. See also Narrow.
Counter
The white space within characters such as b, p, d, and 6.
Descender
The portion of a letter falling below the baseline. For example, the letters g, p, and y have descenders.
Design Axis
Variable typeface attribute, such as weight, width, style, or optical size. See also Optical Size.
Display Type
Typeface that is designed, by its size or weight, to attract attention. Display typefaces are often used as headlines, usually at 14 points or larger.
Downloading
The process of transferring outline font information or PostScript files from the computer to a printer's memory or hard disk.
Fixed Pitch
See Monospace. See also Pitch and Proportional Spacing.
Font
Term generally used to describe a complete collection of letters, figures, symbols, punctuation, and special characters in a particular typeface, but traditionally describes a specific design of an alphabet at one size of one typeface.
Font Cache
Memory reserved for screen font rasterization.
Font Family
See Typeface Family.
Font Foundry
An obsolete utility for DOS that converts Adobe Type 1 fonts into non-scalable bitmap screen and printer fonts for Hewlett-Packard's Windows Printer Control Language (PCL).
Hints
PostScript instructions built into outline fonts that enable character shapes especially subtle curves, printed at small point sizes and low resolutions to print as close to the designed character shape as possible Small point sizes and low resolutions limits the number of pixel choices to reproduce the character's shape as designed.
INF
Information file. Windows file used by ATM to identify a file as a font file. See also AFM and PFM.
Instance
See Multiple Master Instance.
Italic
Typeface designed to be slanted, with varying character stroke thickness and spacing to enhance character readability. See also Bold, Roman and Oblique.
Kern
To change the spacing between letters for optical clarity and aesthetic reasons.
Kerning Pairs
Pairs of letters with predefined kerning definitions. Applications that support pair kerning include PageMaker, QuarkXPress, and FrameMaker. Many text editors (e.g., Microsoft Word, WordPerfect) do not support pair kerning. Adobe fonts include between 100 and 2000 predefined kerning pairs per font. A font's AFM file lists its number of kerning pairs.
Leading
White space or vertical space between lines of type, also referred to as linespacing. Leading is measured in points. The term leading comes from the days of metal type, when strips of lead were used to add space between lines. When specifying type size and leading, typesetters write a fraction in which the type size is the numerator, leading the denominator. For example, 12/14, or 12.14, or twelve on fourteen or twelve over fourteen, describes text formatted in 12 point type and 14 points leading.
Ligature
Two or more characters merged into a single character, most commonly ligatures of the letters f + i and the letters f + l. Ligatures are designed to bring elegance to the document.
Linespacing
See Leading.

Measurements
Type measurements include:

Point
A unit equal to 1/72 inch. 72 points =1 inch. Points are used to specify the vertical size of type.

Pica
A unit equal to 12 points. 6 picas = 1 inch. Picas are often used to specify the width of columns.

Em or em space
A unit of horizontal space equal to a square lead base of the type size. For example, in 10 point type, a standard em is 10 points wide and 10 points high, but em size varies. Em spaces are often used to specify the size of paragraph indents. Originally, an em was the space occupied by a typeface's capital letter M.

En or en space
A unit of horizontal space equal to half of an em space. Originally, an en was the space occupied by a typeface's capital letter N.

MMM
Multiple Master Metrics file for Windows. MMM files are the multiple master font equivalent of the single master font AFM files. See also AFM, PFB, and PSS.

Monospace
Uniform horizontal spacing between characters in a font. The width of each character, including the space character, is exactly the same. Adobe has four monospaced body text fonts (Courier, Prestige Elite, Letter Gothic, and Orator) and three special purpose monospaced fonts (OCR A, OCR B, and MICR). See also Proportional Spacing.

Multiple Master Font
Multiple master fonts are customizable Type 1 fonts. Multiple master typeface characteristics are described in terms of linear design axes such as weight, width, style, and optical size. Although multiple master fonts can be customized in an almost infinite variety between axes, the maximum possible number of axes is four. See also Single Master Font.

Multiple Master Base Font
The multiple master font itself. In Windows, base font files include MMM, PFM, and PFB files.

Multiple Master Instance
A particular rendition of the font described by its coordinates along one or more master design axes. In Windows, instance font files include PFM and PSS files.

Narrow
A typeface that has been compressed to simulate the look of a condensed font. See also Condensed.

Number Fonts
Some typeface families (e.g., Helvetica Neue, Linotype Centennial, PMN Caecilia, Univers) use Frutiger numbers, which quantify type weight and width. In the Frutiger numbering scheme, a two-digit number signifies the weight and amount of compression or extension of the font. The first digit is the weight, with low numbers being light, and high numbers being dark. The second digit indicates both character width and type style. Low numbers designate extended characters and high numbers designate condensed characters. Odd numbers designate roman type styles and even numbers designate italic type styles.

Oblique
A slanted Roman typeface that emulates an italic typeface. See also Italic.

Optical Size
Multiple master design axis designed for readability, with subtle adjustments to letter proportion, weight, contrast, and spacing made to optimize readability at a certain point size.

Outline Font
A file in the PostScript language that contains descriptions of all characters in a typeface. Outline font files enable you to scale (resize) fonts infinitely without loss of definition. See also PFB.

PCL
Printer Control Language. Printer language used by non-PostScript printers (e.g., Hewlett-Packard LaserJet III).

Permanent Status
A description of how fonts reside in the printer memory. Permanent fonts remain in memory until the printer is turned off.

PFB
Printer Font Binary. PFB files are used by Windows, PostScript printers, typesetters, slide printers, ATM, and Font Foundry to generate and print fonts. See also Outline Font.

PFM
Printer Font Metrics. PFMs are used by Windows for on-screen display. When a font has AFM and INF files, ATM combines the AFM and INF files into a PFM file. See also AFM, Bitmap Font and INF.

Pi Font
A font composed of special characters such as symbols or mathematical characters.

Pica
A measure of type equal to 12 points or 1/6th of an inch. See also Measurements.

Pitch
Describes the number of characters printed in a horizontal inch. This terminology dates from the typewriter and daisy-wheel printer eras. The most common pitch values are 10-pitch and 12-pitch. Ten pitch type is called pica and has 10 characters per inch. Twelve pitch type is called elite and has 12 characters per inch. Elite is the most common size in typing. 15 pitch type, not commonly used, is called micro-elite and has 15 characters per inch.

Adobe's four monospaced fonts (Courier, Letter Gothic, Prestige Elite, Orator) can be used as pitch fonts. For 10 pitch, use a 12-point font; for 12 pitch, use a 10-point font; for 15 pitch, use a 8-point font.

Point
A measure of type equal to 1/72 of an inch. See also Measurements.

Point Size
The height of a font, in points, including ascenders and descenders.

PostScript Font
See Type 1 Font.
Primary Instance
One of the set of ready-to-use multiple master instances that constitute a typeface family. See also Multiple Master Instance.
Printer RAM
A printer's random-access memory (RAM). The amount of printer RAM available for font downloading, known as virtual memory (VM), is a fraction of the printer's total RAM. The printer reserves the remaining RAM for page rendering and rasterizing fonts. Printer VM is set by the printer's manufacturer. A typical printer with 2 MB of RAM has approximately 425K of VM available for downloaded fonts.
Proportional Spacing
Variable horizontal spacing between characters in a font. The width of each character, including the space character, varies with the shape of the character. Proportional fonts are easier to read than monospace fonts and are preferred for publishing applications. See also Monospace.
PSS
PostScript Printer Stub. PSS files are the multiple master instance equivalent of the single master and multiple master base font PFB files. See also PFB.
Rasterizing
The process of converting outline font information into a scaleable bitmap image.
Resolution
The number of dots per inch used to create an image onscreen or in print.
Roman
Designates an upright typeface. See also Bold and Italic.
Sans Serif
Typefaces without short lines crossing the main strokes of a character. The word "sans" means "without." See also Serif.
Scaling
Resizing.
Script
Designates typefaces that emulate hand or cursive lettering.
Serif
Typefaces with short lines crossing the main strokes of a character. See also Sans Serif.
Single Master Font
A standard Type 1 font, adjustable only in style (e.g., Roman, italic, bold). See also Multiple Master Font and Design Axis.
Softfont
A typeface that is not resident in printer memory, requiring the printing application to download it to printer memory when you print a document.
Spacing
See Monospace and Proportional Spacing.
Stem
Character's vertical stroke.
TrueType
Font format. TrueType fonts consist of one file that is used for both screen display and printing. ATM does not rasterize TrueType fonts.
Type 1
Font written in the PostScript language. Type 1 fonts are composed of two files, an outline (printer) font and a bitmap (screen) font. Type 1 fonts include hints, unlike Type 3 fonts.
Type 3
Outline font format introduced by Adobe. Type 3 fonts are also called user-defined fonts, and are commonly used to describe complex graphic shapes such as logos. Type 3 fonts do not support hinting.
Type 4
Type 1 font converted and compressed by the Adobe Font Downloader utility for storage on a disk and for downloading to a PostScript Level 1 printer.
Type 42
TrueType fonts that contain PostScript code. When printing standard TrueType fonts to a PostScript printer, the PostScript printer driver converts them to PostScript. The Type 42 font's PostScript code enables the printer's PostScript interpreter to send the font information to the TrueType interpreter without converting the TrueType font to PostScript.
Typeface
A specific or unique design of an alphabet. A typeface describes features such as character thickness, width, angle, letter height, ascender height, and how deep descenders drop below the baseline. Within a family, each style (e.g., Roman, Italic, Bold, Bold italic) is a typeface.
Typeface Family
A range of typeface designs that includes variations such as Roman, Italic, Bold, and Bold italic.
Unimaster Font
See Single Master Font.
Width
The amount of horizontal space required by a character or symbol in a font.
Weight
The heaviness of the characters in a typeface, such as light, medium, or bold.
X-Height
The height of lowercase characters in a font, specifically the letter x, excluding ascenders and descenders.

Multiple Master Fonts General Information

Multiple master fonts are customizable PostScript fonts. The multiple master font format describes a typeface's characteristics using linear design axes, which include weight, width, optical size, and style (i.e., slab, serif). Each design axis has a linear range. For example, Myriad's weight axis range is 1 to 830, and its width axis range is 1 to 700.

Multiple master fonts include a number of primary font instances, preconfigured at differing intersections of their design axes. For example, Myriad includes 15 primary instances, ranging from 215 LT 300 CN (Light Condensed) to 830 BL 700 SE (Black SemiExtended). You use the Font Creator utility to create custom instances.

Multiple master font files, which are larger than single master fonts, require a minimum of 3 MB of printer memory (RAM). PostScript Level 1 printers that don't have the minimum of 3 MB of RAM (e.g., Personal LaserWriter NT, Hewlett-Packard LaserJet with PostScript Level 1 cartridge) are unable to print multiple master fonts.

Adobe multiple master fonts include:

ITC Avant Garde Gothic
Caflisch Script
Ex Ponto
ITC Garamond
Graphite
Jenson
Jimbo
Mezz
Minion
Minion Expert
Myriad
Nueva
Ocean Sans
Penumbra
Sanvit
Tekton
Viva

MULTIPLE MASTER FONT NAMES

All multiple master fonts have MM after the typeface name, with the numeric values of their weight and width added to short axis abbreviations (e.g., MinioMM_578 BD 465 CN 11 OP).

Weight Axis (wt)

XL: ExtraLight
LT: Light
RG: Regular
SB: Semibold
BD: Bold
BL: Black

Width Axis (wd)

XC: ExtraCondensed
CN: Condensed
SC: SemiCondense
NO: Norma
SE: SemiExtended
EX: Extended
XE: ExtraExtended

Optical Size Axis (op)

OP: Optical size (from 6 to 72)

Optical Size

The optical size axis enables you to generate fonts that are optically adjusted for use at specific point sizes. As the optical size increases, the space between the characters (letter fit) tightens, the space within the characters (counters) becomes smaller, the serifs become finer, the overall weight becomes lighter, and the x-height gradually decreases in size. Jenson, Minion, Minion Expert, and Sanvito support optical scaling.

MULTIPLE MASTER FONT REQUIREMENTS

Macintosh

- System 6.0.5 or later
- LaserWriter 6.1 or later printer driver when printing to a PostScript device
- 4 MB RAM (System 7) or 2 MB RAM (System 6)
- Hard disk
- High-density disk drive

Windows

- Windows 3.1 or later or OS/2 1.3 or later
- 4 MB RAM
- Hard disk
- High-density disk drive

Jenson multiple master font for the Macintosh

- Adobe Type Manager (ATM) 3.9 or later
- Adobe PSPrinter 8.3 or later printer driver

PostScript Printer

- 3 MB or more of printer memory (RAM)

Font Name Pronunciation Guide

Pronunciation Key

a	mat, pan
ah	banana, collide, what
aow	how, plow
ay	day, fade, date
ee	beat, evenly, nosebleed
eh	bet, bed, peck
ie	site, side, buy
ih	tip, banish, active
o	bone, know
oo	rule, youth, tool
s	source, less
u	wood, pull
zh	vision, azure

Pronunciation Guide

Font Name	Pronunciation
Aachen Bold	ah'-khehn
Aja	ah'-zha
Berthold Akzidenz Grotesk	behr'-told ahk'-see-dehns grotehsk'
Alexa	ah-lek'-sah
Amigo	ah-mee'-go
Arkona	ahr-ko'-nah
Ariadne	ah-ree-ahd'-nay
Arnold Bîcklin	ahr'-nold bahk'-lihn

Auriol	ah'-ree-ohl
Avenir	ah'-veh-neer
Baker Signet	bay'-kehr sig'-net
Balzano	bahl-zah'-no
Banco	bang'-ko
Barmeno	bahr-may'-no
Bauhaus	baow'-haows
Belwe	bel'-vah or bel'-wee
Benguiat	behn'-gat
Berliner Grotesk	behr'-lihn-ehr gro-tehsk'
New Berolina	behr-o-lee'-nah
Boton	bo-tohn' (with silent n)
Bundesbahn Pi	boon'-dehs-bahn pie
Caflisch Script	kah'-fleesh skrihpt
Caliban	kal'-ee-ban
Castellar	kas-tehl'-ahr
Catull	kah-tuhl'
Centaur	sehn-tahr
ITC Cerigo	sehr-ee'-go
Charlemagne	shahr'-lah-mayn
Charme	shahrm
ITC Cheltenham	chehl'-tehn-ham
Cheq	chehk
Christiana	krihs-tee-ah'-nah
Clairvaux	klehr-vo'
Clarendon	klehr'-ehn-dahn
Cochin	ko-shan' (with silent n)
Colossalis	ko-lah-sal'-ihs
Comenius Antiqua	ko-may'-nee-uhs an-tee'-gwah
Copal	ko-pahl'
Cremona	kray-mo'-nah
Delphin	dehl-phan' (with silent n)
Delta Jaeger	dehl'-tah yay'-gehr
Linotype Didot	dee'-do
DIN Schriften	shrihf'-tehn
Diotima	dee-o'-tee-mah
Duc De Berry	dook deh behr'-ee
Eccentric	ehk-sehn'-trihk
Egyptienne	eh-zhihp-see-ehn'
Ehrhardt	ayr'-hahrt
El Greco	ehl greh'-ko
ITC Eras	eh'-rahs
ITC Esprit	ehs-pree'
Eurostile	yoor'-o-stiel
Excelsior	ehk-sehl'-see-or
Ex Ponto	ehks pahn'-to
Fenice	feh-nee'-cheh
Fette Fraktur	feh'-teh frahk'-toor
Formata	for-mah'-tah
Forte	for'-tay
Friz Quadrata	frihts kwah-drah'-tah
Frutiger	froo'-tih-gehr
Futura	fyoo-tyoor'-uh
Galahad	gal'-ah-had
Simoncini Garamond	see-mahn-chee'-nee gayr'-ah-mahnd
ITC Giovanni	jee-o-vah'-nee
Glypha	glee'-fah
Granjon	grahn-zhon' (silent n's)
Guardi	gwahr'-dee
Hadriano	had-ree-ah'-no
Neue Hammer Unziale	noy'-eh ham'-ehr uhn-zee-al'
Helvetica Inserat	ihn-sehr-aht'
Helvetica Neue	hehl-veh'-tih-kah noy'-eh
Herculanum	hayr-kyoo-la'-num
Hiroshige	heer-o-shee'-geh
Berthold Imago	behr'-told ih-mah'-go
Kabel	kah'-behl
Kigali	kih-gah'-lee
Kino	kee'-no
Koch Antiqua	kohk ahn-tee'-kwah
ITC Korinna	kor-een'-nah
KÅnstler Script	koonst'-lehr skrihpt
ITC Leawood	lee'-wud
Lino	lie'-no
Lubalin	loo'-bah-lihn
Lucida	loo'-sih-dah
Madrone	mah-dro'-nah
Matura	mah-toor'-ah
Medici Script	meh-dee'-chee skrihpt
Melior	mee'-lee-or
Mesquite	mehs-keet'
Minion Cyrillic	mihn'-yun seer-ihl'-ihk
Mistral	mihs-trahl'
ITC Motter Corpus	mah'-tehr kor'-puhs
Myriad	meer'-ee-ahd
Neuland	noy'-lahnd
Neuzeit	noy-tsiet' (rhymes with bite)
Nofret	no'-freht
Novarese	no-vah-reh'-zeh
Nueva	nway'-va
ITC Officina Sans	ah-fih-chee'-nah sans
Ondine	ahn-deen'
Onyx	ah'-nihks
Orator	or'-ah-tohr
Peignot	pehn'-yo
Penumbra	peh-num'-brah
Pepita	peh-pee'-tah
Perpetua	pehr-peht'-choo-ah
Photina	fo-tee'-nah
PMN Caecilia	tseh-tsee'-lee-yah
Poppl-Exquisit	pah'-pul ehks-kwih'-siht
Poppl-Laudatio	pah'-pul lah-dah'-tee-o
Poppl-Pontifex	pah'-pul pahn'-tih-fehks
Poppl-Residenz	pah'-pul rehz-ih-dehnz
Post-MediÑval	post meh-dee-ay'-vahl
Ruzicka Freehand	roo'-zih-kah
Sabon	sah-bon' (with silent n)
Sanvito	sahn-vee'-to
Stempel Schneidler	shtehm'-pul shnied'-lehr
ITC Serif Gothic	sehr'-ihf
Serifa	seh-ree'-fah
Serlio	sayr'-lee-o
ITC Slimbach	slihm'-bahk

Smaragd	shmahr-ahgd'
Tiepolo	tee-eh'-po-lo
Trajan	tray'-jahn
ITC Veljovic	vehl'-yo-vihtch
Versailles	vehr-sie'
Berthold Waulbaum Book	behr'-told vahl'-baowm
ITC Weidemann	vie'-deh-mah
Weiss	vies
Wiesbaden Swing	vees'-bah-dehn
Wilhelm Klingspor Gotisch	veel'-hehlm klihng'-shpor go'-teesh
Wilke	veel'-keh
Wittenberger Fraktur	vee'-tehn-behr-gehr frahk'-toor

Fonts with Revised Menu Names

Many Adobe typeface packages have been revised with new font menu names to provide better compatibility when transferring files between Macintosh and Windows applications. These font name revisions only affect applications that recognize fonts by menu name, and not applications that access fonts by PostScript name (e.g., Adobe Illustrator).

To enable applications that recognize fonts by menu names to recognize fonts in documents created on a different platform, or when printing, replace your old fonts with the new revised fonts, which are listed below.

The fonts Helvetica Narrow, Zapf Chancery, ITC Zapf Dingbats, ITC Avant Garde, and New Century Schoolbook have not been revised, but their font menu names, which differ between platforms, are recognized by most application and printer driver software.

EXPERT COLLECTION FONT REVISIONS

The revisions to the following Adobe Expert Collection typefaces include minor improvements to some characters (e.g., new accent positions), and the addition of some regular capital and lowercase letter characters from the base font's standard character set to the Small Caps & Old Style Figures (SC & OSF) character set.

Revised Adobe Expert Collection typefaces:

- Adobe Caslon Expert
- Adobe Garamond Expert
- Minion Expert
- Utopia Expert

OPTIMA AND ITC ERAS FONT REVISIONS

The revised Optima, package #6, and ITC Eras, package #56, like all other Adobe fonts, are composed of non-hybrid font files, no longer include underscores beneath ordinals, and include improved character shapes for Icelandic glyphs.

Hybrid fonts include different versions of font characters in their font files for different printing resolutions, enabling them to switch between their character sets to accommodate the targeted printer's resolution. Both the Optima and ITC Eras typefaces contain characters with subtle angles and curves that do not reproduce well when printed to low-resolution (i.e., 300 dpi-636 dpi) devices. By creating an alternate character set that replaces the sublime curves with straight edges, these font's were better-looking, but were not typographically accurate, when printed to low-resolution devices. The hybrid Optima uses the font files designed for low-resolution devices when the output device's resolution is 637 dpi or less, and the hybrid Eras font at 601 dpi or less. The revised Optima and ITC Eras font files, which are non-hybrid fonts, include only the typographically-correct character set.

Fonts with Revised Menu Names

Font	Package	Notes
Aachen Bold	34	
Adobe Garamond Expert	101	Windows only
AG Book Rounded	303	Windows only
American Typewriter	10	
Americana Extra Bold	68	
Antique Olive 1	82	
Antique Olive 2	107	
Arnold Boecklin	90	
Benguiat, ITC	11	Windows only
Benguiat Gothic	178	
Bodoni 1 (Poster)	26	
Bodoni 2 (Poster)	118	Windows only
Brush Script	33	Windows only
Caslon	53	Macintosh only
Caslon Open Face	72	Windows only
Century Old Style	22	Windows only
Clarendon Light	64	Macintosh only
Dom Casual	91	Windows only
Eras, ITC	56	Windows only
Eurostile 1	44	Windows only
Fette Fraktur	90	
Fette Fraktur Dfr	90	
Folio	93	Macintosh only
Franklin Gothic	23	
Franklin Gothic 2	103	
Freestyle Script	34	
Friz Quadrata	11	Windows only
Frutiger	73	
Futura 1	39	
Futura 2	46	
Goudy	54	Macintosh only
Grotesque	299	
Helvetica Black	13	
Helvetica Compressed	50	
Helvetica Condensed	14	
Helvetica Inserat	90	
Helvetica Light	13	
Helvetica Neue 1	59	
Helvetica Neue 2	60	
Helvetica Neue 3	61	

Imago	217	Windows only
Hiroshige	89	
Kabel, ITC	57	
Letter Gothic	27	Windows only
Memphis	49	
New Baskerville	18	Windows only
New Caledonia	66	
News Gothic	30	Windows only
Peignot	65	Macintosh only
Serifa	71	
Stempel	75	
Stone Informal	42	Macintosh only
Stone Sans	41	Macintosh only
Stone Serif	40	Macintosh only
Tiffany Heavy	31	
Univers	37	Macintosh only
Univers Condensed	38	Macintosh only
Universal Greek/News	78	Windows only
University Roman	34	
VAG Rounded	95	

Font Creation and Editing Utilities

The following applications can be used to create or modify Type 1 fonts:

- FontMonger
  Adobe Software Corporation
  (800) 783-2737
  Converts Type 1, Type 3, and TrueType fonts between Macintosh and Windows file formats. Enables you to add fractions or composite characters to fonts. Contains drawing tools for creating and editing character outlines. Available for the Macintosh and Windows.
- Fontographer
  Macromedia
  (800) 989-3762
  Font creation and editing utility for Type 1 and TrueType fonts. Fontographer for the Macintosh also supports creating and editing Type 3 and multiple master fonts. Available for the Macintosh and Windows.

MICR and OCR Font Specifications

Adobe distributes one Magnetic Ink Character Recognition (MICR) and two Optical Character Recognition (OCR) typefaces in package number 58. The MICR, OCR-A, and OCR-B fonts are all monospaced characters, except for the alternate "m" character included with OCR-B.

Adobe's MICR, OCR-A, and OCR-B fonts conform to the following industry standards:

- MICR (12 point) conforms to ANSII (American National Standards Institute) X#.2-1970 (R1976)
- OCR-A conforms to ANSI X3.17-1981 (size I)
- OCR-B conforms to ISO (International Organization for Standardization) 1073/II-1976 (E) with 1976 corrections ("letterpress" design, size I)

The ANSI number includes the year the standard was enacted. Revisions since the standard was enacted are indicated by a revision (R) date. Industry standards may have changed since the font's creation or latest revision.

WINDOWS

TrueType Fonts in Windows General Information

The following is a brief overview of TrueType fonts and their features, including comparison with PostScript fonts.

TRUETYPE VS. POSTSCRIPT

TrueType fonts are composed in the TrueImage page description language and are described using quadratic splines. PostScript fonts are composed in the PostScript page description language and are described using Bezier curves. Quadratic splines draw more quickly, but Bezier curves print more defined curves.

A TrueType font is composed of a *.ttf file (the actual font file) and a *.fot file. The *.fot file points to the location of the *.ttf file and contains the font's hinting information. The font files are usually stored in the Fonts directory in the Windows directory (Windows 95) or in the Windows\System directory (Windows 3.1x).

A PostScript Type 1 font is composed of a *.pfm (screen) font file and a *.pfb (printer) font file. PostScript Type 1 font files are installed in the Psfonts directory by default, but you can store them in another location using a font manager (e.g., Adobe Type Manager, FontMinder).

To install a TrueType font in Windows 95:

1. Open the Fonts Control Panel.
2. Choose File > Install New Font.
3. In the Add Fonts dialog box, specify the drive and directory where the fonts you want to add are located.
4. Select the fonts you want to install from the List of Fonts, then click OK.

To install a TrueType font in Windows 3.1x:

1. Open the Fonts Control Panel.
2. Click Add.
3. Specify the drive and directory where the fonts you want to add are located.
4. Select the fonts you want to install from the list of available fonts, then click OK.

DISPLAY AND PRINTING

TrueType fonts are designed to display and print clearly at any point size. When you print TrueType fonts to a PostScript printer, the printer driver usually converts them to PostScript-compatible fonts (e.g., Type 1). When the driver converts the fonts from the TrueImage language to the PostScript language, some font information may be lost or altered slightly, including font hinting and stroke widths.

However, when you print to a TrueImage PostScript printer, which uses native TrueType information, or to a printer containing a TrueType rasterizer (e.g., Apple LaserWriter Pro 600 and 630, Apple Personal LaserWriter NTR), the driver does not convert the fonts, enabling them to print with no alteration.

PCL printer drivers send TrueType font information directly to the printer. Some PCL printer drivers (e.g., LaserJet II & III, LaserJet 4) enable you to send TrueType fonts to the printer as bitmapped images instead. Consult your printer driver documentation for instructions.

When both the TrueType and PostScript version of the same font are installed, you may get unexpected display and printing results (e.g., unexpected character spacing, unexpected line and page breaks) because a PostScript font's character spacing may not be identical to an equivalent TrueType font's character spacing. When you will be printing to a non-PostScript (e.g., PCL) or TrueImage device, TrueType fonts provide the most accurate on-screen representation of the printed output. When you will be printing to a PostScript device, composing and viewing a document using the PostScript font and ATM will provide the most accurate on-screen representation of the printed output.

HINTING

Hints are instructions built into outline fonts that enable character shapes, especially subtle curves printed at small point sizes and low resolutions, to print as close to the designed character shape as possible. TrueType fonts contain complex hinting information. TrueType fonts can hint each character, different sizes of a character, and rotated text.

WIN.INI FILE

When you add a font, the Fonts Control Panel adds a line to the [fonts] section of the Win.ini file that references the TrueType font name and the corresponding *.fot file. For example:

```
[fonts]
Arial (TrueType)=ARIAL.FOT
```

Windows uses the *.fot file to locate the *.ttf file. Both the *.fot file and its corresponding *.ttf file must be installed for each entry in the [fonts] section for Windows to display or print the font as expected.

SYSTEM PERFORMANCE

Generally, the more fonts you install on your system, the longer it will take to start applications and perform commands (e.g., Open, Print). Also, since each added font requires a reference in the Win.ini file, a large number of fonts can cause the Win.ini file to grow too large. The Win.ini file has a maximum allowable file size of 64K, but keeping it 32K or smaller enables your system to run more efficiently and may prevent errors. When the size of the Win.ini file exceeds 32K, Windows or applications running in Windows may behave unpredictably.

RAM CACHE

Windows creates a RAM cache (i.e., memory reserved for screen font display) to store TrueType font glyphs as they are used, which requires less memory than storing an entire font.

MAC OS

TrueType Fonts on the Macintosh General Information

The following is a brief overview of TrueType fonts and their features, including a comparison with PostScript fonts.

TRUETYPE FONTS VS. POSTSCRIPT FONTS

TrueType fonts are composed in the TrueImage page description language and are described using quadratic splines, while PostScript fonts are composed in the Post-Script page description language and are described using Bezier curves. Quadratic splines draw more quickly, but Bezier curves print more defined curves.

A TrueType font is composed of a single file that is used for both display and printing. TrueType fonts icons display in the Finder as a dog-eared page with three letter "A"s in progressively larger sizes, and their filenames do not include a point size.

A PostScript Type 1 font has two components: a bitmap (screen) font file and an outline (printer) font file. PostScript bitmap font icons appear in the Finder as a dog-eared page with the letter "A," and their filenames include a point size (e.g., Times 10, Geneva 14). Adobe PostScript outline font icons appear in the Finder as a letter "A" in front of horizontal lines. Outline fonts created by other companies may have different icons.

On the Macintosh, both TrueType and PostScript Type 1 bitmap font files are stored in suitcases. PostScript Type 1 outline font files are stored loose in the same folder you store your suitcases in.

To install a TrueType font in the default location, copy the font file or suitcase from the original disk to the Fonts folder in the System Folder. You can also install font files in other locations using a font manager (e.g., Adobe Type Manager 4.0, Symantec Suitcase).

DISPLAY AND PRINTING

TrueType fonts are designed to display and print clearly at any point size. When you print TrueType fonts to a QuickDraw printer (e.g., Apple StyleWriter, Hewlett Packard DeskJet), the QuickDraw information used by the Macintosh for display is sent directly to the printer. When you print TrueType fonts to a PostScript printer, the printer driver usually converts them to PostScript-compatible fonts (e.g., Type 1). During this conversion some font information may be lost or altered slightly, including font hinting and stroke widths. However, when you print to a TrueImage

PostScript printer, which uses native TrueType information, or to a printer containing a TrueType rasterizer (e.g., Apple LaserWriter Pro 600 and 630, Apple Personal LaserWriter NTR), the driver does not convert the fonts, enabling them to print with no alteration.

If both the TrueType and PostScript version of the same font are installed, you may get unexpected display and printing results (e.g., unexpected character spacing, unexpected line and page breaks) because a PostScript font's character spacing may not be identical to an equivalent TrueType font's character spacing. If you will be printing to a QuickDraw or TrueImage device, TrueType fonts provide the most accurate representation on screen of the printed output. If you will be printing to a PostScript device, composing and viewing a document using the PostScript font and ATM will provide the most accurate representation on screen of the printed output.

HINTING

Hints are instructions built into outline fonts that enable character shapes, especially subtle curves printed at small point sizes and low resolutions, to print as close to the designed character shape as possible. TrueType fonts contain complex hinting information: they can hint each character, different sizes of a character, and rotated text.

RESOURCES

Every Macintosh file contains resources, which are components of the file that contain programming information. TrueType fonts have an SFNT resource and a FOND resource. The SFNT resource contains scaleable outline data and advanced typographic functions (e.g., automatic glyph substitution for fractions and ligatures, alternate character styles, kerning and tracking, optical alignment, multiple design styles, and variable width and weight). The FOND resource specifies fractional character widths, pair kern information, and the font's name.

PostScript Type 1 and Type 3 Fonts General Information

PostScript fonts are available in a variety of formats, the most common of which are the Type 1 and Type 3 formats. Adobe Corporation developed the PostScript Type 1 font specification, which was originally a proprietary format, and produces and distributes many Type 1 typefaces. Adobe released the Type 1 font specification to third-party font manufacturers provided that all Type 1 fonts adhere to the PostScript Type 1 font specification. Adobe also developed the Type 3 specification and made it available to third-party font manufacturers, but has never produced or distributed Type 3 fonts.

TYPE 1 FONTS

Type 1 fonts contain defined character shapes in an encoded PostScript format and contain hints in their character definitions. Hinting enables font outlines to be reproduced (e.g., printed) while maintaining the font's shape at low resolutions. For example, hinting improves the printed appearance of small text printed to a 300dpi PostScript printer.

Advantages of Type 1 fonts include:

- Outline (printer) font files contain more precise definitions than Type 3 outline font files, enabling Type 1 fonts to print with greater detail.
- Support residing in a printer's ROM, enabling you to print faster.
- Compatible with Adobe Type Manager (ATM), which creates smooth display at any point size using the Type 1 outline font file.
- Compatible with Adobe Type Reunion, which organizes fonts by family in application font menus.
- Require less printer memory and download faster than Type 3 fonts.

TYPE 3 FONTS

Type 3 fonts contain user-defined character shapes in standard PostScript format, which includes the BuildGlyph or BuildChar values in the font dictionary.

Advantages of Type 3 fonts include:

- Character shapes defined using ordinary PostScript language routines, so they are easy to create.
- Support characters described using complex composite characters, gray strokes, and gray fills.

DISTINGUISHING TYPE 1 FROM TYPE 3 FONTS

You can distinguish PostScript Type 1 and Type 3 fonts by comparing font file icons, comparing display, checking the font file's PostScript code in a text editor, or checking the font file's resource fork using a resource editing application (e.g., ResEdit).

To determine if your font is a Type 1 or a Type 3 font:

Open the folder containing the font's outline file (e.g., the Fonts folder in the System Folder). View the files by icon by choosing View > By Icon. An Adobe Type 1 font file icon displays a hollow capital letter "A" on a background of horizontal lines. Type 3 font files, TrueType font files, and Type 1 font files from a vendor other than Adobe display with another icon.

OR: With ATM enabled, open an application, type some text and apply a font size that does not have a corresponding bitmap (screen) font installed (e.g., 73 point) or view the font at a high magnification (e.g., 400%). Because ATM smoothes only Type 1 fonts, Type 3 fonts appear jagged (i.e., bitmapped).

OR: Open the font's outline file in a text editor (e.g., Microsoft Word). If the open file contains no text, the font is a Type 1 font. If the file contains text (i.e., PostScript code), search for the first occurrence of "FontType". If the font type is "3 def", the font is a Type 3 font.

OR: Open the font's outline file in a resource editing application (e.g., ResEdit). Type 1 font files contain font data in the Resource fork. Type 3 font files contain font data in the Data fork, so Type 3 font files contain a small amount of data (e.g., only the POST resource) in the Resource fork.

Adobe Type On Call®

Unexpected Results

MAC OS / WINDOWS

Browser Does Not Display Typeface Sample and Toolbar Buttons Are Dimmed

ISSUE

After you launch the Adobe Type Browser 2.2 or earlier to view and print typeface samples, no text sample of a type family appears. The Browser toolbar buttons (i.e., Display, Text, Font Info, Print, Purchase) are dimmed.

SOLUTION

Select an individual typeface in the Adobe Type Browser, rather than a typeface family:

1. Double-click a typeface family name (e.g., Adobe Garamond) to display the individual typefaces within the family.
2. Select a typeface (e.g., Semibold) within the family.

ADDITIONAL INFORMATION

In the Adobe Type Browser 2.2 or earlier, you must select an individual typeface to view a typeface sample and access the toolbar buttons. The Browser toolbar buttons (i.e., Display, Text, Font Info, Print, Purchase) are dimmed when a type family or package, instead of an individual typeface, is selected.

To select a typeface family in the Adobe Type Browser 2.0 on the Macintosh, which defaults to the Help menu, choose View > Families.

Can't Copy Black-and-White Initial Caps Files from Type on Call 4.1

ISSUE

After you unlock then copy an Aridi Initial Caps package (e.g., Aridi Initial Caps 1) from the Type On Call 4.1 CD-ROM, Type On Call copies the color Initial Cap files, but not the black-and-white files.

SOLUTION

Copy the black-and-white Initial Cap files from the Initial Caps installation disks, available from Adobe Customer Services.

ADDITIONAL INFORMATION

Because of disk space limitations, the Type On Call 4.1 CD-ROM includes only the color Initial Caps files, and not the black-and-white files. The Initial Caps installation disks include both the color and the black-and-white Initial Caps files.

Type On Call 3.x Accept Button Dimmed After Entering Access Code

ISSUE

The Adobe Type On Call 3.0x Accept button is dimmed after you enter an access code to unlock fonts.

SOLUTIONS

Do one or more of the following:

A. Reenter the access key exactly as it was generated by the Type On Call unlocking facility.

B. Make sure the Customer Key that displays in the Type On Call Control Panel is the same Customer Key used to generate the access key.

C. Obtain a new access key from the Type On Call unlocking facility. Do not close the Type On Call Control Panel before you enter the new access key.

D. Upgrade to Type On Call 4.0 or later, then unlock and install the fonts from Type On Call 4.0.

ADDITIONAL INFORMATION

Unless the Access key from the Type On Call database is entered exactly as it was generated by the Type On Call unlocking facility, the Accept button in the Type On Call control panel is dimmed.

If the Customer Key that displays in the Type On Call Control Panel does not exactly match the Customer Key the access key was created with, the access key is invalid and the Accept button remains dimmed. Entering a new access key generated from the displayed Customer Key may enable the Accept button.

You must enter an access key for Type On Call 3.0x before closing the Type On Call Control Panel. If you close the control panel, if your Macintosh shuts down unexpectedly (e.g., freeze, system error), or if you restart your Macintosh before you enter the access key, the access key becomes invalid and you must obtain a new one.

Type On Call 4.0 and later use the Adobe Purchaser, which you can close without invalidating your access keys, instead of a control panel to unlock and copy fonts.

MAC OS

Put Fonts Here Button Dimmed in Purchaser for Type On Call 4.0

ISSUE

After you click the Choose Folder button in the Adobe Purchaser 4.0 Preferences dialog box, Purchaser dims the Put Fonts Here button.

SOLUTIONS

Press the Option key while clicking on the Choose Folder button in the Preferences dialog box.

OR: Use Extensions Manager, which is included with System 7.5x, to disable Norton Utilities Directory Assistance II. Or, remove the Norton Utilities Directory Assistance II system extension document from the Extensions folder in the System Folder, then restart the Macintosh.

NOTE: Other installed extensions or control panels may cause Purchaser to dim the Put Fonts Here button. Run Type On Call and Purchaser with all extensions off to verify that added extensions or control panels are not the cause. To turn all extensions off upon startup in System 7, restart the computer while holding the Shift key until the message "Welcome to Macintosh. Extensions Off." appears.

ADDITIONAL INFORMATION

Directory Assistance II, which is included with Symantec Norton Utilities, is an extension that modifies dialog boxes. Holding down the Option key while accessing a dialog box in any application disables Directory Assistance II.

Application Errors

WINDOWS

Error "...not using your original CD-ROM" Unlocking Fonts in Type on Call 4.1

ISSUE

After entering your access key and clicking Unlock in Adobe Purchaser's Registration Order window, Type on Call 4.1 returns the error "You are not using your original CD-ROM."

SOLUTION

Remove Type On Call 4.1, select another video driver (e.g., Standard VGA), reinstall Type On Call 4.1, then obtain new access codes for previously unlocked fonts:

1. Insert the Type On Call CD-ROM into the CD-ROM drive.
2. Launch the Type On Call Backup/Restore Utility (RESTBKUP.EXE) from the Type On Call CD-ROM.
3. In the Type On Call Backup/Restore Utility dialog box, click Uninstall.
4. In the TOC Uninstall dialog box, click OK.
5. After successfully removing Type On Call, click OK in the Success window, then click Exit.
6. Right-click on the desktop, then choose Properties from the pop-up menu.
7. In the Display Properties dialog box, click the Settings tab, then click the Change Display Type button.
8. Note the Adapter Type, then click Change.
9. In the Select Device dialog box, select the Show All Devices option.
10. Select the Standard Display Types option from the top of the Manufacturers scroll box.
11. Select the Standard Display Adapter (VGA) option from the Models scroll box, then click OK.
12. Note the Monitor Type, then click Change.
13. In the Select Device dialog box, select the Show All Devices option.
14. Select the Standard Monitor Types option from the top of the Manufacturers scroll box.
15. Select another video driver (e.g., Standard VGA 640x-480) from the Models scroll box, then click OK.
16. Restart Windows 95.
17. Reinstall Type On Call 4.1, then select your original video driver.
18. Contact Adobe Customer Services to obtain new access keys for previously unlocked fonts.

ADDITIONAL INFORMATION

The Type On Call 4.1 Installer (INSTALL.EXE) is incompatible with some video drivers (e.g., Cirrus Logic, Trident, Trio, STB) in Windows 95. After installing Type On Call 4.1 in Windows 95, entering your access key and clicking Unlock in Adobe Purchaser's Registration Order window causes Type On Call to return the error "You are not using your original CD-ROM" when an incompatible video driver is installed. Temporarily selecting a compatible video driver (e.g., Standard VGA) enables you to successfully install Type On Call 4.1.

Error "Maximum of 999 orders" When Starting Purchaser in Windows NT 4.0

ISSUE

When you start the Adobe Purchaser after installing Type On Call 4.x in Windows NT 4.0, the Purchaser returns the error, "There is a maximum of 999 orders. Contact Adobe for assistance."

SOLUTION

Create a file named "Pend.000" in the Toc4/Pend directory or "Prev.000" in the Toc4/Prev directory:

1. Open the Pend or Prev subdirectory in the Toc4 directory. 2. Choose View > Options. 3. Cick the View tab in the Options dialog box.
4. Deselect Hide File Extensions For Known File Type, then click OK.
5. Choose File > New > Text Document.
6. Name the file "Pend.000" or "Prev.000".
7. Click Yes when the Rename dialog box appears with the alert, "If you change a filename extension, the file may become unusable."

ADDITIONAL INFORMATION

When you start the Purchaser, it looks for Pend.* and Prev.* (e.g., Pend.001, Prev.001) files in the Pend and Prev subdirectories in the Toc4 directory to determine the number of the last order. When the Purchaser cannot locate either of these files, it may return the error, "There is a maximum of 999 orders." When you add a Pend.000 file to the Pend directory or a Prev.000 file to the Prev directory, the Purchaser starts without returning the error and creates a sequential pending order (i.e., Pend.001 or Prev001). Creating a Pend.000 file or a Prev.000 file will not affect future font orders (e.g., 30 free fonts included with Type On Call).

MAC OS

Error "Error while accessing [fontname]" When Copying Fonts from Type On Call 4.0

ISSUE

When you unlock and copy fonts, or copy previously unlocked fonts from the Type On Call 4.0 CD-ROM, Type On Call returns the error, "Error while accessing [fontname]."

SOLUTIONS

Copy the fonts into a destination (e.g., Adobe Type On Call Products folder) other than the Fonts folder.

OR: When the Adobe Type On Call Products folder created during Type On Call installation does not exist on the targeted hard disk, create a new destination folder. To change the destination folder for copied fonts:

1. Open the Adobe Purchaser located on the Type On Call CD-ROM.
2. Choose Setup > Software Setup.
3. In the Preferences dialog box, click Choose Folder.
4. Select the Adobe Type On Call Products folder or the desired destination folder.
5. Click Put Fonts Here, then click OK to close the Preferences dialog box.
6. Recopy the desired fonts.

ADDITIONAL INFORMATION

The Finder application copies files from one volume to another, and after copying screen fonts into the Fonts folder in the System Folder, makes the new fonts available to applications. When unlocking and coping fonts, or copying previously unlocked fonts, from the Type On Call 4.0 CD-ROM into the Fonts folder in the System Folder, the Finder attempts to copy the fonts from one volume to another and make the fonts available to applications at the same time, resulting in the system error "Error while accessing [fontname]."

To prevent the "Error while accessing [fontname]." error, enable the Finder to copy the fonts from one volume to another then make the fonts available to applications as two separate tasks by choosing a destination folder other than the Fonts folder for copying unlocked fonts. After copying fonts onto the destination volume, move the fonts from the chosen destination folder into the Fonts folder.

Error "-43" or "AFM File Not on CD-ROM" Copying Multiple Master Font from Type On Call

ISSUE

When copying a multiple master font from the Type On Call 4.x Purchaser, the error message "Error -43 File Not Found" or "Sorry, but the AFM file for this font is not on the CD-ROM. Please contact Adobe Systems if you need the AFM file." occurs. Single master fonts copy without error.

SOLUTION

Disable the Copy AFMs option in the Type On Call 4.x Purchaser, then copy the multiple master font:

1. In the Purchaser, choose Setup > Software Setup (Type On Call 4.0x) or Setup > Setup Information (Type On Call 4.1).
2. Deselect Copy AFMs, then click OK.

ADDITIONAL INFORMATION

Because multiple master fonts do not have AFM files, the error "Error -43 File Not Found" or "Sorry, but the AFM file for this font is not on the CD-ROM. Please contact Adobe Systems if you need the AFM file." occurs when you copy multiple master fonts from the Type On Call 4.x Purchaser with the Copy AFMs option selected.

Installation Issues

WINDOWS

Error "Win.ini is Dangerously Large" Installing Fonts from Type On Call 4.0

ISSUE

When you try to copy and install unlocked products from the Adobe Purchaser on the Type On Call 4.0x CD-ROM, the Purchaser returns the error "Win.ini is Dangerously Large. Files in this package will only be copied." The Purchaser copies the font files to the hard disk in the specified directory (e.g., C:\Psfonts).

SOLUTIONS

Use Adobe Type Manager (ATM) to install the fonts copied from Type On Call 4.0x.

OR: If you have fewer than 200 fonts installed in ATM, make sure the Win.ini "softfonts=xxx" references correctly reflect the number of installed fonts by removing all your installed fonts from ATM, removing font references from the Win.ini and Atm.ini files, then re-adding your fonts in ATM:

In ATM 4.0:

1. Make backup copies of the Win.ini and Atm.ini files.
2. In ATM, export your sets (ATM Deluxe only) and remove all installed fonts. For instructions, see Additional Information.
3. Open the Win.ini file, located in the Windows directory, in a text editor that can save in text-only format (e.g., Notepad, WordPad).
4. Delete any lines that begin with "softfont" (e.g., softfonts=20).
5. Delete all lines that refer to an MFD file (e.g., ADMFDFile=C:\Windows\Ad434af1\ Mfd).
6. Save the Win.ini file in text-only format.
7. Open the Atm.ini file, located in the Windows directory, in a text editor that can save in text-only format (e.g., NotePad, WordPad).
8. Delete any lines in the [Fonts] section (e.g., "Helvetica=C:\Psfonts\Pfm\Hv______.pfm; C:\Psfonts\Hv-______.pfb").
9. Save the Atm.ini file in text-only format.
10. Delete all Atmfonts.qlc files, then restart Windows.
11. In ATM, re-add the problem fonts. For instructions, see Additional Information.
12. Choose Start > Find > Files or Folders, then locate the Win.ini file in the Windows directory. Check the size of the Win.ini file in the search results window and make sure it is smaller than 32K. If the Win.ini file is greater than 32K, make a backup of the file, then open the original Win.ini in a text editor that can save in text-only format and remove lines or sections no longer needed.

In ATM 3.0x:

1. Make backup copies of the Win.ini and Atm.ini files.
2. In the ATM Control Panel, select all fonts in the Installed ATM Fonts list and click Remove.
3. In the Remove Fonts dialog box, select No Confirmation to Remove Fonts if you don't want the dialog box to appear for each font you remove, then click Yes or Yes to All. Do not select Delete Fonts from Disk unless you want to delete the font files from your system.
4. Open the Win.ini file, located in the Windows directory, in a text editor that can save in text-only format (e.g., NotePad, Windows Write).
5. Delete any lines that begin with "softfont" (e.g., softfonts=200).
6. When using Windows 95, delete all lines that refer to an MFD file (e.g., ADMFDFile=c:\windows\ad434af1-\mfd).
7. Save the Win.ini file in text-only format.
8. Open the Atm.ini file, located in the Windows directory, in a text editor that can save in text-only format (e.g., NotePad, Windows Write).
9. Delete any lines in the [Fonts] section (e.g., "Helvetica=c:\psfonts\pfm\HV______.PFM; c:\psfonts\HV-______.PFB").
10. Save the Atm.ini file in text-only format.
11. Delete all Atmfonts.qlc files, then restart Windows.
12. Open the ATM Control Panel, then click Add.
13. In the Add Fonts dialog box, locate the drive and directory where your fonts are located (e.g., C:\psfonts\pfm, A:\psfonts).
14. Select the fonts you want to install from the list of available fonts, then click Add.
15. Choose Start > Find > Files or Folders (Windows 95) or open File Manager and choose Search > Find (Windows 3.1x), then locate the Win.ini file in the Windows directory. Check the size of the Win.ini file in the search results window and make sure it is smaller than 32K. If the Win.ini file is larger than 32K, make a backup of the file, then open the original Win.ini in a text editor that can save in text-only format and remove lines or sections no longer needed.

ADDITIONAL INFORMATION

The Adobe Purchaser reads each [PostScript, port] section in the Win.ini file to locate any "softfonts=xxx" references when you try to copy and install font files. Regardless of the actual size of the Win.ini file, when any "softfonts=xxx" reference specifies a number of 200 or higher, the Purchaser returns the error "Win.ini is Dangerously Large. Files in this package will only be copied." Then the Adobe Purchaser copies unlocked fonts onto the hard disk but does not install them into ATM or into the Win.ini file. You can install the fonts in ATM after they have been copied.

When you have Autodownload selected in the Purchaser's Unlock and Copy dialog box and you have a Microsoft PostScript printer driver installed, the Purchaser adds a reference to the Win.ini file indicating the number and location of your font files for the Microsoft driver. A large number of font references can cause the Win.ini file to grow too large, which can cause a variety of system problems. The Win.ini file has a maximum allowable file size of 64K, but keeping it 32K or smaller enables your system to run more efficiently and may prevent errors. When the size of the Win.ini file exceeds 32K or 64K, Windows or applications running in Windows may behave unpredictably.

To export your sets in ATM Deluxe 4.0:

1. In ATM, click the Sets tab.
2. Select one or more sets to export.
3. Choose File > Export.
4. In the Export dialog box, specify a filename and location for the AFS file, then click Save.

To remove your fonts in ATM 4.0:

1. In the All Font Sets pane of the Sets tab (ATM Deluxe 4.0) or the Fonts tab (ATM 4.0), select the fonts you want to remove, then click Remove.
2. In the Remove Font dialog box, select the Remove Fonts from All Set and Master Font List option, select the Remove Font Files from Disk option if you are reinstalling your fonts from the original installation disks, then click Yes or Yes to All.

To re-add your fonts in ATM 4.0:

1. Click the Add Fonts tab (ATM Deluxe 4.0) or the Fonts tab (ATM 4.0), then select Browse for Fonts from the Source pop-up menu.
2. Navigate to the drive and directory where your fonts files are located (e.g., C:\Psfonts\Pfm, A:\Fontdisk).
3. Select the fonts you want to add from the Source pane scroll box then click Add.

To import your sets in ATM Deluxe 4.0:

1. With Browse for Fonts still selected in the Source pop-up menu, navigate to the drive and directory where your AFS file is located. ATM lists the sets you exported in the AFS file.
2. Select the sets you want to import, then click Add.
3. Remove any duplicate fonts outside your sets by selecting them and clicking Remove.

Error "File not found..." Installing Type On Call 4.1

ISSUE

After clicking an install language (e.g., English, French) when installing Type On Call 4.1 in Windows 95, the Type On Call Installer returns the error "File not found on CD-ROM drive."

SOLUTION

Remove Type On Call 4.1, select another video driver (e.g., Standard VGA), reinstall Type On Call 4.1, then obtain new access codes for previously unlocked fonts:

In Windows 95:

1. Insert the Type On Call CD-ROM into the CD-ROM drive.
2. Launch the Type On Call Backup/Restore Utility (Restbkup.exe) from the Type On Call CD-ROM.
3. In the Type On Call Backup/Restore Utility dialog box, click Uninstall.
4. In the TOC Uninstall dialog box, click OK.
5. After successfully removing Type On Call, click OK in the Success window, then click Exit.
6. Right-click on the desktop, then choose Properties from the pop-up menu.
7. In the Display Properties dialog box, click the Settings tab, then click the Change Display Type button.
8. Note the Adapter Type, then click Change.
9. In the Select Device dialog box, select the Show All Devices option.
10. Select the Standard Display Types option from the top of the Manufacturers scroll box.
11. Select the Standard Display Adapter (VGA) option from the Models scroll box, then click OK.
12. Note the Monitor Type, then click Change.
13. In the Select Device dialog box, select the Show All Devices option.
14. Select the Standard Monitor Types option from the top of the Manufacturers scroll box.
15. Select another video driver (e.g., Standard VGA 640x-480) from the Models scroll box, then click OK.
16. Restart Windows 95.
17. Reinstall Type On Call 4.1, then select your original video driver.
18. Contact Adobe Customer Services to obtain new access keys for previously unlocked fonts.

In Windows 3.1x:

1. Insert the Type On Call CD-ROM into the CD-ROM drive.
2. Launch the Type On Call Backup/Restore Utility (Restbkup.exe) from the Type On Call CD-ROM.
3. In the Type On Call Backup/Restore Utility dialog box, click Uninstall.
4. In the TOC Uninstall dialog box, click OK.
5. After successfully removing Type On Call, click OK in the Success window, then click Exit.
6. Make sure your Windows installation disks are available.
7. Make a backup copy of the System.ini file, located in the Windows directory.
8. In the Main group in Program Manager, double-click Windows Setup.
9. In Windows Setup, choose Options > Change System Settings.
10. In the Change System Settings dialog box, select VGA from the Display pop-up menu, then click OK.
11. Follow the on-screen instructions to install the VGA video driver, inserting Windows installation disks if prompted.
12. Restart Windows.
13. Reinstall Type On Call 4.1, then select your original video driver.
14. Contact Adobe Customer Services to obtain new access keys for previously unlocked fonts.

ADDITIONAL INFORMATION

The Type On Call 4.1 Installer (Install.exe) is incompatible with some video drivers (e.g., Cirrus Logic, Trident, Trio, STB) in Windows 95 and Windows 3.1x. When you install Type On Call 4.1 on a computer with an incompatible video driver, the error "File not found on CD-ROM drive" appears after you click an install language. Using a compatible video driver (e.g., Standard VGA) enables the Type On Call 4.1 Installer to successfully install Type On Call 4.1.

Error "Invalid Customer Key" Installing Type On Call 4.1

ISSUE

After an Adobe Customer Services representative enters your Customer Key in the Type On Call unlocking database, the Type On Call 4.1 Installer returns the error "Invalid Customer Key."

SOLUTION

Remove Type On Call 4.1, select another video driver (e.g., Standard VGA), reinstall Type On Call 4.1, then obtain new access codes for previously unlocked fonts:

1. Insert the Type On Call CD-ROM into the CD-ROM drive.
2. Launch the Type On Call Backup/Restore Utility (RESTBKUP.EXE) from the Type On Call CD-ROM.
3. In the Type On Call Backup/Restore Utility dialog box, click Uninstall.
4. In the TOC Uninstall dialog box, click OK.
5. After successfully removing Type On Call, click OK in the Success window, then click Exit.
6. Right-click on the desktop, then choose Properties from the pop-up menu.
7. In the Display Properties dialog box, click the Settings tab, then click the Change Display Type button.
8. Note the Adapter Type, then click Change.
9. In the Select Device dialog box, select the Show All Devices option.
10. Select the Standard Display Types option from the top of the Manufacturers scroll box.
11. Select the Standard Display Adapter (VGA) option from the Models scroll box, then click OK.
12. Note the Monitor Type, then click Change.
13. In the Select Device dialog box, select the Show All Devices option.
14. Select the Standard Monitor Types option from the top of the Manufacturers scroll box.
15. Select another video driver (e.g., Standard VGA 640x480) from the Models scroll box, then click OK.
16. Restart Windows 95.
17. Reinstall TOC 4.1, then select your original video driver.
18. Contact Adobe Customer Services to obtain new access keys for previously unlocked fonts.

ADDITIONAL INFORMATION

The Type On Call 4.1 Installer (INSTALL.EXE) is incompatible with some video drivers (e.g., Cirrus Logic, Trident, Trio, STB) in Windows 95. After unlocking your Type On Call 4.1 database, the Type On Call Installer returns the error "Invalid Customer Key" when an incompatible video driver is installed in Windows 95. Using a compatible video driver (e.g., Standard VGA) enables the Type On Call 4.1 Installer to successfully install Type On Call 4.1.

General Information

MAC OS

Suitcase Filename Designations in Font Packages

Some suitcases in 900-series typeface collections include a two- or three-letter designation (e.g., PS1, VP) at the end of the filename. These designation filenames indicate these suitcases include a different group of bitmap (screen) font files than the originally released suitcase (e.g., the suitcase Bodoni VP contains bitmap fonts only for Bodoni Poster Compressed, while the suitcase Bodoni 2 contains bitmap fonts for Bodoni Bold Condensed, Bodoni Book, Bodoni Book Italic, Bodoni Poster Compressed, and Bodoni Poster Italic). The following collections include suitcases with filename designations.

Special Font Package Designations

Pkg. #	Collection Name	Designation
900-00	Value Pack	VP
902	Type Basics	TB
903	Variety Pack	VR
904	Charleston Collection	CC
905	Jam Pack	JP
909	Originals Deluxe Sampler	ODS
951	Illustrator Fonts	AI
952	PostScript Supplement 1	PS1
953	PostScript Supplement 2	PS2
955	PostScript Supplement 3 Part 1	PS3
956	PostScript Supplement 3 Part 2	PS3
958	PostScript Supplement 4 Part 1	PS4
959	PostScript Supplement 4 Part 2	PS4
961	Premiere Fonts	AP

Adobe Type Manager®

The Deluxe version of Adobe Type Manager 4.0 software was released in February of 1997 for Mac OS and Windows platforms. Originally developed in the late 1980s to get the "jaggies" out of on-screen display and dot-matrix printers, ATM 4 has advanced now to incorporate font activation, font smoothing, font substitution and the ability to custom-organize all of your Type 1 and TrueType fonts. Millions of computer users on all platforms use ATM software to provide crisp, clear type at any point size on Adobe PostScript and non-PostScript printers alike.

Contents

Adobe Type Manager®

Feature Techniques

WINDOWS

Exporting Sets and Removing and Re-adding Fonts in ATM Deluxe 4.0

To troubleshoot font display or printing problems when using ATM Deluxe 4.0, you may need to remove all your installed fonts and reinstall them. Before you remove fonts, you may want to export your sets so you can reimport them after re-adding the fonts, rather than recreating the sets.

When you export sets, Adobe Type Manager (ATM) creates an ATM Font Set (AFS) file, which contains a list of the fonts included in the sets and their font file locations. An AFS file can contain information from one set or multiple sets. When you import a set, ATM confirms the location of the font files. If you have installed your font files in another location or moved them, you will need to specify the new location when importing a set.

To export your sets:

1. In ATM, click the Sets tab.
2. Select one or more sets to export.
3. Choose File > Export.
4. In the Export dialog box, specify a filename and location for the AFS file, then click Save.

To remove your fonts:

1. In the All Font Sets pane of the Sets tab, select the fonts you want to remove, then click Remove.
2. In the Remove Font dialog box, select Remove Fonts from All Set and Master Font List, select Remove Font Files from Disk if you are reinstalling your fonts from the original installation disks, then click Yes or Yes to All.

To re-add your fonts:

1. Click the Add Fonts tab, then select Browse for Fonts from the Source pop-up menu.
2. Navigate to the drive and directory where your fonts files are located (e.g., C:\Psfonts\Pfm, A:\Fontdisk).
3. Select the fonts you want to add from the Source pane scrollbox, then click Add.

To import your sets:

1. With Browse for Fonts still selected in the Source pop-up menu, navigate to the drive and directory where your AFS file is located. ATM lists the sets you exported in the AFS file.
2. Select the sets you want to import, then click Add.
3. Remove any duplicate fonts outside your sets by selecting them and clicking Remove.

ATM 3.02 and Earlier Control Panel Settings General Information

Adobe Type Manager (ATM) 3.02 and earlier have several settings that enable you to control and enhance ATM's performance.

VERSION NUMBER

The version number indicates which version is of Adobe Type Manager (ATM) is running (e.g., 3.02). If the version number displays "Inactive," ATM is disabled.

ON/OFF BUTTONS

The On and Off buttons turn ATM on or off. If you change this setting, you must exit and restart Windows for the change to take effect. When ATM is on, it displays Type 1 fonts on-screen and sends Type 1 fonts to your printer. When ATM is turned off, only fonts installed in other font managers (e.g., TrueType fonts installed in the Fonts Control Panel) appear on-screen and in font menus.

FONT CACHE

ATM's Font Cache is an allotment of memory that ATM uses to store font data. When ATM has insufficient memory in the Font Cache to create or display a font, the font appears bitmapped or does not display.

The default size of the Font Cache is 256K. You should increase this size to 512K or more when displaying a document that uses five or more typefaces or uses a multiple master typeface (e.g., Jenson, Ex Ponto, Tekton).

You can adjust the size of the font cache in the ATM Control Panel, clicking the up or down arrows to increase or decrease its size. The changes do not take effect until you restart Windows.

USE PREBUILT OR RESIDENT FONTS

The Use Prebuilt or Resident Fonts option enables ATM to use bitmap fonts installed in Windows and printer-resident fonts instead of ATM-installed fonts. Using prebuilt or resident fonts enables applications to display and print documents more quickly.

If an application supports auto-kerning, ATM-installed fonts will be kerned, but prebuilt or resident fonts will not.

Some printer-resident fonts look different than the ATM-installed Type 1 fonts. For example, ATM-installed Courier will look different than the Courier resident in Hewlett-Packard laser printers. If you want your document to use the ATM-installed font, deselect the Use Prebuilt or Resident Fonts option and restart Windows before working on a document or printing.

PRINT ATM FONTS AS GRAPHICS

When the Print ATM Fonts as Graphics option is selected, ATM sends fonts to the printer as graphic images and does not use downloadable fonts. Printing time may increase when using this option.

Setting Up ATM to Download Softfonts to PostScript Printers

To print PostScript fonts, the printer requires the PosScript font's file. Most PostScript printers have between 15 to 40 PostScript font files installed in their ROM (i.e., resident fonts). To print a non-resident PostScript font, you install the font's file on your system. When printing a non-resident PostScript font, your printer driver locates the PostScript font's file on your system, then downloads the font's file to your printer.

The method for setting up your system to download non-resident PostScript fonts, or softfonts, depends on which printer driver you are using. When using a Microsoft PostScript printer driver, you add softfont references to the Win.ini file. When using the Adobe PostScript printer driver (AdobePS), you add softfont references to the Atm.ini file, since it does not read softfont references in the Win.ini file for printing.

INSTALLING POSTSCRIPT FONTS

The Microsoft Windows PostScript printer driver (i.e., Pscript.drv), and printer drivers based on it (e.g., Lexps.drv), read softfont references in the [PostScript,<port>] section of the Win.ini file. When a font file is referenced as a softfont in the [PostScript,<port>] section of the Win.ini file, the Microsoft printer driver downloads the font to the printer when you print a document using that font. You can set up Adobe Type Manager (ATM) to automatically add font references to the Win.ini file when you add (i.e., install) fonts, or you can add softfont references manually.

When you add fonts, the options you select in ATM and the printer drivers you have installed determine what ATM adds to your Win.ini file. When you add fonts in ATM with an ATM download option selected, ATM adds font file references to each [PostScript,<port>] section of the Win.ini file that uses a separate port. If you have installed printers on different ports (e.g., LPT1, LPT2, FILE), regardless of whether these printers are connected to your computer, ATM adds a reference under each port section for every active font on your system. Each line ATM adds to your Win.ini file increases its file size. The Win.ini file has a maximum allowable file size of 64K, but keeping it 32K or smaller enables your system to run more efficiently and may prevent errors. When the size of the Win.ini file exceeds 32K or 64K, Windows or applications running in Windows may behave unpredictably.

USING ATM TO SET UP SOFTFONTS TO DOWNLOAD

You can set up ATM to automatically add softfont references to the Win.ini file. In ATM 4.0, you can specify whether ATM adds both metrics and outline file references, only metrics references, or neither. ATM 3.0x adds all softfont references, including both metrics and outline file references. When you have a Microsoft PostScript printer driver installed, ATM enables you to add font references to the Win.ini file.

To set up ATM 4.0 to automatically add font references to the Win.ini file:

1. In ATM, click the Settings tab, then click MS PostScript Driver.
2. Select one of the following options:
   - Mark as Autodownload

   When this option is selected, ATM adds metrics and outline file references to the Win.ini file for each [PostScript,<port>] section. Select this option to make sure your printer driver downloads fonts to the printer.
   - Mark Fonts as Resident in PostScript Printer

   When this option is selected, ATM adds only metrics references to the Win.ini file for each [PostScript,-<port>] section. Select this option for printer-resident fonts.
   - Mark as Not to Be Installed

   When this option is selected, ATM adds no softfont references to the Win.ini file for each [PostScript,<port>] section and sends only font characters required for printing to the printer. Select this option to minimize the file size of the Win.ini file.
3. Click OK.
4. Click the Add Fonts tab, select the fonts you want to add, then click Add.

To set up ATM 3.0x to automatically add font references to the Win.ini file:

1. In the ATM Control Panel, click Add.
2. In the Add Fonts dialog box, select the Autodownload for PostScript Driver option, select the fonts you want to add, then click Add.

MANUALLY SETTING UP SOFTFONTS TO DOWNLOAD

You can manually add softfont references to a [PostScript,-<port>] section of the Win.ini file. For example, when adding printer-resident fonts in ATM 3.0x, you can manually add references to font metrics files only. By manually adding only the softfont references you need, you can minimize the file size of the Win.ini file.

Before manually adding softfont references , determine the locations and filenames of your fonts. Font filename prefixes often do not contain the font's actual name (e.g., Akzidenz Grotesk font files begin with GF, Centaur font files begin with NR). See the document Fntnames.pdf on the Adobe Type On Call CD-ROM for a complete listing of Adobe font filenames.

To manually add softfont references to the Win.ini file:

1. Make a backup copy of the Win.ini file located in the Windows directory.
2. Open the original Win.ini file in a text editor that can save in text-only format (e.g., WordPad, Notepad, Windows Write).
3. Type the line "softfonts=x", where "x" is the number of font references you are adding, as the first line in the [PostScript,<port>] section for the printer to which you are printing (i.e., the first line after the section header, or the first line after the line "ATM=placeholder" if present).
4. Type softfont references for each font file in the format "softfontx=c:\psfonts\pfm\filename,c:\psfonts\filename", where "x" is the sequential number of the font reference. Type each new reference on a new line, and assign the next consecutive number to it. Do not add space characters between letter characters. For example:

```
[PostScript,LPT1]
softfonts=8
softfont1=c:\psfonts\pfm\gn______.pfm,c:\psfonts
  \gn______.pfb
softfont2=c:\psfonts\pfm\gnb_____.pfm,c:\psfonts
  \gnb_____.pfb
softfont3=c:\psfonts\pfm\gnbi____.pfm,c:\psfonts
  \gnbi____.pfb
softfont4=c:\psfonts\pfm\gni_____.pfm,c:\psfonts
  \gni_____.pfb
softfont5=c:\psfonts\pfm\mtr_____.pfm,c:\psfonts
  \mtr_____.pfb
softfont6=c:\psfonts\pfm\mtb_____.pfm,c:\psfonts
  \mtb_____.pfb
softfont7=c:\psfonts\pfm\mtbi____.pfm,c:\psfonts
  \mtbi____.pfb
softfont8=c:\psfonts\pfm\mti_____.pfm,c:\psfonts
  \mti_____.pfb
```

5. Save the Win.ini file in text-only format.
6. Restart Windows.

Troubleshooting Jagged PostScript Font Display with ATM 3.0x in Windows

Adobe Type Manager (ATM) 3.0x creates smooth display of PostScript fonts at any point size using the PostScript font's outline (printer) font file. When ATM cannot display a PostScript font, the font displays bitmapped (i.e., jagged) or text formatted with the font does not display.

A variety of causes can prevent ATM from displaying a PostScript font—the outline font file may be damaged or unavailable (e.g., not installed, not in the expected location), or ATM may be damaged or unable to locate one of its support files. To determine what's preventing your fonts from displaying smoothly, use the troubleshooting steps below.

OVERVIEW OF POSTSCRIPT FONTS AND ATM

Before you begin troubleshooting, you should understand the difference between PostScript Type 1 fonts and TrueType fonts.

PostScript Type 1 fonts are composed of two files: a Printer Font Metrics (PFM) file and a Printer Font Binary (PFB) file. Multiple master base fonts and instances use a Multiple Master Metrics (MMM) file instead of a PFM file, and a multiple master instance creates a PostScript Printer Stub (PSS) file.

PFM and MMM files, located in the Psfonts\Pfm subdirectory, are used to display the font on screen. PFB (or "outline") and PSS files, located in the Psfonts directory, are used for printing and by ATM to display fonts smoothly on screen.

Unlike PostScript fonts, TrueType fonts consist of only one font file, used for both display and printing. You can install and remove TrueType fonts in the Fonts Control Panel.

Without ATM, Windows displays PostScript fonts by scaling the PFM file. Resizing a bitmap font reproduces the general shape of the font, but may cause the font to display with extreme pixelation (i.e., jagged), depending on the size of available bitmap font files and the requested display size. TrueType fonts, on the other hand, display smoothly at any point size.

To PostScript prevent fonts from displaying with extreme pixelation, ATM rasterizes (i.e., converts outline font information into a scaleable bitmap image) PostScript PFB files. ATM supports rasterizing PostScript Type 1 fonts that adhere to the Adobe Type 1 font specification. ATM does not support rasterizing PostScript Type 3 fonts, TrueType fonts, and PostScript fonts that do not adhere to the Adobe Type 1 font specification.

MAKING SURE ATM IS ACTIVE

Your first step in troubleshooting jagged PostScript font display in Windows is to determine if ATM is active. PostScript fonts added in ATM will display jagged when ATM is turned off.

To make sure ATM is active, open the ATM Control Panel by choosing Start > Programs > Main (Windows 95) or by double-clicking the ATM Control Panel icon in the Main Group in Program Manager (Windows 3.1x). When ATM is active, the ATM version (e.g., 3.02) displays in the upper-left corner of the ATM Control Panel. If ATM is active, move to the Defining the Problem section.

When ATM is inactive, "Inactive" displays instead of the version number. To activate ATM, do one or more of the following:

A. Select On, exit the ATM Control Panel, and restart Windows. Then reopen the ATM Control Panel to see if ATM is active.

B. Make sure all the ATM files are installed. The ATM Installer installs files into the Windows and the Windows\System directories. Make sure the following files are installed in the Windows directory:

```
Atmcntrl.exe
Atm.ini
```

Make sure the following files are installed in the Windows\System subdirectory:

```
Atm32.dll
Atm16.dll
Atmsys.drv
```

If any of these files is missing, or if some of your files have a different extension (e.g., *.ndl instead of *.dll), exit Windows, delete the installed ATM files, and reinstall ATM from the original installation disks.

C. Make sure ATM is referenced in the System.ini file. In addition to adding files to the Windows and Windows\System directories, the ATM installer modifies the System.ini file so that ATM is loaded when you start Windows. Make sure the System.ini contains the correct ATM information:

1. Open the System.ini file, located in the Windows directory, in a text editor that can save in text-only format (e.g., Windows Write).
2. In the [Boot] section, modify the line:

   ```
   system.drv=system.drv
   ```

   to read:

   ```
   system.drv=atmsys.drv
   ```

3. In the [Boot] section, add the line:

   ```
   atm.system.drv=system.drv
   ```

4. Save the System.ini file in text-only format, then restart Windows.

D. Reinstall ATM from the original installation disks. When ATM is installed correctly, it is loaded and active when you start Windows.

DEFINING THE PROBLEM

Once you've made sure ATM is active, your next step is to determine the extent of the problem. Because you'll be removing all your installed ATM fonts in the next section and you won't have fonts installed to test with, it's important you define the problem completely before you begin troubleshooting.

Begin isolating the problem by applying another font, and then comparing how different fonts display. Does only one PostScript font display jagged, do multiple PostScript font display jagged, or do all PostScript fonts display jagged?

If one or more PostScript font displays jagged, but others display smoothly, the problem may be caused by a damaged font, or unavailable font files. If all your PostScript fonts display jagged, ATM is the most likely cause; it may be damaged or unable to locate one of its support files.

Before troubleshooting your fonts or ATM, follow the steps in the Removing All Fonts and Font References section to remove old font information.

REMOVING ALL FONTS AND FONT REFERENCES

Once you have determined the extent of the problem, your next step is to do some general Windows font troubleshooting by removing all your fonts from ATM, then removing all font references from the Win.ini file and the Atm.ini file. Once you've cleaned up the Win.ini file and the Atm.ini file, you'll re-add your fonts a few at a time to continue troubleshooting.

Remove All Installed ATM Fonts

Font troubleshooting includes a clean installation of fonts. Remove your old fonts from ATM first:

1. In the ATM Control Panel, select all the installed fonts from the Installed ATM Fonts list.
2. Click Remove.
3. In the Remove Fonts dialog box, select No Confirmation to Remove Fonts if you don't want the dialog box to appear for each font you remove, then click Yes or Yes to All. Do not select Delete Fonts from Disk unless you want to delete the font files from your system.

Remove Font References in the Win.ini File

1. Open the Win.ini file, located in the Windows directory, in a text editor that can save in text-only format (e.g., NotePad, Windows Write).
2. Delete all lines that begin "softfont" (e.g., softfonts=20).
3. In Windows 95, delete all lines that refer to an MFD file (e.g., ADMFDFile=C:\Windows\Ad434af1.mfd).
4. Save the Win.ini file in text-only format.

Remove Font References in the Atm.ini File

1. Open the Atm.ini file, located in the Windows directory, in a text editor that can save in text-only format (e.g., Windows Write).
2. Delete any lines in the [Fonts] section (e.g., "Helvetica=C:\Psfonts\Pfm\Hv______.pfm; C:\Psfonts\Hv______.pfb").
3. Save the Atm.ini file in text-only format, then restart Windows.

READDING FONTS IN THE ATM CONTROL PANEL

Now that you've removed your fonts and the references to them in your system files, install fresh copies of the fonts into the ATM Control Panel using the original font disks. To start, add just a few fonts.

If only some of your fonts display jagged, add just those. If all your fonts display jagged, start by adding just five fonts. Once you have solved the problem, you can add the remaining fonts.

To add fonts in ATM in the ATM Control Panel:

1. In the ATM Control Panel, click Add.
2. In the Add Fonts dialog box, locate the drive and directory where your fonts are located (e.g., C:\Psfonts\Pfm, A:\Psfonts).
3. Select the fonts you want to install from the list of available fonts, then click Add.

Re-adding fonts may enable ATM to display them as expected. If your fonts do not display correctly after re-adding them, move to the Troubleshooting Jagged Font Display After You've Removed and Reinstalled Fonts section.

TROUBLESHOOTING JAGGED FONT DISPLAY AFTER YOU'VE REMOVED AND REINSTALLED FONTS

ATM cannot display a PostScript font smoothly on screen when:

- the font's PFB file is not installed
- the font file is damaged
- ATM has an insufficient Font Cache
- both the TrueType and PostScript version of the font are installed
- an earlier version of the font file is installed
- the Atmfonts.qlc file is damaged
- other font utilities prevent ATM from locating a font's outline font files
- ATM is damaged

Begin troubleshooting by first reinstalling the font or fonts that display jagged. Then, increase the Font Cache, remove TrueType versions of installed PostScript fonts, and update to current versions of your font files. If fonts still display jagged after doing those steps, continue by deleting any Atmfonts.qlc files and disabling other font utilities. As a last resort, reinstall ATM.

Make Sure PFM and PFB Files Are Installed

ATM copies font files into the C:\Psfonts and C:\Psfonts\Pfm directories by default. Check those directories to make sure a PFM file and a PFB file are installed for each font. For example, for the font Helvetica, make sure the Hv_______.pfb file is located in the C:\Psfonts directory and the Hv_______.pfm file is located in the C:\Psfonts\Pfm directory.

Font filename prefixes often do not resemble the font's actual name (e.g., Akzidenz Grotesk font files begin with GF, Centaur font files begin with NR). See the document Fntnames.pdf on the Type On Call CD-ROM for a complete listing of Adobe font filenames.

Increase the Font Cache

ATM's Font Cache is an allotment of memory that ATM uses to store the fonts it has rasterized. When the Font Cache's size is insufficient to create or display a font, the font displays bitmapped or does not display at all.

To change the size of the Font Cache, click the up or down arrow for the Font Cache in the ATM Control Panel, then restart Windows. ATM's default Font Cache size is 256K. Increase the size of the Font Cache to 512K or more when you use a multiple master typeface (e.g., Jenson, Ex Ponto, Tekton) or more than four typefaces in a document.

Remove TrueType Font Files

When both the TrueType and PostScript version of a font are installed (e.g., Helvetica), ATM may be unable to locate the PostScript font's outline font file. Make sure only the PostScript version of the font is installed. Add and remove the TrueType versions of your PostScript fonts using the Fonts Control Panel.

Update the Font Files

ATM 3.0x and later include an updated rasterizer for rendering smooth fonts to the screen. To work with ATM 3.0x's updated rasterizer, PostScript Type 1 fonts must adhere to the Type 1 font specification. Some earlier Type 1 fonts (e.g., fonts created in 1988 or earlier) do not adhere to the most recent version of the Type 1 font specification, causing them to display bitmapped on screen when ATM 3.0x or later is installed. When ATM 3.0x or later is installed, some fonts that do adhere to the PostScript Type 1 font specification may display more bitmapped than when ATM 2.6 and earlier is installed because of the ATM 3.0x and later's updated rasterizer.

When using ATM 3.0x or later, obtain an updated version of your font from the font's manufacturer to ensure your font adheres to the latest Type 1 font specification.

ATM 2.6 and earlier do not require PostScript Type 1 fonts that adhere to the Type 1 font specification for smooth screen display.

Delete All Atmfonts.qlc Files

The Atmfonts.qlc file contains rasterization information on the last several fonts used, enabling ATM to rasterize fonts more quickly. When the Atmfonts.qlc file becomes damaged or multiple Atmfonts.qlc files are present on the system, ATM may be unable to rasterize fonts as expected.

When you delete the Atmfonts.qlc file, ATM creates a new one the next time you launch Windows. The file is located in the Psfonts directory by default, but duplicates may exist in other locations. You can search for and delete every Atmfonts.qlc file using the Windows Explorer (Windows 95) or File Manager (Windows 3.1x).

Disable Other Font Utilities

Other font management or rasterizing utilities (e.g., FontMinder) may prevent ATM from loading or locating a font's outline font files. Make sure ATM is not conflicting with other font utilities by disabling them and installing your fonts in ATM.

Reinstall ATM

When ATM is damaged it may be unable to load or display a PostScript font. To make sure ATM isn't damaged, reinstall it from the original disks.

DISPLAY LIMITATIONS

The smoothness with which ATM can display a font is limited by the resolution of your monitor. Because the resolution of most monitors (e.g., 70 to 85 dpi) is much lower than that of most PostScript printers (e.g., 300 dpi, 600 dpi), fonts print smoother to PostScript printers than they display. Fonts with elaborate curved edges or delicate character strokes (e.g., Eras, Boulevard, Bauhaus, script fonts) appear more jagged than fonts with milder curves and heavier character strokes (e.g., Helvetica, Palatino).

To determine if your fonts display bitmapped because of their design or your monitor's resolution, compare the smoothness of your font on-screen to similar curves of an object, when ATM is disabled, or when displayed on a high-resolution monitor. If the curves of a font character and an object display with the same amount of jaggedness, or if a font's jaggedness increases substantially when ATM is disabled, ATM is displaying the font as smoothly as possible on your monitor. You can enable fonts to display smoother by increasing the resolution of your monitor, or by viewing your fonts at a higher magnification.

Compare Text to a Curved Line

1. In an application that creates curved PostScript paths (e.g., Adobe PageMaker, Adobe Illustrator), apply the PostScript font to the "O" character.
2. Draw an ellipse or a curved path whose shape and line weight emulates the curve of the character next to the text block.
3. Compare the jaggedness of the curves in the drawn object to that of the font character.

Compare Font Display with ATM Enabled and Disabled

1. In application that supports large point sizes (e.g., Adobe PageMaker, Adobe Illustrator 6.0), create 150-point text and apply the PostScript font (e.g., Anna) in a new document, then save the document.
2. Compare the smoothness of the font when ATM is enabled and disabled. To disable ATM, select Off in the ATM Control Panel, then restart Windows.

Increase the Resolution Setting of Your Monitor

When using a monitor that supports different resolution settings, select a higher resolution monitor setting (e.g., select 1024 x 768) in the Display Control Panel.

Troubleshooting Jagged PostScript Font Display with ATM 4.0 in Windows 95

Adobe Type Manager Deluxe (ATM) 4.0 creates smooth display of PostScript fonts at any point size using the PostScript font's outline (printer) font file. When ATM cannot display a PostScript font, the font displays bitmapped (i.e., jagged) or text to which the font is applied does not display.

There are a variety of reasons that ATM might be unable to display a PostScript font—the outline font file may be damaged or unavailable (e.g., not installed, not in the expected location), or ATM may be damaged or unable to locate one of its support files. To determine what's preventing your fonts from displaying smoothly, use the troubleshooting steps below.

OVERVIEW OF POSTSCRIPT FONTS AND ATM

Before you begin troubleshooting, you should understand the difference between PostScript Type 1 fonts and TrueType fonts.

PostScript Type 1 fonts are composed of two files: a Printer Font Metrics (PFM) file and a Printer Font Binary (PFB) file. Multiple master base fonts and instances use a Multiple Master Metrics (MMM) file instead of a PFM file, and multiple master instances use a PostScript Printer Stub (PSS) file instead of a PFB file.

PFM and MMM files, located in the Psfonts\Pfm subdirectory, are used to display the font on screen. PFB (or "outline") and PSS files, located in the Psfonts directory, are used for printing and by ATM to display fonts smoothly on screen.

Unlike PostScript fonts, TrueType fonts consist of only one font file, used for both display and printing.

Without ATM, Windows displays PostScript fonts by scaling the PFM (or "bitmap") file. Resizing a bitmap font reproduces the general shape of the font, but may cause the font to display with extreme pixelation (i.e., jagged edges), depending on the size of available bitmap font files and the requested display size.

To prevent fonts from displaying with extreme pixel-ation, ATM rasterizes (i.e., converts outline font information into a scaleable bitmap image) PostScript PFB files, which enables the fonts to display smoothly at any point size. ATM can rasterize PostScript Type 1 fonts that adhere to the Adobe Type 1 font specification. ATM cannot rasterize PostScript Type 3 fonts, TrueType fonts, and PostScript fonts that do not adhere to the Adobe Type 1 font specification.

In addition to rasterizing fonts, ATM 4.0 can further smooth on-screen font edges using anti-aliasing (i.e., blending colors along an edge).

DISPLAY LIMITATIONS

The smoothness with which ATM can display a font is limited by the resolution of your monitor. Because the resolution of most monitors (e.g., 70 to 85 dpi) is much lower than that of most PostScript printers (e.g., 300 dpi, 600 dpi), fonts print smoother to PostScript printers than they display. Fonts with elaborate curved edges or delicate character strokes (e.g., Eras, Boulevard, Bauhaus, script fonts) appear more jagged than fonts with milder curves and heavier character strokes (e.g., Helvetica, Palatino).

To compensate for limited monitor resolution, you can enable ATM 4.0's Smooth Font Edges On Screen option (i.e., anti-aliasing). When enabling the Smooth Font Edges On Screen option improves PostScript font display, ATM is displaying the fonts as smoothly as possible on your monitor. If enabling the Smooth Font Edges On Screen option does not smooth PostScript font display, move to the Making Sure ATM Is Active section.

To determine if your fonts display bitmapped because of their design or your monitor's resolution when ATM's Smooth Font Edges On Screen option is not enabled, compare the smoothness of your font on-screen to similar curves of an object, when ATM is disabled, or when displayed on a high-resolution monitor. If the curves of a font character and an object display with the same amount of jaggedness, or if a font's jaggedness increases substantially when ATM is disabled, ATM is displaying the font as smoothly as possible on your monitor. You can enable fonts to display smoother by increasing the resolution of your monitor, or by viewing your fonts at a higher magnification.

Compare Text to a Curved Line

1. In an application that creates curved PostScript paths (e.g., Adobe PageMaker, Adobe Illustrator), apply the

PostScript font to the "O" character.
2. Draw an ellipse or a curved path whose shape and line weight emulates the curve of the character next to the text block.
3. Compare the jaggedness of the curves in the drawn object to that of the font character.

Compare Font Display with ATM Enabled and Disabled

1. In application that supports large point sizes (e.g., Adobe PageMaker, Adobe Illustrator 6.0), create 150-point text and apply the PostScript font (e.g., Anna) in a new document, then save the document.
2. Compare the smoothness of the font when ATM is enabled and disabled. To disable ATM, select Off in ATM, then restart Windows.

Enabling ATM's Font Smoothing

1. In ATM, click the Settings tab, then click Advanced.
2. In the Advanced Settings dialog box, select the Smooth Font Edges on Screen option, then click OK.

Increase the Resolution Setting of Your Monitor

When using a monitor that supports different resolution settings, select a higher resolution monitor setting (e.g., select 1024 x 768) in the Display Control Panel.

MAKING SURE ATM IS ACTIVE

Your first step in troubleshooting jagged PostScript font display in Windows is to determine if ATM is active. PostScript fonts added in ATM will display jagged when ATM is turned off.

To make sure ATM is active, open ATM by choosing Start > Programs > Adobe > Adobe Type Manager Deluxe. In ATM, choose Help > About Adobe Type Manager. When ATM is active, the About windows displays the current Dynamic Link Library (DLL) file version number in the "DLL" line. If ATM is active, move to the Defining the Problem section.

When ATM is inactive, About windows displays "ATM System is inactive." in the "DLL" line. To activate ATM, do one or more of the following:

A. Turn ATM on. If ATM is set to Off, click the Settings tab, select On in the ATM System section, exit ATM, and restart Windows. Then reopen ATM to see if it is active.

B. Make sure all the ATM files are installed. The ATM Installer installs files into the Psfonts, Windows, and Windows\System directories. Make sure the following file is installed in the Psfonts directory:

```
Atmfm.exe
```

Make sure the following files are installed in the Windows directory:

```
Atmreg.atm
Atm.ini
```

Make sure the following files are installed in the Windows\System directory:

```
Atm32.dll
Atmsys.drv
```

If any of these files is missing, or if some of your files have a different extension (e.g., *.ndl instead of *.dll), exit Windows, delete the installed ATM files, and reinstall ATM from the original installation disks.

C. Make sure ATM is referenced in the System.ini file. In addition to adding files to the Psfonts, Windows and Windows\System directories, the ATM installer modifies the System.ini file so that ATM is loaded when you start Windows. Make sure the System.ini contains the correct ATM information:

1. Open the System.ini file, located in the Windows directory, in a text editor that can save in text-only format (e.g., Windows Write).
2. In the [Boot] section, modify the line:
```
system.drv=system.drv
```
to read:
```
system.drv=atmsys.drv
```
3. In the [Boot] section, add the line:
```
atm.system.drv=system.drv
```
4. Save the System.ini file in text-only format, then restart Windows.

D. Reinstall ATM from the CD-ROM. If ATM is installed correctly, it will be loaded and active when you start Windows.

DEFINING THE PROBLEM

Once you've made sure ATM is active, your next step is to determine the extent of the problem. Because you'll be removing all your installed ATM fonts in the next section and you won't have fonts installed to test with, it's important you define the problem completely before you begin troubleshooting.

Begin isolating the problem by applying another font, and then comparing how different fonts display. Does only one PostScript font display jagged, do multiple PostScript font display jagged, or do all PostScript fonts display jagged?

When one or more PostScript font displays jagged, but others display smoothly, the problem may be caused by a damaged font, or unavailable font files. When all your PostScript fonts display jagged, ATM is the most likely cause; it may be damaged or unable to locate one of its support files.

Before troubleshooting your fonts or ATM, follow the steps in the Removing All Fonts and Font References section to remove old font information.

REMOVING ALL FONTS AND FONT REFERENCES

Once you have determined the extent of the problem, your next step is to do some general Windows font troubleshooting by removing all your fonts from ATM, then removing all font references from the Win.ini file and the Atm.ini file. Before you remove fonts, you may want to export your sets so you can reimport them after re-adding the fonts, rather than recreating the sets. Once you've cleaned up the Win.ini file and the Atm.ini file, you'll re-add your fonts a few at a time to continue troubleshooting.

Remove All Installed ATM Fonts

To export your sets:

1. In ATM, click the Sets tab.

2. Select one or more sets to export.
3. Choose File > Export.
4. In the Export dialog box, specify a filename and location for the AFS file, then click Save.

To remove your fonts:

1. In the All Font Sets pane of the Sets tab, select the fonts you want to remove, then click Remove.
2. In the Remove Font dialog box, select Remove Fonts from All Set and Master Font List, select Remove Font Files from Disk if you are reinstalling your fonts from the original installation disks, then click Yes or Yes to All.

Remove Font References in the Win.ini File

1. Open the Win.ini file, located in the Windows directory, in a text editor that can save in text-only format (e.g., NotePad, Windows Write).
2. Delete all lines that begin "softfont" (e.g., softfonts=20).
3. In Windows 95, delete all lines that refer to an MFD file (e.g., ADMFDFile=C:\WINDOWS\AD434AF1.MFD).
4. Save the Win.ini file in text-only format.

Remove Font References in the Atm.ini File

1. Open the Atm.ini file, located in the Windows directory, in a text editor that can save in text-only format (e.g., Windows Write).
2. Delete any lines in the [Fonts] section (e.g., "Helvetica=C:\Psfonts\Pfm\Hv______.pfm; C:\Psfonts\Hv-______.pfb").
3. Save the Atm.ini file in text-only format, then restart Windows.

RE-ADDING FONTS IN ATM

Now that you've removed your fonts and the references to them in your system files, install fresh copies of the fonts into ATM using the original font disks. To start, add just a few fonts.

If only some of your fonts display jagged, add just those. If all your fonts display jagged, start by adding just five fonts. Once you have solved the problem, you can add the remaining fonts.

To re-add your fonts:

1. Click the Add Fonts tab, then select Browse for Fonts from the Source pop-up menu.
2. Navigate to the drive and directory where your fonts files are located (e.g., C:\Psfonts\Pfm, A:\Fontdisk).
3. Select the fonts you want to add from the Source pane scroll box then click Add.

To import your sets:

1. With Browse for Fonts still selected in the Source pop-up menu, navigate to the drive and directory where your AFS file is located. ATM lists the sets you exported in the AFS file.
2. Select the sets you want to import, then click Add.
3. Remove any duplicate fonts outside your sets by selecting them and clicking Remove.

Re-adding fonts may enable ATM to display them as expected. If your fonts do not display correctly after re-adding them, move to the Troubleshooting Jagged Font Display After You've Removed and Reinstalled Fonts section.

TROUBLESHOOTING JAGGED FONT DISPLAY AFTER YOU'VE REMOVED AND REINSTALLED FONTS

ATM is unable to display a PostScript font smoothly on screen when:

- The font's PFB file is not installed.
- The font file is damaged.
- ATM has an insufficient Font Cache.
- Both the TrueType and PostScript version of the font are installed.
- An earlier version of the font file is installed.
- The Atmfonts.qlc file is damaged.
- Other font utilities prevent ATM from locating a font's outline font files.
- ATM is damaged.

Begin troubleshooting by first reinstalling the font or fonts that display jagged. Then, increase the Font Cache, remove TrueType versions of installed PostScript fonts, and update to current versions of your font files. If fonts still display jagged after doing those steps, continue by deleting any Atmfonts.qlc files and disabling other font utilities. As a last resort, reinstall ATM.

Make Sure PFM and PFB Files Are Installed

ATM copies font files into the C:\Psfonts and C:\Psfonts\Pfm directories by default. Check those directories to make sure a PFM file and a PFB file are installed for each font. For example, for the font Helvetica, make sure the Hv______.pfb file is located in the C:\Psfonts directory and the Hv______.pfm file is located in the C:\Psfonts\Pfm directory.

Font filename prefixes often do not resemble the font's actual name (e.g., Akzidenz Grotesk font files begin with GF, Centaur font files begin with NR). See the document Fntnames.pdf on the Type On Call CD-ROM for a complete listing of Adobe font filenames.

Increase the Font Cache

ATM's Font Cache is an allotment of memory that ATM uses to store the fonts it has rasterized. When the Font Cache's size is insufficient to create or display a font, the font displays bitmapped or does not display at all.

To change the size of the Font Cache, click the Settings tab, click the up or down arrow for the Font Cache, then restart Windows. ATM's default Font Cache size is 256K. Increase the size of the Font Cache to 512K or more when using a multiple master typeface (e.g., Jenson, Ex Ponto, Tekton) or more than four typefaces in a document.

Remove TrueType Font Files

When both the TrueType and PostScript version of a font are installed (e.g., Helvetica), ATM may be unable to locate the PostScript font's outline font file. Make sure only the PostScript version of the font is installed. To remove TrueType fonts installed in ATM:

1. In the All Font Sets pane of the Sets tab, select the fonts you want to remove, then click Remove.
2. In the Remove Font dialog box, select Remove Fonts from All Sets and Master Font List, select Remove Font Files from Disk if desired, then click Yes or Yes to All.

Update the Font Files
ATM 4.0 includes an updated rasterizer for rendering smooth fonts to the screen. To work with ATM 4.0's updated rasterizer, PostScript Type 1 fonts must adhere to the Type 1 font specification. Some earlier Type 1 fonts (e.g., fonts created in 1988 or earlier) do not adhere to the most recent version of the Type 1 font specification, causing them to display bitmapped on screen when ATM 4.0 is installed. When ATM 4.0 or later is installed, some fonts that do adhere to the PostScript Type 1 font specification may display more bitmapped than when ATM 3.0x and earlier is installed because of the ATM 4.0's updated rasterizer.

When using ATM 4.0, obtain an updated version of your font from the font's manufacturer to ensure your font adheres to the latest Type 1 font specification.

Delete All Atmfonts.qlc Files
The Atmfonts.qlc file contains rasterization information on the last several fonts used, enabling ATM to rasterize fonts more quickly. When the Atmfonts.qlc file becomes damaged or multiple Atmfonts.qlc files are present on the system, ATM may be unable to rasterize fonts as expected.

When you delete the Atmfonts.qlc file, ATM creates a new one the next time you launch Windows. The file is located in the Psfonts directory by default, but duplicates may exist in other locations. You can search for and delete every Atmfonts.qlc file using the Windows Explorer.

Disable Other Font Utilities
Other font management or rasterizing utilities (e.g., FontMinder) may prevent ATM from loading or locating a font's outline font files. Make sure ATM is not conflicting with other font utilities by disabling them and installing your fonts in ATM.

Reinstall ATM
When ATM is damaged it may be unable to load or display a PostScript font. To make sure ATM isn't damaged, reinstall it from the original disks.

MAC OS

Troubleshooting Jagged PostScript Font Display on the Macintosh

Adobe Type Manager (ATM) creates smooth display of PostScript fonts at any point size using PostScript outline (printer) fonts. When ATM cannot display a PostScript font, the font displays bitmapped (i.e., jagged) or text formatted with the font does not display.

A variety of causes can prevent ATM from displaying a PostScript font—the outline font file may be damaged or unavailable (e.g., not installed, not in the expected location), or ATM may be damaged or unable to locate one of its support files. To determine what's preventing your fonts from displaying smoothly, use the troubleshooting steps below.

OVERVIEW OF POSTSCRIPT FONTS AND ATM

Before you begin troubleshooting, you should understand the difference between PostScript Type 1 fonts and TrueType fonts.

PostScript fonts are composed of two files: a bitmap (screen) font and a PostScript outline (printer) font file. Bitmap fonts are used to display the font on screen. Outline fonts are used for printing and for display by ATM.

PostScript bitmap font icons appear in the Finder as a dog-eared page with the letter "A," and their filenames include a point size (e.g., Times 10, Geneva 14). In System 7.1 or later, bitmap fonts are installed in the Fonts folder in the System Folder. In System 7.0.x, bitmap fonts are installed in the System suitcase in the System Folder.

Adobe PostScript outline font icons appear in the Finder as a letter "A" in front of horizontal lines (outline fonts created by other companies may have different icons). Most PostScript font files are named using the first five characters of the font followed by the first three characters of each style (e.g., HelveBol, CouriObl, Symbo, TimesBolIta), and do not include a point size. In System 7.1 or later, outline fonts are installed in the Fonts folder in the System Folder. In System 7.0.x, outline fonts are installed in the Extensions folder in the System Folder.

Unlike PostScript fonts, TrueType fonts consist of only one font file, used for both display and printing. TrueType fonts icons display in the Finder as a dog-eared page with three letter "A"s in progressively larger sizes, and their filenames do not include a point size. In System 7.1 or later, TrueType fonts are installed in the Fonts folder in the System Folder.

Without ATM, the system displays PostScript fonts by scaling the bitmap font file. Resizing a bitmap font reproduces the general shape of the font, but may cause the font to display with extreme pixelation (i.e., jagged), depending on the size of available bitmap font files and the requested display size.

To prevent fonts from displaying with extreme pixelation, ATM rasterizes PostScript outline fonts (i.e., converts outline font information into a scaleable bitmap image) to enable fonts to display smoothly at any point size. ATM supports rasterizing PostScript fonts that adhere to the Adobe Type 1 font specification. ATM does not support rasterizing PostScript Type 3 fonts, TrueType fonts, and PostScript fonts that do not adhere to the Adobe Type 1 font specification.

DEFINING THE PROBLEM

The first step in troubleshooting jagged font display is to determine the exact symptoms of the problem. Begin isolating the problem by applying another font to the text, then comparing how different fonts display. Does only one PostScript font display jagged, do multiple PostScript font display jagged, or do all PostScript fonts display jagged?

If one or more PostScript font displays jagged, but others display smoothly, the problem may be caused by a damaged font or unavailable font files. If all your PostScript fonts display jagged, ATM is the most likely cause: it may be damaged or unable to locate one of its support files.

After determining the exact symptoms of your font display problem, you now have more clues to narrow down the cause of your problem, and you can begin troubleshooting your exact symptoms.

SINGLE OR SEVERAL POSTSCRIPT FONTS DISPLAY JAGGED

ATM cannot display a PostScript font smoothly when the printer font file is not installed, when the font file or the Fonts folder is damaged, when ATM has an insufficient Font Cache, when both the TrueType and PostScript version of the font are installed, or when an earlier version of the font file is installed. Begin troubleshooting by first reinstalling the font, then recreating the fonts folder, next increasing the Font Cache, then removing duplicate TrueType fonts, and finally by updating your font file.

Reinstall the Font

Make sure the PostScript font is not damaged and ATM can locate it by removing the font and reinstalling it from the original disks.

To reinstall a PostScript font in System 7.1 or later:

1. Quit all applications.
2. Open the Fonts folder in the System Folder.
3. Choose View > Select By Name.
4. Remove the outline and bitmap font files from the Fonts folder in the System Folder.
5. Reinstall the outline and bitmap font files from the original disks into the Fonts folder in the System Folder.

To reinstall a PostScript font in System 7.0x:

1. Quit all applications.
2. Remove the PostScript outline fonts from the Extensions folder in the System Folder.
3. Remove bitmap font suitcases from the System suitcase in the System Folder.
4. Reinstall PostScript outline fonts from the original disks into the Extensions folder in the System Folder.
5. Reinstall bitmap font suitcases from the original disks into the System suitcase in the System Folder.

Recreate the Fonts Folder

If you're using System 7.1 or later, the Fonts folder containing your fonts may be damaged, preventing ATM from locating the outline font file. To make sure your Fonts folder is not damaged, remove then recreate it.

To recreate the System 7.1 or later Fonts folder:

1. Move the Fonts folder from the System Folder to the desktop, then restart the Macintosh. After the Macintosh restarts, a new, empty Fonts folder is created in the System Folder.
2. Move font files from the old Fonts folder into the new Fonts folder in the System Folder.

Increase the Font Cache

ATM's Font Cache is an allotment of memory that ATM uses to store the fonts it has rasterized. When the Font Cache is too small to create or display a font, the font displays bitmapped or does not display.

ATM's default Font Cache size is 256K. You should increase the size of the Font Cache to 512K or more when your documents include a multiple master typeface (e.g., Jenson, Ex Ponto, Tekton) or more than four typefaces on a page. To change the size of the Font Cache, click the up or down arrows for the Font Cache in the ATM control panel, then restart your Macintosh.

Remove TrueType Font Files

If both the TrueType and PostScript version of a font are installed (e.g., Helvetica), ATM may be unable to locate the font's outline font file.

To determine if the TrueType version of the font is installed, open the folder or suitcase containing the font, then compare files. Your PostScript bitmap font files include a number (e.g., point size) in their filenames—those filenames without numbers are your TrueType font files. When you view the files by icon (choose View > by Icon), TrueType fonts display as dog-eared page with three letter "A"s. If you have both the TrueType and PostScript version of your font installed, remove the TrueType font.

Update the Font Files

ATM 3.8.x and later include an updated rasterizer for rendering fonts to the screen. To work with ATM 3.8.x's updated rasterizer, PostScript Type 1 fonts must adhere to the Type 1 font specification. Some earlier Type 1 fonts do not adhere to the most recent version of the Type 1 font specification, causing them to display bitmapped on screen when ATM 3.8.x or later is installed. Additionally, some fonts that do adhere to the PostScript Type 1 font specification may display more bitmapped with ATM 3.8.x than with ATM 3.6.x, because of ATM 3.8.x and later's updated rasterizer.

If you're using ATM 3.8.x or later, obtain an updated version of your font from the font's manufacturer to ensure it adheres to the latest Type 1 font specification.

ATM 3.6.x and earlier can create smooth display of fonts that do not adhere to the Type 1 font specification.

ALL POSTSCRIPT FONTS DISPLAY JAGGED

When all your PostScript fonts display jagged, ATM itself is your most likely culprit. ATM cannot display PostScript fonts when it is disabled, has an insufficient Font Cache, is damaged, or is conflicting with another font utility. Begin troubleshooting ATM by ensuring it is turned on, then disabling other font utilities and extensions, next reinstalling ATM, and finally increasing the Font Cache.

Make Sure ATM Is Active

Make sure ATM is active by selecting On in the ATM control panel, then restarting your Macintosh. When ATM is enabled, the message "ATM is active" displays under the Off option in the ATM control panel.

Disable Other Font Utilities and Extensions

Other font management or rasterizing utilities (e.g., Symantec Suitcase) may prevent ATM from loading or locating outline fonts. You can determine if a conflict with other font utilities is the cause of your problem by disabling them and installing your fonts into the System Folder, or by removing each utility from the System Folder (e.g., remove the Suitcase extension from the Extensions folder), then restarting your Macintosh. For instructions on installing PostScript fonts, see Reinstall the PostScript Font above.

If, after disabling your font utilities, your fonts still display bitmapped, disable all added extensions. Other extensions may prevent ATM from loading or interfere with ATM's ability to locate outline font files. Use an extensions manager to disable all extensions and control panels except ATM, or remove all extensions and control panels from the System Folder except ATM, then restart your Macintosh.

Reinstall ATM

When ATM is damaged, it may be unable to read, rasterize, or display PostScript fonts. To make sure ATM isn't damaged, reinstall it after first disabling all extensions to prevent them from interfering with the installation.

Increase the Font Cache

ATM's Font Cache is an allotment of memory that ATM uses to store the fonts it has rasterized. When the Font Cache is too small to create or display a font, the font displays bitmapped or does not display.

ATM's default Font Cache size is 256K. You should increase the size of the Font Cache to 512K or more when your documents include a multiple master typeface (e.g., Jenson, Ex Ponto, Tekton) or more than four typefaces on a page. To change the size of the Font Cache, click the up or down arrows for the Font Cache in the ATM control panel, then restart your Macintosh.

DISPLAY LIMITATIONS

The smoothness with which ATM can display a font is limited by the resolution of your monitor. Because the resolution of most monitors (e.g., 70 to 85 dpi) is much lower than that of most PostScript printers (e.g., 300 dpi, 600 dpi), fonts print smoother to PostScript printers than they display. Fonts with elaborate curved edges or delicate character strokes (e.g., Eras, Boulevard, Bauhaus, script fonts) appear more jagged than fonts with milder curves and heavier character strokes (e.g., Helvetica, Palatino).

To determine if your fonts display bitmapped because of their design or your monitor's resolution, compare the smoothness of your font to similar curves of an object, or compare the font display with ATM turned on and off. If the curves of a font character and an object display with the same amount of jaggedness, or if the font's jaggedness increases substantially when you turn off ATM, then ATM is displaying the font as smoothly as possible on your monitor. You can make the fonts display more smoothly by increasing the resolution of your monitor, or by viewing your fonts at a higher magnification.

Compare Text to a Curved Line

1. In an application that creates curved PostScript paths (e.g., Adobe PageMaker, Adobe Illustrator), apply a PostScript font to the "O" character.
2. Draw an ellipse or a curved path whose shape and line weight emulates the curve of the character next to the text block.
3. Compare the jaggedness of the curves in the drawn object to that of the font character.

Compare Font Display with ATM Enabled and Disabled

1. In application that supports large point sizes (e.g., Adobe PageMaker, Adobe Illustrator 6.0), create 150-point text and apply the PostScript font (e.g., Anna) in a new document, then save the document.
2. Compare the smoothness of the font when ATM is enabled and disabled. To disable ATM, select Off in the ATM control panel, then restart your Macintosh.

Increase the Resolution Setting of Your Monitor

If you're using a monitor that supports different resolution settings, select a higher resolution setting (e.g., select 1024 x 768) by clicking Options in the Monitors control panel.

Adobe Type Manager 3.6 New Feature Summary

NEW FEATURE

- Compatible with Fileguard, Spelling CoachPro, early versions of Suitcase 2.0 Filesaver, DecNET Pathworks, Folderbolt, and Dana NetMount extensions.

ISSUES CORRECTED IN LATER VERSIONS

- System error (e.g., freeze) when you print to Hewlett-Packard DeskWriter

  ATM 3.6 is incompatible with the HP DeskWriter 3.8 or earlier printer driver. Use the DeskWriter 3.9 or later printer driver.
- The error "ATM requires more memory or system resources" occurs when you start your Macintosh

  ATM is conflicting with another extension or the system does not have enough memory to load ATM. The only extension known to conflict with ATM 3.6 is Aladdin Systems Spacesaver. To prevent ATM 3.6 and Spacesaver from conflicting, change the order in which they load so that ATM loads before Spacesaver. To change the order that System 7.x loads these two control panel files, move the Spacesaver from the Control Panels folder to the System Folder, or use a utility or extensions manager to specify the load order of your extensions.
- Typecheck error or no output when you print substituted fonts to Apple LaserWriter II NT

  ATM 3.6 does not downloaded font information for substituted fonts created by Adobe SuperATM or Adobe Acrobat to an Apple LaserWriter II NT printer. When you print to a LaserWriter II NT printer, use ATM 3.6.1 or later, or use ATM 3.5.1 or earlier. If you are using Acrobat, install ATM 3.6.1 or later.
- System error (e.g., Bus error) when you start a Macintosh IIcx with an installed TrueVision NuVista+ board

  Enable 32-bit Addressing in the Memory control panel so that ATM 3.6 can run in conjunction with the TrueVision NuVista+ board. For instructions, consult the TrueVision user guide or the Macintosh System user guide.

- System error (e.g., freeze) when you send a fax using Global Village fax software

  ATM 3.6 is incompatible with Global Village fax software when both the 18- and 24-point Helvetica bitmap (i.e., screen) font files are installed. Remove these bitmap font files before using the Global Village fax software.
- Compatibility with Macintosh AV computers

  ATM 3.6 is incompatible with Macintosh AV computers. Use ATM 3.8 or later, which is compatible with Macintosh AV computers.

Unexpected Results

MAC OS / WINDOWS

ATM's Font Smoothing Doesn't Smooth Colored Text

ISSUE

When font smoothing is turned on in Adobe Type Manager (ATM) 4.0 Deluxe or ATM 4.0 Lite, ATM does not smooth the edges of colored text.

SOLUTION

Set the monitor to display more than 256 colors (e.g., True Color, Millions). For instructions, see Additional Information.

ADDITIONAL INFORMATION

When font smoothing (i.e., anti-aliasing) is turned on, ATM creates gradient shades between the color of the text and the background color to smooth the edges of PostScript fonts. If your monitor is displaying only 16 or 256 colors, there are insufficient gradient shades to smooth colored text, so ATM smoothes only black text.

To change monitor settings on the Macintosh:

1. Choose Control Panels from the Apple menu, then open the Monitors control panel.
2. In the Monitors control panel, select Colors.
3. Select Thousands or Millions from the scroll box
4. Close the Monitors control panel.

To change monitor settings in Windows 95:

1. Exit all applications.
2. Right-click the desktop and select Properties from the pop-up menu.
3. Click the Settings tab.
4. Select High Color (16 Bit) or True Color (32 Bit) from the Color Palette pop-up menu.
5. Click OK.
6. Click Yes to restart your computer with the new monitor settings.

TrueType or Type 3 Font Is Not Smoothed When Smooth Font Edges Is Turned On in ATM

ISSUE

When Smooth Font Edges On Screen is turned on in Adobe Type Manager (ATM) 4.0 Deluxe or ATM 4.0 Lite, ATM does not smooth (i.e., anti-alias) text. The text is formatted with a TrueType or PostScript Type 3 font.

SOLUTION

Format the text with a PostScript Type 1 font.

ADDITIONAL INFORMATION

ATM can smooth (i.e., anti-alias) only PostScript Type 1 fonts.

WINDOWS

ATM 3.0x Is Inactive or Doesn't Load in Windows

ISSUE

When you launch Windows 95 or Windows 3.1x, the Adobe Type Manager (ATM) icon displays with an "X" through it or does not display at all. When you open the ATM 3.0x Control Panel, it displays the message "Inactive" instead of the ATM version number (e.g., 3.02). Windows may return the message "Unable to load Atmsys.drv."

SOLUTIONS

Do one or more of the following:

A. Edit the System.ini file to make sure the [Boot] section contains the necessary references to the ATM driver. To edit the System.ini file:
   1. Open the System.ini file, located in the Windows directory, in a text editor that can save in text-only format (e.g., WordPad, Windows Write).
   2. In the [Boot] section, modify the line:
      ```
      system.drv=system.drv
      ```
      to:
      ```
      system.drv=atmsys.drv
      ```
   3. Add the following line to the end of the [Boot] section:
      ```
      atm.system.drv=system.drv
      ```
   4. Save the System.ini file in text-only format, then restart Windows.

B. Make sure all the ATM files are installed and decompressed in the Windows and the Windows\System directories. If any of these files is missing, or if any has a different extension (e.g., .ndl instead of .dll), exit Windows, delete all the installed ATM files, then reinstall ATM from the original installation disks.

   ATM installs the following files in the Windows directory:
   ```
   Atmcntrl.exe
   Atm.ini
   ```

ATM installs the following files in the Windows\System subdirectory:

```
Atm32.dll
Atm16.dll
Atmsys.drv
```

C. Copy the ATM installation files from the ATM disks to your hard disk, then install ATM:

1. In Windows Explorer (Windows 95) or File Manager (Windows 3.1x), create a directory to contain the ATM installation files (e.g., C:\Atm).
2. Copy all the files from the ATM Program Disk to the ATM directory.
3. Copy the Fontdisk file and the entire PSFonts directory from the Font Disk to the ATM directory.
4. Make sure you have the following files in your Atm directory:

```
Atm.cnf
Atm16.nd_
Atm32.nd_
Atmcntrl.ex_
Atmsys.dr_
Fontdisk
Install.cnf
Install.exe
Progdisk
Readme.wri
Techref.wri
Psfonts (directory)
```

5. Double-click the Install.exe file in the ATM directory.

D. Reinstall ATM in Windows 95's Safe mode:

1. Choose Start > Shut Down.
2. In the Shut Down Windows dialog box, select Restart the Computer.
3. When the message "Starting Windows 95" appears, press the F8 key.
4. Select the Safe Mode option (#3), then press Enter.

OR: Reinstall ATM in Windows 3.1x's standard mode with the video driver set to standard VGA and no other applications running. To start Windows 3.1x in standard mode, type the following command at the DOS prompt:

```
win/s
```

For instructions on changing the video driver to VGA, see Additional Information.

E. Make sure the font cache setting in the ATM Control Panel does not exceed the amount of RAM on your system.

F. Install ATM into a directory that does not have a name substantially similar to another directory's name. For example, the name "Windows2" is similar to the name "Windows."

ADDITIONAL INFORMATION

The ATM installer decompresses and renames the ATM files as it installs them and adds references to ATM in the System.ini file. If the installer cannot decompress and rename the ATM files or edit the System.ini file, ATM will be inactive. Reinstalling ATM or manually editing the System.ini file may enable ATM to load as expected.

ATM's Font Cache is an allotment of memory that ATM uses to store font data. The default size of the Font Cache is 256K.

When you try to install ATM into a directory that has a name substantially similar to another directory's name (e.g., "Windows2" and "Windows"), the ATM installer may be unable to install in the expected directory.

To specify the Windows Standard VGA driver in Windows 95:

1. Right-click on the desktop, then select Properties from the pop-up menu.
2. In the Display Properties dialog box, click on the Settings tab, then click the Change Display Type button.
3. Note the selected Adapter Type, then click Change.
4. In the Select Device dialog box, select the Show All Devices option.
5. Select the Standard Display Types option from the top of the Manufacturers scroll box.
6. Select the Standard Display Adapter (VGA) option from the Models scroll box, then click OK.
   NOTE: Standard Display Adapter (VGA) video drivers display only 16 colors. Switch to Super VGA for applications that require a minimum of 256 colors (e.g., Adobe Photoshop 3.0.x).
7. Note the selected Monitor Type, then click Change.
8. In the Select Device dialog box, select the Show All Devices option.
9. Select the Standard Monitor Types option from the top of the Manufacturers scroll box.
10. Select the Standard VGA 640x480 option from the Models scroll box, then click OK.
11. Restart Windows 95.

Specifying the Windows Standard VGA driver in Windows 3.1x:

1. Make sure your Windows installation disks are available.
2. Create a backup copy of the System.ini file.
3. Launch Windows Setup by double-clicking the Windows Setup icon in the Main group of Program Manager, or by choosing File > Run, typing "setup" in the Command line text box, and clicking OK.
4. In Windows Setup, choose Options > Change System Settings.
5. In the Change System Settings dialog box, select VGA from the Display pop-up menu and click OK.
6. Follow the on-screen instructions to install the VGA video driver, inserting Windows installation disks if prompted.
7. Restart Windows.

ATM Inactive and Fonts Unavailable in Windows NT 4.x or Earlier

ISSUE

After you install Adobe Type Manager (ATM) 3.0x or earlier in Windows NT 4.x or earlier, the ATM Control Panel displays the message "Version: ATM Inactive" instead of ATM's version number (e.g., 3.02). The Control Panel's Installed ATM Fonts scroll box may list installed fonts, but those fonts do not list in application font menus.

SOLUTION

Install PostScript Type 1 fonts in Windows NT by adding them using the Fonts Control Panel, which converts them to TrueType fonts.

DISCLAIMER: Adobe Technical Support does not support the Windows NT Fonts Control Panel's conversion procedure or PostScript Type 1 fonts you have converted to TrueType fonts using the Windows NT Fonts Control Panel. Refer to the Windows NT System Guide or contact Microsoft Windows NT Technical Support for assistance.

ADDITIONAL INFORMATION

ATM 3.0x and earlier is not compatible with Windows NT 4.x and earlier. When you install ATM in Windows NT 4.x or earlier, ATM appears to install, but the ATM Control Panel is inactive and added fonts do not display in application font menus.

You can use PostScript Type 1 fonts in Windows NT by adding them using the Fonts Control Panel. When you install PostScript fonts using the Fonts Control Panel, the Control Panel converts them to TrueType fonts. Because the Fonts Control Panel is unable to convert multiple master fonts, you cannot install multiple master fonts in Windows NT.

The Adobe End-User License Agreement permits you to convert Adobe Type 1 fonts using the Windows NT 4.x Fonts Control Panel, as long as you obey the Scope of Use section of the agreement. You may not sell or distribute the converted fonts.

PostScript Fonts Installed in ATM 3.0x Don't Appear in Any Font Menus

ISSUE

The font family names for PostScript Type 1 fonts (e.g., "AGaramond" for "AGaramond", "AGaramond,BOLD", and "AGaramond,ITALIC") do not appear in any application's Font menu. The fonts are installed in Adobe Type Manager (ATM) 3.0x, and ATM is active (i.e., the ATM Control Panel displays the ATM version).

SOLUTIONS

Do one or more of the following:

A. Deselect the Show Only TrueType Fonts option in Windows' Fonts Control Panel:

In Windows 95:

1. Choose Start > Settings > Control Panel > Fonts.
2. In the Fonts Control Panel, choose View > Options, then click the TrueType tab.
3. Deselect Show Only TrueType Fonts in the Programs on My Computer, then click OK.

In Windows 3.1x:

1. Open the Fonts Control Panel, then click TrueType.
2. Deselect Show Only TrueType Fonts in Applications, then click OK.

B. Remove all installed fonts, remove references to the fonts in the Win.ini and Atm.ini files, delete any Atmfonts.qlc files, then re-add fonts in ATM from the original font disks:

1. Open the ATM Control Panel, select the fonts you want to remove from the list of Installed ATM Fonts, then click Remove. In the Remove Fonts dialog box, select No Confirmation to Remove Fonts if you don't want the dialog box to appear for each font you remove. Select Delete Fonts from Disk only if you want to delete the font files from your system. Click OK to remove the fonts.
2. Delete any duplicate Win.ini files (i.e., Win.ini files not located in the Windows directory), then make a backup copy of the Win.ini file in the Windows directory. Open the original Win.ini file in a text editor that can save in text-only format (e.g., Windows Write, NotePad). Delete all the lines that begin "softfont" (e.g., softfonts=20). In Windows 95, also delete any lines that refer to an MFD file (e.g., ADMFDFile=C:\WINDOWS\AD434AF1.MFD). Save the Win.ini file in text-only format.
3. Delete any duplicate Atm.ini files (i.e., Atm.ini files not located in the Windows directory), then make a backup copy of the Atm.ini file in the Windows directory. Open the original Atm.ini file in a text editor that can save in text-only format (e.g., Windows Write, NotePad). Delete all lines, if there are any, in the [Fonts] section (e.g., "Helvetica=C:\Psfonts\-Pfm\Hv______.pfm; C:\Psfonts\Hv______.pfb"). Save the Atm.ini file in text-only format, then restart Windows.
4. Delete all Atmfonts.qlc files.
5. Open the ATM Control Panel, then click Add. In the Add Fonts dialog box, choose the drive and directory where your fonts are located (e.g., A:\Pssfonts). Select the fonts you want to install from the list of available fonts, then click Add.

ADDITIONAL INFORMATION

When the Show Only TrueType Fonts option is selected in the Fonts Control Panel, PostScript Type 1 fonts installed in ATM do not appear in application Font menus. Deselecting the Show Only TrueType fonts option enables PostScript fonts to display in font menus.

An improperly installed font, a damaged font file, or multiple or damaged Win.ini, Atm.ini, or Atmfonts.qlc files or font references can prevent fonts from displaying in font menus. Removing fonts from ATM, removing font references from the Win.ini and Atm.ini files and deleting Atmfonts.qlc files, then readding fonts may enable fonts to appear in application font menus.

The Atmfonts.qlc file contains screen display information for the last several fonts used, enabling ATM to display fonts more quickly. If you delete the Atmfonts.qlc file, ATM creates a new one the next time you launch Windows. The file is located in the Psfonts directory by default, but duplicates may exist in other locations. You can search for and delete every Atmfonts.qlc file using the Windows Explorer (Windows 95) or the File Manager (Windows 3.1x).

PostScript Font Family Names Installed in ATM 4.0 Don't Appear in Any Font Menus

ISSUE

The font family names of PostScript Type 1 fonts installed in ATM Deluxe 4.0 (e.g., "AGaramond" for "AGaramond", "AGaramond,Bold", and "AGaramond,Italic") do not appear in any application's font menu when ATM is active.

SOLUTIONS

Do one or more of the following:

A. Deselect the Show Only TrueType Fonts option in the Fonts Control Panel:
   1. Choose Start > Settings > Control Panel.
   2. Open the Fonts Control Panel.
   3. Choose View > Options, then click the TrueType tab.
   4. Deselect Show Only TrueType Fonts in the Programs on My Computer, then click OK.

B. Remove all your installed fonts from ATM, remove font references from the Win.ini file and the Atm.ini file, re-add the problem font in ATM, then check the size of the Win.ini file. Before you remove fonts, you may want to export your sets so you can reimport them after re-adding the fonts, rather than recreating the sets:
   1. Make backup copies of the Win.ini and Atm.ini files, located in the Windows directory.
   2. In ATM, export your sets and remove all installed fonts. For instructions, see Additional Information.
   3. Open the Win.ini file in a text editor that can save in text-only format (e.g., Notepad, WordPad).
   4. Delete any lines that begin with "softfont" (e.g., softfonts=20).
   5. Delete all lines that refer to an MFD file (e.g., ADMFDFile=C:\Windows\Ad434af1\Mfd).
   6. Save the Win.ini file in text-only format.
   7. Open the Atm.ini file in a text editor that can save in text-only format (e.g., NotePad, WordPad).
   8. Delete any lines in the [Fonts] section (e.g., "Helvetica=C:\Psfonts\Pfm\Hv______.pfm; C:\Psfonts\Hv-______.pfb").
   9. Save the Atm.ini file in text-only format.
   10. Delete all Atmfonts.qlc files, then restart Windows.
   11. Re-add your fonts in ATM. For instructions, see Additional Information.

ADDITIONAL INFORMATION

When the Show Only TrueType Fonts option is selected in the Fonts Control Panel, PostScript Type 1 fonts installed in ATM do not appear in application font menus. An improperly installed font, a damaged font file, or multiple or damaged Win.ini, Atm.ini, or Atmfonts.qlc files or font references can also prevent fonts from displaying in font menus.

The Atmfonts.qlc file contains rasterization information on the last several fonts used, which enables ATM to rasterize fonts more quickly. When you delete the Atmfonts.qlc file, ATM creates a new one the next time you launch Windows. The file is located in the Psfonts directory by default, but duplicates may exist in other locations. You can search for and delete every Atmfonts.qlc file using the Windows Explorer.

To export your sets:

1. In ATM, click the Sets tab.
2. Select one or more sets to export.
3. Choose File > Export.
4. In the Export dialog box, specify a filename and location for the AFS file, then click Save.

To remove your fonts:

1. In the All Font Sets pane of the Sets tab, select the fonts you want to remove, then click Remove.
2. In the Remove Font dialog box, select Remove Fonts from All Set and Master Font List, select Remove Font Files from Disk if you are reinstalling your fonts from the original installation disks, then click Yes or Yes to All.

To re-add your fonts:

1. Click the Add Fonts tab, then select Browse for Fonts from the Source pop-up menu.
2. Navigate to the drive and directory where your fonts files are located (e.g., C:\Psfonts\Pfm, A:\Fontdisk).
3. Select the fonts you want to add from the Source pane scrollbox, then click Add.

To import your sets:

1. With Browse for Fonts still selected in the Source pop-up menu, navigate to the drive and directory where your AFS file is located. ATM lists the sets you exported in the AFS file.
2. Select the sets you want to import, then click Add.
3. Remove any duplicate fonts outside your sets by selecting them and clicking Remove.

MAC OS

Error "AdobeSanMM or AdobeSerMM is not installed" on Startup or When Launching Application

ISSUE

When you start your Macintosh or launch an application in System 7.1x, Adobe Type Manager (ATM) returns the error "AdobeSanMM or AdobeSerMM is not installed. Please install from your master disks." The substitution fonts Adobe Sans MM and Adobe Serif MM or Adobe SansX MM and Adobe Serif MM are installed in the Fonts folder in the System Folder.

SOLUTIONS

Do one or more of the following:

A. Move the AdobeSanMM and AdobeSerMM outline fonts files from the Fonts folder into the System Folder, then restart the Macintosh.

B. Reinstall the substitution fonts by installing SuperATM, Acrobat Reader, Acrobat Exchange, or Acrobat Distiller.

C. Upgrade to System 7.5 or later.

ADDITIONAL INFORMATION

When ATM is unable to locate the Adobe Sans MM or Adobe Serif MM substitution fonts, it returns an error when you start the Macintosh or launch an application. ATM may be unable to locate outline font files installed in System 7.1's Fonts folder in the System Folder. Moving the outline font files from the Fonts folder to the System Folder, reinstalling the fonts, or upgrading the System 7.5 or later may enable ATM to find the font files as expected.

ATM Deluxe Autoactivation Doesn't Work When Opening Document

ISSUE

When you open a document containing a font that is installed but inactive in Adobe Type Manager (ATM) Deluxe 4.0, ATM does not automatically activate the font for the application. The Enable Auto-Activation option is selected in the ATM control panel's Advanced Settings pane.

SOLUTIONS

If you are using PageMaker 5.x or 6.x, enable ATM font matching and disable PANOSE font matching:

1. Choose File > Preferences.
2. In the Preferences dialog box, click Map Fonts.
3. In the Map Fonts dialog box, select the ATM Font Matching option (PageMaker 6.x) or the SuperATM Font Matching option (PageMaker 5.0x).
4. Deselect the PANOSE Font Matching option, then click OK.
5. Click OK to close the Preferences dialog box.

OR: Activate the font manually in ATM Deluxe.

OR: Open the document in an application that requests a font by its name, not by its ID number. To determine how the version of your application requests font information, see its documentation or contact the manufacturer.

ADDITIONAL INFORMATION

ATM Deluxe can autoactivate fonts installed in ATM but not active when an application requests a font by name. ATM cannot autoactivate fonts for those applications (e.g., SimpleText, Stickies) that request a font by its ID number.

ATM can autoactivate fonts for PageMaker only when the PANOSE Font Matching option is deselected and the ATM Font Matching option (PageMaker 6.x) or the SuperATM Font Matching option (PageMaker 5.x) is selected in the Map Fonts dialog box. If the PANOSE Font Matching option is selected, PageMaker uses PANOSE font matching instead of ATM font matching.

ATM Displays Plain Typeface as Stylized Typeface in QuickDraw GX

ISSUE

When running in QuickDraw GX, ATM 3.8.x and 3.9 display a plain typeface (e.g., Times) as a stylized typeface (e.g., Times Bold, Times italic). The plain typeface is not installed.

SOLUTIONS

Install the plain typeface's screen and printer font files.

OR: To prevent ATM 3.8.x and 3.9 from displaying a plain typeface using a substitute stylized typeface, apply the plain typeface to text before applying the stylized typeface to text.

ADDITIONAL INFORMATION

In QuickDraw GX, ATM 3.8.x and 3.9 display text formatted with a plain typeface in a stylized typeface (i.e., bold, italic) when the plain typeface is not installed and the stylized typeface was applied to text in the document before the plain typeface. For example, in a document containing two text blocks, the first formatted in Stone Serif Bold Italic and the second formatted in Stone Serif, ATM 3.8.x and 3.9 display the second text block in Stone Serif Bold Italic instead of Stone Serif when Stone Serif is not installed.

When ATM 3.8.x and ATM 3.9 display a missing plain typeface in a stylized typeface, the type formatted with the plain typeface may appear with unexpected word and letter spacing because ATM displays the text using the plain typeface's letter spacing definitions, instead of the stylized typeface's letter spacing definitions.

Fonts Display as Bitmaps Using ATM, Suitcase, and System 7.5.2

ISSUE

Fonts are displayed as a bitmap (i.e., jagged) and either print as a bitmap or substitute to Courier when you're using

Adobe Type Manager (ATM), Symantec Suitcase II 2.1.4 or earlier, and System 7.5.2.

SOLUTIONS
Use Suitcase II 2.1.4p3 or later, which is available from Symantec.
OR: Move all fonts into the Fonts folder in the System Folder.

ADDITIONAL INFORMATION
System 7.5.2 maps paths to printer fonts differently than previous versions of Macintosh system software. Suitcase 2.1.4 does not support System 7.5.2's method of mapping paths to printer fonts, causing Suitcase not to locate printer fonts when System 7.5.2 is installed.

Suitcase 2.1.4p3 supports System 7.5.2's method of mapping paths to printer fonts.

Moving the fonts to the Fonts folder in the System Folder enables the system to access them directly, rather than by accessing them using Suitcase.

Substitute for Missing Fonts Option Dimmed in ATM Control Panel

ISSUE
The Substitute for Missing Fonts option (i.e., the option that enables SuperATM functionality) is dimmed in the Adobe Type Manager (ATM) 3.5.x or later Control Panel.

SOLUTIONS
Do one or more of the following:
A. Make sure SuperATM's ATM Font Database file (i.e., 1 MB or larger) is installed in the System Folder. If SuperATM's ATM Font Database is not installed, install it from the original SuperATM disk set.
B. When using SuperATM 3.5.x or 3.6.x, make sure SuperATM has been personalized (i.e., serial number has been entered in the Personalization dialog box in the ATM control panel) and that the serial number is not being used for another copy of SuperATM installed on a different computer on the same network.

ADDITIONAL INFORMATION
The Substitute for Missing Fonts option is available in the ATM control panel when SuperATM's ATM Font Database file (i.e., 1 MB or larger) is installed in the System Folder. The Substitute for Missing Fonts option enables SuperATM to generate substitute fonts when the fonts a document contains are not installed.

SuperATM 3.5.x and 3.6.x require you to enter a serial number in the Personalization dialog box that appears when opening the ATM Control Panel. When no serial number is entered in the Personalization dialog box, the alert "Adobe Type Manager will not do font substitution until you personalize your copy of ATM" appears. The Substitute for Missing Fonts check box is dimmed until SuperATM is personalized.

SuperATM 3.5.x and 3.6.x include built-in network copy detection. When SuperATM 3.5.x or 3.6.x detects another copy of SuperATM using a duplicate serial number on another Macintosh on the same network, it generates the error "Adobe Type Manager cannot do font substitution because a copy of ATM with your serial number is already in use by [User Name]" or "Adobe Type Manager cannot do font substitution because there are already X people running copies of ATM with this serial number." The Substitute for Missing Fonts option is dimmed when SuperATM detects another copy of SuperATM using the same serial number.

Acrobat's ATM Font Database file (i.e., smaller than 100K) does not enable the Substitute for Missing Fonts option.

SuperATM Does Not Substitute Fonts Troubleshooting Guide

ISSUE
When you open a document containing Adobe PostScript fonts that are not installed, SuperATM does not substitute fonts as expected (e.g., the fonts substitute to Courier).

SOLUTIONS
Do one or more of the following:
A. Verify that the SuperATM component files are installed in the expected locations. For SuperATM component file names and installed locations, see Additional Information.
B. Select the Substitute for Missing Fonts option in the ATM control panel, then restart the Macintosh.
C. Select On in the ATM control panel, then restart the Macintosh.
D. Reinstall SuperATM from the original installation disks.
E. Make sure your application supports SuperATM font substitution. For a list of applications that support SuperATM font substitution, refer to the ReadMe file included with SuperATM.
F. Make sure the original document contains Adobe PostScript fonts, not PostScript fonts from another manufacturer.

ADDITIONAL INFORMATION
SuperATM cannot generate substitute fonts when:
- one of its component files is missing or damaged
- the ATM control panel does not have the Substitute for Missing Font option selected or is turned off
- an application does not support font substitution
- the document contains non-Adobe PostScript fonts

Both SuperATM and the Adobe Acrobat products install a read-only ATM Font Database file into the System Folder. SuperATM's ATM Font Database file contains the font substitution information for most of Adobe's typefaces. The file size of SuperATM's Font Database file is larger than 1 MB, while Acrobat's ATM Font Database file size is smaller than 100K, since it contains substitution information for only the Acrobat applications. SuperATM can generate substitute fonts only for those fonts whose substitution information is included in its ATM Font Database file.

SuperATM can generate substitute fonts that simulate most Adobe typefaces, mimicking an actual font's character shapes and line spacing. Because SuperATM's substituted fonts are not intended to replace the actual fonts, character shapes may not exactly match those of the actual font on-screen or when you print them.

SuperATM Substitutes with Only Serif or Only Sans Serif Fonts

ISSUE

When the Substitute For Missing Fonts option is selected in the Adobe Type Manager (ATM) control panel, Adobe SuperATM generates a serif font to display a missing sans serif font, or a sans serif font to display a missing serif font.

SYMPTOM

Adobe Acrobat Exchange 1.0 is installed.

SOLUTIONS

Set Acrobat Exchange 1.0 preferences to display missing fonts using both serif and sans serif substitution fonts:

1. In Acrobat Exchange, choose Edit > Preferences.
2. Set the Font Substitution option to Both Serif and Sans, then click OK.
3. Quit Acrobat Exchange and restart the computer.

OR: Upgrade to Acrobat Exchange 2.0 or later.

ADDITIONAL INFORMATION

The Acrobat Exchange 1.0 Font Substitution preferences option overrides SuperATM's, which changes how SuperATM displays missing fonts in all applications. When the Serif Only option or the Sans Only option is selected for Exchange's Font Substitution preference, SuperATM displays missing fonts with either a serif or sans serif substitute font. When the Both Serif and Sans option is selected, SuperATM displays missing fonts using both serif and sans serif substitution fonts.

The Font Substitution preference in Acrobat Exchange 2.0 does not affect how SuperATM displays missing fonts in other applications.

ATM Control Panel Doesn't Load During Startup

ISSUE

ATM does not load during startup as expected.

SOLUTIONS

Do one or more of the following:

A. Remove all but one of the installed extension management utilities (e.g., Extensions Manager, Conflict Catcher).

B. Make sure only one copy of ATM is installed.

C. Make sure the ATM control panel is located in the Control Panels folder in the System Folder.

ADDITIONAL INFORMATION

More than one installed extension management utility may prevent ATM from loading during startup because the system software honors the settings of only one installed extension management control panel. For example, NOW Startup Manager settings override the settings of Apple's Extensions Manager.

When multiple copies of the ATM control panel are installed, or when the ATM control panel is not installed in the Control Panels folder in the System Folder, ATM does not load during startup as expected.

Message "Font Substitution Will be Shut Down" Appears in SuperATM 3.6.2 and Earlier

ISSUE

The message "Font substitution will be shut down." appears when using Adobe SuperATM 3.6.2 or earlier on a Macintosh connected to a network.

SOLUTIONS

Reinstall SuperATM using a different serial number.

OR: Upgrade to SuperATM 3.8 or later.

OR: Install SuperATM on only one Macintosh connected to the network.

ADDITIONAL INFORMATION

SuperATM 3.6.2 and earlier includes a Network Copy Detection scheme that prevents multiple copies of SuperATM with the same serial number from running on a network. When multiple copies with the same serial number are installed on a network, font substitution is disabled for all but the copy that was launched first.

Network Copy Detection is based on the serial number entered in the ATM control panel. At startup, and every thirty minutes while SuperATM is running, SuperATM queries the network for copies with the same serial number.

Adobe Type Manager (ATM) and SuperATM 3.8 and later do not include Network Copy Detection.

Application Errors

WINDOWS

Error "Cannot open file" When Exporting Font Set from ATM Deluxe to Network Drive

ISSUE

When exporting a set to a network drive, Adobe Type Manager (ATM) Deluxe 4.0 returns the error, "Cannot open file:

[drive]:\[directory]\[set filename]." The set's name contains 9 or more characters or a space character (e.g., Starter Set).

SOLUTIONS
Change the set's name so it contains 8 or fewer characters and no space characters.
OR: Export the set to a local drive, then copy the exported file to the network drive.

ADDITIONAL INFORMATION
When exporting a set, ATM Deluxe uses Windows 95's common Save As dialog box, which does not support saving files with long filenames (i.e., names containing 9 or more characters or containing space characters) to a network drive. The Save As dialog box does support saving files with long filenames to a local hard drive.

Error "An application has accessed an invalid TrueType font" Selecting TrueType Font in Authorware 3.0

ISSUE
When you select a TrueType font in Macromedia Authorware 3.0, Authorware returns the error, "An application has accessed an invalid TrueType font" appears. Then, all TrueType fonts disappear from the font list in Authorware and all other applications.

SYMPTOM
Adobe Type Manager (ATM) 3.x is installed.

SOLUTIONS
Update to Authorware 3.01, which is available from Macromedia.
OR: Restart Windows to make TrueType fonts available to other Windows applications.

ADDITIONAL INFORMATION
Authorware 3.0 is incompatible with ATM 3.x. Authorware 3.01 is compatible with ATM 3.x.

Error "Warning wpt0015: Old File does not exist." When Updating to ATM 3.02

ISSUE
The error "Warning wpt0015: Old File does not exist." appears when updating Adobe Type Manager (ATM) 3.0 or ATM 3.01 using the ATM 3.02 Updater.

SOLUTIONS
Update ATM 3.0 or ATM 3.01 using the ATM 3.02 Updater created 8/25/95.
OR: Reinstall ATM 3.0 or ATM 3.01 from the ATM program disks, then update ATM using the ATM 3.02 Updater created 8/24/95 or later.

ADDITIONAL INFORMATION
When updating ATM 3.0 or ATM 3.01 using the ATM 3.02 Updater created 8/24/95 when all ATM component files are not installed (e.g., ATM16.DLL or ATM32.DLL file is missing) causes the ATM 3.02 Updater to return the error "Warning wpt0015: Old File does not exist." The ATM 3.0.2 Updater created 8/24/95 updates Adobe Type Manager's ATM16.DLL, ATM32.DLL, ATMSYS.DRV, and ATMCNTRL.EXE files.

The ATM 3.02 Updater created 8/25/95 updates installed ATM 3.0 or 3.01 files, but does not require Adobe Type Manager's ATM16.DLL, ATM32.DLL, ATMSYS.DRV, and ATMCNTRL.EXE files to update ATM 3.0 or ATM 3.01.

Error "Cannot create instance name" After Clicking Create in ATM 3.0

ISSUE
After you click Create in the ATM Control Panel to create a multiple master instance using the Font Creator utility, Adobe Type Manager (ATM) 3.0 returns the error "Cannot create instance name."

SOLUTIONS
Use ATM 3.01 or later.
OR: Restart Windows, then reinstall the multiple master font.

ADDITIONAL INFORMATION
Because the Font Creator utility, which is included with ATM 3.0, is unable to create a multiple master instance for a multiple master font that was removed then reinstalled during the same Windows session, clicking Create in the ATM 3.0 Control Panel causes the Font Creator utility to return the error "Cannot create instance name." Restarting Windows then reinstalling the multiple master font enables the Font Creator utility to create the multiple master instance.

MAC OS

Error "ATM requires more memory or additional system resources" on Startup

ISSUE
When starting the Macintosh, the error "ATM requires more memory or additional system resources" appears.

SOLUTIONS
Do one or more of the following:
A. When using Adobe Type Manager (ATM) 3.8.x or ATM 3.9 on a Power Macintosh, change the Virtual Memory and Modern Memory Manager settings in the Memory control panel, then restart the computer. For example, when the Virtual Memory option is Off and the Mod-

ern Memory Manager is On, set the Virtual Memory option to On and the Modern Memory option to Off, then restart.

B. When your hard disk has been formatted by FWB Toolkit RTK 1.8, reformat using the FWB Toolkit HDT 2.0 or later. For instructions, consult the FWB documentation or contact FWB.

C. Reinstall ATM:
When using ATM 3.8.x or ATM 3.9 on a Power Macintosh or a Macintosh with the Power Macintosh upgrade card installed, install ATM for the 68000-series Macintosh:
1. Insert the ATM Program Disk, then launch the ATM & Font Installer.
2. In the ATM & Font Installer window, select Custom Install from the pop-up menu.
3. In the Check Features To Be Installed list, select ATM For 68020/030/040, then click Install.
NOTE: Running ATM for the 68000-series Macintosh on a Power Macintosh causes the alert "Adobe Type Manager will run much faster if you install a PowerMac version" to occur on startup, which cannot be disabled.

OR: When using ATM 3.7, reinstall ATM 3.7 or later.
OR: When using ATM 3.6.x, delete ATM's driver files (i.e., ~ATM 68000, 68020/030, 68020/030/040) installed in the System Folder, reinstall ATM 3.6.x, then restart the computer.
OR: When using ATM 3.5 or earlier, upgrade to ATM 3.6 or later.

D. Recreate the ATM Temp.ATM file by doing one or more of the following:
A. Recreate the Preferences folder:
1. Move the Preferences folder from the System Folder to another location (e.g., desktop).
2. Restart the Macintosh. The Finder creates a new Preferences folder and new System preferences files on startup.
3. Move the new System preferences files (e.g., Finder Preferences) from the new Preferences folder in the System Folder to another location (e.g., new folder on the desktop, Trash without emptying the Trash).
4. Open the old Preferences folder, choose Edit > Select All, then move the selected preferences files into the new Preferences folder in the System Folder.
5. Restart your Macintosh.
6. Delete the new System preferences files copied to another location (e.g., new folder on the desktop, Trash).

B. Use Symantec Anti-Virus to locate and remove damaged ATM Temp.ATM files, then restart the computer to create a new ATM Temp.ATM file.

C. Use ResEdit to change the ATM Temp.ATM file to a visible file, remove the ATM Temp.ATM file, then restart:
1. In ResEdit, choose File > Get File/Folder Info.
2. In the Get File/Folder Info dialog box, locate the ATM Temp.ATM file in the Preferences folder in the System Folder, then click Get Info.
3. In the Get Info dialog box, deselect the Invisible option.
4. Choose File > Save, then close ResEdit.
5. Remove the ATM Temp.ATM file from the Preferences file in the System Folder, then restart the computer.

NOTE: Other extensions or control panels may prevent ATM from loading. Run ATM with all extensions off by using an extensions manager to disable all extensions and control panels except ATM or by removing all extensions and control panels from the System Folder except ATM then restarting the computer to verify that added extensions or control panels are not the cause.

ADDITIONAL INFORMATION

The error "ATM requires more memory or additional system resources" may occur when starting Power Macintosh computers when ATM 3.8.x or ATM 3.9 is installed. Changing the Virtual Memory and Modern Memory Manager settings in the Memory Control Panel, or installing ATM for the 68000-series Macintosh, may prevent the error from occurring and enable ATM to load as expected.

FWB Toolkit HDT is compatible with ATM, but FWB Toolkit RTK 1.8 is incompatible with ATM. Reformatting your hard disk using FWB Toolkit HDT prevents the error "ATM requires more memory or additional system resources" and enables ATM to load as expected.

The error "ATM requires more memory or additional system resources" occurs on startup when the ATM Temp.-ATM file, the ATM control panel, or the ATM driver file is damaged, or when there is an extension conflict.

ATM Temp.ATM is an invisible, temporary file that ATM creates and locates in the Preferences folder in the System Folder. SuperATM and Acrobat use the ATM Temp.ATM file to store font substitution information. When the ATM Temp.ATM file is damaged, creating a new Preferences folder or deleting the ATM Temp.ATM file enables ATM to create a new ATM Temp.ATM file on startup.

ATM 3.5 and earlier are incompatible with DECNet, Dayna DOS Mounter, Norton FileSaver, Suitcase 1.2.10 or earlier running in System 7.0.x, or Suitcase 2.1.2 running in System 7.1 or later. Starting a Macintosh with ATM 3.5 or earlier and one of these utilities installed causes the error "ATM requires more memory or additional system resources." to occur.

Error "Substitution fonts necessary for Acrobat or SuperATM are missing" During Startup

ISSUE

When Adobe Type Manager (ATM) 3.8.2 or later is installed, ATM returns the alert "The substitution fonts necessary for

Acrobat or SuperATM are missing. Please re-install either software package." during startup.

SOLUTIONS

Install the Adobe Sans MM and Adobe Serif MM font files included with SuperATM 3.8.x or 3.9, Acrobat Reader 2.0.1 or later, or Acrobat Exchange 2.0.1 or later into the Fonts folder in the System Folder.

OR: When not using SuperATM, Acrobat Reader, or Acrobat Exchange, remove the ATM Font Database file from the System Folder.

ADDITIONAL INFORMATION

ATM 3.8.2 and later try to locate the Adobe Sans MM and Adobe Serif MM fonts during startup when the ATM Font Database file is installed in the System Folder. When ATM is unable to locate the Adobe Sans MM and Adobe Serif MM font files, it returns the error "The substitution fonts necessary for Acrobat or SuperATM are missing. Please reinstall either software package." Installing the Adobe Sans MM and Adobe Serif MM font files in the System Folder or removing the ATM Font Database file from the System Folder enables ATM to launch without returning the error.

Both SuperATM and the Adobe Acrobat products install a read-only ATM Font Database file into the System Folder. SuperATM's ATM Font Database file contains the font substitution information for most of Adobe's typefaces including height, weight, and pair kerning information. The file size of SuperATM's Font Database file is larger than 1 MB, while Acrobat's ATM Font Database file size is smaller than 100K, since it contains substitution information for only the Acrobat applications. SuperATM can generate substitute fonts only for those fonts whose substitution information is included in its ATM Font Database file.

SuperATM uses the Adobe Sans MM and Adobe Serif MM multiple master fonts to generate substitute fonts. Because Adobe Sans MM and Adobe Serif MM are used for substitution only, they do not display in application font menus.

Error "ATM Requires...'AdobeSansMM' or 'AdobeSansXMM'" During Startup

ISSUE

During startup, Adobe Type Manager (ATM) returns the error "Adobe Type Manager requires the multiple master font 'AdobeSansMM' or 'AdobeSansXMM' or in order to render substitution fonts correctly. Please install this font from your master disks."

SOLUTIONS

When using SuperATM 3.8.x, reinstall the AdobeSansMM substitution fonts from the original SuperATM installation disks.

OR: When using SuperATM 3.5.x or 3.6.x, reinstall the AdobeSansXMM substitution font from the original SuperATM installation disks.

ADDITIONAL INFORMATION

In order to perform font substitution, SuperATM 3.8.x requires the AdobeSansMM multiple master fonts, and Super-ATM 3.5.x and 3.6.x require the AdobeSansXMM multiple master font. When the AdobeSansMM or the AdobeSansXMM font is not installed, SuperATM cannot generate a substitute font and returns an error.

Error "...system software, ATM and substitution fonts not synchronized" Launching Acrobat

ISSUE

When starting, Adobe Acrobat Reader, Adobe Acrobat Exchange, or Adobe Acrobat Distiller return the error "The current versions of system software, ATM and substitution fonts are not synchronized. Reinstall Acrobat."

SOLUTIONS

When SuperATM is installed:

1. Restart with all extensions disabled. To quickly disable added or nonessential extensions, restart with the Shift key held down until the message "Welcome to Macintosh. Extensions off." appears, or use an extensions manager.
2. Remove the ATM control panel from the Control Panels folder in the System Folder.
3. Remove the substitution fonts (e.g., Adobe Serif MM and Adobe Sans[X] MM) from the Fonts folder in the System Folder.
4. Remove the ATM Font Database file from the System Folder.
5. Reinstall SuperATM from the original SuperATM installation disks.

OR: When SuperATM is not installed:

1. Restart with all extensions disabled. To quickly disable added or nonessential extensions, restart with the Shift key held down until the message "Welcome to Macintosh. Extensions off." appears, or use an extensions manager.
2. Remove the ATM control panel from the Control Panels folder in the System Folder.
3. Remove the substitution fonts (e.g., Adobe Serif MM and Adobe Sans[X] MM) from the Fonts folder in the System Folder.
4. Remove the ATM Font Database file located in the System Folder.
5. Reinstall Acrobat Reader, Exchange, or Distiller from the original installation disks.

ADDITIONAL INFORMATION

When Adobe Type Manager (ATM) is installed with an incompatible version of the ATM Font Database file or substitution fonts, Acrobat Reader, Acrobat Exchange, or Acrobat Distiller return the error "The current versions of system software, ATM and substitution fonts are not synchronized. Reinstall Acrobat." when starting.

Both SuperATM and the Adobe Acrobat products install a read-only ATM Font Database file into the System

Folder. SuperATM's ATM Font Database file contains the font substitution information, including height, weight, and pair kerning for most of Adobe's typefaces. The file size of SuperATM's Font Database file is larger than 1 MB, while Acrobat's ATM Font Database file size is smaller than 100K since it contains substitution information for only the Acrobat applications. SuperATM can generate substitute fonts only for those fonts whose substitution information is included in its ATM Font Database file.

System Errors

WINDOWS

GPF in Atmfm.exe When Printing Set Index in ATM Deluxe 4.0

ISSUE

When you print a set index in Adobe Type Manager Deluxe (ATM) 4.0, Windows returns a General Protection Fault in Atmfm.exe. Only part of the set index prints.

SOLUTIONS

Do one or both of the following:

A. Make sure the Win.ini file is smaller than 32K. For more information, refer to the Microsoft Windows User's Guide, or contact Microsoft Technical Support.

B. Remove damaged fonts from the set, then print the set index. ATM prints the fonts in a set index in alphabetical order, so the fonts listed alphabetically after the last font that printed as expected are the most likely to be damaged. For instructions on removing fonts, refer to the ATM Deluxe 4.0 online Help.

ADDITIONAL INFORMATION

ATM may be unable to print a set index (i.e., a list and samples of all the fonts in a font set) when the Win.ini file is larger than 32K. The Win.ini file has a maximum allowable file size of 64K, but keeping it 32K or smaller enables your system to run more efficiently and may prevent errors. When the size of the Win.ini file exceeds 32K or 64K, Windows or applications running in Windows may behave unpredictably.

ATM may also be unable to print a complete set index when the set contains one or more damaged fonts. Removing and reinstalling damaged fonts in a set may enable ATM to print the entire set index without error.

GPF Error When ATM 2.x or 3.0x Is Installed Troubleshooting Guide

ISSUE

When Adobe Type Manager (ATM) 2.x or 3.0x is installed, the system returns a General Protection Fault (GPF) error.

SOLUTIONS

Do one or more of the following:

A. Turn off ATM in the ATM Control Panel, then restart Windows.

B. Upgrade to ATM 3.0x or later.

C. Adjust the amount of memory available to ATM and the system by doing one or more of the following:
   A. When viewing or printing more than four single master or three multiple master typefaces on a page, increase the Font Cache setting in the ATM Control Panel to 250K-1000K.
   B. When ATM uses memory that other applications or the system requires, decrease the Font Cache setting in the ATM Control Panel to no lower than 125K.
   C. Remove PostScript fonts using ATM to reduce the number of PostScript fonts installed.
   D. Exit applications not in use.

D. Toggle the Print ATM Fonts as Graphics option in the ATM Control Panel (i.e., select it when it is deselected, or deselect it when it is selected).

E. Deinstall all PostScript fonts in the ATM Control Panel, then delete duplicate Atm.ini files.

F. If duplicate Atmcntrl.exe files are installed, remove ATM from the system, then reinstall ATM.

G. Move the Atmcntrl.exe and Atm.ini files into the Windows directory.

H. Recreate the Atmfonts.qlc file by deleting all copies of the Atmfonts.qlc file, then restarting Windows.

I. Remove then reinstall all PostScript fonts in the ATM Control Panel:
   1. Make a backup copy of the Atm.ini and Win.ini files, located in the Windows directory.
   2. In the ATM Control Panel, select all fonts in the Installed ATM Fonts list box, then click Remove.
   3. In the alert box that appears, deselect Delete Fonts from Disk, which is deselected by default, then click Yes to remove each font.
   4. Delete the Atm.ini file located in the Windows directory and the Atmfonts.qlc file located in the Psfonts or Windows directory, then restart Windows. ATM creates a new Atm.ini file and Atmfonts.qlc file.
   5. Reinstall PostScript fonts by clicking Add in the ATM Control Panel.

J. Deinstall ATM, then reinstall ATM. For instructions, see Related Records.

   NOTE: Memory-resident (TSR) program, system, and hardware conflicts can also cause General Protection Fault (GPF) errors.

ADDITIONAL INFORMATION

When ATM uses memory that other applications or the system requires, a General Protection Fault (GPF) error occurs. Decreasing the size of ATM's Font Cache decreases the amount of memory ATM uses to store bitmap typefaces for screen display, and increases the amount of memory available to the system and other applications. After you decrease the size of ATM's Font Cache, using multiple typefaces in a document may require memory for ATM to create a bitmap typeface that is unavailable in ATM's Font Cache.

When ATM prints fonts as graphics, the printer receives fonts as a graphic rather than as PostScript code.

The Atmfonts.qlc file is a defaults file containing information on the PostScript fonts installed in ATM. When multiple copies of the Atmfonts.qlc file are installed or if the file is damaged, a GPF error can occur. When you exit Windows, ATM creates a new Atmfonts.qlc file if it cannot locate an existing Atmfonts.qlc file.

Removing and then reinstalling PostScript fonts in ATM forces ATM to create a new Atm.ini and Atmfonts.qlc file, with both files containing identical and accurate PostScript font information. Before deleting the Atm.ini file, deinstall all PostScript fonts from the ATM Control Panel to prevent font substitution caused by different or inaccurate information in the Atm.ini file and Win.ini file.

Error "Cannot find Atm32.ndl" or " Copying Atm??.ndl failed" When Starting Windows on Network

ISSUE

When you start Windows 3.1x, it returns the error, "Cannot find Atm32.ndl." or "Cannot copy Atm32.ndl." or "Adobe Type Manager. Copying file Atm??.ndl failed." Windows is installed on a network, and ATM 3.0x and 32-bit Novell network software (i.e., Novell NetWare Client 32) or non-Novell network software are installed.

SOLUTION

Install the non-network Atmsys.drv file, which is available from Adobe Technical Support:

1. Unzip the compressed non-network Atmsys.drv file, which is named Atmsys.zip.
2. Delete the existing Atmsys.drv file from the Windows\System directory.
2. Delete the Atm16.ndl or Atm16.dll file, if present.
3. Move the unzipped Atmsys.drv file into the Windows\System directory.
5. Restart Windows.

ADDITIONAL INFORMATION

The Atmsys.drv file included with ATM 3.0x is incompatible with NetWare Client 32 network software and non-Novell network software, which prevents Windows from loading ATM when it starts, causing it to return the error, "Cannot find Atm32.ndl." or "Cannot copy Atm32.ndl." or "Adobe Type Manager. Copying file Atm??.ndl failed." Using the non-network Atmsys.drv file with NetWare Client 32 network software or non-Novell network software enables Windows to load ATM when it starts.

NetWare Client 32 includes NetWare Loadable Modules that replace the Virtual Loadable Modules used in the 16-bit version of NetWare. NetWare Client 32 improves network performance by providing 32-bit access to network services and resources.

Opening ATM 4.0 Causes Windows 95 to Restart or Freeze

ISSUE

When you open Adobe Type Manager Deluxe 4.0 (ATM), Windows 95 restarts or freezes. Quarterdeck QEMM 8.0 or earlier is installed.

SOLUTIONS

Disable QEMM and use Himem.sys as the memory manager. For instructions, see Additional Information.
OR: Use QEMM 8.0.1 or later.

ADDITIONAL INFORMATION

ATM 4.0 and QEMM 8.0 and earlier are incompatible, causing Windows 95 to restart when you start ATM with the QEMM memory management software is installed. Disabling QEMM enables ATM to start as expected.

To disable QEMM 8.0 and use Himem.sys as the memory manager:

1. Make a backup copy of the Config.sys file located in the root directory of the C: drive (i.e., C:\Config.sys).
2. In Explorer, note the location of the Himem.sys file that has the most recent date.
3. Open the Config.sys file in a text editor that can save in text-only format (e.g., WordPad, Notepad).
4. Locate the following line:
   DEVICE=QEMM386
5. Type "REM" in front of the "DEVICE=QEMM386" line to prevent the system from reading the line (i.e., remark it out). For example:
   `REM DEVICE=QEMM386`
6. Type the following text below the "REM DEVICE=QEMM386" line:
   `DEVICE=C:\WINDOWS\HIMEM.SYS`
   where C:\Windows\Himem.sys is the path to the Himem.sys file that has the most recent date.
7. Save the Config.sys file in text-only format, then restart the computer.

MAC OS

PrintShop Deluxe 1.1.1 Freezes When ATM 3.8.x Is Installed

ISSUE

Broderbund PrintShop Deluxe 1.1.1 freezes after you format text with a PostScript font when Adobe Type Manager (ATM) 3.8.x is installed.

SOLUTION

Upgrade to PrintShop Deluxe 1.1.2 or later.

OR: Disable ATM by selecting Off in the ATM control panel and restarting the Macintosh.

ADDITIONAL INFORMATION

PrintShop Deluxe 1.1.1 is incompatible with ATM 3.8.x, causing it to freeze after you format text with a PostScript font when ATM 3.8.x is installed. PrintShop 1.1.2 or later is compatible with ATM 3.8.x.

Error "Type 15" Choosing Font from Font Menu

ISSUE

After choosing a PostScript font from a font menu, the system returns the error "The application 'unknown' has unexpectedly quit, because an error of type 15 occurred." QuickDraw GX and ATM 3.8.1 or earlier are installed.

SOLUTIONS

Enable the PostScript Type 1 font to be QuickDraw GX-compatible using the Type 1 Enabler utility, included with System 7.5.

OR: Use ATM 3.8.2 or later.

OR: Remove QuickDraw GX. For instructions, see Additional Information.

ADDITIONAL INFORMATION

Because PostScript Type 1 fonts are not QuickDraw GX-compatible, you must convert (i.e., enable) them using the QuickDraw GX Type 1 Enabler utility. When you select an unenabled PostScript Type 1 font from an application's font menu when both QuickDraw GX and ATM 3.8.1 or earlier are installed, the system returns the error "The application 'unknown' has unexpectedly quit, because an error of type 15 occurred."

ATM 3.8.2 and later use PostScript Type 1 (i.e., unenabled) fonts for display when QuickDraw GX is installed, but do not support printing unenabled fonts using a QuickDraw GX printer driver.

To remove QuickDraw GX:

Remove or disable QuickDraw GX system files, restore PostScript Type 1 fonts, then setup a PostScript printer:

1. Remove QuickDraw GX system files and restore standard Macintosh printing for all applications:
    1. Launch the Apple Installer on the QuickDraw GX Install disk by double-clicking on the Install QuickDraw GX installer control file.
    2. Select Custom Remove from the pop-up menu in the installer dialog box.
    3. Select the Base QuickDraw GX Software for This Macintosh, Base QuickDraw GX Software for Any Macintosh, QuickDraw GX Utilities, ATM for QuickDraw GX, and All QuickDraw GX Drivers for Apple Printers Custom Remove options.
    4. Set the Destination Disk to the volume containing the system software. Use the Switch Disk button to select another disk when your system software is installed on an attached volume.
    5. Click the Remove button.
    6. Restart the Macintosh.

    OR: Disable the QuickDraw GX and PrinterShare GX system extensions using Extensions Manager:
    1. Open the Extensions Manager control panel.
    2. Deselect the QuickDraw GX and PrinterShare GX system extensions, then restart the Macintosh.

    OR: Manually remove the QuickDraw GX and PrinterShare GX system files located in the Extensions folder in the System Folder.
2. Restore PostScript Type 1 fonts:
    1. Move all enabled font suitcases, located in the Fonts folder in the System Folder by default, to a different location. Enabled suitcases contain converted TrueType versions of the Type 1 PostScript font in addition to the bitmap (screen) fonts.
    2. Move fonts contained in the Archived Type 1 Fonts folder, located in the System Folder, into the Fonts folder, and delete the empty Archived Type 1 Fonts folder.
    3. Move other fonts enabled using the Type 1 Enabler application to another folder not accessed by any font management utility (e.g., Suitcase). Move the original archived copy of the Type 1 font back to the desired folder to make it available to the font management utility.
    4. Reinstall Adobe Type Manager versions other than ATM/GX 3.7.
3. Set up a PostScript printer in the Chooser:
    1. In the Chooser, select the Adobe PSPrinter 8.x or Apple LaserWriter 8.x printer driver icon.
    2. Select a PostScript printer from the Select a PostScript Printer list, then click Setup.
    3. Set up the PostScript printer by clicking Setup, clicking Auto Setup in the Current Printer Description file (PPD) Selected dialog box, then clicking OK. An icon appears to the left of the printer's name in the Chooser indicating it is set up using the PostScript printer driver.

    NOTE: After selecting Auto Setup, the LaserWriter 8.x printer driver locates the PostScript Printer Description (PPD) file for the printer. When the PostScript printer driver is unable to locate a corresponding PPD file, select the Select PPD option then choose a PPD file for your printer or click Use Generic in the Select a PostScript Printer Description File dialog box.

System Error (e.g., Freeze) After Installing ATM and Restarting Macintosh AV

ISSUE

A System error (e.g., freeze) occurs when restarting after installing Adobe Type Manager (ATM) 3.6.1 and earlier on a Macintosh with an Audio Video card (e.g., Macintosh 840 AV).

SOLUTION
Install ATM 3.8.1 or later.

ADDITIONAL INFORMATION
Because ATM 3.6.1 or earlier is not compatible with Audio Video cards, restarting a Macintosh with an Audio Video card when ATM 3.6.1 or earlier is installed results in a system error (e.g., freeze).

ATM 3.8.1 and later are compatible with Macintosh models that include Audio Video cards.

Unable to Start Power Macintosh With SuperATM Installed

ISSUE
The Power Macintosh returns a system error (e.g., freeze) during startup when Adobe SuperATM 3.5 is installed.

SOLUTION
Restart the Macintosh with all extensions off, then install the SuperATM 3.6.x or later control panel. To quickly disable added or non-essential extensions, restart with the Shift key held down until the message "Welcome to Macintosh. Extensions off." appears.

ADDITIONAL INFORMATION
Because SuperATM 3.5 is not compatible with Power Macintoshes, the Macintosh returns a system error during startup when loading the SuperATM 3.5 ATM control panel. SuperATM 3.6.x or later is compatible with Power Macintoshes. The Adobe Sans and Adobe Serif multiple master substitution fonts and the ATM Font Database file included with SuperATM 3.5 are compatible with Power Macintoshes.

Error "Unimplemented trap" Launching Omnipage 5.0

ISSUE
The system error "Unimplemented trap" occurs when launching Caere Omnipage 5.x.

SOLUTIONS
Disable ATM 3.8.1 before launching Omnipage 5.x.
OR: Do one or more of the following:
A. Install Adobe Type Manager (ATM) 3.8.2 or later.
B. When using Omnipage 5.x and ATM 3.8.2 with a Micro-tek scanner, install Microtek Scan Extension 1.3 or later scanner driver, which is available from Microtek.

ADDITIONAL INFORMATION
ATM 3.8.1 and earlier are not compatible with many scanner drivers (e.g., Microtek Scan Extension 1.3). Launching Omnipage 5.x when ATM 3.8.1 or earlier and a scanner driver are installed causes the system error "Unimplemented trap" to occur.

ATM 3.8.2 is not compatible with the Microtek Scan Extension 1.2.9 or earlier. Launching Omnipage 5.x when ATM 3.8.2 or earlier and the Microtek Scan Extension 1.2.9 or earlier are installed causes the system error "Unimplemented trap" to occur.

Error "ATM could not be started" When Opening ATM 4.0

ISSUE
When you open the Adobe Type Manager (ATM) 4.0 control panel in System 7.5.3 or 7.5.5, the system returns the errors, "ATM could not be started because it is out of memory. Error -108" and "Application unknown has unexpectedly quit due to an error of type 25." The DayStar PowerPro 100 Mhz PowerPC accelerator board is installed.

SOLUTIONS
Use System 7.5.1.
OR: Use ATM 3.9.

ADDITIONAL INFORMATION
The DayStar PowerPro accelerator board is incompatible with System 7.5.3 and 7.5.5, causing the system to return an error when you open the ATM 4.0 control panel. The DayStar PowerPro accelerator board is compatible with System 7.5.1.

Printing Problems

WINDOWS

Print Option Dimmed in Applications Running in Windows 3.1

ISSUE
When running an application in Windows 3.1, the File > Print command is dimmed in all applications. The Generic / Text Only printer driver is selected as the default printer and ATM 2.02 or earlier is turned on in the ATM Control Panel.

SOLUTIONS
Use ATM 2.5 or later.
OR: Disable ATM 2.02 or earlier by selecting Off in the ATM Control Panel, then restart Windows.
OR: Print using the Windows 3.0 Generic printer driver.

ADDITIONAL INFORMATION
ATM 2.02 and earlier are not compatible with the Windows 3.1 Generic / Text Only printer driver. After selecting

the Windows 3.1 Generic / Text Only printer driver as the default printer driver, and turning ATM 2.02 or earlier on in the ATM Control Panel, the Print command is dimmed in all applications' File menu.

Headers and Footers Print in Unexpected Font from Notes and Netscape

ISSUE

Headers and footers print in an unexpected font (i.e., in a different font than the body text font) from Lotus Notes 3.3 and earlier and Netscape Navigator 2.0 and earlier.

SOLUTION

Modify the [Fonts] section of the ATM.INI file so the font you want headers and footers to print with is the first font listed:

1. Open the ATM.INI file, located in the Windows directory, in a text editor that can save in text-only format (e.g., Microsoft Word, Windows Write).
2. In the [Fonts] section, select the lines that refer to the font you want headers and footers to print with. For example, if you want headers and footers to print in Helvetica, select the following lines:

```
Helvetica=c:\psfonts\pfm\hv______.pfm,c:\psfonts-
  \hv______.pfb
Helvetica,BOLD=c:\psfonts\pfm\hvb_____.pfm,c:\psfonts-
  \hvb_____.pfb
Helvetica,BOLDITALIC=c:\psfonts\pfm\hvbo___.pfm,c:\psfonts-
  \hvbo_____.pfb
Helvetica,ITALIC=c:\psfonts\pfm\hvo_____.pfm,c:\psfonts-
  \hvo_____.pfb
```

3. Cut and paste the selected lines to the beginning of the [Fonts] section.
4. Save the ATM.INI file in text-only format.
5. Restart Windows.

ADDITIONAL INFORMATION

Because Lotus Notes 3.3 and earlier and Netscape 2.0 and earlier do not enable you to specify a font for printing headers and footers, they use the first font supplied by Windows. When ATM is active, the first font Windows supplies to Notes and Netscape is the first font listed in the [Fonts] section of the ATM.INI file (e.g., Anna), excluding AdobeSanMM and AdobeSerMM. When you move the lines that refer to the font you want headers and footers to print with (e.g., Helvetica) to the beginning of the [Fonts] section of the ATM.INI, Windows supplies that font to Notes and Netscape for printing headers and footers.

PostScript Fonts Don't Print to Lexmark Printers

ISSUE

When printing to a Lexmark PostScript printer (e.g., Optra R Plus), PostScript fonts installed in Adobe Type Manager (ATM) 3.0x or earlier print as the printer's default font (e.g., Courier, Times).

SOLUTION

Add a reference for your Lexmark printer in the ATM.INI file, then remove and readd PostScript (i.e., Type 1) fonts in the ATM control panel:

1. Make a backup of the ATM.INI file, located in the Windows directory.
2. Open the original ATM.INI file in a text editor that can save in text-only format (e.g., Windows Write, Notepad).
3. Add the following lines to the end of the ATM.INI file, exactly as shown:

```
[PSDriverNames]
lexps=Yes
```

4. Save the ATM.INI file in text-only format.
5. Restart Windows.
6. Open the ATM Control Panel.
7. Select fonts in the installed ATM fonts list, then click Remove.
8. Click Add.
9. In the Add ATM Fonts dialog box, select Autodownload for PostScript Printer.
10. Locate and select the desired PostScript fonts, then click Add.
11. Close the ATM control panel, then restart Windows.

ADDITIONAL INFORMATION

By default, Lexmark PostScript printers do not support printing PostScript fonts installed using ATM 3.0x or earlier. Adding a reference for your Lexmark PostScript printer to the ATM.INI file, then removing and readding PostScript fonts in the ATM control panel, enables your Lexmark printer to print PostScript fonts.

Bold or Italic TrueType Font Prints Plain to HP LaserJet 4 or 5 from Windows 95

ISSUE

A TrueType font formatted with a bold or italic type style prints in a normal (roman) type style to a Hewlett-Packard LaserJet 4 or 5 series printer. You are using a Windows 95 PCL printer driver (e.g., Unidriver 4.00 with mini-driver 3.78) and Adobe Type Manager 3.0x or earlier is active.

SOLUTIONS

Download TrueType fonts as bitmap soft fonts, instead of as outline soft fonts:

1. Choose Start > Settings > Printers.
2. Right-click on the HP LaserJet 4 or HP LaserJet 5 icon, then select Properties from the pop-up menu.
3. In the Properties dialog box, click the Fonts tab.
4. Select the Download TrueType Fonts as Bitmap Soft Fonts option, instead of the default Download TrueType Fonts as Outline Soft Fonts option.

OR: Install the stylized (i.e., bold or italic) TrueType font in the Fonts Control Panel.

OR: Turn off ATM in the ATM Control Panel, then restart Windows.
OR: Print to a PostScript printer.

ADDITIONAL INFORMATION
When you print a stylized TrueType font to an HP LaserJet 4 or 5 using the LaserJet PCL printer driver for Windows 95, the font prints normal (roman) if the printer driver's Download TrueType Fonts as Outline Soft Fonts option is selected, ATM 3.0x or earlier is enabled, and the stylized TrueType font is not installed.

MAC OS

System or PostScript Error Printing SuperATM Substitution Fonts

ISSUE
A system error or PostScript error occurs when you print a document that uses SuperATM multiple master substitution fonts (i.e., Adobe Sans, Adobe Serif).

SOLUTIONS
Do one or more of the following:
A. Choose File > Page Setup, then select Unlimited Downloadable Fonts in a Document.
B. Format the text with an installed TrueType or PostScript Type 1 font.
C. Print to a PostScript printer using a licensed Adobe PostScript interpreter, rather than a non-Adobe PostScript interpreter (i.e., PostScript clone).
D. If your printer has 2 megabytes (MB) of RAM or less, increase the printer's RAM.
E. When printing to an Apple Personal LaserWriter NT, contact the printer manufacturer for a motherboard upgrade to update the printer to a Personal LaserWriter NTR.
F. When printing to a Hewlett-Packard printer with a PostScript Level 1 cartridge, upgrade to a PostScript level 2 cartridge.

ADDITIONAL INFORMATION
A system or PostScript error may occur when you print a SuperATM substitution font if there is insufficient memory to print SuperATM's fonts, or if your printer does not support multiple master technology.

Apple Personal LaserWriter NT printers, Hewlett-Packard printers using a PostScript level 1 cartridge, and some PostScript clones do not support multiple master technology. PostScript clones interpret PostScript code using a modified version of the Adobe PostScript language, which may cause unexpected printing results. Manufacturers of PostScript clones include Everex, Imagen, GCC, Harlequin, LaserMaster, Lexmark, Newgen, Pacific Page, QMS, and Xante.

Error "ATM fonts cannot be printed" When Printing to LaserWriter Select 300

ISSUE
When printing to an Apple LaserWriter Select 300 using GrayShare with Adobe Type Manager (ATM) 3.5 or later (i.e., SuperATM) installed, the error "The ATM fonts in this document cannot be printed. Canceling print job." appears.

SOLUTIONS
Disable GrayShare. For instructions on disabling GrayShare, consult the documentation included with your GrayShare software.
OR: Print to a PostScript printer.

ADDITIONAL INFORMATION
When printing a file containing PostScript fonts to a QuickDraw printer with ATM installed, ATM sends rasterized PostScript font information to the printer. Because ATM 3.5 or later is not compatible with GrayShare, ATM cannot download rasterized PostScript font information when GrayShare is active, and returns the error "The ATM fonts in this document cannot be printed. Canceling print job."

The Apple LaserWriter Select 300 is a QuickDraw printer that connects directly to a Macintosh. GrayShare allows an Apple LaserWriter Select 300 to be shared by other Macintosh computers on the same network using File Sharing.

Memory-Related Error When Printing from Power Macintosh with ATM 3.8.x or Earlier Installed

ISSUE
When printing using the Apple LaserWriter 8.x or Adobe PSPrinter 8.x printer driver from an application running on a Power Macintosh with Adobe Type Manager (ATM) 3.8.x or earlier installed, the application returns a low-memory error (e.g., "Out of memory, restart application," "Insufficient memory," "Memory is extremely low").

SOLUTIONS
Upgrade to ATM 3.9.
OR: Quit, then relaunch the application.
OR: Allocate more memory to the application.
OR: Print using the LaserWriter 7.x printer driver.

ADDITIONAL INFORMATION
When printing using the LaserWriter 8.x or PSPrinter 8.x printer driver from a Power Macintosh, ATM 3.8.x incorrectly uses 1K of the application's memory for each downloadable font. When ATM has insufficient memory to download multiple fonts in a document, the application returns a memory error (e.g., "Out of memory, restart application," "Insufficient memory," "Memory is extremely low").

Quitting then relaunching an application resets and defragments the application's allocated memory.

ATM 3.9 does not use the application's memory to download fonts when the application is printing a document containing PostScript fonts.

Installation Issues

WINDOWS

Copying ATM Installation Files from Type On Call 4.x to Network Server or Floppy Disk

Adobe Type Manager (ATM) 3.0x, or PC Type Utilities, is a free utility included on the Type On Call 4.x CD-ROM. When you register Type On Call, you can unlock ATM and copy the ATM installation files to your hard disk by clicking Copy Unlocked Products in the Adobe Purchaser and then copying the PC Type Utilities. You can also copy the ATM installation files to a network server or a disk set so that you can install ATM on a workstation without a CD-ROM drive.

For information about Windows font filenames, see the Fntnames.pdf file in the Document directory on the Type On Call CD-ROM. For instructions on using ATM, see the Usrguide.pdf file in the Document directory on the Type On Call CD-ROM.

WINDOWS 95

To copy the ATM installation files from Type On Call 4.x to a network server or floppy disk and then install ATM:

1. Install Type On Call 4.x on a workstation using Windows 95.
2. In the Adobe Purchaser, register Type On Call and order any font you want to install, then click Copy Unlocked Products in the Order window.
3. In the All Orders window, select 601-00 PC Type Utilities and any other font packages you want to copy, then click Copy.
4. When Type On Call returns the message "The product 'Adobe Type Manager (PC Font Utilities)' has been copied... You may now install the application." in the Software Successfully Copied dialog box, choose Start > Programs > Windows Explorer. Do not click Install Application or Close (Type On Call 4.1) or Exit (Type On Call 4.0x) in the Software Successfully Copied dialog box.
5. In Windows Explorer, navigate to the ATM subdirectory in the Toc4\Data subdirectory (Type On Call 4.1) or to the Toc4\Data\Pc subdirectory (Type On Call 4.0x). The ATM subdirectory contains the ATM 3.0x installation files and the Psfonts subdirectory containing the PostScript Type 1 fonts included with ATM.
6. To install ATM from a network server, copy the ATM subdirectory to the desired location on the network server.

   OR: To install ATM from two 1.4MB floppy disks, copy the ATM subdirectory contents, without the Psfonts subdirectory, onto the first disk, then copy the Psfonts subdirectory onto the second disk.
7. Choose File > Close to exit Explorer.
8. In Adobe Purchaser's Software Successfully Copied dialog box, click Close (Type On Call 4.1) or Exit (Type On Call 4.0x). Adobe Purchaser automatically deletes the ATM installation files from the Toc4\Data\Atm (Type On Call 4.1) or Toc4\Data\Pc\Atm (Type On Call 4.0x) subdirectory on your hard disk.
9. Copy additional font files (e.g., other fonts you copied from the Type On Call CD-ROM) from the Psfonts and Psfonts\Pfm subdirectories to the network server or floppy disks.
10. To install ATM on another workstation from a network server, choose Start > Run. Click Browse in the Run dialog box, locate the Install.exe file in the directory on the network server where you copied the ATM files, then click OK.

    OR: To install ATM from floppy disks, in the Explorer create a directory named Atm at the root level of the hard disk (i.e., C:\Atm), then copy the contents of both floppy disks into the new Atm directory. The new Atm directory should contain the ATM installation files and the Psfonts subdirectory. Choose Start > Run, type "c:\atm\install.exe" in the Command Line text box, then click OK.
11. Install fonts in ATM from the network server or from disks.

WINDOWS 3.1X

To copy the ATM installation files from Type On Call 4.x to a network server or floppy disk and then install ATM:

1. Install Type On Call 4.x on a workstation using Windows 3.1x.
2. In the Adobe Purchaser, register Type On Call and order any fonts you want to install, then click Copy Unlocked Products in the Order window.
3. In the All Orders window, select 601-00 PC Type Utilities and any other font packages you want to copy, then click Copy.
4. When Type On Call returns the message "The product 'Adobe Type Manager (PC Font Utilities)' has been copied... You may now install the application." in the Software Successfully Copied dialog box, press Alt + Tab to switch to Program Manager, then start File Manager from the Main group. Do not click Install Application or Close (Type On Call 4.1) or Exit (Type On Call 4.0x) in the Software Successfully Copied dialog box.
5. In File Manager, navigate to the ATM subdirectory in the Toc4\Data subdirectory (Type On Call 4.1) or to the Toc4\Data\Pc subdirectory (Type On Call 4.0x). The ATM subdirectory contains the ATM 3.0x installation files and the Psfonts subdirectory containing the PostScript Type 1 fonts included with ATM.
6. To install ATM from a network server, copy the ATM

subdirectory to the desired location on the network server.

OR: To install ATM from two 1.4MB floppy disks, copy the ATM subdirectory contents, without the Psfonts subdirectory, onto the first disk, then copy the Psfonts subdirectory onto the second disk.

7. Choose File > Exit to exit File Manager, then press Alt + Tab to switch back to the Adobe Purchaser.
8. In the Adobe Purchaser's Software Successfully Copied dialog box, click Close (Type On Call 4.1) or Exit (Type On Call 4.0x). Adobe Purchaser automatically deletes the ATM installation files from the Toc4\Data\Atm (Type On Call 4.1) or Toc4\Data\Pc\Atm (Type On Call 4.0x) subdirectory on your hard disk.
9. Copy additional font files (e.g., other fonts you copied from the Type On Call CD-ROM) from the Psfonts and Psfonts\Pfm subdirectories to the network server or floppy disks.
10. To install ATM on another workstation from a network server, choose File > Run in Program Manager, click Browse in the Run dialog box, locate the Install.exe file in the directory on the network server where you copied the ATM files, and then click OK.

    OR: To install ATM from floppy disks, in File Manager create a directory named Atm at the root level of the hard disk (i.e., C:\Atm), then copy the contents of both floppy disks into the new Atm directory. The new Atm directory should contain the ATM installation files and the Psfonts subdirectory. In Program Manager choose File > Run, type "c:\atm\install.exe" in the Command Line text box, then click OK.
11. Install fonts in ATM from the network server or from disks.

ATM Deluxe 4.0 Doesn't Install or Behave as Expected

ISSUE

Adobe Type Manager (ATM) Deluxe 4.0 does not install (e.g., the installer freezes), or installs but doesn't behave as expected.

SYMPTOMS

After you activate a PostScript or TrueType font, it does not list in application font menus.

After you deactivate a PostScript or TrueType font, the deactivated font appears in application font menus.

When you print to a PostScript printer, it substitutes a PostScript font that appears in font menus with its default font (e.g., Courier).

TrueType font names spontaneously appear outside of font sets in ATM Deluxe.

ATM Deluxe displays a red "x" next to a TrueType font name.

Fonts do not autoactivate as expected in applications that support autoactivation.

SOLUTION

Uninstall ATM, remove unnecessary fonts and font references, set a printer driver as the default, then reinstall ATM:

1. Uninstall ATM Deluxe 4.0 by clicking the Settings tab in ATM, clicking Uninstall ATM, then following the on-screen instructions. After uninstalling ATM, restart Windows.
2. Remove any remaining ATM files. For instructions, see Additional Information.
3. Temporarily move TrueType font files, except for those TrueType fonts installed by Windows 95, from the Windows\Fonts directory to another location. For a list of the TrueType fonts installed by Windows 95, see Additional Information.

   NOTE: Windows 95 installs several hidden font files (e.g., Marlett.ttf, Dosapp.fon, Vgafix.fon) that do not appear in Windows Explorer or in the Fonts Control Panel, but may appear in font management utilities (e.g., Ares FontMinder). Windows requires these hidden font files to run so do not delete them or remove them from the Fonts directory.
4. Remove unnecessary font keys from the Registry in the Registry editor. For instructions, see Additional Information.
5. Remove unnecessary softfont references from the Win.ini file. For instructions, see Additional Information.
6. Remove duplicate printers or printers you do not regularly print with by choosing Start > Settings > Printers, right-clicking the appropriate printer, then selecting Delete from the pop-up menu.
7. Select a printer as your default printer by choosing Start > Settings > Printers, right-clicking the appropriate printer, then selecting Set As Default from the pop-up menu.
8. Reinstall ATM Deluxe.
9. Create a Windows TrueType Fonts set so you can easily determine which fonts you cannot disable. For instructions, see Additional Information.

ADDITIONAL INFORMATION

ATM enables you to add, remove, activate, and deactivate both PostScript and TrueType fonts in Windows 95. A variety of causes can prevent ATM from installing, from activating or deactivating a font, or from listing a font in application font menus. These causes include previously installed ATM files that prevent ATM's installation, damaged or missing font files, a damaged ATM application, or missing ATM support files. Uninstalling ATM, removing unnecessary fonts and font references, setting a printer driver as the default printer, and then reinstalling ATM enables ATM to install or activate and deactivate fonts as expected.

ATM cannot deactivate or autoactivate TrueType fonts located in the Windows\Fonts directory. When you add TrueType fonts in ATM, it creates an Atmfonts subdirectory within the Windows\Fonts directory, from which it can activate and deactivate these fonts.

Unnecessary or invalid keys (i.e., references) in the Registry can cause fonts to appear in application font menus after you deactivated them in ATM. Unnecessary or invalid softfont (i.e., PostScript font) references in the Win.ini file can cause fonts to appear in application font menus after you deactivate them or not to appear after you activate them. Removing these references enables you to activate, deactivate, and move fonts as expected.

When you activate or deactivate fonts in ATM, the selected default printer can affect which fonts display in application font menus. If you activate fonts when ATM is set up to download fonts for one or more Microsoft PostScript printer drivers, ATM adds font references to the Win.ini file. Each font reference in the Win.ini file increases its file size, which also increases the possibility of system problems. The Win.ini file has a maximum allowable file size of 64K, but a Win.ini file size of 32K or smaller enables your system to run more efficiently. To prevent ATM from adding unnecessary font references, remove duplicate or seldom used Microsoft PostScript printer drivers, then set up one of your printers as the default printer before you reinstall ATM.

After you reinstall ATM, it creates a Starter Set containing the TrueType fonts installed in the Windows\Fonts directory and the PostScript fonts included with ATM. You can make a set containing the TrueType fonts installed by Windows 95 so you can easily recognize which fonts you cannot deactivate, then remove those fonts from the Starter Set. Use the Add from Font Sets option, which adds fonts to a new set, but does not copy the font files to another directory, to make sure ATM does not copy the TrueType font files installed by Windows 95 from the Windows\Fonts directory to another location.

Windows 95 installs the following TrueType fonts:

```
Font (Filename)
Arial (Arial.ttf)
Arial Bold (Arialbd.ttf)
Arial Bold Italic (Arialbi.ttf)
Arial Italic (Ariali.ttf)
Courier 10,12,15 (Courf.fon)
Courier New (Cour.ttf)
Courier New Bold (Courbd.ttf)
Courier New Bold Italic (Courbi.ttf)
Courier New Italic (Couri.ttf)
Modern (Modern.fon)
MS Sans Serif 8,10,12,14,18,24 (Sseriff.fon)
MS Serif 8,10,12,14,18,24 (Seriff.fon)
Small Fonts (Smallf.fon)
Symbol (Symbol.ttf)
Symbol 8,10,12,14,18,24 (Symbolf.fon)
Times New Roman (Times.ttf)
Times New Roman Bold (Timesbd.ttf)
Times New Roman Bold Italic (Timesbi.ttf)
Times New Roman Italic (Timesi.ttf)
WingDings (Wingding.ttf)
```

To remove ATM files:

1. Choose Start > Find > Files or Folders.
2. Enter "atm*.*" in the Named text box, then click Find Now.
3. Delete the following files if they appear in the search results window:

```
Atmfm.exe
Atmcntrl.exe
Atmsys.drv
Atm.ini
Atm32.dll
Atm16.dll
Atmfonts.qlc
```

To remove unnecessary font keys from the Registry in the Registry editor:

1. Choose Start > Run.
2. Type "regedit" in the Open text box and then click OK.
3. Make a backup copy of the Registry by choosing Registry > Export Registry File, choosing a location and name for the backup file in the Export Registry File dialog box, then clicking Save.
4. Open the Hkey_Local_Machine \Software\Microsoft\Windows\CurrentVersion key (i.e., directory), select the PostScriptFonts key, then press the Delete key to delete it.
5. Open the Fonts key, select the keys for all fonts except for the one named "Default" and the TrueType fonts installed by Windows 95, then press Delete to delete them.
6. Exit the Registry Editor, which automatically saves your changes to the Registry.

To remove unnecessary softfont references from the Win.ini file:

1. Make a backup copy of the Win.ini file located in the Windows directory.
2. Open the original Win.ini file in a text editor that can save in text-only format (e.g., Notepad, WordPad).
3. Delete all lines that begin with the word "softfont" or refer to an MFD file (e.g., Admfdfile=C:\Windows\Ad434af1\Mfd).
4. Save the Win.ini file in text-only format.
5. Restart Windows.

To create a new set containing only the TrueType fonts installed by Windows 95 in ATM:

1. In ATM, click the Add Fonts tab.
2. In the Add Fonts pane, double-click New Set in the Destination column.
3. In the New Set dialog box, type a name for your new set (e.g., "Windows TT Fonts"), select the Activate New Set option, then click OK.
4. Select Add From Font Sets from the Source pop-up menu.
5. Double-click the Starter Set in the Source column to display its contents.
6. Add the following fonts from the Starter Set into your new set by dragging them from the Source column to your new set in the Destination column:

```
Arial
Arial Bold
Arial Bold Italic
```

```
Arial Italic
Courier New
Courier New Bold
Courier New Bold Italic
Courier New Italic
Symbol
Times New Roman
Times New Roman Bold
Times New Roman Bold Italic
Times New Roman Italic
WingDings
```

7. Remove the fonts you added to your new set from the Starter Set.
8. Add or move your other fonts into sets as desired.

Error "Cannot create directory" Installing ATM Deluxe 4.0

ISSUE

When you try to install Adobe Type Manager Deluxe 4.0 (ATM), the installer returns the error "Cannot create directory." You specified the Windows\Fonts directory as the target directory for ATM files or PostScript font files.

SOLUTION

Specify a target directory other than the Windows\Fonts subdirectory (e.g., Psfonts, Windows\Fonts\ATMFolder).

ADDITIONAL INFORMATION

Because Windows 95 only allows you to install TrueType fonts in the Windows\Fonts subdirectory, the ATM installer cannot install ATM files or PostScript font files in that directory.

If the ATM installer locates an Atm.ini file from a previous installation that specifies the Windows\Fonts directory as the target directory for PostScript font files, it attempts to install font files in that location.

The default directory locations for ATM files are:

```
File Directory
ATM Font Manager (Atmfm.exe) Psfonts
PostScript font outline files Psfonts
PostScript font metrics files Psfonts\Pfm
Font substitution database (Atmsubst.atm)
  Psfonts
```

Manually Removing ATM 4.0 Deluxe

Adobe Type Manager (ATM) 4.0 Deluxe includes an Uninstall option in its Settings pane. However, when you are unable to access the Uninstall option (e.g., ATM won't start), you can remove ATM manually by removing ATM entries from the System.ini file and the Windows 95 Registry, deleting the ATM files, and removing softfont references from the Win.ini file. The Win.ini file contains softfont references for printers that use a Microsoft Windows PostScript printer driver, which you need to remove before you re-add fonts in ATM.

Before removing ATM, start Windows 95 in Safe Mode so that Windows doesn't load ATM. To start in Safe Mode, press the F8 key when the message, "Starting Windows 95" appears, then select Safe Mode from the startup menu.

To remove references to ATM from the System.ini file:

1. Make a backup copy of the System.ini file, which is located in the Windows directory. 2. Open the original System.ini file in a text editor that can save in text-only format (e.g., Notepad, WordPad).
3. In the [Boot] section, edit the system.drv=atmsys.drv line to read:
   `system.drv=system.drv`
4. Delete the line:
   `atm.system.drv=system.drv`
5. Save the System.ini file as text-only.

To remove references to ATM in the Registry:

1. Choose Start > Run.
2. Type "regedit" in the Open text box and click OK.
3. Make a backup copy of the Registry by choosing Registry > Export Registry File, choosing a location and name for the backup file in the Export Registry File dialog box, then clicking Save.
4. Open the Hkey_Local_Machine \Software\Adobe key (i.e., directory), select the Adobe Type Manager key, then press the Delete key to delete it.
5. Exit the Registry Editor, which automatically saves your changes to the Registry.

To delete ATM system files:

NOTE: The following files may be in directories other than those listed. Choose Start > Find > Files or Folders and search for files named "atm*.*" to locate files stored in other directories.

1. Delete the following files from the Windows directory:
   ```
   Atm.ini
   Atmreg.atm
   Atm.cnf
   ```
2. Delete the following files from the Windows\System directory:
   ```
   Atm32.dll
   Atmsys.drv
   ```
3. Delete the following files from the Psfonts directory:
   ```
   Atmfm.exe
   Atmsubst.atm
   Atmfont.qlc
   Atm[xxx].hlp (where [xxx] indicates the
     localized language)
   Atm[xxx].gid (where [xxx] indicates the
     localized language)
   Atm[xxx].cnt (where [xxx] indicates the
     localized language)
   Atm[xxx].fts (where [xxx] indicates the
     localized language)
   ```
4. Delete any ATM Font Set (AFS) files (i.e., files with an .afs extension) from your hard drive. AFS files can be stored in any directory.

To remove softfont references from the Win.ini file:

1. Make a backup copy of the Win.ini file, which is located in the Windows directory.
2. Open the original Win.ini file in a text editor that saves in text-only format (e.g., Notepad, WordPad).
3. Delete any line that begins with the word "softfont" from each [PostScript,<port>] section (e.g., [PostScript, FILE], [PostScript, LPT1]).
4. Save the Win.ini file as text-only and restart Windows.

General Information

MAC OS / WINDOWS

ATM 4.0 Deluxe and ATM 4.0 Lite Feature Summary

Features with a plus sign (+) are available for both the Macintosh and Windows.

ATM 4.0 Deluxe and ATM 4.0 Lite for the Macintosh

- Adjust character cache size
- Anti-alias (i.e., smooth) PostScript fonts +
- Create multiple master instances +
- Disable smoothing at screen font point sizes
- Position characters at subpixel level
- Preserve line spacing or character shapes
- Print multiple master sample
- Substitute for missing Adobe PostScript fonts +, **
  ** Only available in ATM 4.0 Lite when SuperATM was previously installed and SuperATM's ATM Font Database file and substitution fonts are installed in the System Folder.

ATM 4.0 Deluxe for the Macintosh

- Activate or deactivate fonts without deinstalling +
- Autoactivate fonts by application
- Autoactivate fonts for all applications (i.e., global) +
- Automount server containing fonts to activate
- Create, activate, and deactivate sets +
- Customize sample sheet text +
  - Display or print a sample of a font when you double-click font file +
  - Export sets for use on other workstations +
  - Find installed font file +
  - List sets in which a font is installed +
  - Print indexes of installed PostScript and TrueType fonts +
  - Print samples of PostScript and TrueType fonts +
  - Specify the CD-ROM to insert when activating a CD-ROM font
  - Store active fonts outside the Fonts folder +
  - Verify and report on a font file
  - Warn about multiple copies of font files when activating

ATM 4.0 Deluxe and ATM 4.0 Lite for Windows 95

- Anti-alias (i.e., smooth) PostScript fonts +
- Create multiple master instances +
- Display PostScript fonts as graphics
- Install PostScript fonts onto hard disk
- Print PostScript fonts as graphics
- Set up PostScript fonts to download to PostScript printer
- Use prebuilt or resident fonts for display and printing

ATM 4.0 Deluxe for Windows 95

- Activate or deactivate fonts without deinstalling +
- Autoactivate fonts for all applications (i.e., global) +
- Create, activate, and deactivate sets +
- Customize sample sheet text +
- Display or print a sample of a font when you double-click font file +
- Export sets for use on other workstations +
- Find installed font file +
- Install TrueType fonts onto hard disk
- List sets in which a font is installed +
- Print indexes of installed PostScript and TrueType fonts +
- Print multiple master sample +
- Print samples of PostScript and TrueType fonts +
- Store active fonts outside the Fonts or Psfonts directory +
- Substitute for missing Adobe PostScript fonts +

MAC OS

ATM 3.9 and Earlier and PostScript Fonts General Information

Adobe Type Manager (ATM) 3.9 and earlier create smooth display of PostScript fonts at any point size using the PostScript font's outline (printer) font file. When ATM cannot display a PostScript font, the font displays bitmapped (i.e., jagged) or text with the font applied does not display.

Without ATM, the system displays PostScript fonts by scaling the bitmap font file. Resizing a bitmap font reproduces the general shape of the font, but may cause the font to display with extreme pixelation (i.e., jagged), depending on the size of available bitmap font files and the requested display size.

To prevent fonts from displaying with extreme pixelation, ATM rasterizes PostScript outline fonts (i.e., converts outline font information into a scaleable bitmap image) to enable fonts to display smoothly at any point size. ATM supports rasterizing PostScript fonts that adhere to the Adobe Type 1 font specification. ATM does not support rasterizing PostScript Type 3 fonts, TrueType fonts, and PostScript fonts that do not adhere to the Adobe Type 1 font specification.

POSTSCRIPT FONT FILES

PostScript fonts are composed of two files: a bitmap (screen) font and a PostScript outline (printer) font file. Bitmap fonts are used to display the font on screen. Outline fonts are used for printing and for display by ATM.

BITMAP FONTS

Bitmap fonts, also called screen fonts, provide bitmap representations of characters at specific sizes for screen display, usually 10, 12, 14, 18, and 24 point sizes. They also contain kerning information and information the system uses to display the font's name in the font menus.

Bitmap fonts appear in the Finder as a dog-eared page with the letter "A," and their filenames include a point size (e.g., Times 10, Geneva 14). In System 7.1 or later, bitmap fonts are installed in the Fonts folder in the System Folder. In System 7.0.x, bitmap fonts are installed in the System suitcase in the System Folder.

OUTLINE FONTS

PostScript outline fonts, also called printer fonts, contain mathematical descriptions in the PostScript page description language for each character designed for the typeface.

Adobe PostScript outline font icons appear in the Finder as a letter "A" in front of horizontal lines. Most PostScript font files are named using the first five characters of the font followed by the first three characters of each style (e.g., HelveBol, CouriObl, Symbo, TimesBolIta), and do not include a point size. In System 7.1 or later, outline fonts are installed in the Fonts folder in the System Folder. In System 7.0.x, outline fonts are installed in the Extensions folder in the System Folder.

TRUETYPE FONT FILES

Unlike PostScript fonts, TrueType fonts consist of only one font file, used for both display and printing. TrueType fonts icons display in the Finder as a dog-eared page with three letter "A"s in progressively larger sizes, and their filenames do not include a point size. In System 7.1 or later, TrueType fonts are installed in the Fonts folder in the System Folder.

When both the TrueType and PostScript version of a font are installed (e.g., Helvetica), ATM may be unable to locate the PostScript font's outline font file, causing jagged font display or problems when printing. To avoid conflicts, remove the TrueType font file or the PostScript font files from the System Folder.

Adobe Type Reunion®

Unexpected Results

MAC OS

Font Names Display as Unusual Characters or Aren't Complete

ISSUE

Font names display in an application's font menu as unusual characters (e.g., boxes, symbols) or aren't complete (e.g., Helv instead of Helvetica). Adobe Type Reunion 1. x is installed.

SOLUTIONS

Do one or more of the following:

A. Disable all extensions that display font names in their respective typefaces (e.g., NOW Menus WYSIWYG, Symantec Suitcase, PopChar), then restart the Macintosh.

B. Disable all extensions except Type Reunion 1.x, then restart the Macintosh.

C. Remove, then reinstall Type Reunion 1.x.

1. Remove the Type Reunion extension from the Extensions folder in the System Folder.
2. Remove the Type Reunion Data preferences file from the Preferences folder in the System Folder.
3. Reinstall Type Reunion from the original disk set, then restart the Macintosh.

D. Verify that installed fonts and the Fonts folder are not damaged by reinstalling fonts and recreating the Fonts folder in System 7.1 or later:

1. Move the Fonts folder from the System Folder onto the desktop.
2. Restart the Macintosh. When the Macintosh restarts, a new, empty Fonts folder is created in the System Folder.
3. Move fonts, one a time, from the old Fonts folder located on the desktop into the new Fonts folder located in the System Folder.
4. After moving a font into the new Fonts folder, launch an application (e.g., Adobe PageMaker) and display its font menu.
5. Repeat steps 3-4 until a font moved into the Fonts folder displays incorrectly in the application's font menu.
6. Delete and reinstall the damaged bitmap (screen) and outline (printer) font files from the original disks.

ADDITIONAL INFORMATION
When an extension that displays font names in their respective typefaces is installed, expert fonts (e.g., Minion Expert, Garamond Expert) may display unexpected characters (e.g., boxes, symbols) in an application's font menu, or the extension may conflict with Type Reunion, causing fonts to display unexpected characters. Disabling the extension enables the font to display in the font menu as expected.

When Type Reunion 1.x conflicts with another extension, or when the Type Reunion Data preferences file, the Type Reunion extension, the Fonts folder or one or more fonts is damaged, font names in an application's font menu display incompletely or as unusual characters (e.g., boxes, symbols).

Type Reunion 1.x is a system extension that groups installed PostScript bitmap fonts by family in an application's font menu.

Unexpected Typeface Applied from Font Menu

ISSUE
After applying a typeface from an application's font menu to text when Adobe Type Reunion is installed, the text displays or prints in an unexpected typeface (e.g., after choosing typeface Helvetica Regular from the font menu, text displays and prints in the typeface Hobo).

SOLUTIONS
Do one or more of the following:

A. Disable Adobe Type Reunion, then choose the font.

B. Remove, then reinstall Type Reunion 1.0.3 or later:
   1. Delete the Type Reunion file located in the Extensions folder in the System Folder.
   2. Delete the Type Reunion Data file located in the Preferences folder in the System Folder.
   3. Install Type Reunion from the original disk set or from the Adobe Type On Call 4.0 or later CD-ROM.

C. When using Symantec Suitcase and Type Reunion, disable the "Update Existing Font Menus When a Font Suitcase Is Opened or Closed" option in the Suitcase control panel:
   1. In the Suitcase control panel, choose Suitcase > Preferences > Fonts.
   2. In the Fonts dialog box, deselect the "Update Existing Font Menus When a Font Suitcase Is Opened or Closed" option, then click OK.
   3. Restart the Macintosh.

D. Remove and reinstall bitmap (screen) fonts from the original disks to ensure the fonts are not damaged:
   1. Quit all open applications.
   2. Remove all bitmap font suitcases from the Fonts folder in the System Folder (System 7.1 and later) or from the System suitcase in the System Folder (System 7.0.x).
   3. Install new copies of bitmap font suitcases into the Fonts folder in the System Folder (System 7.1 and later) or into the System suitcase in the System Folder (System 7.0.x).

E. When using Microsoft Word 5.x or later, select a font by choosing Format > Font, instead of selecting a font from the font pop-up menu on the ribbon.

NOTE: Other installed extensions or control panels may interfere when selecting fonts from an application's font menu. Run with all extensions off to verify that added extensions or control panels are not the cause. To turn all extensions off upon startup in System 7, restart the computer while holding the Shift key until the message "Welcome to Macintosh. Extensions Off." appears.

ADDITIONAL INFORMATION
An extension conflict or a damaged Type Reunion file, Type Reunion Data file, or bitmap (screen) font can cause an application to apply a typeface other than the typeface you selected from the font menu.

Adobe Type Reunion organizes font families into submenus. When you disable Type Reunion, typefaces list in alphabetical order in font menus. Because Type Reunion and other font management extensions (e.g., Suitcase) do not modify the font list in Microsoft Word 5.x and later's Fonts dialog box, typefaces applied from the Fonts dialog box display and print as expected.

Suitcase's "Update Existing Font Menus When a Font Suitcase Is Opened or Closed" option enables applications to update their font menus when you open or close a suitcase (i.e., you do not have to restart an application for changes to display). Because Type Reunion is unable to modify a font menu when another extension is modifying the same font menu, selecting Suitcase's "Update Existing Font Menus When a Font Suitcase Is Opened or Closed" option while Type Reunion is enabled may cause text in your document to disappear or to print in a different typeface.

Bitmap fonts are available in the Bitmaps folder on the Type on Call 4.0x or later CD-ROM, from the Adobe Online services on CompuServe, America Online, the Adobe BBS, and the Adobe home page on the World Wide Web.

Font Above or Below Chosen Font is Selected in Font Menu

ISSUE
When you choose a font in an application's font menu, the font above or below it is selected instead.

SOLUTION
Delete the Adobe Type Reunion Data file, located in the Preferences folder in the System Folder.

NOTE: Other installed system extensions or control panel documents may interfere with font selection. Run with extensions off to verify that added extensions are not the cause. To turn extensions off upon startup in System 7, restart the computer with the Shift key held down until the message "Welcome to Macintosh, Extensions Off" appears.

ADDITIONAL INFORMATION

The Type Reunion Data file keeps track of installed fonts. When the Type Reunion Data file becomes damaged, the font listed above or below the font chosen in font menu may be selected. Deleting the existing Type Reunion Data file forces Type Reunion to generate a new Type Reunion Data file, either when the Macintosh is restarted or when an application is launched.

Font Name Appears Twice in Font Menu

ISSUE

A font appears twice in an application's font menu when Adobe Type Reunion is installed.

SOLUTIONS

If you're using Adobe Type Manager (ATM) 3.5 or later, install Type Reunion 1.1 or later.

OR: Temporarily disable Type Reunion by holding down the Shift key while accessing the font menu.

OR: Delete the Type Reunion Data file from in the Preferences folder in the System Folder, then restart the Macintosh. Type Reunion creates a new Type Reunion Data file when the computer is restarted.

OR: When using System 7.1 or later:

1. Double-click on the font suitcase for the font that appears twice.
2. Close the font suitcase and delete the Type Reunion Data file.
3. Rebuild the desktop file by holding down the Command and Option keys while restarting the computer. Keep the keys held down until you receive the message, "Are you sure you want to rebuild the desktop file on the disk '[diskname]'? Comments in info windows will be lost," then click OK.

OR: In System 7.1 or later, create a new Fonts folder by moving the current Fonts folder out of the System Folder to the desktop and restarting the computer. Then move fonts from the previous Fonts folder into the new Fonts folder, which is created by the system after restart.

NOTE: Other installed extensions or control panels may interfere with Type Reunion's ability to modify the fonts menu. Run Type Reunion without added extensions to verify that added extensions are not the cause. For instructions, see Related Records.

ADDITIONAL INFORMATION

When the Type Reunion Data file has become damaged, font names do not display correctly. Deleting the Type Reunion Data file enables Type Reunion to create a new Type Reunion Data file.

Fonts Don't Display in Their Typefaces When MenuFonts and Type Reunion 1.x Are Installed

ISSUE

When both MenuFonts and Adobe Type Reunion 1.x are installed, fonts do not appear in application font menus in their own typefaces (e.g., Garamond font name does not appear in the Garamond typeface), as expected.

SOLUTIONS

Use Type Reunion 2.0 Deluxe.

OR: Hold down the Shift key before accessing the font menu to temporarily disable Type Reunion.

OR: Prevent the application from using Type Reunion by pressing the Shift key immediately after you start the application, keeping the Shift key held down until the application is open.

ADDITIONAL INFORMATION

Type Reunion 2.0 Deluxe and MenuFonts display fonts in their actual typefaces in application font menus. Type Reunion 1.x, which does not displays fonts in their actual typefaces, overrides the MenuFonts option, preventing MenuFonts from displaying fonts in their typefaces. Temporarily disabling Type Reunion 1.x enables MenuFonts to display fonts in their actual typefaces.

System Errors

MAC OS

Type 1 Errors After Installing Type Reunion 1.x Troubleshooting Guide

If you receive a Type 1 system error after installing Adobe Type Reunion 1.x, the error may be caused by extension conflicts, damaged bitmap font files, or a damaged Type Reunion extension or Type Reunion Data file. Troubleshooting extension conflicts, reinstalling font files, or removing and then reinstalling Type On Call may enable Type Reunion to run without error.

TROUBLESHOOTING EXTENSION CONFLICTS

Conflicts with other installed extensions or control panels may interfere with Type Reunion and cause the system to return a Type 1 error. To verify that added extensions or control panels are not the cause, run Type Reunion with all other extensions disabled.

To disable other extensions:

1. Quit all applications.
2. Move your Extensions and Control Panels folders from the System Folder to another location (e.g., desktop).

3. Restart the Macintosh. The system creates new, empty Extensions and Control Panels folders in the System Folder.
4. Install Type Reunion from its installation original disk into the new Extensions folder.
5. Restart the Macintosh.

If Type Reunion works as expected when other extensions are disabled, one or more other extensions are conflicting with it. Add your extensions and control panels back into your System Folder a few at a time to see which combination causes the conflict.

REINSTALLING FONT FILES

Because Type Reunion gets its menu information from bitmap font files, a damaged bitmap font file can cause a Type 1 error when Type Reunion tries to use it. Removing font files and then reinstalling them from the original disk set may eliminate the error.

To reinstall fonts in System 7.1 or later:

1. Quit all applications.
2. Move the Fonts folder from the System Folder to another location (e.g., desktop).
3. Restart the Macintosh. The system creates a new, empty Fonts folder in the System Folder.
4. Install the fonts into the new Fonts folder from the original installation disks.

To reinstall fonts in System 7.0 and 7.0.1:

1. Quit all applications.
2. Open the System suitcase in the System Folder and move all font suitcases in it to another location (e.g., desktop).
3. Install the fonts into the System suitcase from the original installation disks.
4. Close the System suitcase.

To reinstall fonts in System 6.x:

1. Quit all applications.
2. Launch Font/DA Mover 3.8 or later, then open the System file.
3. Remove the fonts from the System file, then close Font/DA Mover.
4. Restart the Macintosh.
5. Using Font/DA Mover, install the fonts into the System file from the original installation disks.

REMOVING AND REINSTALLING TYPE REUNION

A damaged Type Reunion extension or Type Reunion Data file can cause the system to return a Type 1 error. Removing and reinstalling Type Reunion may eliminate the error.

To reinstall Type Reunion in System 7.x:

1. Remove the Type Reunion file from the Extensions folder in the System Folder.
2. Remove the Type Reunion Data file from the Preferences folder in the System Folder.
3. Install Type Reunion from the original installation disk into the Extensions folder.
4. Restart the Macintosh.

To reinstall Type Reunion in System 6.x

1. Remove the Type Reunion file and the Type Reunion Data file from the System Folder.
2. Install Type Reunion from the original installation disk into the System Folder.
3. Restart the Macintosh.

Installation Issues

MAC OS

System Performance Slows with Type Reunion 2.0 Deluxe Installed

ISSUE

After you install Adobe Type Reunion 2.0 Deluxe, system performance slows (e.g., the screen redraws slowly). You have created many groups (e.g., 100) or groups containing many typefaces (e.g., 200 or more) in Type Reunion.

SOLUTIONS

Do one or more of the following:

A. Reduce the number of groups.
B. Reduce the number of typefaces in each group.

ADDITIONAL INFORMATION

Creating a large number of groups or adding many typefaces to a group in Type Reunion causes system performance to slow. A font suitcase may contain many typefaces.

Disabling Type Reunion 2.x or Earlier

You can disable Adobe Type Reunion 2.x or earlier for all applications during startup, for a single application when you start an application, or for displaying the font list in an application when you select a font menu. After you disable Type Reunion, it does not group font families, so fonts appear in your font menus in alphabetical order by font name (e.g., Helvetica Bold appears as B Helvetica Bold). After you disable Type Reunion 2.0 Deluxe, it does not display fonts in their typefaces, group fonts, display customized font names, or display recently used fonts in font menus.

To re-enable Type Reunion, restart your Macintosh or application, or select a font menu, without holding down the appropriate key to disable Type Reunion.

DISABLING TYPE REUNION 2.0 DELUXE

You can specify the key you want to use to disable Type Reunion 2.0 Deluxe in the General tab of the Adobe Type Reunion control panel.

To disable Type Reunion during startup, hold down the disabling key you specified immediately after the system begins to load your extensions (e.g., when icons begin to appear across the bottom of your screen). If Type Reunion has been successfully disabled, the Type Reunion icon appears with an "x" on it.

To disable Type Reunion for an application, hold down the disabling key you specified immediately after you start the application, keeping it held down until the application is open.

To disable Type Reunion for an application's font menu, hold down the disabling key you specified and select the font menu. You can release the key when the application's font menu appears.

DISABLING TYPE REUNION 1.X

Use the Shift key to disable Type Reunion 1.x.

To disable Type Reunion during startup, hold down the either the Shift key or the mouse button immediately after the system begins to load your extensions (e.g., when icons begin to appear across the bottom of your screen). If Type Reunion has been successfully disabled, the Type Reunion icon appears with an "x" on it.

To disable Type Reunion for an application, hold down the Shift key immediately after you start the application, keeping it held down until the application is open.

To disable Type Reunion for an application's font menu, hold down the Shift key and select the font menu. You can release the Shift key when the application's font menu appears.

Font Families Aren't Merged After Installing Type Reunion

ISSUE

After you install Adobe Type Reunion, font families are not merged in the font menu (e.g., in the font menu, members of the Helvetica font family are listed separately instead of under a Helvetica submenu).

SOLUTIONS

When running System 7.x, update to Adobe Type Reunion 1.0.3 or later.

OR: Remove the PopChar control panel document, which is located in the Extensions folder in the System Folder (System 7.x) or in the System Folder (System 6.x) and restart the Macintosh.

NOTE: Other installed system extensions (INITs) or control panel documents (CDevs) may interfere with the ability of Type Reunion to merge font families in the font menu. Run with the extensions off to verify that added extensions are not the cause. To turn extensions off upon startup in System 7.x, restart the computer holding the Shift key down until the message "Welcome to Macintosh, Extensions Off" appears.

ADDITIONAL INFORMATION

Adobe Type Reunion 1.02 and earlier is not supported by System 7.x and does not merge font families when running under System 7.x. Adobe Type Reunion 1.0.3 or later supports System 7.x, enabling merged fonts families to list in the font menu.

The PopChar control panel document conflicts and is incompatible with Adobe Type Reunion 1.0.3 or earlier.

No Type Style Submenu After Installing Type Reunion Troubleshooting Guide

ISSUE

Submenus containing type styles (e.g., regular, italic) do not appear by font names listed in the font menu after installing Adobe Type Reunion 1.2 or earlier.

SOLUTIONS

Do one or more if the following:

A. Install more than one type style for each PostScript bitmap (screen) font.
B. Install PostScript fonts instead of TrueType fonts.
C. Reinstall bitmap fonts that have had type styles previously merged with Font Harmony.
D. Reinstall bitmap fonts to ensure the fonts are not damaged.
E. Use only PostScript fonts that follow standard font and type style naming conventions.
F. Reduce the amount of installed fonts to free up system menu resources.
G. Delete the "Type Reunion Data" file, located in the Preferences folder, and restart the Macintosh.

ADDITIONAL INFORMATION

The Adobe Type Reunion System Extension groups PostScript Type 1 and Type 3 bitmap font families together in the font menu and creates submenus that contain installed type styles for each font family. A submenu will not be created for fonts that have only one type style installed.

Type Reunion merges TrueType font families together in the font menu, but does not create a submenu containing type styles next to the TrueType font's name. When there is not PostScript equivalent installed for a TrueType font, type styles may be selected from an applications type style menu or dialog box, when available.

Font Harmony is an application that merges style variations of PostScript font families, allowing only one name to appear for the font family in the font menu. Type Reunion cannot create a submenu containing PostScript fonts with type styles that have been previously merged with Font Harmony. To use Type Reunion, the font merged using Font Harmony must be removed and the original font reinstalled.

Creators of PostScript fonts use their own naming conventions for typefaces and type style variations. Type Reunion tries to account for all known naming conventions, but some fonts contain non-standard PostScript names and may not be merged in the font menu as expected.

When some PostScript font families are merging as expected in the font menu while others are not, there may not be enough system menu resources available. The maximum number of menus the Macintosh system software allows in an application is 235. The total number of submenus available to Type Reunion is 235 minus the number of menus used by an application. Because the number of menus varies between applications, Type Reunion is able to display more submenus in some applications than in others. To reduce the number of menus needed by Type reunion, reduce the number of installed fonts.

When the "Type Reunion Data" file is damaged, font families may not be merged or submenus with type styles may not display as expected. To generate a new "Type Reunion Data" file, delete the existing "Type Reunion Data" file, located in the Preferences folder in the System Folder (System 7.x) or in the System Folder (System 6.0.x), and restart the Macintosh.

General Information

MAC OS

Adobe Type Reunion 2.0 Deluxe New Features

Adobe Type Reunion 2.0 Deluxe is a control panel that groups your installed PostScript fonts by family in an application's font menu. Like Type Reunion 1.x, it groups fonts by creating a type style submenu for each font family that has more than one installed type style (e.g., Helvetica Bold, Helvetica Italic). Unlike Type Reunion 1.x, Type Reunion 2.0 has a variety of other features.

NOTE: Some applications may not support all of Type Reunion's features.

NEW FEATURES

- Activates ATM Deluxe sets from an application's font menu

  You can activate a set created in Adobe Type Manager (ATM) Deluxe from within an application's font menu, without opening the ATM control panel. - Disables itself for applications with which it's incompatible

  You can disable Type Reunion for applications that do not support Type Reunion's features. Type Reunion includes a set of applications for which it is automatically disabled, and you can add other applications to the set.
- Displays fonts in actual typefaces

  Type Reunion can display fonts in their actual typefaces in the font menu. You can individually disable this feature for fonts that are hard to read in their typefaces (e.g., symbols, expert sets, ornaments).
- Divides an application's font menu into sections

  Type Reunion divides an application's font menu into sections. From top to bottom, the sections list the most recently used fonts, active fonts, font groups, and options to open Type Reunion, ATM 4.0 Deluxe, and ATM sets.
- Enables you to define font groups, and display or hide them

  Type Reunion can create custom collections, or groups, of fonts in font menus. Groups can help you organize and shorten your font menus. Type Reunion groups are independent of ATM Deluxe's sets, or sets created in any other font management application (e.g., Symantec Suitcase, MasterJuggler). You can switch between groups to display the fonts you need directly in your font menu or in a submenu. You can also show or hide the inactive fonts in any group's submenu.
- Enables you to open Type Reunion and ATM control panels from an application's font menu Type Reunion lists options in the font menu to open the Type Reunion or ATM control panel.
- Enables you to specify disabling key Like Type Reunion 1.x, you can disable Type Reunion 2.0 for all applications when you start your Macintosh, for an application when you start it, or for a font menu when you select it. Unlike Type Reunion 1.x, Type Reunion 2.0 enables you to specify the disabling key.
- Enables you to specify preferred names

  You can specify a preferred name that appears in your font menu. For example, you can specify the name "Graphite Light Narrow" for the multiple master instance "GraphMM_237LT310NR." Specifying a preferred name in Type Reunion does not alter the actual font file's name.
- Lists recently-used fonts

  You can specify whether and how many recently-used fonts display in the font menu. The list of recently-used fonts is specific to each application, and is recreated each time you start the application.

Adobe Type Reunion 1.x General Information

Adobe Type Reunion 1.x is a system extension that groups installed PostScript bitmap fonts by family in an application's font menu. It groups fonts by creating a type style submenu for each font family that has more than one installed type style (e.g., Helvetica bold, Helvetica italic).

To install Adobe Type Reunion, move the Adobe Type Reunion system extension into the Extensions folder in the System Folder (System 7.x) or into the System Folder (System 6.0x), then restart the Macintosh.

Once installed, Adobe Type Reunion creates the Type Reunion Data file in the Preferences folder in the System Folder (System 7.x) or in the System Folder (System 6.0.x). The Type Reunion Data file contains a current list of all fonts installed in the system.

General Issues

The articles in this appendix cover general system issues for optimizing and troubleshooting Windows, Mac OS, and UNIX platforms as they relate to Adobe software. This information includes explanations of common system errors and methods for configuring system components.

Contents

General Issues

All Platforms

MAC OS / WINDOWS / UNIX

Obtaining Device Profiles (Precision Transforms) Not Included with PageMaker 6.0

A device profile in the Kodak Precision Color Management System is called a Precision Transform (PT). Adobe PageMaker 6.0 includes many common PTs. The PageMaker 6.0 CD-ROM contains more PTs than the installation disks. You can obtain PTs for devices not available on the CD-ROM or installation disks in the following ways:

- Create a device profile for your monitor using the Kodak Monitor Installer utility in the Utilities folder in the PageMaker 6.0 folder on your hard drive. Instructions for the utility are in the "Monitor Installer Readme" file that accompanies it.
- Contact the manufacturer of your device.
- Purchase a device profile from the Adobe Plug-in Source at 800-685-3547. See the list below for available profiles.
- Purchase the Precision Input Color Characterization application from Kodak to create profiles for input devices (e.g., monitor).
- Have Kodak create a custom profile for your device. For information about solutions offered by Kodak, call the Color Management Systems Customer Operations Center at 800-23-KODAK (800-235-6325).

The following device profiles are available from the Adobe Plug-In Source. Prices range from $49 to $400; for specific pricing information, contact the Adobe Plug-In Source at 800-685-3547:

Starter Pack
CMYK Pro Pack
3M Matchprint
Euro Matchprint
Agfa Proof
Dupont Cromalin
Dupont Water Proof
Enco Pressmatch
Fuji ColorArt
Fuji Color Art-Japan
Kodak Approval
Kodak Contract
Kodak Signature
Kodak Peripherals Pack
Starter Pack Access Plus
Precision ICS
DayStar Color Match (Macintosh only)
DayStar Colorimeter24 (Macintosh only)
Newspaper Ad Litho
Calcomp 6613PS
Apple Color Printer (Macintosh only)
Tektronic Phaser 200
QMS Colorscript 100
Canon BJC 600
Canon BJC 800
Epson Stylus
HP ColorSmart
HP1200C
IBM LEXMARK
Fargo Primera
Fargo PrimeraPRO
Fargo Pictura 310
HP Color LaserJet
HP DesignJet 650C
SuperMac Proof Pos (Macintosh only)
Tektronic Phaser III

Digital Film Recorders General Information

Whether you send your completed document or presentation to a slide imaging service or create slides in-house, it's important to have a clear understanding of how film recorders work and the variables involved in getting the highest quality slides possible.

ANALOG VS. DIGITAL FILM RECORDERS

A film recorder is a light-tight box that houses a controller card, an internal monochrome cathode ray tube (CRT) monitor, a filter, and a 35mm camera back. There are two types of film recorders: analog and digital.

Analog Film Recorders

Analog film recorders are the simpler and faster of the two, as well as the least expensive. In an analog recorder, the internal cathode ray tube displays the color image directly from your computer's monitor, and the built-in camera takes a photograph of the display. The imaging times for analog recorders are fast, but the quality of the slide is limited by the relatively low resolution of your computer's video signal.

Digital film recorders
Digital film recorders produce a sharper quality slide and utilize a more complex imaging process. The software running the film recorder analyzes and separates the image to be photographed. The highest quality output is achieved with digital film recorder imaging.

PRINTING TO A DIGITAL FILM RECORDER
Your completed document or presentation is first converted to the recorder's native control language. This is accomplished by printing through a Chooser-level driver or by exporting your document or presentation and opening the image file in a special processing application included with the film recorder.

The converted file is object-oriented and must be converted to bitmap data understood by the film recorder. The processing software first converts the image into bitmap information, then separates it into a red, green, and blue image. During this process, fonts may also be substituted with the film recorder's proprietary fonts and graduated backgrounds into the film recorder's proprietary graduation routines. Each red, green, and blue image, or "pass," is digitized as a high-resolution bitmap image. The more complex the image, the longer it will take the software to complete this digitization.

Each pass is downloaded sequentially to the film recorder. The recorder converts the individual passes into video signals. Before each pass is displayed on the film recorder's internal CRT, a color wheel containing red, green, and blue gel filters rotates into position in front of the CRT. The CRT is a monochrome monitor, displaying only the elements needed for each color filter. A photograph is taken through the red filter, then the green filter, and then through the blue filter.

Each of the three color passes is exposed to film, one on top of the other, in a triple exposure that creates a composite color image. The result is a negative image.

The 35mm film is developed, then cut and mounted into slide holders.

FILM RECORDER RESOLUTION
The film recorder's resolution depends on three things: the size of the internal CRT, the number of pixels per inch, and the pixel size. The standard resolution of 35mm slide film is 4000 x 2000 lines or pixels for a resolution of 4K. This is the highest resolution that the light-sensitive particles on standard 35mm film can achieve.
Addressable Resolution
When literature specifies a film recorder's resolution at 2K or 4K, it is usually referring to the film recorder's addressable resolution. The maximum number of pixels (or lines) the recorder circuitry can internally process is the addressable resolution. Film recorders with a resolution of 4K have 4,096 pixels horizontally and 2,732 vertically available, or addressable; those with a 2K resolution have 2,048 pixels horizontally and 1,366 pixels vertically available.

Resolvable Resolution
Most important to the final clarity of your slides is the actual number of dots or pixels that can be exposed on the film by the film recorder, limiting the amount of detail that can print on your slides. This is the resolvable resolution, determined by the size of the internal CRT divided by the dot size (in millimeters). A high-resolution film recorder has a large CRT, about 7 inches (177.8m) horizontally, with a small dot size, about 0.04mm, and can reproduce an image at 4,445 lines per inch. (177.8mm / .04mm = 4445 or 4K resolvable resolution.)

Film recorders that have a much lower resolvable resolution than addressable resolution will cause the large dots to overlap and obscure each other, resulting in fuzzy slides. Generally, good-looking slides are a matter of personal preference and intended purpose. The methods for imaging slides are simple, but there are a number of other considerations besides film resolution, which affect the quality of your slides.

COLOR
After resolution, clear and accurate color is the most important component of a good slide. Film recorders assign 8 bits of color information for each pixel of the red, green, and blue component images. Most film recorders support 24-bit color for a total of 16.7 million theoretical colors. 16.7 million colors is more than the human eye is able to distinguish. Color differences and problems can arise due to the differences between the way photographic film and the human eye process color information.
Color Variances
Color is perceived differently by each person and the same slide can look different to the same person in a different setting. Colors are generated by mixtures of light wavelengths as well as pure light wavelengths. For example, one yellow wavelength produces the color yellow or the combination of green and red wavelengths can also produce the color yellow. Ambient light plays a crucial role in the perception of color. Because of varying light wavelength, it's difficult to match the colors on your monitor whose phosphors emit one set of wavelengths, with those of your film recorder whose CRT and filter combination emits another set of wavelengths.

With 16.7 million colors, your computer can theoretically generate all possible combinations of integer values from 0 to 65,535 for each of the three subtractive primary colors (red, green, and blue). But these are purely mathematical combinations and don't take into account the variability of human perception to color mixing. Adding equal amounts of one color to different colors may not make the new colors look equally different to the human eye.

Some film recorders attempt to compensate for the visual differences of digital color by compressing various sections of the spectrum, so that more colors may map to, for example, green than to either red or blue. This means that the recorder effectively bunches colors up in some parts of the spectrum as it spreads them out in other parts. This bunching of colors to correct for digital colors may produce more visible transition steps between shade gradations, or banding. To get around this, some film recorders use a mathematical "dodge," which is an increase of the number of output bits to 11 per color, or 33 bits total. Increasing the output to 11 bits maintains a smooth mapping function, even though only 8 bits per color is still addressed.

FILM

Each film recorder manufacturer calibrates its film recorder to properly expose one or more types of slide film. Professional quality film is specifically recommended by most film recorder manufacturers for use in their film recorders, and must be kept refrigerated during storage. To minimize color variations due to different emulsion batches, try to shoot all the slides in a single presentation from the same roll of film or from the same emulsion batch number. Professional films list the emulsion batch number on the film's box. If the film is out of date, or was stored improperly, image quality will be affected.

The film's development process may also affect the final quality of slide color. Professional photo labs will use fresh chemicals and closely monitor processing temperatures and times to assure the greatest consistency in your slide colors.

Color Look-up Tables and Calibration

Film emulsion is designed to be visually uniform, but different types of film have different responses to light. Some films are more sensitive to blue while others are more sensitive to red. One of the most critical aspects of film recorder engineering is the development of the film recorder's electronic color look-up table that maps the digitized images' red, green, and blue values to red, green, and blue beam intensities. Each film recorder's color look-up table is specifically fine-tuned for one or more particular kind of film.

FONTS

Most film recorders come with their own set of printer (outline) fonts, or fonts that they support. The fonts Times, Helvetica, and Symbol are supported by all film recorders. Additional fonts are usually available for purchase. Using unsupported fonts or imaging to a low-resolution film recorder can produce bitmap (jagged or fuzzy) type. Some film recorders are compatible with Adobe Type Manager, which enables outline fonts to image smoothly at any size.

When digitizing the image, the film recorder software replaces the screen font with its corresponding outline font. The quality of the imaged type is directly related to the resolvable resolution of the film recorder.

COMMON ISSUES DUE TO THE FILM RECORDER'S IMAGING SOFTWARE

- Banding (visible transition steps between shade gradations).
- Vignetting (too abrupt a transition between top and bottom colors, color gradation compressed in the middle of the gradation).
- Fringing, flaring, or bleeding (two colors overlap and mix at their borders, usually resulting in a white line).
- Poor color balance (a red, green, or blue cast on gray gradient backgrounds).
- Inconsistent color density or "color drift" (without regular color calibration of the film recorder are likely to be slightly different on each slide).
- Poor color saturation or dull colors (saturation is the depth of color intensity). Zero saturation is white, or no color, and maximum saturation is the deepest or most intense color possible.

COMMON ISSUES DUE TO THE FILM RECORDER'S IMAGING HARDWARE

The electronics that control the placement of the beam must correctly compensate for non-linearities in the CRT, as well as for optical distortions introduced by the filters, by the camera lens, and by any mirrors that the recorder uses.

Scan Resolution Guidelines

The number of samples per inch (spi) determines the scan resolution of an image. A scan resolution that is too low results in a low-quality image. A scan resolution that is too high increases the file size and printing time, without increasing the image's quality. A black-and-white (i.e., 1-bit) image's scan resolution should be equal to or greater than the final output device's printer resolution measured in dots per inch (dpi).

When scaling an image, the effective resolution changes. When you create a bitmap or scan image, the number of pixels is fixed. When you scale that image, the number of pixels does not change. Because the same number of pixels must fit into an area that is smaller or larger than the original, the pixel density of the scaled image changes. For example, when a photograph with a scan resolution of 300 spi is scaled to 200%, its scan resolution decreases to 150 spi.

Use the following guidelines to determine the resolution of a grayscale or color bitmap image that is high enough to avoid pixelization (jagged or digital image), but low enough for efficient files.

SCAN RESOLUTION FORMULA FOR IMAGES AT 100 PERCENT

Use a spi twice the line screen frequency you'll assign to the image. Screen frequency is measured in lines per inch (lpi).

```
lpi x 2 = spi
```

For example: 120 lpi x 2 = 240 spi

SCAN RESOLUTION FORMULA FOR SCALED IMAGES

Line screen frequency times 2, times final width, divided by original width equals the spi.

```
lpi x 2 x (final width) / (original width) =
  spi
```

For example: 120 lpi x 2 x 5 inches (final) = 1200 / 4 = 300 spi

Capturing Screen Images on the Macintosh and in Windows General Information

Both the Macintosh and Windows enable you to capture an image of the current screen display. The images are low-resolution—72 pixels per inch (ppi) on the Macintosh and 96 ppi in Windows. Other third-party utilities, however, such as Hijaak 95 or Flash-It, enable you to control the resolution of screen snapshots.

To capture a screen image on the Macintosh, press Command + Shift + 3. The Macintosh creates a bitmap PICT image at the root level of the hard disk and names the image "Picturexx," where xx is an incremental number.

To capture an image of the entire screen in Windows, press the PrintScreen key. To capture a screen image of the window that is currently active, press Alt + PrintScreen. Windows copies a bitmap (.bmp) image to the Windows clipboard. You can then paste the image into any application that supports bitmap images.

NOTE: If you experience problems using the system's screen capture feature, contact the manufacturer of the operating system. If you experience problems using a third-party utility to capture a screen image, contact the utility manufacturer.

CIE Color Standard General Information

The CIE (Commission International de l'Eclairage or International Commission on Illumination) is an international standards organization begun in 1931. CIE has published a number of colorimetric standards systems called CIE color. These are physical and perceptual based systems where any two colors with the same CIE numbers are perceptually indistinguishable when viewed under standard lighting conditions.

All CIE color models are based on the CIE XYZ color model (CIEXYZ) developed in 1931 and are device independent. The X, Y, and Z are abstract color primaries, similar to Red, Green, and Blue (RGB). When the phosphor RGB primaries and the white point temperature are known, the RGB color values can be converted directly into XYZ color values and vice versa. An RGB color is dependent on the device primaries (monitor phosphors) and white point to distinguish what its color looks like.

More recent CIE models are considered to be perceptually uniform and are referred to as uniform color models. Perceptually uniform means that a unit change in any one of that model's components is perceived by a standard observer to be the minimum perceptible change of a uniform amount in the view color. These uniform color models, LAB and LUV (CIELAB and CIELUV), besides being perceptually uniform, are also known as white point independent as the white point is not adjusted for when converting into these spaces.

With a CIE color and information about a color output device, it is possible to represent that color on the device as accurately as its color gamut allows. CIE colors use specific conditions for color specification, which include standard light sources, standard viewing conditions, and a standard observer.

In the Munsell Color System, or the ISCC NBS (Inter-Society Color Council, National Bureau of Standards), colors are subjectively compared, where the CIE approach is objective. The name of this objective approach is the Commission Internationale d'Eclairage, Uniform Chromaticity Scale (CIE UCS), and the approach does use a uvL space for color reproduction.

Desktop Color Separation (DCS) General Information

Desktop Color Separation (DCS) is an enhancement to the Encapsulated PostScript (EPS) graphic file format. DCS has the ability to manage the entire color separation process on the desktop, reducing production time, and can be implemented without purchasing additional specialized equipment. DCS files describe a pre-separated image using one or more files when adhering to DCS Specification 2.0, or five files when adhering to DCS Specification 1.0. All DCS files include a main EPS file that contains comments specifying the filename and location of the image's high-resolution separation files. You can import, crop, and resize an image saved as a DCS file in a page layout application.

There are two types of applications involved in DCS: DCS Producers and DCS Consumers. DCS Producer applications produce color separations from bitmap images and paint applications capable of working with EPS separation files (e.g., Adobe Photoshop). DCS Consumer applications are desktop publishing and page layout applications (e.g., Adobe PageMaker, QuarkXPress). When you print separations of a document containing a DCS file, the DCS Consumer application locates and prints the high-resolution separation files.

The main DCS file, as an enhanced EPS file, may contain a full-color composite representation of the image saved as a PICT file in the main file's resource fork. Using this PICT file, applications can display a preview of the DCS file on-screen, enabling you to view and manipulate the composite image in the DCS Consumer application (e.g., Adobe PageMaker). When a composite of the image is not described in the main DCS file's PostScript code, the printing application may download the PICT file screen preview to the printer as a composite image for proofing.

The main DCS file contains the following information in the EPS file's header:

- location of the cyan, magenta, yellow, and black EPS files (optional)
- which separation files are needed
- composite image information used to print a composite of the image

The DCS Specification 2.0 supports these new features:

- Option to create multiple- or single-file DCS files

  DCS Specification 2.0 supports the option of creating a single-file DCS file by including the separation files in the main DCS file or a multiple-file DCS file by saving each separation file externally and including a pointer to the separation files in the main DCS file. DCS Specification 1.0 only supports multiple-file DCS files by saving each separation file externally and including a pointer to the separation files in the main DCS file.

- Pointing to separation files that reside on a non-local file system

  DCS Specification 2.0 supports pointing to separation files that resides on a non-local system in the main DCS file. DCS Specification 1.0 supports pointing only to separation files that are accessible using the standard file system.

- Ability to specify additional separation files

  DCS Specification 2.0 can point to more than four separation files, enabling the inclusion of spot color separation files in addition to the four process color separation files (i.e., cyan, magenta, yellow, and black).

  - More capable "%%PlateFile" comment

  The "%%PlateFile" comment enables DCS files to support either single- or multiple-file DCS files and to support additional separation files. The "%%PlateFile" comment replaces the "%%DocumentProcessColors" and "%%[color]Plate" comments, and has two different forms, depending on whether you create a single- or multiple-file DCS file.

SPECIFYING NON-PRINTING SEPARATIONS

Depending on the image, one or more separation files may not be needed. For example, when an image contains no cyan and therefore does not need a cyan separation file, a DCS Producer application can create an empty cyan file, which contains no image information. When printing a DCS file that includes or points to an empty separation file, a DCS Consumer application can avoid printing the empty separation file. DCS files contain the following line that specifies which separation files are needed:

```
%%DocumentProcessColors: cyan magenta yellow
  black
```

SUPPRESSING DOT GAIN COMPENSATION

When a DCS file does not include the "%%SuppressDotGainCompensation" comment, an application may send a transfer function to the printer before sending the separation files to correct for the printer's non-linear gray scale rendering characteristics. If your DCS Producer application creates a DCS file that has dot gain compensation built-in, the DCS file should include the "%%SuppressDotGainCompensation" comment. When the DCS file includes the "%%SuppressDotGainCompensation" comment, the DCS file should also include the screen angle, frequency, and dot function itself, rather than relying on the printer's default settings at print time. The "%%SuppressDotGainCompensation" comment is located in the main DCS file before the comments specifying the location of the separation files, and is followed by composite image information.

Difference Between Object-oriented and Bitmap Graphics

There are two basic types of computer graphics: bitmap and object-oriented (vector).

BITMAP GRAPHICS

Bitmap graphics are similar to a mosaic made from tiny tiles. The tiles are called pixels (derived from "picture elements"). Lines are created by connecting pixels, and all shapes are filled and outlined with pixels.

The mosaic nature of bitmap graphics can produce undesirable results when you move, enlarge, or rotate the image. For example, enlarging a bitmap graphic causes it to appear as if the small tiles have been replaced with larger tiles, resulting in a blocky or jagged appearance.

When you print bitmap graphics, the printer reproduces the image exactly as it is stored, in its tiled form. The effective resolution of the printed page is directly dependent on the resolution of the bitmap. Coarse bitmap graphics are just as coarse or jagged whether printed on a 300 dpi printer or on a 2,540 dpi imagesetter. Fine bitmap images look as good printed to a 300 dpi printer as they do to a 2,540 dpi imagesetter. When enlarging a bitmap image, the pixels become larger, thereby decreasing print quality.

OBJECT-ORIENTED GRAPHICS

Object-oriented (vector) graphics overcome many of the bitmap image's limitations. Object-oriented images are composed of mathematically described objects and paths, sometimes referred to as vectors. Object-oriented graphics aren't a set of tiles, but rather a list of drawing instructions describing menu choices and mouse movements. You can enlarge, reduce, rotate, reshape and refill objects and the program redraws them without any loss of quality.

Object-oriented images are resolution independent. The quality (resolution) of a graphic printed to a 2,540 dpi imagesetter is higher than that of the same graphic printer to a 300 dpi printer. Instead of dictating where each "tile" should appear, the program mathematically describes the object and lets the printer produce it at the highest resolution possible. Because object oriented graphics are described mathematically, their print quality is not affected by resizing.

Dot Gain Compensation General Information

Dot gain occurs when ink bleeds or spreads as it is absorbed by the paper during the commercial printing process, enlarging the halftone dots. The amount of dot gain is dependent upon the type of paper being used. Traditionally, a highly absorbent paper, like newsprint, will have a high dot gain, while a less absorbent paper, like coated stock, will have much less gain.

Other factors that contribute to dot size variance:

- When film is processed from an imagesetter, the strength of the beam and condition of the chemicals can affect the development process, resulting in a poorly calibrated output and variance in the dot size.

- When a printing plate is "burned," variance in the dot size can occur.
- During the actual printing process not directly related to paper absorption, dot variance is affected by the ink coverage on the printing press.

Each of the above factors can influence the dot variance in either direction; i.e., you can have dot loss as well as dot gain. By exact definition, dot gain is different from these other types of dot variances since it is consistent within a certain type of paper and can be compensated for when the film is produced.

Dot gain can be compensated for before or while printing plates are burned. The exposure used to burn the plates can be shortened, or after the film is assembled it can be duplicated, and the exposure of this duplicated film receives is slightly less to create a smaller dot on the film. When printed, the smaller dot will enlarge back to its original size due to the absorption of ink in the paper.

Halftone Primer

Photographic images can blend smoothly, displaying grays in an uninterrupted flow from light to dark. But printing presses can't use dozens of different gray inks; they must use black ink alone to reproduce photographic images. To accomplish that, presses print small black dots close together. The human eye blurs the dots and interprets them as shades of gray. This process of using individual, solid-colored dots to simulate shades of gray is called "halftoning."

To make a printing plate directly from a photograph, a wire screen is used to break up the original image into dots. Finer screens create smaller dots, producing images with better "resolution."

Computer laser printers also use the halftone technique to make gray images. Laser printers have a fixed dot size, expressed as "dots per inch" or dpi. To create halftones, the dots must be grouped into clusters or halftone "cells." The number of shades of gray that we can print is limited by the dpi and the maximum size cell we're willing to accept.

A cell with four dots would be quite small—only four times bigger than a single dot. There are five possible four-dot cells, thus five possible shades of gray:

```
XX  XX  XO  OO  OO   XX  XO  OX  OX
 OO
black ————————> white
```

In these examples, an "x" represents a black dot and an "o" is the white paper we see when no dot is printed.

Five shades of gray might work for some special effects. But for normal images, we need at least twenty-five shades of gray. A 5-by-5 dot cell can create twenty-six shades of gray. On a 300 dpi printer, we'll get 60 of those 5-by-5 cells per inch. Our image will look more natural, but the cells will be very obvious because they are over six times larger than 2-by-2 cells.

The human eye can easily see individual cells printed in neat horizontal rows. By turning the rows on a forty-five degree angle, the cells blend together better and the image looks more realistic. To create the impression that our laser printed cells have been rotated, we have to leave some dots unused. That reduces our cell count from 60 to 53 on a 300 dpi printer.

Because halftone cells are used in rows or lines, the number of cells per inch is often expressed as "line frequency," "lines per inch," or lpi. The term "screen frequency" is sometimes used for lpi, even though there is no physical screen in a laser printer.

To get a better resolution image, you must increase the line frequency. To do that while keeping the number of grays reasonably high, you have to be able to print more dots per inch. Newer laser printers and third-party enhancement products can print at 600 dpi or higher. To get production-quality halftones, you need a high dpi device like an imagesetter. They start at 1200 dpi and go up to 3300 dpi.

Quality magazines often print halftones at 133 lpi. Using a 3300 dpi imagesetter, you get a 25-by-25 halftone cell at 133 lpi, enough dots for 626 shades of gray. As a practical matter, the current PostScript standard is limited to 256 shades of gray.

To reproduce color photographs, the same halftone system is used. Four colors (cyan, magenta, yellow and black) can be combined to reproduce most of the colors the human eye can see. Different halftone line angles are used for each color to minimize the effects of the many colored dots forming unwanted wave patterns called "moire." Products such as PageMaker can change the line frequency and the angle of the halftone cell lines for special effects.

Kodak PhotoCD General Information

Each Kodak PhotoCD includes the following directories:

- The CDI directory, which is reserved, along with the files it contains, for CD-I (Compact Disc Interactive) use.
- A Photo_cd directory, which contains the Images directory, which contains all Image Pack files.
- A PhotoCD may also contain additional information, determined by the operator, using the capability of the Kodak PCD Data Manager and Kodak PCD Writer. Files that are commonly included on PhotoCD discs are the Overview.pcd, Rights, Info.pcd, and Startup.pcd files.
- PhotoCD discs contains five resolutions of each image. The resolutions in pixels of PhotoCD images are:
- Base/16 = 128 x 192 (extracted for thumbnail during cataloging)
- Base/4 = 256 x 384 (lower-resolution version)
- Base = 512 x 768 (for NTSC and PAL systems)
- 4Base = 1024 x 1536 (intended for high-definition television)
- 16Base = 2048 x 3072 (for high-quality hard-copy devices such as the Kodak PCD Printer)

SINGLE-SESSION, MULTI-SESSION, DUAL-SPEED CD ROM DRIVES

Because PhotoCD disks can contain over 100 images at five resolutions, or more images at fewer resolutions, it is necessary to be able to write to the disk multiple times, since each roll of film is a single write session. To view these additional sessions on the disc, you need a multi-session CD-ROM drive. Most new CD-ROM drives are multi-session compatible, and older CD-ROM drives may be upgraded to be multi-session compatible. When using a single-session CD-ROM drive, you can view only the first PhotoCD session. Most older CD-ROM drives are compatible with single-session discs when using the supported version of the driver software.

Unlike hard disks, which are divided into many small data tracks, a CD-ROM disk contains a single data track that spirals from the center of the disk outward. To read this track at a constant speed, the CD-ROM drive adjusts the rotational speed. The data transfer rate for audio CD must be 150, which limits the speed for single-speed CD-ROM drives, but these CD-ROM drives can transfer data faster. With dual-speed or multi-speed technology, the CD-ROM drive doubles the rotational speed (300K/second) when reading data, and spins the disc at two linear velocities, one when playing audio and the other when reading data.

MAKING A PHOTOCD

Making a PhotoCD requires specialized software and hardware. After making a PhotoCD, you can view the images on the PhotoCD on a television using a PhotoCD player, print the images at a photofinisher, and view or manipulate the images in a PhotoCD-compatible application.

To make a PhotoCD:

1. Scan the film.

   The PhotoCD Film Scanner scans 35mm film and slides and produces an RGB digital image at a resolution of 2048 lines by 3072 pixels. This equals 18 MB of data per photo frame, which is far more information than can be used on the finished PhotoCD.
2. Encode, subsample, and decompose each image.

   The Kodak PCD Data Manager converts the RGB image data to Photo YCC data. Then it subsamples and halves the chrominance portion of the image without perceptible loss of quality, leaving the luminance data unchanged. Finally, it decomposes the image into five components so the image can be retrieved at the appropriate resolution for the output device.
3. Write each image to disc.

   The Kodak PCD Data Manager writes each scanned image to an Image Pac file, which enables the scanned images to be retrieved at five different resolutions. The lowest resolution (128 by 192 pixel) image is a separate file, named "Overview Pac," which is commonly used as a table of contents for the PhotoCD.
4. Make an index print of all images.

   The imaging workstation automatically prints the contents of the Overview Pac to create an index print showing all the images on the disc, which is included on the PhotoCD. When using a multi-session disc, the index print also shows all earlier sessions. When the PhotoCD disc already contains images from earlier sessions, the Overview Pac and Index Print also includes the images from those sessions.

Making Backup Copies of Installation Disks

Most application's installation utility searches for specific files in specific locations on specific disks. When creating backup copies of your installation disks, regardless of which method you choose to make the backup copies, ensure the backup disks are identical to the original disks by checking the disk's name and the files and folders it contains. Following are a few disk copying methods that enable you to create backup disks easily.

MACINTOSH

To make a backup of installation disks:

Use Apple's Disk Copy utility, available from Apple, CompuServe, and America Online, by following the instructions included in the utility.

OR: Use the system's disk-to-disk copy feature:

1. Insert the source disk, or the disk you want to back up, into the disk drive.
2. Choose Special > Eject Disk (Command + E) to eject the disk, which ejects the disks but dims the disk's icon on the desktop.
3. Insert the destination disk, or an empty disk, into the disk drive.
4. Drag the dimmed disk icon of your source disk onto your destination's disks icon.
5. After clicking Okay to confirm the copy, follow the system's prompts to insert the disk it needs into the drive to copy the contents of the source disk onto the destination disk.
6. Give the backup disk the same name as the original disk by carefully typing the new name, checking capitalization and spaces, or by copying and pasting the name.

OR: Copy the contents of the disk manually:

1. Insert the original disk, then open the disk when the disk's window does not open automatically by double-clicking it.
2. Because many application's first installation disk may automatically open a folder located on the disk, ensure you are viewing the contents of the original disk in the disk's window, and not the window of a folder on the disk, by ensuring the window's name is the same as the original disk's name.
3. With the original disk's main window active, choose Edit > Select All, then choose Edit > Copy.
4. Insert the destination disk, then open the disk when the disk's window does not open automatically by double-clicking it.
5. With an empty and active open destination disk main window, choose Edit > Paste.

WINDOWS 3.1X

To make a backup of installation disks:

Use File Manager's Copy Disk command:

1. In File Manager, choose Disk > Copy Disk.
2. Follow the on-screen instructions. The Copy Disk dialog box enables you to specify the source and destination disks, which may be the same or a different drive designator (e.g., A:\).

OR: Use the DOS command DISKCOPY:

1. Exit Windows.
2. At the C: prompt, type:
   `diskcopy [source]: [destination]:`
   where [source] is the drive designator for the disk you want to back up and [destination] is the drive designator for an empty disk.
   OR: When the source and destination are the same drive designator, type only the source disk after the DISKCOPY command. For example, type:
   `diskcopy a:`
   NOTE: When you add the switch /v at the end of the DISKCOPY command (e.g., DISKCOPY/V), DOS verifies data as it copies it, which slows the copying process.
3. Press Enter.

Measurement System Equivalents for Common Page Sizes

MEASUREMENT SYSTEM EQUIVALENTS

1 inch = 25.4 millimeters = 6 picas = 5c7.6 ciceros = 72 points
1 millimeter = .395 inches = 0p2.9 picas = 0c2.7 ciceros
1 pica = .167 inches = 4.233 millimeters = 0c11.3 ciceros = 12 points
1 cicero = .178 inches = 4.51 millimeters = 1p0.8 picas

COMMON PAGE SIZE MEASUREMENT SYSTEM EQUIVALENTS

Letter Page
inches: 8.5 x 11
millimeters: 215.9 x 279.4
picas: 51 x 66
ciceros: 47c10.3 x 61c11.2

Legal Page
inches: 8.5 x 14
millimeters: 215.9 x 355.6
picas: 51 x 84
ciceros: 47c10.3 x 78c9.8

Tabloid Page
inches: 11 x 17
millimeters: 279.4 x 431.8
picas: 66 x 102
ciceros: 61c11.2 x 95c8.5

A3 Page
inches: 11.693 x 16.535
millimeters: 297 x 420
picas: 70p1.9 x 99p2.6
ciceros: 65c10 x 93c1.1

A4 Page
inches: 8.268 x 11.693
millimeters: 210 x 297
picas: 49p7.3 x 70p1.9
ciceros: 46c6.6 x 65c10

A4small Page
inches: 8.267717 x 11.69291
millimeters: 210 x 297
picas: 49p7.275 x 70p1.889
ciceros: 46c6.6 x 65c10

A5 Page
inches: 5.827 x 8.268
millimeters: 148 x 210
picas: 34p11.6 x 49p7.3
ciceros: 32c9.7 x 46c6.6

B4 Page
inches: 9.842519 x 13.89763
millimeters: 250 x 253
picas: 59p0.661 x 83p4.629
ciceros: 55c4.9 x 78c2.9

B5 Page
inches: 6.929 x 9.842
millimeters: 176 x 250
picas: 41p6.9 x 59p0.7
ciceros: 39c0.1 x 55c4.9

Open Prepress Interface (OPI) General Information

Open Prepress Interface (OPI) is an extension of the PostScript page-description language that enables you to design pages with low-resolution images, then replace those images with high-resolution images when printing separations. By using low-resolution images for page layout (e.g., in Adobe PageMaker or QuarkXPress), you can reduce the size of your page layout file and reduce processing time when you work in the file.

The OPI workflow is as follows:

1. A prepress service provider scans an image at high resolution and stores it on an OPI server.
2. Customized software creates a low-resolution, "for position only" (FPO) copy of the scan. The FPO image is tagged with a PostScript comment that links it to the original high-resolution scan.
3. You use the FPO image in your page layout application, positioning and manipulating it (e.g., cropping, resizing) as desired.
4. You or your service provider print your page layout file to disk as a PostScript file.
5. Your service provider uses a prepress application (e.g., Luminous Color Central) that prints the PostScript file, reads the OPI comments, and automatically substitutes the high-resolution versions of the images before imaging separations.

OPI originally supported only TIFF (Tagged Image File Format) images. It was later expanded to support EPS (Encapsulated PostScript) and DCS (Desktop Color Separation) images.

DCS images, whose format is an enhancement of the EPS format, consist of five files: a composite FPO image file and four color-separated image files, one each for the cyan, magenta, yellow and black image separations. The main file includes comments that give the file names and locations of the separation files.

Some OPI systems are proprietary and only work with that vendor's equipment. Some OPI servers run platforms other than the Macintosh (e.g., UNIX).

OPI and DCS Desktop Color Separation Method Comparison

OPI (Open Prepress Interface), introduced by the Aldus Corporation, and DCS (Desktop Color Separation), introduced by Quark Inc., produce plate-ready color separations of entire publications, including images.

DCS IMAGES

The DCS format consists of five EPS files: a main file and four pre-separation files, one each for the cyan, magenta, yellow and black image data. The main file contains the screen version and information about where to find the other four files. During separations to a PostScript printer, the page layout program reads the DCS comments in the main file and assigns the cyan, magenta, yellow, and black files to their corresponding separation files.

TIFF IMAGES

Applications that support OPI comments, such as PageMaker, are not limited to pre-separated images. Printing to disk creates a PostScript file and embeds OPI comments which define the image file's location. This separation file is then printed as separations through a desktop color separation program, such as Aldus PrePrint, to a PostScript printer.

Advantages of the OPI Method of Separation over DCS

1. Because DCS produces five EPS files per image, it uses approximately three times the disk space of one TIFF with OPI.
2. Any post-layout changes to a DCS image requires reseparating then replacing the image, making it a very time consuming process. With OPI, changes can be made anytime during or after the page layout stage.
3. OPI gives you the option to separate your images with a high-end prepress system, while DCS is strictly a desktop solution.

A DCS-compatible system separates only text and graphics. For a color photograph to be process color separated, a DCS-aware page layout program, such as QuarkXPress, requires that all images are saved in a pre-separated format (i.e., DCS, CMYK TIFF).

OPI is a more flexible separation solution. An OPI compatible separation system demands more time spent in software development for software to be able read and separate entire PostScript files, including text, graphics, and images.

TIFF Image Resolution and Resampling General Information

RESOLUTION

Resolution or pixel density is the number of pixels or dots per linear inch of an image. An image needs to have a sufficient resolution to mimic the dot pattern of a halftone. An image that has an insufficient resolution will have a reduced range of grayscale or colors. Low resolution will be more noticeable on curved edges and fine patterns. Aldus PrePrint and Adobe Photoshop can display the image width measured in pixels for determining resolution.

RESAMPLING

Resampling or changing pixel density changes the resolution of an image. The higher the resolution, the larger the image's file size. Lowering the resolution is done for images that are large for regular layout work to accommodate handling the file and managing disk space and decreasing long print times when proofing on a laser printer. When the publication is ready for high resolution output, the high resolution images are relinked.

To resample an image in Adobe Photoshop:

1. Choose Image > Image Size.
2. In the Image Size dialog box, enter the desired values in the New Size fields for Width, Height, and Resolution.

Transparent vs. Opaque Images General Information

An image file's format determines whether the white area in an image can be transparent or opaque.

BILEVEL TIFF IMAGES

Bilevel (i.e., 1-bit, black-and-white, line art) TIFF images use values that allow for only on (black) pixels or off (white) pixels. No other values are possible. There is no information within the TIFF file format to designate "transparent" or "opaque." Applications determine whether the off pixels will be opaque or transparent.

Dithered TIFF Images

Dithered (i.e., halftone or pre-screened) TIFF images contain only black or white pixels arranged in patterns to create the illusion of gray at a fixed resolution. They use only on (black) and off (white) pixels. The eye blends these dots together for shades of gray. NOTE: Bilevel or 1-bit TIFF images import into PageMaker with the off pixels transparent.

GRAYSCALE TIFF IMAGES

Grayscale TIFF images describe each pixel as a shade of four to 256 grays. These dots hold information about the gray levels of the image rather than forming patterns to simulate gray shades. The white pixels are always opaque as they are defined as a shade of gray.

COLOR TIFF IMAGES

Color TIFF images describe each pixel as a color. RGB TIFF images describe colors using red, blue, and green values. CMYK TIFF images describe colors using cyan, magenta, yellow, and black values. Palette TIFF images are similar to grayscale images except that they use an index to map colors into an existing RGB color look-up table. The white pixels are always opaque in color images as they are defined as a shade of color.

PAINT-TYPE GRAPHICS

Like bilevel (1-bit) TIFF images, paint-type graphics have color values that allow only on (black) pixels or off (white) pixels. No other gray values are possible. Applications determine whether the off pixels will be opaque or transparent. The resolution of paint-type graphics are always 72 dots per inch.

Using OLE General Information

Editing a linked OLE (object linking and embedding) object in an OLE client application requires you open both the OLE server application (e.g., Chart 1.0, ChartMaker 1.0, Microsoft Excel) and the OLE client application (e.g., Persuasion 3.0, PageMaker 5.0). When you frequently create and edit OLE objects, keeping the original object open in the background saves you the time it takes you to relaunch the OLE server application when you want to create or edit the OLE object. The number of objects you can keep open is limited by your computer's available memory.

After you create an OLE object, choose File > Update. Without closing or quitting, return to the client application by choosing it from the Application menu, located on the right of the menu bar, or by clicking on a visible part of the client application window. The OLE-linked object appears in the client application. To edit the object, double-click on it in the client application.

When infrequently creating or editing OLE objects, quit from the OLE server application to make more memory available memory to other applications. To decrease the time it takes a server application to start, use a computer with a faster processor or reduce the number of installed fonts.

Windows

GENERAL INFORMATION

Troubleshooting General Protection Faults (GPFs) in Windows 3.1

General Protection Faults (GPFs) can be caused by anything from low-level DOS problems, to memory conflicts between device drivers, software, and hardware components, to corrupt elements in specific files. Diagnosing their causes is not always an easy task.

While there are many known factors that cause General Protection Fault errors, and solutions for those errors, there are no definitive cures for GPFs. Follow these DOS, Windows, and Adobe PageMaker tips to diagnose and prevent errors. Adobe Technical Support uses these techniques successfully in supporting the Windows 3.1 versions of PageMaker, Adobe Illustrator, Adobe Persuasion, and Adobe Photoshop. Read this entire document before proceeding.

You may note symptoms that match your problem and be able to correct the problem with only a few steps. If you don't recognize your problem here and you experience GPFs regularly, we recommend that you first carry out the DOS and Windows steps, then go back to work in Windows as usual. If the errors persist, tackle the PageMaker steps. Finally, if none of these steps work, try the more drastic steps listed at the end of this document.

While the wording of the General Protection Fault error message appears to point to a particular application, the application mentioned may or may not be the cause of the error. Because many of these errors are based on memory-management conflicts, it is possible that whatever application is running or loading at that time is caught in the middle of whatever action is not functioning properly. Sometimes the error message, module and address point out the origin of the problem right away. While such an error may only occur in one application, it does not necessarily mean that application is causing the error. It may be the only application that is large enough or memory-intensive enough to activate some other problem.

Many GPFs are one-time occurrences and are no cause for concern. Restart your computer and attempt the same action again. If the error repeats consistently, begin the troubleshooting process.

BASIC DOS HYGIENE

General Protection Faults occur most often on computers that aren't receiving consistent basic maintenance. To ensure your computer is running as efficiently as possible, do one or more of the following:

A. Always restart your computer after receiving a GPF to refresh your computer's memory; if you don't restart, the problem may snowball.

B. Use the DOS CHKDSK command to check for lost allocation units. CHKDSK scans your hard disk for bad sectors, lost allocation units, and lost chains. If CHKDSK finds any of these, you can decide later whether to delete them (typing CHKDSK/F gives you the option to delete or save these files). CHKDSK should be run on each drive if you have partitioned or multiple hard drives.

C. Free up disk space. Low disk space may cause GPFs. Your computer should have a minimum of 2 megabytes (MB) of free disk space whenever you are running Windows; if you have a partitioned hard disk, there should be at least 2 MB free on the volume where the Temp directory is located. When you work in an application, a copy of your data file is stored temporarily in that disk space, and, if you use Print Manager, your print jobs reside there temporarily as well, so you need enough space to accommodate those tasks. Adobe Technical Support recommends that you have 10 -12 MB of free hard disk space available when working with PageMaker 5.0 or later.

D. Make sure your computer has enough memory. If DOS 5.0 or later is installed, type "mem" at the DOS prompt to see how much memory is available. PageMaker 5.0x requires you have 4 MB of random-access memory (RAM) on your system. PageMaker 6.0 requires you have 10 MB of RAM on your system.

E. Make sure there's a Set Temp= line in the Autoexec.bat file and that it points to a valid drive and directory.
NOTE: Certain commands in the Autoexec.bat file, such as WIN or MENU, prevent any subsequent lines in that file from being read. If a Path or Temp statement follows such an entry, move it above the line in question. If there are multiple Path or Temp lines in the Autoexec.bat file, only the last one (before a command such as WIN or MENU) will be read.

F. Delete any temporary files by typing "del *.tmp" at the DOS prompt for the Temp directory (e.g., C:\Temp); do not delete *.tmp files while running Windows or from the DOS prompt within Windows. A buildup of temporary files may cause GPFs.
NOTE: If there is no Set Temp= line in the Autoexec.bat file or it points to an invalid directory, search for and delete temporary files in the Windows directory, or in the root directory. Temp files whose names are PM50-xxx.tmp or PM6.0xxx.tmp, where "xxx" is a three-digit number, may be openable copies of PageMaker publications that no longer open. For more information, see step D in Publication-specific General Protection Faults.

G. Change the settings in the Smartdrv.exe disk-caching utility. For example, adding the line "c:\windows\-smartdrv.exe /C /L" to the Autoexec.bat file puts SMARTDrive into low memory and writes all write-behind information to your hard drive. For more information, refer to the Microsoft Windows User's Guide.

BASIC WINDOWS HYGIENE

To ensure Windows is running as efficiently as possible, do one or more of the following:

A. Make sure there is only one Win.ini file on the system and that it's located in the Windows directory. If there is more than one Win.ini file on your system, find and rename all the Win.ini files, except the one in the Windows directory, then exit and restart Windows.

B. Check for multiple copies of other system files. You need one and only one copy of every system file to run Windows - multiple copies can cause problems on your system. Some of the files that might be duplicated on your system are the System.ini, Autoexec.bat, printer drivers, and other drivers.

C. Make sure you only have one version of Windows installed.

D. Turn off type managers. Running more than one type manager at the same time or running a damaged or outdated type manager may cause GPFs. Turn off all type managers and restart Windows to see if you still get an error. If you're using multiple type managers, try running each type manager separately, and then in combination, to see if one is causing problems. Call the manufacturer of the type manager in question for additional suggestions.

E. Ensure your screen fonts aren't damaged. Screen fonts can be installed through a type manager or through Windows. To check the Windows screen fonts, open the Windows Control Panel and double-click on the Fonts icon to display your list of installed screen fonts. Click on the name of each font to see if it displays properly in the box below. If any font causes a GPF, gives an error or doesn't display, delete the font and reinstall it.

F. Run Windows in Standard mode. To do this, exit Windows and type "win/s" at the DOS prompt. If the error does not occur in Standard mode, you may have a damaged permanent swap file or one that is larger than the size recommended by Windows. For information about deleting and recreating permanent Swap files, refer to your Windows documentation. NOTE Windows for Workgroups cannot run in Standard mode.

G. Run Windows by typing "win/D:X" at a DOS prompt. If this eliminates the GPF, you may have a mapping conflict in a particular adapter segment of memory. Adding the line "EMMExclude=A000-EFFF" under the [386Enh] section of the System.ini file can keep this memory segment from being used by Windows.
NOTE: Make a backup copy of your Win.ini and System.ini files before making changes.

H. Change the resolution of your video card. If you are running a high-resolution card, change the driver setting to Standard VGA and run the program again. Some high-resolution cards are not written to Windows specifications, and may have interface problems with complex Windows applications. If changing the video driver fixes the problem, contact your video card manufacturer to see if updated drivers are available.

I. Rename the font summary file if you're using a PCL printer. This file is named FSxxport.PCL, where "xx" is the printer driver identifier and "port" is the name of the port your printer is using (such as LPT1 or COM2). The next time you use that printer, the file will be rebuilt.

J. Make sure you have a proper target device as a default in your applications. Sometimes a default may be set to a printer that has been removed, or to a driver that is damaged. Change to a different default to see if the problem is corrected.

USING THE ERROR MESSAGE TO IDENTIFY THE CULPRIT

If the GPF always occurs in a particular file at a similar address, it is possible that the file is the culprit. Determine the origin of the file and proceed from there.

If the file is a component of a type manager or another utility that runs in the background, disable that utility and see if the error occurs. If not, reinstall that utility, or contact the utility's manufacturer for additional help. If the GPF occurs in a printer driver file, check for multiples of that file on your hard drive as outlined in the Basic Windows Hygiene section. If there are no duplicates, remove the printer from the Windows Control Panel. Then exit Windows and delete the printer driver file and any of its components from the hard drive. (For example, if the problem is with an Apple LaserWriter Plus PostScript printer, delete the Pscript.drv file and the corresponding *.wpd file). Restart Windows to see if you still get a GPF in that file. If not, reinstall the printer driver. If the problem reoccurs, contact the supplier of that printer driver (usually Microsoft or the printer manufacturer) for additional help.

PAGEMAKER HYGIENE

If General Protection Faults always occur when trying to launch PageMaker and the DOS and Windows solutions do not solve the problem, do one or more of the following:

A. When using PageMaker 5.0x and running no other Aldus products (e.g., Aldus FreeHand, Persuasion), delete all the .DLL files in the ALDUS directory and single file copy them using the Aldus Setup or PM5 Setup application. For instructions on using the Aldus Setup or PM5 Setup single file copy function, see Related Records.

B. Exit PageMaker and rename PageMaker's defaults files. When using PageMaker 5.0x, rename the PM5.cnf, PM5filt.cnf, and Ppds.cnf files in the Aldus\Usenglsh directory. Also rename the Panose.bin file in the Windows directory. When using PageMaker 6.0, rename the PM6.cnf, PM6filt.cnf, and Ppds.cnf files in the PM6\Rsrc\Usenglsh directory. Also rename the Panose.bin file in the PM6\Rrsc directory. Default files contain setup information for various functions in PageMaker (e.g., page layout options). Renaming a defaults file makes it unavailable to PageMaker, but the file remains on your hard drive so you can return to it later if necessary. When PageMaker cannot find a defaults file, it creates a new one using the system defaults. If the GPF doesn't occur after you rename the defaults file, your defaults file was damaged.

C. Delete and reinstall the PageMaker application files. You can delete everything in the PM5 or PM6 directory once you've moved any data files you have stored in these directories into a different directory.

PUBLICATION-SPECIFIC GENERAL PROTECTION FAULTS

If a GPF occurs consistently in a single PageMaker publication, do one or more of the following:

A. Exit PageMaker and rename PageMaker's defaults files. When using PageMaker 5.0x, rename the PM5.cnf, PM5filt.cnf, and Ppds.cnf files in the Aldus\Usenglsh directory. Also rename the Panose.bin file in the Windows directory. When using PageMaker 6.0, rename the PM6.cnf, PM6filt.cnf, and Ppds.cnf files in the PM6\Rsrc\Usenglsh directory. Also rename the Panose.bin file in the PM6\Rsrc directory.

Default files contain setup information for various functions in PageMaker (e.g., page layout options). Renaming a defaults file makes it unavailable to PageMaker, but the file remains on your hard drive so you can return to it later if necessary. When PageMaker cannot find a defaults file, it creates a new one using the system defaults. If the GPF doesn't occur after you rename the defaults file, your defaults file was damaged.

B. Determine whether the GPFs occur in a particular publication, page, or object. If the error occurs on any page in a publication, for example, the entire publication may be damaged. If the error occurs when clicking on an individual object, that object may be damaged.

C. If the GPF occurs when opening a particular publication, prevent PageMaker from displaying your publication:
   1. Launch PageMaker. With no publications open, resize the PageMaker window so only PageMaker's menu bar displays.
   2. Open your publication and choose File > Page Setup (PageMaker 5.0x) or File > Document Setup (PageMaker 6.0), then reselect the appropriate printer from the Compose To pop-up menu and click OK.
   3. Perform a Diagnostic Recompose (hold down the Control and Shift keys while choosing Type > Hyphenation), then save the publication to a new name.
   4. Resize the window to display the page.
   5. If the error still occurs, restart the computer, launch PageMaker and resize its window, and open the publication again.
   6. Choose File > Preferences, then select Gray Out as the Graphics option and click OK.
   7. Resize the PageMaker window and replace the graphics on the affected page.

D. When you cannot open a particular publication, try to open a temporary copy of it. When an error occurs while a publication is open, PageMaker attempts to save a copy of the publication to disk as a temporary (.tmp) file. The file is named PM50xxx.tmp or PM60xxx.tmp (where "xxx" is a three-digit number), and its date and time corresponds to the time the error occurred. If you locate such a file, choose File > Open in PageMaker, select All Files, then select the temporary file.

ADDITIONAL TROUBLESHOOTING

If GPFs persist after trying all these steps, there may be a driver or program running in the background that is causing the problem. Whenever you start your computer, it looks to the Autoexec.bat file and Config.sys file to launch drivers for mice, scanners, networks, and other devices. These programs are launched at startup and are active in the background so they're available whenever you need them. Consequently, they occupy a portion of memory whenever your computer is turned on.

Many General Protection Faults occur because different programs try to access the same portion of your computer's memory. The only way to determine if one of these programs is causing GPFs is to disable it, then restart your computer and see if errors still occur. To troubleshoot driver and other problems within your Autoexec.bat or Config.sys file, start your computer using a bootable floppy disk with minimal system configuration information. If your errors happen throughout Windows and none of the troubleshooting in this record alleviates them, it may help to delete and reinstall Windows. When you reinstall Windows, you can either keep a backup of your Win.ini file and add your Windows program sections to it manually, or you can reinstall your Windows programs for a fresh start.

Missing Files or Directories on CD-ROM in File Manager

ISSUE

Windows File Manager doesn't list all files and directories on a CD-ROM.

SOLUTION

Change the Mscdex.exe file's cache size in the Autoexec.bat file:

1. Make a backup copy of the Autoexec.bat file, which is located in the root directory.
2. Open the original Autoexec.bat file in a text editor that can save in text-only format (e.g., Windows Write, Notepad).
3. Locate the Mscdex.exe line. For example:
   `C:\DOS\Mscdex.exe /M:10 /D:CPQCD001`
4. Change the value following "/m:" to 24. For example:
   `C:\DOS\Mscdex.exe /M:24 /D:CPQCD001`
5. Save in text-only format, then restart the computer.

ADDITIONAL INFORMATION

The Microsoft CD-ROM 2.2 extension (Mscdex.exe) uses a portion of the Windows 3.1 SMARTDrive memory cache to operate. The default Mscdex.exe cache size is adequate for accessing directories on most CD-ROM volumes. When a CD-ROM contains more directories than Mscdex.exe can access using the memory in the cache, File Manager may not list all directories or files on the CD-ROM. Increasing the Mscdex.exe cache size in the Autoexec.bat file to 24K of random-access memory (RAM) enables File Manager to access more files and directories on CD-ROM volumes containing large directories.

Printers, Ports, and Printer Drivers

WHY YOUR PRINTER TYPE MATTERS

While PageMaker will print to any printer that has a printer driver for the current version of Windows, the strategies used by different printers offer different advantages and disadvantages. All printers have two parts: the marking engine, and the page description language which tells the marking engine what to do. The marking engine provides the physical apparatus that puts the image on the page; most printers are categorized by the type of marking engine they use. The page description language translates PageMaker's descriptions of objects on a page into commands that the printer can implement. Often, this information is contained in the printer driver.

LASER PRINTERS

The word "laser" tells us the type of marking engine in your printer, but not the page description language your printer uses. Laser printers work like copy machines. A single laser beam records the image of the page and projects the image onto a drum. Light from the laser beam hits the drum, the area becomes charged and toner (or "ink") distributed over the drum is attracted to the charge. Paper with a negative charge then rolls around the drum picking up the oppositely charged toner particles, heat is applied, and the toner is fused to the paper. Laser printed information is clear and smooth because the resolution is relatively high (normally, 300 or 600 dots per inch [dpi]).

The two main types of laser printers available today, PCL and PostScript, are differentiated by their page description languages. Each offers different advantages and disadvantages and therefore, significantly different capabilities as far as PageMaker is concerned. We'll look at each one separately.

PCL PRINTERS

Printer Command Language (PCL) is the page description language used by Hewlett-Packard LaserJet printers and those that emulate them. There are two versions of the PCL language used in laser printers today (earlier versions of the language are used by printers with other types of marking engines).

PCL 4 was used by the HP LaserJet through HP LaserJet II printers. All PCL 4 printers treat both text and graphics as bitmaps. PCL 4 printers generally don't boast a wide variety of built-in fonts. Bitmapped downloadable soft fonts are supported, but to use these fonts, you have to purchase and install each size, style, and typeface you may want to use. Although these fonts print nicely at resolutions up to 300 dpi, it can take some work to get them set up properly.

When a PCL 4 printer prints a page, text and graphics are processed in independent bands. Text comes first; once all of the text has been processed, all other information is processed and placed on top of it. While this works just fine for most print jobs, unfortunately it means there's no way to print reversed text with these printers. Furthermore, the rigid structure of PCL 4 fonts makes it impossible to print text that has been rotated or text to which PageMaker's "Set width" feature has been applied. However, some font managers such as Adobe Type Manager and the TrueType manager that comes with Windows 3.1 can simulate set width, reversed, and rotated text by sending the font information down as a graphic representation. If you are using a Type manager, make sure that your Graphics Resolution option is set to 300 dpi in the printer driver. You can also select Print TrueType as graphics in the printer driver in order to print reversed text successfully.

PCL 5, an updated version of the page description language, solves the problems of reversed and rotated text while offering a great deal of additional flexibility. The PCL 5 language is used by the Hewlett-Packard Laser Jet III printers. PCL 5 printers support scalable fonts; which means that as long as you have the scalable font correctly installed, you can print that font at any point size. Another important advantage offered by PCL 5 printers is that the graphic and text bands are no longer processed separately, making it possible for these printers to support reversed text. However, Windows 3.1 does not fully utilize the text banding process with the Hewlett-Packard LaserJet III series of printers. Because Windows 3.1 does not fully utilize the text banding process to print set width, rotated, or reversed type you must still rely on a type manager and ensure that your fonts print as graphics. The LaserJet 4 series of printers should print revered text and rotated graphics but may still have problems with set width.

PCL 5 printers are backwards-compatible and support all of the fonts used by PCL 4 printers. Neither PCL 4 nor PCL 5 printers support color printing.

POSTSCRIPT PRINTERS

The PostScript page description language was developed by Adobe Systems. In addition to supporting scalable outline fonts, the PostScript language offers more sophisticated type capabilities than other printer description languages. PostScript offers many other advantages as well: in addition to supporting sophisticated color separation capabilities, you can print at resolutions up to 3600 dpi. One of the most widely used graphic formats on both the Macintosh and IBM-compatibles is EPS, or Encapsulated PostScript. Only PostScript printers can offer full support for this graphic format.

PostScript is considered by most publishing and graphic arts professionals to be the industry standard, in large part due to the flexibility it offers. Your publishing requirements may not demand a PostScript printer, but should you need to produce typeset quality documents from the desktop, PostScript is an option you should consider. It's also useful to know that 300 dpi color PostScript printers are available.

INKJET PRINTERS

InkJet-type printers use small jets to propel ink—either black, colored, or a combination—onto paper. While these printers are generally inexpensive and work reliably with Windows, they can't print EPS graphics and they require soft fonts which can't be used by other printer types (again, unless a type manager is used). These printers are also usually 300 dpi and both black and white and color inkjet printers are currently available.

DOT MATRIX PRINTERS

Dot matrix printers have more in common with traditional typewriters than the other printers we've discussed here. On a dot matrix printer, a printhead hammers through a ribbon to force a printed dot onto the page. As it moves back and forth across the paper, line by line, the pattern of dots eventually resembles the image of the page displayed on your monitor. Dot matrix printers don't require printer fonts, but when used with a type manager such as ATM, they provide an inexpensive proofing option. Both black and white and color dot matrix printers are currently available. Newer more complex versions of software may not fully support these printers.

PRINTER PORTS

Ports allow you to communicate with peripheral devices (e.g., scanners, printers, or modems) by electronically communicating data (in the form of bits and bytes) through a cable. Whenever you print from PageMaker, you'll do so through one of the ports on your computer. There are two types of ports: serial and parallel. Understanding how they differ will help you to determine which one is most appropriate for the type of communication you plan to do.

Parallel ports use eight separate conductors or lines and transmit one bit of data at a time through each of the eight conductors. These eight bits add up to one byte; the fact that data is transmitted over multiple paths makes it fairly fast, simple, and (electronically speaking) uncomplicated. Most Windows users favor this method. Parallel ports are called LPT1, LPT2, and LPT3 and usually have 25-pin connections. Parallel cables can be up to ten feet long.

Serial ports transfer data sequentially through a single conductor bit by bit (literally). Serial ports are slower than parallel ports, but the cabling they require is less expensive. Serial ports are called COM1, COM2, and COM3 and usually have 9-pin connections. Serial cables can be up to 50 feet long.

While all of your physical ports are either parallel or serial, Windows offers the FILE port as an additional option. The FILE port offers an easy way to create files that contain all of the data that would have been sent to a printer. These files can then be taken to another computer (often a service bureau) where they can be printed without worry about font or other system-specific conflicts.

NOTE: PageMaker 5.0x does not require the use of the FILE port to create a PostScript or EPS file. This can be done by opening PageMaker's Options printing dialog box and selecting Write Postscript to File.

WHY PORTS MATTER TO WINDOWS

Under Windows, a printer selection or target printer can be any printer driver assigned to any port. Because Windows makes it possible for you to work with both hypothetical and real printers and for you to have more than one printer installed for each port (though only one can be active at a time), things can get a little confusing. All you really need to know is that Windows uses ports as a way of organizing the printers you have available. Because fonts are installed for specific printers, keeping track of your ports can help you know where your fonts are.

The Win.ini file has a [ports] section which lists all the available ports; the list of available ports in the Printers Control Panel is based on this listing. The Win.ini file will also have a [Printer,Port] section for each printer you've installed; you can have as many as 15. These can be different devices, or multiple instances of the same device with various configurations, such as different ports. This flexibility makes it easier to set up your publications without having to constantly reconfigure your printers.

If you change a printer to a different port, a new [Printer,Port] section will be added to the Win.ini file. If you have downloadable fonts installed for a PostScript printer on COM1, but you change the printer to another port, you'll need to reinstall your fonts for the new [Printer,Port] combination.

PRINTER DRIVERS

The printer driver is the software that serves as the translator or interface between your Windows applications and your printer. Without the right printer driver, Windows won't take advantage of your printer's features (such as built in-fonts).

The driver "translates" the information which makes up your page into signals that the printer can understand. The signals are then sent via a communications port to the printer, where they're interpreted and turned into marks on paper. The printer driver contains information about the attributes of a printer (e.g., paper sizes supported, resident fonts, etc.) which helps PageMaker (and other applications) take advantage of the printer's features. Printer drivers are designed for use by any Windows application.

One of your installed printers should be selected as your default printer in the Control Panel. If no printer name shows up in the Default Printer scroll box, You'll get the error message "Unable to load printer driver." when you try to print from PageMaker 5.0x.

COMPOSING FOR YOUR PRINTERS

When you enter Page Setup dialog box in PageMaker 5.0x, you have the ability to make changes to the setup of your printer driver. Any time you leave the Printer Setup dialog box, PageMaker assumes you have made a change in the setup and, just to be sure, it asks if you want to recompose your publication. When this happens, you'll see the message "Recompose entire publication for x printer?" If you haven't made changes, or the changes shouldn't affect the output (e.g. portrait to landscape), you can press "Cancel."

Sometimes, though, recomposing can help you out. Being targeted or composed for the current printer means your system can take advantage of installed fonts, graphics resolution, and other printer-specific options and gives you the benefit of anything specific for that printer that you've taken the time to set up. While PageMaker can compose a publication without benefit of printer driver (i.e. without being targeted for a specific printer), you'll get the best and most consistent results if you are properly composed or targeted. PageMaker 5.0 automatically recomposes your publication without asking you for permission when you open up the Page Setup dialog box and select a different printer, then click OK.

If you have made changes to the printer setup, you'll want PageMaker to look again at all those changes and act accordingly, making sure your new choices are viable and determining whether all of the necessary components are available.

Specifying the Standard VGA Video Driver in Windows 3.1x

To specify the Windows Standard VGA driver in Windows 3.1x:

1. Make sure your Windows installation disks are available.
2. Create a backup copy of the SYSTEM.INI file.
3. Launch Windows Setup by double-clicking the Windows Setup icon in the Main group of Program Manager, or by choosing File > Run, typing "SETUP" in the Command line text box, and clicking OK.
4. In Windows Setup, choose Options > Change System Settings.
5. In the Change System Settings dialog box, select VGA from the Display pop-up menu and click OK.
6. Follow the on-screen instructions to install the VGA video driver, inserting Windows installation disks if prompted.
7. Restart Windows.

You can restore the original video driver in DOS using the DOS version of Windows Setup, or by replacing the existing SYSTEM.INI file with a backup of the SYSTEM.INI file (e.g., SYSTEM.BAK). In Windows, you can restore the original video driver by restoring the backup copy of the SYSTEM.INI file in File Manager. When Windows displays incorrectly (e.g. distorted), you can use key commands in Windows to change the video driver selected in Windows Setup.

To change video drivers from the DOS version of Windows Setup:

1. At the C:\ prompt, type "CD WINDOWS" to change to the WINDOWS directory.
2. Type "SETUP" and press Enter .
3. In Windows Setup, press the up or down arrow keys to select the Display option and press Enter.
4. Press the up or down arrow keys to select the desired video driver and press Enter.
5. Select the Complete Changes option and press Enter.
6. Follow the prompts to install the selected video driver, then start Windows.

To restore the backup copy of the SYSTEM.INI file in DOS:

1. From the DOS prompt, type "CD WINDOWS" to change to the WINDOWS directory.
2. Rename the existing SYSTEM.INI file in the WINDOWS directory by typing the following text and pressing Enter:

```
REN SYSTEM.INI SYSTEM.ABC
```

where SYSTEM.ABC is the new name of the SYSTEM-.INI file. Do not rename the existing SYSTEM.INI file with the same name as your backup copy of the SYSTEM.INI file (e.g., .BAK).

3. Copy the backup SYSTEM.INI file into the Windows directory and rename it SYSTEM.INI by typing the following text and pressing Enter:

```
REN A:\SYSTEM.BAK C:\WINDOWS\SYSTEM.INI
```

where A:\ SYSTEM.BAK is the driver letter, path name, and file name of the backup copy.

4. Restart Windows.

To replace the updated SYSTEM.INI file with the backup SYSTEM.INI file in Windows:

1. Double-click the File Manager icon in the Main group of Program Manager.
2. Select the backup SYSTEM.INI file (e.g., SYSTEM.BAK), then choose File > Copy.
3. In the Copy dialog box, type C:\WINDOWS\SYSTEM-.INI in the To text box, then click OK.
4. When the Confirm File Replace dialog box appears, click Yes to replace the SYSTEM.INI file with the backup SYSTEM.INI file.
5. Exit File Manager and restart Windows.

To change the video driver selected in the Windows version of Windows Setup using keyboard commands:

1. Launch Windows, then press Alt + F to choose the File menu.
2. Press R to open the Run dialog box.
3. In the Run dialog box, type SETUP and press Enter.
4. In Windows Setup, press Alt + O to choose the Options menu, then press C to select Change System Settings.
5. In the Change System Settings dialog box, type V to select VGA from the Display pop-up menu, then press Enter.
6. Press the Spacebar to select the currently installed driver.
7. Press the spacebar to restart Windows.

Restoring the Windows 95 Registry

In rare situations when the Windows 95 Registry is badly corrupted, you can recreate the Registry from copies of the User.dat and System.dat files. This procedure will restore the Registry using backups of these files generated by Windows. The backup of the Registry files is current as of the last time you launched Windows successfully.

DISCLAIMER: This procedure is not supported by Adobe Systems Incorporated and is only provided as a guideline. Experience working with system files and making command-line entries at DOS is highly recommended. Performing these steps incorrectly could cause further system damage, and the system could fail to start. In the event of problems, contact Microsoft Corporation.

To restore the Registry from a Windows session:

1. Choose Start > Shut Down.
2. Select Restart the Computer in MS-DOS Mode, and click Yes.
3. At the DOS prompt, type the following commands, pressing Enter after each line:

```
attrib -h -r -s system.dat
attrib -h -r -s system.da0
copy system.da0 system.dat
attrib -h -r -s user.dat
attrib -h -r -s user.da0
copy user da0 user.dat
```

4. Restart your computer.

To restore the Registry from the DOS prompt:

1. Switch to your Windows 95 directory.
2. Type the following commands, pressing Enter after each line:

```
attrib -h -r -s system.dat
attrib -h -r -s system.da0
copy system.da0 system.dat
attrib -h -r -s user.dat
attrib -h -r -s user.da0
copy user da0 user.dat
```

3. Restart your computer.

Specifying the Windows Standard VGA Driver in Windows 95

To specify the Windows Standard VGA driver in Windows 95:

1. Right-click on the desktop, then select Properties from the pop-up menu.
2. In the Display Properties dialog box, click on the Settings tab, then click the Change Display Type button.
3. Note the selected Adapter Type, then click Change.
4. In the Select Device dialog box, select the Show All Devices option.
5. Select the Standard Display Types option from the top of the Manufacturers scroll box.
6. Select the Standard Display Adapter (VGA) option from the Models scroll box, then click OK.
   NOTE: Standard Display Adapter (VGA) video drivers display only 16 colors. Switch to Super VGA for applications that require a minimum of 256 colors.
7. Note the selected Monitor Type, then click Change.
8. In the Select Device dialog box, select the Show All Devices option.
9. Select the Standard Monitor Types option from the top of the Manufacturers scroll box.
10. Select the Standard VGA 640x480 option from the Models scroll box, then click OK.
11. Restart Windows 95.

When the Windows 95 Standard Display Adapter (VGA) driver or the Super VGA driver is damaged or is not installed, reinstall the driver from the Windows 95 CD-ROM.

To install the VGA driver:

Copy the VGA.DRV file (size 50.8K, date 7/11/95) from the DRIVERS\DISPLAY\VGA directory on the Windows 95 CD-ROM to the WINDOWS\SYSTEM directory on your startup disk, then restart Windows 95.

To install the Super VGA driver:

1. Insert the Windows 95 CD-ROM in the CD-ROM drive.
2. Restart the computer in MS-DOS mode.
3. At the DOS prompt, type the following text:
   ```
   EXTRACT E:\WIN95\WIN95_04CAB FRAMEBUF.DRV/L
     C:\WINDOWS\SYSTEM
   ```
   where "E:" is the CD-ROM drive indicator.
4. Restart the computer.

Setting Program Manager as Default Workspace

ISSUE

Errors installing Aldus applications when using a third-party desktop applications (e.g., Norton Desktop, TabWorks).

SOLUTIONS

Replace the third-party desktop with the Windows Program Manager. To do this temporarily for the current Windows session:

In the File Manager, double-click on PROGMAN.EXE in the WINDOWS directory.

OR: Choose "Run..." from whatever shell you are using (usually under the File menu), and type "C:\Windows\Progman.exe" (where C: is the drive where Windows is located).

OR: To make Windows Program Manager the default desktop when Windows is launched, modify your SYSTEM.INI file to make Windows recognize Program Manager as the shell:

1. Make a backup copy of the SYSTEM.INI file.
2. Using a text editor (e.g., SysEdit, Windows Notepad, or DOS Edit) open the original SYSTEM.INI file.
3. In the [Boot] section of the SYSTEM.INI file, locate the line that begins "Shell=," and modify it to read:
   ```
   Shell=progman.exe
   ```
4. Save changes to the file, exit and restart Windows.

NOTE: To return to your original desktop application, rename the backup copy of the SYSTEM.INI file (e.g., SYSTEM.OLD) to SYSTEM.INI.

ADDITIONAL INFORMATION

Some third-party desktop applications don't emulate the Program Manager correctly, causing problems for Windows applications, which are expecting certain responses from the Program Manager, particularly during installation.

Changing the Default Working Folder in Windows 95

To change the folder that an application defaults to when opening, placing, or saving a file in Windows 95:

1. Exit the application.
2. Right-click on the taskbar, then choose Properties.
3. Click the Start Menu Programs tab, then click Advanced.
4. In the Exploring window, double-click the Programs folder.
5. Double-click on the folder containing the application whose default working folder you want to change.
6. Right-click the application's icon, then choose Properties.
7. In the Properties dialog box, click the Shortcut tab.
8. In the Start In text box, enter the pathname of the desired default working folder, then click Apply.

Generating a System Resource Report in Windows 95

Windows 95 is able to print a System Resource Report, which is a summary of your computer hardware and the resources used by each hardware device. Adobe technical support can use this information to troubleshoot system issues and recreate your system's configuration. You can deliver the report to a technical support specialist by faxing or mailing a printed copy, or by uploading the report file to the Adobe BBS.

To create a System Resource Report in Windows 95:

1. Right-click on My Computer, then choose Properties from the pop-up menu.
3. Click the Device Manager tab in the System Properties dialog box.
4. Select Computer at the top of the list, then click Print.
5. In the Print dialog box, select the All Devices and System Summary option.
6. Click OK to print the file to your printer, or select Print to File before clicking OK to create a report (.PRN) file.

The System Resource Report includes:

- System Summary (e.g., Windows version number, processor type)
- IRQ Summary (e.g., keyboard type, communications port)
- I/O Port Summary (e.g., memory access)
- Upper Memory Usage Summary (e.g., which drivers are using upper memory)
- DMA Channel Usage Summary (e.g., memory access)
- Memory Summary (i.e., conventional and extended memory)
- Disk Drive Info (e.g., types of disk drives)
- System Device Info (e.g., device drivers)

Making a Bootable Floppy Disk in Windows 3.1x

When starting, DOS-based computers read several files from a disk drive, usually an internal hard disk. However, if the hard disk is damaged, you can start the computer from a floppy disk. You may also boot from a floppy disk to eliminate variables when troubleshooting system or application errors. A floppy disk created for this purpose is called a "bootable" or "system" floppy disk. Several files must be added to a floppy disk to make it bootable.

NOTE: Most DOS-based computers can only boot from a floppy disk in the A: drive. If a computer has more than one floppy drive, the other drives may not have the same physical characteristics as the A: drive. Whenever possible, make a bootable floppy in the computer's A: drive. If you use another computer or drive to create a bootable disk, be sure the disk format is compatible with the A: drive of the computer to be booted from the floppy.

MAKING A BOOTABLE FLOPPY FROM A DOS PROMPT

NOTE: Formatting will erase all the information on the disk being formatted.

To create a floppy disk from a DOS prompt, type the following command:

```
FORMAT A: /s
```

The "/s" switch tells DOS to create a "boot sector" on the floppy disk and copy three additional files necessary for DOS to function.

MAKING A BOOTABLE FLOPPY FROM WINDOWS

NOTE: Formatting will erase all the information on the disk being formatted.

1. Open the Windows File Manager and choose Disk > Make System Disk.
2. Insert a disk into the A: drive
3. Click Yes when prompted "Are you sure you want to copy system files onto the disk in drive A:?"

AUTOEXEC.BAT AND CONFIG.SYS FILES

Using the DOS COPY command from the DOS prompt or the Copy command in File Manager, copy the Autoexec.bat and Config.sys files from the root directory of the hard drive to the boot floppy. These files may contain information necessary to successfully boot the computer. DOS looks for these files only in the root directory of the disk from which it boots. If you boot from a floppy in A:, DOS will not find the Autoexec.bat and Config.sys files on the hard drive.

If you're using Double Space, a hard disk compression utility included with DOS version 6.0 and later, copy the Dblspace.bin file to the boot floppy. Without this file, DOS won't be able to read the hard disk that's been compressed using Double Space. The Config.sys file will also contain a reference to Dblspace.sys. If you want to boot without accessing any files on the hard disk, copy the Dblspace.sys file to the boot floppy also, and make the necessary changes to the copy of Config.sys file on the floppy.

Changes to the Autoexec.bat File

Make sure you edit the Autoexec.bat file on the floppy disk, not the one on the hard drive.

Using a text editor that saves in text-only format (e.g., Windows Notepad, MS-DOS Editor), open the Autoexec.bat file on the boot floppy. To make a "minimum" Autoexec.bat file, remark out all but the following lines, then save the file in text-only format:

```
PROMPT $p$g
PATH=C:\;C:\DOS;C:\WINDOWS
SET TEMP=C:\TEMP
```

Type "rem " at the beginning of the line to remark it out. Remarking out a line prevents it from being read by DOS. Make sure you don't remark out any lines necessary to boot your computer.

Changes to the Config.sys File

Make sure you edit the Config.sys file on the floppy drive, not the one on the hard drive.

Using a text editor that saves in text-only format (e.g., Windows Notepad, MS-DOS Editor), open the Config.sys file on the boot floppy. To make a "minimum" Config.sys file, remark out all but the following lines, then save the file in text-only format:

```
DEVICE=C:\WINDOWS\HIMEM.SYS
FILES=50
BUFFERS=20
STACKS=9,256
```

Type "rem " at the beginning of the line to remark it out. Remarking out a line prevents it from being read by DOS. Make sure you don't remark out any lines necessary to boot your computer.

BOOTING FROM THE FLOPPY DISK

Place the disk in the A: drive and press the reset switch. If the computer has no reset switch, remove any disks from the floppy drives and turn off the computer. Wait at least fifteen seconds for the hard disk drive to come to a complete stop. Insert the boot floppy in the A: drive and turn on the power switch.

Startup Menu Options in Windows 95

The Windows 95 Startup menu is a graphical interface for the MSDOS.SYS file. It provides options that change which startup files are processed when the system loads, enabling you to systematically isolate startup problems. Windows 95 displays the Startup menu when the system fails to load, or when you press the F8 key while the "Starting Windows 95" message displays. Other keyboard shortcuts for particular startup options enable you to bypass the Startup menu completely.

NORMAL

Normal mode loads all startup files and Registry values.

LOGGED

Logged mode loads all startup files and Registry values. All startup actions (i.e., successful loading of device drivers) are added sequentially to the BOOTLOG.TXT file.

SAFE MODE

Safe Mode loads Windows 95 with the minimum complement of device drivers (i.e., mouse, keyboard, and VGA display). When you start in Safe Mode, the Registry, the CONFIG.SYS file, and the AUTOEXEC.BAT file do not load. No network support is available.

You can start in Safe Mode by pressing the F5 key while the "Starting Windows 95" message displays.

SAFE MODE WITH NETWORK SUPPORT

Safe Mode with Network Support loads Windows 95 with the minimum complement of device drivers (i.e., mouse, keyboard, and VGA display). When you start in Safe Mode with Network Support, network device drivers and the Registry load, but not the CONFIG.SYS, or AUTOEXEC.BAT files.

You can start in Safe Mode with Network Support by pressing the F6 key while the "Starting Windows 95" message displays.

STEP-BY-STEP CONFIRMATION

Step-by-Step Confirmation enables you to select whether or not to process each startup file (i.e., the AUTOEXEC.BAT file).

COMMAND PROMPT ONLY

Command Prompt Only loads the operating system components of Windows 95. All startup files are processed, including the Registry and the CONFIG.SYS and AUTOEXEC.BAT files. The system then displays a command prompt rather than loading WIN.COM and starting Windows 95.

SAFE MODE COMMAND PROMPT ONLY

Safe Mode Command Prompt Only loads Windows 95 with the minimum complement of device drivers (i.e., mouse, keyboard, and VGA display). When you start in Safe Mode Command Prompt Only, the Registry and the CONFIG.SYS and AUTOEXEC.BAT files do not load. No network support is available. The system displays a command prompt rather than loading WIN.COM and starting Windows 95.

You can start in Safe Mode Command Prompt Only by pressing Shift + F5 while the "Starting Windows 95" message displays.

PREVIOUS VERSION OF MS-DOS

Previous Version of MS-DOS loads the version of the operating system previously installed on the computer. This option is only available when the computer is configured for dual booting (i.e., both Windows 3.1x and Windows 95 are installed, and the line "Multiboot=1" is present in the MSDOS.SYS file). Dual-boot configurations require MS-DOS 5.0 and later.

You can start in Previous Version of MS-DOS by pressing the F4 key while the "Starting Windows 95" message display.

EMF Spooling in Windows 95 General Information

When spooling to a PCL printer, Windows 95 creates an Enhanced Metafile Format (EMF) file, which is a device-independent rendering of a print job. EMF spooling enables Windows 95 to create device-dependent rendering in the background. Windows 95 does not support EMF spooling when printing to a PostScript printer.

When EMF spooling is enabled, an application passes the print job to the Graphical Device Interface (GDI). The GDI queries the targeted printer driver to determine if the EMF format is supported. When EMF is supported by the printer, the GDI renders the EMF file to the Windows-95\Spool directory. After the GDI spools the EMF file to disk, it returns control of the application to you. The Print Processor and the printer driver then render the EMF file into a device-dependent print file. This EMF or raw data file is sent to the router, which forwards the file to the appropriate service provider (e.g., local printer, network printer) through the 32-bit protect-mode VxD, VCOMM.

When Print Directly to the Printer is selected in the Spool Settings dialog box, EMF spooling is disabled and GDI does not create an EMF file.

To disable EMF Spooling:

1. Choose Start > Settings > Printers.
2. Right-click the desired printer, then choose Properties.
3. In the Properties dialog box, select the Detail, then click Spool Settings.
4. In the Spool Settings dialog box, select RAW from the Spool data format pop-up menu.
5. Click OK, then close the Properties dialog box.

Determining Win32s Component Version

To determine the version number of the installed Win32s component:

Locate the version number listed under the [Win32s] section in the WIN32S.INI file:

1. Open the WIN32S.INI file, located in the WINDOWS\-SYSTEM directory, in a text editor (e.g., Windows Write, Notepad).
2. Locate the version line under the [Win32s] section. For example:

```
[Win32s]
Version=1.30.167.0
```

OR: Determine the version by the WIN32S16.DLL file's date. The Win32s 1.30.167.0 (i.e., Win32s 1.3a) or later WIN32S16.DLL file has a date of 10/19/95 or later.

SW: Windows 3.1 VM Swap File General Information

When you run Windows 3.1 in 386 Enhanced mode, Windows uses free hard disk space as virtual memory (VM). Windows calls this cache of hard disk a "VM swapfile."

The swapfile can be configured as temporary or permanent. You can modify or remove either of these types of swapfiles at any time. To determine or modify the type of swapfile on your computer:

1. Open the Control Panel in the Main group of Program Manager.
2. Double-click on 386 Enhanced.
3. Click Virtual Memory to see the type and size of your swapfile.

4. Use the Change button to modify it if necessary.

Temporary swapfiles are created when Windows launches, and then deleted when Windows closes. The name of this temporary swap file is "Win386.swp." Although temporary swap files are usually deleted when you exit Windows, a temporary swap file might be left on your hard disk if your computer stops running unexpectedly. You can safely delete the Win386.swp file if Windows is not running (i.e., in DOS).

Permanent swapfiles are created the first time Windows starts, and are not deleted when Windows closes. A permanent swap file consists of two files: Spart.par and 386-spart.par. The Spart.par file is a read-only file in your Windows directory; the 386spart.par file is a hidden file in the root directory of the drive displayed under Current Settings in the Virtual Memory dialog box. Do not delete, move, or rename these files.

Since Windows accesses the swapfile frequently, it can become damaged. A damaged VM swapfile causes generic Windows errors (i.e., General Protection Faults) when you perform functions requiring large amounts of memory (e.g., when you run several applications concurrently, use a large or complex application).

To repair or recreate a damaged swapfile:

1. Open the Control Panel in the Main group of Program Manager.
2. Double-click on 386 Enhanced.
3. Click Virtual Memory, then click Change.
4. Set the Type option to None.
5. Click OK, then click OK again to restart Windows.

After removing the swapfile, try to recreate the errors that were occurring. If the errors do not reoccur, recreate the swapfile.

To recreate the swapfile:

1. Open the Control Panel in the Main group of Program Manager.
2. Double-click on 386 Enhanced.
3. Click Virtual Memory, then click Change.
4. Set the Type option to Permanent or Temporary.
5. Click OK, then click OK again to restart Windows.

NOTE: Do not set the swapfile to a compressed or stacked hard disk. If you're using the Doublespace feature of DOS 6.x, you may already have "virtual" drives.

Installing Manufacturer and Model Specific Video Drivers in Windows 95 General Information

When Windows 95 detects new hardware, it may load generic video drivers for cards that use a standard chip-set (e.g., MGA, Cirrus Logic, Tseng, S3) even when manufacturer and model-specific drivers are available on the Windows 95 CD-ROM. When Windows 95 uses generic drivers for video cards, the operating environment can become unstable and cause errors.

Installing or reinstalling Windows 95-compatible drivers that specify the manufacturer and model of your video card ensures the most stable environment for all programs.

To install a Windows 95-compatible video driver that specifies the manufacturer and model of your video card:

1. Choose Start > Settings > Control Panels.
2. Double-click the Display Control Panel.
3. Select the Settings tab.
4. Click Change Display Type.
5. Click Change in the Adapter Type section.
6. Install a driver that specifies the manufacturer and model of your video card:

   If you have a driver from your video card manufacturer, click the Have Disk button.

   OR: If you do not have a driver from your video card manufacturer, select a video driver provided on the Windows 95 CD-ROM by selecting the Show All Devices option. Scroll through the list of Manufacturers and Models and select your specific video card manufacturer and model. Click OK. Windows will prompt you to insert the Windows 95 CD-ROM.

   OR: If the manufacturer or model of your video card is not listed in Manufacturers and Models, contact your video card manufacturer for a Windows 95-compatible driver.
7. Restart the computer.

Clipboard or Spooler Error Message Troubleshooting Guide

ISSUE

When you perform an action that requires an application to save a temporary file (e.g., printing using Print Manager, opening a template, copying to the clipboard, using the Build Booklet Addition), the application returns an error indicating that the action could not be completed.

SYMPTOMS

PageMaker errors include:

"Internal error: Cannot copy to clipboard."

"Cannot create internal clipboard."

"Waiting for spooler to empty its print buffer."

SOLUTION

Determine on which volume (e.g., internal hard disk) the application is saving the temporary file, then ensure there is sufficient space on that volume for the temporary file. For instructions, see Additional Information.

ADDITIONAL INFORMATION

Windows operations can require as much as 10 MB of available space. When there is insufficient disk space for the temporary file, redirect the temporary file to a disk with sufficient space.

To determine where PageMaker is saving temporary files:

1. Double-click on the Aldus Setup icon in the Aldus group. When the Open dialog box displays with the message "Setup requires a .CTL file to install options..." click Cancel. The Aldus Setup Main Window appears.

2. Choose Diagnostic > Display Current Environment to display a list of DOS environment labels in the Aldus Setup Log window.
3. In the Aldus Setup Log dialog box, the line "TEMP=" is the path to the directory where the temporary files are being stored. For example, "TEMP=C:\WINDOWS-\TEMP" indicates the temporary file is being stored in Windows\Temp subdirectory. When there is no "TEMP-=" line, the temporary files are written into the Windows directory (Windows 3.1 or later) or the root directory (Windows 3.0 or earlier).

To determine how much free disk space is available:

1. Double-click on the Aldus Setup icon in the Aldus group. When the Open dialog box displays with the message "Setup requires a .CTL file to install options..." click Cancel." The Aldus Setup Main Window appears.
2. Choose Diagnostics > Display Hard Disk Info to list the total disk space and free disk space on each hard disk partition. For example:

Disk	*Total disk space*	*Free disk space*
`C:(FIXED)`	`220000 Kilobytes`	`890 Kilobytes [0%]`
`D:(FIXED)`	`100000 Kilobytes`	`45000 Kilobytes [45%]`

In this example, the C hard disk is full as 0% of its available disk space free, while the D disk has 45% of its disk space free.

To increase the amount of free disk on a volume, do one or more of the following:

A. Delete existing temporary files and lost allocation units:
   1. Exit Windows.
   2. At the DOS prompt, change to the temporary directory by typing:
      `CD xx`
      where "xx" is the path to the temporary directory:
   3. At the temporary directory, delete existing temporary files by typing:
      `del *.tmp`
   4. Type "CD\" to return to the root directory.
   5. Type "chkdsk/f" at the DOS prompt to check how much free disk space is available, where the line begins "Bytes available on disk." When the message "xxx lost allocation units found in xxx chains. Convert lost chains to files?" appears, type "Y."
      NOTE: Typing "Y" for yes creates *.Chk files in the root directory that you can open in a text editor and save them if necessary. Delete the *.Chk files that you don't need. Typing "N" for no deletes all lost allocation units, which may yield unexpected results (e.g., unable to start Windows).

B. Delete unneeded items from the volume by redirecting temporary files:
   1. Change to a new disk by typing that drive's indicator followed by a colon (e.g., D:) at the DOS prompt, then press Enter. You can type "CD\" to change to the root directory of the disk, if necessary.
   2. Type "MD TEMP" at the DOS prompt, then press Enter to create a Temp directory in the root directory of the disk.
      NOTE: When the Temp directory already exists, DOS returns the message "Directory Already Exists."
   3. Change to the C drive by typing "C:" at the DOS prompt and then pressing Enter.
   4. Make a backup copy of the Autoexec.bat file by typing the following at the DOS prompt:
      `COPY AUTOEXEC.BAT AUTOEXEC.OLD`
   5. Start Windows.
   6. In Windows Program Manager, choose File > Run. In the Run dialog box, type "sysedit" for the command line, then click OK. The System Configuration Editor window opens, containing four system files and listing the Autoexec.bat file first.
   7. In the Autoexec.bat file, locate the "TEMP=" line, select all text on that line except for "TEMP=" and then type "D:\Temp" as the new pathname.
   8. Save the Autoexec.bat file and then exit the System Configuration Editor.
   9. Exit Windows and then restart the computer.

Contents of the Windows 95 Msdos.sys File General Information

Msdos.sys is a file used by the operating system to locate Windows 95 files (e.g., the Windows Registry) and to tailor the Windows 95 startup process. The file contains two sections, a [Paths] section, and an [Options] section, each with entries that the operating system reads during the startup process. The Windows 95 setup program saves this file into the root level of the computer's boot drive, and assigns it hidden and read-only file attributes.

The Msdos.sys file also contains other information (e.g., the text "The following lines are required for compatibility with other programs" followed by a series of "X"s).

If the Msdos.sys file is not present in the root level of the computer's boot drive, Windows 95 will not start.

(PATHS) SECTION

`HostWinBootDrv=`

The HostWinBootDrv= entry sets the location of the root level of the startup drive. The default value for this entry is "c."

`WinBootDir=`

The WinBootDir= entry sets the location of the Windows 95 operating system startup files. You select this value (e.g., c:\win95) during the Windows 95 installation process.

`WinDir=`

The WinDir= entry sets the location of the Windows 95 directory. You select this value (e.g., c:\win95) during the Windows 95 installation process.

(OPTIONS) SECTION

`BootDelay=`

The BootDelay= entry sets the amount of time in seconds that the "Starting Windows" message displays during the startup process. The default value for this entry is "2."

`BootFailSafe=`

The BootFailSafe= entry determines whether or not Windows 95 starts in Safe Mode. The default value, "0," enables Windows 95 to start normally, and a value of "1" starts Windows 95 in Safe Mode.

`BootGUI=`

The BootGUI= entry determines whether or not the Windows 95 Graphic User Interface (GUI) loads at startup. A value of "0" displays a command prompt after startup, and the default value, "1," loads the Windows 95 GUI.

`BootKeys=`

The BootKeys= entry determines whether or not you can use function keys to choose startup options (i.e., F4, F5, F6, F8). The default value, "1," enables the use of function keys at startup, and a value of "0" disables the use of function keys at startup.

`BootMenu=`

The BootMenu= entry determines whether or not the startup menu will display when starting Windows 95. The default value, "0," keeps the startup menu from displaying automatically at startup, and a value of "1," displays the startup menu automatically.

`BootMenuDefault=`

The BootMenuDefault= entry sets the default option displayed in the startup menu. This option defaults to "4" if Windows 95 failed to start at last startup.

`BootMenuDelay=`

The BootMenuDelay= entry represents the amount of time in seconds that the startup menu displays before automatically starting Windows 95. If the number of seconds elapses without intervention, Windows 95 starts using the BootMenuDefault= setting.

`BootMulti=`

The BootMulti= entry determines whether or not your computer can start using Windows 95 as well as the previous operating system. The default value, "0," prevents the system from starting in anything other than Windows 95, and a value of "1" enables the system to start in either Windows 95 or the previous operating system.

`BootWarn=`

The BootWarn= entry determines whether or not the Safe Mode warning message displays when you start Windows 95 in Safe Mode. The default value, "1," enables the warning message, and a value of "0" disables the warning message.

`BootWin=`

The BootWin= entry determines which operating system loads by default in a multi-boot configuration. The default value, "1," enables Windows 95 to load as the default operating system. A value of "0" disables Windows 95 from loading as the default operating system.

`DoubleBuffer=`

The DoubleBuffer= entry determines whether or not the operating system enables double-buffering support. The default value, "0," disables double-buffering support. A value of "1" enables double-buffering for double-buffering-dependent SCSI devices, and a value of "2" enables double-buffering support for all devices.

`DBLSpace=`

A value of "1" for the DBLSpace= entry forces the operating system to load the dblspace.bin file, which enables DoubleSpace hard disk compression. A value of "0" for this entry prevents the dblspace.bin file from loading.

`DRVSpace=`

A value of "1" for the DRVSpace= entry forces the operating system to load the drvspace.bin file, which enables DoubleSpace hard disk compression. A value of "0" for this entry prevents the drvspace.bin file from loading.

`LoadTop=`

A value of "1" for the LoadTop= entry forces the operating system to load the command.com and drvspace.bin (or dblspace.bin) at the top of the first 640K memory segment. A value of "0" for this entry prevents the command.com and drvspace.bin (or dblspace.bin) from loading at the top of the first 640K memory segment.

`Logo=`

The Logo= entry determines whether or not the Windows 95 logo appears at startup. The default value, "1," enables the logo to display at startup, and a value of "0" prevents the logo from displaying.

`Network=`

The Network= entry determines whether or not "Safe Mode with Network Support" appears as a startup menu option. The default value "0," indicates no network was present when you installed Windows 95, and "Safe Mode with Network Support" does not appear as a startup menu option. A value of "1" indicates a network was present when you installed Windows 95, and "Safe Mode with Network Support" appears as a startup menu option.

Creating or Printing Text File That Contains Directory's Contents

To create a text file containing the contents of a directory:

1. Type the following command at the DOS prompt:
   `dir > pathname\filename`
   for example, typing the command "dir *.ini > c:\timbuk2\dir.txt" creates a text file named "Dir.txt" containing a listing of the .INI files in the Timbuk2 directory.
2. To view the file, open the Dir.txt file in a text editor (e.g., Notepad, Write, Microsoft Word).

To print a text file containing the contents of a directory directly to the printer:

In DOS, navigate to the directory and type the command below, then press the Enter key:

`Dir > lptl`

where "lpt1" is the printer port (e.g., lpt2, com1, com2) to which the file is being sent.

Mac OS

GENERAL INFORMATION

System Error Type 11 on Macintosh or Power Macintosh

ISSUE
Random (i.e., intermittent) system error "Type 11" appears on a Macintosh or Power Macintosh computer.

SOLUTIONS
For Power Macintosh computers, ensure the cache card is not the cause by removing the cache card.
OR: Do one or more of the following:

A. Continue troubleshooting the Type 11 system error, ruling out software causes first (e.g., extension conflicts, Memory control panel settings), then hardware causes (e.g., SCSI conflicts, memory (RAM) modules, monitor connection, video card, NuBus cards, cache card, third-party RAM, cache RAM, Cache SIMM).
   NOTE: When troubleshooting other hardware conflicts, contact an Apple reseller or the hardware manufacturer for assistance. Starting the Power Macintosh without the video card in the Processor Direct Slot (PDS) can damage the computer. Contact Apple User Assistance or an authorized Apple reseller for hardware support.
B. Update the SCSI drivers:
   1. Restart the computer from the "Disk Tools" disk (included with the System 7 installation disk set) or the "System Tools" disk (included with System 6.0.x installation disk set).
   2. Launch the HDSC Setup application by double-clicking on its icon.
   3. Click the "Drive" button until the SCSI drive (hard disk) is selected.
      NOTE: The message "Drive selection failed. Unable to locate a suitable drive connected to the SCSI port." is returned when the hard disk is formatted with a non-Apple utility (e.g., Norton Utilities, MacTools, Symantec Tools for Macintosh, StorWare). Click "Continue" in the message dialog box to quit HDSC Setup and use the SCSI drive updating utility included with the formatting utility.
   4. Click the "Update" button to install updated SCSI drivers to each SCSI disk (e.g., hard disk, cartridge, optical).
   5. Choose "Quit" from the File menu.
C. Use Disk First Aid to check the hard disk's directory tree:
   1. Restart the computer from the "Disk Tools" disk (included with the System 7 installation disk set) or the "System Tools" disk (included with System 6.0.x installation disk set).
   2. Launch the Disk First Aid application by double-clicking on its icon.
   3. Select or open the hard drive to be verified.
   4. Click "Verify" to check the disk or "Repair" to check and repair the disk. When "Verify" is clicked, Disk First Aid checks the disk. If any problems are encountered, Disk First Aid asks if you wish to repair it. Always repair the disk when prompted.
   5. Choose "Quit" from the File menu.

ADDITIONAL INFORMATION
The Type 11 system error is a miscellaneous hardware exception error that generally indicates a hardware conflict, but system software and extension conflicts can be the cause. Ruling out software conflicts before troubleshooting hardware conflicts is recommended by Apple User Assistance.

Cache cards installed in some Power Macintosh computers may cause a Type 11 system error, but Apple User Assistance has not found a direct cause. Cache cards "cache" or store the most recently executed System commands and actions for easy retrieval by the System, resulting in faster performance.

According to the Apple Tech Info Library record entitled Power Macintosh: Meaning of Error Type 11 (2/95), "more Type 11 errors may occur on a Power Macintosh computer because of problems with the software based 68K emulator. The emulator allows the RISC processor to run older Macintosh software. If the emulator gets corrupted while loading into in RAM, then some of the failures caused by this are reported as Type 11 or Hardware Exception errors. The emulator can get corrupted by incompatible software or faulty hardware."

Troubleshooting System Errors on the Macintosh

Bombs and crashes are going to happen on the Macintosh. No software is error-free—neither the system software itself, nor your favorite application, utility, or font. While hardware problems can cause system errors, with the Macintosh they're the exception rather than the rule. The most likely cause of a system error is damaged or incompatible software.

Solving the problems that plague your computer doesn't require a degree in computer science. All you really need is time and patience. First make sure the symptoms of your problem are really indicative of a system error. Then eliminate the most common causes. If the error persists, continue the process of elimination, first by ruling out damaged or conflicting extensions, then damaged application software, and finally damaged system software.

A QUICK OVERVIEW OF YOUR MACINTOSH SOFTWARE
You should be familiar with the three basic types of software that run on your Macintosh. The first is system software (e.g., System 7.5). System software is the most important software on your Macintosh—it's what makes your Macintosh a Macintosh. Your CPU, disk drive, monitor, and the software you install all depend on the system software to perform their basic functions.

The second type of software is application software. You spend most of your day laying out pages, word-processing, illustrating, or number crunching in applications like Adobe PageMaker, Microsoft Word, Adobe Illustrator, and Microsoft Excel.

And finally there are extensions. The term "extensions," introduced with System 7, describes file that extend or enhance your system software. Extensions include control panel documents (e.g., Adobe Type Manager) and system extension documents that start, or initialize, when you startup your Macintosh (e.g., Adobe Type Reunion).

DEFINING THE PROBLEM

The system software, application software, and extensions running on your Macintosh must all get along with each other at any given time. When they don't, your Macintosh lets you know by returning a system error.

You can recognize a system error by:

- The error message or error code number it displays.

  System errors fall into two categories: bombs and alerts. System bombs are the most serious. These include a bomb icon in their dialog box and signal a low-level, or basic operating routine, problem. The message (e.g., "Sorry, a system error occurred," "Application 'unknown' has unexpectedly quit.") and identifying error code number (e.g., "Type 1," "-36") in system bomb dialog boxes vary depending on the system error that occurred and the version of your system software. System alerts, which include the exclamation point in a triangle icon, can be equally disabling, but they are not as serious: your system just wants to make you aware of something. The content of the alert message generally points you to the source of the problem. Typical problems range from a full disk to an AppleTalk error.
- The symptom of your problem.

  If your Macintosh freezes or displays an incomplete or flickering dialog box, or if your system is endlessly processing, chances are a system error occurred. Your Macintosh is unable to properly display a system error dialog box when the cause of the system error prevents it from doing so.

When a system error occurs, write down the exact message or symptom and note the circumstances of the error. When does the error occur? Only in this file or in others, too? If the error occurs only in one file, then the file is most likely causing the problem. Does it occur only in this application or others? If the error occurs in more than one application, including the desktop (i.e., the Finder application), you can bet it's a system error, and not an application error. If system errors occur randomly, this is also important. But you will want to verify that they do occur randomly, so taking good notes is especially helpful.

CHECK THESE COMMON CAUSES FIRST

If you've determined that the problem you're experiencing is indeed a system error, begin troubleshooting the cause of your system error by checking your setup against these common causes.

What's New?

Determine if anything new has been added to your Macintosh prior to the system error. For example, if you've added a new control panel document to your system, move it out of the System Folder, then restart your Macintosh. Repeat the actions that triggered the system error. If everything works, you've found the cause of the error.

What's Changed?

Perhaps during spring cleaning you accidentally moved or deleted an important file or two. Is everything where it belongs?

Are There Any Duplicate Files?

Duplicate files, programs, and application resources are easily created when you update software or install a new system. The updated application may not be able to use the older version's file of the same name. Did you follow the installation instructions for the software update? If not, the system, your application, or an extension may be reading the wrong file by mistake.

Is Your Older Application Compatible With Your Newer System Software?

New variables enter the picture when a new version of system software or new hardware is introduced. System 7 and Power Macintosh models introduce many new features. You can bet the extensions your system software installs are compatible with these new features, but is everything else? Older applications or extensions may not be.

How's Your Memory?

Low memory errors, or system errors caused by insufficient memory, can be harder to resolve than other kinds of errors because they seem more random. They can be caused by a variety of things—too many windows open at the same time, extensions and fonts taking up memory your system or applications need for other tasks, or damaged software.

If your application doesn't have enough memory, increasing the amount of memory allocated to your application should solve the problem. How much memory you allocate depends on the amount of memory you have available and the number of other applications you want to open at the same time. Start by increasing memory allocation by 50 percent or so and see what happens.

To change an application's allocated memory:

1. Quit the application.
2. Select the application's icon in the Finder. Make sure you don't select an alias of the application or the folder containing the application.
3. Choose File > Get Info.
4. In the application's Get Info dialog box, enter a higher value in the Preferred Size (System 7.1 and later) or the Current Size (System 7.0.x) text box.

RULE OUT DAMAGED OR CONFLICTING EXTENSIONS

When you install Macintosh system software, you also install the extensions included with it (e.g., General, Keyboards, Monitors, Mouse, Sound). The installer puts control panel documents in the Control Panels folder in the System Folder, and system extension documents in the Extensions folder in the System Folder. You can also customize your Macintosh with extensions created by other companies (e.g., Adobe Type Manager, Now Utilities). If these added extensions conflict with other software or with each other, or if they're damaged, system errors are likely to occur. You can rule out the greatest number of variables—and the most likely cause of a system error—by isolating added or nonessential extensions first.

To determine if a damaged or conflicting extension is causing your system error, first disable all your added or nonessential extensions, then try to recreate the error. If the system error doesn't reoccur, you can isolate which extensions are the cause and resolve the conflict. If the problem persists, then you know these extensions are not the cause of your system error, and you have two variables left to tackle: the active application and the system software itself. Keep your added extensions out of the picture (turned off) until you find the cause of your system error so they don't interfere when you reinstall your application or system software.

Disabling Added Extensions

You can disable extensions several different ways in System 7: you can restart the Macintosh while holding down the Shift key, use the Extensions Manager control panel included with System 7.5 and later, or manually remove extensions from the System Folder. The method you choose to disable added or suspect extensions will depend on your troubleshooting needs. For example, when troubleshooting a system error that occurs only in a single application, you'll need to disable all added extensions except those required by the application (e.g., QuickTime).

To quickly determine if a damaged or conflicting extension is the cause of your problem, disable added or nonessential extensions by restarting with the Shift key held down or by using an extensions manager. Disabling extensions by restarting with the Shift key held down or by using an extensions manager may not disable all added or nonessential extensions, so if your problem reoccurs after using either method, you can make sure extensions are not the cause of your problem by manually disabling them before troubleshooting other causes.

To disable extensions by holding the Shift key while restarting:
Hold down the Shift key and choose Special > Restart. Keep the Shift key held down until the system displays the message "Welcome to Macintosh. Extensions off." Non-Apple keyboards may not support disabling extensions by restarting with the Shift key held down. Extensions may not be disabled if an extension conflict is preventing the system from disabling extensions.

To use the Extensions Manager control panel:

1. Open the Extensions Manager control panel.
2. Either individually select the extensions you want to disable, or select the System 7.5 Only or System 7.5.3 option from the Sets pop-up menu.
3. Restart your Macintosh.

To manually disable extensions and force the system to create a new Control Panels and Extensions folder:
When manually disabling your added or nonessential extensions, you can remove the Extensions and Control Panels folders, including the extension files they contain, from the System Folder to make sure these folders are not damaged and are not the cause of your problem.

To manually disable extensions:

1. Move the Control Panels and Extensions folders, and, if desired, the Fonts and Preferences folders, from the System Folder to a new location (e.g., desktop).
2. Restart your Macintosh. The system searches for system preferences files and the Control Panels, Extensions, Fonts, and Preferences folders in the System Folder. When your system cannot find the folders or system preferences files it needs in the System Folder, it creates new ones.
3. When your problem occurs when working in a single application, enable only those extensions that application requires to launch or run (e.g., QuickTime) by moving them from your previous Control Panels or Extensions folders into your new, empty Control Panels or Extensions folders in the System Folder.
4. Restart your Macintosh.

Isolating Conflicting Extensions

After disabling your added extensions, try to recreate the system error. If it doesn't reoccur, it's time to isolate which extensions are causing the problem. If the error does reoccur, you can move on to testing your application and system software.

To isolate which extensions are damaged or conflicting, re-enable one or several at a time, starting with your favorites. You can re-enable them using Extension Manager or by manually moving them back into your System Folder. If you disabled your extensions by restarting with the Shift key held down, you'll need to disable your extensions either manually or by using the Extensions Manager control panel to isolate the offending extension. When moving files back into the System Folder, you can drag their icon onto the System Folder icon in the Finder to let System 7 automatically return them to their proper location in the System Folder.

After each move, restart the Macintosh and try to recreate the system error. If your system error doesn't reoccur, add another extension. Once the error occurs after adding an extension, leave it in the System Folder then remove all other added extensions so that your system and application are running with only that extension installed. If, after you restart, the system error reoccurs, you've found the culprit. If the error does not reoccur, you'll know your system error is caused by a combination of extensions, and not that single extension.

Resolving Extension Conflicts

You have several choices to resolve problems caused by a damaged or conflicting extension, or combination of extensions. Which solution you choose depends on your needs and which extension is causing the problem.

To resolve extension conflicts, do one or more of the following:

A. Modify the extension.

A setting in a control panel may be causing a conflict. Try changing current settings to see if they're the cause of your problem.

B. Replace the extension.

Rule out a damaged extension by deleting the extension, then reinstalling a new copy from the original installation disks. When deleting the extension, make sure you also delete its support files (e.g., preferences file).

C. Reinstall files used by the extension.

The conflict may not be caused by the extension, but by a damaged file it uses. For example, font management extensions (e.g., Suitcase, MasterJuggler) read font suitcases. The cause of your problem may be a damaged font suitcase, or a font file contained in the suitcase. In this example, you can prevent the font management extension from reading all font suitcases to determine if this prevents your problem from reoccurring. If it does, you'll need to isolate which font suitcase, or font file in a suitcase, is the cause, then reinstall that file.

D. Change the loading order of your extensions.

The order in which your extensions load may be the cause of your conflict. When you start up your Mac, the system loads, in alphabetical order, first your system extension files located in the Extensions folder, then control panel files located in the Control panel folder, and finally both system extension and control panel files located in the System Folder. To change the order in which your system loads an extension, change its name (e.g., add a character at the beginning of an extension's filename). Extensions files whose names begin with a non-Roman character (e.g., dash, tilde, pound sign) load either first or last, depending on the character.

E. Update the conflicting extension.

Check with the extension's developer to see if there is an updated version available, or if they have other information that may help you resolve your problem.

F. Run without the conflicting extension.

Until an update is available, you may have to run without an extension when it doesn't support, or conflicts with, newer software you're running.

RULE OUT DAMAGED APPLICATION SOFTWARE

If your system error occurs in a single application, the next step is to make sure the application itself is not damaged by reinstalling it. To guarantee a successful installation and brand new application software, remove your application and its support files, then reinstall it while keeping your added extensions disabled.

First check inside the application's folder and move personal documents you want to save to another location. Next, throw away the application's folder and its contents, which should include only the application and its support files. Also throw away any of its support files located in the System Folder. Then, with all your added extensions disabled, reinstall your application. Use your application's original installation disks to reinstall, when possible, to ensure backup disks aren't the problem.

After you reinstall your application, you can assume your application is not damaged and is now above suspicion. So if, after you launch the reinstalled application, you can still recreate the system error, move on to the last software variable, the system software itself.

REINSTALL SYSTEM SOFTWARE

Reinstalling system software is the only surefire way to know if damaged system software is causing your system error. If your system error does not reoccur after you reinstall the system software, you know damaged system software was the culprit.

As when reinstalling an application, you want to ensure you do a clean install or install 100% new system software. System 7.5.x's installer includes the Clean Install option, which makes installing new system software easy. When you reinstall System 7.1.x and 7.0.x you'll need to do a clean install manually.

After reinstalling your new system software, but before moving back customizing files (e.g., application support files, added extensions) into the System Folder, try to recreate your system error. When your system error occurs in a single application, you'll need to move the files that application needs in the System Folder back into the System Folder before trying to recreate the system error. If the system error does not reoccur at this point, you know your newly-installed system software, and any application support files you moved back into the System Folder to test for the error, are not the cause. Continue troubleshooting by moving the rest of you customizing files back into your System Folder, then trying to recreate the error. If your system reoccurs at this point, you'll need to isolate which of these files is damaged or incompatible and causing your system error.

Reinstalling System 7

You'll need your Macintosh system CD-ROM or installation disks to reinstall your system software. While the process of reinstalling your system software consists of simple steps, pay attention when moving your files around, both before and after you reinstall your system software.

To reinstall System 7.5.x:

1. Disable your current system by moving the Finder file from your System Folder to another location (e.g., desktop), then restart your Macintosh. A disk icon with a blinking question mark should appear in the middle of your screen, indicating your Macintosh cannot find system software (an active system), which is expected.
   NOTE: If your Macintosh starts up as normally after you've disabled your system, you may have another system installed. Search for and remove any duplicate System or Finder files, then move the remaining System or Finder file to the desktop and restart again.
2. Insert your system CD-ROM or installation disk containing the system's Installer.
3. Open the Installer by double-clicking it.

4. In the Installer's welcome screen, click Continue.
5. In the System 7.5 Installer window, select the Easy installation option, or select the Custom installation option and the items you want to install, then press Command + Shift + K.
6. In the Select Type of Installation dialog box, select Install New System Folder, then click OK.
7. In the System 7.5 Installer window, the Install button is now the Clean Install button. Click Clean Install, then continue with the installation by following the on-screen instructions.
8. When you're done installing new system software, you'll find the contents of your original System Folder in the new folder named Previous System Folder.

To reinstall System 7.1.x or 7.0.x:

1. Disable your current system by moving the Finder file from your System Folder to another location (e.g., desktop).
2. Rename your System Folder (e.g., "Old Folder") to keep the installer from finding it.
3. Restart your Macintosh by choosing Special > Restart. While restarting, your Macintosh ejects the startup disk then displays a disk icon with a blinking question in the middle of your screen, indicating it cannot find system software (an active system), which is expected.
   NOTE: If your Macintosh starts up normally after you've disabled your system, you may have another system installed. Search for and remove any duplicate System or Finder files, then move the remaining System or Finder file to the desktop and restart again.
4. Insert your system CD-ROM or installation disk containing the system's Installer.
5. Follow the on-screen instructions to reinstall your system software.
6. When reinstallation is complete, restart your Macintosh. Your Macintosh ejects the system installation disk while restarting. After restarting, a new System Folder containing new system files, and your renamed System Folder with its contents intact, are installed on your Macintosh.

Moving Application Files to Your New System Folder

After reinstalling your system software, test whether reinstalling the system software solved your problem. When your system error only occurs when you run a single application, move only that application's support files from your original System Folder (e.g., Previous System Folder) to your new System Folder before you try recreating your system error.

If your system error does not reoccur at this point, your newly-installed system software, and perhaps an application's support files, is above suspicion. Continue troubleshooting by moving your remaining customizing files (e.g., fonts, control panels, system extensions, application support files) from your original System Folder (e.g., Previous System Folder, Old Folder) to your new System Folder, trying to recreate your system error after you move each set of files. If your system error reoccurs at this point, you'll need to isolate the damaged or incompatible file causing the problem.

When moving your customizing files from your original System Folder to your new System Folder, open and compare the files, and the contents of folders in your old and new System Folders. Move only those items that were not installed by the system software, and for which there is no duplicate in the new System Folder. This ensures you don't replace your newly installed system files with your old system files, which may be damaged. If you're using System 7.1 or later, copy into the new System suitcase file only those sounds that aren't already there. If you're using System 7.0.x, copy only those bitmap (screen) fonts and sounds that aren't already there.

If, when you move items into your new System Folder, you get a message telling you an item with that name already exists and asking whether you want to replace it with the item you're moving, click Cancel. Then go back and review the names of the files or contents of the folder you are moving to see if they duplicate items already in your new System Folder.

After moving the files you need into your new System Folder, delete your original System Folder containing duplicate or unwanted items by dragging it to the Trash, then emptying the Trash.

HARDWARE, THE LAST RESORT

If you've made it this far, you've got a healthy system on your Macintosh, and neither your application nor your extensions are conflicting with each other or with the system, so there's not much software troubleshooting left that you can do on your own. To leave no stone unturned before calling Technical Support for your hardware or software problem, try these last tests.

You can check your hard disk's formatting, defragment and optimize the files on your hard disk, and check for damaged sectors on your hard disk using a Macintosh disk utility. To check your startup volume (i.e., the hard disk containing your system software), restart your Macintosh from a disk containing system software, then open the Macintosh disk utility.

Run Disk First Aid, a disk checking utility provided by Apple on the system CD-ROM or Disk Tools disk, which can tell you if it encounters any minor formatting problems on your disk. To run Disk First Aid, open the utility and click Verify. When using a hard disk manufactured by a company other than Apple, you may need to use a utility supplied by your disk manufacturer to check formatting problems. You can test your disk for damage and update your driver using Drive Setup or HD SCSI Setup, which are also included with your system software.

You can use other Macintosh disk utilities, such as MacTools or Norton Utilities for the Macintosh, to defragment and optimize your hard disk, check for damaged sectors, and check for other formatting problems that the Macintosh disk utilities included with your system software don't check for. Other Macintosh disk utilities can find damaged sectors on your disk, and prevent other files from being written to the damaged sectors they find.

If you suspect you have a SCSI device connection problem, turn off your Macintosh and all connected SCSI devices, disconnect all your SCSI devices, then restart your Macintosh and try to recreate your system error. If your system error doesn't reoccur, your connected SCSI devices are the cause. You can try connecting each device individually and reconnecting your SCSI chain by trying to recreate the error after you connect each new device, to isolate the problem. Remember to turn off both your Macintosh and SCSI devices before connecting or reconnecting them. For instructions on connecting SCSI devices to your Macintosh, see the User Guide included with your Macintosh and your SCSI device.

If your system error occurs after you've ruled out software causes and the hardware causes that you can, it's time to call for expert help. Tell the support technician about the systematic troubleshooting you've completed. The work you've done will enable them to concentrate on other ways to resolve your system errors.

MINIMIZING SYSTEM ERRORS

You can't prevent all system errors, but you can be ready for them. Here are some maintenance chores and emergency tools that can help you minimize system errors on your Macintosh.

- Always create backup copies of your system software, applications, extensions, and fonts, just as you do with your personal files.
- Always have a complete set of your system installation disks nearby, including a disk you can use as a startup disk (i.e., a disk containing system software).
- Defragment and optimize your hard disk using software designed for this, such as MacTools or Norton Utilities for the Macintosh.
- Rebuild your desktop file often.
- Run virus detection software regularly.
- Make sure you know what's installed on your computer and what's in your System Folder. Learn what each item is for—not all the new options and files of the system software are essential. A little more hard disk space may be handy, and your Macintosh will be faster.
- Read about how the Macintosh thinks and works. Read the user manuals included with your Macintosh and system software. There are also many good books available that explain the inside workings of the Macintosh. Manuals and books can help you understand why different kinds of errors occur. The wise Macintosh trouble-shooter takes advantage of all resources.

EMERGENCY TACTICS

The guidelines above are designed to help get to the cause of a system error. But the same logic can also help you to work around a system error until you have time to systematically troubleshoot it properly.

For example, if you desperately need to print your publication, but a system error prevents the print job whose deadline was two hours ago, try printing without extensions. If you can now print, print away—but first make sure your fonts are installed in the System Folder. You can go back later to find the extension or combination of extensions that are the culprit. Use these tactics to get past the message, but remember, you will eventually have to go back and find the cause.

Memory Requirements for OLE 2.0 on Macintosh and Power Macintosh General Information

Object Linking and Embedding (OLE) 2.0 is comprised of the Microsoft OLE Extension and other associated files. These files require different amounts of memory when installed on a Power Macintosh or 68000-series Macintosh, and load into memory at different times on the two systems.

OLE 2.0 MEMORY REQUIREMENTS ON A POWER MACINTOSH

OLE 2.0 requires a minimum of 1200K of RAM to run on the Power Macintosh. OLE loads into the system heap (i.e., system memory) during startup on the Power Macintosh, so the amount of memory used by the Power Macintosh System increases by 1200K when OLE 2.0 is installed.

OLE 2.0 MEMORY REQUIREMENTS ON A 68000-SERIES MACINTOSH

OLE 2.0 requires a minimum of 600K of RAM to run on a 68000-series Macintosh. OLE loads into the system heap only when needed (e.g., when a client application creates an embedded object) and unloads when finished. After OLE unloads, the amount of memory added to the system heap remains allocated to the system heap (i.e., the system heap is still 600K larger than it was before OLE loaded).

TRACKING MEMORY REQUIREMENTS AND ALLOCATIONS

To track memory usage, use the "About this Macintosh" command in the Apple menu at the Finder.

Unlike applications, whose memory allocations are defined in the application's "Get Info" dialog box, the System's memory allocation (i.e., system heap) is dynamic. The Macintosh operating system determines how much memory it will need during startup and adjusts usage within the heap as necessary.

Since OLE loads into the system heap on a Power Macintosh during startup, there is no need to calculate the amount of memory available for OLE. Conversely, OLE loads only when needed on a 68000-series Macintosh, so the largest unused block of memory (as noted in the "About this Macintosh" dialog box) must be at least 600K.

Preventing the largest unused block of memory never falls below 1000K ensures that the Macintosh doesn't run out of memory, thus preventing system errors. To increase the amount of memory available in your System heap, adjust application memory allocations, quit applications not currently in use, disable unneeded Extensions, install additional memory, or use virtual memory. Any of these options may impact performance of specific applications or the System in general.

USING OLE 2.0 WITH ADOBE PAGEMAKER 6.0

For best results when using Adobe PageMaker 6.0, follow the memory management suggestions on pages 13-14 of the Adobe PageMaker 6.0 Getting Started guide. These recommendations allow adequate memory to be available for OLE, the Macintosh operating system, PageMaker, and other applications.

Reinstalling System 7.x Software

Reinstalling system software is the only sure-fire way to know if a system error is caused by damaged system software. If your system error does not reoccur after you reinstall the system software, you know damaged system software was the cause. System 7.5.x's installer includes a Clean Install option, which makes installing 100% new system software easy. When you reinstall System 7.1.x and 7.0.x, you'll need to do a clean install manually.

You'll need your Macintosh system CD-ROM or installation disks to reinstall your system software. While the process of reinstalling your system software consists of simple steps, pay attention when moving your files around, both before and after you reinstall your system software.

To reinstall System 7.5.x:

1. Disable your current system by moving the Finder file from your System Folder to another location (e.g., desktop), then restart your Macintosh. A disk icon with a blinking question mark should appear in the middle of your screen, indicating your Macintosh cannot find system software (an active system), which is expected.
   NOTE: If your Macintosh starts up as normally after you've disabled your system, you may have another system installed. Search for and remove any duplicate System or Finder files, then move the remaining System or Finder file to the desktop and restart again.
2. Insert your system CD-ROM or installation disk containing the system's Installer.
3. Open the Installer by double-clicking it.
4. In the Installer's welcome screen, click Continue.
5. In the System 7.5 Installer window, select the Easy installation option, or select the Custom installation option and the items you want to install, then press Command + Shift + K.
6. In the Select Type of Installation dialog box, select Install New System Folder, then click OK.
7. In the System 7.5 Installer window, the Install button is now the Clean Install button. Click Clean Install, then continue with the installation by following the on-screen instructions.
8. When you're done installing new system software, you'll find the contents of your original System Folder in the new folder named Previous System Folder.

To reinstall System 7.1.x or 7.0.x:

1. Disable your current system by moving the Finder file from your System Folder to another location (e.g., desktop).
2. Rename your System Folder (e.g., "Old Folder") to keep the installer from finding it.
3. Restart your Macintosh by choosing Special > Restart. While restarting, your Macintosh ejects the startup disk and then displays a disk icon with a blinking question mark in the middle of your screen, indicating it cannot find system software (an active system), which is expected.
   NOTE: If your Macintosh starts up normally after you've disabled your system, you may have another system installed. Search for and remove any duplicate System or Finder files, then move the remaining System or Finder file to the desktop and restart again.
4. Insert your system CD-ROM or installation disk containing the system's Installer.
5. Follow the on-screen instructions to reinstall your system software.
6. When reinstallation is complete, restart your Macintosh. Your Macintosh ejects the system installation disk while restarting. After restarting, a new System Folder containing new system files, and your renamed System Folder with its contents intact, are installed on your Macintosh.

MOVING APPLICATION FILES TO YOUR NEW SYSTEM FOLDER

When moving your customizing files from your original System Folder to your new System Folder, open and compare the files, and the contents of folders in your old and new System Folders. Move only those items that were not installed by the system software, and for which there is no duplicate in the new System Folder. This ensures you don't replace your newly installed system files with your old system files, which may be damaged. If you're using System 7.1 or later, copy into the new System suitcase file only those sounds that aren't already there. If you're using System 7.0.x, copy only those bitmap (screen) fonts and sounds that aren't already there.

If, when you move items into your new System Folder, you get a message telling you an item with that name already exists and asking whether you want to replace it with the item you're moving, click Cancel. Then go back and review the names of the files or contents of the folder you are moving to see if they duplicate items already in your new System Folder.

After moving the files you need into your new System Folder, delete your original System Folder containing duplicate or unwanted items by dragging it to the Trash, then emptying the Trash.

After reinstalling your system software to solve a system error problem, you can test whether reinstalling the system software solved your problem. When your system error only occurs when you run a single application, move only that application's support files from your original System Folder (e.g., Previous System Folder) to your new System Folder before you try recreating your system error.

If your system error does not reoccur at this point, your newly-installed system software, and perhaps an application's support files, is above suspicion. Continue troubleshooting by moving your remaining customizing files (e.g., fonts, control panels, system extensions, application support files) from your original System Folder (e.g., Previous System Folder, Old Folder) to your new System Folder, trying to recreate your system error after you move each set of files. If your system error reoccurs at this point, you'll need to isolate the damaged or incompatible file causing the problem.

Error "There is not enough memory to open..." When Launching an Application

ISSUE

When you launch an application running in System 7.x, the system returns a memory-related error.

SYMPTOMS

The system returns one of the following memory-related errors:

- "There is not enough memory to open '[Name of application]' ([x]K needed, [x]K available). To make more memory available, try quitting [name of application]."
- "There is not enough memory to open '[Name of application]' ([x]K needed, [x]K available). To make more memory available, try quitting the [x] applications that are currently open."

SOLUTIONS

Do one or more of the following:

A. Quit all open applications before launching the desired application.

B. Decrease the amount of memory allocated to the application:
   1. Select the application's icon by clicking it once, then choose File > Get Info.
   2. Decrease the value for Preferred or Minimum size (System 7.1 or later) or Current size (System 7.0x), then close the dialog box.
   3. Launch the application.

C. Turn on Virtual Memory in the Memory control panel, then specify a value that exceeds the total amount of memory required to run both the System and the desired application. For instructions on calculating the amount of memory needed to run both the System and an application, see Additional Information.

D. Delete the application preferences file (e.g., Adobe Photoshop 3.0 Prefs), located in the Preferences folder in the System Folder.

E. Install more random-access memory (RAM) or a RAM extension utility (e.g., Connectix RAM Doubler).

F. Restart the Macintosh to defragment memory.

ADDITIONAL INFORMATION

The Macintosh system returns an error when there is not enough memory available to launch an application. A damaged preferences file may cause an invalid memory error message to occur when launching an application.

To calculate the amount of memory (in kilobytes) required to run both the system software and an application:

1. Choose About This Macintosh from the Apple menu.
2. Note the Total Memory value, which is the amount of available RAM, and the System Software value, which is the amount of memory required to run the system software.
3. Select the application's icon by clicking it once, then choose File > Get Info.
4. Note the Preferred size (System 7.1 or later) or the Current size (System 7.0x), which indicates the amount of memory needed to run the application.
5. Add the amount of memory required to run the system software with the amount of memory required to run the application. If this sum is greater than the amount of available RAM, there is not enough memory to run both the system software and the application.

Optimizing and Maintaining a Macintosh Computer General Information

Over time, changes inherently occur to software and hardware on a Macintosh computer that can lead to performance loss and system problems (e.g., system errors), which include:

- System software and fonts, because they are used continuously, are likely to become damaged; other software can also become damaged.
- SCSI disk drivers can become damaged or may be incompatible with a system software upgrade.
- Hard disk sectors can become damaged.
- Software (e.g., applications, control panel documents, extensions, fonts) may be incompatible.

Optimizing you computer and preventing software and hard disk damage ensures it runs as efficiently as possible. To ensure your computer runs as efficiently, at least every two to three months, perform the following procedures designed to optimize performance and limit issues related to conflicting or damaged software and hardware. Some of these procedures may require software utilities not included with the system software.

MAINTENANCE PROCEDURES

1. Update all SCSI drivers to ensure they are undamaged and compatible with the current system. For instructions, see Updating SCSI Drivers.
2. Use Apple's Disk First Aid to ensure that the disks' directory trees are undamaged. For instructions, see Using Disk First Aid.
3. Use a third-party disk utility (e.g. Norton Utilities, MacTools, Symantec Tools for Macintosh) to ensure damaged sectors are tagged as unusable. For instructions, refer to the utility's documentation.

4. Reinstall the system software using the most current Apple Macintosh system software by choosing to perform a clean install (i.e., installing new system software into a new System Folder, instead of installing over the existing system software). Reinstall any Apple hardware and system software updates you've installed that are still required by the installed system version.
5. Use a third-party disk utility (e.g., Norton Utilities, MacTools) to optimize or defragment the hard disk. For instructions, refer to the utility's documentation.
6. Rebuild the desktop file by holding down the Command and Option keys while choosing Special > Restart. Keep the keys held down until you receive the message "Are you sure you want to rebuild the Desktop file on the disk '[diskname]'? Comments in info windows will be lost," then click OK.
7. Ensure all installed software is compatible with the installed system software version and that it is undamaged by reinstalling the software.

OPTIMIZATION PROCEDURES

1. Disable Virtual Memory in the Memory control panel. When needed, install more RAM instead of using Virtual Memory as Virtual Memory is slower than RAM.
2. Remove all unnecessary control panels and system extensions. Ensure extensions or control panels used to run SCSI devices (e.g., hard disk, cartridge, optical disk drives) are compatible with the version of the system software installed.
3. Disable fonts you are not using by removing them from the System Folder or by using a font management utility (e.g., Fifth Generation Systems' Suitcase).
4. Use a software and hardware diagnostics utility (e.g., Snooper, MacEKG) to identify potential or existing conflicts. For instructions, refer to the utility's documentation.
5. For Power Macintosh computers, ensure Modern Memory Manager is enabled in the Memory control panel and that as much of the installed software as possible is written specifically for the Power Macintosh.

UPDATING SCSI DRIVERS

1. Start up your Mac from the Disk Tools disk, included with your system installation disks or CD-ROM, or from the CD-ROM that includes system software and the HDSC Setup application.
2. Launch the HDSC Setup application.
3. Click Drive until your SCSI drive (hard disk) is selected. NOTE: On a disk that has been formatted with a third-party disk utility (e.g. Norton Utilities, MacTools, Symantec Tools for Macintosh), HDSC Setup returns the message "Drive selection failed. Unable to locate a suitable drive connected to the SCSI port." Clicking Continue quits HDSC Setup. To update all SCSI drivers to ensure they are undamaged and compatible with the current system, use the Disk Tools disk from that utility's disk set. For instructions, refer to the utility's documentation.
4. Click Update to install updated SCSI drivers to each SCSI disk (i.e., hard disk, cartridge, optical).
5. Choose File > Quit.

USING DISK FIRST AID

1. Start up your Mac from the Disk Tools disk, included with your system installation disks or CD-ROM, or from the CD-ROM that includes system software and the Disk First Aid application.
2. Launch the Disk First Aid application.
3. Select or open the drive to be verified or repaired.
4. Click Verify to check the disk, or click Repair to check and repair the disk. When you click Verify, Disk First Aid will tell you if there is a problem with the disk and will ask you if you wish to repair it. Always repair the disk if prompted.
5. Choose File > Quit.

Printing Problems Troubleshooting Guide

When you are experiencing printing problems from a Macintosh application, there are several steps you can take to help determine the cause. To troubleshoot printing problems, follow the suggestions below in the order that they appear.

DISABLE BACKGROUND PRINTING

When Background Printing is enabled, the application first spools the print file to the hard disk, then PrintMonitor sends the file to the printer. Spooling the print file to the hard disk enables the printing application to process your print file in the background and the system to return primary control of the computer to you. When the PrintMonitor application runs out of memory or is damaged, printing errors or no output occurs.

To disable Background printing:

1. Open the Chooser from the Apple menu.
2. In the Chooser window, select the printer driver icon for your output device.
3. Select Off for Background Printing, then close the Chooser window.

If your file prints as expected when background printing is disabled, allocate more memory to the PrintMonitor application in the PrintMonitor's Get Info dialog box, re-enable Background Printing in the Chooser, then try printing again. If your printing problem reoccurs after you allocate more memory to PrintMonitor, reinstall your printing software from the system software installation disks or from the disks included with your printer.

If your file does not print after disabling background printing, continue troubleshooting.

DETERMINE IF THE PROBLEM OCCURS ONLY IN ONE FILE

Open a new file in the application from which you are having trouble printing. In the new file, type a few characters or draw a simple element (e.g., box, line) on the page, then try to print. If the new file prints, your original file may be damaged, may contain a damaged element or font, or may need to be simplified. If your original file is damaged, you may be able to salvage your work by opening the file you are having trouble printing, selecting all the elements, and then copying and pasting these into a new file. If the file containing the pasted elements prints successfully, save this file and use it as your working file.

If the file containing the pasted elements does not print, determine if the problem is due to one or more damaged element in the file. To isolate a damaged element, delete one element and then print the document, repeating this process until you can print the file. The last element you delete before the file prints is most likely the cause of your printing problem or your file may be too complex.

If the isolated element is an imported graphic, try re-importing the graphic into your file. If this does solve your printing problem, re-export the graphic from the application in which you created it, in the same format or in a different format, and then re-import it into your file. If the graphic still prevents the file from printing, determine whether the graphic prints from your application by placing it in a new file. If the graphic prints as the only element in a new file, the graphic may be complex, and when combining it with other elements on a page, it requires more memory to print than is available.

If the isolated element is text, you may have a damaged font. To verify whether a font is damaged, apply a different font to the text and try printing again. If the file prints, reinstall the font from the original or backup installation disks. If your printing problem reoccurs after you reinstall the font, too many downloadable fonts in your file may be preventing your file from printing.

To simplify files created in applications that can import multiple graphic files and formats (e.g., PageMaker 5.0x) use fewer imported graphics or fewer downloadable fonts. If your application can generate complex elements (e.g., Adobe Illustrator), use fewer points on a path, reduce the number of items that have been copied or cloned multiple times, or simplify customized fills or gradients.

If a new file containing only simple elements or text does not print, continue troubleshooting.

TRY PRINTING FROM A DIFFERENT APPLICATION

If you are able to print from a different application, the application from which you are unable to print may be damaged or have a damaged resource. Determine if your printing problem is caused by a damaged application preferences file (e.g., PM5.0 Defaults file, Adobe Illustrator 5.5 Prefs file) by deleting it. Deleting an application's preferences file enables most applications to generate a new preferences file the next time it starts. If printing problems recur after you delete the preferences file, reinstall your application from the original installation disks with all non-Apple or nonessential extensions disabled.

If you are unable to print from a different application or if you are unable to print after you reinstall your application, continue troubleshooting.

REINSTALL OR UPGRADE YOUR PRINTER DRIVER

The printer driver is responsible for sending your application's files to the printer. When printing to a PostScript printer, ensure you are printing using the printer driver recommended by your printer's manufacturer. If your printer driver is damaged or incompatible, your print jobs may fail, generating various printing errors or no output. If you are unsure whether your printer software is the most current version available , contact your printer's manufacturer. After ensuring you are using an up-to-date printer driver, disable all extensions, then reinstall the printer driver from the installation disks included with your printer or from your system software installation disks.

PPD files can also become damaged, resulting in printing problems. When using the Adobe PSPrinter 8.x printer driver or the Apple LaserWriter 8.x printer driver, select a PostScript Printer Description (PPD) file that describes your printer, a similar printer, or use a generic PPD file by selecting Use Generic in the Setup dialog box in the Chooser.

To setup the Adobe PSPrinter 8.x printer driver or the Apple LaserWriter 8.x printer driver to use the Generic PPD file:

1. Open the Chooser from the Apple menu.
2. In the Chooser window, select the Adobe PSPrinter 8.x printer driver or the Apple LaserWriter 8.x printer driver icon.
3. Select your target printer in the right-hand window.
4. Click Setup.
5. In the Setup dialog box, click Select PPD.
6. In the Select a PostScript Printer Description File dialog box, click Use Generic.
7. In the Setup dialog box, click OK.

If you are unable to print after you reinstall your printer driver or when you select the Generic PPD file in the Chooser, continue troubleshooting.

REINSTALL YOUR SYSTEM SOFTWARE

If you still are unable to print, reinstall your system software by performing a clean install (i.e., installing new system software into a new System Folder, instead of installing over the existing system software in the System Folder). When using System 7.5's Clean Install feature, the installer renames the existing System Folder "Previous System Folder" and then installs new system software into a new System Folder.

Items Missing from Apple Menu

ISSUE

One or more folders or files in the Apple Menu Items folder in the System Folder do not display in the Apple menu.

SOLUTION

Reduce the number of folders or files in the Apple Menu Items folder to 52 or fewer by deleting them or by grouping them in folders within the Apple Menu Items folder.

ADDITIONAL INFORMATION

The Apple Menu only displays the first 52 files or folders located in the Apple Menu Items folder in the System folder.

To determine the number of items in the Apple Menu Items folder:

1. Open the Apple Menu Items folder in the System Folder.
2. Choose View > By Icon. The number of items in the folder displays in the upper-left corner of the Apple Menu Items window.

Turning Off Extensions Without Disabling an Apple CD-ROM

When you turn off extensions on your Macintosh by pressing the Shift key while restarting, all extensions are disabled, included those needed by your Apple CD-ROM drive. Without these extensions, the drive cannot load or read CD-ROM discs. To turn off extensions without disabling those needed by your Apple CD-ROM drive, use an extensions manager or manually remove extensions and control panels from the System Folder.

The Apple CD-ROM drive uses the Apple CD-ROM, Apple Photo Access, Audio CD Access, Foreign File Access, High Sierra File Access, and ISO 9660 File Access extensions. Your System Folder may not contain all of these extensions, but should contain the Apple CD-ROM and Foreign File Access extensions.

To disable all extension except the Apple CD-ROM extensions using Extensions Manager (System 7.5.x and later):

1. Open the Extensions Manager control panel.
2. Select the All Off option from the Sets pop-up menu.
3. Select the CD-ROM extensions (e.g., Apple CD-ROM, Foreign File Access) in the scrollbox.
4. Close the Extensions Manager control panel and restart the Macintosh.

To manually disable all extensions except the Apple CD-ROM extensions:

1. Create a new folder on the desktop and name it "Disabled Extensions."
2. Move the all extensions except the CD-ROM extensions (e.g., Apple CD-ROM, Foreign File Access) from the Extensions folder in the System Folder to the Disabled Extensions folder on the desktop.
3. Create a new folder on the desktop and name it "Disabled Control Panels."
4. Move all control panels from the Control Panels folder in the System Folder to the Disabled Control Panels folder on the desktop.
5. Restart the Macintosh.

Error "Could not find application program" After Selecting PPD in Chooser

ISSUE

After you select a PostScript Printer Description (PPD) file in the Chooser, the system returns the error "Could not find the application program that created the document named '[PPD name]'. To open the document, select an alternate program with or without translation."

SOLUTIONS

In the Macintosh Easy Open control panel, select Off for Automatic Document Translation.

OR: Remove the Word for Word MEO extension from the Extensions folder in the System Folder, then restart the Macintosh.

OR: Use the printer driver's Auto Setup feature to select the PPD file:

1. Select a printer driver (e.g., LaserWriter 8, PSPrinter) in the left scrollbox of the Chooser.
2. Select the printer you want to set up from the right scrollbox.
3. Click Setup (when using the LaserWriter 8.2.1 printer driver, press the Command key while clicking Setup).
4. In the Setup dialog box, click Auto Setup.
5. When setup is complete, click OK, then close the Chooser.

OR: When the error message appears and Macintosh Easy Open displays a list of available applications, select Chooser:

1. When the error message appears, deselect the Show Only Recommended Choices option to display alternate program options. Do not select the Chooser with Adobe Translation option.
2. Select Chooser, then click Open.
3. Click OK, then close the Chooser.

ADDITIONAL INFORMATION

When the Word for Word MEO extension is installed and Automatic Document Translation is enabled in the Macintosh Easy Open control panel, the error "Could not find the application program... select an alternate program with or without translation." appears after you select a PPD file in the Chooser. Disabling Automatic Document Translation in the Macintosh Easy Open control panel or removing the Word for Word MEO extension enables you to select a PPD file without error.

Using the printer driver's Auto Setup feature bypasses Macintosh Easy Open's translation options, preventing the error from occurring.

Selecting Chooser for the Macintosh Easy Open translation option instructs Macintosh Easy Open to enable the Chooser to select the PPD file without translation. After you select the Chooser option, Macintosh Easy Open stores that selection in its Macintosh Easy Open Preferences file.

Macintosh Easy Open enables you to choose an alternate application to open a document when the application that created it cannot be found. Macintosh Easy Open 1.1.1, for use with System 7.5, includes a Macintosh Easy Open control panel. Macintosh Easy Open 1.0.x, for use with System 7.1.x, includes both a Macintosh Easy Open Setup control panel and a Macintosh Easy Open extension.

Macintosh Easy Open is installed automatically with some applications (e.g., Adobe Word for Word, Aldus Fetch 1.2) and with an Easy Install of System 7.5. You can perform a custom installation of Word for Word and select not to install Macintosh Easy Open or the Word for Word MEO extension.

Memory or System Error Launching Application on Performa or LC

ISSUE
When launching Adobe PageMaker, Adobe Chart, Adobe Photoshop, or Adobe Illustrator, the application returns a system error (e.g., "Out of Memory," Type 1, Type 11).

SYMPTOMS
The application is installed on a Macintosh computer with a PowerPC 603 processor (i.e., Macintosh 5200 LC series, Performa 5200 series, Performa 6200 series, and only Power Macintosh 6200 sold outside the United States). The application has sufficient memory available to launch.

SOLUTION
Install the Macintosh Easy Open 1.1.1 or later control panel in the Control Panels folder located in the System Folder, then restart the Macintosh. The Macintosh Easy Open control panel is included on the Apple Performa 5200 or 6200 series CD-ROM or is available from Apple Computer.

ADDITIONAL INFORMATION
The Macintosh Easy Open control panel is pre-installed with Mac OS (Macintosh operating system) 7.5.1 on all 5200 and 6200 series Macintosh Performa and LC models. PageMaker, Chart, Photoshop, and Illustrator require Macintosh Easy Open located in the Control Panels folder in the System Folder to launch, but do not require the Automatic Document Translation feature enabled. It is unknown why PageMaker, Chart, Photoshop, and Illustrator require Macintosh Easy Open to launch.

When launching PageMaker, Chart, Photoshop, or Illustrator when the Macintosh Easy Open control panel is not located in the Control Panels folder, or after starting the Macintosh without the Macintosh Easy Open control panel enabled (i.e., restarting with the Shift key held down, turning off Macintosh Easy Open using Extension Manager), the Mac OS returns the error "-108 Storage Allocator Error (Ran out of memory [not enough room in heap zone])" informing the application that memory is full, regardless of how much memory is available. Each application displays its own version of the -108 system error. For example:

- "Cannot start PageMaker. Out of memory. 7527:108" occurs when launching PageMaker 6.0x for the Macintosh or for the Power Macintosh.
- "System Error. Adobe PageMaker 5.0. Type 11." occurs when launching PageMaker 5.0x for the Power Macintosh.
- "The application 'unknown' has unexpectedly quit, because an error of Type 1 occurred." occurs when launching PageMaker 5.0 for the Macintosh.
- "Could not complete your request because there is not enough memory (RAM)." when launching Photoshop 2.5.x or Photoshop 3.0.x.
- "Adobe Illustrator can't run because there isn't enough memory." when launching Illustrator 5.x.

Unable to Dismount CD-ROM in System 7.5

ISSUE
You cannot dismount a CD-ROM volume (i.e., eject the CD-ROM by dragging it to the Trash). The CD-ROM is mounted on a Macintosh running System 7.5 with File Sharing enabled.

SOLUTIONS
Disable File Sharing in the Sharing Setup control panel.
OR: Install System 7.5.1 or later.
OR: Install the File Sharing Extension 7.6.1.

ADDITIONAL INFORMATION
CD-ROM volumes cannot be dismounted when File Sharing Extension 7.1.1 is enabled in System 7.5. The File Sharing Extension 7.1.1 is included with System 7.5.

File Sharing Extension 7.6.1, included with System 7.5.1, enables CD-ROM volumes to be dismounted while File Sharing is enabled.

System Error When Printing Large File from Macintosh with PCI Local Bus

ISSUE
A system error (e.g., freeze) occurs when printing a large file (i.e., 5 MB or larger) using the Apple LaserWriter 8.3.1 or the Adobe PSPrinter 8.3 printer driver from a Macintosh with a Peripheral Component Interconnect (PCI) local bus (e.g., Power Macintosh 9500, 8500, 7500, 7200).

SOLUTIONS
Print using the LaserWriter 8.3.2 or later printer driver.
OR: Print from a Macintosh with a NuBus, instead of a PCI, local bus (e.g., Power Macintosh 8100, 7100).
OR: Reduce the file size of the document to 4 MB or smaller.

ADDITIONAL INFORMATION
Because the LaserWriter 8.3.1 and the PSPrinter 8.3 printer drivers are not compatible with the Peripheral Component Interconnect (PCI) local bus, printing on a PCI local bus Macintosh model using the LaserWriter 8.3.1 and the PSPrinter 8.3 printer drivers causes a system error. LaserWriter 8.3.2 and later is compatible with the Peripheral Component Interconnect (PCI) local bus Macintosh models.

Isolating Extension Conflicts in System 7.1 and Later

Extensions enable you to customize your Macintosh by extending or enhancing your system software. In System 7.x, the term "extensions" refers to both system extension files (e.g., AppleShare, File Sharing Extension) and control panel files (e.g., Macintosh Easy Open, Monitors). When you start your Mac, the system software loads extensions in alphabetical order. The system searches first for system extension files in the Extensions folder, then control panel files in the Control Panels folder, and finally both system extension and control panel files in the System Folder. After your system loads extensions, they're enabled, unless you have disabled them by selecting this option in their control panel windows.

When an extension is damaged or conflicts with one or more of your other installed extensions, the application you are running, or your system software, one or more of the following symptoms occurs:

- system error (e.g., dialog box displaying an error message, freeze, endless processing)
- slow performance
- unexpected behavior
- unsuccessful software installation

When troubleshooting these symptoms, you can eliminate the greatest number of variables, and the most likely cause, by disabling your extensions. For example, if you receive a system error while working in an application, and you have customized your system software by adding four control panel files and four system extension files, you have ten variables to troubleshoot. If your symptoms reoccur after disabling your added extensions, you know that these eight variables are not the cause. When your symptoms do not reoccur after disabling your added extensions, you know that these extensions are the cause of your problem, and you can begin isolating the damaged or conflicting extension, or combination of extensions.

DISABLING EXTENSIONS OVERVIEW

When troubleshooting damaged or conflicting extensions, the method you choose to disable added or suspect extensions will depend on your troubleshooting needs. For example, when troubleshooting a system error that occurs only in a single application, you'll need to disable all added extensions except those required by the application (e.g., QuickTime).

To disable added extensions, you can:

- Restart your Macintosh with the Shift key held down.

  You can disable extensions in System 7.0 and later by restarting while holding down the Shift key. Because this method of disabling extensions does not enable you to select which extensions you want to disable, use this method for troubleshooting extension conflicts when you don't require a specific extension installed (e.g., CD-ROM driver, QuickTime). Keyboards manufactured by a company other than Apple may use a different method for restarting with extensions disabled.
- Use an extensions manager.

  An extensions manager (e.g., Apple Extensions Manager, Casady & Greene Conflict Catcher, Now Startup Manager) enables you to selectively disable extensions, but any extension you use to disable other extensions is suspect itself. Most extensions managers support the same features as Apple Extensions Manager, included with System 7.5 and later, and they may also support additional features.
- Manually move extensions out of the System Folder.

  Disabling extensions by manually moving them out of the System Folder enables you to selectively choose which extensions you want to disable. This method of disabling extensions takes time and requires you to be familiar with the contents of your System Folder, but does give you complete control over the extensions you disable.

DISABLING EXTENSIONS

To quickly determine if a damaged or conflicting extension is the cause of your problem, disable added or nonessential extensions by restarting with the Shift key held down or by using an extensions manager. Disabling extensions by restarting with the Shift key held down or by using an extensions manager may not disable all added or nonessential extensions, so if your problem reoccurs after using either method, you can make sure extensions are not the cause of your problem by manually disabling them before troubleshooting other causes.

Restarting with the Shift Key Down

Restarting with the Shift key held down in System 7.0 and later disables added or nonessential extensions, including some extensions installed with your system software (e.g., Apple CD-ROM).

To disable extensions by restarting with the Shift key held down, restart your Macintosh by choosing Special > Restart, then hold down the Shift key. Keep the Shift key held down until your system displays the message "Welcome to Macintosh. Extensions off." To re-enable your extensions, restart without holding down the Shift key.

Using Extensions Manager

The Extensions Manager control panel, included with System 7.5 and later, enables you to select which extensions, or set of extensions, you want to disable. To enable or disable extensions in the Extensions Manager control panel, click to the left of the extension's name to display or remove the check mark, or enable a set of extensions using the Sets pop-up menu. After you restart your Macintosh, Extensions Manager enables an extension only when it has a check mark next to its name, and moves disabled extensions into the Extensions (Disabled) or Control Panels (Disabled) folder it creates.

To disable extensions using the Extensions Manager control panel:

1. In the Extensions Manager control panel, select the extensions you want to disable:

Select System 7.5.x or System 7.5 Only from the Sets pop-up menu to disable all extensions except those included with your system software.
OR: Select All Off from the Sets pop-up menu to disable all extensions that Extensions Manager can disable.
OR: Selectively disable extensions by clicking to the left of an extension's name to remove the check mark.
2. Close the Extensions Manager control panel.
3. Restart your Macintosh.

Manually Disabling Extensions in System 7.1 and Later

When manually disabling your added or nonessential extensions, you can remove the Extensions and Control Panels folders, including the extension files they contain, from the System Folder to make sure these folders are not damaged and are not the cause of your problem. When you remove the Extensions and Control Panel folders, you can also remove the Fonts and Preferences folders, including the files they contain, to make sure these folders are not damaged and the cause of your problem. You can also make sure the Fonts and Preferences folders are not damaged later when you troubleshoot damaged application or system software.

To manually disable extensions:

1. Move the Control Panels and Extensions folders, and, if desired, the Fonts and Preferences folders, from the System Folder to a new location (e.g., desktop).
2. Restart your Macintosh. The system searches for system preferences files and the Control Panels, Extensions, Fonts, and Preferences folders in the System Folder. When your system cannot find the folders or system preferences files it needs in the System Folder, it creates new ones.
3. When your problem occurs when working in a single application, enable only those extensions that application requires to launch or run (e.g., QuickTime) by moving them from your previous Control Panels or Extensions folders into your new, empty Control Panels or Extensions folders in the System Folder.
4. Restart your Macintosh.

ISOLATING EXTENSION CONFLICTS

After disabling extensions, try to recreate your problem. If your problem reoccurs, your problem is caused by other software or hardware causes. If your problem does not reoccur, it was caused by a damaged or conflicting extension, and you'll need to determine which extension is the culprit by selectively re-enabling your extensions. You can re-enable them by using Extensions Manager or by manually moving them back into your System Folder. If you disabled your extensions by restarting with the Shift key held down, you'll need to disable them manually or by using an extension manager before isolating which extension is the cause of your problem.

To isolate which extension is the cause of your problem, re-enable them one or a few at a time, then try to recreate your problem. For example, you can re-enable them beginning with those included with your system software followed by your favorites, or you can add two at time in alphabetical order. While re-enabling extensions, keep track of which extensions files you just added. You can use label colors to keep track of which extension files you have added back. For example, you can assign the color orange to all extensions files before you begin adding them back into your System Folder, then change the label color of each extension file after you add it back.

When the problem reoccurs after adding an extension, leave it in the System Folder, then remove all other extensions so that your system and application are running with only that extension installed. If, after you restart, the problem reoccurs, you've found the culprit. If the problem doesn't reoccur, you'll know it is caused by a combination of extensions, and not that single extension. You can further determine which combination of extensions is the cause of your problem.

When your problem does not occur after re-enabling all your extensions, and you have manually disabled extensions by removing the Control Panels and Extensions folder, and perhaps the Fonts and Preferences folders, your problem may have been caused by a damaged folder, or by a damaged font or preferences file. If you've removed your Fonts and Preferences folders, you'll need to move back your font files from the previous Fonts folder into the newly created Fonts folder, and your preferences files from the previous Preferences folder into the newly created Preferences folder, one or a few at a time, trying to recreate the problem after each move. Only move font files or preference files that do not already exist in the newly created Fonts or Preferences folder. If your problem occurs after you move a font or preferences file back, the cause of your problem is most likely a damaged file, so you'll need to reinstall the file. To reinstall a damaged preference file, either launch the application that uses the file to force it to recreate its preferences file, or reinstall the application that uses the preferences file.

RESOLVING EXTENSION CONFLICTS

You have several choices to resolve problems caused by a damaged or conflicting extension. Which solution you choose depends on your needs and which extension is causing the problem.

To resolve extension conflicts, do one of the following:

A. Modify the extension.
   A setting in a control panel may be causing a conflict. Try changing current settings to see if they're the cause of your problem.
B. Replace the extension.
   Rule out a damaged extension by deleting the extension, then reinstalling a new copy from the original installation disks. When deleting the extension, make sure you also delete its support files (e.g., preferences file).
C. Reinstall files used by the extension.
   The conflict may not be caused by the extension, but by a damaged file it uses. For example, font management extensions (e.g., Suitcase, MasterJuggler) read font suitcases. The cause of your problem may be a dam-

aged font suitcase, or a font file contained in the suitcase. In this example, you can prevent the font management extension from reading all font suitcases to determine if this prevents your problem from reoccurring. If it does, you'll need to isolate which font suitcase, or font file in a suitcase, is the cause, then reinstall that file.

D. Change the loading order of your extensions.

The order in which your extensions load may be the cause of your conflict. When you start up your Mac, the system loads, in alphabetical order, first your system extension files located in the Extensions folder, then control panel files located in the Control panel folder, and finally both system extension and control panel files located in the System Folder. To change the order in which your system loads an extension, change its name (e.g., add a character at the beginning of an extension's filename). Extensions files whose names begin with a non-Roman character (e.g., dash, tilde, pound sign) load either first or last, depending on the character.

E. Update the conflicting extension.

Check with the extension's developer to see if there is an updated version available, or if they have other information that may help you resolve your problem.

F. Run without the conflicting extension.

Until an update is available, you may have to run without an extension when it doesn't support, or conflicts with, newer software you're running.

Incorrect Spacing Printing Monospace Fonts

ISSUE

The spacing between characters or words formatted with a monospace font (e.g., Courier, Letter Gothic) prints differently than it displays on screen. Lines of text print longer than they display, and underlines don't extend to the end of the text.

SOLUTION

Use ResEdit to change the FOND resource for the monospace screen (bitmap) font:

DISCLAIMER: This procedure is not supported by Adobe Systems or Apple Computer and is only provided as a guideline. It is recommended you have some experience using ResEdit, since it has the capability of changing or removing any resource from any file. If the wrong resource is modified the system could be damaged and require reinstallation. Keep backup copies of original documents. In the event of any problems, revert to original system configuration or remove the modified font and reinstall the original.

1. Remove the screen font from the Fonts folder in the System Folder, then restart the Macintosh. If the font is loading from a font management utility (e.g., Suitcase II, MasterJuggler), disable it in the utility.
2. Launch ResEdit.
3. Locate and open the screen font.
4. Open the Fond resource.
5. Locate and open the font.
6. In this dialog box, change the Flag Word line from "$C000" to "$0000."

ADDITIONAL INFORMATION

Most fonts on the Macintosh vary the space between characters to accommodate thinner letters (e.g., "l" or "i"). Monospace fonts, however, use the same amount of space between every character (e.g., the letter "l" has the same width as the letter "o"). A flaw in some monospace screen fonts causes applications that use fractional width information (e.g., PageMaker) to display the fonts differently than they print.

PRAM General Information

Parameter Random Access Memory (PRAM) contains 20 to 256 bytes (number varies by model of Macintosh) of default information located in the computer's clock chip. The clock chip is powered by a battery when the Macintosh is turned off so that default and user settings are present the next time the Macintosh is restarted.

PRAM contains values for the validity status of the clock chip, node ID hint for modem port (9600 baud, 8 data bits, 2 stop bits, no parity), node ID hint for printer port, use types, modem port configuration stop bits, printer port configuration, printer connection, alarm setting, time, date, monitor colors, application font number minus 1, auto-key threshold, auto-key rate, printer port connection, monitor colors, speaker volume, double-click time, caret-blink time, mouse scaling, preferred system start-up disk, network setting (network defaults to local talk), and menu blink.

Because the clock chip is very difficult to access, the stored PRAM values are copied into low memory at System startup. This copying process is a hardware action done at startup, meaning System software is not involved. These copied PRAM values can be read and changed by using the Control Panel Device "General Controls." At shutdown, these values are written back to the clock chip.

ZAPPING THE PRAM

PRAM values can be reset to the default settings in the clock chip and then recopied into low memory. Restting PRAM values, often referred to as "zapping" the PRAM, resets the Macintosh's PRAM to default settings that include settings in the Monitors and Network control panels.

According to Apple Corporation, there is no value in resetting the PRAM as a troubleshooting tool for software problems. There have been a few, unconfirmed reports that resetting the PRAM helped to reset a NuBus video card when the monitor displays only static. These reports are not verifiable and there are no PRAM values or settings for NuBus slots. The only proven time resetting the PRAM may be of benefit is if your Macintosh fails to boot under any circumstances.

To reset PRAM in System 7.x:

1. Reboot the Macintosh and hold down Command + Option + P + R before the "Welcome to Macintosh" screen appears.
2. Keep the keys depressed until the Macintosh has finished starting up.

To reset PRAM in System 6.x:

Hold down Command + Option + Shift and choose Control Panel from the Apple menu.

Deinstalling QuickDraw GX General Information

To deinstall QuickDraw GX, remove QuickDraw GX system files, restore Type 1 fonts, and setup a PostScript printer.

REMOVING QUICKDRAW GX SYSTEM FILES

To remove QuickDraw GX and restore standard Macintosh printing for all applications:

1. Start the Apple Installer on the QuickDraw GX Install disk by double-clicking on the Install QuickDraw GX installer control file.
2. Choose Custom Remove from the pop-up menu in the installer dialog box.
3. Select the Base QuickDraw GX Software for this Macintosh, Base QuickDraw GX Software for any Macintosh, QuickDraw GX Utilities, ATM for QuickDraw GX, All QuickDraw GX Drivers for Apple Printers options for Custom Remove.
4. Set the Destination Disk to the disk containing the System software; use the Switch Disk button to select another disk, if your System is on another attached hard disk.
5. Click the Remove button. When complete, restart the Macintosh.

RESTORING TYPE 1 FONTS

To restore Type 1 PostScript fonts:

1. Move all enabled font suitcases, located in the Fonts folder in the System Folder by default, to a different location. Enabled suitcases contain converted TrueType versions of the Type 1 PostScript font in addition to the bitmap (screen) fonts.
2. Move fonts contained in the Archived Type 1 Fonts folder, located in the System Folder, into the Fonts folder, and delete the empty Archived Type 1 Fonts folder.
3. Move other fonts enabled using the Type 1 Enabler application to another folder not accessed by any font management utility (e.g., Suitcase). Move the original archived copy of the Type 1 font back to the desired folder to make it available to the font management utility.
4. Reinstall Adobe Type Manager versions other than ATM/GX 3.7.

SETTING UP A POSTSCRIPT PRINTER

To set up a PostScript printer in the Chooser:

1. Choose the Chooser from the Apple menu, then click the LaserWriter 8.x driver icon.
2. Select a PostScript printer from the Select a PostScript Printer list and click Setup.
3. Set up the PostScript printer by clicking Setup, clicking Auto Setup in the Current Printer Description File (PPD) Selected dialog box then clicking OK. An icon appears to the left of the printer's name in the Chooser indicating it is set up using the LaserWriter 8 printer driver.

   NOTE: When you click Auto Setup, the LaserWriter 8.x printer driver locates the PostScript Printer Description (PPD) file for the printer. If the LaserWriter 8.x printer driver is unable to locate a corresponding PPD file, click Select PPD and choose another appropriate PPD file, or click Use Generic in the Select a PostScript Printer Description File dialog box.

To disable the QuickDraw GX and PrinterShare GX system extensions, use the Extensions Manager:

1. Choose Control Panels from the Apple menu and double-click the Extensions Manager control panel.
2. Deselect the QuickDraw GX and PrinterShare GX system extensions and restart.

   OR: Manually remove the QuickDraw GX and PrinterShare GX system.

Checking for Damaged Disks

When you install an application or move a file from a disk onto a destination volume (e.g., hard disk), damaged disks or media errors prevent you from installing or copying the file.

High-density disk drives can read both low- and high-density disks; low-density disk drives can read only low-density disks. The Macintosh Plus, SE, and II computer models include only low-density disk drives; high-density disk drives are optional for the Macintosh IIx and SE/30 computer models.

Newer Macintosh models (e.g., PowerBooks) use disk drives built to different specifications than older Macintosh models (e.g., Macintosh II). Many software companies create installation disks using disk-duplication machines, some of which create disks that adhere to older drive specifications. Drives built to the newer specifications are unable to read these disks and, when attempting to do so, return an error indicating damaged media. Copying the contents of the installation disks onto disks formatted with the newer specification drive enables newer disk drives to read the disks.

To check disks for damage or media errors, copy the contents of the disks to another volume:

1. Create an empty folder on the destination volume.
2. Insert the disk to be checked for damage.
3. Select the disk's icon and drag it onto the empty folder. The disk's contents are copied into a folder named the same as the disk.
4. Note any errors that occur while the system copies files from the disk to the destination volume.

Copying files from the installation disk to another volume uses the system's file verification routines to check for media errors, where "I/O" refers to "input/output;" "input" meaning read and "output" meaning write. When the system encounters a media error, it returns one of the following errors:

- "Cannot read. Error -36" or "The file [file name] could not be read and was skipped. Do you want to continue copying?"
  Indicates a file cannot be copied from the disk or read because a media error on the disk was encountered (i.e., the file being copied is located on a damaged or bad sector on the disk).
- "Cannot write. Error -36"
  Indicates the files cannot be copied to the disk or written on the destination volume because a media error on the destination volume was encountered (i.e., the file is being copied or written to a damaged or bad sector on the destination volume).
- "I/O Error (-36)"
  Indicates a media error was encountered.
- "This disk is damaged, do you want to initialize it?"
  Indicates the inserted disk is damaged.
- "This is not a Macintosh disk, do you want to initialize it?"
  Indicates the inserted disk is damaged, is not formatted for the Macintosh, or is not compatible with the floppy drive (i.e., low-density disk drives cannot read high-density disks).

Printing Using a QuickDraw Printer Driver General Information

When printing to a QuickDraw device, QuickDraw printer drivers use the Macintosh computer's memory (RAM) to process output to QuickDraw devices (e.g., printers, fax modems, film recorders). When an application prints, it sends the document's information to the QuickDraw printer driver, which processes and converts the information into the format required by the QuickDraw device.

When processing, the QuickDraw printer driver requests the amount of memory (RAM) it needs from the system to print the document. The system then allocates available memory from the system heap, which is a portion of memory reserved for the system, to the printer driver. The Macintosh determines the size of the system heap when it starts, then loads code segments, resources, and document data (e.g., control panels, system extensions, fonts, parts of the system software) into the system heap. When the size of the system heap is too small, the QuickDraw printer driver may not have enough memory to print. To increase the amount of memory reserved for the system heap, and the amount of memory available to a QuickDraw printer driver, quit unneeded applications, remove unneeded fonts, and disable unnecessary extensions (i.e., control panel and system extension files).

Because QuickDraw printer drivers use available memory in the system heap, allocating more memory to a QuickDraw printer driver is not possible, and allocating more memory to the printing application does not increase the amount of memory available to a QuickDraw printer driver or improve print performance. Some applications (e.g., PageMaker 5.0x) resample image data before sending the image data to the printer driver, which may decrease print times to QuickDraw printers. Increasing an application's memory partition may decrease the application's processing time for images, but does not decrease overall print times to QuickDraw printers.

When printing to a QuickDraw printer with Background Printing enabled in the Chooser, applications send printing information to a file on the hard disk in the PrintMonitor Documents folder. PrintMonitor then sends the printing information contained in the file to the QuickDraw printer driver.

Unopenable Files Previously Opened, Saved, or Copied over Network Troubleshooting Guide

ISSUE

When you open a file in the application that created it, an application error (e.g., PageMaker's "Fatal error") or system error (e.g., "Unexpectedly quit," "Type 1," freeze) occurs. The file was opened, saved, or copied over a network (e.g., AppleShare, File Sharing, Novell).

SOLUTIONS

For a temporary solution, do one or more of the following:

A. Use the openable backup copy of the file from a local hard disk (e.g., internal hard disk).

B. Recreate the file using backup copies. Avoid repeating actions known to cause or precede the error (e.g., copying or saving files between certain servers or workstations), if possible.

C. Save the file often, making incremental backup copies.

To prevent files from becoming unopenable or damaged, do one or more of the following:

A. Check the disk's formatting and SCSI drivers, and then optimize, defragment, and check the disk for bad sectors (i.e., damaged media) using Disk First Aid (included with your system software) and another disk utilities (e.g., MacTools, Norton Utilities for Macintosh).

B. Isolate the network cause for damaged files (e.g., damaged system software, extension conflicts, network card problem, network problems) with the network administrator, if possible. For instructions, see Additional Information.

ADDITIONAL INFORMATION

When a file that is saved, opened, or copied over a network only, and not on local hard disks, is damaged, the damage is not caused by the application that saved or opened the file . Applications use system functions to save files. The application is aware of location of the saved file, but is unaware of whether the file is saved on a local hard disk or to a remote disk (e.g., file server). When copying files from volume to volume in the Finder, only the Finder application is involved.

When saving files to a server or other shared volume, applications (e.g., Adobe PageMaker) save and write files using the same system routines they use to save file on a local hard disk or floppy disk by using the system to perform the save. The system and network's ability to write the file properly depends on software and hardware variables outside of the application.

Many variables, including file servers, routers, bridges, network cards, software, cables, connectors, power cables, and power supplies, can prevent data from being transmitted accurately and completely. When a network data transmission problem exists, it's possible for a network to verify that it received all information when it was not. When these bits of data are not recovered, files are written incorrectly. Depending on where the damage occurs in the file, it can cause the file to be unopenable by the application that created it.

If a network problem exists, PageMaker publications are more likely to be damaged when you choose the Save As command (or the Save command when the Smaller save preference is selected), which forces PageMaker to rewrite the entire publication. This process increases the amount of network and hard disk activity (e.g., transmitting a file or writing a file to disk), increasing the opportunities for errors to occur. PageMaker's Save command or Faster save preference is similar to other application's quick save features.

Chances of recovering an unopenable file are low, but once the problem's cause is discovered, you can prevent file damage that causes unopenable files. Complex data structures (e.g., PageMaker publications) are not inherently fragile, but because of the complexity of the files, the application requires the data be in the expected order or structure. Damaged files caused by the application that created them usually affects more than one file, regardless of where the files are located (e.g., local hard disk, network server).

File recovery utilities assume damaged media is the cause of unopenable files, not damaged file data. Disk utilities can repair disks, but most are unable to repair damaged file data. They may know basic characteristics about any one application's file structure, but do not know details of the file structure, as this is typically proprietary information.

To isolate network causes of unopenable files, do one or more of the following:

A. Determine the symptoms of the problem:
- Determine the symptom (e.g., error message, unexpected behavior) that occurs when you open the file.
- Verify the unopenable files have been accessed remotely (i.e., across the network) to eliminate file- or application-specific causes.
- If the unopenable file is a template or a copy of another file, open the original file to determine when the damaged occurred.
- Determine if unopenable files have occurred previously or when you could open all files to check for environmental changes at these times.
- Once you save a file to a remote volume, determine the elapse of time before the file is unopenable.

B. Attempt to recover the unopenable file:
1. Copy the file from the remote volume (e.g., network server) to the local hard disk. If a read error occurs, a media error has been detected on the remote volume, and the file is damaged.
2. Open the file on the local hard disk. If you cannot open the file on the local hard disk, the file is damaged.
3. If you can open the file on the local hard disk, have the network administrator check the write privileges for all workstations experiencing the problem. Some applications (e.g., PageMaker) cannot open locked files (the Locked option is selected in the file's Get Info dialog box) or files residing on a shared volume that is write-protected.

C. Isolate network issues:
1. Use a workstation that enables you to open file that were opened, saved, or copied over a network to compare the hardware and software differences between workstations.
2. Determine if whole zones, sections, or groups of the network are unable to open files opened, saved, or copied over a network to isolate network problems localized to a specific part of the network. Once you localize the network problem, the network administrator can check Ethernet cards, routers, bridges, hubs, cables, and local connections for specific problems.
3. When multiple servers exist on the network, determine on which servers or volumes unopenable files occur. Isolate the server and one Macintosh that can open files by setting up a mini-network consisting of one server and one workstation, then determine if the unopenable file occur over a period of time.
4. When you can open files on a local hard disk, but not from a server, have the network administrator verify the write privileges for all workstations.
5. Check the network's wiring, especially when it has been rewired recently, and any other network changes. Crossed data and power cables can disrupt the transmission of data, potentially causing false verification of data being written.
6. For further troubleshooting by the network administrator, determine the network configuration (e.g., type of server, type of network, brand and model of network cards installed on the workstations, mixed or linked network using a combination of servers and network).

SCSI Chain Troubleshooting Guide

ISSUE

Macintosh doesn't start up when SCSI devices (e.g., external hard drive, removable drive, CD-ROM drive, scanner, film recorder) are connected.

External hard drive, removable drive, CD-ROM drive or other desktop mountable hardware do not show up on the desktop.

Scanner, Film Recorder or other SCSI connected devices do not act like they are connected to the Macintosh, unable to access them using their software.

A System error (e.g., Bus Error, ID=1) occurs only when a SCSI device is connected and it has been determined that software is not the cause of the system error.

Random lines appear through scanned TIFF graphics.

SOLUTIONS

Do one or more of the following:

A. Check the SCSI Devices Number and Connection:
   1. Make sure all power is off to the Macintosh and all devices. Failure to do so before changing the SCSI chain can result in voltage spikes that can damage the equipment.
   2. Verify that all connectors are fastened tightly, and correctly (i.e., ensure cable connector's pins are not bent). The first and last devices on a SCSI chain should be terminated. (The Macintosh IIfx requires a special black terminator).
   3. Check the SCSI address on the device (usually on the back of the device next to the SCSI port).

      No two devices may have the same SCSI ID #. Most devices allow you to choose a SCSI ID number from 1 - 6. SCSI ID number 0 is reserved for the internal hard drive, SCSI ID number 7 is reserved for the Macintosh itself.
   4. Ensure all SCSI devices are turned on before starting the Macintosh computer to allow time for the SCSI devices to warm up and be accessible by the time the Macintosh checks the SCSI chain. Some SCSI devices require a system Extension to properly access or mount the SCSI device.

B. Remove termination.

C. Use a shorter or longer cable. The longest recommended cable length is 19.6 feet for the entire SCSI chain. Excessive cable length may result in "echoing," or signals not terminating.

D. Connect one SCSI device at a time. Check for a conflict between each combination of the SCSI devices.

E. Change the physical order of devices on the SCSI chain in an organized way. For example, move the first device to the end of the chain (changing the termination). If that doesn't eliminate the problem, move the current first device to the end of the chain, and so on.

F. A SCSI device may be damaged (e.g., loose cable connectors, improper or damaged terminators, excessive SCSI cabling). Remove one of the devices from the SCSI chain. One of the SCSI devices may be allowing static electricity to enter the Macintosh and cause errant behavior.

G. Move all SCSI devices physically away from each other to ensure electromagnetic fields created by power supplies are not entering the SCSI chain.

ADDITIONAL INFORMATION

SCSI stands for Small Computer System Interface (pronounced "Scuzzy"). The SCSI port is used to connect peripheral devices to a Macintosh. Each device is connected in a series to the Macintosh, called a "daisy chain" or "chain." Apple recommends that the first and last devices are terminated.

The Macintosh looks at SCSI ID #7 first and then goes in order from SCSI ID #5, #4, #3, #2, and #1, with ID #0 being last. Shareware programs like SCSI Probe, SCSI Tools and SCSI Evaluator allow you to view what is connected on the SCSI chain. They are useful programs for making SCSI devices mount. Some SCSI devices do not have a switch for setting the SCSI ID # and are either hard coded with a SCSI ID # or have software that comes with the device for setting the SCSI ID #.

All Macintosh computers since the Macintosh Plus have an Apple standard SCSI port (25 pin to 50 pin wide SCSI interface), Apple PowerBooks use a special SCSI cable called HDI30 (50 pin to 50 pin tiny square connector). Many SCSI devices can be connected together with a standard 50 pin to 50 pin peripheral SCSI cable.

SCSI terminators are plugs that fit into SCSI ports. Their function is to keep signals from echoing back and forth along the SCSI cabling. There will be problems with echoing with a faster Macintosh, increased number of connected SCSI devices, longer cable lengths, and SCSI devices located too near another. Some SCSI devices have a termination switch for terminating the SCSI device. These devices do not need SCSI terminator plugs for termination. SCSI devices that are self terminating must be the last SCSI device on the chain. The Macintosh IIfx requires a special black external terminator at the end of the SCSI chain. No device in the SCSI chain maybe internally terminated, except for the internal hard drive.

Removable hard disk drives and tape drives may not be connected on the same SCSI chain. The SCSI interface only allows for one backup channel. If you connect both only one is likely to work correctly.

To choose the startup disk, select the Startup Disk Control Panels in System 7. In System 6, choose "Set Startup" under the Special menu.

Communication signals along the SCSI chain are often disrupted by noise. Terminators have resistors placed at either end of the SCSI chain to supress noise. Most Macintosh computers have an internal hard drive that is already actively terminated. Adding any additional SCSI devices requires an additional terminator to be placed at the end of the SCSI chain.

The 100- and 500-series PowerBook models have internal terminators that aren't powered like most desktop Macintosh models, where the terminator is only effective for the internal hard drive termination. Adding external SCSI devices to PowerBooks requires the use of two external terminators instead of one. Many SCSI devices have internal active or "powered" termination that can substitute for the second terminator.

When none of the SCSI devices provide powered termination, a powered terminator must be used. Powered terminators usually have lights to indicate the status of the connection. APS technology has a powered terminator called SCSI Sentry. PowerBook Duos have an active termination (powered) in its docking bay, and doesn't need a second terminator for connecting to external SCSI devices.

Capturing Video on the Macintosh General Information

When capturing video on a computer, any software or hardware impediments decrease the quality of the captured video. The following is a list of recommendations for optimizing performance on the Macintosh to achieve the best possible quality when capturing video.

- Disable AppleTalk in the Network control panel.
- Disable Virtual Memory in the Memory control panel.
- Enable 32-bit addressing in the Memory control panel when using a Macintosh without built-in 32-bit addressing.
- Create a 32KB disk cache.
- Load only a minimal set of Extensions when capturing video, disabling any Extension that runs in the background.
- Quit all applications and utilities.
- Allocate as much memory to Premiere as possible.
- Keep media in drives (e.g., diskettes in disk drives, CD-ROMs in CD-ROM drives) to prevent polling interrupts.
- Use a single monitor set to 13" display. Dual monitors and larger displays use more memory for screen display when capturing.
- Turn off idle SCSI devices.
- Use a high-performance video disk or disk array, with a 3 to 6MB per second sustained data transfer rate.
- When possible, use a Fast-SCSI-2 controller.
- Defragment the video hard disk frequently. A fragmented disk slows performance significantly.
- Enable the Dynamic Quantization adjustment when using a video capture board with this feature, and limit the board's data transfer rate to match the sustained data rates of the hard disk.
- Capture audio separately from video using time code, then relink the audio tracks to video tracks in the video editing application (e.g., Adobe Premiere). Capturing audio with video requires extra sound processing, which degrades the quality of the captured video.
- When capturing audio, select "Off While Recording" from the "Speaker" popup menu in the "Sound Input" dialog box of the Sound control panel.
- Light video properly. Material filmed in low light is noisy and difficult to compress.
- The following hardware upgrades, listed in descending order, provide the best performance increases on a Macintosh: a faster hard disk, more RAM, a faster processor.

Error "The memory size must be less than 1,000,000K" When Allocating Memory to an Application

ISSUE

When you enter a value of 1,000,000 or larger in the Preferred Size text box of an application's Info dialog box, the system returns the error, "The memory size must be less than 1,000,000K."

SOLUTION

Set the Preferred Size to a value less than 1,000,000K.

ADDITIONAL INFORMATION

The Macintosh Operating System cannot allocate more than 999,999K (approximately one gigabyte) of memory to any application.

You can access an application's Info dialog box by selecting the application's icon in the Finder and choosing File > Get Info. You can allocate more or less memory to an application by changing the number in the Preferred Size text box in the Memory Requirements section of the application's Info dialog box. How much memory you allocate to any application depends on the amount of memory your computer has available and the number of other applications you want to open at the same time.

32-bit QuickDraw General Information

QuickDraw is the family of routines in the Macintosh Toolbox that are used to draw rectangles, rounded corner rectangles, arcs, wedges, polygons, and PICT graphics on the Macintosh screen and QuickDraw imaging devices.

Color QuickDraw is a library of extensions to standard QuickDraw that provides support for color displays (e.g., PixelMaps). The ability of a Macintosh to support Color QuickDraw is a function of the processor in use. Color QuickDraw is available in Macintosh computers that use the 68020, 68030, or 68040 processor. Macintosh computers that use the 68000 processor do not support Color QuickDraw and thus, do not support color monitors.

32-BIT QUICKDRAW

32-Bit QuickDraw is a library of extensions to the Color QuickDraw family providing support for drawing to 32-bit color monitors. With System 6.x, the 32-Bit QuickDraw Startup document (INIT) is necessary for Macintosh II computers with ROM (read-only memory) sets issued prior to the Macintosh IIci (i.e., Macintosh II, IIx, IIcx, SE/30) as these Macintosh models do not have 32-Bit QuickDraw in ROM. 32-Bit QuickDraw version 1.2 (issued with System software 6.0.5) fixed some known issues in the Macintosh IIci series ROM. System 7.x does not install the 32-Bit QuickDraw INIT as it is built into the system software.

Black-and-white QuickDraw Macintosh computers (68000 processor), which include the Macintosh Plus, SE, or Portable models, ignore the 32-Bit QuickDraw INIT.

Accent Mark Displays Next to Instead of Above Extended or Special Character

ISSUE

After you type an extended character (e.g., character with a grave accent, diaeresis accent, acute accent, or diaeresis accent), the accent mark is next to, rather than above the character.

SOLUTION

Disable Caps Lock by press the Caps Lock key.

ADDITIONAL INFORMATION

Extended or composite characters are included in and vary by font. To type an extended characters, you press Option + [key varies] then type a letter (i.e., a vowel or letter "n"). For example, typing Option + u , u generates a udiaeresis (,), typing Option + `, e generates an egrave (Ë). When you press the Cap Locks key, which provides the same function as pressing the Shift key, while typing extended characters, the Shift key is added to the pressed key sequence, preventing the extended characters from appearing on-screen.

Apple LaserWriter 8.x and Adobe PSPrinter 8.x Printer Driver New Features

The Apple LaserWriter 8.x printer driver is developed by Adobe Systems for Apple Computer. Adobe also distributes the printer driver under the name Adobe PSPrinter 8.x, with only slight differences between the two. Some new features require that you select an option in an application's Print or Page Setup dialog box. Because some applications customize their printing dialog boxes, or modify how the driver functions (e.g., PageMaker 5.0x), not all of the features listed below are available in all applications.

NEW FEATURES

PPD file support

PPD file support at the printer driver level allows the printing application to take advantage of special features of a particular printer, such as resolution enhancement technology, multiple paper trays and output bins, duplexing, and custom paper sizes.

The LaserWriter 8.0 and PSPrinter 8.0 printer driver supports specification 4.0 PPD files, the LaserWriter 8.1.1 printer driver supports specification 4.0 and 4.1 PPD files.

Two-pass design

When printing through the LaserWriter 8.x or PSPrinter 8.x printer driver, the print job is first spooled to disk, regardless of whether Background Printing is enabled. During spooling or the first pass, the driver notes font usage, memory requirements, and repeated objects. On the second pass, the spooled file is then read again by the printer driver, where it may modify the PostScript code based on the driver's notes during the first pass for efficiency before sending the file to the printer. Even though each print job is read (or printed) twice, the optimizations for efficiency during the second pass do decrease overall print times.

Level 2 PostScript Support

The LaserWriter 8.x or PSPrinter 8.x printer driver can determine if the targeted device is a PostScript level 2 device by reading the PPD file that used to set up the printer. When printing to a level 2 PostScript device, it will use more efficient level 2 PostScript commands available when generating the PostScript code.

Use of Printer Queries

When the LaserWriter 8.x or PSPrinter 8.x printer driver prints to a printer connected directly to the computer with background printing disabled, it queries the printer for the following: PostScript Level, PostScript version, binary data protocol support, TrueType rasterizer presence, and font availability.

When checking for fonts, the driver downloads a list of fonts needed to print the current job and asks the printer to return the availability of each of those needed fonts. This avoids long delays waiting for the printer's entire font catalog to be returned. Because the LaserWriter 8.x printer driver is able to query for fonts, custom printer files are generally not required when printing to laser printers. If printing through a network spooler or if background printing is enabled, the LaserWriter 8.x printer driver relies on the font information listed in the selected PPD file. RAM or hard disk-resident fonts will be downloaded from the Macintosh in this case.

The displayed icon next to the printer's name is determined by information that Auto Setup gathers during the printer query. If Auto Setup cannot connect to the printer, or if Auto Setup is never run (e.g., "Select PPD" is used instead of Auto Setup), the default LaserWriter 8.0 icon is displayed. The LaserWriter 8.0 icon is used for laser printers, the magnifying glass icon is used for imagesetters, and the rainbow icon is used for color devices.

Support for Callback Functions

The driver contains a robust applications programmer interface for allowing other applications to customize how the driver functions. For instance, PageMaker 5.0x suppresses most of the driver's normal functions and uses the driver mainly as an I/O channel to printer. PageMaker 5.0x does use the LaserWriter 8.x or PSPrinter 8.x printer driver's new ability of returning fonts to the printing application. The LaserWriter 7.x and earlier printer drivers did not have an applications programmer interface.

Ability to print EPS-to-disk The LaserWriter 8.x or

PSPrinter 8.x printer driver allows a document to be printed to disk as an EPS file, in addition to printing to disk as a PostScript file. Two screen previews are offered for printer driver generated EPS files: Mac Standard Preview (black-and-white bitmap), and Mac Enhanced Preview. Mac Enhanced Preview contains font information ATM can use to render smooth text in the screen preview at high resolution. Mac Enhanced Previews will create EPS files whose file size is much larger on disk than Mac Standard Preview EPS files.

Support for PostScript-to-fax boards

When a PostScript device is equipped with a fax option (e.g., Compaq PageMarq 15, Apple Select 360), the LaserWriter 8.x printer driver can output to fax rather than paper. If the driver detects a fax board in the printer during setup, an additional fax option appears in the Print dialog box. If faxing to a similarly-equipped printer, the fax board can send PostScript, and the receiving printer will print the job as high-resolution PostScript (the PostScript file describing the page is sent over and rasterized at the destination printer).

Improved Error Handling

When you choose Options in a printing dialog box, enhanced error handling options are enabled. These options include the ability to print a detailed report about a specific error message received.

Simple Imposition Features

The option to print two or four pages to a page is available in the pop-up menu in a Page Setup dialog box. Pages are scaled to fit the selected paper.

Support for RLE-compressed Bitmap Graphics

When printing to a PostScript level 2 device, the driver can use Run Length Encoding (RLE) compression to decrease network transmission times to the printer. PostScript Level 2 devices include the decompression software in the printer's ROM.

Apple Logo Character Doesn't Print

ISSUE

The Apple Logo character (Option + Shift + k) displays correctly on screen, but prints as a blank space or unexpected character.

SOLUTION

Reformat the Apple Logo character using a different font (e.g., Chicago Symbol, EncycloFont, JottQuick, or JottQuickLight) when printing to a non-Apple PostScript printer.

ADDITIONAL INFORMATION

The Apple Logo character (Option + Shift + k) does not print directly to non-Apple PostScript printers as this character is a registered trademark of Apple Computer, Inc., available exclusively on Apple PostScript printers. Printers without this character in their ROM based Symbol font produce a blank space or unexpected character for the Option + Shift + k key combination in most fonts.

Chicago Symbol (shareware), EncycloFont (shareware), JottQuick, or JottQuickLight fonts print the Apple Logo character on all printers as the PostScript outline of the Apple Logo character is designed in the font.

Apple Macintosh Speech Recognition System General Information

Apple's speech recognition system available on some Macintosh computers (e.g., Centris 660AV, Quadra 840AV) allows the Macintosh computer to recognize verbal commands corresponding to available menu commands and dialog box buttons, provided there are no duplicates.

All applications and the system software are compatible with and can respond to speech input.

With Apple's Speech Macro editor or QuicKeys, the Macintosh computer can respond to new commands to trigger specific macros. Anything you can automate with the Speech Macro Editor or CE Software QuicKeys, you can automate using speech recognition.

ENABLING SPEECH RECOGNITION

Speech recognition is activated in the "Speech Setup" Control Panel. When the text indicates that the computer is ready, you must say, in a normal, clear voice, "Computer, hello."

BASIC PRE-PROGRAMMED FUNCTIONS

These functions are built into the speech recognition software. You must give all spoken commands in the format, "Computer, blah-blah-blah," where "blah-blah-blah" is the function to be performed.

SPOKEN COMMANDS AND WHAT THEY DO:

"Hello" Computer replies "Hello, welcome to Macintosh."

"What day is it?" Computer announces the date.

"What time is it?" Computer announces the time.

"Zoom window" Clicks the zoom box in the active window.

"Close window" Clicks the close box in the active window.

"Close all windows" Closes all windows when the Finder is active.

"Print x copies" Prints specified number of copies.

"Print page x" Prints specified page.

"Print from x to x" Prints specified page ranges.

"Is file sharing on?" Answers file sharing is "on," "off," or "starting up."

"Start file sharing" Activates file sharing.

"Stop file sharing" De-activates file sharing.

"Open x" Opens x from the Apple menu.

"Switch to x" Switches from the current application to x (providing x is open).

"Restart" Asks for confirmation, then restarts.

"Shut Down" Asks for confirmation, then shuts down.

"[Menu command]" Performs the menu command, but may not work when: a menu item is not available (because a modifier key or other action must be performed first), there are identical menu items in different menus, a menu item includes unpronounceable characters or is represented by an icon, a menu item is in the Help (?) menu.

"[Dialog box button]" Clicks the desired button in a dialog box. The computer will not understand this spoken command when the status window is covering the button (move the window and try again) or a button name is unpronounceable.

"[Speakable Item]" Opens the item or the item's alias located in the Speakable Items Folder.

SPEAKABLE ITEMS FOLDER

You can put an alias of an item, or the item itself, in the Speakable Items folder, and open the item by speaking its name. If you add or delete items while speech recognition is enabled, turn speech recognition off and back on again so the computer recognizes the new items. To avoid slowing performance, no more than 30 items in the folder is recommended.

Default Speakable Items Folder Commands:

"Open General Controls"
"Open Monitors"
"Open Print Monitor"
"Open Sound"
"Open Speech Macro Editor"
"Open Speech Setup"
"Open TeachText"
"Open the Apple Extras folder"
"Open the Apple Menu Items folder"
"Open Control Panels"
"Open the Extensions folder"
"Open the Fonts folder"
"Open the System Folder"

SPEECH MACRO EDITOR

Using the Speech Macro Editor, users can create speech macros, which the computer executes when you say the macro's name.

TROUBLESHOOTING

If you have problems with speech recognition, try a basic pre-programmed function such as "Hello." If the computer does not respond, "Hello, welcome to Macintosh," try moving the slider control in the Speech Setup control panel slightly toward tolerant.

Apple PhotoGrade General Information

PhotoGrade technology, used by the Apple LaserWriter IIf and IIg printers, produces finer halftones than conventional 300 dots per inch (dpi) printers.

PHOTOGRADE

Apple PhotoGrade technology allows up to 65 levels of gray on a 300 dots per inch (dpi) output device by varying the size and pattern of dots used to create the shades of gray. The more variations in the size and pattern of the dots, the smoother the gray. Using this flexible 300 dpi grid, it is possible to create a unique pattern of halftone cells for each level of gray. Fixed grid devices such as the LaserWriter II NTX are limited to 33 shades of gray.

GRAYS AVAILABLE USING PHOTOGRADE

The number of available grays will vary with the screen ruling, measured as lines per inch (lpi). The higher the lpi, the finer the dot pattern, decreasing the number of available grays. The lower the lpi, the coarser the screen, increasing the number of available grays.

Five screen ruling settings are available through the LaserWriter Utility to control the way PhotoGrade is used. The slide bar indicates Maximum Grays"for 53 lpi, and Maximum Resolution for 150 lpi.

53 lpi at 45 degrees (far left hand side of slide bar)
75 lpi at 0 degrees
83 lpi at 56 degrees (middle setting)
106 lpi at 45 degrees (default)
150 lpi at 0 degrees (far right hand side of slide bar)

PRINTER MEMORY REQUIREMENTS

5 MB of RAM

Minimum required for PhotoGrade output on A4 or letter size page.

Minimum required for non-PhotoGrade output on legal page size.

8 MB of RAM

Minimum required for PhotoGrade output on legal size page.

2 MB of RAM

Maximum image area of 7.7-by-10.1 inches (PhotoGrade inactive).

The amount of installed printer memory is printed on the LaserWriter IIf or IIg startup page. If the startup page has been disabled, it can be turned on using the LaserWriter Utility.

High line screens or complex illustrations require more printer RAM. If there is insufficient memory to image with PhotoGrade, the printer will turn PhotoGrade off, limiting output to a maximum of 33 shades of gray.

Error "Could not start application because of error type -199 has occurred"

ISSUE

When you starting an application, the system returns the error "Could not start application because of error type -199 has occurred." The application does not start.

SOLUTIONS

Do one or more of the following:

A. Ensure that a matching install disk set is being used to install the application (e.g., all install disks are high-density).

B. Ensure the hard disk is formatted properly, especially after updating to System 7 software:

For Apple hard disks, use Apple's Disk First Aid or Apple HD SC Setup (located on the "Disk Tools" or "System Tools" disk). In most cases, Apple's Disk First Aid will find minor problems and will be able to repair them.

OR: For non-Apple hard disks, use the utilities included with the hard disk to update the drive for the system software. With System 7 software, ensure the utilities are System 7 compatible.

OR: For Rodime hard disks, use the Cobra Utilities disk which contains a utility for this hard drive. For instructions, see Additional Information.

NOTE: Incompatible system extensions (INITs) or control panel documents (CDevs) or a damaged application may also cause random system errors or freezes. Run the application with the extensions off to verify that added extensions are not the cause. To turn extensions off upon startup in System 7, restart computer holding the Shift key down until the message "Welcome to Macintosh, Extensions Off" appears.

ADDITIONAL INFORMATION

The Aldus Installer/Utility is unable to detect a mismatched disk set and return a message when installing an application. Instead, after installation when the necessary files are not properly installed, the system returns the error "Could not start application because of error type -199 has occurred." For example, substituting a high-density (1.44 MB) Disk 2 for the low-density (800K) Disk 2 in a PageMaker 5.0 low-density install disk set will install the PageMaker 5.0 application incorrectly. The PageMaker 5.0 License Pack is available using a high-density Disk 2 only.

The "-199" error may occur when you install an application on a system on which System 7 software was installed over system 6.x software. System 7 software formats hard disks slightly differently than did System 6.x software. After installing System 7 software, it is recommended to run Apple's Disk First Aid to ensure the hard drive is formatted properly. The system error "-199" is a resource manager error: "mapReadErr: map inconsistent with operation."

To Check Rodime Hard Disks Using Cobra Driver Utility:

1. Restart the machine with Cobra Utilities floppy disk, which comes with Rodime Cobra hard drive.
2. Open the application "Cobra driver utility" or similarly named application.
3. In the dialog box, select the hard drive at the top of the window and click Update.
4. Press Shift + N.
5. Click OK in the warning dialog that says changes will not take effect until the next restart.
6. Quit, then restart the computer from the hard drive.

Error "Disk full" When Printing with the LaserWriter 8.x Printer Driver

ISSUE

When you print a document using the LaserWriter 8.x or Adobe PSPrinter 8.x printer driver, the system returns an error message indicating that the document could not be printed because the hard disk is full. For example, in Adobe Illustrator 5.0 the system returns the error "The spool file could not be saved because there was not enough disk space." Clicking OK in the message box results in the error "The disk is full. ID=-34."

SOLUTIONS

Make sure there is adequate disk space for the print spool file by doing one or more of the following:

A. Move or delete files from the startup disk.

B. Change the location of the spool file to a hard disk with more free space:

1. Create a folder called "Printing Temp Folder" on the disk where you want the spool file to be saved.
2. While the Printing Temp Folder is still selected, choose File > Make Alias.
3. Move the folder alias to the Extensions folder in the System Folder on the startup drive.
4. If you're using LaserWriter 8.x, rename the folder alias "Printing Temp Folder" (i.e., remove " alias" from the folder name). If you're using PSPrinter 8.x, name the folder "PSPrinter Temp Folder."

ADDITIONAL INFORMATION

LaserWriter 8.x and PSPrinter 8.x save temporary print files in the System Folder before sending print jobs to the printer, even when background printing is disabled in the Chooser. The disk space required is approximately equal to the size of the original file plus any linked graphics. When you print separations, multiply the publication size by the number of separations.

Error "Unable to locate the PPD file..." After Clicking Auto Setup in Chooser

ISSUE

When you click Auto Setup to set up a printer for the Apple LaserWriter 8.x driver in the Chooser, the system returns the error "Unable to locate the PPD file [Name of printer and version] or [Name of printer]." No PPD file is selected.

SOLUTIONS

Manually select a PPD file for the printer by clicking the Select PPD button in the error dialog box, or by clicking More Choices in the setup dialog box and then clicking Select PPD.

NOTE: If the correct PPD file for the printer is unavailable, select an existing PPD file that describes a similar printer.

ADDITIONAL INFORMATION

The Auto Setup feature of the LaserWriter 8.x printer driver automatically selects the appropriate file for the targeted printer. To do so, it queries the printer for its product name and PostScript version, then searches for a PPD file in the Printer Descriptions folder that matches this information (e.g., "MyPrinter v.47.0"). If none of the PPD files match the name the LaserWriter driver is searching for exactly (e.g., the name is spelled differently or is missing spaces), the driver is unable to select a PPD file and prompts you to select one manually.

Error "...Macintosh cannot use any more fonts at this time..." When Installing Screen Fonts Under System 7.1

ISSUE

When you install screen fonts under System 7.1 or later, the system returns the error "The Macintosh cannot use any more fonts at this time; only 128 fonts can be used at once."

SOLUTIONS

Do one or more of the following:

A. Install screen fonts outside the Fonts folder and use a font manager (e.g., Suitcase or MasterJuggler) to access the fonts.

B. Install System 7.01 or earlier.

C. Ensure there are 128 or fewer font suitcases installed in the Fonts folder in the System Folder.

ADDITIONAL INFORMATION

System 7.1 and later uses a Fonts folder in the System Folder to hold font resources. The Fonts folder can only address 128 font suitcases. Exceeding 128 font suitcases can cause unpredictable font behavior, including font menus displaying incorrectly.

A font suitcase can contain more than one font.

Index

Adobe Acrobat PDF

WINDOWS

MAC OS

UNIX

Acrobat Reader

WINDOWS

MAC OS

Acrobat Exchange

WINDOWS

MAC OS

UNIX

Acrobat Distiller

WINDOWS

MAC OS

UNIX

Acrobat Catalog

WINDOWS

MAC OS

UNIX

Acrobat Capture

WINDOWS

Acrobat PDF Writer

WINDOWS

MAC OS

UNIX

Adobe After Effects

WINDOWS

MAC OS

Adobe FrameMaker

WINDOWS

System Errors 128

Printing Problems 135

Installation Issues 139

General Information 143

UNIX

Feature Techniques 104

Unexpected Results 113

Adobe Illustrator

WINDOWS

Adobe Dimensions

MAC OS

Adobe Streamline

WINDOWS

MAC OS

Adobe PageMaker

WINDOWS

MAC OS

System Errors 335

Printing Problems 344

Adobe PageMill

MAC OS

Adobe SiteMill

MAC OS

Adobe Persuasion

WINDOWS

Adobe Photoshop

WINDOWS

Adobe PhotoDeluxe

WINDOWS

MAC OS

Adobe PostScript

WINDOWS

Adobe PSPrinter

Adobe Premiere

WINDOWS

MAC OS

Adobe Type Library

WINDOWS

MAC OS

Adobe Type On Call

WINDOWS

MAC OS

Adobe Type Manager

WINDOWS

Adobe Type Reunion

MAC OS

General Issues

WINDOWS

Colophon

Text design by David Bullen. Text is set in Adobe Minion, designed by Robert Slimbach. Titles and heads are set in Adobe Myriad, a multiple master typeface designed by Robert Slimbach and Carol Twombly. Computer code is set in Prestige 12, designed by Clayton Smith in 1953, issued by Monotype/Bitstream. Typesetting by Hans Hansen.

Pre-press and printing by GAC Shepard Poorman, Indianapolis, Indiana. Printed on acid-free #60 Cougar Natural using soy-based inks.

Production Notes:
This book was produced for Adobe Press using Adobe PageMaker 6.5, Claris FileMaker Pro 3.0, Adobe Acrobat 3.0, and Adobe Photoshop 4.

The articles in this book came from the Adobe Customer Support's technical database, from the archives of Adobe Magazine, and from various files and servers upon Adobe's Intranet. Articles were first compiled and sorted using FileMaker Pro. Then using AppleScript, the database records were exported to single text files for each chapter, and concatenated with style tags to automatically embed the appropriate paragraph formatting instructions. These text files were imported into PageMaker reading the style tags, and then PageMaker scripts were used to automate several hundred typesetting manipulations as well as to create page elements such as running heads, thumbtabs, and tips formatting.

After pages were created, the final layouts were distilled into high-resolution Acrobat files via PostScript specially prepared by PageMaker. The Acrobat files were then uploaded to the printer's ftp site via the Internet. Pre-press consisted of printing directly from Acrobat to a computer-to-plate (filmless) platemaker after running the files through an imposition program.

PageMaker also output normal resolution PDF (Acrobat) files for the CD. These PDF files were distilled with embedded links and actions from PageMaker for the Adobe FAQ CD. The CD was compiled and, indexed with Acrobat Catalog, by Tom McIntire.

What's on the Adobe FAQ CD

This CD has been engineered to work on both MacOS and Windows-based computers. It consists of the following:

- A Home Page file "FAQhome.pdf"
- Adobe Acrobat Reader 3.0 (with Search)
- Adobe FAQ & UFAQ Chapter Files
- Adobe File Library

Adobe Acrobat

To access the files on the CD you will need Adobe Acrobat 3.0.

1. If you already have Adobe Acrobat Exchange 3.0, open "FAQhome.pdf" directly.
2. If you already have Adobe Acrobat Reader 3.0, but do not wish to digitally search the 2100 pages of FAQs on the CD, then open "FAQhome.pdf" directly.
3. If you wish to search the 2100 pages of FAQs on the CD, and do not have Acrobat Exchange 3, then install Acrobat Reader 3.0 (with Search) according to the instuctions within the Acrobat Reader directory or folder. This version of Acrobat Reader has a special search plug-in. It will work with the same functionality on any other Acrobat or PDF file you may already possess.

FAQhome.pdf

Once you have installed Adobe Acrobat, open this file. It will provide a CD home page for your exploration. It contains hyperlinks to all the files on the CD, accesss to Acrobat's search engine, and Web hyperlinks to link to www.adobe.com. The more you use the CD the more handy this "home page" file will become.

Adobe FAQ and UFAQ

The CD contains PDF versions of all the chapters within this paper book. In addition, the CD contains another 1300 pages of Unabridged FAQs. You must have Adobe Acrobat 3 installed to view, search, or print any of the FAQ or UFAQ files (previous versions of Acrobat may not work). You can use the "FAQhome.pdf" file to access these files, or you can open their directories and folders. See the "Introduction," at the beginning of this book, for more background on the UFAQ.

Adobe File Library

The File Library contains hundreds of updates, software patches, and other genuinely useful files. You can use the "FAQhome.pdf" file to access these files, or you can open the File Library's directory or folder.